McDougal, Littell
Literature

PURPLE LEVEL
Yellow Level
Blue Level
Orange Level
Green Level
Red Level

FLORIS, 1964. *Bernard Cohen.*
Tate Gallery, London.

McDougal, Littell
Literature

Purple Level

English Literature

Robert C. Granner
Adlai E. Stevenson High School
Prairie View, Illinois

Malcolm E. Stern
English Department Head
Evanston Township High School

McDougal, Littell & Company
Evanston, Illinois
New York   Dallas   Sacramento

Consultants

Louis J. Benedict, English Department Chair, Madison High School, San Diego, California

Phyllis H. Dunning, English Department Head, R. J. Reynolds High School, Winston-Salem, North Carolina

Beverly Pollock, Language Arts Department Head, Bainbridge High School, Bainbridge, Georgia

Frances M. Russell, Director of English, Winchester Public Schools, Winchester, Massachusetts

Frances Snow, English Supervisor, Winston-Salem/Forsyth County Schools, Winston-Salem, North Carolina

Robert Squires, English Department Head, Oneonta High School, Oneonta, New York

Special Contributors

George Bodmer, English Department, Indiana University Northwest, Gary, Indiana

Laurie A. Braun, writer and editor, La Grange, Illinois

Julie West Johnson, English Department, New Trier Township High School, Winnetka, Illinois

Ted Johnson, English Department, Indiana University Northwest, Gary, Indiana

Ken Lawless, English Department, The State University College of Arts and Sciences, Plattsburgh, New York

Susan Schaffrath, Curriculum Specialist in Language Arts and Literature, Chicago, Illinois

Marilyn Sherman, teacher and writer, Wilmette, Illinois

Acknowledgments

African Universities Press: For "Telephone Conversation" by Wole Soyinka, from *Reflections: Nigerian Prose and Verse*, edited by Frances Ademola, 1968. Angus & Robertson (UK) Ltd.: For "Eve to Her Daughters" by Judith Wright, from *The Other Half.* Atheneum Publishers, Inc.: For "Wine," translated by Bernice Grohskopf in *From Age to Age*; copyright © 1968 by Bernice Grohskopf. Brandt & Brandt Literary Agents, Inc.: For "Follow My Fancy" by Joan Aiken, from *The Green Flash*, Holt, Rinehart & Winston, Inc.; copyright © 1971 by Joan Aiken. Curtis Brown Ltd.: For "A Sunrise on the Veld" by Doris Lessing, from *Nine African Stories*; reprinted by kind permission of Curtis Brown Ltd., on behalf of Doris Lessing; copyright Doris Lessing 1951. Carcanet Press Limited: For "The Computer's First Christmas Card" by Edwin Morgan, from *Poems of Thirty Years*; copyright © 1982 Edwin Morgan. Joan Daves: For "The Idealist" by Frank O'Connor, from *The Stories of Frank O'Connor*; copyright © 1950, 1956 by Frank O'Connor. Devin-Adair Publishers, Old Greenwich, CT: For an excerpt from *The Book of Margery Kemp*
continued on page 994

ISBN: 0-88343-270-6

Contents

Staff Credits

Editorial Director: Joy Littell
Administrative Editor: Kathleen Laya
Managing Editor: Geraldine Macsai
Associate Editor: Zana Courser
Rights and Permissions: Irma Rosenberg
Associate Designer: Kenneth M. Izzi

Editor-in-Chief: Joseph F. Littell

McDougal, Littell
Literature

English Literature

THE MAN, SYMBOL OF ST. MATTHEW. *The Book of Durrow.*
The Board of Trinity College, Dublin.

Unit 1

The Anglo-Saxon Period (449–1066)

THE SNETTISHAM TORQUE. *First Century* B.C.
Courtesy of the Trustees of the British Museum.

The Anglo-Saxon Heritage

The Anglo-Saxon Period spans six centuries, most of which falls within a time that historians call the "Dark Ages." This period was marked by bloody conflicts, ignorance, violence, and barbarism. Yet it was also a time of creativity and dynamic change. Arts and crafts flourished, and communication and trade took place among local communities and later between Britain and continental Europe. Pagan ideas and practices gradually gave way to Christian ideals and to a concern with Christian ethical values. During this period, English emerged as a language, and writers began to express ideas in many ways no less profound or "inspired" than those expressed in the twentieth century.

BRITAIN BEFORE THE ANGLO-SAXONS

Julius Caesar made a brief visit to Britain as early as 55 B.C., but it was nearly a century later before the Romans established a military outpost on this remote island, occupied at that time by Celtic tribes. Not much is known about these early Britons except that they were a warlike people who had begun to invade the island about 600 B.C.

The highly organized Romans dominated the Britons, driving some groups off to remote regions in the West (Wales) and North (Scotland) and making others slaves. Within twenty-five years, much of Britain was subdued. The Romans then began to integrate tribal leaders into their provincial system, while the majority of remaining Britons settled down to ordinary daily lives.

The Romans, who were skilled engineers, built military fortifications such as Hadrian's Wall in the North, as well as elaborate baths, villas, amphitheaters, and stone roads between key military posts. Perhaps even more important, however, the Romans brought a system of laws and a unity of government to Britain. They also planted the seeds of a religion that was germinating and spreading throughout the entire western world.

In A.D. 410 the sack of Rome by German barbarians signaled the end of Roman rule in Britain. The Roman legions were recalled to defend a crumbling Empire at home, leaving the islands open to full-scale invasion by the Germanic tribes who had been raiding the coast of Roman Britain for decades.

THE GERMANIC INVASIONS

The Jutes, a Germanic tribe from the Danish peninsula, were the first to arrive, conquering the province of Kent in A.D. 449. They were followed by the Saxons and the Angles, tribes from the northern Germanic plain. The fierce, virile marauders wantonly destroyed much of the Roman civilization and either enslaved the Britons or drove them into the inaccessible highlands of the North and West.

Weakened by Roman dominance, the Britons in the southeast did not put up a sustained fight. However, in the fifth or sixth century one Celtic chief won a minor victory over the Saxons before being driven West. This chief might have been the legendary King Arthur.

The steady infiltration of tribes into Britain continued for over a hundred years. By the middle of the sixth century, the invaders, now known collectively as Anglo-Saxons, were established in various parts of Britain. Their culture became the basis for "Angle-land," or "English," culture; their gutteral, vigorous language became the spoken language of the people, the language now known as Old English.

ANGLO-SAXON SOCIETY

The Anglo-Saxon conquerors brought to Britain a passionate loyalty to king and kinsmen, strict tribal codes of conduct, and a love of action and adventure. Their outlook was essentially fatalistic. Life was a struggle to be endured; evil and death were inescapable realities; and fame was the only true immortality. Their religion was an informal system of god-heroes with few priests and formal rituals and no hierarchical organization.

Although illiterate and often crude, the Anglo-Saxons had an innate intellectual curiosity and an appreciation for beauty. They also were a remarkably adaptable people, gradually assimilating many of the customs, arts, and laws of conquered peoples, while retaining their uniquely Germanic traditions and values. In time, the pagan Anglo-Saxons adapted to the Christian religion, which had been introduced in Britain before the Germanic invasions of the Celtic-Roman island.

THE ESTABLISHMENT OF CHRISTIANITY

When Christianity spread through the Roman empire in the first century A.D., the effect was felt even in far-off Britain. No one knows exactly when the first missionaries arrived, but by A.D. 300 the number of Christians on the island was significant. In 597 Augustine, a monk, landed in Kent, having been sent by Pope Gregory to do missionary work. King Aethelbert of Kent was married to Bertha, a Christian woman who had come to England from France. Bertha evidently had a profound influence on her husband, for when Augustine arrived, Aethelbert was quite ready for conversion. He is said to have been baptized in Canterbury, in a tiny church called St. Martins, supposedly built during the Roman occupation. Augustine established a monastery there and became the first of many famous Archbishops of Canterbury.

The influence of the Roman Church was felt throughout Britain. The Celtic Christians in the North, however, did not recognize the authority of the Pope. For their leadership these Christians looked west to Ireland, to the home of the learned monks who had converted them to Christianity. Representatives of the Roman and Celtic churches met in 664 at Whitby Abbey, a monastery in Yorkshire, to settle their disputes. The outcome of this conference was that Britain became a province of the Roman Church. The island was unified under one religious system and through this system was joined to the rest of Europe.

THE CHURCH AS A CULTURAL FORCE

Through the influence of the Church, the Anglo-Saxon system of justice was modified and refined. Courts of law superseded the old pagan laws of vengeance and blood feuds. The clergy and nobles began to use written contracts and agreements.

The monasteries were the centers of intellectual, literary, artistic, and social activity in Anglo-Saxon Britain. The monks cared for the poor, sick, friendless, and orphaned and provided a refuge for travelers and scholars. Monastic scholars imported books from the Continent, which were then painstakingly copied by the monks. Original works were written, mostly in scholarly Latin, but with occasional lines and later entire pieces in Old English. Schools were provided, at least occasionally, for the very young. The earliest recorded history of the English people comes from the churchmen at the monasteries. The greatest of these monks was the Venerable Bede (673–735), author of *Ecclesiastical History of the English People.* As a historian, Bede is regarded as the "father of English history."

THE DANISH INVASIONS AND KING ALFRED

During the late eighth and ninth centuries, Britain was invaded by the warlike Danes, or Vikings. These plundering raiders destroyed monasteries with their precious stores of manuscripts and threatened to obliterate all traces of cultural refinement. After nearly a century of violence, Alfred the Great led a successful campaign against the Danes.

The crisis of invasion temporarily abated, King Alfred sought to raise the level of culture by providing for the establishment of schools and the rebuilding of monasteries. A well educated man, he translated Latin works into English and encouraged others to do the same and to produce original works in English. During Alfred's time, English history was systematically recorded in a series of chronicles, which were the first historical records kept in English. Wise in politics and government, able in war and sensitive to the intellectual and cultural needs of his people, Alfred puts to rest any notion that the so-called "Dark Ages" were lacking "bright stars."

ANGLO-SAXON LITERATURE

Anglo-Saxon literature reflects the somber temperament of these Germanic people and the bleak environment in which they lived. Not much of the imagery of brief English summers appears in this literature; winter prevails, and spring comes slowly, if at all. The Anglo-Saxons were serious minded, and the reader finds little humor in their literature. Life was difficult, and most of the stories and poems of this period present heroic struggles in which only the strong survive.

Oral tradition was the earliest mode of literary expression. The Anglo-Saxons gathered in great "mead halls" where kings and nobles lavishly entertained friends and strangers alike, often to celebrate successful battles or expeditions. The favorite drink was mead, a potent liquor made of fermented honey and water, often with spices, fruit, and malt, which was drunk from beautifully wrought cups and bowls. The scop, a professional singer or minstrel, entertained the company with retellings of stories and poems about the exploits of tribal heroes. The king's warriors and comrades and sometimes the king himself also sang of their own adventures.

Virtually all written literature of the Anglo-Saxon period dates from Christian times. Anglo-Saxon literature, however, is far from uniformly Christian. The oral tradition, reflecting essentially pagan values, endured for many centuries. Heroic epics such as *Beowulf* eventually were synthesized and recorded by unknown Christian writers, yet they celebrate the traditional Anglo-Saxon virtues of loyalty, courage, and strength and the heroic adventures of early Germanic warriors.

Beowulf represents the most familiar of the Anglo-Saxon poetic forms, the heroic epic. Another form, the elegiac lyric, also recalls the glories of the past. "The Seafarer" is one of the few surviving Anglo-Saxon poems of this type. Also among the remnants of Anglo-Saxon literature are riddles, a kind of folklore that exhibits a delight in sound, rhythm, and imagination.

The poems of monks such as Caedmon and Cynewulf deal with themes and subjects from the Bible and Church tradition, yet they are distinctly Germanic in their fascination with the sea and with heroic deeds. Written in Old English, these poems are similar in imagery, rhythm, and spirit to the literature derived from Anglo-Saxon oral tradition.

Prose developed much later than poetry. The *Anglo-Saxon Chronicle*, initiated in the ninth century by King Alfred, and the Old English translation of Bede's *History* are classic examples of Anglo-Saxon prose style. Much of this early prose is a somewhat dull recital of events, year by year, but it is still an invaluable source of information to the historian. Of more interest to the general reader are the writings of Aelfric, many of whose sermons and translations were commissioned by church leaders as a means of teaching Christianity and moral values to the monks. *A Colloquy* provides a unique view of ordinary Anglo-Saxon working people, unlike the aristocratic subjects of traditional Anglo-Saxon poetry.

Literature

- Caedmon composes hymn telling glory of creation
- Poet Cynewulf writes Old English poems

400   500   600

History

- Britain becomes province of Roman Church after Synod of Whitby
- Muhammad organizes commonwealth of Islam
- Muhammad dies
- Germanic tribes begin conquest of Britain
- German barbarians sack Rome, ending Roman rule in Britain
- St. Augustine arrives in Britain as first Christian missionary

SUTTON HOO: AN ARCHAEOLOGICAL TREASURE

The Prologue to *Beowulf* describes "... jeweled helmets,/ Hooked swords and ... armor/carried from the ends of the earth. . . ." These precious ornaments adorn Shild's funeral vessel, a ring-prowed fighting ship that is put out to sea with its "motionless cargo," the body of the king.

When British archaeologists uncovered an ancient burial mound at Sutton Hoo in 1939, they found such a ship, dating from the mid-seventh century A.D., about a century before the composition of *Beowulf*. The ship measures eighty-six feet long and fourteen feet in the beam. Some six feet longer than any of the later Viking ships yet discovered, it is a large, open, sea-going vessel propelled by thirty-eight oarsmen and steered by a large paddle over the stern.

The burial mound includes objects of the highest quality: magnificent shields, helmets, buckles, and drinking horns, exquisitely decorated purses inlaid with jewels, and many varieties of gold and silver coins. These ornamental "grave goods" might represent things that the dead king would need in his future life, or they might symbolize the nobility of his social position while he lived. The treasures unearthed at Sutton Hoo are the most valuable antiquities of the Anglo-Saxon period ever dug from British soil.

- The *Exeter Book*, containing "The Seafarer," copied

- Christian poet composes *Beowulf*

- Bede's *History* is translated into Old English

- Bede completes *Ecclesiastical History of the English People* in Latin

- Alfred the Great (849–899) translates Pope Gregory's *History of the World* and Boethius's *Consolation of Philosophy*

- *Anglo-Saxon Chronicles* begin to be recorded

| | 800 | 900 | 1000 |

- Danes first invade Britain, beginning century of raids

- Moslems conquer Spain

- Alfred defeats Danes, ending century of violence

- Norsemen under Leif Ericson land in North America

- Alfred becomes King of Britain

- Vikings invade Britain

- Pope crowns Charlemagne Emperor of the West in Rome

The Development of the English Language

OLD ENGLISH

English is the only truly global language, the mother tongue of more than three hundred million people and the native language of countries that cover one-fifth of the globe. Although Mandarin, the main language of China, is spoken by more people, English is in many ways the dominant medium of communication of the twentieth century. It is the language of international airline pilots, the most frequently studied second language, and the leading language of trade and diplomacy. The vocabulary of English is truly international, for it has incorporated extensive borrowings from other languages.

The Indo-European Base for English

About three-thousand languages are in use today, some spoken by millions of people, others spoken only by a few thousand. English can be traced back to Indo-European, the most prevalent prehistoric language. The name Indo-European suggests the geographic range of this language family, which eventually spread east to India and throughout Europe. Scholars theorize that the Indo-Europeans spoke a single language throughout the New Stone Age but that migrations broke up the unity by the time of the Bronze Age, about 3000 B.C. The distinct languages that evolved gradually from Indo-European included Latin, Greek, and the Germanic languages of Northern Europe.

The Germanic Roots of English

The original inhabitants of Britain spoke a Celtic language, which was a derivative of Indo-European. Between the first and fourth centuries, during Roman rule of the island, the common people spoke Celtic, while the imperial ruling class spoke Latin. When the Roman legions withdrew in the fifth century, Germanic tribes from the continent invaded, bringing a new language, which supplanted the language of the Celts. Domination by these Germanic tribes was complete, and very few Celtic words were absorbed into the language of the conquerors. The tribes, called Angles, Saxons, and Jutes, spoke a Germanic dialect derived from Indo-European; this dialect became the basis for English. The most powerful tribe, the Angles, gave its name to the language, "Angleish," or English.

Old English in Perspective

The language spoken in England from the beginning of the Germanic invasions in 449 until the Norman Conquest in 1066 is commonly called Old English. It is distinguished from Middle English, which was used from about 1066 until about 1485, and Modern English, which has developed since. These divisions are approximate signposts, for language evolves as constantly as a river flows. Old English is entirely different from Modern English and cannot be understood without considerable study, but similarities are discernible. For example, in Modern English, Mark 12:1 reads, "A certain man planted a vineyard," and in Old English, "Sum monn him plantode wingeard."

The Germanic Heritage

Old English was a remarkably pure Germanic tongue in the early centuries. For the most part, the Angol-Saxons stubbornly resisted a foreign word when a term existed in their own language, and they formed new words by compounding rather than by borrowing. Old English was also strongly Germanic in grammar. As in modern German, words had inflectional endings. Word order was flexible, for the ending of a word, rather than its placement in a sentence, described its grammatical relation to other words. The following literal translation of the Lord's Prayer demonstrates the Germanic traits of Old English:

Fæder ūre, þū þe eart on heofonum, si þīn nama gahalgod.
(Father our, thou that art on heavens, be thy name hallowed.)
Tōbecume þīn rīce.
(Become thy rich.)
Gewurþe ðīn willa on eorðan swā swā on heofonum.
(Worth thy will on earth so so on heavens.)

The Scandinavian Influence

When the Danes invaded the country in the eighth and ninth centuries the purity of Old English came under assault. Because the Scandinavian tribes were related to the Anglo-Saxons ethnically and linguistically, no fundamental change occurred. However, many new words from the Old Norse language of the Danes, such as *egg*, *dirt*, *sky*, *wrong*, *low*, *take*, *window*, and *get*, were assimilated, along with crucial pronouns such as *they*, *their*, and *them*. While the Scandinavian influence was extensive, contributing not only key nouns, verbs, and pronouns but also phrases, word orders, and irregular verb forms, eventually the newcomers were absorbed into the Anglo-Saxon culture.

The Latin Influence

A more significant contribution to English was made by Latin, the language reintroduced by the missionaries who began to arrive in Britain in 597. After the spread of Christianity, the Latin language of the church played a large part in the legal and intellectual life of the time. Scribes who learned Latin used the Latin alphabet to preserve the literature of the Old English vernacular. Earlier, the runic alphabet with its mysterious symbols had been used.

Borrowings from Latin were on a massive scale and included religious words, such as *alter*, *martyr*, *mass*, *priest*, and *angel*, as well as words for education, such as *school*, *grammar*, and *science*. Latin words also were adopted for new items coming into use, as with *sock*, *cap*, and *mat*, as well as for many foods, including *radish*, *beet*, and *pear*.

The Enduring Heritage of Old English

The development of Old English over six centuries was overshadowed by the drastic change that occurred after the Norman Conquest in 1066, when Old English was altered fundamentally and forever. Essentially, though, Old English has not died out, for it still lives at the very heart of the English language, as surely as earlier generations endure in their descendants. Despite changes in pronunciation, Old English words are part of everyday speech. Most of the common, brief words in contemporary English derive directly from Old English; for example, *a*, *the*, *to*, *from*, *out*, *at*, *eye*, *nose*, *cat*, *eat*, *play*, *go*, *house*, *man*, and *woman*. Words related to natural elements and cycles often are rooted in Old English: *morning*, *night*, *rain*, *sun*, *moon*, *year*, *sleep*, *life*, and *death*.

It would be virtually impossible to speak or write in English without using words from Old English. For modern-day speakers of English, language establishes their kinship with Beowulf and Hrothgar, with all the peasants, princes, bards, and scribes who lived and spoke and wrote a millenium and more ago.

RECONSTRUCTED HELMET WITH GOLD ORNAMENT. *Sutton Hoo.*
Courtesy of the Trustees of the British Museum.

from **Beowulf**   *Translated by Burton Raffel*

The epic Beowulf *probably was first recorded in the eighth century by English monks. The heroic deeds recalled in the epic, however, supposedly took place during the third or fourth century, in the area that is now northern Germany, Denmark, and southern Sweden. The heroes of* Beowulf *are Geats and Danes, tribes that shared a common Germanic heritage and a common heroic tradition with the Anglo-Saxon conquerors of Britain. Through the Anglo-Saxons,* Beowulf, *a distinctly Germanic hero, became the great epic hero of the English people.*

Prologue

   Hear me! We've heard of Danish heroes,
Ancient kings and the glory they cut
For themselves, swinging mighty swords!
   How Shild[1] made slaves of soldiers from every
Land, crowds of captives he'd beaten   5
Into terror; he'd traveled to Denmark alone,
An abandoned child, but changed his own fate,
Lived to be rich and much honored. He ruled
Lands on all sides: wherever the sea
Would take them his soldiers sailed, returned   10
With tribute and obedience. There was a brave
King! And he gave them more than his glory,
Conceived a son for the Danes, a new leader
Allowed them by the grace of God. They had lived,
Before his coming, kingless and miserable;   15
Now the Lord of all life, Ruler
Of glory, blessed them with a prince, Beo,[2]
Whose power and fame soon spread through the world.
Shild's strong son was the glory of Denmark;
His father's warriors were wound round his heart   20
With golden rings, bound to their prince
By his father's treasure. So young men build
The future, wisely open-handed in peace,
Protected in war; so warriors earn
Their fame, and wealth is shaped with a sword.   25

---

1. **Shild** (Scyld): a Danish king who had arrived in Denmark as a child alone in a ship loaded with treasures.
2. **Beo** (bā' ō): grandfather of the Danish King, Hrothgar.

When his time was come the old king died,
Still strong but called to the Lord's hands.
His comrades carried him down to the shore,
Bore him as their leader had asked, their lord
And companion, while words could move on his tongue.   30
Shild's reign had been long; he'd ruled them well.
There in the harbor was a ring-prowed fighting
Ship, its timbers icy, waiting,
And there they brought the belovèd body
Of their ring-giving lord, and laid him near   35
The mast. Next to that noble corpse
They heaped up treasures, jeweled helmets,
Hooked swords and coats of mail, armor
Carried from the ends of the earth: no ship
Had ever sailed so brightly fitted,   40
No king sent forth more deeply mourned.
Forced to set him adrift, floating
As far as the tide might run, they refused
To give him less from their hoards of gold
Than those who'd shipped him away, an orphan   45
And a beggar, to cross the waves alone.
High up over his head they flew
His shining banner, then sadly let
The water pull at the ship, watched it
Slowly sliding to where neither rulers   50
Nor heroes nor anyone can say whose hands
Opened to take that motionless cargo.
    Then Beo was king in that Danish castle,
Shild's son ruling as long as his father
And as loved, a famous lord of men.   55
And he in turn gave his people a son,
The great Healfdane,[3] a fierce fighter
Who led the Danes to the end of his long
Life and left them four children,
Three princes to guide them in battle, Hergar   60
And Hrothgar and Halga the Good, and one daughter,
Yrs, who was given to Onela, king
Of the Swedes, and became his wife and their queen.
    Then Hrothgar, taking the throne, led
The Danes to such glory that comrades and kinsmen   65
Swore by his sword, and young men swelled
His armies, and he thought of greatness and resolved
To build a hall that would hold his mighty
Band and reach higher toward Heaven than anything

---

3. **Healfdane** (hā′ alf den ə): half Dane. Apparently Hrothgar's mother was a foreigner.

That had ever been known to the sons of men. 70
And in that hall he'd divide the spoils
Of their victories, to old and young what they'd earned
In battle, but leaving the common pastures
Untouched, and taking no lives. The work
Was ordered, the timbers tied and shaped 75
By the hosts that Hrothgar ruled. It was quickly
Ready, that most beautiful of dwellings, built
As he'd wanted, and then he whose word was obeyed
All over the earth named it Herot.[4]
His boast come true he commanded a banquet, 80
Opened out his treasure-full hands.
That towering place, gabled and huge,
Stood waiting for time to pass, for war
To begin, for flames to leap as high
As the feud that would light them, and for Herot to burn. 85

Grendel

   A powerful monster, living down
In the darkness, growled in pain, impatient
As day after day the music rang
Loud in that hall, the harp's rejoicing
Call and the poet's clear songs, sung 5
Of the ancient beginnings of us all, recalling
The Almighty making the earth, shaping
These beautiful plains marked off by oceans,
Then proudly setting the sun and moon
To glow across the land and light it; 10
The corners of the earth were made lovely with trees
And leaves, made quick with life, with each
Of the nations who now move on its face. And then
As now warriors sang of their pleasure:
So Hrothgar's men lived happy in his hall 15
Till the monster stirred, that demon, that fiend,
Grendel, who haunted the moors,[1] the wild
Marshes, and made his home in a hell
Not hell but earth. He was spawned in that slime,
Conceived by a pair of those monsters born 20

---

4. **Herot** (hā′ ə rot).
  1. **moors:** wasteland.

Of Cain,[2] murderous creatures banished
By God, punished forever for the crime
Of Abel's death. The Almighty drove
Those demons out, and their exile was bitter,
Shut away from men; they split   25
Into a thousand forms of evil—spirits
And fiends, goblins, monsters, giants,
A brood forever opposing the Lord's
Will, and again and again defeated. . . .
    When darkness had dropped, Grendel   30
Went up to Herot, wondering what the warriors
Would do in that hall when their drinking was done.
He found them sprawled in sleep, suspecting
Nothing, their dreams undisturbed. The monster's
Thoughts were as quick as his greed or his claws: 35
He slipped through the door and there in the silence
Snatched up thirty men, smashed them
Unknowing in their beds and ran out with their bodies,
The blood dripping behind him, back
To his lair, delighted with his night's slaughter.   40
    At daybreak, with the sun's first light, they saw
How well he had worked, and in that gray morning
Broke their long feast with tears and laments
For the dead. Hrothgar, their lord, sat joyless
In Herot, a mighty prince mourning   45
The fate of his lost friends and companions,
Knowing by its tracks that some demon had torn
His followers apart. He wept, fearing
The beginning might not be the end. And that night
Grendel came again, so set   50
On murder that no crime could ever be enough,
No savage assault quench his lust
For evil. Then each warrior tried
To escape him, searched for rest in different
Beds, as far from Herot as they could find,   55
Seeing how Grendel hunted when they slept.
Distance was safety; the only survivors
Were those who fled him. Hate had triumphed.
    So Grendel ruled, fought with the righteous,
One against many, and won; so Herot   60
Stood empty, and stayed deserted for years,
Twelve winters of grief for Hrothgar, king
Of the Danes, sorrow heaped at his door

---

2. **Cain:** son of Adam and Eve. According to the Bible story (Genesis 4), he killed his brother
Abel and was cursed by God.

By hell-forged hands. His misery leaped
The seas, was told and sung in all 65
Men's ears: how Grendel's hatred began,
How the monster relished his savage war
On the Danes, keeping the bloody feud
Alive, seeking no peace, offering
No truce, accepting no settlement, no price 70
In gold or land, and paying the living
For one crime only with another. No one
Waited for reparation from his plundering claws:
That shadow of death hunted in the darkness,
Stalked Hrothgar's warriors, old 75
And young, lying in waiting, hidden
In mist, invisibly following them from the edge
Of the marsh, always there, unseen.
  So mankind's enemy continued his crimes,
Killing as often as he could, coming 80
Alone, bloodthirsty and horrible. Though he lived
In Herot, when the night hid him, he never
Dared to touch king Hrothgar's glorious
Throne, protected by God—God,
Whose love Grendel could not know. But Hrothgar's 85
Heart was bent. The best and most noble
Of his council debated remedies, sat
In secret sessions, talking of terror
And wondering what the bravest of warriors could do.
And sometimes they sacrificed to the old stone gods, 90
Made heathen vows, hoping for Hell's
Support, the Devil's guidance in driving
Their affliction off. That was their way,
And the heathen's only hope, Hell
Always in their hearts, knowing neither God 95
Nor His passing as He walks through our world, the Lord
Of Heaven and earth; their ears could not hear
His praise nor know His glory. Let them
Beware, those who are thrust into danger,
Clutched at by trouble, yet can carry no solace 100
In their hearts, cannot hope to be better! Hail
To those who will rise to God, drop off
Their dead bodies and seek our Father's peace! . . .

  So the living sorrow of Healfdane's son
Simmered, bitter and fresh, and no wisdom 105
Or strength could break it: that agony hung
On king and people alike, harsh
And unending, violent and cruel, and evil.

In his far-off home Beowulf, Higlac's[3]
Follower and the strongest of the Geats—greater   110
And stronger than anyone anywhere in this world—
Heard how Grendel filled nights with horror
And quickly commanded a boat fitted out,
Proclaiming that he'd go to that famous king,
Would sail across the sea to Hrothgar,   115
Now when help was needed. None
Of the wise ones regretted his going, much
As he was loved by the Geats: the omens were good,
And they urged the adventure on. So Beowulf
Chose the mightiest men he could find,   120
The bravest and best of the Geats, fourteen
In all, and led them down to their boat;
He knew the sea, would point the prow
Straight to that distant Danish shore.

Beowulf

   Reaching the rock-steep cliffs of the Danish shore, Beowulf and his men are
escorted to Herot, where Beowulf greets the great lord of the Danes.

            "Hail, Hrothgar!
Higlac is my cousin and my king; the days
Of my youth have been filled with glory. Now Grendel's
Name has echoed in our land: sailors
Have brought us stories of Herot, the best   5
Of all mead-halls,[1] deserted and useless when the moon
Hangs in skies the sun had lit,
Light and life fleeing together.
My people have said, the wisest, most knowing
And best of them, that my duty was to go to the Danes'   10
Great king. They have seen my strength for themselves,
Have watched me rise from the darkness of war,
Dripping with my enemies' blood. I drove
Five great giants into chains, chased

---

3. **Higlac** (hĭg' ə lăk): king of the Geats (gā' ats). The Geats were a Scandinavian tribe living
on a Danish island and in Sweden.
  1. **mead-hall:** The metaphor reflects the idea that the chief purpose of a hall such as Herot
was as a place for men to feast in.

Part II
21 –30

All of that race from the earth. I swam 15
In the blackness of night, hunting monsters
Out of the ocean, and killing them one
By one; death was my errand and the fate
They had earned. Now Grendel and I are called
Together, and I've come. Grant me, then, 20
Lord and protector of this noble place,
A single request! I have come so far,
Oh shelterer of warriors and your people's loved friend,
That this one favor you should not refuse me—
That I, alone and with the help of my men, 25
May purge all evil from this hall. I have heard,
Too, that the monster's scorn of men
Is so great that he needs no weapons and fears none.
Nor will I. My lord Higlac
Might think less of me if I let my sword 30
Go where my feet were afraid to, if I hid
Behind some broad linden shield:[2] my hands
Alone shall fight for me, struggle for life
Against the monster. God must decide
Who will be given to death's cold grip. 35
Grendel's plan, I think, will be
What it has been before, to invade this hall
And gorge his belly with our bodies. If he can,
If he can. And I think, if my time will have come,
There'll be nothing to mourn over, no corpse to prepare 40
For its grave: Grendel will carry our bloody
Flesh to the moors, crunch on our bones
And smear torn scraps of our skin on the walls
Of his den. No, I expect no Danes
Will fret about sewing our shrouds, if he wins. 45
And if death does take me, send the hammered
Mail of my armor to Higlac, return
The inheritance I had from Hrethel, and he
From Wayland. Fate will unwind as it must!" . . .

Then Hrothgar's men gave places to the Geats, 50
Yielded benches to the brave visitors
And led them to the feast. The keeper of the mead
Came carrying out the carved flasks,
And poured that bright sweetness. A poet
Sang, from time to time, in a clear 55
Pure voice. Danes and visiting Geats
Celebrated as one, drank and rejoiced. . . .

---

2. **linden shield:** Linden is the wood of a lime tree.

Then Hrothgar left that hall, the Danes'
Great protector, followed by his court; the queen
Had preceded him and he went to lie at her side,   60
Seek sleep near his wife. It was said that God
Himself had set a sentinel in Herot,
Brought Beowulf as a guard against Grendel and a shield
Behind whom the king could safely rest.
And Beowulf was ready, firm with our Lord's   65
High favor and his own bold courage and strength.
   He stripped off his mail shirt, his helmet, his sword
Hammered from the hardest iron, and handed
All his weapons and armor to a servant,
Ordered his war-gear guarded till morning.   70
And then, standing beside his bed,
He exclaimed:
              "Grendel is no braver, no stronger
Than I am! I could kill him with my sword; I shall not,
Easy as it would be. This fiend is a bold   75
And famous fighter, but his claws and teeth
Scratching at my shield, his clumsy fists
Beating at my sword blade, would be helpless. I will meet him
With my hands empty—unless his heart
Fails him, seeing a soldier waiting   80
Weaponless, unafraid. Let God in His wisdom
Extend His hand where He wills, reward
Whom He chooses!"
              Then the Geats' great chief dropped
His head to his pillow, and around him, as ready   85
As they could be, lay the soldiers who had crossed the sea
At his side, each of them sure that he was lost
To the home he loved, to the high-walled towns
And the friends he had left behind where both he
And they had been raised. Each thought of the Danes   90
Murdered by Grendel in a hall where Geats
And not Danes now slept. But God's dread-loom
Was woven with defeat for the monster, good fortune
For the Geats; help against Grendel was with them,
And through the might of a single man   95
They would win. Who doubts that God in His wisdom
And strength holds the earth forever
In His hands? Out in the darkness the monster
Began to walk. The warriors slept
In that gabled hall where they hoped that He   100
Would keep them safe from evil, guard them
From death till the end of their days was determined

And the thread should be broken. But Beowulf lay wakeful,
Watching, waiting, eager to meet
His enemy, and angry at the thought of his coming.   105

The Battle with Grendel

   Out from the marsh, from the foot of misty
Hills and bogs, bearing God's hatred,
Grendel came, hoping to kill
Anyone he could trap on this trip to high Herot.
He moved quickly through the cloudy night,   5
Up from his swampland, sliding silently
Toward that gold-shining hall. He had visited Hrothgar's
Home before, knew the way—
But never, before nor after that night,
Found Herot defended so firmly, his reception   10
So harsh. He journeyed, forever joyless,
Straight to the door, then snapped it open,
Tore its iron fasteners with a touch
And rushed angrily over the threshold.
He strode quickly across the inlaid   15
Floor, snarling and fierce: his eyes
Gleamed in the darkness, burned with a gruesome
Light. Then he stopped, seeing the hall
Crowded with sleeping warriors, stuffed
With rows of young soldiers resting together.   20
And his heart laughed, he relished the sight,
Intended to tear the life from those bodies
By morning: the monster's mind was hot
With the thought of food and the feasting his belly
Would soon know. But fate, that night, intended   25
Grendel to gnaw the broken bones
Of his last human supper. Human
Eyes were watching his evil steps,
Waiting to see his swift hard claws.
Grendel snatched at the first Geat   30
He came to, ripped him apart, cut
His body to bits with powerful jaws,
Drank the blood from his veins and bolted
Him down, hands and feet; death
And Grendel's great teeth came together,   35

Snapping life shut. Then he stepped to another
Still body, clutched at Beowulf with his claws,
Grasped at a strong-hearted wakeful sleeper
—And was instantly seized himself, claws
Bent back as Beowulf leaned up on one arm.   40
   That shepherd of evil, guardian of crime,
Knew at once that nowhere on earth
Had he met a man whose hands were harder;
His mind was flooded with fear—but nothing
Could take his talons and himself from that tight   45
Hard grip. Grendel's one thought was to run
From Beowulf, flee back to his marsh and hide there:
This was a different Herot than the hall he had emptied.
But Higlac's follower remembered his final
Boast and, standing erect, stopped   50
The monster's flight, fastened those claws
In his fists till they cracked, clutched Grendel
Closer. The infamous killer fought
For his freedom, wanting no flesh but retreat,
Desiring nothing but escape; his claws   55
Had been caught, he was trapped. That trip to Herot
Was a miserable journey for the writhing monster!
   The high hall rang, its roof boards swayed,
And Danes shook with terror. Down
The aisles the battle swept, angry   60
And wild. Herot trembled, wonderfully
Built to withstand the blows, the struggling
Great bodies beating at its beautiful walls;
Shaped and fastened with iron, inside
And out, artfully worked, the building   65
Stood firm. Its benches rattled, fell
To the floor, gold-covered boards grating
As Grendel and Beowulf battled across them.
Hrothgar's wise men had fashioned Herot
To stand forever; only fire,   70
They had planned, could shatter what such skill had put
Together, swallow in hot flames such splendor
Of ivory and iron and wood. Suddenly
The sounds changed, the Danes started
In new terror, cowering in their beds as the terrible   75
Screams of the Almighty's enemy sang
In the darkness, the horrible shrieks of pain
And defeat, the tears torn out of Grendel's
Taut throat, hell's captive caught in the arms
Of him who of all the men on earth   80
Was the strongest. . . .

That mighty protector of men
Meant to hold the monster till its life
Leaped out, knowing the fiend was no use
To anyone in Denmark. All of Beowulf's   85
Band had jumped from their beds, ancestral
Swords raised and ready, determined
To protect their prince if they could. Their courage
Was great but all wasted: they could hack at Grendel
From every side, trying to open   90
A path for his evil soul, but their points
Could not hurt him, the sharpest and hardest iron
Could not scratch at his skin, for that sin-stained demon
Had bewitched all men's weapons, laid spells
That blunted every mortal man's blade.   95
And yet his time had come, his days
Were over, his death near; down
To hell he would go, swept groaning and helpless
To the waiting hands of still worse fiends.
Now he discovered—once the afflictor   100
Of men, tormentor of their days—what it meant
To feud with Almighty God: Grendel
Saw that his strength was deserting him, his claws
Bound fast, Higlac's brave follower tearing at
His hands. The monster's hatred rose higher,   105
But his power had gone. He twisted in pain,
And the bleeding sinews deep in his shoulder
Snapped, muscle and bone split
And broke. The battle was over, Beowulf
Had been granted new glory: Grendel escaped,   110
But wounded as he was could flee to his den,
His miserable hole at the bottom of the marsh,
Only to die, to wait for the end
Of all his days. And after that bloody
Combat the Danes laughed with delight.   115
He who had come to them from across the sea,
Bold and strong-minded, had driven affliction
Off, purged Herot clean. He was happy,
Now, with that night's fierce work; the Danes
Had been served as he'd boasted he'd serve them; Beowulf,   120
A prince of the Geats, had killed Grendel,
Ended the grief, the sorrow, the suffering
Forced on Hrothgar's helpless people
By a bloodthirsty fiend. No Dane doubted
The victory, for the proof, hanging high   125
From the rafters where Beowulf had hung it, was the monster's
Arm, claw and shoulder and all. . . .

And then, in the morning, crowds surrounded
Herot, warriors coming to that hall
From faraway lands, princes and leaders 130
Of men hurrying to behold the monster's
Great staggering tracks. They gaped with no sense
Of sorrow, felt no regret for his suffering,
Went tracing his bloody footprints, his beaten
And lonely flight, to the edge of the lake 135
Where he'd dragged his corpselike way, doomed
And already weary of his vanishing life.
The water was bloody, steaming and boiling
In horrible pounding waves, heat
Sucked from his magic veins; but the swirling 140
Surf had covered his death, hidden
Deep in murky darkness his miserable
End, as hell opened to receive him.
    Then old and young rejoiced, turned back
From that happy pilgrimage, mounted their hardhooved 145
Horses, high-spirited stallions, and rode them
Slowly toward Herot again, retelling
Beowulf's bravery as they jogged along.
And over and over they swore that nowhere
On earth or under the spreading sky 150
Or between the seas, neither south nor north,
Was there a warrior worthier to rule over men.

Getting at Meaning

PROLOGUE

1. Who is Shild? What kind of person is he? Support your conclusions with evidence from the selection.

2. Describe Shild's burial. What do the burial rituals suggest about the cultural values of the Danes?

3. Trace the genealogy from Shild to Hrothgar. What seems to be Hrothgar's major talent?

GRENDEL

4. What contrast is established in the "poet's song" that begins this section? What is the effect of this contrast?

5. How is the existence of Grendel explained?

6. Describe Grendel's assaults on Herot. How long do they last? What is their result?

7. "The bloody feud" refers to the war between Grendel and the Danes and also indirectly to an ancient war between good and evil. If Grendel is evil, what evidence suggests that Hrothgar is on the side of "good"?

BEOWULF

8. What are your first impressions of Beowulf, based on his opening address to Hrothgar?

9. What are the conditions under which Beowulf will fight Grendel?

10. In what sense is Beowulf proud? In what sense is he humble?

THE BATTLE WITH GRENDEL

11. In which lines is the reader told who is going to win the battle? What words and phrases create an ominous atmosphere at the beginning of this section?

12. What evidence in this section supports the conclusion that ". . . of all the men on earth/ [Beowulf] Was the strongest?"

Grendel's Mother

Beowulf's fame grows, and as the years pass, the Danes become dangerously
complacent. Although one monster has died, another still lives.
Grendel's mother, living in a murky cold lake, has brooded on her loss
until, finally, she emerges from her den bent on revenge.

. . . So she reached Herot,
Where the Danes slept as though already dead;
Her visit ended their good fortune, reversed
The bright vane of their luck. No female, no matter
How fierce, could have come with a man's strength,   5
Fought with the power and courage men fight with,
Smashing their shining swords, their bloody,
Hammer-forged blades onto boar-headed helmets,
Slashing and stabbing with the sharpest of points.
The soldiers raised their shields and drew   10
Those gleaming swords, swung them above
The piled-up benches, leaving their mail shirts
And their helmets where they'd lain when the terror took hold
    of them.
To save her life she moved still faster,
Took a single victim and fled from the hall,   15
Running to the moors, discovered, but her supper
Assured, sheltered in her dripping claws.
She'd taken Hrothgar's closest friend,
The man he most loved of all men on earth;
She'd killed a glorious soldier, cut   20
A noble life short. No Geat could have stopped her:
Beowulf and his band had been given better
Beds; sleep had come to them in a different
Hall. Then all Herot burst into shouts:
She had carried off Grendel's claw. Sorrow   25
Had returned to Denmark. They'd traded deaths,
Danes and monsters, and no one had won,
Both had lost!
        The wise old king
Trembled in anger and grief, his dearest   30
Friend and adviser dead. Beowulf
Was sent for at once: a messenger went swiftly
To his rooms and brought him. He came, his band
About him, as dawn was breaking through,
The best of all warriors, walking to where Hrothgar   35
Sat waiting, the gray-haired king wondering
If God would ever end this misery.

Part 3
31-40

The Geats tramped quickly through the hall; their steps
Beat and echoed in the silence. Beowulf
Rehearsed the words he would want with Hrothgar;   40
He'd ask the Danes' great lord if all
Were at peace, if the night had passed quietly.
                    Beowulf spoke:
  "Let your sorrow end! It is better for us all
To avenge our friends, not mourn them forever.   45
Each of us will come to the end of this life
On earth; he who can earn it should fight
For the glory of his name; fame after death
Is the noblest of goals. Arise, guardian
Of this kingdom, let us go, as quickly as we can,   50
And have a look at this lady monster.
I promise you this: she'll find no shelter,
No hole in the ground, no towering tree,
No deep bottom of a lake, where her sins can hide.
Be patient for one more day of misery;   55
I ask for no longer."
               The old king leaped
To his feet, gave thanks to God for such words.
Then Hrothgar's horse was brought, saddled
And bridled. The Danes' wise ruler rode,   60
Stately and splendid; shield-bearing soldiers
Marched at his side. The monster's tracks
Led them through the forest; they followed her heavy
Feet, that had swept straight across
The shadowy waste land, her burden the lifeless   65
Body of the best of Hrothgar's men.
The trail took them up towering, rocky
Hills, and over narrow, winding
Paths they had never seen, down steep
And slippery cliffs where creatures from deep   70
In the earth hid in their holes. Hrothgar
Rode in front, with a few of his most knowing
Men, to find their way. Then suddenly,
Where clumps of trees bent across
Cold gray stones, they came to a dismal   75
Wood; below them was the lake, its water
Bloody and bubbling. And the Danes shivered, . . .
  They could see the water crawling with snakes,
Fantastic serpents swimming in the boiling
Lake, and sea beasts lying on the rocks   80
—The kind that infest the ocean, in the early
Dawn, often ending some ship's
Journey with their wild jaws. They rushed

Angrily out of sight, when the battle horns blew.
Beowulf aimed an arrow at one   85
Of the beasts, swimming sluggishly away,
And the point pierced its hide, stabbed
To its heart; its life leaked out, death
Swept it off. Quickly, before
The dying monster could escape, they hooked   90
Its thrashing body with their curved boar-spears,
Fought it to land, drew it up on the bluff,
Then stood and stared at the incredible waveroamer,
Covered with strange scales and horrible. Then Beowulf
Began to fasten on his armor,   95
Not afraid for his life but knowing the woven
Mail, with its hammered links, could save
That life when he lowered himself into the lake,
Keep slimy monsters' claws from snatching at
His heart, preserve him for the battle he was sent   100
To fight. Hrothgar's helmet would defend him;
That ancient, shining treasure, encircled
With hard-rolled metal, set there by some smith's
Long dead hand, would block all battle
Swords, stop all blades from cutting at him   105
When he'd swum toward the bottom, gone down in the surging
Water, deep toward the swirling sands.
And Unferth[1] helped him, Hrothgar's courtier
Lent him a famous weapon, a fine,
Hilted old sword named Hrunting; it had   110
An iron blade, etched and shining
And hardened in blood. No one who'd worn it
Into battle, swung it in dangerous places,
Daring and brave, had ever been deserted—
Nor was Beowulf's journey the first time it was taken   115
To an enemy's camp, or asked to support
Some hero's courage and win him glory.
Unferth had tried to forget his greeting
To Beowulf, his drunken speech of welcome;
A mighty warrior, he lent his weapon   120
To a better one. Only Beowulf would risk
His life in that lake; Unferth was afraid,
Gave up that chance to work wonders, win glory
And a hero's fame. But Beowulf and fear
Were strangers; he stood ready to dive into battle. . . .   125
    Then Edgetho's[2] brave son spoke:

---

1. **Unferth** (un' fãrth).
2. **Edgetho:** Beowulf's father.

"Remember,
Hrothgar, Oh knowing king, now
When my danger is near, the warm words we uttered,
And if your enemy should end my life   130
Then be, oh generous prince, forever
The father and protector of all whom I leave
Behind me, here in your hands, my belovèd
Comrades left with no leader, their leader
Dead. And the precious gifts you gave me,   135
My friend, send them to Higlac. May he see
In their golden brightness, the Geats' great lord
Gazing at your treasure, that here in Denmark
I found a noble protector, a giver
Of rings whose rewards I won and briefly   140
Relished. And you, Unferth, let
My famous old sword stay in your hands:
I shall shape glory with Hrunting, or death
Will hurry me from this earth!"
                          As his words ended   145
He leaped into the lake, would not wait for anyone's
Answer; the heaving water covered him
Over. For hours he sank through the waves;
At last he saw the mud of the bottom.
And all at once the greedy she-wolf   150
Who'd ruled those waters for half a hundred
Years discovered him, saw that a creature
From above had come to explore the bottom
Of her wet world. She welcomed him in her claws,
Clutched at him savagely but could not harm him,   155
Tried to work her fingers through the tight
Ring-woven mail on his breast, but tore
And scratched in vain. Then she carried him, armor
And sword and all, to her home; he struggled
To free his weapon, and failed. The fight   160
Brought other monsters swimming to see
Her catch, a host of sea beasts who beat at
His mail shirt, stabbing with tusks and teeth
As they followed along. Then he realized, suddenly,
That she'd brought him into someone's battle-hall,   165
And there the water's heat could not hurt him,
Nor anything in the lake attack him through
The building's high-arching roof. A brilliant
Light burned all around him, the lake
Itself like a fiery flame.   170
                    Then he saw
The mighty water witch, and swung his sword,

His ring-marked blade, straight at her head;
The iron sang its fierce song,
Sang Beowulf's strength. But her guest 175
Discovered that no sword could slice her evil
Skin, that Hrunting could not hurt her, was useless
Now when he needed it. They wrestled, she ripped
And tore and clawed at him, bit holes in his helmet,
And that too failed him; for the first time in years 180
Of being worn to war it would earn no glory;
It was the last time anyone would wear it. But Beowulf
Longed only for fame, leaped back
Into battle. He tossed his sword aside,
Angry; the steel-edged blade lay where 185
He'd dropped it. If weapons were useless he'd use
His hands, the strength in his fingers. So fame
Comes to the men who mean to win it
And care about nothing else! He raised
His arms and seized her by the shoulder; anger 190
Doubled his strength, he threw her to the floor.
She fell, Grendel's fierce mother, and the Geats'
Proud prince was ready to leap on her. But she rose
At once and repaid him with her clutching claws,
Wildly tearing at him. He was weary, that best 195
And strongest of soldiers; his feet stumbled
And in an instant she had him down, held helpless.
Squatting with her weight on his stomach, she drew
A dagger, brown with dried blood, and prepared
To avenge her only son. But he was stretched 200
On his back, and her stabbing blade was blunted
By the woven mail shirt he wore on his chest.
The hammered links held; the point
Could not touch him. He'd have traveled to the bottom of
      the earth,
Edgetho's son, and died there, if that shining 205
Woven metal had not helped—and Holy
God, who sent him victory, gave judgment
For truth and right, Ruler of the Heavens,
Once Beowulf was back on his feet and fighting.
   Then he saw, hanging on the wall, a heavy 210
Sword, hammered by giants, strong
And blessed with their magic, the best of all weapons
But so massive that no ordinary man could lift
Its carved and decorated length. He drew it
From its scabbard, broke the chain on its hilt, 215
And then, savage, now, angry
And desperate, lifted it high over his head

And struck with all the strength he had left,
Caught her in the neck and cut it through,
Broke bones and all. Her body fell   220
To the floor, lifeless, the sword was wet
With her blood, and Beowulf rejoiced at the sight.
    The brilliant light shone, suddenly,
As though burning in that hall, and as bright as Heaven's
Own candle, lit in the sky. He looked   225
At her home, then following along the wall
Went walking, his hands tight on the sword,
His heart still angry. He was hunting another
Dead monster, and took his weapon with him
For final revenge against Grendel's vicious   230
Attacks, his nighttime raids, over
And over, coming to Herot when Hrothgar's
Men slept, killing them in their beds,
Eating some on the spot, fifteen
Or more, and running to his loathsome moor   235
With another such sickening meal waiting
In his pouch. But Beowulf repaid him for those visits,
Found him lying dead in his corner,
Armless, exactly as that fierce fighter
Had sent him out from Herot, then struck off   240
His head with a single swift blow. The body
Jerked for the last time, then lay still.
    The wise old warriors who surrounded Hrothgar,
Like him staring into the monsters' lake,
Saw the waves surging and blood   245
Spurting through. They spoke about Beowulf,
All the graybeards, whispered together
And said that hope was gone, that the hero
Had lost fame and his life at once, and would never
Return to the living, come back as triumphant   250
As he had left; almost all agreed that Grendel's
Mighty mother, the she-wolf, had killed him.
The sun slid over past noon, went further
Down. The Danes gave up, left
The lake and went home, Hrothgar with them.   255
The Geats stayed, sat sadly, watching,
Imagining they saw their lord but not believing
They would ever see him again.
                              —Then the sword
Melted, blood-soaked, dripping down   260
Like water, disappearing like ice when the world's
Eternal Lord loosens invisible
Fetters and unwinds icicles and frost

As only He can, He who rules
Time and seasons, He who is truly   265
God. The monsters' hall was full of
Rich treasures, but all that Beowulf took
Was Grendel's head and the hilt of the giants'
Jeweled sword; the rest of that ring-marked
Blade had dissolved in Grendel's steaming   270
Blood, boiling even after his death.
And then the battle's only survivor
Swam up and away from those silent corpses;
The water was calm and clean, the whole
Huge lake peaceful once the demons who'd lived in it   275
Were dead.
              Then that noble protector of all seamen
Swam to land, rejoicing in the heavy
Burdens he was bringing with him. He
And all his glorious band of Geats   280
Thanked God that their leader had come back unharmed;
They left the lake together. The Geats
Carried Beowulf's helmet, and his mail shirt.
Behind them the water slowly thickened
As the monsters' blood came seeping up.   285
They walked quickly, happily, across
Roads all of them remembered, left
The lake and the cliffs alongside it, brave men
Staggering under the weight of Grendel's skull,
Too heavy for fewer than four of them to handle—   290
Two on each side of the spear jammed through it—
Yet proud of their ugly load and determined
That the Danes, seated in Herot, should see it.
Soon, fourteen Geats arrived
At the hall, bold and warlike, and with Beowulf,   295
Their lord and leader, they walked on the mead-hall
Green. Then the Geats' brave prince entered
Herot, covered with glory for the daring
Battles he had fought; he sought Hrothgar
To salute him and show Grendel's head.   300
He carried that terrible trophy by the hair,
Brought it straight to where the Danes sat,
Drinking, the queen among them. It was a weird
And wonderful sight, and the warriors stared. . . .

   Beowulf spoke: 305
              "Hrothgar! Behold,
Great Healfdane's son, this glorious sign
Of victory, brought you by joyful Geats.

My life was almost lost, fighting for it,
Struggling under water: I'd have been dead at once,   310
And the fight finished, the she-devil victorious,
If our Father in Heaven had not helped me. Hrunting,
Unferth's noble weapon, could do nothing,
Nor could I, until the Ruler of the world
Showed me, hanging shining and beautiful   315
On a wall, a mighty old sword—so God
Gives guidance to those who can find it from no one
Else. I used the weapon He had offered me,
Drew it and, when I could, swung it, killed
The monstrous hag in her own home.   320
Then the ring-marked blade burned away,
As that boiling blood spilled out. I carried
Off all that was left, this hilt.
I've avenged their crimes, and the Danes they've killed.
And I promise you that whoever sleeps in Herot   325
—You, your brave soldiers, anyone
Of all the people in Denmark, old
Or young—they, and you, may now sleep
Without fear of either monster, mother   330
Or son."
         Then he gave the golden sword hilt
To Hrothgar, who held it in his wrinkled hands
And stared at what giants had made, and monsters
Owned; it was his, an ancient weapon
Shaped by wonderful smiths, now that Grendel   335
And his evil mother had been driven from the earth,
God's enemies scattered and dead. That best
Of swords belonged to the best of Denmark's
Rulers, the wisest ring-giver Danish
Warriors had ever known. The old king   340
Bent close to the handle of the ancient relic,
And saw written there the story of ancient wars
Between good and evil, the opening of the waters,
The Flood sweeping giants away, how they suffered
And died, that race who hated the Ruler   345
Of us all and received judgment from His hands,
Surging waves that found them wherever
They fled.[3] And Hrothgar saw runic letters[4]
Clearly carved in that shining hilt,

---

3. **The Flood . . . wherever they fled:** a universal deluge, recorded in the Bible as having
occurred during the days of Noah (Genesis 7). The flood was a sign of God's wrath because of
man's disobedience.
4. **runic letters:** the characters of certain ancient alphabets.

Spelling its original owner's name, 350
He for whom it was made, with its twisted
Handle and snakelike carvings. Then he spoke,
Healfdane's son, and everyone was silent.
  "What I say, speaking from a full memory
And after a life spent in seeking 355
What was right for my people, is this: this prince
Of the Geats, Beowulf, was born a better
Man! Your fame is everywhere, my friend,
Reaches to the ends of the earth, and you hold it in your
        heart wisely,
Patient with your strength and our weakness. What I said
        I will do, I will do, 360
In the name of the friendship we've sworn. Your strength
        must solace your people,
Now, and mine no longer. . . .

The Fire Dragon

    Beowulf becomes King of the Danes and rules in peace and prosperity for fifty
years. A spirit of complacency prevails, until a fierce fire dragon awakens from
its darkness and dreams, striking terror throughout the kingdom.

                           . . . The beast
Had slept in a huge stone tower, with a hidden
Path beneath; a man stumbled on
The entrance, went in, discovered the ancient
Treasure, the pagan jewels and gold 5
The dragon had been guarding, and dazzled and greedy
Stole a gem-studded cup, and fled.
But now the dragon hid nothing, neither
The theft nor itself; it swept through the darkness,
And all Geatland knew its anger. . . . 10
    Vomiting fire and smoke, the dragon
Burned down their homes. They watched in horror
As the flames rose up: the angry monster
Meant to leave nothing alive. And the signs
Of its anger flickered and glowed in the darkness, 15
Visible for miles, tokens of its hate
And its cruelty, spread like a warning to the Geats

Part 3
31-40

Who had broken its rest. Then it hurried back
To its tower, to its hidden treasure, before dawn
Could come. It had wrapped its flames around   20
The Geats; now it trusted in stone
Walls, and its strength, to protect it. But they would not.
   Then they came to Beowulf, their king, and announced
That his hall, his throne, the best of buildings,
Had melted away in the dragon's burning   25
Breath. Their words brought misery, Beowulf's
Sorrow beat at his heart: he accused
Himself of breaking God's law, of bringing
The Almighty's anger down on his people.
Reproach pounded in his breast, gloomy   30
And dark, and the world seemed a different place.
But the hall was gone, the dragon's molten
Breath had licked across it, burned it
To ashes, near the shore it had guarded. The Geats
Deserved revenge; Beowulf, their leader   35
And lord, began to plan it, ordered
A battle-shield shaped of iron, knowing that
Wood would be useless, that no linden shield
Could help him, protect him, in the flaming heat
Of the beast's breath. That noble prince   40
Would end his days on earth, soon,
Would leave this brief life, but would take the dragon
With him, tear it from the heaped-up treasure
It had guarded so long. And he'd go to it alone,
Scorning to lead soldiers against such   45
An enemy: . . . "And now I shall fight
For this treasure, fight with both hand and sword."
   And Beowulf uttered his final boast:
   "I've never known fear; as a youth I fought
In endless battles. I am old, now,   50
But I will fight again, seek fame still,
If the dragon hiding in his tower dares
To face me."
                Then he said farewell to his followers,
Each in his turn, for the last time: 55
   "I'd use no sword, no weapon, if this beast
Could be killed without it, crushed to death
Like Grendel, gripped in my hands and torn
Limb from limb. But his breath will be burning
Hot, poison will pour from his tongue.   60
I feel no shame, with shield and sword
And armor, against this monster: when he comes to me
I mean to stand, not run from his shooting

Flames, stand till fate decides
Which of us wins. My heart is firm,   65
My hands calm: I need no hot
Words. Wait for me close by, my friends.
We shall see, soon, who will survive
This bloody battle, stand when the fighting
Is done. No one else could do   70
What I mean to, here, no man but me
Could hope to defeat this monster. No one
Could try. And this dragon's treasure, his gold
And everything hidden in that tower, will be mine
Or war will sweep me to a bitter death!"   75
   Then Beowulf rose, still brave, still strong,
And with his shield at his side, and a mail shirt on his breast,
Strode calmly, confidently, toward the tower, under
The rocky cliffs: no coward could have walked there!
And then he who'd endured dozens of desperate   80
Battles, who'd stood boldly while swords and shields
Clashed, the best of kings, saw
Huge stone arches and felt the heat
Of the dragon's breath, flooding down
Through the hidden entrance, too hot for anyone   85
To stand, a streaming current of fire
And smoke that blocked all passage. And the Geats'
Lord and leader, angry, lowered
His sword and roared out a battle cry,
A call so loud and clear that it reached through   90
The hoary[1] rock, hung in the dragon's
Ear. The beast rose, angry,
Knowing a man had come—and then nothing
But war could have followed. Its breath came first,
A steaming cloud pouring from the stone,   95
Then the earth itself shook. Beowulf
Swung his shield into place, held it
In front of him, facing the entrance. The dragon
Coiled and uncoiled, its heart urging it
Into battle. Beowulf's ancient sword   100
Was waiting, unsheathed, his sharp and gleaming
Blade. The beast came closer; both of them
Were ready, each set on slaughter. The Geats'
Great prince stood firm, unmoving, prepared
Behind his high shield, waiting in his shining   105
Armor. The monster came quickly toward him,
Pouring out fire and smoke, hurrying

---

1. **hoary** (hō′ rē): gray or white with age.

To its fate. Flames beat at the iron
Shield, and for a time it held, protected
Beowulf as he'd planned; then it began to melt, 110
And for the first time in his life that famous prince
Fought with fate against him, with glory
Denied him. He knew it, but he raised his sword
And struck at the dragon's scaly hide.
The ancient blade broke, bit into 115
The monster's skin, drew blood, but cracked
And failed him before it went deep enough, helped him
Less than he needed. The dragon leaped
With pain, thrashed and beat at him, spouting
Murderous flames, spreading them everywhere. 120
And the Geats' ring-giver did not boast of glorious
Victories in other wars: his weapon
Had failed him, deserted him, now when he needed it
Most, that excellent sword. Edgetho's
Famous son stared at death, 125
Unwilling to leave this world, to exchange it
For a dwelling in some distant place—a journey
Into darkness that all men must make, as death
Ends their few brief hours on earth.
   Quickly, the dragon came at him, encouraged 130
As Beowulf fell back; its breath flared,
And he suffered, wrapped around in swirling
Flames—a king, before, but now
A beaten warrior. None of his comrades
Came to him, helped him, his brave and noble 135
Followers; they ran for their lives, fled
Deep in a wood. And only one of them
Remained, stood there, miserable, remembering,
As a good man must, what kinship should mean.
   His name was Wiglaf,[2] he was Wexstan's son 140
And a good soldier; his family had been Swedish,
Once. Watching Beowulf, he could see
How his king was suffering, burning. . . .
   Then he ran to his king, crying encouragement
As he dove through the dragon's deadly fumes: 145
   "Belovèd Beowulf, remember how you boasted,
Once, that nothing in the world would ever
Destroy your fame: fight to keep it,
Now, be strong and brave, my noble
King, protecting life and fame 150
Together. My sword will fight at your side!"

---

2. **Wiglaf:** Beowulf's "cousin" or near relative.

The dragon heard him, the man-hating monster,
And was angry; shining with surging flames
It came for him, anxious to return his visit.
Waves of fire swept at his shield   155
And the edge began to burn. His mail shirt
Could not help him, but before his hands dropped
The blazing wood Wiglaf jumped
Behind Beowulf's shield; his own was burned
To ashes. Then the famous old hero, remembering   160
Days of glory, lifted what was left
Of Nagling, his ancient sword, and swung it
With all his strength, smashed the gray
Blade into the beast's head. But then Nagling
Broke to pieces, as iron always   165
Had in Beowulf's hands. His arms
Were too strong, the hardest blade could not help him,
The most wonderfully worked. He carried them to war
But fate had decreed that the Geats' great king
Would be no better for any weapon.   170
    Then the monster charged again, vomiting
Fire, wild with pain, rushed out
Fierce and dreadful, its fear forgotten.
Watching for its chance it drove its tusks
Into Beowulf's neck; he staggered, the blood   175
Came flooding forth, fell like rain. . . .

    And then when Beowulf needed him most
Wiglaf showed his courage, his strength
And skill, and the boldness he was born with. Ignoring
The dragon's head, he helped his lord   180
By striking lower down. The sword
Sank in; his hand was burned, but the shining
Blade had done its work, the dragon's
Belching flames began to flicker
And die away. And Beowulf drew   185
His battle-sharp dagger: the blood-stained old king
Still knew what he was doing. Quickly, he cut
The beast in half, slit it apart.
It fell, their courage had killed it, two noble
Cousins had joined in the dragon's death.   190
Yet what they did all men must do
When the time comes! But the triumph was the last
Beowulf would ever earn, the end
Of greatness and life together. The wound
In his neck began to swell and grow;   195
He could feel something stirring, burning

In his veins, a stinging venom, and knew
The beast's fangs had left it. He fumbled
Along the wall, found a slab
Of stone, and dropped down; above him he saw   200
Huge stone arches and heavy posts,
Holding up the roof of that giant hall.
Then Wiglaf's gentle hands bathed
The blood-stained prince, his glorious lord,
Weary of war, and loosened his helmet.   205

The Death of Beowulf

   Beowulf spoke, in spite of the swollen,
Livid wound, knowing he'd unwound
His string of days on earth, seen
As much as God would grant him; all worldly
Pleasure was gone, as life would go,   5
Soon:
     "I'd leave my armor to my son,
Now, if God had given me an heir,
A child born of my body, his life
Created from mine. I've worn this crown   10
For fifty winters: no neighboring people
Have tried to threaten the Geats, sent soldiers
Against us or talked of terror. My days
Have gone by as fate willed, waiting
For its word to be spoken, ruling as well   15
As I knew how, swearing no unholy oaths,
Seeking no lying wars. I can leave
This life happy; I can die, here,
Knowing the Lord of all life has never
Watched me wash my sword in blood   20
Born of my own family. Belovèd
Wiglaf, go, quickly, find
The dragon's treasure: we've taken its life,
But its gold is ours, too.[1] Hurry,
Bring me ancient silver, precious   25
Jewels, shining armor and gems,
Before I die. Death will be softer,

---

1. **". . . its gold is ours, too"**: In Anglo-Saxon times the spoils of war belonged to the
victorious king, who apportioned them among his fighters.

Leaving life and this people I've ruled
So long, if I look at this last of all prizes."

Then Wexstan's son went in, as quickly   30
As he could, did as the dying Beowulf
Asked, entered the inner darkness
Of the tower, went with his mail shirt and his sword.
Flushed with victory he groped his way,
A brave young warrior, and suddenly saw   35
Piles of gleaming gold, precious
Gems, scattered on the floor, cups
And bracelets, rusty old helmets, beautifully
Made but rotting with no hands to rub
And polish them. They lay where the dragon left them;   40
It had flown in the darkness, once, before fighting
Its final battle. (So gold can easily
Triumph, defeat the strongest of men,
No matter how deep it is hidden!) And he saw,
Hanging high above, a golden   45
Banner, woven by the best of weavers
And beautiful. And over everything he saw
A strange light, shining everywhere,
On walls and floor and treasure. Nothing
Moved, no other monsters appeared;   50
He took what he wanted, all the treasures
That pleased his eye, heavy plates
And golden cups and the glorious banner,
Loaded his arms with all they could hold.
Beowulf's dagger, his iron blade,   55
Had finished the fire-spitting terror
That once protected tower and treasures
Alike; the gray-bearded lord of the Geats
Had ended those flying, burning raids
Forever.   60
          Then Wiglaf went back, anxious
To return while Beowulf was alive, to bring him
Treasure they'd won together. He ran,
Hoping his wounded king, weak
And dying, had not left the world too soon.   65
Then he brought their treasure to Beowulf, and found
His famous king bloody, gasping
For breath. But Wiglaf sprinkled water
Over his lord, until the words
Deep in his breast broke through and were heard.   70
Beholding the treasure he spoke, haltingly:
   "For this, this gold, these jewels, I thank

Our Father in Heaven, Ruler of the Earth—
For all of this, that His grace has given me,
Allowed me to bring to my people while breath   75
Still came to my lips. I sold my life
For this treasure, and I sold it well. Take
What I leave, Wiglaf, lead my people,
Help them; my time is gone. Have
The brave Geats build me a tomb,   80
When the funeral flames have burned me, and build it
Here, at the water's edge, high
On this spit of land, so sailors can see
This tower, and remember my name, and call it
Beowulf's tower, and boats in the darkness   85
And mist, crossing the sea, will know it."
      Then that brave king gave the golden
Necklace from around his throat to Wiglaf,
Gave him his gold-covered helmet, and his rings,
And his mail shirt, and ordered him to use them well: 90
      "You're the last of all our far-flung family.
Fate has swept our race away,
Taken warriors in their strength and led them
To the death that was waiting. And now I follow them."
      The old man's mouth was silent, spoke   95
No more, had said as much as it could;
He would sleep in the fire, soon. His soul
Left his flesh, flew to glory. . . .
                  Then the warriors rose,
Walked slowly down from the cliff, stared   100
At those wonderful sights, stood weeping as they saw
Beowulf dead on the sand, their bold
Ring-giver resting in his last bed;
He'd reached the end of his days, their mighty
War-king, the great lord of the Geats,   105
Gone to a glorious death. But they saw
The dragon first, stretched in front
Of its tower, a strange, scaly beast
Gleaming a dozen colors dulled and
Scorched in its own heat. From end   110
To end fifty feet, it had flown
In the silent darkness, a swift traveler
Tasting the air, then gliding down
To its den. Death held it in his hands;
It would guard no caves, no towers, keep   115
No treasures like the cups, the precious plates
Spread where it lay, silver and brass
Encrusted and rotting, eaten away

As though buried in the earth for a thousand winters.
And all this ancient hoard, huge   120
And golden, was wound around with a spell:
No man could enter the tower, open
Hidden doors, unless the Lord
Of Victories, He who watches over men,
Almighty God Himself, was moved   125
To let him enter, and him alone. . . .

   Then the Geats built the tower, as Beowulf
Had asked, strong and tall, so sailors
Could find it from far and wide; working
For ten long days they made his monument,   130
Sealed his ashes in walls as straight
And high as wise and willing hands
Could raise them. And the riches he and Wiglaf
Had won from the dragon, rings, necklaces,
Ancient, hammered armor—all   135
The treasures they'd taken were left there, too,
Silver and jewels buried in the sandy
Ground, back in the earth, again
And forever hidden and useless to men.
And then twelve of the bravest Geats   140
Rode their horses around the tower,
Telling their sorrow, telling stories
Of their dead king and his greatness, his glory,
Praising him for heroic deeds, for a life
As noble as his name. So should all men   145
Raise up words for their lords, warm
With love, when their shield and protector leaves
His body behind, sends his soul
On high. And so Beowulf's followers
Rode, mourning their belovèd leader,   150
Crying that no better king had ever
Lived, no prince so mild, no man
So open to his people, so deserving of praise.

Getting at Meaning

GRENDEL'S MOTHER

1. In what sense have the Danes and the monsters now "traded deaths"?

2. What does Beowulf say about vengeance and fame in this scene? What do his statements indicate about traditional Anglo-Saxon values?

3. Describe Beowulf's battle gear. How does this protection help him in his fight with Grendel's mother? With what weapon does he slay her? What else does he do with the same weaponry?

4. What does Beowulf bring back to the Danes as proof of victory over Grendel's mother?

5. What inscriptions does Hrothgar find on the sword that Beowulf presents to him?

THE FIRE DRAGON

6. Why does the dragon awaken in anger? Why does Beowulf feel that he must have broken God's law? How, then, does he justify the Geats' revenge?

7. How does Beowulf's preparation for battle differ from that preceding his earlier encounters with Grendel and Grendel's mother?

8. How does Beowulf know that fate is not with him in this battle?

9. In what ways does Wiglaf come to Beowulf's aid? Why does he help the old king? How does the dragon die?

THE DEATH OF BEOWULF

10. What does Beowulf wish to see before his death? What is the implication of the comment, ". . . gold can easily/Triumph, defeat the strongest of men"?

11. What is your impression of Beowulf at his death? In what ways is his attitude toward death an honorable one?

12. How does the tower, built in memory of Beowulf, reflect a traditional orientation to the sea?

Developing Skills in Reading Literature

1. **Epic.** *Beowulf* is an epic, a long narrative poem that describes heroic deeds in a formal, "ceremonial" style. Like all narrative poems, an epic tells a story, generally in chronological order.

All epics share common characteristics. First, the hero, the main character, is of noble birth or at least of high social position. Often the hero is a prominent historical or legendary figure. Second, the setting is vast, involving entire races, the world, or the universe. Third, the action consists of deeds requiring great courage and valor. Sometimes supernatural forces— gods or demons—help or hinder the actions of the hero, who might also possess superhuman capabilities.

In addition, a few structural characteristics are common to most epics. Often, the speaker begins by stating a theme, a controlling idea or message, or by invoking a Muse, or higher power, for inspiration. Then the narrative begins, usually without any presentation of background information. The reader or listener is plunged immediately into the midst of a crisis. Epics frequently include long formal speeches and "catalogs," or lists, describing warriors, battles, or objects, such as Shild's burial ship.

Explain how *Beowulf* exemplifies the characteristics of an epic, citing specific examples from the text whenever possible.

2. **Speaker.** In poetry, the speaker is the voice that "talks" to the reader or listener. Speaker and poet are not necessarily synonymous, although a poet may choose to speak in his or her own voice. A poet also may create a separate voice, or persona; for example, a poet may write a poem as if it were spoken by an element of nature such as the wind or a river.

The speaker in this epic is a Christian working with essentially pagan material. What evidence in the epic suggests a Christian perspective? Cite several specific examples. How do you explain the presence of Christian values and teachings in a traditional Germanic epic?

3. **Hero and Tragic Hero.** The term *hero* commonly refers to the main character, masculine or feminine, in a work of fiction or drama. A traditional hero possesses "good" qualities that enable him or her to triumph over a villain who is "bad."

The term *tragic hero* was first used by the Greek philosopher Aristotle in his *Poetics*. This term refers to a central character who is dignified or noble in some way; however, because of a character defect called a tragic flaw, the character makes a fatal error in judgment that brings about his or her own downfall. Often, tragic flaws are admirable qualities carried to excess. For example, confidence might become selfish pride; self-assurance might turn into arrogance. According to Aristotle, tragic heroes perceive, before their downfall, how they have contributed to their own destruction.

List the qualities and the actions that make Beowulf a hero. Is he a tragic hero, according to Aristotle's definition? Be prepared to explain your answer.

4. **Stereotype.** A stereotype, or stock character, is a simplified character who represents a certain clearly recognizable type of person; for example, a typical hero or villain. In what ways is Beowulf a stereotypical hero? In what ways are Grendel, Grendel's mother, and the dragon stereotypical villains? How does Beowulf depart from the hero stereotype? How are the monsters atypical villains?

5. **Anglo-Saxon Poetry: Kenning.** A kenning is a miniature riddle, an implied comparison usually with two parts and often hyphenated. For example, God's "dread-loom" means God's plan. The comparison between planning and weaving and the awe inspired by the plan are communicated in the hyphenated compound "dread-loom." Explain what each of these kennings might mean:

shepherd of evil (The Battle with Grendel, line 41)
waveroamer (Grendel's Mother, line 93)
water witch (Grendel's Mother, line 172)
Heaven's/Own candle (Grendel's Mother, lines 224–25)
ring-giver (Grendel's Mother, line 339)

What do these kennings suggest about Anglo-Saxon society?

6. **Anglo-Saxon Poetry: Sound Patterns.** Anglo-Saxon poetry has a strong rhythm, or cadence, that makes it easily chanted or sung. Unity is achieved by means of alliteration, the repetition of consonant sounds at the beginnings of words. Lines are divided into two parts by a caesura, or pause, with each part having two accented syllables. In Old English, a caesura is indicated visually by a space between the

two parts of a line. Usually, an accented syllable in the first part alliterates with one or both accented syllables in the second part; for example:

Out from the *m*arsh, ‖ from the foot of *m*isty
Hills and *b*ogs, ‖ *b*earing God's hatred,
Grendel came, ‖ hoping to *k*ill
Anyone he could *tr*ap ‖ on this *tr*ip to high Herot.

Choose a block of four other lines from the text and analyze their rhythm and alliterative pattern.

7. **Theme.** On a symbolic level, the great conflict in *Beowulf* is between good and evil, with Beowulf the representative of good and the monsters the representatives of evil. What qualities of Beowulf are "good" qualities? What qualities of the monsters are "evil" qualities? What consequences does Beowulf experience as a result of his battles with the monsters? Is the "good" represented by Beowulf totally triumphant? What, then, does the epic imply about the distinctions between good and evil? About the struggle between these opposing forces?

Developing Vocabulary

Inferring Word Meaning. Using context clues, write an appropriate definition for each italicized word in the following sentences. Refer to the text of *Beowulf* if necessary to examine the broader context of each word. Check your definitions against those in a dictionary.

1. ". . . [they]/Broke their long feast with tears and *laments*/For the dead." (Grendel, lines 43–44)
2. "Let them/Beware, those who are thrust into danger . . . yet can carry no *solace*/In their hearts. . . ." (Grendel, lines 98–101)
3. ". . . I expect no Danes/Will fret about sewing our *shrouds*, if he wins." (Beowulf, lines 44–45)
4. ". . . the Danes started/In new terror, *cowering* in their beds. . . ." (The Battle with Grendel, lines 74–75)
5. "[Beowulf] had driven affliction/Off, *purged* Herot clean." (The Battle with Grendel, lines 117–18)
6. "He drew it [the sword]/From its *scabbard*, broke the chain on its *hilt*. . . ." (Grendel's Mother, lines 214–15)

7. "*Reproach* pounded in his breast, gloomy/And dark. . . ." (The Fire Dragon, lines 30–31)

8. "Beowulf spoke, in spite of the swollen,/*Livid* wound. . . ." (The Death of Beowulf, lines 1–2)

Developing Writing Skills

1. **Using Comparisons and Contrasts.** Beowulf is the ideal Anglo-Saxon hero. He is strong, fearless, bold, loyal, and stoic in his acceptance of fate. In a well developed composition, compare and contrast Beowulf's qualities with those of a twentieth-century hero such as John F. Kennedy or Dr. Martin Luther King, Jr. In your conclusion, comment on how the qualities of each hero reflect the values of his or her society.

2. **Analyzing Characters.** Beowulf possesses many of the same qualities as contemporary superheroes such as Superman. Grendel, on the other hand, shares the characteristics of "supervillains" such as Darth Vadar. In a brief composition, identify the qualities that either Beowulf or Grendel has in common with several superheroes or supervillains. Note human as well as superhuman characteristics and weaknesses as well as strengths. Conclude by generalizing about the concept of "superhero" or "supervillain" in Anglo-Saxon and contemporary society.

A shoulder clasp. *Sutton Hoo.*
Courtesy, The British Museum.

from **Grendel** *John Gardner*

The novel Grendel, *written in the twentieth century, sheds new light on stereotyped roles and attitudes in* Beowulf. *This chapter from the novel begins as Grendel enters the great meadhall where he will have his fatal confrontation with the Germanic hero.*

I touch the door with my fingertips and it bursts, for all its fire-forged[1] bands—it jumps away like a terrified deer—and I plunge into the silent, hearth-lit hall with a laugh that I wouldn't much care to wake up to myself. I trample the planks that a moment before protected the hall like a hand raised in horror to a terrified mouth (sheer poetry, ah!) and the broken hinges rattle like swords down the timbered walls. The Geats are stones, and whether it's because they're numb with terror or stiff from too much mead, I cannot tell. I am swollen with excitement, bloodlust, and joy and a strange fear that mingle in my chest like the twisting rage of a bone-fire.[2] I step onto the brightly shining floor and angrily advance on them. They're all asleep, the whole company! I can hardly believe my luck, and my wild heart laughs, but I let out no sound. Swiftly, softly, I will move from bed to bed and destroy them all, swallow every last man. I am blazing, half-crazy with joy. For pure, mad prank, I snatch a cloth from the nearest table and tie it around my neck to make a napkin. I delay no longer. I seize up a sleeping man, tear at him hungrily, bite through his bone-locks[3] and suck hot, slippery blood. He goes down in huge morsels, head, chest, hips, legs, even the hands and feet. My face and arms are wet, matted. The napkin is sopping. The dark floor steams. I move on at once and I reach for another one (whispering, whispering, chewing the universe down to words), and I seize a wrist. A shock goes through me. Mistake!

It's a trick! His eyes are open, were open all the time, cold-bloodedly watching to see how I work. The eyes nail me now as his hand nails down my arm. I jump back without thinking (whispering wildly: *jump back without thinking*). Now he's out of his bed, his hand still closed like a dragon's jaws on mine. Nowhere on middle-earth,[4] I realize, have I encountered a grip like his. My whole arm's on fire, incredible, searing pain—it's as if his crushing fingers are charged like fangs with poison. I scream, facing him, grotesquely shaking hands—dear long-lost brother, kinsman-thane[5]—and the timbered hall screams back at me. I feel the bones go, ground from their sockets, and I scream again. I am suddenly awake. The long pale dream, my history, falls away. The meadhall is alive, great cavernous belly, gold-adorned, bloodstained, howling back at me, lit by the flickering fire in the stranger's eyes. He has wings. Is it possible? And yet it's true: out of his shoulders come terrible fiery wings. I jerk my head, trying to drive out illusion. The world is what it is and always was. That's our hope, our chance. Yet even in times of catastrophe

---

1. **fire-forged:** This and other hyphenated word clusters are examples of kennings, a metaphorical device common to Anglo-Saxon poetry.
2. **bone-fire:** an interesting archaic use of the original form of the word *bonfire.* In this case, it is an ancient place where the bones of sacrificial animals were burned for fuel.
3. **bone-locks:** a "kenning" for the joints of human limbs.
4. **middle-earth:** the human world, halfway between heaven and hell.
5. **thane:** warrior.

we people it with tricks. Grendel, Grendel, hold fast to what is true!

Suddenly, darkness. My sanity has won. He's only a man; I can escape him. I plan. I feel the plan moving inside me like thaw-time waters rising between cliffs. When I'm ready, I give a ferocious kick—but something's wrong: I am spinning—*Wa!*—falling through bottomless space—*Wa!*—snatching at the huge twisted roots of an oak . . . a blinding flash of fire . . . no, darkness. I concentrate. I have fallen! Slipped on blood. He viciously twists my arm behind my back. By accident, it comes to me, I have given him a greater advantage. I could laugh. *Woe, woe!*

And now something worse. He's whispering—spilling words like showers of sleet, his mouth three inches from my ear. I will not listen. I continue whispering. As long as I whisper myself I need not hear. His syllables lick at me, chilly fire. His syllables lick at me, chilly fire. His syllables lick at me, chilly fire. His syllables lick . . .

A meaningless swirl in the stream of time, a temporary gathering of bits, a few random specks, a cloud . . . Complexities: green dust, purple dust, gold. Additional refinements: sensitive dust, copulating dust . . .

The world is my bone-cave, I shall not want[6] . . . (He laughs as he whispers. I roll my eyes back. Flames slip out at the corners of his mouth.) *As you see it it is, while the seeing lasts, dark nightmare-history, time-as-coffin; but where the water was rigid there will be fish, and men will survive on their flesh till spring. It's coming, my brother. Believe it or not. Though you murder the world, turn plains to stone, transmogrify*[7] *life into I and it, strong searching roots will crack your cave and rain will cleanse it: The world will burn green, sperm build again. My promise. Time is the mind, the hand that makes (fingers on harpstrings, hero-swords, the acts, the eyes of queens). By that I kill you.*

I do not listen. I am sick at heart. I have been betrayed before by talk like that.

"Mama!" I bawl. Shapes vague as lurking seaweed surround us. My vision clears. The stranger's companions encircle us, useless swords. I could laugh if it weren't for the pain that makes me howl. And yet I address him, whispering, whimpering, whining.

"If you win, it's by mindless chance. Make no mistake. First you tricked me, and then I slipped. Accident."

He answers with a twist that hurls me forward screaming. The thanes make way. I fall against a table and smash it, and wall timbers crack. And still he whispers.

Grendel, Grendel! You make the world by whispers, second by second. Are you blind to that? Whether you make it a grave or a garden of roses is not the point. Feel the wall: is it not hard? He smashes me against it, breaks open my forehead. *Hard, yes! Observe the hardness, write it down in careful runes. Now sing of walls! Sing!*

I howl.

Sing!

"I'm singing!"

Sing words! Sing raving hymns!

"You're crazy. Ow!"

Sing!

"I sing of walls," I howl. "Hooray for the hardness of walls!"

Terrible, he whispers. *Terrible*. He laughs and lets out fire.

"You're crazy," I say. "If you think I created that wall that cracked my head, you're a lunatic."

Sing walls, he hisses.

I have no choice.

The wall will fall to the wind as
    the windy hill
will fall, and all things thought in
    former times:

---

6. **"The world . . . want"**: a parody of "The Lord is my Shepherd, I shall not want" from Psalm 23. Here "my bone cave" probably means "my source of energy" or possibly "my possession."

7. **transmogrify**: (trans mäg′ rə fi′): to change strangely or grotesquely in appearance or form.

Nothing made remains, nor man
  remembers.
And these towns shall be called
  the shining towns!

Better, he whispers. *That's better.* He
laughs again, and the nasty laugh admits I'm
slyer than he guessed.

He's crazy. I understand him all right, make
no mistake. Understand his lunatic theory of
matter and mind, the chilly intellect, the hot
imagination, blocks and builder, reality as
stress. Nevertheless, it was by accident that
he got my arm behind me. He penetrated no
mysteries. He was lucky. If I'd known he was
awake, if I'd known there was blood on the
floor when I gave him that kick . . .

The room goes suddenly white, as if struck
by lightning. I stare down, amazed. He has
torn off my arm at the shoulder! Blood pours
down where the limb was. I cry, I bawl like a
baby. He stretches his blinding white wings
and breathes out fire. I run for the door and
through it. I move like wind. I stumble and
fall, get up again. I'll die! I howl. The night is
aflame with winged men. *No, no! Think!* I
come suddenly awake once more from the
nightmare. Darkness. I really will die! Every
rock, every tree, every crystal of snow cries
out cold-blooded objectness. Cold, sharp outlines, everything around me: distinct, detached as dead men. I understand. "Mama!" I
bellow. "Mama, Mama! I'm dying!" But her
love is history. His whispering follows me
into the woods, though I've outrun him. "It
was an accident," I bellow back. I will cling to
what is true. "Blind, mindless, mechanical.
Mere logic of chance." I am weak from loss of
blood. No one follows me now. I stumble
again and with my one weak arm I cling to the
huge twisted roots of an oak. I look down past
stars to a terrifying darkness. I seem to recognize the place, but it's impossible. "Accident," I whisper. I will fall. I seem to desire
the fall, and though I fight it with all my will I
know in advance that I can't win. Standing

baffled, quaking with fear, three feet from the
edge of a nightmare cliff, I find myself, incredibly, moving toward it. I look down, down,
into bottomless blackness, feeling the dark
power moving in me like an ocean current,
some monster inside me, deep sea wonder,
dread night monarch astir in his cave, moving
me slowly to my voluntary tumble into death.

Again sight clears. I am slick with blood. I
discover I no longer feel pain. Animals gather
around me, enemies of old, to watch me die. I
give them what I hope will appear a sheepish
smile. My heart booms terror. Will the last of
my life slide out if I let out breath? They
watch with mindless, indifferent eyes, as
calm and midnight black as the chasm below
me.

Is it joy I feel?

They watch on, evil, incredibly stupid, enjoying my destruction.

"Poor Grendel's had an accident," I whisper. *"So may you all."*

Getting at Meaning

1. What is Grendel's impression of himself as he
"plunge(s)" into the meadhall? How do parenthetical
remarks such as "sheer poetry, ah!" emphasize that
impression?

2. Describe Grendel's initial response to Beowulf.
What action of Beowulf disturbs Grendel the most?
Why is this action so threatening?

3. Beginning with *"A meaningless swirl in the
stream of time . . . ,"* most of the italicized text presents Beowulf's thoughts and words. How is his view
of the world essentially different from that of Grendel?

4. What does Grendel mean when he says, "I will
cling to what is true"? What does he think is accidental? How does he feel as he stands on the brink of the
"nightmare cliff"? What is the meaning of his final
words, *"So may you all"*?

5. Describe Grendel as he is portrayed in this
selection. How does the monster here differ from the
Grendel of *Beowulf*?

Developing Skills in Reading Literature

1. **Figurative Language.** Figurative language communicates ideas beyond the literal meanings of the words. Writers use figurative language to strengthen the impact of their ideas, to achieve freshness of expression, and to create pictoral effects. Some figures of speech, or specific kinds of figurative language, illustrate similarities in otherwise dissimilar things.

Following are the definitions of five figures of speech, along with examples drawn from the abundant figurative language in this selection. Be prepared to explain each example.

a. A metaphor is an implied comparison that imaginatively identifies one object or idea with another.
"The meadhall is alive, great cavernous belly. . . ."
"Time is the mind. . . ."

A kenning is a compressed metaphor.
"thaw-time" "time-as-coffin"

b. A simile compares two objects or ideas directly, using *like* or *as*.
"They watch with . . . eyes as calm and midnight black as the chasm below me."

c. Personification is a figure of speech that endows an animal, idea, or other inanimate object with human characteristics.
". . . every crystal of snow cries out cold-blooded objectness."

d. A hyperbole is an exaggeration used to emphasize an idea or to produce a comic effect.
". . . I reach for another one . . . chewing the universe down to words. . . ."

e. Onomatopoeia commonly refers to the use of echoic words such as *hiss* and *buzz* that, in their pronunciations, suggest their specific meanings. A more sophisticated use of the device is made by skilled writers who create effects through the sounds of words and phrases.
". . . I am spinning—*Wa!*—falling through bottomless space—*Wa!* . . ." (echoic word)

". . . chilly fire. His syllables lick at me, chilly fire. His syllables lick. . . ." (sound effect)

Now, find in the selection additional examples of each figure of speech.

2. **Parody.** A parody imitates or burlesques another, usually serious, work or type of literature, often adding a new dimension or depth of insight to the original work. Some parodies are characterized by broad humor and obvious ridicule of the subject. In others the humor is subtle and the mockery secondary to the primary purpose of broadening understanding.

This selection parodies the section of *Beowulf* in which the hero battles Grendel. Identify the similarities in language and sound patterns between the original work and the parody. What other characteristics of the heroic epic does the writer of *Grendel* imitate? How are these characteristics exaggerated? Explain how each of the following differs in the two selections:

Tone, the attitude of the writer toward the subject
Mood, the response of the reader
Treatment of character

How does this account of Grendel's experience change your view of *Beowulf?* What does the writer of *Grendel* suggest about good and evil? truth and falsehood? reality and illusion? What seems to be Gardner's purpose in parodying the epic?

3. **Style.** Style refers to how a selection is written, the distinctive way that a writer expresses ideas. In this selection, the use of parenthetical remarks is a stylistic characteristic. So is the unusual variety in sentence structure. Notice, too, the short exclamatory phrases and single words punctuated as sentences and expletives such as *Wa!* and *Woe!* Explain how each of these elements of style affects the reader.

Developing Vocabulary

Using a Dictionary. The following words, frequently confused, are useful ones to know when talking about literature. Study the sentences in which the words are used. Write a clear definition of each word, consulting a dictionary as necessary. Then write critical and factual statements about this or the preceding selection, using at least three of these words at least once.

1. illusion: Grendel saw an illusion of Beowulf with "terrible fiery wings."

2. allusion: "The world is my bone-cave, I shall not want . . ." is not only a parody but also an allusion to the opening lines of Psalm 23.

3. delusion: Grendel suffered from the delusion that Beowulf was no more powerful than he was.

4. elusive: Grendel's grasp of reality was highly elusive.

Developing Writing Skills

1. **Writing a Parody.** Have you ever read a story or seen a film in which the hero was just a little too heroic to be real, causing your sympathy to shift to the villain? Perhaps that was one of John Gardner's reactions to *Beowulf*. Choose another "classic" such as *Julius Caesar* or a contemporary film such as *Star Wars*. Write a parody of one scene, using some of the same techniques as used by Gardner in *Grendel*. Remember, exaggeration and reversal of roles are key factors in writing an effective parody.

2. **Supporting an Opinion.** Some critics argue that humorous imitations of serious works of literature hinder the reader's ability to appreciate the truth or the beauty of the original. Others say that parodies help the audience to understand and to appreciate the originals even more. Using Gardner's parody of *Beowulf* as an example and your own reactions as a guide, write a well developed paragraph in which you defend one of these points of view.

Reconstructed eagle from a shield. *Sutton Hoo. Courtesy, The British Museum.*

The Seafarer   *Translated by Burton Raffel*

*"The Seafarer," an anonymous poem probably composed early in the eighth
century, was found in the* Exeter Book, *a collection of Anglo-Saxon poetry given
to the Exeter Cathedral in Devonshire during the eleventh century. In this poem
an old sailor recalls the loneliness and hardship of life at sea while also describing
the fascination of the sea.*

This tale is true, and mine. It tells
How the sea took me, swept me back
And forth in sorrow and fear and pain,
Showed me suffering in a hundred ships,
In a thousand ports, and in me. It tells   5
Of smashing surf when I sweated in the cold
Of an anxious watch, perched in the bow
As it dashed under cliffs. My feet were cast
In icy bands, bound with frost,
With frozen chains, and hardship groaned   10
Around my heart. Hunger tore
At my sea-weary soul. No man sheltered
On the quiet fairness of earth can feel
How wretched I was, drifting through winter
On an ice-cold sea, whirled in sorrow,   15
Alone in a world blown clear of love,
Hung with icicles. The hailstorms flew.
The only sound was the roaring sea,
The freezing waves. The song of the swan[1]
Might serve for pleasure, the cry of the sea-fowl,   20
The death-noise of birds instead of laughter,
The mewing of gulls instead of mead.
Storms beat on the rocky cliffs and were echoed
By icy-feathered terns[2] and the eagle's screams;
No kinsman could offer comfort there,   25
To a soul left drowning in desolation.
     And who could believe, knowing but
The passion of cities, swelled proud with wine
And no taste of misfortune, how often, how wearily,
I put myself back on the paths of the sea.   30

---

1. **"song of the swan":** the swan makes sounds or "sings" only at the
moment of death.
2. **tern:** a sea-bird, like a gull.

Night would blacken; it would snow from the north;
Frost bound the earth and hail would fall,
The coldest seeds. And how my heart
Would begin to beat, knowing once more
The salt waves tossing and the towering sea! 35
The time for journeys would come and my soul
Called me eagerly out, sent me over
The horizon, seeking foreigners' homes.
      But there isn't a man on earth so proud,
So born to greatness, so bold with his youth, 40
Grown so brave, or so graced by God,
That he feels no fear as the sails unfurl,
Wondering what Fate has willed and will do.
No harps ring in his heart, no rewards,
No passion for women, no worldly pleasures, 45
Nothing, only the ocean's heave;
But longing wraps itself around him.
Orchards blossom, the towns bloom,
Fields grow lovely as the world springs fresh,
And all these admonish that willing mind 50
Leaping to journeys, always set
In thoughts traveling on a quickening[3] tide.
So summer's sentinel, the cuckoo, sings
In his murmuring voice, and our hearts mourn
As he urges. Who could understand, 55
In ignorant ease, what we others suffer
As the paths of exile stretch endlessly on?
      And yet my heart wanders away,
My soul roams with the sea, the whales'
Home, wandering to the widest corners 60
Of the world, returning ravenous with desire,
Flying solitary, screaming, exciting me
To the open ocean, breaking oaths
On the curve of a wave.
              Thus the joys of God
Are fervent with life, where life itself 65
Fades quickly into the earth. The wealth
Of the world neither reaches to Heaven nor remains.
No man has ever faced the dawn
Certain which of Fate's three threats
Would fall: illness, or age, or an enemy's 70
Sword, snatching the life from his soul.
The praise the living pour on the dead
Flowers from reputation: plant

---

3. **quickening:** life-giving.

An earthly life of profit reaped
Even from hatred and rancor,[4] of bravery   75
Flung in the devil's face, and death
Can only bring you earthly praise
And a song to celebrate a place
With the angels, life eternally blessed
In the hosts of Heaven.
                The days are gone   80
When the kingdoms of earth flourished in glory;
Now there are no rulers, no emperors,
No givers of gold, as once there were,
When wonderful things were worked among them
And they lived in lordly magnificence.   85
Those powers have vanished, those pleasures are dead.
The weakest survives and the world continues,
Kept spinning by toil. All glory is tarnished.
The world's honor ages and shrinks,
Bent like the men who mold it. Their faces   90
Blanch as time advances, their beards
Wither and they mourn the memory of friends.
The sons of princes, sown in the dust.
The soul stripped of its flesh knows nothing
Of sweetness or sour, feels no pain,   95
Bends neither its hand nor its brain. A brother
Opens his palms and pours down gold
On his kinsman's grave, strewing his coffin
With treasures intended for Heaven, but nothing
Golden shakes the wrath of God   100
For a soul overflowing with sin, and nothing
Hidden on earth rises to Heaven.
            We all fear God. He turns the earth,
He set it swinging firmly in space,
Gave life to the world and light to the sky.   105
Death leaps at the fools who forget their God.
He who lives humbly has angels from Heaven
To carry him courage and strength and belief.
A man must conquer pride, not kill it,
Be firm with his fellows, chaste for himself,   110
Treat all the world as the world deserves,
With love or with hate but never with harm,
Though an enemy seek to scorch him in hell,
Or set the flames of a funeral pyre[5]
Under his lord. Fate is stronger   115

Viking Pendant Crucifix.
*Statens Historiska Museum,
Stockholm.*

---

4. **rancor:** bitter resentment.
5. **pyre:** fire, especially for cremation.

And God mightier than any man's mind.
Our thoughts should turn to where our home is,
Consider the ways of coming there,
Then strive for sure permission for us
To rise to that eternal joy,   120
That life born in the love of God
And the hope of Heaven. Praise the Holy
Grace of Him who honored us,
Eternal, unchanging creator of earth. Amen.

Getting at Meaning

1. In the first sixty-four lines, the speaker describes the hardships he has suffered at sea. What are these hardships? Despite the hardships, how does the speaker feel about the sea? With what phrases and lines does he describe these feelings?

2. In line 64 the speaker seems to change the subject. In the following lines he compares the joys of heavenly life with the transience of earthly life. What examples does he give of the follies of earthly life? What is his final conclusion about what is enduring and valuable? How does this conclusion relate to his personal experiences as a sailor, described in the first part of the poem?

3. Summarize the advice in lines 103–124. What are the two meanings of *home* in line 117? How do the meanings of this word help to unify the poem? What other key words and ideas create unity throughout this poem?

Developing Skills in Reading Literature

1. **Lyric and Elegy.** Lyric poetry originally was a song chanted to the accompaniment of a lyre. Now, a lyric is any short poem that expresses one speaker's thoughts and feelings. An elegy is a kind of lyric poetry. In a narrow sense, it is a lament mourning someone's death. Broadly speaking, it is any thoughtful poem on a meditative theme. "The Seafarer" is lyrical in that it expresses the speaker's feelings. In what sense is it also elegiac? Explain.

2. **Analogy.** An analogy is a point by point comparison between two dissimilar objects or ideas for the purpose of clarifying the less familiar of the two

subjects. An analogy in lines 48–57 compares the lure of the sea for the land-bound mariner to the life-giving force in nature and the call of summer's first cuckoo. Study these lines and explain the points of comparison in your own words. What specifically is the speaker's purpose in presenting this analogy?

3. **Denotation and Connotation.** The denotative meaning of a word is its exact dictionary definition. A word has only limited denotative meaning, while it can have variant shades of connotative meaning. Connotative meanings, the emotional responses evoked by a word, may be private and personal, the result of individual experience; they may reflect the experience of a group, such as a race or a nationality; or they may be universal. Connotation often is a key device used by a poet to communicate meaning. Explain the connotations of the italicized words in these lines from "The Seafarer."

a. ". . . breaking *oaths*/On the curve of a wave. . . ." (lines 63–64)

b. ". . . Thus the joys of God/Are fervent with *life*, where *life* itself/Fades quickly into the earth. . . ." (lines 64–66) Note that *life* is used in two different senses.

c. ". . . nothing/*Golden* shakes the wrath of God" (lines 99–100)

d. "Our thoughts should turn to where our *home* is," (line 117)

4. **Imagery.** Imagery is the literary term used to describe words and phrases that appeal to one or more of the five senses. Figurative language can create images; however, not all images are figures of speech. Identify at least ten images in this selection and explain

their sensory appeal. Then comment on the effect created by the imagery.

5. **Theme.** Theme can refer to the main idea in a work of literature or to its message. What message is presented by the speaker in this poem? How does this message reflect the Christian influence in Anglo-Saxon England?

Developing Writing Skills

Comparing or Contrasting Two Poems. In the poem that follows, John Masefield, an early twentieth century poet laureate, demonstrates traditional British fascination with the sea. After reading the poem, write a composition comparing or contrasting it with ''The Seafarer'' in three specific ways. You may wish to focus on the poets' treatment of subject matter, their use of language, and the mood each creates. In your conclusion comment on the similarities or differences in the themes of the two poems.

A Wanderer's Song

A wind's in the heart of me, a fire's in my heels,
I am tired of brick and stone and rumbling wagon-wheels;
I hunger for the sea's edge, the limits of the land,
Where the wild old Atlantic is shouting on the sand.

Oh I'll be going, leaving the noises of the street,
To where a lifting foresail-foot is yanking at the sheet;[1]
To a windy, tossing anchorage where yawls and ketches ride,
Oh I'll be going, going, until I meet the tide.

And first I'll hear the sea-wind, the mewing of the gulls,
The clucking, sucking of the sea about the rusty hulls,
The songs at the capstan in the hooker warping out,[2]
And then the heart of me'll know I'm there or there-about.

Oh I am tired of brick and stone, the heart of me is sick,
For windy green, unquiet sea, the realm of Moby Dick;[3]
And I'll be going, going, from the roaring of the wheels,
For a wind's in the heart of me, a fire's in my heels.

1. **foresail-foot . . . sheet:** the bottom of the lowest sail is tugging at the rope which controls the angle at which the sail is set. 2. **hooker warping out:** movement of the ship (hooker) by ropes fastened to something fixed. 3. **Moby Dick:** the great white whale in Herman Melville's novel of the same name.

A Viking ship known as the Gokstad ship. ©*University Museum of National Antiquities, Oslo.*

Anglo-Saxon Riddles   *Anonymous*

The Exeter Book *contains almost one hundred riddles, some witty, some picturesque, some crude, some so obscure that the reader could never hope to guess their meanings. The following riddles are among those that are challenging but not incomprehensible to the twentieth-century reader.*

1

I war with the wind, with the waves I wrestle;
I must battle with both when the bottom I seek,
My strange habitation by surges o'er-roofed.
I am strong in the strife, while still I remain;
As soon as I stir, they are stronger than I.
They wrench and they wrest, till I run from my foes;
What was put in my keeping they carry away.
If my back be not broken, I baffle them still;
The rocks are my helpers, when hard I am pressed;
Grimly I grip them. Guess what I'm called. *Anchor*

2

My beak is below, I burrow and nose
Under the ground. I go as I'm guided
By my master the farmer, old foe of the forest;
Bent and bowed, at my back he walks,
Forward pushing me over the field;
Sows on my path where I've passed along.
I came from the wood, a wagon carried me;
I was fitted with skill, I am full of wonders.
As grubbing I go, there's green on one side,
But black on the other my path is seen.
A curious prong pierces my back; *Plow*
Beneath me in front, another grows down
And forward pointing is fixed to my head.

3

The wave, over the wave, a weird thing I saw,
through-wrought,[1] and wonderfully ornate:
a wonder on the wave—water became bone. *Iceberg*

---

1. **wrought:** "worked" as in wrought iron.

4

Wounded I am, and weary with fighting;
Gashed by the iron, gored by the point of it,
Sick of battle-work, battered and scarred.
Many a fearful fight have I seen, when
Hope there was none, or help in the thick of it,
Ere I was down and fordone in the fray.
Offspring of hammers, hardest of battle-blades,
Smithed in forges, fell on me savagely,
Doomed to bear the brunt and the shock of it,
Fierce encounter of clashing foes.
Leech[1] cannot heal my hurts with his simples,
Salves for my sores have I sought in vain.
Blade-cuts dolorous,[2] deep in the side of me,
Daily and nightly redouble my wounds.

5

I wear gray, woven over
With bright and gleaming gems. I bring
The stupid to folly's paths, fool
The ignorant with sin, urge all useless
Roads and ruin the rest. I can't
Explain their madness, for I push them to error
And pick their brains, yet they praise me more
For each seduction. Their dullness will be sorrow,
When they lead their souls on high, unless
They learn to walk wisely, and without my help.

---

1. **leech:** in Anglo-Saxon times, a doctor or "blood-letter."
2. **dolorous:** causing pain or sorrow.

Getting at Meaning

What is the subject of each riddle?

Developing Skills in Reading Literature

Anglo-Saxon Poetry. These riddles evidence the characteristics of Anglo-Saxon epic poetry. Choose one riddle and prepare to explain how its language and sound patterns conform to the kind of heroic poetry exemplified by *Beowulf*. If you notice variations on the traditional form, be ready to point these out as well.

Developing Writing Skills

Writing a Riddle. Try your skills at writing a riddle or two, using the Anglo-Saxon samples as models. Employ at least one kenning, more if possible.

Unit Review *The Anglo-Saxon Period*

Understanding the Unit

1. The excerpt from *Grendel* abounds in figurative language that strengthens the narrative and enables the reader to picture the action. Examine *Beowulf*, "The Seafarer," and the riddles, and find several examples of metaphor, simile, personification, hyperbole, and onomatopoeia. Be prepared to explain the effect created by each figure of speech.

2. The imagery in "The Seafarer" reveals both a fascination with the sea and a fear of the sea that was characteristic of most Anglo-Saxons. Examine *Beowulf* and identify several passages describing the sea that reveal similar attitudes. What does the imagery in these passages add to the narrative as a whole? How does it affect the reader?

3. The speaker in *Beowulf* plays quite a different role from that of the speaker in "The Seafarer." Which of the two speakers takes a more detached, or objective, view of the subject? Which is more involved in the subject? What are the differing effects upon the reader?

4. The wealth of references to arts and crafts, to ritual, and to pageantry in the literature of the Anglo-Saxons makes it clear that these people had an innate love of beauty and a strong desire to create order out of chaos. Find examples of these references in several of the selections. Be prepared to explain what each example reveals about the Anglo-Saxons.

5. One of the most significant factors in the development of Anglo-Saxon society was the coming of Christianity to England. The advent of Christianity affected law and order and introduced new ethical values and religious teachings. One Christian idea was that it is better to be humble than to be proud or arrogant. Another was that, even though earthly life is of little lasting value, there is always hope for the future in a newer and richer heavenly life. Look for evidence of these ideas both in *Beowulf* and in "The Seafarer." What other Christian ethical values and religious teachings do you find in each of these selections?

6. In addition to revealing a love of beauty and well defined moral codes, the literature of this period also shows that the Anglo-Saxons valued self-discipline, obedience, and common sense. Look for evidence of these values in *Beowulf* and in "The Seafarer." Why do you think that these qualities were especially important to the Anglo-Saxon people?

Writing

1. *Beowulf* is considered the great English epic, not only because it relates the deeds of a national hero, but also because it reveals on a grand scale the major values of a particular period in English history. Review the characteristics of an epic. Then choose a work that might be considered the great American epic. It could be a novel, a film, a play, or a nonfiction piece. Write a well developed essay in which you discuss the epic characteristics and proportions of your example.

2. George K. Anderson, in *The Literature of the Anglo-Saxons,* makes this comment about *Beowulf.*

> To the modern reader it is inevitably the pagan elements in Old English literature that make it most attractive. The story of strong men championing the cause of their people is always moving. To the sophisticated reader, moreover, there is always something of a paradoxical fascination in the contemplation of the primitive or near primitive. Then, too, the mysteriousness of pagan Anglo-Saxon times, the struggle of the hardy Vikings against their natural and unnatural foes, the spectacle of the ruthless survival of the fittest—these have in them raw drama, which cannot fail to exert a special romantic appeal.

Write an essay in which you discuss this quotation in light of your own reactions to *Beowulf.* Which scenes were most appealing? What seemed pagan and mysterious? What moments were grippingly dramatic? What actions excessively ruthless? In your discussion, try to use literary terms such as *tone, mood, epic, hero,* and *tragic hero.*

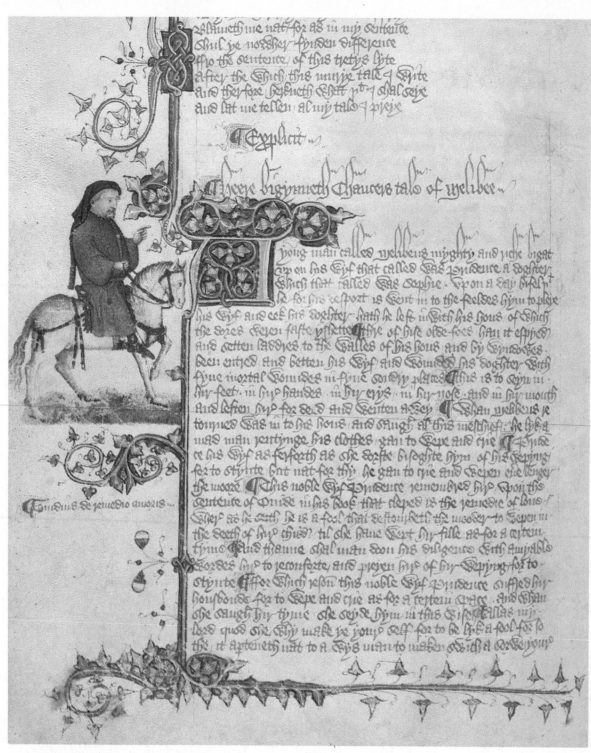

THE ELLESMERE MANUSCRIPT OF THE CANTERBURY TALES (detail), 1400–1410.
Henry E. Huntington Library and Art Gallery.
San Marino, California.

Unit 2
The Medieval Period (1066–1485)

GEOFFREY CHAUCER. *Anonymous.*
National Portrait Gallery, London.

Medieval England

THE NORMAN CONQUEST

In 1066 a well armed, highly trained army led by William, Duke of Normandy, defeated Harold, King of England, at the Battle of Hastings. This event, and the subsequent occupation of England by the Normans, marked the end of the Anglo-Saxon Period and the beginning of the Medieval Period.

The Normans were descendents of the Viking invaders of northwestern France who had become influential throughout western Europe. Demonstrating the aggressiveness and resourcefulness of their ancestors, the Normans were shrewd in the courtroom, exacting in the counting house, skilled in the marketplace, and fearsome on the battlefield. Although they were never more than a ruling minority in England, the Norman presence radically transformed the government, the economic system, the church, and even the language of this Anglo-Saxon land.

THE REIGN OF WILLIAM THE CONQUEROR

William the Conqueror, the most powerful duke in France, ruled England with strength and efficiency. An intelligent, energetic, and thorough administrator, William centralized power by appointing representatives to collect taxes, supervise legal and administrative matters, and organize the military. These representatives were directly responsible to the king, bypassing the Anglo-Saxon earls whose power had equaled or surpassed that of most English kings. To eliminate arguments and establish a firm basis for awarding confiscated lands, William ordered an extensive survey of all property, the results of which were recorded in the *Domesday Book* in 1086.

THE FEUDAL SYSTEM

William introduced into England the system of reciprocal loyalties called feudalism. A feudal king owned all of the land and distributed fiefs, or tracts of land, to his loyal followers in exchange for their service and obedience. These powerful nobles, or barons, gave parcels of land to lesser nobles who promised service and loyalty in return and so forth until the portions of land were too small to be subdivided. In William's system all vassals, or holders of land, owed military service directly to the king, an innovation that assured the continued strength of the monarchy.

About one person in thirty belonged to the nobility or clergy. A small percentage of the population was made up of freemen who were independent farmers, shopkeepers, tradesmen, and hired laborers. Most people were serfs, a class consisting of slaves and lower class freemen under the old Anglo-Saxon system. Serfs worked for a lord in exchange for protection and the right to farm a small plot of land. They lived in wretched poverty, doomed to remain on the land on which they were born, unable to marry or even to visit a relative without permission of the lord, required to "donate" labor and a portion of their meager crops to the lord and his family.

The feudal system dominated the early Medieval Period. Not until the thirteenth and fourteenth centuries did political, social, and economic conditions converge to undermine the system so firmly established by the Conqueror.

THE MONARCHY AFTER WILLIAM

Several able kings consolidated and extended the achievements of William the Conqueror. Henry I, who reigned from 1100 to 1135 and was a notably efficient administrator, further systematized the government. His grandson Henry II, who reigned from 1154 to 1189, reformed and standardized the haphazard legal system, establishing the basis for common law, still the foundation of English justice. Edward I reigned from 1272 to 1307 and was considered the first truly English king after the Conquest. He introduced more legal reforms and encouraged the development of Parliament, the representative body that became an official part of the government in 1295.

Under mediocre and weak kings, England reverted to periods of anarchy, marked by bloodshed, destruction, economic chaos, and baronial uprisings. In 1215, near the end of the seventeen-year reign of the greedy, vengeful King John, the barons forced the king to approve the Magna Carta, a document that implies limitations on royal privilege and certain rights of nobles and commoners. One important provision is the granting to any accused person a trial by a jury of peers. The signing of the Magna Carta was a dramatic event in the gradual trend toward curtailment of royal power that is evident throughout the Medieval Period.

THE MEDIEVAL CHURCH

The Roman Catholic Church was the unifying force of the age, as well as one of England's most powerful institutions. As in the Anglo-Saxon Period, clergy and scholars at the abbeys performed the traditional services of educating clergy and nobles and of writing, translating, copying, gathering, and storing manuscripts. Many of these institutions also were vast estates within the feudal system, administered by worldly, well educated abbots and abbesses. Churchmen also held civil offices and served as advisors to the crown.

The Church was the impetus behind the explosion of architectural creativity during the Medieval Period. The cathedrals and other church buildings constructed between 1066 and 1200 were Romanesque in style, with arches, domes, thick walls, and small windows. Many of the new churches replaced sturdy, plain Anglo-Saxon churches, which were torn down to make way for the more graceful Norman styles. In the later Gothic style, interiors became important. Church officials and lay benefactors commissioned artists to create stained glass, paintings, mosaics, and sculpted statues to decorate these buildings.

From the late eleventh to the early thirteenth centuries, the Church sponsored a series of Crusades to recapture the Holy Land from the Moslems. Some English nobles and their retinues, notably King Richard the Lion-Hearted, participated in the Crusades. Their major impact on England, however, had to do with the opening of new avenues of trade and the introduction of new ideas, foods (rice, sugar, apricots), and fabrics (cotton, damask) into England.

Even in the early Middle Ages, the tremendous influence and wealth of the Church inspired the jealousy of England's nobility and led to a long series of secret power plays and open clashes between clergy and barons, bishops and kings, and popes and kings. The issues often concerned the Church's right to tax English subjects, the position of Church courts within the British legal system, and the right of the monarch to appoint English bishops. At stake was control—over revenue, over government, and over the lives of ordinary Englishmen.

By the late Middle Ages, the Church's political and secular hold on England had weakened, a result of social and economic factors within the country and also of factors within the church itself. Notorious scandals, abuses of clerical privilege, feuding cardinals, and a series of popes allied with Continental princes had undermined respect for the Church among all the English classes. Reformers within the Church responded to the need for spiritual renewal. Among them was John Wycliffe, a dynamic scholar and theologian who supervised the first complete translation of the Bible into

English, a task completed in the late fourteenth century. That Wycliffe gained the protection and support of both ruling barons and commoners by defying papal authority and by criticizing the luxury of the monasteries demonstrates the growing resentment of the Church as an institution.

THE GROWTH OF TOWNS

Raising sheep for wool was an important occupation in Medieval England. At first, raw wool was exported for processing and weaving into cloth. In the mid-fourteenth century domestic woolen mills were established and towns grew up around the centers of production. With the towns came a newly prosperous middle class and opportunities for serfs and other farm laborers to escape agrarian life.

Merchants and tradespeople, both men and women, organized into guilds to control prices and quality and to provide for the political, social, and religious needs of their members. Under the guild training system, apprentices and journeymen worked and lived with master craftsmen until they were ready to take their places among the middle class of the town.

Towns also became the centers of creative and artistic activity. Magnificent guildhalls and imposing churches were constructed, each providing years of work for skilled craftsmen and their assistants. Fairs, markets, and carnivals stimulated economic and social life and cultural life as well. At these gatherings traveling singers called troubadors, storytellers, and local and itinerant performers entertained the crowds.

A few towns were centers of education. At first, all schools were church-affiliated and all teachers were clergy. Later, lay lecturers taught groups of students for a small fee. Eventually, the teachers organized into a guild, called a *universitas.* One center of scholarly activity evolved into Oxford University, which was formally chartered in 1248 as an institution offering studies in theology and the liberal arts.

THE DECLINE OF FEUDALISM

The development of the wool industry, the establishment of guilds, and the growth of towns were factors in the decline of feudalism. So was the Black Death, a kind of bubonic plague that struck England in 1348. Within two years, more than a third of the population had died. An immediate result of this epidemic was a shortage of laborers. Responding to the new availability of jobs, serfs left the land to work in towns and on neighboring estates. Workers realized their new value and demanded better working conditions and higher wages.

In 1381 Jack Straw and Wat Tyler led the Peasants' Revolt, protesting a tax that was disproportionately hard on the poor. Although the revolt failed, it demonstrated a new awareness of the rights of common people and a spirit of rebelliousness alien to the feudal system.

Another factor in the decline of feudalism was the Hundred Years' War, a series of wars fought between the English and the French from 1339 to 1453. At first the English, with their cannon and longbows, dominated the fighting and captured vast territories in France. The French, however, won the later battles, and England lost almost all its French lands.

During the wars, loyalty subtly shifted from the feudal lords to the emerging national state. Also, the wars were expensive and kings had to rely heavily on Parliament to raise revenues through taxation. Parliament thus increased in power relative to the monarchy.

Following the Hundred Years' War, rivalry between the House of York, represented by the white rose, and the House of Lancaster,

Literature

- Popular ballads are composed

- Geoffrey of Monmouth writes *History of the Kings of Britain*

- *Domesday Book* records results of property survey ordered by William the Conqueror

1066   1100   1200

History

- Henry I becomes King
- Henry II becomes King
- Founding of Cambridge University

- First Crusades undertaken to recapture Holy Land from Moslems
- Beginnings of Oxford University

- Construction on Tower of London begins
- Thomas à Becket murdered

- Westminster Abbey completed

- Norman conquest at Battle of Hastings marks end of Anglo-Saxon period

- Magna Carta is approved, beginning trend to curtail royal power

- William the Conqueror introduces feudalism in England

represented by the red rose, led to the Wars of the Roses. This bloody struggle for the throne lasted for thirty years, from 1455 to 1485, and decimated the ranks of the nobility. Finally, Henry Tudor defeated King Richard III and gained the support of both houses. The crowning of Henry VII, the first Tudor monarch, is generally considered the event that signaled the end of the Medieval Period.

LITERATURE IN THE MEDIEVAL PERIOD

For nearly three hundred years after the Norman Conquest, little literature of consequence was produced in England. Latin was the language used by the clergy, scholars, and lawyers. The feudal nobles spoke and wrote in Norman French. Only the middle and lower classes spoke English. Few of these people were literate, and the early traditions were oral and dramatic.

One of the most popular forms of literature in the Medieval Period was the ballad, a narrative song. Ballads told of common folks and of characters and events from legend and folklore. Popular also were mystery plays, based on stories from the Bible, and miracle plays, which portrayed the lives of saints. Although these plays probably were written first in Latin for special church services, they eventually were written in English and performed outside churches,

- Chaucer writes elegy *Book of the Duchess*
- Anonymous composition of *Sir Gawain and the Green Knight*
- First mention of Robin Hood in songs
- Anonymous poet composes *Piers Plowman*
- *Second Shepherds' Play* performed as medieval mystery play
- Chaucer (*ca.* 1343–1400) begins *Canterbury Tales*
- John Wycliffe supervises first complete translation of Bible into English

- Caxton's printing press set up at Westminster
- Thomas Malory's *morte d'Arthur* printed
- *Everyman*, morality play, appears

1300   1400   1500

- Outbreak of Hundred Years' War between English and French
- Black Death plague reduces English population by one-third
- Thomas Aquinas's *Summa Theologiae* reconciles reason and religion
- Peasants' Revolt breaks out, furthering decline of serfdom
- Edward I becomes King, introducing legal reforms and encouraging development of Parliament
- Parliament established
- Henry V wins Battle of Agincourt, leading to English conquest of France
- English burn Joan of Arc at Rouen
- The Wars of the Roses begin

in towns, and in inns. During the later Middle Ages audiences enjoyed morality plays, allegorical dramas intended to teach ethical and moral values. An enduring morality play is *Everyman*, in which characters represent virtues and vices.

The most famous writer of the Medieval Period, the "Father of English Literature," was Geoffrey Chaucer (1340?-1400), a poet who demonstrated the potential of Middle English as a literary language.

Drawing on sources as diverse as French poetry, English songs, Greek classics, contemporary Italian tales, and Aesop's fables, Chaucer created a masterful blend of old and new, using the natural rhythms of the spoken language. *The Canterbury Tales*, his preeminent work, attests to his innate ability as a storyteller, to his keen sense of humor, and to his sharp eye for detail. Of "The Prologue" to these tales, Nevill Coghill wrote: "It [The Prologue] is the concise portrait of an entire nation, high and low, old and young, male and female, lay and clerical, learned and ignorant, rogue and righteous, land and sea, town and country. . . ."

Around 1362 *The Vision of William Concerning Piers the Plowman (Piers Plowman)*, a long allegorical poem in Middle English, first appeared. The poem describes major historical events, such as the Hundred Years' War, the Black Death, and the Peasants' Revolt, and also presents a picture of ordinary everyday life. *Piers Plowman* is probably the first poem of social protest in English literature, showing an unusual sympathy for the plight of the poor. William Langland generally is credited with authorship of the alliterative poem.

The courtly tradition of the Medieval Period was expressed in the romance, an adventurous tale that celebrates the courage and loyalty of the knight who obeys his king and honors womanhood. Romantic heroes practiced the code of chivalry and the code of courtly love, elaborate rules of conduct based on the assumptions that ladies were fair and devout, knights uniformly gallant, manners impeccable, and jousting the way to feminine favor. Early romances were related by troubadors or minstrels, first in France and later in Norman England. By the late Middle Ages, an entire body of romances concerned the legendary hero King Arthur and the Knights of the Round Table. Thomas Malory (?-1471) retold the tales in *Morte d'Arthur* (printed in 1485), the first version of the Arthurian legends written in English prose.

William Caxton (1424?-1491) had a tremendous influence on the preservation of English literature. A respected translator, Caxton traveled extensively in Europe and probably learned the printing trade in Germany. After returning to England, he opened his own printing business. Before his death fifteen years later, he had printed practically all of the English literature available at the time, including *Morte d'Arthur* and *The Canterbury Tales*.

The Development of the English Language

MIDDLE ENGLISH

The English language changed more during the four centuries after 1066 than it did during any period before or since. The language of this period is referred to as Middle English.

The French Inheritance

The precipitating event in the transition from Old English to Middle English was the Norman Conquest in 1066. Following the decisive defeat at the Battle of Hastings, French became the language of the aristocratic ruling class in England. Norman French was a dialect of Old French, which belonged to the Indo-European language family.

The elimination of the English court and the displacement of the English aristocracy destroyed the linguistic unity of the country. The majority of the middle and lower classes continued to speak their native English, but they spoke various dialects, which tended to become increasingly disperate.

Meanwhile, French words entered English by the thousands, particularly words dealing with law and government, such as *attorney, judge, jury, crime, mayor, crown,* and *court.* Other words were adopted from French to describe the arts (*beauty, image, palace, pillar*), cooking (*blanch, mince, stew, roast*), fashion (*dress, boot, frock, pleat*), and religion (*preach, saint, sermon, baptize*). Often, instead of replacing an Anglo-Saxon word, the French term existed alongside the Old English, as with the French *residence* and the native *home* or the French *purchase* and the Anglo-Saxon *buy.*

In general, when large groups of people must communicate in languages that are unfamiliar, usages tend to become simplified. In medieval England, this tendency to simplify hastened the elimination of grammatical endings and gender distinctions from Old English words, a process already evident before the Conquest. Consequently, word order assumed more importance; Middle English sentences began to look more like Modern English sentences, with the subject preceding the verb and the verb preceding the object, as in "I see a lake" or "Mary loves John."

For three centuries, the literature of England was trilingual, with Latin as the language of learning, French of the aristocracy, and English of the masses. Of great importance is the fact that, despite the magnitude of the changes in English, its grammar, syntax, and pronunciation survived. Moreover, because Anglo-Saxon culture remained strong, English was preserved in literature. Works were passed on through the oral tradition and later were written in the various dialects of Middle English.

The Standardization of English

By the late 1200's, there were five major regional dialects, although some scholars say that the differences in spelling were so great that each writer created his or her own dialect. Pronunciation varied greatly from place to place, and so did such basic elements as personal pronouns. Consider the variations in the phrase "she loves" in the five dialects of Middle English:

Northern: scho loves
East Midland: sche loveth
West Midland: scho loveth
Southeastern (Kentish): he loveth
Southern (Southwestern): heo loveth

Out of this chaos of dialects, English re-emerged as a national language in the thirteenth and fourteenth centuries. When King John lost Normandy to the French in 1204, an important link to the Continent was broken. Later, the rise of the middle class and the evolution of Parliament slowly eroded the power of the French-speaking aristocracy, and by the 1300's the balance had tipped in favor of English. In 1362, Parliament declared English the official language of the legal system. In 1399, when Henry IV seized the throne, he became the first monarch since the Norman Conquest whose mother tongue was English. Later in the 1400's, due primarily to increased nationalism, upward mobility, and other factors, English replaced French as the language even of the aristocracy. Finally, by 1500, the triumph of English in England was assured.

Of the several Middle English dialects, the one that prevailed to become the basis for Modern English was the East Midland dialect. Descended primarily from the Mercian dialect of Old English, it was the dialect spoken in London, the political and cultural capital of the country. It was also the language of Geoffrey Chaucer, the founder of modern English literature.

A force for standardizing English came at the end of the Medieval Period with the invention of movable type in Germany and its subsequent introduction in England. Printing brought stability in spelling and usage to written English and ensured the dominance of the language of London. In spoken English, regional dialects retained their significance for some time—for example, Sir Walter Raleigh spoke with a Devon accent in the seventeenth century—but written English was largely standardized by the late 1400's.

English of the Late Medieval Period

To contemporary speakers of English, the English of the early Medieval Period looks and sounds like a foreign language. For example, the following was written in 1230 in the West Midland dialect:

In þis ilke burh wes wuniende a meiden
swiðe ȝung of ȝeres, twa wone of
twenti, feier & freolich o wlite & o
westum.
(In this same town was dwelling a maiden
very young in years—two lacking of
twenty—fair and noble in appearance and
form.)

By the late 1300's, Chaucer was writing poetry that can be understood by most people who know Modern English, as seen in this passage from "The Nun's Priest's Tale":

I kan not love a coward, by my feith
For certes, whatso any woman seith,
We alle desiren, if it mighte bee,
To han housbondes hardy, wise, and free.

Furthermore, while diversity of dialects was a hallmark of Middle English, by 1500 a newly standardized English, blended with French, had emerged. In fact, Chaucer's wish, written in the epilogue for *Troilus and Cressida*, seemed attainable:

Go, lytle booke,
And for ther is so gret diversite
In Englissh, and in writyng of oure tonge,
So I pray I god that non myswrite thee,
Ne thee mys-metre for defaute of tonge,
And wherever thee may be rede,
I pray god thee may be understoode.

Geoffrey Chaucer
1340?–1400

Geoffrey Chaucer, one of the greatest poets of the English language, was born around 1340 to a family of prosperous wine and leather merchants living in London. Through family connections, he became a page in the household of King Edward III's son, where his education prepared him for service in the royal court. Bilingual in English and French, Chaucer also learned Latin and Italian and read both classic and contemporary works in these languages.

As a young soldier Chaucer was sent to France to fight in an engagement of the Hundred Years' War. He was taken prisoner and later released when his ransom was paid in part by the king. Back in England, Chaucer became a royal courtier, representing the king on important diplomatic missions to Flanders, France, Italy, and Spain.

Through reading and travel, Chaucer experienced European literature and culture. French romantic literature had reached its zenith in the *Romance of the Rose*, a poetic expression of the code of courtly love. Chaucer translated this romance into English and imitated its form and spirit in *Book of the Duchess*, his first noteworthy poem.

In Italy in the 1370's, Chaucer came into contact with the budding Renaissance, a resurgence of artistic and literary creativity. He studied the works of Dante, Petrarch, and Boccaccio, writers who influenced the subjects, structure, and philosophy of his later writings. During this period the demands of his career limited his writing time, although he did polish his skills as a poet. He also found time to mingle with the common folks, swapping tales and drinking ale, immersed in the vitality of medieval life.

Chaucer died on October 25, 1400, and was buried in Westminster Abbey. The remains of the "Father of English Literature" still lie in what is now called the Poet's Corner, the first poet to be so honored.

The Canterbury Tales is Chaucer's great accomplishment, a testament to his passion for life and to his mastery of the English language. According to "The Prologue," thirty pilgrims gather at the Tab-

GEOFFREY CHAUCER (detail). *Anonymous.*
National Portrait Gallery, London.

ard Inn in Southwark, about to embark on a pilgrimage to the shrine of Thomas à Becket in Canterbury. They agree to have a storytelling contest on the journey, with the host of the Tabard acting as director and judge. Each pilgrim was to tell four stories, two on the way to Canterbury and two on the return trip. However, Chaucer died having completed only twenty-four tales.

Chaucer's pilgrims encompass the entire spectrum of fourteenth-century English society—nobility and clergy, merchants and tradesmen, professionals and laborers. His characters are both individual and universal, drawn from the Middle Ages yet representative of the human beings in all times and places. The frame story employed by Chaucer encompasses a variety of literary genres, among them romance, allegory, religious biography, beast fable, and sermon. The style of the tales is conversational; the vocabulary is colloquial; the detail is vivid; and, in short, each tale fits the teller. Evident in the tales is a sense of the complexities that engaged the medieval mind: the relationship between free will and destiny, the requirements of salvation, the meaning of happiness, the importance of love both human and divine.

The Canterbury Tales *Translated by Nevill Coghill*

The Prologe

Here biginneth the Book of the Tales of Caunterbury

Whan that Aprill with his shourës sotë[1]
The droghte of Marche hath percëd to the rotë,
And bathëd every veyne in swich licour
Of which vertu engendrëd is the flour;
Whan Zephirus eek[2] with his swetë breeth   5
Inspirëd hath in every holt[3] and heeth
The tendrë croppës, and the yongë sonnë
Hath in the Ram his halfe cours y-ronnë,
And smalë fowlës maken melodyë,
That slepen al the night with open yë   10
(So priketh hem Nature in hir corages):[4]
Than longen folk to goon on pilgrimages
And palmers for to seken straungë strondës,[5]
To fernë halwës, couthe in sondry londës;
And specially, from every shirës endë   15
Of Engelond, to Caunterbury they wendë,
The holy blisful martir for to sekë.
That hem hath holpen, whan that they were sekë.
   Bifel that in that seson on a day,
In Southwerk at the Tabard as I lay   20
Redy to wenden on my pilgrimagë
To Caunterbury with ful devout coragë,[6]
At night was come into that hostelryë
Wel nyne and twenty in a companyë
Of sondry folk, by aventure y-fallë   25
In felawshipe, and pilgrims were they allë,
That toward Caunterbury wolden rydë.
The chambrës and the stablës weren wydë,
And wel we weren esëd attë bestë.
And shortly, whan the sonnë was to restë,   30
So hadde I spoken with hem everichon,[7]
That I was of hir[8] felawshipe anon,
And madë forward erly for to rysë,
To take our wey, ther as I yow devysë.[9] . . .

1. **sotë:** sweet.

2. **eek:** also.
3. **holt:** wood.

4. **corages:** heart.

5. **strondës:** strands.

6. **coragë:** heart.

7. **everichon:** everyone.
8. **hir:** their.

9. **devysë:** tell.

In "The Prologue" a pilgrim introduces the other pilgrims with whom he will journey to Canterbury and establishes the framework within which the pilgrims will relate their tales. The opening lines of "The Prologue" are printed in both the original Middle English and Modern English.

The Prologue

Here begins the Book of the Canterbury Tales

When the sweet showers of April fall and shoot
Down through the drought of March to pierce the root,
Bathing every vein in liquid power
From which there springs the engendering of the flower,
When also Zephyrus[1] with his sweet breath   5
Exhales an air in every grove and heath
Upon the tender shoots, and the young sun
His half-course in the sign of the *Ram* has run,
And the small fowl are making melody
That sleep away the night with open eye   10
(So nature pricks them and their heart engages)
Then people long to go on pilgrimages
And palmers[2] long to seek the stranger strands
Of far-off saints, hallowed in sundry lands,
And specially, from every shire's end   15
In England, down to Canterbury they wend
To seek the holy blissful martyr,[3] quick
In giving help to them when they were sick.
  It happened in that season that one day
In Southwark,[4] at *The Tabard*, as I lay   20
Ready to go on pilgrimage and start
For Canterbury, most devout at heart,
At night there came into that hostelry
Some nine and twenty in a company
Of sundry folk happening then to fall   25
In fellowship, and they were pilgrims all
That towards Canterbury meant to ride.
The rooms and stables of the inn were wide;
They made us easy, all was of the best.
And shortly, when the sun had gone to rest,   30
By speaking to them all upon the trip
I was admitted to their fellowship
And promised to rise early and take the way
To Canterbury, as you heard me say.

1. **Zephyrus** (zef' ər əs): the gentle west wind.

2. **palmers:** persons who visited the Holy Land.

3. **martyr:** Thomas à Becket, Archbishop of Canterbury, murdered in 1170.

4. **Southwark** (sŭth' ark): a suburb of London.

CHAUCER (detail). *Ellesmere Ms. Huntington Library, San Marino, Calif.*

But none the less, while I have time and space, 35
Before my story takes a further pace,
It seems a reasonable thing to say
What their condition was, the full array
Of each of them, as it appeared to me,
According to profession and degree, 40
And what apparel they were riding in;
And at a Knight I therefore will begin.

There was a *Knight*, a most distinguished man,
Who from the day on which he first began
To ride abroad had followed chivalry, 45
Truth, honor, greatness of heart and courtesy.
He had done nobly in his sovereign's war
And ridden into battle, no man more,
As well in Christian as in heathen places,
And ever honored for his noble graces. 50
He saw the town of Alexandria[5] fall;
Often, at feasts, the highest place of all
Among the nations fell to him in Prussia.
In Lithuania he had fought, and Russia,
No Christian man so often, of his rank. 55
And he was in Granada when they sank
The town of Algeciras, also in
North Africa, right through Benamarin;
And in Armenia he had been as well
And fought when Ayas and Attalia fell, 60
For all along the Mediterranean coast
He had embarked with many a noble host.
In fifteen mortal battles he had been
And jousted for our faith at Tramissene
Thrice in the lists, and always killed his man. 65
This same distinguished knight had led the van
Once with the Bey of Balat, doing work
For him against another heathen Turk;
He was of sovereign value in all eyes.
And though so much distinguished, he was wise 70
And in his bearing modest as a maid.
He never yet a boorish thing had said
In all his life to any, come what might;
He was a true, a perfect gentle-knight.
Speaking of his appearance, he possessed 75
Fine horses, but he was not gaily dressed.

---

5. **Alexandria:** a battle in 1365.

He wore a fustian[6] tunic stained and dark
With smudges where his armor had left mark;
Just home from service, he had joined our ranks
To do his pilgrimage and render thanks.   80

    He had his son with him, a fine young *Squire*,
A lover and cadet, a lad of fire
With curly locks, as if they had been pressed.
He was some twenty years of age, I guessed.
In stature he was of a moderate length,   85
With wonderful agility and strength.
He'd seen some service with the cavalry
In Flanders and Artois and Picardy
And had done valiantly in little space
Of time, in hope to win his lady's grace.   90
He was embroidered like a meadow bright
And full of freshest flowers, red and white.
Singing he was, or fluting all the day;
He was as fresh as is the month of May.
Short was his gown, the sleeves were long and wide;   95
He knew the way to sit a horse and ride.
He could make songs and poems and recite,
Knew how to joust and dance, to draw and write.
He loved so hotly that till dawn grew pale
He slept as little as a nightingale.   100
Courteous he was, lowly and serviceable,
And carved to serve his father at the table.

    There was a *Yeoman* with him at his side,
No other servant; so he chose to ride.
This Yeoman wore a coat and hood of green,   105
And peacock-feathered arrows, bright and keen
And neatly sheathed, hung at his belt the while
—For he could dress his gear in yeoman style,
His arrows never drooped their feathers low—
And in his hand he bore a mighty bow.   110
His head was like a nut, his face was brown.
He knew the whole of woodcraft up and down.
A saucy brace was on his arm to ward
It from the bow-string, and a shield and sword
Hung at one side, and at the other slipped   115
A jaunty dirk,[7] spear-sharp and well-equipped.
A medal of St. Christopher he wore

THE SQUIRE (detail).
Ellesmere Ms.
Huntington Library,
San Marino, Calif.

---

6. **fustian:** a coarse, sturdy cloth of cotton and flax.
7. **dirk:** a dagger.

Of shining silver on his breast, and bore
A hunting-horn, well slung and burnished clean,
That dangled from a baldrick[8] of bright green. 120
He was a proper forester I guess.

There also was a *Nun*, a Prioress;
Simple her way of smiling was and coy.
Her greatest oath was only "By St. Loy!"[9]
And she was known as Madam Eglantyne. 125
And well she sang a service, with a fine
Intoning through her nose, as was most seemly,
And she spoke daintily in French, extremely,
After the school of Stratford-atte-Bowe;
French in the Paris style she did not know. 130
At meat her manners were well taught withal;
No morsel from her lips did she let fall,
Nor dipped her fingers in the sauce too deep;
But she could carry a morsel up and keep
The smallest drop from falling on her breast. 135
For courtliness she had a special zest.
And she would wipe her upper lip so clean
That not a trace of grease was to be seen
Upon the cup when she had drunk; to eat,
She reached a hand sedately for the meat. 140
She certainly was very entertaining,
Pleasant and friendly in her ways, and straining
To counterfeit a courtly kind of grace,
A stately bearing fitting to her place,
And to seem dignified in all her dealings. 145
As for her sympathies and tender feelings,
She was so charitably solicitous
She used to weep if she but saw a mouse
Caught in a trap, if it were dead or bleeding.
And she had little dogs she would be feeding 150
With roasted flesh, or milk, or fine white bread.
Sorely she wept if one of them were dead
Or someone took a stick and made it smart;
She was all sentiment and tender heart.
Her veil was gathered in a seemly way, 155
Her nose was elegant, her eyes glass-gray;
Her mouth was very small, but soft and red,
And certainly she had a well-shaped head,

THE PRIORESS (detail).
Ellesmere Ms.
Huntington Library,
San Marino, Calif.

---

8. **baldrick:** an ornamented leather belt worn across the chest to support
a sword.
9. **St. Loy:** a French saint.

Almost a span across the brows, I own;
She was indeed by no means undergrown.
Her cloak, I noticed, had a graceful charm.
She wore a coral trinket on her arm,
A set of beads, the gaudies[10] tricked in green,
Whence hung a golden brooch of brightest sheen
On which there first was graven a crowned *A*,
And lower, *Amor vincit omnia.*[11]
　Another *Nun*, the chaplain at her cell,
Was riding with her, and *three Priests* as well.

160

165

THE SECOND NUN (detail).
Ellesmere Ms.
Huntington Library,
San Marino, Calif.

　There was a *Monk*, a leader of the fashions;
Inspecting farms and hunting were his passions,
A manly man, to be an Abbot able,
Many the dainty horses in his stable;
His bridle, when he rode, a man might hear
Jingling in a whistling wind as clear,
Aye, and as loud as does the chapel bell
Where my lord Monk was Prior of the cell.
The Rule of good St. Benet or St. Maur
As old and strict he tended to ignore;
He let go by the things of yesterday
And followed the new world's more spacious way.
He did not rate that text at a plucked hen
Which says that hunters are not holy men
And that a monk uncloistered is a mere
Fish out of water, flapping on the pier,
That is to say a monk out of his cloister.
That was a text he held not worth an oyster;
And I said I agreed with his opinion;
What! Study until reason lost dominion
Poring on books in cloisters? Must he toil
As Austin[12] bade and till the very soil?
Was he to leave the world upon the shelf?
Let Austin have his labor to himself.
　This Monk was therefore a good man to horse;
Greyhounds he had, as swift as birds, to course.
Hunting a hare or riding at a fence
Was all his fun, he spared for no expense.
I saw his sleeves were garnished at the hand
With fine gray fur, the finest in the land,
And where his hood was fastened at his chin

170

175

180

185

190

195

THE NUN'S PRIEST (detail).
Ellesmere Ms.
Huntington Library,
San Marino, Calif.

---

10. **gaudies:** Every eleventh bead on a rosary stands for a *paternoster* (Lord's prayer). A gaud is green and a bit larger than the rest.
11. ***Amor vincit omnia*** Latin: "Love Conquers All."
12. **Austin:** An English version of St. Augustine's name.

He had a wrought-gold cunningly fashioned pin; 200
Into a lover's knot it seemed to pass.
His head was bald and shone as any glass,
So did his face, as if it had been greased.
He was a fat and personable priest;
His bright eyes rolled, they never seemed to settle, 205
And glittered like the flames beneath a kettle;
Supple his boots, his horse in fine condition.
He was a prelate fit for exhibition,
He was not pale like a tormented soul.
He liked a fat swan best, and roasted whole. 210
His palfrey[13] was as brown as is a berry.

　　There was a *Friar*, a wanton one and merry,
A Limiter,[14] a very festive fellow.
In all Four Orders[15] there was none so mellow
As he in flattery and dalliant speech. 215
He'd fixed up many a marriage, giving each
Of his young women what he could afford her.
He was a noble pillar to his Order.
Highly beloved and intimate was he
With Country folk wherever he might be, 220
And worthy city women with possessions;
For he was qualified to hear confessions,
Or so he said, with more than priestly scope;
He had a special license from the Pope.
Sweetly he heard his penitents at shrift[16] 225
With pleasant absolution, for a gift.
He was an easy man in penance-giving
Where he could hope to make a decent living;
It's a sure sign whenever gifts are given
To a poor Order that a man's well shriven, 230
And should he give enough he knew in verity
The penitent repented in sincerity.
For many a fellow is so hard of heart
He cannot weep, for all his inward smart.
Therefore instead of weeping and of prayer 235
One should give silver for a poor Friar's care.
He kept his tippet[17] stuffed with pins for curls,

---

13. **palfrey:** saddle horse.
14. **Limiter:** a begging friar who was given a specific district in which to beg.
15. **Four Orders:** The four orders of begging friars were the Dominicans, the Franciscans, the Carmelites, and the Austin Friars.
16. **shrift:** confession to a priest.
17. **tippet:** a long stole worn by clergymen.

And pocket-knives, to give to pretty girls.
And certainly his voice was gay and sturdy,
For he sang well and played the hurdy-gurdy.[18]   240
At sing-songs he was champion of the hour.
His neck was whiter than a lily-flower
But strong enough to butt a bruiser down.
He knew the taverns well in every town
And every innkeeper and barmaid too   245
Better than lepers, beggars and that crew,
For in so eminent a man as he
It was not fitting with the dignity
Of his position dealing with such scum.
It isn't decent, nothing good can come   250
Of having truck with slum-and-gutter dwellers,
But only with the rich and victual-sellers.
But anywhere a profit might accrue
Courteous he was and lowly of service too.
Natural gifts like his were hard to match.   255
He was the finest beggar of his batch,
And, for his begging-district, payed a rent;
His brethren did no poaching where he went.
For though a widow mightn't have a shoe,
So pleasant was his holy how-d'ye-do   260
He got his farthing from her just the same
Before he left, and so his income came
To more than he laid out. And how he romped,
Just like a puppy! He was ever prompt
To arbitrate disputes on settling days   265
(For a small fee) in many helpful ways,
Not then appearing as your cloistered scholar
With threadbare habit hardly worth a dollar,
But much more like a Doctor or a Pope.
Of double-worsted was the semi-cope[19]   270
Upon his shoulders, and the swelling fold
About him, like a bell about its mold
When it is casting, rounded out his dress.
He lisped a little out of wantonness
To make his English sweet upon his tongue.   275
When he had played his harp, or having sung,
His eyes would twinkle in his head as bright
As any star upon a frosty night.
This worthy's name was Hubert, it appeared.

18. **hurdy-gurdy:** a medieval instrument shaped like a lute and played by cranking a wheel.
19. **semi-cope:** a cape.

There was a *Merchant* with a forking beard
And motley dress; high on his horse he sat,
Upon his head a Flemish beaver hat
And on his feet daintily buckled boots.
He told of his opinions and pursuits
In solemn tones, and how he never lost.
The sea should be kept free at any cost
(He thought) upon the Harwich-Holland ranges.
He was expert at dabbling in exchanges.
This estimable Merchant so had set
His wits to work, none knew he was in debt,
He was so stately in negotiation,
Loan, bargain, and commercial obligation.
He was an excellent fellow all the same;
To tell the truth I do not know his name.

There was an *Oxford Cleric* too, a student,
Long given to Logic, longer than was prudent;
The horse he had was leaner than a rake,
And he was not too fat, I undertake,
But had a hollow look, a sober air;
The thread upon his overcoat was bare.
He had found no preferment in the church
And he was too unworldly to make search.
He thought far more of having by his bed
His twenty books all bound in black and red,
Of Aristotle and philosophy
Than of gay music, fiddles or finery.
Though a philosopher, as I have told,
He had not found the stone for making gold.
Whatever money from his friends he took
He spent on learning or another book
And prayed for them most earnestly, returning
Thanks to them thus for paying for his learning.
His only care was study, and indeed
He never spoke a word more than was need,
Formal at that, respectful in the extreme,
Short, to the point, and lofty in his theme.
The thought of moral virtue filled his speech
And he would gladly learn, and gladly teach.

A *Sergeant at the Law* who paid his calls,
Wary and wise, for clients at St. Paul's[20]

280

285

290

295

300

305

310

315

320

THE MERCHANT (detail).
Ellesmere Ms.
Huntington Library,
San Marino, Calif.

---

20. **St. Paul's:** Lawyers used to meet for consultation at the portico of St. Paul's cathedral.

There also was, of noted excellence.
Discreet he was, a man to reverence,
Or so he seemed, his sayings were so wise.
He often had been Justice of Assize
By letters patent, and in full commission. 325
His fame and learning and his high position
Had won him many a robe and many a fee.
There was no such conveyancer[21] as he;
All was fee-simple to his strong digestion,
Not one conveyance could be called in question. 330
Though there was none so busy as was he
He was less busy than he seemed to be.
He knew of every judgment, case, and crime
Recorded ever since King William's time.
He could dictate defenses or draft deeds; 335
No one could pinch a comma from his screeds,[22]
And he knew every statute off by rote.
He wore a homely parti-colored coat
Girt with a silken belt of pin-stripe stuff;
Of his appearance I have said enough. 340

   A land-owner, a *Franklin*,[23] had appeared;
White as a daisy-petal was his beard.
A sanguine man, high-colored and benign,
He loved a morning sop of cake in wine.
He lived for pleasure and had always done, 345
For he was Epicurus'[24] very son,
In whose opinion sensual delight
Was the one true felicity in sight.
As noted as St. Julian was for bounty
He made his household free to all the County. 350
His bread, his ale were finest of the fine
And no one had a better stock of wine.
His house was never short of bake-meat pies,
Of fish and flesh, and these in such supplies
It positively snowed with meat and drink 355
And all the dainties that a man could think.
According to the seasons of the year
Changes of dish were ordered to appear.
He kept fat partridges in coops, beyond,

THE FRANKLIN (detail).
Ellesmere Ms.
Huntington Library,
San Marino, Calif.

---

21. **conveyancer:** one who prepares papers for the transfer of real estate or property.
22. **screeds:** long, monotonous documents.
23. **Franklin:** a landowner who is free by birth but not a noble.
24. **Epicurus** (ep' ə kyoor' əs): a Greek philosopher who taught that the pursuit of pleasure is the goal of living.

Many a bream and pike were in his pond.   360
Woe to the cook whose sauces had no sting
Or who was unprepared in anything!
And in his hall a table stood arrayed
And ready all day long, with places laid.
As Justice at the Sessions none stood higher;   365
He often had been Member for the Shire.
A dagger and a little purse of silk
Hung at his girdle, white as morning milk.
As Sheriff he checked audit, every entry.
He was a model among landed gentry.   370

    A *Haberdasher*, a *Dyer*, a *Carpenter*,
A *Weaver* and a *Carpet-maker* were
Among our ranks, all in the livery
Of one impressive guild-fraternity.
They were so trim and fresh their gear would pass   375
For new. Their knives were not tricked out with brass
But wrought with purest silver, which avouches
A like display on girdles and on pouches.
Each seemed a worthy burgess, fit to grace
A guild-hall with a seat upon the dais.   380
Their wisdom would have justified a plan
To make each one of them an alderman;
They had the capital and revenue,
Besides their wives declared it was their due.
And if they did not think so, then they ought;   385
To be called *"Madam"* is a glorious thought,
And so is going to church and being seen
Having your mantle carried like a queen.

    They had a *Cook* with them who stood alone
For boiling chicken with a marrow-bone,   390
Sharp flavoring-powder and a spice for savor.
He could distinguish London ale by flavor,
And he could roast and seethe and broil and fry,
Make good thick soup and bake a tasty pie.
But a great pity, as it seemed to me,   395
Was that he had an ulcer on his knee.
As for blancmange,[25] he made it with the best.

    There was a *Skipper* hailing from far west;
He came from Dartmouth, so I understood.
He rode a farmer's horse as best he could,   400

---

25. **blancmange** (blə mänzh´): a dish of chopped chicken or fish with rice.

In a woolen gown that reached his knee.
A dagger on a lanyard falling free
Hung from his neck under his arm and down.
The summer heat had tanned his color brown,
And certainly he was an excellent fellow.   405
Many a draught of vintage, red and yellow,
He'd drawn at Bordeaux, while the vintner slept.
Few were the rules his tender conscience kept.
If, when he fought, the enemy vessel sank,
He sent his prisoners home; they walked the plank.   410
As for his skill in reckoning his tides,
Currents and many another risk besides,
Moons, harbors, pilots, he had such dispatch
That none from Hull to Carthage was his match.
Hardy he was, prudent in undertaking;   415
His beard in many a tempest had its shaking,
And he knew all the havens as they were
From Gottland to the Cape of Finisterre,[26]
And every creek in Brittany and Spain;
The barge he owned was called *The Maudelayne*.   420

    A *Doctor* too emerged as we proceeded;
No one alive could talk as well as he did
On points of medicine and of surgery,
For, being grounded in astronomy,
He watched his patient's favorable star   425
And, by his Natural Magic, knew what are
The lucky hours and planetary degrees
For making charms and magic effigies.
The cause of every malady you'd got
He knew, and whether dry, cold, moist or hot;[27]   430
He knew their seat, their humor and condition.
He was a perfect practicing physician.
These causes being known for what they were,
He gave the man his medicine then and there.
All his apothecaries in a tribe   435
Were ready with the drugs he would prescribe,
And each made money from the other's guile;
They had been friendly for a goodish while.
He was well-versed in Esculapius too
And what Hippocrates and Rufus knew   440
And Dioscorides, now dead and gone,

---

26. **From Gottland . . . Finisterre:** from Sweden to Spain.
27. **He knew . . . hot:** The body was thought to be composed of equal portions of earth, water, fire, and ice.

Galen and Rhazes, Hali, Serapion,
Averroes, Avicenna, Constantine,
Scotch Bernard, John of Gaddesden, Gilbertine.
In his own diet he observed some measure;   445
There were no superfluities for pleasure,
Only digestives, nutritives and such.
He did not read the Bible very much.
In blood-red garments, slashed with bluish-gray
And lined with taffeta, he rode his way;   450
Yet he was rather close as to expenses
And kept the gold he won in pestilences.
Gold stimulates the heart, or so we're told.
He therefore had a special love of gold.

    A worthy *woman* from beside *Bath* city   455
Was with us, somewhat deaf, which was a pity.
In making cloth she showed so great a bent
She bettered those of Ypres and of Ghent.[28]
In all the parish not a dame dared stir
Towards the altar steps in front of her,   460
And if indeed they did, so wrath was she
As to be quite put out of charity.
Her kerchiefs were of finely woven ground;
I dared have sworn they weighed a good ten pound,
The ones she wore on Sunday, on her head.   465
Her hose were of the finest scarlet red
And gartered tight; her shoes were soft and new.
Bold was her face, handsome, and red in hue.
A worthy woman all her life, what's more
She'd have five husbands, all at the church door,   470
Apart from other company in youth;
No need just now to speak of that, forsooth.
And she had thrice been to Jerusalem,
Seen many strange rivers and passed over them;
She'd been to Rome and also to Boulogne,   475
St. James of Compostella and Cologne,
And she was skilled in wandering by the way.
She had gap-teeth, set widely, truth to say.
Easily on an ambling horse she sat
Well wimpled up, and on her head a hat   480
As broad as is a buckler or a shield;
She had a flowing mantle that concealed
Large hips, her heels spurred sharply under that.
In company she liked to laugh and chat

THE WIFE OF BATH (detail).
Ellesmere Ms.
Huntington Library,
San Marino, Calif.

---

28. **Ypres and Ghent:** centers of Flemish wool trade.

And knew the remedies for love's mischances,   485
An art in which she knew the oldest dances.

  A holy-minded man of good renown
There was, and poor, the *Parson* to a town,
Yet he was rich in holy thought and work.
He also was a learned man, a clerk,   490
Who truly knew Christ's gospel and would preach it
Devoutly to parishioners, and teach it.
Benign and wonderfully diligent,
And patient when adversity was sent
(For so he proved in great adversity)   495
He much disliked extorting tithe or fee,
Nay rather he preferred beyond a doubt
Giving to poor parishioners round about
From his own goods and Easter offerings.
He found sufficiency in little things.   500
Wide was his parish, with houses far asunder,
Yet he neglected not in rain or thunder,
In sickness or in grief, to pay a call
On the remotest whether great or small
Upon his feet, and in his hand a stave.[29]   505
This noble example to his sheep he gave,
First following the word before he taught it,
And it was from the gospel he had caught it.
This little proverb he would add thereto
That if gold rust, what then will iron do?   510
For if a priest be foul in whom we trust
No wonder that a common man should rust;
And shame it is to see—let priests take stock—
A shitten shepherd and a snowy flock.
The true example that a priest should give   515
Is one of cleanness, how the sheep should live.
He did not set his benefice to hire
And leave his sheep encumbered in the mire
Or run to London to earn easy bread
By singing masses for the wealthy dead,   520
Or find some Brotherhood and get enrolled.
He stayed at home and watched over his fold
So that no wolf should make the sheep miscarry.
He was a shepherd and no mercenary.
Holy and virtuous he was, but then   525
Never contemptuous of sinful men,
Never disdainful, never too proud or fine,

---

29. **stave:** a staff.

But was discreet in teaching and benign.
His business was to show a fair behavior
And draw men thus to Heaven and their Savior,   530
Unless indeed a man were obstinate;
And such, whether of high or low estate,
He put to sharp rebuke to say the least.
    I think there never was a better priest.
He sought no pomp or glory in his dealings,   535
No scrupulosity had spiced his feelings.
Christ and His Twelve Apostles and their lore
He taught, but followed it himself before.

    There was a *Plowman* with him there, his brother.
Many a load of dung one time or other   540
He must have carted through the morning dew.
He was an honest worker, good and true,
Living in peace and perfect charity,
And, as the gospel bade him, so did he,
Loving God best with all his heart and mind   545
And then his neighbor as himself, repined
At no misfortune, slacked for no content,
For steadily about his work he went
To thrash his corn, to dig or to manure
Or make a ditch; and he would help the poor   550
For love of Christ and never take a penny
If he could help it, and, as prompt as any,
He paid his tithes in full when they were due
On what he owned, and on his earnings too.
He wore a tabard[30] smock and rode a mare.   555

    There was a *Reeve*, also a *Miller*, there,
A College *Manciple* from the Inns of Court,
A papal *Pardoner* and, in close consort,
A Church-Court *Summoner*, riding at a trot,
And finally myself—that was the lot.   560

    The *Miller* was a chap of sixteen stone,
A great stout fellow big in brawn and bone.
He did well out of them, for he could go
And win the ram at any wrestling show.
Broad, knotty and short-shouldered, he would boast   565
He could heave any door off hinge and post,
Or take a run and break it with his head.
His beard, like any sow or fox, was red

THE MILLER (detail).
*Ellesmere Ms.
Huntington Library,
San Marino, Calif.*

---

30. **tabard:** a short jacket.

And broad as well, as though it were a spade;
And, at its very tip, his nose displayed   570
A wart on which there stood a tuft of hair
Red as the bristles in an old sow's ear.
His nostrils were as black as they were wide,
He had a sword and buckler at his side,
His mighty mouth was like a furnace door.   575
A wrangler and buffoon, he had a store
Of tavern stories, filthy in the main.
His was a master-hand at stealing grain.
He felt it with his thumb and thus he knew
Its quality and took three times his due—   580
A thumb of gold, by God, to gauge an oat!
He wore a hood of blue and a white coat.
He liked to play his bagpipes up and down
And that was how he brought us out of town.

   The *Manciple*[31] came from the Inner Temple;   585
All caterers might follow his example
In buying victuals; he was never rash
Whether he bought on credit or paid cash.
He used to watch the market most precisely
And got in first, and so he did quite nicely.   590
Now isn't it a marvel of God's grace
That an illiterate fellow can outpace
The wisdom of a heap of learned men?
His masters—he had more than thirty then—
All versed in the abstrusest legal knowledge,   595
Could have produced a dozen from their College
Fit to be stewards in land and rents and game
To any Peer in England you could name,
And show him how to live on what he had
Debt-free (unless of course the Peer were mad)   600
Or be as frugal as he might desire,
And they were fit to help about the Shire
In any legal case there was to try;
And yet this Manciple could wipe their eye.

   The *Reeve*[32] was old and choleric and thin;   605
His beard was shaven closely to the skin,
His shorn hair came abruptly to a stop
Above his ears, and he was docked on top
Just like a priest in front; his legs were lean,

---

31. **Manciple:** a purchasing agent.
32. **Reeve:** a minor official or steward on an estate.

Like sticks they were, no calf was to be seen.   610
He kept his bins and garners very trim;
No auditor could gain a point on him.
And he could judge by watching drought and rain
The yield he might expect from seed and grain.
His master's sheep, his animals and hens,   615
Pigs, horses, dairies, stores and cattle-pens
Were wholly trusted to his government.
And he was under contract to present
The accounts, right from his master's earliest years.
No one had ever caught him in arrears.   620
No bailiff, serf, or herdsman dared to kick,
He knew their dodges, knew their every trick;
Feared like the plague he was, by those beneath.
He had a lovely dwelling on a heath,
Shadowed in green by trees above the sward.   625
A better hand at bargains than his lord,
He had grown rich and had a store of treasure
Well tucked away, yet out it came to pleasure
His lord with subtle loans or gifts of goods,
To earn his thanks and even coats and hoods.   630
When young he'd learnt a useful trade and still
He was a carpenter of first-rate skill.
The stallion-cob he rode at a slow trot
Was dapple-gray and bore the name of Scot.
He wore an overcoat of bluish shade   635
And rather long; he had a rusty blade
Slung at his side. He came, as I heard tell,
From Norfolk, near a place called Baldeswell.
His coat was tucked under his belt and splayed.
He rode the hindmost of our cavalcade.   640

    There was a *Summoner*[33] with us in the place
Who had a fire-red cherubinny face,
For he had carbuncles. His eyes were narrow,
He was as hot and lecherous as a sparrow.
Black, scabby brows he had, and a thin beard.   645
Children were afraid when he appeared.
No quicksilver, lead ointments, tartar creams,
Boracic, no, nor brimstone, so it seems,
Could make a salve that had the power to bite,
Clean up or cure his whelks[34] of knobby white   650
Or purge the pimples sitting on his cheeks.

---

33. **Summoner:** one paid to summon sinners to church courts.
34. **whelks:** pimples.

Garlic he loved, and onions too, and leeks,
And drinking strong red wine till all was hazy.
Then he would shout and jabber as if crazy,
And wouldn't speak a word except in Latin   655
When he was drunk, such tags as he was pat in;
He only had a few, say two or three
That he had mugged up out of some decree;
No wonder, for he heard them every day.
And, as you know, a man can teach a jay   660
To call out "Walter" better than the Pope.
But had you tried to test his wits and grope
For more, you'd have found nothing in the bag.
Then *"Questio quid juris"*[35] was his tag.
He was a gentle varlet[36] and a kind one,   665
No better fellow if you went to find one.
He would allow—just for a quart of wine—
Any good lad to keep a concubine
A twelvemonth, and dispense it altogether!
Yet he could pluck a finch to leave no feather;   670
And if he found some rascal with a maid
He would instruct him not to be afraid
In such a case of the Archdeacon's curse
(Unless the rascal's soul were in his purse)
For in his purse the punishment should be.   675
"Purse is the good Archdeacon's Hell," said he.
But well I know he lied in what he said;
A curse should put a guilty man in dread,
For curses kill, as shriving brings, salvation.
We should beware of excommunication.   680
Thus, by mere threat, this fellow could possess
The boys and girls of all the Diocese,
He knew their secrets and they went in dread.
He wore a garland set upon his head
Large as the holly-bush upon a stake   685
Outside an ale-house, and he had a cake,
A round one, which it was his joke to wield
As if it were intended for a shield.

   He and a gentle *Pardoner*[37] rode together,
A bird from Charing Cross of the same feather,   690
Just back from visiting the Court of Rome.

---

35. **Questio quid juris** *Latin:* "The question is, what is the point in law?"
36. **varlet:** rascal, knave.
37. **Pardoner:** one who has the authority from the Pope to sell pardons and indulgences.

THE PARDONER (detail).
Ellesmere Ms.
Huntington Library,
San Marino, Calif.

He loudly sang *"Come hither, love, come home!"*
The Summoner sang deep seconds to this song,
No trumpet ever sounded half so strong.
This Pardoner had hair as yellow as wax 695
Hanging down smoothly like a hank of flax.
In driblets fell his locks behind his head
Down to his shoulders which they overspread;
Thinly they fell, like rat-tails, one by one.
He wore no hood upon his head, for fun; 700
The hood inside his wallet had been stowed,
He aimed at riding in the latest mode;
But for a little cap his head was bare
And he had bulging eye-balls, like a hare.
He'd sewed a holy relic on his cap; 705
His wallet lay before him on his lap,
Brimful of pardons come from Rome all hot.
He had the same small voice a goat has got.
His chin no beard had harbored, nor would harbor,
Smoother than ever chin was left by barber. 710
I judge he was a gelding, or a mare.
As to his trade, from Berwick down to Ware
There was no pardoner of equal grace,
For in his trunk he had a pillow-case
Which he asserted was Our Lady's veil. 715
He said he had a gobbet[38] of the sail
Saint Peter had the time when he made bold
To walk the waves, till Jesu Christ took hold.
He had a cross of metal set with stones
And, in a glass, a rubble of pigs' bones. 720
And with these relics, any time he found
Some poor up-country parson to astound,
On one short day, in money down, he drew
More than the parson in a month or two,
And by his flatteries and prevarication 725
Made monkeys of the priest and congregation.
But still to do him justice first and last
In church he was a noble ecclesiast.
How well he read a lesson or told a story!
But best of all he sang an Offertory, 730
For well he knew that when that song was sung
He'd have to preach and tune his honey-tongue
And (well he could) win silver from the crowd.
That's why he sang so merrily and loud.

---

38. **gobbet:** a piece, or chunk.

Now I have told you shortly, in a clause, 735
The rank, the array, the number and the cause
Of our assembly in this company
In Southwark, at that high-class hostelry
Known as *The Tabard*, close beside *The Bell*.
And now the time has come for me to tell 740
How we behaved that evening; I'll begin
After we had alighted at the Inn.
Then I'll report our journey, stage by stage,
All the remainder of our pilgrimage.
But first I beg of you, in courtesy, 745
Not to condemn me as unmannerly
If I speak plainly and with no concealings
And give account of all their words and dealings,
Using their very phrases as they fell.
For certainly, as you all know so well, 750
He who repeats a tale after a man
Is bound to say, as nearly as he can,
Each single word, if he remembers it,
However rudely spoken or unfit,
Or else the tale he tells will be untrue, 755
The things invented and the phrases new.
He may not flinch although it were his brother,
If he says one word he must say the other.
And Christ Himself spoke broad in Holy Writ,
And as you know there's nothing there unfit, 760
And Plato says, for those with power to read,
"The word should be as cousin to the deed."
Further I beg you to forgive it me
If I neglect the order and degree
And what is due to rank in what I've planned. 765
I'm short of wit as you will understand.

Our *Host*[39] gave us great welcome; everyone
Was given a place and supper was begun.
He served the finest victuals you could think,
The wine was strong and we were glad to drink. 770
A very striking man our Host withal,
And fit to be a marshal in a hall.
His eyes were bright, his girth a little wide;
There is no finer burgess in Cheapside.
Bold in his speech, yet wise and full of tact, 775
There was no manly attribute he lacked,

---

39. **Host:** Harry Bailly, who owned an inn in Southwark in Chaucer's day.

What's more he was a merry-hearted man.
After our meal he jokingly began
To talk of sport, and, among other things
After we'd settled up our reckonings,   780
He said as follows: "Truly, gentlemen,
You're very welcome and I can't think when
—Upon my word I'm telling you no lie—
I've seen a gathering here that looked so spry,
No, not this year, as in this tavern now.   785
I'd think you up some fun if I knew how.
And, as it happens, a thought has just occurred
And it will cost you nothing, on my word.
You're off to Canterbury—well, God speed!
Blessed St. Thomas answer to your need!   790
And I don't doubt, before the journey's done
You mean to while the time in tales and fun.
Indeed, there's little pleasure for your bones
Riding along and all as dumb as stones.
So let me then propose for your enjoyment,   795
Just as I said, a suitable employment.
And if my notion suits and you agree
And promise to submit yourselves to me
Playing your parts exactly as I say
Tomorrow as you ride along the way,   800
Then by my father's soul (and he is dead)
If you don't like it you can have my head!
Hold up your hands, and not another word."
    Well, our consent of course was not deferred,
It seemed not worth a serious debate;   805
We all agreed to it at any rate
And bade him issue what commands he would.
"My lords," he said, "now listen for your good,
And please don't treat my notion with disdain.
This is the point, to make it short and plain.   810
Each one of you shall help to make things slip
By telling two stories on the outward trip
To Canterbury, that's what I intend,
And, on the homeward way to journey's end
Another two, tales from the days of old;   815
And then the man whose story is best told,
That is to say who gives the fullest measure
Of good morality and general pleasure,
He shall be given a supper, paid by all,
Here in this tavern, in this very hall,   820
When we come back again from Canterbury.
And in the hope to keep you bright and merry

I'll go along with you myself and ride
All at my own expense and serve as guide.
I'll be the judge, and those who won't obey   825
Shall pay for what we spend upon the way.
Now if you all agree to what you've heard
Tell me at once without another word,
And I will make arrangements early for it."
   Of course we all agreed, in fact we swore it   830
Delightedly, and made entreaty too
That he should act as he proposed to do,
Become our Governor in short, and be
Judge of our tales and general referee,
And set the supper at a certain price.   835
We promised to be ruled by his advice
Come high, come low; unanimously thus
We set him up in judgment over us.
More wine was fetched, the business being done;
We drank it off and up went everyone   840
To bed without a moment of delay.
   Early next morning at the spring of day
Up rose our Host and roused us like a cock,
Gathering us together in a flock,
And off we rode, at slightly faster pace   845
Than walking, to St.Thomas' watering-place;
And there our Host drew up, began to ease
His horse, and said, "Now, listen if you please,
My lords! Remember what you promised me.
If evensong and matins will agree   850
Let's see who shall be first to tell a tale.
And as I hope to drink good wine and ale
I'll be your judge. The rebel who disobeys,
However much the journey costs, he pays.
Now draw for cut and then we can depart;   855
The man who draws the shortest cut shall start. . . .

Getting at Meaning

1. Which of the pilgrims belong to each of these five categories: nobility, clergy, professionals, craftsmen, servants and laborers? Which of the pilgrims are part of the old feudal system? Which belong to the emerging middle class?

2. The first pilgrim is ". . . a true, a perfect gentle-knight." How does the description of the Knight support this conclusion? Which phrases or lines summarize each of the following characters: Merchant, Sergeant, Clerk, Franklin, Parson, Plowman, Summoner?

3. Which pilgrims are unscrupulous? Explain your choices.

4. What character types are represented among the pilgrims? Are these character types evident in contemporary life? Explain your answer.

5. Only three women embark on the pilgrimage. Discuss reasons why Chaucer might have included these particular women.

6. What are the rules of the storytelling contest, as explained by the Host?

Developing Skills in Reading Literature

1. **Characterization.** "The Prologue" is primarily a series of character sketches created through carefully selected details. These details include precise words and phrases that describe physical appearance; for example, the Doctor wore ". . . blood-red garments, slashed with bluish-gray/And lined with taffeta. . . ." Details also describe the actions and accomplishments of each pilgrim, as in the sketch of the Oxford Clerk: "Whatever money from his friends he took/He spent on learning or another book." Comments by the speaker provide additional information about many of the characters; for instance, the speaker calls the Parson "Benign and wonderfully diligent."

Similes, too, create vivid impressions of both appearance and inner qualities. These similes describe two of the pilgrims:

Squire: He was embroidered like a meadow bright
And full of freshest flowers, red and white.
Pardoner: This Pardoner had hair as yellow as wax
Hanging down smoothly like a hank of flax.

Chose five of the pilgrims and analyze each description, identifying the significant details and commenting on their effect.

2. **Meter.** Meter is the repetition of a regular rhythmic unit in a line of poetry. Each unit of meter is known as a foot, with each foot having one stressed and one or two unstressed syllables. One type of metrical foot is the iamb, one unstressed syllable followed by a stressed syllable (˘ ´). A line of poetry consisting of iambs would be named for the type of foot (iambic) and also for the number of feet in the line; for example, monometer (one foot), trimeter (three feet), or hexameter (six feet). Iambic pentameter is the most common metrical pattern in English poetry, for it closely approximates the natural cadence of the spoken language.

The process of determining meter is known as scanning. For example, these two lines from "The Prologue" are scanned as follows:

Ĭt hap/penĕd ĭn/thăt seá/sŏn thát/one dáy

Ĭn South/wărk, aí/The Tab/ard, aś/Ĭ láy

Select one character sketch from "The Prologue" and scan each line. Notice that the regularity of the meter is not apparent as you read the sketch aloud, due to pauses for punctuation, to the emphasis of key words, and to the continuity of thought from one line to the next.

3. **Rhyme, Couplet, and Heroic Couplet.** When two consecutive lines of poetry end with rhyming words, words whose accented vowels and all succeeding sounds are identical, the lines are called a couplet. When their meter is iambic pentameter, the lines constitute a heroic couplet. Chaucer introduced the heroic couplet into English literature.

Examine a ten-line unit of "The Prologue" and analyze the heroic couplets within the unit. You might encounter two lines ending with words that rhyme imprecisely; for example breath and heath. This kind of rhyme is called off-rhyme, near-rhyme, imperfect rhyme, slant rhyme, or sprung rhyme. Some off-rhymes result from changes in the pronunciations of words, others from a poet's intent to vary a regular metrical pattern.

4. Tone. The details in a literary work and the way that these details are presented reveal the writer's tone. Among the many possible tones are sarcastic, sympathetic, objective, and condescending. Think about the human weaknesses exhibited by the pilgrims. What is Chaucer's attitude toward these weaknesses? What is his attitude toward the clergy? Which pilgrims does he seem to admire the most? Characterize the overall tone of "The Prologue."

Developing Writing Skills

1. **Writing a Character Sketch.** Although the Host is not described in as much detail as the other pilgrims, the reader does learn a great deal about him. Write a one-paragraph character sketch of the Host, based on the descriptive details in "The Prologue" and on the inferences you might make from the Host's words and actions.

2. **Writing Heroic Couplets.** Select a contemporary entertainer, politician, statesman, or athlete, and write a poetic description of that person in heroic couplets. Use the character sketches in "The Prologue" as a model.

3. **Writing an Explanation.** Imagine that you are the Host at The Tabard and that your tables each seat four guests. Select twelve pilgrims and assign four to each of three tables. In a composition explain your reasons for seating each group of pilgrims together.

THE CANTERBURY PILGRIMS LEAVING CANTERBURY.
British Museum.

The Nun's Priest's Tale

The Knight, who drew the shortest cut, told the first tale, followed by the Miller, the Reeve, the Cook, the Sergeant at the Law, the Skipper, and the Prioress. The speaker himself tells two tales, and then the Monk presents his tale. The Host, feeling the need for a change of pace, asks Sir John, the Nun's Priest, to tell a merry tale that will "make our trouble pack." Sir John does just that and teaches a lesson as well.

Once, long ago, there dwelt a poor old widow
In a small cottage by a little meadow
Beside a grove and standing in a dale.
This widow-woman of whom I tell my tale
Since the sad day when last she was a wife   5
Had led a very patient, simple life.
Little she had in capital or rent,
But still by making do with what God sent
She kept herself and her two daughters going.
Three hefty sows—no more—were all her showing.   10
Three cows as well; there was a sheep called Molly.
   Sooty her hall, her kitchen melancholy.
And there she ate full many a slender meal;
There was no *sauce piquante*[1] to spice her veal,
No dainty morsel ever passed her throat,   15
According to her cloth she cut her coat.
Repletion never left her in disquiet
And all her physic was a temperate diet,
Hard work for exercise and heart's content.
And rich man's gout did nothing to prevent   20
Her dancing, apoplexy[2] struck her not;
She drank no wine, nor white nor red had got.
Her board was mostly served with white and black,
Milk and brown bread, in which she found no lack;
Broiled bacon or an egg or two were common,   25
She was in fact a sort of dairy-woman.
   She had a yard that was enclosed about
By a stockade and a dry ditch without,
In which she kept a cock called Chanticleer.
In all the land for crowing he'd no peer;   30

---

1. *sauce piquante* (pē' kənt) *French:* a sharp sauce.
2. **apoplexy:** a stroke.

His voice was jollier than the organ blowing
In church on Sundays, he was great at crowing.
Far, far more regular than any clock
Or abbey bell the crowing of this cock.
The equinoctial wheel and its position   35
At each ascent he knew by intuition;
At every hour—fifteen degrees of movement—
He crowed so well there could be no improvement.
His comb was redder than fine coral, tall
And battlemented like a castle wall,   40
His bill was black and shone as bright as jet,
Like azure were his legs and they were set
On azure toes with nails of lily white,
Like burnished gold his feathers, flaming bright.
    This gentlecock was master in some measure   45
Of seven hens, all there to do his pleasure.
They were his sisters and his paramours,
Colored like him in all particulars;
She with the loveliest dyes upon her throat
Was known as gracious Lady Pertelote.   50
Courteous she was, discreet and debonair,
Companionable too, and took such care
In her deportment, since she was seven days old
She held the heart of Chanticleer controlled,
Locked up securely in her every limb;   55
O such a happiness his love to him!
And such a joy it was to hear them sing,
As when the glorious sun began to spring,
In sweet accord *My Love is far from land*[3]
—For in those far off days I understand   60
All birds and animals could speak and sing.
    Now it befell, as dawn began to spring,
When Chanticleer and Pertelote and all
His wives were perched in this poor widow's hall
(Fair Pertelote was next him on the perch),   65
This Chanticleer began to groan and lurch
Like someone sorely troubled by a dream,
And Pertelote who heard him roar and scream
Was quite aghast and said, "O dearest heart,
What's ailing you? Why do you groan and start?   70
Fie, what a sleeper! What a noise to make!"
"Madam," he said, "I beg you not to take
Offense, but by the Lord I had a dream

---

3. *My Love is far from land:* the first line of a popular song.

So terrible just now I had to scream;
I still can feel my heart racing from fear.   75
God turn my dream to good and guard all here,
And keep my body out of durance[4] vile!
I dreamt that roaming up and down a while
Within our yard I saw a kind of beast,
A sort of hound that tried or seemed at least   80
To try and seize me—would have killed me dead!
His color was a blend of yellow and red,
His ears and tail were tipped with sable fur
Unlike the rest; he was a russet cur.
Small was his snout, his eyes were glowing bright.   85
It was enough to make one die of fright.
That was no doubt what made me groan and swoon."
    "For shame," she said, "you timorous poltroon!
Alas, what cowardice! By God above,
You've forfeited my heart and lost my love.   90
I cannot love a coward, come what may.
For certainly, whatever we may say,
All women long—and O that it might be!—
For husbands tough, dependable and free,
Secret, discreet, no niggard,[5] not a fool   95
That boasts and then will find his courage cool
At every trifling thing! By God above,
How dare you say for shame, and to your love,
That anything at all was to be feared?
Have you no manly heart to match your beard?   100
And can a dream reduce you to such terror?
Dreams are a vanity, God knows, pure error.
Dreams are engendered in the too-replete
From vapors in the belly, which compete
With others, too abundant, swollen tight.   105
    "No doubt the redness in your dream tonight
Comes from the superfluity and force
Of the red choler in your blood. Of course;
That is what puts a dreamer in the dread
Of crimsoned arrows, fires flaming red,   110
Of great red monsters making as to fight him,
And big red whelps and little ones to bite him;
Just so the black and melancholy vapors
Will set a sleeper shrieking, cutting capers
And swearing that black bears, black bulls as well,   115
Or blackest fiends are haling him to Hell.

---

4. **durance:** long imprisonment.
5. **niggard:** miser.

And there are other vapors that I know
That on a sleeping man will work their woe,
But I'll pass on as lightly as I can.
   "Take Cato now, that was so wise a man,   120
Did he not say, 'Take no account of dreams'?
Now, sir," she said, "on flying from these beams,
For love of God do take some laxative;
Upon my soul that's the advice to give
For melancholy choler; let me urge   125
You free yourself from vapors with a purge.
And that you may have no excuse to tarry
By saying this town has no apothecary,
I shall myself instruct you and prescribe
Herbs that will cure all vapors of that tribe,   130
Herbs from our very farmyard! You will find
Their natural property is to unbind
And purge you well beneath and well above.
Now don't forget it, dear, for God's own love!
Your face is choleric and shows distension;   135
Be careful lest the sun in his ascension
Should catch you full of humors, hot and many.
And if he does, my dear, I'll lay a penny
It means a bout of fever or a breath
Of tertian ague.[6] You may catch your death.   140
   "Worms for a day or two I'll have to give
As a digestive, then your laxative.
Centaury, fumitory, caper-spurge
And hellebore will make a splendid purge;
And then there's laurel or the blackthorn berry,   145
Ground-ivy too that makes our yard so merry;
Peck them right up, my dear, and swallow whole.
Be happy, husband, by your father's soul!
Don't be afraid of dreams. I'll say no more."
   "Madam," he said, "I thank you for your lore,   150
But with regard to Cato all the same,
His wisdom has, no doubt, a certain fame,
But though he said that we should take no heed
Of dreams, by God in ancient books I read
Of many a man of more authority   155
Than ever Cato was, believe you me,
Who say the very opposite is true
And prove their theories by experience too.
Dreams have quite often been significations

---

6. **tertian ague:** a form of malaria.

As well of triumphs as of tribulations   160
That people undergo in this our life.
This needs no argument at all, dear wife,
The proof is all too manifest indeed.
   "One of the greatest authors one can read
Says thus: there were two comrades once who went   165
On pilgrimage, sincere in their intent.
And as it happened they had reached a town
Where such a throng was milling up and down,
And yet so scanty the accommodation,
They could not find themselves a habitation,   170
No, not a cottage that could lodge them both;
And so they separated, very loath,
Under constraint of this necessity
And each went off to find some hostelry,
And lodge whatever way his luck might fall.   175
   "The first of them found refuge in a stall
Down in a yard, with oxen and a plow.
His friend found lodging for himself somehow
Elsewhere, by accident or destiny
Which governs all of us equally.   180
   "Now it so happened, long ere it was day,
This fellow had a dream, and as he lay
In bed it seemed he heard his comrade call,
'Help! I am lying in an ox's stall
And shall tonight be murdered as I lie.   185
Help me, dear brother, help or I shall die!
Come in all haste!' Such were the words he spoke;
The dreamer, lost in terror, then awoke.
But once awake he paid it no attention,
Turned over and dismissed it as invention,   190
It was a dream, he thought, a fantasy.
And twice he dreamt this dream successively.
   "Yet a third time his comrade came again,
Or seemed to come, and said, 'I have been slain.
Look, look! my wounds are bleeding wide and deep.   195
Rise early in the morning, break your sleep
And go to the west gate. You there shall see
A cart all loaded up with dung,' said he,
'And in that dung my body has been hidden.
Boldly arrest that cart as you are bidden.   200
It was my money that they killed me for.'
   "He told him every detail, sighing sore,
And pitiful in feature, pale of hue.
This dream, believe me, Madam, turned out true;
For in the dawn as soon as it was light,   205

He went to where his friend had spent the night;
And when he came upon the cattle-stall
He looked about him and began to call.
    "The innkeeper, appearing thereupon,
Quickly gave answer, 'Sir, your friend has gone.   210
He left the town a little after dawn.'
The man began to feel suspicious, drawn
By memories of his dream—the western gate,
The dung-cart—off he went, he would not wait
Towards the western entry. There he found,   215
Seemingly on its way to dung some ground,
A dung-cart loaded on the very plan
Described so closely by the murdered man.
So he began to shout courageously
For right and vengeance on the felony,   220
'My friend's been killed! There's been a foul attack,
He's in that cart and gaping on his back!
Fetch the authorities, get the sheriff down
—Whosever job it is to run the town—
Help! My companion's murdered, sent to glory!'   225
    "What need I add to finish off the story?
People ran out and cast the cart to ground,
And in the middle of the dung they found
The murdered man. The corpse was fresh and new.
    "O blessed God, that art so just and true,   230
Thus thou revealest murder! As we say,
'Murder will out.' We see it day by day.
Murder's a foul, abominable treason,
So loathsome to God's justice, to God's reason,
He will not suffer its concealment. True,   235
Things may lie hidden for a year or two,
But still 'Murder will out,' that's my conclusion.
    "All the town officers in great confusion
Seized on the carter and they gave him hell,
And then they racked the innkeeper as well,   240
And both confessed. And then they took the wrecks
And there and then they hanged them by their necks.
    "By this we see that dreams are to be dreaded.
And in the selfsame book I find embedded,
Right in the very chapter after this   245
(I'm not inventing, as I hope for bliss)
The story of two men who started out
To cross the sea—for merchandise no doubt—
But as the winds were contrary they waited.
It was a pleasant town, I should have stated,   250
Merrily grouped about the haven-side.

A few days later with the evening tide
The wind veered round so as to suit them best;
They were delighted and they went to rest
Meaning to sail next morning early. Well,   255
To one of them a miracle befell.
　　"This man as he lay sleeping, it would seem,
Just before dawn, had an astounding dream.
He thought a man was standing by his bed
Commanding him to wait, and thus he said: 260
'If you set sail to-morrow as you intend,
You will be drowned. My tale is at an end.'
　　"He woke and told his friend what had occurred
And begged him that the journey be deferred
At least a day, implored him not to start.   265
But his companion, lying there apart,
Began to laugh and treat him to derision.
'I'm not afraid,' he said, 'of any vision,
To let it interfere with my affairs;
A straw for all your dreamings and your scares.   270
Dreams are just empty nonsense, merest japes;[7]
Why, people dream all day of owls and apes,
All sorts of trash that can't be understood,
Things that have never happened and never could.
But as I see you mean to stay behind   275
And miss the tide for willful sloth of mind
God knows I'm sorry for it, but good day!'
And so he took his leave and went his way.
　　"And yet, before they'd covered half the trip
—I don't know what went wrong—there was a rip   280
And by some accident the ship went down,
Her bottom rent,[8] all hands aboard to drown
In sight of all the vessels at her side
That had put out upon the selfsame tide.
　　"So, my dear Pertelote, if you discern   285
The force of these examples you may learn
One never should be careless about dreams,
For undeniably I say it seems
That many are a sign of trouble breeding.
　　"Now, take St. Kenelm's life which I've been reading;   · 290
He was Kenulphus' son, the noble King
Of Mercia. Now, St. Kenelm dreamt a thing
Shortly before they murdered him one day.
He saw his murder in a dream, I say.

---

7. **japes:** jokes.
8. **rent:** ripped, torn.

His nurse expounded it and gave her reason   295
On every point and warned him against treason.
But as the saint was only seven years old
All that she said about it left him cold.
He was so holy, how could visions hurt?
　　"By God, I willingly would give my shirt   300
To have you read his legend as I've read it;
And, Madam Pertelote, upon my credit,
Macrobius wrote of dreams and can explain us
The vision of young Scipio Africanus,
And he affirms that dreams can give a due   305
Warning of things that later on come true.
　　"And then there's the Old Testament—a manual
Well worth your study; see the *Book of Daniel*.
Did Daniel think a dream was vanity?
Read about Joseph too and you will see   310
That many dreams—I do not say that all—
Give cognizance of what is to befall.
　　"Look at Lord Pharaoh, king of Egypt! Look
At what befell his butler and his cook.
Did not their visions have a certain force?   315
But those who study history of course
Meet many dreams that set them wondering.
　　"What about Croesus too, the Lydian king,
Who dreamt that he was sitting in a tree,
Meaning he would be hanged? It had to be.   320
　　"Or take Andromache, great Hector's wife;
The day on which he was to lose his life
She dreamt about, the very night before,
And realized that if Hector went to war
He would be lost that very day in battle.   325
She warned him; he dismissed it all as prattle
And sallied forth to fight, being self-willed,
And there he met Achilles and was killed.
The tale is long and somewhat overdrawn,
And anyhow it's very nearly dawn,   330
So let me say in very brief conclusion
My dream undoubtedly foretells confusion,
It bodes me ill, I say. And, furthermore,
Upon your laxatives I set no store,
For they are venomous. I've suffered by them   335
Often enough before and I defy them.
　　"And now, let's talk of fun and stop all this.
Dear Madam, as I hope for Heaven's bliss,
Of one thing God has sent me plenteous grace,
For when I see the beauty of your face,   340

That scarlet loveliness about your eyes,
All thought of terror and confusion dies.
For it's as certain as the Creed, I know,
Mulier est hominis confusio
(A Latin tag, dear Madam, meaning this: 345
'Woman is man's delight and all his bliss'), . . ."
 And with that word he flew down from the beams,
For it was day, and down his hens flew all,
And with a chuck he gave the troupe a call
For he had found a seed upon the floor.   350
Royal he was, he was afraid no more.
He feathered Pertelote in wanton play
And trod her twenty times ere prime of day.
Grim as a lion's was his manly frown
As on his toes he sauntered up and down;   355
He scarcely deigned to set his foot to ground
And every time a seed of corn was found
He gave a chuck, and up his wives ran all.
Thus royal as a prince who strides his hall
Leave we this Chanticleer engaged on feeding   360
And pass to the adventure that was breeding.
 Now when the month in which the world began,
March, the first month, when God created man,
Was over, and the thirty-second day
Thereafter ended, on the third of May,   365
It happened that Chanticleer in all his pride,
His seven wives attendant at his side,
Cast his eyes upward to the blazing sun,
Which in the sign of *Taurus* then had run
His twenty-one degrees and somewhat more,   370
And knew by nature and no other lore
That it was nine o'clock. With blissful voice
He crew triumphantly and said, "Rejoice,
Behold the sun! The sun is up, my seven.
Look, it has climbed forty degrees in heaven,   375
Forty degrees and one in fact, by this.
Dear Madam Pertelote, my earthly bliss,
Hark to those blissful birds and how they sing!
Look at those pretty flowers, how they spring!
Solace and revel fill my heart!" He laughed.   380
 But in that moment Fate let fly her shaft;
Ever the latter end of joy is woe,
God knows that worldly joy is swift to go.
A rhetorician with a flair for style
Could chronicle this maxim in his file   385

Of Notable Remarks with safe conviction.
Then let the wise give ear; this is no fiction.
   My story is as true, I undertake,
As that of good Sir Lancelot du Lake
Who held all women in such high esteem.   390
Let me return full circle to my theme.
   A coal-tipped fox of sly iniquity
That had been lurking round the grove for three
Long years, that very night burst through and passed
Stockade and hedge, as Providence forecast,   395
Into the yard where Chanticleer the Fair
Was wont, with all his ladies, to repair.
Still in a bed of cabbages he lay
Until about the middle of the day
Watching the cock and waiting for his cue,   400
As all these homicides so gladly do
That lie about in wait to murder men.
O false assassin, lurking in thy den!
O new Iscariot, new Ganelon!
And O Greek Sinon,[9] thou whose treachery won   405
Troy town and brought it utterly to sorrow!
O Chanticleer, accursed be that morrow
That brought thee to the yard from thy high beams!
Thou hadst been warned, and truly, by thy dreams
That this would be a perilous day for thee.   410
   But that which God's foreknowledge can foresee
Must needs occur, as certain men of learning
Have said. Ask any scholar of discerning;
He'll say the Schools are filled with altercation
On this vexed matter of predestination,   415
Long bandied by a hundred thousand men.
How can I sift it to the bottom then?
The Holy Doctor St. Augustine shines
In this, and there is Bishop Bradwardine's[10]
Authority, Boethius'[11] too, decreeing   420
Whether the fact of God's divine foreseeing
Constrains me to perform a certain act
—And by "constraint" I mean the simple fact
Of mere compulsion by necessity—

---

9. **Sinon:** the Greek who tricked King Priam into admitting the Trojan horse to Troy.
10. **Bishop Bradwardine:** contemporary theologian.
11. **Boethius:** an esteemed philosopher and musician whose work Chaucer translated.

Or whether a free choice is granted me   425
To do a given act or not to do it,
Though, ere it was accomplished, God foreknew it,
Or whether Providence is not so stringent
And merely makes necessity contingent.
   But I decline discussion of the matter;   430
My tale is of a cock and of the clatter
That came of following his wife's advice
To walk about his yard on the precise
Morning after the dream of which I told.
   O women's counsel is so often cold!   435
A woman's counsel brought us first to woe,
Made Adam out of Paradise to go,
Where he had been so merry, so well at ease.
But, for I know not whom it may displease
If I suggest that women are to blame,   440
Pass over that; I only speak in game.
Read the authorities to know about
What has been said of women; you'll find out.
These are the cock's words, and not mine, I'm giving;
I think no harm of any woman living.   445
   Merrily in her dust-bath in the sand
Lay Pertelote. Her sisters were at hand
Basking in sunlight. Chanticleer sang free,
More merrily than a mermaid in the sea
(For *Physiologus* reports the thing   450
And says how well and merrily they sing).
And so it happened as he cast his eye
Towards the cabbage at a butterfly
It fell upon the fox there, lying low.
Gone was all inclination then to crow.   455
"Cok cok," he cried, giving a sudden start,
As one who feels a terror at his heart,
For natural instinct teaches beasts to flee
The moment they perceive an enemy,
Though they had never met with it before.   460
   This Chanticleer was shaken to the core
And would have fled. The fox was quick to say
However, "Sir! Whither so fast away?
Are you afraid of me that am your friend?
It would be worse than fiendish to intend   465
Some violence or villainy upon you;
Dear sir, I was not even spying on you!
Truly I came to do no other thing
Than just to lie and listen to you sing.
You have as merry a voice as God has given   470

To any angel in the courts of Heaven;
To that you add a musical sense as strong
As had Boethius who was skilled in song.
My Lord your Father (God receive his soul!),
Your mother too—how courtly, what control!—   475
Have honored my poor house, to my great ease;
And you, sir, too, I should be glad to please.
For, when it comes to singing, I'll say this
(Else may these eyes of mine be barred from bliss),
There never was a singer I would rather   480
Have heard at dawn than your respected father.
All that he sang came welling from his soul
And how he put his voice under control!
The pains he took to keep his eyes tight shut
In concentration—then the tip-toe strut,   485
The slender neck stretched out, the delicate beak!
No singer could approach him in technique
Or rival him in song, still less surpass.
I've read the story in *Burnel the Ass*,[12]
Among some other verses, of a cock   490
Whose leg in youth was broken by a knock
A clergyman's son had given him, and for this
He made the father lose his benefice.
But certainly there's no comparison
Between the subtlety of such an one   495
And the discretion of your father's art
And wisdom. Oh, for charity of heart,
Can you not emulate your sire and sing?"
    This Chanticleer began to beat a wing
As one incapable of smelling treason,   500
So wholly had this flattery ravished reason.
Alas, my lords! there's many a sycophant[13]
And flatterer that fill your courts with cant
And give more pleasure with their zeal forsooth
Than he who speaks in soberness and truth.   505
Read what *Ecclesiasticus*[14] records
Of flatterers. 'Ware treachery, my lords!
    This Chanticleer stood high upon his toes,
He stretched his neck, his eyes began to close,

---

12. **Burnel the Ass:** a poem by Wireker about a priest's son who mistreats a
rooster and the rooster's revenge.
13. **sycophant** (sik' ə fənt): one who attempts to win favor by flattery.
14. **Ecclesiasticus:** a book of proverbs in The Apocrypha. Not a reference to
Ecclesiastes in the Old Testament.

His beak to open; with his eyes shut tight 510
He then began to sing with all his might.
   Sir Russel Fox then leapt to the attack,
Grabbing his gorge he flung him o'er his back
And off he bore him to the woods, the brute,
And for the moment there was no pursuit. 515
   O Destiny that may not be evaded!
Alas that Chanticleer had so paraded!
Alas that he had flown down from the beams!
O that his wife took no account of dreams!
And on a Friday, too, to risk their necks! 520
O Venus, goddess of the joys of sex,
Since Chanticleer thy mysteries professed
And in thy service always did his best,
And more for pleasure than to multiply
His kind, on thine own day is he to die? 525
   O Geoffrey,[15] thou my dear and sovereign master
Who, when they brought King Richard to disaster
And shot him dead, lamented so his death,
Would that I had thy skill, thy gracious breath,
To chide a Friday half so well as you! 530
(For he was killed upon a Friday too.)
Then I could fashion you a rhapsody
For Chanticleer in dread and agony.
   Sure never such a cry or lamentation
Was made by ladies of high Trojan station, 535
When Ilium fell and Pyrrhus with his sword
Grabbed Priam by the beard, their king and lord,
And slew him there as the *Aeneid* tells,
As what was uttered by those hens. Their yells
Surpassed them all in palpitating fear 540
When they beheld the rape of Chanticleer.
Dame Pertelote emitted sovereign shrieks
That echoed up in anguish to the peaks
Louder than those extorted from the wife
Of Hasdrubal[16] when he had lost his life 545
And Carthage all in flame and ashes lay.
She was so full of torment and dismay
That in the very flames she chose her part
And burnt to ashes with a steadfast heart.
O woeful hens, louder your shrieks and higher 550
Than those of Roman matrons when the fire

---

15. **Geoffrey:** a reference to Geoffrey de Vinsauf, a writer.
16. **Hasdrubal** (haz' dru bəl): a Carthaginian general killed by the Romans in 146 B.C.

Consumed their husbands, senators of Rome,
When Nero burnt their city and their home,
Beyond a doubt that Nero was their bale![17]
   Now let me turn again to tell my tale;   555
This blessed widow and her daughters two
Heard all these hens in clamor and halloo
And, rushing to the door at all this shrieking,
They saw the fox towards the covert streaking
And, on his shoulder, Chanticleer stretched flat.   560
'Look, look!' they cried. 'O mercy, look at that!
Ha! Ha! the fox!' and after him they ran,
And stick in hand ran many a serving man,
Ran Coll our dog, ran Talbot, Bran and Shaggy,
And with a distaff in her hand ran Maggie,   565
Ran cow and calf and ran the very hogs
In terror at the barking of the dogs;
The men and women shouted, ran and cursed,
They ran so hard they thought their hearts would burst;
They yelled like fiends in Hell, ducks left the water   570
Quacking and flapping as on point of slaughter,
Up flew the geese in terror over the trees,
Out of the hive came forth the swarm of bees;
So hideous was the noise—God bless us all,
Jack Straw[18] and all his followers in their brawl   575
Were never half so shrill, for all their noise,
When they were murdering those Flemish boys,
As that day's hue and cry upon the fox.
They grabbed up trumpets made of brass and box,
Of horn and bone, on which they blew and pooped,   580
And therewithal they shouted and they whooped
So that it seemed the very heavens would fall.
   And now, good people, pay attention all.
See how Dame Fortune quickly changes side
And robs her enemy of hope and pride!   585
This cock that lay upon the fox's back
In all his dread contrived to give a quack
And said, 'Sir Fox, if I were you, as God's
My witness, I would round upon these clods
And shout, "Turn back, you saucy bumpkins all!   590
A very pestilence upon you fall!
Now that I have in safety reached the wood
Do what you like, the cock is mine for good;
I'll eat him there in spite of everyone."

---

17. **bale:** sorrow.
18. **Jack Straw:** one of the leaders in the Peasant Revolt in 1381.

The fox replying, 'Faith, it shall be done!'   595
Opened his mouth and spoke. The nimble bird,
Breaking away upon the uttered word,
Flew high into the treetops on the spot.
And when the fox perceived where he had got,
"Alas," he cried, "alas, my Chanticleer,   600
I've done you grievous wrong, indeed I fear
I must have frightened you; I grabbed too hard
When I caught hold and took you from the yard.
But, sir, I meant no harm, don't be offended,
Come down and I'll explain what I intended;   605
So help me God I'll tell the truth—on oath!"
"No," said the cock, "and curses on us both,
And first on me if I were such a dunce
As let you fool me oftener than once.
Never again, for all your flattering lies,   610
You'll coax a song to make me blink my eyes;
And as for those who blink when they should look,
God blot them from his Everlasting Book!"
"Nay, rather," said the fox, "his plagues be flung
On all who chatter that should hold their tongue."   615
   Lo, such it is not to be on your guard
Against the flatterers of the world, or yard,
And if you think my story is absurd,
A foolish trifle of a beast and bird,
A fable of a fox, a cock, a hen,   620
Take hold upon the moral, gentlemen.
   St. Paul himself, a saint of great discerning,
Says that all things are written for our learning;
So take the grain and let the chaff be still.
And, gracious Father, if it be thy will   625
As saith my Savior, make us all good men,
And bring us to his heavenly bliss.
                    Amen.

Getting at Meaning

1. Describe the widow, her family, and her farm. Describe Chanticleer. Note the contrast between these two descriptions.

2. How does Chanticleer defend his reaction to the dream? On what basis does Pertelote dismiss the dream? What does she prescribe for Chanticleer?

3. How is Chanticleer trapped and caught?

4. How does Chanticleer escape? Why can he persuade Sir Russel Fox so easily?

5. At the end of the tale, the Nun's Priest tells his listeners to "Take hold upon the moral." What is the moral? Is there more than one moral? Explain.

Developing Skills in Reading Literature

1. **Mock Epic.** An epic is a long narrative poem in which the characters and the action are of heroic proportions. A mock epic treats a trivial matter on a heroic scale, generally with a humorous effect. Find evidence in this tale to support the contention that it is a mock epic.

2. **Irony.** Irony is a contrast between appearance and actuality. Irony of situation occurs when what is expected (appearance) is different from what actually exists or happens (actuality). What is ironic about the way that Chanticleer escapes? How does the irony relate to the moral of the tale?

3. **Fable.** A fable is a brief tale that conveys a moral or a principle of behavior. The characters generally are animals who speak and act like human beings while retaining their animal traits. Fables often are based on folklore and contain supernatural and other unusual occurrences. In what ways does this fable fit these criteria? Does it deviate from the traditional simple fable? Explain your answers.

Developing Writing Skills

1. **Explaining an Idea.** One source for this tale is an ancient fable by Aesop. Chaucer's version, however, is distinctly medieval. In a brief composition identify the elements that place the tale squarely in the fourteenth century. Cite specific examples from the text to support your general statements.

2. **Writing a Tale.** Write an original tale in heroic couplets. Use as a model the Nun's Priest's fable or another tale from *The Canterbury Tales*.

DETAIL OF A SHAWL. *Chinese, nineteenth century. Victoria and Albert Museum, Crown copyright.*

English and Scottish Ballads

A traditional folk ballad is a song that tells a story. Early English and Scottish ballads transmitted from one generation to the next the rich folklore indigenous to both town and countryside. Singers created these songs anew at each rendering, and the ballads varied according to performer, locale, audience, and era. Minstrels and troubadors often sang ballads that were elaborate, studied retellings of earlier folk ballads.

Ballads recall dramatic events involving both ordinary people and legendary heroes. Popular subjects include tragic love, domestic conflicts, disastrous wars and shipwrecks, sensational crimes, and the exploits of enterprising outlaws. Later ballads celebrate historical events and the romantic heroes of an earlier chivalrous age. Revenge, rebellion, envy, betrayal, remorse, loyalty, patriotism, and superstition all find thematic expression in the ballad.

The structure and language of the ballad are simple, befitting its origins in oral tradition. A folk ballad focuses on one incident, beginning in the midst of a crisis and proceeding directly to the resolution, with sketchy background information, character development, and descriptive detail, and few transitional passages. Events are related objectively with dialogue being a major narrative device. Absent in the folk ballad is the personal voice of the speaker and the richness of imagery and figurative language typical of most poetry.

The ballad is structured in four-line stanzas, with second and fourth lines that rhyme and that often are slightly shorter than the first and third lines. The lines are heavily accented, and the stanzas contain repetition, of words, phrases, lines, and ideas. These structural and sound devices made the early ballads musically appealing and easy to remember.

An extensive collection of traditional ballads was not available until the mid-eighteenth century when Thomas Percy published *Reliques of Ancient English Poetry* (1765). This collection sparked a renewed interest in the ballad and imitations of the ballad form by contemporary poets. In the next century, Francis Child published *The English and Scottish Popular Ballads* (1882-1898), the definitive collection of folk ballads, some of which originated as early as the fourteenth century.

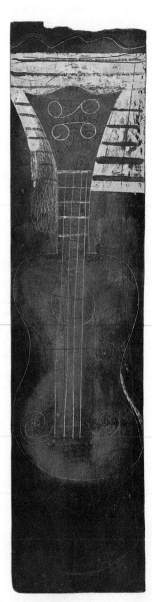

GUITAR, 1933. *Ben Nicholson. Tate Gallery, London.*

The Robin Hood ballads exemplify the type of ballad created by medieval minstrels to glorify a family or a segment of society. Robin Hood is the quintessential English yeoman, decent, self-respecting, chivalrous, devout, and carefree. As a defender of the weak and an enemy of the oppressor, he typifies balladry's beloved outlaw. Like all medieval ballads, these selections are of anonymous authorship and exist in several forms, none of which has been ascertained as the original.

Robin Hood and Allen-a-Dale

Come listen to me, you gallants so free,
   All you that loves mirth for to hear,
And I will you tell of a bold outlaw,
   That lived in Nottinghamshire.

As Robin Hood in the forest stood,   5
   All under the greenwood tree,
There was he ware of a brave young man
   As fine as fine might be.

The youngster was clothed in scarlet red,
   In scarlet fine and gay,   10
And he did frisk it over the plain,
   And chanted a roundelay.

As Robin Hood next morning stood,
   Amongst the leaves so gay,
There did he espy the same young man   15
   Come drooping along the way.

The scarlet he wore the day before,
   It was clean cast away;
And every step he fetcht a sigh,
   "Alack and a well a day!"   20

Then stepped forth brave Little John,
   And Nick the miller's son,
Which made the young man bend his bow,
   When as he see them come.

"Stand off, stand off," the young man said,   25
  "What is your will with me?"
"You must come before our master straight,
  Under yon greenwood tree."

And when he came bold Robin before,
  Robin asked him courteously,   30
"O hast thou any money to spare
  For my merry men and me?"

"I have no money," the young man said,
  "But five shillings and a ring;
And that I have kept this seven long years,   35
  To have it at my wedding.

"Yesterday I should have married a maid,
  But now she is from me tane,
And chosen to be an old knight's delight,
  Whereby my poor heart is slain."   40

"What is thy name?" then said Robin Hood,
  "Come tell me, without any fail."
"By the faith of my body," then said the young man,
  "My name it is Allen-a-Dale."

"What wilt thou give me," said Robin Hood,   45
  "In ready gold or fee,
To help thee to thy true-love again,
  And deliver her unto thee?"

"I have no money," then quoth the young man,
  "No ready gold nor fee.   50
But I will swear upon a book
  Thy true servant for to be."

"How many miles is it to thy true-love?
  Come tell me without any guile."
"By the faith of my body," then said the young man,   55
  "It is but five little mile."

Then Robin he hasted over the plain,
  He did neither stint nor lin,
Until he came unto the church
  Where Allen should keep his wedding.   60

"What dost thou do here?" the bishop he said,
  "I prethee now tell to me."
"I am a bold harper,"[1] quoth Robin Hood,
  "And the best in the north countrey."

"O welcome, O welcome," the bishop he said,   65
  "That music best pleaseth me."
"You shall have no music," quoth Robin Hood,
  "Till the bride and the bridegroom I see."

With that came in a wealthy knight,
  Which was both grave and old,
And after him a finikin[2] lass,   70
  Did shine like glistering gold.

"This is no fit match," quoth bold Robin Hood,
  "That you do seem to make here;
For since we are come into the church,
  The bride she shall choose her own dear."   75

Then Robin Hood put his horn to his mouth,
  And blew blasts two or three;
When four and twenty bowmen bold
  Came leaping over the lea.   80

And when they came into the churchyard,
  Marching all on a row,
The first man was Allen-a-Dale,
  To give bold Robin his bow.

"This is thy true-love," Robin he said,   85
  "Young Allen, as I hear say;
And you shall be married at this same time,
  Before we depart away."

---

1. **harper:** a traditional disguise as a minstrel.
2. **finikin:** well-dressed.

"That shall not be," the bishop he said,
    "For thy word shall not stand;   90
They shall be three times askt in the church,[3]
    As the law is of our land."

Robin Hood pulled off the bishop's coat,
    And put it upon Little John;
"By the faith of my body," then Robin said,   95
    "This cloath doth make thee a man."

When Little John went into the quire,
    The people began for to laugh;
He askt them seven times in the church,
    Lest three times should not be enough.   100

"Who gives me this maid?" then said Little John;
    Quoth Robin, "That do I,
And he that doth take her from Allen-a-Dale
    Full dearly he shall her buy."

And thus having ended this merry wedding,   105
    The bride lookt as fresh as a queen,
And so they returned to the merry greenwood,
    Amongst the leaves so green.

Robin Hood's Death and Burial

When Robin Hood and Little John
    Down a down a down a down
Went oer yon bank of broom,
    Said Robin Hood bold to Little John,
We have shot for many a pound.   5
    Hey down a down a down a down!

But I am not able to shoot one shot more,
    My broad arrows will not flee;
But I have a cousin lives down below,
    Please God, she will bleed me.   10

---

3. **three times ... church:** The banns must be read on three consecutive Sundays.

Now Robin he is to fair Kirkly gone,
   As fast as he can win;
But before he came there, as we do hear,
   He was taken very ill.

And when he came to fair Kirkly-hall,   15
   He knockd all at the ring,
But none was so ready as his cousin herself
   For to let bold Robin in.

"Will you please to sit down, cousin Robin,"
     she said,
   "And drink some beer with me?"   20
"No, I will neither eat nor drink,
   Till I am blooded by thee."

"Well, I have a room, cousin Robin," she said,
   "Which you did never see,
And if you please to walk therein,   25
   You blooded by me shall be."

She took him by the lily-white hand,
   And led him to a private room,
And there she blooded bold Robin Hood,
   While one drop of blood would run down.   30

She blooded him in a vein of the arm,
   And locked him up in the room;
There did he bleed all the live-long day,
   Until the next day at noon.

He then bethought him of a casement there,   35
   Thinking for to get down;
But was so weak he could not leap,
   He could not get him down.

He then bethought him of his bugle-horn,
   Which hung low down to his knee;   40
He set his horn unto his mouth,
   And blew out weak blasts three.

Then Little John, when hearing him,
   As he sat under a tree,
"I fear my master is now near dead,   45
   He blows so wearily."

Then Little John to fair Kirkly is gone,
　　As fast as he can dree;
But when he came to Kirkly-hall,
　　He broke locks two or three;　　　　　　　　　50

Until he came bold Robin to see,
　　Then he fell on his knee;
"A boon,[1] a boon," cries Little John,
　　"Master, I beg of thee."

"What is that boon," said Robin Hood,　　　　　55
　　"Little John, thou begs of me?"
"It is to burn fair Kirkly-hall,
　　And all their nunnery."

"Now nay, now nay," quoth Robin Hood,
　　"That boon I'll not grant thee;　　　　　　　60
I never hurt woman in all my life,
　　Nor men in woman's company.

"I never hurt fair maid in all my time,
　　Nor at mine end shall it be;
But give me my bent bow in my hand,　　　　　65
　　And a broad arrow I'll let flee
And where this arrow is taken up,
　　There shall my grave digged be.

"Lay me a green sod under my head,
　　And another at my feet;　　　　　　　　　　70
And lay my bent bow by my side,
　　Which was my music sweet;
And make my grave of gravel and green.
　　Which is most right and meet.

"Let me have length and breadth enough,　　　75
　　With a green sod under my head;
Then they may say, when I am dead
　　'Here lies bold Robin Hood.'"

These words they readily granted him,
　　Which did bold Robin please;　　　　　　　　80
And there they buried bold Robin Hood,
　　Within the fair Kirkleys.

---

1. **boon:** favor.

1. Who is Little John? What role does he play in each ballad?

2. How does Robin Hood receive Allen-a-Dale? Describe Allen and his problem. What does he offer Robin in gratitude for his help?

3. How does Robin solve Allen's problem?

4. What symptoms of failing health does Robin experience? To whom does he turn for help? What is done to him?

5. How does Little John react to Robin's plight?

What does he want to do? Why does Robin refuse his "boon"? How does Robin determine his burial spot?

Developing Skills in Reading Literature

Ballad. Review the characteristics of the ballad that are presented in the introduction to the medieval ballad. Then analyze the content, structure, rhythm, and language of the two Robin Hood ballads as they illustrate these characteristics. Use quotations from the ballads in your explanation.

Barbara Allen's Cruelty

This Scottish ballad has more than ninety known versions, with variations on the same basic story.

In Scarlet town, where I was born,
    There was a fair maid dwellin',
Made every youth cry *Well-a-way!*
    Her name was Barbara Allen.

All in the merry month of May,   5
    When green buds they were swellin',
Young Jemmy Grove on his deathbed lay,
    For love of Barbara Allen.

He sent his man in to her then,
    To the town where she was dwellin';   10
"O haste and come to my master dear,
    If your name be Barbara Allen."

So slowly, slowly rase she up,
    And slowly she came nigh him,
And when she drew the curtain by—   15
    "Young man, I think you're dyin'."

"O it's I am sick and very very sick,
    And it's all for Barbara Allen."—
"O the better for me ye'se never be,
    Tho' your heart's blood were a-spillin'!"   20

"O dinna ye mind, young man," says she,
　"When the red wine ye were fillin',
That ye made the healths go round and round,
　And slighted Barbara Allen?"

He turn'd his face unto the wall,　　　　　　　　25
　And death was with him dealin':
"Adieu, adieu, my dear friends all,
　And be kind to Barbara Allen!"

As she was walking o'er the fields,
　She heard the dead-bell knellin';　　　　　　30
And every jow the dead-bell gave
　Cried "Woe to Barbara Allen."

"O mother, mother, make my bed,
　O make it saft and narrow:
My love has died for me today,　　　　　　　35
　I'll die for him tomorrow.

"Farewell," she said, "ye virgins all,
　And shun the fault I fell in:
Henceforth take warning by the fall
　Of cruel Barbara Allen."　　　　　　　　　40

Getting at Meaning

1. Why does Jemmy Grove send for Barbara Allen? What is wrong with him?

2. For what does Barbara Allen admonish Jemmy Grove? What happens to both lovers? What is the meaning of Barbara Allen's warning?

Developing Skills in Reading Literature

Ballad. "Barbara Allen's Cruelty" is a folk ballad, which arose from the traditions of the common people, while the two Robin Hood ballads are minstrel ballads, created primarily by minstrels possibly from folklore. Examine the length, language, patterns of repetition, narrative characteristics, and descriptive detail of the three ballads, and think about their subjects and probable purposes. What similarities are evident in both kinds of ballads? What differences are apparent? What factors might account for these differences?

Developing Writing Skills

Using Comparisons and Contrasts. Find two other versions of "Barbara Allen's Cruelty" and, in a five-paragraph composition, compare and contrast the versions. Note specifically the similarities and variations among them.

Lord Randal

This ballad typifies the kind of folk ballad that recounts a sensational crime.

"O where have you been, Lord Randal, my son?
O where have you been, my handsome young man?"—
"I have been to the greenwood; O make my bed soon,
For I'm weary with hunting, and fain would lie down."

"And what met ye there, Lord Randal, my son?   5
And what met ye there, my handsome young man?"—
"I met with my true love; O make my bed soon,
For I'm weary with hunting, and fain would lie down."

"And what did she give you, Lord Randal, my son?
And what did she give you, my handsome young man?"—   10
"Eels fried in a pan; O make my bed soon,
For I'm weary with hunting, and fain would lie down."

"What color were they, Lord Randal, my son?
What color were they, my handsome young man?"—
"They were speckled and blotched; O make my bed soon,   15
For I'm weary with hunting, and fain would lie down."

"O where did she get them, Lord Randal, my son?
O where did she get them, my handsome young man?"—
"From hedges and ditches; O make my bed soon,
For I'm weary with hunting, and fain would lie down."   20

"O where are your bloodhounds, Lord Randal, my son?
O where are your bloodhounds, my handsome young man?"—
"They swelled and they died; Mother, make my bed soon,
For I'm sick at the heart, and I fain would lie down."

"O that was strong poison, Lord Randal, my son!   25
O that was strong poison, my handsome young man!"—
"O yes, I am poisoned; So make my bed soon,
For I'm sick at the heart, and I fain would lie down."

With whom is Lord Randal talking? What has been done to him? by whom?

Developing Skills in Reading Literature

1. **Incremental Repetition.** The repetition of a line or lines with a slight change is called incremental repetition. In this ballad incremental repetition is the organizing principle. Explain how the technique functions in each verse.

2. **Refrain.** A refrain is the repetition of a line or lines in a regular pattern throughout a song or poem. Generally a refrain appears at the ends of succeeding verses or stanzas. What are the two refrains in this ballad? How does the change in the refrain relate to the unfolding of the story? What part of the first refrain is retained in the second? What new meaning do the words take on?

Bonny George Campbell

The border between England and Scotland was the scene of heated skirmishes between powerful feuding clans. The ballads that tell of the triumphs and tragedies surrounding these conflicts are sometimes called the "border ballads."

High upon Highlands[1]
    And low upon Tay,[2]
Bonny George Campbell
    Rade out on a day.

Saddled and bridled   5
    And gallant rade he:
Hame cam[3] his guid horse,
    But never cam he.

Out cam his auld mither,
    Greeting fu' sair,[4]   10
And out cam his bonny bride,
    Riving[5] her hair.

Saddled and bridled
    And booted rade he:
Toom[6] hame cam the saddle,   15
    But never cam he.

"My meadow lies green,
    And my corn is unshorn,
My barn is to build,
    And my babe is unborn."   20

Saddled and bridled
    And booted rade he;
Toom hame cam the saddle,
    But never cam he.

---

1. **Highlands:** northern Scotland.
2. **Tay:** river in Scotland.
3. **Hame cam:** home came.
4. **Greeting fu' sair:** weeping profusely.
5. **Riving:** tearing.
6. **Toom:** empty.

1. Why does George Campbell leave his family? What happens to him? Explain.

2. Who grieves for him in the second to the last verse?

Ballad. Review the characteristics of the standard ballad stanza explained in the introduction to these ballads. Then examine each ballad that you have read so far in the unit and determine whether it follows the traditional pattern. For ballads that have a different form, suggest reasons to account for the variations.

Get Up and Bar the Door

This ballad represents the large body of ballads whose humor derives from ludicrous domestic struggles.

It fell about the Martinmas[1] time,
   And a gay time it was then,
When our goodwife got puddings[2] to make,
   She's boild them in the pan.

The wind sae cauld blew south and north,   5
   And blew into the floor;
Quoth our goodman to our goodwife,
   "Gae out and bar the door."

"My hand is in my hussyfskap,[3]
   Goodman, as ye may see;   10
An it should nae be barrd this hundred year,
   It's no be barrd for me."

They make a paction[4] tween them twa,
   They made it firm and sure,
That the first word whaeer[5] shoud speak,   15
   Shoud rise and bar the door.

---

1. **Martinmas:** November 11.
2. **puddings:** sausages.
3. **hussyfskap:** household chores.
4. **paction:** agreement.
5. **whaeer:** whoever.

Then by there came two gentlemen,
  At twelve o'clock at night,
And they could neither see house nor hall,
  Nor coal nor candlelight.   20

"Now whether is this a rich man's house,
  Or whether it is a poor?"
But neer a word wad ane o' them speak,
  For barring of the door.

And first they ate the white puddings,   25
  And then they ate the black;
Tho muckle⁶ thought the goodwife to
    hersel,
  Yet neer a word she spake.

Then said the one unto the other,
  "Here, man, tak ye my knife;   30
Do ye tak aff the auld man's beard,
  And I'll kiss the goodwife."

"But there's nae water in the house,
  And what shall we do than?"
"What ails ye at the pudding broo,⁷   35
  That boils into the pan?"

O up then started our goodman,
  An angry man was he;
"Will ye kiss my wife before my een,
  And scad⁸ me wi pudding bree?"⁹   40

Then up and started our goodwife,
  Gied three skips on the floor;
"Goodman, you've spoken the foremost
    word;
  Get up and bar the door."

---

6. **muckle:** a great deal.
7. **What . . . broo:** Why not use the boiling pudding water?
8. **scad:** scald.
9. **bree:** broth.

Getting at Meaning

1. Why won't either the husband or wife "Gae out and bar the door"?
2. Who are the "two gentlemen"? How do they break the stalemate between husband and wife?

Developing Skills in Reading Literature

Humor. Think about the goodman and the goodwife, the original situation, the threats of the two gentlemen and the goodman's reaction to them, and the goodwife's final triumph. Then explain how exaggeration and irony create the humor of this ballad.

Developing Writing Skills

1. **Writing an Explanation.** Locate a contemporary ballad, either a traditional ballad that is still popular or a ballad of modern origin. Write a composition explaining how the ballad exemplifies the same characteristics as the ballads you have just studied.
2. **Writing a Ballad.** Select a subject that interests you and write a ballad using the traditional form. Be sure to include a refrain. Prepare to present the ballad either alone or with a partner or group.

Margery Kempe
1373?–1438?

Margery Kempe was a literary pioneer whose autobiography, *The Book of Margery Kempe,* was among the first works of this genre in English literature. Born around 1373, the daughter of John Brunham, the mayor of Lynne, Norfolk, Margery received little formal education. At age twenty she married John Kempe, a tax collector. After giving birth to the first of her fourteen children, she experienced psychological disturbances; she hallucinated and raved deliriously. She associated her eventual recovery with a vision of Christ and dedicated herself to becoming a religious mystic.

Kempe was caught in a classic dilemma: be a housewife and mother or follow her calling as a religious visionary. In pursuing the latter, she traveled extensively in England, Europe, and the Holy Land, directed, as she explained, by the will of God as revealed in her visions. A compassionate woman, Kempe comforted the afflicted and advised prelates. Rather than gratitude, however, she met with ridicule and even imprisonment as a heretic.

As Kempe grew older, she decided to record her life story. She chose as her first scribe a man who was probably not much more educated than she. He died shortly after starting the writing, and she selected a literate priest as her second scribe. Eventually a third man named Salthows prepared the text that was finished around 1450, about twelve years after Kempe's death. To her scribes, Kempe dictated accounts of her visits to Dame Julian in Norwich and to the maid of St. Birgitte in Rome. She described the last months of her husband's life, childbirth, problems with her children and with housekeeping, friendships with other women, and her ecstatic visions.

A few excerpts of Kempe's autobiography were printed around 1500. Most of the work, however, was lost for nearly five hundred years. Not until 1936 did Colonel M. E. Butler-Bowdon publish the full text of the autobiography, the first by a woman in English literature.

from The Book of Margery Kempe

Her Marriage and Illness After Childbirth. She Recovers.

When this creature was twenty years of age, or some deal more, she was married to a worshipful burgess (of Lynne) and was with child within a short time, as nature would. And after she had conceived, she was belabored with great accesses till the child was born and then, what with the labor she had in childing, and the sickness going before, she despaired of her life, weening[1] she might not live. And then she sent for her ghostly father,[2] for she had a thing on her conscience which she had never shewn before that time in all her life. For she was ever hindered by her enemy, the devil, evermore saying to her that whilst she was in good health she needed no confession, but to do penance by herself alone and all should be forgiven, for God is merciful enough. And therefore this creature oftentimes did great penance in fasting on bread and water, and other deeds of alms with devout prayers, save she would not shew that in confession.

And when she was at any time sick or dis-eased, the devil said in her mind that she should be damned because she was not shriven[3] of that default. Wherefore after her child was born, she, not trusting to live, sent for her ghostly father, as is said before, in full will to be shriven of all her lifetime, as near as she could. And when she came to the point for to say that thing which she had so long concealed, her confessor was a little too hasty and began sharply to reprove her, before she had fully said her intent, and so she would no more say for aught he might do. Anon,[4] for the dread she had of damnation on the one side, and his sharp reproving of her on the other side, this creature went out of her mind and was wondrously vexed and labored with spirits for half a year, eight weeks, and odd days.

And in this time she saw, as she thought, devils opening their mouths all inflamed with burning waves of fire, as if they would have swallowed her in, sometimes ramping at her, sometimes threatening her, pulling her and hauling her, night and day during the aforesaid time. Also the devils cried upon her with great threatenings, and bade her that she should forsake Christendom, her faith, and deny her God, His Mother and all the Saints in Heaven, her good works and all good virtues, her father, her mother and all her friends. And so she did. She slandered her husband, her friends and her own self. She said many a wicked word, and many a cruel word; she knew no virtue nor goodness; she desired all wickedness; like as the spirits tempted her to say and do, so she said and did. She would have destroyed herself many a time at their stirrings and have been damned with them in Hell, and in witness thereof, she bit her own hand so violently, that the mark was seen all her life after.

And also she rived[5] the skin on her body against her heart with her nails spitefully, for she had no other instruments, and worse she would have done, but that she was bound and kept with strength day and night so that she might not have her will. And when she had long been labored in these and many other temptations, so that men weened she should never have escaped or lived, then on a time as she lay alone and her keepers were from her, Our Merciful Lord Jesus Christ, ever to be trusted, worshipped be His Name, never forsaking His servant in time of need, appeared

---

1. **weening:** thinking.
2. **ghostly father:** priest.
3. **shriven:** forgiven.
4. **Anon:** soon.
5. **rived:** tore.

to His creature who had forsaken Him, in the likeness of a man, most seemly, most beauteous and most amiable that ever might be seen with man's eye, clad in a mantle of purple silk, sitting upon her bedside, looking upon her with so blessed a face that she was strengthened in all her spirit, and said to her these words:

"Daughter, why hast thou forsaken Me, and I forsook never thee?"

And anon, as He said these words, she saw verily how the air opened as bright as any lightning. And He rose up into the air, not right hastily and quickly, but fair and easily, so that she might well behold Him in the air till it was closed again.

And anon this creature became calmed in her wits and reason, as well as ever she was before, and prayed her husband as soon as he came to her, that she might have the keys of the buttery[6] to take her meat and drink as she had done before. Her maidens and her keepers counseled him that he should deliver her no keys, as they said she would but give away such goods as there were, for she knew not what she said, as they weened.

Nevertheless, her husband ever having tenderness and compassion for her, commanded that they should deliver to her the keys; and she took her meat and drink as her bodily strength would serve her, and knew her friends and her household and all others that came to see how Our Lord Jesus Christ had wrought His grace in her, so blessed may He be, Who ever is near in tribulation. When men think He is far from them, He is full near by His grace. Afterwards, this creature did all other occupations as fell to her to do, wisely and soberly enough, save she knew not verily the call of Our Lord.

---

6. **buttery:** pantry.

Getting at Meaning

1. What explanation does Kempe give for her insanity? What symptoms does she display? How is her illness treated?

2. What experience returns Kempe to sanity? Who is the first to believe that she has recovered?

Developing Skills in Reading Literature

1. **Autobiography.** An autobiography is the story of a person's life created by that person. Autobiographical writing reveals both the qualities of the subject and the characteristics of the society in which the subject lives or once lived. What generalizations can you make about Kempe's personality and character after reading this part of her autobiography? What are her conceptions of the devil and of God? What seems to be the role of religion in Kempe's time? What seems to be the conception of the causes and cures of emotional illness? What can you deduce about medical care from this excerpt?

2. **Point of View.** Point of view can mean a person's unique way of looking at things. In a general sense, the point of view of this autobiography is Margery Kempe's, for the selection presents her perceptions of reality. Notice that Kempe is referred to as "this creature," suggesting a certain pity or contempt for her. Whose point of view might this phrase represent, that of Kempe or of the scribe recording her story?

In literature, the term *point of view* refers specifically to the narrative method used to present a prose selection. Most autobiographies are written in the first person, using the pronouns *I* and *we*. This selection, however, is written in the third person, with the pronouns *she* and *her*. What might account for this unusual narrative method?

Developing Writing Skills

Narrating an Autobiographical Incident. Write one chapter of your autobiography. Limit your focus by first deciding on a time framework; for example, one year of school, one particular summer, one important vacation, one significant relationship, or one memorable job. Then describe one significant episode that occurred within that framework.

Sir Gawain and the Green Knight

Sir Gawain and the Green Knight, believed by some scholars to be the work of the so-called Pearl Poet, first appeared about 1370. In its original Middle English form, *Sir Gawain* is a poem of more than 2500 lines, which are divided into 101 stanzas grouped into four major sections. The alliterative verse is similar to that of *Beowulf*, reflecting the revival of interest in native English poetry that took place during the fourteenth century.

Sir Gawain is a narrative rich in the Arthurian legend and the chivalric code. This code represented a fusion of Christian and military ideals as the basis for gentlemanly conduct. The chief chivalric virtues were piety, bravery, loyalty, and honor. The most important of these was probably loyalty. The chivalrous knight was loyal to God, to his master, and to the mistress of his heart. Besides the battlefield, the tournament was the chief arena in which knights demonstrated the virtues of chivalry.

Sir Lancelot sometimes is considered the perfect knight; however, in the early Arthurian tradition that role belonged to Sir Gawain. He was the greatest of the Knights of the Round Table, famous for his physical prowess, courtesy, and integrity. His encounter with the Green Knight forces him to acknowledge his human weakness and his failure to live up to the knightly ideal.

A CLASH BETWEEN MOUNTED KNIGHTS.
Ill. Ms. Roy (16GVI-F.178).
British Library Board.

from Sir Gawain and the Green Knight

Translated by Y. R. Ponsor

Chapter 1

Winter lay upon the land. Cold held forest and field in its grim clutch, and in the night sky the stars glittered like gems. The wolf slid from shadow to shadow, stalking hapless prey, falling upon the unwary with death in his fangs. Deep in caverns the great trolls and other monsters mumbled in uneasy sleep, seeking warmth. Over moor and fen[1] the mists rose and fell, and strange sounds troubled the chill silence.

But on the hill, lights gleamed in the castle. In the court of Camelot were gathered all the brothers-in-arms of the Table Round and their fair highborn ladies to celebrate the Christmas season. A full fifteen days it was then, a time of merriment and mirth and rich revel. Laughter rang loud through the halls, and all the music and delight that the mind of man might devise. With merrymaking and glee the company welcomed the New Year, exchanging gifts and calling out glad Noel.

On this New Year's day, fresh and crisp-cold, twice the usual number of celebrants crowded the great hall; and the most noble, the fairest, and most famous was Arthur himself, the most honorable man who ever ruled a court or led an army into battle. This king was a man of the greatest good will and generosity of soul, and it would be difficult to imagine a bolder company than that one gathered in the castle on the hill.

Among the group on the high dais facing the great hall lined with tables of noble knights was Guenevere, Arthur's wife, the comeliest maid, the gracious lady of the gleaming gray eyes. Her silken garments sparkled with rich jewels, and her golden hair shone as softly as her eyes. With her sat the young Gawain, with Agravaine the Stronghand on the other side; both were the king's nephews and worthy knights who had proved their prowess many times in test and trial. At the head of the table sat the chief of all bishops in Cornwall, the saintly Bedwin, and with him, Urien's son Iwain.

But Arthur, full of his own happiness and childlike in his joy, would not sit until all were served. For most of all he loved life, its joys and its adventures, and his eager brain and young blood would not allow him to lie abed or sit around lazily. And besides, he had taken upon himself a vow that on this special day of all days, he would not eat until a rare tale of ancestors and arms and high adventure were told, or some grand marvel might be devised, or a challenge of knights to join in jeopardy, jousting life for life as fortune might favor. So he stood before the high table, speaking of trifles and laughing at the noise and fine festival of his free men as the first course was announced with the crackling of trumpets, with drums and tuneful pipers. In the corner a bard awakened the lute and many a heart lifted with his touch upon the strings. Then came the platters piled high with fine food, venison and other meats, and great bowls of soup, and a plenty of strong beer and fine red wine. And all drank and ate as much as they wanted.

Hardly had the first course been finished when the great hall door crashed open and in rode a terrifying knight. He must have been the hugest man on earth, so broad and thick from neck to waist, so long of leg and strong of arm that I half thought him a giant, except for his fine features of face. Everyone knows that giants are hideous to look upon, besides being fearful in size. At sight of him, all in the

---

1. **fen:** bog, marsh.

hall fell silent, struck dumb by this apparition. For this bold man, from toe to top, in clothes and in countenance, was bright green.

Believe me: all garbed in green, this man, and all his trappings. He wore a tight coat with a heavy mantle adorned with ermine, the same fur lining the hood that had fallen from his head and lay upon his shoulders. Green were the stockings on his legs, and decorated with gold embroidery, and bright golden spurs on his feet, and shoes with upturned toes. His belt was set with gleaming jewels, all emerald green, and indeed they were scattered over all his array and that of his horse, the saddle and bridle and reins, all gaudy in gold and green. The trappings of the horse, the breast-cloth and bits and bridle, even the stirrups in which he stood, all were enameled and gleamed goldenly, and the green gems glittered like the eyes of a cat. The steed itself which he straddled was a great heavy horse, hard to hold; and it was the same green as the man who rode it.

Gloriously was this man outfitted in green, and the hair of his head as green as his horse. It fanned out full and fell to his shoulders, and he had a heavy beard which reached his chest. It gleamed green upon the leather tunic. Such a pair had never before been seen on earth, nor since that time! Everyone said he looked as bright as a flash of lightning, and, indeed, who could withstand his stroke! He wore neither helm nor hauberk[2]—no, no coat of mail did he wear, nor want!—and he carried no weapons, neither spear nor shield to smite or to save. But in his hand he carried a bough of holly, that branch which is greenest when all others are bare; and in his other hand an ax, heavy and horrid, a cruel weapon right out of a nightmare. The head measured at least an arm's length, and was of green steel worked with gold, the bit burnished bright, the broad edge honed to shear as closely as a sharp razor. The steel of the haft which he held in his hand was wrapped with iron wire to its very end, graven with green in delicate design. A thong bound it about and fastened at the head where it was tasseled and braided with bright green.

This knight moved through the great hall's silent crowd right up to the high table, and he feared no danger, greeted no one, but looked straight ahead. Then he reined in his horse and faced the room. He stared boldly at the knights, looking them up and down, and his voice thundered when he spoke.

"Where is the leader of this company? I would like to see him and to speak in courtesy with him, as the rules of chivalry require."

He waited and looked at them and considered who might among this company be the most renowned.

Everyone stared at him in wonder, marveling as to what his appearance might mean, how such a knight and such a horse might be such a strange color, green as growing grass, and glowing with enamel and gold. Everyone studied him as he sat there on his horse, and they walked cautiously around him with all the wonder in the world as to what he might do. Many strange things had they seen, but never any such as this. Possibly a phantom, or some fey[3] creature, they deemed him to be, for green is a magic color. But all of these brave knights feared to question him and, stunned at his voice, were dumbstruck. A heavy silence filled the royal chamber, and all those who had been chattering sat as if caught in a dream—some, I suppose, out of politeness, some out of uneasiness, and some in fear, but let another man decide which!

Then Arthur, standing before the dais, greeted him, and bowed courteously, for he was never rude, and said,

"Fair knight, welcome to this place. I am Arthur, the chief of this company. Alight and rest, I beg you, and whatsoever your will may be, we shall be glad to learn."

---

2. **hauberk:** a long tunic made of chain mail.
3. **fey:** enchanted.

"No, God is my witness that to waste time in idle talk is not my errand," replied the knight. "But your fame, lord, is raised high, and through town and countryside you are regarded as the best and bravest ever to ride in battle gear, the noblest and the finest of the world's kind. You are all known to be valiant in dealing with all sorts of adventures, and your hall is known for courtliness. Many tales of this company have reached my ears, and that is what has brought me hither at this special time.

"You may see by this branch which I bear here that I have come in peace, seeking no trouble; for had I fared forth in a frame of mind to fight, I would have brought helm and hauberk, and shield and bright-shining spear, and other weapons to wield also. But because I seek no strife, I am dressed as you see. But if you are as brave as everyone says, you will gladly grant me the game that I ask as a guest's right."

And Arthur answered, "Gentle knight, if you crave combat, you will not fail to find it here."

"No, I seek no contest, as I have told you, especially since I see on these benches only beardless children! If I were geared up for fighting and mounted on my high steed, there is no man here who could match me." And he looked upon them with scorn. "I seek in this court only a Christmas game, for it is Yule and the New Year, and the time to exchange gifts. If there should be any in this hall who considers himself brave enough in heart, hot enough in blood, or quick enough of wit that he would dare exchange stroke for stroke with me, let him come forth. I will give him as my gift this fine heavy ax—heavy enough it is to do his will!—and I shall take the first blow as bare as here I sit. If any of these fine warriors may be so bold as to accept my challenge, let him step forth and seize this weapon. I quit-claim it forever, and he may keep it as his own, and I shall kneel before him and stand him a stroke. And then you will grant me the right to deal him an equal blow, though I will give him respite of a year and a day. Now let any man who so dares speak quickly."

Chapter 2

If the people had been astonished at first, now they all, high and low throughout the hall, sat as if turned to stone. The knight on his steed twisted in the saddle, his red eyes flashing around the room, his green hair flying with each movement of his head. Then he sat still, staring at them and stroking his beard as the silence lengthened. When no one spoke, he stood in his stirrups and, shaking his fist above his head, he shouted at them.

"What is this? Is this Arthur's court and castle, of which the whole world sings praises? Where now is your pride? Where is your fighting spirit? Where now your fierceness and fame and all your fine words? Now is the reputation and glory of the Round Table overthrown by the mere words of one man, without a single blow being struck, because you are afraid to answer!"

Then the blood shot for shame into Arthur's face, and he turned as angry as a stormwind, as indeed did all of them. Men muttered and surged forward in anger, half-rising from their places, white with wrath. But Arthur held up his hand and sprang to face the green man.

"Sir, by heaven! Seek no further! As you in your own folly have asked, so shall it be! No man here is afraid of your boasts. Give me your ax, and with God's help, I shall break every bone in your body. I myself accept your challenge and will meet your terms."

The Green Knight laughed aloud and leaped lightly from his horse and landed before Arthur, taller by head and shoulders than any man in the court. The king seized the ax and gripped the handle tightly and waved it about, striking this way and that to test its feel. The knight calmly removed his mantle and then his short coat, no more dismayed by the threatening blows than if some man had brought him a glass of wine.

Then Gawain, who sat by the queen, called out, "I beseech you, uncle, to grant me a kindness. Let this contest be mine. Gentle lord, give me permission to leave this table and stand in your place there. If I may without discourtesy—if my liege lady will not take it amiss—I would presume to counsel you before your royal court." He stood up and spoke clearly. "I think it is not seemly that such a challenge should be raised in this high chamber, much less that you yourself should so valiantly choose to answer it while so many brave warriors remain on these benches. No better men can be found on any field of battle, nor any more skillful in arms. All men know that I am the least brave, and the feeblest of wit, and the least deserving to be of this company. In truth, it is only because I am your nephew that I am worthy at all; I know no bounty but your blood in my body. And since this business is so foolish and trivial, none of it should concern you at all.

"So I ask: Let it come to me, and if I fail in its performance, then the fault is in me and no blame shall fall on this court."

Arthur moved from table to table consulting with his nobles, as is the custom in such cases, and all agreed that the king should retire from the contest and give Gawain the game.

Gawain turned and bowed to the gray-eyed Guenevere and she smiled on him, and he came down from the dais and, kneeling before his king, he received the ax from Arthur's hands. And Arthur smiled affectionately upon him and raised his hand and asked God's blessing, praying that both Gawain's heart and his hand should be strong.

"Be careful, nephew," he said softly, "and set yourself for the stroke. If you direct it properly, I am sure that you will be able to bear the burden of the blow which he will later inflict." And Arthur removed himself and went and leaned against the edge of the dais and watched eagerly.

Gawain walked, ax in hand, to the Green Knight, who had been waiting patiently. He looked upon Gawain and he said, "Now, let us reaffirm our bargain before we go on. But first I would ask you, sir, what is your name?"

"I am Gawain," the young man said. "It is Gawain who gives you this blow, whatever may happen afterwards. One year from now, you may return the favor with whatever weapon you wish, asking leave of no one else."

"By God," shouted the other, "it pleases me greatly that I should receive this blow from your hands. You have rightly repeated the covenant which I made with your king— except that you must seek me, friend, wheresoever you think I may be found, pledging to come alone, and return to me such wages as you deal to me today before this court."

"And where shall I look for you? Where is your home? I know neither your kingdom nor your name, kith nor kin. Tell me your realm and name and I shall certainly find you. That I swear on my honor."

"No," said the green man, "nothing more is necessary now. But I promise that when I have taken your blow, if you strike squarely, then I will tell you how to find me so that you may fulfill our bargain."

Then he laughed.

"If I do not speak, then so much the better for you; you can stay in your own land and light no wayfarer's fires. But enough! Take up your weapon and let us see how you handle an ax!"

"Sir," said Gawain, "I will," and he stroked the edge of the ax.

The Green Knight knelt on the floor and bent his head and gathered his long, thick hair in one hand and drew it over the crown of his head. His bare neck shone whitely. Gawain set himself, left foot forward on the floor. He grasped the ax and lifted it aloft, and he brought it down like a lightning bolt upon the bare neck. The sharp steel sliced through the pale flesh and sundered the bones and sheared it in half, and the steel blade buried itself in the floor with a great ringing crash.

The fair head flew from the shoulders and rolled about near the tables, and some of the knights kicked at it with their feet, a grim, grisly game. Blood burst from the body, red gleaming on green. The knight did not falter or fall, but at once he sprang up on his strong legs and jumped into the crowd and snatched up his head by the hair and lifted it high for all to see. Then, striding to his horse, he caught up the reins, stepped into the stirrups and sat aloft, still holding his head high in one hand.

And they say that he sat in his saddle as though nothing whatever ailed him, headless though he was. He twisted from side to side, turning that hideous, still-bleeding body in the saddle. Those who watched in fear were even more horrified to see that he was about to speak.

He turned the grim face toward the high table, and the head lifted up its eyelids and looked at them. Then it looked at Gawain and the mouth moved and the lips spoke.

"Look to it, Gawain, that you do as you have sworn, and seek faithfully until you find me. All men know me as the knight of the Green Chapel. To the Green Chapel you must come, I charge you, to receive such a blow as you have dealt here to me today. You will find me if you try. If you fail to come, coward shall you be called by the whole world."

With a quick movement he pulled his horse around and fled through the great door, still head-in-hand, and the fire from the hooves of his flint-shod steed flashed through the hall. What native land he would return to, none there knew, any more than they knew from whence he had come. In a moment a roar of astonishment filled the hall, and Arthur and Gawain burst into laughter at the strange event. All agreed that it had been a marvel among men.

Although Arthur, ever the wise king, had a great uneasiness in his heart, he did not let a hint of it be seen, but he spoke to his queen with courtly speech.

"Dearest lady, let not today dismay you. Often such a magic and wondrous event occurs at this season, along with the music of minstrels and the laughter of lovely ladies and brave knights."

And he touched her hand gently and gazed into her eyes. Then he sat back, looked around the room, and cried out, "Now at last I may address myself to my dinner, for I have certainly seen a marvel, I must admit."

He smiled at Gawain with love shining on his fair face and he said, "Hang up your ax, nephew, it has done its work for today." And it was placed on the wall above the high table where all might admire and wonder at the sight and the strange adventure. Then they sat down again at the tables, each to his place, king and knights, and the servants brought double portions of all the best dishes and with all manner of good will they passed the rest of the evening.

But be sure, Sir Gawain, that fear does not cause you to fail in this test, this challenge which you yourself have taken into your own hands!

The year passes rapidly and soon Sir Gawain sets out to find the Knight of the Green Chapel. Near Christmas he stops at a castle where the lord offers him hospitality and an opportunity to rest before his encounter with the Green Knight.

Each day the lord departs to hunt, while Gawain remains behind with the lady of the castle, who seems intent on seducing the young knight. The men have agreed to exchange what each has won during the day, and so, at the end of the first day, the lord gives Gawain a deer, and Gawain gives the lord a kiss. The second night the lord gives Gawain a boar's head; Gawain gives him two kisses. On the third evening, the lord gives Gawain a fox. Gawain gives the lord three kisses but not the magical green silk scarf that the lady has given him as protection. True to the chivalric code, Gawain has not betrayed the lord; however, he feels guilty about keeping the green scarf. He wears it as he rides out from the castle to his rendezvous with the Knight of the Green Chapel.

At a bubbling brook Gawain hears someone sharpening a scythe; the person turns out to be the Green Knight. Gawain offers himself to the knight who moves as if to deliver a fatal blow to Gawain's neck. Gawain flinches slightly, and the Green Knight reproaches him for his cowardice.

Gawain asks for a second chance. Again the Green Knight brings down his ax but stops before the blade hits Gawain. This time Gawain does not flinch. The Green Knight then tells Gawain to bare his throat. Gawain complies and the Green Knight nicks his neck. Gawain leaps up and prepares to defend himself, as he has now fulfilled the terms of their agreement.

Chapter 11

The Green Knight turned from him and leaned upon his ax, set the shaft to the ground and leaned upon the blade and looked at the lad who waited there. How steadfast, how fearless, and how bold he looked, how ready for battle! And he was pleased in his heart. He laughed with a ringing voice and spoke happily with the lad.

"Bold knight, upon this field of honor be not so fierce! No man here has used you dishonorably, nor treated you discourteously, but only as the decree at Arthur's court allowed. I owed you a stroke and you took it, so hold yourself well paid. I release you of any remnant of all other rights. If I had been more nimble, perhaps I could have wrought you a more harmful blow. First, I merely menaced you with a pretended blow and cut you with no cruel blade. That was for the agreement we made on that first night when you faithfully gave me the day's gains, as an honest man would. That second pretended blow was for the second day when you kissed my dear wife, which kisses you gave to me. And for both of those I offered you but two scant blows without scathe. For an honorable man is true to his word and he needs fear no danger.

"But on the third day you failed in that honor, and therefore you took that tap on the neck."

He looked at Gawain steadily, and Gawain at him, still as stone. And the green man continued.

"It is my garment you wear, that green silken girdle. My own wife offered it to you, I know. Ah, I know all about those kisses and your character also, and the wooing of my wife! I wrought all this myself. I sent her to test you. Truly I think that you must be the most faultless man that ever walked the earth. As a pearl in purity is to white peas, so is Gawain in virtue to all famous knights. But you fell short a little there, sir; you failed in faith. But it was not for intrigue, nor for lawless lust either, but because you loved your life, and I cannot blame you for that."

Gawain still stood like one stunned, so aggrieved with embarrassment that he cried for anguish inside. All the blood of his body burned in his face and he shrank for shame as the green man talked. He took off his helm and held it in his hands. At last he spoke wrathfully.

"Cursed be both cowardice and covetousness! In them is villainy and vice that destroys virtue!" And he caught up the pentangle and tore it loose and flung it roughly down. "Lo!—there is breaking of faith. Foul be its fall! I coveted my life and cowardice led me into fault for fear of your blow, made me forsake my nature, the generosity and loyalty that are a true knight's." And he bowed his head and wept bitterly. "Now am I false indeed and from fear have I fallen into treachery and deceit. Both bring only sorrow and shame. I confess to you, sir, here on this spot, that I have indeed been false to you in my conduct. If you will but allow me to regain your good will, I shall guard against its happening again."

Then the Green Knight laughed and said amiably: "I consider it entirely acquitted, any harm that I had. You have confessed freely and are aware of your failing and you have stood the sharp penance of my sword. I hold you cleansed of that fault and made as pure as if you had never transgressed since your birth. And I give you, sir, as a gift, that very scarf, as green as my own robe." He touched the silk at Gawain's waist lightly, and laid an arm across his shoulders.

"Sir Gawain, you may think upon this particular contest as you fare forth among the great and chivalrous knights of this world. Let this be the clear token of the adventure of the Green Chapel." Then he laughed and said merrily, "Now, you shall in this New Year come back again to my dwelling and we shall revel away the remainder of this festal time. With my wife, I promise, we shall certainly reconcile you, she who you thought was your keen enemy."

"No," said Gawain, and he took up his helm and looked sadly at the green man. "This has been a sorrowful journey. Good fortune betide you and may He who ordains all honor grant it to you! And commend me to that gracious lady, your comely companion, and the other lady, both the honored ladies who so cunningly beguiled this knight with their tricks.

"It is no great marvel to be made a fool of or to be won to sorrow through the wiles of a woman; for so was Adam, the first man on earth beguiled; and Solomon by many and various women; and Samson also, Delilah dealt him his wyrd! David was deluded by Bathsheba and suffered much woe. All these men were brought to disaster by woman's wiles.

"It would be a great gain to love them and yet to believe them not. But no man can do that. For these were the noblest men of old, all blessed above other men and yet they were all beguiled by women with whom they had dealings. To find myself in that company I think must be excused." Then he shook off sad thoughts.

"But your girdle I will accept with a right good will, not for the bright gold, nor for its magic—" here Gawain blushed again—"nor for the silk or fringed sides, nay, not for worth nor worship nor noble works. But as a symbol of my transgression I shall keep it always with me, a reminder, when I ride in renown, of the fault and frailty of feeble flesh, how susceptible it is to the stains of evil. And when pride of prowess inflates me, the sight of this will humble my heart.

"But one request I make, if it does not displease you: Since you are the lord of that land where I stayed with such pleasure, thanks to you, will you tell me your name? Only that and no more?"

"That I shall, certainly," replied the green man. "I am called Bercilak de Hautdesert in this land. Through the power of Morgan leFay, who lives in my house and has the skill of magical lore, all of this has happened. Morgan, the beautiful, the mistress of Merlin —many men has she taken, for she has had love dealings with that excellent wizard who knows all the knights of your court. Morgan the goddess is also her name. There is none so high in power or pride that she cannot tame!

"She sent me in that manner to your royal court in order to test the pride of its men, to see if the reputation of the Round Table were true. She sent me in that strange way to take away your wits and to frighten the fair Guenevere, to make her die with fear at the sight of that man who spoke with his head in his hand before that Table High. She took the form of that old one in my house, the ancient lady; she is in fact your aunt, the half-sister of Arthur, daughter of the Duchess of Tintagel, that lady upon whom the mighty Uther later fathered Arthur, who is your king.

"Therefore I entreat you, dear man, to come to your aunt and rejoice in my house. My court loves you, and I do as well, indeed, as any man under heaven."

SIR GAWAIN BEHEADS THE GREEN KNIGHT,
WATCHED BY KING ARTHUR AND QUEEN GUINEVERE.
Ill. Ms., late fourteenth century. British Museum.

And thus at last he came to the court, did Gawain the good knight.

Happiness sped through those halls when it was learned that Gawain had returned. Everyone thought it was a fine thing, indeed, and somewhat unlooked for. The king kissed the knight and the queen did also, and many knights sought him out to salute him and make inquiry of his wayfaring fortune. And he told the wondrous tale and confessed everything that had happened, the adventure at the chapel, the good will of the green man, the love of the lady, and the silk that he wore. He showed them the scar that he bore on his neck, the sign of his shameful disloyalty to the green man. He suffered when he told them and groaned with grief and mortification, and the blood burned in his face for shame when he spoke of it.

"Lo, lord," said Gawain to Arthur, as he held forth the silk, "here is the band of blame which I bear like the scar on my neck. This is the offense and the loss, the cowardice and covetousness that caught me there. This is the symbol of falsity in which I was taken. I will wear it all my life, for no one may hide his misdeed, nor may he undo it. Once guilt has touched a man, he is never free of it again."

And the king comforted the knight and all the court laughed and lovingly agreed on the spot that each man of the Table Round should henceforth wear such a baldric, the slanting ribbon of bright green, for the sake of that beloved man, and they would wear it with delight. And so it came to be accorded as the renown of the court and always afterwards anyone who wore it was especially honored.

So in Arthur's day this adventure occurred, as books of romance will witness. Many strange and curious wonders have happened in Britain since the days of Brutus whose race came from Troy. But surely this tale of Gawain and his contest with the Green Knight in a trial of honor and faith is one of the most wondrous.

But Gawain still refused. He would not under any conditions. So they embraced in friendship and saluted each other as fine princes and parted right there in the cold. Gawain, mounted on his fine horse, hastened homeward to Arthur's court and the Green Knight wended wheresoever he would.

Gawain rode then through many wild ways in the world on Gringolet. He had been given back his life, a fine gift indeed, and many a thought he gave to that strange event as he traveled. Sometimes he harbored in a house and sometimes out of doors. He had many adventures in the valley and he vanquished many, but I will not take time to tell all that in this tale.

The wound in his neck healed and he wore the green belt fastened like a baldric at his side, tied under his left arm, the end in a knot, as token of the fact that he was guilty of sin.

Getting at Meaning

CHAPTER 1

1. Describe the time and place of the action. How does the description in the opening paragraph contrast with the description of Arthur's court?

2. What picture of King Arthur is created in this chapter? What vow has he taken?

3. What stranger enters King Arthur's hall? What does he carry in each hand? What is the reaction of Arthur's court? Why do they react this way?

4. What "Christmas game" does the Green Knight wish to play? How does his request relate to Arthur's vow?

CHAPTER 2

5. Who answers the Green Knight's challenge? Why?

6. How does Sir Gawain feel about his membership in the Round Table? Do his actions reinforce or negate his expressed feelings? Explain.

7. To what covenant does Sir Gawain agree? What does Gawain then do to the Green Knight?

8. What are the Green Knight's parting words to Gawain? What are Arthur's observations on this incident?

CHAPTER 11

9. What is the identity of the Green Knight? How do the Green Knight's blows correspond to the events that happened at his castle?

10. How does Gawain feel about himself, even after the Green Knight praises his virtue? Why does Gawain refuse the hospitality of the Green Knight?

11. Who is behind the scheme to test King Arthur's knights?

12. When Gawain returns to Arthur's court, how is he received? What do all of the knights agree to wear? Why?

Developing Skills in Reading Literature

1. **Romance.** A romance is a fictional narrative that is set in the past and that deals with the adventures of a hero or group of heroes. The characters in a romance are idealized, at least to some degree, as is the era in which the action takes place. Sir Gawain, for example, is an idealized knight who practices almost perfectly the chivalric virtues. How does he demonstrate his piety? bravery? loyalty? honor? How is he an ideal Christian? An ideal soldier? Why does the reign of King Arthur, seem an ideal period of history?

2. **Allusion.** An allusion is a reference to a literary or historical person, place, or event with which the reader is expected to be familiar. In Chapter 11 Sir Gawain tells the Green Knight that many great men have succumbed to the wiles of women. He presents several allusions to illustrate his point. Explain each of these allusions. What view of women is implied in these allusions? How does this view contrast with the idealized woman of chivalry?

3. **Symbol.** A symbol is a person, place, or object that represents something beyond itself. When the Green Knight enters Arthur's hall, he is carrying a bough of holly. What does the holly symbolize? Find other symbols in the selection and explain their symbolic meanings.

Developing Vocabulary

Word Origins. Compile from this selection a list of at least ten words that are related in some way to the medieval romance; for example, *castle* and *knight*. Look up the origins of these words in a dictionary. Which words originate in Old French? which in Old English? Draw at least one generalization based on the information that you learn.

Developing Writing Skills

1. **Writing an Explanation.** The romance as a literary genre is as attractive to contemporary readers as it was to the people of medieval England and France. In a well developed paragraph, suggest possible reasons for the enduring appeal of this form.

2. **Analyzing Satire.** *A Connecticut Yankee in King Arthur's Court* by Mark Twain is the story of a nineteenth-century American who returns to medieval England. Locate and read this classic. Then write a composition discussing the way that Twain satirizes the chivalric ideal.

Introduction to Medieval Literature

John Steinbeck

John Steinbeck is a major American writer whose reputation derives from novels that portray the struggles of ordinary people caught in the Great Depression of the 1930's. His classic works include The Grapes of Wrath, Tortilla Flat, Of Mice and Men, *and* The Red Pony. *Coexisting with Steinbeck's perceptive understanding of his own society was a lifelong fascination with the Arthurian legends of Sir Thomas Malory. His translation of* Morte d'Arthur, *titled* The Acts of King Arthur and His Noble Knights, *has given contemporary readers accessibility to these legends and also a sense of the vigor and beauty of Malory's tales. Following is Steinbeck's introduction to this work.*

Some people there are who, being grown, forget the horrible task of learning to read. It is perhaps the greatest single effort that the human undertakes, and he or she must do it as a child. An adult is rarely successful in the undertaking—the reduction of experience to a set of symbols. For a thousand thousand years these humans have existed and they have only learned this trick—this magic—in the final ten thousand of the thousand thousand.

I do not know how usual my experience is, but I have seen in my children the appalled agony of trying to learn to read. They, at least, have my experience.

I remember that words—written or printed —were devils, and books, because they gave me pain, were my enemies.

Some literature was in the air around me. The Bible I absorbed through my skin. My uncles exuded Shakespeare, and *Pilgrim's Progress* was mixed with my mother's milk. But these things came into my ears. They were sounds, rhythms, figures. Books were printed demons—the tongs and thumbscrews of outrageous persecution. And then, one day, an aunt gave me a book and fatuously ignored my resentment. I stared at the black print with hatred, and then, gradually, the pages opened and let me in. The magic happened. The Bible and Shakespeare and *Pilgrim's Progress* belonged to everyone. But this was mine—It was a cut version of the Caxton *Morte d'Arthur* of Thomas Malory. I loved the old spelling of the words—and the words no longer used. Perhaps a passionate love for the English language opened to me from this one book. I was delighted to find out paradoxes—that *cleave* means both to stick together and to cut apart; that *host* means both an enemy and a welcoming friend; that *king* and *gens* (people) stem from the same root. For a long time, I had a secret language—*yclept* and *hyght, wist*—and *accord* meaning peace, and *entente* meaning purpose, and *fyaunce* meaning promise. Moving my lips, I pronounced the letter known as *thorn, p,* like a "p," which it resembles, instead of like a "th." But in my town, the first word of Ye Olde Pye Shoppe was pronounced "yee," so I guess my betters were no better off than I. It was much later that I discovered that "y" had been substituted for the lost *p*. But beyond the glorious and secret words— "And when the chylde is borne lete it be delyvered to me at yonder privy posterne uncrystened"—oddly enough I knew the words from whispering them to myself. The very strangeness of the language *dyd me enchante*, and vaulted me into an ancient scene.

And in that scene were all the vices that

ever were—and courage and sadness and frustration, but particularly gallantry—perhaps the only single quality of man that the West has invented. I think my sense of right and wrong, my feeling of noblesse oblige, and any thought I may have against the oppressor and for the oppressed, came from this secret book. It did not outrage my sensibilities as nearly all the children's books did. It did not seem strange to me that Uther Pendragon wanted the wife of his vassal and took her by trickery. I was not frightened to find that there were evil knights, as well as noble ones. In my own town there were men who wore the clothes of virtue whom I knew to be bad. In pain or sorrow or confusion, I went back to my magic book. Children are violent and cruel—and good—and I was all of these—and all of these were in the secret book. If I could not choose my way at the crossroads of love and loyalty, neither could Lancelot. I could understand the darkness of Mordred because he was in me too; and there was some Galahad in me, but perhaps not enough. The Grail feeling was there, however, deep-planted, and perhaps always will be.

Later, because the spell persisted, I went to the sources—to the *Black Book of Caermarthen*, to "The Mabinogion and Other Welsh Tales" from the *Red Book of Hergist*, to *De Excidio Britanniae* by Gildas, to *Giraldus Cambrensis Historia Britonum*, and to many of the "Frensshe" books Malory speaks of. And with the sources, I read the scholarly diggings and scrabblings—Chambers, Sommer, Gollancz, Saintsbury—but I always came back to Malory, or perhaps I should say to Caxton's Malory, since that was the only Malory there was until a little over thirty years ago, when it was announced that an unknown Malory manuscript had been discovered in the Fellows Library of Winchester College. The discovery excited me but, being no scholar but only an enthusiast, I had neither the opportunity nor the qualification to inspect the find until in 1947 Eugène Vinaver, Professor of French Language and Literature at the University of Manchester, edited his great three-volume edition of the works of Sir Thomas Malory, for Oxford University, taken from the Winchester manu-

SHIELD OF PARADE. *Flemish, late fifteenth century. Inscription on scroll reads "Vous ou la mort" (You or death). British Museum.*

script. No better man could have been chosen for the work than Professor Vinaver, with his great knowledge, not only of the "Frensshe" books, but also of the Welsh, Irish, Scottish, Breton, and English sources. He has brought to the work, beyond his scholarly approach, the feeling of wonder and delight so often lacking in a schoolman's methodology.

For a long time I have wanted to bring to present-day usage the stories of King Arthur and the Knights of the Round Table. These stories are alive even in those of us who have not read them. And, in our day, we are perhaps impatient with the old words and the stately rhythms of Malory. My own first and continuing enchantment with these things is not generally shared. I wanted to set them down in plain present-day speech for my own young sons, and for other sons not so young— to set the stories down in meaning as they were written, leaving out nothing and adding nothing—perhaps to compete with the moving pictures, the comic-strip travesties which are the only available source for those children and others of today who are impatient with the difficulties of Malory's spelling and use of archaic words. If I can do this and keep the wonder and the magic, I shall be pleased and gratified. In no sense do I wish to rewrite Malory, or reduce him, or change him, or soften or sentimentalize him. I believe the stories are great enough to survive my tampering, which at best will make the history available to more readers, and at worst can't hurt Malory very much. At long last, I am abandoning the Caxton of my first love for the Winchester, which seems to me more knee-deep in Malory than Caxton was. I am indebted to Professor Eugène Vinaver for his making the Winchester manuscript available.

For my own part, I can only ask that my readers include me in the request of Sir Thomas Malory when he says: "And I pray you all that redyth this tale to pray for him that this wrote that God sende hym good delyverance and sone and hastely—Amen."

Getting at Meaning

1. According to Steinbeck, what was the result of his receiving *Morte d'Arthur* as a gift?

2. How did the human vices and virtues depicted in *Morte d'Arthur* reflect Steinbeck's own world?

3. Why did Steinbeck want to translate Malory? What promises did he make regarding his translation?

Developing Skills in Reading Literature

Essay. The essay is a brief nonfiction composition that offers an opinion on a subject. Essays often are classified as descriptive, narrative, or expository, although most essays blend two or all three writing techniques. What specifically is the subject of Steinbeck's essay? What seems to be his purpose in regard to this subject? How might the essay be classified? What techniques does Steinbeck employ? When discussing techniques, refer to passages in the essay as examples.

Developing Vocabulary

French Phrases in English. Steinbeck uses the term *noblesse oblige* in this essay. Locate the phrase in an etymological dictionary, then answer these questions:

What is the literal translation of the phrase?
What is its meaning as used by Steinbeck?
What is the origin of the term?
How does *noblesse oblige* relate to the tales of chivalry that so impressed Steinbeck?

Developing Writing Skills

Combining Narration and Exposition. Choose one book that captivated your imagination as a child. Write an essay in which you describe the way that the book came into your hands, identify the aspects of the book that were particularly fascinating, and assess the immediate and permanent influence of the book on you.

Sir Thomas Malory
?–1471?

Born around 1400 of prosperous parents, Thomas Malory had a checkered career. He fought in the Hundred Years' War, was knighted around 1442, and was elected to Parliament in 1445. He then became embroiled in the political intrigue and violent conflicts that preceded the outbreak of the Wars of the Roses. A supporter of the Lancastrian claim to the throne, Malory was imprisoned repeatedly by the Yorkist government on a variety of charges. Most scholars believe that Malory wrote his only work, *Morte d'Arthur*, during a prison term that began in 1451 and ended with his death in Newgate Prison in 1471.

Malory's sources for his collection of Arthurian legends probably included English and French poems, French prose romances, and popular folk tales from the oral literature of medieval England. Malory's text consists of eight tales, beginning with Arthur's birth and ending with his death and the dispersal of the Knights of the Round Table. The work is a typical romance, replete with tales of giants, sorcerers, and damsels in distress and imbued with the ideals of medieval chivalry: piety, loyalty, courage, and honor.

Morte d'Arthur was an immediate success, for it allowed readers to escape temporarily from the turbulent reality of the late Middle Ages into Arthur's idyllic Camelot. The work still endures as the definitive English version of the Arthurian legends. The following twentieth-century translation of Malory's Middle English work tells of Arthur's birth and his ascension to the throne.

QUEEN GUINEVERE, 1858. *William Morris. Tate Gallery, London.*

from **Morte d'Arthur**   *Translated by John Steinbeck*

When Uther Pendragon was king of England his vassal, the Duke of Cornwall, was reported to have committed acts of war against the land. Then Uther ordered the duke to attend his court and to bring with him his wife, Igraine, who was famed for her wisdom and beauty.

When the duke arrived before the king, the great lords of the council made peace between them so that the king offered his friendship and his hospitality. Then Uther looked at the Lady Igraine and saw that she was as beautiful as he had heard. He loved her and desired her and begged her to lie with him, but Igraine was a faithful wife and she refused the king.

She spoke privately to the duke, her husband, saying, "I believe that you were not sent for because of transgression. The king has planned to dishonor you through me. Therefore I beg you, my husband, that we may creep away from this danger and ride in the night to our own castle, for the king will not tolerate my refusal."

And, as she wished, they went away so secretly that neither the king nor his council were aware of their going.

When Uther discovered their flight he was filled with rage. He called the lords together and told them of the duke's treachery. The noble council, seeing and fearing his anger, advised the king to send messengers ordering the duke and Igraine to return at once, for, they said, "If he should refuse your summons, it will be your duty and your right to make war against him and destroy him."

And it was so done. The messengers galloped after the duke and came back with the curt reply that neither his wife nor he would return.

Then the enraged Uther sent a second message advising the duke to defend himself, because within forty days the king would drag him from his strongest castle.

Thus warned, the duke provisioned and armed his two best fortresses. He sent Igraine to the castle of Tintagel on the high cliffs above the sea, while he himself defended Terrabil, a thick-walled fort with many gates and secret doors.

King Uther gathered an army and marched against the duke. He pitched his tents about the Castle Terrabil and laid siege to it. In the assault and fierce defense, many good men were killed, but neither side could gain the advantage until at last Uther fell sick from anger and frustration and from longing for the fair Igraine.

Then the noble knight Sir Ulfius went to Uther's tent and asked the nature of his illness.

"I will tell you," said the king. "I am sick from anger and from love and there are no medicines for those."

"My lord," Sir Ulfius said, "I shall go in search of Merlin the Wizard. That wise and clever man can brew a remedy to make your heart glad." And Sir Ulfius rode out to look for Merlin.

Now Merlin was a wise and subtle man with strange and secret powers of prophecy and those deceptions of the ordinary and the obvious which are called magic. Merlin knew the winding channels of the human mind, and also he was aware that a simple open man is most receptive when he is mystified, and Merlin delighted in mystery. Therefore, as if by chance, the searching knight Sir Ulfius came upon a ragged beggar in his path who asked him whom he sought.

The knight was not accustomed to be questioned by such a one, and he did not deign to reply.

Then the ragged man laughed and said, "There's no need to tell me. I know. You are looking for Merlin. Look no further. I am Merlin."

"You—? You are a beggar," said Sir Ulfius.

Merlin chuckled at his joke. "I am also Merlin," he said. "And if King Uther will promise me the reward I wish, I shall give him what his heart desires. And the gift I wish will be more to his honor and profit than to mine."

Sir Ulfius was wonderstruck and he said, "If this is true and if your demand is reasonable, I can promise that you shall have it."

"Ride back to the king then; I will follow you as quickly as I can."

Then Sir Ulfius was glad, and he turned about and put his horse to great speed until he came at last to the tent where Uther lay ill, and he told the king he had found Merlin.

"Where is he?" the king demanded.

"My lord," said Ulfius, "he is afoot. He will come as soon as he can," and at that moment he saw that Merlin was already standing in the entrance of the tent, and Merlin smiled, for he took joy in causing wonder.

Uther saw him and welcomed him and Merlin said brusquely, "Sir, I know every corner of your heart and mind. And if you will swear by your anointed kingship to grant me my wish, you shall have what I know your heart desires."

And so great was Uther's eagerness that he swore by the four Evangelists to keep his promise.

Then Merlin said, "Sir, this is my desire. The first time you make love to Igraine she will conceive a child by you. When that child is born it must be given to me to do with as I

wish. But I do promise that this will be to your honor and to the child's advantage. Do you agree?"

"It shall be as you wish," said the king.

"Then rise and make yourself ready," Merlin said. "This very night you will lie with Igraine in the castle of Tintagel by the sea."

"How can that be?" the king asked.

And Merlin said, "By my arts I will cause her to believe that you are the duke, her husband. Sir Ulfius and I will go with you, but we will wear the appearance of two of the duke's trusted knights. I must warn you, though, when you come to the castle, speak as little as possible or you may be discovered. Say that you are weary and ill and get quickly to bed. And, in the morning, mind you do not rise until I come for you. Now make ready, for Tintagel is ten miles from here."

They prepared themselves and mounted and rode away. But the duke, from the walls of the castle Terrabil, saw King Uther ride away from the siege lines, and knowing the king's forces to be leaderless, he waited until nightfall and then attacked in force from the gates of the castle; and in the fight the duke was killed, a full three hours before the king arrived at Tintagel.

When Uther and Merlin and Sir Ulfius rode through the starlit darkness toward the sea, the fog moved restlessly over the moors like wispy ghosts in floating clothes. Half-formed mist people crept with them, and the forms of riders grew changeable, like figures of cloud. When they came to the guarded gates of Tintagel on its high sharp rock above the whispering sea, the sentries saluted the recognized forms of the duke, and Sir Brastias and Sir Jordanus, two of his trusted men. And in the dim passages of the castle the Lady Igraine welcomed her husband and dutifully led him to her chamber. Then King Uther lay with Igraine, and that night she conceived a child.

When daylight came, Merlin appeared as he had promised. And in the misty light Uther kissed the lady Igraine and hastily departed.

The sleepy sentries opened the gates to their supposed lord and his retainers, and the three rode away into the mist of morning.

And later, when news came to Igraine that her husband was dead, and had been dead when the form of him came to lie with her, she was troubled and filled with sad wonder. But she was alone now and afraid, and she mourned her lord in private and did not speak of it.

Now that the duke was dead, the true reason for the war was lost, and the king's barons begged him to make peace with Igraine. The king smiled secretly and let himself be persuaded. He asked Sir Ulfius to arrange a meeting, and very soon the lady and the king came together.

Then Sir Ulfius spoke to the barons in the presence of the king and Igraine. "What can be wrong here?" he said. "Our king is a strong and lusty knight and he is wifeless. My lady Igraine is wise and beautiful"—he paused and then continued—"and free to marry. It would be a joy to all of us if the king would consent to make Igraine his queen."

Then the barons shouted their agreement and urged the king to make it so. And, like the lusty knight he was, Uther allowed himself to be persuaded, and in all haste and with joy and mirth they were married in the morning.

Igraine had three daughters by the duke, and the wedding fever spread, at Uther's wish and suggestion. King Lot of Lothian and Orkney married the eldest daughter Margawse, and King Nentres of Garlot wedded the second daughter, Elaine. Igraine's third daughter, Morgan le Fay, was too young for marriage. She was put to school in a nunnery, and there she learned so much of magic and necromancy that she became a mistress of these secret matters.

Then, within half a year, Queen Igraine grew great with her coming child. And one night, as Uther lay beside her, he tested her truthfulness and her innocence. He asked her by the faith she owed him who was the father of her child, and the queen was deeply troubled to answer.

Uther said, "Do not be dismayed. Only tell me the truth and I shall love you the more for it no matter what it is."

"Sir," said Igraine, "I will indeed tell you the truth although I do not understand it. On the night when my husband was killed, and after he was dead, if the reports of his knights are true, there came to me in my castle of Tintagel a man exactly like my husband in speech and appearance—and in other ways. And with him came two of his knights known to me: Sir Brastias and Sir Jordanus. And so I went to bed with him as I ought to with my lord. And on that night, I swear unto God, this child was conceived. I am puzzled, my lord, for it cannot have been the duke. And I do not know or understand more than this."

Then King Uther was glad, for he found his queen truthful. He cried out, "That is the exact truth as you tell it. For it was I myself who came to you in the likeness of your husband. It was arranged by the secret device of Merlin. Therefore, do not be puzzled or frightened any longer, for I am the father of your child."

And the queen was easier, for she had been deeply troubled by the mystery.

Not long after this Merlin came to the king saying, "Sir, the time draws near. We must plan for the rearing of your child when it is born."

"I remember my promise," said Uther. "It shall be as you advise."

Then Merlin said, "I suggest then one of your lords who is a faithful and an honorable man. His name is Sir Ector, and he has lands and castles in many parts of England and Wales. Send for this man to come to you. And if you are satisfied, require of him that he put his own child to nurse with another woman so that his wife may suckle yours. And when your child is born, as you promised, it must be delivered to me, unchristened and unnamed; and I will take it away secretly, to Sir Ector."

When Sir Ector came to Uther he promised to rear the child, and because of this the king gave him great rewards of lands.

And when Queen Igraine came to be delivered, the king commanded the knights and two ladies to wrap the child in cloth of gold and to carry him through a little postern gate and give him to a poor man who would be waiting there.

Thus was the child delivered to Merlin, who carried it to Sir Ector, and his wife nursed the baby at her own breast. Then Merlin brought a holy man to christen the child and it was named Arthur.

Within two years of the birth of Arthur, a wasting sickness fell on Uther Pendragon. Then, seeing the king helpless, his enemies raided the realm and overthrew his knights and killed many of his people. And Merlin sent to the king and said gruffly, "You do not have the right to lie here in your bed, no matter what your illness. You must go into the field to lead your men, even if you are carried there in a horse litter, for your enemies will never be defeated until you yourself are there. Only then will you win a victory."

King Uther agreed to this, and his knights carried him out and placed him on a litter between two horses, and in this way he led his army against his enemies. At St. Albans they met a great force of invaders from the north and joined battle. And on that day Sir Ulfius and Sir Brastias performed great deeds of arms, and King Uther's men took heart and attacked with fury and killed many of the enemy and put the rest to flight. When it was over, the king returned to London to celebrate his victory. But his strength was gone and he fell into a coma, and for three days and nights he was paralyzed and could not speak. His barons were sad and apprehensive and they askd Merlin what they should do.

Then Merlin said, "Only God has the remedy. But if all of you will come before the king tomorrow in the morning, I shall through the help of God try to make him speak." And in the morning the barons gathered and Merlin approached the bed where the king lay and cried aloud, "Sir, is it your will that your son, Arthur, shall be king when you are dead?"

Then Uther Pendragon turned and struggled and at last he was able to say in the hearing of all his barons, "I give Arthur God's blessing and mine. I ask that he pray for my soul." Then Uther gathered his strength and he cried, "If Arthur does not rightly and honorably claim the crown of England, he will forfeit my blessing." And with that the king fell back and very soon he died.

King Uther was interred with all the ceremony proper for a king, and his queen, the fair Igraine, and all his barons mourned for him. His court was filled with sorrow, and for a long time there was no King of England. Then danger arose everywhere, on the borders from outside enemies and within the realm from ambitious lords. The barons surrounded themselves with armed men, and many of them wished to take the crown for themselves. In this anarchy no man was safe, and the laws were forgotten, so that at last Merlin went to the Archbishop of Canterbury and advised him to issue a call to all the lords and all the gentlemen of arms in the kingdom to gather in London by Christmas on pain of excommunication. It was believed that since Jesus was born on Christmas Eve, He might on that holy night give some miraculous sign who should rightly be king of the realm. When the archbishop's message was sent out to the lords and knights, many of them were moved by the call and purified their lives so that their prayers might be more acceptable to God.

In the greatest church in London, perhaps St. Paul's, the lords and knights gathered to pray long before dawn. And when matins and first Mass were over, there was seen in the churchyard, in a place nearest the high altar, a great block of marble, and in the marble was set a steel anvil in which a sword was driven. In letters of gold was written:

WHOEVER PULLS THIS SWORD
FROM THIS STONE AND ANVIL
IS KING OF ALL ENGLAND
BY RIGHT OF BIRTH.

The people were amazed and carried the news of the miracle to the archbishop, who said, "Go back into the church and pray to God. And let no man touch the sword until High Mass is sung." And this they did, but when the service was over all the lords went to look at the stone and the sword, and some tried to draw out the blade, but no one could move it.

"The man is not here who will draw this sword," said the archbishop, "but do not doubt that God will make him known. Until that happens," he went on, "I suggest that ten knights, men of good fame, be appointed to guard this sword."

And it was so ordered and further proclaimed that any man who wished might try to release the sword. For New Year's Day a great tournament was planned, and this was designed by the archbishop to keep the lords and knights together, for he reckoned that God would at that time make known who should win the sword.

On New Year's Day, when holy service was over, the knights and barons rode to the field where some would joust—two armored men riding in single combat, each seeking to unhorse his opponent. Others joined the tourney, a military sport wherein chosen groups of armed and mounted men engaged in general melee. By these sports the knights and barons kept themselves hard and practiced for war and also won honor and renown for bravery and expertness with horse, with shield, with lance and sword, for all the barons and the knights were fighting men.

It happened that Sir Ector, who was the lord of lands nearby to London, rode in for the jousting, and with him came his son Sir Kay, only made a knight at Allhallows of that year, and also young Arthur came, who had been reared in Sir Ector's house and who was Sir Kay's foster brother. As they rode toward the jousting field, Sir Kay discovered that he had forgotten his sword at his father's lodging, and he asked young Arthur to ride back for it.

"I will do it gladly," said Arthur, and he turned his horse and galloped back to bring his foster brother's sword to him. But when he came to the lodging he found it empty and locked up, for everyone had gone out to see the jousting.

Then Arthur was angry and he said to himself, "Very well, I will ride to the churchyard and take the sword that is sticking in the stone there. I do not want my brother, Sir Kay, to be without a sword today."

When he came to the churchyard, Arthur dismounted and tied his horse to the stile and walked to the tent, and he found no guardian knights there, for they too had gone to the jousting. Then Arthur grasped the sword by its handle and easily and fiercely drew it from the anvil and the stone, and he mounted his horse and rode quickly until he overtook Sir Kay and gave him the sword.

As soon as Sir Kay saw the sword, he knew it came from the stone and he went quickly to his father and held it out to him. "Sir, look here! I have the sword of the stone, and therefore I must be King of England."

Sir Ector recognized the sword and he called Arthur and Sir Kay to him and all three returned quickly to church. And there Sir Ector made Sir Kay swear how he had got the sword.

"My brother, Arthur, brought it to me," Sir Kay answered.

Then Sir Ector turned to Arthur. "And how did you get this sword?"

Arthur said, "When I rode back for my brother's sword, I found no one at home, so I could not get it. I did not want my brother to be without a sword, and so I came here and took the sword from the stone for him."

"Were there no knights here guarding the sword?" Sir Ector asked.

"No, sir," said Arthur. "There was no one here."

Sir Ector was silent for a time and then he said, "I understand now that you must be king of this land."

"Why should that be?" said Arthur. "For what reason should I be king?"

"My lord," Sir Ector said, "God has willed that only the man who can draw this sword from this stone shall be the rightful king of this land. Now let me see whether you can put the sword back as it was and then draw it out again."

"That is not difficult," said Arthur, and he drove the blade into the anvil. Then Sir Ector tried to draw it out and he could not, and he told Sir Kay to try. Sir Kay pulled at the sword with all his might, and he could not move it.

"Now it is your turn," said Sir Ector to Arthur.

"I will," said Arthur. And he drew the sword out easily.

Then Sir Ector and Sir Kay kneeled down on the earth before him.

And Arthur cried, "What is this? My own dear father and my brother, why do you kneel to me?"

Sir Ector said, "My lord Arthur, I am not your father nor of your blood. I believe that you are of nobler blood than I." Then Sir Ector told Arthur how he had taken him to rear and by Uther's order. And he told him how it was Merlin's doing.

When he heard that Sir Ector was not his father, Arthur was sad and even more sad when Sir Ector said, "Sir, will you be my good and gracious lord when you are king?"

"Why should I not be?" Arthur cried. "I owe you more than anyone in the world, you and your wife, my good lady mother who nursed me and kept me as though I were her own. And if, as you say, it is God's will that I must be king—ask anything of me! I will not fail you."

"My lord," said Sir Ector, "I shall ask only one thing of you, that you will make my son Sir Kay, your foster brother, seneschal[1] and keeper of your lands."

"That shall be done and more," Arthur said. "On my honor, no other man but Sir Kay shall have that office while I live."

Then they three went to the archbishop and told him how the sword had been drawn from the stone, and by his order all of the barons gathered again to try to draw the sword, and all failed except Arthur.

Then many of the lords were jealous and angry, and they said it was an insult and a shame that the realm should be governed by a boy who was not of royal blood. The decision was put off until Candlemas,[2] when all the barons agreed to meet again. Ten knights were delegated to watch over the sword and the stone. A tent was put up to shelter it, and five knights were on guard at all times.

At Candlemas an even greater number of lords gathered to try for the sword, and no one could draw it. But Arthur, as he had done before, drew it without effort. Then the angry barons put it off until the high feast of Easter, and again only Arthur could draw the sword. Some of the great lords were opposed to Arthur as king, and they delayed the final test until the feast of Pentecost.[3] Such was their anger that Arthur's life was in danger. The Archbishop of Canterbury by Merlin's advice gathered those knights whom Uther Pendragon had loved and trusted most. Such men as Sir Bawdewyn of Bretagne, Sir Kaynes, Sir Ulfius, and Sir Brastias, all these and many more stayed near to Arthur day and night to protect him until the feast of Pentecost.

When Pentecost had come, a great gathering assembled and all manner of men struggled to pull the sword from the stone and no one succeeded. Then Arthur mounted the stone with all the lords and common people

---

1. **seneschal:** an official in a medieval noble household in charge of servants.
2. **Candlemas:** a church festival celebrated on February 2.
3. **Pentecost:** the seventh Sunday after Easter.

watching him, and he drew the sword easily out and held it up to them. The common people were convinced, and they cried with one great shout, "We want Arthur for our king without any more delay. We see that God wills him to be king, and we will kill anyone who stands in his way."

And with that both rich and poor kneeled down and begged Arthur's pardon for having delayed so long. Arthur forgave them, and then he took the sword in his hands and placed it on the high altar. The archbishop took the sword and touched Arthur on the shoulder and made him a knight. Then Arthur swore an oath to all the lords and commons that he would be a just and true king to them all the days of his life. . . .

HEAD OF KING ARTHUR (detail), ca. 1385. Nicolas Bataille. From The Nine Heroes Tapestries. The Metropolitan Museum of Art, The Cloisters Collections. Munsey Fund, 1932.

Getting at Meaning

1. What interest does Uther Pendragon have in the Duke of Cornwall and Lady Igraine? When the war against the Duke is at a stalemate, from whom does Sir Ulfius seek help? Why?

2. What are Merlin's instructions to Uther? What is Merlin's ultimate goal? What is Sir Ector's role in Merlin's plan?

3. How does Lady Igraine conform to the chivalric ideal?

4. As Uther suffers his final illness, how does he demonstrate his courage and devotion to duty?

5. What is the position of the barons in the society depicted in this selection? Explain your answer.

6. Describe the way that Arthur becomes king.

Developing Skills in Reading Literature

Character. The character of Merlin appears consistently in the Arthurian legends, although the portrayals vary according to the prevailing attitude toward witchcraft and magic. In some versions, Merlin is demonic; in others he is a wise counselor. Characterize the Merlin of Malory's romance, using specific evidence from the text to support your conclusions. What attitude toward magic is evident in this excerpt?

Unit Review *The Medieval Period*

Understanding the Unit

1. Despite various hardships, people who lived during the Medieval Period retained a sense of humor, which is evident in their literature. Review the selections in this unit and identify examples of humor. Be sure to note subtle humor as well as the more obvious examples.

2. The code of chivalry was important in the literature of the Medieval Period. Which literary works reflect aspects of the chivalric code? How is the code integrated into the literature?

3. Discuss the treatment of death in "Robin Hood's Death and Burial," "Lord Randal," "Barbara Allen's Cruelty," and "Bonny George Campbell."

4. What is the role of women in medieval society, as presented in *The Canterbury Tales,* the ballads, and *The Book of Margery Kempe?*

5. Compare the subject matter of Margery Kempe with that of the other medieval writers represented in this unit.

Writing

1. Write an essay in which you compare and contrast the excerpts from *Sir Gawain and the Green Knight* and *Morte d'Arthur.* As preparation for writing, think about the answers to these questions: What aspects of the Arthurian legend are treated in each selection? How do Sir Gawain and Arthur live up to the ideals of the chivalric code? How are these heroes different? What similarities do you find in the adventures of the two heroes? What elements are different?

2. Chaucer has written vivid character sketches of the Canterbury pilgrims. Review the various techniques that he used. Then choose a character from another selection in the unit—for example, Robin Hood, Sir Gawain, King Arthur, or Merlin—and write a sketch of that character using Chaucer's methods of characterization.

3. Both Beowulf and King Arthur are heroes. In an essay, compare and contrast these heroes, discussing their ancestry, challenges, character traits, and reactions to disappointment and adversity.

4. Research the legendary hero Robin Hood to answer these questions: Was there really such a person? Why have so many ballads and stories been written about him? Present the results of your research in an informally documented essay.

ELIZABETH I, (THE DITCHLEY PORTRAIT), *c.* 1592.
Marcus Gheeraerts, the Younger.
National Portrait Gallery, London.

Unit 3
The Renaissance (1485–1660)

HENRY VIII. *Hans Holbein.*
Galleria Nazionale di Arte Antica, Rome.
Scala/Art Resource.

Renaissance England

At certain times in history a series of chance factors converge to cause dramatic shifts in human values and perceptions. One such shift occurred in Italy about the middle of the fourteenth century and initiated a period in European history known as the Renaissance. The Renaissance, which literally means "rebirth" or "revival," was marked by a surge of creative energy and the emergence of a world view more modern than medieval. From its source in southern Europe, the Renaissance spread north throughout Europe in the mid-fifteenth century and brought new vitality to English life during the sixteenth century.

THE RENAISSANCE SPIRIT

The Renaissance spirit manifested itself differently in each region. However, certain fundamental characteristics remained constant. One was the tendency toward secularism. During the Middle Ages, the world was conceived as a place in which human beings prepared for life after death. Thus the church was the focal point of society. Renaissance Europeans were more worldly. They delighted in art and literature, in the beauty of nature, in human impulses, and in a new sense of mastery over the world. Renaissance scholars looked to the achievements of the pre-Christian past. They studied ancient Greek and Latin texts and advocated the imitation of classical styles in literature, art, and education.

Closely related to secularism was the Renaissance emphasis on the individual and on the importance of developing human potential. The ideal "Renaissance man" was a person who cultivated his innate capabilities to the fullest. He was a many-faceted individual who might be an engineer, philosopher, and painter or an architect, astronomer, and poet. Perceiving himself as the center of his own universe, he synthesized the emotional, rational, social, and spiritual forces in his life into a harmonious balance.

The natural result of secularism and individualism was a general revolt against authority. Renaissance Europeans were less likely than their medieval counterparts to conform to the dictates of Church and government or to accept as unquestioned truth the theories of medieval scientists.

The Renaissance was an expansionist age that pushed back the scholarly, psychological, and geographical boundaries of the medieval world. The translations of ancient Greek and Latin texts brought new knowledge of astronomy, botany, medicine, physics, and mathematics, which in turn stimulated scientific investigation. Technological advances in printing led to a laity more literate than that of the Middle Ages and more cognizant of new ideas. Innovations in shipbuilding and the invention of navigational devices spurred trade and made possible geographical expansion. The discovery of a route to the East around Africa and the exploration of America brought some Europeans new wealth and leisure and profoundly altered the narrow medieval perceptions of the world.

The factors that contributed to the decline of feudalism set the stage for the Renaissance in England. Not until the restoration of domestic stability after the Wars of the Roses, however, did the spirit of the Renaissance take hold and flourish there.

THE TUDOR MONARCHS

In 1485, at Bosworth Field, Henry Tudor defeated Richard III and assumed the throne as King Henry VII, the first Tudor monarch. Henry was not a colorful king, but he was a shrewd leader who exercised strong central authority at home and careful strategy abroad. He directed the negotiation of favorable commercial treaties with other European countries and appropriated revenues to build the merchant fleet that later became the major source of England's rise to power. During Henry's reign, exploratory expeditions penetrated North America and established the English claims to this continent.

When Henry VII died in 1509, his son Henry became king. Henry VIII was a true Renaissance prince, a skilled athlete, dashingly handsome, magnetic in personality, an excellent dancer and musician, well educated in French, Italian, and Latin. As king he wielded power equal to that of any monarch in Europe. His subjects were fervidly nationalistic and loyal, even when Henry defied the authority of the Roman Catholic Church.

During the reign of Henry VIII, the Reformation, or Protestant Revolt, plunged parts of Europe into bloody conflict. England, however, remained Catholic until Henry became obsessed with having a male heir to the throne. After eighteen years of marriage, he and his Spanish queen Catherine had only one surviving child, a daughter. Now, he was attracted to Anne Boleyn, a young lady of the court who he thought would produce the desired son. Failing in his attempt to obtain an annulment from the Church in Rome, Henry declared himself Supreme Head of the English Church, received a "divorce" from a church court, and married Anne.

At another period in history, Henry's break with Rome might have caused serious domestic problems. However, Englishmen in general had long resented the Church's power and wealth and the widespread abuses of clerical privilege. Reformers had been active in England since the Middle Ages, and a succession of English monarchs had opposed the Popes on various issues. By now, the average Englishman felt stronger loyalty to king and country than to the institutional church. Given these factors, Parliament in 1534 willingly passed the Act of Supremacy, which established a national church with the king as its head. At its inception, the new Church of England, or Anglican Church, was not Protestant but was essentially the Roman Catholic Church, without ties to Rome.

Although the majority of nobles and commoners supported Henry, at least outwardly, a few held out against him and paid for their opposition with their lives. Among them was Sir Thomas More, Henry's Chancellor and the writer of *Utopia*, an example of early Renaissance literature.

Henry VIII died in 1547, widowing his sixth wife and leaving his frail, sickly ten-year-old son as the heir to the English throne. The six-year reign of King Edward VI is noteworthy because of the spread of Protestantism throughout England. The English Reformation, which had begun as a political movement, assumed a strong religious direction at this point. The Book of Common Prayer was published, and the official beliefs of the Church of England were clarified.

Edward's successor attempted to stem the tide of Protestantism and to reinstate Catholicism as the national religion. Mary, Henry's eldest child, was half Spanish and a fervent Roman Catholic. She married her cousin, Philip II of Spain, and together they drove Protestant leaders out of England and ordered Protestants burned at the stake as heretics. Queen Mary's fanatical religious persecutions met with fierce opposition from the English whose traditional hatred of the Spanish now embraced all Catholics. "Bloody Mary" was highly unpopular and at her death in 1558, after a five-year reign of terror, most of her subjects looked forward to a change.

THE ELIZABETHAN ERA

Elizabeth, the unwanted daughter of Henry VIII and Anne Boleyn, ascended the throne in 1558 and ruled triumphantly for almost half a century. Her reign is the most glorious period in English history, a time of unprecedented prosperity, artistic achievement, and international prestige. Under Elizabeth, England experienced the full flowering of the Renaissance.

Vain and headstrong, Elizabeth also was practical and disciplined, a brilliant scholar, educated in Latin and Greek, and keenly interested in art and literature. Although she loved pomp and pageantry, she was basically frugal and intent on balancing the national budget. As a ruler, Elizabeth was a consummate politician, exercising absolute authority while remaining sensitive to public opinion and respectful of the forms of Parliamentary government.

In the matter of religion, Elizabeth took a middle-of-the-road position. She reinstated the Anglican Church as the national church and ended religious persecution. Elizabeth's church encompassed both a high church, which was similar to the Roman Catholic Church, and a low church, whose members wanted to "purify" the English church of Catholicism. Although neither uncompromising Catholics nor radical Protestants approved of this church, they tolerated it as a stable buffer zone between extremist groups.

In foreign policy, Elizabeth was a shrewd diplomat and strategist who managed to maintain some semblance of peace throughout most of her reign. One of her first acts was to extricate England from draining, pointless Continental wars and from the unpopular Spanish alliance. Then for over twenty years she used the possibility of her own marriage to the utmost advantage, feigning interest first in one European prince then another.

Expert advisors convinced Elizabeth that the path to prosperity lay across the seas in the rich resources of the New World. Spain, however, dominated the seas with her magnificent Armada. To weaken the Spanish navy and to enrich the English treasury, Elizabeth privately funded pirate raids on the Spanish fleet while publicly apologizing to Spain for the unlawful acts of these sea dogs.

For twenty-five years, English pirates preyed on Spanish colonial shipping. Finally in 1588 the Spanish king dispatched the entire Armada, the strongest invasion fleet ever mounted against the English navy. The smaller, more maneuverable English ships, aided by a violent storm, nearly destroyed the Spanish fleet. Elizabeth was now the undisputed leader of the strongest nation in Europe. For the remainder of her reign, England seemed the ideal Renaissance kingdom, a model of social order. Religious controversies, political divisiveness, and economic disruptions were suppressed or ignored in the interests of national unity and out of respect for the beloved queen.

THE STRUGGLE BETWEEN CROWN AND PARLIAMENT

Elizabeth's death in 1603 marked the end of the powerful Tudor monarchy and the beginning of the weaker Stuart dynasty. Stuart

England witnessed both colonial expansion and a series of wrenching civil disturbances that established the House of Commons as the true center of power.

The first Stuart monarch was Elizabeth's cousin James IV of Scotland, who became James I of England. James was intelligent, well educated, and peace loving, but he was overly confident to the point of arrogance. His monumental lack of tact provoked a French minister to call him "the wisest fool in Christendom." James's son Charles I, who ascended the throne in 1625, also was autocratic and uncompromising. Both father and son believed in the divine right of kings, and they considered themselves God's representatives in all religious and civil matters.

The Stuart kings met with rising hostility among the English people and within the Puritan-dominated House of Commons. This attitude was the result of forces that had been building since the days of Elizabeth, of the kings' own blunders and also of the typical Renaissance view of authority and absolutism. The first conflict between crown and Parliament erupted when James demanded that the Puritans and other religious groups practice the rituals of high church liturgy. The Puritans, who wanted to simplify doctrine and ritual, were outraged. They were even more incensed when James released imprisoned Catholic priests and relaxed the fines placed upon the Catholic clergy, for they suspected that the Spanish were behind these moves. The split between king and people widened under Charles, who swore to make the Puritans conform or "hurry them out of the land."

A second conflict centered around the Stuart kings' chronic need for money. By the beginning of the seventeenth century, because of inflation and a decline in revenue from royal lands, the Stuart kings could not balance the budget. The Puritans in the House of Commons, who were shocked at the scandals and extravagance of the Stuart court, refused to legislate additional revenues. James and Charles both tried to circumvent Parliament by imposing royal import duties, extorting loans from merchants, and selling titles of nobility.

Although there were occasional periods of truce between the House of Commons and the monarchy, the relationship continued to deteriorate until in 1629 Parliament dissolved in a bitter dispute over religious services and illegal customs collections by royal officials. During the next eleven years Charles governed without Parliament and continued to incur the anger and resentment of the people by his autocratic policies. The religious, political, and economic unrest of this period stimulated emigration to British North America, particularly among nonconforming worshippers and government critics. The Stuart years were England's first years of major colonial expansion.

THE PURITAN REVOLUTION

When the Bishop of Edinburgh tried to use a new Anglican prayer book in a Scottish Presbyterian service, an angry woman threw a stool at him. This incident touched off a riot in which rebels seized Edinburgh Castle, abolished high church rule, and rejected the authority of the king. Faced with rebellion, Charles reconvened Parliament in 1640, hoping to get enough money for an army to suppress the Scots. The House of Commons responded by stripping the king of his power as head of the Anglican Church and by ordering the execution of his chief minister and archbishop. Charles tried to arrest the ringleaders in this political revolt, but the spirit of dissent was too strong, and both sides began to prepare for civil war.

The Civil War was an ideological rather than a class or regional struggle. In general, however, the conservative north and west and the nobility supported the king, while the middle class town dwellers and country squires tended to side with the Puritan Parliament. Under the skilled leadership of a gentleman named Oliver Cromwell, the Puritans formed a devout, well disciplined army of "Roundheads," so called because of their closely cropped hair. The royal army was composed mainly of long-haired, devil-may-care aristocrats known as "Cavaliers." The Puritans soundly defeated the royal forces in 1645, and within a year Charles surrendered. Cromwell's army, now in control of the government, ordered the execution of the king and retaliatory measures against royal supporters, Anglicans, and Catholics.

Cromwell ruled England as a military dictator, first at the head of the Commonwealth, then as Lord Protector for Life. He ordered theaters closed and festivals and most other forms of recreation suspended. He declared Sunday a day of prayer when even walking for pleasure was forbidden. When Cromwell died in 1658, his son inherited his father's title, but he was unable to control quarreling generals, discontented government officials, and a restive public.

The Cromwellian government had proved no less autocratic than the Stuarts, and, by 1660, almost everyone wanted a return to the old constitutional rule, with a king or queen, a House of Lords, and a House of Commons. Early that year, a special session of Parliament invited the exiled Charles II, the son of the executed king, to assume the throne. The restoration of the monarchy marks the official end of the Renaissance Period in English history.

RENAISSANCE LITERATURE: THE ELIZABETHAN AGE

During the Renaissance the creative energy of the English people burst forth into the greatest harvest of literature the western world had yet known. The center of literary activity was London, by the late 1500's a bustling city of over 100,000 with the largest population of middle-class citizens in all of Europe. The many printing presses and publishers there found an audience eager for popular romances, religious tracts, accounts of travels, sensational "news stories," political pamphlets, literary criticism, and the earliest novels. Readers and listeners, poets and playwrights all delighted in the vigor and beauty of the English language.

The glittering Elizabethan court was a focus of poetic creativity. Members of the court vied with one another to see who could create the most highly polished, technically perfect poems. The appreciative audience for these lyrics was the elite artistic and social circle that surrounded the queen. The queen herself wrote lyrics, and she patronized favorite poets and rewarded courtiers for eloquent poetic tributes. Among her proteges were poets Sir Philip Sidney and Sir Walter Raleigh; among those who courted her favor with little success was Edmund Spenser who wrote the epic *The Faerie Queen* (1590) in honor of Elizabeth.

Elizabethan poetry evidences a major shift away from the mood and subjects of medieval poetry. Now in vogue were quiet, contented pastorals, in which carefree nymphs and shepherds cavort in idyllic rural settings. Also popular were lyrics that express passionate desire for a beautiful, intriguing, and elusive woman. The poetry of this period appeals to the intellect as well as to the emotions, blending the classical reverence for truth with the Renaissance appreciation for beauty.

The Elizabethans viewed nature as intricate, complex, and beautiful. To them, however, the natural world was a subject not for imitation but for improvement by creative minds. Nature provided raw material to be shaped into works of art. The greater the intricacy or "artificiality" of the result, the more admired the artistry of the poet. Elizabethan poets thus created ingenious metaphors, elaborate allegories, and complex analogies, often within the strictures of the sonnet, originally an Italian verse form.

The secular subjects, light-hearted spirit, and sensuality typical of Elizabethan lyrics incurred the wrath of pious Puritans who called this imaginative literature the "work of the devil."

ELIZABETHAN AND SEVENTEENTH-CENTURY DRAMA

The greatest literary achievement of the English Renaissance was Elizabethan drama, a genre that emerged from three sources. One was the medieval miracle, mystery, and morality plays performed in churches, inns, and private homes and outdoors in towns and rural marketplaces. A second source was the popular entertainment provided by itinerant minstrels, jugglers, acrobats, and actors. By the sixteenth century, some noble families maintained their own companies of actors who doubled as household servants. To amuse their aristocratic patrons, these companies frequently presented brief farcical "interludes" that ridiculed the manners and customs of the commoners. A third source was the Latin and Greek dramas that were revived during the Renaissance and studied at university centers such as Oxford and Cambridge.

Among the early Elizabethan playwrights was Christopher Marlowe, who first exploited the potential of the English language as a dramatic medium. His tragedies and satires show the kind of psychological probing that is a hallmark of the finest Elizabethan and seventeenth-century dramas. One playwright influenced by Marlowe was William Shakespeare, whose plays represent the height of the English dramatic tradition. Shakespeare's *Macbeth* appears in this unit, preceded by a detailed description of the enormously popular Elizabethan theatre.

In retrospect, Shakespeare dominates the theatre of the late sixteenth and early seventeenth centuries. In the early 1600's, however, the comedies of a rugged, boisterous poet and playwright named Ben Jonson were equally admired. His plays provided a satiric, somewhat cynical commentary on lives of ordinary Londoners. Jonson's masques were especially popular among aristocratic and royal audiences, who flocked to the spectacular pageants with their elaborate scenery, costumes, music, and dance.

THE POETRY AND PROSE OF THE SEVENTEENTH CENTURY

The literature of the seventeenth century begins to reflect a certain dissatisfaction with the extravagance, romance, and enthusiasm of the Elizabethan Age. Also evident is a general tone of melancholy, a growing sense of disquiet that parallels the political polarization of the era.

As a poet, Ben Jonson revolted against the romantic style of Elizabethan lyrics and imitated the grace, craftsmanship, and forms of classical poetry. Jonson's followers, the "Tribe of Ben," were sophisticated young Cavaliers, among them Robert Herrick, Robert

Lovelace, and Sir John Suckling. Cavalier poetry is light-hearted, charming, witty, and sometimes cynical and licentious. It deals mainly with themes of love, war, chivalry, and loyalty to the throne.

A second major style in seventeenth-century poetry was introduced by John Donne whose intense poems are characterized by elaborate metaphors and paradoxical imagery and by thoughts of death, physical love, and religious devotion. Whereas Jonson and the Cavaliers tended to treat limited, human subjects, Donne and other "metaphysical poets" tried to encompass the vastness of the universe and to express an awareness of life's complexities and contradictions.

Significant in the development of English prose are the essays of Sir Francis Bacon. In a compact, clear style, Bacon explores the controversial new views of the world and of the cosmos postulated by Renaissance philosophers and scientists.

Literature

- Sir Thomas More (1478-1535) publishes *Utopia*
- Luther begins translation of the Bible into German
- William Tyndale's English translation of Bible replaces Wycliffe's as dominant version
- First complete edition of the Bible is printed in England
- First edition of *The Book of Common Prayer* is published in England

	1485	1500	1550

History

- Columbus discovers America
- Leonardo da Vinci begins *The Last Supper*
- Sir Thomas More is executed
- Anne Boleyn is executed
- Henry VIII dies
- Henry Tudor defeats Richard III and assumes throne as Henry VII, first Tudor King
- Vasco da Gama discovers sea route to India
- Mary I becomes Queen of England
- Michelangelo begins work on Sistine Chapel
- Henry VIII assumes throne
- Elizabeth I becomes Queen
- Martin Luther posts 95 Theses, beginning Protestant Reformation
- Henry VIII, excommunicated by Pope, completes break with Roman Church
- Parliament passes Act of Supremacy, declaring King as head of English Church

A book that has done more to mold English prose style than any other book ever written is the *King James Authorized Bible* (1611). This translation, which was the first to make extensive use of Greek and Hebrew texts, represents the combined efforts of fifty leading Biblical scholars, both Anglican and Puritan.

The last of the great English Renaissance men was John Milton, the only major Puritan writer of the seventeenth century. His concerns are not only different from those of his contemporaries, but also more complex, grandiose, passionate, devotional, and universal than almost any other English writer. Using the classics as stylistic and thematic inspiration, he ignores the raging religious and political controversies of his time and speaks to an unborn audience of the future. In his personal life and in his epic masterpiece *Paradise Lost* (1667), he demonstrates the triumph of human over nature that characterizes the spirit of the English Renaissance.

- To avoid censorship, James Burbage builds first London theater outside city limits
- Holinshed's *Chronicles* published
- Edmund Spenser (1552-1599) publishes *The Shepheard's Calendar*
- Douay-Rheims translation of the Bible
- Sir Philip Sidney (1554-1586) dies
- Christopher Marlowe (1564-1593) writes *Dr. Faustus*
- Jane Anger writes *Her Protection for Women*
- Edmund Spenser (1552-1599) publishes first books of *The Faerie Queene*
- Shakespeare (1564-1616) writes *Henry VI*, parts 2 and 3
- Globe Theater is built
- Shakespeare (1564-1616) completes *Macbeth*

- *King James Bible* published
- Original Globe Theater burns down
- Ben Jonson (1572-1637) is appointed poet laureate, publishes *Works*
- Sir John Suckling (1609-1642) publishes poems
- First publication of *Songs and Sonnets* of John Donne (1572-1631)
- Robert Herrick (1591-1674) publishes poetry
- Richard Lovelace (1618-1657) publishes "To Lucasta"

- John Milton (1608-1674) becomes blind

	1600	1650	1660

- Sir Walter Raleigh sends colonists to Roanoke Island
- English defeat Spanish Armada
- Elizabeth I dies
- James I, first of Stuart line, becomes King
- First permanent English colony in America established at Jamestown
- Pilgrims establish colony at Plymouth, Massachusetts
- Civil War begins between Royalists and Puritans
- Puritan Commonwealth begins in Britain
- Charles II assumes throne, restoring monarchy and ending Commonwealth

The Development of the English Language

THE EARLY MODERN PERIOD

With the Renaissance came the transition to early Modern English. By the late fifteenth century, English had evolved to a stage in which its sounds and appearance would seem familiar to modern-day speakers of English.

The Great Vowel Shift and Other Changes

The most significant development in spoken English was the Great Vowel Shift. This shift, a slow evolution that occurred over centuries but was most evident from about 1400 to about 1600, involved changes in the pronunciations of words. The long vowel sounds changed from the ones used in Middle English to the ones still used today. The sound *ee* in Chaucer's time became today's long *i* sound, as in *time*. Similarly, the sound of long *o*, pronounced like the *a* in *law*, and the sound of long *a*, pronounced like the *a* in *father*, evolved to their modern pronunciations. The sounds of diphthongs also changed. In Middle English, *house* rhymed with *moose*, while *moon* was pronounced "moan," and *meat* was pronounced "met." The Great Vowel Shift was largely completed by 1700; consequently, modern speakers pronounce the words of Shakespeare much as he himself said them.

Along with the changes in vowel sounds came other changes in pronunciation. The final *-e* on words such as *came* and *like*, pronounced as a separate syllable in Chaucer's time, fell silent by Shakespeare's. Likewise, the final *-ed* on verbs, pronounced as an extra syllable in Middle English, lost its full syllabic value and became slurred. *Laughed*, for instance, would have had two complete syllables for a speaker of the fourteenth century ("laf′ ed") but only one for a speaker of the late sixteenth ("laff′d").

During the transition from Middle English to Modern English, an additional change occurred in the endings of words. While speakers and writers of Middle English had formed plurals of nouns by adding *-n* or *-en*, those using early Modern English adopted *-s*, as the standard sign of the plural.

Printing, introduced in England by William Caxton during the Great Vowel Shift, helped to preserve Middle English spellings, even though the pronunciation of words changed. English thus was left with bewildering discrepancies between spelling and sound. Even today, foreigners learning the language often complain of these quirks, and native speakers are challenged by the inconsistencies of English spelling.

The Rebirth of Ancient Learning

A major influence on English during the Renaissance was the revival of classical learning, stimulated by the increased availability of books. While the rebirth of interest in classical works had broad cultural significance, linguistically its chief impact was the massive influx of words from Latin and Greek. Ironically, although the Romans had ruled Britain for centuries and Latin had been the language of the church when it dominated learning in the Medieval Period, the greatest surge of Latin words into English occurred during the sixteenth century. Many Latin words entered the language in a pure and unaltered form: *item, explicit, minor, pauper, proviso*, and *simile* are examples. Other words were adapted from Latin; for example, *perspicere* became *perspective*, and *integrare* became *integrate*. Language scholars today estimate that one-fourth to one-fifth of all words in a Latin dictionary eventually found their way into English, either directly or through French words based on Latin.

Greek words, including *catastrophe, anonymous, criterion, lexicon,* and *tonic,* also entered English at this time. Scholars deliberately attempted to enrich English with words from classical languages, and so many of the Latin and Greek words adopted during this period express abstract ideas.

The Growth of English Vocabulary

The Renaissance is recognized as a time of tremendous vocabulary expansion. Along with words from Latin and Greek, words from French and Italian were also widely incorporated. French words crept in with the resurgence of interest in French literature. Among these words were *bigot, genteel, ticket, vogue.* Similarly, the artistic importance of Italy during the Renaissance led to increased travel there, and among the souvenirs brought back were words such as *balcony, cameo, stanza, violin,* and *volcano.*

The Elizabethan era was also a great age of exploration, commerce, and colonization. Many words came to English from the languages of other major seafaring nations. From Dutch, for example, came *yacht, landscape, sketch,* and *dock.* From Spanish came *banana, bravado, mosquito, potato,* and *tobacco.* With the beginnings of the British Empire, words from America such as *skunk, canoe,* and *moccasin* were added, and English slowly began its course toward becoming a global tongue.

The wholesale adoption of words during the Renaissance enriched English with many synonyms from different linguistic sources. Another lasting legacy is the vast spectrum of words—concrete and abstract, short and long, simple and elegant—with which writers can fulfill their aims.

English Nationalism and the English Tongue

The Elizabethan era was a time of fierce patriotism, of intense pride in being English. That pride manifested itself in love of the English language. Consequently, the practice of classical borrowing infuriated many language purists, who ridiculed the new words as "inkhorn," or pedantic, words. Among the surviving words dubbed "inkhorn" during the Renaissance are *defunct, egregious, inflate, spurious, audacious, ingenious,* and *relinquish.* A leader in the movement to rely on native words, Sir John Cheke, wrote, "Our own tung should be written cleane and pure, unmixt and unmangeled with borrowing of other tunges."

During the Renaissance the English language revealed its potential for sheer brilliance. It was the period of the King James Bible, the era of Spenser and Milton, Marlowe and Jonson, Shakespeare and Donne. Their genius showed the virtuosity and versatility of the tongue, its orchestral sweep and splendor.

A contemporary of Shakespeare's, educator Robert Mulcaster, expressed the common belief that English had reached a glorious peak: "I take this present period of our English tongue to be the very height thereof, because I find it so excellently well fined, . . . Whatsoever shall become of the English state, the English tongue cannot prove fairer than it is at this day." Despite the many outstanding works produced in subsequent centuries, and despite the natural prejudice of each generation for the images that give utterance to its unique dreams, Mulcaster's opinion is widely recognized as the plain truth.

Sir Thomas Wyatt

1503–1542

THOMAS WYATT (drawing). *Hans Holbein.*
Copyright Reserved by Her Majesty, The Queen.

Sir Thomas Wyatt was a courtier, diplomat, and amateur poet who introduced the sonnet into English literature. The sonnet became the dominant poetic form of the Elizabethan Age and a distinctively English mode of expression.

Born into an upper-class family, Wyatt grew up in the same household as Anne Boleyn, the ill-fated wife of Henry VIII. Sometimes in favor and sometimes out of favor with the whimsical king, Wyatt spent most of his adult life at court in royal service. He was a great favorite, handsome, multilingual, a skilled musician. Considering the rumor that Wyatt had once been Anne Boleyn's lover, it is not surprising that the jealous king was suspicious of the popular young courtier. King Henry ordered Wyatt imprisoned in the Tower of London twice, both times accusing him of treason and threatening him with execution. Each time, however, Wyatt was pardoned, and he continued to serve the king in a variety of roles, among them clerk of the royal jewels and Ambassador to Spain. As a member of the diplomatic corps, Wyatt visited a number of cultural centers throughout Europe and developed a lifelong interest in Latin verse forms and in Italian literature, some of which he translated into English. Because he was primarily a diplomat, Wyatt wrote lyrics only in his leisure time to amuse himself and the other cultivated ladies and gentlemen of the court. He also wrote songs to be sung to the accompaniment of a lute; his song "My Lute, Awake!" is included in this unit.

Wyatt is considered the most innovative poet of the early Renaissance. He is often associated with Henry Howard, Earl of Surrey, and the two are sometimes credited with the development of the first "true" English sonnets. Actually, although their poetry is often published together, Surrey was simply Wyatt's young disciple. It was Wyatt who perfected the sonnet form, thus preparing the way for the polished verse of the Elizabethan era.

Wyatt sought to bring order and dignity to English poetry by imitating the strict metrical patterns and classical forms used by Petrarch, an Italian poet of the fourteenth century. Wyatt's sonnets show the influence of the Petrarchan style, yet they are innovative as well. Not only did Wyatt take liberties with the form of the Italian sonnet, but he also introduced a personal note into his poetry by describing his own sufferings from the cruelty of a current mistress. Wyatt's theme of unrequited love, evident in both his sonnets and his songs, was to become a major theme of Elizabethan lyrics. Besides a personal quality, Wyatt's sonnets and songs are distinctive for their dramatic intensity, sensitivity, and ironic wit.

My Lute, Awake!

My lute, awake! Perform the last
Labor that thou and I shall waste,
And end that I have now begun;
For when this song is sung and past,
My lute, be still, for I have done.   5

As to be heard where ear is none,
As lead to grave in marble stone,[1]
My song may pierce her heart as soon.
Should we then sigh or sing or moan?
No, no, my lute, for I have done.   10

The rocks do not so cruelly
Repulse the waves continually
As she my suit and affection.
So that I am past remedy,
Whereby my lute and I have done.   15

Proud of the spoil that thou hast got
Of simple hearts, thorough love's shot;[2]
By whom, unkind, thou hast them won,
Think not he hath his bow forgot,
Although my lute and I have done.   20

Vengeance shall fall on thy disdain
That makest but game on earnest pain.
Think not alone under the sun
Unquit to cause thy lovers plain,[3]
Although my lute and I have done.   25

Perchance thee lie withered and old
The winter nights that are so cold,
Plaining[4] in vain unto the moon.
Thy wishes then dare not be told.
Care then who list,[5] for I have done.   30

And then may chance thee to repent
The time that thou hast lost and spent
To cause thy lovers sigh and swoon.
Then shalt thou know beauty but lent,
And wish and want as I have done.   35

Now cease, my lute. This is the last
Labor that thou and I shall waste,
And ended is that we begun.
Now is this song both sung and past;
My lute, be still, for I have done.   40

---

1. **As to be . . . stone:** when sound can be heard with no ear to hear it or when soft lead is able to carve hard marble.
2. **love's shot:** the arrow of Cupid, Greek god of love.
3. **plain:** complain.
4. **plaining:** complaining.
5. **list:** listen.

Whoso List To Hunt

Whoso list[1] to hunt, I know where is an hind,[2]
But as for me—alas, I may no more.
The vain travail hath wearied me so sore,
I am of them that farthest cometh behind.
Yet may I, by no means, my wearied mind   5
Draw from the deer; but as she fleeth afore,
Fainting I follow. I leave off therefore,
Since in a net I seek to hold the wind.
Who list her hunt, I put him out of doubt,
As well as I, may spend his time in vain.   10
And graven[3] with diamonds in letters plain
There is written, her fair neck round about:
Noli me tangere,[4] for Caesar's I am,
And wild for to hold, though I seem tame.

---

1. **Whoso list:** whoever likes.
2. **hind:** a female deer.
3. **graven:** engraved.
4. ***Noli me tangere,*** *Latin:* "Do not touch me." This sonnet is said to refer to Anne Boleyn, with whom Wyatt was in love. Anne was the wife of Henry VIII, King of England.

Getting at Meaning

MY LUTE, AWAKE!

1. What is the speaker's attitude toward his former lover? Which of her qualities does he emphasize? What possible future does he predict for her?

2. Each stanza in this song ends with a similar line, or refrain. What subtle changes in wording are apparent in the refrain? What idea or attitude is emphasized by the refrain?

WHOSO LIST TO HUNT

3. How do you know that the subject of this poem is a woman, not a deer? Does the speaker feel that it is worthwhile to pursue the woman? Why then does he do so?

4. The footnote for the Latin message in line 13 gives important information about the sonnet. To whom or to what does "Caesar" probably refer in the same line?

5. What is the common theme in these two works by Wyatt?

Developing Skills in Reading Literature

1. **Tone.** Compare the tone of these two selections. Which speaker is more objective, more detached from the situation he describes? Which speaker is more embittered, more subjectively involved in the situation? Would you describe these speakers as emotionally stable? Explain.

2. **Sonnet.** A sonnet is a lyric poem of fourteen lines, commonly written in iambic pentameter. The two standard sonnet types in English poetry are the Italian sonnet and the English sonnet.

a. **The Italian, or Petrarchan, sonnet** was introduced into English poetry by Sir Thomas Wyatt. This type of sonnet is divided into two parts, called the octave (the first eight lines) and the sestet (the last six lines). The usual rhyme scheme for the octave is *a b b a a b b a.* (These letters represent the pattern of end rhyme.) The rhyme scheme for the sestet may be *c d e c d e, c d c c d c,* or a similar variation. Even in the earliest English versions of this form, the rhyme scheme of the sestet varies considerably, and the last two lines often rhyme.

In the Italian sonnet, the octave generally presents a problem, states a proposition, or raises a question; the sestet presents a resolution, either solving the problem or commenting on the subject.

b. **The English, or Shakespearean, sonnet** is structured in four sections: three quatrains (four-line units) and a final couplet. The typical rhyme scheme is *a b a b c d c d e f e f g g.* In the English sonnet, as in the Italian sonnet, a problem or situation often is presented in the octave and resolved in the sestet, with the rhymed couplet at the end of the sonnet providing a final commentary on the subject.

Many variations of the original Italian form developed because of the difficulties of adhering to a strict metrical pattern while at the same time achieving unity, coherence, and sense. Notice, for example, that the first line of Wyatt's Italian sonnet "Whoso List To Hunt" deviates from the customary iambic pentameter. What is this deviation? Does the sonnet contain any other variances in traditional meter? in the Petrarchan rhyme scheme? What idea is presented in the octave? What shift in idea occurs at the beginning of the sestet? How does the sestet relate in meaning to the octave?

Edmund Spenser

1552–1599

Edmund Spenser was one of the chief lyricists of the early English Renaissance, a poet whose unique blending of classical forms with the natural rhythms of the English language resulted in a fluid, graceful style that later poets imitated but seldom duplicated. Spenser's failure to achieve the enthusiastic support of Queen Elizabeth caused him great distress, and perhaps it was this failure that turned him increasingly from the real world to the world of imagination. His facility with language and his scholarly mind earned him the recognition of his contemporaries and of later poets as well, causing him to be dubbed the "poet's poet."

The son of a London clothmaker, Spenser was educated at Cambridge University on a scholarship provided to "poor deserving scholars." As a student he read widely and became an expert in Latin, Greek, French, and Italian literature. Through his university friends, he secured a position with the Earl of Leicester, Robert Dudley, who introduced him to several members of the royal court, including Dudley's nephew Sir Philip Sidney and the flamboyant Sir Walter Raleigh. Spenser dedicated a number of works to Sidney, including *The Shepherd's Calendar* (1579) in which the lyrics are grouped according to the months of the year.

Raleigh encouraged Spenser to continue writing his masterpiece *The Faerie Queene* (1590-1596) and to present the unfinished draft to Elizabeth for her approval. The queen was flattered by the compliment of having such a monumental work written in her honor and pleased at Spenser's glorification of England and the English language. She granted him a small pension, but she did not confer upon him the full patronage that he desired. Discouraged, he returned to his home, an old castle in Ireland, where he remained for seventeen years. When his castle was burned to the ground during an Irish rebellion, he was forced to return to London where he died a pauper, still unrecognized by the queen. He was buried in the Poets' Corner in Westminster Abbey, next to Geoffrey Chaucer.

EDMUND SPENSER. *Benjamin Wilson.*
By permission of the Master and Fellows, Pembroke College, Cambridge.

The Faerie Queene, the longest epic poem in English Literature, is an extraordinarily complex and abstract allegory in which the poet borrows from classical, medieval, and Christian traditions to create a rich pageant of Elizabethan life and a philosophical contemplation of morality and human values. Each book tells the story of a knight in the service of Gloriana (Queen Elizabeth) who personifies one of the virtues of the perfect gentleman, according to Aristotle. The six virtues represented are holiness, temperance, chastity, friendship, justice, and courtesy. Each of *The Faerie Queene*'s six books contains more than five thousand lines, and Spenser had intended to write at least six more books of comparable length.

Besides *The Faerie Queene*, Spenser is admired for his contribution to the development of the English sonnet. His best known collection of sonnets is *Amoretti* (1595), "little love poems." This work was inspired by his passion for a young lady known only as Rosalind, who had apparently spurned the poet, thus feeding his prevailing mood of despair. The three sonnets from *Amoretti* that are included in this unit describe the pain of earthly love.

Sonnet 26

Sweet is the rose, but grows upon a briar;
  Sweet is the juniper, but sharp his bough,[1]
  Sweet is the eglantine, but pricketh near;
  Sweet is the fir bloom, but his branch is rough;
Sweet is the cypress, but his rind is tough;   5
Sweet is the nut, but bitter is his pill;[2]
Sweet is the broom flower, but yet sour enough;
And sweet is moly,[3] but his root is ill.
So every sweet with sour is tempered still,[4]
That maketh it be coveted the more: 10
For easy things, that may be got at will,
Most sorts of men do set but little store.
  Why then should I account of little pain,
  That endless pleasure shall unto me gain!

Rhyme scheme: This pattern is characteristic of Spenser, who developed his own interlocking rhymes.

1. **his bough:** *Bough* was pronounced to rhyme with *rough. His* was used instead of our present-day *its*.
2. **pill:** center or core.
3. **moly:** an herb with white blossoms and a black root, thought to have magical powers.

Sonnet 30

My love is like to ice, and I to fire:
How comes it then that this her cold so great
Is not dissolved through my so hot desire,
But harder grows the more I her entreat?
Or how comes it that my exceeding heat   5
Is not allayed by her heart-frozen cold,
But that I burn much more in boiling sweat,
And feel my flames augmented manifold?
What more miraculous thing may be told,
That fire, which all things melts, should harden ice,   10
And ice, which is congealed with senseless cold,
Should kindle fire by wonderful device?
Such is the power of love in gentle mind,
That it can alter all the course of kind![1]

---

1. **kind:** nature.

PORTRAIT OF AN UNKNOWN MAN, 1588. *Nicholas Hilliard. Victoria and Albert Museum, Crown Copyright.*

Sonnet 67

Like as a huntsman after weary chase,
Seeing the game from him escaped away,
Sits down to rest him in some shady place,
With panting hounds, beguilèd of their prey:
So, after long pursuit and vain assay,[1]   5
When I all weary had the chase forsook,
The gentle deer returned the selfsame way,
Thinking to quench her thirst at the next brook.
There she, beholding me with milder look,
Sought not to fly, but fearless still did bide,   10
Till I in hand her yet half trembling took,
And with her own good will her firmly tied.
    Strange thing, me seemed, to see a beast so wild
    So goodly won, with her own will beguiled.

---

1. **assay:** attempt.

Easter

Most glorious Lord of life, that on this day,
    Didst make thy triumph over death and sin:
And having harrowed[1] hell, didst bring away
    Captivity thence captive us to win:
    This joyous day, dear Lord, with joy begin,   5
And grant that we, for whom thou diddest die,
    Being with thy dear blood clean washed from sin,
May live forever in felicity.
And that thy love we weighing worthily,
    May likewise love thee for the same again: 10
And for thy sake that all like dear didst buy,[2]
    With love may one another entertain.
        So let us love, dear love, like as we ought,
        Love is the lesson which the Lord us taught.

---

1. **harrowed:** destroyed.
2. **that all . . . buy:** who paid dearly for all alike.

Getting at Meaning

SONNET 26

1. What apparent contradiction is expressed in the octave of this sonnet? What is the result of this contradiction, as explained in the sestet?

2. Paraphrase the comment made in the final two lines.

SONNET 30

3. What is the strange effect of love upon nature, according to the final lines of this sonnet? How is the effect illustrated in the rest of the sonnet?

SONNET 67

4. What is the central comparison in this sonnet?

5. What "strange thing" puzzles the lover in the final couplet?

EASTER

6. How has the Lord taught the lesson of love mentioned in the closing line of this sonnet?

7. What does the speaker hope for in his future life on Earth?

Developing Skills in Reading Literature

1. **Sonnet and Spenserian Stanza.** Spenser was familiar with the Italian sonnets of Petrarch and with the sonnets of Wyatt and Surrey. Like Wyatt, Spenser varied the sonnet form to make it his own. Examine these sonnets by Spenser and identify elements that are characteristic of both the Italian and the English types. Be sure to chart the rhyme scheme of each poem as a first step in analyzing the forms of the poems.

For the epic *The Faerie Queene* Spenser invented the so-called "Spenserian stanza," a nine-line stanza with eight lines of iambic pentameter followed by a ninth line containing two additional syllables. The rhyme scheme follows the pattern *a b a b b c b c c*. Identify similarities between this stanza form and the sonnet forms used by Spenser. Be prepared to explain your findings.

2. **Sonnet Sequence.** Toward the end of the fifteenth century, it became fashionable to write a series of sonnets dealing with one subject. Such a series is called a sonnet sequence or sonnet cycle. A common subject for a sonnet sequence was love for a beautiful but unattainable woman. The woman was rarely a real person or one whom the poet was seriously interested in pursuing. Often, she simply represented the poet's Muse, or inspiration.

Examine Sonnets 26, 30, and 67, which are part of the sonnet sequence *Amoretti*. Identify the idea that unifies the three sonnets. Although you do not have the entire sequence available, the three examples illustrate a certain progression of idea. Comment on the development of this idea. For example, do you observe changes, however subtle, in the speaker's feelings toward his lover? Explain.

Developing Vocabulary

Inferring Word Meaning. From your understanding of these sonnets, draw inferences or conclusions as to what each of these words means.

1. "Sonnet 26," line 9: tempered
2. "Sonnet 30," line 6: allayed
3. "Sonnet 30," line 11: congealed
4. "Sonnet 67," line 4: beguiled
5. "Easter," line 8: felicity

Sir Philip Sidney
1554–1586

Soldier, statesman, scientist, musician, critic, and poet, Sir Philip Sidney was viewed by many of his contemporaries as the ideal Renaissance man and as the epitome of knighthood. Scholars now consider him the finest prose writer and among the most talented poets of the Elizabethan Age.

Named for his godfather Philip II of Spain, Sidney came from a family well known at court. His uncle the Earl of Leicester was Queen Elizabeth's most trusted advisor. Sidney loved learning as a child and at eleven wrote letters to his father in both French and Latin. Educated at private academies and at Oxford University, he traveled extensively on the Continent where he made important contacts with famous writers, scholars, and statesmen. He then returned to London, a young man well versed in the latest European literary and artistic achievements, and was received into Elizabeth's charmed inner circle.

Seemingly a casual man about town, Sidney actually was deeply concerned with religious and political issues. Like his friend Sir Francis Drake, a renowned sea dog, he had a keen interest in exploration and in maintaining England's supremacy over Spain. Sidney also was committed to the Protestant cause, and he campaigned actively against Spanish support of English Catholics. So strong were his Protestant convictions that he voluntarily joined a cavalry force in Holland, fighting for the Dutch Protestants against Spain. During one attack, while leading a force of five hundred English horsemen against the Spaniards, Sir Philip was killed. His body was brought back to London where he was buried with highest military honors at St. Paul's Cathedral.

Writing poetry for Sidney, as for many courtiers, was a private activity, with poems being shared informally among friends. His circle included the young Edmund Spenser, whom he had met during his student days and with whom he shared a lifelong friendship and affection for literature. None of Sidney's literary work was published during his lifetime, but both his poetry and his prose

SIR PHILIP SIDNEY. *Anonymous.*
National Portrait Gallery, London.

were read in manuscript copies. Among his most famous works is a long prose romance titled *Arcadia* (1590), which relates in rambling style the adventures of princes in battles, tournaments, and chivalric escapades. The influence of this romance was considerable; Shakespeare, for example, based several episodes from his plays on Sidney's work.

Astrophel and Stella (1591), a collection of 108 sonnets and eleven songs, is perhaps Sidney's best known work. The early poems in this sequence— the first complete sonnet sequence in English— were written simply as literary exercises, patterned after the Italian sonnet. The later sonnets, however, express the poet's passionate obsession with Penelope, the fourteen-year-old daughter of the Earl of Essex, who is the Stella of the sonnets. Although Sidney never married Penelope, he continued to exalt his love for her. Two of the sonnets from Sidney's much imitated sequence—Sonnet 31 and Sonnet 39—are included in this unit.

Sonnet 31

With how sad steps, O Moon, thou climb'st the skies!
How silently, and with how wan a face!
What, may it be that even in heavenly place
That busy archer[1] his sharp arrows tries?
Sure, if that long-with-love-acquainted eyes   5
Can judge of love, thou feel'st a lover's case.
I read it in thy looks; thy languished grace,
To me, that feel the like, thy state descries.[2]
Then, even of fellowship, O Moon, tell me,
Is constant love deemed there but want of wit?[3]   10
Are beauties there as proud as here they be?
Do they above love to be loved, and yet
Those lovers scorn whom that love doth possess?
Do they call virtue there ungratefulness?

---

1. **busy archer:** Cupid, god of love.
2. **descries:** reveals, betrays.
3. **wit:** intelligence, good sense.

Sonnet 39

Come, Sleep! O Sleep, the certain knot of peace,
The baiting place[1] of wit, the balm of woe,
The poor man's wealth, the prisoner's release,
The indifferent judge between the high and low;
With shield of proof shield me from out of the prease[2]   5
Of those fierce darts Despair at me doth throw:
O make in me those civil wars to cease;
I will good tribute pay, if thou do so.
Take thou of me smooth pillows, sweetest bed.
A chamber deaf to noise and blind to light,   10
A rosy garland and a weary head:
And if these things, as being thine by right,
Move not thy heavy grace, thou shalt in me,
Livelier than elsewhere, Stella's image see.

---

1. **baiting place:** place of refreshment.
2. **prease:** crowd.

Heart Exchange

My true love hath my heart, and I have his,
By just exchange one for the other given:
I hold his dear, and mine he cannot miss;
There never was a bargain better driven.
His heart in me keeps me and him in one;   5
My heart in him his thoughts and senses guides:
He loves my heart, for once it was his own;
I cherish his, because in me it bides.
His heart his wound received from my sight;
My heart was wounded with his wounded heart;   10
For, as from me on him his hurt did light,
So still methought in me his hurt did smart:
Both equal hurt in this change sought our bliss:
My true love hath my heart and I have his.

FRANCES, COUNTESS OF SOMERSET. *Anonymous.*
Victoria and Albert Museum, Crown Copyright.

Getting at Meaning

SONNET 31

1. In the octave of this sonnet, the speaker personifies the moon. What are the human emotions attributed to the moon? What has caused them?

2. In the sestet of this sonnet, the speaker asks a series of questions. Rephrase these questions in your own words.

SONNET 39

3. What is the nature of the "civil wars" that are raging within the speaker?

4. According to the speaker, what will happen if sleep does not come?

HEART EXCHANGE

5. What new idea is introduced in line 9 of the poem? How does the tone of the sonnet change? How is the meaning of the last line different from that of the opening line?

6. Who might the speaker be in this sonnet?

Developing Skills in Reading Literature

1. **Sonnet: Form and Meaning.** Identify the sonnet form of each of these sonnets. Notice that each one ends with a final couplet. Describe the function of each couplet in relation to the theme of the sonnet.

Although the rhyme scheme and the structure of the sonnet may seem to be highly contrived, the best poets make skillful use of the form to emphasize tone or to reinforce themes. For example, the changing rhyme scheme in the third quatrain of "Sonnet 31" seems to coincide not only with a new look at the moon but also with an increased sense of urgency on the part of the speaker. Identify the patterns of rhyme and the structural divisions—octave, sestet, quatrains, couplets—within each of these sonnets. Then, look for ways in which rhyme scheme and structure reflect and reinforce thematic ideas.

2. **Apostrophe.** An apostrophe is a figure of speech in which a thing or some abstract quality or a nonexistent or absent person is addressed as though present. How do both "Sonnet 31" and "Sonnet 39" illustrate this device?

3. **Paradox and Oxymoron.** A paradox is a statement that seems to be contradictory or ridiculous but is actually quite true. A special kind of paradox is the oxymoron, which brings together two contradictory terms for sharp emphasis; for example, "wise fool" or "eloquent silence." Find additional examples of oxymoron in "Sonnet 39."

4. **Rhetorical Question.** A question that is asked only for dramatic effect, with no answer expected, is known as a rhetorical question. Comment on the effect created by the rhetorical questions in "Sonnet 31."

Developing Vocabulary

Using a Dictionary. Find each of the following words in the sonnets of Sir Philip Sidney. Then look up the words in a dictionary and find the definition for each word as it is used in the sonnet. Finally, write a sentence using each word in the same sense.

1. "Sonnet 31," line 7: languished
2. "Sonnet 31," line 9: fellowship
3. "Sonnet 39," line 4: indifferent
4. "Sonnet 39," line 13: grace
5. "Sonnet 39," line 14: image

Christopher Marlowe

1564–1593

The dramatic writing of Christopher Marlowe was the most fresh and lively of his day, and it transformed the British theatre. Yet there was a secret side to this writer, which cut short his career and his life.

Marlowe's father was a Canterbury shoemaker, and young Marlowe attended a school that encouraged the writing of poetry and plays. The nature of his scholarship suggests that Marlowe was expected to become an Anglican priest. He attended Corpus Christi College in Cambridge where he earned bachelor's and master's degrees and abandoned for good any intention of entering the ministry. Due to his large number of absences, college authorities were not at first going to grant his master's degree. A letter from the queen's Privy Council, however, explained that Marlowe was traveling in France, among other places, on business important to the British government. This letter indicates that even as a student he was active in the British secret service.

Marlowe began writing plays while he was in college. The year he graduated he wrote *Tamburlaine* (1587), a tragedy about Timur the Lame, a fourteenth-century conqueror of Asia and Europe. This was the only play published during his lifetime. Although Marlowe's career as a playwright lasted only six years, he profoundly influenced the language, the plots, and the characterizations of Elizabethan drama. He demonstrated that blank verse was not necessarily stiff and wooden but could sound natural and graceful. In *Tamburlaine*, *Doctor Faustus*, and *Edward II*, Marlowe probed the psychology of his main characters, thus creating the first modern tragedies. *The Jew of Malta* merged the violent and the comic, which also became typical of the plays that followed. In his poetry, too, Marlowe took old forms and gave them new dimensions. *Hero and Leander* (published 1598), for example, is a masterpiece within the tradition of English narrative poetry; his lyrics are modeled after the Italian pastoral.

As a writer and intellectual, Marlowe was one of a small group of freethinkers who were led by Sir Walter Raleigh. Their discussions and writings questioned all aspects of life, including religion, which led to the charge that Marlowe was an atheist. Marlowe had shared quarters with fellow playwright Thomas Kyd, who was arrested and tortured for treason in 1593. When some freethinking and anti-church writings were found in their lodgings, Kyd blamed Marlowe. Marlowe was arrested, but he was protected by the government from prosecution, suggesting that he had continued his spying activities. It is possible that his arrest had embarrassed his employers, for while dining at a pub with three other known spies and conspirators, he was murdered. He died at the age of twenty-nine, vilified by some as a traitor and blasphemer, praised by others as a dramatic and poetic genius.

The Passionate Shepherd to His Love

Come live with me and be my Love,
And we will all the pleasures prove[1]
That hills and valleys, dales and fields,
Or woods or steepy mountain yields.

And we will sit upon the rocks,   5
And see the shepherds feed their flocks
By shallow rivers, to whose falls
Melodious birds sing madrigals.

And I will make thee beds of roses
And a thousand fragrant posies;   10
A cap of flowers, and a kirtle[2]
Embroidered all with leaves of myrtle.

A gown made of the finest wool
Which from our pretty lambs we pull;
Fair-linèd slippers for the cold,   15
With buckles of the purest gold.

A belt of straw and ivy-buds
With coral clasps and amber studs:
And if these pleasures may thee move,
Come live with me and be my Love.   20

The shepherd swains shall dance and sing
For thy delight each May morning:
If these delights thy mind may move,
Then live with me and be my Love.

---

1. **prove:** experience.
2. **kirtle:** skirt.

Sir Walter Raleigh
1552?–1618

SIR WALTER RALEIGH, 1588. *Anonymous.*
National Portrait Gallery, London.

A true Renaissance man, Sir Walter Raleigh tried just about everything possible in his world. As a statesman, writer, courtier, scientist, soldier, adventurer, and explorer, he lived a life more of action than of contemplation.

Born in Devon, England, Raleigh gravitated to the center of activity even as a young man. Before college he fought on the side of the Huguenots, the French Protestants, in the civil war in France. He later attended Oriel College in Oxford and studied law in the Middle Temple in London. When he helped put down the Irish rebels in Munster in 1580 and criticized English policy in Ireland, he attracted the attention of Queen Elizabeth I. Known as the Virgin Queen, Elizabeth never married, probably in part to prevent England from falling under the control of a foreign-born king. She did form close relationships with those who served her, and Sir Walter Raleigh became the queen's favorite courtier. From 1582 on, he was granted valuable land in Ireland and lucrative licenses to trade wine, cloth, and tin. He was also made an admiral, knighted in 1585, and appointed governor of Jersey, a Channel island. Between 1584 and 1589 Raleigh sponsored the establishment of the ill-fated Roanoke Colony in present-day North Carolina.

When Raleigh married in 1588, he kept it a secret from the jealous queen. The birth of his son in 1592 could not be so easily concealed, however, and Raleigh and his wife were imprisoned in the Tower of London. He was able to buy their freedom when an investment in a profiteering venture paid off. The queen encouraged such attacks against Spanish merchant ships, and Raleigh made a fortune as a profiteer.

Raleigh never regained his position at court. He read widely and studied mathematics, navigation, chemistry, and medicine. He also wrote history and poetry, though few of his poems survive. For a time, a group of freethinkers of all classes and tastes centered around him. This group included Christopher Marlowe, with whom Raleigh frequently debated religious topics.

In 1595 Raleigh led an expedition to Guyana in Spanish South America. An account of his adventures was published as *The Discoverie of Guinana* (1596). Unfortunately, the politics in England changed, and Spain became an ally under James I. Raleigh again fell into royal disfavor. His enemies accused him of trying to overthrow the king, and he was imprisoned in the Tower of London, this time for thirteen years (1614). Although the king did not pardon Raleigh, he was released from prison and given permission to return to South America to find gold. Once there, his soldiers quarreled with the local authorities and burned a town. As a consequence Raleigh was executed by order of the king.

The Nymph's Reply to the Shepherd

If all the world and love were young,
And truth in every shepherd's tongue,
These pretty pleasures might me move
To live with thee and be thy Love.

But Time drives flocks from field to fold;   5
When rivers rage and rocks grow cold;
And Philomel[1] becometh dumb;
The rest complains of cares to come.

The flowers do fade, and wanton fields
To wayward Winter reckoning yields: 10
A honey tongue, a heart of gall,
Is fancy's spring, but sorrow's fall.

Thy gowns, thy shoes, thy beds of roses,
Thy cap, thy kirtle, and thy posies,
Soon break, soon wither—soon forgotten,   15
In folly ripe, in reason rotten.

Thy belt of straw and ivy-buds,
Thy coral clasps and amber studs,—
All these in me no means can move
To come to thee and be thy Love.   20

But could youth last, and love still breed,
Had joys no date,[2] nor age no need,
Then these delights my mind might move
To live with thee and be thy Love.

---

1. **Philomel:** the nightingale.
2. **date:** ending.

Getting at Meaning

THE PASSIONATE SHEPHERD TO HIS LOVE

1. What gifts does the shepherd offer to his love? Which of these gifts are unrealistic? Which are not?

2. Notice the poet's use of repetition in lines 1 and 2, 19 and 20, and 23 and 24. What is the effect of this repetition?

THE NYMPH'S REPLY TO THE SHEPHERD

1. With what accusation does the nymph begin the poem? How does she further insult the shepherd?

2. Does the nymph seem to change her attitude in the last stanza? If so, how?

Developing Skills in Reading Literature

1. **Pastoral.** A pastoral is a poem that treats of shepherds and rustic life, usually in an idealized manner. During the Renaissance, the pastoral became highly stylized, with poets speaking as if they and their friends were simple shepherds and ephemeral spirits of nature. The form of the Renaissance pastoral also is artificial, with meters and rhyme schemes characteristic of formal court poetry. The language is equally unnatural, for the rustics often speak in courtly language more appropriate to the drawing room than to the countryside.

Find examples of both pastoral and courtly imagery in these two poems. What is the meter and rhyme scheme of each poem? Is this form more suited to pastoral or to courtly poetry? Which of these poems seems closer in tone to the idyllic pastoral? Explain your answers.

2. **Speaker.** Without any familiarity with Elizabethan poetry or with the biographical details of Marlowe's life, you might at first assume that the writer of "The Passionate Shepherd to His Love" actually is a shepherd. The fact that the poet has created a speaker who exists within this poem alone becomes obvious only when you notice the courtly imagery. In Raleigh's poem the distinction between poet and speaker is immediately apparent. Why is this so? What is the speaker's attitude toward her subject? Does this attitude differ from that of the poet? Explain your answer.

THE MONTH OF APRIL. *Simon Benninck. From the* Benninck Book of Hours. *The Cooper Bridgeman Library Ltd. Victoria and Albert Museum, London.*

Elizabeth I

1533–1603

"I have the heart of a man, not of a woman, and I am not afraid of anything," Elizabeth once said. It was this indomitable quality, along with her sharp intelligence and the lessons she learned during her lonely and precarious early life, that enabled Elizabeth to become one of the greatest sovereigns that ever ruled England.

The daughter of Henry VIII and his second queen, Anne Boleyn, Elizabeth was born in 1533 and declared illegitimate three years later, just before Henry ordered her mother beheaded. Five years later, her stepmother Queen Catherine Howard met the same fate. These two traumatic events may explain in part Elizabeth's firm resolve never to marry, expressed to friends after her stepmother's execution and adhered to her entire life.

Elizabeth grew up in the shadow of her brother, Edward, and her sister, Mary, both of whom were destined to occupy the throne. She learned early to be extremely circumspect, to avoid any hint of entanglement in political and religious intrigue, and to bend to circumstances in matters that did not compromise her principles. During the years of bloody reprisals against Protestants, she outwardly renounced her religion, although she continued to be the rallying point for English Protestants.

When Mary died in 1558, the English people, tired of religious persecution, Spanish influence, and the dangers of civil war, enthusiastically welcomed the accession of twenty-five-year-old Elizabeth. An astute judge of character, Elizabeth chose as advisors men of brilliance, prudence, and absolute loyalty. With their help she guided England through turbulent years during which disgruntled Catholics, devious foreign kings, and determined popes waited for an opportunity to topple the Protestant monarch.

Elizabeth was a strong, independent ruler in the tradition of the Tudors. Always able to sense the heart and the mind of her people, she inspired in them unprecedented pride and devotion and an exhilarating confidence in the capabilities of England as a nation. Near the end of her life, she summarized her relationship with her subjects,

ELIZABETH I. Zuccari.
Pinacoteca, Siena. Scala/Art Resource.

saying, "Though God hath raised me high, yet I count this the glory of my crown, that I have reigned with your loves."

The image of Elizabeth is familiar, with her startlingly red hair and pale skin, and her fondness for jewels, huge ruffs, and elaborate finery. She was careful of her health and "could hunt all day, dance or watch pageants all night." Elizabeth had been well educated by a series of tutors and acquired early a love of learning. She wrote lyrics, translated classics, and spoke Latin, French, Spanish, Italian, and Flemish. Part of her importance to literary history is due to the fact that she granted her protection to actors and theatrical companies and encouraged dramatists by ordering command performances of new and popular plays. Furthermore, she filled her court with men and women who shone in every category of human activity, and her personality, while it could be cruel or fickle in the political realm, appealed as strongly to the poets of her age as it did to all her subjects.

On her deathbed in March, 1603, Elizabeth acknowledged James VI of Scotland as her heir, assuring a succession as orderly as had been her reign.

When I Was Fair and Young

When I was fair and young, and favor gracèd me,
    Of many was I sought, their mistress for to be;
But I did scorn them all, and answered them therefore,
    "Go, go, go, seek some otherwhere,
        Impòrtune me no more!"   5

How many weeping eyes I made to pine with woe,
    How many sighing hearts, I have no skill to show;
Yet I the prouder grew, and answered them therefore,
    "Go, go, go, seek some otherwhere,
        Impòrtune me no more!"   10

Then spake fair Venus' son, that proud victorious boy,[1]
    And said, "Fine dame, since that you be so coy,
I will so pluck your plumes that you shall say no more,
    'Go, go, go, seek some otherwhere,
        Impòrtune me no more!'   15

When he had spake these words, such change grew in my breast,
    That neither night nor day since that, I could take any rest,
Then lo! I did repent that I had said before,
    "Go, go, go, seek some otherwhere,
        Impòrtune me no more!"   20

---

1. **Venus' son . . . boy:** Venus and her son Cupid were the patrons of lovers in Classical mythology.

Getting at Meaning

1. What is the speaker's attitude toward herself? toward her former suitors? How has her attitude changed?

2. In what sense might this poem be autobiographical?

Developing Skills in Reading Literature

Theme. Unrequited love is a common subject in the lyrics of the early Renaissance. The best poets of the period, however, do not restrict themselves to personal accounts of lovesickness and melancholy. Some deal with universal themes such as the inevitable passage of time and its toll upon the human being. Others reveal the artificiality of courtly poetry, in which the object of love is always young and beautiful. Some poets are critical of court life; others simply portray the foibles of courtly conventions, with wit and irony.

To what extent does this lyric convey a universal theme? What other lyrics in this unit present a similar theme? What differences do you note among these lyrics in the treatment of the theme?

William Shakespeare

1564–1616

WILLIAM SHAKESPEARE. *Chandos. National Portrait Gallery, London.*

William Shakespeare is surely the greatest writer the western world has ever produced, a dramatist and poet whose works transcend time and place to explore what is universal in the human experience. As stated by fellow dramatist Ben Jonson, Shakespeare is "not of an age, but for all time."

The facts concerning Shakespeare's life are scarce, primarily because as a playwright his works rather than his life were the focus of attention. Only on the manuscripts of his later plays is his name even mentioned. Not until thirty or forty years after his death was a biography attempted. By that time, most of his contemporaries were dead, and biographers had to reconstruct his life story from a few court and church records and much educated guessing.

Shakespeare was born in Stratford, Warwickshire, an idyllic rural town on the banks of the gentle Avon River. John Shakespeare, William's father, had settled in Stratford around 1550 and had become a glove maker. He was active in local politics and served at various times as an alderman, constable, town chamberlain, and mayor. His wife, Mary Arden Shakespeare, was a wealthy woman whose lineage could be traced to William the Conqueror. The first two children born to the Shakespeares died; then in 1564 William was born. An accurate record of his baptism gives the date as April 26. Because babies usually were baptized two or three days after their births, most scholars establish Shakespeare's birth date as April 23. Choice of this date may also have been influenced by the fact that April 23 is the birthday of England's patron Saint George.

William probably entered the Stratford grammar school at the age of seven where he studied Latin grammar, composition, and literature for six days a week. Virtually no other subjects, with the possible exception of Greek, were included in the curriculum. The reading and writing of English were taught at home, and spelling was done phonetically. Shakespeare most likely supplemented his formal education with a great deal of reading, of both classic and contemporary works. As a boy he no doubt saw many touring companies perform in the Stratford village square, performances that may have piqued his interest in theatre.

On November 17, 1582, William Shakspere [sic], then eighteen, applied for a license to marry Anne Hathwey [sic], eight years his elder. Six months later Susanna was born; in 1585 their twins, Hamnet and Judith, were baptized. Little is known of Shakespeare's life during the seven years from 1585 to 1592. Scholars speculate that he might have been a schoolmaster, dyer, soldier, apothecary, printer, notary, or horsetender for theatergoers; however, none of these occupations has ever been verified.

By 1592 Shakespeare was living in London, without his family, and was an acclaimed actor and established playwright. His first histories, *Henry VI, 1, 2,* and *3* (1589–92) had been well received, and *Richard III* (1592–93) was playing to packed houses. Clearly, London in the Renaissance was the right place for a talented dramatist. Four theaters were in operation, and the audience for plays was large and enthusiastic.

From the beginning, Shakespeare showed himself to be a master of dramatic language and a major experimenter with spoken English. In his plays he skillfully combined formal diction with slang, prose with poetry. He was clever and imaginative in his use of language, playing on ambiguities, connotations, and double meanings and creating vivid images and figures of speech. He drew upon an enormous vocabulary that has been estimated at 24,000 words, as compared to the average person's 3,000 words.

Elizabethan audiences responded strongly to Shakespeare's memorable characters, who emerge even today as flesh-and-blood human beings with all the virtues and vices that dignify and afflict humanity. As a playwright, Shakespeare was both perceptive and sympathetic. He understood human psychology, and he shaped and interpreted his material without moralizing or imposing judgments.

In 1593 the plague struck London. Having no way to explain the pestilence, the clergy blamed the evils of society, represented by the theater, and demanded that all theaters be shuttered. For two years, most actors had no choice but to tour the country markets and rural towns performing for small unsophisticated audiences.

Shakespeare stayed in London and directed his talent to poetry. After completing *Venus and Adonis* (1593) and *The Rape of Lucrece* (1594), two long poems dedicated to his patron the Earl of Southampton, he began writing sonnets. In 1609 a sonnet sequence consisting of 154 individual poems was first printed by Thomas Thorpe, a London publisher. In this sequence Shakespeare perfected the form of the English sonnet and demonstrated his mastery of the final summarizing couplet.

The first 126 Shakespearean sonnets are addressed to a beautiful young man who is encouraged to marry so that his type can be continued in his children. The themes of these sonnets deal with the entire spectrum of human emotions and values: love, honor, jealousy, fidelity, ingratitude, reconciliation. Sonnets 127-152 are addressed to a dark woman whom the speaker loves passionately. The last two sonnets are conventional love poems about Cupid.

For years, scholars have tried to relate the sonnets to Shakespeare's private life. William Wordsworth, the Romantic poet, wrote:

Scorn not the sonnet; Critic, you frowned,
Mindless of its just honor; with this key
Shakespeare unlocked his heart.

To date, however, no one has produced solid evidence that the sonnets are autobiographical.

When the theaters were reopened, Shakespeare once again wrote plays for repertory performance, producing two to four plays per year, for a total of thirty-seven plays in a little more than twenty years. At this time he joined Lord Chamberlain's Men (later, the King's Men), a prestigious acting company that was led by Richard Burbage, one of the greatest actors in England and a favorite of the Elizabethan court. In 1599 several members of Chamberlain's company, including Shakespeare, opened the Globe Theater, the finest theater in London.

During these busy, productive years, Shakespeare wrote comedies such as *The Taming of the Shrew* (1593–94) and *A Midsummer Night's Dream* (1595–96) and histories such as *Richard II* (1595–96) and *King John* (1596–97). As an artist he was supremely original; however, he did draw upon contemporary and classic sources for themes, plots, characters, and poetic inspiration. These sources include the works of classic dramatists and poets, English morality drama, Italian Renaissance drama and prose, popular prose fiction, the plays of Christopher Marlowe, and the masques of Ben Jonson.

In the late 1590's Shakespeare seemed to undergo a change of mood, perhaps resulting from the death of his only son in 1596, from the political intrigue that caused the demise of several friends, or from the challenge to his acting company by a rival group. For whatever reason, Shakespeare turned from history and comedy to tragedy. *Julius Caesar* appeared in 1599, followed by *Hamlet* (1600–01), *Othello* (1604–05), *King Lear* (1605–1606), and *Macbeth* (1606). These plays are considered among his greatest works.

The Globe Theater was closed again in 1608 because of the plague. When it reopened, *Cymbeline* (1609–10), *The Winter's Tale* (1610–11), and *The Tempest* (1611–12) were performed. The nature of this last group of tragicomedies suggests a return to tranquility and optimism in Shakespeare's life. In 1613 *Henry VIII*, written to glorify the birth of Elizabeth, was performed at the Globe. Cannons were discharged in a royal salute; unfortunately, the thatched roof of the theater caught fire and the building burned to the ground.

Shakespeare had become a wealthy landowner with property in both Stratford and London. In 1611 he retired to his home, New Place, in Stratford, where he died on April 23, 1616, of unknown causes. He was buried in the chancel of the Strat- ford church. Keenly aware of the practice of digging up old bones to make way for new ones, he issued this solemn warning in his epitaph:

> Good friend, for Jesus' sake forbear
> To dig the dust enclosed here.
> Blest be the man that spares these stones,
> And curst be he that moves my bones.

From an enlarged drawing of an extensive view of London, 1647. Engraved by Hollar. Folger Shakespeare Library.

Sonnet 18

Shall I compare thee to a summer's day?
Thou art more lovely and more temperate:
Rough winds do shake the darling buds of May,
And summer's lease hath all too short a date:
Sometime too hot the eye of heaven shines,   5
And often is his gold complexion dimmed;
And every fair from fair sometime declines,
By chance or nature's changing course untrimmed;[1]
But thy eternal summer shall not fade,
Nor lose possession of that fair thou owest;[2]   10
Nor shall Death brag thou wander'st in his shade,
When in eternal lines to time thou growest:
   So long as men can breathe, or eyes can see,
   So long lives this, and this gives life to thee.

---

1. **untrimmed:** shorn of beauty.
2. **owest:** ownest.

Sonnet 29

When, in disgrace with fortune and men's eyes,
I all alone beweep my outcast state,[1]
And trouble deaf heaven with my bootless[2] cries
And look upon myself and curse my fate,
Wishing me like to one more rich in hope,   5
Featured like him, like him with friends possessed,
Desiring this man's art and that man's scope,
With what I most enjoy contented least;
Yet in these thoughts myself almost despising,
Haply I think on thee,—and then my state,   10
Like to the lark at break of day arising
From sullen earth, sings hymns at heaven's gate;
   For thy sweet love remembered such wealth brings
   That then I scorn to change my state with kings.

---

1. **state:** condition.
2. **bootless:** futile.

Sonnet 30

When to the sessions[1] of sweet silent thought
I summon up remembrance of things past,
I sigh the lack of many a thing I sought,
And with old woes new wail[2] my dear time's waste:
Then can I drown an eye, unused to flow,   5
For precious friends hid in death's dateless[3] night,
And weep afresh love's long since cancelled woe,
And moan the expense[4] of many a vanished sight:
Then can I grieve at grievances foregone,[5]
And heavily from woe to woe tell o'er[6]   10
The sad account of fore-bemoaned moan,
Which I new pay as if not paid before.
   But if the while I think on thee, dear friend,
   All losses are restored and sorrows end.

---

1. **sessions:** sittings of a law court.
2. **new wail:** lament anew.
3. **dateless:** everlasting.
4. **expense:** loss.
5. **foregone:** long past.
6. **tell o'er:** count up.

Sonnet 73

That time of year thou mayst in me behold
When yellow leaves, or none, or few, do hang
Upon those boughs which shake against the cold,
Bare ruined choirs,[1] where late the sweet birds sang.
In me thou see'st the twilight of such day   5
As after sunset fadeth in the west,
Which by and by black night doth take away,
Death's second self, that seals up all in rest.
In me thou see'st the glowing of such fire
That on the ashes of his youth doth lie,   10
As the death-bed whereon it must expire,
Consumed with that which it was nourished by.[2]
  This thou perceivest, which makes thy love more strong,
  To love that well which thou must leave ere long.

---

1. **choirs:** that part of the church where services are conducted.
2. **Consumed . . . by:** suffocated by the ashes of the wood that fired its flame.

Sonnet 116

Let me not to the marriage of true minds
Admit impediments.[1] Love is not love
Which alters when it alteration finds,
Or bends with the remover to remove.
Oh, no! it is an ever-fixèd mark   5
That looks on tempests and is never shaken;
It is the star[2] to every wandering bark,[3]
Whose worth's unknown, although his height be taken.
Love's not Time's fool, though rosy lips and cheeks
Within his bending sickle's compass come;   10
Love alters not with his brief hours and weeks,
But bears it out even to the edge of doom.[4]
  If this be error and upon me proved,
  I never writ, nor no man ever loved.

---

1. **impediment:** reasons for not allowing a marriage to proceed.
2. **star:** the North Star.
3. **bark:** a ship.
4. **doom:** Doomsday.

Sonnet 130

My mistress' eyes are nothing like the sun,
Coral is far more red than her lips' red.
If snow be white, why then her breasts are dun,
If hairs be wires, black wires grow on her head.
I have seen roses damasked,[1] red and white,   5
But no such roses see I in her cheeks.
And in some perfumes is there more delight
Than in the breath that from my mistress reeks.[2]
I love to hear her speak, yet well I know
That music hath a far more pleasing sound.   10
I grant I never saw a goddess go,[3]
My mistress, when she walks, treads on the ground.
   And yet, by Heaven, I think my love as rare
   As any she belied with false compare.

---

1. **damasked:** variegated.
2. **reeks:** emanates.
3. **go:** walk.

Getting at Meaning

SONNET 18

1. How does the speaker answer the opening question?

2. To what does "this" refer in line 14? How does "this" give life to the beloved? What then is the meaning of the sestet?

SONNET 29

3. What contrasting feelings are described by the speaker in this sonnet? What causes a change in feeling? How does the speaker feel by the end of the sonnet?

SONNET 30

4. What losses and sorrows are described by the speaker in this sonnet? According to the speaker, how powerful is friendship?

SONNET 73

5. With what season is the speaker compared in the first quatrain? What should the reader conclude about the speaker's age? How do the comparisons in the second and third quatrains reinforce this conclusion? How do the comparisons relate to the concluding couplet?

SONNET 116

6. Describe the type of love that the speaker of this sonnet admires. What is the relationship between love and time, according to the speaker?

SONNET 130

7. Describe the speaker's mistress. How does this woman contrast with the ideal Renaissance lady? What does the speaker achieve through this unconventional description? What reversal takes place in the couplet?

Developing Skills in Reading Literature

1. **Sonnet.** Choose one of these sonnets by Shakespeare and analyze its meter and rhyme scheme. Study the way that the ideas in the sonnet are presented and developed. Then suggest reasons why Shakespeare is considered the undisputed master of the English sonnet.

2. **Symbol and Mood.** Symbols succinctly communicate abstract, complex ideas. They also function in relation to the other elements within a work of literature. In "Sonnet 29" the lark is used as a symbol. What does this bird generally symbolize? How does the symbolic use of the lark in this sonnet reinforce the mood of the sestet? Why would the symbol be inappropriate in the octave? Explain.

3. **Theme.** Shakespeare's sonnets have universal themes, themes that appeal to readers in all times and places. To discover the theme in a Shakespearean sonnet, the reader should examine carefully the concluding couplet. Note in these sonnets that the couplet is set apart visually and that it comments on the first twelve lines. Occasionally a concluding couplet resembles an epigram, a pithy, pointed, concise saying. Reread each sonnet and explain how the couplet restates, emphasizes, or comments on the universal theme. Which of the sonnets share a common theme?

4. **Metaphor and Simile.** Shakespeare used metaphors and similes extensively in his sonnets. Examine each sonnet presented in this unit and identify a metaphor or simile. Discuss the specific function of each figure of speech; for example, to reinforce a shift in mood or to clarify an abstract idea. Then comment on the way that the metaphor or simile helps to bring out the theme of the sonnet.

Developing Writing Skills

Using Comparisons and Contrasts. Choose one sonnet by Shakespeare and one by either Spenser or Sidney. Write an essay in which you compare and contrast the two poems, considering the following elements: meter, rhyme scheme, structure, tone, imagery, figurative language, and theme.

Interior of the Swan Theater.
BBC Hulton Picture Library/Bettmann Archive.

The Globe Theater

In 1576 James Burbage built a theater in the London suburbs. This first English playhouse was called simply "the Theater." Shortly, other theaters were constructed, also outside the city limits to escape the stringent licensing requirements and capricious closings imposed by the London city fathers. In late 1598, because of a dispute over the Theater's lease, the Lord Chamberlain's Men, including Shakespeare, bought land south of the Thames River, tore down the Theater, transported the materials to the new site, and started work on the Globe Theater. In seven months, the finest theater in England was ready for its first performances.

Information about the Globe and other Elizabethan playhouses comes mainly from sketches and woodcuts, building contracts, and stage directions and other references within plays. The Globe was unusual in that it was octagonal in shape, with five sections used by the spectators and three by the actors and stage crew. Each section of the frame structure was approximately thirty-six feet long and had a thatched straw roof that was thirty-three feet above the ground. The five spectator sections each housed three tiers of galleries. In the center of the "wooden O" was an open-air courtyard, surrounded by the galleries.

On performance days, a flag flew over the Globe Theater. Spectators crossed the Thames River from central London and entered the Globe through a door facing the stage. If a spectator wished to stand in the yard and watch the play, the entry fee was one penny. These patrons were called "groundlings," and frequently they were the most boisterous and least educated of all the theatergoers. If a spectator wished to sit in the upper gallery, he or she paid another penny. A third penny bought a cushioned seat in the first gallery, considered the best seat in the house. No one could purchase a reserved seat, so spectators tended to arrive early and to be waiting expectantly for performances to begin. A sell-out crowd probably meant that nearly two thousand people were packed into the small theater.

The stage at the Globe differed considerably from most modern stages. It jutted out into the yard and was surrounded by spectators on three sides. There was no curtain or artificial lighting. On either side of the stage were doors for entrances and exits. Over the stage supported by two pillars was the "shadow," a canopy that sheltered the players from the rain. Trapdoors in the stage were used for the appearances of ghosts and spirits and for the disappearances of bodies. Behind the main stage was an inner stage called the "tiring house," where indoor scenes that required props were played. The inner stage might become a tavern, a prison, a tomb, or a throne room. Behind the inner stage was a door and a staircase to the "chamber" on the second level. The chamber and its projecting balcony were used for scenes requiring two levels, such as the balcony scene in *Romeo and Juliet*. On the third level was another chamber, used for musicians and occasionally for scenes. At the very top was a turret where stage hands created sound effects. From the turret were fired the cannons that ignited the Globe in 1613.

DRAMA IN SHAKESPEAREAN ENGLAND

The early English theaters possessed an intimacy that does not exist in most modern theaters. The players and the groundlings were within "spitting" distance of each other. At times, young gallants even lounged on the stage. Audiences became emotionally involved in performances, openly demonstrating their pleasure, sorrow, disappointment, and anger. They cheered, booed, hissed, and on occasion threw rotten vegetables. They roundly applauded agile sword fighting, and expected dramatic sound effects such as blares of trumpets, rolls of drums, and claps of thunder.

The audience was forced to rely heavily on imagination, for there was little scenery and young boys played the women's roles. A few props often suggested entire scenes; props included chairs, tables, thrones, beds, torches, armor, swords, shields, animal skins, and pig bladders filled with blood for realistic death scenes. The language of a play was all-important, for it evoked the spectators' imaginations, allowing them to enter the world of the play, to follow the action, and to understand nuances of character.

Shakespeare was keenly aware of his audience. People of all classes attended the theater regularly: students, courtiers, adventurers, merchants, tradesmen, apprentices, servants, and laborers, along with opportunistic thieves and pickpockets. The only Londoners who were conspicuously absent were the Puritans, who objected to all "frivolous" entertainments, and the royal family, who attended private performances.

Shakespeare knew well the capabilities and limitations of the theater building and of the acting company for whom he wrote his plays. This company drew from a repertory of plays, which they acted on a rotating basis, with the most popular plays being repeated often. New plays were added to the repertory each year, and the least popular plays were dropped. Regular patrons of the Globe became familiar with the plots, actors, dramatic conventions, and language of Shakespeare's plays, thus increasing their ability to appreciate and to respond to these dramatic masterpieces.

THE TRAGEDY OF *MACBETH*

Shakespeare probably wrote *Macbeth* in 1606 at the request of King James I, who was the patron of the King's Men, the playwright's company. The play might have been commissioned as an entertainment for the state visit of King Christian of Denmark, which occurred in the summer of that year. The King's Men first performed *Macbeth* either in the paved courtyard or in the great hall at Hampton Court, a royal palace up the Thames river from London.

Shakespeare wrote *Macbeth* in a few weeks, drawing mainly from two stories in Holinshed's *Chronicles,* a popular history text. One story described the reign of Macbeth, a twelfth-century Scottish king with a reputation as a blood-thirsty tyrant. The other story concerned the murder of King Duff by Donwald, who was prodded by his ambitious wife. Shakespeare also wove into his plot the tradition that the Stuart kings were descended from a nobleman named Banquo and the legend that witches once appeared to a Scottish king and predicted his future.

Macbeth is Shakespeare's shortest play, possibly in deference to King James's dislike of long plays. As suited to its brevity, the play has a quality of compression, of tautness and foreboding, right from the beginning. As the drama unfolds, the spectators, and readers, witness the paramount crime of regicide. Yet they also witness a human drama, as the murderers suffer the consequences of their actions. The humanization of the characters coupled with powerful poetic language make this play more tragedy than history, more universal than specific to time and place.

THE BEAR GARDEN AND THE GLOBE THEATER. *Folger Shakespeare Library.*

ELLEN TERRY AS LADY MACBETH, 1888. *John Singer Sargent.*
National Portrait Gallery, London.

Macbeth

CHARACTERS

Duncan, King of Scotland
Malcolm ⎱
Donalbain ⎰ his sons
Macbeth ⎱
Banquo ⎰ Generals of the Scottish Army
Macduff ⎱
Lennox
Ross
Menteith ⎰ Noblemen of Scotland
Angus
Caithness
Fleance, son of Banquo
Siward, Earl of Northumberland,
  General of the English forces
Young Siward, his son
Seyton, an Officer attending on Macbeth
Boy, son of Macduff
A Captain
An English Doctor
A Scottish Doctor
A Porter
An Old Man
Lady Macbeth
Lady Macduff
A Gentlewoman attending on Lady Macbeth
Hecate, goddess of witchcraft
Three Witches
The Ghost of Banquo
Apparitions
Lords, Gentlemen, Officers, Soldiers, Murderers,
  Messengers, Attendants

The Time: The eleventh century
The Place: Scotland and England

Act One

Scene 1

[*Three witches discuss when and where they will meet Macbeth.*]

[*Scotland. An open place.*]

[*Thunder and lightning. Enter three* Witches.]

First Witch. When shall we three meet again
    In thunder, lightning, or in rain?
Second Witch. When the hurlyburly's[1] done,
    When the battle's lost and won.
Third Witch. That will be ere the set of sun.   5
First Witch. Where the place?
Second Witch.   Upon the heath.
Third Witch. There to meet with Macbeth.
First Witch. I come, Graymalkin![2]
Second Witch. Paddock[3] calls.   10
Third Witch.   Anon!
All. Fair is foul, and foul is fair.
    Hover through the fog and filthy air.

[*Exeunt.*]

Scene 2

[*Macbeth, King Duncan's cousin, has been dispatched to put down an uprising in the west of Scotland. The king learns of Macbeth's victory over the rebel Macdonwald and over Norwegian invaders, aided by the traitorous Thane of Cawdor. Duncan orders the Thane's death and awards his title to Macbeth.*]

[*A camp near Forres.*]

[*Alarum*[1] *within. Enter Duncan, Malcolm, Donalbain, Lennox, with* Attendants, *meeting a bleeding* Sergeant.]

Duncan. What bloody man is that? He can report,
    As seemeth by his plight, of the revolt
    The newest state.

---

1. **hurlyburly:** disorder, commotion. 2. **Graymalkin:** common name for a cat; the First Witch's demon spirit. 3. **Paddock:** toad; the Second Witch's demon spirit.
  1. **Alarum:** a trumpet call to arms.

Malcolm.   This is the sergeant
  Who like a good and hardy soldier fought   5
  'Gainst my captivity. Hail, brave friend!
  Say to the King the knowledge of the broil
  As thou didst leave it.
Sergeant.   Doubtful it stood,
  As two spent swimmers that do cling together   10
  And choke their art.² The merciless Macdonwald
  (Worthy to be a rebel, for to that
  The multiplying villainies of nature
  Do swarm upon him) from the Western Isles
  Of kerns and gallowglasses³ is supplied;   15
  And Fortune, on his damnèd quarrel smiling,
  Showed like a rebel's whore. But all's too weak;
  For brave Macbeth (well he deserves that name),
  Disdaining Fortune, with his brandished steel,
  Which smoked with bloody execution   20
  (Like valor's minion⁴), carvèd out his passage
  Till he faced the slave;
  Which ne'er shook hands nor bade farewell to him
  Till he unseamed him⁵ from the nave to the chops
  And fixed his head upon our battlements.   25
Duncan. O valiant cousin! worthy gentleman!
Sergeant. As whence the sun 'gins his reflection⁶
  Shipwracking storms and direful thunders break,
  So from that spring whence comfort seemed to come
  Discomfort swells. Mark, King of Scotland, mark.   30
  No sooner justice had, with valor armed,
  Compelled these skipping kerns to trust their heels
  But the Norweyan lord, surveying vantage,⁷
  With furbished arms and new supplies of men,
  Began a fresh assault.   35
Duncan.   Dismayed not this
  Our captains, Macbeth and Banquo?
Sergeant.   Yes,
  As sparrows eagles, or the hare the lion.
  If I say sooth,⁸ I must report they were   40
  As cannons overcharged with double cracks,⁹ so they
  Doubly redoubled strokes upon the foe.
  Except they meant to bathe in reeking¹⁰ wounds,
  Or memorize another Golgotha,¹¹

---

2. **art:** skill. 3. **kerns . . . gallowglasses:** Irish soldiers. The kerns fought on foot; the gallowglasses were armed with an ax and fought on horses. 4. **minion:** darling, favorite. 5. **unseamed him:** cut Macdonwald open from his navel to his jaws. 6. **whence . . . reflection:** rises. 7. **Norweyan . . . vantage:** the King of Norway, seeing a good opportunity. 8. **sooth:** truth. 9. **overcharged . . . cracks:** loaded with two cannon balls. 10. **reeking:** steaming. 11. **memorize another Golgotha:** create a slaughter that would make the place as famous as Golgotha, "the Place of the Skull," where Christ was crucified.

I cannot tell— 45

But I am faint; my gashes cry for help.

Duncan. So well thy words become thee as thy wounds;

They smack of honor both. Go get him surgeons.

[*Exit* Sergeant, *attended.*]

[*Enter* Ross.]

Who comes here?

Malcolm.   The worthy Thane[12] of Ross. 50

Lennox. What a haste looks through his eyes! So should he look

That seems to speak things strange.

Ross.   God save the King!

Duncan. Whence cam'st thou, worthy thane?

Ross.   From Fife, great King, 55

Where the Norweyan banners flout[13] the sky

And fan our people cold. Norway himself,

With terrible numbers,

Assisted by that most disloyal traitor

The Thane of Cawdor, began a dismal conflict, 60

Till that Bellona's bridegroom,[14] lapped in proof,[15]

Confronted him with self-comparisons,

Point against point, rebellious arm 'gainst arm,

Curbing his lavish[16] spirit; and to conclude,

The victory fell on us. 65

Duncan.   Great happiness!

Ross.   That now

Sweno, the Norways' king, craves composition;[17]

Nor would we deign him burial of his men

Till he disbursèd, at Saint Colme's Inch,[18] 70

Ten thousand dollars to our general use.

Duncan. No more that Thane of Cawdor shall deceive

Our bosom interest.[19] Go pronounce his present[20] death

And with his former title greet Macbeth.

Ross. I'll see it done. 75

Duncan. What he hath lost noble Macbeth hath won.

[*Exeunt.*]

---

12. **Thane:** a Scottish title for a clan chief, comparable to an English earl. 13. **flout:** defy. 14. **Bellona's bridegroom:** the mate of the Roman goddess of war, a reference to Macbeth. 15. **lapped in proof:** dressed in armor. 16. **lavish:** undisciplined. 17. **composition:** a treaty of peace. 18. **Saint Colme's Inch:** the Island of St. Columba in the Firth of Forth (now known as Inchcolin). 19. **bosom interest:** my dearest concerns. 20. **present:** immediate.

Scene 3

[The three witches discuss their evil deeds while waiting for Macbeth. The witches hail Macbeth as Thane of Glamis, his official title, Thane of Cawdor, and "King hereafter." They tell Banquo that he will father kings but will not be a king, and then they vanish. As Macbeth and Banquo are puzzling over the strange predictions, Ross and Angus arrive and inform Macbeth that he is now the Thane of Cawdor. Macbeth is intrigued at this fulfillment of the witches' prophecy and ponders his future, deciding to let fate rule his destiny.]

[A heath near Forres.]

[Thunder. Enter the three Witches.*]*

First Witch. Where hast thou been, sister?
Second Witch. Killing swine.[1]
Third Witch. Sister, where thou?
First Witch. A sailor's wife had chestnuts in her lap
    And mounched and mounched and mounched. "Give me," quoth I.   5
    "Aroint thee,[2] witch!" the rump-fed[3] ronyon[4] cries.
    Her husband's to Aleppo gone, master o' the *Tiger;*[5]
    But in a sieve I'll thither sail
    And, like a rat without a tail,
    I'll do, I'll do, and I'll do.   10
Second Witch. I'll give thee a wind.
First Witch. Th' art kind.
Third Witch. And I another.
First Witch. I myself have all the other,
    And the very ports they blow,   15
    All the quarters that they know
    I' the shipman's card.[6]
    I'll drain him dry as hay.
    Sleep shall neither night nor day
    Hang upon his penthouse lid.[7]   20
    He shall live a man forbid.[8]
    Weary sev'nights,[9] nine times nine,
    Shall he dwindle, peak,[10] and pine.
    Though his bark[11] cannot be lost,
    Yet it shall be tempest-tost.   25
    Look what I have.

---

1. **killing swine:** witches were commonly accused of killing the neighbor's pigs. 2. **Aroint thee:** be off! 3. **rump-fed:** fat-rumped. 4. **ronyon:** good-for-nothing. 5. **Her . . . Tiger:** Aleppo, Syria, was famous as a trading center; *Tiger* was the name of several merchant ships. 6. **shipman's card:** compass. 7. **penthouse lid:** eyelid. 8. **forbid:** under a curse. 9. **sev' nights:** weeks. 10. **peak:** grow thin. 11. **bark:** ship.

Second Witch. Show me! show me!
First Witch. Here I have a pilot's thumb,
    Wracked as homeward he did come.

                                                              [Drum within.]

Third Witch. A drum, a drum!   30
    Macbeth doth come.
All. The Weird Sisters, hand in hand,
    Posters[12] of the sea and land,
    Thus do go about, about,
    Thrice to thine, and thrice to mine,   35
    And thrice again, to make up nine.
    Peace! The charm's wound up.

    [Enter Macbeth and Banquo.]

Macbeth. So foul and fair a day I have not seen.
Banquo. How far is't called to Forres? What are these,
    So withered, and so wild in their attire,   40
    That look not like the inhabitants o' the earth,
    And yet are on't? Live you? or are you aught
    That man may question? You seem to understand me,
    By each at once her choppy[13] finger laying
    Upon her skinny lips. You should be women,   45
    And yet your beards[14] forbid me to interpret
    That you are so.
Macbeth. Speak, if you can. What are you?
First Witch. All hail, Macbeth! Hail to thee, Thane of Glamis!
Second Witch. All hail, Macbeth! Hail to thee, Thane of Cawdor!   50
Third Witch. All hail, Macbeth, that shalt be King hereafter!
Banquo. Good sir, why do you start and seem to fear
    Things that do sound so fair? I' the name of truth,
    Are ye fantastical,[15] or that indeed
    Which outwardly ye show? My noble partner   55
    You greet with present grace and great prediction
    Of noble having[16] and of royal hope,
    That he seems rapt withal. To me you speak not.
    If you can look into the seeds of time
    And say which grain will grow and which will not,   60
    Speak then to me, who neither beg nor fear
    Your favors nor your hate.
First Witch. Hail!

---

12. **Posters:** quick travelers. 13. **choppy:** chapped. 14. **yet your beards:** for a woman to have a beard was sinister. 15. **fantastical:** creatures of the imagination. 16. **having:** possessions.

Second Witch. Hail!

Third Witch. Hail!

First Witch. Lesser than Macbeth, and greater.

Second Witch. Not so happy, yet much happier.

Third Witch. Thou shalt get[17] kings, though thou be none.
    So all hail, Macbeth and Banquo!

First Witch. Banquo and Macbeth, all hail!   70

Macbeth. Stay, you imperfect speakers, tell me more!
    By Sinel's[18] death I know I am Thane of Glamis,
    But how of Cawdor? The Thane of Cawdor lives,
    A prosperous gentleman; and to be King
    Stands not within the prospect of belief,   75
    No more than to be Cawdor. Say from whence
    You owe[19] this strange intelligence, or why
    Upon this blasted heath you stop our way
    With such prophetic greeting. Speak, I charge you.

                                      [Witches *vanish.*]   80

Banquo. The earth hath bubbles, as the water has,
    And these are of them. Whither are they vanished?

Macbeth. Into the air, and what seemed corporal[20] melted
    As breath into the wind. Would they had stayed!

Banquo. Were such things here as we do speak about?
    Or have we eaten on the insane root[21]   85
    That takes the reason prisoner?

Macbeth. Your children shall be kings.

Banquo.   You shall be King.

Macbeth. And Thane of Cawdor too. Went it not so?

Banquo. To the selfsame tune and words. Who's here?   90

    [*Enter* Ross *and* Angus.]

Ross. The King hath happily received, Macbeth,
    The news of thy success; and when he reads
    Thy personal venture in the rebels' fight,
    His wonders and his praises do contend
    Which should be thine or his. Silenced[22] with that,   95
    In viewing o'er the rest o' the selfsame day,
    He finds thee in the stout Norweyan ranks,
    Nothing afeard of what thyself didst make,
    Strange images of death. As thick as hail
    Came post with post,[23] and every one did bear   100

---

17. **get:** beget.　18. **Sinel:** Macbeth's father.　19. **owe:** own.　20. **corporal:** of bodily substance.　21. **insane root:** henbane or hemlock, thought to cause insanity.　22. **Silenced:** speechless with admiration.　23. **post with post:** messengers came one after the other.

Thy praises in his kingdom's great defense
And poured them down before him.
Angus.   We are sent
To give thee from our royal master thanks;
Only to herald thee into his sight,   105
Not pay thee.
Ross. And for an earnest²⁴ of a greater honor,
He bade me, from him, call thee Thane of Cawdor;
In which addition,²⁵ hail, most worthy Thane!
For it is thine.   110
Banquo.   What, can the devil speak true?
Macbeth. The Thane of Cawdor lives. Why do you dress me
In borrowed robes?
Angus.   Who was the Thane lives yet,
But under heavy judgment bears that life   115
Which he deserves to lose. Whether he was combined
With those of Norway, or did line²⁶ the rebel
With hidden help and vantage, or that with both
He labored in his country's wrack,²⁷ I know not;
But treasons capital,²⁸ confessed and proved,   120
Have overthrown him.
Macbeth. [*Aside*] Glamis, and Thane of Cawdor!
The greatest is behind.²⁹ [*To* Ross *and* Angus] Thanks for your pains.
[*Aside to* Banquo] Do you not hope your children shall be kings,
When those that gave the Thane of Cawdor to me   125
Promised no less to them?
Banquo. [*Aside to* Macbeth] That, trusted home,³⁰
Might yet enkindle³¹ you unto the crown,
Besides the Thane of Cawdor. But 'tis strange!
And oftentimes, to win us to our harm,   130
The instruments of darkness tell us truths,
Win us with honest trifles, to betray's
In deepest consequence.³²—
Cousins, a word, I pray you.
Macbeth.   [*Aside*] Two truths are told,   135
As happy prologues to the swelling act
Of the imperial theme.³³—I thank you, gentlemen.—
[*Aside*] This supernatural soliciting
Cannot be ill; cannot be good. If ill,
Why hath it given me earnest³⁴ of success,   140
Commencing in a truth? I am Thane of Cawdor.

---

24. **earnest:** partial payment on a contract—a sample of greater honor yet to come.   25. **addition:** title of honor.   26. **line:** support.   27. **wrack:** ruin.   28. **capital:** deserving death.   29. **behind:** to follow.   30. **home:** fully.   31. **enkindle:** encourage you to hope for.   32. **consequence:** in matters of great importance.   33. **imperial theme:** that Macbeth will be king. 34. **earnest:** tangible evidence.

If good, why do I yield to that suggestion
Whose horrid image doth unfix my hair
And make my seated heart knock at my ribs
Against the use of nature?[35] Present fears   145
Are less than horrible imaginings.
My thought, whose murder yet is but fantastical,[36]
Shakes so my single[37] state of man that function
Is smothered in surmise and nothing is
But what is not.   150
Banquo.   Look how our partner's rapt.
Macbeth. [*Aside*] If chance will have me King, why, chance may crown me,
    Without my stir.
Banquo.   New honors come upon him,
    Like our strange garments,[38] cleave not to their mold   155
    But with the aid of use.
Macbeth.   [*Aside*] Come what come may,
    Time and the hour runs through the roughest day.
Banquo. Worthy Macbeth, we stay[39] upon your leisure.
Macbeth. Give me your favor.[40] My dull brain was wrought   160
    With things forgotten. Kind gentlemen, your pains[41]
    Are registered where every day I turn
    The leaf to read them. Let us toward the King.
    [*Aside to* Banquo] Think upon what hath chanced, and, at more time,[42]
    The interim having weighed it, let us speak   165
    Our free[43] hearts each to other.
Banquo. Very gladly.
Macbeth. Till then, enough.—Come, friends.

                                                                    [*Exeunt.*]

---

35. **Against . . . nature:** in an unnatural way. 36. **fantastical:** imagined. 37. **single:** undivided. 38. **strange garments:** like
a new suit of clothes. 39. **stay:** wait. 40. **favor:** indulgence. 41. **pains:** troubles. 42. **at more time:** when there is more
time. 43. **free:** frank.

Scene 4

[*King Duncan's son Malcolm describes the execution of the Thane of Cawdor. Macbeth, Banquo, Ross, and Angus arrive at the palace. The king thanks Macbeth and Banquo for their support, and Macbeth reaffirms his loyalty to the king. Duncan then announces that Malcolm will be his heir and that he intends to visit Inverness, Macbeth's castle. Macbeth leaves to prepare for the king's visit, acknowledging "black and deep desires" regarding the crown.*]

[*Forres. The Palace.*]

[*Flourish.*[1] *Enter* Duncan, Lennox, Malcolm, Donalbain, *and* Attendants.]

Duncan. Is execution done on Cawdor? Are not
    Those in commission[2] yet returned?
Malcolm.   My liege,
    They are not yet come back. But I have spoke
    With one that saw him die; who did report   5
    That very frankly he confessed his treasons,

---

1. **Flourish:** trumpet fanfare.   2. **Those in commission:** the executioners.

Implored your Highness' pardon, and set forth
A deep repentance. Nothing in his life
Became him like the leaving it. He died
As one that had been studied³ in his death   10
To throw away the dearest thing he owed⁴
As 'twere a careless trifle.
Duncan.   There's no art
To find the mind's construction⁵ in the face.
He was a gentleman on whom I built   15
An absolute trust.

     [*Enter* Macbeth, Banquo, Ross, *and* Angus.]

              O worthiest cousin,
The sin of my ingratitude even now
Was heavy on me! Thou art so far before
That swiftest wing of recompense is slow   20
To overtake thee. Would thou hadst less deserved,
That the proportion both of thanks and payment
Might have been mine! Only I have left to say,
More is thy due than more than all can pay.
Macbeth. The service and the loyalty I owe,   25
In doing it pays itself. Your Highness' part
Is to receive our duties; and our duties
Are to your throne and state children and servants,
Which do but what they should by doing everything
Safe toward your love and honor.   30
Duncan.   Welcome hither.
I have begun to plant thee and will labor
To make thee full of growing. Noble Banquo,
That hast no less deserved, nor must be known
No less to have done so, let me infold thee   35
And hold thee to my heart.
Banquo.   There if I grow,
The harvest is your own.
Duncan.   My plenteous joys,
Wanton⁶ in fullness, seek to hide themselves   40
In drops of sorrow. Sons, kinsmen, thanes,
And you whose places are the nearest, know
We will establish our estate⁷ upon
Our eldest, Malcolm, whom we name hereafter
The Prince of Cumberland; which honor must   45
Not unaccompanied invest him only,

---

3. **studied:** rehearsed.   4. **owed:** owned.   5. **the . . . construction:** a person's character.   6. **Wanton:** unrestrained.
7. **estate:** throne.

But signs of nobleness, like stars, shall shine
On all deservers. From hence to Inverness,[8]
And bind us further to you.
Macbeth. The rest is labor, which is not used for you.   50
I'll be myself the harbinger,[9] and make joyful
The hearing of my wife with your approach;
So, humbly take my leave.
Duncan.   My worthy Cawdor!
Macbeth. [*Aside*] The Prince of Cumberland! That is a step   55
On which I must fall down, or else o'erleap,
For in my way it lies. Stars, hide your fires!
Let not light see my black and deep desires.
The eye wink at[10] the hand; yet let that be,
Which the eye fears, when it is done, to see.   60

                [*Exit.*]

Duncan. True, worthy Banquo: he is full so valiant,
And in his commendations I am fed;
It is a banquet to me. Let's after him,
Whose care is gone before to bid us welcome.
It is a peerless kinsman.   65

           [*Flourish. Exeunt.*]

Scene 5   [*Lady Macbeth reads a letter from Macbeth in which he informs
her of the witches' prophecy and of its partial fulfillment.
Desperate for Macbeth to be king, Lady Macbeth questions
whether he is ruthless enough to seize the crown and resolves to
push him into decisive action. A messenger announces Duncan's
forthcoming visit. Lady Macbeth implores the evil spirits to make
her cruel and remorseless for her role in Duncan's murder.
Macbeth arrives, and Lady Macbeth urges him to behave
naturally and to leave the rest up to her.*]

[*Inverness. Macbeth's Castle.*]

[*Enter* Lady Macbeth, *alone, with a letter.*]

Lady Macbeth. [*Reads*] "They met me in the day of success; and I have learned
by the perfect'st report they have more in them than mortal knowledge. When
I burned in desire to question them further, they made themselves air, into
which they vanished. Whiles I stood rapt in the wonder of it, came missives[1]

---

8. **Inverness:** Macbeth's castle. 9. **harbinger:** an official of the court who goes before the King to arrange lodging and
entertainment. 10. **wink at:** refuse to see.
 1. **missives:** messengers.

from the King, who all-hailed me Thane of Cawdor, by which title, before,   5
these Weird Sisters saluted me, and referred me to the coming on of time with
'Hail, King that shalt be!' This have I thought good to deliver thee, my dearest
partner of greatness, that thou mightst not lose the dues of rejoicing by being
ignorant of what greatness is promised thee. Lay it to thy heart, and farewell."

Glamis thou art, and Cawdor, and shalt be   10
What thou art promised. Yet do I fear thy nature.
It is too full o' the milk of human kindness
To catch the nearest way. Thou wouldst be great;
Art not without ambition, but without
The illness² should attend it. What thou wouldst highly,   15
That wouldst thou holily; wouldst not play false,
And yet wouldst wrongly win.³ Thou'ldst have, great Glamis,
That which cries "Thus thou must do," if thou have it;
And that⁴ which rather thou dost fear to do
Than wishest should be undone. Hie⁵ thee hither,   20
That I may pour my spirits in thine ear
And chastise with the valor of my tongue
All that impedes thee from the golden round⁶
Which fate and metaphysical⁷ aid doth seem
To have thee crowned withal.   25

[*Enter a* Messenger.]

        What is your tidings?
Messenger. The King comes here tonight.
Lady Macbeth.   Thou'rt mad to say it!
Is not thy master with him? who, were't so,
Would have informed for preparation.   30
Messenger. So please you, it is true. Our Thane is coming.
One of my fellows had the speed of him,⁸
Who, almost dead for breath, had scarcely more
Than would make up his message.
Lady Macbeth.   Give him tending;   35
He brings great news.

                            [*Exit* Messenger.]

        The raven himself is hoarse
That croaks the fatal entrance of Duncan
Under my battlements. Come, you spirits
That tend on mortal⁹ thoughts, unsex me here,   40

2. **illness:** wickedness.   3. **wrongly win:** he wants things he can only get through wrongdoing.   4. **that:** Duncan's
death.   5. **Hie:** hasten.   6. **golden round:** the crown.   7. **metaphysical:** supernatural.   8. **had . . . him:** overtook him.
9. **mortal:** deadly.

And fill me, from the crown to the toe, top-full
Of direst cruelty! Make thick my blood;
Stop up the access and passage to remorse,
That no compunctious visitings of nature[10]
Shake my fell[11] purpose nor keep peace between   45
The effect and it! Come to my woman's breasts
And take my milk for gall,[12] you murd'ring ministers,
Wherever in your sightless[13] substances
You wait on nature's mischief! Come, thick night,
And pall[14] thee in the dunnest[15] smoke of hell,   50
That my keen knife see not the wound it makes,
Nor heaven peep through the blanket of the dark
To cry "Hold, hold!"

    [*Enter* Macbeth.]

                Great Glamis! worthy Cawdor!
Greater than both, by the all-hail hereafter!   55
Thy letters have transported me beyond
This ignorant present, and I feel now
The future in the instant.
Macbeth.   My dearest love,
Duncan comes here tonight.   60
Lady Macbeth.   And when goes hence?
Macbeth. Tomorrow, as he purposes.
Lady Macbeth.   O, never
Shall sun that morrow see!
Your face, my Thane, is as a book where men   65
May read strange matters. To beguile[16] the time,
Look like the time; bear welcome in your eye,
Your hand, your tongue; look like the innocent flower,
But be the serpent under't. He that's coming
Must be provided for; and you shall put   70
This night's great business into my dispatch,[17]
Which shall to all our nights and days to come
Give solely sovereign sway and masterdom.
Macbeth. We will speak further.
Lady Macbeth.   Only look up clear.[18]   75
To alter favor ever is to fear.[19]
Leave all the rest to me.

                             [*Exeunt.*]

---

10. **compunctious . . . nature:** natural pangs of conscience.   11. **fell:** deadly.   12. **gall:** bitterness.   13. **sightless:** invisible.   14. **pall:** shroud.   15. **dunnest:** darkest.   16. **beguile:** deceive.   17. **dispatch:** Duncan's murder and the crown for Macbeth.   18. **look up clear:** look innocent.   19. **To . . . fear:** to change countenance is to show fear.

Nicholas Pennell (Macbeth), Roberta Maxwell (Lady Macbeth) in *Macbeth*. Stratford Festival, 1983.

Scene 6

[*King Duncan arrives at Inverness and is greeted warmly by Lady Macbeth.*]

[*The same. Before Macbeth's Castle.*]

[*Hautboys¹ and torches. Enter* Duncan, Malcolm, Donalbain, Banquo, Lennox, Macduff, Ross, Angus, *and* Attendants.]

Duncan. This castle hath a pleasant seat. The air
Nimbly² and sweetly recommends itself
Unto our gentle³ senses.

---

1. **Hautboys:** oboes. 2. **nimbly:** briskly. 3. **gentle:** soothed.

Banquo.   This guest of summer,
The temple-haunting martlet,[4] does approve[5]
By his loved mansionry[6] that the heaven's breath
Smells wooingly here. No jutty, frieze,[7]
Buttress, nor coign of vantage,[8] but this bird
Hath made his pendent bed and procreant cradle.
Where they most breed and haunt, I have observed
The air is delicate.

     [*Enter* Lady Macbeth.]

Duncan.   See, see, our honored hostess!
The love that follows us sometime is our trouble,
Which still we thank as love. Herein I teach you
How you shall bid God 'ield[9] us for your pains
And thank us for your trouble.
Lady Macbeth.   All our service
In every point twice done, and then done double,
Were poor and single[10] business to contend
Against those honors deep and broad wherewith
Your Majesty loads our house. For those of old,
And the late dignities heaped up to them,
We rest[11] your hermits.[12]
Duncan.   Where's the Thane of Cawdor?
We coursed[13] him at the heels and had a purpose
To be his purveyor;[14] but he rides well,
And his great love, sharp as his spur, hath holp[15] him
To his home before us. Fair and noble hostess,
We are your guest tonight.
Lady Macbeth.   Your servants ever
Have theirs, themselves, and what is theirs, in compt,[16]
To make their audit at your Highness' pleasure,
Still[17] to return your own.
Duncan.   Give me your hand;
Conduct me to mine host. We love him highly
And shall continue our graces towards him.
By your leave, hostess.

                                                [*Exeunt.*]

Lines: 5, 10, 15, 20, 25, 30, 35

---

4. **martlet:** martin, a bird of the swallow family. 5. **approve:** show. 6. **loved mansionry:** favorite nesting place. 7. **jutty, frieze:** projections. 8. **coign of vantage:** convenient corner. 9. **God 'ield:** God reward. Duncan points out that he should be rewarded and thanked because his love for them is his reason for being there. 10. **single:** weak. 11. **rest:** remain. 12. **hermits:** beadsmen, who pray for the soul of a benefactor. 13. **coursed:** followed. 14. **purveyor:** an officer who went ahead to make the needed preparations. 15. **holp:** helped. 16. **compt:** account. 17. **Still:** always.

Scene 7

[Macbeth faces a dilemma: honor his guest, kinsman, and king or realize his ambition. He fears the consequences of murder, especially the condemnation of society. Lady Macbeth taunts him for his cowardice and outlines her plan: ply the king's chamberlains with drink and then murder the unguarded Duncan, making it appear as if the chamberlains committed the crime. Macbeth agrees to proceed with the plan.]

[The same. Macbeth's Castle.]

[Hautboys. Torches. Enter a Sewer,[1] *and divers* Servants *with dishes and service, and pass over the stage. Then enter* Macbeth.]

Macbeth. If it were done when 'tis done, then 'twere well
It were done quickly. If the assassination
Could trammel up[2] the consequence, and catch,
With his surcease,[3] success, that but this blow
Might be the be-all and the end-all here,   5
But[4] here, upon this bank and shoal of time,
We'ld jump[5] the life to come. But in these cases
We still have judgment here, that we but teach
Bloody instructions, which, being taught, return
To plague the inventor. This even-handed justice   10
Commends[6] the ingredience of our poisoned chalice[7]
To our own lips. He's here in double trust:
First, as I am his kinsman and his subject,
Strong both against the deed; then, as his host,
Who should against his murderer shut the door,   15
Not bear the knife myself. Besides, this Duncan
Hath borne his faculties[8] so meek, hath been
So clear[9] in his great office, that his virtues
Will plead like angels, trumpet-tongued, against
The deep damnation of his taking-off;   20
And pity, like a naked new-born babe,
Striding the blast, or heaven's cherubin, horsed
Upon the sightless couriers[10] of the air,
Shall blow the horrid deed in every eye,
That tears shall drown the wind. I have no spur   25
To prick the sides of my intent, but only
Vaulting ambition, which o'erleaps itself
And falls on the other—[11]

[Enter Lady Macbeth.]

---

1. **Sewer:** steward. 2. **trammel up:** entangle in a net. 3. **his surcease:** Duncan's death. 4. **But:** even. 5. **jump:** risk. 6. **Commends:** offers. 7. **chalice:** cup. 8. **faculties:** powers. 9. **clear:** blameless. 10. **sightless couriers:** invisible messengers, i.e., the winds. 11. **other:** i.e., side.

How now? What news?

Lady Macbeth. He has almost supped. Why have you left the chamber? 30

Macbeth. Hath he asked for me?

Lady Macbeth. Know you not he has?

Macbeth. We will proceed no further in this business.
He hath honored me of late, and I have bought
Golden opinions from all sorts of people, 35
Which would be worn now in their newest gloss,
Not cast aside so soon.

Lady Macbeth. Was the hope drunk
Wherein you dressed yourself? Hath it slept since?
And wakes it now to look so green and pale 40
At what it did so freely? From this time
Such I account thy love. Art thou afeard
To be the same in thine own act and valor
As thou art in desire? Wouldst thou have that
Which thou esteem'st the ornament of life,[12] 45
And live a coward in thine own esteem,
Letting "I dare not" wait upon "I would,"
Like the poor cat i' the adage?[13]

Macbeth. Prithee peace!
I dare do all that may become a man. 50
Who dares do more is none.[14]

Lady Macbeth. What beast was't then
That made you break this enterprise to me?
When you durst[15] do it, then you were a man;
And to be more than what you were, you would 55
Be so much more the man. Nor time nor place
Did then adhere, and yet you would make both.
They have made themselves, and that their[16] fitness now
Does unmake you. I have given suck, and know
How tender 'tis to love the babe that milks me. 60
I would, while it was smiling in my face,
Have plucked my nipple from his boneless gums
And dashed the brains out, had I so sworn as you
Have done to this.

Macbeth. If we should fail? 65

Lady Macbeth. We fail?
But screw your courage to the sticking place,
And we'll not fail. When Duncan is asleep
(Whereto the rather shall his day's hard journey
Soundly invite him), his two chamberlains 70

---

12. **ornament of life:** the crown. 13. **the poor cat i' the adage:** a common proverb of the cat who would eat fish but who would not get its feet wet. 14. **none:** an animal. 15. **durst:** dared. 16. **that their:** their very.

Will I with wine and wassail[17] so convince[18]
That memory, the warder of the brain,
Shall be a fume, and the receipt of reason
A limbeck only.[19] When in swinish sleep
Their drenchèd natures lie as in a death,   75
What cannot you and I perform upon
The unguarded Duncan? what not put upon
His spongy[20] officers, who shall bear the guilt
Of our great quell?[21]

Macbeth.   Bring forth men-children only,   80
For thy undaunted mettle[22] should compose
Nothing but males. Will it not be received,
When we have marked with blood those sleepy two
Of his own chamber and used their very daggers,
That they have done't?   85

Lady Macbeth.   Who dares receive it other,
As we shall make our griefs and clamor roar
Upon his death?

Macbeth.   I am settled and bend up[23]
Each corporal agent to this terrible feat.   90
Away, and mock the time with fairest show;
False face must hide what the false heart doth know.

                                                    [*Exeunt.*]

---

17. **wassail:** carousing. 18. **convince:** overcome. 19. **receipt . . . only:** reason will become like a still *(limbec)*, distilling only confused thoughts. 20. **spongy:** that soak up drink like a sponge. 21. **quell:** murder. 22. **mettle:** spirit. 23. **bend up:** stretch tight, as a strung bow.

Act One

Getting at Meaning

Scene 1

1. What atmosphere is established in this scene?

Scene 2

2. Why is King Duncan so pleased with Macbeth?
3. What impression do you have of Macbeth from this scene?

Scene 3

4. What impression of the witches do you form from this scene? How might they represent past, present, and future?
5. How do Macbeth and Banquo react to the witches' prophecies? What warning does Banquo give Macbeth? Does Macbeth heed his warning? Why, or why not?

Scene 4

6. What apparently is the relationship between King Duncan and Macbeth, as suggested by their conversation? How does Macbeth's final passage of dialogue shed new light on the relationship?

Scene 5

7. How does Lady Macbeth react to her husband's letter? Describe Lady Macbeth, referring to specific actions that illustrate the qualities you identify.

Scene 6

8. Describe the striking contrast between appearance and reality in this scene.

Scene 7

9. According to Macbeth's speech at the beginning of this scene, how does he feel about Duncan's assassination? What is the "double trust" under which Duncan is in the castle? What "spur" motivates Macbeth?

10. Macbeth tells his wife flatly, "We will proceed no further in this business." However, Lady Macbeth changes his mind completely. Describe the arguments by which she persuades him to carry out her plan.

11. What are Lady Macbeth's exact plans for murdering Duncan and for hiding her and her husband's guilt?

12. Both Macbeth and Lady Macbeth are ambitious. However, even at this early point in the play, there is a qualitative difference in their characters. Describe this difference.

Developing Skills in Reading Literature

1. **Meter and Blank Verse.** Blank verse is unrhymed poetry written in iambic pentameter. Most of *Macbeth* is written in blank verse, which sounds graceful and natural because it closely reflects the rhythm of spoken English. Select a passage of dialogue spoken by a major character such as Macbeth, Banquo, Lady Macbeth, or Duncan. Scan the passage to see if it is truly blank verse. (Some lines may be partial lines or may vary slightly from this meter.) Now, scan the witches' dialogue and identify the rhyme scheme. How is the pattern of their dialogue different from that of blank verse? What effect is created by the meter and rhyme scheme of the witches' lines?

2. **Echoing.** To reinforce key ideas, the characters in this play repeat certain words and phrases, sometimes with slightly different meanings. This technique is called echoing. Note the echoing in these lines:

If it were done when 'tis done, then 'twere well
It were done quickly. . . ." (Scene 7, lines 1–2)

How is the meaning of *done* slightly different each time the word is used? What idea is emphasized through this echoing?

The word *done* is echoed repeatedly throughout the play, often in conjunction with the word *deed*. The effect is a dirge-like sound that recalls the telling of a death knell and that alliterates with the word *death*.

3. **Foreshadowing.** Foreshadowing is a writer's use of hints and clues to indicate events that will occur later in the work. The use of this technique creates suspense and in drama piques the interest of the

audience. How does the line "Fair is foul, and foul is fair" foreshadow the events that follow in Act One? How might Banquo's warning to Macbeth also be foreshadowing?

4. **Exposition.** Exposition is a detailed explanation, often at the beginning of a literary work, that provides pertinent background information. In drama, the opening scenes present exposition. In the first three scenes of *Macbeth,* what important information does the audience learn?

5. **Soliloquy.** A soliloquy is a speech given by a character while she or he is either alone on stage or among characters who are ignored temporarily. The purpose of a soliloquy is to let the audience know what the character is thinking and planning. What does the audience learn about Lady Macbeth from her soliloquy in Scene 5, lines 36–53? about Macbeth from his soliloquy in Scene 7, lines 1–28?

6. **Aside.** An aside is a remark spoken by one character to another that other characters on stage are not supposed to hear. Sometimes an aside is directed to the audience. Notice the use of asides in Scene 3, lines 126–177. How are the asides spoken by Macbeth to Banquo different from those addressed to the audience? What is the effect of the asides in this scene?

7. **Protagonist and Antagonist.** A protagonist is the main character in a literary work. A protagonist can be heroic or common, rich or poor, good or evil. The force or person opposing the protagonist is the antagonist. The antagonist might be an external force such as nature, society, or another character, or an internal force within the protagonist. At this point in the play, who has emerged as the protagonist? Who or what might possibly be the antagonist? Give reasons for your choice or choices.

8. **Irony.** Dramatic irony occurs when the words or acts of a character convey a meaning unperceived by himself or herself but understood by the audience.

What is the dramatic irony in King Duncan's reference to Macbeth as "a peerless kinsman"? What other ironies are evident in Act One?

9. **Imagery and Mood.** At the beginning of Act One, the witches say, "Fair is foul, and foul is fair./ Hover through the fog and filthy air." This statement introduces contrasting images of darkness and light, which are extended not only through Act One but also throughout the entire play. A second key image in the play is introduced in King Duncan's question at the beginning of Scene 2: "What bloody man is that?" Images of darkness and light and of blood and violence stimulate feelings of apprehension, confusion, and gloom right from the opening scenes of the play.

Trace the images of darkness and light and of blood and violence throughout Act One. Comment on how each recurrence of the images intensifies both the mood and the meaning of the passage.

10. **Theme.** Major themes in a work are sometimes introduced early in a play; as the action continues, the theme is further developed and clarified. In this play the idea of destiny and free will is presented early. In Act One who seems to represent destiny? What pivotal choice does Macbeth make? Is this choice a free choice or is it inevitable? Is Macbeth aware of other possible choices? of the consequences of his decision? At this point in the play, what is within Macbeth's control? What is beyond his control? In answering these questions, support your opinions with evidence from the play.

Developing Writing Skills

Writing a Paraphrase. Rewrite in your own words Macbeth's speech in Scene 3, lines 141–156. Then discuss the way that the poetic language of this passage intensifies the dramatic impact of the character's statements.

Act Two

Scene 1

[*It is past midnight as a troubled Banquo and his son Fleance prepare for bed. Banquo admits to Macbeth that he has been thinking about the witches' prophecies. Macbeth feigns indifference but suggests that the two might meet to discuss the implications of the predictions. In responding, Banquo indicates his intention of remaining honorable and loyal to the king. Alone, Macbeth envisions a bloody dagger leading him to King Duncan. When he hears the ringing of a bell, Macbeth knows that it is time to proceed to the king's chambers.*]

[*Court of Macbeth's Castle.*]

[*Enter* Banquo, *and* Fleance *with a torch before him.*]

Banquo. How goes the night, boy?
Fleance. The moon is down; I have not heard the clock.
Banquo. And she goes down at twelve.
Fleance.   I take't, 'tis later, sir.
Banquo. Hold, take my sword. There's husbandry[1] in heaven;   5
   Their candles are all out. Take thee that too.[2]
   A heavy summons[3] lies like lead upon me,
   And yet I would not sleep. Merciful powers,
   Restrain in me the cursèd thoughts that nature
   Gives way to in repose!   10

[*Enter* Macbeth, *and a* Servant *with a torch.*]

                Give me my sword.
   Who's there?
Macbeth. A friend.
Banquo. What, sir, not yet at rest? The King's abed.
   He hath been in unusual pleasure and   15
   Sent forth great largess[4] to your offices.[5]
   This diamond he greets your wife withal
   By the name of most kind hostess, and shut up[6]
   In measureless content.

---

1. **husbandry:** thrift. 2. **Take thee that too:** Since Fleance has taken his sword, Banquo asks him to take his dagger also. 3. **heavy summons:** weariness. 4. **largess:** gifts of money. 5. **offices:** servants' quarters. 6. **shut up:** retired to his room.

Macbeth.   Being unprepared,   20
  Our will became the servant to defect,
  Which else should free have wrought.[7]
Banquo.   All's well.
  I dreamt last night of the three Weird Sisters.
  To you they have showed some truth.   25
Macbeth.   I think not of them.
  Yet when we can entreat an hour to serve,
  We would spend it in some words upon that business,
  If you would grant the time.
Banquo.   At your kind'st leisure.   30
Macbeth. If you shall cleave to my consent,[8] when 'tis,
  It shall make honor for you.
Banquo.   So I lose none
  In seeking to augment it but still keep
  My bosom franchised[9] and allegiance clear,   35
  I shall be counseled.[10]
Macbeth.   Good repose the while!
Banquo. Thanks, sir. The like to you!

                                  [*Exeunt* Banquo *and* Fleance.]

Macbeth. Go bid thy mistress, when my drink is ready,
  She strike upon the bell. Get thee to bed.   40

                                 [*Exit* Servant.]

  Is this a dagger which I see before me,
  The handle toward my hand? Come, let me clutch thee!
  I have thee not, and yet I see thee still.
  Art thou not, fatal vision, sensible[11]
  To feeling as to sight? or art thou but   45
  A dagger of the mind, a false creation,
  Proceeding from the heat-oppressèd brain?
  I see thee yet, in form as palpable[12]
  As this which now I draw.
  Thou marshal'st[13] me the way that I was going,   50
  And such an instrument I was to use.
  Mine eyes are made the fools o' the other senses,
  Or else worth all the rest. I see thee still;
  And on thy blade and dudgeon[14] gouts[15] of blood,
  Which was not so before. There's no such thing.   55
  It is the bloody business which informs[16]

---

7. **Being . . . wrought:** As we were unprepared, our entertainment was not as lavish as we would have wished.   8. **cleave to my consent:** be my ally.   9. **bosom franchised:** conscience clear.   10. **I shall be counseled:** I will be ready to listen. 11. **sensible:** tangible.   12. **palpable:** clear.   13. **marshal'st:** leadest.   14. **dudgeon:** handle.   15. **gouts:** drops. 16. **informs:** creates forms.

Thus to mine eyes. Now o'er the one half-world
Nature seems dead, and wicked dreams abuse[17]
The curtained sleep. Witchcraft celebrates
Pale Hecate's[18] offerings; and withered murder, 60
Alarumed by his sentinel, the wolf,
Whose howl's his watch,[19] thus with his stealthy pace,
With Tarquin's ravishing strides,[20] towards his design
Moves like a ghost. Thou sure and firm-set earth,
Hear not my steps which way they walk, for fear 65
Thy very stones prate of my whereabout
And take the present horror[21] from the time,
Which now suits[22] with it. Whiles I threat, he lives;
Words to the heat of deeds too cold breath gives.

[*A bell rings.*]

I go, and it is done. The bell invites me. 70
Hear it not, Duncan, for it is a knell
That summons thee to heaven, or to hell.

[*Exit.*]

Scene 2

[*After seeing that the chamberlains are drunk and heavily drugged, Lady Macbeth awaits Macbeth. Macbeth returns from Duncan's chamber with the bloody daggers, horrified that he has actually murdered the king. He imagines that he has heard a voice saying, "Macbeth shall sleep no more!" Macbeth refuses to return to the scene of the murder, so Lady Macbeth plants the bloody daggers in the king's chamber to incriminate the chamberlains. A knocking at the south entry begins, and Lady Macbeth insists that they go immediately to their own chamber and pretend to have been asleep. Macbeth already is beginning to regret the murder.*]

[*The same.*]

[*Enter* Lady Macbeth.]

Lady Macbeth. That which hath made them drunk hath made me bold;
What hath quenched them hath given me fire. Hark! Peace!

---

17. **abuse:** deceive.   18. **Hecate:** goddess of witchcraft.   19. **howl's . . . watch:** who tells the time by howling.
20. **Tarquin's ravishing strides:** Tarquin, the last King of Rome, overcame the chaste Lucrece while she slept.
21. **present horror:** the silence of midnight.   22. **suits:** matches.

It was the owl that shrieked, the fatal bellman[1]
Which gives the stern'st good-night. He is about it.
The doors are open, and the surfeited grooms[2]
Do mock their charge[3] with snores. I have drugged their possets,[4]
That death and nature do contend about them
Whether they live or die.

Macbeth. [*Within*] Who's there? What, ho?

Lady Macbeth. Alack, I am afraid they have awaked,
And 'tis not done! The attempt, and not the deed,
Confounds[5] us. Hark! I laid their daggers ready;
He could not miss 'em. Had he not resembled
My father as he slept, I had done't.

[*Enter* Macbeth.]

                      My husband!

Macbeth. I have done the deed. Didst thou not hear a noise?

Lady Macbeth. I heard the owl scream and the crickets cry.
Did not you speak?

Macbeth.   When?

Lady Macbeth.   Now.

Macbeth.   As I descended?

Lady Macbeth. Ay.

Macbeth. Hark!
Who lies i' the second chamber?

Lady Macbeth.   Donalbain.

Macbeth. This is a sorry sight. [*Looking on his hands.*]

Lady Macbeth. A foolish thought, to say a sorry sight.

Macbeth. There's one did laugh in's sleep, and one cried "Murder!"
That they did wake each other. I stood and heard them.
But they did say their prayers and addressed them
Again to sleep.

Lady Macbeth.   There are two lodged together.

Macbeth. One cried "God bless us!" and "Amen!" the other,
As they had seen me with these hangman's hands,[6]
List'ning their fear. I could not say "Amen!"
When they did say "God bless us!"

Lady Macbeth. Consider it not so deeply.

Macbeth. But wherefore could not I pronounce "Amen"?
I had most need of blessing, and "Amen"
Stuck in my throat.

---

1. **fatal bellman:** at midnight on the night before an execution, a bellman rang a handbell outside the cell of the condemned, bidding him think on his sins. 2. **surfeited grooms:** overfed servants. 3. **charge:** duty, i.e., protecting the King. 4. **possets:** a warm drink of milk and ale taken at bedtime. 5. **Confounds:** destroys. 6. **hangman's hands:** the state executioner had to hang the victims and also draw and quarter them.

Lady Macbeth.   These deeds must not be thought

After these ways. So, it will make us mad.

Macbeth. Methought I heard a voice cry "Sleep no more!

Macbeth does murder sleep"—the innocent sleep,

Sleep that knits up the raveled sleave[7] of care,   45

The death of each day's life, sore labor's bath,

Balm of hurt minds, great nature's second course,[8]

Chief nourisher in life's feast.

Lady Macbeth.   What do you mean?

Macbeth. Still it cried "Sleep no more!" to all the house;   50

"Glamis hath murdered sleep, and therefore Cawdor

Shall sleep no more! Macbeth shall sleep no more!"

Lady Macbeth. Who was it that thus cried? Why, worthy Thane,

You do unbend[9] your noble strength to think

So brainsickly of things. Go get some water   55

And wash this filthy witness[10] from your hand.

Why did you bring these daggers from the place?

They must lie there. Go carry them and smear

The sleepy grooms with blood.

Macbeth.   I'll go no more.   60

I am afraid to think what I have done;

Look on't again I dare not.

Lady Macbeth.   Infirm of purpose!

Give me the daggers. The sleeping and the dead

Are but as pictures. 'Tis the eye of childhood   65

That fears a painted devil. If he do bleed,

I'll gild the faces of the grooms withal,

For it must seem their guilt.

                                        [Exit. Knocking within.]

Macbeth.   Whence is that knocking?

How is't with me when every noise appals me?   70

What hands are here? Ha! they pluck out mine eyes!

Will all great Neptune's ocean wash this blood

Clean from my hand? No. This my hand will rather

The multitudinous seas incarnadine,[11]

Making the green one red.   75

     [Reenter Lady Macbeth.]

Lady Macbeth. My hands are of your color, but I shame

To wear a heart so white. *[Knock.]* I hear a knocking

---

7. **raveled sleave:** tangled skein.   8. **second course:** main part of the meal.   9. **unbend:** relax.   10. **witness:** evidence.   11. **incarnadine:** make red.

At the south entry. Retire we to our chamber.
A little water clears us of this deed.
How easy is it then! Your constancy[12]   80
Hath left you unattended. [*Knock.*] Hark! more knocking.
Get on your nightgown,[13] lest occasion call us
And show us to be watchers.[14] Be not lost
So poorly in your thoughts.
Macbeth. To know my deed, 'twere best not know myself.   85

[*Knock.*]

Wake Duncan with thy knocking! I would thou couldst!

[*Exeunt.*]

Scene 3   [*The drunken porter imagines that he is welcoming sinners at
                    hell's gate. Finally, he opens the gate for Lennox and Macduff,
                    who listen to the porter's discourse on drink. Macbeth leads the
                    two noblemen to the king's quarters. As Macbeth and Lennox
                    discuss the ominous happenings of the night, Macduff enters the
                    king's chamber and discovers the murder. Lennox and Macbeth
                    go to the murder scene where the enraged Macbeth kills the
                    chamberlains. Aroused by the commotion, the rest of the
                    household and the guests react to the news of the king's murder.
                    Lady Macbeth collapses, and the nobles agree to investigate the
                    treasonous act. Donalbain and Malcolm, the king's sons, decide
                    to flee the dangerous situation in Scotland. Donalbain will go to
                    Ireland, Malcolm to England.*]

[*The same.*]

[*Knocking within. Enter a* Porter.]

Porter. Here's a knocking indeed! If a man were porter of hell gate, he should have
  old turning the key.[1] [*Knock.*] Knock, knock, knock! Who's there, i' the name of
  Belzebub? Here's a farmer that hanged himself on the expectation of plenty.[2]
  Come in time! Have napkins enow[3] about you; here you'll sweat for't. [*Knock.*]
  Knock, knock! Who's there, in the other devil's name? Faith, here's an equivoca-   5
  tor,[4] that could swear in both the scales against either scale; who committed
  treason enough for God's sake, yet could not equivocate to heaven. O, come in,
  equivocator! [*Knock.*] Knock, knock, knock! Who's there? Faith, here's an

---

12. **constancy:** firm purpose. 13. **nightgown:** dressing gown. 14. **watchers:** awake.
  1. **turning the key:** opening the door. 2. **Here's . . . plenty:** the farmer feared over-production and low prices for the
crops. 3. **napkins enow:** towels enough. 4. **equivocator:** one who gives an answer that can be taken two ways.

Mervyn Blake (Porter) in *Macbeth*. Stratford Festival, 1983.

English tailor come hither for stealing out of a French hose.[5] Come in, tailor. Here you may roast your goose.[6] [*Knock.*] Knock, knock! Never at quiet! What are you? But this place is too cold for hell. I'll devil-porter it no further. I had thought to have let in some of all professions that go the primrose way[7] to the everlasting bonfire. [*Knock.*] Anon, anon! [*Opens the gate.*] I pray you remember the porter.

[*Enter* Macduff *and* Lennox.]

Macduff. Was it so late, friend, ere you went to bed,
    That you do lie so late?
Porter. Faith, sir, we were carousing till the second cock;[8] and drink, sir, is a great provoker.
Macduff. I believe drink gave thee the lie last night.

---

5. **English . . . French hose:** French hose were breeches. It is a double theft of the fashion and the material.   6. **goose:** tailor's pressing iron.   7. **primrose way:** the pleasant path to Hell.   8. **second cock:** 3 A.M.

Porter. That it did, sir, i' the very throat on me; but I requited[9] him for his lie; 20
and, I think, being too strong for him, though he took up my legs sometime, yet I
made a shift to cast him.[10]
Macduff. Is thy master stirring?

[*Enter* Macbeth.]

Our knocking has awaked him; here he comes.
Lennox. Good morrow, noble sir. 25
Macbeth.   Good morrow, both.
Macduff. Is the King stirring, worthy Thane?
Macbeth.   Not yet.
Macduff. He did command me to call timely on him;
I have almost slipped the hour. 30
Macbeth.   I'll bring you to him.
Macduff. I know this is a joyful trouble to you;
But yet 'tis one.
Macbeth. The labor we delight in physics[11] pain.
This is the door. 35
Macduff.   I'll make so bold to call,
For 'tis my limited service.[12]

                                        [*Exit.*]

Lennox. Goes the King hence today?
Macbeth.   He does; he did appoint so.
Lennox. The night has been unruly. Where we lay, 40
Our chimneys were blown down; and, as they say,
Lamentings heard i' the air, strange screams of death,
And prophesying, with accents terrible,
Of dire combustion[13] and confused events
New hatched to the woeful time. The obscure bird[14] 45
Clamored the livelong night. Some say the earth
Was feverous and did shake.
Macbeth.   'Twas a rough night.
Lennox. My young remembrance cannot parallel
A fellow to it. 50

[*Reenter* Macduff.]

Macduff. O horror, horror, horror! Tongue nor heart
Cannot conceive nor name thee!
Macbeth and Lennox.   What's the matter?
Macduff. Confusion now hath made his masterpiece!
Most sacrilegious murder hath broke open 55

---

9. **requited:** repaid.   10. **made . . . him:** managed to throw up.   11. **physics:** cures.   12. **limited service:** appointed
duty.   13. **dire combustion:** terrible uproar.   14. **obscure bird:** owl. *Obscure* means "dark," the owl being nocturnal.

The Lord's anointed temple[15] and stole thence
The life o' the building!
Macbeth.   What is't you say? the life?
Lennox. Mean you his Majesty?
Macduff. Approach the chamber, and destroy your sight   60
With a new Gorgon.[16] Do not bid me speak.
See, and then speak yourselves.

                                        [*Exeunt* Macbeth *and* Lennox.]
                         Awake, awake!
Ring the alarum bell. Murder and treason!
Banquo and Donalbain! Malcolm! awake!   65
Shake off this downy sleep, death's counterfeit,
And look on death itself! Up, up, and see
The great doom's image![17] Malcolm! Banquo!
As from your graves rise up and walk like sprites[18]
To countenance[19] this horror! Ring the bell!   70

[*Bell rings.*]

    [*Enter* Lady Macbeth.]

Lady Macbeth. What's the business,
    That such a hideous trumpet calls to parley
    The sleepers of the house? Speak, speak!
Macduff.   O gentle lady,
    'Tis not for you to hear what I can speak!   75
    The repetition in a woman's ear
    Would murder as it fell.

    [*Enter* Banquo.]

        O Banquo, Banquo,
    Our royal master's murdered!
Lady Macbeth.   Woe, alas!   80
    What, in our house?
Banquo.   Too cruel anywhere.
    Dear Duff, I prithee contradict thyself
    And say it is not so.

    [*Enter* Macbeth, Lennox, *and* Ross.]

Macbeth. Had I but died an hour before this chance,   85
    I had lived a blessèd time; for from this instant
    There's nothing serious in mortality;

---

15. **The Lord's anointed temple:** the King's body.   16. **Gorgon:** the snake-headed monster Medusa, who turned to stone anyone who looked upon it.   17. **great . . . image:** the picture of Doomsday.   18. **sprites:** ghosts.   19. **countenance:** to be in keeping with.

All is but toys;²⁰ renown and grace²¹ is dead;
The wine of life is drawn, and the mere lees
Is left this vault²² to brag of.

    [*Enter* Malcolm *and* Donalbain.]   90

Donalbain. What is amiss?
Macbeth.   You are, and do not know't.
  The spring, the head, the fountain of your blood
  Is stopped, the very source of it is stopped
Macduff. Your royal father's murdered.   95
Malcolm.   O, by whom?
Lennox. Those of his chamber, as it seemed, had done't.
  Their hands and faces were all badged²³ with blood;
  So were their daggers, which unwiped we found
  Upon their pillows.   100
  They stared and were distracted. No man's life
  Was to be trusted with them.
Macbeth. O, yet I do repent me of my fury
  That I did kill them.
Macduff.   Wherefore did you so?   105
Macbeth. Who can be wise, amazed,²⁴ temp'rate, and furious,
  Loyal and neutral, in a moment? No man.
  The expedition²⁵ of my violent love
  Outrun the pauser,²⁶ reason. Here lay Duncan,
  His silver skin laced with his golden blood,   110
  And his gashed stabs looked like a breach in nature
  For ruin's wasteful entrance; there, the murderers,
  Steeped in the colors of their trade, their daggers
  Unmannerly breeched with gore.²⁷ Who could refrain
  That had a heart to love and in that heart   115
  Courage to make's love known?
Lady Macbeth.   Help me hence, ho!
Macduff. Look to the lady.
Malcolm. [*Aside to* Donalbain] Why do we hold our tongues,
  That most may claim this argument²⁸ for ours?   120
Donalbain. [*Aside to* Malcolm] What should be spoken here,
  Where our fate, hid in an auger hole,²⁹
  May rush and seize us? Let's away,
  Our tears are not yet brewed.
Malcolm. [*Aside to* Donalbain] Nor our strong sorrow   125
  Upon the foot of motion.

---

20. **toys:** trifles. 21. **grace:** honor. 22. **vault:** universe. 23. **badged:** marked. 24. **amazed:** shocked. 25. **expedition:** hasty action. 26. **pauser:** restrainer. 27. **Unmannerly . . . gore:** covered with blood rather than sheaths. 28. **argument:** business. 29. **auger hole:** a tiny hole, i.e., a small event may destroy us.

Banquo.   Look to the lady.

[Lady Macbeth *is carried out.*]

  And when we have our naked frailties hid,
  That suffer in exposure, let us meet
  And question this most bloody piece of work,   130
  To know it further. Fears and scruples[30] shake us.
  In the great hand of God I stand, and thence
  Against the undivulged pretense[31] I fight
  Of treasonous malice.
Macduff.   And so do I.   135
All.   So all.
Macbeth. Let's briefly[32] put on manly readiness
  And meet i' the hall together.
All.   Well contented.

                    [*Exeunt all but* Malcolm *and* Donalbain.]

Malcolm. What will you do? Let's not consort with them.   140
  To show an unfelt sorrow is an office
  Which the false man does easy. I'll to England.
Donalbain. To Ireland I. Our separated fortune[33]
  Shall keep us both the safer. Where we are,
  There's daggers in men's smiles; the near in blood,   145
  The nearer bloody.[34]
Malcolm.   This murderous shaft that's shot
  Hath not yet lighted, and our safest way
  Is to avoid the aim. Therefore to horse!
  And let us not be dainty[35] of leave-taking   150
  But shift away. There's warrant in that theft
  Which steals itself when there's no mercy left.[36]

                             [*Exeunt.*]

Scene 4   [*An old man and Ross discuss King Duncan's murder and the natural phenomena that reflect the horror of the deed. Macduff reports that Malcolm and Donalbain are suspected of enlisting the chamberlains to murder their father. Macbeth has been named Duncan's successor and is to be crowned at Scone. Ross will attend the ceremony, while Macduff will return to Fife, already uneasy about Macbeth's reign.*]

---

30. **scruples:** doubts. 31. **pretense:** purpose. 32. **briefly:** quickly. 33. **fortune:** ways. 34. **near . . . bloody:** the nearer we are related to a man, the nearer we are to his destruction. 35. **dainty:** particular. 36. **There's . . . left:** we are justified in stealing away under these circumstances.

[*Outside Macbeth's Castle.*]

[*Enter* Ross *with an* Old Man.]

Old Man. Threescore and ten I can remember well;
    Within the volume of which time I have seen
    Hours dreadful and things strange; but this sore[1] night
    Hath trifled former knowings.
Ross.   Ah, good father,   5
    Thou seest the heavens, as troubled with man's act,
    Threaten his bloody stage. By the clock 'tis day,
    And yet dark night strangles the traveling lamp.[2]
    Is't night's predominance,[3] or the day's shame,[4]
    That darkness does the face of earth entomb   10
    When living light should kiss it?
Old Man.   'Tis unnatural,
    Even like the deed that's done. On Tuesday last
    A falcon, tow'ring in her pride of place,
    Was by a mousing owl hawked at and killed.   15
Ross. And Duncan's horses (a thing most strange and certain),
    Beauteous and swift, the minions[5] of their race,
    Turned wild in nature, broke their stalls, flung out,
    Contending 'gainst obedience, as they would make
    War with mankind.   20
Old Man.   'Tis said they eat each other.
Ross. They did so, to the amazement of mine eyes
    That looked upon't.

    [*Enter* Macduff.]

      Here comes the good Macduff.
    How goes the world, sir, now?   25
Macduff.   Why, see you not?
Ross. Is't known who did this more than bloody deed?
Macduff. Those that Macbeth hath slain.
Ross.   Alas, the day!
    What good could they pretend?[6]   30
Macduff.   They were suborned.[7]
    Malcolm and Donalbain, the King's two sons,
    Are stol'n away and fled, which puts upon them
    Suspicion of the deed.

---

1. **sore:** terrible. 2. **strangles . . . lamp:** blots out the sun. 3. **predominance:** supremacy. 4. **day's shame:** the day is ashamed of this dreadful deed. 5. **minions:** darlings. 6. **pretend:** intend. 7. **suborned:** bribed.

Ross.   'Gainst nature still!   35
    Thriftless ambition, that will raven up[8]
    Thine own live's means! Then 'tis most like
    The sovereignty will fall upon Macbeth.
Macduff. He is already named, and gone to Scone[9]
    To be invested.   40
Ross.   Where is Duncan's body?
Macduff. Carried to Colmekill,[10]
    The sacred storehouse of his predecessors
    And guardian of their bones.
Ross.   Will you to Scone?   45
Macduff. No, cousin, I'll to Fife.
Ross.   Well, I will thither.
Macduff. Well, may you see things well done there.[11] Adieu,
    Lest our old robes sit easier than our new![12]
Ross. Farewell, father.   50
Old Man. God's benison[13] go with you, and with those
    That would make good of bad, and friends of foes!

                                        [Exeunt.]

---

8. **raven up:** devour greedily. 9. **Scone:** the traditional site of the coronation of Scottish Kings. 10. **Colmekill:** Iona, the ancient burial place of the Scottish Kings. 11. **may . . . there:** Macduff is uneasy about the future with Macbeth as King. 12. **Lest . . . new:** Macbeth's reign may be harsher than Duncan's. 13. **benison:** blessing.

Act Two

Getting at Meaning

Scene 1

1. With what words does Banquo reaffirm his loyalty to the king? What lie does Macbeth tell Banquo? Why is Banquo's reaction to the witches' prophecies so different from that of Macbeth?

2. Consider the implications of the dagger hallucination. What does Macbeth mean by the "fatal vision" of the dagger? by a "dagger of the mind"?

3. Why is Macbeth's allusion to Tarquin in line 64 particularly appropriate?

Scene 2

4. Describe the murder of Duncan as recounted by Macbeth. Why is he unable to say "Amen"?

5. Macbeth imagines that a voice speaks to him. What message is spoken? How does Macbeth interpret this message?

6. Why must Lady Macbeth return the bloody daggers to Duncan's chambers? How do Macbeth and

Lady Macbeth differ in their reactions to the murder? What does Macbeth wish at the end of this scene?

Scene 3

7. What dual purpose does the porter serve at the beginning of this scene?

8. Who are Macbeth's second and third victims? What reason does he give for killing them?

9. Why does Lady Macbeth faint? Explain your answer.

10. Why do Malcolm and Donalbain secretly leave Macbeth's castle? Where do they go?

Scene 4

11. Why are Malcolm and Donalbain suspects in the murder of their father? What motive is attributed to them? Why is this accusation ironic?

12. As described in Scenes 3 and 4, how does nature reflect human events? What idea is emphasized by these references to nature?

Developing Skills in Reading Literature

1. **Figurative Language.** Like all of Shakespeare's poems and plays, *Macbeth* is rich in figures of speech, such as simile, metaphor, and personification. Examine the following lines from Act Two to identify the figures of speech that they contain. Then comment on the effectiveness of figurative language in heightening the dramatic impact of the scenes.

    a. Scene 1, lines 1–5   e. Scene 3, lines 54–62
    b. Scene 1, lines 41–72   f. Scene 3, lines 92–94
    c. Scene 2, lines 43–48   g. Scene 4, lines 5–11
    d. Scene 2, lines 63–68

2. **Comic Relief.** Comic relief is a humorous scene, incident, or speech that is included in a serious drama to provide respite from emotional intensity.

Comic relief allows the audience to internalize what has just happened and to prepare emotionally for the events to come. When a play is studied in its entirety, comic relief often can be seen as deepening through contrast of thematically significant events.

The exchange between the porter and Macduff and Lennox at the beginning of Scene 3 is an example of comic relief. What has just happened prior to this scene? How does the character of the porter break the dramatic tension? What kind of humor does he interject? What immediately follows the humorous exchange? The impact of what event is sharpened through comic relief?

3. **Characterization: Soliloquy and Dialogue.** The soliloquies spoken by Macbeth and Lady Macbeth are important contributions to the development of their characters. In Act Two, Macbeth's dagger soliloquy is significant, for it appears just before the murder of Duncan. What striking contrasts are presented in the soliloquy? what blood imagery? what elements of the supernatural? What is Macbeth's state of mind, as revealed by the soliloquy? How has he changed since Act One?

In Act Two, Scene 2, immediately after the murder of Duncan, Macbeth and Lady Macbeth exchange dialogue that suggests the impact of the murder on both of them. How is this dialogue different at first from the exchanges between these two characters earlier in the play? What apparently is the reaction of both characters to the murder? Who seems to recover more quickly? What does this suggest about the character? Explain, using evidence from the play.

4. **Imagery, Symbol, and Character.** In this act the images of light and darkness recur; however, it is the image of blood that dominates the act, along with the contrasting image of water. Blood and water, in fact, are elevated to the level of symbols, communicating abstract as well as sensory meanings.

After the murder of Duncan, Macbeth says:

> Will all great Neptune's ocean wash this blood
> Clean from my hand? No. This hand will rather
> The multitudinous sea incarnadine,
> Making the green one red.

What is the symbolic meaning of blood in this passage? What does water symbolize for Macbeth?

In the same scene, Lady Macbeth reacts to the same situation—hands stained with Duncan's blood—in a literal, pragmatic way. She says, "A little water clears us of this deed." What does this statement indicate about her character? How is Macbeth different from Lady Macbeth? Does he realize the ramifications of his act? Why does Lady Macbeth's statement seem ironic when contrasted with Macbeth's words? Explain.

Act Three

Scene 1

[*Banquo voices his suspicions about Macbeth's role in Duncan's murder and expresses hope that the witches' prophecy about his own children will be fulfilled. Macbeth requests that Banquo attend a state banquet, and Banquo explains that he and Fleance will be away on business until evening. Macbeth is tormented by the idea that Banquo's descendants and not his own will occupy the throne. He persuades two vengeful murderers to kill Banquo and Fleance.*]

[*Forres. The Palace.*]

[*Enter* Banquo.]

Banquo. Thou hast it now—King, Cawdor, Glamis, all,
    As the Weird Women promised; and I fear
    Thou play'dst most foully for't. Yet it was said
    It should not stand[1] in thy posterity,
    But that myself should be the root and father   5
    Of many kings. If there come truth from them
    (As upon thee, Macbeth, their speeches shine),
    Why, by the verities on thee made good,
    May they not be my oracles as well
    And set me up in hope? But hush, no more!   10

[*Sennet[2] sounded. Enter* Macbeth, *as King;* Lady Macbeth, *as Queen,* Lennox, Ross, Lords, Ladies, *and* Attendants.]

Macbeth. Here's our chief guest.
Lady Macbeth.   If he had been forgotten,
    It had been as a gap in our great feast,
    And all-thing[3] unbecoming.
Macbeth. Tonight we hold a solemn[4] supper, sir,   15
    And I'll request your presence.
Banquo.   Let your Highness
    Command upon me, to the which my duties
    Are with a most indissoluble tie
    For ever knit.   20
Macbeth.   Ride you this afternoon?
Banquo. Ay, my good lord.

---

1. **stand:** continue. 2. **Sennet:** a trumpet call announcing the approach of important persons. 3. **all-thing:** every way.
4. **solemn:** ceremonious.

Macbeth. We should have else desired your good advice
(Which still hath been both grave and prosperous)⁵
In this day's council; but we'll take tomorrow.   25
Is't far you ride?
Banquo. As far, my lord, as will fill up the time
'Twixt this and supper. Go not my horse the better,
I must become a borrower of the night
For a dark hour or twain.   30
Macbeth.   Fail not our feast.
Banquo. My Lord, I will not.
Macbeth. We hear our bloody cousins are bestowed
In England and in Ireland, not confessing
Their cruel parricide, filling their hearers   35
With strange invention. But of that tomorrow,
When therewithal we shall have cause of state
Craving us jointly.⁶ Hie you to horse. Adieu,
Till you return at night. Goes Fleance with you?
Banquo. Ay, my good lord. Our time does call upon's.⁷   40
Macbeth. I wish your horses swift and sure of foot,
And so I do commend you to their backs.
Farewell.

                                                    [*Exit* Banquo.]

Let every man be master of his time
Till seven at night. To make society   45
The sweeter welcome, we will keep ourself⁸
Till supper time alone. While⁹ then, God be with you!

                            [*Exeunt all but* Macbeth *and a* Servant.]

Sirrah, a word with you. Attend¹⁰ those men
Our pleasure?
Servant. They are, my lord, without the palace gate.   50
Macbeth. Bring them before us.

                                                   [*Exit* Servant.]

                    To be thus¹¹ is nothing,
But to be safely thus. Our fears in Banquo
Stick deep, and in his royalty of nature¹²
Reigns that which would¹³ be feared. 'Tis much he dares,   55
And to that dauntless temper of his mind
He hath a wisdom that doth guide his valor
To act in safety. There is none but he
Whose being I do fear; and under him
My genius is rebuked, as it is said   60
Mark Antony's was by Cæsar. He chid the Sisters

---

5. **grave and prosperous:** serious and profitable.   6. **Craving us jointly:** demanding the attention of both of us.
7. **Our . . . upon's:** our business is urgent.   8. **ourself:** the royal plural.   9. **While:** until.   10. **Attend:** await.   11. **To be thus:** to have gained the throne.   12. **royalty of nature:** kingly nature.   13. **would:** should.

When first they put the name of King upon me,
And bade them speak to him. Then, prophet-like,
They hailed him father to a line of kings.
Upon my head they placed a fruitless crown 65
And put a barren scepter in my gripe,[14]
Thence to be wrenched with an unlineal hand,
No son of mine succeeding. If't be so,
For Banquo's issue have I filed[15] my mind;
For them the gracious Duncan have I murdered; 70
Put rancors[16] in the vessel of my peace
Only for them, and mine eternal jewel[17]
Given to the common enemy of man[18]
To make them kings, the seed of Banquo kings!
Rather than so, come, Fate, into the list,[19] 75
And champion me to the utterance![20] Who's there?

[*Enter* Servant *and two* Murderers.]

Now go to the door and stay there till we call.

[*Exit* Servant.]

Was it not yesterday we spoke together?
Murderers. It was, so please your Highness.
Macbeth.   Well then, now 80
Have you considered of my speeches? Know
That it was he, in the times past, which held you
So under fortune, which you thought had been
Our innocent self. This I made good[21] to you
In our last conference, passed in probation[22] with you 85
How you were borne in hand,[23] how crossed; the instruments;
Who wrought with them; and all things else that might
To half a soul[24] and to a notion[25] crazed
Say "Thus did Banquo."
First Murderer.   You made it known to us. 90
Macbeth. I did so; and went further, which is now
Our point of second meeting. Do you find
Your patience so predominant in your nature
That you can let this go? Are you so gospeled[26]
To pray for this good man and for his issue, 95
Whose heavy hand hath bowed you to the grave
And beggared yours for ever?
First Murderer.   We are men, my liege.

---

14. **gripe:** grip. 15. **filed:** defiled. 16. **rancors:** bitterness. 17. **eternal jewel:** immortal soul. 18. **common . . . man:** the
Devil. 19. **list:** place of combat. 20. **champion . . . utterance:** fight in combat to the death. 21. **made good:**
demonstrated. 22. **passed in probation:** proved. 23. **borne in hand:** deceived. 24. **half a soul:** halfwit. 25. **notion:**
mind. 26. **so gospeled:** such a good Christian.

Macbeth. Ay, in the catalogue ye go for men,
    As hounds and greyhounds, mongrels, spaniels, curs,   100
    Shoughs, water-rugs,[27] and demi-wolves are clept[28]
    All by the name of dogs. The valued file[29]
    Distinguishes the swift, the slow, the subtle,
    The housekeeper, the hunter, every one
    According to the gift which bounteous nature   105
    Hath in him closed; whereby he does receive
    Particular addition,[30] from the bill
    That writes them all alike; and so of men.
    Now, if you have a station in the file,[31]
    Not i' the worst rank of manhood, say't;   110
    And I will put that business in your bosoms
    Whose execution takes your enemy off,
    Grapples you to the heart and love of us,
    Who wear our health but sickly in his life,[32]
    Which in his death were perfect.   115
Second Murderer.   I am one, my liege,
    Whom the vile blows and buffets of the world
    Have so incensed that I am reckless what
    I do to spite the world.
First Murderer.   And I another,   120
    So weary with disasters, tugged with fortune,
    That I would set my life on any chance,
    To mend it or be rid on't.
Macbeth.   Both of you
    Know Banquo was your enemy.   125
Murderers.   True, my lord.
Macbeth. So is he mine, and in such bloody distance[33]
    That every minute of his being thrusts
    Against my near'st of life;[34] and though I could
    With barefaced power sweep him from my sight   130
    And bid my will avouch[35] it, yet I must not,
    For certain friends that are both his and mine,
    Whose loves I may not drop, but wail his fall[36]
    Who I myself struck down. And thence it is
    That I to your assistance do make love,   135
    Masking the business from the common eye
    For sundry weighty reasons.
Second Murderer.   We shall, my lord,
    Perform what you command us.
First Murderer.   Though our lives—   140

---

27. **Shoughs, water-rugs:** two types of dogs. 28. **clept:** called. 29. **valued file:** list of those valued. 30. **Particular addition:** a distinguishing title. 31. **station . . . file:** place. 32. **in his life:** so long as he is alive. 33. **distance:** disagreement. 34. **near'st of life:** very existence. 35. **avouch:** justify. 36. **wail his fall:** must pretend to lament his death.

Macbeth. Your spirits shine through you. Within this hour at most
    I will advise you where to plant yourselves,
    Acquaint you with the perfect spy o' the time,[37]
    The moment on't; for't must be done tonight,
    And something[38] from the palace (always thought   145
    That I require a clearness),[39] and with him,
    To leave no rubs[40] nor botches in the work,
    Fleance his son, that keeps him company,
    Whose absence is no less material to me
    Than is his father's, must embrace the fate   150
    Of that dark hour. Resolve yourselves apart;[41]
    I'll come to you anon.
Murderers.   We are resolved, my lord.
Macbeth. I'll call upon you straight.[42] Abide within.

                              [Exeunt Murderers.]

    It is concluded. Banquo, thy soul's flight,   155
    If it find heaven, must find it out tonight.

                                   [Exit.]

Scene 2

[Although Lady Macbeth has realized her ambition to be Queen, she is discontented and restless. Macbeth reveals similar feelings of torment and insecurity and admits to being afflicted by terrible dreams. Lady Macbeth and Macbeth urge each other to mask their emotions for their guests. Macbeth keeps secret his plan for the murder of Banquo and Fleance, but he alludes to bloody deeds that will take place under the cover of darkness.]

[The Palace.]

[Enter Lady Macbeth *and a* Servant.]

Lady Macbeth. Is Banquo gone from court?
Servant. Ay, madam, but returns again tonight.
Lady Macbeth. Say to the King I would attend his leisure
    For a few words.
Servant.   Madam, I will.   5

                                [Exit.]

Lady Macbeth.   Naught's had, all's spent,
    Where our desire is got without content.
    'Tis safer to be that which we destroy

---

37. **the . . . time:** exact moment. 38. **something:** some distance. 39. **a clearness:** be free of implication. 40. **rubs:** impediments. 41. **Resolve . . . apart:** decide by yourselves. 42. **straight:** immediately.

Than by destruction dwell in doubtful joy.

[*Enter* Macbeth.]

How now, my lord? Why do you keep alone,   10
Of sorriest fancies your companions making,
Using those thoughts which should indeed have died
With them they think on? Things without all remedy
Should be without regard. What's done is done.
Macbeth. We have scotched¹ the snake, not killed it.   15
She'll close² and be herself, whilst our poor malice
Remains in danger of her former tooth.³
But let the frame of things disjoint, both the worlds suffer,⁴
Ere we will eat our meal in fear and sleep
In the affliction of these terrible dreams   20
That shake us nightly. Better be with the dead,
Whom we, to gain our peace, have sent to peace,
Than on the torture of the mind to lie
In restless ecstasy.⁵ Duncan is in his grave;
After life's fitful fever he sleeps well.   25
Treason has done his worst: nor steel nor poison,
Malice domestic, foreign levy, nothing,
Can touch him further.
Lady Macbeth.   Come on.
Gentle my lord, sleek o'er your rugged looks;   30
Be bright and jovial among your guests tonight.
Macbeth. So shall I, love; and so, I pray, be you.
Let your remembrance apply to Banquo;
Present him eminence⁶ both with eye and tongue:
Unsafe the while, that⁷ we   35
Must lave⁸ our honors in these flattering streams
And make our faces vizards⁹ to our hearts,
Disguising what they are.
Lady Macbeth.   You must leave this.
Macbeth. O, full of scorpions is my mind, dear wife!   40
Thou know'st that Banquo, and his Fleance, lives.
Lady Macbeth. But in them Nature's copy's not eterne.¹⁰
Macbeth. There's comfort yet; they are assailable.
Then be thou jocund. Ere the bat hath flown
His cloistered flight, ere to black Hecate's summons   45
The shard-borne¹¹ beetle with his drowsy hums
Hath rung night's yawning peal, there shall be done
A deed of dreadful note.

---

1. **scotched:** wounded slightly. 2. **close:** heal. 3. **whilst . . . tooth:** while we for all of our hatred are in as great a danger as before. 4. **let . . . suffer:** let the universe fall to pieces, let heaven and earth perish. 5. **ecstasy:** madness. 6. **Present him eminence:** make much of him. 7. **Unsafe . . . that:** we are not safe so long as. 8. **lave:** wash. 9. **vizards:** masks. 10. **in . . . eterne:** they will not live forever. 11. **shard-borne:** borne on scaly wings.

Lady Macbeth.   What's to be done?

Macbeth. Be innocent of the knowledge, dearest chuck,[12]   50
    Till thou applaud the deed. Come, seeling[13] night,
    Scarf[14] up the tender eye of pitiful day,
    And with thy bloody and invisible hand
    Cancel and tear to pieces that great bond[15]
    Which keeps me pale! Light thickens, and the crow   55
    Makes wing to the rooky[16] wood.
    Good things of day begin to droop and drowse,
    Whiles night's black agents to their preys do rouse.
    Thou marvell'st at my words; but hold thee still:
    Things bad begun make strong themselves by ill.   60
    So prithee go with me.

                                                        [Exeunt.]

Scene 3

    *[The two murderers, joined by a third, ambush Banquo and
    Fleance, killing Banquo but allowing Fleance to escape.]*

[A park near the Palace.]

[Enter three Murderers.]

First Murderer. But who did bid thee join with us?

Third Murderer.   Macbeth.

Second Murderer. He needs not our mistrust, since he delivers
    Our offices,[1] and what we have to do,
    To the direction just.[2]   5

First Murderer.   Then stand with us.
    The west yet glimmers with some streaks of day.
    Now spurs the lated[3] traveler apace
    To gain the timely inn, and near approaches
    The subject of our watch.   10

Third Murderer.   Hark! I hear horses.

Banquo. *[Within]* Give us a light there, ho!

Second Murderer.   Then 'tis he! The rest
    That are within the note of expectation[4]
    Already are i' the court.   15

First Murderer.   His horses go about.[5]

---

12. **chuck:** chick. 13. **seeling:** blinding. 14. **Scarf up:** blindfold. 15. **great bond:** Banquo's life. 16. **rooky:** murky.

    1. **offices:** duties. 2. **To . . . just:** in exact detail. 3. **lated:** belated. 4. **within . . . expectation:** on the list of expected guests. 5. **His . . . about:** his horses have been put up for the night.

Third Murderer. Almost a mile; but he does usually,
   So all men do, from hence to the palace gate
   Make it their walk.

   [*Enter* Banquo, *and* Fleance *with a torch.*]

Second Murderer.   A light, a light!   20
Third Murderer.   'Tis he.
First Murderer. Stand to't.
Banquo. It will be rain tonight.
First Murderer.   Let it come down!

[*They set upon* Banquo.]

Banquo. O, treachery! Fly, good Fleance, fly, fly, fly!   25
   Thou mayst revenge. O slave!

   [*Dies.* Fleance *escapes.*]

Third Murderer. Who did strike out the light?
First Murderer.   Was't not the way?
Third Murderer. There's but one down; the son is fled.
Second Murderer.   We have lost   30
   Best half of our affair.
First Murderer. Well, let's away, and say how much is done.

                                 [*Exeunt.*]

Scene 4

[*As the banquet begins, one of the murderers reports to Macbeth that Banquo is dead but that Fleance has escaped. When Macbeth returns to the banquet table, he sees the bloody ghost of Banquo in his place. Lady Macbeth explains her husband's strange behavior as a malady that he has suffered since childhood and tells the guests to ignore him. However, when Macbeth continues to talk about murder and death and to address the apparition, Lady Macbeth dismisses the gathering. Alone, they discuss Macduff's absence from the banquet, and Macbeth plans to consult with the witches the next day. Lady Macbeth attributes his agitation to lack of sleep, Macbeth to his inexperience in violent acts.*]

[*Hall in the Palace.*]

[*Banquet prepared. Enter* Macbeth, Lady Macbeth, Ross, Lennox, Lords, *and* Attendants.]

Macbeth. You know your own degrees,[1] sit down. At first
    And last the hearty welcome.
Lords.   Thanks to your Majesty.
Macbeth. Ourself will mingle with society
    And play the humble host.   5
    Our hostess keeps her state,[2] but in best time
    We will require her welcome.
Lady Macbeth. Pronounce it for me, sir, to all our friends,
    For my heart speaks they are welcome.

[First Murderer *appears at the door.*]

Macbeth. See, they encounter thee with their hearts' thanks.   10
    Both sides are even:[3] here I'll sit i' the midst.
    Be large in mirth;[4] anon we'll drink a measure[5]
    The table round. [*Moves toward* Murderer *at door.*]
    There's blood upon thy face.
Murderer. 'Tis Banquo's then.   15
Macbeth. 'Tis better thee without than he within.
    Is he dispatched?
Murderer. My lord, his throat is cut. That I did for him.
Macbeth. Thou art the best o' the cutthroats! Yet he's good
    That did the like for Fleance. If thou didst it,   20
    Thou art the nonpareil.[6]
Murderer.   Most royal sir,
    Fleance is scaped.
Macbeth. [*Aside*] Then comes my fit again. I had else been perfect;
    Whole as the marble, founded as the rock,   25
    As broad and general[7] as the casing[8] air.
    But now I am cabined, cribbed, confined, bound in
    To saucy doubts and fears.—But Banquo's safe?[9]
Murderer. Ay, my good lord. Safe in a ditch he bides,
    With twenty trenchèd gashes on his head,   30
    The least a death to nature.
Macbeth.   Thanks for that!
    There the grown serpent lies; the worm[10] that's fled
    Hath nature that in time will venom breed,
    No teeth for the present. Get thee gone. Tomorrow   35
    We'll hear ourselves again.[11]

[*Exit* Murderer.]

---

1. **your own degrees:** at a state banquet each guest sits according to his rank.   2. **keeps her state:** sits on her throne apart.   3. **even:** equal.   4. **large in mirth:** unrestrained in your enjoyment.   5. **measure:** toast.   6. **nonpareil:** unequaled.   7. **broad and general:** free and unlimited.   8. **casing:** surrounding.   9. **safe:** no longer to be feared.   10. **worm:** little serpent, i.e., Fleance.   11. **hear . . . again:** speak together.

Roberta Maxwell (Lady Macbeth), Nicholas Pennell (Macbeth)
in *Macbeth*. Stratford Festival, 1983.

Lady Macbeth. My royal lord,
You do not give the cheer. The feast is sold
That is not often vouched, while 'tis a-making,
'Tis given with welcome. To feed were best at home.
From thence, the sauce to meat is ceremony;[12]   40
Meeting were bare without it.

[*Enter the* Ghost of Banquo, *and sits in* Macbeth's *place.*]

Macbeth. Sweet remembrancer!
Now good digestion wait on appetite,
And health on both!   45
Lennox. May't please your Highness sit.
Macbeth. Here had we now our country's honor, roofed,[13]
Were the graced[14] person of our Banquo present;
Who may I rather challenge for unkindness
Than pity for mischance![15]   50

---

12. **feast . . . ceremony:** there is no hospitality at a feast where the guests are not made welcome. Without welcome, it is a mere bought dinner. Ceremony should accompany a feast away from home.   13. **our . . . roofed:** all of the best men in Scotland are under our roof.   14. **graced:** honored.   15. **Who . . . mischance:** whose absence, I hope, is through discourtesy and not because of an accident.

Ross. His absence, sir,
   Lays blame upon his promise. Please't your Highness
   To grace us with your royal company?
Macbeth. The table's full.
Lennox. Here is a place reserved, sir. 55
Macbeth. Where?
Lennox. Here, my good lord. What is't that moves your Highness?
Macbeth. Which of you have done this?
Lords. What, my good lord?
Macbeth. Thou canst not say I did it. Never shake 60
   Thy gory locks at me.
Ross. Gentlemen, rise. His Highness is not well.
Lady Macbeth. Sit, worthy friends. My lord is often thus,
   And hath been from his youth. Pray you keep seat.
   The fit is momentary; upon a thought[16] 65
   He will again be well. If much you note him,
   You shall offend him and extend his passion.[17]
   Feed, and regard him not.—Are you a man?
Macbeth. Ay, and a bold one, that dare look on that
   Which might appal the devil. 70
Lady Macbeth. O proper stuff!
   This is the very painting of your fear.
   This is the air-drawn dagger which you said
   Led you to Duncan. O, these flaws[18] and starts
   (Imposters to true fear)[19] would well become 75
   A woman's story at a winter's fire,
   Authorized by her grandam. Shame itself!
   Why do you make such faces? When all's done,
   You look but on a stool.
Macbeth. Prithee see there! behold! look! lo! How say you? 80
   Why, what care I? If thou canst nod, speak too.
   If charnel houses[20] and our graves must send
   Those that we bury back, our monuments
   Shall be the maws of kites.[21]

                                        [*Ghost vanishes.*]
Lady Macbeth. What, quite unmanned in folly? 85
Macbeth. If I stand here, I saw him.
Lady Macbeth. Fie, for shame!
Macbeth. Blood hath been shed ere now, i' the olden time,
   Ere humane statute purged the gentle weal;[22]

---

16. **upon a thought:** quickly. 17. **passion:** fit. 18. **flaws:** storms of emotion. 19. **Imposters to true fear:** a case of nerves, not fear. 20. **charnel houses:** places where human bones were stored. 21. **maws of kites:** stomachs of birds of prey. 22. **Ere . . . weal:** before humane laws civilized the state.

Ay, and since too, murders have been performed 90
Too terrible for the ear. The time has been
That, when the brains were out, the man would die,
And there an end! But now they rise again,
With twenty mortal murders on their crowns,[23]
And push us from our stools. This is more strange 95
Than such a murder is.
Lady Macbeth.   My worthy lord,
Your noble friends do lack you.
Macbeth.   I do forget.
Do not muse at me, my most worthy friends. 100
I have a strange infirmity, which is nothing
To those that know me. Come, love and health to all!
Then I'll sit down. Give me some wine, fill full.

    [*Reenter* Ghost.]

I drink to the general joy o' the whole table,
And to our dear friend Banquo, whom we miss. 105
Would he were here! To all, and him, we thirst,
And all to all.[24]
Lords.   Our duties, and the pledge.
Macbeth. Avaunt,[25] and quit my sight! Let the earth hide thee!
Thy bones are marrowless, thy blood is cold; 110
Thou hast no speculation[26] in those eyes
Which thou dost glare with!
Lady Macbeth.   Think of this, good peers,
But as a thing of custom. 'Tis no other.
Only it spoils the pleasure of the time. 115
Macbeth. What man dare, I dare.
Approach thou like the rugged Russian bear,
The armed rhinoceros, or the Hyrcan[27] tiger;
Take any shape but that,[28] and my firm nerves
Shall never tremble. Or be alive again 125
And dare me to the desert[29] with thy sword.
If trembling I inhabit[30] then, protest me
The baby of a girl. Hence, horrible shadow!
Unreal mock'ry, hence!
                              [Ghost *vanishes*.] 125
              Why, so! Being gone,
I am a man again. Pray you sit still.

---

23. **twenty . . . crowns:** twenty deadly wounds on their heads.   24. **All . . . all:** I toast all and especially Banquo.
25. **Avaunt:** be gone!   26. **speculation:** power of sight.   27. **Hyrcan:** Hyrcania was a desert area south of the Caspian Sea.
28. **that:** the shape of Banquo.   29. **desert:** a place where neither of us could escape.   30. **inhabit:** stay at home.

Lady Macbeth. You have displaced the mirth, broke the good meeting
    With most admired[31] disorder.
Macbeth.   Can such things be,
    And overcome[32] us like a summer's cloud   130
    Without our special wonder? You make me strange
    Even to the disposition that I owe,[33]
    When now I think you can behold such sights
    And keep the natural ruby of your cheeks
    When mine is blanched with fear.   135
Ross.   What sights, my lord?
Lady Macbeth. I pray you speak not. He grows worse and worse;
    Question enrages him. At once, good night.
    Stand not upon the order of your going,[34]
    But go at once.   140
Lennox.   Good night, and better health
    Attend his Majesty!
Lady Macbeth.   A kind good night to all!

                          [*Exeunt* Lords *and* Attendants.]

Macbeth. It will have blood, they say: blood will have blood.
    Stones have been known to move and trees to speak;   145
    Augures[35] and understood relations[36] have
    By maggot-pies[37] and choughs[38] and rooks brought forth
    The secret'st man of blood.[39] What is the night?
Lady Macbeth. Almost at odds with morning, which is which.
Macbeth. How say'st thou that Macduff denies his person   150
    At our great bidding?
Lady Macbeth.   Did you send to him, sir?
Macbeth. I hear it by the way; but I will send.
    There's not a one of them but in his house
    I keep a servant feed.[40] I will tomorrow   155
    (And betimes I will) to the Weird Sisters.
    More shall they speak; for now I am bent[41] to know
    By the worst means the worst. For mine own good
    All causes shall give way. I am in blood
    Stepped in so far that, should I wade no more,   160
    Returning were as tedious as go o'er.
    Strange things I have in head, that will to hand,
    Which must be acted ere they may be scanned.[42]
Lady Macbeth. You lack the season[43] of all natures, sleep.
Macbeth. Come, we'll to sleep. My strange and self-abuse[44]   165

---

31. **admired:** amazing. 32. **overcome:** come over. 33. **owe:** possess. 34. **Stand . . . going:** dispense with formality in going. 35. **Augures:** omens. 36. **understood relations:** the relation between the omen and what it signifies. 37. **maggot-pies:** magpies. 38. **choughs:** crows. 39. **man of blood:** murderer. 40. **feed:** in my pay as a spy. 41. **bent:** eager. 42. **scanned:** examined. 43. **season:** preservative. 44. **self-abuse:** self-deception.

Is the initiate fear[45] that wants hard use.
We are yet but young in deed.   *[Exeunt.]*

Scene 5

[Scholars believe that this scene was not written by Shakespeare but was a later interpolation from The Witch *by Thomas Middleton. In this scene, Hecate, goddess of sorcery and witchcraft, upbraids the three witches for dealing with Macbeth independently. She orders them to meet her to plan his downfall.]*

[A heath.]

[Thunder. Enter the three Witches, *meeting* Hecate.]

First Witch. Why, how now, Hecate? You look angerly.
Hecate. Have I not reason, beldams[1] as you are,
  Saucy and overbold? How did you dare
  To trade and traffic with Macbeth
  In riddles and affairs of death;   5
  And I, the mistress of your charms,
  The close contriver[2] of all harms,
  Was never called to bear my part
  Or show the glory of our art?
  And, which is worse, all you have done   10
  Hath been but for a wayward son,
  Spiteful and wrathful, who, as others do,
  Loves for his own ends, not for you.
  But make amends now. Get you gone
  And at the pit of Acheron[3]   15
  Meet me i' the morning. Thither he
  Will come to know his destiny.
  Your vessels and your spells provide,
  Your charms and everything beside.
  I am for the air. This night I'll spend   20
  Unto a dismal and a fatal end.
  Great business must be wrought ere noon.
  Upon the corner of the moon
  There hangs a vap'rous drop profound.
  I'll catch it ere it come to ground;   25
  And that, distilled by magic sleights,[4]

---

45. **initiate fear:** novice's fear, i.e., when I have more experience in murder I shall not be troubled with ghosts.
  1. **beldams:** hags. 2. **close contriver:** secret inventor. 3. **Acheron:** Hell. 4. **sleights:** devices.

Shall raise such artificial sprites
As by the strength of their illusion
Shall draw him on to his confusion.[5]
He shall spurn fate, scorn death, and bear   30
His hopes 'bove wisdom, grace,[6] and fear;
And you all know security[7]
Is mortals' chiefest enemy.

[*Music and a song within: "Come away, come away," etc.*]

Hark! I am called. My little spirit, see,
Sits in a foggy cloud and stays for me.   35

[*Exit.*]

First Witch. Come, let's make haste. She'll soon be back again.

[*Exeunt.*]

Scene 6

[*Lennox and another nobleman review the events surrounding the
murders of Duncan and Banquo, suggesting that Macbeth is both
a murderer and a tyrant. They reveal in their conversation that
Macduff has followed Malcolm to the English court of King
Edward, where Macduff is soliciting military aid against Macbeth,
and that Macbeth, angered by Macduff's rebuff of his summons,
also is preparing for war.*]

[*Forres. The Palace.*]

[*Enter* Lennox *and another* Lord.]

Lennox. My former speeches have but hit your thoughts,
Which can interpret farther.[1] Only I say
Things have been strangely borne.[2] The gracious Duncan
Was pitied of Macbeth. Marry,[3] he was dead!
And the right valiant Banquo walked too late;   5
Whom, you may say (if't please you) Fleance killed,
For Fleance fled. Men must not walk too late.
Who cannot want[4] the thought how monstrous
It was for Malcolm and for Donalbain
To kill their gracious father? Damnèd fact!   10
How it did grieve Macbeth! Did he not straight,
In pious rage, the two delinquents tear,
That were the slaves of drink and thralls[5] of sleep?

---

5. **confusion:** destruction. 6. **grace:** virtue. 7. **security:** false sense of safety.
    1. **Which . . . farther:** from which you can draw your own conclusions. 2. **borne:** managed. 3. **Marry:** a mild
oath. 4. **want:** be without. 5. **thralls:** slaves.

Was not that nobly done? Ay, and wisely too!
For 'twould have angered any heart alive   15
To hear the men deny't. So that I say
He has borne all things well; and I do think
That, had he Duncan's sons under his key
(As, an't please heaven, he shall not), they should find
What 'twere to kill a father. So should Fleance.   20
But peace! for from broad words,⁶ and 'cause he failed
His presence at the tyrant's feast, I hear
Macduff lives in disgrace. Sir, can you tell
Where he bestows himself?

Lord.   The son of Duncan,   25
From whom this tyrant holds the due of birth,⁷
Lives in the English court, and is received
Of the most pious Edward⁸ with such grace
That the malevolence of fortune nothing
Takes from his high respect.⁹·Thither Macduff   30
Is gone to pray the holy King upon his aid¹⁰
To wake Northumberland and warlike Siward;
That by the help of these (with Him above
To ratify the work) we may again
Give to our tables meat, sleep to our nights,   35
Free from our feasts and banquets bloody knives,¹¹
Do faithful homage and receive free honors—¹²
All which we pine for now. And this report
Hath so exasperate the King that he
Prepares for some attempt of war.   40

Lennox.   Sent he to Macduff?
Lord. He did; and with an absolute "Sir, not I!"
The cloudy¹³ messenger turns me his back
And hums, as who should say, "You'll rue the time
That clogs¹⁴ me with this answer."   45

Lennox.   And that well might
Advise him to a caution t' hold what distance
His wisdom can provide. Some holy angel
Fly to the court of England and unfold
His message ere he come, that a swift blessing   50
May soon return to this our suffering country
Under a hand accursed!

Lord.   I'll send my prayers with him.

                                                [Exeunt.]

---

6. **broad words:** unguarded talk.   7. **holds . . . birth:** withholds the birthright.   8. **Edward:** King Edward the Confessor,
regarded as a saintly person.   9. **That . . . respect:** in spite of his misfortunes he is held in the highest respect.   10. **upon his
aid:** on behalf of Malcolm.   11. **Free . . . knives:** restore order to the court so banquets no longer are occasions for murder.
12. **free honors:** honors bestowed on free men and not for rewards for crimes.   13. **cloudy:** surly.   14. **clogs:** hinders.

Act Three
Getting at Meaning

Scene 1

1. What hope does Banquo maintain? How is Banquo treated by Macbeth and Lady Macbeth? How does he respond?

2. Why does Macbeth fear Banquo? Does Macbeth truly believe the witches' prophecy? Explain.

3. How does Macbeth persuade the murderers to kill Banquo and Fleance? What is his reason for wanting to keep secret his connection with the murderers?

Scene 2

4. What is ironic about Lady Macbeth's statement, "What's done is done"?

5. Compare and contrast the feelings of Macbeth and Lady Macbeth in this scene. What changes do you perceive in Macbeth?

6. How does Macbeth now feel about Duncan? How do these feelings contrast with his feelings before the murder?

Scene 3

7. Explain the meaning of the murderer's statement, "We have lost/Best half of our affair."

8. How do the images of light and dark function in this scene?

Scene 4

9. How does Macbeth behave at the banquet? What does his behavior suggest about his emotional state? How does Lady Macbeth handle the situation?

10. What is the significance of Fleance's escape?

11. What does Macbeth plan for the day after the banquet? Why? Does he tell Lady Macbeth what he plans to do? What does this suggest about their relationship?

12. Explain the following lines in relation to the development of Macbeth as a character: "I am in blood/Stepped in so far that should I wade no more,/Returning were as tedious as go o'er."

Scene 5

13. Contrast the atmosphere of this scene with that of the preceding scene. Does Scene 5 develop the action of the play? Explain.

Scene 6

14. What specific events and persons are discussed by Lennox and another lord in this scene?

Developing Skills in Reading Literature

1. **Irony.** Verbal irony occurs when a character says one thing but in actuality means something quite different. Discuss the verbal ironies in Lennox's opening speech in Scene 6. Then reread the first forty-four lines of Scene 1. Find examples of irony in these lines.

2. **Conflict.** A conflict in dramatic or narrative literature is a struggle between opposing forces. The conflict that determines the main action of a work is between the protagonist and one or more antagonists. Who or what has emerged as the main antagonist in this play? How then would you describe the primary conflict? What secondary conflicts have developed? Have any of these conflicts been resolved? Explain.

3. **Rising Action, Climax, and Falling Action.** The climax is the point of highest suspense in a play, the point at which the fortunes of the protagonist are at their height. In a tragedy the climax generally occurs in the third act. The events that build to the climax constitute the rising action. The decline in the fortunes of the protagonist after the climax is called the falling action. What is the climax in *Macbeth*? Give reasons for your answer, and quote lines that suggest a shift in Macbeth's fortunes. What events lead up to the climax? What speeches and events in Act Three begin the falling action?

Developing Writing Skills

1. **Analyzing Scenes.** In the dagger scene and the banquet scene, Macbeth experiences hallucinations. Consider the circumstances that precede each scene. Then compare and contrast the two scenes in a well developed essay.

2. **Supporting an Opinion.** In Scene 3 a third murderer appears. The identity of that murderer is an enigma of *Macbeth*, speculated about by scholars but never established with any certainty. Who do you think is the third murderer? Write an essay explaining your choice.

Act Four

Scene 1

[*The three witches prepare a potion in a boiling cauldron. At Macbeth's request, they conjure up three apparitions. The first, an armed head, warns Macbeth to be wary of Macduff. Next, a bloody child assures Macbeth that no one born of woman can harm him. Then a child wearing a crown and holding a tree tells him that he will not be defeated until Birnam Wood moves to Dunsinane Hill. Macbeth demands to know whether Banquo's descendants will be the kings of Scotland. His answer is a procession of eight kings, with a final vision of Banquo pointing to the line. Lennox tells Macbeth that Macduff has fled to England, and Macbeth resolves to slaughter the rebel's family.*]

[*A cavern. In the middle, a boiling cauldron.*]

[*Thunder. Enter the three* Witches.]

First Witch. Thrice the brinded[1] cat hath mewed.
Second Witch. Thrice, and once the hedge-pig whined.
Third Witch. Harpier[2] cries; 'tis time, 'tis time.
First Witch. Round about the cauldron go;
  In the poisoned entrails throw. 5
  Toad, that under cold stone
  Days and nights has thirty-one
  Swelt'red venom sleeping got,
  Boil thou first i' the charmed pot.
All. Double, double, toil and trouble; 10
  Fire burn, and cauldron bubble.
Second Witch. Fillet of a fenny snake,[3]
  In the cauldron boil and bake;
  Eye of newt, and toe of frog,
  Wool of bat, and tongue of dog, 15
  Adder's fork, and blindworm's[4] sting,
  Lizard's leg, and howlet's[5] wing;
  For a charm of pow'rful trouble
  Like a hell-broth boil and bubble.
All. Double, double, toil and trouble; 20
  Fire burn, and cauldron bubble.
Third Witch. Scale of dragon, tooth of wolf,
  Witch's mummy,[6] maw and gulf[7]

---

1. **brinded:** striped. 2. **Harpier:** the Third Witch's evil spirit. 3. **fenny snake:** snake from a marsh. 4. **blindworm:** small, legless lizard. 5. **howlet:** small owl. 6. **Witch's mummy:** part of a mummified body. 7. **maw and gulf:** belly and gullet.

Of the ravined[8] salt-sea shark,
Root of hemlock, digged i' the dark;[9]   25
Liver of blaspheming Jew,
Gall of goat, and slips of yew
Slivered in the moon's eclipse;
Nose of Turk and Tartar's lips;
Finger of birth-strangled babe   30
Ditch-delivered by a drab:[10]
Make the gruel thick and slab.[11]
Add thereto a tiger's chaudron[12]
For the ingredience of our cauldron.
All. Double, double, toil and trouble;   35
Fire burn, and cauldron bubble.
Second Witch. Cool it with a baboon's blood,
Then the charm is firm and good.

[*Enter* Hecate, *to the other three* Witches.]

Hecate. O, well done! I commend your pains,
And every one shall share i' the gains.   40
And now about the cauldron sing
Like elves and fairies in a ring,
Enchanting all that you put in.

[*Music and a song: "Black spirit," etc. Exit* Hecate.]

Second Witch. By the pricking of my thumbs,
Something wicked this way comes.   45
Open locks,
Whoever knocks!

[*Enter* Macbeth.]

Macbeth. How now, you secret, black, and midnight hags?
What is't you do?
All.   A deed without a name.   50
Macbeth. I conjure you by that which you profess[13]
(Howe'er you come to know it), answer me.
Though you untie the winds and let them fight
Against the churches; though the yesty[14] waves
Confound[15] and swallow navigation up;   55
Though bladed corn be lodged[16] and trees blown down;
Though castles topple on their warders' heads;

---

8. **ravined:** voracious. 9. **digged i' the dark:** dug at night. Midnight was the best time to gather herbs for magical uses. 10. **drab:** whore. 11. **slab:** like thick mud. 12. **chaudron:** entrails. 13. **by . . . profess:** by your witchcraft. 14. **yesty:** foaming. 15. **Confound:** destroy. 16. **bladed . . . lodged:** ripe corn be beaten flat.

Though palaces and pyramids do slope
Their heads to their foundations; though the treasure
Of nature's germens[17] tumble all together,   60
Even till destruction sicken—answer me
To what I ask you.
First Witch.   Speak.
Second Witch.   Demand.
Third Witch.   We'll answer.   65
First Witch. Say, if th' hadst rather hear it from our mouths
Or from our masters.
Macbeth.   Call 'em! Let me see 'em.
First Witch. Pour in sow's blood, that hath eaten
Her nine farrow;[18] grease that's sweaten   70
From the murderer's gibbet[19] throw
Into the flame.
All.   Come, high or low;
Thyself and office[20] deftly show!

[*Thunder.* First Apparition: *an* Armed Head.[21]]

---

17. **germens:** seeds. 18. **farrow:** offspring. 19. **gibbet:** gallows where bodies of executed criminals were left hanging as a warning. 20. **office:** function. 21. **Armed Head:** symbol of Macduff.

Nicholas Pennell (Macbeth), Seana McKenna, Paddy Companaro, Elizabeth Leigh-Milne (Witches) in *Macbeth.* Stratford Festival, 1983.

Macbeth. Tell me, thou unknown power—   75
First Witch.   He knows thy thought.
   Hear his speech, but say thou naught.
First Apparition. Macbeth! Macbeth! Macbeth! Beware Macduff;
   Beware the Thane of Fife. Dismiss me. Enough.

                                         [He descends.]

Macbeth. Whate'er thou art, for thy good caution thanks!   80
   Thou hast harped[22] my fear aright. But one word more—
First Witch. He will not be commanded. Here's another,
   More potent than the first.

         [Thunder. Second Apparition: a Bloody Child.[23]]

Second Apparition. Macbeth! Macbeth! Macbeth!
Macbeth. Had I three ears, I'ld hear thee.   85
Second Apparition. Be bloody, bold, and resolute; laugh to scorn
   The pow'r of man, for none of woman born
   Shall harm Macbeth.

                                            [Descends.]

Macbeth. Then live, Macduff. What need I fear of thee?
   But yet I'll make assurance double sure   90
   And take a bond of fate.[24] Thou shalt not live!
   That I may tell pale-hearted fear it lies
   And sleep in spite of thunder.

    [Thunder. Third Apparition: a Child Crowned,[25] *with a tree in his hand.]*

                              What is this
   That rises like the issue of a king   95
   And wears upon his baby-brow the round
   And top of sovereignty?[26]
All.   Listen, but speak not to't.
Third Apparition. Be lion-mettled, proud, and take no care
   Who chafes, who frets, or where conspirers are.   100
   Macbeth shall never vanquished be until
   Great Birnam Wood to high Dunsinane Hill
   Shall come against him.

                                            [Descends.]

Macbeth.   That will never be.
   Who can impress[27] the forest, bid the tree   105
   Unfix his earth-bound root? Sweet bodements,[28] good!
   Rebellious dead rise never till the Wood
   Of Birnam rise, and our high-placed Macbeth

---

22. **harped:** hit upon. 23. **Bloody Child:** Macduff at birth. 24. **bond of fate:** force fate to keep the agreement. 25. **Child Crowned:** symbol of Malcolm. 26. **round . . . sovereignty:** crown. 27. **impress:** conscript. 28. **bodements:** prophecies.

Shall live the lease of nature,[29] pay his breath
To time and mortal custom. Yet my heart   110
Throbs to know one thing. Tell me, if your art
Call tell so much—shall Banquo's issue ever
Reign in this kingdom?
All.   Seek to know no more.
Macbeth. I will be satisfied. Deny me this,   115
And an eternal curse fall on you! Let me know.
Why sinks that cauldron? and what noise[30] is this?

[*Hautboys.*]

First Witch. Show!
Second Witch. Show!
Third Witch. Show!   120
All. Show his eyes, and grieve his heart!
Come like shadows, so depart!

[*A show of eight Kings,*[31] *the last with a glass*[32] *in his hand; Banquo's ghost*
following.]

Macbeth. Thou art too like the spirit of Banquo. Down!
Thy crown does sear mine eyeballs. And thy hair,
Thou other gold-bound brow, is like the first.   125
A third is like the former. Filthy hags!
Why do you show me this? A fourth? Start, eyes!
What, will the line stretch out to the crack of doom?
Another yet? A seventh? I'll see no more.
And yet the eighth appears, who bears a glass   130
Which shows me many more; and some I see
That twofold balls and treble scepters[33] carry.
Horrible sight! Now I see 'tis true;
For the blood-boltered[34] Banquo smiles upon me
And points at them for his. [*Apparitions* vanish] What? Is this so? 135
First Witch. Ay, sir, all this is so. But why
Stands Macbeth thus amazedly?
Come, sisters, cheer we up his sprites[35]
And show the best of our delights.
I'll charm the air to give a sound   140
While you perform your antic round,[36]
That this great king may kindly say
Our duties did his welcome pay.

[*Music. The* Witches *dance, and vanish.*]

---

29. **lease of nature:** his natural span of life. 30. **noise:** a common word for music. 31. **A . . . Kings:** a dumb show, figures
passing silently across the back of the stage. 32. **glass:** mirror. 33. **twofold . . . scepters:** the insignia of Ireland, Scotland,
and England, united in 1603 when Scotland's James VI (descended from Banquo) became James I of England.
34. **blood-boltered:** hair matted with blood. 35. **sprites:** spirits. 36. **antic round:** fantastic dance.

Macbeth. Where are they? Gone? Let this pernicious hour
   Stand aye accursèd in the calendar!   145
   Come in, without there!

   [Enter Lennox.]

Lennox. What's your Grace's will?
Macbeth. Saw you the Weird Sisters?
Lennox.   No, my lord.
Macbeth. Came they not by you?   150
Lennox.   No indeed, my lord.
Macbeth. Infected be the air whereon they ride,
   And damned all those that trust them! I did hear
   The galloping of horse. Who was't came by?
Lennox. 'Tis two or three, my lord, that bring you word   155
   Macduff is fled to England.
Macbeth.   Fled to England?
Lennox. Ay, my good lord.
Macbeth. *[Aside]* Time, thou anticipat'st my dread exploits.
   The flighty purpose never is o'ertook   160
   Unless the deed go with it.[37] From this moment
   The very firstlings[38] of my heart shall be
   The firstlings of my hand. And even now,
   To crown my thoughts with acts, be it thought and done!
   The castle of Macduff I will surprise,   165
   Seize upon Fife, give to the edge o' the sword
   His wife, his babes, and all unfortunate souls
   That trace[39] him in his line. No boasting like a fool!
   This deed I'll do before this purpose cool.
   But no more sights!—Where are these gentlemen?   170
   Come, bring me where they are.

                              [Exeunt.]

Scene 2   *[Ross visits his kinswoman Lady Macduff and assures her of her*
                   husband's wisdom and courage. Lady Macduff, still believing that
                   Macduff deserted his family out of fear, tells her son that his
                   father was a traitor who is now dead. A messenger warns Lady
                   Macduff to flee, but she has no time to act on his warning. The
                   murderers sent by Macbeth stab Macduff's son and prepare to kill
                   the rest of the family.]

---

37. **The . . . it:** the plan is never fulfilled unless carried out immediately. 38. **firstlings:** first fruits. 39. **trace:** follow.

[*Fife. Macduff's Castle.*]

[*Enter* Lady Macduff, *her* Son, *and* Ross.]

Lady Macduff. What had he done to make him fly the land?
Ross. You must have patience, madam.
Lady Macduff.   He had none.
  His flight was madness. When our actions do not,
  Our fears do make us traitors.   5
Ross.   You know not
  Whether it was his wisdom or his fear.
Lady Macduff. Wisdom? To leave his wife, to leave his babes,
  His mansion, and his titles,[1] in a place
  From whence himself does fly? He loves us not,   10
  He wants the natural touch.[2] For the poor wren,
  (The most diminutive of birds) will fight,
  Her young ones in her nest, against the owl.
  All is the fear, and nothing is the love,
  As little is the wisdom, where the flight   15
  So runs against all reason.

---

1. **titles:** possessions.   2. **He . . . touch:** lacks the natural instinct to protect his family.

Mary Haney (Lady Macduff), Joel Silver (Macduff's son),
Shaun Austin-Olsen (Ross) in *Macbeth.* Stratford Festival, 1983.

Ross.   My dearest coz,[3]
I pray you school[4] yourself. But for your husband,
He is noble, wise, judicious, and best knows
The fits o' the season.[5] I dare not speak much further;   20
But cruel are the times, when we are traitors
And do not know ourselves;[6] when we hold rumor
From what we fear, yet know not what we fear,[7]
But float upon a wild and violent sea
Each way and move[8]—I take my leave of you.   25
Shall not be long but I'll be here again.
Things at the worst will cease, or else climb upward
To what they were before.—My pretty cousin,
Blessing upon you!
Lady Macduff. Fathered he is, and yet he's fatherless.   30
Ross. I am so much a fool, should I stay longer,
It would be my disgrace and your discomfort.
I take my leave at once.

                                                             [*Exit.*]

Lady Macduff.   Sirrah, your father's dead;
And what will you do now? How will you live?   35
Son. As birds do, mother.
Lady Macduff.   What, with worms and flies?
Son. With what I get, I mean; and so do they.
Lady Macduff. Poor bird! thou'dst never fear the net nor lime,[9]
The pitfall nor the gin.[10]   40
Son. Why should I, mother? Poor birds they are not set for.[11]
My father is not dead, for all your saying.
Lady Macduff. Yes, he is dead. How wilt thou do for a father?
Son. Nay, how will you do for a husband?
Lady Macduff. Why, I can buy me twenty at any market.   45
Son. Then you'll buy 'em to sell[12] again.
Lady Macduff. Thou speak'st with all thy wit; and yet, i' faith,
With wit enough for thee.[13]
Son. Was my father a traitor, mother?
Lady Macduff. Ay, that he was!   50
Son. What is a traitor?
Lady Macduff. Why, one that swears, and lies.
Son. And be all traitors that do so?
Lady Macduff. Every one that does so is a traitor and must be hanged.
Son. And must they all be hanged that swear and lie?   55
Lady Macduff. Every one.

---

3. **coz:** cousin. 4. **school:** control. 5. **fits . . . season:** sudden changes in the times. 6. **when . . . ourselves:** we are treated as traitors for no reason. 7. **when . . . fear:** believe our fears. 8. **But . . . move:** like a powerless ship in a storm, tossed from here to there. 9. **lime:** birdlime, a sticky substance used to trap birds. 10. **gin:** snare. 11. **Poor . . . for:** no one sets a trap for a poor bird. 12. **sell:** betray. 13. **wit . . . thee:** a great deal of intelligence in so young a child.

Son. Who must hang them?

Lady Macduff. Why, the honest men.

Son. Then the liars and swearers are fools; for there are liars and swearers enow[14]
    to beat the honest men and hang up them. 60

Lady Macduff. Now God help thee, poor monkey!
    But how wilt thou do for a father?

Son. If he were dead, you'ld weep for him. If you would not, it were a good sign
    that I should quickly have a new father.

Lady Macduff. Poor prattler, how thou talk'st! 65

[*Enter a* Messenger.]

Messenger. Bless you, fair dame! I am not to you known,
    Though in your state of honor I am perfect.[15]
    I doubt[16] some danger does approach you nearly.
    If you will take a homely[17] man's advice,
    Be not found here. Hence with your little ones! 70
    To fright you thus methinks I am too savage;
    To do worse to you were fell[18] cruelty,
    Which is too nigh your person. Heaven preserve you!
    I dare abide no longer.

                                                       [*Exit.*]

Lady Macduff.   Whither should I fly? 75
    I have done no harm. But I remember now
    I am in this earthly world, where to do harm
    Is often laudable, to do good sometime
    Accounted dangerous folly. Why then, alas,
    Do I put up that womanly defense 80
    To say I have done no harm?—What are these faces?

[*Enter* Murderers.]

Murderers. Where is your husband?

Lady Macduff. I hope, in no place so unsanctified
    Where such as thou mayst find him.

Murderers.   He's a traitor. 85

Son. Thou liest, thou shag-eared villain![19]

Murderers.   What, you egg![20] [*Stabbing him.*]
    Young fry[21] of treachery!

Son.   He has killed me, mother.
    Run away, I pray you! 90

                                      [*Dies.*]
    [*Exit* Lady Macduff, *crying "Murder!" followed by* Murderers.]

---

14. **enow:** enough. 15. **Though . . . perfect:** I know you to be an honorable person. 16. **doubt:** fear. 17. **homely:**
simple. 18. **fell:** fierce. 19. **shag-eared:** hairy-eared. 20. **egg:** unhatched traitor. 21. **fry:** spawn.

Scene 3

[*Macduff tries to persuade Malcolm to seize the throne of Scotland, describing vividly the deplorable condition of the country under the tyrannical Macbeth. At first Malcolm mistrusts Macduff's motives. However, he eventually is convinced of Macduff's integrity and informs him that Siward, Earl of Northumberland, already has dispatched ten thousand troops to Scotland. Ross then tells Macduff of the slaughter of his family. Wild with grief, Macduff swears to avenge their murders.*]

[*England. Before the King's Palace.*]

[*Enter* Malcolm *and* Macduff.]

Malcolm. Let us seek out some desolate shade, and there
    Weep our sad bosoms empty.
Macduff.   Let us rather
    Hold fast the mortal[1] sword and, like good men,
    Bestride our downfall'n birthdom.[2] Each new morn   5
    New widows howl, new orphans cry, new sorrows
    Strike heaven on the face, that it resounds
    As if it felt with Scotland and yelled out
    Like syllable of dolor.[3]
Malcolm.   What I believe, I'll wail;   10
    What know, believe; and what I can redress,
    As I shall find the time to friend,[4] I will.
    What you have spoke, it may be so perchance.
    This tyrant, whose sole[5] name blisters our tongues,
    Was once thought honest;[6] you have loved him well;   15
    He hath not touched you yet. I am young; but something
    You may discern of him through me, and wisdom[7]
    To offer up a weak, poor, innocent lamb
    T' appease an angry god.
Macduff. I am not treacherous.   20
Malcolm.   But Macbeth is.
    A good and virtuous nature may recoil
    In an imperial charge.[8] But I shall crave your pardon.
    That which you are, my thoughts cannot transpose.
    Angels are bright still, though the brightest[9] fell.   25
    Though all things foul would wear the brows of grace,
    Yet grace must still look so.[10]
Macduff.   I have lost my hopes.
Malcolm. Perchance even there where I did find my doubts.

---

1. **mortal:** deadly. 2. **Bestride . . . birthdom:** fight to protect our country. 3. **Like . . . dolor:** even the heavens resound as if echoing the cries of Scotland. 4. **the time to friend:** time to be friendly. 5. **sole:** very. 6. **honest:** honorable.
7. **You . . . wisdom:** by betraying me to him you might think it wise. 8. **A . . . charge:** even a good man may degenerate and do wicked deeds if ordered by a King. 9. **the brightest:** Lucifer. 10. **still look so:** still appear as goodness.

Why in that rawness[11] left you wife and child,   30
Those precious motives,[12] those strong knots of love,
Without leave-taking? I pray you,
Let not my jealousies be your dishonors,
But mine own safeties.[13] You may be rightly just,
Whatever I shall think.   35
Macduff.   Bleed, bleed, poor country!
Great tyranny, lay thou thy basis sure,
For goodness dare not check thee! Wear thou thy wrongs;
The title is affeered![14] Fare thee well, lord.
I would not be the villain that thou think'st   40
For the whole space that's in the tyrant's grasp
And the rich East to boot.
Malcolm.   Be not offended.
I speak not as in absolute fear of you.
I think our country sinks beneath the yoke;   45
It weeps, it bleeds, and each new day a gash
Is added to her wounds. I think withal
There would be hands uplifted in my right;
And here from gracious England[15] have I offer
Of goodly thousands. But, for all this,   50
When I shall tread upon the tyrant's head
Or wear it on my sword, yet my poor country
Shall have more vices than it had before,
More suffer and more sundry ways than ever,
By him that shall succeed.   55
Macduff.   What should he be?
Malcolm. It is myself I mean; in whom I know
All the particulars of vice so grafted
That, when they shall be opened, black Macbeth
Will seem as pure as snow, and the poor state   60
Esteem him as a lamb, being compared
With my confineless[16] harms.
Macduff.   Not in the legions
Of horrid hell can come a devil more damned
In evils to top Macbeth.   65
Malcolm.   I grant him bloody,
Luxurious,[17] avaricious, false, deceitful,
Sudden, malicious, smacking of every sin
That has a name. But there's no bottom, none,
In my voluptuousness.[18] Your wives, your daughters,   70
Your matrons, and your maids could not fill up

---

11. **rawness:** unprotected state. 12. **motives:** inspirations. 13. **Let . . . safeties:** my suspicions are not meant to insult you, but rather to protect me. 14. **The . . . affeered:** legal right is confirmed. 15. **gracious England:** the English King, Edward the Confessor. 16. **confineless:** unlimited. 17. **Luxurious:** lustful. 18. **voluptuousness:** lust.

The cistern of my lust; and my desire
All continent impediments[19] would o'erbear
That did oppose my will. Better Macbeth
Than such an one to reign.   75
Macduff.   Boundless intemperance
In nature is a tyranny. It hath been
The untimely emptying of the happy throne
And fall of many kings. But fear not yet
To take upon you what is yours. You may   80
Convey your pleasures in a spacious plenty,[20]
And yet seem cold[21]—the time you may so hoodwink.
We have willing dames enough. There cannot be
That vulture in you to devour so many
As will to greatness dedicate themselves,   85
Finding it so inclined.
Malcolm.   With this there grows
In my most ill-composed affection[22] such
A stanchless[23] avarice that, were I King,
I should cut off the nobles for their lands,
Desire his jewels, and this other's house,   90
And my more-having would be as a sauce
To make me hunger more, that I should forge[24]
Quarrels unjust against the good and loyal,
Destroying them for wealth.
Macduff.   This avarice   95
Sticks deeper, grows with more pernicious root
Than summer-seeming[25] lust; and it hath been
The sword of[26] our slain kings. Yet do not fear.
Scotland hath foisons[27] to fill up your will   100
Of your mere own.[28] All these are portable,[29]
With other graces weighed.
Malcolm. But I have none. The king-becoming graces,
As justice, verity, temp'rance, stableness,
Bounty, perseverance, mercy, lowliness,   105
Devotion, patience, courage, fortitude,
I have no relish of them, but abound
In the division of each several crime,
Acting it many ways. Nay, had I pow'r, I should
Pour the sweet milk of concord into hell,   110
Uproar the universal peace, confound
All unity on earth.

---

19. **continent impediments:** restraints. 20. **Convey . . . plenty:** find plenty of room in which to indulge your pleasures secretly. 21. **cold:** chaste. 22. **affection:** disposition. 23. **stanchless:** insatiable. 24. **forge:** fabricate. 25. **summer-seeming:** which lasts for only the summer season. 26. **sword of:** which has killed. 27. **foisons:** plenty. 28. **mere own:** own property. 29. **portable:** bearable.

Macduff.   O Scotland, Scotland!

Malcolm. If such a one be fit to govern, speak.
I am as I have spoken.   115

Macduff.   Fit to govern?
No, not to live. O nation miserable,
With an untitled[30] tyrant bloody-scept'red,
When shalt thou see thy wholesome days again,
Since that the truest issue of thy throne   120
By his own interdiction[31] stands accursed
And does blaspheme his breed?[32] Thy royal father
Was a most sainted king; the queen that bore thee,
Oft'ner upon her knees than on her feet,
Died every day she lived.[33] Fare thee well!   125
These evils thou repeat'st upon thyself
Have banished me from Scotland. O my breast,
Thy hope ends here!

Malcolm.   Macduff, this noble passion,
Child of integrity, hath from my soul   130
Wiped the black scruples, reconciled my thoughts
To thy good truth and honor. Devilish Macbeth
By many of these trains[34] hath sought to win me
Into his power; and modest wisdom plucks me
From over-credulous haste; but God above   135
Deal between thee and me! for even now
I put myself to thy direction and
Unspeak mine own detraction, here abjure
The taints and blames I laid upon myself
For strangers to my nature. I am yet   140
Unknown to woman, never was forsworn,[35]
Scarcely have coveted what was mine own,
At no time broke my faith, would not betray
The devil to his fellow, and delight
No less in truth than life. My first false speaking   145
Was this upon myself. What I am truly,
Is thine and my poor country's to command;
Whither indeed, before thy here-approach,
Old Siward with ten thousand warlike men
Already at a point[36] was setting forth.   150
Now we'll together; and the chance of goodness
Be like our warranted quarrel![37] Why are you silent?

Macduff. Such welcome and unwelcome things at once
'Tis hard to reconcile.

---

30. **untitled:** having no legal right to be king. 31. **interdiction:** exclusion. 32. **blaspheme his breed:** slander his ancestors.
33. **Died . . . lived:** lived continually in a state of grace. 34. **trains:** enticements. 35. **was forsworn:** broke my oath.
36. **at a point:** ready for action. 37. **the chance . . . quarrel:** may our chance of good luck equal the justice of our cause.

[*Enter a* Doctor.]

Malcolm. Well, more anon. Comes the King forth, I pray you?   155
Doctor. Ay, sir. There are a crew of wretched souls
    That stay his cure.[38] Their malady convinces
    The great assay of art;[39] but at his touch,
    Such sanctity hath heaven given his hand,
    They presently amend.   160
Malcolm.   I thank you, doctor.

                                       [*Exit* Doctor.]

Macduff. What's the disease he means?
Malcolm.   'Tis called the evil:[40]
    A most miraculous work in this good king,
    Which often since my here-remain in England   165
    I have seen him do. How he solicits heaven
    Himself best knows; but strangely-visited people,
    All swol'n[41] and ulcerous, pitiful to the eye,
    The mere[42] despair of surgery, he cures,
    Hanging a golden stamp[43] about their necks,   170
    Put on with holy prayers; and 'tis spoken,
    To the succeeding royalty he leaves
    The healing benediction. With this strange virtue,
    He hath a heavenly gift of prophecy,
    And sundry blessings hang about his throne   175
    That speak him full of grace.

[*Enter* Ross.]

Macduff.   See who comes here.
Malcolm. My countryman; but yet I know him not.
Macduff. My ever gentle[44] cousin, welcome hither.
Malcolm. I know him now. Good God betimes[45] remove   180
    The means[46] that makes us strangers!
Ross.   Sir, amen.
Macduff. Stands Scotland where it did?
Ross.   Alas, poor country,
    Almost afraid to know itself! It cannot   185
    Be called our mother, but our grave; where nothing,
    But who knows nothing, is once seen to smile;
    Where sighs and groans, and shrieks that rent the air,
    Are made, not marked;[47] where violent sorrow seems

---

38. **stay his cure:** wait for him to cure them. 39. **convinces . . . art:** defeats medicine's best efforts. 40. **the evil:** scrofula, a skin disease. Edward the Confessor used to help those afflicted by touching them, which he was believed to have bequeathed to his successors. 41. **swol'n:** swollen. 42. **mere:** absolute. 43. **stamp:** medal. 44. **gentle:** noble. 45. **betimes:** soon. 46. **The means:** Macbeth, the cause of our separation. 47. **made, not marked:** so common as to be unnoticed.

A modern ecstasy.[48] The dead man's knell
Is there scarce asked for who; and good men's lives
Expire before the flowers in their caps,
Dying or ere they sicken.[49]

Macduff.   O, relation
Too nice,[50] and yet too true!

Malcolm.   What's the newest grief?

Ross. That of an hour's age doth hiss the speaker;[51]
Each minute teems[52] a new one.

Macduff.   How does my wife?

Ross. Why, well.

Macduff.   And all my children?

Ross.   Well too.

Macduff. The tyrant has not battered at their peace?

Ross. No, they were well at peace when I did leave 'em.

Macduff. Be not a niggard[53] of your speech. How goes't?

Ross. When I came hither to transport the tidings
Which I have heavily[54] borne, there ran a rumor
Of many worthy fellows that were out;[55]
Which was to my belief witnessed[56] the rather
For that I saw the tyrant's power[57] afoot.
Now is the time of help. Your eye in Scotland
Would create soldiers, make our women fight
To doff[58] their dire distresses.

Malcolm.   Be't their comfort
We are coming thither. Gracious England hath
Lent us good Siward and ten thousand men.
An older and a better soldier none
That Christendom gives out.

Ross.   Would I could answer
This comfort with the like! But I have words
That would be howled out in the desert air,
Where hearing should not latch[59] them.

Macduff.   What concern they?
The general cause? or is it a fee-grief[60]
Due to some single breast?

Ross.   No mind that's honest
But in it shares some woe, though the main part
Pertains to you alone.

Macduff.   If it be mine,
Keep it not from me, quickly let me have it.

190

195

200

205

210

215

220

225

230

---

48. **modern ecstasy:** ordinary emotion.   49. **or . . . sicken:** before they are sick, i.e., unnatural deaths of violence.   50. **nice:** exact.   51. **That . . . speaker:** earns the teller nothing but hisses for repeating an old story.   52. **teems:** gives birth to. 53. **niggard:** sparing.   54. **heavily:** sorrowfully.   55. **out:** in rebellion.   56. **witnessed:** confirmed.   57. **power:** army. 58. **doff:** put off.   59. **latch:** catch.   60. **fee-grief:** private sorrow.

Ross. Let not your ears despise my tongue for ever,
    Which shall possess them with the heaviest[61] sound
    That ever yet they heard.
Macduff.   Humh! I guess at it.
Ross. Your castle is surprised; your wife and babes   235
    Savagely slaughtered. To relate the manner
    Were, on the quarry[62] of these murdered deer,
    To add the death of you.
Malcolm.   Merciful heaven!
    What man! Ne'er pull your hat upon your brows.   240
    Give sorrow words. The grief that does not speak
    Whispers the o'erfraught heart[63] and bids it break.
Macduff. My children too?
Ross.   Wife, children, servants, all
    That could be found.   245
Macduff.   And I must be from thence?
    My wife killed too?
Ross.   I have said.
Malcolm.   Be comforted.
    Let's make us med'cines of our great revenge   250
    To cure this deadly grief.
Macduff. He has no children. All my pretty ones?
    Did you say all? O hell-kite! All?
    What, all my pretty chickens and their dam
    At one fell swoop?   255
Malcolm. Dispute it[64] like a man.
Macduff.   I shall do so;
    But I must also feel it as a man.
    I cannot but remember such things were
    That were most precious to me. Did heaven look on   260
    And would not take their part? Sinful Macduff,
    They were all struck for thee! Naught[65] that I am,
    Not for their own demerits, but for mine,
    Fell slaughter on their souls. Heaven rest them now!
Malcolm. Be this the whetstone of your sword. Let grief   265
    Convert to anger; blunt not the heart, enrage it.
Macduff. O, I could play the woman with mine eyes
    And braggart with my tongue! But, gentle heavens,
    Cut short all intermission. Front to front[66]
    Bring thou this fiend of Scotland and myself.   270
    Within my sword's length set him. If he scape,
    Heaven forgive him too!

---

61. **heaviest:** saddest.   62. **quarry:** heap of slain deer after the hunt.   63. **o'erfraught:** overladen.   64. **Dispute it:** strive
against.   65. **Naught:** worthless.   66. **Front to front:** face to face.

Malcolm.   This tune goes manly.
    Come, go we to the King. Our power is ready;
    Our lack is nothing but our leave.[67] Macbeth   275
    Is ripe for shaking, and the pow'rs above
    Put on their instruments.[68] Receive what cheer you may.
    The night is long that never finds the day.

                                                          [Exeunt.]

---

67. **Our . . . leave:** all we need is the King's permission to go.   68. **Put . . . instruments:** prepare for action.

Act Four

Getting at Meaning

Scene 1

1. What is Macbeth's attitude toward the witches? How does this attitude contrast with that shown by Macbeth in his first encounter with them? What does this change in attitude show about the deterioration of his character?

2. How does Macbeth react to each apparition that the witches conjure up?

3. How is Macbeth changing, as indicated by the passage in which he orders the murder of Macduff's family?

Scene 2

4. In her conversations with Ross and with her son, of what does Lady Macduff accuse her husband?

5. How does the dialogue between Lady Macduff and her son intensify reader response to their murders?

6. How is Lady Macduff similar to Lady Macbeth? different from Lady Macbeth?

Scene 3

7. What qualities of leadership does Malcolm reveal in his encounter with Macduff? How does Malcolm test Macduff?

8. What is the significance of the scene in which a doctor describes King Edward's power of healing?

9. How does Macduff respond to the news of his family's massacre?

Developing Skills in Reading Literature

Unity. Unity refers to the harmonious blend of elements in a literary work and also to the internal consistency of elements such as mood, tone, character, and language. If part of a work is written in a different style, if a character behaves inexplicably, or if any element is even subtly incongruous with the rest of the work, the unity of that work suffers. An interpolation into an existing work by another writer nearly always violates unity in some way, for few writers can duplicate perfectly another's unique style, and a well constructed work is complete unto itself.

Most modern critics believe that Act Three, Scene 5 and the speeches of Hecate, lines 75 and 76, and lines 140–147 in Act Four, Scene 1, were not written by Shakespeare but by Thomas Middleton. In fact, the song in Act Three, Scene 5, appears in *The Witch* by Middleton. Examine carefully this interpolated material, and contrast these passages with other scenes involving the witches. Discuss the differences, answering these questions as you do so: Do the interpolated passages advance the action of the play? Are they consistent with the mood that Shakespeare has created? What differences in style do you note? Assess the impact of the interpolated passages on the unity of the play. Do the passages disrupt the play in any significant way? Explain.

Developing Vocabulary

Understanding Changes in Language. Following are listed twenty-eight words, along with the definitions that appear in the footnotes for Acts One through Four. The meanings of some of these words have changed drastically since the early seventeenth century. For other words, the meanings used by Shakespeare are now antiquated or less common, although these meanings still are included in dictionary entries. Give the most common contemporary definition for each word, using a dictionary if necessary. For words whose meanings have changed significantly, note any relationship between the older and the more contemporary meanings.

1. reeking: steaming
2. lavish: undisciplined
3. forbid: under a curse
4. peak: grow thin
5. owe: own
7. free: frank
6. line: support
8. illness: wickedness
9. single: weak
10. convince: overcome
11. quell: murder
12. sensible: tangible
13. palpable: clear
14. abuse: deceive
15. confounds: destroys
16. pretense: purpose
17. sore: terrible
18. pretend: intend
19. ecstasy: madness
20. measure: toast
21. passion: fit
22. flaws: storms of emotion
23. confusion: destruction
24. cloudy: surly
25. homely: simple
26. luxurious: lustful
27. mere: absolute
28. nice: exact

Now, examine the footnotes for Acts One through Four, and identify words that are no longer used in contemporary speech and writing or that have changed notably in spelling. Suggest words that are now used in their place.

Act Five

Scene 1   *[A sleepwalking Lady Macbeth is observed by a concerned gentlewoman and a doctor. Lady Macbeth appears to be washing her hands of imagined blood. She talks incoherently of the murdered Duncan, Lady Macduff, and Banquo. The doctor concludes that Lady Macbeth needs spiritual not medical help and suggests that the gentlewoman watch her carefully.]*

[*Dunsinane. Macbeth's Castle.*]

[*Enter a* Doctor of Physic *and a* Waiting Gentlewoman.]

Doctor. I have two nights watched with you, but can perceive no truth in your report. When was it she last walked?

Gentlewoman. Since his Majesty went into the field¹ I have seen her rise from her bed, throw her nightgown upon her, unlock her closet,² take forth paper, fold it, write upon't, read it, afterwards seal it, and again return to bed; yet all this while   5 in a most fast sleep.

Doctor. A great perturbation in nature, to receive at once the benefit of sleep and do the effects of watching!³ In this slumb'ry agitation, besides her walking and other actual performances, what (at any time) have you heard her say?

Gentlewoman. That, sir, which I will not report after her.   10

Doctor. You may to me, and 'tis most meet you should.

Gentlewoman. Neither to you nor any one, having no witness to confirm my speech.

[*Enter* Lady Macbeth, *with a taper.*⁴]

Lo you, here she comes! This is her very guise,⁵ and, upon my life, fast asleep! Observe her; stand close.⁶   15

Doctor. How came she by that light?

Gentlewoman. Why, it stood by her. She has light by her continually. 'Tis her command.

Doctor. You see her eyes are open.

Gentlewoman. Ay, but their sense is shut.   20

Doctor. What is it she does now? Look how she rubs her hands.

Gentlewoman. It is an accustomed action with her, to seem thus washing her hands. I have known her continue in this a quarter of an hour.

Lady Macbeth. Yet here's a spot.

Doctor. Hark, she speaks! I will set down what comes from her, to satisfy my   25 remembrance the more strongly.

Lady Macbeth. Out, damned spot! out, I say! One; two. Why then 'tis time to do't. Hell is murky. Fie, my lord, fie! a soldier, and afeard? What need we fear who

---

1. **into the field:** out with the army. 2. **closet:** a chest for private belongings. 3. **do . . . watching:** behave as if awake. 4. **taper:** candle. 5. **guise:** custom. 6. **close:** hidden.

Roberta Maxwell (Lady Macbeth) in *Macbeth*.
Stratford Festival, 1983.

knows it, when none can call our pow'r to accompt?[7] Yet who would have
thought the old man to have had so much blood in him? 30

Doctor. Do you mark that?

Lady Macbeth. The Thane of Fife had a wife. Where is she now? What, will these
hands ne'er be clean? No more o' that, my lord, no more o' that! You mar all with
this starting.

Doctor. Go to, go to![8] You have known what you should not. 35

Gentlewoman. She has spoke what she should not, I am sure of that. Heaven knows
what she has known.

Lady Macbeth. Here's the smell of the blood still. All the perfumes of Arabia will
not sweeten this little hand. Oh, oh, oh!

Doctor. What a sigh is there! The heart is sorely charged.[9] 40

Gentlewoman. I would not have such a heart in my bosom for the dignity of the
whole body.

Doctor. Well, well, well.

Gentlewoman. Pray God it be, sir.

Doctor. This disease is beyond my practice. Yet I have known those which have 45
walked in their sleep who have died holily in their beds.

---

7. **accompt:** account.   8. **Go to:** for shame.   9. **charged:** burdened.

Lady Macbeth. Wash your hands, put on your nightgown, look not so pale! I tell you
    yet again, Banquo's buried. He cannot come out on's grave.

Doctor. Even so?

Lady Macbeth. To bed, to bed! There's knocking at the gate. Come, come, come,   50
    come, give me your hand! What's done cannot be undone. To bed, to bed, to bed!

                                                               [Exit.]

Doctor. Will she go now to bed?

Gentlewoman. Directly.

Doctor. Foul whisp'rings are abroad. Unnatural deeds
    Do breed unnatural troubles. Infected minds   55
    To their deaf pillows will discharge their secrets.
    More needs she the divine than the physician.
    God, God forgive us all! Look after her;
    Remove from her the means of all annoyance,[10]
    And still keep eyes upon her. So good night.   60
    My mind she has mated,[11] and amazed[12] my sight.
    I think, but dare not speak.

Gentlewoman.   Good night, good doctor.   *[Exeunt.]*

Scene 2   *[The Scottish rebels are approaching Birnam Wood where they
                        will join the English forces led by Malcolm, Macduff, and Siward,
                        Earl of Northumberland. Macbeth awaits at Dunsinane, in
                        command of an army that is bound to him by duty not love.]*

[The country near Dunsinane.]

[Drum and Colors.[1] Enter Menteith, Caithness, Angus, Lennox, Soldiers.*]*

Menteith. The English pow'r is near, led on by Malcolm,
    His uncle Siward, and the good Macduff.
    Revenges burn in them; for their dear causes
    Would to the bleeding and the grim alarm[2]
    Excite the mortified[3] man.   5

Angus.   Near Birnam Wood
    Shall we well meet them; that way are they coming.

Caithness. Who knows if Donalbain be with his brother?

Lennox. For certain, sir, he is not. I have a file[4]
    Of all the gentry. There is Siward's son   10
    And many unrough[5] youths that even now
    Protest their first of manhood.[6]

Menteith.   What does the tyrant?

---

10. **annoyance:** harm. 11. **mated:** confounded. 12. **amazed:** confused.

  1. **drum and colors:** a drummer and a soldier with a flag. 2. **alarm:** call to arms. 3. **mortified:** half dead. 4. **file:**
list. 5. **unrough:** beardless. 6. **Protest . . . manhood:** show that they have hardly reached manhood.

Caithness. Great Dunsinane he strongly fortifies.
    Some say he's mad; others, that lesser hate him, 15
    Do call it valiant fury; but for certain
    He cannot buckle his distempered cause
    Within the belt of rule.[7]
Angus.   Now does he feel
    His secret murders sticking on his hands. 20
    Now minutely[8] revolts upbraid his faith-breach.[9]
    Those he commands move only in command,
    Nothing in love. Now does he feel his title
    Hang loose about him, like a giant's robe
    Upon a dwarfish thief. 25
Menteith.   Who then shall blame
    His pestered[10] senses to recoil and start,
    When all that is within him does condemn
    Itself for being there?
Caithness.   Well, march we on 30
    To give obedience where 'tis truly owed.
    Meet we the med'cine of the sickly weal;[11]
    And with him pour we in our country's purge
    Each drop of us.
Lennox.   Or so much as it needs 35
    To dew[12] the sovereign flower[13] and drown the weeds.
    Make we our march towards Birnam.   *[Exeunt, marching.]*

---

7. **buckle . . . rule:** he can not keep his evil cause under control.   8. **minutely:** every minute.   9. **faith-breach:** disloyalty.
10. **pestered:** troubled.   11. **Meet . . . weal:** that which will heal the commonwealth, namely, Malcolm and his
party.   12. **dew:** water.   13. **sovereign flower:** Malcolm.

Scene 3

[*Macbeth interprets the witches' apparitions to mean that he will be neither killed nor defeated. After he hears of the huge English army he faces, Macbeth expresses profound disillusionment and a willingness to die. Lady Macbeth's doctor reports that he cannot rid her of disturbing hallucinations. Macbeth prepares for battle.*]

[*Dunsinane. A room in the Castle.*]

[*Enter* Macbeth, Doctor, *and* Attendants.]

Macbeth. Bring me no more reports. Let them fly all!
Till Birnam Wood remove to Dunsinane,
I cannot taint[1] with fear. What's the boy Malcolm?
Was he not born of woman? The spirits that know
All mortal consequences[2] have pronounced me thus: 5
"Fear not, Macbeth. No man that's born of woman
Shall e'er have power upon thee." Then fly, false thanes,
And mingle with the English epicures.[3]
The mind I sway by[4] and the heart I bear
Shall never sag with doubt nor shake with fear.   10

   [*Enter* Servant.]

The devil damn thee black,[5] thou cream-faced loon![6]
Where got'st thou that goose look?
Servant. There is ten thousand—
Macbeth.   Geese, villain?
Servant.   Soldiers, sir.   15
Macbeth. Go prick thy face and over-red thy fear,
Thou lily-livered boy. What soldiers, patch?[7]
Death of thy soul! Those linen[8] cheeks of thine
Are counselors to fear. What soldiers, whey-face?
Servant. The English force, so please you.   20
Macbeth. Take thy face hence.   [*Exit* Servant.]
            Seyton!—I am sick at heart,
When I behold—Seyton, I say!—This push[9]
Will cheer me ever, or disseat[10] me now.
I have lived long enough. My way of life   25
Is fallen into the sere,[11] the yellow leaf;
And that which should accompany old age,
As honor, love, obedience, troops of friends,
I must not look to have; but, in their stead,
Curses not loud but deep, mouth-honor,[12] breath,   30

---

1. **taint:** be infected. 2. **All . . . consequences:** human fate. 3. **epicures:** gluttons, i.e., not soldiers. 4. **sway by:** rule myself with. 5. **The . . . black:** Black was the devil's color. It was believed that when he captured a soul, the body turned black. 6. **loon:** stupid rascal. 7. **patch:** fool. 8. **linen:** pale as linen. 9. **push:** attack. 10. **disseat:** unseat. 11. **sere:** dry and withered. 12. **mouth-honor:** honor in words only, not deeds.

Which the poor heart would fain[13] deny, and dare not.
Seyton!

    [*Enter* Seyton.]

Seyton. What's your gracious pleasure?
Macbeth.   What news more?
Seyton. All is confirmed, my lord, which was reported.   35
Macbeth. I'll fight, till from my bones my flesh be hacked.
    Give me my armor.
Seyton.   'Tis not needed yet.
Macbeth. I'll put it on.
    Send out mo[14] horses, skirr[15] the country round;   40
    Hang those that talk of fear. Give me mine armor.
    How does your patient, doctor?
Doctor.   Not so sick, my lord,
    As she is troubled with thick-coming fancies
    That keep her from her rest.   45
Macbeth.   Cure her of that!
    Canst thou not minister to a mind diseased,
    Pluck from the memory a rooted sorrow,
    Raze out[16] the written troubles of the brain,
    And with some sweet oblivious antidote[17]   50
    Cleanse the stuffed bosom of that perilous stuff
    Which weighs upon the heart?
Doctor.   Therein the patient
    Must minister to himself.
Macbeth. Throw physic to the dogs, I'll none of it!—   55
    Come, put mine armor on. Give me my staff.
    Seyton, send out.—Doctor, the thanes fly from me.—
    Come, sir, dispatch.—If thou couldst, doctor, cast
    The water of my land,[18] find her disease,
    And purge it to a sound and pristine[19] health,   60
    I would applaud thee to the very echo,
    That should applaud again.—Pull't off, I say.—[20]
    What rhubarb, senna,[21] or what purgative drug,
    Would scour these English hence? Hear'st thou of them?
Doctor. Ay, my good lord. Your royal preparation   65
    Makes us hear something.
Macbeth.   Bring it after me!
    I will not be afraid of death and bane[22]
    Till Birnam Forest come to Dunsinane.
Doctor. [*Aside*] Were I from Dunsinane away and clear,   70
    Profit again should hardly draw me here.   [*Exeunt.*]

---

13. **fain:** gladly. 14. **mo:** more. 15. **skirr:** scour. 16. **Raze out:** erase. 17. **oblivious antidote:** medicine producing oblivion. 18. **cast . . . water:** diagnose the illness. 19. **pristine:** former. 20. **Pull . . . say:** Macbeth orders Seyton to pull off part of his armor that has been put on wrong in his haste. 21. **senna:** purgative herb. 22. **bane:** destruction.

Scene 4

[*The English army led by Malcolm, Macduff, and Siward have joined the Scottish rebels near Birnam Wood. Malcolm orders each soldier to cut a branch from a tree and to hold it before him as he approaches Dunsinane.*]

[*Country near Birnam Wood.*]

[*Drum and Colors. Enter* Malcolm, Siward, Macduff, Siward's Son, Menteith, Caithness, Angus, Lennox, Ross, *and* Soldiers *marching.*]

Malcolm. Cousins, I hope the days are near at hand
    That chambers[1] will be safe.
Menteith.   We doubt it nothing.
Siward. What wood is this before us?
Menteith.   The wood of Birnam.   5
Malcolm. Let every soldier hew him down a bough
    And bear't before him. Thereby shall we shadow[2]
    The numbers of our host and make discovery[3]
    Err in report of us.
Soldiers.   It shall be done.   10
Siward. We learn no other but the confident tyrant
    Keeps still in Dunsinane and will endure
    Our setting down[4] before't.
Malcolm.   'Tis his main hope;
    For where there is advantage[5] to be given,   15
    Both more and less[6] have given him the revolt;
    And none serve with him but constrained[7] things,
    Whose hearts are absent too.
Macduff.   Let our just censures
    Attend the true event,[8] and put we on   20
    Industrious soldiership.
Siward.   The time approaches
    That will with due decision make us know
    What we shall say we have, and what we owe.[9]
    Thoughts speculative their unsure hopes relate,   25
    But certain issue strokes must arbitrate;[10]
    Towards which advance the war.

                        [*Exeunt, marching.*]

---

1. **That . . . chambers:** a man will have nothing to fear in his own home.   2. **shadow:** conceal.   3. **discovery:** Macbeth's lookouts.   4. **setting down:** siege.   5. **advantage:** opportunity.   6. **more and less:** greater and lesser; all classes. 7. **constrained:** forced.   8. **Let . . . event:** before we predict the result, let us await the outcome.   9. **owe:** possess. 10. **But . . . arbitrate:** the outcome will be determined by the blows.

Scene 5

[When Macbeth learns of Lady Macbeth's death, he comments on the brevity and emptiness of life, for his sensitivity has been dulled by his terrible deeds. A messenger reports that a grove of trees seems to be moving toward Dunsinane. Macbeth realizes that he might have misinterpreted the witches' predictions.]

[Dunsinane. Within the Castle.]

[Enter Macbeth, Seyton, and Soldiers, with Drum and Colors.]

Macbeth. Hang out our banners on the outward walls.
The cry is still, "They come!" Our castle's strength
Will laugh a siege to scorn. Here let them lie
Till famine and the ague[1] eat them up.
Were they not forced[2] with those that should be ours,[3]   5
We might have met them dareful,[4] beard to beard,
And beat them backward home.

[A cry within of women.]

                         What is that noise?
Seyton. It is the cry of women, my good lord.

                                          [Exit.]
Macbeth. I have almost forgot the taste of fears.   10
The time has been, my senses would have cooled
To hear a night-shriek, and my fell of hair[5]
Would at a dismal treatise[6] rouse and stir
As life were in't. I have supped full with horrors.
Direness,[7] familiar to my slaughterous thoughts,   15
Cannot once start[8] me.

[Reenter Seyton.]

                        Wherefore was that cry?
Seyton. The Queen, my lord, is dead.
Macbeth. She should have died hereafter;[9]
There would have been a time for such a word.   20
Tomorrow, and tomorrow, and tomorrow
Creeps in this petty pace from day to day
To the last syllable of recorded time;
And all our yesterdays have lighted fools
The way to dusty death. Out, out, brief candle!   25
Life's but a walking shadow, a poor player,

---

1. **ague:** fever. 2. **forced:** reinforced. 3. **those . . . ours:** deserters. 4. **dareful:** defiantly. 5. **my . . . hair:** the hair on my scalp. 6. **dismal treatise:** tale of horror. 7. **Direness:** horror. 8. **start:** move. 9. **She . . . hereafter:** She would have died at some other time.

That struts and frets his hour upon the stage
And then is heard no more. It is a tale
Told by an idiot, full of sound and fury,
Signifying nothing.   30

    [Enter a Messenger.]

Thou com'st to use thy tongue. Thy story quickly!
Messenger. Gracious my lord,
  I should report that which I say I saw,
  But know not how to do't.
Macbeth.   Well, say, sir!   35
Messenger. As I did stand my watch upon the hill,
  I looked toward Birnam, and anon methought
  The wood began to move.
Macbeth.   Liar and slave!
Messenger. Let me endure your wrath if't be not so.   40
  Within this three mile may you see it coming;
  I say, a moving grove.
Macbeth.   If thou speak'st false,
  Upon the next tree shalt thou hang alive,
  Till famine cling[10] thee. If thy speech be sooth,[11]   45
  I care not if thou dost for me as much.
  I pull in resolution,[12] and begin
  To doubt[13] the equivocation[14] of the fiend,
  That lies like truth. "Fear not, till Birnam Wood
  Do come to Dunsinane!" and now a wood   50
  Comes toward Dunsinane. Arm, arm, and out!
  If this which he avouches does appear,
  There is nor flying hence nor tarrying here.
  I 'gin to be aweary of the sun,
  And wish the estate o' the world were now undone.   55
  Ring the alarum bell! Blow wind, come wrack,[15]
  At least we'll die with harness[16] on our back!   *[Exeunt.]*

Scene 6   *[Malcolm orders the soldiers to discard their camouflage and attack.]*

[Dunsinane. Before the Castle.]

[Drum and Colors. Enter Malcolm, Siward, Macduff, *and their* Army, *with boughs.]*

---

10. **cling:** wither.   11. **sooth:** truth.   12. **resolution:** courage.   13. **doubt:** fear.   14. **equivocation:** double talk.   15. **wrack:** wreck.   16. **harness:** armor.

Malcolm. Now near enough. Your leavy[1] screens throw down
    And show like those you are.[2] You, worthy uncle,
    Shall with my cousin, your right noble son,
    Lead our first battle.[3] Worthy Macduff and we
    Shall take upon's what else remains to do,   5
    According to our order.
Siward.   Fare you well.
    Do we but find the tyrant's power tonight,
    Let us be beaten if we cannot fight.
Macduff. Make all our trumpets speak, give them all breath,   10
    Those clamorous harbingers[4] of blood and death.

                                         [*Exeunt. Alarums continued.*]

Scene 7   [*Macbeth slays young Siward. Macduff seeks Macbeth, intent on
                          avenging the deaths of his family. Siward reports that Macbeth's
                          soldiers have surrendered and that many have joined the attackers.*]

[*Another part of the field.*]

[*Enter Macbeth.*]

Macbeth. They have tied me to a stake. I cannot fly,
    But bearlike I must fight the course.[1] What's he
    That was not born of woman? Such a one
    Am I to fear, or none.

        [*Enter Young Siward.*]

Young Siward. What is thy name?   5
Macbeth.   Thou'lt be afraid to hear it.
Young Siward. No; though thou call'st thyself a hotter name
    Than any is in hell.
Macbeth.   My name's Macbeth.
Young Siward. The devil himself could not pronounce a title   10
    More hateful to mine ear.
Macbeth.   No, nor more fearful.
Young Siward. Thou liest, abhorred tyrant! With my sword
    I'll prove the lie thou speak'st.

[*Fight, and* Young Siward *slain.*]

Macbeth.   Thou wast born of woman.   15
    But swords I smile at, weapons laugh to scorn,
    Brandished by man that's of a woman born.   [*Exit.*]

---

1. **leavy:** leafy. 2. **And . . . are:** discard the camouflage and be yourselves. 3. **battle:** division. 4. **harbingers:** messengers.
   1. **They . . . course:** in bearbaiting the bear was tied to a stake while dogs attacked him.

[*Alarums. Enter Macduff.*]

Macduff. That way the noise is. Tyrant, show thy face!
    If thou beest slain and with no stroke of mine,
    My wife and children's ghosts will haunt me still.   20
    I cannot strike at wretched kerns, whose arms
    Are hired to bear their staves.² Either thou, Macbeth,
    Or else my sword with an unbattered edge
    I sheathe again undeeded.³ There thou shouldst be.
    By this great clatter one of greatest note   25
    Seems bruited.⁴ Let me find him, Fortune!
    And more I beg not.   [*Exit. Alarums.*]

        [*Enter Malcolm and Siward.*]

Siward. This way, my lord. The castle's gently rendered:⁵
    The tyrant's people on both sides do fight;
    The noble thanes do bravely in the war;   30
    The day almost itself professes yours,
    And little is to do.
Malcolm.   We have met with foes
    That strike beside us.⁶
Siward.   Enter, sir, the castle.   35

                   [*Exeunt. Alarum.*]

Scene 8

[*Macbeth refuses to fight Macduff, feeling that he already has killed too many of this family. He tells Macduff that no one born of woman will prevail against him. Macduff reveals that he was ripped from his mother's womb, thus not born naturally. To avoid humiliation, Macbeth chooses to fight Macduff, although he now knows he will be killed. As Ross, Siward, and Malcolm talk about young Siward's noble death, Macduff enters, carrying Macbeth's severed head. Malcolm is proclaimed King of Scotland. He rewards his supporters and invites them to his coronation.*]

[*Another part of the field.*]

[*Enter Macbeth.*]

Macbeth. Why should I play the Roman fool and die
    On mine own sword?¹ Whiles I see lives,² the gashes
    Do better upon them.

---

2. **staves:** spears.   3. **undeeded:** not used.   4. **bruited:** revealed by the noise.   5. **gently rendered:** easily surrendered.
6. **beside us:** on our side.
  1. **play . . . sword:** like Brutus or Cassius, who committed suicide in the moment of defeat.   2. **lives:** enemies.

[*Enter* Macduff.]

Macduff.   Turn, hellhound, turn!
Macbeth. Of all men else I have avoided thee.   5
    But get thee back! My soul is too much charged
    With blood of thine already.
Macduff.   I have no words;
    My voice is in my sword, thou bloodier villain
    Than terms can give thee out!   10

[*Fight. Alarum.*]

Macbeth.   Thou losest labor.
    As easy mayst thou the intrenchant[3] air
    With thy keen sword impress[4] as make me bleed.
    Let fall thy blade on vulnerable crests.
    I bear a charmèd life, which must not yield   15
    To one of woman born.
Macduff.   Despair thy charm!
    And let the angel whom thou still hast served
    Tell thee, Macduff was from his mother's womb
    Untimely ripped.   20
Macbeth. Accursed be that tongue that tells me so,
    For it hath cowed my better part of man!
    And be these juggling fiends no more believed,
    That palter[5] with us in a double sense,
    That keep the word of promise to our ear   25
    And break it to our hope! I'll not fight with thee!
Macduff. Then yield thee, coward,
    And live to be the show and gaze o' the time!
    We'll have thee, as our rarer monsters are,
    Painted upon a pole,[6] and underwrit   30
    "Here may you see the tyrant."
Macbeth.   I will not yield,
    To kiss the ground before young Malcolm's feet
    And to be baited with the rabble's curse.
    Though Birnam Wood be come to Dunsinane,   35
    And thou opposed, being of no woman born,
    Yet I will try the last. Before my body
    I throw my warlike shield. Lay on, Macduff,
    And damned be him that first cries "Hold, enough!"

[*Exeunt fighting. Alarums.*]

[*Retreat and flourish. Enter, with Drum and Colors,* Malcolm, Siward, Ross, Thanes, *and* Soldiers.]

---

3. **intrenchant:** that cannot be cut.   4. **impress:** make an impression on.   5. **palter:** juggle.   6. **Painted . . . pole:** your likeness painted on a placard and set on a pole for all to see.

Malcolm. I would the friends we miss were safe arrived.   40
Siward. Some must go off;[7] and yet, by these I see,
   So great a day as this is cheaply bought.[8]
Malcolm. Macduff is missing, and your noble son.
Ross. Your son, my lord, has paid a soldier's debt.
   He only lived but till he was a man,   45
   The which no sooner had his prowess confirmed
   In the unshrinking station[9] where he fought
   But like a man he died.
Siward.   Then he is dead?
Ross. Ay, and brought off the field. Your cause of sorrow   50
   Must not be measured by his worth, for then
   It hath no end.
Siward.   Had he his hurts before?
Ross. Ay, on the front.
Siward.   Why then, God's soldier be he!   55
   Had I as many sons as I have hairs,
   I would not wish them to a fairer death.
   And so his knell is knolled.
Malcolm.   He's worth more sorrow,
   And that I'll spend for him.   60
Siward.   He's worth no more.
   They say he parted well and paid his score,
   And so, God be with him! Here comes newer comfort.

     [*Reenter* Macduff, *with* Macbeth's *head.*]

Macduff. Hail, King! for so thou art. Behold where stands
   The usurper's cursèd head. The time is free.[10]   65
   I see thee compassed with thy kingdom's pearl,[11]
   That speak my salutation in their minds;
   Whose voices I desire aloud with mine—
   Hail, King of Scotland!
All.   Hail, King of Scotland! [*Flourish.*]   70
Malcolm. We shall not spend a large expense of time
   Before we reckon with your several[12] loves
   And make us even with you.[13] My Thanes and kinsmen,
   Henceforth be Earls, the first that ever Scotland
   In such an honor named. What's more to do   75
   Which would be planted newly with the time—
   As calling home our exiled friends abroad
   That fled the snares of watchful tyranny,
   Producing forth[14] the cruel ministers

---

7. **go off:** die. 8. **cheaply bought:** few casualties. 9. **unshrinking station:** the spot where he held his ground and fought it out. 10. **The . . . free:** liberty is restored. 11. **I . . . pearl:** surrounded by the pearl of the kingdom, the noblest Scots. 12. **several:** separate. 13. **make . . . you:** pay you what we owe. 14. **producing forth:** bring from hiding.

Of this dead butcher and his fiendlike queen,   80
Who (as 'tis thought) by self and violent hands[15]
Took off her life—this, and what needful else
That calls upon us, by the grace of Grace
We will perform in measure,[16] time, and place.
So thanks to all at once and to each one,   85
Whom we invite to see us crowned at Scone.

[Flourish. Exeunt omnes.]

---

15. **self . . . hands:** committed suicide.   16. **measure:** full measure.

Act Five

Getting at Meaning

Scene 1

1. What is the mental state of Lady Macbeth during the sleepwalking scene? Why does she carry a candle? What does she do as she walks? What seems to bother her the most? What does the doctor fear will happen?

2. When Lady Macbeth says, "All the perfumes of Arabia will not sweeten this little hand," she is echoing a thought expressed by Macbeth in Act Two, Scene 2. What are Macbeth's exact words? What are they both saying? How is Lady Macbeth's statement different from her comment about water made immediately after the murder?

Scene 2

3. What does this scene reveal about Macbeth as a person and as a ruler?

Scene 3

4. Why does Macbeth no longer fear death? How does he feel about old age?

5. How does Macbeth respond to the doctor's report regarding Lady Macbeth's ill health?

Scene 4

6. Relate this scene to the prophecies given to Macbeth through the apparitions.

Scene 5

7. When Macbeth hears the cry of women, he responds by commenting on his feelings. What does

he say? Is he aware of the changes that have taken place within him? Explain.

8. Why does Macbeth respond with such indifference to Lady Macbeth's death?

9. What does the "Tomorrow, and tomorrow, and tomorrow" soliloquy reveal about Macbeth?

10. How does this scene show Macbeth's increasing desperation?

Scene 6

11. What is Malcolm's position among the nobles, as suggested in this scene?

Scene 7

12. What tactical error does Macbeth make? What happens as a result?

Scene 8

13. Why does Macbeth still have confidence when he first encounters Macduff? How does Macbeth react to Macduff's revelation regarding his birth?

14. How does Macbeth's final act show that he still possesses a trace of his former nobility? Is death the ultimate disaster for Macbeth? Explain.

15. What are Malcolm's first acts as the new king of Scotland? What kind of king will he most likely be? Support your answer with evidence from the play.

Developing Skills in Reading Literature

1. **Allusion.** Reread lines 1–3 in Scene 8. What is the classical allusion in these lines? What attitude is

revealed through the way that Macbeth presents the allusion?

2. **Metaphor and Soliloquy.** Study the soliloquy in Scene 5 that begins "Tomorrow, and tomorrow, and tomorrow." Identify the metaphors that describe life as Macbeth now sees it. The final sentence which begins "It is a tale/Told by an idiot . . . ," is an interpolation by another writer. What differences do you note between this sentence and the rest of the soliloquy?

3. **Falling Action and Dénouement.** The dénouement is the final resolution of a plot, the conclusion of the falling action. Summarize the falling action that takes place in Acts Four and Five. What is the dénouement?

4. **Motif.** A recurring word, phrase, image, object, idea, or action in a work of literature is called a motif. Motifs function as unifying devices and often relate directly to one or more major themes. The motifs in *Macbeth* include the repetition of the word *done,* the image of ill-fitting clothing, and the idea of sleep and sleeplessness. What other motifs are introduced and developed in this play? Select one and trace its appearances throughout the play. Then identify the main idea that is emphasized by the motif.

5. **Tragedy.** A tragedy is a literary work that recounts the downfall of a dignified, superior character who is involved in historically or socially significant events. The main character, or tragic hero, has a tragic flaw, the quality that leads to his or her destruction. The events in a tragic plot are set in motion by a decision that often is an error in judgment caused by the tragic flaw. The succeeding events are linked in a cause-effect relationship and lead inexorably to a disastrous conclusion. Tragedy arouses both pity and fear, pity for the doomed hero and fear for all humans who are subject to the same forces and weaknesses as the tragic hero.

How is Macbeth a superior character? What is his tragic flaw? What fatal decision does he make? Trace the chain of events that results from this decision. Do you pity Macbeth? Why? How do you feel at the end of the tragedy?

6. **Theme.** Two important themes of this play involve the concept of free will and the effect of violence. Think about the role of the witches in relation to Macbeth's actions. Do the witches control Macbeth?

Do they undermine his free will? To what degree are Macbeth's actions determined by circumstances outside his control? To what degree are they determined by his own choices? Explain your conclusions. Next, think about how their bloody deeds affect Macbeth and Lady Macbeth. What happens to them morally? emotionally? physically? What happens to their relationship? Cite evidence from the play to support your answers. Then write two thematic statements, one relating to destiny and free will, the other to the effect of violence. Finally, think about the concepts of nobility and treachery, loyalty and ambition, good and evil, guilt and innocence, reality and illusion, law and order brought out in this play. Write two or more additional thematic statements.

Developing Writing Skills

1. **Analyzing Main Characters.** An audience learns about each character in a play through the words and actions of that character and through the comments of the other characters. Trace the development of Macbeth through all five acts, describing both his character and the methods of characterization employed. In a second essay, do the same with the character of Lady Macbeth. Quote specific lines from the play.

2. **Describing a Character.** Shakespeare was a genius at characterization, creating memorable minor as well as major characters. Choose one character from these four minor characters in *Macbeth*: Banquo, Duncan, Malcolm, Macduff. Write a character sketch in which you describe specific character traits as they are indicated by the words and actions of the character and of other characters in relation to your subject. Quote lines and cite other evidence from the play to support your conclusions.

3. **Analyzing an Element of Plot.** Consider the importance of the supernatural in *Macbeth*. Do the prophecies and apparitions determine events? precipitate events? reflect internal states? Of what are they symbolic? How do they make the play more than a story about the rise and fall of an obscure Scottish king? Are supernatural elements integral to the development of plot? of character and setting? of mood? of theme? Organize your ideas, then write an essay analyzing the role of the supernatural in this play.

Francis Bacon

1561–1626

Francis Bacon, lawyer, statesman, scientist, philosopher, and writer, is considered the father of the English essay. In his essays, he applied his philosophical principles to everyday life and provided his readers with practical guidelines for personal, social, and civic harmony.

Bacon was the son of the Lord Keeper of the Seal and a nephew of Queen Elizabeth's principal minister. He attended Cambridge University for two years, then lived in Paris for a time in the household of the English ambassador to France. Returning to England in 1579, he embarked on a long, distinguished, and often turbulent legal and political career. Despite temporary setbacks and disappointments, he rose steadily in royal service and in 1595 was appointed one of the queen's "learned counsels." He served Elizabeth's successor with equal diligence and loyalty, becoming James I's spokesman in Parliament, solicitor general, attorney general, and in 1618 lord chancellor, the highest judicial position in England. Three years later, Bacon's political career was destroyed when he was charged with—and admitted—accepting bribes. Although he denied that these bribes influenced his decisions, he was removed from his office, banished from the court, and imprisoned briefly.

Forced to retire from public life, Bacon directed his full attention to literature, philosophy, and science. In 1626, curious about the preservative effects of refrigeration, Bacon killed a hen and painstakingly stuffed it with snow. Damp and chilled during this experiment, he developed the bronchitis from which he died on April 9, 1626.

Bacon was a prolific writer, even during his years of public service, producing letters, scientific notebooks, fiction, drama, speeches, political and legal papers, essays, and philosophical treatises and texts. His works include *The Advancement of Learning* (1605), in which he reviews and classifies all the branches of knowledge and defends the value of learning, and *New Atlantis*, published posthumously in 1627, a fictional depiction of a

SIR FRANCES BACON. *Anonymous.*
National Portrait Gallery, London.

utopian colony of scholars who implement Bacon's philosophy.

Bacon's literary fame is based on his *Essays*, first published in 1597 and later in 1612 and 1625. In these essays he comments on the nature of human behavior and motivation, generalizing about what humans do and what they ought to do. Derived from Bacon's observations of life, his concepts are expressed in prose that is concise, balanced, structured, and enriched with the stylistic complexity typical of Elizabethan writing. Bacon's essays reflect the Renaissance ideal, a man whose interests embraced all life on earth and whose grand vision encompassed both the material and the spiritual dimensions of the universe.

Of Studies

Studies serve for delight, for ornament, and for ability. Their chief use for delight is in privateness and retiring; for ornament, is in discourse; and for ability, is in the judgment and disposition of business. For expert men can execute, and perhaps judge of particulars, one by one; but the general counsels, and the plots and marshaling of affairs come best from those that are learned. To spend too much time in studies is sloth; to use them too much for ornament is affectation; to make judgment wholly by their rules is the humor[1] of a scholar. They perfect nature, and are perfected by experience: for natural abilities are like natural plants, that need pruning by study; and studies themselves do give forth directions too much at large, except they be bounded in by experience. Crafty men contemn studies, simple men admire them, and wise men use them; for they teach not their own use; but that is a wisdom without them and above them, won by observation. Read not to contradict and confute, nor to believe and take for granted, nor to find talk and discourse, but to weigh and consider. Some books are to be tasted, others to be swallowed, and some few to be chewed and digested; that is, some books are to be read only in parts; others to be read, but not curiously;[2] and some few to be read wholly, and with diligence and attention. Some books also may be read by deputy, and extracts made of them by others; but that would[3] be only in the less important arguments and the meaner sort of books; else distilled books are, like common distilled waters,[4] flashy[5] things. Reading maketh a full man; conference a ready man; and writing an exact man. And, therefore, if a man write little, he had need have a great memory; if he confer little, he had need have a present wit;[6] and if he read little, he had need have much cunning, to seem to know that he doth not. Histories make men wise; poets, witty; the mathematics, subtile; natural philosophy, deep; moral, grave; logic and rhetoric, able to contend. *Abeunt studia in mores.*[7] Nay, there is no stond[8] or impediment in the wit but may be wrought out by fit studies, like as diseases of the body may have appropriate exercises. Bowling is good for the stone and reins,[9] shooting for the lungs and breast, gentle walking for the stomach, riding for the head, and the like. So if a man's wit be wandering, let him study the mathematics; for in demonstrations, if his wit be called away never so little, he must begin again. If his wit be not apt to distinguish or find differences, let him study the schoolmen; for they are *Cymini sectores.*[10] If he be not apt to beat over[11] matters, and to call up one thing to prove and illustrate another, let him study the lawyer's cases. So every defect of the mind may have a special receipt.[12]

---

1. **humor:** whim, disposition.
2. **curiously:** carefully, thoroughly.
3. **would:** should.
4. **common distilled waters:** herbal home remedies.
5. **flashy:** insipid, flat.
6. **wit:** intelligence.
7. ***Abeunt studia in mores*** *Latin:* Studies pass into and influence manners.
8. **stond:** stoppage.
9. **stone and reins:** gallbladder and kidneys.
10. ***Cymini sectores*** *Latin:* splitters of hairs.
11. **beat over:** reason through.
12. **receipt:** remedy, prescription.

Of Marriage and Single Life

He that hath wife and children hath given hostages to fortune; for they are impediments to great enterprises, either of virtue or mischief. Certainly, the best works, and of greatest merit for the public, have proceeded from the unmarried or childless men, which both in affection and means have married and endowed the public. Yet it were great reason that those that have children should have greatest care of future times; unto which they know they must transmit their dearest pledges. Some there are, who though they lead a single life, yet their thoughts do end with themselves, and account future times impertinences.[1] Nay, there are some other that account wife and children but as bills of charges. Nay more, there are some foolish rich covetous men that take a pride in having no children, because they may be thought so much the richer. For perhaps they have heard some talk: "Such an one is a great rich man," and another except to it: "Yea, but he hath a great charge of children"; as if it were an abatement[2] to his riches. But the most ordinary cause of a single life is liberty; especially in certain self-pleasing and humorous[3] minds, which are so sensible of every restraint, as they will go near to think their girdles and garters to be bonds and shackles. Unmarried men are best friends, best masters, best servants; but not always best subjects; for they are light to run away; and almost all fugitives are of that condition. A single life doth well with churchmen; for charity will hardly water the ground where it must first fill a pool. It is indifferent for judges and magistrates; for if they be facile and corrupt, you shall have a servant five times worse than a wife. For soldiers, I find the generals commonly in their hortatives[4] put men in mind of their wives and children; and I think the despising of marriage amongst the Turks maketh the vulgar soldier more base. Certainly wife and children are a kind of discipline of humanity; and single men, though they be many times more charitable, because their means are less exhaust, yet, on the other side, they are more cruel and hardhearted (good to make severe inquisitors), because their tenderness is not so oft called upon. Grave natures, led by custom, and therefore constant, are commonly loving husbands; as was said of Ulysses, *Vetulam suam praetulit immortalitati.*[5] Chaste women are often proud and froward,[6] as presuming upon the merit of their chastity. It is one of the best bonds both of chastity and obedience in the wife, if she think her husband wise; which she will never do if she find him jealous. Wives are young men's mistresses; companions for middle age; and old men's nurses. So as a man may have a quarrel to marry when he will. But yet he was reputed one of the wise men, that made answer to the question, when a man should marry? "A young man not yet, an elder man not at all." It is often seen that bad husbands have very good wives; whether it be that it raiseth the price of their husbands' kindness when it comes; or that the wives take a pride in their patience. But this never fails, if the bad husbands were of their own choosing, against their friends' consent; for then they will be sure to make good their own folly.

---

1. **impertinences:** irrelevances.
2. **abatement:** reduction.
3. **humorous:** whimsical.
4. **hortatives:** urgings to do good deeds.
5. ***Vetulam suam praetulit immortalitari*** *Latin:* He preferred his own wife to immortality.
6. **froward:** not easily controlled.

Getting at Meaning

OF STUDIES

1. According to Bacon, what purposes do studies serve? What warning does he present regarding over-dependence on studies?

2. What is the proper approach to books suggested in this essay? What is the value of reading? of writing? of discussion?

3. What is the effect of various kinds of studies on the student?

OF MARRIAGE AND SINGLE LIFE

4. According to Bacon, what are the advantages of marriage to the individual and to society? What are the advantages of single life?

5. What are Bacon's observations about the relationship between husband and wife?

6. Which does Bacon admire more, the married or the single life? Support your answer with reasons derived from the essay.

Developing Skills in Reading Literature

1. **Style.** Bacon's literary style is characterized by the complementary qualities of balance and emphasis, achieved through the skillful use of four techniques.

a. **Parallelism.** Parallelism is the expression of ideas of equal worth in the same grammatical form. For example, Bacon begins "Of Studies" with the sentence, "Studies serve for delight, for ornament, and for ability." Parallelism can occur within one sentence, as in the example, or among succeeding sentences of identical construction.

b. **Structure.** Structure is the way in which a work of literature is put together. In "Of Marriage and Single Life" Bacon repeatedly juxtaposes ideas, as when he asserts on one hand that families are "impediments to great enterprises" and on the other hand that men with children "have greatest care of future times."

c. **Anaphora.** Anaphora is the repetition or near repetition of words, phrases, or sentences, often at the beginnings of succeeding sentences, clauses, or para-

graphs. For example, in "Of Studies" Bacon repeats "some books" at the beginnings of three independent clauses.

d. **Aphorism.** An aphorism is a brief statement that expresses a truth about life, such as, "Reading maketh a full man; conference a ready man; and writing an exact man."

Find additional examples of these stylistic characteristics in these two essays. For each, identify the idea that is emphasized through the technique. Be sure to note overlapping techniques; for example, an aphorism might be expressed in a series of parallel constructions.

2. **Figurative Language.** These two essays contain both similes and metaphors, figurative language that emphasizes Bacon's ideas and that reflects the Renaissance mind. Identify at least three examples of figurative language, and explain what they suggest to you about Bacon's world.

3. **Essay.** The essay is a flexible genre whose purpose might be to instruct, persuade, or entertain the reader or to analyze or offer commentary on a subject. Essays are described as either formal or informal, depending primarily on subject and tone and on the presentation and development of ideas. What is the purpose of Bacon's essays? What characteristics make them examples of formal essays?

Developing Writing Skills

1. **Writing an Explanation.** In a brief essay explain the meaning of this statement: "Some books are to be tasted, others to be swallowed, and some few to be chewed and digested. . . ." Tell what kinds of books you would put in each category and why.

2. **Writing a Formal Essay.** Choose a serious subject for an essay, either one of Bacon's subjects or a current topic such as nuclear arms, defense spending, or American families. Organize your ideas, then write a formal essay that incorporates several of Bacon's stylistic techniques. Be sure to maintain consistency of tone and to develop your topic point by point, using examples and figurative language where appropriate.

from **Her Protection for Women** *Jane Anger*

One of the earliest examples of protest writing is Her Protection for Women *(1589) by Jane Anger. Nothing is known of the life of Jane Anger. Some scholars believe that her name is a pseudonym. What can be determined is that Anger was an ardent defender of women, for in* Her Protection for Women *she attacks an anti-feminist work and the men responsible for such writing. An emotional writer, Anger explained her motivation for writing the* Protection *when she wrote, ". . . it was ANGER that did write it."*

To *defend them against the scandalous reports of a late surfeiting lover, and all other like venerians that complain so to be overcloyed with women's kindness. 1589.*

To all women in general, and gentle reader whatsoever.

Fie on the falsehood of men, whose minds go oft a madding, and whose tongues can not so soon be wagging, but straight they fall a railing. Was there ever any so abused, so slandered, so railed upon, or so wickedly handled undeservedly as are we women?

A Protection for Women, Etc.

The desire that every man has to show his true vein in writing is unspeakable, and their minds are so carried away with the manner, as no care at all is had of the matter. They run so into rhetoric as often times they overrun the bounds of their own wits and go they know not whither. If they have stretched their invention so hard on a last as it is at a stand, there remains but one help, which is to write of us women. If they may once encroach so far into our presence as they may but see the lining of our outermost garment, they straight think that Apollo[1] honors them in yielding so good a supply to refresh their sore overburdened heads, through studying for matters to indite[2] of. And, therefore, that the god may see how thankfully they receive his liberality (their wits whetted, and their brains almost broken with botching his bounty), they fall straight to dispraising and slandering our silly[3] sex. But judge what the cause should be of this their so great malice towards simple women. Doubtless the weakness of our wits, and our honest bashfulness, by reason whereof they suppose that there is not one amongst us who can or dare reprove their slanders and false reproaches. . . . They have been so daintily fed with our good natures that, like jades (their stomachs are grown so queasy), they surfeit of our kindness. If we will not suffer them to smell on our smocks, they will snatch at our petticoats. But if our honest natures cannot sway with that uncivil kind of jesting then we are coy, yet if we bear with their rudeness, and be somewhat modestly familiar with them, they will straight make matter of nothing, blaring abroad that they have surfeited with love, and then their wits must be shown in telling the manner how.

Among the innumerable number of books to that purpose of late (unlooked for), the new surfeit of an old lover (sent abroad to warn those which are of his own kind from catching the like disease) came by chance to my hands, which, because as well women as men are desirous of novelties, I willingly read over. Neither did the ending thereof less please me

---

1. **Apollo:** in Classical mythology the god of music, poetry, prophecy, and medicine, represented as exemplifying manly youth and beauty.
2. **indite:** to express or describe in prose or verse.
3. **silly:** helpless.

than the beginning, for I was so carried away with the conceit of the Gentleman as that I was quite out of the book, before I thought I had been in the midst thereof: . . . The chief matters therein contained were of two sorts: the one in the dispraise of man's folly, and the other, invective against our sex, their folly proceeding of their own flattery joined with fancy, and our faults are through our folly, with which is some faith.

The greatest fault that does remain in us women is that we are too credulous, for could we flatter as they can dissemble, and use our wits well, as they can their tongues ill, then never would any of them complain of surfeiting. But if we women be so, so perilous cattle, as they term us, I marvel that the gods made not fidelity as well a man, as they created her a woman, and all the moral virtues of their masculine sex, as of the feminine kind, except their deities knew that there was some sovereignty in us women which could not be in them men. But least some snatching fellow should catch me before I fall to the ground (and say they will adorn my head with a feather, affirming that I roam beyond reason, seeing it is most manifest that the man is the head of the woman, and that therefore we ought to be guided by them), I prevent them with this answer. The gods, knowing that the minds of mankind would be aspiring, and having thoroughly viewed the wonderful virtues wherewith women are enriched, least they should provoke us to pride, and so confound us with Lucifer,[4] they bestowed the supremacy over us to man, that of the coxcomb[5] he might only boast, and therefore, for God's sake, let them keep it.

Euthydemus made six kinds of women, and I will approve that there are so many of men, which be poor and rich, bad and good, foul and fair. There are men which are snout-fair, whose faces look like a cream-pot, and yet those are not the fair men I speak of. But I mean those whose conditions are free from knavery, and I term those foul that have neither civility nor honesty. Of these sorts there are none good, none rich, or fair long. But if we do desire to have them good, we must always tie them to the manger and diet their greedy paunches, otherwise they will surfeit. What shall I say? Wealth makes them lavish, wit knavish, beauty effeminate, poverty deceitful, and deformity ugly. Therefore, of me take this counsel:

Esteem of men as of a broken reed,
Mistrust them still, and then you well shall
    speed.

---

4. **Lucifer:** Satan, who was cast out of heaven for leading the revolt of the angels against God.
5. **coxcomb:** a silly, vain, foppish fellow.

Getting at Meaning

1. What is the purpose of *Her Protection for Women,* as stated by the writer?

2. What dilemma does the woman face in dealing with men, according to Anger?

3. What positive qualities of women are brought out in this excerpt? What negative qualities of men are described or implied by Anger?

4. What can be inferred about the work that Anger is responding to? Cite specific statements from the *Protection* to support your answer.

Developing Skills in Reading Literature

Persuasion. Protest writing is essentially persuasive writing, for it attempts to convince the reader to accept the writer's ideas or point of view. One characteristic of persuasive writing is a strong emotional appeal. For the writing to be effective, however, the emotional appeal must be balanced with a logical, intellectual approach. In this essay, what words and phrases have definite emotional overtones? What sentences or passages evoke emotional reactions? What information and arguments elicit intellectual agreement? Does Jane Anger achieve the delicate balance between the emotional and the intellectual? Could she have changed her essay to make it more persuasive? Explain.

Developing Vocabulary

Archaic Words. Look up *speed* in a dictionary and note the definitions that no longer fit contemporary usage. Then reread the couplet that ends this selection. Explain the message in these lines in light of the probable meaning of *speed* in the second line.

Developing Writing Skills

1. **Using Comparisons and Contrasts.** Recall the views of men and women presented by Francis Bacon in "Of Marriage and Single Life." Then write an essay comparing and contrasting his views with those of Anger. In your conclusion, try to generalize about how these two writers seem to view humanity in general.

2. **Developing an Argument.** Select a public issue about which you have strong feelings; for example, nuclear disarmament, civil rights, drunk driving legislation, or environmental protection. Narrow and refine your topic. Then write an essay in which you protest the current situation and attempt to persuade the reader to consider and perhaps accept your point of view.

SIR ANTHONY MILDMAY, 1596: Nicholas Hilliard.
Cleveland Museum of Art.
Purchase from the J. H. Wade Fund.

Translations of the Bible

During the Anglo-Saxon and early Medieval periods, sections of the Bible were translated into English. However, no complete translation existed until John Wycliffe and his followers translated both Old and New Testaments into Middle English. The Wycliffe Bible, which first appeared in 1382, was based on the Vulgate, the official Latin Bible of the Roman Catholic Church. Not everyone agreed with Wycliffe that people should have access to the Bible in their own language. Officials both within and outside the Church objected to his work, charging that independent reading of the Bible would weaken the authority of the clergy. The scarcity of hand-copied manuscripts and limited literacy, too, precluded the widespread distribution and use of the Wycliffe translation.

William Tyndale, a leader in the English Reformation, recognized the need for a translation that would be available for all to read and study. When the Bishop of London refused to support the project, Tyndale went to Germany in 1524 to start his work. King Henry VIII pressured his European friends to withdraw their support from Tyndale. However, he continued to translate, completing the New Testament and parts of the Old Testament between 1525 and 1535. King Henry lifted his ban on the Tyndale Bible in 1535, and the translation was then printed and circulated in England.

The only English translation of the Bible for Roman Catholics was the Douay-Rheims Version, which was translated by exiled priests living in France and was published in 1582 (New Testament) and 1609–10 (Old Testament). This translation was intended primarily for use by the clergy. The basic source was the Latin Vulgate, not the original Greek and Hebrew texts. Although the language of the Douay-Rheims Bible was generally plain, simple English, the translators did use words foreign to English readers in an attempt to insure accuracy and to remain close to the Latin original.

When James became King of England in 1603, Puritan leaders petitioned him to support a new translation of the Bible. Although King James bore no great love for the Puritans, he agreed that English worshippers needed a better translation than the one in popular use. In 1604, he appointed fifty-four of England's most famous scholars and theologians for the task. The group organized into committees and allocated responsibility for research and revision. Instructions to the committees were clear: revise rather than offer a complete new translation; create a lectern Bible, one to be read aloud in church services; use original Greek and Hebrew texts; borrow from Medieval Latin translations and from English translations as needed.

The *King James Authorized Bible* was printed in 1611. This masterpiece of the Renaissance was the principal Protestant Bible in English for over three hundred years and still remains the most important and influential of all the English translations. The beautiful images, graceful simplicity, and measured cadences of the King James Bible make it as much a literary as a religious work.

Since 1946 representatives of the major Protestant denominations in England have been working on a complete new translation of the Bible. The New Testament portion of this translation was published in 1961 under the title *The New English Bible.* For this translation, prominent Biblical scholars and literary advisors collaborated with the official committees and panels in translating ancient Greek texts into the grammar, vocabulary, and rhythms of contemporary English. The translators' emphasis was primarily on clarity and accuracy and secondarily on the preservation of the literary beauty of the original Greek. In many respects *The New English Bible* truly is new, for it incorporates the findings of twentieth-century Biblical scholarship and is based in part on manuscripts unavailable to earlier translators.

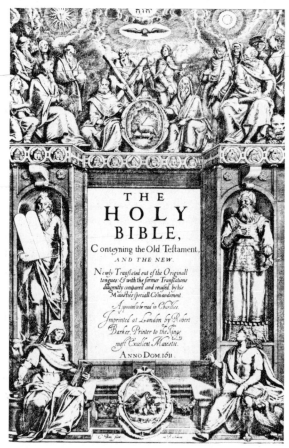

KING JAMES BIBLE FRONTIS, 1611.
Folger Shakespeare Library.

The King James Bible
from The Book of Genesis

The Creation

Chapter 1

In the beginning God created the heaven and the earth.

2 And the earth was without form, and void; and darkness was upon the face of the deep. And the Spirit of God moved upon the face of the waters.

3 And God said, Let there be light: and there was light.

4 And God saw the light, that it was good: and God divided the light from the darkness.

5 And God called the light Day, and the darkness he called Night. And the evening and the morning were the first day.

6 And God said, Let there be a firmament in the midst of the waters, and let it divide the waters from the waters.

7 And God made the firmament, and divided the waters which were under the firmament from the waters which were above the firmament: and it was so.

8 And God called the firmament Heaven. And the evening and the morning were the second day.

9 And God said, Let the waters under the heaven be gathered together unto one place, and let the dry land appear: and it was so.

10 And God called the dry land Earth; and the gathering together of the waters called he Seas: and God saw that it was good.

11 And God said, Let the earth bring forth grass, the herb yielding seed, and the fruit tree yielding fruit after his kind, whose seed is in itself, upon the earth: and it was so.

12 And the earth brought forth grass, and herb yielding seed after his kind, and the tree yielding fruit, whose seed was in itself, after his kind: and God saw that it was good.

13 And the evening and the morning were the third day.

14 And God said, Let there be lights in the firmament of the heaven to divide the day from the night; and let them be for signs, and for seasons, and for days, and years.

15 And let them be for lights in the firmament of the heaven to give light upon the earth: and it was so.

16 And God made two great lights; the greater light to rule the day, and the lesser light to rule the night: he made the stars also.

17 And God set them in the firmament of the heaven to give light upon the earth.

18 And to rule over the day and over the night, and to divide the light from the darkness: and God saw that it was good.

19 And the evening and the morning were the fourth day.

20 And God said, Let the waters bring forth abundantly the moving creature that hath

life, and fowl that may fly above the earth in the open firmament of heaven.

21 And God created great whales, and every living creature that moveth, which the waters brought forth abundantly, after their kind, and every winged fowl after his kind: and God saw that it was good.

22 And God blessed them, saying, Be fruitful, and multiply, and fill the waters in the seas, and let fowl multiply in the earth.

23 And the evening and the morning were the fifth day.

24 And God said, Let the earth bring forth the living creature after his kind, cattle, and creeping thing, and beast of the earth after his kind: and it was so.

25 And God made the beast of the earth after his kind, and cattle after their kind, and every thing that creepeth upon the earth after his kind: and God saw that it was good.

26 And God said, Let us make man in our image, after our likeness: and let them have dominion over the fish of the sea, and over the fowl of the air, and over the cattle, and over all the earth, and over every creeping thing that creepeth upon the earth.

27 So God created man in his own image, in the image of God created he him; male and female created he them.

28 And God blessed them, and God said unto them, Be fruitful, and multiply, and replenish the earth, and subdue it: and have dominion over the fish of the sea, and over the fowl of the air, and over every living thing that moveth upon the earth.

29 And God said, Behold, I have given you every herb bearing seed, which is upon the face of all the earth, and every tree, in the which is the fruit of a tree yielding seed; to you it shall be for meat.

30 And to every beast of the earth, and to every fowl of the air, and to every thing that creepeth upon the earth, wherein there is life, I have given every green herb for meat: and it was so.

31 And God saw every thing that he had made, and, behold, it was very good. And the evening and the morning were the sixth day.

Chapter 2

Thus the heavens and the earth were finished, and all the host of them.

2 And on the seventh day God ended his work which he had made; and he rested on the seventh day from all his work which he had made.

3 And God blessed the seventh day, and sanctified it: because that in it he had rested from all his work which God created and made.

4 These are the generations of the heavens and of the earth when they were created, in the day that the Lord God made the earth and the heavens,

5 And every plant of the field before it was in the earth, and every herb of the field before it grew: for the Lord God had not caused it to rain upon the earth, and there was not a man to till the ground.

6 But there went up a mist from the earth, and watered the whole face of the ground.

7 And the Lord God formed man of the dust of the ground, and breathed into his nostrils the breath of life; and man became a living soul.

8 And the Lord God planted a garden eastward in Eden; and there he put the man whom he had formed.

9 And out of the ground made the Lord God to grow every tree that is pleasant to the sight, and good for food; the tree of life also in the midst of the garden, and the tree of knowledge of good and evil.

10 And a river went out of Eden to water the garden; and from thence it was parted, and became into four heads.

11 The name of the first is Pison: that is it which compasseth the whole land of Havilah, where there is gold;

12 And the gold of that land is good: there is bdellium and the onyx stone.

13 And the name of the second river is Gihon: the same is it that compasseth the whole land of Ethiopia.

14 And the name of the third river is Hiddekel: that is it which goeth toward the east of Assyria. And the fourth river is Euphrates.

15 And the Lord God took the man, and put him into the garden of Eden to dress it and to keep it.

16 And the Lord God commanded the man, saying, Of every tree of the garden thou mayest freely eat:

17 But of the tree of the knowledge of good and evil, thou shalt not eat of it: for in the day that thou eatest thereof thou shalt surely die.

18 And the Lord God said, It is not good that the man should be alone; I will make him an help meet for him.

19 And out of the ground the Lord God formed every beast of the field, and every fowl of the air; and brought them unto Adam to see what he would call them: and whatsoever Adam called every living creature, that was the name thereof.

20 And Adam gave names to all cattle, and to the fowl of the air, and to every beast of the field; but for Adam there was not found an help meet for him.

21 And the Lord God caused a deep sleep to fall upon Adam, and he slept: and he took one of his ribs, and closed up the flesh instead thereof;

22 And the rib which the Lord God had taken from man, made he a woman, and brought her unto the man.

23 And Adam said, This is now bone of my bones, and flesh of my flesh: she shall be called Woman, because she was taken out of Man.

24 Therefore shall a man leave his father and his mother, and shall cleave unto his wife: and they shall be one flesh.

25 And they were both naked, the man and his wife, and were not ashamed.

Chapter 3

Now the serpent was more subtil than any beast of the field which the Lord God had made. And he said unto the woman, Yea, hath God said, Ye shall not eat of every tree of the garden?

2 And the woman said unto the serpent, We may eat of the fruit of the trees of the garden:

3 But of the fruit of the tree which is in the midst of the garden, God hath said, Ye shall not eat of it, neither shall ye touch it, lest ye die.

4 And the serpent said unto the woman, Ye shall not surely die:

5 For God doth know that in the day ye eat thereof, then your eyes shall be opened, and ye shall be as gods, knowing good and evil.

6 And when the woman saw that the tree was good for food, and that it was pleasant to the eyes, and a tree to be desired to make one wise, she took of the fruit thereof, and did eat, and gave also unto her husband with her; and he did eat.

7 And the eyes of them both were opened, and they knew that they were naked; and they sewed fig leaves together, and made themselves aprons.

8 And they heard the voice of the Lord God walking in the garden in the cool of the day: and Adam and his wife hid themselves from the presence of the Lord God amongst the trees of the garden.

9 And the Lord God called unto Adam, and said unto him, Where art thou?

10 And he said, I heard thy voice in the garden, and I was afraid, because I was naked; and I hid myself.

11 And he said, Who told thee that thou wast naked? Hast thou eaten of the tree, whereof I commanded thee that thou shouldest not eat?

12 And the man said, The woman whom thou gavest to be with me, she gave me of the tree, and I did eat.

13 And the Lord God said unto the woman, What is this that thou hast done? And the woman said, The serpent beguiled me, and I did eat.

14 And the Lord God said unto the serpent, Because thou hast done this, thou art cursed above all cattle, and above every beast of the field; upon thy belly shalt thou go, and dust shalt thou eat all the days of thy life:

15 And I will put enmity between thee and the woman, and between thy seed and her seed; it shall bruise thy head, and thou shalt bruise his heel.

16 Unto the woman he said, I will greatly multiply thy sorrow and thy conception; in sorrow thou shalt bring forth children; and thy desire shall be to thy husband, and he shall rule over thee.

17 And unto Adam he said, Because thou hast hearkened unto the voice of thy wife, and hast eaten of the tree, of which I commanded thee, saying, Thou shalt not eat of it: cursed is the ground for thy sake; in sorrow shalt thou eat of it all the days of thy life;

18 Thorns also and thistles shall it bring forth to thee; and thou shalt eat the herb of the field;

19 In the sweat of thy face shalt thou eat bread, till thou return unto the ground; for out of it wast thou taken: for dust thou art, and unto dust shalt thou return.

20 And Adam called his wife's name Eve; because she was the mother of all living.

21 Unto Adam also and to his wife did the Lord God make coats of skins, and clothed them.

22 And the Lord God said, Behold, the man is become as one of us, to know good and evil: and now, lest he put forth his hand, and take also of the tree of life, and eat, and live for ever:

23 Therefore the Lord God sent him forth from the garden of Eden, to till the ground from whence he was taken.

24 So he drove out the man; and he placed at the east of the garden of Eden Cherubims, and a flaming sword which turned every way, to keep the way of the tree of life.

Noah and the Flood

Chapter 7

And the Lord said unto Noah, Come thou and all thy house into the ark; for thee have I seen righteous before me in this generation.

2 Of every clean beast thou shalt take to thee by sevens, the male and his female: and of beasts that are not clean by two, the male and his female.

3 Of fowls also of the air by sevens, the male and the female; to keep seed alive upon the face of all the earth.

4 For yet seven days, and I will cause it to rain upon the earth forty days and forty nights; and every living substance that I have made will I destroy from off the face of the earth.

5 And Noah did according unto all that the Lord commanded him.

6 And Noah was six hundred years old when the flood of waters was upon the earth.

7 And Noah went in, and his sons, and his wife, and his sons' wives with him, into the ark, because of the waters of the flood.

8 Of clean beasts, and of beasts that are not clean, and of fowls, and of every thing that creepeth upon the earth,

9 There went in two and two unto Noah into the ark, the male and the female, as God had commanded Noah.

10 And it came to pass after seven days, that the waters of the flood were upon the earth.

11 In the six hundredth year of Noah's life, in the second month, the seventeenth day of the month, the same day were all the foun-

tains of the great deep broken up, and the windows of heaven were opened.

12 And the rain was upon the earth forty days and forty nights.

13 In the selfsame day entered Noah, and Shem, and Ham, and Japheth, the sons of Noah, and Noah's wife, and the three wives of his sons with them, into the ark;

14 They, and every beast after his kind, and all the cattle after their kind, and every creeping thing that creepeth upon the earth after his kind, and every fowl after his kind, every bird of every sort.

15 And they went in unto Noah into the ark, two and two of all flesh, wherein is the breath of life.

16 And they that went in, went in male and female of all flesh, as God had commanded him: and the Lord shut him in.

17 And the flood was forty days upon the earth; and the waters increased, and bare up the ark, and it was lift up above the earth.

18 And the waters prevailed, and were increased greatly upon the earth; and the ark went upon the face of the waters.

19 And the waters prevailed exceedingly upon the earth; and all the high hills, that were under the whole heaven, were covered.

20 Fifteen cubits upward did the waters prevail; and the mountains were covered.

21 And all flesh died that moved upon the earth, both of fowl, and of cattle, and of beast, and of every creeping thing that creepeth upon the earth, and every man:

22 All in whose nostrils was the breath of life, of all that was in the dry land, died.

23 And every living substance was destroyed which was upon the face of the ground, both man, and cattle, and the creeping things, and the fowl of the heaven; and they were destroyed from the earth: and Noah only remained alive, and they that were with him in the ark.

24 And the waters prevailed upon the earth an hundred and fifty days.

Chapter 8

And God remembered Noah, and every living thing, and all the cattle that was with him in the ark: and God made a wind to pass over the earth, and the waters assuaged;

2 The fountains also of the deep and the windows of heaven were stopped, and the rain from heaven was restrained;

3 And the waters returned from off the earth continually: and after the end of the hundred and fifty days the waters were abated.

4 And the ark rested in the seventh month, on the seventeenth day of the month, upon the mountains of Ararat.

5 And the waters decreased continually until the tenth month: in the tenth month, on the first day of the month, were the tops of the mountains seen.

6 And it came to pass at the end of forty days, that Noah opened the window of the ark which he had made:

7 And he sent forth a raven, which went forth to and fro, until the waters were dried up from off the earth.

8 Also he sent forth a dove from him, to see if the waters were abated from off the face of the ground;

9 But the dove found no rest for the sole of her foot, and she returned unto him into the ark, for the waters were on the face of the whole earth: then he put forth his hand, and took her, and pulled her in unto him into the ark.

10 And he stayed yet other seven days; and again he sent forth the dove out of the ark;

11 And the dove came in to him in the evening; and, lo, in her mouth was an olive leaf pluckt off: so Noah knew that the waters were abated from off the earth.

12 And he stayed yet other seven days; and sent forth the dove; which returned not again unto him any more.

13 And it came to pass in the six hundredth and first year, in the first month, the first day

of the month, the waters were dried up from off the earth: and Noah removed the covering of the ark, and looked, and, behold, the face of the ground was dry.

14 And in the second month, on the seven and twentieth day of the month, was the earth dried.

15 And God spake unto Noah, saying,

16 Go forth of the ark, thou, and thy wife, and thy sons, and thy sons' wives with thee.

17 Bring forth with thee every living thing that is with thee, of all flesh, both of fowl, and of cattle, and of every creeping thing that creepeth upon the earth; that they may breed abundantly in the earth, and be fruitful, and multiply upon the earth.

18 And Noah went forth, and his sons, and his wife, and his sons' wives with him:

19 Every beast, every creeping thing, and every fowl, and whatsoever creepeth upon the earth, after their kinds, went forth out of the ark.

20 And Noah builded an altar unto the Lord; and took of every clean beast, and of every clean fowl, and offered burnt offerings on the altar.

21 And the Lord smelled a sweet savour; and the Lord said in his heart, I will not again curse the ground any more for man's sake; for the imagination of man's heart is evil from his youth; neither will I again smite any more every thing living, as I have done.

22 While the earth remaineth, seedtime and harvest, and cold and heat, and summer and winter, and day and night shall not cease.

Getting at Meaning

1. What familiar Bible stories are recounted in these chapters from The Book of Genesis?

2. What themes, or messages, are presented in these chapters from the Bible?

Developing Skills in Reading Literature

1. **Style: Repetition.** Repetition is a literary technique, used in both poetry and prose, in which a sound, word, phrase, image, line, or grammatical construction is repeated once, several times, or throughout a work. Repetition reinforces meaning and creates an appealing rhythm. The way that repetition is used is one of the many elements that constitute the style of a literary work. Specific types of repetition common in prose include alliteration, anaphora, and parallelism. Assonance, the repetition of a vowel sound within words, and consonance, the repetition of a consonant sound within words, also are types of repetition.

Select a block of at least thirty lines from one of the chapters in The Book of Genesis, and identify and classify the repetitive devices used. Then suggest how repetition makes the passage more effective and memorable.

2. **Imagery.** Images abound in The Book of Genesis. In the opening chapters, images of light and darkness and nature and fertility prevail. After the fall of Adam and Eve, the images change to dust and dryness, and in the story of Noah, the images are concerned mainly with water, animals, and numbers. Identify examples of particularly striking images in these chapters of Genesis. To what senses do the images appeal? What is their overall effect within the context of each chapter? How do the images relate to the subject of the chapter?

Developing Writing Skills

Using Comparisons and Contrasts. Locate other accounts of creation in collections of poetry, mythology, and legends. Choose one and compare and contrast it with the account in the *King James Authorized Bible*. Focus not only on what is said but also on how it is said, on imagery, tone, and poetic devices. Conclude by commenting on the concepts of life and of the deity that emerge from each selection.

Psalm 23

A Psalm of David

The Lord is my shepherd; I shall not want.

2 He maketh me to lie down in green pastures: he leadeth me beside the still waters.

3 He restoreth my soul: he leadeth me in the paths of righteousness for his name's sake.

4 Yea, though I walk through the valley of the shadow of death, I will fear no evil: for thou art with me; thy rod and thy staff they comfort me.

5 Thou preparest a table before me in the presence of mine enemies: thou anointest my head with oil; my cup runneth over.

6 Surely goodness and mercy shall follow me all the days of my life: and I will dwell in the house of the Lord for ever.

Psalm 100

A Psalm of Praise

Make a joyful noise unto the Lord, all ye lands.

2 Serve the Lord with gladness: come before his presence with singing.

3 Know ye that the Lord he is God: it is he that hath made us, and not we ourselves; we are his people, and the sheep of his pasture.

4 Enter into his gates with thanksgiving, and into his courts with praise: be thankful unto him, and bless his name.

5 For the Lord is good; his mercy is everlasting; and his truth endureth to all generations.

Getting at Meaning

What qualities of God are emphasized in these psalms? What relationship between God and human beings is projected in each?

Developing Skills in Reading Literature

Metaphor. The same metaphor is used in both of these psalms to describe the relationship between God and human beings. What is the basic metaphor? Cite the lines in which the metaphor is presented in each psalm. What concept of the deity is emphasized by this metaphor? what concept of human beings? of the earth?

From Ecclesiastes

Chapter 3

To every thing there is a season, and a time to every purpose under the heaven:

2 A time to be born, and a time to die; a time to plant, and a time to pluck up that which is planted;

3 A time to kill, and a time to heal; a time to break down, and a time to build up;

4 A time to weep, and a time to laugh; a time to mourn, and a time to dance;

5 A time to cast away stones, and a time to gather stones together; a time to embrace, and a time to refrain from embracing;

6 A time to get, and a time to lose; a time to keep, and a time to cast away;

7 A time to rend, and a time to sew; a time to keep silence, and a time to speak;

8 A time to love, and a time to hate; a time of war, and a time of peace.

LADY MARGARET BEAUFORT. *Anonymous.*
National Portrait Gallery, London.

Getting at Meaning

What one idea is supported by the numerous examples in this passage?

Developing Skills in Reading Literature

Repetition and Theme. How does the repetition of the word *time* reinforce the theme of this selection? What parallel grammatical structure is repeated in verses 2–8? What new parallel structure is introduced in verse 8? Describe the rhythmic effect created by the repetitions in this excerpt. In what ways does repetition intensify the impact of the message on the reader or listener?

Developing Vocabulary

Context Clue: Contrast. Each verse of this excerpt from *Ecclesiastes* sets up contrasts, generally utilizing words and phrases with opposite or nearly opposite meanings; for example, *born* and *die, kill* and *heal.* Apply this understanding to determine the definition of *rend* in verse 7.

Development of the English Language Through Biblical Translations of I Corinthians Chapter 13

from The Second Wycliffite Version

If I speke with tungis of men and of aungels, and I have not charite, I am maad as bras sownynge, or a cymbal tynklynge. 2 And if I have prophecie, and knowe alle mysteries, and al kunnynge, and if I have al feith, so that I meve hillis fro her place, and I have not charite, I am nought. 3 And if I departe alle my goodis in to the metis of pore men, and if I bitake my bodi, so that I brenne, and if I have not charite, it profitith to me no thing. 4 Charite is pacient, it is benygne; charite envyeth not, it doith not wickidli, it is not blowun, 5 it is not coveytouse, it sekith not tho thingis that ben hise owne, it is not stirid to wrathe, it thenkith not yvel, 6 it joyeth not on wickidnesse, but it joyeth togidere to treuthe; 7 it suffrith alle thingis, it bileveth alle thingis, it hopith alle thingis, it susteyneth alle thingis. Charite fallith nevere doun, 8 whether prophecies schulen be voided, ethir langagis schulen ceesse, ethir science schal be distried. 9 For a parti we knowun, and a parti we prophecien; 10 but whanne that schal come that is parfit, that thing that is of parti schal be avoidid. 11 Whanne I was a litil child, I spak as a litil child, I undurstood as a litil child, I thoughte as a litil child; but whanne I was maad a man, I avoidide tho thingis that weren of a litil child. 12 And we seen now bi a myrour in derknesse, but thanne face to face; now I knowe of parti, but thanne I schal knowe, as I am knowun. 13 And now dwellen feith, hope, and charite, these thre; but the most of these is charite.

c.1395

from Tyndale's Translation

Though I spake with the tonges of men and angels, and yet had no love, I were even as soundynge brasse: or as a tynklynge cymball. 2 And though I coulde prophesy, and understode all secretes, and all knowledge: yee, yf I had all fayth, so that I coulde move mountayns oute of ther places, and yet had no love, I were nothinge. 3 And though I bestowed all my gooddes to fede the poore, and though I gave my body even that I burned, and yet had no love, it profeteth me nothinge.

4 Love suffreth longe and is corteous. Love envieth not. Love doth not frowardly, swelleth not, 5 dealeth not dishonestly, seketh not her awne, is not

provoked to anger, thinketh not evyll, 6 rejoyseth not in iniquite: but rejoyseth in the trueth, 7 suffreth all thinges, beleveth all thinges, hopeth all thinges, endureth in all thinges. 8 Though that prophesyinge fayle, other tonges shall cease, or knowledge vanysshe awaye, yet love falleth never awaye.

9 For oure knowledge is unparfect and oure prophesyinge is unperfect. 10 But when that which is parfect, is come, then that which is unparfect, shall be done awaye. 11 When I was a chylde, I spake as a chylde, I understode as a chylde, I ymagened as a chylde. But assone as I was a man, I put away chyldeshnes. 12 Now we se in a glasse, even in a darke speakynge: but then shall we se face to face. Now I knowe unparfectly: but then shall I knowe even as I am knowen. 13 Now abydeth fayth, hope, and love, even these thre: but the chefe of these is love.

1525; revised 1535

from The Douay-Rheims Version

If I speake with the tonges of men and of Angels, and have not charitie: I am become as sounding brasse, or a tinkling cymbal. 2 And if I should have prophecie, and knew al mysteries, and al knowledge, and if I should have al faith so that I could remove mountaines, and have not charitie, I am nothing. 3 And if I should distribute al my goods to be meate for the poore, and if I should deliver my body so that I burne, and have not charitie, it doth profit me nothing. 4 Charitie is patient, is benigne: Charitie envieth not, dealeth not perversly: is not puffed up, 5 is not ambitious, seeketh not her owne, is not provoked to anger, thinketh not evil: 6 rejoyceth not upon iniquitie, but rejoyceth with the truth: 7 suffereth al things, beleeveth al things, hopeth al things, beareth al things. 8 Charitie never falleth away: whether prophecies shal be made voide, or tonges shal cease, or knowledge shal be destroied. 9 For in part we know, and in part we prophecie. 10 But when that shal come that is perfect, that shal be made voide that is in part. 11 When I was a litle one, I spake as a litle one, I understood as a litle one, I thought as a litle one. But when I was made a man, I did away the things that belonged to a litle one. 12 We see now by a glasse in a darke sort: but then face to face. Now I know in part: but then I shal know as also I am knowen. 13 And now there remaine, faith, hope, charitie, these three, but the greater of these is charitie.

1582

from The King James Authorized Version

Though I speak with the tongues of men and of angels, and have not charity, I am become as sounding brass, or a tinkling cymbal. 2 And though I have the gift of prophecy, and understand all mysteries, and all knowledge; and though

I have all faith, so that I could remove mountains, and have no charity, I am nothing. 3 And though I bestow all my goods to feed the poor, and though I give my body to be burned, and have not charity, it profiteth me nothing. 4 Charity suffereth long, and is kind; charity envieth not; charity vaunteth not itself, is not puffed up, 5 doth not behave itself unseemly, seeketh not her own, is not easily provoked, thinketh no evil; 6 rejoiceth not in iniquity, but rejoiceth in the truth; 7 beareth all things, believeth all things, hopeth all things, endureth all things. 8 Charity never faileth: but whether there be prophecies they shall fail; whether there be tongues, they shall cease; whether there be knowledge, it shall vanish away. 9 For we know in part, and we prophesy in part. 10 But when that which is perfect is come, then that which is in part shall be done away. 11 When I was a child, I spake as a child, I understood as a child, I thought as a child: but when I became a man, I put away childish things. 12 For now we see through a glass, darkly; but then face to face: now I know in part; but then shall I know even as also I am known. 13 And now abideth faith, hope, charity, these three; but the greatest of these is charity.

1611, in edition of 1873

from **The New English Bible**

I may speak in tongues of men or of angels, but if I am without love, am a sounding gong or a clanging cymbal. I may have the gift of prophecy, and know every hidden truth; I may have faith strong enough to move 2 mountains; but if I have no love, I am nothing. I may dole out all I possess, or even give my body to be burnt, but if I have no love, I am none the 3 better.

Love is patient; love is kind and envies no one. Love is never boastful, nor conceited, nor rude; never selfish, not quick to take offence. Love keeps 4 no score of wrongs; does not gloat over other men's sins, but delights in the 5 truth. There is nothing love cannot face; there is no limit to its faith, its 6 hope, and its endurance. 7

Love will never come to an end. Are there prophets? their work will be over. Are there tongues of ecstasy? they will cease. Is there knowledge? 8 it will vanish away; for our knowledge and our prophecy alike are partial, and the partial vanishes when wholeness comes. When I was a child, my 9 speech, my outlook, and my thoughts were all childish. When I grew up, 10 I had finished with childish things. Now we see only puzzling reflections 11 in a mirror, but then we shall see face to face. My knowledge now is partial; 12 then it will be whole, like God's knowledge of me. In a word, there are three 13 things that last for ever: faith, hope, and love; but the greatest of them all is love.

1961

JOB, HIS WIFE AND HIS FRIENDS, 1786. *William Blake.*
Tate Gallery, London.

Getting at Meaning

Describe briefly the message in *I Corinthians.*

Developing Skills in Reading Literature

Language Development. In examining these five translations, a movement from Middle English to Modern English to the English of the twentieth century is discernible. For example, in comparing the excerpt from the Wycliffe Bible with the one from the Tyndale translation, you notice that Tyndale's spellings of words such as *angels* and *brasse* are closer to Modern English but that he still retains the *-th* ending on many verbs. Identify other similarities and differences in the spellings, vocabulary, structure, and ways of expressing ideas in these two versions of *I Corinthians*. Try to generalize about the changes in language that have taken place in the 140 years that separate the two translations. Do the same kind of comparison between the Douay-Rheims version and the King James version and then between the King James version and *The New English Bible* version. Focus on the language rather than on the writing styles, for style differs even among translators who are contemporaries.

John Donne
1572–1631

John Donne, whose writing is characterized by paradoxes, was something of a paradox himself. He was a poet turned preacher, a sensualist and scholar, a lover and a mystic, a doubter and a believer. He was both dramatic and introspective, worldly and spiritual. Steeped in medieval learning, he was at the same time open to all the fresh currents of seventeenth-century science and discovery. Critics say that Donne "married passion to reason," that he "thought with his body and felt with his mind," and that his "major themes were woman and God," or actually himself in relation to each.

The eldest son of a prosperous tradesman, Donne was born in London in 1572. His grandfather was John Heywood, a well known satirist and epigramist, and his mother was related by marriage to Sir Thomas More, Chancellor of England under Henry VIII. As Roman Catholics the family suffered persecution during Queen Elizabeth's reign. Donne's uncle was imprisoned for conspiring with the Jesuits, and his brother, arrested for concealing a priest, died in Newgate prison.

When he was only eleven, Donne was sent to Oxford University and spent three years there, and three more at Cambridge University, but as a Catholic he could not earn a degree. He then traveled in Spain and Italy, and in the early 1590's studied law, languages, and theology at the Inns of Court in London. The poetry he wrote as a student reveals his preoccupations: the joys of physical pleasure and the urgent question of finding a true religion. These early poems attracted a coterie of ardent admirers, who circulated the poems and later ones as well in manuscript form.

In 1596 and 1597 Donne participated in naval expeditions to Cádiz and the Azores, along with other gentlemen adventurers aspiring to careers in public service. In 1598 Donne became secretary to the powerful Sir Thomas Egerton, Lord Keeper of the Great Seal. Then, just as a brilliant career in the field of diplomacy seemed open to him, Donne fell in love with Anne More, Egerton's sixteen-year-old niece, and the two were secretly married.

JOHN DONNE (after Isaac Oliver). *Anonymous. National Portrait Gallery, London.*

Her enraged father had Donne arrested and dismissed from his post, dashing his hopes for worldly success.

For some years King James I had been interested in the young poet as an important recruit in the cause of Protestantism. The king pressured Donne to become a clergyman, which he finally did in 1615. Within six years Donne was named dean of St. Paul's Cathedral, where he achieved fame as a compelling preacher. In his sermons, of which 160 have been preserved, and in his *Devotions Upon Emergent Occasions* (1623), Donne refers often to his own life, his fears, his past sins. His prose is full of wit and poetic language even while it is preoccupied with death, decay, and damnation.

Nearing the end of his life and already an invalid, Donne ordered a monument and posed for the sculptor wearing a funeral shroud. On the first Friday in Lent, he rose from his deathbed to preach before the king in St. Paul's, his famous final sermon on the subject of his own earthly end: *Death's Duel.* He died peacefully on March 31, 1631.

Song

Sweetest love, I do not go
  For weariness of thee,
Nor in hope the world can show
  A fitter love for me;
    But since that I   5
Must die at last, 'tis best,
To use myself in jest
  Thus by feigned deaths to die.[1]

Yesternight the sun went hence,
  And yet is here today;   10
He hath no desire nor sense,
  Nor half so short a way.[2]
    Then fear not me,[3]
But believe that I shall make
Speedier journeys, since I take   15
  More wings and spurs than he.

O how feeble is man's power,
  That if good fortune fall,
Cannot add another hour,
  Nor a lost hour recall!   20
    But come bad chance,[4]
And we join to it our strength,
And we teach it art and length,
  Itself o'er us to advance.

When thou sigh'st, thou sigh'st not wind,   25
  But sigh'st my soul away;
When thou weep'st unkindly kind,
  My life's blood doth decay.
    It cannot be
That thou lov'st me as thou say'st,   30
If in thine my life thou waste;
  Thou are the best of me.

Let not thy divining heart
  Forethink me any ill;
Destiny may take thy part,   35
  And may thy fears fulfill;
    But think that we
Are but turned aside to sleep;
They who one another keep
  Alive, ne'er parted be.   40

---

1. **Thus by . . . die:** to accustom oneself to death in a joking manner by pretended deaths.
2. **Nor . . . way:** nor so short a way to go as I have.
3. **fear not me:** fear not for me.
4. **bad chance:** bad luck.

Getting at Meaning

1. The speaker gives reasons why his beloved should not grieve at his absence. What are these reasons?

2. According to the speaker, what is the effect of good fortune? of bad fortune?

3. Why won't the lovers in this poem ever be parted?

Developing Skills in Reading Literature

1. **Rhyme Scheme and Meter.** What is the rhyme scheme of this poem? Is it consistent throughout the poem? Scan the first three stanzas. Is the meter of each stanza regular? Is the metrical pattern consistent from one stanza to the next? How would you describe the overall rhythm created by the meter and rhyme scheme?

2. **Personification, Metaphor, and Allusion.** Donne often weaves several types of poetic language into a rich tapestry of meaning. In the second stanza of this poem, for example, he employs personification, metaphor, and allusion to bring out the idea that the speaker will return quickly. Identify the ways that the sun is personified in this stanza. Why is it appropriate that the lover compare himself to the sun? The phrase

"wings and spurs" used in relation to the sun is an allusion to a Greek myth. Research the myths about the sun. Then explain this allusion.

3. **Oxymoron.** In line 27 Donne uses the oxymoron "unkindly kind." To whom does this phrase refer? What does it mean? How does its meaning relate to the rest of the poem?

Developing Vocabulary

Multiple Meanings of Words. Look up *divine* in a dictionary. Then reread line 33. What meanings of *divine* fit the phrase "divining heart"? What meanings are suggested by the entire phrase?

The Canonization

For God's sake, hold your tongue, and let me love,
   Or chide my palsy, or my gout,
My five gray hairs, or ruined fortune flout,
   With wealth your state, your mind with arts improve,
     Take you a course,[2] get you a place,[3]   5
     Observe his Honor, or his Grace,[4]
Or the King's real, or his stamped face[5]
     Contemplate; what you will, approve,[6]
     So you will let me love.

Alas, alas, who's injured by my love?   10
   What merchant's ships have my sighs drowned?
Who says my tears have overflowed his ground?
   When did my colds a forward spring remove?[7]
     When did the heats which my veins fill
     Add one more to the plaguy bill?[8]   15
Soldiers find wars, and lawyers find out still
   Litigious men, which quarrels move,
   Though she and I do love.

---

1. **Canonization:** declaring a deceased person to be a saint; also, making something divine.
2. **Take . . . course:** find a way of advancing yourself.
3. **place:** a job.
4. **Observe . . . Grace:** get to know a lord or bishop.
5. **stamped face:** the likeness of the King stamped on coins.
6. **approve:** try out.
7. **forward . . . remove:** hold back an early spring.
8. **plaguy bill:** lists of those who died of the plague.

Call us what you will, we are made such by love;
   Call her one, me another fly,[9]   20
We are tapers too, and at our own cost die,[10]
   And we in us find the eagle and the dove,[11]
    The phoenix riddle[12] hath more wit[13]
By us; we two being one, are it.
So to one neutral thing both sexes fit.   25
  We die and rise the same, and prove
  Mysterious by this love.

We can die by it, if not live by love,
  And if unfit for tombs and hearse
Our legend be, it will be fit for verse;   30
   And if no piece of chronicle we prove,
    We'll build in sonnets pretty rooms;
    As well a well-wrought urn becomes
The greatest ashes, as half-acre tombs,
   And by these hymns, all shall approve   35
   Us canonized for love:[14]

And thus invoke us; "You whom reverend love
  Made one another's hermitage;
You, to whom love was peace, that now is rage;
   Who did the whole world's soul contract, and drove   40
   Into the glasses of your eyes[15]
    (So made such mirrors and such spies,
That they did all to you epitomize)
   Countries, towns, courts: beg from above
   A pattern of your love!"   45

---

9. **fly:** The taper-fly burns itself to death by approaching a flame.

10. **We . . . die:** Dying was a popular metaphor for consummation of physical love. This line refers to the then popular belief that lovers shorten their lives by lovemaking.

11. **eagle . . . dove:** the masculine and the feminine.

12. **phoenix riddle:** the mystery of the legendary bird, which contained both sexes, burned itself to death, and then rose again from its own ashes.

13. **hath more wit:** makes more sense.

14. **And if no . . . for love:** If our love is not recorded in history, and if we do not have any children, then the love will be immortalized in verse.

15. **drove . . . eyes:** forced into each other's eyes by intense stares. For the lovers, their love was the whole world.

Getting at Meaning

1. Who or what is canonized in this poem?

2. In the first stanza the speaker addresses an unnamed person. What is the speaker's message?

3. What is the speaker's view of love, as presented in the second and third stanzas?

4. What is the power of poetry, as described in the fourth stanza?

5. What is the connotation of *invoke*? Explain the invocation in the fifth stanza.

Developing Skills in Reading Literature

1. **Unity: Meter, Rhyme, Repetition.** Meter, rhyme, and repetition are tools used by a poet to create and reinforce unity. Scan the meter, and chart the rhyme scheme of this poem. Are both patterns consistent throughout the poem? How are the stanzas connected through the rhyme scheme? What key word is repeated at the ends of lines in each stanza? Why is this a significant repetition, given the subject of the poem?

2. **Rhetorical Question.** Note the use of rhetorical questions in the second stanza. The first question presents a controlling idea; the questions that follow develop the idea. What is the general focus of the supporting questions? What idea about love, introduced in the first stanza, do the rhetorical questions reinforce?

3. **Metaphor, Symbol, and Allusion.** The poetic language in the third stanza is multi-layered and complex, interweaving metaphor, symbol, and allusion. The speaker compares himself and his lover to the taper-fly, which is drawn to the flame that destroys it. What does flame symbolize for the lovers? How is the lovers' "flame" destructive? How does the allusion to the phoenix riddle continue the idea of destruction by fire? What opposite idea is embodied by the phoenix? In what lines does the speaker identify himself and his lover with the phoenix? How is martyrdom in a religious sense related to the same idea of death and rebirth? How does martyrdom relate to canonization?

The fusion of the individual lovers is another key idea in this stanza. The eagle and the dove symbolize the masculine and the feminine, both of which are contained in the phoenix. Notice that the idea of fusion is not clear when the eagle and the dove are first mentioned. In what lines does the idea become clear? What sacrifice must the lovers make? What happens to their masculinity and femininity? How does this relate to sainthood and divinity?

4. **Title and Theme.** Often the title of a poem provides a clue to its theme. The title becomes especially important when the poem is as complicated and difficult as this one by Donne. Think about the meaning of "The Canonization," and review what Donne says about love in each stanza. For the fourth and fifth stanzas, try to relate the message about love to the idea of canonization, as was done in the preceding exercise for the third stanza. Then formulate a thematic statement for the entire poem.

from **Meditation 17**

Nunc lento sonitu dicunt, Morieris.
(Now, this bell tolling softly for another,
says to me, Thou must die.)

Perchance he for whom this bell tolls may be so ill as that he knows not it tolls for him; and perchance I may think myself so much better than I am as that they who are about me and see my state may have caused it to toll for me, and I know not that.

The church is catholic, universal, so are all her actions; all that she does belongs to all. When she baptizes a child, that action concerns me; for that child is thereby connected to that body which is my head too, and ingrafted into that body whereof I am a member.[1] And when she buries a man, that action concerns me: all mankind is of one author, and is one volume. When one man dies, one chapter is not torn out of the book, but translated into a better language; and every chapter must be so translated. God employs several translators; some pieces are translated by age, some by sickness, some by war, some by justice; but God's hand is in every translation, and his hand shall bind up all our scattered leaves again for that library where every book shall lie open to one another.

As therefore the bell that rings to a sermon calls not upon the preacher only but upon the congregation to come, so this bell calls us all; but how much more me who am brought so near the door by this sickness! There was a contention as far as a suit[2]—in which piety and dignity, religion and estimation,[3] were mingled—which of the religious orders should ring to prayers first in the morning; and it was determined that they should ring first that rose earliest.

If we understand aright the dignity of this bell that tolls for our evening prayer, we would be glad to make it ours by rising early, in that application, that it might be ours as well as his, whose indeed it is.

The bell doth toll for him that thinks it doth; and though it intermit again, yet from that minute that that occasion wrought upon him he is united to God.

Who casts not up his eye to the sun when it rises? but who takes off his eye from a comet when that breaks out? Who bends not his ear to any bell which upon any occasion rings? but who can remove it from that bell which is passing a piece of himself out of this world?

No man is an island entire of itself; every man is a piece of the continent, a part of the main.[4] If a clod be washed away by the sea, Europe is the less, as well as if a promontory were, as well as if a manor of thy friend's or of thine own were. Any man's death diminishes me, because I am involved in mankind, and therefore never send to know for whom the bell tolls; it tolls for thee. . . .

---

1. **member:** the Christian church is the head of all men, as well as a body made up of its members.
2. **suit:** a lawsuit.
3. **estimation:** self-esteem.
4. **main:** mainland.

Getting at Meaning

1. What kind of bell precipitates Donne's meditation? To what other kinds of tollings does Donne refer in this selection?

2. When Donne wrote "Meditation 17," he was recovering from a serious illness. What influence might his condition have had on the meditation?

3. How does Donne illustrate the idea that an individual does not exist in isolation? Use quotations from the selection to support your answer.

4. Explain in your own words the last paragraph of this excerpt.

5. What is Donne's attitude toward death, as suggested in this selection?

Developing Skills in Reading Literature

Analogy. Donne draws an analogy between the translation of a book and death. Find the analogy and explain its points of comparison. What view of life emerges from the analogy? what view of humanity? of the relationship between God and humanity?

Developing Vocabulary

Understanding Changes in Language. This selection is easier to read than the excerpt from the Wycliffe Bible, for Donne wrote in Modern English. What characteristics, however, distinguish this selection from the Modern English of contemporary writers? Are the differences mainly in vocabulary? spelling? sentence structures? idioms? Explain.

Developing Writing Skills

Narrating an Autobiographical Incident. Donne contends that no one lives in isolation, that "No man is an island." Write an essay in which you describe a personal experience that illustrates this theme.

Holy Sonnet 4   *John Donne*

At the round earth's imagined corners,[1] blow
Your trumpets, angels; and arise, arise
From death, you numberless infinities
Of souls, and to your scattered bodies go;
All whom the flood did, and fire shall, o'erthrow,   5
All whom war, dearth, age, agues,[2] tyrannies,
Despair, law, chance hath slain, and you whose eyes
Shall behold God, and never taste death's woe.[3]
But let them sleep, Lord, and me mourn a space;
For, if above all these, my sins abound,   10
'Tis late to ask abundance of Thy grace
When we are there. Here on this lowly ground,
Teach me how to repent; for that's as good
As if Thou hadst sealed my pardon with Thy blood.

---

1. **imagined corners:** The old flat maps of the world depicted angels blowing trumpets from the four corners.
2. **agues:** fevers.
3. **you . . . woe:** those still alive at the Last Judgment who will be judged without having died.

Holy Sonnet 6   *John Donne*

Death, be not proud, though some have called thee
Mighty and dreadful, for thou art not so;
For those whom thou think'st thou dost overthrow
Die not, poor Death, nor yet canst thou kill me.
From rest and sleep, which but thy pictures be,   5
Much pleasure; then from thee much more must flow,[1]
And soonest our best men with thee do go,
Rest of their bones, and soul's delivery.
Thou art slave to fate, chance, kings, and desperate men,
And dost with poison, war, and sickness dwell,   10
And poppy[2] or charms can make us sleep as well
And better than thy stroke; why swell'st[3] thou then?
One short sleep past, we wake eternally
And death shall be no more; Death, thou shalt die.

---

1. **From rest . . . flow:** If we derive pleasure from rest and sleep, which are
only images of death, we should derive much more from actual death.
2. **poppy:** opium, a narcotic drug.
3. **swell'st:** that is, with pride.

THE SALTONSTALL FAMILY, ca. 1637. David Des Granges.
Tate Gallery, London.

Getting at Meaning

HOLY SONNET 4

1. What is the subject of the octave?

2. What does the speaker mean by this line: "But let them sleep, Lord, and me mourn a space"? Why does the speaker make this request?

3. What is the speaker's concept of repentence?

HOLY SONNET 6

4. Describe the speaker's attitude toward death. In what ways is this view of death reinforced throughout the sonnet?

5. Explain the meaning of the final two lines.

Developing Skills in Reading Literature

1. **Sonnet.** Review the characteristics of the Italian sonnet. Then explain how each of these sonnets exemplifies these characteristics. Answer the following questions in your explanation: Are the poems written in the usual sonnet meter? What are their rhyme schemes? What off-rhymes do you detect? What is the relationship between octave and sestet in "Holy Sonnet 4"? in "Holy Sonnet 6"? How does the final couplet function in each sonnet?

Besides their form, these two sonnets share certain unifying characteristics. What tone characterizes the octaves of both sonnets? the sestets? What common themes connect the two sonnets?

2. **Personification and Paradox.** Trace the personification of death throughout "Holy Sonnet 6," quoting words and phrases from the poem. How does personification diminish the power and might of death for the reader? Why is the statement "Death, thou shalt die" an appropriate culmination to the personification in this poem? Notice that this statement is an example of both personification and paradox. Why is the statement an apparent contradiction? What underlying truth is emphasized by the paradox?

Developing Writing Skills

1. **Using Comparisons and Contrasts.** Write an essay in which you compare and contrast one of Donne's sonnets with a sonnet by Sidney or Spenser. Consider structure, tone, subject, and figurative language.

2. **Using Comparisons.** Write an essay in which you compare "Holy Sonnet 6" with "Psalm 23." Describe similarities in mood, tone, figurative language, form, and theme.

Ben Jonson
1572–1637

Ben Jonson was one of the most learned of Renaissance writers and the first to systematically infuse into English literature the spirit of the classics. He revolutionized the theatre, inspired an entire "tribe" of imitators, and wrote some of the finest lyrics in the English language.

Jonson was born in London in 1572. His father, an impoverished minister, died two months before his son was born. His mother, apparently a spirited and energetic woman, married a bricklayer when the boy was two. After some preliminary schooling, Jonson was admitted to Westminster, a large and prestigious public school headed by William Camden, a prominent Elizabethan scholar. From Camden, Jonson learned classical literature as well as the habits of scholarship that were to put him on equal terms with the foremost scholars of his time.

Jonson was only eight years younger than Shakespeare and, like Shakespeare, he began his career in the theater as both an actor and playwright. When his acting seemed less than brilliant, the theater manager assigned Jonson to his "stable" of playwrights. Satire, which was just emerging as a popular dramatic form, was a form well suited to Jonson's original ideas, combative nature, and scathing wit. The first play on which he collaborated so enraged the authorities that they ordered all the playhouses closed and Jonson imprisoned for several months. The next year his quarrelsome temperament got him into trouble again when he killed an actor in a duel. He was jailed and barely escaped the gallows.

Jonson became famous with the comedy *Every Man in His Humour* (1598), based on the medieval idea that four bodily fluids, or "humours," determine a person's health and disposition. Even more successful was *Every Man out of His Humour* (1599), which like its predecessor was performed by Shakespeare's company at the Globe Theater. The same group produced later plays such as *Volpone, the Fox* (1606) and *The Alchemist* (1610). Jonson's popular comedies and his few successful tragedies were strongly influenced by classical drama. His comedies included the kinds of stock characters typical of Latin comedy; his tragedies adhered to Aristotle's rules regarding dramatic unity and historical accuracy.

Jonson was a many-sided man. A scholarly perfectionist, he also frequented taverns such as the Mermaid or the Devil. A man great in bulk, with what he called his "mountain belly" and "rocky face," he was a lively conversationalist who knew well his city and most of its important citizens. He dictated literary taste to his fellow patrons, criticized, quarreled, and reconciled with other writers, and attracted an admiring group of young poets who were proud to be called his "sons, sealed to the tribe of Benjamin."

Jonson achieved legendary status even in his own time, yet his life encompassed tragedy as well as success. A fire destroyed his great library, one of the finest collections in England. His later plays were failures, to the obvious delight of his critics. Ill health and finally paralytic strokes plagued his last years and ended the brilliant exchanges at the taverns. His writings, though, continued to exert an influence well into the eighteenth century.

BEN JONSON (after Van Blyenberch). *Anonymous. Granger Collection.*

On My First Daughter

Here lies to each her parents' ruth,[1]
Mary, the daughter of their youth:
Yet, all heaven's gifts, being heaven's due,
It makes the father, less, to rue.
At six months end, she parted hence   5
With safety of her innocence;
Whose soul heaven's Queen, (whose name she bears)
In comfort of her mother's tears,
Hath placed amongst her virgin-train:
Where, while that severed doth remain,   10
This grave partakes the fleshly birth,
Which cover lightly, gentle earth.

---

1. **ruth:** sorrow, grief, remorse.

On My First Son

Farewell, thou child of my right hand, and joy;
My sin was too much hope of thee, loved boy.
Seven years thou wert lent to me, and I thee pay,
Exacted by thy fate, on the just day.
O, could I lose all father now. For why   5
Will man lament the state he should envy?
To have so soon 'scaped world's, and flesh's, rage,
And if no other misery, yet age?
Rest in soft peace, and, asked, say here doth lie
Ben Jonson, his best piece of poetry.   10
For whose sake, henceforth, all his vows be such,
As what he loves may never like too much.

---

1. **child . . . hand:** The Hebrew name Benjamin means literally "son of my right hand." Jonson's son died of the plague in 1603.
2. **just:** exact.
3. **lose . . . father:** lose the feeling of being a father.

Getting at Meaning

1. What human feelings about the children and about their deaths are expressed by the speaker in these poems?

2. In each poem the speaker suggests that parents do not really possess their children. Quote the lines in each poem that express this idea.

3. From what thought does the speaker in each poem draw comfort?

4. Which line suggests that the speaker views his son as his most perfect creation? What might account for the fact that he seems to grieve more for his son than for his daughter?

Developing Skills in Reading Literature

1. **Elegy.** Each poem is an elegy in the narrow sense of the term: a poetic tribute to a person, usually someone who has died recently. In both poems Jonson laments the deaths of his children. Describe the tone of each poem, using several adjectives. Is the tone exactly the same in each poem? Is the tone of each appropriate to an elegy? Explain.

Choose one poem and analyze the way that tone has been achieved. Factors to consider include rhythm, meter, and the connotations of words and phrases.

2. **Couplet.** Both "On My First Daughter" and "On My First Son" are written in couplets. However, Jonson's use of the couplet is somewhat different in each poem. Notice that each couplet in "On My First Son" is self-contained, or "closed." This kind of unit is characteristic of the heroic couplet, the form in which the poem is written. Compare and contrast this use of couplets as closed units with the use of couplets in "On My First Daughter," citing lines from the poem to support your conclusions. Then comment on how the couplet form seems to suit the overall rhythm, tone, and development of idea in both poems.

THOMAS PEARTREE. *Thomas Gainsborough.*
Ipswich Borough Council Museums.

Song, to Celia

Drink to me only with thine eyes,
    And I will pledge with mine;
Or leave a kiss but in the cup,
    And I'll not look for wine.
The thirst that from the soul doth rise   5
    Doth ask a drink divine;
But might I of Jove's nectar sup,
    I would not change for thine.

I sent thee late a rosy wreath,
    Not so much honoring thee   10
As giving it a hope, that there
    It could not withered be.
But thou thereon didst only breathe,
    And sent'st it back to me;
Since when it grows, and smells, I swear,   15
    Not of itself but thee.

Getting at Meaning

1. How does the speaker feel about Celia? What seems to be the purpose of the poem?

2. For what does the speaker's soul thirst? What will best satisfy his thirst?

3. What is Celia's effect on the wreath? Why?

Developing Skills in Reading Literature

1. **Conceit.** A conceit is an extended metaphor that is more elaborate, formal, and ingeniously clever than the ordinary metaphor. The conceit in the first stanza deals with the idea of drinking and nourishment. Analyze this conceit, explaining the various points of comparison. Then examine the conceit in the second stanza in which the speaker describes his lover as a source of life. How does this stanza suggest the idea of youth, life, and vitality?

2. **Dramatic Lyric.** A dramatic lyric is a lyric poem in which the speaker addresses one or more listeners. What is essentially dramatic about this kind of poem? What dramatic qualities are evidenced by "Song, to Celia"? How does the title of the poem link it to the origins of the lyric and to drama in its broadest sense?

Developing Writing Skills

Writing a Dramatic Lyric. Write a short dramatic lyric in which you celebrate love, friendship, or kinship. Include at least one extended metaphor that brings out your feelings about the subject. Model your verse form on that of Jonson in "Song, to Celia," varying meter and rhyme to fit the development of your ideas.

Robert Herrick

1591–1674

Robert Herrick, one of the most original and accomplished of the Cavalier poets, created appealing lyrics that celebrate the sweetness of life and love. His timeless poems are light, charming, sensual, and consistently true to human emotion. Their language and proportions are classically elegant, reflecting the influence of Greek and Latin models and of Ben Jonson, Herrick's mentor.

The son of a goldsmith, Herrick was born in London in 1591, the sixth of seven children. After the death of their father, the Herrick children became the wards of their uncle, who was jeweler to the king and the richest goldsmith in England. The uncle paid for Herrick's education at Westminster School, and in 1607 apprenticed the young man as a goldsmith. When it became clear that this trade did not suit him, Herrick received his uncle's permission to enter St. John's College at Cambridge University, where he received a bachelor's degree in 1617 and a master's degree in 1620. Three years later he was ordained an Anglican minister.

In time Herrick became chaplain to the colorful and controversial Duke of Buckingham. After Buckingham was murdered in 1628, Charles I appointed Herrick to a country parish in the west of England. For the next eighteen years, he served as rector in the hamlet of Dean Prior, in Devonshire. Pining for the excitement of London, he complained in various poems of "dull Devonshire," which he "loathed." Ironically, though, Herrick was at his best when describing his rural environment. In one poem he wrote:

I sing of brooks, of blossoms, birds and bowers:
Of April, May, of June and July flowers.
I sing of May-poles, hock-carts, wassails,
　　wakes,
Of bridegroom, brides and of their bridal cakes.
I write of youth, of love . . .

Herrick loved London, and it was there, in his thirties, that he fell under the spell of Ben Jonson. Like the young well born gentlemen with whom he socialized in the inns and taverns, he was happy to be numbered among the "tribe of Ben." Herrick

read the classical poets, consorted with writers and musicians, acquired influential patrons, and wrote poetry, which circulated in manuscript form and earned him a reputation as a fashionable poet.

Herrick supported the king, not Parliament during the civil war. As a consequence, he was expelled from his parish in 1646. Not too unhappily, after his "long and irksome banishment" in "the dull confines of the drooping West," he returned to London where he lived on the charity of rich relatives and friends. In 1648 *Hesperides,* his one great book, was published. This volume contains more than eleven hundred lyrics of consistently high quality, filled with things typically English: country life, rustic customs, spring beauty, and maidens named Julia, Corinna, and Anthea. Published along with *Hesperides* was *His Noble Numbers,* a collection of about three hundred poems on religious subjects.

When the monarchy was restored, Herrick, now past seventy, was sent back to his old country vicarage at Dean Prior. There he lived out his life peacefully among the farmers and country gentry, with his maid and his pets: a hen, a spaniel, a goose, a cat, a cow, a lamb, and a pig that he trained to drink from a tankard. He died in 1674 at the age of eighty-three.

Delight in Disorder

A sweet disorder in the dress
Kindles in clothes a wantonness:
A lawn about the shoulders thrown
Into a fine distraction;
An erring lace, which here and there   5
Enthralls the crimson stomacher;[1]
A cuff neglectful, and thereby
Ribbands to flow confusedly;
A winning wave (deserving note)
In the tempestuous petticoat;   10
A careless shoestring, in whose tie
I see a wild civility;
Do more bewitch me than when art
Is too precise in every part.

---

1. **stomacher:** an ornamented, triangular piece of cloth
worn as a covering for the chest and abdomen.

To the Virgins, To Make Much of Time

Gather ye rosebuds while ye may,
　　Old Time is still a-flying;
And this same flower that smiles today,
　　Tomorrow will be dying.

The glorious lamp of heaven, the sun,   5
　　The higher he's a-getting;
The sooner will his race be run,
　　And nearer he's to setting.

That age is best which is the first,
　　When youth and blood are warmer;   10
But being spent, the worse, and worst
　　Times, still succeed the former.

Then be not coy, but use your time;
　　And while ye may, go marry:
For having lost but once your prime,   15
　　You may forever tarry.

PORTRAIT OF A YOUNG MAN. *Nicholas Hilliard.*
Victoria and Albert Museum, Crown Copyright.

Getting at Meaning

DELIGHT IN DISORDER

1. What specific signs of disorder does the speaker name? What impression do these disorders create for the speaker?

2. The word *art* in the final couplet refers to the art of dressing and also to the broader concept of art. Explain what the speaker means by these lines.

TO THE VIRGINS, TO MAKE MUCH OF TIME

3. A popular theme in Cavalier poetry is the need to live for the moment. This philosophy is summarized by the Latin expression *carpe diem,* literally, "seize the day." Quote lines from the poem that express this idea.

4. What is the speaker's attitude toward time? What examples from nature bring out this attitude?

Developing Skills in Reading Literature

1. **Meter and Rhyme Scheme.** In "Delight in Disorder" Herrick expresses the idea that art, which includes poetry, should not be too perfect. Examine the meter and rhyme scheme of each poem, and determine whether he has implemented this philosophy. Note any major or minor inconsistencies that lend a certain imprecision to the verse forms.

2. **Alliteration, Assonance, and Consonance.** Find in these poems examples of the sound devices alliteration, assonance, and consonance. What are their specific effects within the poems? In which poem do these devices seem more important? Explain.

3. **Personification and Symbol.** In both poems personification is an important device, closely connected to symbolism. Identify the personifications in these poems, and then explain the symbolic meanings of the personified objects. Are all the subjects of personification symbols as well? If not, suggest reasons related to the nature of symbols.

Richard Lovelace
1618–1657

The poems of Richard Lovelace typify the Cavalier spirit in English poetry. Lovelace himself was a prototypical Cavalier: a courtier and a soldier, a poet and a lover, a scholar and a musician, a connoisseur of painting, and one of the handsomest men in England. He died young, having written several lyrics that are as fine as any by the Cavalier poets.

Lovelace came from a landed family with a long tradition of military distinction. His father, Sir William Lovelace, who had been knighted by James I, was killed in 1628 while serving in Holland. Young Richard was then ten, the eldest in a large family. In 1634 he entered Oxford University and two years later was granted a master's degree at the request of one of the queen's ladies who was impressed with his "most amiable and beautiful person, innate modesty, virtue, and courtly deportment."

In 1639 and 1640 Lovelace served as ensign and then as captain in what were known as the Bishops' Wars, two brief campaigns against the rebellious Scots. By now he was not only a courtier and a country gentleman but one of the most distinguished of a group of court poets patronized by Queen Henrietta, consort of Charles.

When the rupture between king and Parliament took place in 1642, Lovelace presented to the House of Commons a petition in the king's favor from a group of Kentish royalists. For this he was imprisoned for seven weeks, during which time he wrote his most famous lyric, "To Althea, from Prison." He was released on payment of a large bail, but he was still a prisoner on parole and prevented from leaving London through most of the civil war. Nevertheless he managed to render considerable service to the king's cause. He was also generous to a number of scholars and musicians and numbered among his friends and associates poets Andrew Marvell and Sir John Suckling.

Finally, in 1645, Lovelace rejoined the military, fighting first in England and then in France against the Spanish. Badly wounded at Dunkirk, he returned to England in 1648 with his brother Dudley,

RICHARD LOVELACE, 1794. *Anonymous.* *Brown Brothers.*

who had served under him. In the spring of that year an uprising in Kent was suppressed by Parliamentary forces, and both brothers were imprisoned by the Puritan government. During this second imprisonment, Lovelace collected and revised a volume of poems, published in 1649 under the title of *Lucasta.* The name comes from the Latin phrase *lux casta,* meaning "pure light."

Lovelace was released from prison after the execution of Charles I, but he had depleted his fortune "in useless efforts to serve his sovereign." He spent the remaining ten years of his life in obscurity, poverty, and depression, living in a London slum, dependent on the charity of his friends.

While he was alive, Lovelace's poems were praised by his friends and set to music by eminent composers. After his death, though, his work was almost forgotten. More than a hundred years later it was revived by Bishop Bercy in his *Reliques of Ancient English Poetry* (1765).

To Lucasta, on Going to the Wars

Tell me not, sweet, I am unkind,
    That from the nunnery
Of thy chaste breast and quiet mind
    To war and arms I fly.

True, a new mistress now I chase,   5
    The first foe in the field;
And with a stronger faith embrace
    A sword, a horse, a shield.

Yet this inconstancy is such
    As you too shall adore;   10
I could not love thee, dear, so much,
    Loved I not honor more.

Getting at Meaning

1. What is the speaker asking of Lucasta?

2. What inconstancy does the speaker urge Lucasta to accept?

3. What is the relationship between love and honor, according to the speaker?

Developing Skills in Reading Literature

1. **Personification.** How is war personified in this poem? What words and phrases extend the personification? What image of war is created through the figure of speech? How does this image relate to the theme, or message, that emerges in the third stanza?

2. **Imagery.** Compare and contrast the imagery of the first stanza with that of the second stanza. The images relate to the main concerns of the Cavaliers. What are these concerns? What is the typical Cavalier attitude toward each?

Sir John Suckling
1609–1642

Sir John Suckling has been called "the central diamond on the Cavalier chain." He was many things: wit, rake, lover, gambler, soldier, and poet. He was a courtier capable of both courage and cowardice, a servant of the king and a member of Parliament, a conspirator, fugitive, exile, and suicide. In his poetry, Suckling was a master of the light touch, of spontaneity and colloquial directness, of reckless, careless ease. Like Lovelace, he produced several lyrics that are timeless celebrations of the Cavalier spirit.

Suckling was born in Middlesex, the eldest son of Sir John Suckling and Martha Cranfield, sister of the first Earl of Middlesex. His father held a number of important and lucrative government posts, including secretary of state and privy councilor. At fourteen young Suckling was sent to Trinity College, Cambridge University, and left four years later without a degree to continue his studies at Gray's Inn. His close friends already included the poets Thomas Carew and Richard Lovelace.

When Sir John the elder died in 1628, leaving Suckling heir to his great estate, the young man set out on a tour of Europe, visiting France, Italy, and the Netherlands. When he returned to England two years later, he was knighted by Charles I. He then fought briefly in the Thirty Years' War before becoming part of King Charles's extravagant court. Suckling was rich, handsome, and generous, and his gift for poetry especially commended him to Charles and Queen Henrietta. He was also a great gallant, the best bowler and the best cardplayer at court, and such a gambler that "no shopkeeper would trust him for sixpence." He is said to have invented the game of cribbage and bowled away his sisters' money on the Picadilly bowling green.

Often ostentatious and profligate, Suckling spent unprecedented amounts of money staging his four plays in the manner of court masques. In the tragedy *Aglaura* (1635), even the lace on the actors' coats was of real gold and silver. He also spent a substantial portion of his dwindling fortune raising a troop of a hundred horsemen and outfitting them in gorgeous white and scarlet uniforms for what turned out to be a disastrous expedition to Scotland.

As the civil war approached, Suckling is said to have worked hard to prevent a break between king and Parliament. He became a member of Parliament in 1640 and advised the king to redress grievances before it was too late. As the situation worsened, Suckling became involved in a doomed plot to rescue the king's impeached minister, the Earl of Stafford, from the Tower of London and to bring French troops to the king's rescue. The plan was betrayed, and Suckling fled to Paris along with his fellow conspirators.

According to one account of his death, Suckling had run through all his fortune, and now, exiled in an alien land, he chose not to live out his life in obscure poverty. In May or June of 1642, he took poison and ended his own life.

Why So Pale and Wan

Why so pale and wan, fond lover?
   Prithee, why so pale?
Will, when looking well can't move her,
   Looking ill prevail?
   Prithee, why so pale?   5

Why so dull and mute, young sinner?
   Prithee, why so mute?
Will, when speaking well can't win her,
   Saying nothing do 't?
   Prithee, why so mute?   10

Quit, quit for shame! This will not move;
   This cannot take her.
If of herself she will not love,
   Nothing can make her:
   The devil take her!   15

The Constant Lover

Out upon it! I have loved
   Three whole days together!
And am like to love three more,
   If it prove fair weather.

Time shall molt away his wings   5
   Ere he shall discover
In the whole wide world again
   Such a constant lover.

But the spite on 't is, no praise
   Is due at all to me: 10
Love with me had made no stays,
   Had it any been but she.

Had it any been but she,
   And that very face,
There had been at least ere this   15
   A dozen dozen in her place.

Getting at Meaning

WHY SO PALE AND WAN

1. What advice does the speaker offer the "fond lover"?

2. What do the last three lines suggest about the efficacy of a lover's suit?

THE CONSTANT LOVER

3. How long has the speaker been in love? How does the speaker view this brief span of time?

4. What two meanings of the word *constant* fit the speaker of this poem? Which meaning is ironic? Does the speaker seem to be aware of the irony?

5. What rather dubious compliment does the speaker give his lover? Is his attitude any different from that at the beginning of this poem? Explain.

6. What impression of the speaker emerges from this poem?

Developing Skills in Reading Literature

1. **Tone.** The tone of these poems is typically Cavalier. What attitude toward love and toward woman is evident in the poems? How does this attitude compare with the medieval chivalric ideal? to the attitude of the Elizabethan lyricists?

2. **Repetition.** Note how certain phrases and lines are repeated in these poems. How do the repetitions reinforce the unity within and between stanzas? How does repetition reinforce the rhythm of the poems? the development of their themes?

Developing Writing Skills

Explaining an Idea. Almost every Cavalier poet was concerned with the passage of time. In an essay discuss the way this theme is manifested in the poems by Herrick, Lovelace, and Suckling. Note both common attitudes and differences in the treatment of this theme.

Andrew Marvell

1621–1678

Andrew Marvell was known in his own time as a fierce satirist and pamphleteer who was devoted to political and religious causes. He is remembered now for brilliant lyrics that combine the perceptiveness of the metaphysicals with the wit and grace of the Cavaliers.

Marvell's father, also named Andrew, was rector in the town of Winestead, Yorkshire, where young Andrew was born. When he was three, his father became master of the nearby Hull Grammar School. Marvell studied there until he was thirteen and then entered Trinity College, Cambridge. He left the university at one point to become a Roman Catholic, but within months he was discovered by his father in a London bookseller's shop and returned to school and to Anglicanism. Two of his early poems, one in Latin and one in Greek, appeared in a Cambridge anthology in 1637. In 1640 his father was drowned while crossing a river. On the small inheritance he received, Marvell traveled for four years, visiting Holland, France, Italy, and Spain, and learning the languages of these countries.

Marvell never again left the Church of England, but he came to admire many of the Puritan virtues and saw in Oliver Cromwell a man of destiny, perhaps an ideal civic leader who could rule without personal ambition. One of his best poems is the "Horatian Ode Upon Cromwell's Return from Ireland." It is interesting that the most famous lines of this poem are a tribute to the nobility of the dethroned and beheaded Charles I.

In his late twenties, from 1650 to 1652, Marvell spent probably the two happiest years of his life, at Nunappleton, the Yorkshire estate of the Cromwellian general, Lord Fairfax. Here he wrote most of his best lyrics, including his "garden poems." It may have been through Fairfax that Marvell met John Milton, who was to become his great friend. In 1653 Milton, who was Cromwell's Latin Secretary, praised Marvell as "a man of singular desert for the state to make use of" and

ANDREW MARVELL, 1655–1660. *Anonymous.*
National Portrait Gallery, London.

recommended that Marvell be appointed his assistant. The post was given to another, but four years later it fell vacant again; this time Marvell was appointed. He held his civil service post for three years during which time he wrote many political poems honoring Cromwell and the Commonwealth.

An important strand of Marvell's career began in 1659, when he was elected to Parliament from Hull, his boyhood home in Yorkshire. Until his death nearly twenty years later, he represented the town efficiently and honestly, sending home to his constituents a series of four hundred news letters. Over the years Marvell's hostility to the king's policies grew, and he became known as the most formidable pamphleteer and satirist of the opposition. In 1677 his *Account of the Growth of Popery and Absolute Government in England*, an attack on the king and the court, resulted in a reward being offered for the apprehension of its anonymous author. When Marvell died in London the following year, some suspected that he had been poisoned. The actual cause of his death, however, was improper medical treatment for malaria.

To His Coy Mistress

Had we but world enough, and time,
This coyness, lady, were no crime.
We would sit down, and think which way
To walk, and pass our long love's day.
Thou by the Indian Ganges' side   5
Shouldst rubies find: I by the tide
Of Humber[1] would complain[2] I would
Love you ten years before the flood,[3]
And you should, if you please, refuse
Till the conversion of the Jews,[4]   10
My vegetable[5] love should grow
Vaster than empires and more slow;
An hundred years should go to praise
Thine eyes, and on thy forehead gaze;
Two hundred to adore each breast,   15
But thirty thousand to the rest;
An age at least to every part,
And the last age should show your heart,
For, lady, you deserve this state;[6]
Nor would I love at lower rate.   20

But at my back I always hear
Time's wingèd chariot hurrying near;
And yonder all before us lie
Deserts of vast eternity.
Thy beauty shall no more be found,   25
Nor in thy marble vault shall sound
My echoing song; then worms shall try
That long preserved virginity;
And your quaint honor turn to dust.
And into ashes all my lust: 30
The grave's a fine and private place,
But none, I think, do there embrace.
Now therefore, while the youthful hue
Sits on thy skin like morning dew,
And while thy willing soul transpires[7]   35
At every pore with instant fires,
Now let us sport us while we may,
And now, like amorous birds of prey,
Rather at once our time devour
Than languish in his slow-chapped[8] power,   40
Let us roll all our strength and all
Our sweetness up into one ball,
And tear our pleasures with rough strife
Thorough[9] the iron gates of life:
Thus, though we cannot make our sun   45
Stand still, yet we will make him run.

---

1. **Humber:** a river in Marvell's home town.
2. **complain:** sing plaintive long songs.
3. **flood:** the Biblical flood.
4. **conversion . . . Jews:** It was believed that this would occur just before the Last Judgment and the end of the world.
5. **vegetable:** in the sense of living growth.
6. **state:** dignity.
7. **transpires:** breathes.
8. **slow-chapped:** slow-jawed.
9. **Thorough:** through.

Getting at Meaning

1. What are the connotations of the word *coy*? How would the speaker court his coy mistress if time allowed?

2. What frightening realization is expressed in the first two lines of the second stanza?

3. What plea does the speaker present to his mistress in the second stanza? With what reasons does he support his plea?

4. What change in the natural order does the speaker suggest in the last two lines? What is the figurative meaning of these lines?

Developing Skills in Reading Literature

1. **Meter and Theme.** The meter of this poem is iambic tetrameter, a line that is relatively short for English verse. In general, what rhythmic effect is created by this meter? How does the meter reflect the speaker's feelings? What effect is created by the use of this meter in the first stanza, when the speaker is describing an ideal situation? Now, think about the theme of this poem, its message about life and time. Why is the meter appropriate to this theme?

2. **Figurative Language.** Marvell uses metaphor, hyperbole, simile, and personification in this poem. Explain the extended metaphor and the hyperbole in the first stanza. What effect does Marvell achieve by his use of these devices? Identify the personifications, simile, and metaphors in the second stanza. Then comment on why Marvell is considered an original, forceful poet.

3. **Imagery.** The impression created by the imagery in the second stanza contrasts with that created by the imagery in the first stanza. What impression is communicated in the first stanza? Notice how the images of beauty and of death are intermingled in the second stanza. Cite several words and phrases that connote beauty and passion and several that connote death and decay. What overall response does the imagery of the stanza evoke? What concept of reality emerges?

The imagery throughout this poem reinforces the logical argument that is presented by the speaker. What are the tenets of this argument? Would the argument be convincing even without the imagery that goes along with it? Explain.

YOUNG MAN LEANING AGAINST A TREE, 1590.
Sir Isaac Oliver. Queen's Gallery.

John Milton
1608–1674

John Milton decided early in life that he would become an important poet, a goal that he achieved without question. Amidst tempestuous political and religious controversy, he produced work that places him among the giants of English literature and among the most erudite interpreters of Puritan thought. Desiring to "justify God's ways to man," Milton created *Paradise Lost*, the finest epic poem in the English language.

Milton was born in 1608, when Shakespeare was still alive, when many other illustrious figures of Queen Elizabeth's reign still walked the streets of London, and when Ben Jonson was holding his "merry meetings" at the nearby Mermaid Tavern. Milton's father was a convert to Protestantism who had come to London after being disinherited for abandoning the Roman Catholic faith. He had become a fairly prosperous notary and moneylender and also was an accomplished musician and amateur poet. He exposed young Milton to education and to culture, and, although the father had originally expected his son to enter the ministry, he encouraged the boy to pursue his chosen vocation of scholar and poet.

As a student Milton applied himself eagerly to his studies, often reading until midnight. At sixteen he entered Christ's College, Cambridge, already aware of his poetic genius. He was uncomfortable with the university's medieval methods and a bit scornful of his fellow students and masters, being suspended at one point for disagreeing with his tutor. In addition to his formal studies, Milton read widely and wrote verse in Latin and English, conscious of his calling to dedicate his life to poetry. At twenty-one he wrote one of his finest poems, "On the Morning of Christ's Nativity." Soon after, he wrote the charming companion poems "L'Allegro" and "Il Penseroso" and a sonnet on Shakespeare, which was published in 1632, the year that he received his master's degree. Even these early poems demonstrate the grand themes and forceful language that characterize Milton's later masterpieces.

JOHN MILTON, 1629. *Anonymous.*
National Portrait Gallery, London.

At the age of twenty-four, Milton moved to the village of Horton, in Buckinghamshire, where his father had retired and where he spent six happy years in peaceful rural surroundings, reading Greek and Latin classics, studying music and mathematics, and writing poetry and drama. From this period came "Lycidas," a heartfelt elegy in which he grapples with the mystery of life and death, and *Comus*, a masque about the great conflict between good and evil.

In 1638 Milton left for a long tour of the Continent. He met Galileo in Italy and wrote a number of sonnets in Italian and Latin. He had intended to visit Sicily and Greece, but when he learned of the impending civil war in England, he decided to return to London. There, he devoted his energy to educating two nephews and to writing pamphlets in the cause of religious and civil liberty and in support of the Puritan reformation of the Anglican Church.

In 1642, when he was thirty-four, Milton married Mary Powell, a girl of seventeen whose father had owed a debt to Milton's father. Her lively temperament and royalist background ill-suited her for life with this sober and scholarly man. She soon returned to her family for an extended visit, during which time Milton wrote his famous pamphlets on divorce. Two years later, Mary's family arranged a reconciliation, and she returned and bore Milton three daughters and a son (who died in infancy) before she died in childbirth at the age of twenty-six.

Milton's public stand in favor of divorce had aroused such passionate opposition that he wrote in 1644 his most eloquent and enduring piece of prose "Areopagitica," an attack on censorship of the press and a plea for toleration of divergent opinions.

For many years Milton had planned to write an epic, but he deferred the work, undertaking instead massive projects such as the creation of a Latin dictionary and the writing of a history of England. When King Charles was beheaded in January, 1649, Milton immediately came to the defense of the regicides. In his first political pamphlet, "The Tenure of Kings and Magistrates," he claimed the right of the people to "call to account a Tyrant or wicked King." He then accepted the post of Cromwell's Latin Secretary, putting off again the execution of his poetic masterpiece. He continued to turn out his thundering pamphlets, in Latin and English, in defense of execution of the king and in support of Puritan ideals. The most notable are his *Defence of the People of England* (1651) and *The Second Defence . . .* (1654). He undertook the latter despite his failing eyesight, and by the time he had finished it, he was totally blind. In a sonnet on his blindness he accepted his condition, writing, "They also serve who only stand and wait." He continued his duties for the government, later assisted by his friend, poet Andrew Marvell, and he wrote one last desperate appeal in 1660 on the eve of the restoration of the monarchy. When Charles II took the throne, Milton was spared hanging, perhaps because of his blindness and the influence of friends such as Marvell.

In 1658 Milton finally began serious work on *Paradise Lost,* dictating twenty or thirty lines at a time to paid assistants, friends, and relatives. His three motherless daughters, somewhat neglected, poorly educated, and forced to read to their father in six or seven unfamiliar languages, showed signs of rebellion. Milton decided to remarry, choosing as a partner Elizabeth Minshull, who suited him well and who assumed the task of raising his children. *Paradise Lost,* which he had had in mind since he was nineteen and which he had written in his fifties, finally was finished in 1663 and was published in ten volumes in 1667.

According to some sources, Milton had compiled a list of nearly one hundred subjects to explore as possibilities for his great epic. Discarding all of these, he chose an event that was significant in both Biblical and human history: the fall of human beings from God's grace.

Using *Genesis* as his basic source, Milton describes a civil war that takes place in heaven when God appoints His Son to the seat of honor, a seat coveted by the archangel Satan. When Satan and his band of rebel angels are defeated and exiled to hell, Satan vows to corrupt man, God's latest creation. This he accomplishes through the temptation of Eve. As the last book ends, Adam and Eve leave the Garden of Eden, holding hands. Their punishment has been softened by the promise of a Messiah; *Paradise Regained,* finished two years after *Paradise Lost,* describes the fulfillment of this promise.

In *Paradise Lost* Milton probes the relationship between free will and destiny, freedom and responsibility. His treatment of this theme is appropriately grand, in the tradition of Homer and Virgil whose classic epics were his models. *Paradise Lost* is written in long, flowing sentences in blank verse that is a perfect fusion of rhythm, sound, and image.

Milton's last great work, a return to the dramatic form, was *Samson Agonistes,* which is written in the severe style of Greek tragedy and which considers the nature of despair and spiritual strength. Milton spent his remaining years quietly with his young wife, rising early, passing his days in work, with music and friends for diversion, enjoying a pipe and a little wine, and receiving distinguished visitors. He was sometimes seen being led through the streets, dressed neatly in black. He died at the age of sixty-five, in November, 1674.

On His Having Arrived at the Age of Twenty-Three

How soon hath Time, the subtle thief of youth,
    Stolen on his wing my three and twentieth year!
    My hasting days fly on with full career,
    But my late spring no bud or blossom[1] showeth.
Perhaps my semblance might deceive the truth,   5
    That I to manhood am arrived so near,
    And inward ripeness doth much less appear,
    That some more timely-happy spirits[2] endueth.[3]
Yet be it less or more, or soon or slow,
    It shall be still[4] in strictest measure even[5]   10
    To that same lot, however mean or high,
Toward which Time leads me, and the will of Heaven;
    All is, if I have grace to use it so,
    As ever[6] in my great Taskmaster's eye.

---

1. **blossom:** poetry.
2. **spirits:** people of the same age who seem to be better poets.
3. **endueth:** endoweth.
4. **still:** forever.
5. **even:** adequate.
6. **ever:** eternity.

To the Lord General Cromwell

On the Proposals of Certain Ministers at
the Committee for Propagation of the Gospel

Cromwell, our chief of men, who through a cloud
Not of war only, but detractions rude,[1]
Guided by faith and matchless fortitude,
To peace and truth thy glorious way hast plowed,
And on the neck of crownèd Fortune proud   5
Hast reared God's trophies[2] and his work pursued,
While Darwen stream with blood of Scots inbrued,
And Dunbar field resounds thy praises loud,
And Worcester's[3] laureate wreath; yet much remains
To conquer still; Peace hath her victories   10
No less renowned than war, new foes arise
Threatening to bind our souls with secular chains.
Help us to save free conscience from the paw
Of hireling wolves whose Gospel is their maw.[4]

---

1. **detractions rude:** Many of Cromwell's followers were angry because he did not carry religious reform far enough for them.
2. **God's trophies:** Milton believed that the soldiers of the Commonwealth had succeeded in bringing about religious reform.
3. **Darwen . . . Dunbar . . . Worcester:** three sites of battle won under Cromwell's generalship.
4. **wolves . . . maw:** Milton thought that some Puritans wanted to take over after Cromwell's victories and set up another official church. He compares them to wolves that want to get everything into their "maws" or stomachs.

On His Blindness

When I consider how my light is spent,
  Ere half my days, in this dark world and wide.
  And that one talent[1] which is death to hide
  Lodged with me useless, though my soul more bent
To serve therewith my Maker, and present   5
  My true account, lest he, returning, chide.
  "Doth God exact day labor, light denied?"
  I fondly[2] ask; but Patience, to prevent
That murmur, soon replies: "God doth not need
  Either man's work or his own gifts; who best   10
  Bear his mild yoke, they serve him best; his state
Is kingly—thousands[3] at his bidding speed
  And post o'er land and ocean without rest;
  They also serve who only stand and wait."

---

1. **talent:** a Biblical reference to the parable of the talents in Matthew. A servant who has hidden his one talent, or coin, in the earth, is reprimanded for not putting it to good use.
2. **fondly:** foolishly.
3. **thousands:** of angels.

MILTON AT 62, 1670. *W. Faithorne.*
National Portrait Gallery, London.

Getting at Meaning

ON HIS HAVING ARRIVED AT THE AGE OF TWENTY-THREE

1. What does the speaker lament in the octave of this sonnet?

2. The speaker compares his "inward ripeness" with his literary output. In what phrase does he establish a comparison between his own age and a time of year? What phrase both extends this metaphor and refers to his productivity?

3. Who will direct the speaker's destiny, as explained in the sestet?

4. How does the speaker's concept of time differ in the octave and the sestet? What difference in focus between the two parts of the sonnet accounts for the difference in the concept of time?

TO THE LORD GENERAL CROMWELL

5. What kinds of information does the speaker give about Cromwell in the octave? What shift occurs at the beginning of the sestet?

6. What new foe does the speaker oppose? Why? Quote phrases from the sonnet that suggest an answer to this question.

ON HIS BLINDNESS

7. Aside from the Biblical meaning, what is the one talent referred to in line 3? Why is this talent "useless"?

8. How has blindness affected the speaker's relationship with God?

9. What does Patience explain to the speaker? What solace can he gather from the last line?

Developing Skills in Reading Literature

1. **Sonnet.** Milton's sonnets are in the Italian, or Petrarchan, form, with slight variances among the rhyme schemes of the sestets. Chart the rhyme schemes of the three sonnets. Do all the octaves conform to the strict Italian form? The sestets of which two sonnets have similar rhyme schemes? How do these rhyme schemes differ? What typically English characteristic appears in one sonnet?

For each sonnet explain in general terms the relationship between the octave and the sestet. What kind of idea does the poet present in the octave? What does the poet do with the idea in the sestet?

2. **Tone.** "On His Having Arrived at the Age of Twenty-Three" and "On His Blindness" deal with personal issues, while "To the Lord General Cromwell" praises a public figure. What differences in tone do you note between these two kinds of sonnets? In each sonnet identify key words and phrases whose connotations help to establish the tone of the poem. Then consider this question: How might Milton's purpose for writing each sonnet have influenced his tone?

3. **Allusion.** In "To the Lord General Cromwell" Milton alludes to *Matthew* 7:15. Look up this passage from the Bible, and then discuss the meaning of the concluding couplet in light of this allusion.

4. **Theme.** Milton was a deeply religious man, committed to the Puritan cause. As a consequence, religious themes abound in his poetry. For each sonnet, formulate a statement of theme that summarizes the religious message in the poem. Notice that Milton writes of both personal faith and religion as a political force. Why is this understandable, given the times in which he lived?

Developing Writing Skills

1. **Using Comparisons and Contrasts.** Both "On His Having Arrived at the Age of Twenty-Three" and "On His Blindness" are concerned with Milton's talent and accomplishments, but these two sonnets were written more than twenty years apart. Write an essay in which you compare and contrast the sonnets. Include the answers to these questions in your essay: How have the facts in Milton's life changed? Has his attitude toward his talent changed? Is his attitude toward God the same or different?

2. **Using Contrasts.** Select a sonnet by Wyatt, and in a well organized essay discuss the differences between this sonnet and the two by Milton. In your conclusion generalize about the differences that result from the gradual perfection of the sonnet form and those that are related to the skill and talent of the two poets.

from **Paradise Lost**

from **Book I**

Milton begins by invoking the Heavenly Muse for inspiration and by stating his purpose for writing the epic. He then begins to describe the fall of Satan.

Of man's first disobedience, and the fruit
Of that forbidden tree, whose mortal taste
Brought death into the world, and all our woe,
With loss of Eden, till one greater Man[1]
Restore us, and regain the blissful seat,   5
Sing, Heavenly Muse,[2] that on the secret top
Of Oreb, or of Sinai,[3] didst inspire
That shepherd,[4] who first taught the chosen seed
In the beginning how the Heavens and Earth
Rose out of Chaos;[5] or if Sion hill[6]   10
Delight thee more, and Siloa's brook[7] that flowed
Fast by the oracle of God, I thence
Invoke thy aid to my adventurous song,
That with no middle flight intends to soar
Above the Aonian mount,[8] while it pursues   15
Things unattempted yet in prose or rhyme.
And chiefly thou, O Spirit,[9] that dost prefer
Before all temples the upright heart and pure,
Instruct me, for thou know'st; thou from the first
Wast present, and with mighty wings outspread   20
Dovelike sat'st brooding on the vast abyss
And mad'st it pregnant: what in me is dark
Illumine, what is low raise and support;

---

1. **Man:** Christ, the Messiah.
2. **Heavenly Muse:** Milton invokes Urania, named later in the poem, the muse of astronomy and sacred poetry, to help him write his epic.
3. **Oreb . . . Sinai:** alternate names for the mountain where Moses received the Law from God.
4. **shepherd:** Moses.
5. **in . . . Chaos:** Moses was believed to have written the first five books of the Bible.
6. **Sion hill:** a hill in Jerusalem on which the temple was built.
7. **Siloa's brook:** a stream that flowed near the temple on Sion hill.
8. **Aonian Mount:** Mount Helicon in Greek mythology, where the Muses lived.
9. **Spirit:** divine inspiration.

That to the highth[10] of this great argument
I may assert Eternal Providence,   25
And justify the ways of God to men.
   Say first, for Heaven hides nothing from thy view,
Nor the deep tract of Hell, say first what cause
Moved our grand[11] parents in that happy state,
Favored of Heaven so highly, to fall off   30
From their Creator, and transgress his will
For one restraint,[12] lords of the world besides?
Who first seduced them to that foul revolt?
The infernal Serpent; he it was, whose guile,
Stirred up with envy and revenge, deceived   35
The mother of mankind, what time his pride[13]
Had cast him out from Heaven, with all his host
Of rebel angels, by whose aid aspiring
To set himself in glory above his peers,
He trusted to have equaled the Most High,   40
If he opposed; and with ambitious aim
Against the throne and monarchy of God,
Raised impious war in Heaven and battle proud
With vain attempt. Him the Almighty Power
Hurled headlong flaming from the ethereal sky   45
With hideous ruin and combustion down
To bottomless perdition, there to dwell
In adamantine[14] chains and penal fire,
Who durst defy the Omnipotent to arms.
Nine times the space that measures day and night   50
To mortal men, he with his horrid crew
Lay vanquished, rolling in the fiery gulf,
Confounded though immortal. But his doom
Reserved him to more wrath; for now the thought
Both of lost happiness and lasting pain   55
Torments him; round he throws his baleful eyes,
That witnessed huge affliction and dismay
Mixed with obdúrate pride and steadfast hate; . . .

   The setting now switches to Hell where Satan revels in his new status
as supreme ruler.

---

10. **highth:** height.
11. **grand:** first.
12. **restraint:** God's command that Adam and Eve should not eat the fruit of the tree
of knowledge.
13. **pride:** Satan's sin, the most deadly of the Seven Deadly Sins.
14. **adamantine:** hard as a diamond, unbreakable.

from **Book I** (*second excerpt*)

. . . "Is this the region, this the soil, the clime,"
Said then the lost Archangel,[15] "this the seat
That we must change for Heaven, this mournful gloom
For that celestial light? Be it so, since he
Who now is sovran[16] can dispose and bid   5
What shall be right: farthest from him is best,
Whom reason hath equalled, force hath made supreme
Above his equals. Farewell, happy fields,
Where joy for ever dwells! Hail, horrors! hail,
Infernal World! and thou, profoundest Hell,   10
Receive thy new possessor—one who brings
A mind not to be changed by place or time.
The mind is its own place, and in itself
Can make a Heaven of Hell, a Hell of Heaven.
What matter where, if I be still the same,   15
And what I should be, all but less than he
Whom thunder hath made greater? Here at least
We shall be free; the Almighty hath not built
Here for his envy, will not drive us hence;
Here we may reign secure, and, in my choice,   20
To reign is worth ambition, though in Hell:
Better to reign in Hell than serve in Heaven.
But wherefore let we then our faithful friends,
The associates and co-partners of our loss,
Lie thus astonished on the oblivious pool,   25
And call them not to share with us their part
In this unhappy mansion, or once more
With rallied arms to try what may be yet
Regained in Heaven, or what more lost in Hell?"

The remainder of Book I deals with the rebellion of the fallen angels,
Satan's acknowledged need for guile in the battle with God, and the
building of Pandemonium, Satan's great palace. Book II is set in Hell
where Satan and his followers decide to battle God through His human
creation. Book III details Satan's journey to the newly created world. God
is fully aware of Satan's plan, knows that Satan will succeed, and shares
this information with His Son, who offers Himself as ransom for the
human race. God accepts His Son's offer. As Book IV opens, Satan
struggles with the concepts of evil and power. Finally, he decides that his
good is to do evil. He arrives at the Garden of Eden and sees Adam and
Eve.

---

15. **lost Archangel:** Satan.

from **Book IV**

                 . . . the Fiend[1]
Saw undelighted all delight, all kind
Of living creatures, new to sight and strange.
Two of far nobler shape, erect and tall,
Godlike erect, with native honor clad   5
In naked majesty, seemed lords of all,
And worthy seemed, for in their looks divine
The image of their glorious Maker shone,
Truth, wisdom, sanctitude severe and pure—
Severe, but in true filial freedom placed,   10
Whence true authority in men: though both
Not equal, as their sex not equal seemed;
For contemplation he and valor formed,
For softness she and sweet attractive grace;
He for God only, she for God in him.   15
His fair large front and eye sublime[2] declared
Absolute rule, and hyacinthine[3] locks
Round from his parted forelock manly hung
Clustering, but not beneath his shoulders broad:
She, as a veil down to the slender waist,   20
Her unadorned golden tresses wore
Dishevelled, but in wanton ringlets waved
As the vine curls her tendrils,[4] which implied
Subjection, but required with gentle sway,
And by her yielded, by him best received,   25
Yielded with coy[5] submission, modest pride,
And sweet, reluctant, amorous delay.
Nor those mysterious parts were then concealed;
Then was not guilty shame—dishonest[6] Shame
Of Nature's works, Honor dishonorable,   30
Sin-bred, how have ye troubled all mankind
With shows instead, mere shows of seeming pure,
And banished from man's life his happiest life,
Simplicity and spotless innocence.

---

1. **Fiend:** Satan.
2. **sublime:** looking upward.
3. **hyacinthine:** In Classical mythology, Hyacinthus was a beautiful youth loved but accidentally killed by Apollo and from whose blood Apollo caused the hyacinth to grow.
4. **tendrils:** long, slender coiling locks.
5. **coy:** shy.
6. **dishonest:** unchaste.

So passed they naked on, nor shunned the sight   35
Of God or Angel, for they thought no ill;
So hand in hand they passed, the loveliest pair
That ever since in love's embraces met—
Adam, the goodliest man of men since born
His sons; the fairest of her daughters Eve. . . .   40
    "Sight hateful, sight tormenting! Thus these two,[7]
Imparadised in one another's arms,
The happier Eden, shall enjoy their fill
Of bliss on bliss, while I to Hell am thrust,
Where neither joy nor love, but fierce desire,[8]   45
Among our other torments not the least,
Still unfulfilled, with pain of longing pines![9]
Yet let me not forget what I have gained
From their own mouths. All is not theirs, it seems;
One fatal tree there stands, of Knowledge called,   50
Forbidden them to taste. Knowledge forbidden?
Suspicious, reasonless. Why should their Lord
Envy them that? Can it be sin to know?
Can it be death? And do they only stand
By ignorance? Is that their happy state,   55
The proof of their obedience and their faith?
O fair foundation laid whereon to build
Their ruin! Hence I will excite their minds
With more desire to know, and to reject
Envious commands, invented with design   60
To keep them low, whom knowledge might exalt
Equal with gods. Aspiring to be such,
They taste and die: what likelier can ensue?
But first with narrow search I must walk round
This garden, and no corner leave unspied;[10]   65
A chance but chance may lead where I may meet
Some wandering Spirit of Heaven, by fountain-side,
Or in thick shade retired, from him to draw
What further would be learned. Live while ye may,
Yet happy pair; enjoy, till I return,   70
Short pleasures, for long woes are to succeed!"
   So saying, his proud step he scornful turned,
But with sly circumspection, and began
Through wood, through waste, o'er hill, o'er dale, his roam. . . .

---

7. **two:** Adam and Eve.
8. **desire:** The devil knew desire but not love.
9. **pines:** makes me pine.
10. **unspied:** unobserved.

EXPULSION FROM PARADISE (detail, fresco). Masaccio.
Santa Maria del Carmine. Florence. Scala/Art Resource.

Getting at Meaning

from BOOK I

1. In the first twenty-six lines, the speaker states both the subject and the purpose of the epic. Quote the lines in which the subject is described and those in which the purpose is stated. Explain both subject and purpose in your own words.

2. What specifically does the speaker ask the Heavenly Muse to do for him? In invoking the Muse, the speaker ranks himself with Moses. Why is this appropriate in light of the stated purpose of the epic?

3. Why was Satan cast out of heaven? What qualities are at the root of his defiance?

4. How does Hell contrast with Heaven? What does Satan observe about Heaven and Hell? Has he changed since his banishment from Heaven? Explain.

from BOOK IV

5. Describe Adam and Eve as Satan sees them the first time. How does the description of Adam and Eve reflect the attitudes of Milton's time about men and women?

6. What about Adam and Eve arouses Satan's hatred, anger, and envy?

7. What has Satan learned from Adam and Eve about the tree of knowledge? Satan reacts by posing a series of rhetorical questions. What do these questions reveal about him?

8. What does Satan plan to do to Adam and Eve? Why does Satan delay acting on his plan in order to walk around the garden?

Developing Skills in Reading Literature

1. **Epic.** As you learned in your study of *Beowulf,* the setting of an epic is vast, often the entire world or universe, the characters are of heroic proportions, and the action transcends the ordinary, often involving superhuman feats or supernatural elements. An epic addresses universal concerns: good and evil, life and death, sin and redemption. Identify specifically the epic qualities in the setting, characters, and plot of *Paradise Lost.* Then explain why the epic is universally appealing, even to non-Christians.

2. **Epic: Structure.** An epic generally begins with an invocation to a muse, a structural characteristic evident in *Paradise Lost.* A second characteristic is the use of *in medias res,* literally "in the middle of things," a technique in which the writer begins in the midst of the action then informs the reader of earlier events through flashbacks and reminiscences. Describe the way that *in medias res* is used by Milton in *Paradise Lost.*

3. **Epic: Style.** As is true of all epics, the style of *Paradise Lost* is lofty and dignified. Milton achieves this style through the grammatical constructions in which he expresses his ideas and through his diction, or choice of words.

Choose one of the following passages from Book I: lines 16–26, lines 44–58, or lines 8–22 in the second excerpt. Study the passage, identifying the sentences that are shaped into lines of blank verse and analyzing their structures. What kinds of sentences does Milton employ? What effect do the sentences create?

Discuss the connotations of the key verbs, nouns, and adjectives in the passage. What words and phrases are particularly striking? How would you describe the sounds of the words and phrases? What overall effect is created by the language in this passage?

Developing Writing Skills

1. **Describing a Character.** Write a sketch of the character Satan as he appears in these excerpts from *Paradise Lost.* In the conclusion of your composition, comment on why this character is so eternally fascinating.

2. **Explaining an Idea.** Consider Milton's comment: "The mind is its own place, and in itself/Can make a Heaven of Hell, a Hell of Heaven." In an essay explain the meaning of this idea, within the context of *Paradise Lost* and as it relates to your own experience and understanding.

3. **Using Comparison and Contrast.** In an essay discuss how the great English epics *Beowulf* and *Paradise Lost* are alike yet different. Consider form, subject, setting, character, theme, and poetic language.

Unit Review *The Renaissance*

Understanding the Unit

1. The selections in this unit encompass a wide range of genres, among them lyric, sonnet, drama, essay, song, sermon, epic, and prose narrative. Generalize about the characteristics of drama, as they are embodied in *Macbeth*. Then identify similarities and differences between the drama of Shakespeare and the other genres in the unit. For example, you might note that both drama and the prose narrative from *Genesis* contain dialogue.

2. The use of the speaker can vary markedly among poems, as demonstrated by the difference between the Elizabethan pastoral and the personal, meditative lyric. Review the poems in the unit, and discuss differences in the ways that the poets have created their speakers.

3. Review the stylistic characteristics of Bacon's essays. Then examine the excerpt from *Her Protection for Women* by Jane Anger and "Meditation 17" by John Donne, and identify the same stylistic characteristics in these essays.

4. Trace the moods of *Macbeth*, listing adjectives that describe the moods precisely. Then note similarities between the moods of this play and of other selections in the unit.

5. *Macbeth,* the chapters from *Genesis,* and *Paradise Lost* all deal with the conflict between good and evil. Discuss the way that this theme is treated in each selection, keeping in mind the following questions: Who or what represents good? evil? What is the nature of good and evil, according to the selection? What form does the conflict between good and evil take? Is the conflict resolved? If so, how?

6. The following works all have religious themes, subjects, or overtones. Discuss how their focus is ultimately human, despite strong religious elements.

Edmund Spenser: "Easter"

John Donne: "Song," "The Canonization,"

"Meditation 17," "Holy Sonnet 4,"

"Holy Sonnet 6"

Ben Jonson: "On My First Daughter"

John Milton: "On His Having Arrived at the Age of Twenty-Three," "On His Blindness,"

Paradise Lost

7. One of the major concerns of the Renaissance writers was the rapid passage of time. Discuss how this theme is treated in the lyrics of the Elizabethans and the Cavalier poets and in the poems of Marvell and Donne.

8. Describe the stereotypical attitude of the Elizabethan lyricists toward women. Then discuss how Queen Elizabeth in her poem and Jane Anger in her essay refute this stereotype.

Writing

1. Select one poem from this unit as a model and write a poem that imitates the form and style of the Renaissance work. Use as your theme one that Shakespeare treated in his sonnets.

2. A. C. Bradley, a Shakespearean scholar, wrote:

So long as Macbeth's imagination is active, we watch him fascinated; we feel suspense, horror, awe, in which are latent, also, admiration and sympathy. But as soon as it is quiescent, these feelings vanish. He is no longer "infirm of purpose": he becomes domineering, even brutal, or he becomes a cool pitiless hypocrite.

In an essay comment on Bradley's analysis of the reader's feelings about Macbeth.

3. Marvell's "To His Coy Mistress" embodies qualities of both the metaphysical and Cavalier schools of poetry. In an essay recall the characteristics of each school and show how these characteristics are reflected in this poem. Focus on form, tone, imagery, and theme, and include references to writers and poems from both the metaphysical and Cavalier schools.

4. The Renaissance has been described as "the rebirth of the human spirit, a realization of the human potential for development." Review the characteristics of the Renaissance spirit described in the introduction to the unit. Then choose the works of one writer included in the unit and in a brief essay explain how these works embody the Renaissance spirit.

THE MORNING WALK, 1785. *Thomas Gainsborough.*
The National Gallery, London.

Unit 4

The Restoration and
the Enlightenment (1660–1798)

THE DISTRESSED POET. *William Hogarth.*
Birmingham City Museum and Art Gallery.

The Age of Reason

In 1660 Charles II assumed the throne of England, ending the Puritan Protectorate. This event, known as the Restoration, ushered in an era of reaction to the authoritarian government of the Puritans and to the religious and political upheavals of the preceding century. For the next twenty-five years, the glittering Stuart court set the tone for the political and social life of the ruling class.

Following the Restoration era, England settled into a long period of relative stability, which lasted throughout most of the eighteenth century. Politically and socially, the status quo prevailed, with Protestantism, Parliamentary rule, and the dominance of the landed aristocracy representing traditional values. Reason, balance, and order permeated political and scientific theory, philosophy, and literature. Paradoxically, this period was also an age of expansion and global influence and of change that in time brought England to the brink of the modern age.

RESTORATION ENGLAND

England in the seventeenth century was primarily an agricultural country with independent farmers, tenants, and farm laborers comprising the majority of the population and country gentry making up most of the aristocracy. London was the commercial, financial, political, and cultural center of England, home to a large middle class and the site of the Restoration court.

Charles had spent much of his exile in France, where he had acquired a taste for the glamor, elegance, and intrigue of the French court. Back in England, he presided over a court in the French style. Both ladies and lords dressed in fine silks and lace-trimmed finery and wore enormous powdered wigs inset with jewels. They performed intricate, stately French dances and attended elaborate balls in honor of the king and his latest mistress.

Although in actuality Charles was clever and astute, he appeared cynical, lazy, and frivolous. His rejection of traditional moral codes scandalized most Englishmen who were church-going, hardworking, and decidedly conservative. It must have seemed to them that God's wrath had been justly aroused when three disasters struck the country: in 1665 the plague killed more than seventy thousand people in London alone; in 1666 a great fire destroyed much of London, leaving two-thirds of the population homeless; in 1667 the Dutch stunned and humiliated the proud English navy by burning and capturing English ships harbored in the Thames River.

England was involved in the war against the Dutch as an ally of France. At this time, France was the most powerful nation in Europe, a potential threat to the balance of power and to England's security at home and in the far off American colonies. Charles, however, was closely tied to France, having a strong affinity both for French court life and for the Catholic religion practiced there. The king's alliance with England's historic enemy alarmed the English and strengthened the determination of Parliament to limit further the power of the monarchy.

POLITICS AND RELIGION IN RESTORATION ENGLAND

The restoration of the monarchy meant the restoration of Parliament and of the established Church of England. Charles, the head of the Anglican Church, favored tolerance, but the Anglican bishops and the country squires in Parliament instituted harsh measures against Protestant dissenters and against Catholics who to them represented French influence. By law, anyone refusing to conform to the Church of England was branded a traitor and was barred from holding public office or attending a university.

Most members of Parliament at first were fervidly royalist. Soon, however, the old rivalries surfaced and Parliament was polarized into two distinct political parties. The royalists, or Tories, supported the traditional monarchy in which the king or queen was the active leader of government. The Tories were mainly the aristocracy and the conservative element of the Anglican Church. Their opponents, the Whigs, opposed the interference of the monarch in government. They favored toleration of religious dissidents and a severing of ties with France. The Whigs included certain powerful nobles, wealthy merchants and financiers, and representatives of the increasingly prosperous middle class.

THE GLORIOUS REVOLUTION

Charles was succeeded in 1685 by his brother James, a blundering, tactless statesman who also was a Catholic determined to reestablish his religion in Protestant England. Highly critical of James's ineptness and fearful of his pro-French and pro-Catholic policies, Whig leaders in Parliament secretly negotiated to replace James with his daughter Mary and her husband, the Dutchman William of Orange. Both William and Mary were Protestant, and William was shrewd, strong-willed, and staunchly anti-French as well. In 1688 James abdicated and fled to the French court, and

William and Mary became the joint monarchs of England. This event is known in history as the Glorious or Bloodless Revolution.

The Revolution Settlement, a series of declarations and acts passed by Parliament, outlined the rights and powers of Parliament, specified the succession of Protestant monarchs, and granted freedom of worship to most English people. The Glorious Revolution marked the final triumph of Parliamentary supremacy and ended once and for all the domination of dissipated royalists in government and the era of violent religious confrontations.

THE MONARCHS OF THE EIGHTEENTH CENTURY

Queen Anne, who ascended the throne at the beginning of the eighteenth century, was the last of the Stuart monarchs and the last monarch for the next half-century to take an active part in government. Although she was stodgy, dull, and often ill, she faithfully tended to her royal duties. During her reign, Scotland was united with England, and Great Britain came into being as a union of England, Wales, Ireland, and Scotland.

Occupying the throne after Anne were two lackluster kings from the German House of Hanover. Both George I and his son George II were more German than English and willingly permitted a predominantly Whig Parliament and Whig ministers to handle all matters of state. During these years, two traditions were established: the monarch as a figurehead and the head of the majority party serving as the chief, or "prime," minister.

The ascendency to the throne of George III, who ruled for sixty years, marked the end of the peaceful coexistence between the monarchy and Parliament. Commonly depicted as the "mad king," George made the great political blunder of determining to rule personally rather than to allow his ministers to act freely in his name. The result was political turmoil and unrest and the eventual loss of the American colonies.

THE ENLIGHTENMENT

The eighteenth century sometimes is called the Enlightenment in reference to the philosophy that prevailed throughout Europe. Immanuel Kant, a German philosopher, defined the Enlightenment as ". . . man's emergence from his nonage." Nonage, or immaturity, he explained, is caused by the failure of human beings to exercise their intelligence rationally to free themselves from outside authority. John Locke, another early Enlightenment philosopher, described an ideal government of checks and balances and asserted the right of citizens to revolt against a government that is intolerant, unfair, or authoritarian.

Utilizing the methodology of scientific inquiry, Enlightenment scholars and intellectuals sought to discover the universal principles governing human nature and the laws of the natural world. They also applied reason and common sense to problems of politics, law, and economics, believing firmly in human perfectability and in the possibility of an ideal society. Philosophers conceived God as a benevolent but distant deity, the mechanic of an orderly, benign universe.

The Enlightenment emphasis on intellectual freedom, human capability, and natural rights provided the philosophical basis for the revolutions in the American colonies and in France and for documents such as the American Declaration of Independence and Constitution. The emphasis on scientific investigation stimulated research and the practical application of scientific theories. The emphasis on the rational and the scientific challenged the traditional Christian concepts of a personal God and of the improbability of earthly happiness. As a result, mainstream religion in the early eighteenth century tended to be dispassionate and often perfunctory. Later in the century, however, an evangelical revival led by John and Charles Wesley gave rise to the new Methodist religion, which in turn inspired a revivalist movement within the Church of England.

UPPER AND MIDDLE CLASS LIFE IN AN ENLIGHTENED AGE

Many in England lived well during the eighteenth century, and a few lived sumptuously. Wealthy aristocrats built dignified "Georgian" country houses with classic lines and stately columns; the houses were surrounded by beautifully tended lawns and gardens. In London gracious townhouses, magnificent public buildings, and splendid churches lined the spacious streets and squares that had been laid out after the Great Fire.

For middle class Londoners, the nearly three thousand coffeehouses served as intellectual, social, and political centers. Businessmen, artists, merchants, lawyers, writers, and some aristocrats gathered daily in their favorite coffeehouses to gossip, conduct business, and discuss literature, political issues, philosophical questions, and scientific theories.

Exquisite artistry made the Enlightenment a great age of English handcraft. Goldsmiths, silversmiths, and other craftsmen transformed even ordinary objects—walls, furniture, cutlery, and tableware—into extraordinary works of art. Furniture modeled on the designs of furniture makers such as Chippendale and Heppelwhite was created by skilled specialists. A designer planned a chair or a table; a carpenter built the basic structure; a sculptor carved the intricate relief patterns; finally, an artist applied paint or gilt or attached delicate inlays and veneers. Rich tapestries often were used to upholster furniture and to cover entire walls.

SOURCES OF AGRICULTURAL AND INDUSTRIAL DEVELOPMENT

Throughout the eighteenth century, and particularly during the reign of George III, profound changes occurred in agriculture and in industry, changes so dramatic and far reaching as to be called revolutions. The roots of these revolutions can be traced back to the late seventeenth century, to the work of scientists who probed the secrets of the physical world.

The most influential of these scientists was Sir Isaac Newton, who formulated the laws of gravity and motion and described the laws in *Mathematical Principles of Natural Philosophy* (1687). This important document inspired a long line of scientists to investigate through experimentation the principles that govern the universe. Astronomers learned that "fixed stars" are actually in motion and that the Milky Way is an immense collection of stars. Chemists isolated hydrogen, discovered carbon dioxide, and converted hydrogen and oxygen into water. Botanists and zoologists categorized literally millions of individual plants and animals.

The Royal Society, chartered by Charles II in 1662, collected and disseminated information on the accomplishments of both theoretical and applied science. Among the practical achievements that contributed to the agricultural and industrial revolutions were new methods for brewing ale, making bricks, hatching eggs, plowing, harvesting, and breeding, and improved scientific instruments, tools, and engines.

THE REVOLUTION IN AGRICULTURE

In the mid-eighteenth century, scientists had discovered new ways to increase productivity. Use of the horse-drawn cultivator and crop rotation to maintain soil fertility were shown to produce higher yields with fewer laborers. Breeding experiments resulted in larger animals; by the end of the century, the size of the average sheep had nearly tripled; the weight of the average cow had doubled.

Farmers with small plots of land could not utilize the new methods. Equipment and fertilizers were expensive, and the old village system of communal fields discouraged individual initiative. The landlords and tenants who could benefit from agricultural innovations joined the common fields into larger tracts, forcing thousands of lesser tenants to abandon their villages. Some emigrated to America or signed on as laborers on large estates. Others migrated to the new factory towns.

THE REVOLUTION IN INDUSTRY

With its many inventions, ample coal and iron, and ready colonial markets, Britain became a pioneer in using machines and steam power to manufacture goods that previously had been made by hand. This change affected the very fabric of English life. Sleepy towns in the north and west, which were close to coal and iron mines and to sources of water power, burgeoned into grimy manufacturing centers. Displaced tenants and farm laborers flocked to the cities, where they crowded into dark, filthy tenements. Male unemployment soared, for women and children were the preferred factory hands. Workers were exploited mercilessly, expected to work long hours for low pay and no benefits. Trade unions were illegal, and it was a criminal offense for workers to band together to improve wages and working conditions. When disgruntled workers rioted, the riots were put down by force. Even Adam Smith, the great proponent of free enterprise, felt compelled to issue this warning in his classic economic text *Wealth of Nations* (1776): "No society can be flourishing and happy of which the far greater part of the members are poor and miserable." The dominant economic philosophy, though, was *laissez faire*, which dictates that government should not restrict the free operation of industry.

The class structure of England shifted during the industrial revolution. Two new classes emerged—wealthy capitalists and poor, landless laborers. As England's economy moved from agricultural to industrial, the influence of the capitalists undermined the long-standing domination of the landed aristocracy in politics, government, and society.

By the end of the eighteenth century, England was both richer and poorer than ever before, a nation with a solid commercial and industrial base and a mass of restless, impoverished workers. She was a nation of reformers agitating for change and of reactionaries panicked by the violent overthrow of the old order in France and the rise of Napoleon Bonaparte. As a world power England was undeniably strong, yet she was also vulnerable to the attacks of jealous rivals. Parliament as an institution ruled the country, but the hereditary aristocracy no longer had quite the same control of Parliament. For most British subjects, the future seemed less certain than at any other time in the eighteenth century.

LITERATURE IN THE AGE OF REASON

The literary style that prevailed during the Restoration period and throughout most of the eighteenth century is called Neoclassicism, or "new classicism." Neoclassical writers believed that the writers of Greece and Rome had discovered the universal truths or "rules" informing life and literature. They modeled their works on the classics, emulating their restraint, rationality, and dignity. Like classical writing, Neoclassical prose and poetry was orderly, clear, concise, unified, and well proportioned. Reflecting the Enlightenment emphasis on society and on the human intellect, Neoclassical writers chose public rather than private themes and avoided emotionalism, imaginative speculation, and expression of personal feelings.

The literature of the Age of Reason can be divided into three periods: the Restoration Age (1660–1700), which begins with the restoration of Charles II and ends with the death of John Dryden, the foremost literary figure of the age; the Augustan Age (1700–1750), also called the Age of Pope after the poet who dominated the literature of the period; and the Age of Johnson (1750–1798), named for Samuel Johnson who set the literary standards of his day.

EARLY NEOCLASSICAL LITERATURE

During the Restoration Age drama flourished once again. Influenced by the French comedy of manners, dramatists portrayed and often satirized the artificial, sophisticated society centered in the Stuart court. Their plays were characterized by stereotyped characters, clever plots, and witty repartee. Equally popular with fashionable audiences were heroic dramas, tragedies, and tragicomedies that featured idealized heroes, virtuous heroines, despicable villains, exciting action, and spectacular staging. While the comedy of manners was written in prose, the heroic drama was written in heroic couplets, the dominant verse form of the Age of Reason.

Both the comedies of manners and the heroic plays appealed primarily to the elite. Attracting a much wider audience was the prose of John Bunyan, who along with John Milton represented the enduring Puritan tradition in Restoration England. Bunyan, a religious dissenter, wrote *The Pilgrim's Progress* (1678), an allegory that extols the Christian virtues of faith, hope, and charity and condemns vices in the form of characters such as Worldly Wiseman, Mr. Live-Loose, and Mr. Hate-Light.

THE HEIGHT OF NEOCLASSICISM

The Augustan Age was so named because writers at that time were acutely aware of imitating Latin literature. They compared London to Rome, referred to the English king as "Augustus," and imitated the works of Virgil and Horace, poets who had lived during the reign of Augustus. The Augustan Age represents the zenith of Neoclassicism. Satire reigned supreme; good taste, temperance, and "correct" behavior constituted the highest ideals; and writing was formal, balanced, realistic, and often moralistic as well.

Alexander Pope was the master of satiric verse. He satirized the dandies and ladies of high society and addressed moral, political, and philosophical issues in poetry remarkable for its polished, witty couplets. Essayists Joseph Addison and Richard Steele were the masters of satiric prose. Acting on a desire to reform the manners and refine the tastes of the general public, they published periodicals comprised of satiric sketches and essays on theatre, literature, politics, and society. In marked contrast to their subdued, sensible, and kindly approach are the incisive satires of Jonathan Swift. Appalled by the hypocrisy and sham he perceived around him, Swift castigated educators, politicians, churchmen, and all categories of human beings for failing to exercise their innate reason.

Neoclassicism dominated the poetry and much of the prose of this period, yet a strain of emotionalism is evident in drama and in the new lengthy works of fiction that captured the imaginations of large numbers of middle-class readers. In drama, domestic tragedies and sentimental comedies were melodramatic and unrealistic but nonetheless emotionally satisfying and consistently popular throughout the eighteenth century. Beginning with loosely constructed, episodic works such as *Robinson Crusoe* (1719) and *Moll Flanders* (1721) by Daniel Defoe, the novel emerged as a narrative genre that encompassed works as varied as the sentimental novels of Samuel Richardson, the rollicking comedies of Tobias Smollett, and the clever, amusing narratives of Laurence Sterne. Henry Fielding produced the bawdy *Tom Jones* (1749) whose hero demonstrates an impulsiveness and an indifference to morality and manners abhorrent to the Neoclassicists and a hard-headed view of life alien to the sentimentalists.

FROM NEOCLASSICISM TO ROMANTICISM

The Age of Johnson was a period of transition that witnessed the waning of Neoclassicism and the first stirrings of Romanticism. Johnson, a poet, critic, journalist, essayist, scholar, and lexicographer, and his biographer James Boswell reaffirmed Neoclassical ideals and deplored the increasing interest among writers in the primitive, exotic, and antiquated; in simple folk and their traditional literature; in country life and the beauties of nature; and in human emotion and personal expression. Despite the warnings of Johnson and other conservative spokesmen, public tastes turned from the classic tradition as interpreted by the writers of the Augustan Age. In drama, the plays of Shakespeare attracted large audiences as did burlesques, melodramas, pantomimes, and the spirited comedies of Richard Sheridan and Oliver Goldsmith. Especially popular near the end of the century were Gothic novels, eerie,

Literature

- Richard Steele (1672-1729) starts publishing *The Tattler*

- Alexander Pope (1688-1744) publishes *Essay On Criticism*

- *The Spectator* first published by Joseph Addison (1672-1719) and Richard Steele (1672-1729)

- Samuel Pepys (1633-1703) begins *Diary*

- John Dryden (1631-1700) is declared poet laureate

- Daniel Defoe (1659?-1731) publishes *Robinson Crusoe*

- John Bunyan (1628-1688) composes *The Pilgrim's Progress* while in prison

---

1660   **1700**

History

- Anne assumes throne of England

- Great Britain is formed by Act of Union between England and Scotland

- Sir Isaac Newton publishes *Mathematical Principles of Natural Philosophy* revolutionizing scientific thought and practice

- Charles II assumes throne of England

- Great Fire of London destroys churches, buildings, and leaves 200,000 homeless

- William and Mary declared joint sovereigns in so-called Glorious Revolution, assuring Protestant rule in England

- James II abdicates throne under pressure from Anglicans

- James II assumes throne of England, raising fears of pro-Catholic policies

mysterious tales set in medieval castles and monasteries and often involving the supernatural.

The eighteenth-century concern with real life was reflected in the great number and variety of nonfiction works, among them biographies, histories, philosophical works, political treatises, letters, travelogues, and memoirs. *The Decline and Fall of the Roman Empire* (1776–1787) by Edward Gibbon represents history at its most lucid and eloquent. The writings of Edmund Burke demonstrate that political writing is not necessarily dull, or pedantic.

The poets of this period best express the undercurrents of Romantic fervor, writing simpler, freer lyrics on subjects close to the human heart. The reflective poetry of Goldsmith and Thomas Gray, the lyrical songs of Robert Burns, and the intensely passionate lyrics of William Blake all anticipate the flowering of Romanticism in the next century.

• Henry Fielding (1707-1754) publishes *Tom Jones*

• Robert Burns (1759-1796) publishes *Poems*

• Thomas Gray (1716-1771) publishes *Elegy Written in a Country Churchyard*

• James Boswell (1740-1795) publishes *Life of Samuel Johnson*

• First edition of letters of Lady Mary Wortley Montague (1689-1762) is published

• William Blake (1757-1827) writes *Songs of Innocence and Experience*

• Samuel Johnson (1709-1784) publishes edition of *Shakespeare*

• Jonathan Swift (1667-1745) publishes *Gulliver's Travels*

• Oliver Goldsmith (1730-1774) writes *She Stoops to Conquer*

• Edward Gibbon (1737-1794) begins *The Decline and Fall of the Roman Empire*

1750 **1800**

• Seven Years' War begins French and English struggle for control of North America

• Adam Smith writes *Wealth of Nations*, criticizing mercantilism

• George III becomes King of Great Britain and Ireland

• Treaty of Paris ends war between Britain and colonies, now declared independent

• Parliament enacts Stamp Act, launching colonial protests against taxation

• George II becomes King of Great Britain and Ireland

• Parliament passes Townshend Acts furthering tensions with American colonies

• French Revolution begins

• Parliament passes Tea Act, leading to Boston Tea Party

• British defeat colonists at Battle of Bunker Hill

The Development of the English Language

THE AGE OF REASON

Two significant features of intellectual history can be seen influencing the evolution of English. One is the "pendulum effect" in which the excesses of one era are balanced with opposite tendencies in the next. During the transitions a kind of equilibrium is established but eventually the new trend becomes exaggerated, sending the "pendulum" swinging back the other way. The exuberant Renaissance followed by the rational, restrained Neoclassical Age demonstrates this "pendulum effect."

A second characteristic of intellectual history is the tendency for thinkers and writers to apply the newest principles of science to other aspects of life, including language. This tendency was evident in the Renaissance and assumed even greater importance in the Neoclassical Period.

The Rule of Reason and the Rise of Science

In 1688 when Parliament ousted the pro-Catholic James II in favor of the staunchly Protestant William and Mary, relative reason returned to England, ending decades of political turmoil. The supremacy of reason and logic was further assured by the influence of Isaac Newton, whose *Mathematical Principles of Natural Philosophy* (1687) explained the physical laws of the universe. John Locke's "Essay Concerning Human Understanding" (1690) provided a philosophical foundation for a Newtonian world view based on reason, logic, and science. Reacting against the freedom of the preceding era, the leaders of the eighteenth century worked toward permanent forms in society and in language.

In this atmosphere, in the words of language historian Lincoln Barnett, "reflective men of letters were clamoring for a kind of language authority that did not yet exist." In 1693, John Dryden expressed the prevailing desire to stabilize and systematize the language: "We have yet no prosodia, not so much as a tolerable dictionary or a grammar, so that our language is in a manner barbarous." In keeping with the desire for order and regulation, for the first time serious efforts were made to standardize the English language, to refine and improve it, as well as to stabilize it in a desirable form.

The Dictionary as Stabilizer

One accomplishment of the period was *A Dictionary of the English Language* by Samuel Johnson, completed in 1755. While attempting to fix pronunciation, preserve language purity, and discover usage, Johnson showed the great variety of English vocabulary and helped to standardize spelling. Although he wrote in the Preface that "it is the duty of the lexicographer to correct or proscribe" imperfections, Johnson realized that language constantly changes. He remarked, "Sounds are too volatile and subtile for legal restraints; to enchain syllables and to lash the wind are equally the undertakings of pride."

The Dream of "Standard English"

What Johnson's dictionary did for vocabulary and spelling, grammarians attempted to do for syntax. In 1762 Robert Lowth published his *Short Introduction to English*

Grammar in which he criticized as anarchic the usage of the greatest writers and pronounced the need for absolute and inflexible laws of grammar, as immutable and sacrosanct as the law of gravity. Lowth and other grammarians attempted to reduce language to rules, judge correctness in matters under dispute, and point out errors. They were not only descriptive, stating how language is used, but also prescriptive, telling how language should be used.

There was a strong movement during this Neoclassical Period to "purify" English. Joseph Addison commented in *The Spectator* that he often wished that certain people "might be set apart as superintendents of our language to hinder any words of a foreign coin from passing among us." In "A Proposal for Correcting, Improving, and Ascertaining the English Tongue" (1712), Jonathan Swift proposed the establishment of an English Academy to set standards for language. Swift unleashed some of his most savage satire against those whose vocabulary included fashionable new clipped words and coinages such as *mob, banter, sham, bully,* and *bamboozle.* He even crusaded to omit contractions and to restore the suffix *-ed* to full syllabic value.

Since the eighteenth century, constant warfare has existed between those who insist that only one kind of English is standard or correct, and those who accept widespread usage as the standard of correctness, with the former faction winning many of the battles, the latter winning most of the wars.

Literary and Scientific Vocabulary

Neoclassical writers admired the Latin language enormously, often relying on Latin as the basis for precise communication. They called their age Augustan, likening it to the reign of Augustus, the time of great Roman writers and thinkers such as Ovid, Horace, and Virgil. Dryden confessed that he often composed phrases in Latin before putting them into English, and Samuel Johnson's writing is often so Latinate that a reader must be virtually bilingual to appreciate the clarity of his thoughts.

Scientists needed new terms to express concepts and to describe their discoveries. They created new scientific meanings for old words and coined new words, often from Latin and Greek roots. Among the new words that were incorporated into the language during the seventeenth century were *vertebra, acid, atmosphere,* and *gravity.* The influx of scientific terminology continued in the eighteenth century, with zoology and botany dominating the first half (*coleoptera, fauna, habitat, pistil*) to be joined in importance by chemistry in the second (*hydrogen, oxygen, molecule*).

English as a Mother Tongue

When the American colonies won their independence in 1781, London ceased to be the capital of the English-speaking world. As American and later Australian English evolved from regional dialects into distinct languages, English became more decentralized than other international languages such as Latin and French, which had maintained single standards of correct usage. By the twentieth century the differences between British English and the English of one former colony had become so marked that critic and playwright Bernard Shaw commented, "England and America are two countries separated by the same language."

John Dryden
1631–1700

JOHN DRYDEN, 1693. *Sir Godfrey Kneller.*
National Portrait Gallery, London.

John Dryden, the literary giant of his day, exerted a profound influence on English literature and language throughout the eighteenth century. In his plays, critical essays, and poems, Dryden established the Neoclassical style, the graceful, clear, succinct, and reserved mode of expression that prevailed for the next century. In recognition of his preeminence among Restoration writers, the era often is referred to as the Age of Dryden.

Born into a strict Puritan family, Dryden experienced severity in his early life, often in the form of floggings both at home and at the exclusive Westminster School. At Cambridge University Dryden pursued classical studies and also developed a lifelong interest in science, which is reflected in the numerous scientific allusions in his poetry. After graduation he moved to London where he gained favor first by supporting Oliver Cromwell and the Commonwealth and then by supporting the restoration of Charles II. Dryden's two poetic tributes to Charles, "Astraea Redux" and "To His Sacred Majesty," initiated a long period of productivity and acclaim.

During the eighteen years between 1662 and 1680, Dryden was primarily a playwright. However, he did write a classic work of literary criticism, *An Essay of Dramatic Poesy* (1668), in which four imaginary writers discuss dramatic principles and techniques and compare contemporary and earlier drama and French and English plays. In 1680 Dryden began to write verse satires castigating liberal factions and praising the established order represented by the king and his Tory supporters. In satires such as "Absalom and Achitophel" (1681) and "Mac Flecknoe" (1682) Dryden demonstrates the wit, urbanity, confidence, and tolerant ease that characterize his finest work.

In deference to his royal patron, Dryden became a Roman Catholic after the accession of James II to the throne. "The Hind and the Panther" (1687), his longest poem, is an elaborate beast fable in defense of the Catholic Church. Appearing the same year was "A Song for St. Cecilia's Day," an ode written to be performed on November 22, the English feast day of St. Cecilia.

In spite of the apparent expediency of his conversion, Dryden remained a faithful Catholic to his death, even during the rule of Protestants William and Mary. During their reign, however, he lost his patronage and his titles. He turned again to drama, but abandoned playwriting after several failures. He spent his last years presiding over lively discussions at Will's Coffeehouse, writing poetry and criticism, translating the works of the Latin poet Virgil, and compiling *Fables Ancient and Modern* (1700), a collection of tales from originals by Ovid, Chaucer, and Boccaccio. Dryden died quietly in 1700 and was buried in the Poets' Corner in Westminster Abbey, next to Geoffrey Chaucer.

A Song for St. Cecilia's Day

I

From harmony, from heavenly harmony
  This universal frame[1] began:
   When Nature underneath a heap
    Of jarring atoms[2] lay,
   And could not heave her head,   5
The tuneful voice was heard from high:
  "Arise, ye more than dead."
Then cold, and hot, and moist, and dry,[3]
In order to their stations leap,
   And Music's power obey.[4]   10
From harmony, from heavenly harmony
  This universal frame began:
  From harmony to harmony
Through all the compass of the notes it ran,
The diapason[5] closing full in Man.   15

II

What passion cannot Music raise and quell!
   When Jubal[6] struck the corded shell,
  His listening brethren stood around,
  And, wondering, on their faces fell
  To worship that celestial sound.   20
Less than a god they thought there could not dwell
  Within the hollow of that shell
  That spoke so sweetly and so well.
What passion cannot Music raise and quell!

---

1. **universal frame:** the totality of all things that exist, the universe.
2. **Nature . . . jarring atoms:** the power or force thought to have brought order out of chaos.
3. **cold . . . dry:** The ancient Greeks believed that all matter was made up of these four elements.
4. **Music's power obey:** Dryden, like Milton, believed that the forces that brought order to the universe were reflected in the mathematical harmony of music.
5. **diapason:** one of the principal stops of an organ, one that covers the complete range of the instrument; the implication here is that Man, too, is the expression of Nature's fullest harmony.
6. **Jubal:** one of Cain's descendents (see Genesis 4:21), the inventor of musical instruments, who is said to have made a harp from a tortoise shell ("corded shell").

III

The trumpet's loud clangor 25
  Excites us to arms,
With shrill notes of anger
  And mortal alarms.
The double double double beat
  Of the thundering drum 30
Cries: "Hark! the foes come;
Charge, charge, 'tis too late to retreat."

IV

The soft complaining flute
In dying notes discovers
The woes of hopeless lovers, 35
Whose dirge is whispered by the
    warbling lute.

V

  Sharp violins proclaim
Their jealous pangs, and desperation,
Fury, frantic indignation,
Depth of pains, and height of passion, 40
  For the fair, disdainful dame.

VI

  But O! what art can teach,
  What human voice can reach,
The sacred organ's praise?
  Notes inspiring holy love, 45
Notes that wing their heavenly ways
  To mend the choirs above.

VII

Orpheus[7] could lead the savage race;
And trees unrooted left their place,
  Sequacious of[8] the lyre; 50
But bright Cecilia raised the wonder higher:
When to her organ[9] vocal breath was given,
  An angel heard, and straight appeared,
  Mistaking earth for heaven.

Grand Chorus

As from the power of sacred lays 55
  The spheres began to move,[10]
And sung the great Creator's praise
  To all the blest above;
So, when the last and dreadful hour[11]
This crumbling pageant[12] shall devour, 60
The trumpet shall be heard on high,
The dead shall live, the living die,
And Music shall untune the sky.[13]

---

7. **Orpheus:** a gifted singer in Greek mythology who could charm not only
savage beasts but also rocks and trees when he played the lyre.
8. **Sequacious of:** following.
9. **organ:** St. Cecilia was said to be the inventor of the pipe organ.
10. **spheres . . . move:** The power of music is said to have put the planets in
motion.
11. **last and dreadful hour:** the Last Judgment.
12. **pageant:** used here as a metaphor comparing the stage performance
honoring St. Cecilia to the existence of life itself in the universe.
13. **Music . . . sky:** At the sound of the last trumpet (see I Corinthians 15:52)
all creation will be judged. Although the universe will be destroyed, Music,
the essence of creation, will still remain.

LUTE PLAYER IN A GARDEN.
Embroidered Textile, English, ca. 1650–75.
The Metropolitan Museum of Art. Rogers Fund, 1929.

Getting at Meaning

1. What are the connotations of *harmony* in the first line of this song? How is the idea suggested in this line expanded in lines 13 and 14?

2. What concept of the deity is suggested in the first stanza? what concept of nature? of the human being's place in the universe? How do these concepts relate to the philosophy of the Enlightenment?

3. With what human emotions is each instrument named in the third, fourth, and fifth stanzas associated? What specific words within the stanzas connote these emotions?

4. In the fifth stanza the speaker indicates that the violin can express sharply contrasting emotions. As it is described in this poem, does all music possess this capacity? Explain.

5. What is the function of the Grand Chorus? As described in this poem, how does music seem to be both a creative and a destructive force? Ultimately, is music associated more closely with life or death? Explain.

Developing Skills in Reading Literature

1. **Ode.** In its original Greek form, an ode was a choral work; it was associated with movement, for the members of the chorus moved dramatically from one side to another to emphasize the rise and fall of emotion. Later, ode came to mean any exalted, complex lyric, written for a specific purpose, that develops one dignified theme. An ode appeals both to the imagination and the intellect and often commemorates an occasion or event or praises a person or element of nature. Structurally, an ode is divided into stanzas that may be identical in form or that may evidence patterned variations in form.

Point out characteristics of the ode in "A Song for St. Cecilia's Day." Consider purpose, subject, tone, diction, form, and theme. How does Dryden's ode resemble the early Greek odes?

2. **Sound Devices.** Dryden's ode was meant to be sung as well as read and has been set to music by many fine composers. Understandably, the sound of the poem is of great importance, particularly in the stanzas that describe music. Identify examples of each of the following sound devices in the third, fourth, and fifth stanzas, and be prepared to discuss the tonal effects created by the devices.

onomatopoeia	repetition	rhythm
assonance	alliteration	rhyme
consonance		

3. **Figurative Language.** This ode is an extended metaphor in which music is compared to a powerful spiritual force. The ode also contains personification, another kind of comparison. Identify several examples of personification, and trace the specific metaphors that extend the basic controlling metaphor. How do these figures of speech contribute to the sense of grandeur appropriate to an ode? How do they enhance the appeal of the poem for readers today?

from The Cock and the Fox

Dreams

The following excerpt is from "The Cock and the Fox," a fable based on "The Nun's Priest's Tale" by Geoffrey Chaucer. In Dryden's version the speaker responds to Chanticleer's terrifying dream by commenting on the nature of dreams.

Dreams are but interludes which fancy[1] makes;
When monarch Reason[2] sleeps, this mimic wakes;
Compounds a medley of disjointed things,
A mob of cobblers, and a court of kings.
Light fumes[3] are merry, grosser fumes are sad;   5
Both are the reasonable soul run mad:
And many monstrous forms in sleep we see,
That neither were, nor are, nor e'er can be.
Sometimes forgotten things long cast behind
Rush forward in the brain, and come to mind.   10
The nurse's legends[4] are for truths received,
And the man dreams but what the boy believed.
Sometimes we but rehearse a former play;
The night restores our actions done by day,
As hounds in sleep will open for their prey.   15
In short the farce of dreams is of a piece,
Chimeras[5] all; and more absurd, or less.

GREEK PLATE, *ca. 520–510* B.C. *Epiktetos.*
The Metropolitan Museum of Art,
Classical Purchase Fund,
Schimmel Foundation, Inc. and
Christos G. Bastis Gifts, 1981.   *351*

---

1. **fancy:** imagination.
2. **monarch Reason:** The Eighteenth Century was known as the Age of Reason; rational thought took precedence over the world of imagination.
3. **fumes:** vapors or "humors"; universal elements, commonly thought in the seventeenth century to influence human behavior and disposition.
4. **nurse's legends:** old-wives' tales, myths.
5. **Chimeras:** in Greek mythology, a fire-breathing monster; here, an impossible or foolish fancy.

Getting at Meaning

1. According to the speaker, what is the relationship between reality and the world of imagination? Cite examples from the excerpt to support your answer.

2. What lines from this excerpt probably are based on the poet's observation of human behavior? Does the poet seem to have insight into human psychology? Explain.

Developing Skills in Reading Literature

1. **Figurative Language.** The poet makes use of metaphor, simile, and personification in this poem in order to portray vividly the world of imagination. Locate examples of these figures of speech, and be prepared to describe the image evoked by each and the relationship between the image and the idea that is being communicated.

2. **Neoclassical Style.** The Neoclassical writers of the eighteenth century developed a style that was characterized by order, logic, symmetry, grace, and good taste. Believing that literature should serve mankind, they created literary works that were meant not only to delight readers but also to instruct them in moral virtues and in the art of "correct" social behavior. To the Neoclassicists, the intellect was more important than the emotions; their prose and poetry, therefore, are coolly polite, witty, and somewhat artificial.

Examine both "A Song for St. Cecilia's Day" and the excerpt from "The Cock and the Fox" to identify characteristics of the Neoclassical style. Comment on both general characteristics and on the specific manifestations of these characteristics within each selection. Which selection is more clearly Neoclassical? What might account for the difference between the two selections?

Developing Writing Skills

Using Comparisons and Contrasts. In a well developed paragraph, compare the excerpt from "The Cock and the Fox" with Chaucer's treatment of the same subject in "The Nun's Priest's Tale." Discuss ways in which the response of each writer to his subject reveals differences between the two historic periods in which they wrote.

Samuel Pepys

1633–1703

It is rare to have such a vivid account of daily life in any period of history as is found in *The Diary of Samuel Pepys* (pronounced "Peeps"). Begun in the historic year of the Restoration, *The Diary* not only records the grandeur of public scenes, such as the king's coronation ceremony and the great London fire of 1666, but also provides candid pictures of the domestic life of a prosperous middle class Londoner.

Pepys, the son of a tailor, received a scholarship to Cambridge University, where he earned bachelor's and master's degrees. He was hired as the personal secretary to his cousin Admiral Edward Montague, later the first Earl of Sandwich. In this role, he accompanied Montague on his mission to bring Charles II back to England from his exile in France. Pepys gives a full account of the crossing in *The Diary*, along with detailed descriptions of the fascinating rituals of court life.

Through his own presence of mind and through influential contacts at court, Pepys obtained an appointment to the Navy Office and eventually became Secretary of the Admiralty. Knowing nothing about the navy, he devoted himself to becoming a naval expert. He attended lectures on shipbuilding, mastered navigational mathematics, and learned the prices of naval supplies. To secure increased appropriations, he ran successfully for Parliament, where he argued the importance of sea power and the necessity for a strengthened navy. Pepys was honest and efficient, ferreting out corruption and establishing an orderly, disciplined administration. As a high ranking Tory minister, though, he had powerful political enemies, who once implicated him in a plot against the king and nearly succeeded in having him executed for treason. Pepys retired after the reign of James II and spent the remaining sixteen years of his life working on his library and collecting information on the history of the navy.

During his busy years as an administrator, Pepys enjoyed an active social life and took a lively interest in art, theatre, and literature. Among his friends were the foremost scholars of his age:

SAMUEL PEPYS, 1666. *J. Hays.*
National Portrait Gallery, London.

scientist Sir Isaac Newton, architect Sir Christopher Wren, writer John Dryden, and other fellow members of the Royal Academy.

The Diary of Samuel Pepys is an invaluable historical document covering the period from January 1, 1660, to May 31, 1669. *The Diary* is also an intimate portrait of an extraordinary personality, a man shrewd in business, keenly observant, and insatiably curious. He is a man engagingly honest about his weaknesses—vanity, stinginess, jealousy, irritability—a quality that gives *The Diary* a unique and enduring charm.

Apparently to insure privacy and the freedom to be completely at ease in describing his personal life, Pepys wrote in an obscure system of shorthand with only proper names in longhand. He bequeathed the six-volume *Diary*, along with the rest of his library, to Cambridge University where it was eventually unearthed and painstakingly deciphered. The first edition was published in 1825, and several editions have been issued since that time.

from The Diary of Samuel Pepys

1660

The Restoration of Charles II

March 16th. To Westminster Hall, where I heard how the Parliament had this day dissolved themselves,[1] and did pass very cheerfully through the Hall, and the Speaker without his mace.[2] The whole Hall was joyful thereat, as well as themselves, and now they begin to talk loud of the King. Tonight I am told, that yesterday, about five o'clock in the afternoon, one came with a ladder to the Great Exchange, and wiped with a brush the inscription that was upon King Charles, and that there was a great bonfire made in the Exchange, and people called out "God bless King Charles the Second!"

May 22nd. News brought that the two Dukes are coming on board, which, by and by, they did, in a Dutch boat, the Duke of York in yellow trimmings, the Duke of Gloucester in grey and red. My Lord[3] went in a boat to meet them, the Captain, myself, and others, standing at the entering port. . . .

All the afternoon the King walked here and there, up and down (quite contrary to what I thought him to have been), very active and stirring. Upon the quarterdeck he fell into discourse of his escape from Worcester, where it made me ready to weep to hear the stories that he told of his difficulties that he had passed through, as his traveling four days and three nights on foot, every step up to his knees in dirt, with nothing but a green coat and a pair of country breeches on, and a pair of country shoes that made him so sore all over his feet, that he could scarce stir. Yet he was forced to run away from a miller and other company, that took them for rogues. His sitting at table at one place, where the master of the house, that had not seen him in eight years, did know him, but kept it private; when at the same table there was one that had been of his own regiment at Worcester, could not know him, but made him drink the King's health, and said that the King was at least four fingers higher than he. At another place he was by some servants of the house made to drink, that they might know him not to be a Roundhead, which they swore he was. In another place at his inn, the master of the house, as the King was standing with his hands upon the back of a chair by the fireside, kneeled down and kissed his hand, privately, saying, that he would not ask him who he was, but bid God bless him whither he was going.

Oct. 13th. I went out to Charing Cross, to see Major General Harrison[4] hanged, drawn, and quartered; which was done there, he looking as cheerful as any man could do in that condition. He was presently cut down, and his head and heart shown to the people, at which there was great shouts of joy. It is said, that he said that he was sure to come shortly at the right hand of Christ to judge them that now had judged him; and that his wife do expect his coming again. Thus it was my chance to see the King beheaded at White Hall,[5] and to see the first blood shed in revenge for the blood of the King at Charing Cross.

---

1. **Parliament . . . themselves:** The Parliament met in 1660 solely to put an end to the Commonwealth and to call Charles II to the throne.
2. **mace:** a staff used as a symbol of authority.
3. **My Lord:** Sir Edward Montague, Pepys's employer, who was in command of the fleet that brought Charles II back to England from his exile in France.
4. **Major General Harrison:** one of the signers of the death warrant for Charles I.
5. **King . . . White Hall:** Pepys had been present at the beheading of Charles I in 1649. He was sixteen at the time.

Within all the afternoon setting up shelves in my study. At night to bed.

1661

Jan. 1st. At the end of the last and the beginning of this year, I do live in one of the houses belonging to the Navy Office, as one of the principal officers,[6] and have done now about half a year. After much trouble with workmen I am now almost settled; my family being, myself, my wife, Jane, Will, Hewer, and Wayneman, my girl's brother. Myself in constant good health, and in a most handsome and thriving condition. Blessed be Almighty God for it. As to things of State.—The King settled, and loved of all.

The Coronation of the King

April 23rd. About four I rose and got to the Abbey,[7] where with a great deal of patience I sat from past four till eleven before the King came in his robes, bareheaded, which was very fine. And after all had placed themselves, there was a sermon and the service; and then in the Quire at the high altar, the King passed through all the ceremonies of the Coronation, which to my great grief I and most in the Abbey could not see. The crown being put upon his head, a great shout began, and he came forth to the throne, and there passed more ceremonies: as taking the oath, and having things read to him by the Bishop; and his lords (who put on their caps as soon as the King put on his crown) and bishops came, and kneeled before him. And three times the King at Arms[8] went to the three open places on the scaffold, and proclaimed, that if any one could show any reason why Charles Stuart should not be King of England, that now he should come and speak. And a General Pardon also was read by the Lord Chancellor, and medals[9] flung up and down by my Lord Cornwallis, of

silver, but I could not come by any. But so great a noise that I could make but little of the music; and indeed, it was lost to everybody. I went out a little while before the King had done all his ceremonies, and went round the Abbey to Westminster Hall, all the way within rails, and 10,000 people, with the ground covered with blue cloth; and scaffolds all the way. Into the Hall I got, where it was very fine with hangings and scaffolds one upon another full of brave ladies; and my wife in one little one, on the right hand. Here I stayed walking up and down, and at last upon one of the side stalls I stood and saw the King come in with all the persons (but the soldiers) that were yesterday in the cavalcade; and a most pleasant sight it was to see them in their several robes. And the King came in with his crown on, and his sceptre in his hand, under a canopy borne up by six silver staves, carried by Barons of the Cinque Ports,[10] and little bells at every end.

And after a long time, he got up to the farther end, and all set themselves down at their several tables; and that was also a brave sight: and the King's first course carried up by the Knights of the Bath. And many fine ceremonies there were of the Heralds leading up people before him, and bowing; and my Lord of Albemarle's going to the kitchen and eating a bit of the first dish that was to go to the King's table. But, above all, were these three Lords, Northumberland, and Suffolk, and the Duke of Ormond, coming before the courses on horseback, and staying so all dinnertime, and at last to bring up the King's Champion,

---

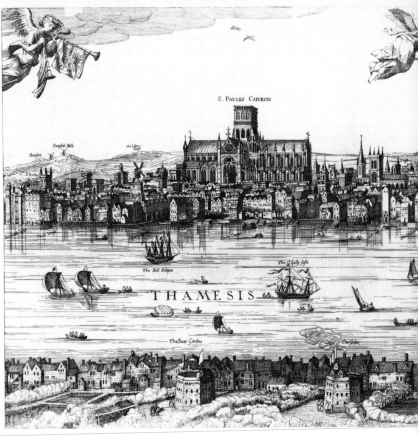

VIEW OF LONDON (engraving), 1616. John Vischer. British Museum.

all in armor on horseback, with his spear and target carried before him. And a Herald proclaims "That if any dare deny Charles Stuart to be lawful King of England, here was a Champion that would fight with him," and with these words, the Champion flings down his gauntlet, and all this he does three times in his going up towards the King's table. At last when he is come, the King drinks to him, and then sends him the cup which is of gold, and he drinks it off, and then rides back again with the cup in his hand.

1666

The Great London Fire

Sept. 2nd. (Lord's day). Some of our maids sitting up late last night to get things ready against our feast today, Jane called us up about three in the morning, to tell us of a great fire they saw in the City. So I rose and slipped on my nightgown, and went to her window, and thought it to be on the backside of Mark Lane at the farthest; but, being unused to such fires as followed, I thought it far enough off; and so went to bed again and to sleep. About seven rose again to dress myself, and there looked out at the window, and saw the fire not so much as it was and further off. So to my closet to set things to rights after yesterday's cleaning.

By and by Jane comes and tells me that she hears that above 300 houses have been burned down tonight by the fire we saw, and that it is now burning down all Fish Street, by London Bridge. So I made myself ready presently, and walked to the Tower,[11] and there got up upon one of the high places, Sir J. Robinson's little

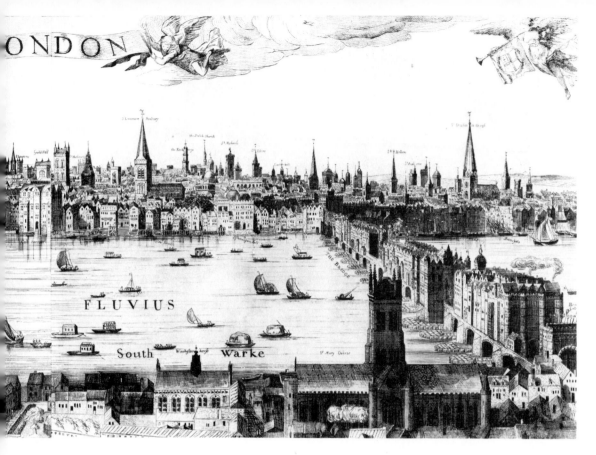

son going up with me; and there I did see the houses at that end of the bridge all on fire, and an infinite great fire on this and the other side the end of the bridge; which, among other people, did trouble me for poor little Michell and our Sarah on the bridge.[12] So down, with my heart full of trouble, to the Lieutenant of the Tower, who tells me that it begun this morning in the King's baker's house in Pudding Lane, and that it hath burned St. Magnus's Church and most part of Fish Street already. So I down to the waterside, and there got a boat and through bridge, and there saw a lamentable fire. Poor Michell's house, as far as the Old Swan, already burned that way, and the fire running further, that in a very little time it got as far as the Steeleyard, while I was there. Everybody endeavoring to remove their goods, and flinging into the river or bringing them into lighters that lay off; poor people staying in their houses as long as till the very fire touched them, and then running into boats, or clambering from one pair of stairs by the waterside to another. And among other things, the poor pigeons, I perceive, were loth to leave their houses, but hovered about the windows and balconys till they were, some of them burned, their wings, and fell down.

At last met my Lord Mayor in Canning Street, like a man spent, with a handkerchief about his neck. To the King's message he cried, like a fainting woman, "Lord! what can I do? I am spent: people will not obey me. I have been pulling down houses; but the fire overtakes us faster than we can do it." That

---

11. **Tower:** the Tower of London.
12. **on the bridge:** Houses lined both sides of the Old London Bridge.

THE GREAT FIRE OF LONDON (engraving), 1666. *The Mansell Collection.*

he needed no more soldiers; and that, for himself, he must go and refresh himself, having been up all night. So he left me, and I him, and walked home, seeing people all almost distracted, and no manner of means used to quench the fire. The houses, too, so very thick thereabouts, and full of matter for burning, as pitch and tar, in Thames Street; and warehouses of oil, and wines, and brandy, and other things.

Having seen as much as I could now, I away to White Hall by appointment, and there walked to St. James's Park, and there met my wife and Creed and Wood and his wife, and walked to my boat; and there upon the water again, and to the fire up and down, it still increasing, and the wind great. So near the fire as we could for smoke; and all over the Thames, with one's face in the wind, you were almost burned with a shower of fire-drops. This is very true; so as houses were burned by these drops and flakes of fire, three or four, nay, five or six houses, one from another. When we could endure no more upon the water, we to a little alehouse on the Bankside, over against the Three Cranes, and there stayed till it was dark almost, and saw the fire grow; and, as it grew darker, churches and houses, as far as we could see up the hill of the City, in a most horrid malicious bloody flame, not like the fine flame of an ordinary fire. We stayed till, it being darkish, we saw the fire as only one entire arch of fire from this to the other side the bridge, and in a bow up the hill for an arch of above a mile long: it made me weep to see it. The churches, houses, and all on fire and flaming at once; and a horrid noise the flames made, and the cracking of houses at their ruin. So home with a sad heart, and there find every body discoursing and lamenting the fire.

Sept. 3rd. About four o'clock in the morning, my Lady Batten sent me a cart to carry away all my money, and plate, and best things, to Sir W. Rider's at Bednal Green. Which I did, riding myself in my nightgown in the cart; and, Lord! to see how the streets and the highways are crowded with people running and riding, and getting of carts at any rate to fetch away things. I find Sir W. Rider tired with being called up all night, and receiving things from several friends. His house full of goods, and much of Sir W. Batten's and Sir W. Penn's. I am eased at my heart to have my treasure so well secured. Then home, with much ado to find a way, nor any sleep all this night to me nor my poor wife.

Sept. 17th. Up betimes, and shaved myself after a week's growth: but, Lord! how ugly I was yesterday and how fine today! By water, seeing the City all the way, a sad sight indeed, much fire being still in.

Sept. 22nd. Now my house is so clean as I never saw it, or any other house in my life, and everything in as good condition as ever before the fire; but with, I believe, about £20[13] cost one way or other, besides about £20 charge in removing my goods, and do not find that I have lost anything but two little pictures of ships and sea, and a little gold frame for one of my sea-cards. My glazier, indeed, is so full of work that I cannot get him to come to perfect my house. In the afternoon I paid for the two lighters that carried my goods to Deptford, and they cost me £8.

1660

Domestic Affairs

Jan. 26th. Home from my office to my Lord's lodgings where my wife had got ready a very fine dinner—viz. a dish of marrow bones; a leg of mutton; a loin of veal; a dish of fowl, three pullets, and two dozen of larks all in a dish; a great tart, a neat's tongue, a dish of anchovies; a dish of prawns and cheese. My company was my father, my uncle Fenner, his two sons, Mr. Pierce, and all their wives, and my brother Tom.

1662

Jan. 1st. Waking this morning out of my sleep on a sudden, I did with my elbow hit my wife a great blow over her face and nose, which waked her with pain, at which I was sorry, and to sleep again.

Jan. 13th. My poor wife rose by five o'clock in the morning, before day, and went to market and bought fowls and many other things for dinner, with which I was highly pleased, and the chine of beef[14] was down also before six o'clock, and my own jack, of which I was doubtful, do carry it very well. Things being put in order, and the cook come, I went to the office, where we sat till noon and then broke up, and I home, whither by and by comes Dr. Clerke and his lady, his sister, and a she-cousin, and Mr. Pierce and his wife, which was all my guests. I had for them, after oysters, at first course, a hash of rabbits, a lamb, and a rare chine of beef. Next a great dish of roasted fowl, cost me about 30s.,[15] and a tart, and then fruit and cheese. My dinner was noble and enough. I had my house mighty clean and neat; my room below with a good fire in it; my dining room above, and my chamber being made a withdrawing chamber; and my wife's a good fire also. I find my new table very proper, and will hold nine or ten people well, but eight with great room. After

---

13. **£20:** An English pound note is currently equal to approximately two dollars and fifty cents.
14. **chine of beef:** a cut of meat containing the backbone.
15. **30s:** thirty shillings; a shilling is equal to five (new) pennies or 1/20 of a pound. The coinage of shillings was discontinued in 1971.

dinner the women to cards in my wife's chamber, and the Dr. and Mr. Pierce in mine, because the dining room smokes unless I keep a good charcoal fire, which I was not then provided with. At night to supper, had a good sack posset[16] and cold meat, and sent my guests away about ten o'clock at night, both them and myself highly pleased with our management of this day; and indeed their company was very fine, and Mrs. Clerke a very witty, fine lady, though a little conceited and proud. I believe this day's feast will cost me near £5.

Oct. 21st. This evening I began to enter my wife in arithmetic, in order to her studying of the globes and she takes it very well, and I hope I shall bring her to understand many fine things.

1667

Jan. 7th. To the Duke's house, and saw *Macbeth*, which, though I saw it lately, yet appears a most excellent play in all respects, but especially in *divertisement*, though it be a deep tragedy; which is a strange perfection in a tragedy, it being most proper here, and suitable.

Feb. 25th. Lay long in bed, talking with pleasure with my poor wife, how she used to make coal fires, and wash my foul clothes with her own hand for me, poor wretch! in our little room at my Lord Sandwich's;[17] for which I ought for ever to love and admire her, and do; and persuade myself she would do the same thing again, if God should reduce us to it.

May 26th (Lord's day). My wife and I to church, where several strangers of good condition come to our pew. After dinner I by water alone to Westminster[18] to the parish church, and there did entertain myself with my perspective glass up and down the church, by which I had the great pleasure of seeing and gazing at a great many very fine women; and what with that, and sleeping, I passed away the time till sermon was done.

May 27th. Abroad, and stopped at the bear garden stairs, there to see a prize fought.[19] But the house so full there was no getting in there, so forced to go through an alehouse into the pit, where the bears are baited; and upon a stool did see them fight, which they did very furiously, a butcher and a waterman. The former had the better all along, till by and by the latter dropped his sword out of his hand, and the butcher, whether not seeing his sword dropped I know not, but did give him a cut over the wrist, so as he was disabled to fight any longer. But, Lord! to see how in a minute the whole stage was full of watermen to revenge the foul play, and the butchers to defend their fellow, though most blamed him; and there they all fell to it to knocking down and cutting many on each side. It was pleasant to see, but that I stood in the pit, and feared that in the tumult I might get some hurt. At last the rabble broke up, and so I away.

1669

Jan. 12th. This evening I observed my wife mighty dull, and I myself was not mighty fond, because of some hard words she did give me at noon, out of a jealousy at my being abroad this morning, which, God knows, it was upon the business of the Office unexpectedly; but I to bed, not thinking but she would come after me. But waking by and by out of a slumber, which I usually fall into presently

---

16. **sack posset:** a hot drink made of milk curdled with ale or wine, usually spiced.
17. **Lord Sandwich:** Sir Edward Montague, Pepys's earlier employer, was the Earl of Sandwich.
18. **I . . . Westminster:** Pepys took a boat up the Thames River from his home to his parish in Westminster.
19. **bear garden . . . prize fought:** Bearbaiting was a common diversion in which dogs were made to torment a chained bear. The bear garden was a rowdy place where violence and common brawling were everyday pastimes.

after my coming into the bed, I found she did not prepare to come to bed, but got fresh candles, and more wood for her fire, it being mighty cold, too. At this being troubled, I after a while prayed her to come to bed, and all my people being gone to bed; so, after an hour or two, she silent, and I now and then praying her to come to bed, she fell out into a fury, that I was a rogue, and false to her. At last, about one o'clock, she came to my side of the bed, and drew my curtaine open, and with the tongs red hot at the ends, made as if she did design to pinch me with them, at which, in dismay, I rose up, and with a few words she laid them down; and did by little and little, very sillily, let all the discourse fall; and about two, but with much seeming difficulty, come to bed, and there lay well all night.

From Pepys's Collection of Caligraphy.
Pepysian Library, Cambridge.

Getting at Meaning

THE RESTORATION OF CHARLES II

1. What attitudes and activities of middle class Londoners are described in the first four excerpts from *The Diary*?

2. What attitude does Pepys seem to take toward public execution? What might account for this attitude?

3. How does Pepys feel about King Charles? Cite evidence from *The Diary* to support your answer.

THE CORONATION OF THE KING

4. How does this account reveal Pepys's highly developed sense of curiosity?

5. What specific details make this account particularly vivid for the reader?

THE GREAT LONDON FIRE

6. Does Pepys seem to take a detached, objective view of the holocaust, or does he seem genuinely upset by it? Cite details to support your opinion.

7. How does Pepys reveal himself to be efficient, prudent, and careful with money?

DOMESTIC AFFAIRS

8. How does Pepys show that he enjoys a comfortable lifestyle in spite of his concern about spending money?

9. What kinds of public and private entertainment does Pepys enjoy? What does his choice of entertainment suggest about him as a person?

10. Describe the relationship between Pepys and his wife, giving details to support your conclusions.

Developing Skills in Reading Literature

1. **Point of View: Objectivity and Subjectivity.** Journalists today are expected to strive for complete objectivity in reporting news events. Objectivity, in this sense, means describing events without indicating feelings and judgments. Subjectivity, on the other hand, means that a writer reveals his or her personal responses to events. Pepys's account of public events combines objective and subjective detail; he blends personal responses with impersonal, detached description and narration. Examine "The Coronation of the King" and "The Great London Fire," and identify passages that are written objectively and those that are primarily subjective. Be alert for words and phrases that imply judgments (for example, "brave ladies" and "lamentable fire") and thus introduce subjectivity into otherwise objective statements.

2. **Autobiographical Narrative.** The autobiographical narrative as a literary form includes formal autobiographies—sustained, reflective, and usually lengthy narratives—and informal accounts such as diaries, memoirs, journals, and letters. Both formal and informal autobiographical writing provides the reader with insight into the writer's motivation, personality, character, and unique point of view and with some sense of the society in which the writer lived. In a few statements, generalize about the picture of Pepys and of his society that emerges from these excerpts from The Diary. What are the characteristics of a diary, as evidenced by these excerpts? What qualities make the Pepys diary a work of literary merit as well as a valuable historical document? Does Pepys seem to have the perceptiveness necessary to the skilled autobiographer? Explain.

Developing Vocabulary

1. **Idioms.** In describing the coronation, Pepys reports that the Champion "flings down his gauntlet."

This phrase can be interpreted both literally and as an idiom, an expression with a meaning quite different from its literal meaning. Look up *gauntlet* in a dictionary to find the literal meaning of the word and the idiomatic meaning of the phrase. Explain both and comment on how the idiomatic meaning might have developed from the literal meaning.

Study the following phrases from The Diary. Are they idioms, or are they to be taken literally? Using context clues, write the meaning of each phrase in your own words.

    a. "fell into discourse" (May 22, 1660)

    b. "pulling down houses" (Sept. 2, 1666)

    c. "with much ado" (Sept. 3, 1666)

2. **Multiple Meanings of Words.** Study the use of the word *quarter* in the following quotations from The Diary. Either by using context clues or by finding the appropriate meaning in a dictionary, write a clear definition of the word as it functions within the compound and then as it is used alone.

"Upon the *quarterdeck* he fell into discourse of his escape. . . ." (May 22, 1660)

". . . to see Major General Harrison hanged, drawn, and *quartered*. . . ." (Oct. 13, 1660)

In these quotations *quarter* is used as part of a compound noun and as a verb. Write sentences using the word as a single noun and as an adjective.

Developing Writing Skills

Describing an Event from Different Points of View. Can you recall witnessing a public event that was either spectacular or devastating? It may have been a rock concert or a terrible automobile accident. A personal friend of the rock star or a family member of an accident victim would probably describe the event subjectively, with an emphasis upon personal reaction. A newspaper reporter, on the other hand, would describe that event objectively, emphasizing what, where, when, why, and how it happened.

Choose an event with which you are familiar and write two paragraphs of description. In the first paragraph, describe the event subjectively, as if you were personally involved. In the second paragraph, describe the same event as if you were a newspaper reporter.

Alexander Pope
1688–1744

Alexander Pope was one of those rare artists who seem to thrive on adversity. Despite enormous obstacles, he became the foremost poet of the Augustan Age, a master of classical form and satiric style. His commentary on the contemporary political, social, and literary scene reaffirmed the classical values of good sense, temperance, geniality, balance, and simplicity, qualities that are evident in his elegant and graceful poetry.

Pope was born in London, the son of a wholesale linen merchant who soon retired and moved the family to the countryside near London. From childhood Pope suffered constant physical pain and deep personal humiliation, a result of tuberculosis of the spine. He never grew more than four feet six inches in height, and he became increasingly more humpbacked throughout his lifetime. Because of his grotesque appearance, he was frequently rejected, both publicly and privately. Besides this, he was brought up as a Roman Catholic at a time when only Protestants could receive the benefits of university education or pursue public careers. For this reason, Pope was largely self-taught, and he learned early to fend for himself in seeking professional prestige and social position.

Pope's genius as a poet was recognized early. His "Pastorals" (1709) were published when he was twenty-one, and *Essay on Criticism* (1711) appeared two years later. A collection of polished epigrams on the art of writing, *Essay on Criticism* addresses the question of how art can best mirror the order of the natural world. When the work was praised by Sir Richard Steele and Joseph Addison, editors of *The Spectator*, Pope's reputation was established once and for all. His next major work was *The Rape of the Lock* (1712, 1714), a mock epic in which he satirizes the false values of society by treating a trivial incident with Homeric grandeur.

Literary friends encouraged young Pope to undertake the massive task of translating first the *Iliad* and then the *Odyssey* of Homer into English, a task that was finally completed in 1726. By this time Pope was well known in aristocratic society and wealthy enough to purchase a lavish villa in

ALEXANDER POPE. *William Haare. National Portrait Gallery, London.*

Twickenham on the Thames River near London. An avid gardener, he planned his own garden and the gardens of friends according to the principles of eighteenth-century classical design.

Pope developed a sharp tongue and a critical attitude toward many of his literary colleagues. Believing that fools were his natural enemies and that his standards were those of civilized society, Pope wrote *The Dunciad* (1728) in which he satirized the critics, booksellers, historians, and writers of his day who had attacked him or whom he considered to be mediocre poets. His snobbishness often backfired, and intellectual arguments with friends sometimes developed into lifelong feuds. Once Pope quarreled with his friend Addison who later appeared in "Epistle to Dr. Arbuthnot" (1735) as the insincere, arbitrary Atticus.

More typical of Pope's personal relationships, however, was his friendship with Martha Blount, an aristocratic lady and fellow Catholic to whom he addressed "Of the Characters of Women" and other notable poems. Although she refused to marry him, he never broke with her, and when he died, he left her most of his estate.

Epistle to Miss Blount, on Her Leaving the Town after the Coronation[1]

As some fond virgin,[2] whom her mother's care
Drags from the town to wholesome country air,
Just when she learns to roll a melting eye,
And hear a spark,[3] yet think no danger nigh,
From the dear man unwilling she must sever,   5
Yet takes one kiss before she parts for ever;
Thus from the world fair Zephalinda[4] flew,
Saw others happy, and with sighs withdrew;
Not that their pleasures caus'd her discontent,
She sigh'd not that they stay'd, but that she went.   10
　　She went to plain work,[5] and to purling[6] brooks,
Old-fashion'd halls, dull aunts, and croaking rooks;[7]
She went from opera, park, assembly, play,
To morning walks, and prayers three hours a-day;
To part her time 'twixt reading and bohea,[8]   15
To muse, and spill her solitary tea,
Or o'er cold coffee trifle with the spoon,
Count the slow clock, and dine exact at noon;
Divert her eyes with pictures in the fire,
Hum half a tune, tell stories to the squire;   20
Up to her godly garret[9] after seven,
There starve and pray, for that's the way to heaven.

1. **after the Coronation:** This poem was written in 1714, the year of Queen Anne's death and the accession to the throne of George II, known popularly as "Augustus." Thus, the poem appropriately sets the tone for what is known as the "Augustan Age" in English literature.
2. **virgin:** a young girl.
3. **spark:** a flirtatious remark.
4. **Zephalinda:** Pope's pet name for Miss Blount.
5. **plain work:** sewing.
6. **purling:** rippling.
7. **croaking rooks:** literally thieving crows, possibly also swindling or "cheating" suitors.
8. **bohea:** a variety of tea.
9. **garret:** an attic.

Some squire, perhaps, you take delight to rack,[10]
Whose game is whist,[11] whose treat a toast in sack;[12]
Who visits with a gun, presents you birds,   25
Then gives a smacking buss, and cries—no words!
Or with his hounds comes hallooing from the stable,
Makes love with nods, and knees beneath a table;
Whose laughs are hearty, though his jests are coarse,
And loves you best of all things—but his horse.   30
   In some fair evening, on your elbow laid,
Your dream of triumphs in the rural shade;
In pensive thought recall the fancied scene,
See coronations rise on every green:
Before you pass the imaginary sights   35
Of lords, and earls, and dukes, and garter'd knights,
While the spread fan o'ershades your closing eyes,
Then give one flirt,[13] and all the vision flies.
Thus vanish sceptres, coronets and balls,
And leave you in lone woods or empty walls!   40
   So when your slave,[14] at some dear idle time,
(Not plagued with headaches or the want of rhyme),
Stands in the streets abstracted from the crew,
And while he seems to study, thinks of you;
Just when his fancy paints[15] your sprightly eyes,   45
Or sees the blush of soft Parthenia[16] rise,
Gay[17] pats my shoulder, and you vanish quite,
Streets, chairs, and coxcombs,[18] rush upon my sight:
Vex'd to be still in town I knit my brow,
Look sour, and hum a tune, as you may now.   50

---

10. **rack:** torture.
11. **whist:** a card game.
12. **sack:** wine.
13. **give one flirt:** close the fan.
14. **your slave:** Pope is referring to himself; he was often plagued with headaches.
15. **paints:** imagines.
16. **Parthenia:** Pope's pet name for Miss Blount's sister.
17. **Gay:** John Gay (1685–1732), English poet and dramatist; composer of *The Beggars' Opera* and Pope's lifelong friend.
18. **coxcombs:** "men-about-town."

Getting at Meaning

1. In another poem, also addressed to Miss Blount, Pope says facetiously,

"Nothing so true as what you once let fall,
'Most Women have no Characters at all'"

What do you suppose Pope meant by this couplet? Do you think it is applicable to Miss Blount as she is described in this poem? Explain.

2. How does Miss Blount's present lifestyle differ from the kind of life that the speaker assumes she would prefer?

3. In the last ten lines of the poem, what does the speaker suggest that he and Miss Blount have in common? How would you describe his feelings for her?

4. Miss Blount is the subject of this poem, but the poem is also a comment on society as a whole. What attitudes, practices, and character types does Pope poke fun at in this poem?

Developing Skills in Reading Literature

1. **Satire.** Satire is a literary technique, used in both prose and poetry, that combines a critical attitude with wit and humor for the purpose of improving society. Wit in satire refers to the writer's skill in phrasing and wordplay and in creating paradoxes and other striking contrasts. The reader responds to wit intellectually, appreciating the satirist's originality and perceiving his or her point. Humor in satire generally derives from incongruities, which cause readers to smile in recognition of the truths revealed by the satirist's words. The two basic types of satire common in English literature are named after the styles of the early Roman poets Horace and Juvenal. Horatian satire is gentle and urbane; it aims to correct by provoking sympathetic laughter. Juvenalian satire is biting and angry; it points with bitterness and indignation to corrupt institutions and human beings.

In "Epistle to Miss Blount" find examples of both wit and humor. Is the poem Horatian or Juvenalian in its tone? Explain your conclusion.

2. **Epistle.** In literature the term *epistle* refers to a formal letter written by an individual and addressed to a particular person or group. An epistle differs from an informal letter in that it is a conscious literary effort rather than a spontaneous, private composition. During the eighteenth century, the epistle was a popular form both in prose and in poetry. Novelists such as Samuel Richardson and Tobias Smollett, for example, used the epistle to carry forward the narrative line and to present the feelings and attitudes of characters.

Pope defined epistle in a narrow sense as a formal letter in verse. Pope's epistles satirized social issues, and, while they usually were addressed to an individual, they actually were intended for the educated public. The epistle form used by Pope might seem somewhat artificial and contrived to the twentieth-century reader. What qualities, however, would have made the form especially appealing to the eighteenth-century reader? What effect does Pope achieve in "Epistle to Miss Blount" by presenting social criticism as commentary on one person's behavior? Why might Pope have used the third person at the beginning of the epistle? What is the effect of shifting to the second person?

3. **Structure.** This epistle is divided into sections, three of which are ten lines in length. Of the remaining two sections, one consists of a scant eight lines and the other extends to twelve lines. Examine the content of these two sections, and try to determine a relationship between the length of each section and its content.

from **Essay on Criticism**

Epigrams

We think our fathers fools, so wise we grow;
Our wiser sons, no doubt, will think us so.

Music resembles poetry, in each
Are nameless graces which no methods teach,
And which a master hand alone can reach.

Of all the causes which conspire to blind
Man's erring judgment, and misguide the mind,
What the weak head with strongest bias rules,
Is pride, the never-failing vice of fools.

True wit is nature to advantage dressed,
What oft was thought, but ne'er so well expressed;
Something, whose truth convinced at sight we find,
That gives us back the image of our mind.

In wit, as nature, what affects our hearts
Is not the exactness of peculiar parts;
'Tis not a lip, or eye, we beauty call,
But the joint force and full result of all.

Trust not yourself; but your defects to know,
Make use of every friend—and every foe.

Good nature and good sense must ever join;
To err is human, to forgive, divine.

Avoid extremes; and shun the fault of such,
Who still are pleased too little or too much.

A little learning is a dangerous thing;
Drink deep, or taste not the Pierian spring:[1]
There shallow draughts intoxicate the brain,
And drinking largely sobers us again.

---

1. **Pierian** (pī ir' ē ən) **spring:** Pieria, the birthplace of the muses;
the source of inspiration.

Getting at Meaning

1. What concept of human nature is evident in these epigrams?

2. What is the relationship between wit and nature as suggested in the epigrams?

3. What elements of Enlightenment philosophy are reflected in Pope's epigrams?

Developing Skills in Reading Literature

Epigram. In ancient Greece an epigram was an inscription, specifically an epitaph or a memorial inscription on a tombstone. Later, epigram came to mean a short poem notable for its conciseness, balance, and clarity. Epigrams are used for various themes and purposes: to express friendship, bereavement, or criticism, for example. Usually written in two parts, an epigram begins with a statement of theme and ends with a conclusion that sharply and tersely makes a point.

The epigrams included here can be grouped into those dealing with human nature and those dealing with artistic expression. What points does Pope make about each subject? Which of the two groups of epigrams seems to be more applicable to the present day? Why might this be so?

Developing Vocabulary

Words from Latin. The following words, which appear in the selections by Pope, contain both Latin roots and prefixes. Use a dictionary to find the literal meaning of each root and prefix. Then be prepared to explain the relationship between the English meaning of the word and its Latin source.

abstract   conspire
divert   intoxicate

Developing Writing Skills

Writing Heroic Couplets. Using Pope's epigrams as models, write several witty sayings of your own in heroic couplets. Remember, heroic couplets are written in iambic pentameter, with five stressed syllables per line.

True Ease in Writing

True ease in writing comes from art, not chance,
As those move easiest who have learned to dance.
'Tis not enough no harshness gives offense,
The sound must seem as Echo to the sense:
Soft is the strain when Zephyr[1] gently blows,   5
And the smooth stream in smoother numbers flows;
But when loud surges lash the sounding shore,
The hoarse, rough verse should like the torrent roar:
When Ajax[2] strives some rock's vast weight to throw,
The line too labors, and the words move slow;   10
Not so, when swift Camilla[3] scours the plain,
Flies o'er the unbending corn, and skims along the main.

---

1. **Zephyr:** the west wind.
2. **Ajax:** legendary Greek hero famous for his strength.
3. **Camilla:** legendary woman warrior.

Getting at Meaning

1. Explain the apparent contradiction in the first line of this poem. How does the second line help to explain the first?

2. According to this poem, what should be the relationship between language and idea in good writing? What examples help to explain this relationship?

Developing Skills in Reading Literature

1. **Poetry: Sound and Sense.** In this poem the speaker says that, in good writing, "The sound must seem as Echo to the sense." Throughout the poem the sounds of the words mirror the ideas expressed. Notice in the following line, for example, how the alliteration of the s sound, the repetition of the m, th, and oo sounds, and the sounds of er and fl reflect the gentleness of a rippling stream:

"And the smooth stream in smoother numbers flows;"

Find three other lines in this poem in which sound echoes sense. Is this blend of sound and sense evident in "Epistle to Miss Blount"? in the two poems by Dryden? Quote lines from each poem to support your answers.

2. **Neoclassical Style.** The following elements of style mark the poems of Pope as particularly characteristic examples of eighteenth-century poetry.

a. **Heroic Couplet.** A heroic couplet is "closed" if the two lines contain a self-contained statement, not dependent on the lines that precede or follow for sense or grammatical completeness. When used in a longer poem, closed couplets are interrelated in meaning, each contributing to the development of theme. As a master of the heroic couplet, Pope was able to achieve variety and flexibility within its structural rigidity. Look for examples of such flexibility in "True Ease in Writing," "Epistle to Miss Blount," and the epigrams. What variations in rhythm do you find? How do these variations reflect shifts in subject matter?

b. **Antithesis.** Antithesis is a figure of speech in which sharply contrasting words, phrases, clauses, or sentences are juxtaposed, as in this line by Pope: "Man proposes, God disposes." True antithesis contrasts both language and ideas for the purpose of emphasizing one main point. Find several examples of antithesis in the selections by Pope, and identify the idea that is emphasized through each.

3. **Imagery.** Writers of the Neoclassical Period tended to focus on the general rather than on the specific, treating their subjects with a certain detachment. This does not mean, however, that imagery, with its concrete, sensual appeal, is absent from neoclassical poetry. In the poems of Alexander Pope, for example, images are counterpointed against a cool, rational tone, resulting in a richly textured balance of aloofness and warmth, loftiness and naturalness. Find several examples of imagery in "True Ease in Writing" and then in "Epistle to Miss Blount." What kinds of images seem especially prevalent? What information from Pope's biography might explain his skill in creating these particular images?

Developing Writing Skills

Explaining an Idea. Write a paragraph in which you restate in your own words Pope's ideas about writing. To illustrate the ideas, provide several comparisons drawn from your experiences and observations. For example, you might compare the desired fusion of sound and sense in a poem to the beautifully integrated movements of a trained athlete.

Joseph Addison
1672–1719

Richard Steele
1672–1729

JOSEPH ADDISON. *Sir Godfrey Kneller.*
National Portrait Gallery, London.

Known primarily for establishing the informal essay as an English literary genre, Joseph Addison and Richard Steele seem inseparably linked. As literary partners and intimate friends for most of their lives, they collaborated in writing and editing *The Tatler* and *The Spectator*, the first popular periodicals and the predecessors of the news magazine. Together, they created a literary form that has remained popular for nearly three centuries.

Addison and Steele first met as teenagers at the Charterhouse School in London. Later, both attended Oxford University, where Addison distinguished himself as a scholar and where Steele revealed a reckless temperament. Leaving the university without a degree, Steele served in the army, then managed a theater, worked for the Whig party as a political writer, and gained a seat in Parliament, which he promptly lost for "uttering seditious libels." When George I came to the throne in 1714 and the Whigs returned to power, Steele was elected once again to Parliament and was knighted by the king.

Addison was quite different from the gregarious, impetuous Steele. Often accused of being cold and arrogant, Addison actually was shy and introverted. Like Steele, he was active in Whig politics; he was appointed an assistant to the Secretary of State for Southern Affairs, secretary to the Lord Lieutenant of Ireland, and eventually Secretary of State, and he served in both the British and Irish Parliaments. During his years of government service, Addison maintained a close friendship with Steele, contributing to Steele's plays and supplying ideas for Steele's political articles.

SIR RICHARD STEELE, 1712. *Jonathan Richardson.*
National Portrait Gallery, London.

In 1709, while Addison was in Ireland, Steele founded *The Tatler*, a periodical smaller in format and more gossipy in character than earlier journals. At first he wanted only to show that ordinary news could be enlivened with the kind of witty commentary appreciated by the patrons of the coffeehouses. In later issues, perhaps because of Addison's influence, he turned to more serious subjects and spoke out against hypocrisy and inefficiency in English society. In an era when women were treated with false chivalry, for example, Steele often supported their cause, believing them as capable of development as men. Although Addison was a frequent contributor to *The Tatler*, he remained anonymous. Not until the two began to collaborate on *The Spectator* in 1711 did Addison and Steele become famous literary partners.

Addison wrote most of the articles for *The Spectator*, nearly all of them ascribed to the amiable Sir Roger de Coverley. In these essays he strove to amuse his audience by gently satirizing contemporary manners and customs while at the same time suggesting virtuous behavior and high morals. The elegance and simplicity of Addison's essays influenced the style of eighteenth-century prose and inspired Samuel Johnson to praise Addison for his "eloquence of form which turns human utterance into literature."

Addison and Steele worked together successfully until 1718 when they quarreled over a political issue. Steele attempted a reconciliation, but Addison died in 1719 before it could be accomplished. Saddened by the loss of his friend and apparently bereft of a stabilizing force in his life, Steele fell heavily in debt and wrote little more of value before his own death ten years later.

from The Spectator

Advantages of Marriage   *Richard Steele*

. . . There is an accidental advantage of marriage which has likewise fallen to my share; I mean having a multitude of children. These I cannot but regard as very great blessings. When I see my little troop before me I rejoice in the additions which I have made to my species, to my country, and to my religion, in having produced such a number of reasonable creatures, citizens, and Christians. I am pleased to see myself thus perpetuated, and as there is no production comparable to that of a human creature, I am more proud of having been the occasion of ten such glorious productions than if I had built a hundred pyramids at my own expense, or published as many volumes of the finest wit and learning. . . . For my own part I can sit in my parlor with great content when I take a review of half a dozen of my little boys mounting upon hobbyhorses, and of as many little girls tutoring their babies, each of them endeavoring to excel the rest, and to do something that may gain my favor and approbation. I cannot question but He who blessed me with so many children will assist my endeavors in providing for them. There is one thing I am able to give each of them, which is a virtuous education.

It is my business to implant in every one of my children the same seeds of industry and the same honest principles. By this means I think I have a fair chance that one or other of them may grow considerable in some or other way of life, whether it be in the army or in the fleet, in trade or in any of the three learned professions; for you must know, Sir, that from long experience and observation I am persuaded of what seems a paradox to most of those with whom I converse—namely, that a man who has many children, and gives them a good education, is more likely to raise a family than he who has but one, notwithstanding he leaves him his whole estate. For this reason I cannot forbear amusing myself with finding out a general, an admiral, or an alderman of London, a divine,[1] a physician, or a lawyer among my little people who are now perhaps in petticoats; and when I see the motherly airs of my little daughters when they are playing with their puppets,[2] I cannot but flatter myself that their husbands and children will be happy in the possession of such wives and mothers.

If you are a father you will not perhaps think this letter impertinent, but if you are a single man you will not know the meaning of it, and probably throw it into the fire. Whatever you determine of it, you may assure yourself that it comes from one who is your most humble servant and well-wisher.

---

1. **divine:** a clergyman
2. **puppets:** dolls.

On Courtship and Marriage   *Joseph Addison*

Those marriages generally abound most with love and constancy that are preceded by a long courtship. The passion should strike root and gather strength before marriage be grafted on it. A long course of hopes and expectations fixes the idea in our minds and habituates us to a fondness of the person beloved.

There is nothing of so great importance to us as the good qualities of one to whom we join ourselves for life; they do not only make our present state agreeable, but often determine our happiness to all eternity. Where the choice is left to friends, the chief point under consideration is an estate; where the parties choose for themselves, their thoughts turn most upon the person. . . .

Before marriage we cannot be too inquisitive and discerning in the faults of the person beloved, nor after it too dim-sighted and superficial. However perfect and accomplished the person appears to you at a distance, you will find many blemishes and imperfections in her humor,[1] upon a more intimate acquaintance, which you never discovered, or perhaps suspected. Here, therefore, discretion and good nature are to show their strength; the first will hinder your thoughts from dwelling on what is disagreeable, the other will raise in you all the tenderness of compassion and humanity, and by degrees soften those very imperfections into beauties.

Marriage enlarges the scene of our happiness and miseries. A marriage of love is pleasant; a marriage of interest easy; and a marriage where both meet happy. A happy marriage has in it all the pleasures of friendship, all the enjoyments of sense and reason, and, indeed, all the sweets of life. Nothing is a greater mark of a degenerate and vicious age than the common ridicule which passes on this state of life. It is, indeed, only happy in those who can look down with scorn or neglect on the impieties of the times, and tread the paths of life together in a constant uniform course of virtue.

---

1. **humor:** disposition or temperament.

Getting at Meaning

ADVANTAGES OF MARRIAGE

1. What relationship between parents and children is suggested in this essay? What is the main duty of parents? What is their ultimate reward?

2. Although Steele's essay was probably inoffensive in his day, it appears chauvinistic and pompous today. Point out lines and phrases from this essay that would tend to offend contemporary men and women.

ON COURTSHIP AND MARRIAGE

3. What are the advantages given by Addison for a long courtship preceding marriage?

4. According to Addison, what constitutes a happy marriage?

5. What attitudes typical of the Enlightenment are evident in this essay and in the essay by Steele?

Developing Skills in Reading Literature

Essay and Style. The informal essay is usually briefer, looser in structure, more relaxed in style, and less serious in subject and tone than the formal essay. Meant primarily to instruct by delighting and entertaining the reader, the informal essay is personal and often humorous and offers one view rather than a complete treatment of a subject.

No two essayists write in the same style. Even Addison and Steele who were literary collaborators reveal very different stylistic characteristics in their essays. Examine the two essays from *The Spectator*, and identify the qualities that make them informal essays. Then compare and contrast the styles of the two essayists, focusing specifically on structure, tone, diction, and the use of antithesis.

Developing Vocabulary

Understanding Changes in Language. In the eighteenth century the vocabulary in Steele's essays was considered quite informal. Because of changes in the language, however, many of his words and expressions now seem formal or even quaintly archaic. Read the following quotations, and look up the italicized words that you do not already know. Then rewrite each quotation in the common language of everyday speech.

1. "I am pleased to see myself *thus perpetuated.* . . ."

2. ". . . each of them *endeavoring to excel* the rest, and to do something that may gain my favor and *approbation.*"

3. "For this reason I cannot *forbear* amusing myself. . . ."

4. "If you are a father you will not perhaps think this letter *impertinent.* . . ."

Developing Writing Skills

Supporting an Opinion. Write an informal essay in which you agree or disagree with one of the values or viewpoints expressed by Addison or Steele. Present reasons to support your opinion.

Lady Mary Wortley Montague
1689–1762

Lady Mary Wortley Montague was a celebrated literary and social figure who was considered the "cleverest woman of her day." A prolific and facile letter writer, Lady Montague demonstrated an uncommonly keen eye for detail, an easy writing style, and a generous measure of the common sense so admired among her contemporaries.

Born in London, the daughter of an earl and a cousin of novelist Henry Fielding, she eloped with Edward Wortley Montague to escape an arranged marriage. When Edward was appointed ambassador to Turkey in 1716, Lady Montague accompanied him to Constantinople. She quickly learned Turk-

ish and wrote her impressions of that exotic country in her journals and in witty and sensitive letters to relatives and friends in England. Known popularly as "the female traveler," Lady Montague was one of the first Western women to live in the Near East and one of the few Europeans of her day to understand and admire Islamic culture.

When the Montagues returned to England in 1718, Lady Montague promoted the Turkish practice of smallpox innoculation, her own beauty having been marred by the disease. The couple settled in Twickenham, near the estate of Alexander Pope with whom Lady Montague carried on an

LADY MARY WORTLEY MONTAGUE WITH HER SON AND ATTENDANTS, 1717.
Attributed to Jean Baptiste Van Mour.
National Portrait Gallery, London.

intimate correspondence until their famous quarrel. She wrote poems, the earliest in imitation of Pope's style, published anonymous essays on feminism, literature, and politics, and translated Latin classics. She also compiled from her journals and correspondence the fifty-two Turkish embassy letters that represent her finest work.

In her volumes of letters, Lady Montague describes her relationship with her husband and discusses in detail the role of women in her society, noting particularly the obstacles faced by learned women. Widely read herself, she often included informal critical remarks on the works of contemporary writers, such as Henry Fielding, Samuel Richardson, and Jonathan Swift.

A Letter to My Sister

I wish, dear sister, that you were as regular in letting me know what passes on your side of the globe as I am careful in endeavoring to amuse you by the account of all I see here that I think worth your notice. You content yourself with telling me over and over, that the town is very dull: it may possibly be dull to you, when every day does not present you with something new; but for me, that am in arrears at least two months' news, all that seems very stale with you would be very fresh and sweet here. Pray let me into more particulars, and I will try to awaken your gratitude by giving you a full and true relation of the novelties of this place, none of which would surprise you more than the sight of my person, as I am now in my Turkish habit,[1] though I believe you would be of my opinion, that 'tis admirably becoming. I intend to send you my picture; in the meantime accept of it here.

The first part of my dress is a pair of drawers, very full, that reach to my shoes, and conceal the legs more modestly than your petticoats. They are of a thin rose-colored damask, brocaded with silver flowers. My shoes are of white kid leather, embroidered with gold. Over this hangs my smock, of a fine white silk gauze, edged with embroidery. This smock has wide sleeves, hanging half way down the arm, and is closed at the neck with a diamond button; but the shape and color of the bosom are very well to be distinguished through it. The *antery* is a waistcoat, made close to the shape, of white and gold damask, with very long sleeves falling back, and fringed with deep gold fringe, and should have diamond or pearl buttons. My *caftan*, of the same stuff with my drawers, is a robe exactly fitted to my shape, and reaching to my feet, with very long straight falling sleeves. Over this is my girdle,[2] of about four fingers broad, which all that can afford it have entirely of diamonds or other precious stones; those who will not be at that expense, have it of exquisite embroidery on satin; but it must be fastened before with a clasp of diamonds. The *curdee* is a loose robe they throw off or put on according to the weather, being of a rich brocade (mine is green and gold), either lined with ermine or sables; the sleeves reach very little below the shoulders. The headdress is composed of a cap, called *talpock*, which is in winter of fine velvet embroidered with pearls or diamonds, and in summer of a light shining silver stuff. This is fixed on one side of the head, hanging a little way down with a gold

---

1. **Turkish habit:** clothing; Lady Montague was especially fond of wearing unusual clothing, and her individuality in dress was frequently criticized in London as the epitome of poor taste.
2. **girdle:** belt.

tassel, and bound on either with a circle of diamonds (as I have seen several) or a rich embroidered handkerchief. On the other side of the head the hair is laid flat; and here the ladies are at liberty to show their fancies: some putting flowers, others a plume of heron's feathers, and, in short, what they please; but the most general fashion is a large bouquet of jewels, made like natural flowers: that is, the buds, of pearl; the roses, of different colored rubies; the jasmins, of diamonds; the jonquils, of topazes, etc., so well set and enameled, 'tis hard to imagine anything of that kind so beautiful. The hair hangs at its full length behind, divided into tresses braided with pearl or ribbon, which is always in great quantity.

I never saw in my life so many fine heads of hair. In one lady's I have counted a hundred and ten of the tresses, all natural; but it must be owned that every kind of beauty is more common here than with us. 'Tis surprising to see a young woman that is not very handsome. They have naturally the most beautiful complexion in the world, and generally large black eyes. I can assure you with great truth, that the court of England (though I believe it is the fairest in Christendom) does not contain so many beauties as are under our protection here. They generally shape their eyebrows, and both Greeks and Turks have a custom of putting round their eyes a black tincture,[3] that, at a distance, by candlelight, adds very much to the blackness of them. I fancy many of our ladies would be overjoyed to know this secret; but 'tis too visible by day. They dye their nails a rose color; but, I own, I can not enough accustom myself to this fashion to find any beauty in it.

As to their morality or good conduct, I can say, like Harlequin,[4] that 'tis just as it is with you; and the Turkish ladies don't commit one sin the less for not being Christians. Now that I am a little acquainted with their ways, I can not forbear admiring either the exemplary discretion or extreme stupidity of all the writers that have given accounts of them. 'Tis very easy to see they have in reality more liberty than we have. No woman, of what rank soever, is permitted to go into the streets without two *murlins*;[5] one that covers her face all but her eyes, and another that hides the whole dress of her head, and hangs half way down her back. Their shapes are also wholly concealed by a thing they call a *ferigee*,[6] which no woman of any sort appears without; this has straight sleeves, that reach to their finger-ends, and it laps all round them, not unlike a riding hood. In winter 'tis of cloth, and in summer of plain stuff or silk. You may guess, then, how effectually this disguises them, so that there is no distinguishing the great lady from her slave. 'Tis impossible for the most jealous husband to know his wife when he meets her; and no man dare touch or follow a woman in the street.

This perpetual masquerade gives them entire liberty of following their inclinations without danger of discovery. The most usual method of intrigue is to send an appointment to the lover to meet the lady at a shop, which are as notoriously convenient as our Indian-houses;[7] and yet, even those who don't make use of them, do not scruple to go buy pennyworths,[8] and tumble over rich goods, which are chiefly to be found among that sort of people. The great ladies seldom let their gallants[9] know who they are; and 'tis so difficult to find it out, that they can very seldom guess at her name, whom they have corresponded with for above half a year together. You may

---

3. **tincture:** dye.
4. **Harlequin** (här' lə kwin): a clownish stock character in a type of improvisational theater that flourished in Italy in the eighteenth century.
5. ***murlins:*** heavy gauze scarves, usually black.
6. ***ferigee*** (fər' ə jē): an outer garment, like a hooded cloak.
7. **Indian-houses:** pawnshops.
8. **pennyworths:** trifles.
9. **gallant** (gə lant'): lover or paramour.

easily imagine the number of faithful wives very small in a country where they have nothing to fear from a lover's indiscretion, since we see so many have the courage to expose themselves to that in this world, and all the threatened punishment of the next, which is never preached to the Turkish damsels. Neither have they much to apprehend from the resentment of their husband; those ladies that are rich having all their money in their own hands.

Upon the whole, I look upon the Turkish women as the only free people in the empire: the very divan[10] pays respect to them; and the Grand-Seignior himself, when a pasha[11] is executed, never violates the privileges of the harem (or women's apartment), which remains unsearched and entire to the widow. They are queens of their slaves, whom the husband has no permission so much as to look upon, except it be an old woman or two that his lady chooses. 'Tis true their law permits them four wives; but there is no instance of a man of quality that makes use of this liberty, or of a woman of rank that would suffer it.

---

10. **divan** (di van'): the royal council.
11. **pasha** (pə shä'): a high ranking civil or military official.

Getting at Meaning

1. What overall impression do you get from the description of Lady Montague's Turkish clothing? How does she create this impression?

2. Lady Montague seems to have developed a certain broadmindedness that must have been unusual for a woman of her day. What moral judgments does she express in this letter that would no doubt have shocked many of her contemporaries in England?

3. What is ironic in Lady Montague's description of Turkish women who are supposedly kept in bondage by authoritarian men? What is implied about the position of women in eighteenth-century England?

Developing Skills in Reading Literature

Epistle. This letter was among the embassy letters that Lady Montague selected, revised, and compiled after her return from Turkey. Although the original letters probably were not intended for a public audience, they became the basis for fifty-two epistles, or literary letters, which were published a year after her death. What details suggest that this letter originated as a private communication? Is the tone more suited to a formal letter or to spontaneous, personal correspondence? What made Lady Montague uniquely qualified to comment on the position of women in English and Turkish societies? What might explain the fact that Lady Montague's letters were enormously popular throughout Europe in the late eighteenth century? Why has their appeal endured?

Developing Writing Skills

Using the Senses in Writing. Lady Montague tells her sister that she will soon send her a picture; meanwhile, she describes herself in such a way that her sister can picture her clearly. Not only does she appeal to the reader's sense of sight, but she also appeals to the sense of touch in language such as "fine velvet," "rich brocade lined with ermine or sables," and "a plume of heron's feathers."

In one paragraph describe a costume or outfit, possibly one from another era or country, a traditional folk dress, or a stage costume worn by a performer. In your description appeal definitely to the sense of sight and also to either touch or hearing.

Jonathan Swift
1667–1745

JONATHAN SWIFT, 1718. C. Jervas. National Portrait Gallery, London.

Swift has been called the only man of his age whose life story resembles a Shakespearean tragedy. His powerful personality contained such fierce contradictions that he inspired both deep devotion and violent enmity. Considered the preeminent satirist of the English language, Swift addressed political, social, economic, and religious issues in writings both playfully witty and wickedly biting.

Swift's parents were English, but his father had moved to Dublin because an older brother, Godwin, was Attorney General of Tipperary. Before Godwin could secure him a position, indeed before his son was born, Swift's father died. Young Jonathan grew up in Dublin on the grudging charity of his Uncle Godwin. An indifferent student, the brilliant but reckless Swift barely earned a degree from Trinity College in 1685. His mother managed to find him an excellent position with a distant cousin, Sir William Temple, a retired politician writing his memoirs at his elegant estate, Moor Park.

During the Moor Park years Swift's literary genius first bloomed with the dazzlingly witty *Tale of a Tub*, a three-part satire that includes the mock epic "Battle of the Books." It was also at Moor Park that he formed a sentimental attachment with a young girl who, like him, lived on the generosity of Temple. Swift was in his early twenties and Ester Johnson about seven when they met, both lonely and feeling like outsiders. After Temple's death, Swift took another parish in Ireland and invited Ester and her companion Mrs. Dingley to live nearby. Swift nicknamed his young friend Stella, which, like Ester, means star.

In London Swift had charmed a young woman named Hester Vonhomrigh, whom he teasingly called Vanessa. Madly in love, Vanessa followed him to Ireland, much to the consternation of Stella who insisted that Swift choose between them. Swift reluctantly agreed to a secret marriage, an arrangement that hardly mollified the spunky Stella. Rumors of Swift's marriage to Stella finally reached Vanessa, who rashly wrote Stella an indignant letter. Infuriated, Stella showed the letter to Swift, who stormed into Vanessa's residence, flung the letter into her face, and left without a word. Broken-hearted, Vanessa died within a few weeks. Stella lived for five more years, the melancholy, unacknowledged wife.

During these years of personal tragedy, Swift created the great works upon which his enduring fame rests. An English Protestant, he won the love of Irish Catholics by defending their liberties in the "Drapier's Letters" (1724), and in the satire "A Modest Proposal" (1729), ". . . the most savagely sustained ironic writing in [English] literature." *Gulliver's Travels*, his undisputed masterpiece, appeared in 1726, to the delight of readers then and since. Enjoyable on one level as a fantasy, *Gulliver's Travels* satirizes the entire spectrum of English society and humanity in all times and places.

Swift's painful last years were blighted by the hereditary insanity that had afflicted his Uncle Godwin. In a last satiric touch, he willed his fortune to endow a lunatic asylum. Buried in St. Patrick's Cathedral in the same coffin as Stella, Swift lies beneath a Latin inscription of his own composition.

A Modest Proposal

For Preventing the Children of Poor People in Ireland from Being a Burden to Their Parents or Country, and for Making Them Beneficial to the Public

It is a melancholy object to those who walk through this great town,[1] or travel in the country, when they see the streets, the roads, and cabin doors crowded with beggars of the female sex, followed by three, four, or six children, all in rags and importuning every passenger for an alms. These mothers, instead of being able to work for their honest livelihood, are forced to employ all their time in strolling to beg sustenance for their helpless infants; who as they grow up either turn thieves, for want of work, or leave their dear native country to fight for the pretender[2] in Spain, or sell themselves to the Barbados.[3]

I think it is agreed by all parties that this prodigious number of children in the arms, or on the backs, or at the heels of their mothers, and frequently of their fathers, is, in the present deplorable state of the kingdom, a very great additional grievance; and therefore whoever could find out a fair, cheap, and easy method of making these children sound, useful members of the commonwealth would deserve so well of the public as to have his statue set up for a preserver of the nation.

But my intention is very far from being confined to provide only for the children of professed beggars: it is of a much greater extent and shall take in the whole number of infants at a certain age who are born of parents in effect as little able to support them as those who demand our charity in the streets.

As to my own part, having turned my thoughts for many years upon this important subject and maturely weighed the several schemes of our projectors, I have always found them grossly mistaken in their computation. It is true, a child just dropped from its dam may be supported by her milk for a solar year, with little other nourishment: at most not above the value of two shillings which the mother may certainly get, or the value in scraps, by her lawful occupation of begging; and it is exactly at one year old that I propose to provide for them in such a manner, as, instead of being a charge upon their parents or the parish, or wanting food and raiment for the rest of their lives, they shall, on the contrary, contribute to the feeding and partly to the clothing of many thousands.

There is likewise another great advantage in my scheme, that it will prevent those voluntary abortions and that horrid practice of women murdering their bastard children, alas! too frequent among us, sacrificing the poor innocent babes, I doubt more to avoid the expense than the shame, which would

---

1. **this great town:** Dublin.
2. **the pretender:** James Stuart (1688–1766), son of James II who had lost the throne to William and Mary in the Revolution of 1688. The young James was the "pretender" or claimant to the throne that his father had lost. He was Roman Catholic, and Ireland was loyal to him.
3. **sell . . . the Barbados** (bär bä' doz): Because of the extreme poverty in Ireland, some of the Irish "sold" themselves to planters and landowners in the West Indies or in North America. They usually agreed to work as "slaves" for a specified number of years.

THE ENRAGED MUSICIAN, 1741. *Engraved by E. Stalker from the original design by William Hogarth. The Mansell Collection.*

move tears and pity in the most savage and inhuman breast.

The number of souls in Ireland being usually reckoned one million and a half, of these I calculate there may be about two hundred thousand couple, whose wives are breeders; from which number I subtract thirty thousand couple, who are able to maintain their own children (although I apprehend there cannot be so many, under the present distresses of the kingdom), but this being granted, there will remain an hundred and seventy thousand breeders. I again subtract fifty thousand for those women who miscarry, or whose children die by accident or disease within the year. There only remains one hundred and twenty thousand children of poor parents annually born. The question therefore is, How this number shall be reared and provided for? which, as I have already said, under the present situation of affairs, is utter-

ly impossible by all the methods hitherto proposed. For we can neither employ them in handicraft or agriculture; we neither build houses (I mean in the country) nor cultivate land: they can very seldom pick up a livelihood by stealing till they arrive at six years old, except where they are of towardly[4] parts; although I confess they learn the rudiments much earlier; during which time they can, however, be properly looked upon only as probationers; as I have been informed by a principal gentleman in the county of Cavan, who protested to me that he never knew above one or two instances under the age of six, even in a part of the kingdom so renowned for the quickest proficiency in that art.

I am assured by our merchants that a boy or a girl before twelve years old is no salable

---

4. **of towardly parts:** easily manageable.

commodity; and even when they come to this age they will not yield above three pounds, or three pounds and half a crown at most, on the exchange; which cannot turn to account either to the parents or kingdom, the charge of nutriment and rags having been at least four times that value.

I shall now therefore humbly propose my own thoughts, which I hope will not be liable to the least objection.

I have been assured by a very knowing American of my acquaintance in London that a young healthy child well nursed is at a year old a most delicious, nourishing, and wholesome food, whether stewed, roasted, baked, or boiled; and I make no doubt that it will equally serve in a fricassee or a ragout.[5]

I do therefore humbly offer it to public consideration that of the hundred and twenty thousand children already computed, twenty thousand may be reserved for breed, whereof only one-fourth part to be males; which is more than we allow to sheep, black cattle, or swine; and my reason is that these children are seldom the fruits of marriage, a circumstance not much regarded by our savages; therefore one male will be sufficient to serve four females. That the remaining hundred thousand may, at a year old, be offered in sale to the persons of quality and fortune through the kingdom; always advising the mother to let them suck plentifully in the last month, so as to render them plump and fat for a good table. A child will make two dishes at an entertainment for friends; and when the family dines alone, the fore or hind quarter will make a reasonable dish, and seasoned with a little pepper or salt will be very good boiled on the fourth day, especially in winter.

I have reckoned upon a medium[6] that a child just born will weigh twelve pounds, and in a solar year, if tolerably nursed, will increase to twenty-eight pounds.

I grant this food will be somewhat dear, and therefore very proper for landlords, who, as they have already devoured most of the par-

ents, seem to have the best title to the children.

Infant's flesh will be in season throughout the year, but more plentifully in March, and a little before and after: for we are told by a grave author, an eminent French physician,[7] that fish being a prolific diet, there are more children born in Roman Catholic countries about nine months after Lent than at any other season; therefore, reckoning a year after Lent, the markets will be more glutted than usual, because the number of popish infants is at least three to one in this kingdom: and therefore it will have one other collateral advantage, by lessening the number of papists among us.

I have already computed the charge of nursing a beggar's child (in which list I reckon all cottagers, laborers, and four-fifths of the farmers) to be about two shillings per annum, rags included; and I believe no gentleman would repine to give ten shillings for the carcass of a good fat child, which, as I have said, will make four dishes of excellent nutritive meat, when he has only some particular friend or his own family to dine with him. Thus the squire will learn to be a good landlord and grow popular among his tenants; the mother will have eight shillings net profit and be fit for work till she produces another child.

Those who are more thrifty (as I must confess the times require) may flay the carcass; the skin of which artifically[8] dressed will make admirable gloves for ladies and summer boots for fine gentlemen.

As to our city of Dublin, shambles[9] may be appointed for this purpose in the most convenient parts of it, and butchers we may be

---

5. **ragout** (ra gōō′): a highly seasoned stew of meat and vegetables.

6. **upon a medium:** on the average.

7. **a grave author . . . physician:** Francois Rabelais (1494–1553), a French satirist who was certainly not a "grave" author.

8. **artifically:** skillfully.

9. **shambles:** slaughterhouses.

assured will not be wanting; although I rather recommend buying the children alive and dressing them hot from the knife as we do roasting pigs.

A very worthy person, a true lover of his country, and whose virtues I highly esteem, was lately pleased, in discoursing on this matter, to offer a refinement upon my scheme. He said that many gentlemen of this kingdom, having of late destroyed their deer, he conceived that the want of venison might be well supplied by the bodies of young lads and maidens, not exceeding fourteen years of age nor under twelve; so great a number of both sexes in every country being now ready to starve for want of work and service; and these to be disposed of by their parents, if alive, or otherwise by their nearest relations. But with due deference to so excellent a friend and so deserving a patriot, I cannot be altogether in his sentiments; for as to the males, my American acquaintance assured me from frequent experience that their flesh was generally tough and lean, like that of our schoolboys, by continual exercise, and their taste disagreeable; and to fatten them would not answer the charge. Then as to the females, it would, I think, with humble submission be a loss to the public, because they soon would become breeders themselves: and besides, it is not improbable that some scrupulous people might be apt to censure such a practice (although indeed very unjustly), as a little bordering upon cruelty; which, I confess, has always been with me the strongest objection against any project, however so well intended.

But in order to justify my friend, he confessed that this expedient was put into his head by the famous Psalmanazar,[10] a native of the island Formosa, who came from thence to London above twenty years ago: and in conversation told my friend that in his country when any young person happened to be put to death, the executioner sold the carcass to persons of quality as a prime dainty; and that in his time the body of a plump girl of fifteen, who was crucified for an attempt to poison the emperor, was sold to his imperial majesty's prime minister of state, and other great mandarins of the court, in joints from the gibbet, at four hundred crowns.[11] Neither indeed can I deny that if the same use were made of several plump girls in this town, who, without one single groat[12] to their fortunes, cannot stir abroad without a chair, and appear at a playhouse and assemblies in foreign fineries which they never will pay for, the kingdom would not be the worse.

Some persons of a desponding spirit are in great concern about that vast number of poor people, who are aged, diseased, or maimed; and I have been desired to employ my thoughts, what course may be taken to ease the nation of so grievous an incumbrance. But I am not in the least pain upon that matter, because it is very well known that they are every day dying and rotting, by cold and famine, and filth and vermin, as fast as can be reasonably expected. And as to the young laborers, they are now in almost as hopeful a condition: they cannot get work, and consequently pine away for want of nourishment to a degree that if at any time they are accidentally hired to common labor, they have not strength to perform it; and thus the country and themselves are happily delivered from the evils to come.

I have too long digressed and therefore shall return to my subject. I think the advantages, by the proposal which I have made, are obvious and many, as well as of the highest importance.

For first, as I have already observed, it would greatly lessen the number of papists,

---

10. **Psalmanazar:** a Frenchman, George Psalmanazer (1679–1763), who came to England pretending to be from the island of Formosa. He wrote a totally fictitious account of cannibalism there, passing it off as a "true" account.

11. **crown:** a British coin (no longer in use) worth about sixty-three cents in U. S. currency.

12. **groat:** a trifling sum.

with whom we are yearly overrun, being the principal breeders of the nation, as well as our most dangerous enemies; and who stay at home on purpose to deliver the kingdom to the pretender, hoping to take their advantage by the absence of so many good Protestants, who have chosen rather to leave their country than stay at home and pay tithes against their conscience to an Episcopal curate.[13]

Secondly, the poorer tenants will have something valuable of their own, which by law may be made liable to distress,[14] and help to pay their landlord's rent; their corn and cattle being already seized, and money a thing unknown.

Thirdly, whereas the maintenance of a hundred thousand children, from two years old and upwards, cannot be computed at less than ten shillings a piece per annum, the nation's stock will be thereby increased fifty thousand pounds per annum, beside the profit of a new dish introduced to the tables of all gentlemen of fortune in the kingdom, who have any refinement in taste. And the money will circulate among ourselves, the goods being entirely of our own growth and manufacture.

Fourthly, the constant breeders, beside the gain of eight shillings sterling per annum by the sale of their children, will be rid of the charge of maintaining them after the first year.

Fifthly, this food would likewise bring great custom to taverns: where the vintners[15] will certainly be so prudent as to procure the best receipts for dressing it to perfection, and consequently have their houses frequented by all the fine gentlemen, who justly value themselves upon their knowledge in good eating: and a skillful cook, who understands how to oblige his guests, will contrive to make it as expensive as they please.

Sixthly, this would be a great inducement to marriage, which all wise nations have either encouraged by rewards or enforced by laws and penalties. It would increase the care and tenderness of mothers toward their children, when they were sure of a settlement for life to the poor babes, provided in some sort by the public, to their annual profit instead of expense. We should see an honest emulation among the married women, which of them could bring the fattest child to the market. Men would become as fond of their wives during the time of their pregnancy as they are now of their mares in foal, their cows in calf, or sows when they are ready to farrow; not offer to beat or kick them (as is too frequent a practice) for fear of a miscarriage.

Many other advantages might be enumerated. For instance, the addition of some thousand carcasses in our exportation of barreled beef, the propagation of swine's flesh, and improvement in the art of making good bacon, so much wanted among us by the great destruction of pigs, too frequent at our tables; which are no way comparable in taste or magnificence to a well grown, fat, yearling child, which roasted whole will make a considerable figure at a lord mayor's feast,[16] or any other public entertainment. But this and many others I omit, being studious of brevity.

Supposing that one thousand families in this city would be constant customers for infants' flesh, besides others who might have it at merry-meetings, particularly weddings and christenings, I compute that Dublin would take off annually about twenty thousand carcasses; and the rest of the kingdom (where probably they will be sold somewhat cheaper) the remaining eighty thousand.

---

13. **Protestants . . . curate:** Swift is attacking absentee landlords, those Irish nobles who chose to live in England and to spend there the income from their Irish property. Much of the poverty in Ireland was attributed to such absentee ownership. Swift is also poking fun at himself here, since he had once been a poor Episcopal curate, or country priest.
14. **distress:** distrain; to seize or to hold property for payment of debts.
15. **vintners:** wine merchants.
16. **Lord Mayor's Feast:** Lord Mayors were expected to celebrate their tenure of office with lavish hospitality.

I can think of no one objection that will possibly be raised against this proposal, unless it should be urged that the number of people will be thereby much lessened in the kingdom. This I freely own, and it was indeed one principal design in offering it to the world. I desire the reader will observe that I calculate my remedy for this one individual kingdom of Ireland, and for no other that ever was, is, or, I think, ever can be upon earth. Therefore let no man talk to me of other expedients: of taxing our absentees at five shillings a pound: of using neither clothes nor household furniture, except what is of our own growth and manufacture: of utterly rejecting the materials and instruments that promote foreign luxury: of curing the expensiveness of pride, vanity, idleness, and gaming in our women: of introducing a vein of parsimony, prudence, and temperance: of learning to love our country in the want of which we differ even from Laplanders and the inhabitants of Topinamboo:[17] of quitting our animosities and factions, nor acting any longer like the Jews, who were murdering one another at the very moment their city was taken:[18] of being a little cautious not to sell our country and conscience for nothing: of teaching landlords to have at least one degree of mercy toward their tenants: lastly, of putting a spirit of honesty, industry, and skill into our shopkeepers; who, if a resolution could now be taken to buy only our native goods, would immediately unite to cheat and exact upon us in the price, the measure, and the goodness, nor could ever yet be brought to make one fair proposal of just dealing, though often and earnestly invited to it.[19]

Therefore, I repeat, let no man talk to me of these and the like expedients, till he has at least some glimpse of hope that there will be ever some hearty and sincere attempt to put them in practice.

But as to myself, having been wearied out for many years with offering vain, idle, visionary thoughts, and at length utterly despairing of success, I fortunately fell upon this proposal; which, as it is wholly new, so it has something solid and real, of no expense and little trouble, full in our own power, and whereby we can incur no danger in disobliging England. For this kind of commodity will not bear exportation, the flesh being of too tender a consistence to admit a long continuance in salt, although perhaps I could name a country which would be glad to eat up our whole nation without it.[20]

After all, I am not so violently bent upon my own opinion as to reject any offer proposed by wise men, which shall be found equally innocent, cheap, easy, and effectual. But before something of that kind shall be advanced in contradiction to my scheme, and offering a better, I desire the author or authors will be pleased maturely to consider two points. First, as things now stand, how they will be able to find food and raiment for an hundred thousand useless mouths and backs. And secondly, there being a round million of creatures in human figure throughout this kingdom, whose whole subsistence put into a common stock would leave them in debt two millions of pounds sterling, adding those who are beggars by profession to the bulk of farmers, cottagers, and laborers, with their wives and children, who are beggars in effect; I desire those politicians, who dislike my overture, and may perhaps be so bold as to attempt an answer, that they will first ask the parents of these mortals, whether they would not at this day think it a great happiness to have been sold for food at a year old in the manner I

---

17. **Topinamboo:** a district in Brazil.
18. **city was taken:** Within the city of Jerusalem in A. D. 70, factions of fanatics were waging bloody civil wars at the very moment the city was taken over by the Roman Emperor, Titus.
19. **often . . . invited to it:** Swift had written pamphlets suggesting all of these "expedients." For the most part they had all been ignored.
20. **a country . . . without it:** Swift is accusing England here of "eating up" the Irish.

prescribe, and thereby have avoided such a perpetual scene of misfortunes as they have since gone through by the oppression of landlords, the impossibility of paying rent without money or trade, the want of common sustenance, with neither house nor clothes to cover them from the inclemencies of the weather, and the most inevitable prospect of entailing the like or greater miseries upon their breed forever.

I profess, in the sincerity of my heart, that I have not the least personal interest in endeavoring to promote this necessary work, having no other motive than the public good of my country, by advancing our trade, providing for infants, relieving the poor, and giving some pleasure to the rich. I have no children by which I can propose to get a single penny; the youngest being nine years old, and my wife past childbearing.

Getting at Meaning

1. What are the major problems besetting Ireland at the time of this writing? Does Swift feel genuine concern over these issues? How do you know?

2. What is the tone of this essay? How do you know that Swift's real feelings are quite different from what they seem to be? Cite specific passages in which it is clear that Swift says one thing but means another. Why do you think he uses this method?

3. Swift makes several references to unnamed outside sources who have given him advice or information. What values do these "experts" profess? Why do you suppose Swift introduced them into his essay?

4. List, in your own words, the so-called advantages of the proposal, as Swift explains them. What is the cumulative effect of presenting these advantages one after another?

5. Why do you suppose Swift chose to call his proposal "modest"? Discuss the relationship between the title and the content of the essay. What is the effect of the title upon the reader?

6. Toward the end of the essay, Swift supposedly rejects a list of alternative solutions to the problem of poverty in Ireland. How do these alternatives reflect values that are totally opposite from those that Swift has been espousing? Does Swift intend his readers to accept the alternative solutions rather than his "proposal"? Justify your answer.

7. In the final paragraph of the essay, Swift pledges his sincerity, saying, ". . . I have . . . no other motive than the public good of my country. . . ." As he has been so obviously "insincere" up to this point, is it safe to believe him now? Explain.

Developing Skills in Reading Literature

1. **Irony.** One of the chief elements in satirical prose and poetry is irony. The ability to recognize irony is a sure test of intelligence and sophistication; those who read only for literal meanings are apt to misinterpret ideas that are expressed ironically. Writers who use irony often seem unemotional and detached from their material, whereas they are more than likely covering up for deeper feelings, sometimes for real outrage and moral indignation. Among the devices by which writers achieve irony are the following:

hyperbole: exaggeration for emphasis or humorous effect

understatement: a statement that says less than is actually or literally true

sarcasm: a critical, contemptuous statement expressed as verbal irony

incongruity: the result of combining inappropriate or incongruous elements

Look for examples of each of these devices in "A Modest Proposal." Explain the contrast in each example between apparent meaning and actual intent.

2. **Verisimilitude.** The appearance, or semblance, of truth in literature is called verisimilitude. Verisimilitude is achieved when a writer presents details, however far-fetched, in such a way as to give them the appearance of truth and to sweep the reader, for the moment at least, into an acceptance of them. Discuss Swift's creation of verisimilitude in "A Modest Proposal." How does he imbue even the most outrageous contentions with a sense of validity? Were you swept into a momentary acceptance of the "truth" of his proposal? Explain.

3. **Style: Diction.** As a stylistic device Swift chooses words that are deliberately shocking to the reader. Examine the italicized words and phrases that follow and explain what is incongruous or shocking, almost horrifying, about each one.

a. ". . . a fair, *cheap,* and easy method of making these children sound, useful members of the commonwealth. . . ."

b. "It is true, a child *just dropped from its dam.* . . ."

c. "I calculate there may be about two hundred thousand couple, whose wives are *breeders.* . . ."

d. ". . . a boy or a girl before twelve years old is *no salable commodity.* . . ."

Find at least five more examples of similar diction in the essay. What does Swift accomplish by using such diction? What, in your opinion, is the most shocking statement in the entire essay? Give reasons for your choice.

4. **Structure.** As is typical of eighteenth-century prose, Swift's essay is clearly structured, with each major idea supported by ample explanatory detail. The essay is divided into five distinct sections, each signaled by a shift in subject matter. Identify these five sections and be prepared to summarize briefly the content of each. Which section is longest? Which provides the most detail? What progression of idea is evident from section to section? Explain.

5. **Theme.** The primary target of this essay is the devastating economic policy imposed by the British government on Ireland. What specifically does Swift imply about economic policy in Ireland? What are some of the secondary targets of this essay? What is Swift's attitude toward the Irish people? Why is his indictment of British policy ironic in light of his feelings about the Irish? What does this suggest about Swift's fundamental political beliefs?

Developing Vocabulary

1. **Inferring Word Meaning.** Locate the following quotations in the essay, and try to determine the meanings of the italicized words from the contexts in which they appear. Check their definitions in a dictionary. Then for each word write a synonym or a short phrase that would fit into the same context.

a. ". . . three, four, or six children, all in rags and *importuning* every passenger for an alms."

b. ". . . mothers . . . are forced to employ all their time in strolling to beg *sustenance* for their helpless infants. . . ."

c. ". . . no gentleman would *repine* to give ten shillings for the *carcass* of a good fat child. . . ."

d. ". . . it is not improbable that some *scrupulous* people might be apt to *censure* such a practice . . . as a little bordering upon cruelty. . . ."

e. "Some persons of a *desponding* spirit are in great concern about that vast number of poor people, who are aged, diseased, or maimed. . . ."

f. "We should see an honest *emulation* among the married women, which of them could bring the fattest child to the market."

2. **Words from Latin.** The Latin words below function in English as root words and as prefixes.

contra- meaning "against" or "opposite"

dis- meaning "away," "opposite of," or "depriving of"

ex- meaning "without," "out of," or "out"

in- or *im-* meaning "not," "in or into," or "very"

pre- meaning "before"

pro- meaning "in favor of," "forward," or "ahead"

sub- meaning "under" or "below"

Look up each of these words from "A Modest Proposal" and define it in terms of its Latin root or prefix.

contradict	impose	procure	proposal
disoblige	induce	profess	subsistence
expedient	prescribe		

Developing Writing Skills

Developing an Argument. Often those who write persuasive essays are aware that they are taking positions that are unpopular. Thus, they present their material in a calm, reasonable manner in order to convince readers who are neutral to accept their ideas, without totally alienating the opposition. Choose a current issue in your school, community, or country, one that is controversial, if possible. Then write a five-paragraph essay in which you state your opinion clearly and support it with facts and reasons. The structure of your argument should be logical, the tone rational, restrained, and sincere.

James Boswell
1740–1795

James Boswell wrote *The Life of Samuel Johnson*, universally admired and hailed by critics as the finest biography ever written. This book seems almost to transcend its own genre, becoming far more than the story of a man's life. Historian Thomas Carlyle put it this way: "It is not speaking with exaggeration, but with strict measured sobriety, to say that this book of Boswell's will give us more real insight into the history of England, during those days, than twenty other books, falsely entitled 'Histories,' which take to themselves that special aim." Given the solidity and magnitude of Boswell's achievement, it is curious that he was considered during his lifetime and for more than a century after his death to be a vain, silly sycophant, a man with no real ability who just happened to latch onto a great man, Samuel Johnson, whose genius was such that even Boswell could write a great book about him. Only in the twentieth century has Boswell's great talent been conceded.

Boswell's father, Lord Auchinleck, was a supreme court judge in Scotland, a substantial figure with an indomitable will and a character as strong as it was stern. In contrast, young Boswell was a spoiled and pampered youth who described himself as "constitutionally unfit for any employment." His father forced him to study law, although Boswell yearned not for legal distinction but for refinement, elegance, and fame. Never happier than when in the presence of a celebrity, he was to spend most of his life basking in reflected glory.

In the autumn of 1762, Boswell began keeping a journal in which he described events, recorded impressions, and reconstructed entire conversations with an immediacy and vividness unparalleled among diarists. He had a zest for life and insatiable curiosity; he also had a talent for eliciting conversation and a prodigious memory for detail, all qualities that are reflected in his writings.

On Monday, May 16, 1763, on his second visit to London, Boswell managed to meet Samuel Johnson, whom he practically idolized. They spoke in the back parlor of a bookseller's shop, and by Boswell's own account Johnson was calm and ponderous while the young man was childish and servile. An instant affinity was established between the two starkly different men. Johnson was a large man, careless about his appearance, deeply religious, sternly moral, politically conservative, with quick wit, impeccable logic, and elegant expression. Boswell was the opposite: small, dandified, dissipated, politically erratic but of a radical bent at times, with no apparent wit, logic, or conversational ability.

After Johnson's death in 1784, Boswell worked hard and long on the biography of Johnson, gathering material, selecting and polishing journal entries, writing and revising, intent upon producing a masterpiece, a "mode of biography, which gives not only a history of Johnson's visible progress through the world, and of his publications, but a view of his mind in his letters and conversations." *The Life of Samuel Johnson* appeared in 1791, an instant success. Four years later, on May 19, 1795, Boswell died after a brief illness. He died believing himself a failure.

from **The Life of Samuel Johnson**

Following are the opening paragraphs of the biography.

To write the Life of him who excelled all mankind in writing the lives of others, and who, whether we consider his extraordinary endowments, or his various works, has been equaled by·few in any age, is an arduous, and may be reckoned in me a presumptuous task.

As I had the honor and happiness of enjoying his friendship for upwards of twenty years; as I had the scheme of writing his life constantly in view; as he was well apprised of this circumstance, and from time to time obligingly satisfied my inquiries, by communicating to me the incidents of his early years; as I acquired a facility in recollecting, and was very assiduous in recording his conversation, of which the extraordinary vigor and vivacity constituted one of the first features of his character; and as I have spared no pains in obtaining materials concerning him, from every quarter where I could discover that they were to be found, and have been favored with the most liberal communications by his friends; I flatter myself that few biographers have entered upon such a work as this with more advantages; independent of literary abilities, in which I am not vain enough to compare myself with some great names who have gone before me in this kind of writing.

Had his other friends been as diligent and ardent as I was, he might have been almost entirely preserved. As it is, I will venture to say that he will be seen in this work more completely than any man who has ever yet lived.

The Dictionary

This excerpt concerns Johnson's life before his first meeting with Boswell. It describes the development of Johnson's Dictionary of the English Language.

The year 1747 is distinguished as the epoch when Johnson's arduous and important work, his *Dictionary of the English Language*, was announced to the world by the publication of its Plan or *Prospectus*.[1]

How long this immense undertaking had been the object of his contemplation, I do not know. I once asked him by what means he had attained to that astonishing knowledge of our language, by which he was enabled to realize a design of such extent, and accumulated difficulty. He told me, that "it was not the effect of particular study; but that it had grown up in his mind insensibly."

That he was fully aware of the arduous nature of the undertaking, he acknowledges; and shows himself perfectly sensible of it in the conclusion of his Plan; but he had a noble consciousness of his own abilities, which enabled him to go on with undaunted spirit.

Dr. Adams[2] found him one day busy at his Dictionary, when the following dialogue ensued. *Adams:* This is a great work, Sir. How

---

1. **Plan or Prospectus:** The outline (Plan) for the dictionary was published twenty-eight years before the publication of the dictionary itself in 1775.
2. **Dr. Adams:** William Adams (1706–1789), a professor at Oxford, where Johnson was a student.

are you to get all the etymologies? *Johnson:* Why, Sir, here is a shelf with Junius, and Skinner,[3] and others; and there is a Welsh gentleman who has published a collection of Welsh proverbs, who will help me with the Welsh. *Adams:* But, Sir, how can you do this in three years? *Johnson:* Sir, I have no doubt that I can do it in three years. *Adams:* But the French Academy, which consists of forty members, took forty years to compile their Dictionary. *Johnson:* Sir, thus it is. This is the proportion. Let me see; forty times forty is sixteen hundred. As three to sixteen hundred, so is the proportion of an Englishman to a Frenchman. With so much ease and pleasantry could he talk of that prodigious labor which he had undertaken to execute.

While the Dictionary was going forward, Johnson lived part of the time in Holborn, part in Gough Square, Fleet Street; and he had an upper room fitted up like a countinghouse for the purpose, in which he gave to the copyists their several tasks. The words, partly taken from other dictionaries, and partly supplied by himself, having been first written down with spaces left between them, he delivered in writing their etymologies, definitions, and various significations. The authorities were copied from the books themselves, in which he had marked the passages with a black lead pencil, the traces of which could easily be effaced. It is remarkable, that he was so attentive in the choice of the passages in which words were authorized, that one may read page after page of his Dictionary with improvement and pleasure; and it should not pass unobserved, that he has quoted no author whose writings had a tendency to hurt sound religion and morality.

The necessary expense of preparing a work of such magnitude for the press, must have been a considerable deduction from the price stipulated to be paid for the copyright. I understand that nothing was allowed by the booksellers on that account; and I remember his telling me that a large portion of it having,

by mistake, been written upon both sides of the paper, so as to be inconvenient for the compositor,[4] it cost him twenty pounds to have it transcribed upon one side only.

Boswell's First Meeting with Johnson

This is to me a memorable year; for in it I had the happiness to obtain the acquaintance of that extraordinary man whose memoirs I am now writing; an acquaintance which I shall ever esteem as one of the most fortunate circumstances in my life. Though then but two-and-twenty, I had for several years read his works with delight and instruction, and had the highest reverence for their author, which had grown up in my fancy into a kind of mysterious veneration.

Mr. Thomas Davies the actor, who then kept a bookseller's shop in Russel Street, Covent Garden, told me that Johnson was very much his friend, and came frequently to his house, where he more than once invited me to meet him; but by some unlucky accident or other he was prevented from coming to us. Mr. Davies recollected several of Johnson's remarkable sayings, and was one of the best of the many imitators of his voice and manner, while relating them. He increased my impatience more and more to see the extraordinary man whose works I highly valued, and whose conversation was reported to be so peculiarly excellent.

At last, on Monday the 16th of May, when I was sitting in Mr. Davies's back parlor, after having drunk tea with him and Mrs. Davies, Johnson unexpectedly came into the shop; and Mr. Davies having perceived him through the glass door in the room in which we were sitting, advancing towards us,—he announced

---

3. **Junius, and Skinner:** writers of books on etymology, the study of the origin and development of words.
4. **compositor:** typesetter.

his awful approach to me, somewhat in the manner of an actor in the part of Horatio, when he addresses Hamlet on the appearance of his father's ghost, "Look, my Lord, it comes." I found that I had a very perfect idea of Johnson's figure, from the portrait of him painted by Sir Joshua Reynolds soon after he had published his Dictionary, in the attitude of sitting in his easy chair in deep meditation, which was the first picture his friend did for him, which Sir Joshua very kindly presented to me. Mr. Davies mentioned my name, and respectfully introduced me to him. I was much agitated; and recollecting his prejudice against the Scotch, of which I had heard much, I said to Davies, "Don't tell where I come from."—"From Scotland," cried Davies, roguishly. "Mr. Johnson, (said I) I do indeed come from Scotland, but I cannot help it." I am willing to flatter myself that I meant this as light pleasantry to sooth and conciliate him, and not as an humiliating abasement at the expense of my country. But however that might be, this speech was somewhat unlucky; for with that quickness of wit for which he was so remarkable, he seized the expression "come from Scotland," which I used in the sense of being of that country; and, as if I had said that I had come away from it, or left it, retorted, "That, Sir, I find, is what a very great many of your countrymen cannot help." This stroke stunned me a good deal; and when we had sat down, I felt myself not a little embarrassed, and apprehensive of what might come next. He then addressed himself to Davies: "What do you think of Garrick?[5] He has refused me an order for the play for Miss Williams,[6] because he knows the house will be full, and that an order would be worth three shillings." Eager to take any opening to get into conversation with him, I ventured to say, "O, Sir, I cannot think Mr. Garrick would grudge such a trifle to you." "Sir, (said he, with a stern look,) I have known David Garrick longer than you have done: and I know no right you have to talk to me on the subject." Perhaps I deserved this check; for it was rather presumptuous in me, an entire stranger, to express any doubt of the justice of his animadversion[7] upon his old acquaintance and pupil. I now felt myself much mortified, and began to think that the hope which I had long indulged of obtaining his acquaintance was blasted. And, in truth, had not my ardor been uncommonly strong, and my resolution uncommonly persevering, so rough a reception might have deterred me forever from making any further attempts. Fortunately, however, I remained upon the field not wholly discomfited; and was soon rewarded by hearing some of his conversation, of which I preserved the following short minute, without marking the questions and observations by which it was produced.

"People (he remarked) may be taken in once, who imagine that an author is greater in private life than other men. Uncommon parts[8] require uncommon opportunities for their exertion.

"In barbarous society, superiority of parts is of real consequence. Great strength or great wisdom is of much value to an individual. But in more polished times there are people to do everything for money; and then there are a number of other superiorities, such as those of birth and fortune, and rank, that dissipate men's attention, and leave no extraordinary share of respect for personal and intellectual superiority. This is wisely ordered by Providence, to preserve some equality among mankind."

---

5. **Garrick:** David Garrick (1717–1779), the famous Shakespearean actor and theater director, Johnson's long-time acquaintance who had once been his pupil in a country school.
6. **Miss Williams:** Anna Williams, the blind daughter of a Welsh physician, and a friend of Johnson's wife. Johnson maintained her in his home until her death.
7. **animadversion** (an am ad vur' zhan): the practice of making critical remarks.
8. **parts:** abilities, qualities, or talents.

"Sir, this book (*The Elements of Criticism*,[9] which he had taken up,) is a pretty essay, and deserves to be held in some estimation, though much of it is chimerical."

Speaking of one who with more than ordinary boldness attacked public measures and the royal family, he said,

"I think he is safe from the law, but he is an abusive scoundrel; and instead of applying to my Lord Chief Justice to punish him, I would send half a dozen footmen and have him well ducked."

"The notion of liberty amuses the people of England, and helps to keep off the *tædium vitæ*.[10] When a butcher tells you that *his heart bleeds for his country*, he has, in fact, no uneasy feeling."

"Sheridan[11] will not succeed at Bath with his oratory. Ridicule has gone down before him, and, I doubt, Derrick[12] is his enemy."

"Derrick may do very well, as long as he can outrun his character; but the moment his character gets up with him, it is all over."

It is, however, but just to record, that some years afterwards, when I reminded him of this sarcasm, he said, "Well, but Derrick has now got a character that he need not run away from."

I was highly pleased with the extraordinary vigor of his conversation, and regretted that I was drawn away from it by an engagement at another place. I had, for a part of the evening, been left alone with him, and had ventured to make an observation now and then, which he received very civilly; so that I was satisfied that though there was a roughness in his manner, there was no ill nature in his disposition. Davies followed me to the door, and when I complained to him a little of the hard blows which the great man had given me, he kindly took upon him to console me by saying, "Don't be uneasy. I can see he likes you very well."

A few days afterwards I called on Davies, and asked him if he thought I might take the liberty of waiting on Mr. Johnson at his Chambers in the Temple.[13] He said I certainly might, and that Mr. Johnson would take it as a compliment. So upon Tuesday the 24th of May, after having been enlivened by the witty sallies of Messieurs Thornton, Wilkes, Churchill, and Lloyd,[14] with whom I had passed the morning, I boldly repaired to Johnson. His Chambers were on the first floor of No. I, Inner Temple Lane, and I entered them with an impression given me by the Reverend Dr. Blair, of Edinburgh, who had been introduced to him not long before, and described his having "found the Giant in his den"; an expression, which, when I came to be pretty well acquainted with Johnson, I repeated to him, and he was diverted at this picturesque account of himself.

He received me very courteously; but, it must be confessed, that his apartment, and furniture, and morning dress, were sufficiently uncouth. His brown suit of clothes looked very rusty; he had on a little old shrivelled unpowdered wig, which was too small for his head; his shirtneck and knees of his breeches were loose; his black worsted stockings ill drawn up; and he had a pair of unbuckled shoes by way of slippers. But all these slovenly particularities were forgotten the moment that he began to talk. Some gentlemen, whom I do not recollect, were sitting with him; and when they went away, I also rose; but he said to me, "Nay, don't go."—"Sir, (said I,) I am afraid that I intrude upon you. It is benevolent

---

9. **The Elements of Criticism:** a book of literary criticism, recently published by Henry Home (1699–1782), a Scottish lord.

10. **taedium vitae** (tē' dē am vi' tē) *Latin:* boredom with life.

11. **Sheridan:** Thomas Sheridan (1719–1788), an actor and teacher of elocution; the father of Richard Brinsley Sheridan, the dramatist.

12. **Derrick:** Samuel Derrick (1724–1769), a minor writer who was master of ceremonies at the oratorical contest at Bath.

13. **Temple:** an area of London in which lawyers lived and where law courts are located.

14. **Thornton . . . Lloyd:** literary friends of Boswell.

to allow me to sit and hear you." He seemed pleased with this compliment, which I sincerely paid him, and answered, "Sir, I am obliged to any man who visits me."

When I rose a second time he again pressed me to stay, which I did.

He told me, that he generally went abroad at four in the afternoon, and seldom came home till two in the morning. I took the liberty to ask if he did not think it wrong to live thus, and not make more use of his great talents. He owned it was a bad habit. On reviewing, at the distance of many years, my journal of this period, I wonder how, at my first visit, I ventured to talk to him so freely, and that he bore it with so much indulgence.

Before we parted, he was so good as to promise to favor me with his company one evening at my lodgings; and, as I took my leave, shook me cordially by the hand. It is almost needless to add, that I felt no little elation at having now so happily established an acquaintance of which I had been so long ambitious.

My readers will, I trust, excuse me for being thus minutely circumstantial, when it is considered that the acquaintance of Dr. Johnson was to me a most valuable acquisition, and laid the foundation of whatever instruction and entertainment they may receive from my collections concerning the great subject of the work which they are now perusing.

In subsequent meetings Johnson and Boswell discussed every imaginable subject at great length. Boswell recalls five of their discussions in the following excerpts.

On the English Language

He found fault with me for using the phrase to *make* money. "Don't you see (said he) the impropriety of it? To *make* money is to *coin* it: you should say *get* money." The phrase, however, is, I think, pretty current. But Johnson was at all times jealous of infractions upon the genuine English language, and prompt to repress colloquial barbarisms; such as, *pledging myself*, for *undertaking; line*, for *department* or *branch*, as, the *civil line*, the *banking line*. He was particularly indignant against the almost universal use of the word *idea* in the sense of *notion* or *opinion*, when it is clear that *idea* can only signify something of which an image can be formed in the mind. We may have an *idea* or *image* of a mountain, a tree, a building; but we cannot surely have an *idea* or *image* of an *argument* or *proposition*. Yet we hear the sages of the law "delivering their *ideas* upon the question under consideration;" and the first speakers in parliament "entirely coinciding in the *idea* which has been ably stated by an honorable member;"—or "reprobating an *idea* unconstitutional, and fraught with the most dangerous consequences to a great and free country." Johnson called this "modern cant."

On Young People and Education

At night, Mr. Johnson and I supped in a private room at the Turk's Head coffeehouse, in the Strand. "I encourage this house (said he); for the mistress of it is a good civil woman, and has not much business."

"Sir, I love the acquaintance of young people; because, in the first place, I don't like to think myself growing old. In the next place, young acquaintances must last longest, if they do last; and then, Sir, young men have more virtue than old men; they have more generous sentiments in every respect. I love the young dogs of this age: they have more wit and humor and knowledge of life than we had; but then the dogs are not so good scholars. Sir, in my early years I read very hard. It is a sad reflection, but a true one, that I knew almost as much at eighteen as I do now. My judgment, to be sure, was not so good; but, I

had all the facts. I remember very well, when I was at Oxford, an old gentleman said to me, 'Young man, ply your book diligently now, and acquire a stock of knowledge; for when years come upon you, you will find that poring upon books will be but an irksome task.'"

He maintained that a boy at school was the happiest of human beings. I supported a different opinion, from which I have never yet varied, that a man is happier; and I enlarged upon the anxiety and sufferings which are endured at school. *Johnson:* "Ah! Sir, a boy's being flogged is not so severe as a man's having the hiss of the world against him. Men have a solicitude about fame; and the greater share they have of it, the more afraid they are of losing it."

We talked of the education of children; and I asked him what he thought was best to teach them first. *Johnson:* "Sir, it is no matter what you teach them first, any more than what leg you shall put into your breeches first. Sir, you may stand disputing which is best to put in first, but in the meantime your breech is bare. Sir, while you are considering which of two things you should teach your child first, another boy has learned them both."

On Eating

At supper this night he talked of good eating with uncommon satisfaction. "Some people (said he,) have a foolish way of not minding, or pretending not to mind, what they eat. For my part, I mind my belly very studiously, and very carefully; for I look upon it, that he who does not mind his belly will hardly mind anything else." I never knew any man who relished good eating more than he did. When at table, he was totally absorbed in the business of the moment; his looks seemed riveted to his plate; nor would he, unless when in very high company, say one word, or even pay the least attention to what was said by others,

till he had satisfied his appetite, which was so fierce, and indulged with such intenseness, that while in the act of eating, the veins of his forehead swelled, and generally a strong perspiration was visible. But it must be owned, that Johnson, though he could be rigidly abstemious, was not a temperate man either in eating or drinking. He could refrain, but he could not use moderately. He told me that he had fasted two days without inconvenience, and that he had never been hungry but once. They who beheld with wonder how much he ate upon all occasions when his dinner was to his taste, could not easily conceive what he must have meant by hunger; and not only was he remarkable for the extraordinary quantity which he ate, but he was, or affected to be, a man of very nice discernment in the science of cookery. He used to descant critically on the dishes which had been at table where he had dined or supped, and to recollect very minutely what he had liked. When invited to dine, even with an intimate friend, he was not pleased if something better than a plain dinner was not prepared for him. I have heard him say on such an occasion, "This was a good dinner enough, to be sure; but it was not a dinner to *ask* a man to."

On American Independence 1776

The doubts which, in my correspondence with him, I had ventured to state as to the justice and wisdom of the conduct of Great Britain towards the American colonies, while

I at the same time requested that he would enable me to inform myself upon that momentous subject, he had altogether disregarded; and had recently published a pamphlet, entitled, "Taxation no Tyranny; an Answer to the Resolutions and Address of the American Congress."

He had long before indulged most unfavorable sentiments of our fellow subjects in America. For, as early as 1769, I was told by Dr. John Campbell, that he had said of them, "Sir, they are a race of convicts, and ought to be thankful for anything we allow them short of hanging."

Of this performance I avoided to talk with him; for I had now formed a clear and settled opinion, that the people of America were well warranted to resist a claim that their fellow subjects in the mother country should have the entire command of their fortunes, by taxing them without their own consent; and the extreme violence which it breathed,[15] appeared to me so unsuitable to the mildness of a Christian philosopher.

On Marriage and Fidelity

*B*oswell: "Pray, Sir, do you not suppose that there are fifty women in the world, with any one of whom a man may be as happy, as with any one woman in particular." *Johnson:* "Ay, Sir, fifty thousand." *Boswell:* "Then, Sir, you are not of opinion with some who imagine that certain men and certain women are made for each other; and that they cannot be happy if they miss their counterparts." *Johnson:* "To be sure not, Sir. I believe marriages would in general be as happy, and often more so, if they were all made by the Lord Chancellor,[16] upon a due consideration of characters and circumstances, without the parties having any choice in the matter. Marriage, Sir, is much more necessary to a man than to a woman; for he is much less able to supply himself with domestic comforts. You will recollect my saying to some ladies the other day, that I had often wondered why young women should marry, as they have so much more freedom, and so much more attention paid to them while unmarried, than when married. I indeed did not mention the *strong* reason for their marrying—the *mechanical* reason." *Boswell:* "Why that *is* a strong one. But does not imagination make it seem much more important than it is in reality? Is it not, to a certain degree, a delusion in us as well as in women?" *Johnson:* "Why yes, Sir; but it is a delusion that is always beginning again." *Boswell:* "I don't know but there is upon the whole more misery than happiness produced by that passion." *Johnson:* "I don't think so, Sir."

I repeated to him an argument of a lady of my acquaintance, who maintained, that her husband's having been guilty of numberless infidelities, released her from conjugal obligations, because they were reciprocal. *Johnson:* "This is miserable stuff, Sir. To the contract of marriage, besides the man and wife, there is a third party—Society; and, if it be considered as a vow—God: and, therefore, it cannot be dissolved by their consent alone. Laws are not made for particular cases, but for men in general. A woman may be unhappy with her husband; but she cannot be freed from him without the approbation of the civil and ecclesiastical power. A man may be unhappy, because he is not so rich as another; but he is not to seize upon another's property with his own hand." *Boswell:* "But, Sir, this lady does not want that the contract should be dissolved; she only argues that she may indulge herself in gallantries with equal freedom as her husband does, provided she takes care not

---

15. **which it breathed:** Boswell refers here to Johnson's treatise denouncing the Americans' rebellion against having been taxed by the British. Johnson was well known for his support of the King against the American "rebels."

16. **Lord Chancellor:** any of a number of high officials in the British government.

to introduce a spurious issue into his family." *Johnson*: "This lady of yours, Sir, I think, is very fit for a brothel."

Boswell concludes the biography by praising Johnson's manners and morals.

His moral precepts are practical; for they are drawn from an intimate acquaintance with human nature. His maxims carry conviction; for they are founded on the basis of common sense, and a very attentive and minute survey of real life. His mind was so full of imagery, that he might have been perpetually a poet; yet it is remarkable, that, however rich his prose is in this respect, his poetical pieces, in general, have not much of that splendor, but are rather distinguished by strong sentiment, and acute observation, conveyed in harmonious and energetic verse, particularly in heroic couplets. Though usually grave, and even awful, in his deportment, he possessed uncommon and peculiar powers of wit and humor; he frequently indulged himself in colloquial pleasantry; and the heartiest merriment was often enjoyed in his company; with this great advantage, that as it was entirely free from any poisonous tincture of vice or impiety, it was salutary to those who shared in it. He had accustomed himself to such accuracy in his common conversation that he at all times expressed his thoughts with great force, and an elegant choice of language, the effect of which was aided by his having a loud voice, and a slow, deliberate utterance. In him were united a most logical head with a most fertile imagination, which gave him an extraordinary advantage in arguing: for he could reason close or wide, as he saw best for the moment. Exulting in his intellectual strength and dexterity, he could, when he pleased, be the greatest sophist[17] that ever contended in the lists of declamation; and, from a spirit of contradiction, and a delight in showing his powers, he would often maintain the wrong side with equal warmth and ingenuity; so that, when there was an audience, his real opinions could seldom be gathered from his talk; though when he was in company with a single friend, he would discuss a subject with genuine fairness: but he was too conscientious to make error permanent and pernicious, by deliberately writing it; and, in all his numerous works, he earnestly inculcated what appeared to him to be the truth; his piety being constant, and the ruling principle of all his conduct.

Such was Samuel Johnson, a man whose talents, acquirements, and virtues, were so extraordinary, that the more his character is considered, the more he will be regarded by the present age, and by posterity, with admiration and reverence.

---

17. **sophist** (säf′ ist): one who is gifted in clever, sometimes devious argument.

Getting at Meaning

1. What does Boswell seem to think of his own abilities at the outset of his project? What other qualities does he reveal in himself in his description of the first meeting with Johnson? What particularly impresses Boswell about Johnson during this first meeting?

2. Johnson's strong opinions made him a controversial figure in his day, heartily admired by some, violently criticized by others. Summarize Johnson's opinions on the following subjects.

a. People who exhibit their talent in order to make money

b. Those who criticize public affairs and the royal family

c. The importance of accuracy in using the English language

d. Whether it is easier to learn as a young person or as an adult

e. The American Colonies

f. Marriage for love or for convenience

Does Boswell disagree with any of Johnson's opinions? Explain.

3. Although Boswell clearly has great respect for Johnson, he does present the negative as well as the positive qualities of his admired subject. What are Johnson's positive qualities, as presented in these excerpts? What are his negative qualities?

4. In his final assessment of Johnson, what attributes particularly admired in the eighteenth century does Boswell note?

Developing Skills in Reading Literature

Biography. In 1683 John Dryden defined biography as the "history of particular men's lives." As it evolved in the eighteenth century, a biography is an accurate history, a comprehensive, well constructed narrative that reveals the subject as a living, breathing human being. The skilled biographer gathers information from journals, letters, documents, interviews, and other reliable sources and then shapes the material into a balanced portrayal of the subject, weaving together anecdotes, description, quotations, reconstructed conversations, and interpretive passages while avoiding intrusive editorial commentary and obvious moralizing. Even when a biographer includes an evaluation of the subject, readers still can draw their own conclusions, given the wealth of detail common in a biography.

What techniques of the biographer are evident in these excerpts by Boswell? How does he manage to portray Johnson as a real human being? Is his a balanced portrayal, as far as you can tell? One characteristic of good biography is objectivity. Can any biography, however, be completely objective? Does Boswell's account seem to be objective? Support your answer with reasons based on the excerpts.

Developing Vocabulary

Synonyms. It is a mistake to assume that synonyms are exactly alike in meaning. They are words with similar meanings, distinguished by differences in connotation and usage. Boswell often reinforces meaning by using synonyms in close proximity. Examine each pair of italicized words in the quotations that follow. Then look up the words in a dictionary and be prepared to tell how the meanings of the words are similar but slightly different and how the synonyms reinforce one another.

a. "Had his other friends been as *diligent* and *ardent* as I was, he might have been almost entirely preserved."

b. "I had . . . the highest *reverence* for their author, which had grown up in my fancy into a kind of mysterious *veneration*."

c. . . . "it must be confessed, that his apartment, and furniture, and morning dress, were sufficiently *uncouth*. . . . But all these *slovenly* particularities were soon forgotten. . . ."

d. "But it must be owned, that Johnson, though he could be rigidly *abstemious,* was not a *temperate* man either in eating or drinking."

e. "Though usually *grave,* and even *aweful,* in his deportment, he possessed uncommon and peculiar powers of wit and humor. . . ."

Developing Writing Skills

Writing a Character Sketch. A character sketch is a kind of biographical writing, more limited in scope than a formal biography and intended to create an impression of the subject. Choose a subject for a character sketch and prepare to write by doing the following:

a. Think about the various facets of the person's character.

b. Decide on the facet to emphasize.

c. List descriptive details, interpretive comments, exchanges of dialogue, and anecdotes that will create one desired impression.

d. Review the list and delete any details that do not relate directly to the facet of your subject that you have chosen to illuminate.

Be sure that your finished character sketch is as rich in detail as is possible within the limitations of the form.

Samuel Johnson

1709–1784

Samuel Johnson wrote *A Dictionary of the English Language,* a stupendous feat that won him an important place in literary history. His essays remain classic examples of the formal, eighteenth-century prose of which he was the acknowledged master. A poet himself, he also wrote graceful biographies of poets and critiques of poems and other literary works. Johnson was more than an accomplished writer; he was the literary dictator of London and the undisputed arbiter of taste for his time.

Born and raised in Lichfield, Johnson's father was a prominent but nearly impoverished bookseller in the midland counties. The family could not afford to send the obviously brilliant boy to one of the famous public schools, so Johnson went to work in his father's shop where he gained vast knowledge by reading his father's books.

Born with scrofula, Johnson was disfigured by the malady, his cheeks deeply scarred, his eyesight badly impaired. Large and enormously strong, he was awkward, subject to tics and inexplicable gestures. A gregarious man of quick wit and generous heart, he was subject to bouts of deep depression and to outbursts of violent temper.

Johnson entered Oxford University on the promise of financial help from a wealthy neighbor. This promise proved to be largely worthless, and the young man was destitute, literally in tatters. With his ungainly figure, eccentric ways, and impressive knowledge, Johnson amazed his professors and his peers, who viewed the ragged scholar with a mixture of mirth and pity, both of which wounded his pride. At twenty, Johnson left college without either a degree or a way to earn a living. For several years he barely survived on teaching and translating jobs and on the occasional charity of people who recognized his extraordinary ability.

At the age of twenty-eight, Johnson walked to London on the faint hope of earning a living by his pen. Within a year, he had achieved a literary reputation with his work for magazines and his poem "London," modeled on a satire by Juvenal. In

SAMUEL JOHNSON, 1756. *Sir Joshua Reynolds. National Portrait Gallery, London.*

1745 eminent booksellers prevailed upon Johnson to produce a dictionary. He agreed, expecting to finish the dictionary by 1750, a date he missed by five years. Almost singlehandedly, Johnson created a work of gigantic proportions, consisting of forty thousand definitions and 114,000 quotations. He believed that the English language is a dynamic, living language that reached its fullest development in the days of Shakespeare. Rather than attempting to "fix the language," he simply defined words as they had been used by the "best writers."

The appearance of *A Dictionary of the English Language* brought Johnson instant fame but meager financial rewards. He was jailed for debt twice during the year that followed its publication, and he continued to earn fees by writing periodical essays on literature, politics, ethics, and social problems, character sketches, book reviews, dedications, and critical introductions.

Johnson once said, "It matters not how a man dies, but how he lives." He did both well. After a long, agonizing illness, he died peacefully, his last words spoken to a little girl who knelt at his bedside: "God bless you, my dear."

from **Preface to Shakespeare**

Shakespeare is, above all writers, at least above all modern writers, the poet of nature; the poet that holds up to his readers a faithful mirror of manners and of life. His characters are not modified by the customs of particular places, unpracticed by the rest of the world; by the peculiarities of studies or professions, which can operate but upon small numbers; or by the accidents of transient fashions or temporary opinions; they are the genuine progeny of common humanity, such as the world will always supply and observation will always find. His persons act and speak by the influence of those general passions and principles by which all minds are agitated and the whole system of life is continued in motion. In the writings of other poets a character is too often an individual; in those of Shakespeare it is commonly a species.

It is from this wide extension of design that so much instruction is derived. It is this which fills the plays of Shakespeare with practical axioms and domestic wisdom. It was said of Euripides[1] that every verse was a precept; and it may be said of Shakespeare that from his works may be collected a system of civil and economical prudence. Yet his real power is not shown in the splendor of particular passages, but by the progress of his fable and the tenor of his dialogue; and he that tries to recommend him by select quotations will succeed like the pedant in Hierocles,[2] who, when he offered his house to sale, carried a brick in his pocket as a specimen.

It will not easily be imagined how much Shakespeare excels in accommodating his sentiments to real life, but by comparing him with other authors. It was observed of the ancient schools of declamation that the more diligently they were frequented, the more was the student disqualified for the world, be-cause he found nothing there which he should ever meet in any other place. The same remark may be applied to every stage but that of Shakespeare. The theater, when it is under any other direction, is peopled by such characters as were never seen, conversing in a language which was never heard, upon topics which will never arise in the commerce of mankind. But the dialogue of this author is often so evidently determined by the incident which produces it, and is pursued with so much ease and simplicity, that it seems scarcely to claim the merit of fiction, but to have been gleaned by diligent selection out of common conversation and common occurrences.

Upon every other stage the universal agent is love, by whose power all good and evil is distributed, and every action quickened or retarded. To bring a lover, a lady, and a rival into the fable; to entangle them in contradictory obligations, perplex them with oppositions of interest, and harass them with violence of desires inconsistent with each other; to make them meet in rapture and part in agony; to fill their mouths with hyperbolical joy and outrageous sorrow; to distress them as nothing human ever was distressed; to deliver them as nothing human ever was delivered—is the business of a modern dramatist. For this probability is violated, life is misrepresented, and language is depraved. But love is only one of many passions, and, as it has no great influence upon the sum of life, it has little operation in the dramas of a poet, who caught

---

1. **Euripides** (yoo rip′ ə dēz): Greek writer of tragedies in the fifth century B.C.
2. **Hierocles** (hī′ ər ə klēz): fifth-century scholar and critic.

his ideas from the living world, and exhibited only what he saw before him. He knew that any other passion, as it was regular or exorbitant, was a cause of happiness or calamity.

Characters thus ample and general were not easily discriminated and preserved, yet perhaps no poet ever kept his personages more distinct from each other. I will not say with Pope that every speech may be assigned to the proper speaker, because many speeches there are which have nothing characteristical; but, perhaps, though some may be equally adapted to every person, it will be difficult to find any that can be properly transferred from the present possessor to another claimant. The choice is right when there is reason for choice.

Other dramatists can only gain attention by hyperbolical or aggravated characters, by fabulous and unexampled excellence or depravity, as the writers of barbarous romances invigorated the reader by a giant and a dwarf; and he that should form his expectations of human affairs from the play, or from the tale, would be equally deceived. Shakespeare has no heroes; his scenes are occupied only by men who act and speak as the reader thinks that he should himself have spoken or acted on the same occasion. Even where the agency is supernatural, the dialogue is level with life. Other writers disguise the most natural passions and most frequent incidents, so that he who contemplates them in the book will not know them in the world. Shakespeare approximates the remote, and familiarizes the wonderful; the event which he represents will not happen, but if it were possible, its effects would be probably such as he has assigned; and it may be said that he has not only shown human nature as it acts in real exigences, but as it would be found in trials to which it cannot be exposed.

This therefore is the praise of Shakespeare, that his drama is the mirror of life; that he who has mazed his imagination in following the phantoms which other writers raise up before him may here be cured of his delirious ecstasies by reading human sentiments in human language, by scenes from which a hermit may estimate the transactions of the world, and a confessor predict the progress of the passions.

Getting at Meaning

1. Johnson calls Shakespeare the "poet of nature." What does he mean by this epithet?

2. According to Johnson, how is Shakespeare's treatment of the subject of love different from that of the dramatists who were Johnson's contemporaries?

3. Johnson says, "Shakespeare has no heroes; his scenes are occupied only by men who act and speak as the reader thinks that he should himself have spoken or acted on the same occasion." Do you agree that Shakespeare's plays lack heroes? Does *Macbeth* fit Johnson's contention, for example? Explain.

4. Summarize Johnson's critical standards as they are implied in the preface.

Developing Skills in Reading Literature

Parallelism. In prose, parallelism can occur in parts of a sentence, in sentences as a whole, within paragraphs, and sometimes among several paragraphs. Parallelism is a structural characteristic of classical literature and also of Neoclassical writing. Examine this selection, and locate examples of parallelism in each of the following:

    prepositional phrases   subordinate clauses
    infinitive phrases   sentences

How does parallelism create clarity, conciseness, and emphasis in this critical preface?

Examine the essays by Steele, Addison, and Swift. What examples of parallelism do you find? Is parallelism a significant stylistic characteristic in any of these prose selections?

MRS. SIDDONS AS THE TRAGIC MUSE. *Sir Joshua Reynolds.*
Henry E. Huntington Library and Art Gallery, San Marino, California.

Letter to Lord Chesterfield

Before beginning the Dictionary, *Johnson appealed to Lord Chesterfield for financial support of the project. Lord Chesterfield ignored the request. Years later, when Johnson had almost finished his work, Chesterfield praised the* Dictionary *enthusiastically and hinted, in articles written for a newspaper, that he would be pleased if it were dedicated to him. Johnson responded in one of the most famous letters in English literature.*

To the Right Honorable
the Earl of Chesterfield

February 7, 1755.

My Lord:

I have lately been informed by the proprietor of *The World,*[1] that two papers, in which my *Dictionary* is recommended to the public, were written by your Lordship. To be so distinguished is an honor which, being very little accustomed to favors from the great, I know not well how to receive, or in what terms to acknowledge.

When, upon some slight encouragement, I first visited your Lordship, I was overpowered, like the rest of mankind, by the enchantment of your address; and I could not forbear to wish that I might boast myself *"Le vainqueur du vainqueur de la terre"*;[2] that I might obtain that regard for which I saw the world contending; but I found my attendance so little encouraged, that neither pride nor modesty would suffer me to continue it. When I had once addressed your Lordship in public, I had exhausted all the art of pleasing which a retired and uncourtly scholar can possess. I had done all that I could; and no man is well pleased to have his all neglected, be it ever so little.

Seven years, my Lord, have now passed, since I waited in your outward rooms, or was repulsed from your door; during which time I have been pushing on my work through difficulties, of which it is useless to complain, and have brought it at last to the verge of publication, without one act of assistance, one word of encouragement, or one smile of favor. Such treatment I did not expect, for I never had a patron[3] before.

The shepherd in Virgil grew at last acquainted with Love, and found him a native of the rocks.[4]

Is not a patron, my Lord, one who looks with unconcern on a man struggling for life in the water, and, when he has reached ground, encumbers him with help? The notice which

---

1. **The World:** a current periodical in which Chesterfield had recently written articles praising Johnson for his work on the *Dictionary.*
2. **Le . . . terre** *French:* the conqueror of the conqueror of the world.
3. **patron:** The patronage system had long been an essential part of the literary scene in England. The reading public was small, and the only way an author could obtain substantial financial return was to secure a patron among the wealthy nobility. Johnson's feisty letter is said to have sounded the death knell for the entire system toward the end of the eighteenth century.
4. **The shepherd . . . rocks:** Johnson makes an allusion here to a passage from the *Eclogues* of Virgil (70–19 B. C.), in which the Latin poet speaks of the cruelty of the god of Love who must have been born among the rocks.

you have been pleased to take of my labors, had it been early, had been kind; but it has been delayed till I am indifferent, and cannot enjoy it; till I am solitary,[5] and cannot impart it; till I am known, and do not want[6] it. I hope it is no very cynical asperity not to confess obligations where no benefit has been received, or to be unwilling that the public should consider me as owing that to a patron, which Providence has enabled me to do for myself.

Having carried on my work thus far with so little obligation to any favorer of learning, I shall not be disappointed though I should conclude it, if less be possible, with less; for I have been long wakened from that dream of hope, in which I once boasted myself with so much exaltation,

My Lord,

    Your Lordship's most humble,
    Most obedient servant,

                  Samuel Johnson.

---

5. **solitary:** Johnson's wife had died before he could finish his *Dictionary*.
6. **want:** need.

SAMUEL JOHNSON (toward the end of his life).
Sir Joshua Reynolds.
National Portrait Gallery, London.

Getting at Meaning

1. What is the tone of this letter to Lord Chesterfield?

2. What does the reader learn of Johnson's character from this letter?

3. What does the comparison between a writer and "a man struggling for life in the water" suggest about both patron and artist?

Developing Skills in Reading Literature

Connotation. The connotations of certain key words in this letter reinforce the contrast between Johnson, the poor, struggling scholar, and Chesterfield, the imperious, indifferent patron of the arts. Examine the words with which Johnson describes himself and his work on the *Dictionary*. What image of Johnson is created by these words? What particularly suggestive words does Johnson use when discussing Lord Chesterfield, his first encounter with Chesterfield, and patrons in general? What attitude on Johnson's part is revealed by these words?

Developing Writing Skills

Writing a Letter. In your examination of the letter to Lord Chesterfield, you discovered several of Johnson's personality traits along with his attitude toward the patronage system. Using this letter as a model, write a letter to someone who has injured you in some way. Be sure that your letter reveals both your personality and your ideas about the major issue involved.

Thomas Gray

1716–1771

Thomas Gray's claim to literary immortality is "Elegy Written in a Country Churchyard," an elegant, melancholy meditation upon death, which Gray revised and reworked for nearly eight years. Instantly popular upon publication in 1751, the poem has defied the vicissitudes of taste, claiming a vast readership in every era.

Gray's father, Philip Gray, was an outwardly respectable businessman who treated his family with alternating brutality and neglect. Thomas became obsessively devoted to his mother, whose brother arranged for the lad to be educated at Eton and Cambridge. At Eton, the serious, bookish youth became the close friend of two brilliant young men with powerful fathers: Richard West, son of the Lord Chancellor of Ireland; and Horace Walpole, son of Sir Robert Walpole, the leading Whig minister. In 1739, Gray accompanied young Walpole on a grand tour of France, Switzerland, and Italy, which ended in a violent quarrel. Eventually they were reconciled, but at the time the sensitive Gray suffered greatly. In 1742 Richard West died early in his twenty-sixth year. This event precipitated Gray's withdrawal into lifelong semi-seclusion at Cambridge, where the reclusive scholar and poet became a living legend.

Among Gray's major works are "Ode on the Spring," "Hymn to Adversity," and "Ode on a Distant Prospect of Eton College." Like "Elegy Written in a Country Churchyard," these poems are transitional works, evidencing a familiarity with Greek and Latin literature typical of Neoclassicism and an interest in nature, in humble villagers, and in Celtic and Norse folklore that foreshadowed Romanticism. The poems, with their melancholy overtones, seem like public statements of Gray's private personality. His letters, however, reveal another side to his nature. In them, the reader meets a happy scholar who loves his work, a warm friend eager to entertain with humorous wordplay or gentle satire. To strangers at Cambridge, Gray appeared to be an odd, hermit-like creature, who spoke with maddening slowness and always wrote with a crow quill, yet to his few intimates he was a warm, charming, rather innocent fellow.

At his death in the summer of 1771, Gray was buried alongside the remains of his mother in the sequestered village churchyard at Stoke Pogis in Buckinghamshire, the setting of his famous elegy.

THOMAS GRAY.
National Portrait Gallery, London.

Elegy Written in a Country Churchyard

The curfew tolls the knell of parting day,
The lowing herd wind slowly o'er the lea,[1]
The plowman homeward plods his weary way,
And leaves the world to darkness and to me.

Now fades the glimmering landscape on the sight,   5
And all the air a solemn stillness holds,
Save where the beetle wheels his droning flight,
And drowsy tinklings lull the distant folds;

Save that from yonder ivy-mantled tower
The moping owl does to the moon complain   10
Of such as, wandering near her secret bower,
Molest her ancient solitary reign.

Beneath those rugged elms, that yew tree's shade,
Where heaves the turf in many a moldering heap,
Each in his narrow cell forever laid,   15
The rude forefathers of the hamlet[2] sleep.

The breezy call of incense-breathing morn,
The swallow twittering from the straw-built shed,
The cock's shrill clarion or the echoing horn,
No more shall rouse them from their lowly bed.   20

For them no more the blazing hearth shall burn,
Or busy housewife ply her evening care:
No children run to lisp their sire's return,
Or climb his knees the envied kiss to share.

Oft did the harvest to their sickle yield,   25
Their furrow oft the stubborn glebe[3] has broke;
How jocund did they drive their team afield!
How bowed the woods beneath their sturdy stroke!

Let not Ambition mock their useful toil,
Their homely joys and destiny obscure;   30
Nor Grandeur hear, with a disdainful smile,
The short and simple annals of the poor.

---

1. **lea:** a meadow or a grassy field.
2. **rude . . . hamlet:** simple village folk.
3. **glebe:** piece of cultivated soil.

The boast of heraldry,[4] the pomp of power,
And all that beauty, all that wealth e'er gave,
Awaits alike the inevitable hour.   35
The paths of glory lead but to the grave.

Nor you, ye Proud, impute to these the fault,
If Memory o'er their tomb no trophies[5] raise,
Where through the long-drawn aisle and fretted vault[6]
The pealing anthem swells the note of praise.   40

Can storied urn[7] or animated[8] bust
Back to its mansion call the fleeting breath?
Can Honor's voice provoke[9] the silent dust,
Or Flattery soothe the dull cold ear of Death?

Perhaps in this neglected spot is laid   45
Some heart once pregnant with celestial fire;
Hands that the rod of empire might have swayed,
Or waked to ecstasy the living lyre.[10]

But Knowledge to their eyes her ample page
Rich with the spoils of time did ne'er unroll;   50
Chill Penury repressed their noble rage,[11]
And froze the genial current[12] of the soul.

Full many a gem of purest ray serene
The dark unfathomed caves of ocean bear:
Full many a flower is born to blush unseen,   55
And waste its sweetness on the desert air.

---

4. **boast of heraldry:** pride in genealogy or family lineage.
5. **trophies:** elaborate stone sculptures.
6. **fretted vault:** the ornamented arched roof of a cathedral ceiling.
7. **storied urn:** In the eighteenth century vases or urns were elaborately decorated with classical paintings or bas-relief sculpture. If the urn were used to hold the ashes of the deceased, the pictures would sometimes depict scenes from the dead person's life.
8. **animated bust:** lifelike sculptures.
9. **provoke:** call forth; arouse.
10. **lyre:** a small stringed instrument sometimes associated with "heavenly" music.
11. **noble rage:** intensity, energy.
12. **genial current:** life-giving force.

Some village Hampden[13] that with dauntless breast
The little tyrant of his fields withstood;
Some mute inglorious Milton here may rest,
Some Cromwell[14] guiltless of his country's blood. 60

The applause of listening senates to command,
The threats of pain and ruin to despise,
To scatter plenty o'er a smiling land,
And read their history in a nation's eyes,[15]

Their lot forbade: nor circumscribed alone   65
Their growing virtues, but their crimes confined;
Forbade to wade through slaughter to a throne,
And shut the gates of mercy on mankind.

The struggling pangs of conscious truth[16] to hide,
To quench the blushes of ingenuous shame,[17]   70
Or heap the shrine of Luxury and Pride
With incense kindled at the Muse's flame.[18]

Far from the madding[19] crowd's ignoble strife
Their sober wishes never learned to stray;
Along the cool sequestered vale of life   75
They kept the noiseless tenor[20] of their way.

Yet even these bones from insult to protect
Some frail memorial[21] still erected nigh,
With uncouth rhymes and shapeless sculpture decked,
Implores the passing tribute of a sigh.   80

Illustration for Gray's "Elegy,"
executed by Bentley for Horace Walpole's
Strawberry Hill edition. *British Library.*

---

13. **Hampden:** John Hampden (1594–1643), a Puritan leader who
defied "the little tyrant," Charles I, in 1636, over unjust taxation.
14. **Cromwell:** Oliver Cromwell, Lord Protector of the Commonwealth from 1653–1658.
15. This entire stanza is to be read as the object of the verb *forbade*,
in the next stanza.
16. **pangs of conscious truth:** conscience.
17. **ingenuous shame:** a naive sense of virtue or nobility.
18. **incense . . . flame:** poetic praise.
19. **madding:** wildly excited or disorderly. Thomas Hardy (1840–
1928), novelist and poet, borrowed this line as the title for his
famous novel, *Far from the Madding Crowd.*
20. **tenor:** tendency or course.
21. **frail memorial:** simple gravestone.

Their name, their years, spelt by the unlettered muse,[22]
The place of fame and elegy supply:
And many a holy text around she strews,
That teach the rustic moralist to die.

For who to dumb Forgetfulness a prey,   85
This pleasing anxious being e'er resigned,
Left the warm precincts of the cheerful day,
Nor cast one longing lingering look behind?[23]

On some fond breast the parting soul relies,
Some pious drops[24] the closing eye requires;   90
Even from the tomb the voice of Nature cries,
Even in our ashes live their wonted[25] fires.

For thee[26] who, mindful of the unhonored dead,
Dost in these lines their artless tale relate;
If chance, by lonely Contemplation led,   95
Some kindred spirit shall inquire thy fate,

Haply some hoary-headed swain[27] may say,
"Oft have we seen him at the peep of dawn,
Brushing with hasty steps the dews away
To meet the sun upon the upland lawn.   100

"There at the foot of yonder nodding beech
That wreathes its old fantastic roots so high,
His listless length at noontide would he stretch,
And pore upon the brook that babbles by.

"Hard by yon wood, now smiling as in scorn,   105
Muttering his wayward fancies he would rove,
Now drooping, woeful wan, like one forlorn,
Or crazed with care, or crossed in hopeless love.

---

22. **unlettered muse:** the goddess who provided inspiration for the uneducated stone carver who made the tombstone.
23. **For who . . . behind:** For who has never been reluctant to leave the warmth and security of his present life in order to resign himself to death or "dumb Forgetfulness"?
24. **drops:** tears.
25. **wonted:** accustomed.
26. **For thee:** for Gray himself.
27. **hoary-headed swain:** aged peasant or shepherd.

Getting at Meaning

A RED, RED ROSE

1. What declarations does the speaker make to his love?

2. What do the exaggerations in this poem suggest about the probable intentions of the speaker?

JOHN ANDERSON, MY JO

3. Who is the speaker in this poem? From what perspective does she speak?

4. What feelings does the speaker convey about John Anderson? How do these feelings differ from the feelings expressed by the speaker in "A Red, Red Rose"? How are the speakers' feelings similar?

5. What is implied by the metaphor contained in the last two lines of the poem?

Developing Skills in Reading Literature

1. **Sound Devices.** "A Red, Red Rose" and "John Anderson, My Jo" exemplify the use of sound devices in lyrics to enhance the musical quality of the lines. Read both poems, noting the absence of harsh sounds. How are softness and gentleness appropriate to the subjects of the songs? Chart the rhyme scheme and scan the meter of each poem. What similarities and differences are apparent? What is musical about the resulting rhythm? In "A Red, Red Rose" what purpose is served by the tightening of the rhyme scheme in the third and fourth stanzas? Notice the repetends in the rhyme schemes of both poems. How do these particular repetends reinforce sound and meaning?

2. **Imagery.** Find examples of figures of speech such as simile, metaphor, and hyperbole in these two songs. Also, look for other images that convey an impression of the beloved in each poem. What attitude toward the beloved is brought out through these images?

3. **Tone and Mood.** The emotionalism of these songs makes them more typical of nineteenth-century Romanticism than of eighteenth-century Neoclassicism. This emotionalism is evident in both the tone and the mood of the lyrics. What are the feelings of the speaker in each lyric? How does each speaker view his or her subject? How do you as a reader respond to the poems? Point out examples of both diction and sound devices that contribute significantly to tone and mood in the poems. Which poem seems more sentimental? What might account for the subtle difference between the two poems?

Developing Writing Skills

Poetry: Avoiding Clichés. The first line of "A Red, Red Rose" was fresh and original in the eighteenth century. Now, however, a comparison between a beloved and a red rose is a cliché, or hackneyed expression. Write a lyric of at least three stanzas on the subject of love. Include four or more interesting similes that maintain the desired tone of the poem. You may speak in your own voice or through a created speaker, and you may address your poem to a real or imaginary person.

To a Louse

On Seeing One on a Lady's Bonnet at Church

Ha! wh' are ye gaun, ye crowlin' ferlie![1]
Your impudence protects you sairly;[2]
I canna say but ye strunt[3] rarely,
   Owre gauze and lace;
Though faith! I fear ye dine but sparely   5
   On sic[4] a place.

Ye ugly, creepin', blastit wonner,[5]
Detested, shunned by saunt an' sinner!
How dare ye set your fit[6] upon her,
   Sae fine a lady?   10
Gae somewhere else, and seek your dinner
   On some poor body.

Swith, in some beggar's haffet squattle;[7]
There ye may creep, and sprawl, and sprattle[8]
Wi'ither kindred jumping cattle,   15
   In shoals and nations;
Where horn nor bane[9] ne'er dare unsettle
   Your thick plantations.

Now haud ye there,[10] ye're out o' sight,
Below the fatt'rels,[11] snug an' tight;   20
Na, faith ye yet! ye'll no be right
   Till ye've got on it,
The very tapmost tow'ring height
   O'Miss's bonnet.

---

1. **crowlin' ferlie** (fĕr' lē): crawling wonder.
2. **sairly** (sĕr' lē): greatly.
3. **strunt**: strut.
4. **sic**: such.
5. **blastit wonner**: blasted wonder.
6. **fit**: foot.
7. **Swith . . . squattle**: Get you gone! Sprawl in some beggar's hovel.
8. **sprattle**: struggle.
9. **horn nor bane**: comb nor poison.
10. **haud ye there**: Stay right where you are!
11. **fatt'rels**: ends of the ribbons on the lady's bonnet.

My sooth! right bauld ye set your nose out,   25
As plump and gray as onie grozet;[12]
O for some rank mercurial rozet,[13]
    Or fell red smeddum![14]
I'd gie you sic a hearty dose o't,
    Wad dress your droddum![15]   30

I wad na been surprised to spy
You on an auld wife's flannen toy;[16]
Or aiblins some bit duddie boy,[17]
    On's wyliecoat;[18]
But Miss's fine Lunardi![19] fie,   35
    How daur ye do 't?

O Jenny, dinna toss your head,
An' set your beauties a' abread![20]
Ye little ken[21] what cursèd speed
    The blastie's makin'!   40
Thae winks and finger ends,[22] I dread,
    Are notice takin'!

O wad some Pow'r the giftie gie us
To see oursels as ithers see us!
It wad frae mony a blunder free us,   45
    And foolish notion:
What airs in dress an' gait wad lea'e us,
    And e'en devotion![23]

---

12. **onie grozet** (grŏz' ĭt): any gooseberry.
13. **mercurial rozet:** a fast-acting rosin; something to make
the louse "stick."
14. **smeddum:** powder.
15. **Wad dress your droddum:** would be the death of you!
16. **flainen toy:** a flannel turban used as a hat.
17. **Or . . . boy:** or perhaps on some little beggar.
18. **on's wyliecoat** (wī' lē kōt): on his flannel vest.
19. **Lunardi:** a famous balloonist for whom a bonnet was
named.
20. **abread:** abroad.
21. **ken:** understand.
22. **Thae winks and finger-ends:** the gossips, glancing and
pointing.
23. **devotion:** artificial piety.

Getting at Meaning

1. What attitude does the speaker in this poem seem to take toward the lady? toward the louse? Is there any similarity in the way he views both of them? Explain.

2. What change in tone occurs in the final stanza of the poem? What is the message of the poem as it is summarized in this stanza?

3. What elements of humor do you find in the poem?

Developing Skills in Reading Literature

1. **Satire.** This poem is one of Burns's early and best known satires. What is the central target of the satire? Is the poem written in the Horatian or the Juvenalian style? What specifically is its tone? In what way is the subject of the poem more characteristic of the Romantic Age than of the Neoclassical Age? Is the social criticism contained in the poem more typically Romantic or Neoclassical? What about the verse form? the diction?

2. **Dialect.** A dialect is the particular variety of language spoken in one place by a distinct group of people. Dialect reflects the colloquialisms, grammatical construction, vocabulary, and unique pronunciations that are distinctive of a region. "To a Louse" is written in the Scottish dialect spoken by Burns and his fellow Scots. Paraphrase the following lines from the poem.

a. "I canna say but ye strunt rarely,
    Owre gauze and lace;"

b. "Na, faith ye yet! ye'll no be right
    Till ye've got on it,"

c. "My sooth! right bauld ye set your nose out,"

d. "O wad some Pow'r the giftie gie us
    To see oursels as others see us!
    It wad frae monie a blunder free us,
    And foolish notion:
    What airs in dress an' gait wad lea'e us,
    And ev'n devotion!"

Study the footnotes, which define difficult vocabulary and explain unusual expressions, and identify words in the poem that are recognizable but are spelled differently than in contemporary standard English. Then read the entire poem aloud, rolling the *r*'s and pronouncing the *a*'s like *ah*'s. Comment briefly on the effect created through the use of dialect.

William Blake
1757–1827

Poet and painter, prophet, mystic, and visionary, William Blake was so unique that critics have been tempted to consider him a mad genius, inspired but irrational. Blake's unconventional works were so at odds with the prevailing tastes of the day that his contemporaries could not appreciate the magnitude of his accomplishment. Only after World War One was Blake widely recognized as a passionately dedicated and astonishingly original artist.

Blake drew a sharp distinction between his "spiritual life" and his "corporeal life," considering the former of paramount importance. His biography reveals an ordinary, uneventful corporeal life, his works an unfettered and fantastic spiritual life. As a revolutionary in the Romantic sense, he sympathized with the American and French causes; as a dissenter in the Puritan tradition, he mistrusted religious and political institutions. Without having witnessed the poverty, grime, and degradation of the new industrial centers, Blake perceived the potential for dehumanization inherent in the industrial system, a view that anticipates the twentieth century.

Son of a London haberdasher, Blake had a natural flair for drawing. At ten, he attended drawing school, and in his free time he haunted art galleries where he was fondly nicknamed the "little connoisseur." When he was fourteen, he began a seven year apprenticeship with engraver James Basire, then studied briefly at the royal Academy of Arts.

In addition to engraving, Blake had learned to paint with water colors. He also had begun to write poems, rejecting the Neoclassical tradition in favor of a simpler style marked by bold figures of speech and striking symbols. His first book of poetry, *Poetical Sketches by W. B.* (1783), was published in the usual fashion. He published all of his subsequent books in a manner quite as extraordinary and unusual as the works themselves. In a process partially invented by Blake, he covered a copper plate with acid-proof wax, then engraved a design that incorporated both the text and illustrations into a harmonious whole. After applying acid to make the design in relief, he printed a page, then painted it with water colors, slowly and laborious-

WILLIAM BLAKE. *Thomas Phillips.*
National Portrait Gallery, London.

ly producing a bound volume. The obsessive dedication to artistic integrity represented by this painstaking procedure has been part of Blake's appeal for his modern enthusiasts. Few copies could be published in this way; for example, only twenty-seven copies of *Songs of Innocence and Experience* (1794-c.1801), a joint edition of Blake's two famous collections of lyrics, are known to exist, and not all of the copies are complete.

After *Songs of Experience*, which includes such mature masterworks as "The Tyger" and "London," Blake's writing became increasingly obscure, marked by prophetic and apocalyptic visions similar to those in *The Book of Thel* (1789), an allegorical poem, and *The Marriage of Heaven and Hell* (1794), a prose work that includes a collection of paradoxical aphorisms titled "Proverbs of Hell." Eventually, Blake abandoned the lyrical style and wrote poems in long unrhymed lines whose rhythm echoes that of the *King James Authorized Bible.*

from **Songs of Innocence**

Introduction

Piping down the valleys wild,
Piping songs of pleasant glee,
On a cloud I saw a child,
And he laughing said to me:

"Pipe a song about a Lamb!"   5
So I piped with merry cheer.
"Piper, pipe that song again;"
So I piped: he wept to hear.

"Drop thy pipe, thy happy pipe;
Sing thy songs of happy cheer:"   10
So I sang the same again,
While he wept with joy to hear.

"Piper, sit thee down and write
In a book, that all may read."
So he vanish'd from my sight,   15
And I pluck'd a hollow reed,

And I made a rural pen,
And I stain'd the water clear,
And I wrote my happy songs
Every child may joy to hear.   20

The Lamb

Little Lamb, who made thee?
  Dost thou know who made thee?
Gave thee life, and bid thee feed,
By the stream and o'er the mead;
Gave thee clothing of delight,   5
Softest clothing, woolly, bright;
Gave thee such a tender voice,
Making all the vales rejoice?
  Little Lamb, who made thee?
  Dost thou know who made thee?   10

Little Lamb, I'll tell thee,
  Little Lamb, I'll tell thee:
He is callèd by thy name,
For He calls Himself a Lamb.
He is meek, and He is mild;   15
He became a little child.
I a child, and thou a lamb,
We are callèd by His name.
  Little Lamb, God bless thee!
  Little Lamb, God bless thee!   20

The Little Boy Lost

"Father! father! where are you going?
O do not walk so fast.
Speak, father, speak to your little boy,
Or else I shall be lost."

The night was dark, no father was there;   5
The child was wet with dew;
The mire was deep, and the child did weep,
And away the vapor[1] flew.

1. **vapor:** here referring to an "aura" or an atmosphere of fear and gloom.

The Little Boy Found

The little boy lost in the lonely fen,[1]
Led by the wand'ring light,
Began to cry; but God, ever nigh,
Appear'd like his father, in white.

He kissèd the child, and by the hand led,   5
And to his mother brought,
Who in sorrow pale, thro' the lonely dale,
Her little boy weeping sought.

1. **fen:** swamp or marsh.

THE FOUR AND TWENTY ELDERS, 1805. *William Blake.*
Tate Gallery, London.

Getting at Meaning

INTRODUCTION

1. Who is the piper in this poem? What is the relationship between piping and writing? What images predominate in the references to the piper's songs?

2. What vision inspires the piper? What does this vision probably represent?

3. In the final stanza the piper suggests that the audience for the songs is "every child." Is this phrase meant to be understood figuratively as well as literally? Explain.

4. After reading this introduction, what kinds of poems do you expect will follow?

THE LAMB

5. The first stanza seems to be a straightforward address to a lamb. What clue suggests that the animal might have a symbolic meaning? Who seems to be speaking in this stanza? What attitude does this speaker take toward the Lamb?

6. In which lines does the speaker identify the Lamb with the Christian Creator? What does the speaker say about the Creator's relationship with humanity? What lines in particular emphasize the unity of the divine, the natural, and the human?

7. What concept of the deity is evident in this poem? How is this concept different from the God of the Enlightenment, as described in the introduction to the unit?

LITTLE BOY LOST AND LITTLE BOY FOUND

8. What images suggest the abstract concepts of fear and hope in these companion poems? In what figurative sense does the speaker use the words *lost* and *found*?

9. In "Little Boy Found" both God and mother show love for the boy. Which of the two proves to be a more effective source of help? Of what does the help consist, literally and figuratively?

10. These poems incorporate the ideas of innocence and experience. Identify lines suggesting that the innocent child is at the mercy of powerful forces and that he inevitably must experience pain and alienation.

Developing Skills in Reading Literature

Symbol. William Blake uses recurring symbols in his poetry to represent certain mystic concepts. He uses the child, for example, to represent the state of innocence, the father to represent the world of experience, and the mother to symbolize the earth or nature. Discuss the function of these symbols in the four selections from *Songs of Innocence*.

In addition to the child, father, and mother symbols, Blake uses several symbols to represent religious concepts, specifically those associated with Christianity. What symbol for Christ, for example, do you find in the poems from *Songs of Innocence*? What is the symbol for God? What concept of the deity is suggested by the use of these particular symbols?

from **Songs of Experience**

Introduction

Hear the voice of the Bard![1]
Who present, past, and future, sees;
Whose ears have heard
The Holy Word
That walk'd among the ancient trees,   5

Calling the lapsèd soul,[2]
And weeping in the evening dew;
That might control
The starry pole,
And fallen, fallen light renew!   10

"O Earth, O Earth, return!
Arise from out the dewy grass;
Night is worn,
And the morn
Rises from the slumberous mass.   15

"Turn away no more;
Why wilt thou turn away.
The starry floor,
The wat'ry shore,
Is giv'n thee till the break of day."   20

---

1. **Bard:** a poet with mystic insight.
2. **lapsed soul:** a soul fallen from grace after Adam and Eve sinned.

The Tyger

Tyger! Tyger![1] burning bright
In the forests of the night,
What immortal hand or eye[2]
Could frame thy fearful symmetry?

In what distant deeps or skies   5
Burnt the fire of thine eyes?
On what wings dare he aspire?
What the hand dare seize the fire?

And what shoulder, and what art,
Could twist the sinews of thy heart?   10
And when thy heart began to beat,
What dread hand? and what dread feet?

What the hammer? what the chain?
In what furnace was thy brain?
What the anvil? what dread grasp   15
Dare its deadly terrors clasp?

When the stars threw down their spears,
And water'd heaven with their tears,[3]
Did he smile his work to see?
Did he who made the Lamb make thee?   20

Tyger! Tyger! burning bright
In the forests of the night,
What immortal hand or eye
Dare frame thy fearful symmetry?

The Fly

Little Fly,
Thy summer's play
My thoughtless hand
Has brush'd away.

Am not I   5
A fly like thee?
Or art not thou
A man like me?

For I dance,
And drink, and sing,   10
Till some blind hand
Shall brush my wing.

If thought is life
And strength and breath,
And the want   15
Of thought is death;

Then am I
A happy fly,
If I live
Or if I die.   20

---

1. **Tyger:** Blake's unique spelling is retained; it seems to emphasize the symbolic quality of the animal.
2. **eye:** pronounced "ee" to rhyme with "symmetry" in the next line.
3. **When . . . tears:** These lines suggest some cosmic disaster associated with divine creativity. In other poems by Blake, these images refer more clearly to the angels who threw down their spears and wept in despair when they fell from Heaven with Satan.

The Clod and the Pebble

"Love seeketh not itself to please,
Nor for itself hath any care,
But for another gives its ease,
And builds a Heaven in Hell's despair."

So sung a little Clod of Clay,   5
Trodden with the cattle's feet,
But a Pebble of the brook
Warbled out these metres meet:

"Love seeketh only Self to please,
To bind another to its delight,   10
Joys in another's loss of ease,
And builds a Hell in Heaven's despite."[1]

---

1. **despite:** contempt or scorn.

Getting at Meaning

INTRODUCTION

1. Contrast the tone and mood of this poem with the tone and mood of the introduction to *Songs of Innocence*.

2. Who is the "Holy Word"? What power does the Word have over the "lapsèd soul"? What is the relationship of the Bard with the Holy Word?

3. What is the Bard's vision, as described in the first stanza? How does the idea of vision contrast with that in the introduction to *Songs of Innocence*? What does this contrast suggest about innocence and experience? Explain.

4. How does the role of the poet implied in this introduction differ from that presented in the introduction to *Songs of Innocence*?

5. What is the view of Earth presented in the third stanza? What might Earth represent? Who is calling to the Earth? From where must the Earth return? In the fourth stanza the Earth is described as turning away. From what or whom?

6. Explain the meaning of the final three lines. How might you interpret "break of day"? What is the message in the last two stanzas of the poem?

7. After reading this introduction, what kinds of poems might you expect to find in *Songs of Experience*?

THE TYGER

8. The Tyger embodies pure, vibrant energy in a dark world. What are the qualities of this form of energy?

9. In the fourth stanza, with what other creative process is the creation of the Tyger connected? What does this metaphor suggest about the Tyger?

10. If the Creator of the Tyger also created the Lamb, what striking contrasts exist in the world? Some critics suggest that the human condition and not a divine force is responsible for the existence of the Tyger. Does the poem provide evidence to support this view? Explain.

11. What idea about the Tyger is suggested by ending the poem with a repetition of the first stanza?

THE FLY

12. What idea is emphasized through the comparison of the speaker with the fly? What is the "blind hand" that will "brush . . . [the]wing" of the speaker?

13. In the final stanzas the speaker ponders the value of awareness, or experience. What conclusion does the speaker draw? With what does the speaker associate innocence?

THE CLOD AND THE PEBBLE

14. This poem suggests the existence of two kinds of love. Characterize both kinds. In what way are innocence and experience illustrated by these two ways of expressing love?

15. What are the contrasting concepts of heaven in the first and third stanzas? Relate these concepts to innocence and experience.

Developing Skills in Reading Literature

1. **Imagery.** Images of light and darkness and water recur throughout the poetry of William Blake. Find several examples of these motifs in the poems from *Songs of Innocence* and *Songs of Experience*. Be prepared to discuss how the images relate to the ideas of innocence and experience.

2. **Symbol and Theme.** Much of Blake's poetry is based on contrasting symbols, such as the clod that stands for unselfishness and the pebble that stands for selfishness. In what way are these two symbols especially appropriate in expressing contrasting ideas? When answering this question, consider the physical properties of the clod and the pebble and relate these physical properties to the concepts symbolized. What awareness of life's contradictions is expressed in this poem? What view of human nature is implied?

The Lamb and the Tyger are similar contrasting symbols. How do these symbols represent the duality of innocence and experience? Which seems to be more closely associated with divinity? The force represented by the Tyger is potentially destructive, yet it burns brightly and consistently, illuminating the night. Comment on the message about experience presented through the Tyger.

3. **Rhetorical Question.** Blake makes effective use of rhetorical questions in his poems. "The Tyger," for example, reverberates with one insistent question after another. What is the effect of this questioning? How does the rhythmic intensity of the questions contribute to the meaning? What other poems in both groups illustrate the use of rhetorical questions? Is the effect similar or different from that in "The Tyger"? Explain.

4. **Enjambment.** Enjambment is the continuation of the sense and grammatical construction of a line of poetry onto the next line or of a couplet or stanza onto the succeeding couplet or stanza. Enjambment creates rhythmic and thematic effects that contrast with the effects achieved by the end-stopped lines typical of the eighteenth-century couplet. Find examples of enjambment between stanzas in the introductory poems and in "The Fly." Then compare Blake's lines with the neat, closed couplets of Pope. What contrasting effects do you note? What does Blake's use of enjambment illustrate about the major literary trend of the late eighteenth century?

Developing Writing Skills

Analyzing Theme. The subtitle for the joint edition of *Songs of Innocence* and *Songs of Experience* published in 1794 is "shewing the Two Contrary States of the Human Soul." The innocence and purity of the first lyrics are in sharp contrast with the awareness of reality and the distortion of the child's imaginary sense in the second group of lyrics. Within the poems themselves are contrary ideas such as joy and sadness, fear and hope, and awareness and ignorance. Write an essay in which you discuss specific contraries and what they communicate about innocence and experience. In your essay refer to the following poems and pairs of poems.

"Introduction" to *Songs of Innocence* and "Introduction" to *Songs of Experience*

"The Lamb" and "The Tyger"

"Little Boy Lost" and "Little Boy Found"

"The Fly"

"The Clod and the Pebble"

Conclude the essay by explaining what you think Blake means by *experience* and what the importance of experience seems to be, relative to innocence.

Unit Review   *The Restoration and the Enlightenment*

Understanding the Unit

1. The late seventeenth and eighteenth centuries witnessed significant changes in literary styles and in subject matter. Examine the selections from the works of Dryden, Pope, and Blake. Then comment on the general progression in subject and treatment of subject represented by these selections.

2. The eighteenth century was a great era of reformers, with many writers speaking out against hypocrisy and sham in society. Review the selections by Lady Montague, Addison, Steele, and Swift. Then explain what faults these writers perceived in society and how they went about correcting them. In discussing each writer's approach, be sure to consider the genre in which he or she wrote and the audience for which the writings were intended.

3. In "True Ease in Writing" Pope discusses the importance of blending sound and sense in poetry. Examine the poems by Gray, Burns, and Blake, and comment on the way that the poems exemplify this basic poetic principle.

4. The selections by Pepys, Addison, Lady Montague, and Boswell all express attitudes toward domestic life in general and toward women in particular. Discuss the views of these writers as they are apparent in the selections.

5. This unit includes several examples of satire, among them Pope's "Epistle to Miss Blount" and Burns's "To a Louse." Compare the targets attacked and the satirical tone of these two poems with the subject matter and tone of "A Modest Proposal."

6. Pepys and Dryden were contemporaries, yet each represents a distinct strain in English literature. Pepys wrote as a means of self-expression, while Dryden wrote for an audience made up of the educated, aristocratic, leisured few. Comment on the way their works reflect this basic difference. Use technical terms such as diction, structure, style, tone, imagery and allusion when noting specific characteristics.

7. "A Song for St. Cecilia's Day" and the songs of Robert Burns are similar in that they are meant to be sung, yet they are also different in a number of ways.

Compare and contrast the poems, discussing elements such as structure, rhythm and other sound devices, figurative language, tone, mood, and diction.

Writing

1. The neoclassic position on art as imitation is clearly stated by Samuel Johnson in this excerpt from a didactic novel titled *Rasselas* (1759).

> The business of the poet is to examine, not the individual, but the species. . . . he does not number the streaks of the tulip, or describe the different shades in the verdure of the forest. He is to exhibit in his portraits of nature such prominent and striking features as recall the original to every mind, and must neglect the minuter discriminations in favor of those which are alike obvious to vigilance and carelessness.

Write an essay in which you discuss how Johnson, the critic, would evaluate several selections from this unit, applying the standard expressed in this passage. Choose a variety of selections from the three periods covered in the unit, including at least one selection by a pre-Romantic poet.

2. Pope's epigrams are still appealing because they express unchanging truths about human nature. Other selections in the unit also express universal truths, either explicitly or implicitly. List several selections and identify a concept in each that remains applicable today. Then choose one selection from your list, and write a well developed paragraph explaining why the concept it illustrates is universally true.

3. Blake is said by critics to be in a category all his own, having more in common with the twentieth century than with the eighteenth or nineteenth. Think about the prevailing attitudes toward the following among your contemporaries and within American society as a whole: human nature, society, good and evil, childhood and adulthood, religion and morality, the mystical and the imaginative. Then write an essay in which you explain connections between Blake's ideas and those of twentieth-century Americans. Draw conclusions about Blake's relevance to readers today.

IN A SHOREHAM GARDEN, 1829. *Samuel Palmer.*
Victoria and Albert Museum, Crown Copyright.

Unit 5

The Romantic Period (1798–1832)

OPHELIA, 1852. *John Everett Millais.*
Tate Gallery, London.

The Romantic Tradition

The Romantic Movement swept the Western world in the late eighteenth and early nineteenth centuries. In general, Romanticism was a revolt against science, authority, materialism, and discipline and an affirmation of individuality, imagination, and national heritage. A natural reaction to the strictures of eighteenth-century thought, Romanticism emerged from the same forces that gave rise to the American and French Revolutions and to agitation for political, social, and economic change. In some countries the impact of Romanticism was profound, affecting the very foundations of society. In others Romanticism pervaded philosophy, music, art, and literature but exerted less dramatic influence on the other facets of national life.

The Romantic Period in English literature covers the years between 1798 and 1832. The liberal, creative Romantic spirit that infused literature, however, did not transform English political, economic, and educational institutions, which remained thoroughly conservative and in many ways more akin to the eighteenth century than to the nineteenth. While intellectuals applauded the American and French experiments in democratic government, the ruling classes were alarmed by the specter of political upheaval and the destruction of social barriers. The dichotomy between artistic ideals and official practice existed throughout most of the Romantic Period, until change finally came as the inevitable result of historical and cultural development.

THE POLITICAL SCENE

England had been unusually stable throughout the eighteenth century. The last years of the Stuart monarchs had been peaceful, and when George I became the first Hanoverian king in 1714, the country was prosperous and well ordered by the standards of the day. When his grandson George III became king in 1760, England was still stable, with no hint of revolution in the air.

George III, later called by the poet Percy Bysshe Shelley "an old, mad, blind, despised, and dying king," ruled England during the French and Indian War and the American and French Revolutions. Many commentators argue that George was chiefly responsible for the American Revolution because of his inflexible and unsympathetic attitude toward the colonists. George III was not a particularly intelligent king, and he was bewildered by the unprecedented political events in America and France. A devoted family man, interested in music, he retreated increasingly into his domestic life, and later, into bouts of insanity. The year before the French Revolution, George suffered a major attack of madness, and in 1811 he was declared totally insane. His son George ruled as Prince Regent until the king's death in 1820.

Although George III was not a distinguished king, several of his ministers were impressive. A prominent statesman at the beginning of his reign was William Pitt, whose policies led to the defeat of the French in India and Canada. Pitt urged conciliation of the American colonies, agreeing to any settlement short of independence. His son, also William Pitt, became Prime Minister in 1783. A liberal Tory, he urged the practice of general elections and the institution of Parliamentary reforms as a way to prevent revolution in England. Another well known statesman who initially shared this goal was Edmund Burke, a Whig politician. His *Reflections on the Revolution in France* (1790), however, attacked the revolution and crystallized opposition to all liberal ideas.

WAR IN EUROPE

Numerous English writers and citizens felt initial sympathy for the French Revolution, but when the moderate revolutionary party fell from power, English sympathy began to dissipate. During the Reign of Terror, radicals massacred and persecuted thousands of French aristocrats and middle-class citizens, to the horror of Englishmen who were all too aware of the mass of restless laborers within their own country. For nearly twenty-five years, all efforts at reform were suppressed in the fear that reform would lead to anarchy as it had in post-revolutionary France.

When France invaded the Netherlands in 1792, Britain entered a war that ultimately involved most of Europe and lasted for over twenty years. During this time, a penniless French aristocrat came up through the ranks of the military and eventually became emperor of France and conqueror of Europe. This man was Napoleon Bonaparte, a brilliant military strategist and charismatic leader who by 1812 had established French control over much of Europe.

In 1812 the United States became implicated in the European conflict in protest against the impressment of American sailors into the British navy, arbitrary searches of ships on the high seas, and other abuses that resulted from England's militant war against

French commerce. The War of 1812 lasted for three years and ended in an American victory over England that had little impact on the balance of power in Europe.

A number of factors contributed to the eventual triumph of England and her allies over the forces of Napoleon. England had superior naval strength, daring admirals such as Horatio Nelson, and determined, experienced sailors. Also, the French economy was in shambles due to decades of war, political upheaval, and economic sanctions by enemy nations. Militarily, Napoleon had over-extended himself, penetrating as far east as Moscow in one of the most disastrous campaigns in military history. By this time, too, most of the unconquered nations and principalities were allied against France, formidable opposition even for Napoleon.

Napoleon abdicated in April, 1814, and was exiled to the Mediterranean island of Elba. Within the year, he escaped, rallied his still-loyal troops, resumed the French throne, and set out to reconquer Europe. British troops under the Duke of Wellington, the "Iron Duke," defeated Napoleon for the last time at Waterloo, in June, 1815. The deposed emperor spent his final days in exile on the remote island of St. Helena, while representatives of the victorious powers attempted to restore order along pre-revolutionary lines.

After the defeat of Napoleon, English foreign policy became more liberal, due in part to the resurgence of the long-dormant liberal spirit, in part to economic self-interest. England supported several South American countries in their revolts against Spain and thus secured lucrative trade arrangements. In the Near East, Russia was threatening to occupy territories that belonged to the disintegrating Turkish Ottoman Empire. When the Greeks rebelled against the Turks, England intervened on the side of the revolutionaries to prevent Russia from annexing Greece and endangering England's Mediterranean trade routes.

THE SOCIAL AND ECONOMIC SCENE

By the beginning of the Romantic Age, England was an industrial as well as an agricultural land with a well established colonial system and a worldwide network of trade. The Industrial and Agricultural Revolutions had brought increased prosperity to the middle and upper classes but degrading poverty to the families employed in the factories and mills. Living and working conditions for industrial laborers were generally appalling. The prevailing economic philosophy in Britain was *laissez faire* capitalism, which dictated that individuals be allowed to pursue their own private interests without legislative interference from the government. Laborers were at the mercy of factory owners, who exacted long hours for low pay. Child labor was common, as were industrial accidents.

The victory over Napoleon enhanced England's prestige, yet war also aggravated the domestic problems associated with industrial development. Once the fighting had ended and British industry no longer needed to supply a large army and navy, businesses folded and unemployment rose precipitously. Discharged veterans swelled the ranks of the unemployed. Agitation through petitions, hunger strikes, and bloody riots mushroomed in the postwar years.

Before the war with France, liberals had achieved progressive legislation that improved the prison system, the criminal code, and trade and customs regulations. During the war years, however, the reactionary mood of the country stifled the thrust toward reform that was a natural outgrowth of Romanticism. After the war, publicity about industrial conditions led reform-minded Britons to seek political changes, specifically, an end to the restrictions on trade unions, laws to protect factory workers, universal suffrage, and above all Parliamentary reforms. The first major reform bill came at the end of the Romantic Period. The Reform Bill of 1832 distributed the seats in Parliament to create more equitable representation, and it granted the franchise to middle-class men. The bill broke the monopoly of the landed gentry in Parliament and laid the groundwork for the reform legislation of the Victorian Period.

ROMANTICISM IN THE ARTS

The Romantic Movement had a great impact on English music, architecture, and art, as well as on literature. The German composer Ludwig von Beethoven effected a Romantic revolution in music that eventually touched England. In architecture the formalism of the eighteenth century gave way to more natural forms, a transformation that affected landscape architecture as well. The rigid geometric patterns of the neoclassical garden were replaced by random shapes and serpentine lines. The landscape architecture of Capability Brown typified the new style, in which fences were buried in ditches known as "ha-has" so that free-flowing vistas would not be interrupted.

The Romantic spirit also was manifested in painting and sculpture. William Blake, the great poet and illustrator, introduced Romanticism into British art. The English landscape painters John Constable and John Turner continued the Romantic tradition by emphasizing the warmth and beauty of nature in their work. Later in the nineteenth century the English Pre-Raphaelite painters continued the Romantic style, with some eccentric changes.

LITERATURE: THE FLOWERING OF ROMANTICISM

The word *Romantic* was first used in Germany in 1798 by the critics Friedrich and August von Schlegel. In many ways Romanticism as a literary style began in Germany, among such *Sturm und Drang* ("storm and stress") writers as Johann Wolfgang von Goethe and Johann Christoph Friedrich von Schiller.

In England the Romantics were writers who revolted against the order, propriety, and traditionalism of the Age of Reason. The Neoclassicists had venerated the literary achievements of the ancient Greek and Roman writers; they had great respect for rules, both in literature and in society, and they wrote about the human being as an integral part of organized society, rather than as an individual. The Romantics, in direct contrast, searched for freer artistic forms, outside the classical tradition. Romantic poets abandoned the measured, witty heroic couplet for the musical rhythms, richly evocative language, and stanza forms of Medieval and Renaissance poetry. Romantic writers concerned themselves with the primitive, the bizarre, the irregular, and the unique, yet they also looked for fresh and lively ways to convey the concrete and the familiar.

To the Romantics the individual was far more interesting than society, and the individual's relationship to nature was of primary concern. They tended to view society as problematic and corrupt, unlike nature, which they perceived as vital and nurturing, a source of beauty, truth, and wisdom. Instead of reason, the Romantics revered emotion and viewed poetry as "the spontaneous overflow of powerful feelings." The lyric poem, with its emphasis on subjective experiences, thoughts, feelings, and desires, was the most popular literary form among the Romantic poets.

The poets William Wordsworth and Samuel Taylor Coleridge ushered in Romanticism with their startling declaration of poetic aims in *Lyrical Ballads* (1798). The two poets had met in 1795, and, along with Wordsworth's sister Dorothy, they were intent on seeking new modes of literary expression. Wordsworth had traveled extensively in both Germany and France, where he had become deeply committed to the revolutionary cause. He became a poet of the common man, writing to capture intimate experiences in natural language, without concern for artificial rules and conventions. For both Wordsworth and Coleridge nature and meditation were linked, with insight into the human experience flowing freely from communion with nature. Coleridge also wrote about the bizarre and the unnatural, reviving the magic, mystery, superstition, and folklore that had characterized earlier literature. Later in life both Wordsworth and Coleridge turned from radical ideals, becoming conservative upholders of traditional political, social, and religious institutions.

Wordsworth and Coleridge are considered "first-generation" Romantics. A "second generation" followed; these poets were Percy Bysshe Shelley, John Keats, and George Gordon, Lord Byron. Full of raw talent, revolutionary optimism, and admiration for Greek and Italian culture, these three poets produced some of the finest lyrics in the English language. All three died young. Keats died at twenty-five of tuberculosis. Shelley eulogized Keats in the poem "Adonais," written only months before Shelley himself died in a boating accident at age twenty-nine. Byron died of fever in Greece at age thirty-six.

The Romantic Period produced two great novelists, Jane Austen and Sir Walter Scott. Austen remained in many ways a neoclassical writer, producing ironic comedies of manners, such as her incomparable *Pride and Prejudice* (1813). Her works, though, contain Romantic elements: a focus on the details of daily life and a preoccupation with character and personality. Scott was a complete Romantic, producing historical novels and narrative verse, such as *Ivanhoe* (1819) and *The Lady of the Lake* (1810), that show a typical Romantic interest in superstitions and legends, in the Medieval Period, and in Scottish history and culture. Just prior to the Romantic Period, William Godwin, a political theorist, wrote what might be called the first "novel of purpose." In *Caleb Williams* (1794) he actively promotes specific political and moral theories. Godwin's daughter Mary Wollstonecraft Shelley married Percy Shelley and herself became a writer. Her novel *Frankenstein* (1817) combines the novel of purpose with a form already popular in England, the Gothic novel of mystery and terror.

The Romantic Age also had its share of essayists, biographers, and journalists. The poets themselves wrote significant critical works, such as Wordsworth's "Preface" to *Lyrical Ballads*, Coleridge's *Biographia Literaria* (1817), and Shelley's *A Defense of Poetry* (1821). Keats's letters are justly famous. Charles Lamb, one of the great English essayists, wrote during this period, as did Leigh Hunt, William Hazlitt, and Thomas DeQuincey, other well known essayists and critics. Like the poets, these writers rebelled against eighteenth-century literary forms and made their prose more personal and casual.

Despite great admiration for Shakespeare, the Romantics did not produce much original drama. Several of the poets did write poetic dramas: Coleridge wrote *Remorse* (1813); Byron, *Manfred: A Dramatic Poem* (1817); and Shelley, *The Cenci, a Tragedy in Five Acts* (1819) and *Prometheus Unbound* (1820). These poems were not successful as drama, however.

Romanticism was the dominant expressive mode in the first

Literature

- Charles and Mary Lamb publish *Tales from Shakespeare* for children

- Goethe publishes first novel in romantic genre

- Sir Walter Scott (1771–18 publishes *The Lady of the Lake*

- Wordsworth and Coleridge publish *Lyrical Ballads* anonymously

- Samuel Taylor Coleridge (1772–1834) publishes "The Rime of the Ancient Mariner" in *Lyrical Ballads*

- William Wordsworth (1770–1850) publishes second edition of *Lyrical Ballads* with famous *Preface*

| 1795 | 1800 | 1805 | 1810 |

History

- Turner, English landscape painter, exhibits his work

- Haydn composes *The Creation*

- Beethoven composes *Symphyony No. 1,* exemplifying romanticism in music

- United Kingdom of Great Britain and Ireland is established

- Napoleon is crowned Emperor

- Lord Nelson defeats French at Trafalgar

half of the nineteenth century and a major artistic strain in the late nineteenth and twentieth centuries. The end of the Romantic Age, however, is set at 1832, the year of the first far-reaching reform bill and of the death of Sir Walter Scott. After that year, gradual shifts in perception and a changing political, social, and economic environment began to temper unabashed Romanticism and to prompt new kinds of creative responses.

- Jane Austen (1775–1816) publishes *Pride and Prejudice*

- Percy Bysshe Shelley (1792–1822) completes *Prometheus Unbound*

- Keats writes major poems between January and September (1819)

- Sir Walter Scott (1771–1832) publishes *Ivanhoe*

- George Gordon, Lord Byron (1788–1824) publishes first two cantos of *Childe Harold's Pilgrimage*

- Charles Lamb (1775–1834) contributes essays to *London Magazine*

- Shelley writes *A Defense of Poetry*

- William Hazlitt (1778–1830) writes essay "My First Acquaintance with Poets"

- Lord Byron joins Greek war for liberation from the Turks

- Leigh Hunt (1784–1859) publishes poem "Story of Rimini"

- Mary Wollstonecraft Shelley (1797–1851) publishes *Frankenstein*

- Coleridge publishes *Biographia Literaria*

- John Keats (1795–1821) publishes first book, *Poems*

1815	1820	1825	1830

- George, Prince of Wales, acts as regent for George III who is declared incurably insane

- Constable, English painter, exhibits works

- George III dies

- U.S. Congress declares war on Britain

- George IV assumes throne

- Napoleon invades Russia

- Monroe Doctrine warns European nations to cease colonization of Western Hemisphere

- Napoleon abdicates and is exiled

- Reform Bill redistributes seats in Parliament

- British forces defeat Napoleon at Waterloo

- Congress of Vienna meets to restore European balance of power

The Development of the English Language

THE ROMANTIC PERIOD

Changes in the English language during the past two hundred years have been more subtle than those during the time of Middle English or during the Great Vowel Shift. Nevertheless, the changes have been broad in scope. The Romantic Period was a period of freedom in literature and in language, a reaction against the rationalism and materialism of the Age of Reason. During this period, the concept of "acceptable" language broadened, and the distance between the language of scholars and of aristocrats and that of the common person narrowed.

English in a Changing Society

At the beginning of the Romantic Period, the American and French Revolutions inspired widespread hopes for more just societies. By the close of the period, the passage of the Reform Bill of 1832 in England and the emergence of Jacksonian democracy in the United States showed that those hopes were not in vain. Democracy and education were forces for change in these societies and also were important factors in the evolution of the language.

Democracy and education are closely entwined. Democratic societies depend upon citizens who can read and write, while education creates expectations among the educated that only democratic institutions can fulfill. During the nineteenth century, previously unschooled segments of society began to receive formal education, which led to a powerful drive toward standardization of the English language. Indeed, during this century standardization was an ideal, and correct usage was not merely admired but revered.

Broadening democracy brought the middle and upper classes closer together in their language. After the first inexpensive newspaper began in 1816, widespread circulation of newspapers had the effect of bringing the spoken standard closer to the written and of making colloquialisms more accepted. With Romanticism and its admiration of the common person came more interest in regional dialects and fresh coinages, as well as a wider use of slang. Lord Byron and other Romantics used colloquialisms in their writing, to the dismay of more conservative critics.

English in America

Geographic and political separation from England resulted in the emergence of a distinct American dialect, and the American nationalistic spirit made patriots eager to assert that American English was every bit as "correct" as British English. As immigration into the United States created an ever-growing polyglot population, the need for a single standard of English increased. Opportunities for upward social mobility provided an incentive to learn the kind of English associated with the upper classes, the English of the powerful and prestigious.

The language spoken in America was already quite different from that spoken in England. However, marked differences in vocabulary did not come until later in the century, when new inventions were given different names on opposite sides of the Atlantic. A Britisher, for example, rides a *lift* and drives a car, whch uses *petrol* and has a *boot* and a *bonnet;* an American rides an *elevator* and puts *gas* in a car, which has a *trunk* and a *hood.* Words and idioms that are characteristic of the English of the United States are known as Americanisms.

Noah Webster's Influence

A major figure in the development of American English was the lexicographer Noah Webster. His *Grammatical Institute of the English Language* appeared in three parts between 1783 and 1785 and established him as the leading American expert on the language. Although he was schooled in neither etymology nor linguistics, his genius for definition made his works enormously successful and vastly influential. Webster's *Elementary Spelling Book* was used in pioneer homes as a weapon against illiteracy, and his *American Dictionary of the English Language* (1828) became an American institution. Through Webster's influence the *u* was eliminated from words such as *colour* and *flavour* and the *k* was omitted from words such as *traffick* and *publick.*

English Around the World

By the end of the Romantic Period westward expansion in the United States had taken English into the interior of North America. The British empire continued to expand, and English became the language of government and international commerce in India and in parts of Southeast Asia, the Far East, and Africa. The language was already well established in the older colonies in the Caribbean, South America, and the South Pacific. British expansion made English an important language in far-reaching areas of the globe, and it swelled English dictionaries with thousands of words borrowed from all parts of the world.

Contact with new territories brought new products and activities and the words to identify them. From India came *cashmere, shampoo, jungle,* and *pajamas.* From Russia came *vodka,* from Turkey *coffee,* from Malaya *bamboo,* and from Haiti *barbecue.* Improved communication and travel reinforced this addition of words until virtually every nation gained representation in the English lexicon.

William Wordsworth

1770–1850

Considered the greatest of the English Romantic poets, William Wordsworth described reality in language so lovely that his poems seem to confer a deeply spiritual beauty on their subjects and through them on their readers and life itself. The sheer beauty of his lines, standing in sharp contrast to the stilted diction of much eighteenth-century poetry, was so striking that Wordsworth seemed to have reinvented poetry. His definition of poetry as "the spontaneous overflow of powerful feelings" that "takes its origin from emotion recollected in tranquillity," although an unconventional idea in its time, now seems to be a self-evident and permanent truth.

Born at Cockermouth in the Lake District of northern England, Wordsworth spent much of his boyhood roaming the countryside. His mother died when he was eight, and his father died five years later, circumstances that may have contributed to the aimlessness of Wordsworth's youth and young manhood. Thanks to his uncle, he went to Cambridge, where he took his degree in 1791. He then went on a walking tour of France, where his youthful enthusiasm was fired by the still-idealistic causes of the Revolution.

The next few years were difficult for Wordsworth. He fell in love with Annette Vallon, who bore him a daughter, Caroline, but circumstances prevented their marrying. As time passed, he and Annette drifted apart. Racked by guilt, disillusioned by the excesses of the French Revolution, ambivalent about virtually everything ("wearied out with contrarieties"), he was on the verge of emotional collapse.

In 1795 Wordsworth settled at Racedown, Dorsetshire, with his beloved sister Dorothy, who was to be a lifelong confidante and emotional bulwark. In June of that year, he was visited by Samuel Taylor Coleridge, who had already discerned greatness in the few poems Wordsworth had published. An instant bond was formed, and the Wordsworths moved to Alfoxden to be near Coleridge. There Wordsworth and Coleridge were in almost daily contact for a year. The result was *Lyrical Ballads*

WILLIAM WORDSWORTH, 1818. *B. R. Haydon.*
National Portrait Gallery, London.

(1798), the appearance of which announced a new literary epoch. Coleridge, whose realm was the supernatural, contributed "The Rime of the Ancient Mariner," while the more prolific Wordsworth, whose realm was common life, contributed many splendid poems, among them "Lines Written a Few Miles Above Tintern Abbey." In 1799 the Wordsworths returned to the Lake District, and in 1802 Wordsworth married Mary Hutchinson, whom he had known since childhood.

During his final forty years, Wordsworth occasionally wrote a splendid poem when moved by powerful emotion, but he only infrequently recaptured the poetic power of his earlier years. Yet even as he wrote less, his fame grew. A new generation, raised on the Romantic taste Wordsworth had helped to create, recognized the genius of works such as "Ode: Intimations of Immortality," and it was considered entirely fitting when he was appointed poet laureate upon the death of Robert Southey in 1843. After a short illness, Wordsworth died on April 23, 1850.

Lines Composed a Few Miles Above Tintern Abbey

On Revisiting the Banks of the Wye During a Tour, July 13, 1798

Tintern Abbey is a ruined monastery in the valley of the Wye River in Monmouthshire, on the Welsh border. Wordsworth had visited these ruins on a walking tour in 1793; five years later he returned with his sister Dorothy.

Five years have passed; five summers, with the length
Of five long winters! and again I hear
These waters, rolling from their mountain springs
With a soft inland murmur.—Once again
Do I behold these steep and lofty cliffs,   5
That on a wild secluded scene impress
Thoughts of more deep seclusion; and connect
The landscape with the quiet of the sky.
The day is come when I again repose
Here, under this dark sycamore, and view   10
These plots of cottage ground, these orchard tufts,
Which at this season, with their unripe fruits,
Are clad in one green hue, and lose themselves
'Mid groves and copses. Once again I see
These hedgerows, hardly hedgerows, little lines   15
Of sportive wood run wild: these pastoral farms,
Green to the very door; and wreaths of smoke
Sent up, in silence, from among the trees!
With some uncertain notice, as might seem
Of vagrant dwellers in the houseless woods,   20
Or of some hermit's cave, where by his fire
The hermit sits alone.
                   These beauteous forms,
Through a long absence, have not been to me
As is a landscape to a blind man's eye:
But oft, in lonely rooms, and 'mid the din   25
Of towns and cities, I have owed to them
In hours of weariness, sensations sweet,
Felt in the blood, and felt along the heart;
And passing even into my purer mind,
With tranquil restoration:—feelings too   30
Of unremembered pleasure: such, perhaps,

TINTERN ABBEY (watercolor), 1834. *J. M. W. Turner.*
Victoria and Albert Museum, Crown Copyright.

As have no slight or trivial influence
On that best portion of a good man's life,
His little, nameless, unremembered acts
Of kindness and of love. Nor less, I trust,   35
To them I may have owed another gift,
Of aspect more sublime; that blessed mood,
In which the burthen of the mystery,
In which the heavy and the weary weight
Of all this unintelligible world,   40
Is lightened:—that serene and blessed mood
In which the affections gently lead us on,—
Until, the breath of this corporeal frame
And even the motion of our human blood
Almost suspended, we are laid asleep   45
In body, and become a living soul:
While with an eye made quiet by thy power
Of harmony, and the deep power of joy,
We see into the life of things.
                              If this
Be but a vain belief, yet, oh! how oft—   50
In darkness and amid the many shapes
Of joyless daylight; when the fretful stir
Unprofitable, and the fever of the world,
Have hung upon the beatings of my heart—
How oft, in spirit, have I turned to thee,   55
O sylvan Wye! thou wanderer through the woods,
How often has my spirit turned to thee!
  And now, with gleams of half-extinguished thought,
With many recognitions dim and faint,
And somewhat of a sad perplexity,   60
The picture of the mind revives again;
While here I stand, not only with the sense
Of present pleasure, but with pleasing thoughts
That in this moment there is life and food
For future years. And so I dare to hope,   65
Though changed, no doubt, from what I was when first
I came among these hills; when like a roe
I bounded o'er the mountains, by the sides
Of the deep rivers, and the lonely streams,
Wherever nature led: more like a man   70
Flying from something that he dreads, than one
Who sought the thing he loved. For nature then
(The coarser pleasures of my boyish days,
And their glad animal movements all gone by)
To me was all in all.—I cannot paint   75
What then I was. The sounding cataract

Haunted me like a passion; the tall rock,
The mountain, and the deep and gloomy wood,
Their colors and their forms, were then to me
An appetite; a feeling and a love,   80
That had no need of a remoter charm,
By thought supplied, nor any interest
Unborrowed from the eye.—That time is past,
And all its aching joys are now no more,
And all its dizzy raptures. Not for this   85
Faint I, nor mourn nor murmur; other gifts
Have followed; for such loss, I would believe,
Abundant recompense. For I have learned
To look on nature, not as in the hour
Of thoughtless youth; but hearing oftentimes   90
The still, sad music of humanity,
Nor harsh nor grating, though of ample power
To chasten and subdue. And I have felt
A presence that disturbs me with the joy
Of elevated thoughts; a sense sublime,   95
Of something far more deeply interfused,
Whose dwelling is the light of setting suns,
And the round ocean and the living air,
And the blue sky, and in the mind of man;
A motion and a spirit, that impels   100
All thinking things, all objects of all thought,
And rolls through all things. Therefore am I still
A lover of the meadows and the woods,
And mountains; and of all that we behold
From this green earth; of all the mighty world   105
Of eye, and ear,—both what they half create,
And what perceive; well pleased to recognize
In nature and the language of the sense,
The anchor of my purest thoughts, the nurse,
The guide, the guardian of my heart, and soul   110
Of all my moral being.
                  Nor perchance,
If I were not thus taught, should I the more
Suffer my genial spirits to decay:
For thou art with me here upon the banks
Of this fair river; thou my dearest friend,[1]   115
My dear, dear friend; and in thy voice I catch
The language of my former heart, and read
My former pleasures in the shooting lights

------

1. **thou . . . friend:** Wordsworth's sister Dorothy.

Of thy wild eyes. Oh! yet a little while
May I behold in thee what I was once, 120
My dear, dear sister! and this prayer I make,
Knowing that Nature never did betray
The heart that loved her; 'tis her privilege,
Through all the years of this our life, to lead
From joy to joy: for she can so inform 125
The mind that is within us, so impress
With quietness and beauty, and so feed
With lofty thoughts, that neither evil tongues,
Rash judgments, nor the sneers of selfish men,
Nor greetings where no kindness is, nor all 130
The dreary intercourse of daily life
Shall e'er prevail against us, or disturb
Our cheerful faith, that all which we behold
Is full of blessings. Therefore let the moon
Shine on thee in thy solitary walk; 135
And let the misty mountain-winds be free
To blow against thee: and, in after years,
When these wild ecstasies shall be matured
Into a sober pleasure; when thy mind
Shall be a mansion for all lovely forms, 140
Thy memory be as a dwelling-place
For all sweet sounds and harmonies; oh! then,
If solitude, or fear, or pain, or grief,
Should be thy portion, with what healing thoughts
Of tender joy wilt thou remember me, 145
And these my exhortations! Nor, perchance—
If I should be where I no more can hear
Thy voice, nor catch from thy wild eyes these gleams
Of past existence—wilt thou then forget
That on the banks of this delightful stream 150
We stood together; and that I, so long
A worshipper of Nature, hither came
Unwearied in that service: rather say
With warmer love—oh! with far deeper zeal
Of holier love. Nor wilt thou then forget 155
That after many wanderings, many years
  Of absence,
These steep woods and lofty cliffs,
And this green pastoral landscape, were to me
More dear, both for themselves and for thy sake!

Getting at Meaning

1. What does the speaker mean by "These beauteous forms" in line 23? How and in what circumstances have they affected him since his last visit?

2. On returning to the scene, what has the speaker lost, compared with his first visit five years earlier? What has he gained in compensation?

3. What does the speaker find significant in his sister's reactions to the scene?

Developing Skills in Reading Literature

1. **Prose and Poetry.** In the "Preface" to *Lyrical Ballads,* Wordsworth states, "My purpose was to imitate, and, as far as possible, to adopt the very language of men." Later, he explains that, except for meter, there is little distinction between good poetry and good prose.

Notice that this poem is written in blank verse, which is used often for long poems, whether dramatic, philosophical, or narrative. Why is blank verse an appropriate form, in light of Wordsworth's stated purpose? How does it suit the pace and mood of the poem? The structural units of this poem are called "verse-paragraphs." How are these groupings of lines similar to paragraphs? Judging from this poem, how might Wordsworth describe "good prose"?

2. **Meter.** One means by which a poet can produce variety in blank verse is by shifting the stresses among the syllables, thus altering the feet. Two variant types of feet in English metrics are the spondee and the pyrrhic. The spondee is made up of two equally accented syllables, as in *dówntówn* or *deép peáce.* The effect is to slow or halt the pace of the line. The pyrrhic, on the other hand, consists of two unstressed syllables, as in *ŏf thĕ.* It tends to speed the line along. Scan the first five lines of this poem. How does Wordsworth vary the rhythm with spondees and pyrrhics? How is this speeding up and slowing down appropriate to the meaning of the lines?

Other ways of producing metrical variety are the caesura and enjambment. Where do caesuras occur in lines 1-5? Which lines are enjambed, or run on? How does line 8 provide a balance or contrast to the metrical variations that precede it? Choose another group of eight or more lines, and analyze the meter, identifying metrical variations and commenting on their overall effect.

3. **Imagery.** The rich imagery in the first section of this poem allows the reader to share the poet's physical perception of the scene and also his tranquil, contemplative response to the scene. Describe the physical setting, as it is re-created through imagery. Then discuss the way that the imagery establishes the tone and the mood of the poem, noting particularly evocative words and phrases.

4. **Theme.** Wordsworth's famous definition of poetry is "the spontaneous overflow of powerful feelings . . . recollected in tranquillity." This poem is concerned with such recollections and with the contrast between innocence and experience. The poet, returning to a remembered scene, feels more strongly the deep spiritual power in nature and its connection with humanity. What passage describes the insights he gained from his earlier recollections? Turning to the present moment, where does the poet best describe the gifts in perception and understanding that have come with the intervening years? What lines include human beings as a part of the poet's vision of nature? In line 91 why might he have used the phrase "the still, sad music" to describe humanity? How does Wordsworth view the value of experience? How does his concept of experience compare with that of William Blake?

Developing Writing Skills

Using Comparisons and Contrasts. Recall a place that is important to you, or that impressed you strongly, and that you have visited more than once. In a "then and now" pattern of development, describe the place as it first seemed to you, and then as it appeared on a later visit. It may be that the place itself changed, or it may be that your feelings about it altered or matured, as did Wordsworth's feelings about the countryside surrounding Tintern Abbey.

I Wandered Lonely As a Cloud

I wandered lonely as a cloud
That floats on high o'er vales and hills,
When all at once I saw a crowd,
A host, of golden daffodils;
Beside the lake, beneath the trees,   5
Fluttering and dancing in the breeze.

Continuous as the stars that shine
And twinkle on the milky way,
They stretched in never-ending line
Along the margin of a bay: 10
Ten thousand saw I at a glance,
Tossing their heads in sprightly dance.

The waves beside them danced; but they
Outdid the sparkling waves in glee:
A poet could not but be gay,   15
In such a jocund company:
I gazed—and gazed—but little thought
What wealth the show to me had brought:

For oft, when on my couch I lie
In vacant or in pensive mood,   20
They flash upon that inward eye
Which is the bliss of solitude;
And then my heart with pleasure fills,
And dances with the daffodils.

Getting at Meaning

1. What is the immediate effect upon the speaker of seeing the daffodils?

2. What is the unexpected effect of the experience?

Developing Skills in Reading Literature

1. **Meter and Rhyme Scheme.** Considering both the kind and the number of feet in each line of this poem, identify the metrical pattern. Then chart the rhyme scheme. Is it the same for each stanza?

In "Preface" to *Lyrical Ballads,* Wordsworth acknowledges the value of meter in ordering ideas and in heightening the pleasure of reading poetry, as long as the meter does not interfere with passion. Comment on the way that this poem exemplifies Wordsworth's critical theory regarding meter.

2. **Personification.** In "Preface" to *Lyrical Ballads,* Wordsworth states, ". . . personifications are utterly rejected, as an ordinary device to elevate the style, and raise it above prose. . . . They are a figure of speech occasionally prompted by passion, and I have made use of them as such." Where is personification ·used in this poem? What qualities does it emphasize in the things being described? Is the personification here "prompted by passion" and thus a justifiable device in the context of the poem? Explain.

3. **Diction.** The opening simile compares the lonely speaker to a floating cloud. Does this suggest a painful kind of loneliness? What words in lines 3 and 4 present an alternative to lonely isolation? What other words in the poem carry forward the idea of happy commingling? What words pick up the idea of loneliness?

What does the phrase "bliss of solitude" suggest about being alone?

4. **Imagery.** Two kinds of images predominate in this poem: images suggesting movement and those suggesting light. Identify these images. What is their effect upon the mood of the poem?

Developing Vocabulary

Word Origins. The speaker, initially lonely, discovers jocund company. Look up the meaning of *jocund* in a dictionary. What other words in the third stanza convey a similar meaning? What is the root origin of *jocund*? Can you find three other words that derive from the same root?

She Was a Phantom of Delight

She[1] was a Phantom of delight
When first she gleamed upon my sight;
A lovely Apparition, sent
To be a moment's ornament;
Her eyes as stars of Twilight fair;   5
Like Twilight's, too, her dusky hair;
But all things else about her drawn
From May-time and the cheerful Dawn;
A dancing Shape, an Image gay,
To haunt, to startle, and waylay.   10

---

1. **She:** Mary Hutchinson, Wordsworth's wife.

I saw her upon nearer view,
A Spirit, yet a Woman too!
Her household motions light and free,
And steps of virgin liberty;
A countenance in which did meet   15
Sweet records, promises as sweet;
A Creature not too bright or good
For human nature's daily food;
For transient sorrows, simple wiles,
Praise, blame, love, kisses, tears, and smiles.   20

And now I see with eye serene
The very pulse of the machine;
A Being breathing thoughtful breath,
A Traveler between life and death;
The reason firm, the temperate will,   25
Endurance, foresight, strength, and skill;
A perfect Woman, nobly planned,
To warn, to comfort, and command;
And yet a Spirit still, and bright
With something of angelic light.   30

Getting at Meaning

1. This poem records several stages in the speaker's perception of the woman. What are these stages? How do they reflect the changes in the speaker's viewpoint? How does the poem's form reinforce the development of idea?

2. What does the speaker mean by "human nature's daily food" in line 18?

3. In line 24 the speaker describes the woman as "A Traveler between life and death." How is this appropriate to the qualities emphasized in the third stanza?

Developing Skills in Reading Literature

1. **Imagery.** On first glimpsing the woman, the speaker sees her as a "phantom of delight." What other words or phrases in the first stanza reinforce this "phantom" image? What does this image suggest about the speaker's reaction to her? Is there any suggestion of this same quality at the end of the poem?

2. **Diction.** Does the diction in the third stanza tend to be abstract or concrete? Do you think this makes the poem more or less effective? Find one unusual phrase that is an exception to this tendency. Explain its meaning and its effect on the reader.

Composed upon Westminster Bridge, September 3, 1802

Earth has not anything to show more fair:
Dull would he be of soul who could pass by
A sight so touching in its majesty:
This City now doth, like a garment, wear
The beauty of the morning; silent, bare,   5
Ships, towers, domes, theaters, and temples lie
Open unto the fields, and to the sky;
All bright and glittering in the smokeless air.
Never did sun more beautifully steep
In his first splendor, valley, rock, or hill;   10
Ne'er saw I, never felt, a calm so deep!
The river glideth at his own sweet will:
Dear God! the very houses seem asleep;
And all that mighty heart is lying still!

The World Is Too Much with Us

The world is too much with us; late and soon,
Getting and spending, we lay waste our powers:
Little we see in Nature that is ours;
We have given our hearts away, a sordid boon![1]
This sea that bares her bosom to the moon;   5
The winds that will be howling at all hours,
And are upgathered now like sleeping flowers;
For this, for everything, we are out of tune;
It moves us not.—Great God! I'd rather be
A Pagan suckled in a creed outworn;   10
So might I, standing on this pleasant lea,
Have glimpses that would make me less forlorn;
Have sight of Proteus rising from the sea;
Or hear old Triton[2] blow his wreathèd horn.

---

1. **boon:** a favor requested.
2. **Proteus** (prō′ tē əs) ... **Triton** (trīt′ n): sea gods in Greek mythology.

London, 1802

Milton! thou shouldst be living at this hour:
England hath need of thee: she is a fen[1]
Of stagnant waters: altar, sword, and pen,
Fireside, the heroic wealth of hall and bower,[2]
Have forfeited their ancient English dower   5
Of inward happiness. We are selfish men;
Oh! raise us up, return to us again;
And give us manners, virtue, freedom, power.
Thy soul was like a Star, and dwelt apart;
Thou hadst a voice whose sound was like the sea: 10
Pure as the naked heavens, majestic, free,
So didst thou travel on life's common way,
In cheerful godliness; and yet thy heart
The lowliest duties on herself did lay.

---

1. **fen:** a bog.
2. **hall and bower:** The hall and bower were the main rooms of large Anglo-Saxon houses.

It Is a Beauteous Evening, Calm and Free

It is a beauteous evening, calm and free,
The holy time is quiet as a Nun
Breathless with adoration; the broad sun
Is sinking down in its tranquillity;
The gentleness of heaven broods o'er the Sea: 5
Listen! the mighty Being is awake,
And doth with his eternal motion make
A sound like thunder—everlastingly.
Dear Child![1] dear Girl! that walkest with me here,
If thou appear untouched by solemn thought,   10
Thy nature is not therefore less divine:
Thou liest in Abraham's bosom[2] all the year;
And worship'st at the Temple's inner shrine,
God being with thee when we know it not.

---

1. **Dear Child:** Wordsworth's daughter Caroline.
2. **in Abraham's bosom:** in the presence of God.

MORTLAKE TERRACE, 1826. J. M. W. Turner.
National Gallery of Art, Washington, D. C.
Andrew W. Mellon Collection, 1937.

Getting at Meaning

COMPOSED UPON WESTMINSTER BRIDGE, SEPTEMBER 3, 1802

1. What is the emotional effect of the scene on the speaker? Where does the poem indicate this?

2. In what way does the speaker establish a relationship between a city scene and the beauty of nature?

3. Explain the phrase "that mighty heart" in line 14. What do the exclamations in this and the preceding line suggest to the reader?

THE WORLD IS TOO MUCH WITH US

4. Do *world* and *nature* mean the same thing in this poem, or different things? How could the world be "too much with us"?

5. Why would the speaker rather be a pagan? What qualities does the speaker seem to attach to the word *pagan*?

LONDON, 1802

6. According to the speaker, what is wrong with England in 1802?

7. Notice, after the semicolon in line 13, the words "and yet." What qualities of Milton are being contrasted in the sestet of the sonnet?

IT IS A BEAUTEOUS EVENING, CALM AND FREE

8. Notice that the octave of this sonnet is concerned with the natural scene, and the sestet is concerned with the child. What do both parts have in common?

9. How is the speaker's response to the experience different from the child's?

10. In lines 6–8, what sound is being described?

Developing Skills in Reading Literature

1. **Sonnet.** Is "Composed upon Westminster Bridge" a Petrarchan (Italian) or a Shakespearean (English) sonnet? In "The World Is Too Much with Us," how does the octave-sestet arrangement coincide with the poem's ideas? What kind of sonnet is "London, 1802"? Does its form reflect its content?

These sonnets do not end with a couplet as do many Elizabethan sonnets. Why might Wordsworth have avoided using the closing couplet?

2. **Personification.** Where in "Composed upon Westminster Bridge" do you find personification? How does it enhance the description of the scene? What quality does it seem to introduce?

3. **Tone.** Part of the effect of "Composed upon Westminster Bridge" lies in the tone that it achieves. How would you characterize that tone, and what words or passages contribute to it? Comment on the similarities in tone among all four sonnets. In which sonnets does the tone deviate most markedly from that of "Composed upon Westminster Bridge"? What might account for this difference in tone?

4. **Theme.** In "Ode: Intimations of Immortality," Wordsworth says that we come into this world from God, "trailing clouds of glory," and that "Heaven lies about us in our infancy." Explain how this idea about the nature of childhood is echoed in "It Is a Beauteous Evening, Calm and Free."

To Wordsworth, Milton embodies the qualities of the ideal poet. What are these qualities, as implied in "London, 1802"? What is the relationship between the poet and society? between the poet and ordinary human beings?

5. **Imagery.** Analyze the imagery of "Composed upon Westminster Bridge" in terms of the qualities of light, sound, and movement. What words and phrases emphasize calm or quiet? How does the imagery contribute to the overall mood of the scene?

In "The World Is Too Much with Us," the speaker would rather be "suckled in a creed outworn" than be out of tune with nature. How does the poem's imagery identify nature as the life force, a source of sustenance and nurturing?

In "London, 1802," note the similes in lines 9–11. What qualities in Milton do they suggest? Is there any similarity between the qualities associated with the sea in this sonnet and in "The World Is Too Much with Us"?

"It Is a Beauteous Evening, Calm and Free," like "Composed upon Westminster Bridge," emphasizes the qualities of calm and quiet and associates energy or movement with water. What qualities does Wordsworth associate with the sea in both "The World Is Too Much with Us" and "It Is a Beauteous Evening, Calm and Free"? In the latter sonnet, point out how the use of religious imagery enhances the poem's theme.

6. **Allusion.** In "The World Is Too Much with Us," what is the effect of alluding to the ancient Greek gods Proteus and Triton? How does this reinforce the pattern of imagery that contrasts "the world" with nature and the sea?

7. **Metonymy.** A figure of speech in which an associated word is substituted for a literal meaning is metonymy. In *Genesis*, when God tells Adam, "In the sweat of thy face shalt thou eat bread," *sweat* stands for "hard labor." Similarly, *crown* can mean "the king." In "London, 1802," where do you find metonymy? What are the literal meanings of these metonyms?

Developing Vocabulary

Word Origins. The derivation and history of a word strongly affect its connotations, which are always important in poetry. The following five words, used in these sonnets, have been in the English language a long time and have interesting derivations.

1. Steep. After deciding on its part of speech in "Composed upon Westminster Bridge," look up the derivation and meaning of *steep*. How does it function as a metaphor in this poem?

2. Boon (as a noun). Using a dictionary, find the language from which it is derived and when and where that language was spoken.

3. Lea. Find its meaning and derivation. Does your dictionary also record its past association with a certain Latin root?

4. Fen. Use a dictionary to find its derivation and the other languages to which its root is related.

5. Brood (as a verb). Note its use in "It Is a Beauteous Evening, Calm and Free." How are its connotations related to its derivation?

Developing Writing Skills

Using Comparisons and Contrasts. Choose two or more of these sonnets and, in several paragraphs, compare and contrast them in terms of theme, imagery, structure, and other elements. For example, how do "The World Is Too Much with Us" and "London, 1802" both express some kind of dissatisfaction and suggest an alternative? How do the views of London contrast in "Composed upon Westminster Bridge" and "London, 1802"? What are the similarities and differences in imagery between "Composed upon Westminster Bridge" and "It Is a Beauteous Evening, Calm and Free"? Are any patterns of imagery or diction apparent in several of these poems?

Samuel Taylor Coleridge
1772–1834

A remarkable poet and thinker, Samuel Taylor Coleridge is best remembered today for "The Rime of the Ancient Mariner," "Christabel," and "Kubla Khan," three poems that deal with demonic and supernatural themes. A consummate craftsman, Coleridge produced musical verse with an exquisite perfection of meter. In addition, no figure was more influential than he in the shift from classic to the Romantic spirit, not solely because of his poetic, critical, and philosophical writings but also because of his extraordinary personal magnetism.

As a schoolboy, Coleridge was precocious, reading the most difficult passages of Virgil for amusement. His delicate health, which plagued him throughout his life, was a serious problem even in his boyhood. Already an excellent scholar when he entered Cambridge, Coleridge did not care for college life. In his third year, in despair over financial difficulties, he fled to London to enlist in the Light Dragoons under the absurd alias Silas Tomkyn Comberback. His brothers found him and with some difficulty secured his discharge, sending him back to Cambridge, though when he left in 1794 he still had no degree. That same year Coleridge met an Oxford student named Robert Southey who was to be his lifelong friend.

In 1795, Coleridge had the extraordinary good fortune to meet William Wordsworth. The two young men had a catalytic effect upon one another, inspiring each other to better work than either had until then done singly. Wordsworth said, "The only wonderful man I ever knew was Coleridge." In 1798, *Lyrical Ballads* appeared, with poems by both Wordsworth and Coleridge, including "The Rime of the Ancient Mariner." During this time of great creativity, personal and financial concerns caused Coleridge to consider supporting himself as a Unitarian minister, but an annuity from Thomas and Josiah Wedgwood, sons of the founder of the pottery firm, enabled Coleridge to devote his life to letters. In September of 1798, accompanied by the Wordsworths, he went to Germany to study philosophy.

SAMUEL TAYLOR COLERIDGE, 1814. Washington Allston. National Portrait Gallery, London.

Coleridge was frequently in severe pain from his physical disabilities. Wordsworth noted that in his pain Coleridge would "throw himself down and writhe like a worm upon the ground." Doctors prescribed laudanum, opium dissolved in alcohol, and it is well known that Coleridge composed "Kubla Khan" in 1797 while under the influence of this drug. By 1800, his dosage having been repeatedly increased to cope with rheumatic attacks, Coleridge was addicted, and for more than fifteen years the gifted man lived miserably, able to write only in fits and starts. He moved frequently, living with friends in London, going to Malta, visiting Rome, until in 1816 he moved in with a Dr. Gillman at Highgate, north of London. Though he seldom left his rooms, they became a kind of literary Mecca, with admirers from England and America flocking to listen to the dazzling conversation of "The Sage of Highgate." *Biographia Literaria* (1817) appeared in the early Highgate years. A blend of autobiographical, philosophical, and critical writing, this two-volume work contains a detailed evaluation of Wordsworth's poetry and affirms Coleridge's fundamental belief in the power of the imagination.

Kubla Khan

Almost as well known as this poem are the circumstances of its composition. According to Coleridge, he had been reading about the building of a summer palace by the great thirteenth-century Mongolian ruler Kubla Khan, when he fell asleep in his chair as a result of a pain-killing drug he had taken. As he slept, he said, "the images [of this poem] rose up before him as things, . . . without any . . . consciousness of effort." On awakening he began writing down the poem but was interrupted at line 54 by a "person on business from Porlock," a nearby village, and afterwards was unable to remember the rest. The result was a "fragment," he said, "a vision in a dream."

In Xanadu[1] did Kubla Khan
A stately pleasure-dome decree:
Where Alph, the sacred river, ran
Through caverns measureless to man
   Down to a sunless sea.   5
So twice five miles of fertile ground
With walls and towers were girdled round:
And there were gardens bright with sinuous rills,
Where blossomed many an incense-bearing tree;
And here were forests ancient as the hills,   10
Enfolding sunny spots of greenery.

But oh! that deep romantic chasm which slanted
Down the green hill athwart a cedarn cover!
A savage place! as holy and enchanted
As e'er beneath a waning moon was haunted   15
By woman wailing for her demon lover!
And from this chasm, with ceaseless turmoil seething,
As if this earth in fast thick pants were breathing,
A mighty fountain momently was forced:
Amid whose swift half-intermitted burst   20
Huge fragments vaulted like rebounding hail,
Or chaffy grain beneath the thresher's flail:
And 'mid these dancing rocks at once and ever
It flung up momently the sacred river.
Five miles meandering with a mazy motion   25
Through wood and dale the sacred river ran,
Then reached the caverns measureless to man,
And sank in tumult to a lifeless ocean:

---

1. **Xanadu** (zăn' ə dōō): an indefinite area of Tartary in Asia.

LADIES ON TERRACE WITH FLUTTERING PIGEONS, 1780.
Rajasthan Bundi.
Victoria and Albert Museum, Crown Copyright.

And 'mid this tumult Kubla heard from far
Ancestral voices prophesying war!   30

   The shadow of the dome of pleasure
   Floated midway on the waves;
   Where was heard the mingled measure
   From the fountain and the caves.
It was a miracle of rare device,   35
A sunny pleasure-dome with caves of ice!

   A damsel with a dulcimer[2]
   In a vision once I saw:
   It was an Abyssinian maid,
   And on her dulcimer she played,   40
   Singing of Mount Abora.[3]
   Could I revive within me
   Her symphony and song,
   To such a deep delight 'twould win me,
That with music loud and long,   45
I would build that dome in air,
That sunny dome! those caves of ice!
And all who heard should see them there,
And all should cry, Beware! Beware!
His flashing eyes, his floating hair!   50
Weave a circle round him thrice,
And close your eyes with holy dread,
For he on honeydew hath fed,
And drunk the milk of Paradise.

---

2. **dulcimer** (dul' sə mər): a musical instrument with metallic wires
played with small hammers.
3. **Mount Abora:** a legendary earthly paradise like Kubla Khan's.

Getting at Meaning

1. Trace the progress of Alph, the sacred river. How and in what kind of place does it originate? Through what kind of area does it flow? What kind of course does it follow? What is its final destination? In your answer refer to specific lines in the poem.

2. Describe the pleasure dome and its setting. Where is the pleasure dome described as a blend of opposites? How does the pleasure-dome figure in the last stanza of the poem?

3. Inspired by a vision of an Abyssinian damsel, what does the speaker hope to do?

4. In the last lines of the poem, the speaker anticipates a reaction. Why should all beware and avert their eyes?

Developing Skills in Reading Literature

1. **Imagery.** In lines 1–11, do you find any similarities to a Biblical paradise? Explain. Notice how the mysterious slanting chasm is described in lines 12–16. Does it seem sinister or attractive or both? What curious blend of imagery is apparent here? Do you find overtones of the romantic? the satanic? the erotic? In lines 17–24, in what way does the language suggest the process of birth and creation? Amid this violence and turmoil, what is being "born"? After the sacred river runs past gardens and scenes of nature, it reaches the "caverns measureless to man," the "sunless sea," the "lifeless ocean." What is suggested by these phrases?

2. **Symbol.** Considering that the Alph is a sacred river that runs through nature to a "lifeless ocean," what might the river symbolize? In what way might the passage of this river represent a kind of panorama of existence?

3. **Structure.** This poem has three parts that could be called the thesis, the antithesis, and the synthesis. The first part presents a vision of a paradise. Then follows a sinister and turbulent contrast. The third part introduces another vision and brings the first two visions together, for the poet who could create such a dome "in air" inspires a "holy dread."

Applying this scheme, where do you think the divisions are in the poem? Where does the antithesis begin? Where does it end? Note that the antithesis returns briefly to the contrasting thesis. What change in meter comes with the beginning of the synthesis? What happens to the metrical pattern in the final ten lines of the poem? What is suggested by the pattern of these lines?

4. **Theme.** This is one of Coleridge's "mystery poems," filled with romantic magic, strongly influenced by the irrational and the unconscious. It can give pleasure without being thoroughly "understood" and can be seen to have meaning and coherence, even as a dream can. In what way does this poem deal with human existence itself, with beginnings and endings and the search for paradise? with the magic of poetic creation and the sacred rivers and chasms of the mind?

5. **Sound Devices.** This poem can be read as a kind of "pure poetry"; its musical language and suggestive imagery can be enjoyed for their own sake. Consider line 25. What technique enhances its sounds? How do the words seem to imitate what they describe? Find several other examples of striking sound effects, created by devices such as alliteration, assonance, consonance, onomatopoeia, rhyme, and rhythmic variations.

Developing Vocabulary

Latin Roots. The prefix *inter-* comes from the Latin word meaning "between" or "among." The word *half-intermitted* occurs in line 20 of this poem. Using a dictionary, establish the meaning of this word in relation to its Latin roots. Do the same for these other words, which also combine *inter-* with Latin roots.

interstice	interject	internuncio
interdict	interpellate	interface
intercede	interpolate	intermittent

The Rime of the Ancient Mariner

This poem opened the 1798 edition of Lyrical Ballads. *The sources of the poem include various travel narratives and a friend's dream about a skeleton ship manned by eerie figures. Wordsworth contributed ideas such as the shooting of the albatross and the navigation of the ship by the dead sailors. The gloss, or commentary in the margin next to the poem, was added by Coleridge in a later edition.*

Argument

How a Ship, having first sailed to the Equator, was driven by storms to the cold Country towards the South Pole; how the Ancient Mariner cruelly and in contempt of the laws of hospitality killed a Seabird and how he was followed by many and strange judgments: and in what manner he came back to his own Country.

Gustav Doré.

Part I

An ancient Mariner
meeteth three
Gallants bidden
to a wedding
feast and
detaineth one.

It is an ancient Mariner,
And he stoppeth one of three.
"By thy long gray beard and glittering eye,
Now wherefore stopp'st thou me?

"The Bridegroom's doors are opened wide,   5
And I am next of kin;
The guests are met, the feast is set;
May'st hear the merry din."

He holds him with his skinny hand;
"There was a ship," quoth he.   10
"Hold off! unhand me, graybeard loon!"
Eftsoons[1] his hand dropped he.

The Wedding Guest is
spellbound by
the eye of the
old seafaring
man and
constrained to
hear his tale.

He holds him with his glittering eye—
The Wedding Guest stood still,
And listens like a three years' child;   15
The Mariner hath his will.

The Wedding Guest sat on a stone;
He cannot choose but hear;
And thus spake on that ancient man,
The bright-eyed Mariner.   20

"The ship was cheered, the harbor cleared,
Merrily did we drop
Below the kirk,[2] below the hill,
Below the lighthouse top.

The Mariner tells
how the ship sailed
southward with
a good wind and
fair weather till
it reached the
Line.[3]

"The Sun came up upon the left,   25
Out of the sea came he—
And he shone bright, and on the right
Went down into the sea.

"Higher and higher every day,
Till over the mast at noon—"   30
The Wedding Guest here beat his breast,
For he heard the loud bassoon.

---

1. **Eftsoons:** quickly.
2. **kirk:** church.
3. **Line:** equator.

*The Wedding Guest
heareth the
bridal music;
but the Mariner
continueth his tale.*
The bride hath paced into the hall,
Red as a rose is she;
Nodding their heads before her goes   35
The merry minstrelsy.

The Wedding Guest he beat his breast,
Yet he cannot choose but hear;
And thus spake on that ancient man,
The bright-eyed Mariner.   40

*The ship driven by a
storm toward
the South Pole.*

"And now the Storm blast came, and he
Was tyrannous and strong.
He struck with his o'ertaking wings,
And chased us south along.

"With sloping masts and dipping prow,   45
As who pursued with yell and blow
Still treads the shadow of his foe,
And forward bends his head,
The ship drove fast, loud roared the blast,
And southward aye we fled.   50

"And now there came both mist and snow,
And it grew wondrous cold;
And ice, mast-high, came floating by,
As green as emerald.

*The land of ice, and
of fearful
sounds, where
no living thing
was to be seen.*

"And through the drifts[4] the snowy clifts[5]   55
Did send a dismal sheen;
Nor shapes of men nor beasts we ken[6]—
The ice was all between.

"The ice was here, the ice was there,
The ice was all around;   60
It cracked and growled, and roared and howled
Like noises in a swound![7]

*Till a great sea bird,
called the Albatross,
came through the snow-fog,
and was received with
great joy and hospitality.*

"At length did cross an Albatross,
Thorough[8] the fog it came;
As if it had been a Christian soul,   65
We hailed it in God's name.

---

4. **drifts:** mists.
5. **clifts:** icebergs.
6. **ken:** saw.
7. **swound:** dream.
8. **Thorough:** through.

"It ate the food it n'er had eat,[9]
And round and round it flew.
The ice did split with a thunder fit;
The helmsman steered us through!   70

"And a good south wind sprung up behind;
The Albatross did follow,
And every day, for food or play,
Came to the mariners' hollo!

"In mist or cloud, on mast or shroud,[10]   75
It perched for vespers[11] nine;
Whiles all the night, through fog-smoke white,
Glimmered the white moonshine."

"God save thee, ancient Mariner!
From the fiends, that plague thee thus!—
Why look'st thou so?"[12]—"With my crossbow   80
I shot the Albatross!

Part II

"The Sun now rose upon the right,[13]
Out of the sea came he,
Still hid in mist, and on the left   85
Went down into the sea.

"And the good south wind still blew behind,
But no sweet bird did follow,
Nor any day for food or play
Came to the mariners' hollo!   90

"And I had done a hellish thing,
And it would work 'em woe;
For all averred, I had killed the bird
That made the breeze to blow.
Ah wretch! said they, the bird to slay,   95
That made the breeze to blow!

---

9. **eat:** pronounced *et*, old form of *eaten*.
10. **shroud:** rope.
11. **vespers:** evening prayers.
12. **God . . . so:** spoken by the wedding guest.
13. **upon the right:** The ship is heading north into the
Pacific after rounding the bottom of South America.

*But when the fog
cleared off, they
justify the same,
and thus make
themselves
accomplices in
the crime.*

"Nor dim nor red, like God's own head,
The glorious Sun uprist;[14]
Then all averred, I had killed the bird
That brought the fog and mist.   100
'Twas right, said they, such birds to slay,
That bring the fog and mist.

*The fair breeze continues;
the ship enters the
Pacific Ocean,
and sails northward, even
till it reaches the Line.*

"The fair breeze blew, the white foam flew,
The furrow[15] followed free;
We were the first that ever burst   105
Into that silent sea.

*The ship hath been
suddenly
becalmed.*

"Down dropped the breeze, the sails dropped
            down,
'Twas sad as sad could be;
And we did speak only to break
The silence of the sea!   110

"All in a hot and copper sky,
The bloody Sun, at noon,
Right up above the mast did stand,
No bigger than the Moon.

"Day after day, day after day,   115
We stuck, nor breath nor motion;
As idle as a painted ship
Upon a painted ocean.

*And the Albatross
begins to be
avenged.*

"Water, water, everywhere,
And all the boards did shrink;   120
Water, water, everywhere,
Nor any drop to drink.

"The very deep did rot; O Christ!
That ever this should be!
Yea, slimy things did crawl with legs   125
Upon the slimy sea.

---

14. **uprist:** arose.
15. **furrow:** wake of the ship.

A Spirit had followed
them: one of the
invisible
inhabitants of
this planet,
neither departed
souls nor angels.
They are very
numerous, and
there is no
climate or
element without
one or more.

The shipmates, in
their sore
distress, would
fain throw the
whole guilt on
the ancient
Mariner, in sign
whereof they
hang the dead
sea bird round
his neck.

"About, about, in reel and rout[16]
The death fires[17] danced at night;
The water, like a witch's oils,
Burnt green and blue and white.   130

"And some in dreams assurèd were
Of the Spirit that plagued us so;
Nine fathom deep he had followed us
From the land of mist and snow.

"And every tongue, through utter drought,   135
Was withered at the root;
We could not speak, no more than if
We had been choked with soot.

"Ah, welladay! what evil looks
Had I from old and young!   140
Instead of the cross, the Albatross
About my neck was hung.

Part III

"There passed a weary time. Each throat
Was parched, and glazed each eye.
A weary time! a weary time!   145
How glazed each weary eye,
When looking westward, I beheld
A something in the sky.

The ancient Mariner
beholdeth a sign
in the element
afar off.

"At first it seemed a little speck,
And then it seemed a mist;   150
It moved and moved, and took at last
A certain shape, I wist.[18]

"A speck, a mist, a shape, I wist!
And still it neared and neared;
As if it dodged a water sprite,   155
It plunged and tacked and veered.

---

16. **rout:** tumultuous crowd.
17. **death fires:** St. Elena's fires. An electrical discharge
often brushes a ship's rigging. Sailors believed it was a
bad omen.
18. **wist:** knew.

At its nearer approach it seemeth him to be a ship, and at a dear ransom he freeth his speech from the bonds of thirst.

"With throats unslaked, with black lips baked,
We could nor laugh nor wail;
Through utter drought all dumb we stood!
I bit my arm, I sucked the blood,   160
And cried, A sail! A sail!

"With throats unslaked, with black lips baked,
Agape they heard me call;
Gramercy![19] they for joy did grin,
And all at once their breath drew in,   165

A flash of joy.

As they were drinking all.

And horror follows. For can it be a ship that comes onward without wind or tide?

"See! see! (I cried) she tacks no more!
Hither to work us weal;[20]
Without a breeze, without a tide,
She steadies with upright keel!   170

"The western wave was all aflame.
The day was well-nigh done!
Almost upon the western wave
Rested the broad bright Sun;
When that strange shape drove suddenly   175
Betwixt us and the Sun.

It seemeth him but the skeleton of a ship.

"And straight the Sun was flecked with bars,
(Heaven's Mother send us grace!)
As if through a dungeon grate he peered
With broad and burning face.   180

"Alas! (thought I, and my heart beat loud)
How fast she nears and nears!
Are those her sails that glance in the Sun,
Like restless gossameres?[21]

And its ribs are seen as bars on the face of the setting Sun. The Specter-Woman and her Death mate, and no other on board the skeleton ship.

"Are those her ribs through which the Sun   185
Did peer, as through a grate?
And is that Woman all her crew?
Is that a Death? and are there two?
Is Death that woman's mate?

---

19. **Gramercy** (grə mûr' sē): great thanks.
20. **work us weal:** help us.
21. **gossameres:** floating webs. The spelling has been changed to rhyme with *nears*.

"Her lips were red, her looks were free,[22]   190
Her locks were yellow as gold.
Her skin was as white as leprosy,

Like vessel, like crew!

The Nightmare Life-in-Death was she,
Who thicks man's blood with cold.

Death and Life-in-Death have diced for the ship's crew, and she (the latter) winneth the ancient Mariner.

"The naked hulk alongside came,   195
And the twain were casting dice;
'The game is done! I've won! I've won!'
Quoth she, and whistles thrice.

No twilight within the courts of the Sun.

"The Sun's rim dips; the stars rush out;
At one stride comes the dark;   200
With far-heard whisper, o'er the sea,
Off shot the specter bark.

"We listened and looked sideways up!
Fear at my heart, as at a cup,

At the rising of the Moon,

My lifeblood seemed to sip!   205
The stars were dim, and thick the night,
The steersman's face by his lamp gleamed white;
From the sails the dew did drip—
Till clomb[23] above the eastern bar
The hornèd[24] Moon, with one bright star   210
Within the nether tip.

One after another,

"One after one, by the star-dogged Moon,[25]
Too quick for groan or sigh,
Each turned his face with a ghastly pang,
And cursed me with his eye,   215

His shipmates drop down dead.

"Four times fifty living men,
(And I heard nor sigh nor groan)
With heavy thump, a lifeless lump,
They dropped down one by one.

But Life-in-Death begins her work on the ancient Mariner.

"The souls did from their bodies fly—   220
They fled to bliss or woe!
And every soul, it passed me by,
Like the whizz of my crossbow!"

---

22. **free:** wild.
23. **clomb:** climbed.
24. **hornèd:** crescent.
25. **star-dogged Moon:** A star dogging the moon was an evil omen to sailors.

Part IV

The Wedding Guest feareth that a Spirit is talking to him.

"I fear thee, ancient Mariner!
I fear thy skinny hand!   225
And thou art long, and lank, and brown,
As is the ribbed sea sand.

"I fear thee and thy glittering eye,
And thy skinny hand, so brown."—

But the ancient Mariner assureth him of his bodily life, and proceedeth to relate his horrible penance.

"Fear not, fear not, thou Wedding Guest!   230
This body dropped not down.

"Alone, alone, all, all alone,
Alone on a wide, wide sea!
And never a saint took pity on
My soul in agony.   235

"The many men, so beautiful!
And they all dead did lie;

He despiseth the creatures of the calm.

And a thousand thousand slimy things
Lived on! and so did I.

And envieth that they should live, and so many lie dead.

"I looked upon the rotting sea,   240
And drew my eyes away;
I looked upon the rotting deck,
And there the dead men lay.

"I looked to heaven, and tried to pray;
But or[26] ever a prayer had gushed,   245
A wicked whisper came, and made
My heart as dry as dust.

"I closed my lids, and kept them close,
And the balls like pulses beat;
For the sky and the sea, and the sea and the sky   250
Lay like a load on my weary eye,
And the dead were at my feet.

But the curse liveth for him in the eye of the dead men.

"The cold sweat melted from their limbs,
Nor rot nor reek did they;
The look with which they looked on me   255
Had never passed away.

---

26. **or:** before.

"An orphan's curse would drag to hell
A spirit from on high;
But oh! more horrible than that
Is a curse in a dead man's eye!   260
Seven days, seven nights, I saw that curse,
And yet I could not die.

"The moving Moon went up the sky,
And nowhere did abide;
Softly she was going up,   265
And a star or two beside—

"Her beams bemocked the sultry main,[27]
Like April hoarfrost spread;
But where the ship's huge shadow lay,
The charmèd water burnt alway   270
A still and awful red.

"Beyond the shadow of the ship,
I watched the water snakes.
They moved in tracks of shining white,
And when they reared, the elfish light   275
Fell off in hoary flakes.

"Within the shadow of the ship
I watched their rich attire;
Blue, glossy green, and velvet black,
They coiled and swam, and every track   280
Was a flash of golden fire.

"Oh happy living things! no tongue
Their beauty might declare.
A spring of love gushed from my heart,
And I blessed them unaware;   285
Sure my kind saint took pity on me,
And I blessed them unaware.

"The selfsame moment I could pray;
And from my neck so free
The Albatross fell off, and sank   290
Like lead into the sea.

---

27. **main:** sea.

THE RIME OF THE ANCIENT MARINER   467

Part V

"O sleep! it is a gentle thing,
Beloved from pole to pole!
To Mary Queen the praise be given!
She sent the gentle sleep from Heaven,   295
That slid into my soul.

"The silly[28] buckets on the deck,
That had so long remained,
I dreamt that they were filled with dew;
And when I awoke, it rained.   300

"My lips were wet, my throat was cold,
My garments all were dank;
Sure I had drunken in my dreams,
And still my body drank.

"I moved, and could not feel my limbs;   305
I was so light—almost
I thought that I had died in sleep,
And was a blessèd ghost.

"And soon I heard a roaring wind.
It did not come anear;   310
But with its sound it shook the sails,
That were so thin and sere.[29]

"The upper air burst into life!
And a hundred fire flags sheen,[30]
To and fro they were hurried about!   315
And to and fro, and in and out,
The wan stars danced between.[31]

"And the coming wind did roar more loud,
And the sails did sigh like sedge;[32]
And the rain poured down from one black cloud;   320
The Moon was at its edge.

---

28. **silly:** empty.
29. **sere:** dried up.
30. **fire flags sheen:** lightning.
31. **The upper air . . . danced between:** the play of the southern lights.
32. **sedge:** tall rushes around ponds and streams.

"The thick black cloud was cleft, and still
The Moon was at its side;
Like waters shot from some high crag,
The lightning fell with never a jag,   325
A river steep and wide.

"The loud wind never reached the ship,
Yet now the ship moved on!
Beneath the lightning and the Moon
The dead men gave a groan.   330

"They groaned, they stirred, they all uprose,
Nor spake, nor moved their eyes;
It had been strange, even in a dream,
To have seen those dead men rise.

"The helmsman steered, the ship moved on;   335
Yet never a breeze upblew;
The mariners all 'gan work the ropes,
Where they were wont[33] to do;
They raised their limbs like lifeless tools—
We were a ghastly crew.   340

"The body of my brother's son
Stood by me, knee to knee:
The body and I pulled at one rope,
But he said nought to me."

"I fear thee, ancient Mariner!"   345
"Be calm, thou Wedding Guest!
'Twas not those souls that fled in pain,
Which to their corses[34] came again,
But a troop of spirits blest;

"For when it dawned—they dropped their arms,   350
And clustered round the mast;
Sweet sounds rose slowly through their mouths,
And from their bodies passed.

"Around, around, flew each sweet sound,
Then darted to the Sun;   355
Slowly the sounds came back again,
Now mixed, now one by one.

---

33. **wont:** accustomed.
34. **corses:** corpses.

"Sometimes a-dropping from the sky
I heard the skylark sing;
Sometimes all little birds that are,   360
How they seemed to fill the sea and air
With their sweet jargoning![35]

"And now 'twas like all instruments,
Now like a lonely flute;
And now it is an angel's song,   365
That makes the heavens be mute.

"It ceased; yet still the sails made on
A pleasant noise till noon,
A noise like of a hidden brook
In the leafy month of June,   370
That to the sleeping woods all night
Singeth a quiet tune.

"Till noon we quietly sailed on,
Yet never a breeze did breathe;
Slowly and smoothly went the ship,   375
Moved onward from beneath.

*The lonesome Spirit
from the South Pole
carries on the ship as far
as the Line, in obedience to
the angelic troop, but still
requireth vengeance.*

"Under the keel nine fathom[36] deep,
From the land of mist and snow,
That Spirit slid; and it was he
That made the ship to go.   380
The sails at noon left off their tune,
And the ship stood still also.

"The Sun, right up above the mast,
Had fixed her to the ocean;
But in a minute she 'gan stir,   385
With a short uneasy motion—
Backwards and forwards half her length
With a short uneasy motion.

"Then like a pawing horse let go,
She made a sudden bound;   390
It flung the blood into my head,
And I fell down in a swound.

---

35. **jargoning:** confusion of sounds.
36. **nine fathom:** fifty-four feet.

The Polar Spirit's
fellow demons, the invisible
inhabitants of the element,
take part in his wrong;
and two of them relate, one
to the other, that penance
long and heavy for the
ancient Mariner hath been
accorded to the Polar Spirit,
who returneth southward.

"How long in that same fit I lay,
I have not to declare;
But ere my living life returned,   395
I heard, and in my soul discerned,
Two voices in the air.

"'Is it he?' quoth one, 'Is this the man?
By him who died on cross,
With his cruel bow he laid full low   400
The harmless Albatross.

"'The Spirit who bideth by himself
In the land of mist and snow,
He loved the bird that loved the man
Who shot him with his bow.'   405

"The other was a softer voice,
As soft as honeydew;
Quoth he, 'The man hath penance done,
And penance more will do.'

Part VI

First Voice
"'But tell me, tell me! speak again,   410
Thy soft response renewing—
What makes that ship drive on so fast?
What is the ocean doing?'

Second Voice
"'Still as a slave before his lord,
The ocean hath no blast;   415
His great bright eye most silently
Up to the Moon is cast—

"'If he may know which way to go;
For she guides him smooth or grim.
See, brother, see! how graciously   420
She looketh down on him.'

First Voice
"'But why drives on that ship so fast,
Without or wave or wind?'

The Mariner hath
been cast into a trance,
for the angelic power
causeth the vessel to drive
northward faster than
human life could endure.

Second Voice

"'The air is cut away before,
And closes from behind.   425

"'Fly, brother, fly! more high, more high!
Or we shall be belated;
For slow and slow that ship will go,
When the Mariner's trance is abated.'

*The supernatural motion
is retarded;
the Mariner awakes,
and his penance
begins anew.*

"I woke, and we were sailing on   430
As in a gentle weather;
'Twas night, calm night, the Moon was high;
The dead men stood together.

"All stood together on the deck,
For a charnel dungeon[37] fitter;   435
All fixed on me their stony eyes,
That in the Moon did glitter.

"The pang, the curse, with which they died,
Had never passed away;
I could not draw my eyes from theirs,   440
Nor turn them up to pray.

*The curse is finally
expiated.*

"And now this spell was snapped; once more
I viewed the ocean green,
And looked far forth, yet little saw
Of what had else been seen—   445

"Like one, that on a lonesome road
Doth walk in fear and dread,
And having once turned round walks on,
And turns no more his head;
Because he knows a frightful fiend   450
Doth close behind him tread.

"But soon there breathed a wind on me,
Nor sound nor motion made;
Its path was not upon the sea,
In ripple or in shade.   455

---

37. **charnel dungeon:** burial vault.

"It raised my hair, it fanned my cheek
Like a meadow-gale of spring—
It mingled strangely with my fears,
Yet it felt like a welcoming.

"Swiftly, swiftly flew the ship,   460
Yet she sailed softly too;
Sweetly, sweetly blew the breeze—
On me alone it blew.

"Oh! dream of joy! is this indeed
The lighthouse top I see?   465
Is this the hill? Is this the kirk?
Is this mine own countree?

"We drifted o'er the harbor bar,
And I with sobs did pray—
O let me be awake, my God!   470
Or let me sleep alway.

"The harbor bay was clear as glass,
So smoothly it was strewn!³⁸
And on the bay the moonlight lay,
And the shadow of the Moon.   475

"The rock shone bright, the kirk no less,
That stands above the rock;
The moonlight steeped in silentness
The steady weathercock.

"And the bay was white with silent light   480

Till, rising from the same,
Full many shapes, that shadows were,
In crimson colors came.

"A little distance from the prow
Those crimson shadows were;   485
I turned my eyes upon the deck—
Oh, Christ, what saw I there!

---

38. **strewn:** spread.

"Each corse lay flat, lifeless and flat,
And, by the holy rood!³⁹
A man all light, a seraph⁴⁰-man   490
On every corse there stood.

*And appear in their
own forms of light.*

"This seraph band, each waved his hand;
It was a heavenly sight!
They stood as signals to the land,
Each one a lovely light;   495

"This seraph band, each waved his hand;
No voice did they impart—
No voice; but oh! the silence sank
Like music on my heart.

"But soon I heard the dash of oars,   500
I heard the Pilot's cheer;
My head was turned perforce away,
And I saw a boat appear.

"The Pilot and the Pilot's boy,
I heard them coming fast;   505
Dear Lord in Heaven! it was a joy
The dead men could not blast.

"I saw a third—I heard his voice;
It is the Hermit good!
He singeth loud his godly hymns   510
That he makes in the wood.
He'll shrieve⁴¹ my soul, he'll wash away
The Albatross's blood.

Part VII

The Hermit of the wood

"This Hermit good lives in that wood
Which slopes down to the sea.   515
How loudly his sweet voice he rears!
He loves to talk with mariners
That come from a far countree.

---

39. **rood:** cross.
40. **seraph:** angel.
41. **shrieve:** absolve from sin.

"He kneels at morn, and noon, and eve—
He hath a cushion plump;   520
It is the moss that wholly hides
The rotted old oak stump.

"The skiff boat neared; I heard them talk,
'Why, this is strange, I trow!42
Where are those lights so many and fair,   525
That signal made but now?'

Approacheth the ship
with wonder.

"'Strange, by my faith!' the Hermit said—
'And they answered not our cheer!43
The planks looked warped! and see those sails,
How thin they are and sere!   530
I never saw aught like to them,
Unless perchance it were

"'Brown skeletons of leaves that lag
My forest brook along,
When the ivy tod44 is heavy with snow,   535
And the owlet whoops to the wolf below,
That eats the she-wolf's young.'

"'Dear Lord! it hath a fiendish look'—
(The Pilot made reply)
'I am afeared'—'Push on, push on!'   540
Said the Hermit cheerily.

"The boat came closer to the ship,
But I nor spake nor stirred;
The boat came close beneath the ship,
And straight45 a sound was heard.   545

The ship suddenly sinketh.

"Under the water it rumbled on,
Still louder and more dread;
It reached the ship, it split the bay;
The ship went down like lead.

---

42. **trow:** believe.
43. **cheer:** call.
44. **ivy tod:** ivy bush.
45. **straight:** immediately.

"Stunned by that loud and dreadful sound,   550
Which sky and ocean smote,
Like one that hath been seven days drowned
My body lay afloat;
But swift as dreams, myself I found
Within the Pilot's boat.   555

"Upon the whirl, where sank the ship,
The boat spun round and round;
And all was still, save that the hill
Was telling of the sound.

"I moved my lips—the Pilot shrieked   560
And fell down in a fit;
The holy Hermit raised his eyes,
And prayed where he did sit.

"I took the oars; the Pilot's boy,
Who now doth crazy go,   565
Laughed loud and long, and all the while
His eyes went to and fro.
'Ha! ha!' quoth he, 'full plain I see,
The Devil knows how to row.'

"And now, all in my own countree,   570
I stood on the firm land!
The Hermit stepped forth from the boat,
And scarcely he could stand.

"'O shrieve me, shrieve me, holy man!"
The Hermit crossed his brow.[46]   575
'Say quick,' quoth he, 'I bid thee say—
What manner of man art thou?'

"Forthwith this frame of mine was wrenched
With a woeful agony,
Which forced me to begin my tale;   580
And then it left me free.

"Since then, at an uncertain hour,
That agony returns;
And till my ghastly tale is told,
This heart within me burns.   585

46. **crossed his brow:** made the sign of the cross on his forehead.

"I pass, like night, from land to land;
I have strange power of speech;
That moment that his face I see
I know the man that must hear me;
To him my tale I teach.   590

"What loud uproar bursts from that door!
The wedding guests are there;
But in the garden bower the bride
And bridemaids singing are;
And hark the little vesper bell,   595
Which biddeth me to prayer!

"O Wedding Guest! this soul hath been
Alone on a wide, wide sea;
So lonely 'twas, that God himself
Scarce seemèd there to be.   600

Gustav Doré.

"O sweeter than the marriage feast,
'Tis sweeter far to me,
To walk together to the kirk
With a goodly company!—

"To walk together to the kirk,   605
And all together pray,
While each to his great Father bends,
Old men, and babes, and loving friends,
And youths and maidens gay!

And to teach by   "Farewell, farewell; but this I tell   610
his own example   To thee, thou Wedding Guest!
love and reverence to   He prayeth well, who loveth well
all things that   Both man and bird and beast.
God made and loveth.

"He prayeth best, who loveth best
All things both great and small;   615
For the dear God who loveth us,
He made and loveth all."

The Mariner, whose eye is bright,
Whose beard with age is hoar,
Is gone; and now the Wedding Guest   620
Turned from the bridegroom's door.

He went like one that hath been stunned,
And is of sense forlorn;
A sadder and a wiser man,
He rose the morrow morn.   625

Getting at Meaning

Part I

1. What aspect of the mariner seems to cast a spell over the wedding guest?

2. Why does the ship sail to "the land of ice and of fearful sounds"? How does the coming of the albatross apparently affect the ship's course?

Part II

3. Why do the mariner's shipmates first condemn his killing of the albatross, then approve of it? Later, why do they hang it on his neck?

4. As the albatross begins to be avenged, what effects are seen in the natural world? What supernatural force is at work?

Part III

5. As a ship nears, how does the mariner manage to cry out? What details reveal it as a ghost ship? Describe the appearance of its crew, and their effect on the mariner and his companions.

Part IV

6. At this point, why is the wedding guest suddenly fearful? How does the mariner reassure him?

7. How long does the mariner suffer "Alone on a wide, wide sea" and under whose curse?

8. What act finally enables the mariner to pray? Was it a spontaneous or a premeditated decision?

Part V

9. How does nature reflect the change in the mariner?

10. With the crew dead, how is the ship manned? What spiritual agencies are involved?

11. Now that he has dropped the guilty weight of the albatross, is the mariner forgiven and released from suffering? Explain.

Part VI

12. At what point in the journey is the curse dispelled?

13. What elements of the supernatural are described in this part of the poem?

Part VII

14. What finally happens to the ship, and how is the mariner saved? Why is the pilot's boy frightened?

15. What service does the hermit perform? What is the mariner's final doom or sentence? What strange power does he have?

16. How does the mariner's tale affect the wedding guest?

Developing Skills in Reading Literature

1. **Literary Ballad.** This poem is a literary ballad, modeled on the English and Scottish popular ballads, which had been part of the literary tradition since the Middle Ages. The literary ballad was a popular form among the Romantic poets, who imitated the techniques and tried to catch the traditional flavor of the folk ballad.

Review the characteristics of the folk ballad described in the introduction to the English and Scottish ballads in Unit 2. Then identify the qualities of the folk ballad that are apparent in "The Rime of the Ancient Mariner." What qualities distinguish this poem from the folk ballad?

2. **Simile.** A common figure of speech in the traditional ballad is the simile, and this poem also abounds with them. Find five similes that seem particularly

effective. Do the similes in this poem seem to function most often in describing character, establishing setting, or advancing plot? Explain.

3. **Imagery.** How much does this poem depend on visualization and the use of color imagery to intensify its effects? What about the appearance and movements of the sun, moon, and stars? Point out passages that are effective pictorially.

Is there any relation between the action in this tale and the image patterns of cold and heat? Images associated with refreshing rain follow those describing parching heat and thirst. How is this contrast significant in the context of the narrative?

4. **Symbol.** Some critics view the albatross as a Christ-symbol or relate the shooting of the albatross to original sin. Do you see any evidence of these connections in the poem? If the mariner is a kind of Adam and his crime represents the fall of mankind, what would the crew symbolize? the ship? the hermit? Apart from any Biblical associations, what might the albatross represent in the context of the poem? Explain the symbolism as it relates to other elements in the poem.

5. **Theme.** Why was it a crime to kill the albatross? Is the prohibition just a matter of kindness to animals? Is superstition involved? If the mariner had killed a crow or a vulture or some other bird of ill omen, would he still have committed a crime? Does the gloss at the end of Part I provide a clue? What passages in the poem suggest that the mariner's spontaneous upwelling of love for the beauty of living things put him into a state of grace and allowed him to do penance for his deed? Develop a thematic statement for this poem that summarizes Coleridge's ideas about the essential relationship between human beings and nature.

Developing Vocabulary

Understanding Changes in Language. In imitating the old ballads, Coleridge deliberately included many archaic usages; for example, "I wist," "I trow," "we ken," and "eftsoons." He also enhanced the poem's flavor with other words that are still current but slightly outside the mainstream of common usage. Record the meaning and/or the derivation of the following words. agape (line 163) bark (line 202) jargoning (line 362) smote (line 551) charnel (line 435)

George Gordon, Lord Byron
1788–1824

"I am such a strange *mélange* of good and evil, that it would be difficult to describe me," Lord Byron once said. Because he is the most glamorous figure in British literature, it is difficult to consider Byron's artistic merit apart from the legend of the man. Handsome, adventurous, restless, melancholy, hedonistic, and self-destructive, Byron himself seems quintessentially modern, yet his poetic style was firmly rooted in the eighteenth century. Although his poetry seldom equals that of contemporaries such as Wordsworth, Coleridge, Keats, and Shelley, it is Byron, not these more innovative writers, who symbolizes the Romantic spirit.

Byron's father, Captain Mad Jack Byron, was a profligate rascal who married Byron's mother for her money, squandered it in a matter of months, then abandoned her and his son. Byron had been born with a clubfoot, and although years of agonizing and often inept treatment left him with but a slight limp, he remained pathologically aware of his disability. This sensitivity contributed both to his shyness among strangers and to his passionate devotion to athletics, including swimming, boxing, riding, and fencing.

When he was ten, Byron became the sixth Lord Byron, entitling him to the ancestral estate of Newstead and to enrollment at fashionable Harrow School and then Cambridge University. He was not rich, however, at least not rich for a Lord, and he squandered much of his inheritance. Byron intended to enter the House of Lords for a political career, but first he tried writing poetry. In 1807 he published an unremarkable, slim volume entitled *Hours of Idleness*. The prestigious *Edinburgh Review* savagely denounced the book, prompting Byron to reply with the satirical *English Bards and Scotch Reviewers* in 1809. Instantly popular, the talk of London, it confirmed Byron in his commitment to a career as a poet.

For the next two years, Byron toured Portugal, Spain, Malta, Greece, and Asia Minor. On this adventurous excursion he gathered material for *Childe Harold's Pilgrimage* (1812–1818), a long, lively poem about the adventures of a brilliant but unhappy young Lord. Back in London in 1812, Byron entered the House of Lords, made a few speeches, and then suddenly found himself famous; *Childe Harold* had become an instant and enormous success.

The sale of Newstead gave Byron a modicum of financial security, and he traveled through Europe. He added cantos to *Childe Harold* and in 1818 began his masterful *Don Juan*, a picaresque verse satire that drew on Byron's own experiences and was widely attacked for its supposed immorality.

In Italy, Byron befriended Shelley, who admired *Don Juan*, and Byron and Shelley became part of the flamboyantly colorful "Pisan Circle" (so named because its members lived in Pisa) of political adventurers. In 1822, Shelley was drowned. The next year, Byron, seeking an opportunity for heroism that would redeem his sullied reputation in the eyes of his countrymen, decided to help the Greeks fight the Turks. Byron was not to see this action, however, for he succumbed to a fever after being caught in a downpour on his daily ride, and he died on April 19, 1824, in Missolonghi, Greece. The Greeks consider him one of their national heroes.

She Walks in Beauty

This poem was inspired by Lady Wilmot Horton, Byron's cousin by marriage, who arrived at a party wearing a black dress with spangles.

She walks in beauty, like the night
  Of cloudless climes and starry skies;
And all that's best of dark and bright
  Meet in her aspect[1] and her eyes:
Thus mellowed to that tender light   5
  Which heaven to gaudy day denies.

One shade the more, one ray the less,
  Had half impaired the nameless grace
Which waves in every raven tress,
  Or softly lightens o'er her face;   10
Where thoughts serenely sweet express
  How pure, how dear their dwelling place.

And on that cheek, and o'er that brow,
  So soft, so calm, yet eloquent,
The smiles that win, the tints that glow,   15
  But tell of days in goodness spent,
A mind at peace with all below,
  A heart whose love is innocent!

---

1. **aspect:** appearance.

Getting at Meaning

1. In the first stanza, to what exactly is the lady's beauty compared? Is it darkness? brightness? What is "that tender light"?

2. In line 8, how would you express the verb *had . . . impaired* in everyday English?

3. What lines in the second stanza describe the lady's "nameless grace" in terms of both darkness and light?

4. In line 17, what do you think is meant by "all below"?

Developing Skills in Reading Literature

1. **Meter and Rhyme Scheme.** What metrical pattern is used in this poem? What is the rhyme scheme? Considering both the form and the content of this poem, what connections do you see between Byron's poem and the Cavalier tradition? the Neoclassic tradition? What characteristics are clearly Romantic?

2. **Sound Devices and Mood.** How do consonance, assonance, and alliteration add to the musical quality of this poem? How do they contribute to the prevailing mood? Cite specific examples from the poem.

3. **Theme.** What does the woman's physical appearance reveal about her? What does this poem suggest about the relation between body and soul? What similar relation is implied in this poem? Does the poem support the Romantic concept of the unity of all creation? Explain.

Developing Vocabulary

Using a Dictionary. Examine more closely three of the words in this poem.

a. While the usual meaning of *aspect* (line 4) is "appearance," the word has another related meaning, old but rare. Find this meaning in a dictionary. Might Byron have had this meaning in mind when writing the poem?

b. The poem refers to "gaudy day" in line 6. What is the noun form of *gaudy* and its derivation? Does your dictionary differentiate among the synonyms of *gaudy*? In the poem, what adjective functions as the antonym of *gaudy*?

c. The word *clime* can mean "climate," but what else does it mean? What usage label (such as "slang" or "obsolete") does your dictionary assign to this word?

So, We'll Go No More A-Roving

So, we'll go no more a-roving
  So late into the night,
Though the heart be still as loving,
  And the moon be still as bright.

For the sword outwears its sheath,   5
  And the soul wears out the breast,
And the heart must pause to breathe,
  And love itself have rest.

Though the night was made for loving,
  And the day returns too soon,   10
Yet we'll go no more a-roving
  By the light of the moon.

Getting at Meaning

1. What kind of roving does the speaker seem to mean?

2. Why does the speaker no longer wish to go a-roving? Is it indifference or something else?

Developing Skills in Reading Literature

1. **Meter.** How many stresses, or strong accents, occur in each line of this poem? Is there variation in the number of weak accents? What is the effect of the meter in the last line?

2. **Tone.** How would you characterize the tone of this poem? How do the clauses beginning with *Though* contribute to this tone? What is the effect of meter in creating the tone?

3. **Theme and Figurative Language.** What is the speaker saying about the nature of passion? How would you express this idea in your own words? How does the speaker express the theme of the poem through figurative language?

Developing Vocabulary

1. **Word Origins.** Look up the etymologies of *rove* and *rover* for an example of how the meanings of separate words can merge or influence each other. Which word is related to archery and which to pirates? Is either of these connotations appropriate in Byron's poem?

2. **Synonyms.** Your dictionary may discuss *rove* as a synonym of *roam*. How do these words differ? Why is *rove* a better choice for this poem?

from Childe Harold's Pilgrimage
Apostrophe to the Ocean

There is a pleasure in the pathless woods,
There is a rapture on the lonely shore,
There is society, where none intrudes,
By the deep sea, and music in its roar;
I love not man the less, but nature more,   5
From these our interviews, in which I steal
From all I may be, or have been before,
To mingle with the universe, and feel
What I can ne'er express, yet cannot all conceal.

Roll on, thou deep and dark blue Ocean—roll!   10
Ten thousand fleets sweep over thee in vain;
Man marks the earth with ruin—his control
Stops with the shore—upon the watery plain
The wrecks are all thy deed, nor doth remain
A shadow of man's ravage,[1] save his own,   15

---

1. **ravage:** destruction.

When, for a moment, like a drop of rain,
He sinks into thy depths with bubbling groan—
Without a grave, unknelled, uncoffined, and unknown.

His steps are not upon thy paths—thy fields
Are not a spoil for him—thou dost arise   20
And shake him from thee; the vile strength he wields
For earth's destruction thou dost all despise,
Spurning him from thy bosom to the skies,
And send'st him, shivering in thy playful spray
And howling, to his gods, where haply[2] lies   25
His petty hope in some near port or bay,
And dashest him again to earth; there let him lay.

The armaments which thunderstrike the walls
Of rock-built cities, bidding nations quake
And monarchs tremble in their capitals,   30
The oak leviathans,[3] whose huge ribs make
Their clay creator[4] the vain title take
Of lord of thee, and arbiter of war—
These are thy toys, and as the snowy flake,
They melt into thy yeast of waves, which mar   35
Alike the Armada's[5] pride, or spoils of Trafalgar.[6]

Thy shores are empires, changed in all save thee—
Assyria, Greece, Rome, Carthage, what are they?
Thy waters washed them power while they were free,
And many a tyrant since; their shores obey   40
The stranger, slave, or savage; their decay
Has dried up realms to deserts—not so thou,
Unchangeable save to thy wild waves' play.
Time writes no wrinkle on thine azure brow;
Such as creation's dawn beheld, thou rollest now.   45

---

2. **haply:** perhaps.
3. **oak leviathans:** large ships.
4. **clay creator:** human beings.
5. **Armada:** The Spanish Armada was defeated by the British fleet in 1588.
6. **Trafalgar:** Lord Nelson led the British fleet to victory over the French and Spanish fleets in 1805.

Thou glorious mirror, where the Almighty's form
Glasses itself in tempest; in all time,
Calm or convulsed—in breeze, or gale, or storm,
Icing the pole, or in the torrid clime
Dark-heaving—boundless, endless, and sublime;   50
The image of eternity, the throne
Of the Invisible; even from out thy slime
The monsters of the deep are made; each zone
Obeys thee; thou goest forth, dread, fathomless, alone.

And I have loved thee, Ocean! and my joy   55
Of youthful sports was on thy breast to be
Borne, like thy bubbles, onward; from a boy
I wantoned with thy breakers[7]—they to me
Were a delight; and if the freshening sea
Made them a terror—'twas a pleasing fear,   60
For I was as it were a child of thee,
And trusted to thy billows far and near,
And laid my hand upon thy mane—as I do here.

---

7. **I . . . breakers:** Byron was a powerful swimmer.

Getting at Meaning

1. What aspect of the ocean does the speaker admire? What basic comparison in the poem dramatizes this quality?

2. Explain "thy fields/Are not a spoil for him." (lines 19–20). What are "thy toys" (line 34)? What qualities of the "clay creator" (line 32) are being referred to here? What other lines suggest the same qualities?

3. Why is the ocean called a "glorious mirror" in line 46?

4. What particular emotions has the ocean inspired in the speaker?

Developing Skills in Reading Literature

1. **Spenserian Stanza.** Chart the rhyme scheme of the stanza form used in this poem. How does this form contribute a sense of unity to the poem? Now scan the meter. What variation is consistent throughout the poem?

A stanza with this rhyme scheme and meter is known as a Spenserian stanza; the line at variance with the others is called an Alexandrine. What is the meter of an Alexandrine? What effect does the Alexandrine seem to have, coming where it does in the stanza?

For *Childe Harold's Pilgrimage*, Byron revised the verse form invented by Edmund Spenser for *The Faerie Queene*, a complex and often philosophical poem glorifying England and Queen Elizabeth. Why does the Spenserian stanza seem an appropriate form, at least for this excerpt from Byron's poem?

2. **Simile and Metaphor.** Explain what quality of the ocean is described or implied by means of the following similes: "like a drop of rain" (line 16), "as the snowy flake" (line 34), and "like thy bubbles" (line 57). What do the metaphors "thy yeast" (line 35) and "thy mane" (line 63) suggest? What view of nature is communicated through these figures of speech?

3. **Tone and Theme.** Read line 10 aloud. How would you describe the tone it conveys? Find other lines that produce a similar effect. In what way is this tone appropriate to the poem's theme?

On This Day I Complete My Thirty-Sixth Year

'Tis time this heart should be unmoved,
   Since others it hath ceased to move:
Yet, though I cannot be beloved,
     Still let me love!

My days are in the yellow leaf;   5
   The flowers and fruits of love are gone;
The worm, the canker, and the grief
     Are mine alone!

The fire that on my bosom preys
   Is lone as some volcanic isle;   10
No torch is kindled at its blaze—
     A funeral pile.

The hope, the fear, the jealous care,
   The exalted portion of the pain
And power of love, I cannot share,   15
     But wear the chain.

But 'tis not *thus*—and 'tis not *here*—
   Such thoughts should shake my soul,
      nor *now*,
Where glory decks the hero's bier,
     Or binds his brow.   20

The sword, the banner, and the field,
   Glory and Greece, around me see!
The Spartan, borne upon his shield,
     Was not more free.

Awake! (not Greece—she *is* awake!)   25
   Awake, my spirit! Think through *whom*
Thy lifeblood tracks its parent lake,
     And then strike home!

Tread those reviving passions down,
   Unworthy manhood!—unto thee   30
Indifferent should the smile or frown
     Of Beauty be.

If thou regret'st thy youth, *why live?*
    The land of honorable death
Is here:—up to the field, and give   35
    Away thy breath!

Seek out—less often sought than found—
    A soldier's grave, for thee the best;
Then look around, and choose thy ground,
    And take thy rest.   40

Getting at Meaning

1. How would you summarize the speaker's complaint in the first four stanzas? Why are "Such thoughts" (line 18) inappropriate?

2. If the speaker is Byron, what biographical facts relate to the content of this poem? Does the poem serve as a fitting epitaph, or tribute, to Byron? Explain.

3. What are "those reviving passions" (line 29)? What is the speaker's attitude toward them?

4. What does the speaker mean when he says, "If thou regret'st thy youth, *why live?*" How does he free himself of the mood expressed in the first 16 lines?

Developing Skills in Reading Literature

1. **Meter.** Scan the meter of this poem. How does a consistent variation in the overall pattern enhance the dramatic effectiveness of each stanza? Contrast the effect with that of the Alexandrine in "Apostrophe to the Ocean."

2. **Figurative Language.** Analyze the fire imagery in the third stanza. What does *volcanic* suggest? What does the metaphor in lines 11 and 12 imply about the speaker's passions?

3. **Internal Rhyme and Theme.** Find the internal rhyme, rhyme within lines of poetry, in the final stanza. What idea does this rhyme underscore? What major theme?

4. **Tone.** How does the tone of the last six stanzas differ from that of the first four? Point out some of the ways the tone is achieved in each group of stanzas. Note particularly the connotations of key words and the way that the poet achieves emphasis and rhythmic variations through punctuation and phrasing. Note also the sounds of the language, created through assonance, consonance, and alliteration.

5. **Speaker.** In both this poem and the excerpt from *Childe Harold's Pilgrimage,* the speakers are identified closely with Byron and with the Byronic hero, a passionate, melancholy, solitary, and typically Romantic character. What qualities of the Byronic hero are implied in these two selections? in the other two poems by Byron?

Developing Writing Skills

Narration: Establishing Tone. The tone and mood of this poem change as the speaker resolves his problem and alters his attitude. In several paragraphs, narrate an event, either real or imagined, during which a character undergoes a change of heart, suffers a disappointment, overcomes depression, or reacts to a surprise. At some point in the narrative, the tone should shift dramatically to reflect the change in the character's feelings. Use either first-person or third-person narration, whichever is more appropriate to your subject.

John Keats

1795–1821

A beloved figure in literature, Keats wrote some of the most beautiful poems in the English language in the few years before his death at the age of twenty-five. "I have lov'd the principle of beauty in all things," he said. There is virtually nothing abstract or intellectual about his poems, which appeal directly to the senses. Keats's friends believed that his writing possesses the same harmonious intensity as Shakespeare's works, an opinion echoed by many critics since.

Keats came from humble origins. His father, who had worked in a livery stable before marrying the boss's daughter, eventually took over the business, which was prosperous enough for the boy to attend Reverend John Clarke's private academy at Enfield. Although small in stature, young Keats was pugnacious, distinguishing himself in fistfights. One of his teachers, seeing that Keats was intellectually gifted, encouraged his reading and introduced him to music and the theatre.

Keats's father died in a riding accident when the boy was eight; his mother died of tuberculosis when he was fourteen. At fifteen his guardian apprenticed Keats to a surgeon, and he began to study medicine. Keats abandoned this career in favor of literature, however, largely due to the encouragement he received from Shelley, Lamb, and Hazlitt, important writers who were part of the circle surrounding Leigh Hunt, an influential man of letters.

Keats's first book, *Poems*, came out in 1817. *Endymion*, an ambitious allegory, followed the next year and was met with reviews that, according to a sentimental but false legend, contributed to the author's early death. *Blackwood's Magazine*, for example, suggested that the surgeon's apprentice stick to his "plasters, pills, and ointment boxes." These reviews were at least in part politically motivated, for Leigh Hunt was an outspoken radical, and Keats was attacked because of his association with Hunt's group. It is unlikely in any case that Keats worried too much over his reviews; he was maturing so fast as an artist that he had his own reservations about his earlier work, and his personal problems were pressing: his brother

JOHN KEATS. *William Hilton (after Joseph Severn). National Portrait Gallery, London.*

George had gone bankrupt in Kentucky, and his younger brother Tom needed his attendance as he wasted away from tuberculosis. On top of all that, Keats fell in love with a pretty, lively girl of eighteen, Fanny Brawne, but their engagement was made impossible by Keats's poverty and by his increasing awareness that he, too, had contracted the disease that had proved fatal to his mother and brother.

In the midst of his emotional distress, Keats in the first ten months of 1819 produced a series of poetic masterworks: his great odes, "The Eve of St. Agnes," "La Belle Dame sans Merci," and numerous sonnets. Graceful, sensuous, musical, these works epitomize English poetry for many readers and are all the more remarkable because they were produced by a poet not yet twenty-four years old.

When Keats began to experience symptoms of tuberculosis, he sought the milder climate of Italy, but the worsening ravages of the disease made his last months what he called "a posthumous existence." In this last as in his earlier adversities, Keats remained gallant, writing letters that grace English literature as his poems had done. He died in Rome on February 23, 1821, and was buried beneath the epitaph he composed: "Here lies one whose name was writ in water."

Ode on a Grecian Urn

Thou still unravished bride of quietness,
   Thou foster child of silence and slow time,
Sylvan historian, who canst thus express
   A flowery tale more sweetly than our rhyme:
What leaf-fringed legend haunts about thy shape   5
   Of deities or mortals, or of both,
      In Tempe[1] or the dales of Arcady?[2]
What men or gods are these? What maidens loath?
   What mad pursuit? What struggle to escape?
      What pipes and timbrels?[3] What wild ecstasy?   10

Heard melodies are sweet, but those unheard
   Are sweeter; therefore, ye soft pipes, play on;
Not to the sensual ear, but, more endeared,
   Pipe to the spirit ditties of no tone.
Fair youth, beneath the trees, thou canst not leave   15
   Thy song, nor ever can those trees be bare;
      Bold Lover, never, never canst thou kiss,
Though winning near the goal—yet, do not grieve;
   She cannot fade, though thou hast not thy bliss,
      Forever wilt thou love, and she be fair!   20

Ah, happy, happy boughs! that cannot shed
   Your leaves, nor ever bid the Spring adieu;
And, happy melodist, unwearièd,
   Forever piping songs forever new;
More happy love! more happy, happy love!   25
   Forever warm and still to be enjoyed,
      Forever panting, and forever young;
All breathing human passion far above,
   That leaves a heart high-sorrowful and cloyed,
      A burning forehead, and a parching tongue.   30

Who are these coming to the sacrifice?
   To what green altar, O mysterious priest,
Lead'st thou that heifer lowing at the skies,
   And all her silken flanks with garlands dressed?

---

1. **Tempe:** a beautiful valley in Greece.
2. **Arcady:** a simple, rustic region in Greece.
3. **timbrels:** ancient tambourines.

What little town by river or seashore,   35
 Or mountain-built with peaceful citadel,
  Is emptied of this folk, this pious morn?
And, little town, thy streets for evermore
 Will silent be; and not a soul to tell
  Why thou art desolate, can e'er return.   40

O Attic[4] shape! Fair attitude! with brede[5]
 Of marble men and maidens overwrought,
With forest branches and the trodden weed;
 Thou, silent form, dost tease us out of thought
As doth eternity. Cold Pastoral.[6]   45
 When old age shall this generation waste,
  Thou shalt remain, in midst of other woe
Than ours, a friend to man, to whom thou say'st,
 "Beauty is truth, truth beauty—that is all
  Ye know on earth, and all ye need to know."   50

---

4. **Attic:** a Grecian shape of elegant simplicity and grace.
5. **brede:** embroidery.
6. **Cold Pastoral:** poem in marble.

Getting at Meaning

1. In the first stanza, why is the urn a "sylvan historian"? What is the "flowery tale" it tells?

2. To what "unheard melodies" does the second stanza refer? Why are they "sweeter" than heard ones?

3. Similarly, the third stanza refers to warmth and passion of two kinds, or on two levels. What are they? What advantages do the lovers on the urn enjoy? What are the limitations of art, as represented by the urn?

4. The urn has caught the warmth and motion of a moment held forever in suspension, and in the fourth stanza the reader is drawn even further into that "eternal present." What part of the scene is not even pictured on the urn and must be imagined? In the last line of the fourth stanza, who or what is "desolate"?

5. What essential contradiction or paradox is indicated by "cold pastoral"? What comparison is implied in this phrase? Briefly explain the comparison.

Developing Skills in Reading Literature

1. **Ode.** The ode, an elaborate kind of lyric poem, deals with a serious theme in language that is dignified as well as enthusiastic and exalted. In what ways does this poem exemplify the characteristics of an ode?

2. **Diction.** Poets can make use of ambiguity, choosing words with various possible meanings. Consider *still* in line 1. In what two senses might this word be understood? How might each be appropriate to the poem's meaning?

3. **Imagery and Structure.** Which stanza contains images suggesting heat? How does the stanza that follows "cool" the temperature? Where does the poem emphasize (unheard) sounds, and where does it emphasize silence? Where is the focus on the depicted scene, and where on the urn itself? Based on the imagery in the poem, can you detect any general pattern, any rising and falling structure?

4. Theme. The poem leads up to the statement, "Beauty is truth, truth beauty." Does this seem to be a contradiction? If so, perhaps the poem tries to resolve this contradiction by presenting the statement from the perspective not of our temporal world but of the urn's immortal one. Try substituting *poetry* for *beauty* and *science* for *truth:* "Poetry is science, science poetry." The Romantics were often concerned with the split between the esthetic (poetry) and the practical (science). What do you think? Are they essentially one?

What is the relationship between art and life, according to this poem? Explain.

In describing unheard melodies and unpictured scenes, the speaker makes a statement about imagination. What message is implied about the power and range of poetic imagination? about a work of art as compared to the creative impulse? Does the message in the final two lines seem to reinforce or contradict these ideas? Explain.

To Autumn

Season of mists and mellow fruitfulness,
    Close bosom-friend of the maturing sun;
Conspiring with him how to load and bless
    With fruit the vines that round the thatch-eaves run;
To bend with apples the mossed cottage-trees,   5
    And fill all fruit with ripeness to the core;
      To swell the gourd, and plump the hazel shells
With a sweet kernel; to set budding more,
    And still more, later flowers for the bees,
    Until they think warm days will never cease,   10
      For Summer has o'er-brimmed their clammy cells.

Who hath not seen thee oft amid thy store?
    Sometimes whoever seeks abroad may find
Thee sitting careless on a granary floor,
    Thy hair soft-lifted by the winnowing wind;   15
Or on a half-reaped furrow sound asleep,
    Drowsed with the fume of poppies, while thy hook
      Spares the next swath and all its twinèd flowers:
And sometimes like a gleaner thou dost keep
    Steady thy laden head across a brook;   20
    Or by a cider-press, with patient look,
      Thou watchest the last oozings hours by hours.

Where are the songs of Spring? Aye, where are they?
 Think not of them, thou hast thy music too—
While barred clouds bloom the soft-dying day,   25
 And touch the stubble-plains with rosy hue;
Then in a wailful choir the small gnats mourn
 Among the river sallows,[1] borne aloft
  Or sinking as the light wind lives or dies;
And full-grown lambs loud bleat from hilly bourn;[2]   30
 Hedge crickets sing; and now with treble soft
 The redbreast whistles from a garden croft;[3]
 And gathering swallows twitter in the skies.

---

1. **sallows:** willow trees.
2. **bourn:** region.
3. **croft:** small enclosed field.

Getting at Meaning

1. What impression of autumn emerges from the description in this poem? What attitude toward spring is implied?

2. Who or what is the subject of the second stanza? How do you know?

Developing Skills in Reading Literature

1. **Imagery.** A remarkable quality of this poem is the richness and profusion of its imagery, the concentrated intensity of its sensuous detail. Can you detect any pattern or organization of the images? What details in each stanza suggest different stages of autumn? Is there any progression in the time of day? Which stanza emphasizes the ripening process? which the harvesting? How difficult is the work? What details carry a touch of melancholy, suggesting the passing of time, the transcience of beauty? On the other hand, where do you find a sense of careless ease? where a feeling that time has no bounds?

The imagery in this poem appeals to all five senses. Find examples of each. Do certain kinds of images predominate in particular stanzas? Do any of the visual images remind you of paintings you have seen?

2. **Personification.** How is autumn personified? How does the personification vary among the stanzas? Do these figures of speech seem realistic, or mythical, or both?

3. **Tone.** Do you find any progression in the tone of this poem? Examine the third stanza. What sort of mixed tone seems to emerge? This stanza demonstrates the ability of poetic language to convey human feelings in all their subtlety and complexity. What details, suggestions, and connotations of words help produce the effect here?

Developing Writing Skills

Analyzing Form. Analyze closely the meter and rhyme scheme of ''To Autumn'' and ''Ode on a Grecian Urn.'' Report your findings in a paragraph or two, noting variations among the stanzas within each ode as well as similarities and differences between the odes. Draw a conclusion about how form reflects content in both poems.

When I Have Fears That I May Cease To Be

When I have fears that I may cease to be
  Before my pen has gleaned my teeming brain,
Before high-pilèd books, in charactery,[1]
  Hold like rich garners the full-ripened grain;
When I behold, upon the night's starred face,   5
  Huge cloudy symbols of a high romance,
And think that I may never live to trace
  Their shadows, with the magic hand of chance;[2]
And when I feel, fair creature of an hour,
  That I shall never look upon thee more,   10
Never have relish in the fairy power
  Of unreflecting love—then on the shore
Of the wide world I stand alone, and think
Till love and fame to nothingness do sink.

---

1. **charactery:** handwriting.
2. **chance:** inspiration.

DEATHBED PORTRAIT OF JOHN KEATS (pen and ink wash).
*By permission of the London Borough of Camden
from the collections at Keats House, Hampstead.*

Bright Star! Would I Were Steadfast As Thou Art

Bright star! would I were steadfast as thou art—
  Not in lone splendor hung aloft the night
And watching, with eternal lids apart,
  Like nature's patient, sleepless Eremite,[1]
The moving waters at their priestlike task   5
  Of pure ablution round earth's human shores,
Or gazing on the new soft-fallen mask
  Of snow upon the mountains and the moors—
No—yet still steadfast, still unchangeable,
  Pillowed upon my fair love's ripening breast,   10
To feel forever its soft fall and swell,
  Awake forever in a sweet unrest,
Still, still to hear her tender-taken breath,
And so live ever—or else swoon to death.

---

1. **Eremite** (er′ ə mīt): hermit.

Solitude

O solitude! if I must with thee dwell,
  Let it not be among the jumbled heap
  Of murky buildings; climb with me the steep,—
Nature's observatory,—whence the dell,
Its flowery slopes, its river's crystal swell,   5
  May seem a span; let me thy vigils keep
  'Mongst boughs pavilion'd, where the deer's swift leap
Startles the wild bee from the foxglove bell.
But though I'll gladly trace these scenes with thee,
  Yet the sweet converse of an innocent mind,   10
  Whose words are images of thoughts refin'd,
Is my soul's pleasure; and it sure must be
  Almost the highest bliss of humankind,
When to thy haunts two kindred spirits flee.

WIVENHOE PARK, ESSEX, 1816. *John Constable.*
National Gallery of Art, Washington, D. C.
Widener Collection.

On First Looking into Chapman's Homer

Keats and Charles C. Clarke spent one October evening reading a translation of Homer by George Chapman, an Elizabethan poet. Keats returned home at dawn, wrote this sonnet, and sent it to Clarke who received it that same morning.

Much have I traveled in the realms of gold,
   And many goodly states and kingdoms seen;
   Round many western islands have I been
Which bards in fealty to Apollo[1] hold.
Oft of one wide expanse had I been told   5
   That deep-browed Homer ruled as his demesne;[2]
   Yet did I never breathe its pure serene[3]
Till I heard Chapman speak out loud and bold.
Then felt I like some watcher of the skies
   When a new planet swims into his ken;   10
Or like stout Cortez[4] when with eagle eyes
   He stared at the Pacific—and all his men
Looked at each other with a wild surmise—
   Silent, upon a peak in Darien.[5]

---

1. **Apollo:** Greek god of poetry and music.
2. **demesne** (di mān´): domain, refers to the *Iliad* and the *Odyssey*.
3. **serene:** clear air.
4. **Cortez:** Balboa, not Cortez, discovered the Pacific Ocean. This is a famous error.
5. **Darien:** located on the Isthmus of Panama.

To One Who Has Been Long in City Pent

To one who has been long in city pent,
'Tis very sweet to look into the fair
And open face of heaven,—to breathe a prayer
Full in the smile of the blue firmament
Who is more happy, when, with heart's content,   5
Fatigued he sinks into some pleasant lair
Of wavy grass, and reads a debonair
And gentle tale of love and languishment?
Returning home at evening, with an ear
Catching the notes of Philomel,[1]—and eye   10
Watching the sailing cloudlet's bright career,
He mourns that day so soon has glided by,
E'en like the passage of an angel's tear
That falls through the clear ether[2] silently.

---

1. **Philomel:** the nightingale.
2. **ether:** sky.

Getting at Meaning

WHEN I HAVE FEARS THAT I MAY CEASE TO BE

1. What is the subject of the verb *hold* in line 4? To what books does the speaker refer? What is the "full-ripened grain"?

2. In line 8, what shadows does the speaker wish to trace? What does "the magic hand of chance" suggest?

3. What is the "fair creature of an hour"?

4. What two things does the speaker sometimes fear?

5. What philosophical conclusion does the speaker arrive at?

BRIGHT STAR! WOULD I WERE STEADFAST AS THOU ART

6. In what ways does the speaker want to be like the star and yet not like it?

7. Describe the state that the speaker wishes for in the poem's last lines.

SOLITUDE

8. What two natural scenes does the speaker recall? Describe them in your own words.

9. Where would the speaker rather not experience solitude? What would be the ideal way to experience it?

ON FIRST LOOKING INTO CHAPMAN'S HOMER

10. In a figurative sense, what kind of traveling has the speaker been doing? What are the "realms of gold"? What is the "wide expanse" in line 5?

11. Which lines suggest that, before reading Chapman's work, the speaker had not read Homer in an adequate translation?

TO ONE WHO HAS BEEN LONG IN CITY PENT

12. In the opening lines, what aspect of nature provides the most relief to one who has been "pent" in the city?

13. What are the touches of melancholy or regret in this sonnet?

Developing Skills in Reading Literature

1. **Sonnet.** Identify the sonnet form of "When I Have Fears" and show how each of the main divisions treats a separate idea. Notice that the poem is all one sentence. How does parallelism add to the symmetry of the poem?

Consider the rhyme scheme and the sense pattern or division of ideas in "Bright Star." Do they coincide? How would you classify the sonnet?

What is the relationship between form and meaning in "Solitude"? in "To One Who Has Been Long in City Pent"?

"On First Looking into Chapman's Homer" has a "before-after" structure. Does it correspond with the rhyme scheme?

2. **Diction.** The diction in "When I Have Fears" helps to establish its tone and meaning. What phrases suggest a rich and profuse imagination? What is the effect of the word *charactery*?

In "Solitude" find a noun that is usually an adjective and a verb that is usually a noun. Suggest possible synonyms for these words. How do their connotations differ from those of the words in the sonnet?

3. **Sound Devices.** In "When I Have Fears" identify the touches of alliteration, the lines containing assonance, and the consonant that seems to recur most often.

In "Bright Star" note the repeated *n* sound in line 2 and the repeated *l*'s, continuing in lines 3 and 4. Note the consonance and assonance in "soft fallen." Where else do vowel and consonant repetitions produce musical effects?

Read aloud line 2 of "Solitude," and comment on the poet's use of vowels. Which vowel sound can be heard quite frequently in this poem?

Note the contrast in sound between the phrases "city pent" and "the fair and open face of heaven." How does this contrast emphasize the opposing meanings? In line 8 of the same poem, what sound effects reinforce the meaning?

4. **Imagery.** In "Bright Star" examine the images in the octave. What qualities predominate? How do they set off by contrast the predominant feeling of the sestet? How do these image patterns underline the poem's ideas?

The images in Keats's poems often have a marvelous specificity. Find a passage in "Solitude" that illustrates this quality.

In "To One Who Has Been Long in City Pent," point out three images that describe the sky as something pure and free.

"On First Looking into Chapman's Homer" ends with an image of the explorer, sighting the Pacific for the first time. How do the images in these four lines help create the remarkable effect of this scene? Is the mistaken identification of Cortez as the discoverer of the Pacific poetically significant? Does it detract from the meaning or impact of the poem?

5. **Caesura.** A caesura results from the interplay between the sense of a line and its rhythm. In the last four lines of "On First Looking into Chapman's Homer," the pauses seem to emphasize the feeling of discovery. Show where the caesuras occur in "Solitude" and in "To One Who Has Been Long in City Pent." What effect do they have on the rhythm of the poems?

6. **Oxymoron.** In "Bright Star" which phrase is an oxymoron? How does the phrase relate to the poem's theme?

Developing Vocabulary

1. **Word Origins and Appropriate Meanings.** The following words from "To One Who Has Been Long in City Pent" have had interesting histories, often involving changes in meaning. Look up their meanings and derivations. You know from a footnote that in this poem *ether* means "sky." Decide for each of the other words which meaning Keats intended.

career	debonair
firmament	ether

The word *pavilion,* used in "Solitude," has an insect in its background. Consult a dictionary to find out how etymology and entomology come together in this

word. Which sense of the word seems most appropriate in the context of this poem?

2. **Synonyms: Connotation.** "Solitude" contains the phrase "murky buildings." Find a dictionary that distinguishes among the synonyms of *dark*. What does *murky* suggest that the others do not?

Developing Writing Skills

1. **Writing a Sonnet.** Working within the arbitrary rules of the sonnet can be both challenging and satisfying, for the form is capable of expressing an idea or emotion in a highly concentrated, dramatic way. To create a sonnet of your own, begin by writing lines in iambic pentameter. You eventually will hit upon a rhyme scheme. Decide then how you will follow through on the English or the Italian form. Remember that a final couplet can provide an epigrammatic close and that a sestet can resolve or comment on an octave. Rework your draft until you are satisfied with the result.

2. **Analyzing Imagery.** Choose one of these sonnets, and in a brief composition analyze the image patterns precisely, showing how they contribute to the tone, mood, and meaning of the poem. For example, in "Bright Star" what kind of images seem to be connected with the star? What about sky imagery in "To One Who Has Been Long in City Pent"? or exploration in "On First Looking into Chapman's Homer"? or romance and imagination in "When I Have Fears"?

3. **Using Comparisons and Contrasts.** In several paragraphs, compare the theme of "Bright Star" with that of "Solitude," or compare the sestet of "Bright Star" with the second and third stanzas of "Ode on a Grecian Urn." In your composition, comment on both similarities and differences.

Letter

February 19, 1818.

Almost any man may, like the spider, spin from his own inwards his own airy Citadel.[1] The points of leaves and twigs on which the spider begins her work are few, and she fills the air with a beautiful circuiting. Man should be content with as few points to tip with the fine web of his soul, and weave a tapestry empyrean[2]—full of symbols for his spiritual eye, of softness for his spiritual touch, of space for his wandering, of distinctness for his luxury.

John Keats

---

1. **Citadel:** fortress, refuge.
2. **empyrean** (em' pī rē' ən): the abode of God.

To Fanny Brawne

July 8th. [Postmark, Newport, 10 July 1819].

My sweet Girl,

Your Letter gave me more delight than anything in the world but yourself could do; indeed I am almost astonished that any absent one should have that luxurious power over my senses which I feel. Even when I am not thinking of you I receive your influence and a tenderer nature stealing upon me. All my thoughts, my unhappiest days and nights, have I find not at all cured me of my love of Beauty, but made it so intense that I am miserable that you are not with me: or rather breathe in that dull sort of patience that cannot be called Life. I never knew before, what such a love as you have made me feel, was; I did not believe in it; my Fancy was afraid of it, lest it should burn me up. But if you will fully love me, though there may be some fire, 'twill not be more than we can bear when moistened and bedewed with Pleasures. You mention "horrid people" and ask me whether it depend upon them whether I see you again. Do understand me, my love, in this. I have so much of you in my heart that I must turn Mentor[1] when I see a chance of harm befalling you. I would never see any thing but Pleasure in your eyes, love on your lips, and Happiness in your steps. I would wish to see you among those amusements suitable to your inclinations and spirits; so that our loves might be a delight in the midst of Pleasures agreeable enough, rather than a resource from vexations and cares. But I doubt much, in case of the worst, whether I shall be philosopher enough to follow my own Lessons: if I saw my resolution give you a pain I could not. Why may I not speak of your Beauty, since without that I could never have lov'd you?—I cannot conceive any beginning of such love as I have for you but Beauty. There may be a sort of love for which, without the least sneer at it, I have the highest respect and can admire it in others: but it has not the richness, the bloom, the full form, the enchantment of love after my own heart. So let me speak of your Beauty, though to my own endangering: if you could be so cruel to me as to try elsewhere its Power. You say you are afraid I shall think you do not love me—in saying this you make me ache the more to be near you. I am at the diligent use of my faculties here, I do not pass a day without sprawling some blank verse or tagging some rhymes; and here I must confess, that (since I am on that subject) I love you the more in that

---

1. **Mentor:** a wise, loyal advisor.

I believe you have liked me for my own sake and for nothing else. I have met with women whom I really think would like to be married to a Poem and to be given away by a Novel. I have seen your Comet, and only wish it was a sign that poor Rice would get well whose illness makes him rather a melancholy companion: and the more so as to conquer his feelings and hide them from me, with a forced Pun. I kissed your writing over in the hope you had indulged me by leaving a trace of honey. What was your dream? Tell it me and I will tell you the interpretation thereof.

Ever yours, my love!

John Keats

Do not accuse me of delay—we have not here an opportunity of sending letters every day. Write speedily.

Getting at Meaning

1. According to the first selection, what might any person build, corresponding to a spider's web?

2. According to Keats, what caused him to love Fanny in the first place? How does he justify this fact? What quality caused him to love her still more?

3. Explain the reference to the other women attracted to Keats.

Developing Skills in Reading Literature

1. **Analogy.** Explain the comparison involving the web of the spider. Then find a similar comparison in the letter to Fanny Brawne. Is this comparison a true analogy or is it a metaphor? Give reasons for your answer.

2. **Parallelism.** In each letter, find an example of parallelism in sentence structure. What ideas are emphasized through this stylistic device?

3. **Diction.** In the first selection, how do the etymology and the connotations of *citadel* affect the meaning? What quality does *empyrean* convey that is appropriate here? In his letter to Fanny Brawne, Keats says that he must "turn Mentor." To what literary character might Keats have been comparing himself? Why might Keats have used the proper rather than the common form of this noun?

4. **Theme.** What can you find in these letters that might help explain why Keats became a poet, as well as his ideas of what poetry can do?

Percy Bysshe Shelley

1792–1822

Heretic and idealistic, Percy Bysshe Shelley dreamed of changing the world for the better, of redeeming sordid life, through love, imagination, and poetry. "Poets are the unacknowledged legislators of the world," he said. Now regarded as one of the greatest of the English Romantic poets, in his lifetime Shelley was scorned and his work was thoroughly ignored.

Scion of Sussex aristocrats, in line for a baronetcy, Shelley was sent to Eton, where he encountered a peculiarly harsh form of tyranny, the cruelty of bullies. Slightly built, no athlete or fighter, he became the butt of crude jests by older boys. At Oxford University he collaborated on a pantheistic pamphlet with the provocative title *The Necessity of Atheism* (1811), for which he was expelled during his freshman year and which alienated him from his father. That same year at the age of nineteen, Shelley eloped from London to Edinburgh with sixteen-year-old Harriet Westbrook and married her despite his belief that marriage was inherently degrading to both partners. Influenced by the radical social philosopher William Godwin, Shelley wrote and had printed privately his first significant poem, *Queen Mab, a Philosophical Poem* (1813), a utopian fantasy in which exploitive institutions wither away as mankind returns to its natural state of virtuous harmony.

Shelley fell in love with Godwin's stunning daughter, Mary. They ran away to France, and Shelley invited his wife to live with them as a devoted sister. Within two years, the distraught Harriet had drowned herself. Ironically, Shelley, who saw himself as a champion of the liberties of mankind, now found that most people in England despised him as an immoral, revolutionary atheist. Denied custody of his two children, he chose a life in exile, marrying Mary Godwin in 1818 and moving to Italy.

Shelley was at the peak of his form in the following years, when he wrote his acknowledged masterpiece *Prometheus Unbound* (1820); *The Cenci, a Tragedy in Five Acts* (1819); *Adonais* (1821), a heartfelt elegy on the death of Keats; *A*

PERCY BYSSHE SHELLEY, 1819. A. Curran. National Portrait Gallery, London.

Defense of Poetry (written 1821, published 1840), a presentation of Shelley's critical theories; and a great quantity of fine lyrics. The Shelleys settled at Pisa and became the center of a group of friends known as the "Pisan Circle," among whom was Lord Byron. Happy and at home in the midst of these charming swashbucklers, the Shelleys dabbled in political intrigue in the name of Italian and Greek liberty, and Shelley continued to write poetry. He was working on *The Triumph of Life* when he and his friend Edward Williams were drowned when a sudden squall swamped their open sailboat in the Gulf of Spezia on July 8, 1822. Shelley was cremated and his ashes were buried in Rome near the grave of Keats.

Shelley's quest for beauty was as passionate as that of Keats, though Shelley sought it in more rarified spheres: Keats took inspiration from tangible things—a Grecian urn, Chapman's translation of Homer—while Shelley found it in fanciful, imaginary realms where idealism was the true reality. His finest lyrics have a flawlessly musical cadence and a pure and ethereal beauty. Matthew Arnold called Shelley "a beautiful and ineffectual angel, beating in the void his luminous wings in vain."

from **A Defense of Poetry**

A poem is the very image of life expressed in its eternal truth. There is this difference between a story and a poem, that a story is a catalog of detached facts, which have no other bond of connection than time, place, circumstance, cause, and effect; the other is the creation of actions according to the unchangeable forms of human nature as existing in the mind of the Creator, which is itself the image of all other minds. The one is partial, and applies only to a definite period of time and a certain combination of events which can never again recur; the other is universal, and contains within itself the germ of a relation to whatever motives or actions have place in the possible varieties of human nature. Time, which destroys the beauty and the use of the story of particular facts, stripped of the poetry which should invest them, augments that of poetry, and forever develops new and wonderful applications of the eternal truth which it contains. . . . A story of particular facts is a mirror which obscures and distorts that which should be beautiful; poetry is a mirror which makes beautiful that which is distorted.

The great secret of morals is love, or a going out of our own nature, and an identification of ourselves with the beautiful which exists in thought, action, or person not our own. A man, to be greatly good, must imagine intensely and comprehensively; he must put himself in the place of another and of many others; the pains and pleasures of his species must become his own. The great instrument of moral good is the imagination; and poetry administers to the effect by acting upon the cause. Poetry enlarges the circumference of the imagination by replenishing it with thoughts of ever new delight, which have the power of attracting and assimilating to their own nature all other thoughts and which form new intervals and interstices whose void forever craves fresh food. Poetry strengthens that faculty which is the organ of the moral nature of man, in the same manner as exercise strengthens a limb.

All high poetry is infinite; it is as the first acorn, which contained all oaks potentially. Veil after veil may be undrawn, and the inmost naked beauty of the meaning never exposed.

Poetry is indeed something divine. It is at once the center and circumference of knowledge; it is that which comprehends all science, and that to which all science must be referred. . . . It is the perfect and consummate surface and bloom of all things; it is as the odor and the color of the rose to the texture of the elements which compose it, as the form and splendor of unfaded beauty to the secrets of anatomy and corruption . . . Poetry is not like reasoning, a power to be exerted according to the determination of the will. A man cannot say, "I will compose poetry." The greatest poet even cannot say it; for the mind in creation is as a fading coal, which some invisible influence, like an inconstant wind, awakens to transitory brightness; this power arises from within, like the color of a flower which fades and changes as it is developed, and the conscious portions of our natures are unprophetic either of its approach or its departure.

Poetry is the record of the best and happiest moments of the happiest and best minds . . . It is as it were the interpenetration of a diviner nature through our own; but its footsteps are like those of a wind over the sea, which the coming calm erases, and whose traces remain only, as on the wrinkled sand which paves it. Poetry redeems from decay the visitations of the divinity in man.

Poetry turns all things to loveliness; it exalts the beauty of that which is most beautiful, and it adds beauty to that which is most deformed; it marries exultation and horror, grief and pleasure, eternity and change; it subdues to union, under its light yoke, all irreconcilable things. It transmutes all that it touches, and every form moving within the radiance of its presence is changed by wondrous sympathy to an incarnation of the spirit which it breathes: its secret alchemy turns to potable gold the poisonous waters which flow from death through life; it strips the veil of familiarity from the world, and lays bare the naked and sleeping beauty, which is the spirit of its forms.

It is impossible to read the compositions of the most celebrated writers of the present day without being startled with the electric life which burns within their words. They measure the circumference and sound the depths of human nature with a comprehensive and all-penetrating spirit, and they are themselves perhaps the most sincerely astonished at its manifestations; for it is less their spirit than the spirit of the age.

Getting at Meaning

1. According to Shelley, why is a poem superior to a story?

2. The second paragraph of this excerpt presents Shelley's theory of "sympathetic imagination." Explain the meaning of this term. What is the relationship among imagination, poetry, and morality?

3. How does Shelley use the word *divine*? What does divinity have to do with the creation of poetry?

4. From where does the inspiration for poetry come, according to Shelley? from the outside? from within? both? Refer to the text to support your answer.

5. Shelley describes the transforming and redeeming quality of poetry. Why is poetry able to exert such power?

of a rose and to "unfaded beauty." What two ways does Shelley suggest that the world may be perceived? What differing aspects of poetic creation are illustrated by a fading coal and a flower? What are the "poisonous waters which flow from death through life"? What do these waters become, in a figurative sense? Explain the image of the wind on the sea. What traces of divine interpenetration remain?

2. **Theme.** Compared with the Puritan view that human nature is essentially corrupt, what would you say is Shelley's view of human nature? of all creation? What concept of the deity is implied in this selection? How does Shelley seem to conceive the role of the poet in society? How do his ideas compare with those of Keats?

Developing Skills in Reading Literature

1. **Figurative Language.** In defining poetry, Shelley relies on some of its devices, such as the imaginative metaphors and similes found in this selection. What meaning is suggested by the food metaphor used in describing the effect of poetry on the imagination? What particular point does Shelley make by comparing poetry to an acorn? Examine the statement in which Shelley compares poetry to the odor and color

Developing Writing Skills

Using Figurative Language. In one paragraph, illustrate Shelley's view about poetic creativity with one or two original similes or metaphors. As an alternative, you might illustrate your own theory regarding the source of human creativity, as it is manifested in poetry, music, sports, or another expressive activity. Try to clarify what seems to be a mysterious process by means of figures of speech.

Ozymandias[1]

I met a traveler from an antique land
Who said: Two vast and trunkless legs of stone
Stand in the desert . . . Near them, on the sand,
Half sunk, a shattered visage lies, whose frown,
And wrinkled lip, and sneer of cold command,   5
Tell that its sculptor well those passions read
Which yet survive, stamped on these lifeless things,
The hand that mocked them, and the heart that fed:
And on the pedestal these words appear:
"My name is Ozymandias, king of kings: 10
Look on my works, ye Mighty, and despair!"
Nothing beside remains. Round the decay
Of that colossal wreck, boundless and bare
The lone and level sands stretch far away.

---

1. Ozymandias (äz ĭ man' dē əs) was the Greek name for Ramses II of
Egypt who ruled from 1292–1225 B.C. He was noted for building palaces
and temples and many statues of himself.

Getting at Meaning

1. Describe the monument as it originally appeared and in its ruined state.

2. What "passions" were read by the sculptor?

3. *Survive* in line 7 is a transitive verb, with *hand* and *heart* as objects. Whose hand? Whose heart? What is the antecedent of *them* in line 8?

Developing Skills in Reading Literature

1. **Speaker.** Who are the two speakers in this poem? What is the effect of having the statue described and the commentary presented by one speaker through another? How does this technique differ from that used in most Romantic poems?

2. **Diction: Connotation.** Can you think of a substitute for the word *antique* in line 1? Would it be as effective? In line 4, why is *visage* a better word than some other synonym of *face*? Why is *colossal* (line 13) an exactly appropriate word? (Hint: the answer lies in its etymology.)

3. **Sonnet.** Which type of sonnet is this poem? How does the idea pattern fit the form?

4. **Irony and Theme.** Comment on the irony in this poem. What contrasts contribute to it? What theme emerges from the irony?

5. **Mood.** Examine the last three lines. How would you describe their mood? How does the imagery contribute to the mood? What about the sound effects?

Ode to the West Wind

I

O wild West Wind, thou breath of Autumn's being,
Thou, from whose unseen presence the leaves dead
Are driven, like ghosts from an enchanter fleeing,

Yellow, and black, and pale, and hectic red,
Pestilence-stricken multitudes: O thou,   5
Who chariotest to their dark wintry bed

The wingèd seeds, where they lie cold and low,
Each like a corpse within its grave, until
Thine azure sister of the Spring[1] shall blow

Her clarion[2] o'er the dreaming earth, and fill   10
(Driving sweet buds like flocks to feed in air)
With living hues and odors plain and hill:

Wild Spirit, which art moving everywhere;
Destroyer and preserver; hear, oh, hear!

II

Thou on whose stream, 'mid the steep sky's commotion,   15
Loose clouds like earth's decaying leaves are shed,
Shook from the tangled boughs of Heaven and Ocean,

Angels[3] of rain and lightning: there are spread
On the blue surface of thine aery surge,
Like the bright hair uplifted from the head   20

Of some fierce Maenad,[4] even from the dim verge
Of the horizon to the zenith's height,
The locks of the approaching storm. Thou dirge

Of the dying year, to which this closing night
Will be the dome of a vast sepulcher,   25
Vaulted with all thy congregated might

---

1. **sister . . . spring:** the reviving south wind of spring.
2. **clarion:** a trumpet with a clear, ringing tone.
3. **Angels:** messengers.
4. **Maenad** (mē′ năd): a priestess of Dionysus, the Greek god of wine and revelry.

Of vapors, from whose solid atmosphere
Black rain, and fire, and hail will burst: oh, hear!

III

Thou who didst waken from his summer dreams
The blue Mediterranean, where he lay,   30
Lulled by the coil of his crystàlline streams,

Beside a pumice[5] isle in Baiae's bay,[6]
And saw in sleep old palaces and towers
Quivering within the wave's intenser day,

All overgrown with azure moss and flowers   35
So sweet, the sense faints picturing them! Thou
For whose path the Atlantic's level powers[7]

Cleave themselves into chasms, while far below
The sea-blooms and the oozy woods which wear
The sapless foliage of the ocean, know   40

Thy voice, and suddenly grow gray with fear,
And tremble and despoil themselves: oh, hear!

IV

If I were a dead leaf thou mightest bear;
If I were a swift cloud to fly with thee;
A wave to pant beneath thy power, and share   45

The impulse of thy strength, only less free
Than thou, O uncontrollable! If even
I were as in my boyhood, and could be

The comrade of thy wanderings over Heaven,
As then, when to outstrip thy skyey speed   50
Scarce seemed a vision;[8] I would ne'er have striven

As thus with thee in prayer in my sore need.
Oh, lift me as a wave, a leaf, a cloud!
I fall upon the thorns of life! I bleed!

---

5. **pumice:** volcanic lava.
6. **Baiae:** an ancient Roman resort.
7. **level powers:** surfaces.
8. **vision:** that is, something impossible to achieve.

A heavy weight of hours has chained and bowed   55
One too like thee: tameless, and swift, and proud.

V

Make me thy lyre,[9] even as the forest is:
What if my leaves are falling like its own!
The tumult of thy mighty harmonies

Will take from both a deep, autumnal tone,   60
Sweet though in sadness. Be thou, Spirit fierce,
My spirit! Be thou me, impetuous one!

Drive my dead thoughts over the universe
Like withered leaves to quicken a new birth!
And, by the incantation of this verse,   65

Scatter, as from an unextinguished hearth
Ashes and sparks, my words among mankind!
Be through my lips to unawakened earth

The trumpet of a prophecy! O Wind,
If Winter comes, can Spring be far behind?   70

---

9. **lyre:** Aeolian lute that makes musical sounds when the wind blows
through it.

Getting at Meaning

1. Identify: "pestilence-stricken multitudes" in line 5; "angels of rain and lightning" in line 18; "both" in line 60.

2. What are the subjects of parts I, II, and III? What do the subjects have in common? In what lines does the speaker identify with each subject?

3. What contrast does the speaker perceive between his boyhood and his present state? Why does he pray to the wind? What is his "sore need" (line 52)?

4. What relationship between speaker and wind is established in part V? What does the wind do literally that the speaker would like to do in a figurative sense?

Developing Skills in Reading Literature

1. **Rhyme Scheme: Terza Rima and Couplet.** Shelley has created an unusual form for this ode, writing in terza rima but rounding off each fourteen-line unit with a couplet, as in a sonnet. Terza rima, originally an Italian stanza form but popular with English poets, has a rhyme scheme of *a b a, b c b, c d c, d e d* and so forth. Note that the middle rhyme of one tercet becomes the first and third rhyme of the following tercet. How does this rhyme scheme, with an added couplet, relate to the content and the overall feeling of Shelley's poem?

2. **Alliteration and Consonance.** One of the consonants most resembling a vowel is *w*, which produces a breathy *oo* sound. Recite aloud, very slowly, the words "wild West Wind," and you will hear a series of *oo*'s along with the other vowels. Why is the effect created by the alliteration of *w* suitable in this poem?

Among the profusion of sound effects in this poem is the repetition of the *s* sound. Read aloud lines 15-17, for example, or lines 50 and 51. Does this hissing effect seem natural, given the subject of the poem, or does it seem overly exaggerated? Explain your answer. Point out two or three other examples of the manipulation of consonants in this poem.

3. **Imagery.** Two image patterns—of death and of wild or violent energy—emerge in parts I and II. Identify the details that make up each of these patterns. How are they both important in understanding the destroying and preserving qualities of the wind?

4. **Figurative Language.** Shelley's metaphors and similes can sometimes be strikingly original. Note the buds of spring compared to flocks in line 11. More challenging is part II, in which the speaker watches an approaching storm that will bring lightning and rain by nightfall. Read the lines closely, and sort out the various figures of speech that combine images of sky, leaves, boughs, ocean, angels, and bright hair. Explain in your own words what is actually being described. (Note: Line 19 refers to a blue sky.)

Finally, explain the figurative language that relates a lyre, the forest, and the speaker in part V.

5. **Symbol.** This poem grew out of Shelley's experience on a windy day near Florence, but the West Wind in the poem is more than an element of weather. Taking into account the image patterns already discussed and the relation between poet and wind established in parts IV and V, summarize what the wind symbolizes for Shelley. Comment on what the meaning of this symbol implies about poetry and poets.

Developing Writing Skills

Using Contrasts. A comparison of Keats's "To Autumn" and this poem reveals interesting differences between the approaches of the two poets. In several paragraphs, summarize the differences in subject and treatment of subject in the two poems.

To a Skylark

Hail to thee, blithe Spirit!
   Bird thou never wert,
That from Heaven, or near it,
   Pourest thy full heart
In profuse strains of unpremeditated art.   5

Higher still and higher
   From the earth thou springest
Like a cloud of fire;
   The blue deep thou wingest,
And singing still dost soar, and soaring ever singest.   10

In the golden lightning
   Of the sunken sun,
O'er which clouds are bright'ning,
   Thou dost float and run;
Like an unbodied joy whose race is just begun.   15

The pale purple even[1]
   Melts around thy flight;
Like a star of Heaven
   In the broad daylight
Thou art unseen, but yet I hear thy shrill delight,   20

Keen as are the arrows
   Of that silver sphere,[2]
Whose intense lamp narrows
   In the white dawn clear,
Until we hardly see—we feel that it is there.   25

---

1. **even:** evening.
2. **silver sphere:** the morning star.

SKYLARK. *Thomas Bewick.*
© *Gordon Fraser Gallery, 1981.*

All the earth and air
   With thy voice is loud,
As, when night is bare,
   From one lonely cloud
The moon rains out her beams, and Heaven is overflowed.   30

What thou art we know not;
   What is most like thee?
From rainbow clouds there flow not
   Drops so bright to see,
As from thy presence showers a rain of melody.   35

Like a Poet hidden
   In the light of thought,
Singing hymns unbidden,
   Till the world is wrought
To sympathy with hopes and fears it heeded not: 40

Like a highborn maiden
   In a palace tower,
Soothing her love-laden
   Soul in secret hour
With music sweet as love, which overflows her bower: 45

Like a glowworm golden
   In a dell of dew,
Scattering unbeholden
   Its aerial hue
Among the flowers and grass, which screen it from the view!   50

Like a rose embowered
   In its own green leaves,
By warm winds deflowered,[3]
   Till the scent it gives
Makes faint with too much sweet those heavy-wingèd
      thieves[4]:   55

Sound of vernal showers
   On the twinkling grass,
Rain-awakened flowers,
   All that ever was
Joyous, and clear, and fresh, thy music doth surpass: 60

---

3. **deflowered:** fully opened.
4. **thieves:** the "warm winds."

Teach us, Sprite or Bird,
    What sweet thoughts are thine;
I have never heard
    Praise of love or wine
That panted forth a flood of rapture so divine.   65

Chorus Hymeneal,[5]
    Or triumphal chant,
Matched with thine, would be all
    But an empty vaunt,[6]
A thing wherein we feel there is some hidden want.   70

What objects are the fountains[7]
    Of thy happy strain?
What fields, or waves, or mountains?
    What shapes of sky or plain?
What love of thine own kind? what ignorance of pain?   75

With thy clear keen joyance
    Languor cannot be;
Shadow of annoyance
    Never came near thee;
Thou lovest—but ne'er knew love's sad satiety.   80

Waking or asleep,
    Thou of death must deem[8]
Things more true and deep
    Than we mortals dream,
Or how could thy notes flow in such a crystal stream?   85

We look before and after,
    And pine for what is not;
Our sincerest laughter
    With some pain is fraught;
Our sweetest songs are those that tell of saddest thought.   90

Yet if[9] we could scorn
    Hate, and pride, and fear;
If we were things born
    Not to shed a tear,
I know not how thy joy we ever should come near.   95

---

5. **Hymeneal:** marriage song. Hymen was the Greek god of marriage.
6. **vaunt:** a boast.
7. **fountains:** sources.
8. **deem:** know.
9. **if:** even if.

Better than all measures
    Of delightful sound
Better than all treasures
    That in books are found,
Thy skill to poet were,[10] thou scorner of the ground!   100

Teach me half the gladness
    That thy brain must know,
Such harmonious madness
    From my lips would flow,
The world should listen then—as I am listening now.   105

---

10. **were:** would be.

Getting at Meaning

1. Where or in what direction is the skylark flying? Describe the scene pictured in lines 11–14. What time of day is it? Why does the skylark seem like a disembodied presence?

2. What effect does the song of the skylark have upon the listener? Cite lines to support your answer.

3. If the bird is a kind of poet of nature, what advantages does it enjoy over mortals? Why is its "unpremeditated art" superior?

4. If it were possible, what would the speaker learn from the skylark? What would be the effect of this knowledge?

5. What does the phrase "harmonious madness" suggest about the nature of poetry?

Developing Skills in Reading Literature

1. **Figurative Language.** In the long series of similes beginning in line 16, which stanzas compare the bird and its song to some kind of light? Which compare the bird with sounds? with things that appeal to other senses? Where is there a suggestion of something secret or unseen? What kind of image is evoked by verbs suggesting a flowing profusion of song?

Explain the rather precise comparison drawn between the bird and the star in lines 18–25.

2. **Theme.** As evident in "Ode to the West Wind,"

Shelley is a poet of prophecy, awaiting the millenium, hoping to awaken the spirit of revolutionary change. Do you see any touches of that quality in "To a Skylark"? What lines in the poem most poignantly express a sense of the mixed state of the human condition, a dissatisfaction with the paradoxes of earthly existence? Do you sympathize with Shelley's feelings? Does he seem unrealistic or utopian?

3. **Imagery.** The Romantics often felt drawn to nature as a source of the spiritual, even the divine. Shelley in particular, in this poem as in "Ode to the West Wind," expresses a yearning to identify with some aspect of the natural world, as if to transcend somehow the limitations of ordinary existence. Like the skylark he is a "scorner of the ground" (line 100). Thus his images often seem on the verge of leaving tangible reality behind. Identify several of these ethereal images in this poem. Is the skylark fully realized as a physical being? If not, how does this relate to the poem's theme?

Developing Writing Skills

Combining Narration and Exposition. Read lines 86–90 of "To a Skylark." In a brief composition, provide several examples from your own experience of the truth of these lines, or write a narrative that illustrates the same point.

Love's Philosophy

The fountains mingle with the river
  And the rivers with the Ocean,
The winds of Heaven mix forever
  With a sweet emotion;
Nothing in the world is single;   5
  All things by a law divine
In one spirit meet and mingle.
  Why not I with thine?—

See the mountains kiss high Heaven
  And the waves clasp one another;   10
No sister-flower would be forgiven
  If it disdained its brother;
And the sunlight clasps the earth
  And the moonbeams kiss the sea:
What is all this sweet work worth   15
  If thou kiss not me?

Getting at Meaning

1. The word *philosophy* implies a rational argument. What is the lover's reasoning in this poem? What is its unstated premise, or underlying assumption?

2. Does the speaker cite any kind of authority in developing this argument?

Developing Skills in Reading Literature

1. **Meter.** In scanning this poem, do you find a regular pattern of stressed syllables? What about unstressed syllables? Is the meter trochaic, with each foot comprised of a stressed followed by an unstressed syllable ($-\smile$)? Find a line that is clearly trochaic. Or is the predominating meter iambic? If so, the extra unstressed syllable at the end of a line produces what is called a feminine ending.

2. **Feminine and Masculine Rhyme.** When rhyme occurs in two consecutive syllables, the second of which is unstressed, it is called feminine rhyme, or multiple rhyme. When only the final accented syllables rhyme, the rhyme is called masculine or perfect rhyme. Find examples of both feminine and masculine rhyme in this poem. What seems to be the effect of each on the rhythm? Why do you suppose that these patterns came to be called feminine and masculine?

3. **Pathetic Fallacy.** Through personification, poets credit nature with human qualities. The portrayal of inanimate nature as having human feelings or character is also known as the pathetic fallacy, especially if it seems false or exaggerated in its emotionalism. The phrase is not always derogatory, however, for response to the pathetic fallacy is partly a matter of taste. Do you find any particularly good examples of the pathetic fallacy in this poem?

4. **Theme.** The virtues of this lyric are mostly superficial; the poem does not invite penetrating analysis or conceal rich thematic complexities. Nevertheless, it does echo a certain Romantic tendency to identify with nature and to see it as a primary source of values. How does this poem illustrate the theme that is worked out more profoundly in "Ode to the West Wind"?

Mary Wollstonecraft Shelley
1797–1851

MARY WOLLSTONECRAFT SHELLEY, 1840. Richard Rothwell.
National Portrait Gallery, London.

Mary Wollstonecraft Shelley's *Frankenstein, or the Modern Prometheus* appeared in 1818, when its author was only twenty-one. Generally regarded as the superlative masterpiece of horror, it has been perennially popular ever since. The enormous success of *Frankenstein*, coupled with the fame of Shelley's husband, Percy Bysshe Shelley, have obscured the other accomplishments of her remarkable life.

Shelley's parents were themselves extraordinary. Her mother, Mary Wollstonecraft, was author of *A Vindication of the Rights of Women*, a stirring feminist manifesto. She died ten days after the birth of Mary, who was then raised by her father, William Godwin, a philosophical anarchist who believed in the possibility of a utopia where repressive institutions such as governments, churches, and marriage would be superfluous.

One of Godwin's most enthusiastic admirers was the young Percy Bysshe Shelley. Although Shelley was already married, when he and Mary met, they fell in love instantly. Shelley's wife was two months pregnant with their second child when he and Mary eloped to France. William Godwin, enraged, became a convert to the sanctimony of matrimony. In 1816 Mary bore a son and named him William in honor of her father. Later that year Shelley's wife drowned herself, and Mary and Shelley were married shortly afterward. In 1817 their daughter, Clara, was born, and that same year Mary wrote *Frankenstein*.

The famous horror tale began as a sort of parlor game. One evening at Lord Byron's villa, a group of friends sat by the fireside telling ghost stories, and Byron sportively suggested that they each write one. The source of Mary's tale was a dream, or what she called "an acute mental vision." Lying in bed, she imagined a monster created by the artificial reanimation of a hideous corpse. "What terrified me will terrify others," she decided; "I need only describe the specter that haunted my midnight pillow." She did it so well that her novel proved more popular than all of her husband's poems. Highly imaginative and poetic, *Franken-*stein is also intellectually ambitious. The book's bleak vision of the darker side of scientific triumph was at odds with the official optimism of the era, yet it struck a responsive chord even then, and in our own century the tale has achieved the stature of prophetic myth.

Tragedy haunted the Shelleys. Within one year, Clara died from dysentery and three-year-old William died after a short illness. The loss of her children left Mary desolate. The birth in 1819 of another son, Percy Florence, helped dispel her depression, but just a few years later, in 1822, her husband drowned in a boating accident. Shelley's will should have provided comfortably for Mary and her infant son, but the poet had been estranged from his father, who considered him scandalously immoral, and Sir Timothy Shelley prevented the execution of the will. Mary was forced to support herself with her pen.

Although none of her subsequent works attained success remotely similar to that of *Frankenstein*, Mary was a prolific writer. She edited her husband's works, wrote biographies for an encyclopedia, contributed to magazines, and wrote two novels, *The Fortunes of Perkin Warbeck* (1830) and *Falkner* (1837).

from The Journal

Oct. 2.—On the 8th of July[1] I finished my journal. This is a curious coincidence. The date still remains—the fatal 8th—a monument to show that all ended then. And I begin again? Oh, never! But several motives induce me, when the day has gone down, and all is silent around me, steeped in sleep, to pen as occasion wills, my reflections and feelings. First, I have no friend. For eight years I communicated, with unlimited freedom, with one whose genius, far transcending mine, awakened and guided my thoughts. I conversed with him; rectified my errors of judgment; obtained new lights from him; and my mind was satisfied. Now I am alone—oh, how alone! The stars may behold my tears, and the winds drink my sighs; but my thoughts are a sealed treasure, which I can confide to none. But can I express all I feel? Can I give words to thoughts and feelings that, as a tempest, hurry me along? Is this the sand that the ever-flowing sea of thought would impress indelibly? Alas! I am alone. No eye answers mine; my voice can with none assume its natural modulation. What a change! O my beloved Shelley! how often during those happy days—happy, though checkered—I thought how superiorly gifted I had been in being united to one to whom I could unveil myself, and who could understand me! Well, then, now I am reduced to these white pages, which I am to blot with dark imagery. As I write, let me think what he would have said if, speaking thus to him, he could have answered me. Yes, my own heart, I would fain know what to think of my desolate state; what you think I ought to do, what to think. I guess you would answer thus:—"Seek to know your own heart, and, learning what it best loves, try to enjoy that." Well, I cast my eyes around, and, look forward to the bounded prospect in view; I ask myself what pleases me there? My child;—so many feelings arise when I think of him, that I turn aside to think no more. Those I most loved are gone forever; those who held the second rank are absent; and among those near me as yet, I trust to the disinterested kindness of one alone. Beneath all this, my imagination never flags. Literary labors, the improvement of my mind, and the enlargement of my ideas, are the only occupations that elevate me from my lethargy; all events seem to lead me to that one point, and the courses of destiny having dragged me to that single resting-place, have left me. Father, mother, friend, husband, children—all made, as it were, the team that conducted me here; and now all, except you, my poor boy (and you are necessary to the continuance of my life), all are gone, and I am left to fulfill my task. So be it.

Sunday, Oct. 21.—I have been so often abused by pretended friends for my lukewarmness in "the good cause," that, though I disdain to answer them, I shall put down here a few thoughts on this subject. I am much of a self-examiner. Vanity is not my fault, I think; if it is, it is uncomfortable vanity, for I have none that teaches me to be satisfied with myself; far otherwise,—and, if I use the word *disdain*, it is that I think my qualities (such as they are) not appreciated from unworthy causes.

---

1. **8th of July:** Percy Bysshe Shelley drowned in the Gulf of Spezzia, Italy, on July 8, 1822.

In the first place, with regard to "the good cause"—the cause of the advancement of freedom and knowledge, of the rights of women, etc.—I am not a person of opinions. I have said elsewhere that human beings differ greatly in this. Some have a passion for reforming the world; others do not cling to particular opinions. That my parents and Shelley were of the former class, makes me respect it. I respect such when joined to real disinterestedness, toleration, and a clear understanding. My accusers, after such as these, appear to me mere drivellers. For myself, I earnestly desire the good and enlightenment of my fellow creatures, and see all, in the present course, tending to the same, and rejoice; but I am not for violent extremes, which only bring on an injurious reaction. I have never written a word in disfavor of liberalism; that I have not supported it openly in writing, arises from the following causes, as far as I know:—

That I have not argumentative powers: I see things pretty clearly, but cannot demonstrate them. Besides, I feel the counter-arguments too strongly. I do not feel that I could say ought to support the cause efficiently; besides that, on some topics (especially with regard to my own sex), I am far from making up my mind. I believe we are sent here to educate ourselves, and that self-denial, and disappointment, and self-control, are a part of our education; that it is not by taking away all restraining law that our improvement is to be achieved; and, though many things need great amendment, I can by no means go so far as my friends would have me. When I feel that I can say what will benefit my fellow-creatures, I will speak: not before.

Then, I recoil from the vulgar abuse of the inimical[2] press. I do more than recoil: proud and sensitive, I act on the defensive—an inglorious position.

To hang back, as I do, brings a penalty. I was nursed and fed with a love of glory. To be something great and good was the precept given me by my Father:[3] Shelley reiterated it.

Alone and poor, I could only be something by joining a party; and there was much in me—the woman's love of looking up, and being guided, and being willing to do anything if any one supported and brought me forward —which would have made me a good partisan. But Shelley died, and I was alone. My Father, from age and domestic circumstances, could not *"me faire valoir."*[4] My total friendlessness, my horror of pushing, and inability to put myself forward unless led, cherished and supported,—all this has sunk me in a state of loneliness no other human being ever before, I believe, endured—except Robinson Crusoe. How many tears and spasms of anguish this solitude has cost me, lies buried in my memory.

If I had raved and ranted about what I did not understand; had I adopted a set of opinions, and propagated them with enthusiasm; had I been careless of attack, and eager for notoriety; then the party to which I belonged had gathered round me, and I had not been alone. But since I had lost Shelley I have no wish to ally myself to the Radicals—they are full of repulsion to me—violent without any sense of Justice—selfish in the extreme— talking without knowledge—rude, envious, and insolent—I wish to have nothing to do with them.

It has been the fashion with these same friends to accuse me of worldliness. There, indeed, in my own heart and conscience, I take a high ground. I may distrust my own judgment too much—be too indolent and too timid; but in conduct I am above merited blame.

I like society; I believe all persons who have any talent (who are in good health) do. The soil that gives forth nothing, may lie ever fallow; but that which produces—however

---

2. **inimical** (in im' ik'l): hostile, unfriendly.
3. **My Father:** William Godwin (1756–1836), a writer and political philosopher.
4. **me faire valoir** *French:* boast about my merits.

humble its product—needs cultivation, change of harvest, refreshing dews, and ripening sun. Books do much; but the living intercourse is the vital heat. Debarred from that, how have I pined and died!

My early friends chose the position of enemies. When I first discovered that a trusted friend had acted falsely by me, I was nearly destroyed. My health was shaken. I remembered thinking, with a burst of agonizing tears, that I should prefer a bed of torture to the unutterable anguish a friend's falsehood engendered. There is no resentment; but the world can never be to me what it was before. Trust, and confidence, and the heart's sincere devotion, are gone.

I sought at that time to make acquaintances—to divert my mind from this anguish. I got entangled in various ways through my ready sympathy and too eager heart; but I never crouched to society—never sought it unworthily. If I have never written to vindicate the rights of women, I have ever befriended women when oppressed. At every risk I have befriended and supported victims to the social system; but I make no boast, for in truth it is simple justice I perform; and so I am still reviled for being worldly.

God grant a happier and a better day is near! Percy—my all-in-all—will, I trust, by his excellent understanding, his clear, bright, sincere spirit and affectionate heart, repay me for sad long years of desolation. His career may lead me into the thick of life or only gild a quiet home. I am content with either, and, as I grow older I grow more fearless for myself—I become firmer in my opinions. The experienced, the suffering, the thoughtful may at last speak unrebuked. If it be the will of God that I live, I may ally my name yet to "the good cause," though I do not expect to please my accusers.

Thus have I put down my thoughts. I may have deceived myself; I may be in the wrong; I try to examine myself; and such as I have written appears to me the exact truth.

Enough of this! The great work of life goes on. Death draws near. To be better after death than in life is one's hope and endeavor—to be so through self-schooling. If I write the above, it is that those who love me may hereafter know that I am not all to blame, nor merit the heavy accusations cast on me for not putting myself forward. *I cannot* do that; it is against my nature. As well cast me from a precipice and rail at me for not flying.

Getting at Meaning

1. Mary Shelley stopped writing her journal on July 8, 1822, the day her husband drowned. Why does she start writing it again? How does it serve her?

2. In her desolate state after Shelley's death, what advice does Mary Shelley imagine he would give her?

3. How does an idea about destiny help Mary Shelley to cope with her loss? What does she decide she must do?

4. In her London entry, sixteen years later, what accusation does Mary Shelley defend herself against? How does she feel that she differs from Shelley and from her own parents?

5. What aspects of Mary Shelley's mind and character prevent her from speaking out as strongly as some would wish? What sacrifice of her own integrity would have made her more popular? Why does she dislike "the Radicals"?

6. Do Mary Shelley's views on various issues seem to you to be liberal or conservative? Refer to the text to support your answer.

Developing Skills in Reading Literature

1. **Autobiographical Narrative: Journal.** Just as artists carry sketchbooks, many writers keep journals,

which sometimes are published. A journal is a form of autobiographical writing in which day-by-day accounts of events, as well as a record of personal impressions, can be kept. Do these entries seem to fit the definition of *journal*? How do you think Mary Shelley's journal may have been useful to her? to students studying her life and period?

2. **Style.** Shelley's style is graceful and direct, but capable of subtlety and complexity. Some sentences may seem formal. In the first paragraph of the London entry she writes, ". . . I think my qualities (such as they are) not appreciated from unworthy causes." How would this statement sound if it were put more directly and without the double negative? Would it lose some of its effect? Is the style perhaps appropriate to her thought?

The first sentence in the sixth paragraph of the London entry reads, ". . . then the party to which I belonged had gathered round me, and I had not been alone." How would you express this statement in a more current idiom?

Shelley's graceful, balanced sentence constructions are evident throughout her journal. In the sixth paragraph of the London entry, find two examples of parallel construction. Can you find others in other parts of the journal?

In effective writing, transitional words and phrases at the beginnings and ends of paragraphs produce smooth logical connections, a coherent flow of ideas. How are the first four paragraphs of the London entry linked by transitional devices? Do you see other instances of skillful transitions?

3. **Figurative Language.** What does Shelley mean when, answering the charge of worldliness, she writes, "I take a high ground"? With what extended metaphor does she express her need for social interaction? What powerful figure of speech does she use to explain her inability to put herself forward? In the Italian entry Shelley draws figures of speech from nature. Identify several of these figures, and explain the ideas that they reinforce.

Developing Vocabulary

Using a Dictionary: Definitions and Word Origins. Mary Shelley describes her days with Shelley as

"happy, though checkered." What does she mean, and what does the word *checkered* have to do with the board game?

Shelley writes, ". . . I would fain know what to think of my desolate state." What does *fain* mean? How does your dictionary label the word?

Shelley says that she has a "disinterested" friend. This word is often confused with *uninterested*. What is the difference in their meanings?

In the next sentence she says that her imagination "never flags." How did *flag* come to be both a verb and a noun?

Shelley says that she "disdains" to answer her accusers. In terms of its root meaning, why is disdain an appropriate word?

Shelley speaks of her accusers as "drivellers." What physical act does this suggest? In its root meaning, what is drivel?

Developing Writing Skills

1. **Writing a Journal.** Writing a journal can cause you to clarify your ideas and feelings, help you to improve your writing in an undemanding context, and give you an interesting, lasting record of your thoughts and feelings. In some sort of permanent book or notebook, start keeping a journal of your activities, ideas, and concerns. Try to get into the habit of writing in it regularly.

2. **Writing a Character Sketch; Writing an Explanation.** Based on these journal entries, and whatever else you may know about Mary Shelley, compose a brief character sketch. Describe her character and temperament, her ideas and priorities.

As an alternative, consider Mary Shelley in the context of feminism today. How might she relate to the contemporary movement? How does she compare with contemporary feminists? Explain your ideas in a brief composition, using material from the journal to support your conclusions.

Charles Lamb

1775–1834

CHARLES LAMB, 1804. *W. Hazlitt.*
National Portrait Gallery, London.

A close friend of Keats, Coleridge, and Wordsworth, Lamb is remembered as a master of the informal essay and as a subtle and profound critic. So vivid were Lamb's descriptions of himself, his oddities, his stutter, his odd eyes, his ragged head, that those who read his writings feel that they know Lamb personally.

A Londoner by birth, Lamb attended the exclusive grammar school Christ's Hospital, where he began his lifelong friendship with Coleridge. When he was seventeen, he took a post as a clerk in the accounting department of the huge East India Company, a job he kept for thirty-three years. He lived at home with his invalid parents and his beloved sister Mary, ten years his senior, who cared for them. In 1796, when Lamb was twenty-two, tragedy struck. In a fit of insanity, Mary stabbed her mother to death and wounded her father. Lamb had himself appointed her guardian so that she would not have to spend her entire life in an asylum, and for the rest of his life he bore this burden. Most of the time Mary was quiet and gracious, and she collaborated on several works with her brother, but periodically the attacks would recur. Critic Walter Pater aptly described the situation as having "something of the fateful domestic horror, of the beautiful heroism and devotedness too, of old Greek tragedy."

Poverty was constant for Lamb and his sister, and he wrote in a variety of forms to supplement his salary. For William Godwin's Juvenile Library series, he and Mary produced *Tales from Shakespeare* (1807) and *The Adventures of Ulysses* (1808). *Tales from Shakespeare* and other writings stimulated interest in Shakespeare and the other Elizabethans among adult readers as well as among children. Lamb collected his prose and poetry into *The Works of Charles Lamb*, which appeared in 1818. This publication was so well received that the editors of *London Magazine* asked him to contribute a series of essays. Using the pen name Elia, Lamb wrote the famous pieces that were collected in book form in 1823 and 1833 and that established him as one of the world's great essayists.

The essays of Elia are thinly disguised autobiography. Lamb's father appears as the character of Lovel, his sister as Cousin Bridget. The deceptively easy charm of the essays is so masterful that casual readers may not realize how skillfully crafted they are nor how original in style. The essays also reveal Lamb's extraordinary range of sentiment and his powers of fancy and his genius at maintaining a delicate balance between the two.

In 1825 Lamb retired from the East India Company. With Mary's attacks becoming more frequent and lasting longer, he and Mary moved from London to country homes in Enfield and then Edmonton. A slight wound from a fall developed into a fatal illness, and Lamb died in December, 1834. Mary lived until 1847.

A Dissertation upon Roast Pig

Mankind, says a Chinese manuscript, which my friend M. was obliging enough to read and explain to me, for the first seventy thousand ages ate their meat raw, clawing or biting it from the living animal, just as they do in Abyssinia to this day. This period is not obscurely hinted at by their great Confucius[1] in the second chapter of his *Mundane Mutations*, where he designates a kind of golden age by the term *Cho-fang*, literally the Cook's Holiday. The manuscript goes on to say, that the art of roasting, or rather broiling (which I take to be the elder brother) was accidentally discovered in the manner following. The swineherd, Ho-ti, having gone out into the woods one morning, as his manner was, to collect mast[2] for his hogs, left his cottage in the care of his eldest son Bo-bo, a great lubberly boy, who being fond of playing with fire, as younkers[3] of his age commonly are, let some sparks escape into a bundle of straw, which kindling quickly, spread the conflagration over every part of their poor mansion, till it was reduced to ashes. Together with the cottage (a sorry antediluvian[4] makeshift of a building, you may think it), what was of much more importance, a fine litter of new farrowed pigs, no less than nine in number, perished. China pigs have been esteemed a luxury all over the East from the remotest periods that we read of. Bo-bo was in the utmost consternation, as you may think, not so much for the sake of the tenement, which his father and he could easily build up again with a few dry branches, and the labor of an hour or two, at any time, as for the loss of the pigs. While he was thinking what he should say to his father, and wringing his hands over the smoking remnants of one of those untimely sufferers, an odor assailed his nostrils, unlike any scent which he had before experienced. What could it proceed from?—not from the burnt cottage—he had smelt that smell before—indeed this was by no means the first accident of the kind which had occurred through the negligence of this unlucky young firebrand. Much less did it resemble that of any known herb, weed, or flower. A premonitory moistening at the same time overflowed his nether[5] lip. He knew not what to think. He next stooped down to feel the pig, if there were any signs of life in it. He burnt his fingers, and to cool them he applied them in his booby fashion to his mouth. Some of the crumbs of the scorched skin had come away with his fingers, and for the first time in his life (in the world's life indeed, for before him no man had known it) he tasted—*crackling!* Again he felt and fumbled at the pig. It did not burn him so much now, still he licked his fingers from a sort of habit. The truth at length broke into his slow understanding, that it was the pig that smelt so, and the pig that tasted so delicious; and surrendering himself up to the newborn pleasure, he fell to tearing up whole handfuls of the scorched skin with the flesh next it, and was cramming it down his throat in his beastly fashion, when his sire entered amid the smoking rafters, armed with retributory cudgel, and finding how affairs stood, began to rain blows upon the young rogue's shoulders, as thick as hailstones, which Bo-bo heeded not any more than if they had been

---

1. **Confucius** (Kən fyōo′ shəs): Chinese philosopher and teacher, 551?–479? B.C.
2. **mast:** beechnuts, acorns, chestnuts, etc.
3. **younker:** a youngster.
4. **antediluvian** (an′ ti də lōo′ vē ən): of the time before the Biblical Flood.
5. **nether:** lower.

flies. The tickling pleasure, which he experienced in his lower regions, had rendered him quite callous to any inconveniences he might feel in those remote quarters. His father might lay on, but he could not beat him from his pig, till he had fairly made an end of it, when, becoming a little more sensible of his situation, something like the following dialogue ensued.

"You graceless whelp, what have you got there devouring? Is it not enough that you have burnt me down three houses with your dog's tricks, and be hanged to you, but you must be eating fire, and I know not what—what have you got there, I say?"

"Oh, father, the pig, the pig, do come and taste how nice the burnt pig eats."

The ears of Ho-ti tingled with horror. He cursed his son, and he cursed himself that ever he should beget a son that should eat burnt pig.

Bo-bo, whose scent was wonderfully sharpened since morning, soon raked out another pig, and fairly rending it asunder, thrust the lesser half by main force into the fists of Ho-ti, still shouting out, "Eat, eat, eat the burnt pig, father, only taste—O Lord"—with such-like barbarous ejaculations, cramming all the while as if he would choke.

Ho-ti trembled in every joint while he grasped the abominable thing, wavering whether he should not put his son to death for an unnatural young monster, when the crackling scorching his fingers, as it had done his son's, and applying the same remedy to them, he in his turn tasted some of its flavor, which, make what sour mouths he would for a pretence, proved not altogether displeasing to him. In conclusion (for the manuscript here is a little tedious) both father and son fairly sat down to the mess, and never left off till they had despatched all that remained of the litter.

Bo-bo was strictly enjoined not to let the secret escape, for the neighbors would certainly have stoned them for a couple of abominable wretches, who could think of improving upon the good meat which God had sent them. Nevertheless, strange stories got about. It was observed that Ho-ti's cottage was burnt down now more frequently than ever. Nothing but fires from this time forward. Some would break out in broad day, others in the night-time. As often as the sow farrowed, so sure was the house of Ho-ti to be in a blaze; and Ho-ti himself, which was the more remarkable, instead of chastising his son, seemed to grow more indulgent to him than ever. At length they were watched, the terrible mystery discovered, and father and son summoned to take their trial at Pekin, then an inconsiderable assize town.[6] Evidence was given, the obnoxious food itself produced in court, and verdict about to be pronounced, when the foreman of the jury begged that some of the burnt pig, of which the culprits stood accused, might be handed into the box. He handled it, and they all handled it, and burning their fingers, as Bo-bo and his father had done before them, and nature prompting to each of them the same remedy, against the face of all the facts, and the clearest charge which judge had ever given—to the surprise of the whole court, townsfolk, strangers, reporters, and all present—without leaving the box, or any manner of consultation whatever, they brought in a simultaneous verdict of Not Guilty.

The judge, who was a shrewd fellow, winked at the manifest iniquity of the decision; and, when the court was dismissed, went privily, and bought up all the pigs that could be had for love or money. In a few days his lordship's town house was observed to be on fire. The thing took wing, and now there was nothing to be seen but fires in every direction. Fuel and pigs grew enormously dear all over the district. The insurance offices one and all shut up shop. People built slighter and slighter every day, until it was feared that the

---

6. **assize town:** a town where court sessions were held periodically to try civil and criminal cases.

very science of architecture would in no long time be lost to the world. Thus this custom of firing houses continued, till in process of time, says my manuscript, a sage rose, like our Locke,[7] who made a discovery, that the flesh of swine, or indeed of any other animal, might be cooked (*burnt*, as they called it) without the necessity of consuming a whole house to dress it. Then first began the rude form of a gridiron. Roasting by the string, or spit, came in a century or two later, I forget in whose dynasty. By such slow degrees, concludes the manuscript, do the most useful, and seemingly the most obvious arts, make their way among mankind.—

Without placing too implicit faith in the account above given, it must be agreed that if a worthy pretext for so dangerous an experiment as setting houses on fire (especially in these days) could be assigned in favor of any culinary object, that pretext and excuse might be found in ROAST PIG.

Of all the delicacies in the whole *mundus edibilis*,[8] I will maintain it to be the most delicate—*princeps obsoniorum*.[9]

I speak not of your grown porkers—things between pig and pork—those hobbledehoys[10] —but a young and tender suckling—under a moon old—guiltless as yet of the sty—with no original speck of the *amor immunditiae*,[11] the hereditary failing of the first parent, yet manifest—his voice as yet not broken, but something between a childish treble, and a grumble—the mild forerunner, or *praeludium*, of a grunt.

He must be roasted. I am not ignorant that our ancestors ate them seethed, or boiled— but what a sacrifice of the exterior tegument!

There is no flavor comparable, I will contend, to that of the crisp, tawny, well-watched, not over-roasted, *crackling*, as it is well called—the very teeth are invited to their share of the pleasure at this banquet in overcoming the coy, brittle resistance—with the adhesive oleaginous—O call it not fat— but an indefinable sweetness growing up to it—the tender blossoming of fat—fat cropped in the bud—taken in the shoot—in the first innocence—the cream and quintessence of the child-pig's yet pure food—the lean, no lean, but a kind of animal manna—or, rather, fat and lean (if it must be so) so blended and running into each other, that both together make but one ambrosian result, or common substance.

Behold him, while he is doing—it seemeth rather a refreshing warmth, than a scorching heat, that he is so passive to. How equably he twirleth round the string!—Now he is just done. To see the extreme sensibility of that tender age, he hath wept out his pretty eyes— radiant jellies—shooting stars.—

See him in the dish, his second cradle, how meek he lieth!—wouldst thou have had this innocent grow up to the grossness and indocility which too often accompany maturer swinehood? Ten to one he would have proved a glutton, a sloven, an obstinate, disagreeable animal—wallowing in all manner of filthy conversation—from these sins he is happily snatched away—

Ere sin could blight, or sorrow fade,
Death came with timely care—[12]

his memory is odoriferous—no clown curseth, while his stomach half rejecteth, the rank bacon—no coal-heaver bolteth him in reeking sausages—he hath a fair sepulcher in the grateful stomach of the judicious epicure —and for such a tomb might be content to die.

---

7. **Locke:** John Locke (1632–1704), English empirical philosopher.
8. *mundus edibilis Latin:* world of edibles.
9. *princeps obsoniorum Latin:* prince of delicacies.
10. **hobbledehoy:** an awkward and gawky adolescent youth.
11. *amor immunditiae Latin:* love of the unclean.
12. **Ere . . . care:** a quotation from Coleridge's "Epitaph on an Infant."

He is the best of sapors.[13] Pineapple is great. She is indeed almost too transcendent—a delight, if not sinful, yet so like to sinning, that really a tender-conscienced person would do well to pause—too ravishing for mortal taste, she woundeth and excoriateth the lips that approach her—like lovers' kisses, she biteth—she is a pleasure bordering on pain from the fierceness and insanity of her relish —but she stoppeth at the palate—she meddleth not with the appetite—and the coarsest hunger might barter her consistently for a mutton chop.

Pig—let me speak his praise—is no less provocative of the appetite, than he is satisfactory to the criticalness of the censorious palate. The strong man may batten[14] on him, and weakling refuseth not his mild juices.

Unlike to mankind's mixed characters, a bundle of virtues and vices, inexplicably intertwisted, and not to be unravelled without hazard, he is—good throughout. No part of him is better or worse than another. He helpeth, as far as his little means extend, all around. He is the least envious of banquets. He is all neighbors' fare.

I am one of those, who freely and ungrudgingly impart a share of the good things of this life which fall to their lot (few as mine are in this kind) to a friend. I protest I take as great an interest in my friend's pleasures, his relishes, and proper satisfactions, as in mine own. "Presents," I often say, "endear Absents." Hares, pheasants, partridges, snipes, barndoor chickens (those "tame villatic[15] fowl"), capons, plovers, brawn,[16] barrels of oysters, I dispense as freely as I receive them. I love to taste them, as it were, upon the tongue of my friend. But a stop must be put somewhere. One would not, like Lear, "give everything." I make my stand upon pig. Methinks it is an ingratitude to the Giver of all good flavors, to extra-domiciliate or send out of the house, slightingly (under pretext of friendship, or I know not what), a blessing so particularly adapted, predestined, I may say, to my individual palate.—It argues an insensibility.

I remember a touch of conscience in this kind at school. My good old aunt, who never parted from me at the end of a holiday without stuffing a sweetmeat, or some nice thing, into my pocket, had dismissed me one evening with a smoking plum-cake, fresh from the oven. On my way to school (it was over London Bridge) a gray-headed old beggar saluted me (I have no doubt at this time of day that he was a counterfeit). I had no pence to console him with, and in the vanity of self-denial, and the very coxcombry[17] of charity, schoolboy-like, I made him a present of—the whole cake! I walked on a little, buoyed up, as one is on such occasions, with a sweet soothing of self-satisfaction; but before I had got to the end of the bridge, my better feelings returned, and I burst into tears, thinking how ungrateful I had been to my good aunt, to go and give her good gift away to a stranger that I had never seen before, and who might be a bad man for aught I knew; and then I thought of the pleasure my aunt would be taking in thinking that I—I myself, and not another— would eat her nice cake—and what should I say to her the next time I saw her—how naughty I was to part with her pretty present! —and the odor of that spicy cake came back upon my recollection, and the pleasure, and the curiosity I had taken in seeing her make it, and her joy when she sent it to the oven, and how disappointed she would feel that I had never had a bit of it in my mouth at last—and I blamed my impertinent spirit of alms-giving, and out-of-place hypocrisy of goodness, and above all I wished never to see the face again of that insidious, good-for-nothing, old gray imposter.

---

13. **sapor** (sāp' ər): taste or flavor.
14. **batten:** fatten.
15. **villatic:** farmyard.
16. **brawn:** cooked boar's flesh.
17. **coxcombry** (käks' kōm rē): silly conceit.

Our ancestors were nice in their method of sacrificing these tender victims. We read of pigs whipped to death with something of a shock, as we hear of any other obsolete custom. The age of discipline is gone by, or it would be curious to inquire (in a philosophical light merely) what effect this process might have towards intenerating and dulcifying[18] a substance, naturally so mild and dulcet as the flesh of young pigs. It looks like refining a violet. Yet we should be cautious, while we condemn the inhumanity, how we censure the wisdom of the practice. It might impart a gusto.—

I remember an hypothesis, argued upon by the young students, when I was at St. Omer's[19] and maintained with much learning and pleasantry on both sides, "Whether, supposing that the flavor of a pig who obtained his death by whipping (*per flagellationem extremam*) superadded a pleasure upon the palate of a man more intense than any possible suffering we can conceive in the animal, is man justified in using that method of putting the animal to death?" I forget the decision.

His sauce should be considered. Decidedly, a few bread crumbs, done up with his liver and brains, and a dash of mild sage. But, banish, dear Mrs. Cook, I beseech you, the whole onion tribe. Barbecue your whole hogs to your palate, steep them in shalots, stuff them out with plantations of the rank and guilty garlic; you cannot poison them, or make them stronger than they are—but consider, he is a weakling—a flower.

---

18. **intenerating and dulcifying:** making tender and sweet.
19. **St. Omer's:** a college conducted by the Jesuits in France for English boys.

PIGS IN THE MEADOW, 1910. *Mela Koehler.*
Postcard published by the Wiener Werkstätte, Austria.
The Metropolitan Museum of Art, New York.

Getting at Meaning

1. In the discovery of roast pig, what was the importance of such factors as ingenuity, carelessness, stupidity, and pure chance? How did people react to the idea at first? How did the idea spread? What is Lamb suggesting about human nature?

2. Are the characters involved in the discovery of roast pig foolish or intelligent? What incidents indicate this?

3. What paragraph serves as a transition from the story in the ancient manuscript to the rest of the essay?

4. How does Lamb rank the taste of roast pig? According to Lamb, why are young pigs tastier?

5. What is the point of Lamb's story about giving his aunt's plum-cake to a beggar?

Developing Skills in Reading Literature

1. **Essay.** An informal essay can deal lightly, often humorously, with personal experiences, opinions, ideas, and prejudices. To what extent does Lamb's essay fit this description?

2. **Style.** You will note in this essay that what might be put simply often is stated in a complex or round-about way. Lamb refers to what is left of a burnt pig as "the smoking remnants of one of those untimely sufferers." Later he remarks that the pig "hath a fair sepulchre in the grateful stomach of the judicious epicure." He resorts to understatement or double negatives, as when he says that the father finds the taste "not altogether displeasing." This style of writing is known as circumlocution ("talking around") or periphrasis. Point out several other good examples of circumlocution. What is the effect of using such a weighty style in telling a basically simple story? In other words, how is the style an integral part of this essay?

Notice also the use of archaic words, such as *curseth, meddleth, refuseth,* the Latin phrases sprin-kled throughout the second part of the essay, and the title "A Dissertation." What type of writing is Lamb imitating? Again, what is the intended effect of contrasting style and subject matter?

Where does Lamb vary this inflated style with much more direct language, or with slang? Is this a disturbing inconsistency or an effective technique?

3. **Stereotype.** Notice that Lamb treats his characters somewhat patronizingly; much of the humor of this essay is at their expense. Have you come across this kind of humor before? What kinds of stock characters do these seem to be? Are they typically Romantic? Explain.

Developing Vocabulary

1. **Word Origins.** Learning the root of a word can help you remember the current meaning of the word when you encounter it in your reading. Record the etymologies of the following words and explain their meanings in relation to their roots.

antediluvian
oleaginous
ambrosian

2. **Multiple Meanings of Words.** Explain the meaning of *dear* in this sentence: "Fuel and pigs grew enormously dear all over the district."

The earlier, more precise definition of *nice* is now often forgotten. What is its meaning in the first sentence of the third from the last paragraph?

Developing Writing Skills

Writing an Informal Essay. On a subject of your choice, write a brief informal essay in which you reveal personal tastes or opinions. You might try to imitate the kinds of humorous effects created by Lamb, or you might present all of your ideas in a straightforward, easygoing manner.

Unit Review *The Romantic Period*

Understanding the Unit

1. Wordsworth defined poetry as "the spontaneous overflow of powerful feelings . . . recollected in tranquillity." What kinds of intense experiences seem to be most valuable for the poets represented in this unit? What kinds of insights have the poets gained from these experiences? Refer to specific poems.

2. In *Biographia Literaria*, Coleridge explained that he and Wordsworth agreed to write two different kinds of poems: ". . . my endeavors should be directed to persons and characters supernatural, or at least romantic [so as to produce] that willing suspension of disbelief . . . which constitutes poetic faith. Mr. Wordsworth, on the other hand, was to . . . give the charm of novelty to things of every day, and to excite a feeling analogous to the supernatural, by awakening the mind's attention from the lethargy of custom and directing it to the loveliness and the wonders of the world before us. . . ." Explain how the poems of Wordsworth and Coleridge illustrate this statement of purpose, referring to specific poems as you do so.

3. As an aspect of nature, the sea is a recurring image in Romantic poetry. What qualities or values are associated with the sea in the following poems: "The World Is Too Much with Us," "It Is a Beauteous Evening, Calm and Free," "The Rime of the Ancient Mariner," "Kubla Khan," "Apostrophe to the Ocean," "Ode to the West Wind," and "Love's Philosophy"? How do these poems illustrate the characteristic Romantic attitude toward nature?

4. The Neoclassical mind tended to seek the divine in the ordered, the restrained, and the proportioned. The Romantics, on the other hand, were more likely to intuit divinity in the vast or the obscure, the wild or infinite. Which poems in the unit illustrate this difference between Neoclassicism and Romanticism?

5. Romanticism often is identified with a yearning to escape the limitations of the actual, the ordinary, the familiar. Different writers, though, sought escape in different ways. From among the selections in the unit, identify those in which the writers escape in the following ways:

a. by focusing on the past, the primitive, the remote in space and time

b. by finding a transcendent reality within the everyday, the familiar

c. by attempting to capture a particular moment and make it eternal

d. by imagining the future

Writing

1. In "Preface" to *Lyrical Ballads,* Wordsworth asks, "What is a poet?" He answers as follows: "He is a man . . . endowed with more lively sensibility, more enthusiasm and tenderness, who has a greater knowledge of human nature, and a more comprehensive soul, than are supposed to be common among mankind; a man pleased with his own passions and volitions, and who rejoices more than other men in the spirit of life that is in him; delighting to contemplate similar volitions and passions as manifested in the goings on of the universe. . . . To these qualities he has added a disposition to be affected more than other men by absent things . . . a greater readiness and power in expressing what he thinks and feels . . . without immediate external excitement."

Explain this expression of poetic theory in your own words. Then discuss the way that Wordsworth himself and at least three other poets in the unit embody this ideal. Refer to specific poems in your essay.

2. A frequent feature of Romanticism is a rejection of intellectualism and "common sense." The result, at its best, fits the definition of Romanticism given by one early critic: "The Renaissance of Wonder." Using the poems of at least four Romantic writers, discuss the "wonder" of Romanticism in a five-paragraph essay.

3. An important concern in Romanticism is the nature of the creative imagination. In a well developed essay discuss the Romantic concept of the creative process as implied in the following selections and in any others that seem relevant: "Ode to the West Wind," "Lines Composed a Few Miles Above Tintern Abbey," "Kubla Khan," and "To a Skylark."

QUEEN VICTORIA, 1900. *B. Müller (after H. Von Angeli, 1899).*
National Portrait Gallery, London.

Unit 6
The Victorian Period (1832–1900)

KING CHARLES SPANIELS, 1845. *Sir Edwin Landseer.*
Tate Gallery, London.

The Age of the Victorians

To most contemporary readers, the term *Victorian* connotes restrictive morality, hypocrisy, pretentiousness, prudery, and stuffy complacency, but these characteristics by no means sum up the era. The Victorian Period was a complex time during which the people of Great Britain experienced enormous changes in virtually every area of life. The period began with bishops in wigs riding in elegant horse-drawn coaches; it ended with motorcars in the streets. One political reform after another forced the old aristocracy to give way reluctantly to increasing democracy. A tremendous religious revival ultimately lost its momentum. The foundations of thought were shaken by the new science, with its revolutionary explanation of the origin of humans. Perhaps most important, there was at the end of the century an undercurrent of social unrest and a realization that, although the Industrial Revolution had brought great prosperity to the country, large segments of the population had suffered in the process.

AN AGE OF REFORM

When Victoria ascended the throne in 1837 at the age of eighteen, the country was emerging from the sternly repressive era that had followed the French Revolution. A series of reform laws had been passed recently, beginning with the Reform Bill of 1832, which was a significant step toward a more representative government. It was followed by the abolition of slavery in 1833 and, also in 1833, the first effective law for the protection of children in factories.

Reforms were sorely needed, for the industrialization had brought abominable working conditions for the majority of factory laborers. Of particular concern was the plight of children. Some children as young as five years of age were hired to drag tubs of coal through mine tunnels for sixteen hours a day.

Although the early reform bills were no panacea, they did mark an increasing concern on the part of the upper and middle classes for the plight of the poor. There was a growing awareness that the combination of industrialization and an enormous population growth had created a situation in which large numbers of citizens were unable to support themselves. One attempt to deal with this problem was the Poor Law of 1834, which created workhouses for the poor. The miserable conditions in these workhouses further demoralized and impoverished the people they were established to help.

Throughout the nineteenth century, the Victorians continued to make progress in social reform. Factory laws were strengthened and model factory towns were built; the Public Health Act of 1848 provided for public parks, public baths, and improved sanitation systems for poor areas. The workers themselves became an effective force in improving living and working conditions; by the 1850's there had been a revival of trade unions, and in 1871 the Trade Union Act legalized unions and gave them the protection of the courts.

While it is true, therefore, that huge injustices existed during the Victorian Period, it is also true that the Victorians made efforts to improve their society. England was the first nation to experience the social evils caused by the Industrial Revolution and was also the first to attempt to deal with them.

POLITICS AND ECONOMICS IN VICTORIAN ENGLAND

A stabilizing influence in the turbulent mid-nineteenth century was Robert Peel who served as Prime Minister from 1841 until his death in 1850. His administration felt the influence of two important groups: the Chartists and the Anti-Corn-Law League. The Chartists, an organization of working class people, drew up a "People's Charter" calling for the extension of the right to vote, the secret ballot, and other legislative reforms. Despite ten years of agitation and much popular support, the Chartists failed to have their program passed by Parliament.

The Anti-Corn-Law League sought to abolish the high tariffs on imported grain, which protected the landowners but kept the price of food artificially high. Serious crop failures in England and the failure of the Irish potato crop in 1845 and 1846 convinced Peel to repeal the controversial Corn Laws, an act that paved the way for free trade. Although free trade could not eradicate poverty, it did help to relieve the immediate economic distress and ushered in two decades of prosperity.

The dominant political personality of mid-Victorian Britain was Viscount Palmerston, who served as Prime Minister from 1855 to 1858 and from 1859 to 1865. By force of his popularity and his adroit political maneuvering, Palmerston was able to pursue policies of foreign intervention even when his wishes opposed those of the court and despite the confused state of British politics. His domestic policies were less aggressive, however, and Palmerston's rule was a time of notable lack of reform. With the death of Palmerston in 1865, the stage was set for the two strong personalities who dominated British politics for much of the rest of the century—William Gladstone, a Liberal, and Benjamin Disraeli, a Conservative.

Gladstone first served as Prime Minister from 1868 to 1874, succeeding Disraeli who had served for only nine months. Gladstone's administration was marked by a series of liberal reforms, including the Irish Land Act of 1870, which provided safeguards to Irish tenant farmers; the Education Act of 1870, the first national act dealing with primary education; the Trade Union Act of 1871; and the Ballot Act of 1871, which introduced the secret ballot. These reforms alienated many factions, and in 1874 Disraeli and the Conservatives took over, to the delight of Queen Victoria who preferred the flamboyant Disraeli to the staid Gladstone.

BRITISH IMPERIALISM

In the early years of his career in Parliament, Disraeli had busied himself with domestic social issues such as slum clearance, public health, and protection of trade unions. As Prime Minister, however, his principal cause was imperialism. In 1875 he managed to acquire for England the controlling interest in the Suez Canal, which provided a shorter trade route to India, a British stronghold since the 1700's. Through clever international diplomacy, Disraeli was also instrumental in obtaining the island of Cyprus and large stretches of land in the Transvaal in South Africa, acquisitions that led eventually to the Boer War (1899–1902) with the South Africans of Dutch descent. Keenly aware of the imperialist fever gripping Britain, Disraeli persuaded Parliament to proclaim Queen Victoria "Empress of India," a title she professed not to want but which she accepted despite heavy opposition.

During the last two decades of the nineteenth century, the Queen and a majority of her subjects believed in the necessity of accepting the "burden" of imperialism. This attitude was described by poet Rudyard Kipling as follows:

> Take up the White Man's burden—
> Send forth the best ye breed—
> Go bind your sons to exile
> To serve your captives' need;
> To wait in heavy harness,
> On fluttered folk and wild—
> Your new-caught, sullen peoples,
> Half-devel and half-child. . . .

AN AGE OF PROGRESS

The Victorian era was a time of industrial and scientific progress, with great strides made in electrical engineering, in the development of machine tools and mass production, and in the creation of vaccines to control contagious diseases. An appropriate tribute to this era of material progress was the Great Exhibition of 1851, the purpose of which was to display "the Works of Industry of All Nations." The pet project of Prince Albert, husband of Queen Victoria, the exhibition was housed in a magnificent "Crystal Palace" with glass walls and towering columns of iron. Here visitors saw collected in one place the marvels of the age—locomotives, steamships, telegraphs, hydraulic presses, and power looms; indoor water closets, bathtubs, and gas cooking ranges; and Cyrus McCormick's reaper, which was to revolutionize agricultural methods in Europe in the decades to come.

Most of those who visited the exhibition shared an optimistic faith in humanity's ability to triumph with the help of material goods. The generally accepted thesis of the day was that human ingenuity could control the world and achieve an earthly paradise.

SCIENCE, RELIGION, AND PHILOSOPHY

Science and technology not only affected the physical world of the Victorians but also had a profound effect on Victorian thought. The new science of the nineteenth century was a major intellectual force that was to shake the very foundations of traditional beliefs. As early as 1830 geologists formulated the theory that the earth had evolved gradually over long periods of time. Most disturbing to Victorians was the work of Charles Darwin, who in *Origin of Species* (1859) proclaimed that all existing species of plant and animal life had evolved into their present form over the course of millions of years by the process of natural selection. Darwin's ideas seemed to contradict the Biblical version of creation and prompted furious debates among theologians and intellectuals.

The majority of people found the notion that human beings "descended from a monkey" simply preposterous and so were not drawn into the controversy until much later. They were concerned instead with a powerful religious revival known as Evangelical Reform. Begun in the eighteenth century by John and Charles Wesley, among others, this movement continued through much of the nineteenth century. Inspired by missionary zeal, Evangelicals built churches, led revival meetings, and preached a message that appealed to the heart of the common people. The movement united the Protestant denominations in an effort not only to convert all of England but also to dispatch representatives of Christianity and white civilization to every part of the world.

Another significant force in Victorian England was the Utilitarian movement, which was based on the philosophy of Jeremy Bentham. Utilitarians believed that the only valid test of all institutions—governmental, religious, and social—is whether they are useful to society, and they defined utility, or usefulness, as "the greatest happiness for the greatest number of people."

One reform movement within the Church of England was the Oxford Movement. Under the leadership of John Henry Newman, this group sought to restore to church worship the dignity of earlier times and to protect the church from encroachment by the state. Newman, who lost his post at Oxford University when he was accused of advocating the high liturgy of Roman Catholicism, ultimately joined the Roman Catholic Church and became Cardinal Newman. The Oxford Group continued to work within the Anglican Church to revive ritual, to beautify church buildings, and to improve church music.

POPULAR CULTURE

Improvements in mass production and in communication made possible the publication of the London *Daily Express*, a popular newspaper that boasted, "No event can occur in the most remote corner of the earth without the *Daily Express* being placed in immediate possession of the fullest details." Improvements in public transportation meant easy access to public entertainment, which included music halls, auctions, band concerts, seaside resorts, cricket and football matches, golf courses, and bicycle paths.

For "respectable" Victorians, entertainment centered in the church and the home. The middle-class Victorian particularly was preoccupied with the comforts of home. The typical middle-class parlor was overcrowded with heavy furniture and knick-knacks, and an accumulation of family photographs was displayed on the piano or organ. On Sundays and festive occasions, the dining room table groaned under the weight of literally dozens of different foods, all prepared by household servants. Middle-class families were generally large, considered a tribute to the father's adequacy as a breadwinner and to the mother's devotion to her family and efficiency as a manager. A few pioneering women took advantage of new educational and professional opportunities, lower-class women worked in factories and mills and as domestic servants, and farm women worked in the fields as they always had; but the great majority of middle-class women applied their energies to domestic tasks, a devotion to duty that emulated the example of Queen Victoria herself.

LATE VICTORIAN BRITAIN

By the closing decades of the Victorian Period, the fervor of the reformers had waned. An awareness of the social ills brought about by industrial expansion created a new mood in the country. The confident optimism that progress was good and that humanity would triumph was tinged by an undercurrent of anxiety about what the future might bring.

On the international scene, England's leadership in the world was no longer unchallenged. The United States had progressed rapidly after the Civil War, and the nations of continental Europe were also fast becoming industrial rivals of Britain. Germany, Belgium, Portugal, Russia, and France all were vying with England for control of the rich resources of Africa and China. The struggle for colonial possessions, along with a complex array of political, economic, social, and historical factors, led to an international arms race that split the great powers. Still, the British felt tremendously proud of their considerable achievements. Symbolic of the feeling in England at this time were the two jubilees of Queen Victoria in 1887 and 1897, which celebrated with imperial pageantry her fiftieth and sixtieth years as Queen. No one could have suspected that England would soon be involved in World War I, a war that would devastate the nation's spirit.

VICTORIAN LITERATURE

British literature of the Victorian Age cannot be characterized by a single distinct style or emphasis on a particular subject. Many Victorian writers protested smugness and hypocrisy; some clung to fading romantic ideals of the past; others wrote realistic interpretations of life.

One major strain was social criticism, with writers focusing on the evils and ugliness they attributed to the Industrial Revolution. Thomas Carlyle, for example, firmly believed that the society of his time was going from bad to worse, that it was nonsense to believe in salvation by machines, gadgets, and physical comforts, and that the prevailing economic doctrine of *laissez-faire* was doomed to failure. John Stuart Mill, another social critic, also was troubled by materialistic values, but his approach was less radical than Carlyle's. Mill's essays reflect a reasonable, analytic approach to the economic and political problems of the period. Two other writers of nonfiction,

John Ruskin and William Morris, stressed the importance of independent thinking and other human values while condemning the industrial age for its emphasis on joyless work and inartistic practicality. Matthew Arnold, who was a poet as well as a literary critic, wrote thoughtful essays in which he deplored the unimaginative materialism of the Victorians.

THE VICTORIAN NOVEL

The novel was an especially popular form of literature in Victorian times. Although many Victorian novelists were also critics, most depended for their livelihood upon the popularity of their works. They, therefore, were not able to be as frank in their criticism of social values as were the poets and essayists. Because reading novels aloud was a popular form of family entertainment, a successful novelist was expected to produce something wholesome, enlightening, and entertaining for every member of the family.

Certainly one of the most popular storytellers of all time is Charles Dickens, whose novels are both entertaining and critical of sham and hypocrisy in Victorian society. In *Oliver Twist* (1838) and *Nicholas Nickleby* (1839), for example, he exposes the shameful treatment of orphans; in *Great Expectations* (1861) he attacks the materialistic values of mid-Victorian society. Another early Victorian novelist, William Makepeace Thackeray, shared Dickens's keen eye for social pretense and gift for revealing character and human conflict. *Vanity Fair* (1848) is Thackeray's best known novel, although *The History of Henry Esmond, Esq.* (1852) is thought by many to be his most perfectly integrated work. The tradition of social criticism established by these novelists is evident throughout the period, culminating in *The Way of All Flesh* (1903) by Samuel Butler, a venomous attack on repressive family life, hypocritical religious practice, and inadequate education.

Early in the Victorian Period, a number of women novelists began to make a name for themselves in what was certainly a male-dominated world. Among these were the Brontë sisters. Emily Brontë's only novel was the masterpiece *Wuthering Heights* (1847), which deals with powerful and sometimes terrifying human emotions. Charlotte Brontë was more prolific as a writer and also became more involved in the external world. Her best known novel, *Jane Eyre* (1847), is an imaginative and compelling tale of human passion. Like the Brontës, Mary Ann Evans found it difficult at first to gain recognition. After assuming the pen name George Eliot, though, she gained fame and was recognized as the first English novelist to incorporate the intellectual ideas of the time into her novels. In her masterpiece, *Middlemarch* (1871–72), Eliot's knowledge of the contemporary scene and her sense of moral virtue are most highly developed.

Toward the end of the century a number of novelists seemed to be more interested in human psychology than in social issues. Two of them, George Meredith and Thomas Hardy, wrote lengthy novels that probed the depths of human behavior. Meredith chose to write comic romances, primarily about male weakness and female strength, such as *The Adventures of Harry Richmond* (1871), while Hardy wrote realistic tales set in his native Wessex, a bleak, somber region steeped in history. Hardy expressed a dark pessimism in powerful works such as *The Return of the Native* (1878), *Tess of the D'Urbervilles* (1891), and *Jude the Obscure* (1895).

In addition to this group of rather introspective writers were others whose novels illustrate the increasing interest in the world at large. Three of these storytellers were Robert Louis Stevenson, Rudyard Kipling, and Joseph Conrad. Stevenson is best known for robust adventure tales often set in the exotic South Seas. Kipling, in writing about life in India, seemed to champion the cause of British imperialism. His point of view contrasts sharply with that of Conrad, who denounced England's attempt to justify its supremacy as an imperial power. Although Conrad's early works were sea stories written in the nineteenth century, his finest novels and stories belong in both spirit and chronology to the twentieth century.

A fascinating writer of this period who celebrated the human imagination was the Reverend Charles L. Dodson, an ordained minister and a mathematics tutor at Oxford who wrote under the pen name Lewis Carroll. His major works, *Alice's Adventures in Wonderland* (1865) and *Through the Looking-Glass* (1872), are complex and sophisticated children's books, rich in parody, irony, and symbolic suggestion.

POETRY AND DRAMA IN VICTORIAN ENGLAND

Victorian poets were extremely diverse in style and subject matter. Even Alfred, Lord Tennyson, the poet laureate of the time who is considered the quintessential Victorian poet, wrote "official" verse in an optimistic mood to please the public and the Queen but was wistfully romantic and melancholy when he expressed his own thoughts and feelings.

The concerns of Victorian poets were not limited to England. Robert Browning and his wife, Elizabeth Barrett Browning, lived most of their lives outside of England, and Robert was often more interested in subjects such as the Italian Renaissance than in what was going on in his native country. Also fascinated by the Italian

Renaissance was Dante Gabriel Rossetti, one of the founders of a group of poets and painters known as the Pre-Raphaelites. The Pre-Raphaelites repudiated Victorian excess and emulated the pure, simple images characteristic of medieval Italian art. The poetry of Christina Rossetti, though less complex than that of her brother, also suggests an interest in symbolism, especially that of religious mysticism, which is quite alien to most Victorians.

Notable in the poetry of the late nineteenth century is a willingness to explore new modes of expression and a mood of pessimism, a sense of tragedy, disappointment, and waste that anticipates the mood of the twentieth century. The poems of Thomas Hardy, for example, consider the human being as subject to dark, uncontrollable forces. In attitude, A. E. Housman is equally fatalistic, although his style is more "modern" than that of Hardy. Gerard Manley Hopkins experimented with language and rhythm, creating poems that are more akin to the poetry of the twen-

---

Literature

- Charles Dickens (1812–1870) publishes first book of short stories
- Dickens publishes *Pickwick Papers*
- Charlotte Brontë (1816–1855) publishes *Jane Eyre*
- Emily Brontë (1818–1848) publishes *Wuthering Heights*
- Christina Rossett (1830–1894) publishes collect of Pre-Raphaelite poetry

- Thomas Carlyle (1795–1881) publishes *Sartor Resartus* in *Fraser's Magazine*
- Robert Browning (1812–1889) publishes "Pippa Passes"
- Elizabeth Barrett Browning (1806–1861) publishes *Sonnets from the Portuguese*
- Tennyson begins *In Memoriam*, an elegy for English essayist Arthur Henry Hallam
- John Ruskin (1819–1900) publishes first volume of *Modern Painters*
- William Makepeace Thackeray (1811–1863) publishes satirical romance, *Barry Lyndon*
- George Eliot (Mary Ann Evans) publishes *Silas Ma*
- Alfred, Lord Tennyson (1809–1892) publishes *Poems*, including "The Lady of Shalott"
- Edward Lear (1812–1888) publishes *Book of Nonsense* for children, popularizing the limerick
- Matthew Arnold (1822–1888) publishes *Poems*

| 1832 | 1840 | 1850 | 1860 |

History

- Victoria becomes Queen of Great Britain and Ireland
- Chartism, political reform movement, begins in Great Britain
- John Stuart Mill (1806–1873) publishe treatise *On Liberty*
- Factory Act legislates protection for children working in factories
- Failure of potato crop causes Great Famine in Ireland
- Civil War breaks out in United State
- British government repeals Corn Laws
- Slavery abolished in the British Empire
- Albert, Prince Consort of Queen Victoria dies
- Dante Gabriel Rossetti establishes Pre-Raphaelite brotherhood
- Charles Darwin pub *Origin of Species*, introducing theory evolution

tieth century than to the poems of his Victorian contemporaries.

The Victorians produced little notable writing for the stage. Not until the end of the period did a few significant dramatists emerge. One was W. S. Gilbert, whose comic operas ridicule artificiality and social hypocrisy with keenness and vitality. The plays of Oscar Wilde have more surface brilliance than Gilbert's operettas, but they are not as sharply satiric. Wilde's popular comedy of manners, *The Importance of Being Earnest* (1895), projects upper-class English society as totally devoid of emotional, moral, and physical reality. George Bernard Shaw, who dominated British drama for much of the twentieth century, wrote his first plays during the Victorian Period, and his fame was beginning to mount during the last five years of the century. Shaw's funny, original plays provided a clear look into the origins of social problems and represented the anti-Victorian tradition that was also apparent in the poetry and fiction of the period.

Lewis Carroll (1832–1898) publishes
Alice's Adventures in Wonderland

George Meredith (1828–1909) publishes
The Adventures of Harry Richmond

Thomas Hardy (1840–1928) publishes
first of his "Wessex" novels

Robert Louis Stevenson (1850–1894)
publishes *Treasure Island*

Arthur Conan Doyle (1859–1930)
introduces Sherlock Holmes character

Oscar Wilde (1854–1900) publishes
The Picture of Dorian Gray

Rudyard Kipling (1865–1936)
publishes *Barrack-Room Ballads*

A.E. Housman
(1859–1936) publishes
A Shropshire Lad

Bernard Shaw
(1856–1950) writes
Arms and the Man

1870	1880	1890	1900

Gladstone becomes
Prime Minister

Irish Land Act safeguards tenant farmers

Trade Union Act legalizes unions and
gives them protection of the courts

Disraeli becomes Prime Minister

Gilbert and Sullivan collaborate
on their first operetta

Disraeli acquires controlling
interest in Suez Canal

Charles Parnell is elected to Parliament and
begins movement for Irish independence

Disraeli secures for Victoria the title Empress of India

British annex Transvaal (the
South African Republic)

Queen Victoria celebrates
her Golden Jubilee

Spanish-American
War begins

Boer War begins

The Development of the English Language

THE VICTORIAN PERIOD

Language does not alter significantly in a span of sixty-eight years, even if the rate of change in the world is dizzying. Still, important trends can be identified. Often they are rooted in the distant past; sometimes they are extended in a later era.

Language and Social Class

During the Victorian Period, the social structure of the English-speaking nations was altered radically by the maturing Industrial Revolution. The initial impact was to intensify the pressure toward a single standard of usage, ostensibly based upon the usage of the upper classes, particularly the British aristocracy. Ironically, the aristocracy was often lax and flexible in its usage because, very simply, it could afford to be.

This was not the case with the new rich, the industrialists who wanted nothing but the best. On the one hand, this new class could afford to purchase mansions, art masterpieces, and the finest education for its children. On the other hand, the new class as a whole was socially insecure, painfully aware of its humble origins, ill at ease among those born to wealth and high station, eager to be taught deportment of every kind: the proper fork to use for the salad, the appropriate tie to wear to the reception, the correct verb form to use for the subjunctive. Language historian Thomas Pyles commented, "There can be no denying that the careless, aristocratic speech heard in eighteenth-century English drawing rooms has been to some extent supplanted by the stilted and unnatural language recommended by schoolmasters and lexicographers to whom the Industrial Revolution gave a new lease on life."

Jargon and Slang

Beyond regional dialects, different professions develop jargon, specialized or technical vocabulary. An educator, for example, might speak of *reading readiness* and *cognitive paradigm*, an economist of *infrastructure* and *stagflation*, a psychologist of *behavior modification* and *overcompensation*. Sometimes the terms become popular coinages.

During Victorian times, a kind of rhyming slang was developed in the Cockney section of London. To some extent, this was a street argot that enabled the Cockneys to converse safely in the presence of the police. It developed, however, into an elaborate, obscure code based on synonyms, rhymes, and associations. For example, the word *china* means "friend" because a friend is a mate, *mate* rhymes with *plate*, and a good plate is china. Similarly, *scarper* means "escape" because a synonym for *escape* is *go*, and *go* rhymes with *flow*; in England, *flow* is associated with Scapa Flow, the waters off the north coast of Scotland, and Cockneys pronounce *Scapa* "scarper."

Some Victorian underworld slang, such as *dimber mort* for "pretty girl" and *rumbeak* for "a judge who takes bribes," did not endure. However, Victorian slang terms included *finniff* for "five dollars," an expression that remained current well into the twentieth century, and *pig* for "police officer," an epithet so closely associated with the 1960's that many people assume it was invented then, rather than a century and more earlier. Other enduring words that were once slang are *joke*, *boom*, *slump*, *fad*, and *grit*.

The proliferation of slang and jargon, to which English seems peculiarly congenial, worked against a single standard of correct English. While strict schoolmasters enforced the rules of grammar with a hickory stick in the classroom, and society matrons enforced the rules of grammar with raised eyebrows in the drawing room, in less formal settings English defied convention. One striking development of the nineteenth century was a more scientific, objective attitude toward slang, in contrast with the opinion expressed by Noah Webster in 1828 that slang is "low, vulgar, unmeaning language."

Victorian Circumlocutions

If convention can regulate the way that people speak, it is well on its way to regulating how they think and behave. No group revealed a better understanding of this process than the Victorians, who used language to police decorum. Victorian propriety decreed that certain words, especially those having sexual connotations, were taboo. Certain anatomical words, such as *belly* and *breast*, were considered inflammatory, as was *legs*, which was replaced with the more neutral *limbs*. The Victorian era was the great age of the euphemism, and language was one way that proper Victorians avoided acknowledging unpleasant realities.

New Coinages

New events, ideas, inventions, and trends all spawn new words; the history of words is the history of humans. Consider the new way of life revealed by these coined words and the date of earliest citation: *refrigerator* (1824), *photography* (1839), *telephone* (1844), *dynamite* (1867), *prohibitionist* (1846), *locomotive* (1825), *coeducation* (1874), *feminist* (1894), *volt* (1873), and *psychiatrist* (1890). The Victorians needed such words, although the English had done without them for more than a thousand years.

Preserving the History of English

One triumph of Victorian England was the publication of the *Oxford English Dictionary*. This dictionary traces the history of words by noting the date of their first use and showing how the meanings of the words have changed through the years. Although work began on this dictionary in 1857, the first of the dictionary's ten volumes did not appear until 1884.

Alfred, Lord Tennyson

1809–1892

The name Alfred, Lord Tennyson is for many readers synonymous with nineteenth-century English poetry. In his carefully wrought poems, Tennyson was a true spokesman for the middle-class Victorian Englishman. He not only reflected the attitudes and morals of the day but also dealt with the doubts and difficulties, such as the problem of the human being's place in a universe that had been redefined by the new science of Darwin and others.

The fourth son in a family of twelve children, Tennyson grew up in the parsonage at Somersby where his father, the rector, tutored his sons in classical and modern languages. Alfred displayed a precocious flair for verse, collaborating with his brother Charles on *Poems by Two Brothers* (1827), which attracted the favorable notice of a group of talented Cambridge undergraduates who called themselves the "Apostles." These gifted young men encouraged Tennyson to become a poet. In 1829 he won the Chancellor's medal for "Timbuctoo," and in 1830 he published his first independent volume, *Poems Chiefly Lyrical*, which won mixed reviews in England but proved more popular in America.

A massive man with a powerful physique, Tennyson was nevertheless shy and was deeply devoted to his few close friends, particularly Arthur Hallam. Hallam was one of the Cambridge "Apostles" and later became engaged to Tennyson's sister. Family problems and financial need forced Tennyson to leave Cambridge without a degree, but he was able to spend part of 1832 traveling with Hallam. The sudden death of Hallam in 1833 overwhelmed Tennyson with grief, prompting him to begin the elegiac *In Memoriam*, which took him seventeen years to complete to his satisfaction.

This was a difficult period for Tennyson. He fell in love with Emily Sellwood in 1836, yet poverty forced a series of postponements to their marriage. Family problems (one brother was insane, another an opium addict), money worries, and ill health plagued Tennyson through the 1840's, but in 1850 his fortune changed. In that year he was named

ALFRED, LORD TENNYSON, 1840. Samuel Lawrence. National Portrait Gallery, London.

poet laureate and finally married Emily Sellwood.

During the remaining forty-two years of Tennyson's life, his fame grew steadily until he became a living legend, one of the most loved, emblematic figures of the age. Among the more popular of his many works were *Idylls of the King* (1859); *Enoch Arden* (1864), a work that American director D. W. Griffith made into two movies; and *Locksley Hall* (1886).

Patriotic and prolific, Tennyson was an ideal poet laureate. Some critics complain that his "official" poems are uneven, yet one of his less highly regarded poems, "The Charge of the Light Brigade," is among the most famous in the English language. Few lines in literature are more widely known than "Theirs not to make reply,/Theirs not to reason why,/Theirs but to do and die."

Tennyson's appearance has been preserved in the pioneering photographs of Julia Cameron, showing him in his characteristic cloak and broadbrimmed hat. The huge man with the gruff ways delighted audiences when he read his poems in a thunderous voice. His compassion, his exquisite sense of beauty, his descriptive powers, his meticulous craftsmanship, his gift for matching the sense and sound of his language, all helped make Tennyson the great poet of his age.

As often through the purple night,
Below the starry clusters bright,
Some bearded meteor, trailing light,
    Moves over still Shalott.

His broad clear brow in sunlight glowed;   100
On burnished hooves his war horse trode;
From underneath his helmet flowed
His coal-black curls as on he rode,
    As he rode down to Camelot.
From the bank and from the river   105
He flashed into the crystal mirror,
"Tirra lirra," by the river
    Sang Sir Lancelot.

She left the web, she left the loom,
She made three paces through the room,   110
She saw the water lily bloom,
She saw the helmet and the plume,
    She looked down to Camelot.
Out flew the web and floated wide;
The mirror cracked from side to side;   115
"The curse is come upon me," cried
    The Lady of Shalott.

Part IV

In the stormy east wind straining,
The pale yellow woods were waning,
The broad stream in his banks complaining,   120
Heavily the low sky raining
    Over towered Camelot;
Down she came and found a boat
Beneath a willow left afloat,
And round about the prow she wrote   125
    The Lady of Shalott.

And down the river's dim expanse
Like some bold seër in a trance,
Seeing all his own mischance—
With a glassy countenance   130
    Did she look to Camelot.
And at the closing of the day
She loosed the chain, and down she lay;
The broad stream bore her far away,
    The Lady of Shalott.   135

Lying, robed in snowy white
That loosely flew to left and right—
The leaves upon her falling light—
Through the noises of the night
    She floated down to Camelot: 140
And as the boathead wound along
The willowy hills and fields among,
They heard her singing her last song,
    The Lady of Shalott.

Heard a carol, mournful, holy,   145
Chanted loudly, chanted lowly,
Till her blood was frozen slowly,
And her eyes were darkened wholly,
    Turned to towered Camelot.
For ere she reached upon the tide   150
The first house by the waterside,
Singing in her song she died,
    The Lady of Shalott.

THE LADY OF SHALOTT, 1888. *John William Waterhouse.*
Tate Gallery, London.

Under tower and balcony,
By garden wall and gallery,   155
A gleaming shape she floated by,
Dead-pale between the houses high,
   Silent into Camelot.
Out upon the wharfs they came,
Knight and burgher,[14] lord and dame,   160
And round the prow they read her name,
   The Lady of Shalott.

Who is this? and what is here?
And in the lighted palace near
Died the sound of royal cheer;   165
And they crossed themselves for fear,
   All the knights at Camelot:
But Lancelot mused a little space;
He said, "She has a lovely face;
God in his mercy lend her grace,   170
   The Lady of Shalott."

---

14. **burgher:** townsman.

Getting at Meaning

1. What two antithetical realms are described in this narrative poem? What contrasts distinguish the two realms? Who represents each of the realms?

2. Why does the Lady of Shalott spend her nights and days weaving? What do the sights in the mirror make her long for? What does she mean when she says, "I am half sick of shadows"?

3. How does the Lady react to the cheerful song and the dazzling reflection of Sir Lancelot? What is the result of her action?

4. How do the villagers react to the sight of the dead Lady of Shalott? What is the significance of Lancelot's reaction?

Developing Skills in Reading Literature

1. **Refrain.** The line or lines that make up the refrain of a poem usually are repeated exactly at the ends of succeeding stanzas. Less common is the refrain technique used in "The Lady of Shalott." Two refrains appear in each stanza and their wording varies somewhat throughout the poem. Trace each refrain, noting the variations in wording. How do the refrains reinforce the narrative? What shifts in mood are emphasized by changes in the wording of the refrains?

2. **Poetry: Sound and Mood.** Examine the feminine rhymes in these opening lines from Part IV. Notice how the sounds of the words suggest an atmosphere of gloom and depression.

In the stormy east wind straining,
The pale yellow woods were waning,
The broad stream in his banks complaining,
Heavily the low sky raining
    Over towered Camelot;

Look through the rest of Part IV and find at least five additional rhymes whose sound contributes to mood. Then look back at Part III and find rhyming words that convey a sense of strength and vitality. Do these tend to be masculine or feminine rhymes?

3. **Symbol.** Critics suggest that the Lady of Shalott as a weaver of fabric is analogous to a poet, a weaver of ideas and images. If the Lady of Shalott does indeed symbolize a poet, then what might her "magic web" symbolize? her mirror? What might be the curse of the poet? What might Camelot and Sir Lancelot symbolize in terms of the creative process? What imprisons a poet? How does a poet break out of this prison? What happens as a consequence, according to this poem? Does anything in the poem negate this symbolic interpretation, or does everything in the poem fit a symbolic analysis? Explain.

4. **Imagery.** Point out images of dazzling light and brilliance in Part III of this poem. How do these images contrast with those in the rest of the poem? What is the significance of this contrast? How does the imagery in Part III correspond to the unfolding of the story?

5. **Narrative Poem.** Like a short story, a narrative poem contains characters; a setting, or time and place of the action; a plot, or plan of action, which builds to a climax; and a point of view, all of which combine to bring out the theme. Examine this poem and be prepared to identify each of these narrative elements. Which elements seem to be most significant? In many ways, this poem is similar to a parable, a brief story that teaches a moral lesson. What lesson is suggested by the fate of the lady? How does Lancelot's reaction to seeing her body reinforce the lesson?

Developing Writing Skills

1. **Writing an Explanation.** In your local or school library find an encyclopedia of myths and legends. Read about the legend of the Lady of Shalott to discover how the curse was placed upon the mysterious lady. Then in a well developed paragraph explain what this legend reveals about the values and customs of the people who originated it. Be sure to credit your source or sources.

2. **Creating a Dominant Impression.** Tennyson uses words and phrases to convey distinct impressions. In "The Eagle" he emphasizes the stark remoteness of the eagle's nest in images such as "clasps the crag," "close to the sun," and "watches from his mountain walls." Similarly, in "The Lady of Shalott" the entire description of Lancelot, from the first "bowshot" of his appearance to his last "flash into the crystal mirror" conveys the impression of speed and light.

Write a paragraph or a poem describing a familiar scene, a person, or an action. Use specific words, phrases, and details to convey a dominant impression.

Ulysses

*Ulysses, the king of Ithaca and a leader in the Trojan War, is the hero of Homer's
Odyssey. In the poem that follows, Tennyson describes the restless longing of the
now aged hero for one last adventure.*

It little profits that an idle king,
By this still hearth, among these barren crags,
Matched with an agèd wife,[1] I mete and dole[2]
Unequal laws[3] unto a savage race,
That hoard, and sleep, and feed, and know not me.   5
I cannot rest from travel; I will drink
Life to the lees. All times I have enjoyed
Greatly, have suffered greatly, both with those
That loved me, and alone; on shore, and when
Through scudding drifts the rainy Hyades[4]   10
Vexed the dim sea. I am become a name;
For always roaming with a hungry heart
Much have I seen and known—cities of men
And manners, climates, councils, governments,
Myself not least, but honored of them all—   15
And drunk delight of battle with my peers,
Far on the ringing plains of windy Troy.
I am a part of all that I have met;
Yet all experience is an arch wherethrough
Gleams that untraveled world whose margin fades   20
Forever and forever when I move.
How dull it is to pause, to make an end,
To rust unburnished, not to shine in use!
As though to breathe were life! Life piled on life
Were all too little, and of one to me   25
Little remains; but every hour is saved
From that eternal silence, something more,
A bringer of new things; and vile it were
For some three suns to store and hoard myself,
And this gray spirit yearning in desire   30
To follow knowledge like a sinking star,

---

1. **aged wife:** Penelope.
2. **meet and dole:** measure and give out.
3. **unequal laws:** unfair laws.
4. **Hayades** (hī′ ə dēz): an open cluster of stars in the constellation Taurus,
thought to cause rain when it rose with the sun.

Beyond the utmost bound of human thought.
　　This is my son, mine own Telemachus,
To whom I leave the scepter and the isle[5]—
Well-loved of me, discerning to fulfill　　　　　　　　　　35
This labor, by slow prudence to make mild
A rugged people, and through soft degrees
Subdue them to the useful and the good.
Most blameless is he, centered in the sphere
Of common duties, decent not to fail　　　　　　　　　　40
In offices of tenderness, and pay
Meet adoration to my household gods,
When I am gone. He works his work, I mine.
　　There lies the port; the vessel puffs her sail;
There gloom the dark, broad seas. My mariners,　　　　45
Souls that have toiled, and wrought, and thought with me—
That ever with a frolic welcome took
The thunder and the sunshine, and opposed
Free hearts, free foreheads—you and I are old;
Old age hath yet his honor and his toil.　　　　　　　　50
Death closes all; but something ere the end,
Some work of noble note, may yet be done,
Not unbecoming men that strove with Gods.
The lights begin to twinkle from the rocks;
The long day wanes; the slow moon climbs; the deep　55
Moans round with many voices. Come, my friends,
'Tis not too late to seek a newer world.
Push off, and sitting well in order smite
The sounding furrows; for my purpose holds
To sail beyond the sunset, and the baths　　　　　　　　60
Of all the western stars, until I die.
It may be that the gulfs will wash us down;
It may be we shall touch the Happy Isles,[6]
And see the great Achilles,[7] whom we knew.
Though much is taken, much abides; and though　　　　65
We are not now that strength which in old days
Moved earth and heaven, that which we are, we are—
One equal temper of heroic hearts,
Made weak by time and fate, but strong in will
To strive, to seek, to find, and not to yield.　　　　　　70

---

5. **This . . . the isle:** Ithaca, an island off the coast of Greece. Telemachus
(tə lĕm′ ə kəs), the son of Ulysses, is to inherit his father's kingdom there.
6. **Happy Isles:** Elysium (i lizh′ ē əm), the dwelling place of virtuous people after
death.
7. **Achilles** (ə kyl′ ēz): the Greek leader with whom Ulysses had fought in the
Trojan War.

ULYSSES DERIDING POLYPHEMUS, 1829. *Joseph Turner. The National Gallery, London.*

Getting at Meaning

1. How does Ulysses feel about his present life? Point out lines that reveal this attitude. What passages best indicate his feelings about his former life of adventure? What does he reveal in lines 19–21 about his view of the future?

2. What is Ulysses's "work," according to the poem? How does his work differ from that of his son?

3. What weaknesses and what strengths does Ulysses recognize in himself? What seems to be Ulysses's attitude toward aging and death? toward life?

Developing Skills in Reading Literature

1. **Dramatic Monologue.** A dramatic monologue is a lyric poem in which a speaker addresses a silent listener in a moment of high intensity or deep emotion. To increase the dramatic impact of the poem, the poet often reveals the motivations as well as the feelings of the speaker. What is shown in this monologue to be Ulysses's prime motivating force? Is it a practical or an impractical motive? Explain. What emotions does Ulysses reveal in the course of his monologue? Who might be the silent, unnamed listener in the poem? Give reasons for your answer.

2. **Tone and Theme.** Ulysses's desire to pursue adventure might be interpreted as a sign of his heroic spirit or as an immature avoidance of responsibility. What seems to be Tennyson's attitude toward Ulysses? What then is the theme of the poem? Support your conclusions by pointing out words and phrases that suggest Tennyson's attitude.

3. **Paradox.** Although Ulysses pledges courageously in the last line of this poem "To strive, to seek, to find, and not to yield," he also speaks earlier of a plaintive desire "To sail beyond the sunset, and the baths/Of all the western stars until I die." What is paradoxical about these seemingly conflicting resolves?

from **In Memoriam**

The death of Tennyson's close friend Arthur Henry Hallam inspired In Memoriam, *an elegy mourning the death of a young man of great talent cut off before he is able to fulfill the promise of his youth.* In Memoriam *contains 133 separate lyrics, three of which are included here.*

27

I envy not in any moods
  The captive void of noble rage,
  The linnet[1] born within the cage,
That never knew the summer woods;

I envy not the beast that takes   5
  His license in the field of time,
  Unfettered by the sense of crime,
To whom a conscience never wakes;

Nor, what may count itself as blest,
  The heart that never plighted troth   10
  But stagnates in the weeds of sloth;
Nor any want-begotten rest.[2]

I hold it true, whate'er befall;
  I feel it, when I sorrow most;
  'Tis better to have loved and lost   15
Than never to have loved at all.

54

O, yet we trust that somehow good
  Will be the final goal of ill,
  To pangs of nature, sins of will,
Defects of doubt, and taints of blood;[3]

---

1. **linnet:** a small songbird.
2. **Nor, what . . . rest:** Neither do I envy the peace of mind that comes from never having pledged love or human affection.
3. **pangs . . . blood:** physical pain, moral crimes, spiritual doubt, and inherited faults.

That nothing walks with aimless feet;
  That not one life shall be destroyed,
  Or cast as rubbish to the void,
When God hath made the pile complete;

That not a worm is cloven in vain;
  That not a moth with vain desire
  Is shriveled in a fruitless fire,
Or but subserves another's gain.

Behold, we know not anything;
  I can but trust that good shall fall
  At last—far off—at last, to all,
And every winter change to spring.

So runs my dream; but what am I?
  An infant crying in the night;
  An infant crying for the light,
And with no language but a cry.

130

Thy voice is on the rolling air;
  I hear thee where the waters run;
  Thou standest in the rising sun,
And in the setting thou art fair.

What art thou then? I cannot guess;
  But though I seem in star and flower
  To feel thee some diffusive power,
I do not therefore love thee less.

My love involves the love before;
  My love is vaster passion now;
  Though mixed with God and Nature thou,
I seem to love thee more and more.

Far off thou art, but ever nigh;
  I have thee still, and I rejoice;
  I prosper, circled with thy voice;
I shall not lose thee though I die.

Getting at Meaning

LYRIC 27

1. What creatures in nature and what human beings does the speaker not envy? What does he value?

2. What connections exist between the first and third stanzas? between the second and fourth stanzas?

3. What aphorism within this lyric summarizes the theme of the poem?

LYRIC 54

4. How does the speaker view the value of natural life? How does he view humankind? What hope does he express for humankind?

5. What view of the speaker emerges in the final stanza? What is the theme of this lyric?

LYRIC 130

6. Whose voice is heard by the speaker in the first stanza? What connection does the speaker make between that voice and his natural surroundings? between that voice and God?

7. What paradoxes are expressed in the final stanza? What purpose do these paradoxes serve?

8. How does the speaker in each lyric seem to resolve his grief? From what does he derive comfort?

Developing Skills in Reading Literature

Elegy. Like many in his day, Tennyson worried about the implications of scientific discoveries and Darwin's theories, about God and the meaning of life. The death of Arthur Hallam caused the poet great personal grief and intensified his struggle to come to terms with the eternal and temporal context of human life. These three lyrics, taken from the beginning, middle, and end of a long elegy, show the development of the poet's thought as he worked his way through overwhelming grief through worry to faith. Trace this development as it is embodied in the subjects and themes of the three lyrics. What does Tennyson ultimately proclaim to be his lasting consolation? What makes these poems elegiac as well as philosophical?

Developing Writing Skills

Using Comparisons and Contrasts. In both lyric 54 of *In Memoriam* and "Flower in the Crannied Wall," Tennyson responds to Darwinian theories such as "survival of the fittest." Read about Darwin's theories in encyclopedias and other reference sources. Then, in a brief essay, explain how Tennyson's ideas compare and contrast with those of Darwin.

Matthew Arnold

1822–1888

Matthew Arnold was not only among the best of the Victorian poets, but also a critic of lasting worth. Many of his best poems deal with the loneliness of mankind in an indifferent universe, bereft of traditional religious certainties.

Arnold's father was Thomas Arnold, a clergyman and educational reformer who gained fame and honor as the headmaster of Rugby School. Arnold attended Rugby before proceeding to Oxford University where he cultivated dandyism and wit and barely passed his exams, though he did win the prestigious Newdigate Prize for a poem on Cromwell. In 1847 Arnold became private secretary to Lord Lansdowne. This led in 1851 to his becoming an inspector of schools, a post he held for thirty-five years.

Arnold published a book of poems anonymously in 1849 and another in 1852. He later withdrew both volumes but included their best works, such as "The Forsaken Merman," in the simply titled *Poems* of 1853, which also included "The Scholar Gypsy." *Poems* established Arnold's reputation. In 1857 he was appointed to the chair of poetry at Oxford, a part-time post he held for ten years. Ironically, Arnold then virtually abandoned poetry in favor of prose, devoting most of his later efforts to criticism. *New Poems* appeared in 1867, but most of them were new only to the public; the most celebrated, "Dover Beach," had been composed around 1851. In his critical essays, Arnold attacked the complacency of his age, its philistinism and provinciality. He believed fervently that true culture had to be based upon nobility of purpose that could be demonstrated by elegance and high style. He staunchly defended free inquiry at a time when many who feared to face the implications of new scientific knowledge wanted to place blind faith in authority.

Arnold admired the calm and restraint of the ancient Greeks, their attempt to avoid excesses of

MATTHEW ARNOLD. *G. F. Watts.*
National Portrait Gallery, London.

passion and reason. In his poetry, he worked diligently to strike a balance between the best of the old and the new. Some critics believe that Arnold failed to achieve that balance, complaining that his rationalism quenches his poetic fire. Arnold the critic commented on Arnold the poet as follows: "It might be fairly urged that I have less poetical sentiment than Tennyson, and less intellectual vigor and abundance than Browning; yet, because I have perhaps more of a fusion of the two than either of them, and have more regularly applied that fusion to the main line of modern development, I am likely enough to have my turn, as they have had theirs." While few rank Arnold's verse with that of Tennyson or Browning, none would deny that Arnold has a secure niche among major English poets.

Dover Beach

The sea is calm tonight,
The tide is full, the moon lies fair
Upon the straits;[1] on the French coast, the light
Gleams and is gone; the cliffs of England stand,
Glimmering and vast, out in the tranquil bay.   5
Come to the window, sweet is the night air!
Only, from the long line of spray
Where the sea meets the moon-blanched land,
Listen! you hear the grating roar
Of pebbles which the waves draw back, and fling,   10
At their return, up the high strand,
Begin and cease, and then again begin,
With tremulous cadence slow, and bring
The eternal note of sadness in.

Sophocles[2] long ago   15
Heard it on the Aegean,[3] and it brought
Into his mind the turbid ebb and flow
Of human misery; we
Find also in the sound a thought,
Hearing it by this distant northern sea.   20

The sea of faith
Was once, too, at the full, and round earth's shore
Lay like the folds of a bright girdle furled.
But now I only hear
Its melancholy, long, withdrawing roar,   25
Retreating, to the breath
Of the night wind, down the vast edges drear
And naked shingles[4] of the world.

---

1. **Straits:** Strait of Dover, the English Channel crossing between England and France.
2. **Sophocles** (säf′ ə klēz): 496?–406 B. C., Greek writer of tragic dramas.
3. **Aegean** (ē jē′ ən): an arm of the Mediterranean Sea.
4. **shingles:** large, waterworn gravel, as found on a shore.

Ah, love, let us be true
To one another! for the world, which seems   30
To lie before us like a land of dreams,
So various, so beautiful, so new,
Hath really neither joy, nor love, nor light,
Nor certitude, nor peace, nor help for pain;
And we are here as on a darkling plain   35
Swept with confused alarms of struggle and flight,
Where ignorant armies clash by night.

Getting at Meaning

1. Describe the setting of the first stanza. How does the speaker respond to the sights and sounds of the evening? to the sound of the waves?

2. What bond with Sophocles does the speaker seem to feel?

3. Explain the reference to the ''sea of faith'' in the third stanza. In what historical sense was the sea of faith once ''at the full''? What has happened, according to the speaker?

4. To whom is this poem addressed? How does the speaker's view of the world affect their relationship? Comment on the connotations of the word *love* in line 29. Does *love* refer only to a single individual, or is the word symbolic as well? Explain. If love endures, what does not last, according to this final stanza?

5. What catastrophe is implied in the last three lines of the poem? What are the connotations of ''darkling plain'' and ''ignorant armies clash by night''?

Developing Skills in Reading Literature

1. **Theme.** In spite of Arnold's professed belief that a poem should not express the personal feelings of the poet, much of his poetry communicates his own anxiety and his disillusionment with the new industrial society. Arnold perceived that radical new scientific theories were threatening the very foundations of traditional religious and philosophical systems and that society on the whole seemed shockingly unaware and complacent in the face of profound change. Comment on how ''Dover Beach'' treats the contrast between appearance and reality, between life as it seems to be and life as it actually is. What ''human misery'' might once have been imagined by Sophocles as inherent in life? What is the unique misery of modern life? What is the only antidote, according to Arnold?

2. **Setting and Mood.** Michael Thorpe, a noted critic, has praised ''Dover Beach'' as a poem that ''perfectly recreates time and place and gives a vital setting to the mood.'' What progression of mood is evident in the poem? Identify the lines in which subtle shifts in mood occur. What details of setting convey the mood of each stanza?

Robert Browning

1812–1889

ROBERT BROWNING, 1858. *Michele Gordigioni.*
National Portrait Gallery, London.

Although he is now considered one of the great Victorian poets, Robert Browning did not always enjoy such acclaim. Both critics and the public found his poems dense and difficult, and before his wife's death in 1861, he was often referred to slightingly as "Mrs. Browning's husband." Only later in life did he become popular. Some, such as members of the Browning Societies, admired his wisdom more than his art, regarding him as a philosopher who had resolved the doubts that troubled his age. Others admired his technical craftsmanship. In the twentieth century poets and critics have hailed Browning as a pioneer.

Browning was born in the London suburb of Camberwell. His father was a bank clerk who loved books, his mother a religious woman who loved music, and with their brilliant son they comprised a remarkable family. Although he attended the University of London for a brief period, Browning's real education took place at home, where he was tutored in languages and music as well as boxing and horsemanship. The extraordinary nature of his household and his education helps explain the difficulty of his poems: he sometimes assumed that all educated people would recognize his often obscure references.

Browning's early literary career was not marked by success. Inspired by the verse of Shelley, Browning published his first poem, "Pauline," when he was twenty-one. It was so savagely reviewed by critic John Stuart Mill that Browning was humiliated, and he resolved to avoid the subjective style of Shelley thereafter. Browning then turned to the theater, and from 1836 to 1846 he was a playwright. His plays failed, but in the writing of them Browning may have discovered his talent for creating dramatic monologues. Among the best known are "Fra Lippo Lippi," "Andrea del Sarto," "The Bishop Orders His Tomb at Saint Praxed's Church," and "My Last Duchess," poems in which characters reveal themselves in their own words, without authorial intrusion.

In 1845, Robert Browning met Elizabeth Barrett, six years his senior and an invalid. Defying her domineering father, she married him and the couple moved to Italy, where they lived happily until her death. Like many English writers, Browning seemed to thrive in the Latin atmosphere and warmer climate of the Mediterranean. *Men and Women*, a vigorous and dynamic work, appeared in 1855. After Elizabeth's death, Browning returned to London to live with his son. His vast epic, *The Ring and the Book*, came out in 1868, when his reputation was belatedly beginning to grow, and the two volumes of *Dramatic Idylls* appeared in 1879 and 1880.

Thomas Hardy called Browning "*the* literary puzzle of the nineteenth century," a puzzle that remains unsolved to this day. His cheerful optimism and unquestioning belief in God are belied by the dark sides of his complex characters. His monologues constitute a portrait gallery whose subjects speak from the fifteenth and sixteenth centuries in language that frequently conceals as many motives and meanings as it reveals. The subjects speak in their own voices, distinct from the voice of the poet, a technique that influenced major poets in the twentieth century.

My Last Duchess

This poem is set during the Italian Renaissance in the palace of the Duke of Ferrara. The Duke is involved in negotiations to marry the daughter of a powerful Count. As the poem begins, the Duke is showing the agent of the Count a portrait of Lucrezia, his late wife.

That's my last Duchess painted on the wall,
Looking as if she were alive. I call
That piece a wonder, now: Frà Pandolf's[1] hands
Worked busily a day, and there she stands.
Will 't please you sit and look at her? I said   5
"Frà Pandolf" by design, for never read
Strangers like you that pictured countenance,
The depth and passion of its earnest glance,
But to myself they turned (since none puts by
The curtain I have drawn for you, but I)   10
And seemed as they would ask me, if they durst,
How such a glance came there; so, not the first
Are you to turn and ask thus. Sir, 'twas not
Her husband's presence only, called that spot
Of joy into the Duchess' cheek; perhaps   15
Frà Pandolf chanced to say, "Her mantle laps
Over my lady's wrist too much," or "Paint
Must never hope to reproduce the faint
Half flush that dies along her throat." Such stuff
Was courtesy, she thought, and cause enough   20
For calling up that spot of joy. She had
A heart—how shall I say?—too soon made glad,
Too easily impressed; she liked whate'er
She looked on, and her looks went everywhere.
Sir, 'twas all one! My favor at her breast,   25
The dropping of the daylight in the West,
The bough of cherries some officious fool
Broke in the orchard for her, the white mule
She rode with round the terrace—all and each
Would draw from her alike the approving speech,   30
Or blush, at least. She thanked men—good! but thanked
Somehow—I know not how—as if she ranked

---

1. **Frà Pandolf:** a fictitious monk (*Frà* means "brother") who is the painter of the portrait.

My gift of a nine-hundred-years-old name
With anybody's gift. Who'd stoop to blame
This sort of trifling? Even had you skill   35
In speech—which I have not—to make your will
Quite clear to such an one, and say, "Just this
Or that in you disgusts me; here you miss,
Or there exceed the mark"—and if she let
Herself be lessoned so, nor plainly set   40
Her wits to yours, forsooth, and made excuse
—E'en then would be some stooping; and I choose
Never to stoop. Oh, sir, she smiled, no doubt,
Whene'er I passed her; but who passed without
Much the same smile? This grew; I gave commands;   45
Then all smiles stopped together. There she stands
As if alive. Will 't please you rise? We'll meet
The company below, then. I repeat,
The Count your master's known munificence
Is ample warrant that no just pretense   50
Of mine for dowry will be disallowed;
Though his fair daughter's self, as I avowed
As starting, is my object. Nay, we'll go
Together down, sir.[2] Notice Neptune,[3] though,
Taming a sea horse, thought a rarity,   55
Which Claus of Innsbruck[4] cast in bronze for me!

SARAH, LADY INNES, 1757. *Thomas Gainsborough.*
Copyright The Frick Collection, New York.

2. **we'll . . . down:** The messenger, apparently standing behind, is encouraged to walk downstairs alongside the Duke.
3. **Neptune:** the Roman god of the sea.
4. **Claus of Innsbruck:** a fictitious sculptor from Austria.

Getting at Meaning

1. The Duke begins speaking genially, but before long he reveals his condescension, egotism, and cruelty. Which lines first suggest these characteristics? Look for further examples of his critical attitude toward his wife's personality. What probably happened to her? How do you know?

2. What do you think is the Duke's main motive in talking with the agent as he does? What does his casual remark about the dowry suggest about him and about his attitude toward his future wife?

3. Why does the Duke call attention to the bronze statue of Neptune? In what way is this statue related to the painting of his wife? In what sense does he value both works of art? What does this suggest about his attitude toward human beings, particularly women?

Developing Skills in Reading Literature

1. **Irony.** The words of a speaker can express meanings that he or she is unaware of but that the reader understands clearly. This kind of dramatic irony creates much of the interest in "My Last Duchess." What is ironic, for example, about the way that the Duke views women? What other examples of dramatic irony do you find?

2. **Characterization.** The use of conversational phrasing and colloquial expressions is characteristic of Browning's style. In this poem, the Duke's speech patterns are an effective means of suggesting his true character and his underlying motivation. Point out several examples of informal language in the poem, and be prepared to discuss what this language reveals about the Duke. What effect results from his frequent hesitancy? Notice the way that informal and formal language intertwine in the poem. At what point is the Duke's language most formal? Why might Browning have chosen to use this kind of language here?

3. **Dramatic Monologue.** A dramatic monologue contains many of the characteristics of drama; for example, action, setting, and characterization through dialogue. Discuss these elements as they appear in Browning's poem, distinguishing between explicit action and the action implied by the speaker, describing the actual setting and the implied setting of the Renaissance, and describing the characters and the methods of characterization employed. How is the reader drawn into the dramatic situation? How does the character of the Duke control the development of the scene?

4. **Title.** Through a title, a poet can highlight a theme, clarify meaning, or add a dimension of understanding for the reader. Sometimes a title yields subtle implications that may or may not have been intended by the poet. Reread the title of Browning's poem, emphasizing the word *last*. What does this reading of the title suggest about the Duke and the situation described in the poem?

Home Thoughts, from Abroad

Oh, to be in England
Now that April's there,
And whoever wakes in England
Sees, some morning, unaware,
That the lowest boughs and the brushwood sheaf   5
Round the elm tree bole are in tiny leaf,
While the chaffinch sings on the orchard bough
In England—now!

And after April, when May follows,
And the whitethroat[1] builds, and all the swallows!   10
Hark, where my blossomed pear tree in the hedge
Leans to the field and scatters on the clover
Blossoms and dewdrops—at the bent spray's edge—
That's the wise thrush; he sings each song twice over,
Lest you should think he never could recapture   15
The first fine careless rapture!
And though the fields look rough with hoary dew,
All will be gay when noontide wakes anew
The buttercups, the little children's dower[2]
—Far brighter than this gaudy melon flower![3]   20

---

1. **brushwood . . . elm tree bole . . . chaffinch . . . whitethroat:** plants and birds characteristic of the English countryside. A "bole" is a tree trunk.
2. **dower:** a special gift.
3. **melon flower:** probably the passionflower, with red, yellow, purple, or white flowers. Characteristic of southerly climates.

A SUMMER'S DAY IN HYDE PARK, 1858. *John Ritchie.*
The Museum of London.

Getting at Meaning

1. What details does the speaker recall about England in the spring? Which details seem to inspire the most delight?

2. According to the speaker, what specific changes take place between April and May?

3. What is the speaker's attitude toward England, as suggested in the final line?

Developing Skills in Reading Literature

Imagery and Theme. How does the image created by the "gaudy melon flower" contrast with the images describing the English spring? How does this contrast reinforce the theme of the poem?

Prospice

Prospice (prō spik'ē) is a Latin word meaning "to look forward." Browning wrote this poem shortly after the death of Elizabeth Barrett Browning.

Fear death?—to feel the fog in my throat,
   The mist in my face,
When the snows begin, and the blasts denote
   I am nearing the place,
The power of the night, the press of the storm,   5
   The post of the foe;
Where he stands, the Arch Fear[1] in a visible form,
   Yet the strong man must go.
For the journey is done and the summit attained,
   And the barriers fall,   10
Though a battle's to fight ere the guerdon[2] be gained,
   The reward of it all.
I was ever a fighter, so—one fight more,
   The best and the last!
I would hate that death bandaged my eyes, and forbore,   15
   And bade me creep past.
No! let me taste the whole of it, fare like my peers,
   The heroes of old,
Bear the brunt, in a minute pay glad life's arrears
   Of pain, darkness, and cold.   20
For sudden the worst turns the best to the brave,
   The black minute's at end,
And the elements' rage, the fiend-voices that rave,
   Shall dwindle, shall blend,
Shall change, shall become first a peace out of pain,   25
   Then a light, then thy breast,
O thou soul of my soul![3] I shall clasp thee again,
   And with God be the rest!

---

1. **Arch Fear:** death.
2. **guerdon:** reward.
3. **soul of my soul:** Mrs. Browning.

Getting at Meaning

1. At the beginning of this poem, the speaker takes the stance of a courageous hero facing a foe. Trace the development of the speaker's feelings up to the moment of death in line 22.

2. What significant change occurs in the final lines of the poem?

3. In an earlier version of this poem, the words "out of pain" in line 25 were "then a joy." Why is "out of pain" more appropriate in the context of the poem?

Developing Skills in Reading Literature

Apostrophe. In the final lines of the poem, the speaker addresses the deceased Elizabeth as his soul. To whom does he speak directly in the first line of the poem? Who or what is addressed in line 17? What differences in tone do you notice at these points in the poem? What is the effect of these tonal shifts?

Developing Writing Skills

Analyzing Theme. Graham Greene, the English novelist and philosopher, wrote, "No one comes to consciousness except through suffering." In a well developed paragraph discuss how this twentieth-century writer might agree or disagree with the ideas expressed in "Prospice."

Elizabeth Barrett Browning

1806–1861

Elizabeth Barrett Browning was one of the most popular poets of her time. Her finest poems, a remarkable series called *Sonnets from the Portuguese*, create an autobiographical record of her legendary love for Robert Browning. The poems in this volume contain passages of exquisite beauty and evidence the poet's intense preoccupation with the lofty, the sublime, the refined, and the elevated, qualities much admired by the Victorians. Although many of Browning's works suffer from excess verbiage and diffuseness, she did produce a small body of poetry of enduring merit, which has earned her a place among the significant Victorian poets.

The daughter of an English country gentleman, Elizabeth Barrett was born at Coxhoe Hall near Durham. She was a precocious child, reading Greek at the age of eight and writing polished verse in her early teens. A friend described her as a "slight delicate figure, with a shower of dark curls falling on each side of a most expressive face, large tender eyes, richly fringed by dark eyelashes, and a smile like a sunbeam." In 1837 she suffered a burst blood vessel in her lungs that nearly proved fatal and left her an invalid, under the total domination of her tyrannical father. In 1838 the Barretts moved to 50 Wimpole Street, London, where her famous courtship with Robert Browning was carried on furtively to escape the watchfully jealous eyes of her father.

Despite Elizabeth's illness and her father's tyranny, in 1846 the lovers were secretly married and moved to Italy. There, Elizabeth's health improved, enabling her to live a normal life. She wrote a great many poems, had a son, and became an ardent supporter of many liberal causes, in particular the cause of Italian liberation. The Brownings' home in Florence, Casa Guidi, became a gathering place for people prominent in politics

ELIZABETH BARRETT BROWNING, 1859. *Field Talfourd. National Portrait Gallery, London.*

and the arts and was the setting for one of her collections, *Casa Guidi Windows* (1851).

Browning wrote *Sonnets from the Portuguese* as a wedding gift for her husband, and the collection has remained popular since its appearance in 1850. Few lines in English poetry are more familiar than the first line of Sonnet 43: "How do I love thee? Let me count the ways." Her most ambitious work was *Aurora Leigh* (1857), an autobiographical novel in blank verse that was popular at the time but is little read today. Her letters, however, still appeal to readers, who respond to their emotional intensity.

from **Sonnets from the Portuguese**

14

If thou must love me, let it be for naught
Except for love's sake only. Do not say
"I love her for her smile—her look—her way
Of speaking gently—for a trick of thought
That falls in well with mine, and certes¹ brought   5
A sense of pleasant ease on such a day"—
For these things in themselves, Belovèd, may
Be changed, or change for thee—and love, so wrought,
May be unwrought so. Neither love me for
Thine own dear pity's wiping my cheeks dry—   10
A creature might forget to weep, who bore
Thy comfort long, and lose thy love thereby!
But love me for love's sake, that evermore
Thou mayst love on, through love's eternity.

43

How do I love thee? Let me count the ways.
I love thee to the depth and breadth and height
My soul can reach, when feeling out of sight
For the ends of Being and ideal Grace.
I love thee to the level of every day's   5
Most quiet need, by sun and candlelight.
I love thee freely, as men strive for Right;
I love thee purely, as they turn from Praise.
I love thee with the passion put to use
In my old griefs, and with my childhood's faith.   10
I love thee with a love I seemed to lose
With my lost saints—I love thee with the breath,
Smiles, tears, of all my life!—and, if God choose,
I shall but love thee better after death.

---

1. **certes:** certainly

Getting at Meaning

SONNET 14

1. What qualities does the speaker not want to be loved for? What reasons does the speaker give?

2. What is meant by the words "love's sake"? What effect is created by the repetition of this phrase at the beginning and at the end of the poem?

SONNET 43

3. How many ways does the speaker claim to love in this sonnet? Are any of the claims impossible or impractical? Why does the speaker make them? What is the quality of love described in this sonnet?

4. What attitude does the speaker express toward religion? What is implied by the phrase "my lost saints"? by "if God choose"?

5. How does the final line of this sonnet echo the sentiment in Robert Browning's "Prospice"?

Developing Skills in Reading Literature

Sonnet Sequence. During their famous courtship, Elizabeth Barrett wrote a series of forty-four sonnets expressing her love for Robert Browning. After their marriage, upon Browning's insistence, the two decided to publish the sonnets under the title *Sonnets from the Portuguese*, a title that was meant to mislead the public into thinking Elizabeth had merely translated the intimate love poems.

Examine sonnets 14 and 43, which are from this sonnet sequence. Are they Petrarchan or Shakespearean in form? What shift in idea takes place between the octave and the sestet of each sonnet? What is the unifying theme of the sequence, as indicated by these two examples? How is the deepening of the poet's love suggested by the two sonnets, one from the beginning of the sequence, the other from the end? What differences in tone, mood, subject, and structure do you find between Browning's sonnets and those written by the Romantic poets?

Developing Vocabulary

Archaic Words. The Victorian poets were especially fond of using archaic or "old-fashioned" words to re-create the spirit of the past. Examine the following italicized words and phrases, which appear in poems you have studied in this unit. Then translate these archaic expressions into contemporary English. Use a dictionary as necessary.

a. "On burnished hooves his war horse *trode;*"

b. "For *ere* she reached upon the tide/The first house by the waterside,"

c. "But Lancelot mused *a little space;*"

d. ". . . I will drink/Life *to the lees.* . . ."

e. "I hold it true, *whate'er befall;*"

f. "Retreating, to the breath/Of the night wind down the vast edges *drear*"

g. "And we are here as on a *darkling* plain"

h. ". . . and if she let/Herself be *lessoned* so, nor plainly set/Her wits to yours, *forsooth,* and made excuse, —E'en then would be some stooping; and I choose/Never to stoop. . . ."

i. "If thou must love me, let it be *for naught*/Except for love's sake only. . . ."

Developing Writing Skills

Supporting an Opinion. Robert Browning said of *Sonnets from the Portuguese:* "These are the finest sonnets in any language since Shakespeare." Others, too, have acclaimed the sonnets as perceptive, well wrought expressions of love. Still other critics have severely criticized the sonnets as too highly emotional, embarrassingly personal in tone, and awkward in their spontaneity. One critic wrote, "The *Sonnets from the Portuguese* cannot be read through today without discomfort, though there are arresting moments." Read at least ten more sonnets from this collection. Then, in a well developed paragraph support or refute one of these opinions.

Christina Rossetti

1830–1894

The exquisite lyrics of Christina Rossetti convey deep religious meaning tinged with melancholy. In *Goblin Market and Other Poems* (1862) she displayed an affinity for the aims of the Pre-Raphaelite movement, but her poetic gift is singular enough to defy any simple historical classification. It is unfortunate that Rossetti is so often considered only in the context of women poets, for by any standard, her poetry is strikingly original and technically perfect.

Christina was the youngest child in the remarkable Rossetti family. Her father was Gabriele Rossetti, an Italian poet and patriot whose turbulent career forced him into exile. He arrived in England in 1824 and in 1831 became Professor of Italian at King's College, London, where he was a recognized authority on Dante. The Rossetti household was a dynamic center for people of liberal politics who hotly debated the controversial topics of the time. The three youngest of the four Rossetti children all gained prominence in the artistic life of England.

Christina's brother Dante Gabriel Rossetti was a poet and painter who in 1848 helped form a group that called itself the Pre-Raphaelite Brotherhood. Both the poets and the painters in the Brotherhood determined to reject the ornate academic formalism of contemporary taste in favor of the simpler, more natural expressive style found in Italy prior to the Renaissance. Another brother, William, was a brilliant critic and editor of *The Germ*, a magazine that exerted an influence far more lasting than the magazine itself. The magazine's four issues presented important early poems by Christina Rossetti, including "The Dream," under her pseudonym Ellen Alleyne.

Christina Rossetti led a quiet life. A devout Anglican, she devoted herself to doing good works for church and charity. Beneath the calm surface, however, Christina suffered emotional turmoil. Her first fiancé became a Roman Catholic, making marriage to him out of the question for her. A second engagement also was broken off, apparently on more vague religious grounds. Many of Rossetti's most moving poems are about the frustrations

CHRISTINA ROSSETTI. *Dante Gabriel Rossetti. British Museum.*

of love, frustrations she knew all too well. Her sonnet sequence "Monna Innominata" ranks as one of the finest expressions in the English language of the timeless poetic theme of unhappy love.

Despite the apparently straightforward simplicity of Rossetti's poetry, a close reading reveals complex religious themes of temptation and redemption. The title poem of *Goblin Market* has been likened in theme and power to Coleridge's "The Rime of the Ancient Mariner." Other volumes published during Rossetti's lifetime were *The Prince's Progress* (1866); *Sing-Song* (1872), a collection of children's verses; *A Pageant and Other Poems* (1881); and *Time Flies* (1885), a reading diary with a poem or thought for each day. A final collection, *New Poems*, appeared posthumously in 1896.

A Birthday

My heart is like a singing bird
    Whose nest is in a watered shoot;
My heart is like an apple tree
    Whose boughs are bent with thickset fruit;
My heart is like a rainbow shell   5
    That paddles in a halcyon[1] sea;
My heart is gladder than all these
    Because my love is come to me.

Raise me a dais of silk and down;
    Hang it with vair[2] and purple dyes;   10
Carve it in doves and pomegranates,
    And peacocks with a hundred eyes;
Work it in gold and silver grapes,
    In leaves and silver fleurs-de-lys;[3]
Because the birthday of my life   15
    Is come, my love is come to me.

---

1. **halcyon:** calm, peaceful.
2. **vair:** fur used for trimming and lining clothes in the Middle Ages.
3. **fleur-de-lys** (flur′ də lē′): flower of the lily, or iris. In medieval heraldry, the pattern of the fleur-de-lys was often used in fine metalwork and in embroidery.

Song

When I am dead, my dearest,
    Sing no sad songs for me;
Plant thou no roses at my head,
    Nor shady cypress tree:
Be the green grass above me   5
    With showers and dewdrops wet;
And if thou wilt, remember,
    And if thou wilt, forget.

I shall not see the shadows,
    I shall not feel the rain;   10
I shall not hear the nightingale
    Sing on, as if in pain;
And dreaming through the twilight
    That doth not rise nor set,
Haply[1] I may remember,   15
    And haply may forget.

---

1. **haply:** by chance.

Getting at Meaning

SONG

1. What attitude toward death does the speaker convey? what view of life?

2. Is this a poem of faith? of philosophical meditation? of imagination? Explain your answer.

A BIRTHDAY

3. In what sense is the word *birthday* used in this poem? What are the speaker's feelings on this day?

4. What gifts does the speaker request in the second stanza? What attitude is conveyed? What is the tone of the entire poem?

Developing Skills in Reading Literature

Imagery and Theme. Christina Rossetti's gift for creating images that are clear and unpretentious and at the same time sharp and unique is apparent in these two poems. Her talent for conveying complex themes through simple imagery becomes equally apparent upon close examination of the poems. What concept of nature informs "Song"? What happens to the relationship between humans and the physical world at death? What concept of the afterlife is implied? How does this differ from the pantheistic beliefs expressed by the Romantics? In "A Birthday" how do the sensory impressions in the first stanza differ from those in the second? What does the poet imply about the relationship between nature and art?

Developing Vocabulary

Words from Greek Mythology. The word *halcyon* comes from a Greek legend about an ancient bird. Look up this word in an etymological dictionary; then explain the relationship between the legend and the present-day meaning of the word.

Developing Writing Skills

Poetry: Using Figurative Language. Write an original poem in which you use a series of metaphors or similes, as Christina Rossetti has done in "A Birthday," to define a feeling such as love, happiness, fear, or loneliness. Use a regular meter and rhyme scheme, not necessarily modeled on the Rossetti poem.

PROSERPINE, 1874. *Dante Gabriel Rossetti. Tate Gallery, London.*

Charles Dickens

1812–1870

Widely considered the greatest English novelist, Charles Dickens created characters so vividly alive that they seem as real as any historical figures: Oliver Twist, Mr. Micawber, Scrooge, Little Nell, and many more. Dickens's striking and compassionate portrayals of the troubled society of his age made him an influential social critic and the champion of the exploited. From the publication of his first novel, *The Pickwick Papers* in 1836 and 1837, his vast popularity has never ebbed. Warmly humorous and endlessly inventive, he charms readers of all intellectual and social strata with rambling tales full of frank sentimentality and humanitarian sympathy.

Dickens drew from life in his writing, and the suffering children of his stories are based upon his own painful experience. His father, John, was a cheerful navy pay clerk whose extravagance and mismanagement of the family income caused him to be sent to prison for debt. As the eldest son, Charles had to leave school at the age of twelve and was sent to earn six shillings a week in a blacking factory, tying blue covers on pots of paste-blacking while rats scurried over his feet. This episode was short-lived, and Charles returned to school in a few months, but it deeply affected the boy. He left school for good when he was fifteen, first becoming a clerk in a solicitor's office and then a court reporter, covering Parliamentary speeches from 1831 to 1836.

Signing himself "Boz," Dickens began contributing stories and essays to periodicals; these were collected in book form in 1836 as *Sketches by Boz*. His literary career was launched. Readers loved his humorous characters who coped with ludicrous incidents, and they were heartened by the dogged cheerfulness of characters who struggled to make merry despite adversity.

The success of the Boz sketches led to the serial publication of *The Pickwick Papers*, which skyrocketed Dickens to fame. Dickens wrote his novels in monthly installments of a few chapters, and his schedule was hectic. In 1837 he wrote *The Pickwick Papers* and *Oliver Twist* in tandem,

CHARLES DICKENS, 1855. *Ary Scheffer.*
National Portrait Gallery, London.

never more than a few days ahead of the printer. *Nicholas Nickleby* followed in 1839. *The Old Curiosity Shop* came out in 1840 and 1841, and when Little Nell died, a wave of grief swept the English-speaking world.

Dickens continued his steady and ambitious production throughout his life. His favorite novel, the partly autobiographical *David Copperfield*, appeared in 1849 and 1850, followed by such masterpieces as *Bleak House* (1853), *Hard Times* (1854), *Little Dorrit* (1857), *A Tale of Two Cities* (1859) and *Great Expectations* (1861). Dickens can be said to have worked himself to death. Troubled by gout and the effects of an 1865 train accident in which he behaved bravely to extricate dead and wounded from the wreckage, he nonetheless continued a grueling schedule of writings and readings until he suffered from severe chest pains and soaring blood pressure. Advised to slow down, Dickens instead increased his pace. He suffered a stroke at dinner on June 8, 1870, and died the next day.

from **The Pickwick Papers**

A Madman's Manuscript

"**Y**es!—a madman's! How that word would have struck to my heart many years ago! How it would have roused the terror that used to come upon me sometimes, sending the blood hissing and tingling through my veins, till the cold dew of fear stood in large drops upon my skin, and my knees knocked together with fright! I like it now though. It's a fine name. Show me the monarch whose angry frown was ever feared[1] like the glare of a madman's eye—whose cord and axe were ever half so sure as a madman's grip. Ho! ho! It's a grand thing to be mad! to be peeped at like a wild lion through the iron bars—to gnash one's teeth and howl through the long still night, to the merry ring of a heavy chain—and to roll and twine among the straw, transported with such brave music. Hurrah for the madhouse! Oh, it's a rare place!

"I remember days when I was *afraid* of being mad; when I used to start from my sleep, and fall upon my knees, and pray to be spared from the curse of my race; when I rushed from the sight of merriment or happiness, to hide myself in some lonely place, and spend the weary hours in watching the progress of the fever that was to consume my brain. I knew that madness was mixed up with my very blood, and the marrow of my bones! that one generation had passed away without the pestilence appearing among them, and that I was the first in whom it would revive. I knew it *must* be so, that so it always had been, and so it ever would be; and when I cowered in some obscure corner of a crowded room, and saw men whisper, and point, and turn their eyes towards me, I knew they were telling each other of the doomed madman; and I slunk away again to mope in solitude.

"I did this for years; long, long years they were. The nights here are long sometimes—very long; but they are nothing to the restless nights and dreadful dreams I had at that time. It makes me cold to remember them. Large dusky forms with sly and jeering faces crouched in the corners of the room and bent over my bed at night, tempting me to madness. They told me in low whispers that the floor of the old house in which my father's father died was stained with his own blood, shed by his own hand in raging madness. I drove my fingers into my ears, but they screamed into my head till the room rang with it, that in one generation before him the madness slumbered, but that his grandfather had lived for years with his hands fettered to the ground to prevent his tearing himself to pieces. I knew they told the truth—I knew it well. I had found it out years before, though they had tried to keep it from me. Ha! ha! I was too cunning for them, madman as they thought me.

"At last it came upon me, and I wondered how I could ever have feared it. I could go into the world now, and laugh and shout with the best among them. I knew I was mad, but they did not even suspect it. How I used to hug myself with delight when I thought of the fine trick I was playing on them after their old pointing and leering when I was not mad, but only dreading that I might one day become so! And how I used to laugh for joy when I was alone, and thought how well I kept my secret, and how quickly my kind friends would have fallen from me if they had known the truth. I

---

1. **was ever feared:** ever conveyed such awesome dread.

could have screamed with ecstasy when I dined alone with some fine roaring fellow, to think how pale he would have turned, and how fast he would have run if he had known that the dear friend who sat close to him, sharpening a bright, glittering knife, was a madman with all the power and half the will to plunge it into his heart. Oh, it was a merry life!

"Riches became mine, wealth poured in upon me, and I rioted in pleasures enhanced a thousandfold to me by the consciousness of my well-kept secret. I inherited an estate. The law—the eagle-eyed law itself—had been deceived, and had handed over disputed thousands to a madman's hands. Where was the wit of the sharp-sighted men of sound mind? Where the dexterity of the lawyers, eager to discover a flaw? The madman's cunning had overreached them all.

"I had money. How I was courted! I spent it profusely. How I was praised! How those three proud, overbearing brothers humbled themselves before me! The old white-headed father, too—such deference—such respect—such devoted friendship—he worshipped me! The old man had a daughter, and the young men a sister; and all the five were poor. I was rich; and when I married the girl, I saw a smile of triumph play upon the faces of her needy relatives as they thought of their well-planned scheme and their fine prize. It was for me to smile. To smile! To laugh outright, and tear my hair, and roll upon the ground with shrieks of merriment. They little thought they had married her to a madman.

"Stay. If they had known it, would they have saved her? A sister's happiness against her husband's gold. The lightest feather I blow into the air, against the gay chain that ornaments my body!

"In one thing I was deceived, with all my cunning. If I had not been mad—for though we madmen are sharp-witted enough, we get bewildered sometimes—I should have known that the girl would rather have been placed, stiff and cold in a dull leaden coffin, than borne an envied bride to my rich, glittering house. I should have known that her heart was with the dark-eyed boy whose name I once heard her breathe in her troubled sleep, and that she had been sacrificed to me to relieve the poverty of the old white-headed man and the haughty brothers.

"I don't remember forms or faces now, but I know the girl was beautiful. I *know* she was; for in the bright moonlight nights, when I start up from my sleep and all is quiet about me, I see, standing still and motionless in one corner of this cell, a slight and wasted figure with long black hair, which streaming down her back, stirs with no earthly wind, and eyes that fix their gaze on me, and never wink or close. Hush! the blood chills at my heart as I write it down—that form is *hers*; the face is very pale and the eyes are glassy bright, but I know them well. That figure never moves; it never frowns and mouths as others do, that fill this place sometimes; but it is much more dreadful to me, even than the spirits that tempted me many years ago—it comes fresh from the grave, and is so very death-like.

"For nearly a year I saw that face grow paler; for nearly a year I saw the tears steal down the mournful cheeks, and never knew the cause. I found it out at last though. They could not keep it from me long. She had never liked me; I had never thought she did: she despised my wealth and hated the splendor in which she lived; but I had not expected that. She loved another. This I had never thought of. Strange feelings came over me, and thought, forced upon me by some secret power, whirled round and round my brain. I did not hate her, though I hated the boy she still wept for. I pitied—yes, I pitied—the wretched life to which her cold and selfish relations had doomed her. I knew that she could not live long; but the thought that before her death she might give birth to some ill-fated being, destined to hand down madness to its offspring, determined me. I resolved to kill her.

"For many weeks I thought of poison, and then of drowning, and then of fire. A fine sight the grand house in flames, and the madman's wife smoldering away to cinders. Think of the jest of a large reward, too, and of some sane man swinging in the wind for a deed he never did, and all through a madman's cunning! I thought often of this, but I gave it up at last. Oh! the pleasure of stropping[2] the razor day after day, feeling the sharp edge, and thinking of the gash one stroke of its thin bright edge would make!

"At last the old spirits who had been with me so often before whispered in my ear that the time was come, and thrust the open razor into my hand. I grasped it firmly, rose softly from the bed, and leaned over my sleeping wife. Her face was buried in her hands. I withdrew them softly, and they fell listlessly on her bosom. She had been weeping, for the traces of the tears were still wet upon her cheek. Her face was calm and placid, and even as I looked upon it, a tranquil smile lighted up her pale features. I laid my hand softly on her shoulder. She started—it was only a passing dream. I leaned forward again. She screamed, and woke.

"One motion of my hand, and she would never again have uttered cry or sound. But I was startled, and drew back. Her eyes were fixed on mine. I knew not how it was, but they cowed and frightened me, and I quailed beneath them. She rose from the bed, still gazing fixedly and steadily on me. I trembled; the razor was in my hand, but I could not move. She made towards the door. As she neared it, she turned, and withdrew her eyes from my face. The spell was broken. I bounded forward and clutched her by the arm. Uttering shriek upon shriek, she sank upon the ground.

"Now I could have killed her without a struggle, but the house was alarmed. I heard the tread of footsteps on the stairs. I replaced the razor in its usual drawer, unfastened the door, and called loudly for assistance.

"They came, and raised her, and placed her on the bed. She lay bereft of animation for hours; and when life, look, and speech returned, her senses had deserted her and she raved wildly and furiously.

"Doctors were called in—great men who rolled up to my door in easy carriages, with fine horses and gaudy servants. They were at her bedside for weeks. They had a great meeting, and consulted together in low and solemn voices in another room. One, the cleverest and most celebrated among them, took me aside, and bidding me prepare for the worst, told me—me, the madman!—that my wife was mad. He stood close beside me at an open window, his eyes looking in my face and his hand laid upon my arm. With one effort, I could have hurled him into the street beneath. It would have been rare sport to have done it; but my secret was at stake, and I let him go. A few days after, they told me I must place her under some restraint, I must provide a keeper for her. I! I went into the open fields where none could hear me, and laughed till the air resounded with my shouts!

"She died next day. The white-headed old man followed her to the grave, and the proud brothers dropped a tear over the insensible corpse of her whose sufferings they had regarded in her lifetime with muscles of iron.[3] All this was food for my secret mirth, and I laughed behind the white handkerchief which I held up to my face as we rode home, till the tears came into my eyes.

"But though I had carried my object and killed her, I was restless and disturbed, and I felt that before long my secret must be known. I could not hide the wild mirth and joy which boiled within me, and made me when I was alone at home, jump up and beat my hands together, and dance round and round, and roar aloud. When I went out, and saw the busy crowds hurrying about the streets, or the theatre, and heard the sound of

---

2. **stropping:** sharpening on a thick leather band.
3. **muscles of iron:** hardness and insensitivity.

from THE PICKWICK PAPERS 577

music, and beheld the people dancing, I felt such glee that I could have rushed among them and torn them to pieces limb from limb and howled in transport.[4] But I ground my teeth, and struck my feet upon the floor, and drove my sharp nails into my hands. I kept it down, and no one knew I was a madman yet.

"I remember—though it's one of the last things I *can* remember, for now I mix up realities with my dreams, and having so much to do, and being always hurried here, have no time to separate the two from some strange confusion in which they get involved—I remember how I let it out at last. Ha! ha! I think I see their frightened looks now, and feel the ease with which I flung them from me, and dashed my clenched fist into their white faces, and then flew like the wind, and left them screaming and shouting far behind. The strength of a giant comes upon me when I think of it. There—see how this iron bar bends beneath my furious wrench. I could snap it like a twig, only there are long galleries here with many doors—I don't think I could find my way along them; and even if I could, I know there are iron gates below which they keep locked and barred. They know what a clever madman I have been, and they are proud to have me here, to show.

"Let me see: yes, I had been out. It was late at night when I reached home, and found the proudest of the three proud brothers waiting to see me—urgent business he said. I recollect it well. I hated that man with all a madman's hate. Many and many a time had my fingers longed to tear him. They told me he was there. I ran swiftly upstairs. He had a word to say to me. I dismissed the servants. It was late, and we were alone together—*for the first time.*

"I kept my eyes carefully from him at first, for I knew what he little thought—and I gloried in the knowledge—that the light of madness gleamed from them like fire. We sat in silence for a few minutes. He spoke at last. My recent dissipation, and strange remarks,

made so soon after his sister's death, were an insult to her memory. Coupling together many circumstances which had at first escaped his observation, he thought I had not treated her well. He wished to know whether he was right in inferring that I meant to cast a reproach upon her memory, and a disrespect upon her family. It was due to the uniform he wore to demand this explanation.

"This man had a commission in the army—a commission purchased with my money and his sister's misery! This was the man who had been foremost in the plot to ensnare me and grasp my wealth. This was the man who had been the main instrument in forcing his sister to wed me, well knowing that her heart was given to that puling boy. Due to *his* uniform! The livery[5] of his degradation! I turned my eyes upon him—I could not help it—but I spoke not a word.

"I saw the sudden change that came upon him beneath my gaze. He was a bold man, but the color faded from his face and he drew back in his chair. I dragged mine nearer to him, and as I laughed—I was very merry then—I saw him shudder. I felt the madness rising within me. He was afraid of me.

"'You were very fond of your sister when she was alive,' I said.—'Very.'

"He looked uneasily round him, and I saw his hand grasp the back of his chair, but he said nothing.

"'You villain,' said I, 'I found you out; I discovered your hellish plots against me; I know her heart was fixed on someone else before you compelled her to marry me. I know it—I know it.'

"He jumped suddenly from his chair, brandishing it aloft, and bid me stand back—for I took care to be getting closer to him all the time I spoke.

"I screamed rather than talked, for I felt tumultuous passions eddying through my

---

4. **in transport:** in ecstasy.
5. **livery:** identifying uniform.

veins, and the old spirits whispering and taunting me to tear his heart out.

"'Damn you,' said I, starting up and rushing upon him. 'I killed her. I am a madman. Down with you. Blood, blood! I will have it!'

"I turned aside with one blow the chair he hurled at me in his terror, and closed with him, and with a heavy crash we rolled upon the floor together.

"It was a fine struggle that; for he was a tall, strong man, fighting for his life; and I, a powerful madman, thirsting to destroy him. I knew no strength could equal mine, and I was right. Right again, though a madman! His struggles grew fainter. I knelt upon his chest, and clasped his brawny throat firmly with both hands. His face grew purple; his eyes were starting from his head, and with protruded tongue he seemed to mock me. I squeezed the tighter.

"The door was suddenly burst open with a loud noise, and a crowd of people rushed forward, crying aloud to each other to secure the madman.

"My secret was out, and my only struggle now was for liberty and freedom. I gained my feet before a hand was on me, threw myself among my assailants, and cleared my way with my strong arm as if I bore a hatchet in my hand, and hewed them down before me. I gained the door, dropped over the banisters, and in an instant was in the street.

"Straight and swift I ran, and no one dared to stop me. I heard the noise of feet behind, and redoubled my speed. It grew fainter and fainter in the distance, and at length died away altogether; but on I bounded, through marsh and rivulet, over fence and wall, with a wild shout which was taken up by the strange beings that flocked around me on every side, and swelled the sound till it pierced the air. I was borne upon the arms of demons who swept along upon the wind and bore down bank and hedge before them and spun me round and round with a rustle and a speed that made my head swim until at last they threw me from them with a violent shock, and I fell heavily upon the earth. When I woke I found myself here—here in this gray cell, where the sunlight seldom comes, and the moon steals in, in rays which only serve to show the dark shadows about me and that silent figure in its old corner. When I lie awake, I can sometimes hear strange shrieks and cries from distant parts of this large place. What they are, I know not; but they neither come from that pale form, nor does it regard them. For from the first shades of dusk till the earliest light of morning, it still stands motionless in the same place, listening to the music of my iron chain, and watching my gambols on my straw bed."

Getting at Meaning

1. What seems unusual about the narrator's attitude toward his madness and toward the madhouse where he is confined?

2. What does the madman think is ironic about his inheritance of a large estate and much money? What indictment against the law does Dickens make?

3. The madman speculates about whether his wife's family would have saved her if they had known of his madness. He says, "A sister's happiness against her husband's gold. The lightest feather I blow into the air, against the gay chain that ornaments my body!" What does he mean by this comparison?

4. In what one way is the madman deceived by his wife's family? How does he finally learn his wife's secret? What is his attitude toward her when he finally learns the secret?

5. The madman resolves to kill his wife. How does he carry out this resolve?

6. As the madman seems to have a foolproof alibi, why do you suppose he eventually confesses his crime? What seems to be beyond the madman's control?

7. Who are the demons who finally capture the madman? Are they real? How do you know? Who or what is the "silent figure in its old corner" of the cell?

Developing Skills in Reading Literature

1. **Unity: Plot.** A work that has unity is cohesive, complete, and self-contained. Although in fiction unity can be achieved through setting, theme, and character, unity is most commonly created through a skillfully structured plot. A unified plot involves a logically related sequence of events that lead to a natural resolution. The interplay of one force upon another, which is the basis for action, is called conflict. Conflict may be internal, within the main character, or external, between the main character and an outside force such as nature, society, another character, or the supernatural. The struggle between opposing forces leads inevitably to a climax, or turning point, which may occur at any point, even at the very end of a story. The plot then is resolved, and the outcome becomes clear to the reader. If the plot is well constructed, nothing will seem out of place; nothing will remain unexplained; every detail will serve some purpose.

Discuss this excerpt from *The Pickwick Papers*, noting any flaws that mar the unity of the plot. Consider the following: Do the events flow easily from one to the other? Is the conclusion logical? What central conflict is the basis for the action? Is the conflict resolved satisfactorily? Does every detail serve some clear purpose? Do the shifts in time from past to present detract from unity or enhance it? Explain.

2. **First-Person Narration.** This story is told in the first person, from the point of view of the madman.

Why is the first-person point of view essential for this story? How would the story change if it were told by another character? by a narrator outside the action?

Developing Vocabulary

Inferring Word Meaning. Try to infer the meaning of each italicized word from the clues in the surrounding sentence and from the broader context in which the word appears. Write a definition for each word, using a dictionary as necessary.

a. "I knew that madness was mixed up with my very blood, and . . . that one generation had passed away without the *pestilence* appearing among them, and that I was the first in whom it would revive."

b. ". . . his grandfather had lived for years with his hands *fettered* to the ground to prevent his tearing himself to pieces."

c. "The old white-headed father, too—such *deference*—such respect—such devoted friendship—he worshipped me!"

d. "Her eyes were fixed on mine. I knew not how it was, but they *cowed* and frightened me, and I *quailed* beneath them."

e. "She lay *bereft* of animation for hours; and when life, look, and speech returned, her senses had deserted her and she raved wildly and furiously."

f. "He jumped suddenly from his chair, *brandishing* it aloft, and bid me stand back. . . ."

Developing Writing Skills

Analyzing Plot. The encounter between the madman and his former brother-in-law is a key incident in this story. In one paragraph discuss the importance of this incident as the climax of the plot. Consider how the major conflict in the story leads up to this incident and how the conflict is resolved as a result of the encounter.

Lewis Carroll
1832–1898

LEWIS CARROLL.
Brown Brothers.

Lewis Carroll, whose real name was Charles Lutwidge Dodgson, was an accomplished mathematician, logician, and photographer, but his enduring popularity is based on a pair of books for children, *Alice's Adventures in Wonderland* (1865) and *Through the Looking-Glass and What Alice Found There* (1872), known together as *Alice in Wonderland.* In these books Dodgson mingled the homely details of everyday life with fantastic absurdities, employing humorous logic and inventive word play to delight adults and children alike.

Dodgson was born at Daresbury near Warrington, his father a clergyman who eventually became Archdeacon of Richmond. Educated at Rugby School and Oxford University, Dodgson took double honors in classics and mathematics. Upon graduation, he was appointed a fellow of Christ Church College, Oxford, where he spent his working life. In 1861, fulfilling a requirement of his fellowship, he was ordained a deacon in the Church of England. He preached only rarely, however, being very shy except in the company of children, with whom he formed many fast friendships and to whom he wrote letters full of warmth and whimsy.

Dodgson's masterpiece began in 1862 as a tale he told for amusement while on a picnic with another Oxford fellow and three daughters of Henry George Liddell, the Dean of Christ Church. Nine-year-old Alice Liddell later persuaded Dodgson to write down the story; he accommodated her with a hand-printed version called *Alice's Adventures Underground.* After being convinced that the story was worthy of publication, Dodgson revised it extensively, adding intricacy upon intricacy to his original version.

The *Alice* books reveal the author's flair for characterization and his inventive genius. The Mad Hatter, the March Hare, the Red Queen, and the White Rabbit are among the most familiar and vivid creations in literature. Some of the songs in the absurd chronicle are parodies, while others are sheer playful nonsense. Dodgson published many puzzles during his life, and the mathematician's love of puzzles is evident in poems such as *Jabberwocky,* which appears in the *Alice* books.

Besides *Alice in Wonderland,* Dodgson as Carroll wrote humorous verse, including the delirious nonsense of *The Hunting of the Snark: An Agony in Eight Fits* (1876). In *Sylvie and Bruno* (1889) and its sequel, *Sylvie and Bruno Concluded* (1893), he tried with mixed success to incorporate Christian philosophy into a story for children; as always, his comic verse is delightful, but the total effect is marred by lapses into mawkish sentiment not found in *Alice in Wonderland.*

Charles Dodgson died and was buried at Guilford. His will divided his estate equally among his surviving brothers and sisters and the children of siblings who had predeceased him.

from **Through the Looking-Glass**

Humpty Dumpty on Words

The egg got larger and larger, and more and more human; when she had come within a few yards of it, she saw that it had eyes and a nose and mouth; and, when she had come close to it, she saw clearly that it was Humpty Dumpty himself. "It can't be anybody else!" she said to herself. "I'm as certain of it as if his name were written all over his face!"

It might have been written a hundred times, easily, on that enormous face. Humpty Dumpty was sitting, with his legs crossed like a Turk, on the top of a high wall—such a narrow one that Alice quite wondered how he could keep his balance—and, as his eyes were steadily fixed in the opposite direction, and he didn't take the least notice of her, she thought he must be a stuffed figure, after all.

"And how exactly like an egg he is!" she said aloud, standing with her hands ready to catch him, for she was every moment expecting him to fall.

"It's *very* provoking," Humpty Dumpty said after a long silence, looking away from Alice as he spoke, "to be called an egg—*very!*"

"I said you *looked* like an egg, Sir," Alice gently explained. "And some eggs are very pretty, you know," she added, hoping to turn her remark into a sort of compliment.

"Some people," said Humpty Dumpty, looking away from her as usual, "have no more sense than a baby!"

Alice didn't know what to say to this; it wasn't at all like conversation, she thought, as he never said anything to *her*; in fact, his last remark was evidently addressed to a tree —so she stood and softly repeated to herself—

Humpty Dumpty sat on a wall:
Humpty Dumpty had a great fall.
All the King's horses and all the King's men
Couldn't put Humpty Dumpty in his place again.

"That last line is much too long for the poetry," she added, almost out loud, forgetting that Humpty Dumpty would hear her.

"Don't stand chattering to yourself like that," Humpty Dumpty said, looking at her for the first time, "but tell me your name and your business."

"My *name* is Alice, but—"

"It's a stupid enough name!" Humpty Dumpty interrupted impatiently. "What does it mean?"

"*Must* a name mean something?" Alice asked doubtfully.

"Of course it must," Humpty Dumpty said with a short laugh; "*my* name means the shape I am—and a good handsome shape it is, too. With a name like yours, you might be any shape, almost."

"Why do you sit out here all alone?" said Alice, not wishing to begin an argument.

"Why, because there's nobody with me!" cried Humpty Dumpty. "Did you think I didn't know the answer to *that*? Ask another."

"Don't you think you'd be safer down on the ground?" Alice went on, not with any idea of making another riddle, but simply in her good-natured anxiety for the queer creature. "That wall is so *very* narrow!"

"What tremendously easy riddles you ask!!" Humpty Dumpty growled out. "Of course I don't think so! Why if ever I *did* fall off—which there's no chance of—but *if* I did—" Here he pursed up his lips, and looked so solemn and grand that Alice could hardly help laughing. "*If* I *did* fall," he went on, "*the King has promised me*—ah, you may turn pale, if you like! You didn't think I was going to say that, did you? *The King has promised me*—*with his very own mouth*—to—to——"

"To send all his horses and all his men," Alice interrupted, rather unwisely.

"Now I declare that's too bad!" Humpty Dumpty cried, breaking into a sudden passion. "You've been listening at doors—and behind trees—and down chimneys—or you couldn't have known it!"

"I haven't indeed!" Alice said very gently. "It's in a book."

"Ah, well! They may write such things in a *book*," Humpty Dumpty said in a calmer tone. "That's what you call a History of England, that is. Now, take a good look at me! I'm one that has spoken to a King, *I* am; mayhap you'll never see such another; and, to show you I'm not proud, you may shake hands with me!" And he grinned almost from ear to ear, as he leant forwards (and as nearly as possible fell off the wall in doing so) and offered Alice his hand. She watched him a little anxiously as she took it. "If he smiled much more the ends of his mouth might meet behind," she thought: "And then I don't know *what* would happen to his head! I'm afraid it would come off!"

"Yes, all his horses and all his men," Humpty Dumpty went on. "They'd pick me up again in a minute, *they* would! However, this conversation is going on a little too fast; let's go back to the last remark but one."

"I'm afraid I can't quite remember it," Alice said, very politely.

"In that case we start afresh," said Humpty Dumpty, "and it's my turn to choose a subject——" ("He talks about it just as if it was a game!" thought Alice.) "So here's a question for you. How old did you say you were?"

Alice made a short calculation, and said, "Seven years and six months."

"Wrong!" Humpty Dumpty exclaimed triumphantly. "You never said a word like it!"

"I thought you meant 'How old *are* you?'" Alice explained

"If I'd meant that, I'd have said it," said Humpty Dumpty.

Alice didn't want to begin another argument, so she said nothing.

"Seven years and six months!" Humpty Dumpty repeated thoughtfully. "An uncomfortable sort of age. Now if you'd asked *my* advice, I'd have said 'Leave off at seven'—— but it's too late now."

"I never ask advice about growing," Alice said indignantly.

"Too proud?" the other enquired.

Alice felt even more indignant at this suggestion. "I mean," she said, "that one can't help growing older."

"One can't, perhaps," said Humpty Dumpty: "but *two* can. With proper assistance, you might have left off at seven."

"What a beautiful belt you've got on!" Alice suddenly remarked. (They had had quite enough of the subject of age, she thought; and, if they really were to take turns in choosing subjects, it was *her* turn now.) "At least," she corrected herself on second thoughts, "a beautiful cravat, I should have said—no, a belt, I mean—I beg your pardon!" she added in dismay, for Humpty Dumpty looked thoroughly offended, and she began to wish she hadn't chosen that subject. "If only I knew," she thought to herself, "which was neck and which was waist!"

Evidently Humpty Dumpty was very angry, though he said nothing for a minute or two. When he *did* speak again, it was in a deep growl.

"It is a—*most*—*provoking*—thing," he said at last, "when a person doesn't know a cravat from a belt!"

"I know it's very ignorant of me!" Alice said, in so humble a tone that Humpty Dumpty relented.

"It's a cravat, child, and a beautiful one, as

you say. It's a present from the White King and Queen. There now!"

"Is it really?" said Alice, quite pleased to find that she *had* chosen a good subject after all.

"They gave it me," Humpty Dumpty continued thoughtfully as he crossed one knee over the other and clasped his hands round it, "they gave it me—for an un-birthday present."

"I beg your pardon?" Alice said with a puzzled air.

"I'm not offended," said Humpty Dumpty.

"I mean, what *is* an un-birthday present?"

"A present given when it isn't your birthday, of course."

Alice considered a little. "I like birthday presents best," she said at last.

"You don't know what you're talking about!" cried Humpty Dumpty. "How many days are there in a year?"

"Three hundred and sixty-five," said Alice.

"And how many birthdays have you?"

"One."

"And if you take one from three hundred and sixty-five what remains?"

"Three hundred and sixty-four, of course."

Humpty Dumpty looked doubtful. "I'd rather see that done on paper," he said.

Alice couldn't help smiling as she took out her memorandum book, and worked the sum for him:

$$\begin{array}{r} 365 \\ \underline{1} \\ \underline{364} \end{array}$$

Humpty Dumpty took the book and looked at it carefully. "That seems to be done right——" he began.

"You're holding it upside down!" Alice interrupted.

"To be sure I was!" Humpty Dumpty said gaily as she turned it round for him. "I thought it looked a little queer. As I was saying, that *seems* to be done right—though I haven't time to look it over thoroughly just now—and that shows that there are three hundred and sixty-four days when you might get un-birthday presents——"

"Certainly," said Alice.

"And only *one* for birthday presents, you know. There's glory for you!"

"I don't know what you mean by 'glory'," Alice said.

Humpty Dumpty smiled contemptuously. "Of course you don't—till I tell you. I meant 'there's a nice knock-down argument for you!'"

"But 'glory' doesn't mean 'a nice knock-down argument'," Alice objected.

"When *I* use a word," Humpty Dumpty said, in rather a scornful tone, "it means just what I choose it to mean—neither more nor less."

"The question is," said Alice, "whether you *can* make words mean so many different things."

"The question is," said Humpty Dumpty, "which is to be master——that's all."

Alice was too much puzzled to say anything, so after a minute Humpty Dumpty began again. "They've a temper, some of them—particularly verbs; they're the proudest—adjectives you can do anything with, but not verbs—however, *I* can manage the whole lot of them! Impenetrability! That's what *I* say!"

"Would you tell me please," said Alice, "what that means?"

"Now you talk like a reasonable child," said Humpty Dumpty, looking very much pleased. "I meant by 'impenetrability' that we've had enough of that subject, and it would be just as well if you'd mention what you mean to do next, as I suppose you don't mean to stop here all the rest of your life."

"That's a great deal to make one word mean," Alice said in a thoughtful tone.

"When I make a word do a lot of work like that," said Humpty Dumpty, "I always pay it extra."

"Oh!" said Alice. She was too much puzzled to make any other remark.

"Ah, you should see 'em come round me of a Saturday night," Humpty Dumpty went on, wagging his head gravely from side to side, "for to get their wages, you know."

(Alice didn't venture to ask what he paid them with; and so you see I can't tell *you*.)

"You seem very clever at explaining words, Sir," said Alice. "Would you kindly tell me the meaning of the poem called 'Jabberwocky'?"

"Let's hear it," said Humpty Dumpty. "I can explain all the poems that ever were invented—and a good many that haven't been invented just yet."

This sounded very hopeful, so Alice repeated the first verse:—

'Twas brillig, and the slithy toves
 Did gyre and gimble in the wabe:
All mimsy were the borogoves,
 And the mome raths outgrabe.

"That's enough to begin with," Humpty Dumpty interrupted; "there are plenty of hard words there. '*Brillig*' means four o'clock in the afternoon—the time when you begin *broiling* things for dinner."

"That'll do very well," said Alice: "and '*slithy*'?"

"Well, '*slithy*' means 'lithe and slimy.' 'Lithe' is the same as 'active.' You see it's like a portmanteau—there are two meanings packed up into one word."

"I see it now," Alice remarked thoughtfully: "and what are '*toves*'?"

"Well, '*toves*' are something like badgers—they're something like lizards—and they're something like corkscrews."

"They must be very curious-looking creatures."

"They are that," said Humpty Dumpty; "also they make their nests under sundials—also they live on cheese."

"And what's to '*gyre*' and to '*gimble*'?"

"To '*gyre*' is to go round and round like a gyroscope. To '*gimble*' is to make holes like a gimlet."

"And '*the wabe*' is the grass plot round a sundial, I suppose?" said Alice, surprised at her own ingenuity.

"Of course it is. It's called '*wabe*' you know, because it goes a long way before it, and a long way behind it—"

"And a long way beyond it on each side," Alice added.

"Exactly so. Well then, '*mimsy*' is 'flimsy and miserable' (there's another portmanteau for you). And a '*borogove*' is a thin shabby-looking bird with its feathers sticking out all round—something like a live mop."

"And then '*mome raths*'?" said Alice. "I'm afraid I'm giving you a great deal of trouble."

"Well, a '*rath*' is a sort of green pig: but '*mome*' I'm not certain about. I think it's short for 'from home'—meaning that they'd lost their way, you know."

"And what does '*outgrabe*' mean?"

"Well, '*outgrabing*' is something between bellowing and whistling, with a kind of sneeze in the middle; however, you'll hear it done, maybe—down in the wood yonder—and, when you've once heard it, you'll be *quite* content. Who's been repeating all that hard stuff to you?"

"I read it in a book," said Alice. "But I *had* some poetry repeated to me much easier than that, by—Tweedledee, I think it was."

"As to poetry, you know," said Humpty Dumpty, stretching out one of his great hands, "*I* can repeat poetry as well as other folk, if it comes to that——"

"Oh, it needn't come to that!" Alice hastily said, hoping to keep him from beginning.

"The piece I'm going to repeat," he went on without noticing her remark, "was written entirely for your amusement."

Alice felt that in that case she really *ought* to listen to it, so she sat down, and said "Thank you" rather sadly.

In winter, when the fields are white,
 I sing this song for your delight——

only I don't sing it," he added, as an explanation.

"I see you don't," said Alice.

"If you can *see* whether I'm singing or not, you've sharper eyes than most," Humpty Dumpty remarked severely. Alice was silent.

> In spring, when woods are getting green,
> I'll try and tell you what I mean:

"Thank you very much," said Alice.

> In summer, when the days are long,
> Perhaps you'll understand the song:
>
> In autumn, when the leaves are brown,
> Take pen and ink, and write it down.

"I will, if I can remember it so long," said Alice.

"You needn't go on making remarks like that," Humpty Dumpty said; "they're not sensible, and they put me out."

> I sent a message to the fish:
> I told them "This is what I wish."
>
> The little fishes of the sea,
> They sent an answer back to me.
>
> The little fishes' answer was
> "We cannot do it, Sir, because——"

"I'm afraid I don't quite understand," said Alice.

"It gets easier further on," Humpty Dumpty replied.

> I sent to them again to say
> "It will be better to obey."
>
> The fishes answered, with a grin
> "Why, what a temper you are in!"
>
> I told them once, I told them twice:
> They would not listen to advice.
>
> I took a kettle large and new,
> Fit for the deed I had to do.

> My heart went hop, my heart went thump:
> I filled the kettle at the pump.
>
> Then some one came to me and said
> "The little fishes are in bed."
>
> I said to him, I said it plain,
> "Then you must wake them up again."
>
> I said it very loud and clear:
> I went and shouted in his ear.

Humpty Dumpty raised his voice almost to a scream as he repeated this verse, and Alice thought, with a shudder, "I wouldn't have been the messenger for *anything!*"

> But he was very stiff and proud:
> He said, "You needn't shout so loud!"
>
> And he was very proud and stiff:
> He said "I'd go and wake them, if——"
>
> I took a corkscrew from the shelf:
> I went to wake them up myself.
>
> And when I found the door was locked,
> I pulled and pushed and kicked and knocked.
>
> And when I found the door was shut,
> I tried to turn the handle, but——

There was a long pause.

"Is that all?" Alice timidly asked.

"That's all," said Humpty Dumpty. "Goodbye."

This was rather sudden, Alice thought; but, after such a *very* strong hint that she ought to be going, she felt that it would hardly be civil to stay. So she got up, and held out her hand. "Goodbye, till we meet again!" she said as cheerfully as she could.

"I shouldn't know you again if we *did* meet," Humpty Dumpty replied in a discontented tone, giving her one of his fingers to shake; "you're so exactly like other people."

"The face is what one goes by, generally," Alice remarked in a thoughtful tone.

"That's just what I complain of," said

Humpty Dumpty. "Your face is the same as everybody has—the two eyes, so——" (marking their places in the air with his thumb) "nose in the middle, mouth under. It's always the same. Now if you had the two eyes on the same side of the nose, for instance—or the mouth at the top—that would be *some* help."

"It wouldn't look nice," Alice objected. But Humpty Dumpty only shut his eyes, and said "Wait till you've tried."

Alice waited a minute to see if he would speak again, but as he never opened his eyes or took any further notice of her, she said "Goodbye!" once more, and, getting no answer to this, she quietly walked away; but she couldn't help saying to herself, as she went, "Of all the unsatisfactory——" (she repeated this aloud, as it was a great comfort to have such a long word to say) "of all the unsatisfactory people I *ever* met——" She never finished the sentence, for at this moment a heavy crash shook the forest from end to end.

ALICE LIDDELL, *the original Alice in Wonderland.*
The Bettmann Archive, Inc.

Jabberwocky

'Twas brillig, and the slithy toves
   Did gyre and gimble in the wabe;
All mimsy were the borogoves,
   And the mome raths outgrabe.

"Beware the Jabberwock, my son!   5
   The jaws that bite, the claws that catch!
Beware the Jubjub bird, and shun
   The frumious Bandersnatch!"

He took his vorpal sword in hand;
   Long time the manxome foe he sought—   10
So rested he by the Tumtum tree,
   And stood awhile in thought.

And, as in uffish thought he stood,
   The Jabberwock, with eyes of flame,
Came whiffling through the tulgey wood,   15
   And burbled as it came!

One, two! One, two! And through and through
   The vorpal blade went snicker-snack!
He left it dead, and with its head
   He went galumphing back.   20

"And hast thou slain the Jabberwock?
   Come to my arms, my beamish boy!
O frabjous day! Callooh! Callay!"
   He chortled in his joy.

'Twas brillig, and the slithy toves   25
   Did gyre and gimble in the wabe;
All mimsy were the borogoves,
   And the mome raths outgrabe.

Getting at Meaning

1. The conversation between Alice and Humpty Dumpty gets off to a bad start when they insult each other. What are their first insults? Do you think they are intentional?

2. What are some of the basic ground rules for a good conversation? How do Alice and Humpty Dumpty fail to adhere to these ground rules? Does this explain in part why the conversation is so unsatisfactory? Explain.

3. The following quotations set forth three standards of Humpty Dumpty's world. Describe the qualities of this world as suggested by the quotations.

a. *"Must* a name mean something?" Alice asked doubtfully.

b. "When *I* use a word," Humpty Dumpty said in a rather scornful tone, "it means just what I choose it to mean—neither more nor less."

c. "I can explain all the poems that ever were invented—and a good many that haven't been invented just yet."

4. What is Humpty Dumpty's view of language? Does he think literally or imaginatively? Explain, supporting your answer with references to the selection.

5. Why does Alice react so negatively to Humpty Dumpty's recitation of his poem? What is the basic difference between these two?

6. Humpty Dumpty explains "Jabberwocky" to Alice. Tell in your own words the "sense" of this poem.

Developing Skills in Reading Literature

1. **Dialogue.** The dialogue in a fictional work advances the action in a definite way and expresses each character's unique personality. No two people speak exactly alike, even though they may have the same cultural backgrounds, and dialogue should reflect even these subtle differences. "Humpty Dumpty on Words" is written almost exclusively in dialogue. Generalize about the differences in the speech patterns of Alice and Humpty Dumpty, quoting lines of dialogue to support your generalizations. What personality traits are suggested by the conversation of

each character? Does all the dialogue in this selection advance the action of the scene? Explain.

2. **Poetry: Nonsense Verse.** Poets who write nonsense verse rely on the same techniques as do more conventional poets. Thus their poems can sound as if they have more meaning than they actually do. Identify the poetic devices used in "Jabberwocky" and the tone and mood of this poem. Why might Carroll have written the poem: To present a "hidden" message? To provide escape? Just to entertain? What might have been the appeal of "Jabberwocky" for the Victorian audience? Does the poem have the same appeal for today's audience? Give reasons for your opinions.

Developing Vocabulary

Portmanteau Words. Words that are concocted by telescoping two words into one are called portmanteau words. The word *portmanteau,* from the French name for a stiff leather suitcase that opens into two compartments like a book, was first used by Lewis Carroll to describe the nonsensical coined words in his poetry. In "Humpty Dumpty on Words" you learn that *slithy* is a combination of *lithe* and *slimy* and that *mimsy* combines *flimsy* and *miserable.* What might be the derivation of the following portmanteau words:

brillig	whiffling
borogoves	tulgey
frumious	galumphing
Bandersnatch	beamish
vorpal	frabjous
uffish	

Developing Writing Skills

1. **Writing Dialogue.** Imagine two students discussing a recent motion picture. One student fails to understand the theme, while the other understands the film but fails to show tolerance for the first student's ignorance. Write a conversation that might take place between these two students. Plan and develop the conversation so that it leads to a natural conclusion. In the dialogue try to reflect differences in personality through variations in speech patterns. Refer to a style

manual or a language arts text if you need to review the mechanics of paragraphing, punctuating, and capitalizing dialogue.

2. **Writing Poetry.** Tongue twisters and nonsense verses of all types are favorite forms for amateur and professional poets alike who enjoy the sounds of words and their rhythmic vitality. Using "Jabberwocky" as a model or following your own pattern, write a poem in which the majority of words and phrases are used in a nonsensical way. Try to coin several portmanteau words. Also, try to convey a particular mood through the sounds of your lines.

The Yellow Bird.

The Dark Blue Bird

The Orange-colour Bird.

The Lilac Bird.

FOUR COMIC BIRDS (Watercolor), 1880. Edward Lear. Intended to provide examples to instruct a child. Victoria and Albert Museum. Crown Copyright.

Gerard Manley Hopkins

1844–1889

GERARD MANLEY HOPKINS.
Oxford University Press.

Gerard Manley Hopkins lived in the nineteenth century, but his poetry belongs to the twentieth. His highly original poems, combining experimental form with intellectual power and deep religious feeling, influenced later poets such as T. S. Eliot and Dylan Thomas.

Hopkins was born at Stratford, Essex (today a part of London). His father, who had published some poetry, had been British consul general in Hawaii. Hopkins studied under several of the most prominent educators of his age, including R. W. Dixon at Highgate School and Benjamin Jowett and Walter Pater at Oxford University, where among his friends was the future poet laureate Robert Bridges.

While studying classics at Balliol College, Oxford, Hopkins was swept up in the enthusiasms of the Oxford Movement, a passionate attempt to reassert traditional religious dogmas in an increasingly skeptical world. Along with many others in the movement, Hopkins turned to Roman Catholicism. This decision cost Hopkins much torment, but in 1866 he was baptized; in 1868 he joined the Society of Jesus, the Jesuits; and in 1877 he was ordained a priest. For several years his parishes were in working-class slums, where he was appalled by the squalor. In 1884 he was appointed professor of Greek literature at University College, Dublin, a mission uncongenial both to his health and to his artistic temperament.

Hopkins felt a terrible tension between his religious vocation and his artistic impulse. He burned his early poems upon entering the Jesuits, feeling that they were inappropriate to a clergyman, and he apparently did not write poetry again until 1875. In that year he composed "The Wreck of the Deutschland" and, not long after, "The Windhover," the first poems in his characteristic style. He continued to write poetry after this, but it was read by only a few friends, including Robert Bridges. Despite their urgings to publish his work, Hopkins refused, and none of his mature work was published in his lifetime.

Hopkins used many devices to portray what he called "inscape," the inner landscape of meaning. He used an irregular pattern of stresses rather than regular metrical feet. He used archaic words as if they were still current and familiar words in unfamiliar contexts. He used unusual word juxtapositions, unconventional word orders, and unexpected imagery. He did not shy from devices long considered shopworn, such as alliteration and the pun, using them to convey layers of meaning. His successful efforts to concentrate meaning give his poems a rich density that demands thoughtful analysis on the part of the reader.

In 1918 Robert Bridges, then poet laureate, published the first collected edition of Hopkins's poems. In 1930 a second edition with a few additional poems appeared, with wider acceptance. In the years since, the originality and power of his poems have been recognized, and Hopkins has come to be regarded as one of the great poets of the English language.

Spring and Fall: To a Young Child

Márgarét, are you gríeving
Over Goldengrove unleaving?
Leáves, líke the things of man, you
With your fresh thoughts care for, can you?[1]
Ah! ás the heart grows older   5
It will come to such sights colder
By and by, nor spare a sigh
Though worlds of wanwood[2] leafmeal[3] lie;
And yet you wíll[4] weep and know why.
Now no matter, child, the name: 10
Sórrow's spríngs áre the same.
Nor[5] mouth had, no nor mind, expressed
What heart heard of, ghost[6] guessed:
It ís the blight man was born for,
It is Margaret you mourn for.   15

---

1. **Leaves . . . can you?** How can you, in your innocence,
grieve over the loss of autumn leaves as if you were
mourning the loss of human life?
2. **wanwood:** a coined word, literally pale wood.
3. **leafmeal:** dry, ground-up leaves.
4. **will:** Accent *will* so that it means "insist upon."
5. **Nor:** Neither.
6. **ghost:** intuition.

Getting at Meaning

1. At what does the speaker express surprise in the
first four lines of the poem?

2. According to the speaker, what will Margaret
experience as she grows older? In lines 10 and 11,
what shift occurs in the progression of idea? How does
the speaker suggest that, in grieving over the coming of
autumn, Margaret is in fact grieving over her own
mortality?

3. According to the speaker, what is the "blight
man was born for"? What does the speaker mean by
the last line, "It is Margaret you mourn for"?

4. What does the title of this poem mean? Do the
words *spring* and *fall* refer only to seasons of the year?
What other connotations do they have within the
poem?

5. What attitude toward life does the speaker seem
to advocate?

Developing Skills in Reading Literature

1. **Diction: Coined Words.** The use of coined
words, sometimes derived from archaic meanings, is a
stylistic characteristic of Hopkins's poetry. W. H.

Gardner, who edited the third edition of Hopkins's poems, explained the meaning of the coined words *wanwood* and *leafmeal* as follows: "I take *wanwood* to be a noun (the meaning 'bloodless' being combined with the older meaning 'dark,' 'livid'). . . . *Leafmeal* I take for an adverb, made by substitution from *piece-meal* on the analogy of Shakespeare's *inch-meal* and *limb-meal*: hence it suggests the leaves falling one by one, then rotting to form pale, mealy fragments." What concept of life is communicated by *wanwood* and *leafmeal*? How do these words affect the tone and mood of the poem? How does Hopkins's use of coined words compare with that of Lewis Carroll?

2. **Sprung Rhythm.** Hopkins attempts to imitate the rhythm of natural speech by disregarding traditional metrical units and patterns. Instead, he creates what is called sprung rhythm, in which a foot is made up of one stressed syllable or of a stressed syllable followed by one, two, or even three unstressed syllables, as in these lines:

> Loók ăt tȟe/ stárs!/ loók,/ loók ŭp ăt tȟe/ sḱies!

> Ó/ loók ăt aĺl tȟe/ fíre-/foĺk/ síttiñg iñ tȟe/ aír!

As additional rhythmic devices, Hopkins uses marked accents, enjambment, unusual phrases, and omission of nonessential words, all of which contribute to the distinctly "modern" sound of his poems. Scan "Spring and Fall: To a Young Child," and identify its characteristic rhythmic devices.

3. **Rhyme Scheme and Theme.** Throughout this poem, Hopkins emphasizes key ideas through end rhyme. For example, *grieving* and *unleaving* emphasize the sadness inherent in life and the unchanging reality of aging and death, two important themes in the poem. Examine the other rhymes, and be prepared to discuss how they reinforce significant themes.

Pied Beauty

Glory be to God for dappled things—
　　For skies of couple-color as a brinded[1] cow;
　　　　For rose-moles all in stipple[2] upon trout that swim;
Fresh-firecoal chestnut-falls; finches' wings;
　　Landscape plotted and pieced—fold[3], fallow, and plow;　　5
　　　　And áll trádes, their gear and tackle and trim.

All things counter, original, spare, strange;
　　Whatever is fickle, freckled (who knows how?)
　　　　With swift, slow; sweet, sour; adazzle, dim;
He fathers-forth[4] whose beauty is past change:　　10
　　　　Praise him.

---

1. **brinded:** brindle; streaked or spotted with a darker color.
2. **rose-moles . . . stipple:** iridescent speckles or spots.
3. **fold:** enclosure for animals.
4. **fathers-forth:** creates.

Getting at Meaning

1. What are "dappled things"? What are the different dappled things for which the speaker praises God? What concept of nature is implied? Is nature an active or a passive force? Explain.

2. What does the speaker suggest about the relationship between God and nature? What is meant by "whose beauty is past change" in line 10? What is paradoxical about God, as He is described in this poem?

Developing Skills in Reading Literature

1. **Imagery and Theme.** Find images in this poem that contrast earth and sky or other opposing concepts. Also look for images that suggest the traditional four elements: earth, water, air, and fire. How do the images suggest a certain changeability and lack of substance along with richness and variety? How do they contrast with the images describing God? What theme is implied through the images in this poem?

2. **Sprung Rhythm.** Scan this poem to illuminate its characteristic sprung rhythm. Does the function of sprung rhythm in this poem differ from that in "Spring and Fall: To a Young Child"? Explain.

3. **Diction.** Hopkins sought an intensity of expression unique among Victorian writers. In doing so, he experimented with language, making hyphenated linguistic units out of different parts of speech and using words as parts of speech different from their usual usage (conversion). Find examples of these techniques in "Pied Beauty." What is the effect of Hopkins's innovative diction?

Developing Writing Skills

Using Comparisons. Hopkins's view of nature is similar in some ways to the attitudes expressed by earlier writers. In a brief essay compare Hopkins's concept and treatment of nature with that of at least one other Victorian writer and of one or two writers from the Romantic Period.

God's Grandeur

The world is charged with the grandeur of God.
  It will flame out, like shining from shook foil;[1]
  It gathers to a greatness, like the ooze of oil
Crushed. Why do men then now not reck his rod?[2]
Generations have trod, have trod, have trod;   5
  And all is seared with trade; bleared, smeared with toil;
  And wears man's smudge and shares man's smell: the soil
Is bare now, nor can foot feel, being shod.

And for all this, nature is never spent;
  There lives the dearest freshness deep down things;   10
And though the last lights off the black West went
  Oh, morning, at the brown brink eastward, springs—
Because the Holy Ghost over the bent
  World broods with warm breast and with ah! bright wings.

---

1. **shook foil:** goldfoil or tinsel.
2. **reck his rod:** reckon with God's authority and obey it.

Getting at Meaning

1. In what sense is God both involved in and apart from the world, according to this poem? What is the meaning of *charged* in the opening line?

2. In lines 4–8 what judgment does the speaker make against human beings? What picture of industrialized England does the speaker present?

3. According to the speaker, why has nature survived destruction by human beings? What image of hope and rejuvenation does nature present?

Developing Skills in Reading Literature

1. **Sonnet and Theme.** Does Hopkins use the Petrarchan or the Shakespearean form for this sonnet? How does the idea presented in the octave take on new meaning in the sestet? Specifically, how does the concept of "God's grandeur" at the end of the poem differ from the concept of God's grandeur in the first eight lines? How is the "black West" described in the octave transformed in the sestet? How is the treatment of the passage of time different in each part of the poem? What theme is brought out through the development of idea from octave to sestet? How does the subject matter of this poem differ from the typical subject matter of earlier sonnets?

2. **Imagery.** Identify contrasting images of light and darkness in the poem. What is the source of light? With what concept is darkness associated? How do these images relate to the theme of the poem?

3. **Diction: Connotation.** An examination of Hopkins's choice of words can lead the reader to appreciate the poet's mastery of language and to understand the message he is communicating. Point out several examples of familiar, "homely" words and also of words that suggest a nurturing quality. Then find examples of phrases that are richly connotative. How would you describe the mood created by the diction in this poem? What concepts of God, of nature, and of human beings are emphasized through the connotations of the words and phrases?

4. **Sound Devices.** Alliteration, internal rhyme, and repetition are used effectively to emphasize the ideas in this poem. Find examples of each of these poetic devices, and discuss how they function to create emphasis.

OMNIBUS LIFE IN LONDON. *William M. Egley.*
Tate Gallery, London.

Thomas Hardy
1840–1928

Thomas Hardy is the foremost English regional novelist and also a major Victorian poet. Seemingly immune to changing literary fashions, Hardy produced prose and poetry that are straightforward and authentic and that possess a rugged integrity still admired by critics and readers. As a novelist, he used gritty realism to portray the tragic ironies of characters struggling against the violent passions of human nature within and indifferent forces of a hostile world without. As a poet, he created ironic anecdotes in verse, often using the rhythm of the ballad to emphasize the timelessness of his themes.

Hardy's birthplace was in southwest England near Dorchester, a region he was to call Wessex in his novels. His father was a builder who loved music. After attending private school at Dorchester, Hardy was apprenticed to an ecclesiastical architect doing restoration there, and later he went to London to study Gothic architecture. Despite the promise he showed in this field, Hardy drifted toward a career in literature. His first published novel, a murder tale titled *Desperate Remedies*, appeared in 1871. After several lesser efforts, *Far From the Madding Crowd* was published serially in 1874, and Hardy was acclaimed as a major novelist.

During the next twenty-two years, Hardy produced a series of novels, many of them among the best examples of the genre in English. *The Return of the Native* came out in 1878 and *The Mayor of Casterbridge* in 1886, the year after he moved into Max Gate, the Dorchester house built according to his own design where he spent the remainder of his life. In 1891 Hardy faced official and unofficial censorship for the supposed immorality of *Tess of the D'Urbervilles*, in which a girl who has an illegitimate baby is hanged for murdering the man she lives with. Readers were incensed that Hardy treated the girl as a human being rather than as a depraved monster. *Jude the Obscure* (1896) was met with an even more hostile reaction, and Hardy, disgusted, abandoned the novel form altogether and turned to poetry.

THOMAS HARDY, 1893. *W. Strang.*
National Portrait Gallery, London.

Hardy's novels have an uncompromising stoicism. His characters are caught in circumstances beyond their control, their tragedies redeemed only by their heroic dignity as their fate overwhelms them. Similarly, Hardy's poetry has none of the self-pity so common in Victorian verse. His tone is stern; he stares into the abyss with perfect equanimity. Hardy's unflinching acceptance of things as they appear, unredeemed by any metaphysical theory to explain away the tragic aspects of existence, struck most of his contemporaries as appallingly pessimistic. Hardy himself denied being a pessimist at all, calling himself a "meliorist," one who believes people must work to ameliorate the human condition.

Hardy died at Max Gate on January 11, 1928. His ashes rest in the Poet's Corner of Westminster Abbey, and his heart lies in the earth at Stinsford near Dorchester.

The Darkling Thrush

I leant upon a coppice gate[1]
  When Frost was specter-gray,
And Winter's dregs made desolate
  The weakening eye of day.
The tangled bine-stems[2] scored the sky   5
  Like strings of broken lyres,
And all mankind that haunted nigh
  Had sought their household fires.

The land's sharp features seemed to be
  The Century's corpse[3] outleant,   10
His crypt the cloudy canopy,
  The wind his death lament.
The ancient pulse of germ[4] and birth
  Was shrunken hard and dry,
And every spirit upon earth   15
  Seemed fervorless as I.

At once a voice arose among
  The bleak twigs overhead
In a full-hearted evensong   20
  Of joy illimited;
An aged thrush, frail, gaunt, and small,
  In blast-beruffled plume,
Had chosen thus to fling his soul
  Upon the growing gloom.

So little cause for carolings   25
  Of such ecstatic sound
Was written on terrestrial things
  Afar or nigh around,
That I could think there trembled through
  His happy good-night air   30
Some blessèd Hope, whereof he knew
  And I was unaware.

---

1. **coppice gate:** a gate within a copse or thicket of shrubs.
2. **bine-stems:** trailing vines of the woodbine.
3. **Century's corpse:** the nineteenth century.
4. **germ:** seed.

Getting at Meaning

1. In the first two stanzas, what attitude does the speaker take toward the nineteenth century? Point out specific lines from the poem that suggest this attitude.

2. What new attitude is introduced in the third stanza? What positive note is sounded at the end of the poem? What is the nature of this positive force?

Developing Skills in Reading Literature

1. **Symbol.** Hardy was a pessimist, deeply troubled about the nature of existence and the presence of evil in the world. Still, he persisted in hoping for the best even while recognizing the worst. In "The Darkling Thrush" the bird introduces this hope. What kind of bird is the thrush? Why is a bird, particularly a thrush, appropriate as a sign of hope? Note, however, the contrast between the words used to describe the thrush itself (*aged, frail, gaunt, small, blast-beruffled*) and those used to describe the thrush's song (*full-hearted, ecstatic*). Clearly the bird's song is the symbol for hope. With what, then, is the bird itself associated? What is the apparent source of the bird's "blessèd Hope"? Why is *hope* capitalized? What does this suggest about the nature of the bird's song?

2. **Personification.** Find several examples of personification in this poem. What contrast exists between the personifications in the first half of the poem and the one example in the second half?

3. **Rhythm and Theme.** Hardy's use of the traditional ballad rhythm seems incongruous for a subject as gloomy as the "death" of a century. Study the poem to see if you can determine Hardy's purpose for choosing the lively rhythm of the ballad. Think, for example, about the melancholy description in the first two stanzas. What does the rhythm suggest, even while the images are unrelentingly depressing? Is the content of the last two stanzas more appropriate to this rhythm? What paradoxical theme is reinforced through the rhythm of the poem?

Ah, Are You Digging on My Grave?

"Ah, are you digging on my grave
  My loved one?—planting rue?"
—"No; yesterday he went to wed
One of the brightest wealth has bred.
'It cannot hurt her now,' he said,   5
  'That I should not be true.'"

"Then who is digging on my grave?
  My nearest dearest kin?"
—"Ah, no; they sit and think, 'What use!
What good will planting flowers produce?   10
No tendance of her mound can loose
  Her spirit from Death's gin.'"[1]

"But someone digs upon my grave?
  My enemy?—prodding sly?"
—"Nay; when she heard you had passed the Gate   15
That shuts on all flesh soon or late,
She thought you no more worth her hate,
  And cares not where you lie."

"Then, who is digging on my grave?
  Say—since I have not guessed!"   20
—"O it is I, my mistress dear,
Your little dog, who still lives near,
And much I hope my movements here
  Have not disturbed your rest?"

"Ah, yes! *You* dig upon my grave . . .   25
  Why flashed it not on me
That one true heart was left behind!
What feeling do we ever find
To equal among humankind
  A dog's fidelity!"   30

"Mistress, I dug upon your grave
  To bury a bone, in case
I should be hungry near this spot
When passing on my daily trot.
I am sorry, but I quite forgot   35
  It was your resting place."

---

1. **gin:** a snare or trap for game.

Getting at Meaning

1. The first speaker in this poem is a young woman who has died. In what stanza do you learn the identity of the second speaker? What advantage is gained by concealing the identity of this speaker?

2. What does the first speaker expect, as indicated by her questions? Is there any significance in the order of her questions? Explain.

3. What attitude toward death is shared by all the "mourners" mentioned in the poem? What is ironic about this attitude?

Developing Skills in Reading Literature

Satire. In this poem Hardy reacts against the romantic notions of some Victorians. Displaying a wry sense of humor, he satirizes typically sentimental ideas about love, loyalty, and death. What are some of these ideas? How does the poet indicate criticism of them? What statement is Hardy making about illusion and reality? What seems to be his view of human nature? Is this satire Horatian or Juvenalian in tone?

Developing Vocabulary

Archaic and Poetic Words. Hardy frequently uses archaic and poetic words, which contrast with his typically simple, homely diction. The following lines from Hardy's poems contain italicized archaic and poetic words. Using a dictionary, provide a more contemporary or common word or phrase for each italicized word.

a. "And all mankind that haunted *nigh*
Had sought their household fires."

b. "The land's sharp features seemed to be
The Century's corpse *outleant*,"

c. "In a full-hearted evensong
Of joy *illimited*;
An aged thrush, frail, gaunt, and small,
In *blast-beruffled* plume,"

d. "Some blessèd Hope, *whereof* he knew
And I was unaware."

e. "Are you digging on my grave
My loved one?—planting *rue*?"

The Man He Killed

"Had he and I but met
  By some old ancient inn,
We should have sat us down to wet
  Right many a nipperkin![1]

"But ranged as infantry,   5
  And staring face to face,
I shot at him as he at me,
  And killed him in his place.

"I shot him dead because—
  Because he was my foe,   10
Just so: my foe of course he was;
  That's clear enough; although

"He thought he'd 'list,[2] perhaps,
  Offhand like—just as I—
Was out of work—had sold his traps[3]—   15
  No other reason why.

"Yes; quaint and curious war is!
  You shoot a fellow down
You'd treat if met where any bar is,
  Or help to half-a-crown."[4]   20

---

1. **nipperkin:** a container holding a half-pint or less of ale.
2. **'list:** enlist.
3. **traps:** small personal belongings.
4. **half-a-crown:** an English coin worth about sixty-three cents in Hardy's day.

Getting at Meaning

1. What social class do both the speaker and the man he killed represent? How do you know?

2. Why does the speaker repeat the word *because* in the third stanza? Does he seem satisfied with the reason he gives in line 11? How do you know?

3. What reasons are given in this poem for becoming a soldier? Do you think that Hardy views these as typical reasons? Explain.

Developing Skills in Reading Literature

Tone. In line 17 the speaker says, "Yes; quaint and curious war is!" Does Hardy actually view war as quaint and curious, or is he understating his real feelings? How does he seem to view the effect of war on natural human impulses? How do the preceding stanzas reinforce the impact of this line? What is the tone of the poem as a whole?

Developing Writing Skills

Analyzing Style. One of Hardy's contemporaries explained that Hardy's style—his unusual phrasings; his use of dialect and of archaic, technical, and compound words; and his metrics and stanza forms—illustrates both a seemingly old-fashioned restrictiveness and an originality of expression that is fresh and forward looking. In a well developed essay discuss this critic's assessment of Hardy's style. Point out examples of stylistic characteristics that recall earlier poetic traditions and those that represent a break with these traditions.

A. E. Housman

1859–1936

An eminent classical scholar, Alfred Edward Housman wrote poems that have the simplicity and directness of ancient Greek poetry. Not a prolific poet, Housman was nonetheless very influential, with many poets attempting to emulate the economy and grace of his short lyrics. In treating the theme of doomed youth and beauty, Housman's mood often goes beyond melancholy to stark fatalism, an ancient attitude he makes immediate by associating it with vivid pictures of the English countryside.

The son of a lawyer, Housman was born in Worcestershire, within sight of the Shropshire countryside he was to portray in his poetry. Although he was a brilliant scholar, he failed his final examination at Oxford University because he was in a state of emotional turmoil. Housman worked as a clerk in the Patent Office for ten years until articles he wrote for journals came to the attention of scholars, and in 1892 he was appointed professor of Latin at University College, London. In 1911 he became professor of Latin and fellow of Trinity College, Cambridge, where he taught almost until his death.

One of the greatest of all Latin scholars, Housman's major scholarly effort was his monumental annotated edition of the writings of Manilius, which appeared between 1903 and 1930. He also produced editions of the works of Lucan and Juvenal and wrote many classical studies.

In a lecture he gave in 1933, *The Name and Nature of Poetry*, Housman expresses his idea that poetry cannot be explained or analyzed, that it is an experience not of the intellect but of the emotions.

During the early months of 1895, Housman composed the sixty-three poems that appeared the

A. E. HOUSMAN, 1926. *F. Dodd.*
National Portrait Gallery, London.

following year as *A Shropshire Lad*. In the clean, lean lines of these poems, Housman explores the favorite theme of doomed youth. His message is that, if it is tragic that youth and beauty are fleeting, there is nobility in enduring this fate with dignity. The fastidious formality of the poems in *A Shropshire Lad* reflects the qualities that made Housman such a formidable classicist.

After *A Shropshire Lad*, more than a quarter of a century passed before another slim volume, *Last Poems* (1922), appeared. After Housman's death his brother published a final volume, *More Poems* (1936).

When I Was One-and-Twenty

When I was one-and-twenty
  I heard a wise man say,
"Give crowns and pounds and guineas,
  But not your heart away;
Give pearls away and rubies   5
  But keep your fancy free."
But I was one-and-twenty,
  No use to talk to me.

When I was one-and-twenty
  I heard him say again,   10
"The heart out of the bosom
  Was never given in vain;
'Tis paid with sighs a plenty
  And sold for endless rue."
And I am two-and-twenty,   15
  And oh, 'tis true, 'tis true.

Getting at Meaning

1. How does the speaker's attitude change between the ages of twenty-one and twenty-two? What probably happened to produce that change?

2. What message is implied in the last two lines of this poem?

Developing Skills in Reading Literature

Poetry: Sound and Sense. The quick rhythm, repetitious rhymes, and clipped, one-syllable words in this poem reflect the spirit and confidence of youth. Note, however, that the pace of the poem shifts abruptly in the second stanza. Where does this change take place? What shift in tone and mood occurs as a result of the change?

To an Athlete Dying Young

The time you won your town the race
We chaired you through the marketplace;
Man and boy stood cheering by,
And home we brought you shoulder-high.

Today, the road all runners come,   5
Shoulder-high we bring you home,
And set you at your threshold down,
Townsman of a stiller town.

Smart lad, to slip betimes away
From fields where glory does not stay   10
And early though the laurel grows
It withers quicker than the rose.

Eyes the shady night has shut
Cannot see the record cut,[1]
And silence sounds no worse than cheers   15
After earth has stopped the ears.

Now you will not swell the rout[2]
Of lads that wore their honors out,
Runners whom renown outran
And the name died before the man.   20

So set, before its echoes fade,
The fleet foot on the sill[3] of shade,
And hold to the low lintel[4] up
The still-defended challenge-cup.

And round that early-laureled head   25
Will flock to gaze the strengthless dead,
And find unwithered on its curls
The garland briefer than a girl's.

---

1. **cut:** broken.
2. **rout:** noisy crowd.
3. **sill:** threshold.
4. **lintel:** top frame of a doorway.

Getting at Meaning

1. What two occasions are compared in the first two stanzas of this poem? How are the occasions both similar and different?

2. Why is the young athlete a "smart lad"? According to the third, fourth, and fifth stanzas, what apparent advantages has he gained from having died? What is the meaning of lines 11 and 12?

3. What "entrance" is described in lines 21–24? What is the "sill of shade"? What reception will greet the athlete?

Developing Skills in Reading Literature

Imagery and Theme. What images in this poem are drawn from Greek and Roman times? How did the Greeks and Romans view athletes and athletic competition? How does their view differ from that of the speaker in this poem? What is the speaker's concept of life? of death? Why are classical images appropriate in developing the theme of this poem?

Is My Team Plowing?

"Is my team plowing,
    That I was used to drive
And hear the harness jingle
    When I was man alive?"

Aye, the horses trample,   5
    The harness jingles now;
No change though you lie under
    The land you used to plow.

"Is football playing
    Along the river shore,   10
With lads to chase the leather,
    Now I stand up no more?"

Aye, the ball is flying,
    The lads play heart and soul;
The goal stands up, the keeper   15
    Stands up to keep the goal.

"Is my girl happy,
    That I thought hard to leave,
And has she tired of weeping
    As she lies down at eve?"   20

Aye, she lies down lightly,
    She lies not down to weep;
Your girl is well contented.
    Be still, my lad, and sleep.

"Is my friend hearty,   25
    Now I am thin and pine,
And has he found to sleep in
    A better bed than mine?"

Yes, lad, I lie easy,
    I lie as lads would choose;   30
I cheer a dead man's sweetheart—
    Never ask me whose.

Getting at Meaning

1. What is the relationship between the two speakers in this poem? What answers does the first speaker seem to expect from the second? What kinds of answers does he get?

2. Why does the third question seem to make the second speaker uneasy?

3. Is there any significance in the order of the questions asked by the first speaker? Explain.

Developing Skills in Reading Literature

Irony. The final stanza prevents this poem from being sentimental or even melodramatic. What ironic twist occurs in this stanza? What is the effect of the irony upon the tone of the entire poem?

Developing Writing Skills

Using Comparisons and Contrasts. This poem, like Hardy's "Ah, Are You Digging on My Grave?" is written as a dialogue. In a well developed essay compare the two poems, noting similarities and differences in the tone, sequence, form, diction, and theme of both poems.

As into the Garden Elizabeth Ran

As into the garden Elizabeth ran
Pursued by the just indignation of Ann,
She trod on an object that lay in her road,
She trod on an object that looked like a toad.

It looked like a toad, and it looked so because   5
A toad was the actual object it was;
And after supporting Elizabeth's tread
It looked like a toad that was visibly dead.

Elizabeth, leaving her footprint behind,
Continued her flight on the wings of the wind,   10
And Ann in her anger was heard to arrive
At the toad that was not any longer alive.

She was heard to arrive, for the firmament rang
With the sound of a scream and the noise of a bang,
As her breath on the breezes she broadly bestowed   15
And fainted away on Elizabeth's toad.

Elizabeth, saved by the sole of her boot,
Escaped her insensible sister's pursuit;
And if ever hereafter she irritates Ann,
She will tread on a toad if she possibly can.   20

TOAD. *Thomas Bewick.*

Getting at Meaning

1. What child-like qualities are exhibited by Elizabeth and Ann?

2. The fourth stanza begins, "She was heard to arrive. . . ." Who heard Ann arrive? What noise accompanies her arrival?

3. Which of the two sisters is more emotional? Which is more rational? Explain your conclusions.

Developing Skills in Reading Literature

1. **Poetry: Sound and Sense.** In this poem Housman uses alliteration, assonance, and other kinds of repetition to reinforce ideas and to create special tonal effects. Find examples of these sound devices and be prepared to discuss how each of them emphasizes an idea within the poem.

This poem is perhaps more regular in its rhythm and rhyme than any of the other poems by Housman. How is its sound similar to that of a nursery rhyme? How does this poem compare in subject to the typical nursery rhyme? Are Ann and Elizabeth stereotypical nursery rhyme children? Explain.

2. **Imagery and Mood.** What images are suggested by each of the following quotations from the poem? How do the images strengthen the mood of the poem?

a. "on the wings of the wind"

b. "for the firmament rang"

c. "As her breath on the breezes she broadly bestowed"

d. "saved by the sole of her boot"

3. **Metaphor.** The future relationship of the two girls is foreshadowed in the last line of the poem. Will Elizabeth "tread on a toad" literally or figuratively? Explain.

Developing Writing Skills

Writing a Narrative Poem. Think of an amusing incident that you have observed, or imagine one that might happen on a playground. Using "As into the Garden Elizabeth Ran" as a model, narrate the incident as if you were telling it to a child. Emphasize rhythmic vitality, include various kinds of repetition, and create imaginative imagery in your poem.

Unit Review *The Victorian Period*

Understanding the Unit

1. Many of the great Victorian writers criticized the society in which they lived. Examine the selections in this unit by Arnold, Dickens, Hopkins, and Hardy. What aspects of Victorian society seem to disturb these writers? How do they express their disturbance? What differences in tone do you find among the selections? Which writers seem most direct in their criticism? Which seem most withdrawn from society? most troubled? most critical?

2. Death and dying seem to be favorite topics for many of the Victorian writers. Examine the selections by Tennyson, the Brownings, Rossetti, Hardy, Hopkins, and Housman. Discuss the ways that these writers treat the subject of death, referring to the tone and mood of specific selections. Then contrast the writers' attitudes toward life, as implied in their treatment of death.

3. The literature of the Victorian Period is many sided and complex. Discuss the wide variety of types and styles of writing represented in this unit, mentioning specific selections as examples. Then think about the literature of the preceding periods. The eighteenth century was an age of formal neoclassical writing; the Romantic Age was the golden age of lyric poetry. Can the Victorian Age be characterized in the same way? Explain.

4. You have already discussed the poetry of Thomas Hardy as it illustrates both a continuation of an older poetic tradition and a break with that tradition. Now examine the poetry of Hopkins and Housman, and discuss the way that their poems demonstrate the same blend of old and new. To what extent do these writers seem bound by traditional subjects, attitudes, and techniques? What elements of originality and freshness do you find in their poems?

5. A number of Victorian poets express ideas about human and divine love in their writings. Discuss the concept of love evident in the poems by Tennyson, Arnold, Elizabeth Barrett Browning, Rossetti, Hardy, and Housman. What similarities and differences do you find among the poets in their attitude toward love?

Writing

1. Some Victorian writers deliberately elude the present by escaping into an imaginative world. Many of these writers, however, only seem to be escaping, for they are actually making indirect observations about real life. Examine the following selections:

Tennyson: "The Lady of Shalott," "Ulysses"
Browning: "My Last Duchess"
Carroll: "Humpty Dumpty on Words," "Jabberwocky"
Hardy: "The Man He Killed"
Housman: "Is My Team Plowing?"

Then discuss the way that these writers make use of imaginative worlds. Are they writing purely to entertain? Are they creating imaginative worlds primarily as a tool for making social commentary? as a way of bringing out universal truths about human life? Conclude your essay by drawing comparisons and contrasts among the selections.

2. John Ruskin, a nineteenth-century critic and "prophet," perceived the entire industrial system as enslaving because it made machines of human beings and destroyed their individuality. In the three-volume treatise *The Stones of Venice* (1851), he wrote:

It is this degradation of the operative into a machine which, more than any other evil of the times, is leading the mass of the nations everywhere into vain, incoherent, destructive struggling for a freedom of which they cannot explain the nature to themselves.

In a brief essay discuss the way that several selections in this unit reflect the same attitude toward industrialization and its effects. Conclude by explaining your own opinion of Ruskin's ideas.

3. Several late Victorian poets are recognized especially for their innovative use of language. Choose two of these poets, and find one poem by each from outside this unit. Then analyze the language in these poems, focusing on specifics such as meter, rhythm, rhyme scheme, sound devices, structure, diction, and imagery. In your analysis point out techniques that make the poems seem more "modern" than those written earlier in the nineteenth century.

WASHING DAY, 1912. *Augustus John.*
Tate Gallery, London.

Unit 7

The Twentieth Century:
New Directions (1900–1939)

VIEW FROM CAMBRIAN ROAD, RICHMOND, 1913. *Spencer Gore.*
Tate Gallery, London.

The Emergence of Modern England

England at the beginning of the twentieth century was the seat of a great global empire. Raw materials from far-flung colonies fueled British industries, and London was the hub of worldwide commercial enterprises. The vast wealth of the empire was protected by the awesome firepower of the splendid British navy. For nearly a hundred years, peace had reigned among the Dominions, for none dared challenge the central authority. Politically, economically, militarily, England was the dominant power, the envy of the world.

EDWARDIAN ENGLAND

When Queen Victoria died in 1901, the crown passed to her eldest son, Albert Edward, then in his sixtieth year. His reign as King Edward VII lasted until 1910, a period known as the Edwardian Era. The Edwardian style was confident and boastful, opulent and excessive, as the titled and the moneyed classes luxuriated in England's last golden era. Although many inequities remained, the working class was better off than it had been since the Industrial Revolution. The reform legislation of the Victorian Period was augmented by new measures to protect workers and their families. These resulted in broader coverage for job-related injuries, minimum wages for certain non-unionized industries, an old-age pension, a government-sponsored employment service, national health and unemployment insurance, and improved housing in industrial regions. Through strikes and the threat of strikes, unions gained safety and wage concessions in key industries such as railroads, shipbuilding, and coal mining.

The Edwardian Era was a grand era for the English, most of whom were terribly proud of the accomplishments of their small island nation. At its worst, this pride spawned moral complacency and smug self-satisfaction, prompting thoughtful writers to try drawing public attention to persistent problems. The concerns of the intellectual minority, however, were generally dismissed as insignificant and overly critical.

THE ROOTS OF CONFLICT

The major watershed in modern history was the Great War, the conflict now called World War I. The domestic and international upheavals that are associated with the war, however, had roots buried deep in the past. The Industrial Revolution had transformed the methods of producing and distributing goods and services, thereby undermining traditional institutions and creating new stresses as emerging groups demanded a fairer share of political and economic power. The tremendous wealth created by the industrial system contributed to polarization among and within nations. Privileged nations and the privileged groups within them organized to protect their favored status, while underprivileged groups sought to change the status quo.

Throughout Europe and the European colonial empires, nationalism was the dominating spirit. One manifestation was the fierce patriotism demonstrated by the citizens of older nations such as England and France. Another was the unification of Italy and of Germany and the subsequent expansion of these new nations into colonial empires. Still another was the unrest among peoples governed by foreign powers and demands for the sovereignty of colonial territories.

THE ROAD TO WAR

A long history of commercial and naval rivalries, conflicting territorial claims in Europe and throughout the world, and efforts to maintain a balance of power in Europe culminated in two powerful alliances: the Triple Alliance of Germany, Austria-Hungary, and Italy and the Triple Entente of England, France, and Russia. Although the professed purpose of these alliances was mutual defense, they created a precarious situation in which all Europe was poised on the brink of war. As tensions mounted, so did nationalist hysteria and the stockpiling of arms, one fueling the other in a seemingly unbreakable cycle. The drift toward war was obvious and inexorable.

The average European seemed complacent about the prospect of war. Few anticipated the horrors of the coming war. The wars of the nineteenth century had been relatively limited conflicts, and most people expected another such war, even hoping it would somehow clear the air. For troops to charge entrenched machine gun emplacements was so obviously suicidal that Europeans assumed their leaders were simply too civilized to order such attacks on a large scale. Socialists, calling the bayonet "a weapon with a worker at both ends," claimed that international working class solidarity would prevent war, that workers would not slaughter one another for the profit of the ruling classes, and that socialist and labor politicians would never vote for war.

On June 28, 1914, Archduke Francis Ferdinand, heir to the

thrones of Austria and Hungary, was assassinated in Sarajevo by a Serbian nationalist. Austria first made demands that would have virtually ended Serbian independence and then declared war on Serbia. In response, the Czar ordered the mobilization of the Russian army. German leaders felt compelled to begin a much more rapid mobilization, which in turn convinced the French and finally the English to declare war. Canada, Australia, New Zealand, and South Africa followed England into war, as did Japan, a nation that coveted German colonies in the Pacific.

WORLD WAR I

Intending to achieve a quick victory in the West before turning against Russia, the German army swept through neutral Belgium, crushing the heroic Belgian army in a matter of days. British and French forces, initially defeated by the Germans, finally stopped the German advance during the first Battle of the Marne, in September, 1914. Both sides dug in, and trench warfare began. In a tragic way, the incredible carnage of the early encounters prolonged the war, for leaders on both sides were unwilling to admit that such terrible suffering, such tremendous losses had been in vain. To the horrors of battleship, submarine, and machine gun, were added the tank, the hand grenade, exploding bullets, barbed wire, and poison gas; yet the stalemate and the sacrifices continued, month after month, year after year. All along the western front, millions of soldiers lived in trenches crawling with vermin and infested with rats, amid mud and garbage and the stench of rotting corpses, until the notion of war as glorious was itself a casualty. At sea, innocent civilians lost their lives as a result of Germany's unrestricted submarine warfare. At home, rabid propaganda intensified the bitterness and the determination to continue fighting.

Russia pulled out of the war in 1918 when the new revolutionary regime signed the ignominious Treaty of Brest Litovsk, in which Russia ceded much of her vast empire. The armistice with Russia enabled the Germans to concentrate all their forces on the western front. By that time, the United States had entered the war, tipping the balance in favor of the English and French.

At the end of the war, Germany was crushed, and France crippled. Russia was in ruins and in the throes of revolution. The United States opted to play no major role on the international scene. The predominant position of England seemed to have been enhanced by the war. Like so many things in the twentieth century, that predominance proved to be an illusion. England won the war, but the England of Victoria and Edward was transformed utterly in the process.

THE AFTERMATH OF WAR

The war had decimated an entire generation of young English men; 750,000 were killed and twice that number wounded. Personal loss and deprivation had touched nearly everyone. The war had cost billions of pounds and had multiplied British debt twelvefold. Commerce was less profitable in the impoverished, disorganized postwar world, and the punitive Treaty of Versailles had destroyed the once lucrative German market. British industry readjusted with difficulty to a peacetime economy, and stiff competition from the United States and Japan further depressed the shipping, mining, and textile industries. Unemployment soared, demoralizing the working class, and steep taxes reduced the spendable income of the middle and upper classes. A sense of disillusionment and cynicism about the future pervaded all levels of society. Groups at home and abroad pressured the government for social, economic, and political changes.

THE POSTWAR POLITICAL SCENE

As a prosperous and stable parliamentary democracy with a largely homogenous population, England suffered rather less dislocation than most societies making the transition into the twentieth century. After the war, however, various elements in British society demanded some of the fruits of victory. Before the war, the struggle for woman suffrage had been bitter, divisive, and violent. During the war years, women temporarily abandoned their fight, putting patriotism before self-interest. Their contributions to the war effort were recognized in 1918 when all women over thirty were allowed to vote. (The age requirement for men was twenty-one.) The struggle for political equality resumed, and in 1928 the law finally granted the vote to men and women on identical terms and removed the prohibition against women members in the House of Commons.

Before the war, the major political parties had been the Conservative and the Liberal; the Labor party, which supported democratic socialism, was third in strength. During the war, all three parties formed a coalition government, but the coalition collapsed soon after the war.

The militant struggle of the workers to maintain their position within the straitened postwar economy was accompanied by a rise in the political power of the Labor party. In the general election of 1922, Labor took second place for the first time in its history. When the Conservative government failed to take decisive action against unemployment, support for the Conservatives dwindled, and in 1924 the first Labor government was formed. For the next sixty years, the struggle was between Conservative and Labor, with the Conservatives predominating through the 1920's and 1930's.

THE IRISH QUESTION

The Irish had never accepted English rule, but the struggle for Irish independence was hampered in the nineteenth century by massive emigration and by the ravages of famine. Nationalist fervor, though, found fertile ground in Ireland by the turn of the century. The war presented the Irish with a dilemma: Why should they fight to defend an empire they hated? Many did fight for that empire, with the ambivalence described by William Butler Yeats in "An Irish Airman Foresees His Death": "Those that I fight I do not hate,/ Those that I guard I do not love." Irish Republican extremists were not ambivalent. They actively courted German support, and on Easter of 1916 a small group of Republican radicals seized much of Dublin, calling for the Irish to rise up against the British. The British dealt so brutally with captured Republican prisoners that sympathy for the Republican movement spread like wildfire. Violence was sporadic until November, 1919, when warfare between the supporters of the Irish Sinn Fein, or "We Ourselves," party and the British constabulary broke out on a large scale. The British sent in the "Black and Tans," who were as savage in their reprisals as were the revolutionaries in their attacks. By 1921 the British and the Sinn Fein agreed to the partitioning of Ireland into north and south and to Dominion status for the southern Irish Free State. Civil war continued for years between those Irish who accepted the Free State and those who demanded a united and independent Ireland. Independence was achieved in 1949; reunification has never been achieved.

EMPIRE AND COMMONWEALTH

The size of the British empire increased substantially at the end of the war, with the acquisition of former German colonies, but the bonds of empire already had begun to loosen as the spirit of nationalism was felt even in distant Africa and Asia and as England granted ever greater degrees of self-determination to subject lands. In India, Palestine, Egypt and elsewhere patriots dreamed, often from British jails, of transforming these colonies into fully independent states. The knotty problems confronting British officials in these lands proved insoluble in the postwar years, and complete independence remained in the future.

Canada, South Africa, Australia, and New Zealand had long been self-governing dominions within the British empire. After the war, the ministers of these dominions made it plain that they wanted more autonomy. British political leaders convened a conference in 1926 at which a resolution was passed declaring the dominions to be "autonomous communities within the British Empire, equal in status, in no way subordinate one to another in any aspect of their domestic or external affairs, though united by a common allegiance to the crown, and freely associated as members of the British Commonwealth of Nations." In other words, these countries were now partners, not possessions, of England.

DEPRESSION AND THE RISE OF DICTATORSHIPS

The paralyzing economic crisis that began with the crash of the American stock market in October, 1929, was global in scope. In Britain, the new crisis further weakened an economy already depressed by over-production and chronic postwar unemployment. The economic collapse threw a million more people out of work, causing terrible hardships and privation.

Dictatorships, established during the twenties and early thirties, gained strength as democratic governments proved inadequate to the challenge of the Great Depression. Josef Stalin had made himself the communist dictator of Russia in the years after Lenin's death in 1924. Benito Mussolini had been fascist dictator of Italy since 1928. The German experiment with democracy ended in 1933 when the Reichstag gave dictatorial powers to Adolph Hitler, the leader of the National Socialist German Labor, or Nazi, Party. As the economic crisis dragged on, Europeans tended to be drawn to the extremes of right and left. It seemed to some at the time that the eventual choice would be between fascist dictatorship and communist dictatorship.

Under Hitler, Germany began to rearm, a violation of the Treaty of Versailles. At first, British reaction was mixed. Some recognized that the treaty had been too harsh and that the total repression of Germany was unrealistic and impractical. Others remembered vividly the horrors of the World War and supported peace at almost any price. A few, some of them very influential, actually admired Hitler's dynamism and shared his anti-communist and anti-semitic views. Most people were more concerned with the economic crisis at home than with foreign policy crises abroad.

A DECADE OF CRISIS

The world situation grew increasingly ominous during the 1930's. Japan invaded first Manchuria and then China. Italy occupied Ethiopia, threatening the balance of colonial power in Africa. Then civil war broke out in Spain. In a way this conflict foreshadowed World War II, for Hitler and Mussolini backed the Spanish rebels while Russia and the International Brigades fought for the republic. Once again, alliances pitted the major powers against each other. The Rome-Berlin Axis, later joined by Japan, opposed the English and French alliance, with Russia as yet uncommitted.

By the late 1930's Britain's situation was precarious. Germany was ahead in the race to rearm. The French were not nearly as formidable as they had been in 1914, while the Americans were isolationists. Russia, another ally from World War I, was communist, and relations were strained at best. England was in a weak position in September, 1938, when Hitler demanded that Czechoslovakia cede part of its territory to Germany. Prime Minister Neville Chamberlain went to Munich, where he acceded to Hitler's demands in order to preserve peace.

Finally alerted to the immediacy of the danger, England began to rearm in earnest. Too late the British tried to woo the Russians into a "peace front." Alarmed by the weakness of Britain and France in the face of German aggression, afraid of having to fight Germany alone, Stalin signed a non-aggression pact with his archenemy Hitler in August, 1939. On September 1, 1939, Hitler's forces invaded Poland, a country that England had pledged to defend. England was again at war. At stake was not global hegemony, but survival itself.

LITERARY CURRENTS

Even at the height of the Victorian and Edwardian Eras, perceptive writers already were anticipating twentieth-century attitudes in their attacks on nationalism and jingoism and in their dissent from the prevailing optimism. Most of these writers chose to remain outside conventional society, establishing the tradition of the "alienated artist," which has been evident throughout the twentieth century. The war validated and accentuated their concerns and changed the entire psychological milieu for readers and writers alike.

The broadened educational opportunities of the late nineteenth and early twentieth centuries had ramifications in the literary world. A large new audience made up of unsophisticated readers created new markets for popular novels and for sensational journalistic writing, while small, select audiences continued to appreciate innovative, subtle poetry and fiction, intellectually rigorous criticism, and serious social commentary. This fragmentation of the reading public and a tremendous variety in literary output has been a consistent characteristic of twentieth century literature.

POETRY, FICTION, AND DRAMA

A majority of the poetry written in the prewar years exemplified an older tradition, tending to be lyrical, sentimental, and pastoral. Poets such as Rupert Brooke carried this romantic view into the early years of the war. For serious poets, the war destroyed forever the possibility of romantic illusions. Poets such as Siegfried Sassoon and Wilfred Owen began to express the bitter ironies and the sense of hopelessness and alienation that came to characterize the entire age.

During these same years, poets such as T. S. Eliot and William Butler Yeats experimented with language and rhythms. Influenced by the innovators of the late Victorian Age, by the poetry of the French Symbolists, by the metaphysical poetry of the seventeenth century, and by the attempts of the Imagists to capture moments in pure, compressed images, Eliot, Yeats, and others wrote an entirely new kind of poetry, intellectually challenging, suggestive, ironic, realistic, and often disquieting. Their poems, along with those of Gerard Manley Hopkins, published posthumously in 1918, inspired later poets such as W. H. Auden, Stephen Spender, C. Day Lewis, and Dylan Thomas to create technically precise poetry rich in nuance and idea.

The novel was the major literary form through the 1930's, with the short story developing as a parallel genre. Reflecting the great variety in tastes, writers produced adventures, romances, mysteries, and science fiction, using exotic as well as more familiar regional settings. Notable in the prewar period were starkly naturalistic works in which characters are subject to forces beyond their control; the new stories of working class life, among them the early works of James Joyce and D. H. Lawrence; and the psychological novels and short stories of Joseph Conrad. The anti-Victorian tradition endured well into the twentieth century, and novelists such as H. G. Wells, Arnold Bennett, and John Galsworthy continued to explore contemporary British society during the early decades.

After World War I novels such as those by Aldous Huxley and Evelyn Waugh became darker and more cynical in tone, befitting the insecurity and disillusionment of the "lost generation." E. M. Forster, Virginia Woolf, and other "Modernist" writers repudiated prewar values and sought new ways to respond to altered realities. During the 1930's literature tended to become politicized, as young writers were attracted to the idealism of the Left and to the solidity of the Right. George Orwell, a socialist with conservative tastes, wrote first anti-imperialist and then anti-communist classics, illustrating the way that many writers developed and changed in response to complex artistic and historical forces.

The quest for new forms and modes of expression that characterized poetry also characterized the novel and the short story. Writers such as James Joyce, Katherine Mansfield, and Virginia Woolf experimented with shifting points of view and with structure, often presenting events through the consciousness of the narrator rather than in chronological sequence. In his more innovative works, Joyce combined myth and symbol into a new kind of reality, existing only within the confines of a fictional world.

No longer able to assume a common set of values, writers as diverse as Woolf, Mansfield, Forster, Joyce, and Lawrence shifted concern to the human being in isolation, to human relationships,

Literature

- E.M. Forster (1879–1970) publishes novel *Where Angels Fear To Tread*
- John Galsworthy (1867–1933) publishes first draft of *The Forsyte Saga*
- John Synge (1871–1909) produces *The Playboy of the Western World*
- H.G. Wells (1866–1946) publishes novel based on his conflicts with Bernard Shaw
- Katherine Mansfield (1888–1923) writes stories for *New Age* magazine

- Bernard Shaw (1856–1950) publishes *Pygmalion*
- Joseph Conrad (1857–1924) publishes "The Secret Sharer"
- Rupert Brooke (1887–1915) publishes "The Soldier"
- James Joyce (1882–1941) publishes *A Portrait of the Artist as a Young Man*
- Siegfried Sassoon (1886–1967) wins acclaim for anti-war writings

1900	1905	1910	1915

History

- Queen Victoria dies
- Edward VII assumes throne
- Anglo-Russian convention settles long-standing differences
- George V becomes King of Great Britain and Ireland
- British establish Union of South Africa as Dominion within British Empire

- Great Britain declares war on Germany
- Archduke Francis Ferdinand is assassinated in Sarajevo, leading to outbreak of World War I
- Germans sink *Lusitania*
- Revolution breaks out in Russia
- Signing Treaty of Brest-Litovsk, Russia pulls out of war
- Women over 30 years old gain the vote in Britain

and to common human strengths and vulnerabilities. Some writers placed characters within a particular social scene, revealing social problems sometimes with shocking frankness.

A new realism also was introduced to the stage, initiating a trend that developed progressively throughout the twentieth century. Dramatist Bernard Shaw turned the popular comedy into a vehicle for incisive, original social satire, brilliant in its perception, scathing in its indictment of lingering Victorianism, and engagingly entertaining in its execution. Also contributing creative vitality to prewar English drama were the playwrights associated with the Abbey Theater in Dublin. These playwrights, among them Yeats, Lady Augusta Gregory, Sean O'Casey, and John Millington Synge, were nationalistic in spirit, celebrating the legends and lore, the culture and politics of the Irish people in language that recalled the island's Celtic heritage.

- William Butler Yeats (1865–1939) publishes "The Wild Swans at Coole"

- T.S. Eliot (1888–1965) publishes "Journey of the Magi"

- Wilfred Owen (1893–1918) poetry is published posthumously

- W.H. Auden (1907–1973) publishes *Poems*

- Virginia Woolf (1882–1941) publishes sketches *Monday or Tuesday*

- Aldous Huxley (1894–1963) publishes *Brave New World*

- Sean O'Casey (1880–1964) completes play about conflict between IRA and British

- Dylan Thomas (1914–1953) publishes *Eighteen Poems*

- D.H. Lawrence (1885–1930) publishes "The Rocking-Horse Winner"

- C.S. Lewis (1893–1963) publishes *Allegory of Love*

1920	1925	1930	1935	1940

- Treaty of Versailles ends World War I

- Conference declares Great Britain and Dominions autonomous communities

- Chamberlain accedes to Hitler's demands regarding Czechoslovakia

- Parliament enacts New Home Rule establishing separate Parliaments for northern and southern Ireland

- Great Depression begins in U.S.

- Germany and U.S.S.R. become allies

- Japanese troops invade China

- Hitler invades Poland, launching World War II

- Southern Ireland is granted Dominion status

- Hitler's Nazi Party wins majority in Reichstag

- Mussolini assumes dictatorial power in Italy

- Italy invades Ethiopia

- U.S.S.R. is formed

- Edward VIII becomes King, but abdicates

- Hitler writes *Mein Kampf*

- George VI becomes King

- Lenin dies

- Spanish Civil War begins

- F.D.R. becomes President

The Development of the English Language

NEW DIRECTIONS

The European world of 1900 seemed remarkably stable, as did the English language, under the restraints of Victorian decorum and the dictates of stern grammarians. However, the two world wars destroyed most of the European dynasties, ensured the end of European imperialism, shattered the illusion of stability, and altered patterns of language. Very simply, the horrors of World War I made the delicacies of Victorian usage seem ludicrous. By the 1920's, there was a new freedom of usage that struck many conservatives as anarchic, a trend that has accelerated since.

The Emergence of Popular Culture

After World War I, the ideas of Karl Marx, Sigmund Freud, and Albert Einstein began to create a new intellectual environment. A new critical vocabulary emerged, first in scholarly journals, later in common currency. At the same time, new patterns of production and distribution resulted in a commercial society and eventually in a popular culture that developed its own idiom, as if oblivious to the traditional restraints of nineteenth-century grammarians. Slang became common in even the most genteel usage, and the role of slang became more prominent in the twentieth century than ever before. In the struggle between esoteric culture and popular culture, the latter was victor. Although intellectuals dominated universities and journals of opinion, in the 1920's the language of popular music was more influential. A speaker of English in the early twentieth century used a language that increasingly reflected the fads and fancies of popular culture.

The Impact of the Electronic Media

Between 1900 and 1940 the impact of electronic communications was first felt. That effect was to become even more important by mid-century. The gramophone created a separate youth culture with a lingo of its own, and movies gave young people new models. After the addition of sound to motion pictures in the 1920's, the cinema provided the example of glib, glamorous speech in the popular wisecrack comedies. Spoken language assumed more significance, and pronunciations and usages became more standardized.

On a more ominous note, the rise of Hitler was facilitated by his flair for using loudspeakers and radio. While the world had seen dictators and demagogues before, twentieth-century propagandists had powerful new weapons for manipulating the emotions.

The Expansion of Vocabulary

One aspect of English that has undergone enormous change during the twentieth century is vocabulary. The number of words in the language has multiplied time and time again, until contemporary English has about one million words, ten times more than in Anglo-Saxon times. Technology is the largest single source of new words. Every new invention, every new device, every new product, and every component and ingredient needs a name. For example, with the development of the automobile came many new words and new meanings, such as *chassis*, *hubcap*, *clutch*, and *convertible*. The technical vocabulary of contemporary English is now larger than the entire English vocabulary at the time of Shakespeare.

The military also introduced many new words to English. During World War I, for example, the words *blimp*, *dud*, *camouflage*, *tank*, and *barrage* were added. With World War II came *parachutist* and *roadblock*, along with new meanings for *alert* and *evacuate*.

How Words Are Created

Most new words adopted in the twentieth century have come from the same sources as in earlier times. Besides borrowing words from other languages, new words also are coined, as from Latin and Greek roots. From the Greek root *tele-*, for instance, came *telescopic*, *teletype*, and *television* in the early twentieth century.

A colorful source of coinages is the acronym, composed from the initials of a phrase. *Radar* (radio detecting and ranging) and *scuba* (self-contained underwater breathing apparatus) are acronyms.

A more common source of new words is affixation, in which suffixes and prefixes are added to English words or roots to create new meanings. *De-*, *post-*, *pre-*, and *sub-*, for example, are prefixes used to create *demoralize*, *postwar*, *pre-release*, and *subtitle* during this period. The suffices *-ation*, *-ence*, *-dom*, *-ist*, and *-er* were used to create *nationalization*, *transference*, *stardom*, *futurist*, and *announcer*.

Compounding is another way to form new words. Compounds are usually self-explanatory, as are *paperback*, *lipstick*, *speedboat*, *newsworthy*, and *hitchhike*, new words in the twentieth century.

Blending creates words by amalgamating current words into new ones. For example, *brunch*, which dates back to 1900, combines *breakfast* and *lunch*, and *smog* comes from *smoke* and *fog*.

Some common words develop from proper nouns. The twentieth century added *limousine* and *hamburger*, named for European cities, just as the nineteenth century had added *diesel*, *bobby*, *bloomers*, and *shrapnel*, words based on the names of inventors or popularizers. Some words owe their origins to deliberate invention as proper names. In the twentieth century, many proprietary trade names became common nouns; for example, *thermos*, *kleenex*, and *bandaid*.

Finally, established words may take on new meanings. In the twentieth century, *broadcast*, *radiator*, and *record*, for example, all acquired new meanings.

The Accelerating Pace of Change

The English that is best known is the English of the present century. Yet in some ways it may be the English that is least understood, the most mysterious and elusive, for scholars lack perspective on their own time. The twentieth century may well be an age of massive change in English usage, although it will be some time before that can be known with certainty.

Society has changed rapidly since World War I, and the language has been a means for people to describe and cope with that change. To a certain degree, language has changed at an equally accelerated pace, particularly in the areas of vocabulary and colloquial expressions. One consequence has been a difficulty in communicating essential emotions and ideas, for language does not always transcend differences in age, education, class, and technical expertise. Language in a way defines both group and individual identity, yet the inherent limitations and evolving nature of language contribute to the problems of identity so apparent in the twentieth century.

Joseph Conrad
1857–1924

Born Jozef Teodor Konrad Nalecz Korzeniowski to parents who were Polish landed gentry, Joseph Conrad became one of the greatest English novelists and short-story writers. Originally admired for his descriptions of sea life and exotic lands, Conrad increasingly has been appreciated for his penetrating exploration of the darker side of human nature. His insightful and technically innovative writing deeply influenced later novelists such as American William Faulkner and Frenchman André Malraux.

Conrad was born in the town of Berdichev in Russian-occupied Poland. His father was a poet and patriot who was exiled to northern Russia for his part in the Polish insurrection of 1863. Conrad's mother died when he was seven; his father died four years later, and the boy was then cared for by a kind and loving uncle in Cracow. Bored by school, Conrad longed to go to sea, and in 1874 he traveled to Marseilles, France, to become a merchant seaman.

In the next four years Conrad's voyages took him to Martinique and the West Indies. What really happened during these years may never be known, although it is believed that Conrad was involved in gun-running, and he became deeply in debt. Episodes from these times found their way into the novels *Nostromo* (1904) and *The Arrow of Gold* (1919).

In 1878 Conrad signed on as a deckhand on a British freighter, and he spent the next sixteen years in the British merchant navy. On his early voyages on British ships he learned English. In 1886 he became a British subject and earned his master mariner's certificate.

In 1887, while on the crew of a steamship that traded among the islands of southeast Asia, Conrad experienced the places described in his early novels and in short stories such as "The Secret Sharer." Conrad began his first novel, *Almayer's Folly*, in London in 1889, but his writing was interrupted when in 1890 he commanded a steamboat up the Congo River into the heart of Africa. He spent four months in the Congo, an experience that permanently damaged his health and shocked him psychologically. He described this profound experi-

JOSEPH CONRAD, 1903. *Sir William Rothenstein. National Portrait Gallery, London.*

ence in *Heart of Darkness* (1902), a classic study in corruption and horror. Conrad resumed work on *Almayer's Folly* in 1891 and finished it in 1894. Although the book met with a cool reception from the public, it and its successor, *Outcast of the Islands* (1896), attracted critical acclaim, and Conrad turned to a full-time career as a writer.

Conrad married in 1896, and the couple settled in southeast England. Life was difficult for Conrad, who continued to be in poor health and was near poverty. He was, however, producing his finest novels, which include *The Nigger of the "Narcissus"* (1897), the story of a dying sailor and how he affects the crew; *Lord Jim* (1900), a study of the corrupting effects of politics on personal relationships; and *Under Western Eyes* (1911), a political novel in which a spy must pretend that he is a revolutionary.

Only after many of his great works had been published did Conrad become financially secure. He also began to gain recognition in England and America, as his serialized novel *Chance* (1913) was a popular success. His fame grew in his late years, but his health never returned. He died on August 3, 1924, after a heart attack.

The Secret Sharer

I

On my right hand there were lines of fishing stakes resembling a mysterious system of half-submerged bamboo fences, incomprehensible in its division of the domain of tropical fishes, and crazy of aspect as if abandoned forever by some nomad tribe of fishermen now gone to the other end of the ocean; for there was no sign of human habitation as far as the eye could reach. To the left a group of barren islets, suggesting ruins of stone walls, towers, and blockhouses, had its foundations set in a blue sea that itself looked solid, so still and stable did it lie below my feet; even the track of light from the westering sun shone smoothly, without that animated glitter which tells of an imperceptible ripple. And when I turned my head to take a parting glance at the tug which had just left us anchored outside the bar, I saw the straight line of the flat shore joined to the stable sea, edge to edge, with a perfect and unmarked closeness, in one leveled floor half brown, half blue under the enormous dome of the sky. Corresponding in their insignificance to the islets of the sea, two small clumps of trees, one on each side of the only fault in the impeccable joint, marked the mouth of the river Meinam we had just left on the first preparatory stage of our homeward journey; and, far back on the inland level, a larger and loftier mass, the grove surrounding the great Paknam pagoda, was the only thing on which the eye could rest from the vain task of exploring the monotonous sweep of the horizon. Here and there gleams as of a few scattered pieces of silver marked the windings of the great river; and on the nearest of them,

just within the bar, the tug steaming right into the land became lost to my sight, hull and funnel and masts, as though the impassive earth had swallowed her up without an effort, without a tremor. My eye followed the light cloud of her smoke, now here, now there, above the plain, according to the devious curves of the stream, but always fainter and farther away, till I lost it at last behind the miter-shaped hill of the great pagoda. And then I was left alone with my ship, anchored at the head of the Gulf of Siam.

She floated at the starting point of a long journey, very still in an immense stillness, the shadows of her spars flung far to the eastward by the setting sun. At that moment I was alone on her decks. There was not a sound in her—and around us nothing moved, nothing lived, not a canoe on the water, not a bird in the air, not a cloud in the sky. In this breathless pause at the threshold of a long passage we seemed to be measuring our fitness for a long and arduous enterprise, the appointed task of both our existences to be carried out, far from all human eyes, with only sky and sea for spectators and for judges.

There must have been some glare in the air to interfere with one's sight, because it was only just before the sun left us that my roaming eyes made out beyond the highest ridges of the principal islet of the group something which did away with the solemnity of perfect solitude. The tide of darkness flowed on swiftly; and with tropical suddenness a swarm of stars came out above the shadowy earth, while I lingered yet, my hand resting lightly on my ship's rail as if on the shoulder of a trusted friend. But, with all that multitude of celestial bodies staring down at one, the comfort of quiet communion with her was gone for good. And there were also disturbing sounds by this time—voices, foot-steps forward; the steward flitted along the main deck, a busily ministering spirit; a hand bell tinkled urgently under the poop deck. . . .

I found my two officers waiting for me near the supper table, in the lighted cuddy.[1] We sat down at once, and as I helped the chief mate, I said:

"Are you aware that there is a ship anchored inside the islands? I saw her mastheads above the ridge as the sun went down."

He raised sharply his simple face, overcharged by a terrible growth of whisker, and emitted his usual ejaculations: "Bless my soul, sir! You don't say so!"

My second mate was a round-cheeked, silent young man, grave beyond his years, I thought; but as our eyes happened to meet I detected a slight quiver on his lips. I looked down at once. It was not my part to encourage sneering on board my ship. It must be said, too, that I knew very little of my officers. In consequence of certain events of no particular significance, except to myself, I had been appointed to the command only a fortnight before. Neither did I know much of the hands forward. All these people had been together for eighteen months or so, and my position was that of the only stranger on board. I mention this because it has some bearing on what is to follow. But what I felt most was my being a stranger to the ship; and if all the truth must be told, I was somewhat of a stranger to myself. The youngest man on board (barring the second mate), and untried as yet by a position of the fullest responsibility, I was willing to take the adequacy of the others for granted. They had simply to be equal to their tasks; but I wondered how far I should turn out faithful to that ideal conception of one's own personality every man sets up for himself secretly.

Meantime the chief mate, with an almost visible effect of collaboration on the part of his round eyes and frightful whiskers, was trying to evolve a theory of the anchored ship. His dominant trait was to take all things into earnest consideration. He was of a painstaking turn of mind. As he used to say, he "liked to account to himself" for practically everything that came in his way, down to a miserable scorpion he had found in his cabin a week before. The why and the wherefore of that scorpion—how it got on board and came to select his room rather than the pantry (which was a dark place and more what a scorpion would be partial to), and how on earth it managed to drown itself in the inkwell of his writing desk—had exercised him infinitely. The ship within the islands was much more easily accounted for; and just as we were about to rise from table he made his pronouncement. She was, he doubted not, a ship from home lately arrived. Probably she drew too much water to cross the bar except at the top of spring tides. Therefore she went into that natural harbor to wait for a few days in preference to remaining in an open roadstead.

"That's so," confirmed the second mate, suddenly, in his slightly hoarse voice. "She draws over twenty feet. She's the Liverpool ship *Sephora* with a cargo of coal. Hundred and twenty-three days from Cardiff."

We looked at him in surprise.

"The tugboat skipper told me when he came on board for your letters, sir," explained the young man. "He expects to take her up the river the day after tomorrow."

After thus overwhelming us with the extent of his information he slipped out of the cabin. The mate observed regretfully that he "could not account for that young fellow's whims." What prevented him telling us all about it at once, he wanted to know.

I detained him as he was making a move. For the last two days the crew had had plenty of hard work, and the night before they had very little sleep. I felt painfully that I—a

---

1. **cuddy:** cabin.

stranger—was doing something unusual when I directed him to let all hands turn in without setting an anchor watch.[2] I proposed to keep on deck myself till one o'clock or thereabouts. I would get the second mate to relieve me at that hour.

"He will turn out the cook and the steward at four," I concluded, "and then give you a call. Of course at the slightest sign of any sort of wind we'll have the hands up and make a start at once."

He concealed his astonishment. "Very well, sir." Outside the cuddy he put his head in the second mate's door to inform him of my unheard-of caprice to take a five hours' anchor watch on myself. I heard the other raise his voice incredulously—"What? The Captain himself?" Then a few more murmurs, a door closed, then another. A few moments later I went on deck.

My strangeness, which had made me sleepless, had prompted that unconventional arrangement, as if I had expected in those solitary hours of the night to get on terms with the ship of which I knew nothing, manned by men of whom I knew very little more. Fast alongside a wharf, littered like any ship in port with a tangle of unrelated things, invaded by unrelated shore people, I had hardly seen her yet properly. Now, as she lay cleared for sea, the stretch of her main deck seemed to me very fine under the stars. Very fine, very roomy for her size, and very inviting. I descended the poop[3] and paced the waist,[4] my mind picturing to myself the coming passage through the Malay Archipelago, down the Indian Ocean, and up the Atlantic. All its phases were familiar enough to me, every characteristic, all the alternatives which were likely to face me on the high seas—everything! . . . except the novel responsibility of command. But I took heart from the reasonable thought that the ship was like other ships, the men like other men, and that the sea was not likely to keep any special surprises expressly for my discomfiture.

Arrived at that comforting conclusion, I bethought myself of a cigar and went below to get it. All was still down there. Everybody at the after end of the ship was sleeping profoundly. I came out again on the quarter-deck, agreeably at ease in my sleeping suit on that warm breathless night, barefooted, a glowing cigar in my teeth, and, going forward, I was met by the profound silence of the fore end of the ship. Only as I passed the door of the forecastle[5] I heard a deep, quiet, trustful sigh of some sleeper inside. And suddenly I rejoiced in the great security of the sea as compared with the unrest of the land, in my choice of that untempted life presenting no disquieting problems, invested with an elementary moral beauty by the absolute straightforwardness of its appeal and by the singleness of its purpose.

The riding light in the forerigging burned with a clear, untroubled, as if symbolic, flame, confident and bright in the mysterious shades of the night. Passing on my way aft along the other side of the ship, I observed that the rope side ladder, put over, no doubt, for the master of the tug when he came to fetch away our letters, had not been hauled in as it should have been. I became annoyed at this, for exactitude in some small matters is the very soul of discipline. Then I reflected that I had myself peremptorily dismissed my officers from duty, and by my own act had prevented the anchor watch being formally set and things properly attended to. I asked myself whether it was wise ever to interfere with the established routine of duties even from the kindest of motives. My action might have made me appear eccentric. Goodness only knew how that absurdly whiskered mate would "account" for my conduct, and what

---

2. **watch:** that part of the ship's crew kept on duty while the ship lies at anchor.
3. **poop:** the stern section.
4. **waist:** the central section.
5. **forecastle** (fōk' s'l): the front part of a merchant ship, where the sailors' quarters are located.

the whole ship thought of that informality of their new captain. I was vexed with myself.

Not from compunction certainly, but, as it were mechanically, I proceeded to get the ladder in myself. Now a side ladder of that sort is a light affair and comes in easily, yet my vigorous tug, which should have brought it flying on board, merely recoiled upon my body in a totally unexpected jerk. What the devil! . . . I was so astounded by the immovableness of that ladder that I remained stock-still, trying to account for it to myself like that imbecile mate of mine. In the end, of course, I put my head over the rail.

The side of the ship made an opaque belt of shadow on the darkling glassy shimmer of the sea. But I saw at once something elongated and pale floating very close to the ladder. Before I could form a guess a faint flash of phosphorescent light, which seemed to issue suddenly from the naked body of a man, flickered in the sleeping water with the elusive, silent play of summer lightning in a night sky. With a gasp I saw revealed to my stare a pair of feet, the long legs, a broad livid back immersed right up to the neck in a greenish cadaverous glow. One hand, awash, clutched the bottom rung of the ladder. He was complete but for the head. A headless corpse! The cigar dropped out of my gaping mouth with a tiny plop and a short hiss quite audible in the absolute stillness of all things under heaven. At that I suppose he raised up his face, a dimly pale oval in the shadow of the ship's side. But even then I could only barely make out down there the shape of his black-haired head. However, it was enough for the horrid, frost-bound sensation which had gripped me about the chest to pass off. The moment of vain exclamations was past, too. I only climbed on the spare spar and leaned over the rail as far as I could, to bring my eyes nearer to that mystery floating alongside.

As he hung by the ladder, like a resting swimmer, the sea lightning played about his limbs at every stir; and he appeared in it ghastly, silvery, fishlike. He remained as mute as a fish, too. He made no motion to get out of the water, either. It was inconceivable that he should not attempt to come on board, and strangely troubling to suspect that perhaps he did not want to. And my first words were prompted by just that troubled incertitude.

"What's the matter?" I asked in my ordinary tone, speaking down to the face upturned exactly under mine.

"Cramp," it answered, no louder. Then slightly anxious, "I say, no need to call anyone."

"I was not going to," I said.

"Are you alone on deck?"

"Yes."

I had somehow the impression that he was on the point of letting go the ladder to swim away beyond my ken—mysterious as he came. But, for the moment, this being appearing as if he had risen from the bottom of the sea (it was certainly the nearest land to the ship) wanted only to know the time. I told him. And he, down there, tentatively:

"I suppose your captain's turned in?"

"I am sure he isn't," I said.

He seemed to struggle with himself, for I heard something like the low, bitter murmur of doubt. "What's the good?" His next words came out with a hesitating effort.

"Look here, my man. Could you call him out quietly?"

I thought the time had come to declare myself.

"*I* am the captain."

I heard a "By Jove!" whispered at the level of the water. The phosphorescence flashed in the swirl of the water all about his limbs, his other hand seized the ladder.

"My name's Leggatt."

The voice was calm and resolute. A good voice. The self-possession of that man had somehow induced a corresponding state in myself. It was very quietly that I remarked:

"You must be a good swimmer."

"Yes. I've been in the water practically since nine o'clock. The question for me now is whether I am to let go this ladder and go on swimming till I sink from exhaustion, or—to come on board here."

I felt this was no mere formula of desperate speech, but a real alternative in the view of a strong soul. I should have gathered from this that he was young; indeed, it is only the young who are ever confronted by such clear issues. But at the time it was pure intuition on my part. A mysterious communication was established already between us two—in the face of that silent, darkened tropical sea. I was young, too; young enough to make no comment. The man in the water began suddenly to climb up the ladder, and I hastened away from the rail to fetch some clothes.

Before entering the cabin I stood still, listening in the lobby at the foot of the stairs. A faint snore came through the closed door of the chief mate's room. The second mate's door was on the hook, but the darkness in there was absolutely soundless. He, too, was young and could sleep like a stone. Remained the steward, but he was not likely to wake up before he was called. I got a sleeping suit out of my room and, coming back on deck, saw the naked man from the sea sitting on the main hatch, glimmering white in the darkness, his elbows on his knees and his head in his hands. In a moment he had concealed his damp body in a sleeping suit of the same gray-stripe pattern as the one I was wearing and followed me like my double on the poop. Together we moved right aft, barefooted, silent.

"What is it?" I asked in a deadened voice, taking the lighted lamp out of the binnacle,[6] and raising it to his face.

"An ugly business."

He had rather regular features; a good mouth; light eyes under somewhat heavy, dark eyebrows; a smooth, square forehead; no growth on his cheeks; a small, brown mustache, and a well-shaped, round chin. His expression was concentrated, meditative, under the inspecting light of the lamp I held up to his face; such as a man thinking hard in solitude might wear. My sleeping suit was just right for his size. A well-knit young fellow of twenty-five at most. He caught his lower lip with the edge of white, even teeth.

"Yes," I said, replacing the lamp in the binnacle. The warm, heavy tropical night closed upon his head again.

"There's a ship over there," he murmured.

"Yes, I know. The *Sephora*. Did you know of us?"

"Hadn't the slightest idea. I am the mate of her—" He paused and corrected himself. "I should say I *was*."

"Aha! Something wrong?"

"Yes. Very wrong indeed. I've killed a man."

"What do you mean? Just now?"

"No, on the passage. Weeks ago. Thirty-nine south. When I say a man—"

"Fit of temper," I suggested, confidently.

The shadowy, dark head, like mine, seemed to nod imperceptibly above the ghostly gray of my sleeping suit. It was, in the night, as though I had been faced by my own reflection in the depths of a somber and immense mirror.

"A pretty thing to have to own up to for a *Conway*[7] boy," murmured my double, distinctly.

"You're a *Conway* boy?"

"I am," he said, as if startled. Then, slowly . . . "Perhaps you too—"

It was so; but being a couple of years older I had left before he joined. After a quick interchange of dates a silence fell; and I thought suddenly of my absurd mate with his terrific whiskers and the "Bless my soul—you don't say so" type of intellect. My double gave me an inkling of his thoughts by saying: "My father's a parson in Norfolk. Do you see me

---

6. **binnacle:** a stand on the deck that holds the compass.
7. *Conway:* a training ship for British student officers.

before a judge and jury on that charge? For myself I can't see the necessity. There are fellows that an angel from heaven—And I am not that. He was one of those creatures that are just simmering all the time with a silly sort of wickedness. Miserable devils that have no business to live at all. He wouldn't do his duty and wouldn't let anybody else do theirs. But what's the good of talking! You know well enough the sort of ill-conditioned snarling cur—"

He appealed to me as if our experiences had been as identical as our clothes. And I knew well enough the pestiferous danger of such a character where there are no means of legal repression. And I knew well enough also that my double there was no homicidal ruffian. I did not think of asking him for details, and he told me the story roughly in brusque, disconnected sentences. I needed no more. I saw it all going on as though I were myself inside that other sleeping suit.

"It happened while we were setting a reefed foresail, at dusk. Reefed foresail! You understand the sort of weather. The only sail we had left to keep the ship running; so you may guess what it had been like for days. Anxious sort of job, that. He gave me some of his cursed insolence at the sheet. I tell you I was overdone with this terrific weather that seemed to have no end to it. Terrific, I tell you—and a deep ship. I believe the fellow himself was half crazed with funk.[8] It was no time for gentlemanly reproof, so I turned round and felled him like an ox. He up and at me. We closed just as an awful sea made for the ship. All hands saw it coming and took to the rigging, but I had him by the throat, and went on shaking him like a rat, the men above us yelling, 'Look out! look out!' Then a crash as if the sky had fallen on my head. They say that for over ten minutes hardly anything was to be seen of the ship—just the three masts and a bit of the forecastle head and of the poop all awash driving along in a smother of foam. It was a miracle that they found us, jammed together behind the forebitts. It's clear that I meant business, because I was holding him by the throat still when they picked us up. He was black in the face. It was too much for them. It seems they rushed us aft together, gripped as we were, screaming 'Murder!' like a lot of lunatics, and broke into the cuddy. And the ship running for her life, touch and go all the time, any minute her last in a sea fit to turn your hair gray only a-looking at it. I understand that the skipper, too, started raving like the rest of them. The man had been deprived of sleep for more than a week, and to have this sprung on him at the height of a furious gale nearly drove him out of his mind. I wonder they didn't fling me overboard after getting the carcass of their precious shipmate out of my fingers. They had rather a job to separate us, I've been told. A sufficiently fierce story to make an old judge and a respectable jury sit up a bit. The first thing I heard when I came to myself was the maddening howling of that endless gale, and on that the voice of the old man. He was hanging on to my bunk, staring into my face out of his sou'wester.[9]

"'Mr. Leggatt, you have killed a man. You can act no longer as chief mate of this ship.'"

His care to subdue his voice made it sound monotonous. He rested a hand on the end of the skylight to steady himself with, and all that time did not stir a limb, so far as I could see. "Nice little tale for a quiet tea party," he concluded in the same tone.

One of my hands, too, rested on the end of the skylight; neither did I stir a limb, so far as I knew. We stood less than a foot from each other. It occurred to me that if old "Bless my soul—you don't say so" were to put his head up the companion and catch sight of us, he would think he was seeing double, or imagine himself come upon a scene of weird witch-

---

8. **funk:** fear, panic.
9. **sou'wester** (sou wes' tər): a sailor's waterproof oilskin coat or hat.

craft; the strange captain having a quiet con-fabulation by the wheel with his own gray ghost. I became very much concerned to pre-vent anything of the sort. I heard the other's soothing undertone.

"My father's a parson in Norfolk," it said. Evidently he had forgotten he had told me this important fact before. Truly a nice little tale.

"You had better slip down into my state-room now," I said, moving off stealthily. My double followed my movements; our bare feet made no sound; I let him in, closed the door with care, and, after giving a call to the second mate, returned on deck for my relief.

"Not much sign of any wind yet," I re-marked when he approached.

"No, sir. Not much," he assented, sleepily, in his hoarse voice, with just enough defer-ence, no more, and barely suppressing a yawn.

"Well, that's all you have to look out for. You have got your orders."

"Yes, sir."

I paced a turn or two on the poop and saw him take up his position face forward with his elbow in the ratlines of the mizzen rigging before I went below. The mate's faint snoring was still going on peacefully. The cuddy lamp was burning over the table on which stood a vase with flowers, a polite attention from the ship's provision merchant—the last flowers we should see for the next three months at the very least. Two bunches of bananas hung from the beam symmetrically, one on each side of the rudder casing. Everything was as before in the ship—except that two of her captain's sleeping suits were simultaneously in use, one motionless in the cuddy, the other keeping very still in the captain's stateroom.

It must be explained here that my cabin had the form of the capital letter L, the door being within the angle and opening into the short part of the letter. A couch was to the left, the bed place to the right; my writing desk and the chronometers' table faced the door. But anyone opening it, unless he stepped right inside, had no view of what I call the long (or vertical) part of the letter. It contained some lockers surmounted by a bookcase; and a few clothes, a thick jacket or two, caps, oilskin coat, and such like, hung on hooks. There was at the bottom of that part a door opening into my bathroom, which could be entered also directly from the saloon.[10] But that way was never used.

The mysterious arrival had discovered the advantage of this particular shape. Entering my room, lighted strongly by a big bulkhead lamp swung on gimbals[11] above my writing desk, I did not see him anywhere till he stepped out quietly from behind the coats hung in the recessed part.

"I heard somebody moving about, and went in there at once," he whispered.

I, too, spoke under my breath.

"Nobody is likely to come in here without knocking and getting permission."

He nodded. His face was thin and the sun-burn faded, as though he had been ill. And no wonder. He had been, I heard presently, kept under arrest in his cabin for nearly seven weeks. But there was nothing sickly in his eyes or in his expression. He was not a bit like me, really; yet, as we stood leaning over my bed place, whispering side by side, with our dark heads together and our backs to the door, anybody bold enough to open it stealthily would have been treated to the uncanny sight of a double captain busy talking in whispers with his other self.

"But all this doesn't tell me how you came to hang on to our side ladder," I inquired, in the hardly audible murmurs we used, after he had told me something more of the proceed-ings on board the *Sephora* once the bad weather was over.

"When we sighted Java Head I had had time to think all those matters out several times

---

10. **saloon:** officer's dining room.
11. **gimbals:** a device that suspends articles in order to keep them horizontal regardless of the ship's motion.

over. I had six weeks of doing nothing else, and with only an hour or so every evening for a tramp on the quarter-deck.''

He whispered, his arms folded on the side of my bed place, staring through the open port. And I could imagine perfectly the manner of this thinking out—a stubborn if not a steadfast operation; something of which I should have been perfectly incapable.

''I reckoned it would be dark before we closed with the land,'' he continued, so low that I had to strain my hearing near as we were to each other, shoulder touching shoulder almost. ''So I asked to speak to the old man. He always seemed very sick when he came to see me—as if he could not look me in the face. You know, that foresail saved the ship. She was too deep to have run long under bare poles. And it was I that managed to set it for him. Anyway, he came. When I had him in my cabin—he stood by the door looking at me as if I had the halter round my neck already—I asked him right away to leave my cabin door unlocked at night while the ship was going through Sunda Straits.[12] There would be the Java coast within two or three miles, off Angier Point. I wanted nothing more. I've had a prize for swimming my second year in the *Conway*.''

''I can believe it,'' I breathed out.

''God only knows why they locked me in every night. To see some of their faces you'd have thought they were afraid I'd go about at night strangling people. Am I a murdering brute? Do I look it? By Jove! If I had been he wouldn't have trusted himself like that into my room. You'll say I might have chucked him aside and bolted out, there and then—it was dark already. Well, no. And for the same reason I wouldn't think of trying to smash the door. There would have been a rush to stop me at the noise, and I did not mean to get into a confounded scrimmage. Somebody else might have got killed—for I would not have broken out only to get chucked back, and I did not want any more of that work. He refused,

looking more sick than ever. He was afraid of the men, and also of that old second mate of his who had been sailing with him for years— a gray-headed old humbug; and his steward, too, had been with him devil knows how long—seventeen years or more—a dogmatic sort of loafer who hated me like poison, just because I was the chief mate. No chief mate ever made more than one voyage in the *Sephora*, you know. Those two old chaps ran the ship. Devil only knows what the skipper wasn't afraid of (all his nerve went to pieces altogether in that hellish spell of bad weather we had)—of what the law would do to him—of his wife, perhaps. Oh, yes! she's on board. Though I don't think she would have meddled. She would have been only too glad to have me out of the ship in any way. The 'brand of Cain' business, don't you see. That's all right. I was ready enough to go off wandering on the face of the earth—and that was price enough to pay for an Abel of that sort. Anyhow, he wouldn't listen to me. 'This thing must take its course. I represent the law here.' He was shaking like a leaf. 'So you won't?' 'No!' 'Then I hope you will be able to sleep on that,' I said, and turned my back on him. 'I wonder that *you* can,' cries he, and locks the door.

''Well after that, I couldn't. Not very well. That was three weeks ago. We have had a slow passage through the Java Sea; drifted about Carimata[13] for ten days. When we anchored here they thought, I suppose, it was all right. The nearest land (and that's five miles) is the ship's destination; the consul would soon set about catching me; and there would have been no object in bolting to these islets there. I don't suppose there's a drop of water on them. I don't know how it was, but tonight that steward, after bringing me my supper,

---

12. **Sunda Straits:** a narrow passage between the islands of Sumatra and Java in the East Indies.
13. **Carimata:** a strait between the islands of Borneo and Billiton that connects the Java Sea and South China Sea.

went out to let me eat it, and left the door unlocked. And I ate it—all there was, too. After I had finished I strolled out on the quarter-deck. I don't know that I meant to do anything. A breath of fresh air was all I wanted, I believe. Then a sudden temptation came over me. I kicked off my slippers and was in the water before I had made up my mind fairly. Somebody heard the splash and they raised an awful hullabaloo. 'He's gone! Lower the boats! He's committed suicide! No, he's swimming.' Certainly I was swimming. It's not so easy for a swimmer like me to commit suicide by drowning. I landed on the nearest islet before the boat left the ship's side. I heard them pulling about in the dark, hailing, and so on, but after a bit they gave up. Everything quieted down and the anchorage became as still as death. I sat down on a stone and began to think. I felt certain they would start searching for me at daylight. There was no place to hide on those stony things—and if there had been, what would have been the good? But now I was clear of that ship, I was not going back. So after a while I took off all my clothes, tied them up in a bundle with a stone inside, and dropped them in the deep water on the outer side of that islet. That was suicide enough for me. Let them think what they liked, but I didn't mean to drown myself. I meant to swim till I sank—but that's not the same thing. I struck out for another of these little islands, and it was from that one that I first saw your riding light. Something to swim for. I went on easily, and on the way I came upon a flat rock a foot or two above water. In the daytime, I dare say, you might make it out with a glass from your poop. I scrambled up on it and rested myself for a bit. Then I made another start. That last spell must have been over a mile."

His whisper was getting fainter and fainter, and all the time he stared straight out through the porthole, in which there was not even a star to be seen. I had not interrupted him. There was something that made comment impossible in his narrative, or perhaps in himself; a sort of feeling, a quality, which I can't find a name for. And when he ceased, all I found was a futile whisper: "So you swam for our light?"

"Yes—straight for it. It was something to swim for. I couldn't see any stars low down because the coast was in the way, and I couldn't see the land, either. The water was like glass. One might have been swimming in a confounded thousand-feet deep cistern with no place for scrambling out anywhere; but what I didn't like was the notion of swimming round and round like a crazed bullock before I gave out; and as I didn't mean to go back . . . No. Do you see me being hauled back, stark naked, off one of these little islands by the scruff of the neck and fighting like a wild beast? Somebody would have got killed for certain, and I did not want any of that. So I went on. Then your ladder—"

"Why didn't you hail the ship?" I asked, a little louder.

He touched my shoulder lightly. Lazy footsteps came right over our heads and stopped. The second mate had crossed from the other side of the poop and might have been hanging over the rail for all we knew.

"He couldn't hear us talking—could he?" My double breathed into my very ear, anxiously.

His anxiety was in answer, a sufficient answer, to the question I had put to him. An answer containing all the difficulty of that situation. I closed the porthole quietly, to make sure. A louder word might have been overheard.

"Who's that?" he whispered then.

"My second mate. But I don't know much more of the fellow than you do."

And I told him a little about myself. I had been appointed to take charge while I least expected anything of the sort, not quite a fortnight ago. I didn't know either the ship or the people. Hadn't had the time in port to look about me or size anybody up. And as to the crew, all they knew was that I was appointed to take the ship home. For the rest, I was almost as much of a stranger on board as himself, I said. And at the moment I felt it most acutely. I felt that it would take very little to make me a suspect person in the eyes of the ship's company.

He had turned about meantime; and we, the two strangers in the ship, faced each other in identical attitudes.

"Your ladder—" he murmured, after a silence. "Who'd have thought of finding a ladder hanging over at night in a ship anchored out here! I felt just then a very unpleasant faintness. After the life I've been leading for nine weeks, anybody would have got out of condition. I wasn't capable of swimming round as far as your rudder chains. And, lo and behold! there was a ladder to get hold of. After I gripped it I said to myself, 'What's the good?' When I saw a man's head looking over I thought I would swim away presently and leave him shouting—in whatever language it was. I didn't mind being looked at. I—I liked it. And then you speaking to me so quietly—as if you had expected me—made me hold on a little longer. It had been a confounded lonely time—I don't mean while swimming. I was glad to talk a little to somebody that didn't belong to the *Sephora*. As to asking for the captain, that was a mere impulse. It could have been no use, with all the ship knowing about me and the other people pretty certain to be round here in the morning. I don't know—I wanted to be seen, to talk with somebody, before I went on. I don't know what I would have said. . . . 'Fine night, isn't it?' or something of the sort."

"Do you think they will be round here presently?" I asked with some incredulity.

"Quite likely," he said, faintly.

He looked extremely haggard all of a sudden. His head rolled on his shoulders.

"H'm. We shall see then. Meantime get into that bed," I whispered. "Want help? There."

It was a rather high bed place with a set of drawers underneath. This amazing swimmer really needed the lift I gave him by seizing his leg. He tumbled in, rolled over on his back, and flung one arm across his eyes. And then, with his face nearly hidden, he must have looked exactly as I used to look in that bed. I gazed upon my other self for a while before drawing across carefully the two green serge curtains which ran on a brass rod. I thought for a moment of pinning them together for greater safety, but I sat down on the couch, and once there I felt unwilling to rise and hunt for a pin. I would do it in a moment. I was extremely tired, in a peculiarly intimate way, by the strain of stealthiness, by the effort of whispering and the general secrecy of this excitement. It was three o'clock by now and I had been on my feet since nine, but I was not sleepy; I could not have gone to sleep. I sat there, fagged out, looking at the curtains, trying to clear my mind of the confused sensation of being in two places at once, and greatly bothered by an exasperating knocking in my head. It was a relief to discover suddenly that it was not in my head at all, but on the outside of the door. Before I could collect myself the words "Come in" were out of my mouth, and the steward entered with a tray, bringing in my morning coffee. I had slept, after all, and I was so frightened that I shouted, "This way! I am here, steward," as though he had been miles away. He put down the tray on the table next the couch and only then said, very quietly, "I can see you are here, sir." I felt him give me a keen look, but I dared not meet his eyes just then. He must have wondered why I had drawn the curtains of my bed before going to sleep on the couch. He went out, hooking the door open as usual.

I heard the crew washing decks above me. I knew I would have been told at once if there had been any wind. Calm, I thought, and I was doubly vexed. Indeed, I felt dual more than ever. The steward reappeared suddenly in the doorway. I jumped up from the couch so quickly that he gave a start.

"What do you want here?"

"Close your port, sir—they are washing decks."

"It is closed," I said, reddening.

"Very well, sir." But he did not move from the doorway and returned my stare in an extraordinary, equivocal manner for a time. Then his eyes wavered, all his expression changed, and in a voice unusually gentle, almost coaxingly:

"May I come in to take the empty cup away, sir?"

"Of course!" I turned my back on him while he popped in and out. Then I unhooked and closed the door and even pushed the bolt. This sort of thing could not go on very long. The cabin was as hot as an oven, too. I took a peep at my double, and discovered that he had not moved, his arm was still over his eyes; but his chest heaved; his hair was wet; his chin glistened with perspiration. I reached over him and opened the port.

"I must show myself on deck," I reflected.

Of course, theoretically, I could do what I liked, with no one to say nay to me within the whole circle of the horizon; but to lock my cabin door and take the key away I did not dare. Directly I put my head out of the companion I saw the group of my two officers, the second mate barefooted, the chief mate in long India-rubber boots, near the break of the poop, and the steward halfway down the poop ladder talking to them eagerly. He happened to catch sight of me and dived, the second ran down on the main deck shouting some order or other, and the chief mate came to meet me, touching his cap.

There was a sort of curiosity in his eye that I did not like. I don't know whether the steward had told him that I was "queer" only, or downright drunk, but I know the man meant to have a good look at me. I watched him coming with a smile which, as he got into point-blank range, took effect and froze his very whiskers. I did not give him time to open his lips.

"Square the yards by lifts and braces before the hands go to breakfast."

It was the first particular order I had given on board that ship; and I stayed on deck to see it executed, too. I had felt the need of asserting myself without loss of time. That sneering young cub got taken down a peg or two on that occasion, and I also seized the opportunity of having a good look at the face of every foremast man as they filed past me to go to the after braces. At breakfast time, eating nothing myself, I presided with such frigid dignity that the two mates were only too glad to escape from the cabin as soon as decency permitted; and all the time the dual working of my mind distracted me almost to the point of insanity. I was constantly watching myself, my secret self, as dependent on my actions as my own personality, sleeping in that bed, behind that door which faced me as I sat at the head of the table. It was very much like being mad, only it was worse because one was aware of it.

I had to shake him for a solid minute, but when at last he opened his eyes it was in the full possession of his senses, with an inquiring look.

"All's well so far," I whispered. "Now you must vanish into the bathroom."

He did so, as noiseless as a ghost, and then I rang for the steward, and facing him boldly, directed him to tidy up my stateroom while I was having my bath—"and be quick about it." As my tone admitted of no excuses, he said, "Yes, sir," and ran off to fetch his dustpan and brushes. I took a bath and did most of my dressing, splashing, and whistling softly for the steward's edification, while the secret sharer of my life stood drawn up bolt upright in that little space, his face looking very sunken in daylight, his eyelids lowered under the stern, dark line of his eyebrows drawn together by a slight frown.

When I left him there to go back to my room the steward was finishing dusting. I sent for the mate and engaged him in some insignificant conversation. It was, as it were, trifling with the terrific character of his whiskers; but my object was to give him the opportunity for a good look at my cabin. And then I could at last shut, with a clear conscience, the door of my stateroom and get my double back into the recessed part. There was nothing else for it. He had to sit still on a small folding stool, half smothered by the heavy coats hanging there. We listened to the steward going into the bathroom out of the saloon, filling the water bottles there, scrubbing the bath, setting things to rights, whisk, bang, clatter—out again into the saloon—turn the key—click. Such was my scheme for keeping my second self invisible. Nothing better could be contrived under the circumstances. And there we sat; I at my writing desk ready to appear busy with some papers, he behind me out of sight of the door. It would not have been prudent to talk in daytime; and I could not have stood the excitement of that queer sense of whispering to myself. Now and then, glancing over my shoulder, I saw him far back there, sitting rigidly on the low stool, his bare feet close together, his arms folded, his head hanging on his breast—and perfectly still. Anybody would have taken him for me.

I was fascinated by it myself. Every moment I had to glance over my shoulder. I was looking at him when a voice outside the door said:

"Beg pardon, sir."

"Well!" . . . I kept my eyes on him, and so when the voice outside the door announced, "There's a ship's boat coming our way, sir," I saw him give a start—the first movement he had made for hours. But he did not raise his bowed head.

"All right. Get the ladder over."

I hesitated. Should I whisper something to him? But what? His immobility seemed to have been never disturbed. What could I tell him he did not know already? . . . Finally I went on deck.

II

The skipper of the *Sephora* had a thin red whisker all round his face, and the sort of complexion that goes with hair of that color; also the particular, rather smeary shade of blue in the eyes. He was not exactly a showy figure; his shoulders were high, his stature but middling—one leg slightly more bandy than the other. He shook hands, looking vaguely around. A spiritless tenacity was his main characteristic, I judged. I behaved with a politeness which seemed to disconcert him. Perhaps he was shy. He mumbled to me as if he were ashamed of what he was saying; gave his name (it was something like Archbold—but at this distance of years I hardly am sure), his ship's name, and a few other particulars of that sort, in the manner of a criminal making a reluctant and doleful confession. He had had terrible weather on the passage out—terrible—terrible—wife aboard, too.

By this time we were seated in the cabin and the steward brought in a tray with a bottle and glasses. "Thanks! No." Never took liquor. Would have some water, though. He drank two tumblerfuls. Terrible thirsty work. Ever since daylight had been exploring the islands round his ship.

"What was that for—fun?" I asked, with an appearance of polite interest.

"No!" He sighed. "Painful duty."

As he persisted in his mumbling and I wanted my double to hear every word, I hit upon the notion of informing him that I regretted to say I was hard of hearing.

"Such a young man, too!" he nodded, keeping his smeary blue, unintelligent eyes fastened upon me. "What was the cause of it—some disease?" he inquired, without the least sympathy and as if he thought that, if so, I'd got no more than I deserved.

"Yes; disease," I admitted in a cheerful tone which seemed to shock him. But my point was gained, because he had to raise his voice to give me his tale. It is not worth while to record that version. It was just over two months since all this had happened, and he had thought so much about it that he seemed completely muddled as to its bearings, but still immensely impressed.

"What would you think of such a thing happening on board your own ship? I've had the *Sephora* for these fifteen years. I am a well-known shipmaster."

He was densely distressed—and perhaps I should have sympathized with him if I had been able to detach my mental vision from the unsuspected sharer of my cabin as though he were my second self. There he was on the other side of the bulkhead, four or five feet from us, no more, as we sat in the saloon. I looked politely at Captain Archbold (if that was his name), but it was the other I saw, in a gray sleeping suit, seated on a low stool, his bare feet close together, his arms folded, and every word said between us falling into the ears of his dark head bowed on his chest.

"I have been at sea now, man and boy, for seven-and-thirty years, and I've never heard of such a thing happening in an English ship. And that it should be my ship. Wife on board, too."

I was hardly listening to him.

"Don't you think," I said, "that the heavy sea which, you told me, came aboard just then might have killed the man? I have seen the sheer weight of a sea kill a man very neatly, by simply breaking his neck."

"Good God!" he uttered, impressively, fixing his smeary blue eyes on me. "The sea! No man killed by the sea ever looked like that." He seemed positively scandalized at my suggestion. And as I gazed at him certainly not prepared for anything original on his part, he advanced his head close to mine and thrust his tongue out at me so suddenly that I couldn't help starting back.

After scoring over my calmness in this graphic way he nodded wisely. If I had seen the sight, he assured me, I would never forget it as long as I lived. The weather was too bad to give the corpse a proper sea burial. So next day at dawn they took it up on the poop, covering its face with a bit of bunting; he read a short prayer, and then, just as it was, in its oilskins and long boots, they launched it amongst those mountainous seas that seemed ready every moment to swallow up the ship herself and the terrified lives on board of her.

"That reefed foresail saved you," I threw in.

"Under God—it did," he exclaimed fervently. "It was by a special mercy, I firmly believe, that it stood some of those hurricane squalls."

"It was the setting of that sail which—" I began.

"God's own hand in it," he interrupted me. "Nothing less could have done it. I don't mind telling you that I hardly dared give the order. It seemed impossible that we could touch anything without losing it, and then our last hope would have been gone."

The terror of that gale was on him yet. I let him go on for a bit, then said, casually—as if returning to a minor subject:

"You were very anxious to give up your mate to the shore people, I believe?"

He was. To the law. His obscure tenacity on that point had in it something incomprehensible and a little awful; something, as it were, mystical, quite apart from his anxiety that he should not be suspected of "countenancing any doings of that sort." Seven-and-thirty virtuous years at sea, of which over twenty of immaculate command, and the last fifteen in the *Sephora*, seemed to have laid him under some pitiless obligation.

"And you know," he went on, groping shame-facedly amongst his feelings, "I did not engage that young fellow. His people had some interest with my owners. I was in a way forced to take him on. He looked very smart, very gentlemanly, and all that. But do you know—I never liked him, somehow. I am a plain man. You see, he wasn't exactly the sort for the chief mate of a ship like the *Sephora*."

I had become so connected in thoughts and impressions with the secret sharer of my cabin that I felt as if I, personally, were being given to understand that I, too, was not the sort that would have done for the chief mate of a ship like the *Sephora*. I had no doubt of it in my mind.

"Not at all the style of man. You understand," he insisted, superfluously, looking hard at me.

I smiled urbanely. He seemed at a loss for a while.

"I suppose I must report a suicide."

"Beg pardon?"

"Sui-cide! That's what I'll have to write to my owners directly I get in."

"Unless you manage to recover him before tomorrow," I assented, dispassionately. . . . "I mean, alive."

He mumbled something which I really did not catch, and I turned my ear to him in a puzzled manner. He fairly bawled:

"The land—I say, the mainland is at least seven miles off my anchorage."

"About that."

My lack of excitement, of curiosity, of surprise, of any sort of pronounced interest, began to arouse his distrust. But except for the felicitous pretense of deafness I had not tried to pretend anything. I had felt utterly incapable of playing the part of ignorance properly, and therefore was afraid to try. It is also certain that he had brought some ready-made suspicions with him, and that he viewed my politeness as a strange and unnatural phenomenon. And yet how else could I have received him? Not heartily! That was impossible for psychological reasons, which I need not state here. My only object was to keep off his inquiries. Surlily? Yes, but surliness might have provoked a point-blank question. From its novelty to him and from its nature, punctilious courtesy was the manner best calculated to restrain the man. But there was the

danger of his breaking through my defense bluntly. I could not, I think, have met him by a direct lie, also for psychological (not moral) reasons. If he had only known how afraid I was of his putting my feeling of identity with the other to the test! But, strangely enough— (I thought of it only afterwards)—I believe that he was not a little disconcerted by the reverse side of that weird situation, by something in me that reminded him of the man he was seeking—suggested a mysterious similitude to the young fellow he had distrusted and disliked from the first.

However that might have been, the silence was not very prolonged. He took another oblique step.

"I reckon I had no more than a two-mile pull to your ship. Not a bit more."

"And quite enough, too, in this awful heat," I said.

Another pause full of mistrust followed. Necessity, they say, is mother of invention, but fear, too, is not barren of ingenious suggestions. And I was afraid he would ask me point-blank for news of my other self.

"Nice little saloon, isn't it?" I remarked, as if noticing for the first time the way his eyes roamed from one closed door to the other. "And very well fitted out, too. Here, for instance," I continued, reaching over the back of my seat negligently and flinging the door open, "is my bathroom."

He made an eager movement, but hardly gave it a glance. I got up, shut the door of the bathroom, and invited him to have a look round, as if I were very proud of my accommodation. He had to rise and be shown round, but he went through the business without any raptures whatever.

"And now we'll have a look at my stateroom," I declared, in a voice as loud as I dared to make it, crossing the cabin to the starboard side with purposely heavy steps.

He followed me in and gazed around. My intelligent double had vanished. I played my part.

"Very convenient—isn't it?"

"Very nice. Very comf . . ." He didn't finish and went out brusquely as if to escape from some unrighteous wiles of mine. But it was not to be. I had been too frightened not to feel vengeful; I felt I had him on the run, and I meant to keep him on the run. My polite insistence must have had something menacing in it, because he gave in suddenly. And I did not let him off a single item; mate's room, pantry, storerooms, the very sail locker which was also under the poop—he had to look into them all. When at last I showed him out on the quarter-deck he drew a long, spiritless sigh, and mumbled dismally that he must really be going back to his ship now. I desired my mate, who had joined us, to see to the captain's boat.

The man of whiskers gave a blast on the whistle which he used to wear hanging round his neck, and yelled, "*Sephora's* away!" My double down there in my cabin must have heard, and certainly could not feel more relieved than I. Four fellows came running out from somewhere forward and went over the side, while my own men, appearing on deck too, lined the rail. I escorted my visitor to the gangway ceremoniously, and nearly overdid it. He was a tenacious beast. On the very ladder he lingered, and in that unique, guiltily conscientious manner of sticking to the point:

"I   say . . . you . . . you   don't   think that——"

I covered his voice loudly:

"Certainly not . . . I am delighted. Good-bye."

I had an idea of what he meant to say, and just saved myself by the privilege of defective hearing. He was too shaken generally to insist, but my mate, close witness of that parting, looked mystified and his face took on a thoughtful cast. As I did not want to appear as if I wished to avoid all communication with my officers, he had the opportunity to address me.

"Seems a very nice man. His boat's crew told our chaps a very extraordinary story, if what I am told by the steward is true. I suppose you had it from the captain, sir?"

"Yes. I had a story from the captain."

"A very horrible affair—isn't it, sir?"

"It is."

"Beats all these tales we hear about murders in Yankee ships."

"I don't think it beats them. I don't think it resembles them in the least."

"Bless my soul—you don't say so! But of course I've no acquaintance whatever with American ships, not I, so I couldn't go against your knowledge. It's horrible enough for me. . . . But the queerest part is that those fellows seemed to have some idea the man was hidden aboard here. They had really. Did you ever hear of such a thing?"

"Preposterous—isn't it?"

We were walking to and fro athwart the quarter-deck. No one of the crew forward could be seen (the day was Sunday), and the mate pursued:

"There was some little dispute about it. Our chaps took offense. 'As if we would harbor a thing like that,' they said. 'Wouldn't you like to look for him in our coalhole?' Quite a tiff. But they made it up in the end. I suppose he did drown himself. Don't you, sir?"

"I don't suppose anything."

"You have no doubt in the matter, sir?"

"None whatever."

I left him suddenly. I felt I was producing a bad impression, but with my double down there it was most trying to be on deck. And it was almost as trying to be below. Altogether a nerve-trying situation. But on the whole I felt less torn in two when I was with him. There was no one in the whole ship whom I dared take into my confidence. Since the hands had got to know his story, it would have been impossible to pass him off for anyone else, and an accidental discovery was to be dreaded now more than ever. . . .

The steward being engaged in laying the table for dinner, we could talk only with our eyes when I first went down. Later in the afternoon we had a cautious try at whispering. The Sunday quietness of the ship was against us; the stillness of air and water around her was against us; the elements, the men were against us—everything was against us in our secret partnership; time itself—for this could not go on forever. The very trust in Providence was, I suppose, denied to his guilt. Shall I confess that this thought cast me down very much? And as to the chapter of accidents which counts for so much in the book of success, I could only hope that it was closed. For what favorable accident could be expected?

"Did you hear everything?" were my first words as soon as we took up our position side by side, leaning over my bed place.

He had. And the proof of it was his earnest whisper, "The man told you he hardly dared to give the order."

I understood the reference to be to that saving foresail.

"Yes. He was afraid of it being lost in the setting."

"I assure you he never gave the order. He may think he did, but he never gave it. He stood there with me on the break of the poop after the main topsail blew away, and whimpered about our last hope—positively whimpered about it and nothing else—and the night coming on! To hear one's skipper go on like that in such weather was enough to drive any fellow out of his mind. It worked me up into a sort of desperation. I just took it into my own hands and went away from him, boiling, and—But what's the use telling you? *You* know! . . . Do you think that if I had not been pretty fierce with them I should have got the men to do anything? Not It! The bo's'n[14] perhaps? Perhaps! It wasn't a heavy sea—it was a sea gone mad! I suppose the end of the world will be something like that; and a man may have the heart to see it coming once and

be done with it—but to have to face it day after day—I don't blame anybody. I was precious little better than the rest. Only—I was an officer of that old coal wagon, anyhow—"

"I quite understand," I conveyed that sincere assurance into his ear. He was out of breath with whispering; I could hear him pant slightly. It was all very simple. The same strung-up force which had given twenty-four men a chance, at least, for their lives, had, in a sort of recoil, crushed an unworthy mutinous existence.

But I had no leisure to weigh the merits of the matter—footsteps in the saloon, a heavy knock. "There's enough wind to get under way with, sir." Here was the call of a new claim upon my thoughts and even upon my feelings.

"Turn the hands up," I cried through the door. "I'll be on deck directly."

I was going out to make the acquaintance of my ship. Before I left the cabin our eyes met—the eyes of the only two strangers on board. I pointed to the recessed part where the little campstool awaited him and laid my finger on my lips. He made a gesture—somewhat vague—a little mysterious, accompanied by a faint smile, as if of regret.

This is not the place to enlarge upon the sensations of a man who feels for the first time a ship move under his feet to his own independent word. In my case they were not unalloyed.[15] I was not wholly alone with my command; for there was that stranger in my cabin. Or rather, I was not completely and wholly with her. Part of me was absent. That mental feeling of being in two places at once affected me physically as if the mood of secrecy had penetrated my very soul. Before an hour had elapsed since the ship had begun to move, having occasion to ask the mate (he stood by my side) to take a compass bearing of

---

14. **bo's' n** (bō' s'n): contracted form of *boatswain*; the petty officer in charge of the deck crew.
15. **unalloyed:** unmixed, unqualified.

the pagoda, I caught myself reaching up to his ear in whispers. I say I caught myself, but enough had escaped to startle the man. I can't describe it otherwise than by saying that he shied. A grave, preoccupied manner, as though he were in possession of some perplexing intelligence, did not leave him henceforth. A little later I moved away from the rail to look at the compass with such a stealthy gait that the helmsman noticed it—and I could not help noticing the unusual roundness of his eyes. These are trifling instances, though it's to no commander's advantage to be suspected of ludicrous eccentricities. But I was also more seriously affected. There are to a seaman certain words, gestures, that should in given conditions come as naturally, as instinctively as the winking of a menaced eye. A certain order should spring on to his lips without thinking; a certain sign should get itself made, so to speak, without reflection. But all unconscious alertness had abandoned me. I had to make an effort of will to recall myself back (from the cabin) to the conditions of the moment. I felt that I was appearing an irresolute commander to those people who were watching me more or less critically.

And, besides, there were the scares. On the second day out, for instance, coming off the deck in the afternoon (I had straw slippers on my bare feet) I stopped at the open pantry door and spoke to the steward. He was doing something there with his back to me. At the sound of my voice he nearly jumped out of his skin, as the saying is, and incidentally broke a cup.

"What on earth's the matter with you?" I asked, astonished.

He was extremely confused. "Beg your pardon, sir. I made sure you were in your cabin."

"You see I wasn't."

"No, sir. I could have sworn I had heard you moving in there not a moment ago. It's most extraordinary . . . very sorry, sir."

I passed on with an inward shudder. I was so identified with my secret double that I did not even mention the fact in those scanty, fearful whispers we exchanged. I suppose he had made some slight noise of some kind or other. It would have been miraculous if he hadn't at one time or another. And yet, haggard as he appeared, he looked always perfectly self-controlled, more than calm—almost invulnerable. On my suggestion he remained almost entirely in the bathroom, which, upon the whole, was the safest place. There could be really no shadow of an excuse for anyone ever wanting to go in there, once the steward had done with it. It was a very tiny place. Sometimes he reclined on the floor, his legs bent, his head sustained on one elbow. At others I would find him on the campstool, sitting in his gray sleeping suit and with his cropped dark hair like a patient, unmoved convict. At night I would smuggle him into my bed place, and we would whisper together, with the regular footfalls of the officer of the watch passing and repassing over our heads. It was an infinitely miserable time. It was lucky that some tins of fine preserves were stowed in a locker in my stateroom; hard bread I could always get hold of; and so he lived on stewed chicken, *pâté de foie gras*,[16] asparagus, cooked oysters, sardines—on all sorts of abominable sham delicacies out of tins. My early-morning coffee he always drank; and it was all I dared do for him in that respect.

Every day there was the horrible maneuvering to go through so that my room and then the bathroom should be done in the usual way. I came to hate the sight of the steward, to abhor the voice of that harmless man. I felt that it was he who would bring on the disaster of discovery. It hung like a sword over our heads.

The fourth day out, I think (we were then working down the east side of the Gulf of Siam, tack for tack, in light winds and smooth

---

16. **pâté de foie gras** (pätä′ də fwä′ grä′) *French:* a paste made of livers of fattened geese.

water)—the fourth day, I say, of this miserable juggling with the unavoidable, as we sat at our evening meal, that man, whose slightest movement I dreaded, after putting down the dishes ran up on deck busily. This could not be dangerous. Presently he came down again; and then it appeared that he had remembered a coat of mine which I had thrown over a rail to dry after having been wetted in a shower which had passed over the ship in the afternoon. Sitting stolidly at the head of the table I became terrified at the sight of the garment on his arm. Of course he made for my door. There was no time to lose.

"Steward," I thundered. My nerves were so shaken that I could not govern my voice and conceal my agitation. This was the sort of thing that made my terrifically whiskered mate tap his forehead with his forefinger. I had detected him using that gesture while talking on deck with a confidential air to the carpenter. It was too far to hear a word, but I had no doubt that this pantomime could only refer to the strange new captain.

"Yes, sir," the pale-faced steward turned resignedly to me. It was this maddening course of being shouted at, checked without rhyme or reason, arbitrarily chased out of my cabin, suddenly called into it, sent flying out of his pantry on incomprehensible errands, that accounted for the growing wretchedness of his expression.

"Where are you going with that coat?"

"To your room, sir."

"Is there another shower coming?"

"I'm sure I don't know, sir. Shall I go up again and see, sir?"

"No! never mind."

My object was attained, as of course my other self in there would have heard everything that passed. During this interlude my two officers never raised their eyes off their respective plates; but the lip of that confounded cub, the second mate, quivered visibly.

I expected the steward to hook my coat on and come out at once. He was very slow about it; but I dominated my nervousness sufficiently not to shout after him. Suddenly I became aware (it could be heard plainly enough) that the fellow for some reason or other was opening the door of the bathroom. It was the end. The place was literally not big enough to swing a cat in. My voice died in my throat and I went stony all over. I expected to hear a yell of surprise and terror, and made a movement, but had not the strength to get on my legs. Everything remained still. Had my second self taken the poor wretch by the throat? I don't know what I could have done next moment if I had not seen the steward come out of my room, close the door, and then stand quietly by the sideboard.

"Saved," I thought. "But, no! Lost! Gone! He was gone!"

I laid my knife and fork down and leaned back in my chair. My head swam. After a while, when sufficiently recovered to speak in a steady voice, I instructed my mate to put the ship round at eight o'clock himself.

"I won't come on deck," I went on. "I think I'll turn in, and unless the wind shifts I don't want to be disturbed before midnight. I feel a bit seedy."

"You did look middling bad a little while ago," the chief mate remarked without showing any great concern.

They both went out, and I stared at the steward clearing the table. There was nothing to be read on that wretched man's face. But why did he avoid my eyes, I asked myself. Then I thought I should like to hear the sound of his voice.

"Steward!"

"Sir!" Startled as usual.

"Where did you hang up that coat?"

"In the bathroom, sir." The usual anxious tone. "It's not quite dry yet, sir."

For some time longer I sat in the cuddy. Had my double vanished as he had come? But of his coming there was an explanation, whereas his disappearance would be inexplicable. . . . I went slowly into my dark room, shut the door, lighted the lamp, and for a time dared not turn round. When at last I did I saw him standing bolt-upright in the narrow recessed part. It would not be true to say I had a shock, but an irresistible doubt of his bodily existence flitted through my mind. Can it be, I asked myself, that he is not visible to other eyes than mine? It was like being haunted. Motionless, with a grave face, he raised his hands slightly at me in a gesture which meant clearly, "Heavens! what a narrow escape!" Narrow indeed. I think I had come creeping quietly as near insanity as any man who has not actually gone over the border. That gesture restrained me, so to speak.

The mate with the terrific whiskers was now putting the ship on the other tack. In the moment of profound silence which follows upon the hands going to their stations I heard on the poop his raised voice: "Hard alee!" and the distant shout of the order repeated on the main-deck. The sails, in that light breeze, made but a faint fluttering noise. It ceased. The ship was coming round slowly: I held my breath in the renewed stillness of expectation; one wouldn't have thought that there was a single living soul on her decks. A sudden brisk shout, "Mainsail haul!" broke the spell, and in the noisy cries and rush overhead of the men running away with the main brace we two, down in my cabin, came together in our usual position by the bed place.

He did not wait for my question. "I heard him fumbling here and just managed to squat myself down in the bath," he whispered to me. "The fellow only opened the door and put his arm in to hang the coat up. All the same—"

"I never thought of that," I whispered back, even more appalled than before at the closeness of the shave, and marveling at that something unyielding in his character which was carrying him through so finely. There was no agitation in his whisper. Whoever was being driven distracted, it was not he. He was

sane. And the proof of his sanity was continued when he took up the whispering again.

"It would never do for me to come to life again."

It was something that a ghost might have said. But what he was alluding to was his old captain's reluctant admission of the theory of suicide. It would obviously serve his turn—if I had understood at all the view which seemed to govern the unalterable purpose of his action.

"You must maroon me as soon as ever you can get amongst these islands off the Cambodge[17] shore," he went on.

"Maroon you! We are not living in a boy's adventure tale," I protested. His scornful whispering took me up.

"We aren't indeed! There's nothing of a boy's tale in this. But there's nothing else for it. I want no more. You don't suppose I am afraid of what can be done to me? Prison or gallows or whatever they may please. But you don't see me coming back to explain such things to an old fellow in a wig and twelve respectable tradesmen, do you? What can they know whether I am guilty or not—or of *what* I am guilty, either? That's my affair. What does the Bible say? 'Driven off the face of the earth.' Very well, I am off the face of the earth now. As I came at night so I shall go."

"Impossible!" I murmured. "You can't."

"Can't? . . . Not naked like a soul on the Day of Judgment. I shall freeze on to this sleeping suit. The Last Day is not yet—and . . . you have understood thoroughly. Didn't you?"

I felt suddenly ashamed of myself. I may say truly that I understood—and my hesitation in letting that man swim away from my ship's side had been a mere sham sentiment, a sort of cowardice.

"It can't be done now till next night," I breathed out. "The ship is on the off-shore tack and the wind may fail us."

---

17. **Cambodge:** Cambodia.

"As long as I know that you understand," he whispered. "But of course you do. It's a great satisfaction to have got somebody to understand. You seem to have been there on purpose." And in the same whisper, as if we two whenever we talked had to say things to each other which were not fit for the world to hear, he added, "It's very wonderful."

We remained side by side talking in our secret way—but sometimes silent or just exchanging a whispered word or two at long intervals. And as usual he stared through the port. A breath of wind came now and again into our faces. The ship might have been moored in dock, so gently and on an even keel she slipped through the water, that did not murmur even at our passage, shadowy and silent like a phantom sea.

At midnight I went on deck, and to my mate's great surprise put the ship round on the other tack. His terrible whiskers flitted round me in silent criticism. I certainly should not have done it if it had been only a question of getting out of that sleepy gulf as quickly as possible. I believe he told the second mate, who relieved him, that it was a great want of judgment. The other only yawned. That intolerable cub shuffled about so sleepily and lolled against the rails in such a slack, improper fashion that I came down on him sharply.

"Aren't you properly awake yet?"

"Yes, sir! I am awake."

"Well, then, be good enough to hold yourself as if you were. And keep a lookout. If there's any current we'll be closing with some islands before daylight."

The east side of the gulf is fringed with islands, some solitary, others in groups. On the blue background of the high coast they seem to float on silvery patches of calm water, arid and gray, or dark green and rounded like clumps of evergreen bushes, with the larger ones, a mile or two long, showing the outlines of ridges, ribs of gray rock under the dank mantle of matted leafage. Unknown to

trade, to travel, almost to geography, the manner of life they harbor is an unsolved secret. There must be villages—settlements of fishermen at least—on the largest of them, and some communication with the world is probably kept up by native craft. But all that forenoon, as we headed for them, fanned along by the faintest of breezes, I saw no sign of man or canoe in the field of the telescope I kept on pointing at the scattered group.

At noon I gave no orders for a change of course, and the mate's whiskers became much concerned and seemed to be offering themselves unduly to my notice. At last I said:

"I am going to stand right in. Quite in—as far as I can take her."

The stare of extreme surprise imparted an air of ferocity also to his eyes, and he looked truly terrific for a moment.

"We're not doing well in the middle of the gulf," I continued, casually. "I am going to look for the land breezes tonight."

"Bless my soul! Do you mean, sir, in the dark amongst the lot of all them islands and reefs and shoals?"

"Well—if there are any regular land breezes at all on this coast one must get close inshore to find them, mustn't one?"

"Bless my soul!" he exclaimed again under his breath. All that afternoon he wore a dreamy, contemplative appearance which in him was a mark of perplexity. After dinner I went into my stateroom as if I meant to take some rest. There we two bent our dark heads over a half-unrolled chart lying on my bed.

"There," I said. "It's got to be Koh-ring. I've been looking at it ever since sunrise. It has got two hills and a low point. It must be inhabited. And on the coast opposite there is what looks like the mouth of a biggish river—with some towns, no doubt, not far up. It's the best chance for you that I can see."

"Anything. Koh-ring let it be."

He looked thoughtfully at the chart as if surveying chances and distances from a lofty height—and following with his eyes his own figure wandering on the blank land of Cochin-China, and then passing off that piece of paper clean out of sight into uncharted regions. And it was as if the ship had two captains to plan her course for her. I had been so worried and restless running up and down that I had not had the patience to dress that day. I had remained in my sleeping suit, with straw slippers and a soft floppy hat. The closeness of the heat in the gulf had been most oppressive, and the crew were used to seeing me wandering in that airy attire.

"She will clear the south point as she heads now," I whispered into his ear. "Goodness only knows when, though, but certainly after dark. I'll edge her in to half a mile, as far as I may be able to judge in the dark—"

"Be careful," he murmured, warningly—and I realized suddenly that all my future, the only future for which I was fit, would perhaps go irretrievably to pieces in any mishap to my first command.

I could not stop a moment longer in the room. I motioned him to get out of sight and made my way on the poop. That unplayful cub had the watch. I walked up and down for a while thinking things out, then beckoned him over.

"Send a couple of hands to open the two quarter-deck ports," I said, mildly.

He actually had the impudence, or else so forgot himself in his wonder at such an incomprehensible order, as to repeat:

"Open the quarter-deck ports! What for, sir?"

"The only reason you need concern yourself about is because I tell you to do so. Have them open wide and fastened properly."

He reddened and went off, but I believe made some jeering remark to the carpenter as to the sensible practice of ventilating a ship's quarter-deck. I know he popped into the mate's cabin to impart the fact to him because the whiskers came on deck, as it were by chance, and stole glances at me from below—for signs of lunacy or drunkenness, I suppose.

A little before supper, feeling more restless than ever, I rejoined, for a moment, my second self. And to find him sitting so quietly was surprising, like something against nature, inhuman.

I developed my plan in a hurried whisper.

"I shall stand in as close as I dare and then put her round. I will presently find means to smuggle you out of here into the sail locker, which communicates with the lobby. But there is an opening, a sort of square for hauling the sails out, which gives straight on the quarter-deck and which is never closed in fine weather, so as to give air to the sails. When the ship's way is deadened in stays and all the hands are aft at the main braces you will have a clear road to slip out and get overboard through the open quarter-deck port. I've had them both fastened up. Use a rope's end to lower yourself into the water so as to avoid a splash—you know. It could be heard and cause some beastly complication."

He kept silent for a while, then whispered, "I understand."

"I won't be there to see you go," I began with an effort. "The rest . . . I only hope I have understood, too."

"You have. From first to last"—and for the first time there seemed to be a faltering, something strained in his whisper. He caught hold of my arm, but the ringing of the supper bell made me start. He didn't though; he only released his grip.

After supper I didn't come below again till well past eight o'clock. The faint, steady breeze was loaded with dew; and the wet, darkened sails held all there was of propelling power in it. The night, clear and starry, sparkled darkly, and the opaque, lightless patches shifting slowly against the low stars were the drifting islets. On the port bow there was a big one more distant and shadowily imposing by the great space of sky it eclipsed.

On opening the door I had a back view of

my very own self looking at a chart. He had come out of the recess and was standing near the table.

"Quite dark enough," I whispered.

He stepped back and leaned against my bed with a level, quiet glance. I sat on the couch. We had nothing to say to each other. Over our heads the officer of the watch moved here and there. Then I heard him move quickly. I knew what that meant. He was making for the companion; and presently his voice was outside my door.

"We are drawing in pretty fast, sir. Land looks rather close."

"Very well," I answered. "I am coming on deck directly."

I waited till he was gone out of the cuddy, then rose. My double moved too. The time had come to exchange our last whispers, for neither of us was ever to hear each other's natural voice.

"Look here!" I opened a drawer and took out three sovereigns. "Take this anyhow. I've got six and I'd give you the lot, only I must keep a little money to buy some fruit and vegetables for the crew from native boats as we go through Sunda Straits."

He shook his head.

"Take it," I urged him, whispering desperately. "No one can tell what—"

He smiled and slapped meaningly the only pocket of the sleeping jacket. It was not safe, certainly. But I produced a large old silk handkerchief of mine, and tying the three pieces of gold in a corner, pressed it on him. He was touched, I supposed, because he took it at last and tied it quickly round his waist under the jacket, on his bare skin.

Our eyes met; several seconds elapsed, till, our glances still mingled, I extended my hand and turned the lamp out. Then I passed through the cuddy, leaving the door of my room wide open. . . . "Steward!"

He was still lingering in the pantry in the greatness of his zeal, giving a rub-up to a plated cruet stand the last thing before going to bed. Being careful not to wake up the mate, whose room was opposite, I spoke in an undertone.

He looked round anxiously. "Sir!"

"Can you get me a little hot water from the galley?"

"I am afraid, sir, the galley fire's been out for some time now."

"Go and see."

He flew up the stairs.

"Now," I whispered, loudly, into the saloon —too loudly, perhaps, but I was afraid I couldn't make a sound. He was by my side in an instant—the double captain slipped past the stairs—through a tiny dark passage . . . a sliding door. We were in the sail locker, scrambling on our knees over the sails. A sudden thought struck me. I saw myself wandering barefooted, bareheaded, the sun beating on my dark poll. I snatched off my floppy hat and tried hurriedly in the dark to ram it on my other self. He dodged and fended off silently. I wonder what he thought had come to me before he understood and suddenly desisted. Our hands met gropingly, lingered united in a steady, motionless clasp for a second. . . . No word was breathed by either of us when they separated.

I was standing quietly by the pantry door when the steward returned.

"Sorry, sir. Kettle barely warm. Shall I light the spirit lamp?"

"Never mind."

I came out on deck slowly. It was now a matter of conscience to shave the land as close as possible—for now he must go overboard whenever the ship was put in stays. Must! There could be no going back for him. After a moment I walked over to leeward and my heart flew into my mouth at the nearness of the land on the bow. Under any other circumstances I would not have held on a minute longer. The second mate had followed me anxiously.

I looked on till I felt I could command my voice.

"She will weather," I said then in a quiet tone.

"Are you going to try that, sir?" he stammered out incredulously.

I took no notice of him and raised my tone just enough to be heard by the helmsman.

"Keep her good full."

"Good full, sir."

The wind fanned my cheek, the sails slept, the world was silent. The strain of watching the dark loom of the land grow bigger and denser was too much for me. I had shut my eyes—because the ship must go closer. She must! The stillness was intolerable. Were we standing still?

When I opened my eyes the second view started my heart with a thump. The black southern hill of Koh-ring seemed to hang right over the ship like a towering fragment of the everlasting night. On that enormous mass of blackness there was not a gleam to be seen, not a sound to be heard. It was gliding irresistibly towards us and yet seemed already within reach of the hand. I saw the vague figures of the watch grouped in the waist, gazing in awed silence.

"Are you going on, sir?" inquired an unsteady voice at my elbow.

I ignored it. I had to go on.

"Keep her full. Don't check her way. That won't do now," I said, warningly.

"I can't see the sails very well," the helmsman answered me, in strange, quavering tones.

Was she close enough? Already she was, I won't say in the shadow of the land, but in the very blackness of it, already swallowed up as it were, gone too close to be recalled, gone from me altogether.

"Give the mate a call," I said to the young man who stood at my elbow as still as death. "And turn all hands up."

My tone had a borrowed loudness reverberated from the height of the land. Several voices cried out together: "We are all on deck, sir."

Then stillness again, with the great shadow gliding closer, towering higher, without a light, without a sound. Such a hush had fallen on the ship that she might have been a bark of the dead floating in slowly under the very gate of Erebus.[18]

"My God! Where are we?"

It was the mate moaning at my elbow. He was thunderstruck, and as it were deprived of the moral support of his whiskers. He clapped his hands and absolutely cried out, "Lost!"

"Be quiet," I said, sternly.

He lowered his tone, but I saw the shadowy gesture of his despair. "What are we doing here?"

"Looking for the land wind."

He made as if to tear his hair, and addressed me recklessly.

"She will never get out. You have done it, sir. I knew it'd end in something like this. She will never weather, and you are too close now to stay. She'll drift ashore before she's round. O my God!"

I caught his arm as he was raising it to batter his poor devoted head, and shook it violently.

"She's ashore already," he wailed, trying to tear himself away.

"Is she? . . . Keep good full there!"

"Good full, sir," cried the helmsman in a frightened, thin, childlike voice.

I hadn't let go the mate's arm and went on shaking it. "Ready about, do you hear? You go forward"—shake—"and stop there"—shake—"and hold your noise"—shake—"and see these head-sheets properly overhauled"—shake, shake—shake.

And all the time I dared not look towards the land lest my heart should fail me. I released my grip at last and he ran forward as if fleeing for dear life.

I wondered what my double there in the sail locker thought of this commotion. He was

18. **Erebus** (er' ə bəs): in Greek mythology the dark place under the earth through which the dead passed before entering Hades.

able to hear everything—and perhaps he was able to understand why, on my conscience, it had to be thus close—no less. My first order "Hard alee!" re-echoed ominously under the towering shadow of Koh-ring as if I had shouted in a mountain gorge. And then I watched the land intently. In that smooth water and light wind it was impossible to feel the ship coming-to. No! I could not feel her. And my second self was making now ready to ship out and lower himself overboard. Perhaps he was gone already . . . ?

The great black mass brooding over our very mastheads began to pivot away from the ship's side silently. And now I forgot the secret stranger ready to depart, and remembered only that I was a total stranger to the ship. I did not know her. Would she do it? How was she to be handled?

I swung the mainyard and waited helplessly. She was perhaps stopped, and her very fate hung in the balance, with the black mass of Koh-ring like the gate of the everlasting night towering over her taffrail.[19] What would she do now? Had she way on her yet? I stepped to the side swiftly, and on the shadowy water I could see nothing except a faint phosphorescent flash revealing the glassy smoothness of the sleeping surface. It was impossible to tell—and I had not learned yet the feel of my ship. Was she moving? What I needed was something easily seen, a piece of paper, which I could throw overboard and watch. I had nothing on me. To run down for it I didn't dare. There was no time. All at once my strained, yearning stare distinguished a white object floating within a yard of the ship's side. White on the black water. A phosphorescent flash passed under it. What was that thing? . . . I recognized my own floppy hat. It must have fallen off his head . . . and he didn't bother. Now I had what I wanted—the saving mark for my eyes. But I hardly thought of my other self, now gone from the ship, to be hidden forever from all friendly faces, to be a fugitive and a vagabond on the earth, with no

brand of the curse on his sane forehead to stay a slaying hand . . . too proud to explain.

And I watched the hat—the expression of my sudden pity for his mere flesh. It had been meant to save his homeless head from the dangers of the sun. And now—behold—it was saving the ship, by serving me for a mark to help out the ignorance of my strangeness. Ha! It was drifting forward, warning me just in time that the ship had gathered sternway.

"Shift the helm," I said in a low voice to the seaman standing still like a statue.

The man's eyes glistened wildly in the binnacle light as he jumped round to the other side and spun round the wheel.

I walked to the break of the poop. On the overshadowed deck all hands stood by the forebraces waiting for my order. The stars ahead seemed to be gliding from right to left. And all was so still in the world that I heard the quiet remark, "She's round," passed in a tone of intense relief between two seamen.

"Let go and haul."

The foreyards ran round with a great noise, amidst cheery cries. And now the frightful whiskers made themselves heard giving various orders. Already the ship was drawing ahead. And I was alone with her. Nothing! no one in the world should stand now between us, throwing a shadow on the way of silent knowledge and mute affection, the perfect communion of a seaman with his first command.

Walking to the taffrail, I was in time to make out, on the very edge of a darkness thrown by a towering black mass like the very gateway of Erebus—yes, I was in time to catch an evanescent glimpse of my white hat left behind to mark the spot where the secret sharer of my cabin and of my thoughts, as though he were my second self, had lowered himself into the water to take his punishment: a free man, a proud swimmer striking out for a new destiny.

---

19. **taffrail:** the rail around the stern of a ship.

THE MUCH RESOUNDING SEA, 1884. *Thomas Moran.*
National Gallery of Art, Washington, D.C. Gift of the Avalon Foundation, 1967.

Getting at Meaning

Part I

1. As the story opens, the captain is in a state of some uncertainty. What is the nature of that uncertainty, and what factors contribute to it? That night, as he walks the deck alone under the stars, how does he feel about his future life on the sea?

2. What initial impression does the captain make on his officers? Why is he vexed with himself for changing the routine and standing watch?

3. From the beginning, the captain feels a strange kinship with Leggatt. When does this bond first become apparent to the captain? What are some of the things the two have in common?

4. What characteristic of the chief mate makes it more difficult for the captain to deceive him? What aspect of the second mate makes him a challenge to the captain's authority?

5. What is it about Leggatt's story and manner that causes the captain—and perhaps the reader—to sympathize with him? What role did he play in saving his former ship?

6. What makes the captain's cabin an ideal hiding place? Why does the captain choose to jeopardize his command by harboring a fugitive?

7. While Leggatt is hidden aboard the ship, he seems to be a kind of "double" of the captain. Identify in Part I several of the numerous narrative and descriptive details that continually reinforce this idea. What might have prompted the captain to deny this association, saying, "He was not a bit like me, really. . . ."?

Part II

8. When the old captain of the *Sephora* comes aboard, what details indicate that the captain-narrator is not in full sympathy with him? Is there something

unkind in the way the narrator treats him? Why does he ask him to shout? How does he avoid telling him the truth? What are the chief characteristics of the old captain?

9. What does the captain mean when, referring to Leggatt's crime, he says, "The same strung-up force which had given twenty-four men a chance, at least, for their lives, had in a sort of recoil, crushed an unworthy mutinous existence"? What new information has Leggatt just revealed about the situation that led to the crime?

10. In what way does the captain's hiding of Leggatt affect the performance of his duties? What specific incidents illustrate this? What is the effect upon the crew—for example, the steward? How does Leggatt's behavior contrast with that of the captain?

11. What does Leggatt mean when he says to the captain, ". . . you have understood thoroughly. Didn't you"? Why does the narrator suddenly feel ashamed of himself?

12. Why does it become "a matter of conscience to shave the land as close as possible"?

13. How does the captain's hat emphasize the identification of Leggatt with the captain?

14. When Leggatt is gone, what is the effect upon the captain's sense of command? How has he changed since the beginning of the story?

15. At the beginning of the story, the captain wonders if he will "turn out faithful to that ideal conception of one's own personality every man sets up for himself secretly." How might he evaluate himself at the end of the story?

Developing Skills in Reading Literature

1. **Short Story.** A short story is a fictional narrative generally about one central action or event, without the large number of characters and wealth of detail typical of longer works of fiction. In a short story elements of fiction, such as plot, character, setting, point of view, and theme, combine to produce one primary effect. Short stories represent a wide variety of types and styles; "The Secret Sharer," for example, is a psychological study of one character. What narrative method does Conrad employ to reveal the mental and emotional state of this character? How would the choice of a different point of view change the effect of the story? Why is an isolated ship an appropriate setting for a story of this type? In what way is a journey an appropriate framework? Notice the way that the characters all exist in relation to the main character. How does this intensify the effect of the story? Does the simplicity of the plot have the same result?

2. **Setting and Mood.** Examine the opening paragraphs of the story, and identify the details that suggest a dreamlike atmosphere, a strange and eerie mood. Then comment on the atmosphere of the final scene, as the captain brings his ship closer and closer to the land. What is similar about the atmosphere when Leggatt first appears and when he slides back into the sea again?

3. **Characterization.** With skill and economy, Conrad has given a distinct identity to each of the several important characters. Notice the means by which he makes each character recognizable to the reader. What distinctive details of physical appearance and manner are associated with the chief mate, the second mate, and the steward? What mixture of qualities seem to belong to the captain of the *Sephora*? In particular, what values or norms does he represent? What is especially significant in the description of Leggatt? As for the captain, this is his first command, and it is mentioned early that he is "at the starting point of a long journey" and "at the threshold of a long passage." How are these details important in understanding the captain? in understanding the story?

4. **Foil.** A foil is a character who provides a striking contrast to another character. The captain of the *Sephora* functions as a foil to the narrator, thus throwing into sharp focus the relationship between the narrator and Leggatt. In what specific ways is the old captain different from the narrator? as an individual? as a ship's captain? What dilemma does the old captain face in regard to Leggatt? How does he solve the dilemma? What is the narrator's dilemma? How is his solution different from that of the captain?

5. **Flashback.** The linear progression of this plot is interrupted by several flashbacks to incidents that

happened before the beginning of the story. How are these flashbacks introduced into the narrative? What specifically do they reveal about the various characters? Given the nature of this short story, could these incidents be presented as effectively in any other way? Explain.

6. **Imagery and Symbol.** On the surface this is a compelling adventure story that also raises some interesting ethical questions. Is it also more than that? Are there meanings, deeper or symbolic implications? If so, the image patterns in the story may offer helpful clues. First, remember that the narrator early in the story says that he is "somewhat of a stranger" to himself. Later he says, "I was constantly watching myself, my secret self, as dependent on my actions as my own personality, sleeping in that bed, behind that door. . . ." Consider that Leggatt has emerged naked from the water and later slips back into the water again, each time at night. What do you think this means, considering that water often is a symbol of the unconscious? Notice that Leggatt and the narrator communicate only in whispers and through nonverbal signals. Why then is their communication so effective? Is it significant that the narrator gives Leggatt his "sleeping suit"—something people wear when they dream—and that later he wears one as well? Recall also that, when Leggatt is first seen in the water, he seems to be "complete but for the head" and gives off a "phosphorescent light." In view of these and other patterns of images, can you suggest a way of interpreting the character of Leggatt symbolically in relation to the narrator? How would you interpret the entire story on a symbolic level? What kind of interior journey has the narrator taken, and what is its final outcome, once he has managed to cast off his "secret self" into the sea?

7. **Allusion.** As the captain is bringing his ship in through the darkness, ever closer to the land, the setting is described as follows: "Such a hush had fallen on the ship that she might have been the bark of the dead floating in slowly under the very gate of Erebus." Why is this allusion appropriate at this point in the story?

When Leggatt is gone, the narrator, struggling to gain control of his ship, has little time to think of his "other self, now gone from the ship, to be hidden forever from all friendly faces, to be a fugitive and a vagabond on the earth, with no brand of the curse on his sane forehead to stay a slaying hand. . . ." To what is he alluding? How does this allusion connect with the reference to Cain and Abel in the first part of the story? Do Cain and Abel represent the same forces as do Leggatt and the narrator? Explain.

8. **Theme.** If, as the text suggests repeatedly, Leggatt can be viewed as the narrator's double, even his "secret self," what side of his character does Leggatt represent? How does this run counter to the narrator's belief, expressed at the beginning of the story, that the sea offers an "untempted life"?

"The Secret Sharer" belongs to a literary tradition in which a character faces a difficult moral dilemma in the context of a ship at sea. Often in such stories there is a clash between different conceptions of justice or between the rights of an individual and of the community. What moral issues has Conrad posed in this story? Has he suggested any clear answers? In judging Leggatt, what mitigating factors might be considered? Which character in the story represents strong traditional values? How do you think Conrad wishes the reader to judge the narrator's action in hiding Leggatt and in endangering his ship and crew? Does Conrad present the narrator as foolish, immature, or admirable, or is the question simply left open?

Developing Writing Skills

Developing an Argument. In a carefully reasoned essay in which you clearly define your principles, argue either for or against the action taken by the narrator in this story. Whichever side you take, be sure to answer the counterarguments that might be offered. As an alternative, imagine that you are involved in a trial in which the captain has been accused of exposing his crew and his ship to unnecessary danger. Put into writing the summation either of the prosecution or the defense.

Saki (Hector Hugh Munro)

1870–1916

Master of the spoof, the parody, and the finely wrought story, the Scottish writer Hector Hugh Munro might be considered the British version of America's O. Henry. His short stories and sketches are brief masterpieces, intended to delight the reader while exposing the follies of humankind.

Munro was born in Akyab, Burma, the son of a Scottish inspector-general of the Burma police. After his mother died when he was two, he was sent with his brother and sister to live under the care of two unmarried aunts in Devonshire, England. The aunts did not understand children, and the Munro children's life was strict and confined. They were considered sickly, especially Hector, and were seldom allowed to play outside by the aunts, who instead took them shopping and gossiping. The children reacted by drawing and cartooning and by staging elaborate practical jokes. Hector later portrayed his aunts and their friends in his stories.

Munro was educated at Exmouth and Bedford grammar schools and later traveled with his father to France, Germany, Austria, and Czechoslovakia. Through his father's influence, he secured a job with the Burma police in 1893, but after thirteen months, recurrent bouts of malaria forced him to resign the position.

Munro recuperated in England and finally moved to London, where he supported himself by writing parodies of British political figures for the *Westminster Gazette*, using the pen name Saki for the first time. Written in the style of Lewis Carroll, these satiric sketches were collected as *The Westminster Alice* in 1902. Meanwhile, Munro researched and wrote his only serious historical work, *The Rise of the Russian Empire* (1900). He joined the staff of *The Morning Post* in 1902, and for six years he served as foreign correspondent in Paris, St. Petersburg, and the Balkans.

Munro returned to England where he continued to contribute sketches to newspapers and to write short stories. His stories are collected in *Reginald* (1904), *Reginald in Russia* (1910), *The Chronicles of Clovis* (1912), and *Beasts and Super-Beasts* (1914). The novel *The Unbearable Bassington* (1912) describes the adventures of a ridiculous but likable hero. Munro's novels, horror tales, and stories catch the nuances of social interaction. His characters, who bear foppish names such as Latimer Springfield, Mrs. Teresa Thropplestance, and the Froplinsons, embody the superficial values and perform the empty rituals of prewar upper-class society. Their drawing room conversations sparkle with the witty phrase and the cutting rejoinder; their whispered words in the hall underscore Munro's pointed but gentle satire.

When England entered World War I, Munro quickly enlisted, even though he was forty-four. A courageous and dedicated soldier, he was killed in battle after returning to his unit still weak from a flare-up of malaria.

Tobermory

It was a chill, rain-washed afternoon of a late August day, that indefinite season when partridges are still in security or cold storage, and there is nothing to hunt—unless one is bounded on the north by the Bristol Channel, in which case one may lawfully gallop after fat red stags. Lady Blemley's house party was not bounded on the north by the Bristol Channel, hence there was a full gathering of her guests round the tea table on this particular afternoon. And, in spite of the blankness of the season and the triteness of the occasion, there was no trace in the company of that fatigued restlessness which means a dread of the pianola[1] and a subdued hankering for auction bridge. The undisguised open-mouthed attention of the entire party was fixed on the homely negative personality of Mr. Cornelius Appin. Of all her guests, he was the one who had come to Lady Blemley with the vaguest reputation. Someone had said he was "clever," and he had got his invitation in the moderate expectation, on the part of his hostess, that some portion at least of his cleverness would be contributed to the general entertainment. Until teatime that day she had been unable to discover in what direction, if any, his cleverness lay. He was neither a wit nor a croquet champion, a hypnotic force nor a begetter of amateur theatricals. Neither did his exterior suggest the sort of man in whom women are willing to pardon a generous measure of mental deficiency. He had subsided into mere Mr. Appin, and the Cornelius seemed a piece of transparent baptismal bluff. And now he was claiming to have launched on the world a discovery beside which the invention of gunpowder, of the printing press, and of steam locomotion were inconsiderable trifles. Science had made bewildering strides in many directions during recent decades, but this thing seemed to belong to the domain of miracle rather than to scientific achievement.

"And do you really ask us to believe," Sir Wilfrid was saying, "that you have discovered a means for instructing animals in the art of human speech, and that dear old Tobermory has proved your first successful pupil?"

"It is a problem at which I have worked for the last seventeen years," said Mr. Appin, "but only during the last eight or nine months have I been rewarded with glimmerings of success. Of course I have experimented with thousands of animals, but latterly only with cats, those wonderful creatures which have assimilated themselves so marvelously with our civilization while retaining all their highly developed feral[2] instincts. Here and there among cats one comes across an outstanding superior intellect, just as one does among the ruck of human beings, and when I made the acquaintance of Tobermory a week ago I saw at once that I was in contact with a 'Beyond-cat' of extraordinary intelligence. I had gone far along the road to success in recent experiments; with Tobermory, as you call him, I have reached the goal."

Mr. Appin concluded his remarkable statement in a voice which he strove to divest of a triumphant inflection. No one said "Rats," though Clovis's lips moved in a monosyllabic contortion which probably invoked those rodents of disbelief.

"And do you mean to say," asked Miss Resker, after a slight pause, "that you have taught Tobermory to say and understand easy sentences of one syllable?"

---

1. **pianola:** a trademark for a kind of player piano.
2. **feral:** untamed, savage.

"My dear Miss Resker," said the wonder worker patiently, "one teaches little children and savages and backward adults in that piecemeal fashion; when one has once solved the problem of making a beginning with an animal of highly developed intelligence one has no need for those halting methods. Tobermory can speak our language with perfect correctness."

This time Clovis very distinctly said, "Beyond-rats!" Sir Wilfrid was more polite, but equally skeptical.

"Hadn't we better have the cat in and judge for ourselves?" suggested Lady Blemley.

Sir Wilfrid went in search of the animal, and the company settled themselves down to the languid expectation of witnessing some more or less adroit drawing-room ventriloquism.

In a minute Sir Wilfrid was back in the room, his face white beneath its tan and his eyes dilated with excitement.

"By Gad, it's true!"

His agitation was unmistakably genuine, and his hearers started forward in a thrill of awakened interest.

Collapsing into an armchair he continued breathlessly: "I found him dozing in the smoking room, and called out to him to come for his tea. He blinked at me in his usual way, and I said, 'Come on, Toby; don't keep us waiting; and, by Gad! he drawled out in a most horribly natural voice that he'd come when he dashed well pleased! I nearly jumped out of my skin!"

Appin had preached to absolutely incredulous hearers; Sir Wilfrid's statement carried instant conviction. A Babel-like[3] chorus of startled exclamation arose, amid which the scientist sat mutely enjoying the first fruit of his stupendous discovery.

In the midst of the clamor Tobermory entered the room and made his way with velvet tread and studied unconcern across to the group seated round the tea table.

A sudden hush of awkwardness and constraint fell on the company. Somehow there seemed an element of embarrassment in addressing on equal terms a domestic cat of acknowledged mental ability.

"Will you have some milk, Tobermory?" asked Lady Blemley in a rather strained voice.

"I don't mind if I do," was the response, couched in a tone of even indifference. A shiver of suppressed excitement went through the listeners, and Lady Blemley might be excused for pouring out the saucerful of milk rather unsteadily.

"I'm afraid I've spilt a good deal of it," she said apologetically.

"After all, it's not my Axminster,"[4] was Tobermory's rejoinder.

Another silence fell on the group, and then Miss Resker, in her best district-visitor manner, asked if the human language had been difficult to learn. Tobermory looked squarely at her for a moment and then fixed his gaze serenely on the middle distance. It was obvious that boring questions lay outside his scheme of life.

"What do you think of human intelligence?" asked Mavis Pellington lamely.

"Of whose intelligence in particular?" asked Tobermory coldly.

"Oh, well, mine for instance," said Mavis, with a feeble laugh.

"You put me in an embarrassing position," said Tobermory, whose tone and attitude certainly did not suggest a shred of embarrassment. "When your inclusion in this house party was suggested Sir Wilfrid protested that you were the most brainless woman of his acquaintance, and that there was a wide distinction between hospitality and the care of the feeble-minded. Lady Blemley replied that your lack of brain power was the precise quality which had earned you your invitation,

---

3. **Babel:** Biblical reference to a city where Noah's descendants tried to build a very high tower and were prevented from doing so by a confusion of tongues.
4. **Axminster:** an expensive carpet.

as you were the only person she could think of who might be idiotic enough to buy their old car. You know, the one they call 'The Envy of Sisyphus,'[5] because it goes quite nicely uphill if you push it."

Lady Blemley's protestations would have had greater effect if she had not casually suggested to Mavis only that morning that the car in question would be just the thing for her down at her Devonshire home.

Major Barfield plunged in heavily to effect a diversion.

"How about your carryings-on with the tortoise-shell puss up at the stables, eh?"

The moment he had said it every one realized the blunder.

"One does not usually discuss these matters in public," said Tobermory frigidly. "From a slight observation of your ways since you've been in this house I should imagine you'd find it inconvenient if I were to shift the conversation on to your own little affairs."

The panic which ensued was not confined to the Major.

"Would you like to go and see if cook has got your dinner ready?" suggested Lady Blemley hurriedly, affecting to ignore the fact that it wanted at least two hours to Tobermory's dinnertime.

"Thanks," said Tobermory, "not quite so soon after my tea. I don't want to die of indigestion."

"Cats have nine lives, you know," said Sir Wilfrid heartily.

"Possibly," answered Tobermory; "but only one liver."

"Adelaide!" said Mrs. Cornett, "do you mean to encourage that cat to go out and gossip about us in the servants' hall?"

The panic had indeed become general. A narrow ornamental balustrade[6] ran in front of most of the bedroom windows at the Towers, and it was recalled with dismay that this had formed a favorite promenade for Tobermory at all hours, whence he could watch the pigeons—and heaven knew what else besides.

If he intended to become reminiscent in his present outspoken strain the effect would be something more than disconcerting. Mrs. Cornett, who spent much time at her toilet table, and whose complexion was reputed to be of a nomadic though punctual disposition, looked as ill at ease as the Major. Miss Scrawen, who wrote fiercely sensuous poetry and led a blameless life, merely displayed irritation; if you are methodical and virtuous in private you don't necessarily want everyone to know it. Bertie van Tahn, who was so depraved at seventeen that he had long ago given up trying to be any worse, turned a dull shade of gardenia white, but he did not commit the error of dashing out of the room like Odo Finsberry, a young gentleman who was understood to be reading for the Church and who was possibly disturbed at the thought of scandals he might hear concerning other people. Clovis had the presence of mind to maintain a composed exterior; privately he was calculating how long it would take to procure a box of fancy mice through the agency of the *Exchange and Mart* as a species of hush money.

Even in a delicate situation like the present, Agnes Resker could not endure to remain too long in the background.

"Why did I ever come down here?" she asked dramatically.

Tobermory immediately accepted the opening.

"Judging by what you said to Mrs. Cornett on the croquet lawn yesterday, you were out for food. You described the Blemleys as the dullest people to stay with that you knew, but said they were clever enough to employ a first-rate cook; otherwise they'd find it difficult to get any one to come down a second time."

---

5. **Sisyphus** (sis' ə fəs): in Greek mythology a greedy king of Corinth doomed forever in Hades to roll uphill a heavy stone that always rolled down again.

6. **balustrade:** a railing.

"There's not a word of truth in it! I appeal to Mrs. Cornett—" exclaimed the discomfited Agnes.

"Mrs. Cornett repeated your remark afterwards to Bertie van Tahn," continued Tobermory, "and said, 'That woman is a regular Hunger Marcher; she'd go anywhere for four square meals a day,' and Bertie van Tahn said—"

At this point the chronicle mercifully ceased. Tobermory had caught a glimpse of the big yellow tom from the Rectory working his way through the shrubbery towards the stable wing. In a flash he had vanished through the open French window.

With the disappearance of his too-brilliant pupil Cornelius Appin found himself beset by a hurricane of bitter upbraiding, anxious inquiry, and frightened entreaty. The responsibility for the situation lay with him, and he must prevent matters from becoming worse. Could Tobermory impart his dangerous gift to other cats? was the first question he had to answer. It was possible, he replied, that he might have initiated his intimate friend the stable puss into his new accomplishment, but it was unlikely that his teaching could have taken a wider range as yet.

"Then," said Mrs. Cornett, "Tobermory may be a valuable cat and a great pet; but I'm sure you'll agree, Adelaide, that both he and the stable cat must be done away with without delay."

"You don't suppose I've enjoyed the last quarter of an hour, do you?" said Lady Blemley bitterly. "My husband and I are very fond of Tobermory—at least, we were before this horrible accomplishment was infused into him; but now, of course, the only thing is to have him destroyed as soon as possible."

"We can put some strychnine in the scraps he always gets at dinnertime," said Sir Wilfrid, "and I will go and drown the stable cat myself. The coachman will be very sore at losing his pet, but I'll say a very catching form of mange[7] has broken out in both cats and we're afraid of it spreading to the kennels."

"But my great discovery!" expostulated Mr. Appin; "after all my years of research and experiment—"

"You can go and experiment on the shorthorns at the farm, who are under proper control," said Mrs. Cornett, "or the elephants at the Zoological Gardens. They're said to be highly intelligent, and they have this recommendation, that they don't come creeping about our bedrooms and under chairs, and so forth."

An archangel ecstatically proclaiming the millennium, and then finding that it clashed unpardonably with Henley and would have to be indefinitely postponed, could hardly have felt more crestfallen than Cornelius Appin at the reception of his wonderful achievement. Public opinion, however, was against him—in fact, had the general voice been consulted on the subject it is probable that a strong minority vote would have been in favor of including him in the strychnine diet.

Defective train arrangements and a nervous desire to see matters brought to a finish prevented an immediate dispersal of the party, but dinner that evening was not a social success. Sir Wilfrid had had rather a trying time with the stable cat and subsequently with the coachman. Agnes Resker ostentatiously limited her repast to a morsel of dry toast, which she bit as though it were a personal enemy, while Mavis Pellington maintained a vindictive silence throughout the meal. Lady Blemley kept up a flow of what she hoped was conversation, but her attention was fixed on the doorway. A plateful of carefully dosed fish scraps was in readiness on the sideboard, but sweets and savory and dessert went their way, and no Tobermory appeared either in the dining room or kitchen.

---

7. **mange:** a skin disease of mammals caused by parasitic mites and characterized by a loss of hair.

The sepulchral dinner was cheerful compared with the subsequent vigil in the smoking room. Eating and drinking had at least supplied a distraction and cloak to the prevailing embarrassment. Bridge was out of the question in the general tension of nerves and tempers, and after Odo Finsberry had given a lugubrious rendering of "Mélisande in the Wood" to a frigid audience, music was tacitly avoided. At eleven the servants went to bed, announcing that the small window in the pantry had been left open as usual for Tobermory's private use. The guests read steadily through the current batch of magazines, and fell back gradually on the "Badminton Library" and bound volumes of *Punch*. Lady Blemley made periodic visits to the pantry, returning each time with an expression of listless depression which forestalled questioning.

At two o'clock Clovis broke the dominating silence.

"He won't turn up tonight. He's probably in the local newspaper office at the present moment, dictating the first installment of his reminiscences. Lady What's-her-name's book won't be in it. It will be the event of the day."

Having made this contribution to the general cheerfulness, Clovis went to bed. At long intervals the various members of the house party followed his example.

The servants taking round the early tea made a uniform announcement in reply to a uniform question. Tobermory had not returned.

Breakfast was, if anything, a more unpleasant function than dinner had been, but before its conclusion the situation was relieved. Tobermory's corpse was brought in from the shrubbery, where a gardener had just discovered it. From the bites on his throat and the yellow fur which coated his claws it was evident that he had fallen in unequal combat with the big tom from the Rectory.

By midday most of the guests had quitted the Towers, and after lunch Lady Blemley had sufficiently recovered her spirits to write an extremely nasty letter to the Rectory about the loss of her valuable pet.

Tobermory had been Appin's one successful pupil, and he was destined to have no successor. A few weeks later an elephant in the Dresden Zoological Garden, which had shown no previous signs of irritability, broke loose and killed an Englishman who had apparently been teasing it. The victim's name was variously reported in the papers as Oppin and Eppelin, but his front name was faithfully rendered Cornelius.

"If he was trying German irregular verbs on the poor beast," said Clovis, "he deserved all he got."

THREE-TAILED CAT CLINGING TO A PEONY BRANCH. *Koma Kyūhakū.*
The Metropolitan Museum of Art.
Bequest of Mrs. H. O. Havemeyer, 1929.
The H. O. Havemeyer Collection.

Getting at Meaning

1. Describe the setting of this story. What is the occasion? Who are the host and hostess? What is "the Towers"? Identify some of the details that indicate the level of society represented.

2. Describe Mr. Cornelius Appin. Why has he been invited? What is meant by his "homely negative personality"? What is there about him that people might find irritating? How do the references to his name also help to characterize him?

3. Why do the people gathered at the country house feel threatened by Tobermory? How would you describe his personality?

4. Why does Tobermory suddenly leave the company to confront the yellow tom from the Rectory?

5. Why is dinner that evening "not a social success"? Why does Agnes Resker ostentatiously limit her repast to a morsel of dry toast?

6. How does the manner of Mr. Appin's death seem to confirm what the reader already knows about him?

Developing Skills in Reading Literature

1. **Narrator and Point of View.** Does the narrator, or person who tells this story, sound like an impersonal outsider or like someone who identifies with the social milieu being described? How does the narrator's verbal style tend to confirm this? Point out several illustrative passages. At whose expense is this story told? How would the story be different if it were told from the first-person point of view of one of the characters? Is the third-person narrator omniscient, or all knowing, or does the narrator adopt a limited point of view, presenting events as experienced by one character? Support your answer with evidence from the story.

2. **Tone.** With its drawing room wit and satire, this story is in the tradition of the comedy of manners, and its humor stems not only from situation but also from character and language. What is funny, for example, about Lady Blemley, Miss Scrawen, Odo Finsberry, Mrs. Cornett, and Agnes Resker?

Next, note the language of the narrator. Mr. Appin is described as follows: "Neither did his exterior suggest the sort of man in whom women are willing to pardon a generous measure of mental deficiency." Mrs. Cornett's complexion "was reputed to be of a nomadic though punctual disposition." If Tobermory "intended to become reminiscent in his present outspoken strain the effect would be something more than disconcerting." What is the meaning of each of these passages, and how does their style affect the tone of the story? Point out one or two other examples.

3. **Short Story.** In terms of substance and complexity, this story clearly lies at the other end of the spectrum from "The Secret Sharer." As different as they are, however, the two stories do exhibit the same basic characteristics of the short story. What are these characteristics, as they are evident in "Tobermory"?

Developing Vocabulary

Finding the Appropriate Meaning. Look up the word *ruck* in a dictionary. Which of its various meanings is the appropriate one in the phrase, "among the ruck of human beings"? Note the etymology of this word, and explain how it came to acquire this particular meaning.

Odo Finsberry is said to be "reading for the Church." This is a particularly British usage of the word *read*. Of the meanings listed in the dictionary which applies in this phrase?

Agnes Resker is "discomfited" by Tobermory's remarks. What would be a synonym for that word in this context?

The final dinner was a "sepulchral" one. What would be another way of describing it? Is it anything like *lugubrious*, which appears a few lines later?

Developing Writing Skills

Writing a Short Story. This story is built around a single idea, like a joke. In fact, it is a kind of elegantly told joke or humorous tale, based on the following idea: What if a cat, when it finally learned to talk, could say only unpleasant or embarrassing things? What might be the outcome? With this in mind, think of some idea, perhaps an outlandish invention, and project its possible consequences in a brief, perhaps humorous tale. Possibly, like Saki, you will be able also to poke fun at a particular social class or group.

D. H. Lawrence
1885–1930

Novelist, poet, short-story writer, and essayist, David Herbert Lawrence explores the world of love between men and women and the cultural, historical, and natural forces that bear on the fulfillment of human potential. A brilliant, imaginative, and emotional writer, Lawrence portrays characters sympathetically, as victims of an inhibiting society, and nature as symbolic of what is vital and nurturing in life.

One of five children, Lawrence was born in a coal mining village in Nottinghamshire, in central England. The conflict between his mother, who had been a teacher and had written poetry, and his father, a crude and uneducated miner, made Lawrence feel keenly the tension between the gentler world of imagination and art and the world of physical labor. In his writing Lawrence often contrasted the physical side of love with the passionless, intellectualized side. While his mother was clearly an early inspiration, he also wrote about his father with gentleness, as in the semi-autobiographical novel *Sons and Lovers* (1913).

Lawrence studied and wrote poems as a child, won a scholarship in high school, earned a certificate as a teacher, and taught elementary school. After his friend Ford Madox Ford helped him publish his first novel, *The White Peacock* (1911), Lawrence quit teaching and devoted himself to writing.

In 1912 Lawrence met Frieda von Richthofen, the aristocratic German wife of a professor. The two fell in love and began a nomadic life together. Their relationship was intensely intimate but often troubled, and Lawrence based much of his fiction on this lifelong love. The couple was married in 1914, when Frieda's divorce became final.

Ill health and disillusionment with England caused Lawrence to travel the world, seeking a hospitable climate. The Lawrences visited and lived in Italy, Sicily, Ceylon, Australia, Mexico, New Mexico, and the South Pacific. Many of these localities and cultures provided Lawrence with inspiration for books.

D. H. LAWRENCE. *The Bettmann Archive, Inc.*

Lawrence's nonfiction, fiction, and poetry all are characterized by strong physical descriptions and by sensitivity to the world of nature. One volume of poems is titled *Birds, Beasts, and Flowers* (1923); other collections include *Tortoises* (1921), *Pansies* (1929), and *Nettles* (1930).

Lawrence often suffered from censorship and public condemnation. An early novel, *The Rainbow* (1915), was banned in England as obscene, and even his literary friends did not appreciate this strikingly original work. His last and most famous book, *Lady Chatterley's Lover*, was not legally published in its entirety in America until 1959. In this novel Lawrence tells the story of a love affair between an aristocratic lady and a gamekeeper in order to show the importance of the physical as well as the emotional side of human relationships. This book did much to expand the range of published material, for courts ruled that it is art and therefore justified in depicting love explicitly.

Lawrence lived his last few years in southern France. He died of tuberculosis in 1930 and was buried in Taos, New Mexico.

The Rocking-Horse Winner

There was a woman who was beautiful, who started with all the advantages, yet she had no luck. She married for love, and the love turned to dust. She had bonny children, yet she felt they had been thrust upon her, and she could not love them. They looked at her coldly, as if they were finding fault with her. And hurriedly she felt she must cover up some fault in herself. Yet what it was that she must cover up she never knew. Nevertheless, when her children were present, she always felt the center of her heart go hard. This troubled her, and in her manner she was all the more gentle and anxious for her children, as if she loved them very much. Only she herself knew that at the center of her heart was a hard little place that could not feel love, no, not for anybody. Everybody else said of her: "She is such a good mother. She adores her children." Only she herself, and her children themselves, knew it was not so. They read it in each other's eyes.

There were a boy and two little girls. They lived in a pleasant house, with a garden, and they had discreet servants, and felt themselves superior to anyone in the neighborhood.

Although they lived in style, they felt always an anxiety in the house. There was never enough money. The mother had a small income, and the father had a small income, but not nearly enough for the social position which they had to keep up. The father went in to town to some office. But though he had good prospects, these prospects never materialized. There was always the grinding sense of the shortage of money, though the style was always kept up.

At last the mother said, "I will see if *I* can't make something." But she did not know where to begin. She racked her brains, and tried this thing and the other, but could not find anything successful. The failure made deep lines come into her face. Her children were growing up, they would have to go to school. There must be more money, there must be more money. The father, who was always very handsome and expensive in his tastes, seemed as if he never *would* be able to do anything worth doing. And the mother, who had a great belief in herself, did not succeed any better, and her tastes were just as expensive.

And so the house came to be haunted by the unspoken phrase: *There must be more money! There must be more money!* The children could hear it all the time, though nobody said it aloud. They heard it at Christmas, when the expensive and splendid toys filled the nursery. Behind the shining modern rocking horse, behind the smart doll's house, a voice would start whispering: "There *must* be more money! There *must* be more money!" And the children would stop playing, to listen for a moment. They would look into each other's eyes, to see if they had all heard. And each one saw in the eyes of the other two that they too had heard. "There *must* be more money! There *must* be more money!"

It came whispering from the springs of the still-swaying rocking horse, and even the horse, bending his wooden, champing head, heard it. The big doll, sitting so pink and smirking in her new pram, could hear it quite plainly, and seemed to be smirking all the more self-consciously because of it. The foolish puppy, too, that took the place of the teddy bear, he was looking so extraordinarily foolish for no other reason but that he heard the secret whisper all over the house: "There *must* be more money!"

Yet nobody ever said it aloud. The whisper was everywhere, and therefore no one spoke it. Just as no one ever says: "We are breathing!" in spite of the fact that breath is coming and going all the time.

"Mother," said the boy Paul one day, "why don't we keep a car of our own? Why do we always use uncle's, or else a taxi?"

"Because we're the poor members of the family," said the mother.

"But why *are* we, mother?"

"Well—I suppose," she said slowly and bitterly, "it's because your father has no luck."

The boy was silent for some time.

"Is luck money, mother?" he asked, rather timidly.

"No, Paul. Not quite. It's what causes you to have money."

"Oh!" said Paul vaguely. "I thought when Uncle Oscar said *filthy lucker*, it meant money."

"*Filthy lucre* does mean money," said the mother. "But it's lucre, not luck."

"Oh!" said the boy. "Then what *is* luck, mother?"

"It's what causes you to have money. If you're lucky you have money. That's why it's better to be born lucky than rich. If you're rich, you may lose your money. But if you're lucky, you will always get more money."

"Oh! Will you? And is father not lucky?"

"Very unlucky, I should say," she said bitterly.

The boy watched her with unsure eyes.

"Why?" he asked.

"I don't know. Nobody ever knows why one person is lucky and another unlucky."

"Don't they? Nobody at all? Does *nobody* know?"

"Perhaps God. But He never tells."

"He ought to, then. And aren't you lucky either, mother?"

"I can't be, if I married an unlucky husband."

"But by yourself, aren't you?"

"I used to think I was, before I married. Now I think I am very unlucky indeed."

"Why?"

"Well—never mind! Perhaps I'm not really," she said.

The child looked at her, to see if she meant it. But he saw, by the lines of her mouth, that she was only trying to hide something from him.

"Well, anyhow," he said stoutly, "I'm a lucky person."

"Why?" said his mother, with a sudden laugh.

He stared at her. He didn't even know why he had said it.

"God told me," he asserted, brazening it out.

"I hope He did, dear!" she said, again with a laugh, but rather bitter.

"He did, mother!"

"Excellent!" said the mother, using one of her husband's exclamations.

The boy saw she did not believe him; or rather, that she paid no attention to his assertion. This angered him somewhere, and made him want to compel her attention.

He went off by himself, vaguely, in a childish way, seeking for the clue to "luck." Absorbed, taking no heed of other people, he went about with a sort of stealth, seeking inwardly for luck. He wanted luck, he wanted it, he wanted it. When the two girls were playing dolls in the nursery, he would sit on his big rocking horse, charging madly into space, with a frenzy that made the little girls peer at him uneasily. Wildly the horse careered, the waving dark hair of the boy tossed, his eyes had a strange glare in them. The little girls dared not speak to him.

When he had ridden to the end of his mad little journey, he climbed down and stood in front of his rocking horse, staring fixedly into its lowered face. Its red mouth was slightly open, its big eye was wide and glassy-bright.

"Now!" he would silently command the snorting steed. "Now, take me to where there is luck! Now take me!"

And he would slash the horse on the neck with the little whip he had asked Uncle Oscar for. He *knew* the horse could take him to where there was luck, if only he forced it. So he would mount again, and start on his furious ride, hoping at last to get there. He knew he could get there.

"You'll break your horse, Paul!" said the nurse.

"He's always riding like that! I wish he'd leave off!" said his elder sister Joan.

But he only glared down on them in silence. Nurse gave him up. She could make nothing of him. Anyhow he was growing beyond her.

One day his mother and his Uncle Oscar came in when he was on one of his furious rides. He did not speak to them.

"Hallo, you young jockey! Riding a winner?" said his uncle.

"Aren't you growing too big for a rocking horse? You're not a very little boy any longer, you know," said his mother.

But Paul only gave a blue glare from his big, rather close-set eyes. He would speak to nobody when he was in full tilt. His mother watched him with an anxious expression on her face.

At last he suddenly stopped forcing his horse into the mechanical gallop, and slid down.

"Well, I got there!" he announced fiercely, his blue eyes still flaring, and his sturdy long legs straddling apart.

"Where did you get to?" asked his mother.

"Where I wanted to go," he flared back at her.

"That's right, son!" said Uncle Oscar. "Don't you stop till you get there. What's the horse's name?"

"He doesn't have a name," said the boy.

"Gets on without all right?" asked the uncle.

"Well, he has different names. He was called Sansovino last week."

"Sansovino, eh? Won the Ascot.[1] How did you know his name?"

"He always talks about horse races with Bassett," said Joan.

The uncle was delighted to find that his small nephew was posted with all the racing news. Bassett, the young gardener, who had been wounded in the left foot in the war and had got his present job through Oscar Cresswell, whose batman[2] he had been, was a perfect blade of the "turf."[3] He lived in the racing events, and the small boy lived with him.

Oscar Cresswell got it all from Bassett.

"Master Paul comes and asks me, so I can't do more than tell him, sir," said Bassett, his face terribly serious, as if he were speaking of religious matters.

"And does he ever put anything on a horse he fancies?"

"Well—I don't want to give him away—he's a young sport, a fine sport, sir. Would you mind asking him himself? He sort of takes a pleasure in it, and perhaps he'd feel I was giving him away, sir, if you don't mind."

Bassett was serious as a church.

The uncle went back to his nephew, and took him off for a ride in the car.

"Say, Paul, old man, do you ever put anything on a horse?" the uncle asked.

The boy watched the handsome man closely.

"Why, do you think I oughtn't to?" he parried.

"Not a bit of it! I thought perhaps you might give me a tip for the Lincoln."

The car sped on into the country, going down to Uncle Oscar's place in Hampshire.

"Honor bright?" said the nephew.

---

1. **Ascot:** a prestigious thoroughbred horse race.
2. **batman:** a military officer's orderly.
3. **turf:** the world of racing.

"Honor bright, son!" said the uncle.

"Well, then, Daffodil."

"Daffodil! I doubt it, sonny. What about Mirza?"

"I only know the winner," said the boy. "That's Daffodil."

"Daffodil, eh?"

There was a pause. Daffodil was an obscure horse comparatively.

"Uncle!"

"Yes, son?"

"You won't let it go any further, will you? I promised Bassett."

"Bassett be damned, old man! What's he got to do with it?"

"We're partners. We've been partners from the first. Uncle, he lent me my first five shillings, which I lost. I promised him, honor bright, it was only between me and him; only you gave me that ten-shilling note I started winning with, so I thought you were lucky. You won't let it go any further, will you?"

The boy gazed at his uncle from those big, hot, blue eyes, set rather close together. The uncle stirred and laughed uneasily.

"Right you are, son! I'll keep your tip private. Daffodil, eh. How much you putting on him?"

"All except twenty pounds," said the boy. "I keep that as reserve."

The uncle thought it a good joke.

"You keep twenty pounds in reserve, do you, you young romancer? What are you betting, then?"

"I'm betting three hundred," said the boy gravely. "But it's between you and me, Uncle Oscar! Honor bright?"

The uncle burst into a roar of laughter.

"It's between you and me all right, you young Nat Gould,"[4] he said, laughing. "But where's your three hundred?"

"Bassett keeps it for me. We're partners."

"You are, are you! And what is Bassett putting on Daffodil?"

"He won't go quite as high as I do, I expect. Perhaps he'll go a hundred and fifty."

"What, pennies?" laughed the uncle.

"Pounds," said the child, with a surprised look at his uncle. "Bassett keeps a bigger reserve than I do."

Between wonder and amusement Uncle Oscar was silent. He pursued the matter no further, but he determined to take his nephew with him to the Lincoln races.

"Now, son," he said, "I'm putting twenty on Mirza, and I'll put five for you on any horse you fancy. What's your pick?"

"Daffodil, uncle."

"No, not the fiver on Daffodil!"

"I should if it was my own fiver," said the child.

"Good! Good! Right you are! A fiver for me and a fiver for you on Daffodil."

The child had never been to a race-meeting before, and his eyes were blue fire. He pursed his mouth tight, and watched. A Frenchman just in front had put his money on Lancelot. Wild with excitement, he flayed his arms up and down, yelling, *Lancelot! Lancelot!* in his French accent.

Daffodil came in first, Lancelot second, Mirza third. The child, flushed and with eyes blazing, was curiously serene. His uncle brought him four five-pound notes, four to one.

"What am I to do with these?" he cried, waving them before the boy's eyes.

"I suppose we'll talk to Bassett," said the boy. "I expect I have fifteen hundred now; and twenty in reserve; and this twenty."

His uncle studied him for some moments.

"Look here, son!" he said. "You're not serious about Bassett and that fifteen hundred, are you?"

"Yes, I am. But it's between you and me, uncle. Honor bright!"

"Honor bright all right, son! But I must talk to Bassett."

"If you'd like to be a partner, uncle, with

---

4. **Nat Gould:** a famous racing authority.

Bassett and me, we could all be partners. Only, you'd have to promise, honor bright, uncle, not to let it go beyond us three. Bassett and I are lucky, and you must be lucky, because it was your ten shillings I started winning with. . . ."

Uncle Oscar took both Bassett and Paul into Richmond Park for an afternoon, and there they talked.

"It's like this, you see, sir," Bassett said. "Master Paul would get me talking about racing events, spinning yarns, you know, sir. And he was always keen on knowing if I'd made or if I'd lost. It's about a year since, now, that I put five shillings on Blush of Dawn for him: and we lost. Then the luck turned, with that ten shillings he had from you: that we put on Singhalese. And since that time, it's been pretty steady, all things considering. What do you say, Master Paul?"

"We're all right when we're sure," said Paul. "It's when we're not quite sure that we go down."

"Oh, but we're careful then," said Bassett.

"But when are you *sure*?" smiled Uncle Oscar.

"It's Master Paul, sir," said Bassett, in a secret, religious voice. "It's as if he had it from heaven. Like Daffodil, now, for the Lincoln. That was as sure as eggs."

"Did you put anything on Daffodil?" asked Oscar Cresswell.

"Yes, sir. I made my bit."

"And my nephew?"

Bassett was obstinately silent, looking at Paul.

"I made twelve hundred, didn't I, Bassett? I told uncle I was putting three hundred on Daffodil."

"That's right," said Bassett, nodding.

"But where's the money?" asked the uncle.

"I keep it safe locked up, sir. Master Paul he can have it any minute he likes to ask for it."

"What, fifteen hundred pounds?"

"And twenty! And *forty*, that is, with the twenty he made on the course."

"It's amazing!" said the uncle.

"If Master Paul offers you to be partners, sir, I would, if I were you: if you'll excuse me," said Bassett.

Oscar Cresswell thought about it.

"I'll see the money," he said.

They drove home again, and, sure enough, Bassett came round to the garden house with fifteen hundred pounds in notes. The twenty pounds reserve was left with Joe Glee, in the Turf Commission deposit.

"You see, it's all right, uncle, when I'm *sure*! Then we go strong, for all we're worth. Don't we, Bassett?"

"We do that, Master Paul."

"And when are you sure?" said the uncle, laughing.

"Oh, well, sometimes I'm *absolutely* sure, like about Daffodil," said the boy; "and sometimes I have an idea; and sometimes I haven't even an idea, have I, Bassett? Then we're careful, because we mostly go down."

"You do, do you! And when you're sure, like about Daffodil, what makes you sure, sonny?"

"Oh, well, I don't know," said the boy uneasily. "I'm sure, you know, uncle; that's all."

"It's as if he had it from heaven, sir," Bassett reiterated.

"I should say so!" said the uncle.

But he became a partner. And when the Leger was coming on Paul was "sure" about Lively Spark, which was a quite inconsiderable horse. The boy insisted on putting a thousand on the horse, Bassett went for five hundred, and Oscar Cresswell two hundred. Lively Spark came in first, and the betting had been ten to one against him. Paul had made ten thousand.

"You see," he said, "I was absolutely sure of him."

Even Oscar Cresswell had cleared two thousand.

"Look here, son," he said, "this sort of thing makes me nervous."

"It needn't, uncle! Perhaps I shan't be sure again for a long time."

"But what are you going to do with your money?" asked the uncle.

"Of course," said the boy, "I started it for mother. She said she had no luck, because father is unlucky, so I thought if I was lucky, it might stop whispering."

"What might stop whispering?"

"Our house. I *hate* our house for whispering."

"What does it whisper?"

"Why—why"—the boy fidgeted—"why, I don't know. But it's always short of money, you know, uncle."

"I know it, son, I know it."

"You know people send mother writs,[5] don't you, uncle?"

"I'm afraid I do," said the uncle.

"And then the house whispers, like people laughing at you behind your back. It's awful, that is! I thought if I was lucky—"

"You might stop it," added the uncle.

The boy watched him with big blue eyes, that had an uncanny cold fire in them, and he said never a word.

"Well, then!" said the uncle. "What are we doing?"

"I shouldn't like mother to know I was lucky," said the boy.

"Why not, son?"

"She'd stop me."

"I don't think she would."

"Oh!"—and the boy writhed in an odd way—"I *don't* want her to know, uncle."

"All right, son! We'll manage it without her knowing."

They managed it very easily. Paul, at the other's suggestion, handed over five thousand pounds to his uncle, who deposited it with the family lawyer, who was then to inform Paul's mother that a relative had put five thousand pounds into his hands, which sum was to be paid out a thousand pounds at a time, on the mother's birthday, for the next five years.

"So she'll have a birthday present of a thousand pounds for five successive years," said Uncle Oscar. "I hope it won't make it all the harder for her later."

Paul's mother had her birthday in November. The house had been "whispering" worse than ever lately, and, even in spite of his luck, Paul could not bear up against it. He was very anxious to see the effect of the birthday letter, telling his mother about the thousand pounds.

When there were no visitors, Paul now took his meals with his parents, as he was beyond the nursery control. His mother went into town nearly every day. She had discovered that she had an odd knack of sketching furs and dress materials, so she worked secretly in the studio of a friend who was the chief "artist" for the leading drapers. She drew the figures of ladies in furs and ladies in silk and sequins for the newspaper advertisements. This young woman artist earned several thousand pounds a year, but Paul's mother only made several hundreds, and she was again dissatisfied. She so wanted to be first in something, and she did not succeed, even in making sketches for drapery advertisements.

She was down to breakfast on the morning of her birthday. Paul watched her face as she read her letters. He knew the lawyer's letter. As his mother read it, her face hardened and became more expressionless. Then a cold, determined look came on her mouth. She hid the letter under the pile of others, and said not a word about it.

"Didn't you have anything nice in the post for your birthday, mother?" said Paul.

"Quite moderately nice," she said, her voice cold and absent.

She went away to town without saying more.

But in the afternoon Uncle Oscar appeared. He said Paul's mother had had a long interview with the lawyer, asking if the whole five

---

5. **writs:** legal papers.

thousand could not be advanced at once, as she was in debt.

"What do you think, uncle?" said the boy.

"I leave it to you, son."

"Oh, let her have it, then! We can get some more with the other," said the boy.

"A bird in the hand is worth two in the bush, laddie!" said Uncle Oscar.

"But I'm sure to *know* for the Grand National; or the Lincolnshire; or else the Derby. I'm sure to know for *one* of them," said Paul.

So Uncle Oscar signed the agreement, and Paul's mother touched the whole five thousand. Then something very curious happened. The voices in the house suddenly went mad, like a chorus of frogs on a spring evening. There were certain new furnishings, and Paul had a tutor. He was *really* going to Eton, his father's school, in the following autumn. There were flowers in the winter, and a blossoming of the luxury Paul's mother had been used to. And yet the voices in the house, behind the sprays of mimosa and almond-blossom, and from under the piles of iridescent cushions, simply trilled and screamed in a sort of ecstasy: "There *must* be more money! Oh-h-h; there *must* be more money. Oh, now, now-w! Now-w-w—there *must* be more money!—more than ever! More than ever!"

It frightened Paul terribly. He studied away at his Latin and Greek with his tutors. But his intense hours were spent with Bassett. The Grand National had gone by: he had not "known," and had lost a hundred pounds. Summer was at hand. He was in agony for the Lincoln. But even for the Lincoln he didn't "know," and he lost fifty pounds. He became wild-eyed and strange, as if something were going to explode in him.

"Let it alone, son! Don't you bother about it!" urged Uncle Oscar. But it was as if the boy couldn't really hear what his uncle was saying.

"I've got to know for the Derby! I've got to know for the Derby!" the child reiterated, his big blue eyes blazing with a sort of madness.

His mother noticed how overwrought he was.

"You'd better go to the seaside. Wouldn't you like to go now to the seaside, instead of waiting? I think you'd better," she said, looking down at him anxiously, her heart curiously heavy because of him.

But the child lifted his uncanny blue eyes.

"I couldn't possibly go before the Derby, mother!" he said. "I couldn't possibly!"

"Why not?" she said, her voice becoming heavy when she was opposed. "Why not? You can still go from the seaside to see the Derby with your Uncle Oscar, if that's what you wish. No need for you to wait here. Besides, I think you care too much about these races. It's a bad sign. My family has been a gambling family, and you won't know till you grow up how much damage it has done. But it has done damage. I shall have to send Bassett away, and ask Uncle Oscar not to talk racing to you, unless you promise to be reasonable about it: go away to the seaside and forget it. You're all nerves!"

"I'll do what you like, mother, so long as you don't send me away till after the Derby," the boy said.

"Send you away from where? Just from this house?"

"Yes," he said, gazing at her.

"Why, you curious child, what makes you care about this house so much, suddenly? I never knew you loved it."

He gazed at her without speaking. He had a secret within a secret, something he had not divulged, even to Bassett or to his Uncle Oscar.

But his mother, after standing undecided and a little bit sullen for some moments, said:

"Very well, then! Don't go to the seaside till after the Derby, if you don't wish it. But promise me you won't let your nerves go to pieces. Promise you won't think so much about horse racing and *events*, as you call them!"

"Oh, no," said the boy casually. "I won't think much about them, mother. You needn't worry. I wouldn't worry, mother, if I were you."

"If you were me and I were you," said his mother, "I wonder what we *should* do!"

"But you know you needn't worry, mother, don't you?" the boy repeated.

"I should be awfully glad to know it," she said wearily.

"Oh, well, you *can*, you know. I mean, you *ought* to know you needn't worry," he insisted.

"Ought I? Then I'll see about it," she said.

Paul's secret of secrets was his wooden horse, that which had no name. Since he was emancipated from a nurse and a nursery governess, he had had his rocking horse removed to his own bedroom at the top of the house.

"Surely, you're too big for a rocking horse!" his mother had remonstrated.

"Well, you see, mother, till I can have a *real* horse, I like to have *some* sort of animal about," had been his quaint answer.

"Do you feel he keeps you company?" she laughed.

"Oh, yes! He's very good, he always keeps me company, when I'm there," said Paul.

So the horse, rather shabby, stood in an arrested prance in the boy's bedroom.

The Derby was drawing near, and the boy grew more and more tense. He hardly heard what was spoken to him, he was very frail, and his eyes were really uncanny. His mother had sudden strange seizures of uneasiness about him. Sometimes, for half an hour, she would feel a sudden anxiety about him that was almost anguish. She wanted to rush to him at once, and know he was safe.

Two nights before the Derby, she was at a big party in town, when one of her rushes of anxiety about her boy, her firstborn, gripped her heart till she could hardly speak. She

fought with the feeling, might and main, for she believed in common sense. But it was too strong. She had to leave the dance and go downstairs to telephone to the country. The children's nursery governess was terribly surprised and startled at being rung up in the night.

"Are the children all right, Miss Wilmot?"

"Oh, yes, they are quite all right."

"Master Paul? Is he all right?"

"He went to bed as right as a trivet. Shall I run up and look at him?"

"No," said Paul's mother reluctantly. "No! Don't trouble. It's all right. Don't sit up. We shall be home fairly soon." She did not want her son's privacy intruded upon.

"Very good," said the governess.

It was about one o'clock when Paul's mother and father drove up to their house. All was still. Paul's mother went to her room and slipped off her white fur cloak. She had told her maid not to wait up for her. She heard her husband downstairs, mixing a whisky and soda.

And then, because of the strange anxiety at her heart, she stole upstairs to her son's room. Noiselessly she went along the upper corridor. Was there a faint noise? What was it?

She stood, with arrested muscles, outside his door, listening. There was a strange, heavy, and yet not loud noise. Her heart stood still. It was a soundless noise, yet rushing and powerful. Something huge, in violent, hushed motion. What was it? What in God's name was it? She ought to know. She felt that she knew the noise. She knew what it was.

Yet she could not place it. She couldn't say what it was. And on and on it went, like a madness.

Softly, frozen with anxiety and fear, she turned the door handle.

The room was dark. Yet in the space near the window, she heard and saw something plunging to and fro. She gazed in fear and amazement.

Then suddenly she switched on the light, and saw her son, in his green pajamas, madly surging on the rocking horse. The blaze of light suddenly lit him up, as he urged the wooden horse, and lit her up, as she stood, blonde, in her dress of pale green and crystal, in the doorway.

"Paul!" she cried. "Whatever are you doing?"

"It's Malabar!" he screamed, in a powerful, strange voice. "It's Malabar!"

His eyes blazed at her for one strange and senseless second, as he ceased urging his wooden horse. Then he fell with a crash to the ground, and she, all her tormented motherhood flooding upon her, rushed to gather him up.

But he was unconscious, and unconscious he remained, with some brain fever. He talked and tossed, and his mother sat stonily by his side.

"Malabar! It's Malabar! Bassett, Basset, I *know*! It's Malabar!"

So the child cried, trying to get up and urge the rocking horse that gave him his inspiration.

"What does he mean by Malabar?" asked the heart-frozen mother.

"I don't know," said the father stonily.

"What does he mean by Malabar?" she asked her brother Oscar.

"It's one of the horses running for the Derby," was the answer.

And, in spite of himself, Oscar Cresswell spoke to Bassett, and himself put a thousand on Malabar: at fourteen to one.

The third day of the illness was critical: they were waiting for a change. The boy, with his rather long, curly hair, was tossing ceaselessly on the pillow. He neither slept nor regained consciousness, and his eyes were like blue stones. His mother sat, feeling her heart had gone, turned actually into a stone.

In the evening, Oscar Cresswell did not come, but Bassett sent a message, saying could he come up for one moment, just one moment? Paul's mother was very angry at the intrusion, but on second thoughts she agreed. The boy was the same. Perhaps Bassett might bring him to consciousness.

The gardener, a shortish fellow with a little brown moustache, and sharp little brown eyes, tiptoed into the room, touched his imaginary cap to Paul's mother, and stole to the bedside, staring with glittering, smallish eyes at the tossing, dying child.

"Master Paul!" he whispered. "Master Paul! Malabar came in first all right, a clean win. I did as you told me. You've made over seventy thousand pounds, you have; you've got over eighty thousand. Malabar came in all right, Master Paul."

"Malabar! Malabar! Did I say Malabar, mother? Did I say Malabar? Do you think I'm lucky, mother? I knew Malabar, didn't I? Over eighty thousand pounds! I call that lucky, don't you, mother? Over eighty thousand pounds! I knew, didn't I know I knew? Malabar came in all right. If I ride my horse till I'm sure, then I tell you, Bassett, you can go as high as you like. Did you go for all you were worth, Bassett?"

"I went a thousand on it, Master Paul."

"I never told you, mother, that if I can ride my horse and *get there*, then I'm absolutely sure—oh, absolutely! Mother, did I ever tell you? I *am* lucky!"

"No, you never did," said the mother.

But the boy died in the night.

And even as he lay dead, his mother heard her brother's voice saying to her: "My God, Hester, you're eighty-odd thousand to the good, and a poor devil of a son to the bad. But, poor devil, poor devil, he's best gone out of a life where he rides his rocking horse to find a winner."

Getting at Meaning

1. Describe the financial and social position of the family in this story. Why do they always need money? What can you tell from the story about their emotional well being?

2. Explain the whispering in the house. Is it caused by a supernatural element? What is meant by this statement: "The whisper was everywhere, and therefore no one spoke it"?

3. Why does Paul at first confuse luck with money? What verbal pun points up his confusion?

4. There is an unhealthy, obsessive quality to the way that Paul rides his rocking horse. What descriptive details indicate this?

5. How does Bassett view Paul's luck? How is this apparent from the gardener's remarks and his demeanor?

6. Explain the mother's reaction to her birthday present. When she receives the full five thousand pounds, "The voices in the house suddenly went mad." Why?

7. What is the meaning of Oscar Cresswell's words at the end of the story?

Developing Skills in Reading Literature

1. **Short Story and Theme.** In what ways does this story resemble a fairy tale? Consider such elements as narrative style as well as plot and character. If this is a kind of fairy tale, does it have a moral? Does it make a statement about luck? money? love? Do Uncle Oscar's final words provide any clue? Is this story realistic as well as fantastic? Explain.

2. **Point of View.** To what extent is the story restricted to objective narration, leaving interpretation to the reader, and to what extent are the minds of any of the characters revealed? How might a different handling of the point of view have affected the story?

3. **Plot: Climax.** What do you think is the most dramatic moment in the story? Why is it so? How does the plot build up the tension to this point? What is

remarkable about the scene as it is presented? What words and phrases contribute to the dramatic effect of the scene? In particular, what verbs, in the present participle form, intensify it even further?

4. **Character.** What kind of a character has Lawrence created in the mother? Consider questions such as these: What is her deficiency? Is it luck? Is something lacking in her nature? in her value system? Is she a wicked mother, as in a fairy tale? Is she shown with any sympathy? Is she to blame for what happens, or is she at the mercy of forces beyond her control? Does she blame others? Is she a victim? Is her characterization simple or complex? Does her character change or is it static?

The father goes "in to town to some office." What else do we learn about him? What kind of a presence is he in the story?

Which character in the story, if any, speaks for the author? In what way?

5. **Characterization: Imagery.** Which of Paul's physical features is emphasized repeatedly? Identify the appearances of this image and the qualities associated with it. How is this image used to suggest Paul's state? Find a similar image used in describing Bassett at the end of the story. What do the references to the mother's heart, both early and later in the story, reveal about her? Does this imagery change in any way after the climax of the story? Explain.

6. **Irony.** What is ironic about (a) Paul's attempt to stop the whispers, (b) the outcome for the mother at the end of the story, and (c) the last words Paul speaks in the story?

Developing Writing Skills

Writing a Definition. Write a brief essay in which you define the concept of luck, as you see it. Do you think that some people are "born lucky"? Illustrate your definition with specific examples, and then apply it, if possible, to Lawrence's story. Does it coincide or differ with the mother's definition?

Katherine Mansfield

1888–1923

Although she lived to be only thirty-four years old, Katherine Mansfield was a master of the short story and developed a distinctive prose style characterized by mood and suggestion rather than by dramatic action.

Born Kathleen Mansfield Beauchamp in Wellington, New Zealand, Mansfield published her first story when she was nine. In 1903 she went to college in London, where she played the cello and edited the literary magazine. She planned a career in music. On her return to New Zealand, she was so unhappy that her father sent her back to London, where she supported herself meagerly with her music. In 1909 she married George Bowden, but she left him after a few days and began reviewing and writing short stories. These early stories were collected in *In a German Pension* (1911).

Also in 1911 Mansfield met the English critic John Middleton Murry, and they began a creative but stormy relationship. She published stories in *Rhythm* and *The Blue Review*, two journals edited by Murry. Mansfield and Murry married in 1919, after Mansfield's divorce from Bowden. The couple stayed for some weeks with Frieda and D. H. Lawrence in 1915, and Lawrence loosely based the main characters in *Women in Love* on the four of them.

Mansfield suffered from ill health and traveled often in search of a favorable climate. Although World War I made travel more difficult, she moved frequently between London, Paris, and Cornwall, writing many articles. Her brother stopped to visit her on his way from New Zealand to France, and he was killed almost immediately when he reached the front. In honor of her brother, Mansfield began writing stories based on memories of her family and of the mood and color of New Zealand. These stories, including "Prelude," were collected in *Bliss and Other Stories* (1920), which finally brought her fame.

Mansfield spent her last years as an invalid, but at the same time she was at the height of her powers as a writer. In the stories collected in *The Garden Party* (1922), she uses psychological revelation and skillful description of social gatherings to portray young people trying to break through the superficiality of upper-middle-class life. Some of these stories achieve the level of poetry in their impressionistic re-creation of scenes and moments. Mansfield recorded her thoughts during her last years in a writer's *Journal*, which Murry edited and issued in 1927, after her death.

Miss Brill

Although it was so brilliantly fine—the blue sky powdered with gold and the great spots of light like white wine splashed over the Jardins Publiques[1]—Miss Brill was glad that she had decided on her fur. The air was motionless, but when you opened your mouth there was just a faint chill, like a chill from a glass of iced water before you sip, and now and again a leaf came drifting—from nowhere, from the sky. Miss Brill put up her hand and touched her fur. Dear little thing! It was nice to feel it again. She had taken it out of its box that afternoon, shaken out the moth powder, given it a good brush, and rubbed the life back into the dim little eyes. "What has been happening to me?" said the sad little eyes. Oh, how sweet it was to see them snap at her again from the red eiderdown![2] . . . But the nose, which was of some black composition, wasn't at all firm. It must have had a knock, somehow. Never mind—a little dab of black sealing wax when the time came—when it was absolutely necessary. . . . Little rogue! Yes, she really felt like that about it. Little rogue biting its tail just by her left ear. She could have taken it off and laid it on her lap and stroked it. She felt a tingling in her hands and arms, but that came from walking, she supposed. And when she breathed, something light and sad—no, not sad, exactly—something gentle seemed to move in her bosom.

There were a number of people out this afternoon, far more than last Sunday. And the band sounded louder and gayer. That was because the Season had begun. For although the band played all the year round on Sundays, out of season it was never the same. It was like someone playing with only the family to listen; it didn't care how it played if there weren't any strangers present. Wasn't the conductor wearing a new coat, too? She was sure it was new. He scraped with his foot and flapped his arms like a rooster about to crow, and the bandsmen sitting in the green rotunda blew out their cheeks and glared at the music. Now there came a little "flutey" bit—very pretty!—a little chain of bright drops. She was sure it would be repeated. It was; she lifted her head and smiled.

Only two people shared her "special" seat: a fine old man in a velvet coat, his hands clasped over a huge carved walking stick, and a big old woman, sitting upright, with a roll of knitting on her embroidered apron. They did not speak. This was disappointing, for Miss Brill always looked forward to the conversation. She had become really quite expert, she thought, at listening as though she didn't listen, at sitting in other people's lives just for a minute while they talked round her.

She glanced, sideways, at the old couple. Perhaps they would go soon. Last Sunday, too, hadn't been as interesting as usual. An Englishman and his wife, he wearing a dreadful Panama hat and she button boots. And she'd gone on the whole time about how she ought to wear spectacles; she knew she needed them; but that it was no good getting any; they'd be sure to break and they'd never keep on. And he'd been so patient. He'd suggested everything—gold rims, the kind that curved round your ears, little pads inside the bridge.

---

1. **Jardins Publiques** (zhär dän' pōō blēk') *French:* Public Gardens.
2. **eiderdown:** a quilt stuffed with the down of the eider duck.

No, nothing would please her. "They'll always be sliding down my nose!" Miss Brill had wanted to shake her.

The old people sat on the bench, still as statues. Never mind, there was always the crowd to watch. To and fro, in front of the flower beds and the band rotunda, the couples and groups paraded, stopped to talk, to greet, to buy a handful of flowers from the old beggar who had his tray fixed to the railings. Little children ran among them, swooping and laughing; little boys with big white silk bows under their chins; little girls, little French dolls, dressed up in velvet and lace. And sometimes a tiny staggerer came suddenly rocking into the open from under the trees, stopped, stared, as suddenly sat down "flop," until its small high-stepping mother, like a young hen, rushed scolding to its rescue. Other people sat on the benches and green chairs, but they were nearly always the same, Sunday after Sunday, and—Miss Brill had often noticed—there was something funny about nearly all of them. They were odd, silent, nearly all old, and from the way they stared they looked as though they'd just come from dark little rooms or even—even cupboards!

Behind the rotunda the slender trees with yellow leaves down drooping, and through them just a line of sea, and beyond the blue sky with gold-veined clouds.

Tum-tum-tum tiddle-um! tiddle-um! tum tiddley-um tum ta! blew the band.

Two young girls in red came by and two young soldiers in blue met them, and they laughed and paired and went off arm in arm. Two peasant women with funny straw hats passed, gravely, leading beautiful smoke-colored donkeys. A cold, pale nun hurried by. A beautiful woman came along and dropped her bunch of violets, and a little boy ran after to hand them to her, and she took them and threw them away as if they'd been poisoned. Dear me! Miss Brill didn't know whether to admire that or not! And now an ermine toque[3]

and a gentleman in gray met just in front of her. He was tall, stiff, dignified, and she was wearing the ermine toque she'd bought when her hair was yellow. Now everything, her hair, her face, even her eyes, was the same color as the shabby ermine, and her hand, in its cleaned glove, lifted to dab her lips, was a tiny yellowish paw. Oh, she was so pleased to see him—delighted! She rather thought they were going to meet that afternoon. She described where she'd been—everywhere, here, there, along by the sea. The day was so charming—didn't he agree? And wouldn't he, perhaps? . . . But he shook his head, lighted a cigarette, slowly breathed a great deep puff into her face and, even while she was still talking and laughing, flicked the match away and walked on. The ermine toque was alone; she smiled more brightly than ever. But even the band seemed to know what she was feeling and played more softly, played tenderly, and the drum beat "The Brute! The Brute!" over and over. What would she do? What was going to happen now? But as Miss Brill wondered, the ermine toque turned, raised her hand as though she'd seen someone else, much nicer, just over there, and pattered away. And the band changed again and played more quickly, more gaily than ever, and the old couple on Miss Brill's seat got up and marched away, and such a funny old man with long whiskers hobbled along in time to the music and was nearly knocked over by four girls walking abreast.

Oh, how fascinating it was! How she enjoyed it! How she loved sitting here, watching it all! It was like a play. It was exactly like a play. Who could believe the sky at the back wasn't painted? But it wasn't till a little brown dog trotted on solemnly and then slowly trotted off, like a little "theatre" dog, a little dog that had been drugged, that Miss Brill discovered what it was that made it so exciting. They were all on the stage. They

---

3. **toque:** a woman's small, round closefitting hat.

weren't only the audience, not only looking on; they were acting. Even she had a part and came every Sunday. No doubt somebody would have noticed if she hadn't been there; she was part of the performance, after all. How strange she'd never thought of it like that before! And yet it explained why she made such a point of starting from home at just the same time each week—so as not to be late for the performance—and it also explained why she had quite a queer, shy feeling at telling her English pupils how she spent her Sunday afternoons. No wonder! Miss Brill nearly laughed out loud. She was on the stage. She thought of the old invalid gentleman to whom she read the newspaper four afternoons a week while he slept in the garden. She had got quite used to the frail head on the cotton pillow, the hollowed eyes, the open mouth, and the high pinched nose. If he'd been dead she mightn't have noticed for weeks; she wouldn't have minded. But suddenly he knew he was having the paper read to him by an actress! "An actress!" The old head lifted; two points of light quivered in the old eyes. "An actress—are ye?" And Miss Brill smoothed the newspaper as though it were the manuscript of her part and said gently: "Yes, I have been an actress for a long time."

The band had been having a rest. Now they started again. And what they played was warm, sunny, yet there was just a faint chill—a something, what was it?—not sadness—no, not sadness—a something that made you want to sing. The tune lifted, lifted, the light shone; and it seemed to Miss Brill that in another moment all of them, all the whole company, would begin singing. The young ones, the laughing ones who were moving together, they would begin, and the men's voices, very resolute and brave, would join them. And then she too, she too, and the others on the benches—they would come in with a kind of accompaniment—something low, that scarcely rose or fell, something so beautiful—moving. . . . And Miss Brill's eyes filled with tears and she looked smiling at all the other members of the company. Yes, we understand, we understand, she thought—though what they understood she didn't know.

Just at that moment a boy and a girl came and sat down where the old couple had been. They were beautifully dressed; they were in love. The hero and heroine, of course, just arrived from his father's yacht. And still soundlessly singing, still with that trembling smile, Miss Brill prepared to listen.

"No, not now," said the girl. "Not here, I can't."

"But why? Because of that stupid old thing at the end there?" asked the boy. "Why does she come here at all—who wants her? Why doesn't she keep her silly old mug at home?"

"It's her fu-fur which is so funny," giggled the girl. "It's exactly like a fried whiting."

"Ah, be off with you!" said the boy in an angry whisper. Then: "Tell me, ma petite chère—"[4]

"No, not here," said the girl. "Not *yet*."

On her way home she usually bought a slice of honey cake at the baker's. It was her Sunday treat. Sometimes there was an almond in her slice, sometimes not. It made a great difference. If there was an almond it was like carrying home a tiny present—a surprise —something that might very well not have been there. She hurried on the almond Sundays and struck the match for the kettle in quite a dashing way.

But today she passed the baker's by, climbed the stairs, went into the little dark room—her room like a cupboard—and sat down on the red eiderdown. She sat there for a long time. The box that the fur came out of was on the bed. She unclasped the necklet quickly; quickly, without looking, laid it inside. But when she put the lid on she thought she heard something crying.

---

4. **ma petite chère** (mà p' tĕt shâr') my little dear.

Getting at Meaning

1. Describe Miss Brill's situation. What does the reader know about her life? What does she do on days of the week other than Sunday? Why is her Sunday routine important to her?

2. Why is this particular Sunday better than usual? What is the season of the year? What details show that Miss Brill is very familiar with the weekly scene?

3. What is Miss Brill's primary interest, and why is the Jardins Publiques on Sunday a good time and place to satisfy it? What particular skill has she developed, and why does it give her such pleasure?

4. What kind of people usually sit on the benches and chairs? What do they tend to have in common with Miss Brill?

5. While sitting on the bench viewing the scene before her, what sudden insight, what new perspective does Miss Brill gain about the world and her relation to it? What one line sums it up? How does it affect her? Who are "all the other members of the company"?

6. When Miss Brill overhears the young couple ridicule her, how is the poignant effect of the scene intensified by contrast with what has come before? How has she become more vulnerable than she might have been?

7. Notice that Miss Brill's feelings, when she reaches her room, are understated. At the end of the story, she thinks she hears "something crying," something that has been mentioned before. What is it? How does it symbolize Miss Brill herself?

tions of a character. Stream of consciousness is both a narrative technique and a method of characterization and is common in the poems, novels, and short stories of the twentieth century. In this story, what does the reader, sharing Miss Brill's inner thoughts and feelings, learn about her? What is shown, for example, in the first five paragraphs, by her thoughts about her fur, the music, her own habit of eavesdropping, the couple who shared her bench the preceding Sunday, and the other people on the benches? What kinds of things does she tend to notice about people, and to what degree does she empathize? What does this indicate about her character? What is the significance of what she does on other days of the week? In general, what are the qualities with which she faces the world and by which she compensates for the fact that she is old and alone? To what extent is she a pathetic character, a helpless victim, ignorant of the cause of his or her pain and who arouses pity, sorrow, sympathy or compassion in the reader?

3. **Imagery.** The mood of a story can be subtly affected by small, almost subliminal details. Find the reference to a "faint chill," which occurs at the beginning of this story. What overtone does this phrase impart to the story? What mixed associations are suggested by the season itself and by the occasional glimpses of nature, as in the first and sixth paragraphs? How do you interpret the references to "cupboards"? Is there any pattern to the imagery of light and darkness?

Developing Skills in Reading Literature

1. **Point of View.** This story is told in the third person, but what is the point of view? Is it omniscient; that is, does the narrator reveal the thoughts and feelings of all the characters? Is there anything the reader is told aside from what Miss Brill sees, hears, feels, and thinks? Is she described at all from the outside? Explain.

2. **Stream of Consciousness and Characterization.** Stream of consciousness is the technique of presenting directly the flow of thoughts, responses, and sensa-

Developing Writing Skills

Analyzing Theme. One of the benefits of literature is that it allows the reader to see the world more clearly, to understand and feel more deeply our common humanity. If a story or a poem is successful, it will leave the reader with some small but perceptible gain in empathy or understanding. With this in mind, describe the effect of this story on you. Does it have a "moral" that might change your life in some way? If you did not like the story, describe its effect and try to analyze the reasons why you reacted negatively.

James Joyce
1882–1941

James Joyce drew on the history and culture of his native Ireland to extend the limits of fiction. A master of the English language, he produced boldly innovative works that plunge readers into the consciousness of the characters and into the mythical worlds signified by Dublin.

Joyce was born to a large family in the Dublin suburb of Rathgar, into an Ireland dominated by England and by the Roman Catholic Church. His mother was strictly religious, and his father was renowned as a colorful character. A strong tenor, a reckless drinker, and an indifferent worker, John Stanislaus Joyce squandered his inheritance and the Joyce family sank into poverty as the years passed. Joyce was sent at first to the best of Jesuit schools, Clongowes Wood College, but he had to withdraw after three years when his family was unable to pay the tuition. He later attended Belvedere College, a Jesuit grammar school, where he was an excellent student, and he earned his bachelor's degree at University College in Dublin.

In June, 1904, Joyce met Nora Barnacle, an unsophisticated but enthusiastic supporter of his literary endeavors. Although Nora was his lifelong love, for years he refused on principle to marry her. With the promise of a job as an English teacher in Zurich, Joyce and Nora moved to Switzerland and later to Trieste. Joyce spent the next thirty-six years struggling to support Nora and their two children, enduring failing eyesight, and trying to get his books published.

Joyce had begun to write short stories for a farmer's magazine, *The Irish Homestead*, in 1904, but his stories were soon judged unsuitable for the magazine's audience. Because he dealt frankly with real people and places and because British law made the printer as well as the writer responsible for an "unfit" book, Joyce did not find another publisher for nearly ten years. In 1914 his stories finally were published under the title *Dubliners*. In *Dubliners* characters struggle with questions of love and religion and with the mundane details of everyday life. These stories typify Joyce's use of "epiphany," a moment or brief episode in which a character reveals his or her true nature.

JAMES JOYCE, 1928. Berenice Abbott. Collection, The Museum of Modern Art, New York. Stephen R. Currier Memorial Fund.

By 1914 *A Portrait of the Artist As a Young Man* was being serialized, and in 1916 it was published in book form. This novel, in which Joyce describes a young man like himself who grows up amid religious crises, begins with baby-talk and ends as the artist leaves Ireland. In *A Portrait of the Artist As a Young Man*, as in *Dubliners*, Ireland is a dreary, depressing place, impoverished both economically and spiritually.

From 1914 to 1921, Joyce wrote his most famous novel, *Ulysses*, which was published chapter by chapter in literary magazines. This masterpiece describes a single day in June, 1904, in Dublin. On one level a modern version of Homer's *Odyssey*, *Ulysses* is also filled with the sights, sounds, and smells of the modern city.

For seventeen years Joyce worked on his long final novel, *Finnegans Wake* (1939). Nearly blind, at times he wrote with crayon on large sheets of paper. A complex and baffling narrative, *Finnegans Wake* is written in a blend of dozens of languages, some extinct, with few recognizable sentences. Through jokes, puns, and coined words, it presents a dreamlike world of Irish history and of the unconscious.

The Boarding House

Mrs. Mooney was a butcher's daughter. She was a woman who was quite able to keep things to herself: a determined woman. She had married her father's foreman and opened a butcher's shop near Spring Gardens. But as soon as his father-in-law was dead Mr. Mooney began to go to the devil. He drank, plundered the till, ran headlong into debt. It was no use making him take the pledge: he was sure to break out again a few days after. By fighting his wife in the presence of customers and by buying bad meat he ruined his business. One night he went for his wife with the cleaver and she had to sleep in a neighbor's house.

After that they lived apart. She went to the priest and got a separation from him with care of the children. She would give him neither money nor food nor house-room; and so he was obliged to enlist himself as a sheriff's man. He was a shabby stooped little drunkard with a white face and a white moustache and white eyebrows, penciled above his little eyes, which were pink-veined and raw; and all day long he sat in the bailiff's room, waiting to be put on a job. Mrs. Mooney, who had taken what remained of her money out of the butcher business and set up a boarding house in Hardwicke Street, was a big imposing woman. Her house had a floating population made up of tourists from Liverpool and the Isle of Man and, occasionally, *artistes* from the music halls. Its resident population was made up of clerks from the city. She governed the house cunningly and firmly, knew when to give credit, when to be stern and when to let things pass. All the resident young men spoke of her as *The Madam*.

Mrs. Mooney's young men paid fifteen shillings a week for board and lodgings (beer or stout at dinner excluded). They shared in common tastes and occupations, and for this reason they were very chummy with one another. They discussed with one another the chances of favorites and outsiders. Jack Mooney, the Madam's son, who was clerk to a commission agent in Fleet Street, had the reputation of being a hard case. He was fond of using soldiers' obscenities: usually he came home in the small hours. When he met his friends he had always a good one to tell them and he was always sure to be on to a good thing—that is to say, a likely horse or a likely *artiste.* He was also handy with the mits and sang comic songs. On Sunday nights there would often be a reunion in Mrs. Mooney's front drawing room. The music-hall *artistes* would oblige; and Sheridan played waltzes and polkas and vamped accompaniments. Polly Mooney, the Madam's daughter, would also sing. She sang:

> I'm a . . . naughty girl.
> You needn't sham:
> You know I am.

Polly was a slim girl of nineteen; she had light soft hair and a small full mouth. Her eyes, which were gray with a shade of green through them, had a habit of glancing upwards when she spoke with anyone, which made her look like a little perverse madonna. Mrs. Mooney had first sent her daughter to be a typist in a corn factor's office but, as a disreputable sheriff's man used to come every other day to the office, asking to be allowed to say a word to his daughter, she had taken her daughter home again and set her to do housework. As Polly was very lively, the intention was to give her the run of the young men. Besides, young men like to feel that there is a young woman not very far away. Polly, of course, flirted with the young men, but Mrs. Mooney, who was a shrewd judge, knew that the young men were only passing the time away: none of them meant business. Things went on so for a long time and Mrs. Mooney began to think of sending Polly back to type-writing when she noticed that something was going on between Polly and one of the young men. She watched the pair and kept her own counsel.

Polly knew that she was being watched, but still her mother's persistent silence could not be misunderstood. There had been no open complicity between mother and daughter, no open understanding but, though people in the house began to talk of the affair, still Mrs. Mooney did not intervene. Polly began to grow a little strange in her manner and the young man was evidently perturbed. At last, when she judged it to be the right moment, Mrs. Mooney intervened. She dealt with moral problems as a cleaver deals with meat: and in this case she had made up her mind.

It was a bright Sunday morning of early summer, promising heat, but with a fresh breeze blowing. All the windows of the boarding house were open, and the lace curtains ballooned gently towards the street beneath the raised sashes. The belfry of George's Church sent out constant peals and worshippers, singly or in groups, traversed the little circus[1] before the church, revealing their purpose by their self-contained demeanor no less than by the little volumes in their gloved hands. Breakfast was over in the boarding house, and the table of the breakfast room was covered with plates on which lay yellow streaks of eggs with morsels of bacon-fat and bacon-rind. Mrs. Mooney sat in the straw armchair and watched the servant Mary remove the breakfast things. She made Mary collect the crusts and pieces of broken bread to help to make Tuesday's bread-pudding. When the table was cleared, the broken bread collected, the sugar and butter safe under lock and key, she began to reconstruct the interview which she had had the night before with Polly. Things were as she had suspected: she had been frank in her questions and Polly had been frank in her answers. Both had been somewhat awkward, of course. She had been made awkward by her not wishing to receive the news in too cavalier a fashion or to seem to have connived, and Polly had been made awkward not merely because allusions of that kind always made her awkward but also because she did not wish it to be thought that in her wise innocence she had divined the intention behind her mother's tolerance.

Mrs. Mooney glanced instinctively at the little gilt clock on the mantelpiece as soon as she had become aware through her revery that the bells of George's Church had stopped ringing. It was seventeen minutes past eleven: she would have lots of time to have the matter out with Mr. Doran and then catch short twelve at Marlborough Street. She was sure she would win. To begin with she had all the weight of social opinion on her side: she was an outraged mother. She had allowed him to live beneath her roof, assuming that he was a man of honor, and he had simply abused her hospitality. He was thirty-four or thirty-five years of age, so that youth could not be pleaded as his excuse; nor could ignorance be his excuse since he was a man who had seen something of the world. He had simply taken advantage of Polly's youth and inexperience: that was evident. The question was: What reparation would he make?

There must be reparation made in such case. It is all very well for the man: he can go his ways as if nothing had happened, having had his moment of pleasure, but the girl has to bear the brunt. Some mothers would be

---

1. **circus:** a circular open place where many streets come together.

content to patch up such an affair for a sum of money; she had known cases of it. But she would not do so. For her, only one reparation could make up for the loss of her daughter's honor: marriage.

She counted all her cards again before sending Mary up to Mr. Doran's room to say that she wished to speak with him. She felt sure she would win. He was a serious young man, not rakish or loud-voiced like the others. If it had been Mr. Sheridan or Mr. Meade or Bantam Lyons her task would have been much harder. She did not think he would face publicity. All the lodgers in the house knew something of the affair; details had been invented by some. Besides, he had been employed for thirteen years in a great Catholic wine-merchant's office and publicity would mean for him, perhaps, the loss of his job. Whereas if he agreed, all might be well. She knew he had a good screw[2] for one thing and she suspected he had a bit of stuff put by.

Nearly the half-hour! She stood up and surveyed herself in the pier glass. The decisive expression of her great florid face satisfied her, and she thought of some mothers she knew who could not get their daughters off their hands.

Mr. Doran was very anxious indeed this Sunday morning. He had made two attempts to shave, but his hand had been so unsteady that he had been obliged to desist. Three days' reddish beard fringed his jaws and every two or three minutes a mist gathered on his glasses so that he had to take them off and polish them with his pocket handkerchief. The recollection of his confession of the night before was a cause of acute pain to him; the priest had drawn out every ridiculous detail of the affair and in the end had so magnified his sin that he was almost thankful at being afforded a loophole of reparation. The harm was done. What could he do now but marry her or run away? He could not brazen it out. The affair would be sure to be talked of and his employer would be certain to hear of it. Dublin is such a small city: everyone knows everyone else's business. He felt his heart leap warmly in his throat as he heard in his excited imagination old Mr. Leonard calling out in his rasping voice: "Send Mr. Doran here, please."

All his long years of service gone for nothing! All his industry and diligence thrown away! As a young man he had sown his wild oats, of course; he had boasted of his freethinking and denied the existence of God to his companions in public houses.[3] But that was all passed and done with . . . nearly. He still bought a copy of *Reynolds's Newspaper* every week, but he attended to his religious duties and for nine-tenths of the year lived a regular life. He had money enough to settle down on; it was not that. But the family would look down on her. First of all there was her disreputable father, and then her mother's boarding house was beginning to get a certain fame. He had a notion that he was being had. He could imagine his friends talking of the affair and laughing. She *was* a little vulgar; sometimes she said "I seen" and "If I had've known." But what would grammar matter if he really loved her? He could not make up his mind whether to like her or despise her for what she had done. Of course he had done it too. His instinct urged him to remain free, not to marry. Once you are married you are done for, it said.

While he was sitting helplessly on the side of the bed in shirt and trousers she tapped lightly at his door and entered. She told him all, that she had made a clean breast of it to her mother and that her mother would speak with him that morning. She cried and threw her arms round his neck, saying:

"O Bob! Bob! What am I to do? What am I to do at all?"

She would put an end to herself, she said.

He comforted her feebly, telling her not to cry, that it would be all right, never fear. He

---

2. **screw:** salary.
3. **public house:** a bar or saloon.

felt against his shirt the agitation of her bosom.

It was not altogether his fault that it had happened. He remembered well, with the curious patient memory of the celibate, the first casual caresses her dress, her breath, her fingers had given him. Then late one night as he was undressing for bed she had tapped at his door, timidly. She wanted to relight her candle at his, for hers had been blown out by a gust. It was her bath night. She wore a loose open combing jacket[4] of printed flannel. Her white instep shone in the opening of her furry slippers and the blood glowed warmly behind her perfumed skin. From her hands and wrists too as she lit and steadied her candle a faint perfume arose.

On nights when he came in very late it was she who warmed up his dinner. He scarcely knew what he was eating, feeling her beside him alone, at night, in the sleeping house. And her thoughtfulness! If the night was anyway cold or wet or windy, there was sure to be a little tumbler of punch ready for him. Perhaps they could be happy together. . . .

They used to go upstairs together on tiptoe, each with a candle, and on the third landing exchange reluctant goodnights. They used to kiss. He remembered well her eyes, the touch of her hand and his delirium. . . .

But delirium passes. He echoed her phrase, applying it to himself: *"What am I to do?"* The instinct of the celibate warned him to hold back. But the sin was there; even his sense of honor told him that reparation must be made for such a sin.

While he was sitting with her on the side of the bed, Mary came to the door and said that the missus wanted to see him in the parlor. He stood up to put on his coat and waistcoat, more helpless than ever. When he was dressed he went over to her to comfort her. It would be all right, never fear. He left her crying on the bed and moaning softly: *"O my God!"*

Going down the stairs his glasses became so dimmed with moisture that he had to take them off and polish them. He longed to ascend through the roof and fly away to another country where he would never hear again of his trouble, and yet a force pushed him downstairs step by step. The implacable faces of his employer and of the Madam stared upon his discomfiture. On the last flight of stairs he passed Jack Mooney who was coming up from the pantry nursing two bottles of *Bass*. They saluted coldly; and the lover's eyes rested for a second or two on a thick bulldog face and a pair of thick short arms. When he reached the foot of the staircase he glanced up and saw Jack regarding him from the door of the return room.

Suddenly he remembered the night when one of the music hall *artistes*, a little blond Londoner, had made a rather free allusion to Polly. The reunion had been almost broken up on account of Jack's violence. Everyone tried to quiet him. The music hall *artiste*, a little paler than usual, kept smiling and saying that there was no harm meant: but Jack kept shouting at him that if any fellow tried that sort of a game on with his sister he'd bloody well put his teeth down his throat, so he would.

Polly sat for a little time on the side of the bed, crying. Then she dried her eyes and went over to the looking glass. She dipped the end of the towel in the water jug and refreshed her eyes with the cool water. She looked at herself in profile and readjusted a hairpin above her ear. Then she went back to the bed again and sat at the foot. She regarded the pillows for a long time, and the sight of them awakened in her mind secret, amiable memories. She rested the nape of her neck against the cool iron bedrail and fell into a reverie. There was no longer any perturbation visible on her face.

She waited on patiently, almost cheerfully, without alarm, her memories gradually giving

---

4. **combing jacket:** a jacket worn to protect clothes from hair combings.

place to hopes and visions of the future. Her hopes and visions were so intricate that she no longer saw the white pillows on which her gaze was fixed or remembered that she was waiting for anything.

At last she heard her mother calling. She started to her feet and ran to the banisters.

"Polly! Polly!"

"Yes, mamma?"

"Come down, dear. Mr. Doran wants to speak to you."

Then she remembered what she had been waiting for.

Getting at Meaning

1. As the story opens, how is Mrs. Mooney characterized in contrast with her husband? How does the story bear out the assessment of Mrs. Mooney as "a determined woman"?

2. Polly, when she becomes involved with Mr. Doran, "knew that she was being watched, but still her mother's persistent silence could not be misunderstood." Explain.

3. "At last, when she judged it to be the right moment, Mrs. Mooney intervened." Why? What was the right moment, and how did she know?

4. Based on the interview Mrs. Mooney has with her daughter, how would you describe the relationship between the two? Has the mother "connived"? What is meant by Polly's "wise innocence"?

5. Mrs. Mooney pictures herself as "an outraged mother" whose guest has "abused her hospitality." Is this the way she actually feels? Explain her concept of "reparation."

6. Why is Mr. Doran "very anxious indeed this Sunday morning," though he does not yet know that Polly has talked to her mother? What conflicting impulses does he feel?

7. Describe and explain Polly's change of mood, as she waits for Mr. Doran. What has she been waiting for? In what ways will "reparation" be made?

Developing Skills in Reading Literature

1. **Point of View.** When a writer summarizes events and conversations rather than presenting them in detail, the narrative method is called panoramic. In the scenic method, on the other hand, actions are presented as they are imagined to occur, often objectively, sometimes as they are seen and understood by a single character. In "The Boarding House" where does Joyce use the panoramic method and where does he use the scenic method? Where is the point of view omniscient? Where is it limited to particular characters? In terms of the effectiveness of the story, what is the result of the progressive shifts in the point of view?

2. **Exposition.** Notice the amount of introductory exposition in this story. How is it relevant? Why is the description of Mr. Mooney included, for example, when he doesn't really appear in the story?

3. **Character.** Does this story tend to show human beings as controlling their destinies, as victims of circumstances or manipulation, or as something in between? Consider whether each main character is (a) doing the acting, (b) being acted upon, or (c) both.

What do these passages reveal about Mrs. Mooney:

"She dealt with moral problems as a cleaver deals with meat. . . ."

"She counted all her cards again before sending Mary up to Mr. Doran's room. . . ."

What motivates her actions? Is she as simple a character as might be suggested by the two quotations? Explain.

This story portrays a critical point in the life of Bob Doran. Why does he make the choice he does, or is it a choice? How has he been influenced by the following factors: his sense of honor, Polly's initiative, his "instinct of the celibate," Mrs. Mooney, Jack Mooney, his employer, his confessor, his family, his own sense of helplessness? Has Joyce depicted realistically the way a choice such as Doran's is made?

Now think about the character of Polly. Are you surprised by her actions at the end of the story? How has Joyce prepared you for this ending?

4. **Tone.** This story deals with sexual attraction against a background of social and religious convention and constraint. Does the imagery reflect this mixture of forces? Comment, for example, on the first part of the paragraph beginning, "It was a bright Sunday morning of early summer. . . ." Earlier, the phrase "perverse madonna" is used to describe Polly. How does the phrase sum up the conflict between sexuality and repression?

Religion is a pervasive force in Irish society, a part of the context in which Joyce's characters exist. Consider how religion functions in the lives of each of the characters in this story. How does Joyce seem to view religion? With what kinds of people do his sympathies seem to lie?

Developing Vocabulary

Word Origins. Words having abstract meanings often derive from origins that are much more concrete. Look up the etymologies of the following words, and explain the relationships between their concrete roots and their abstract meanings.

brunt	delirium
cavalier	florid
connive	

Developing Writing Skills

Using Comparison and Contrast. Paul's mother in "The Rocking-Horse Winner" and Polly's mother in "The Boarding House" are both important characters. In a well developed paragraph, compare and contrast them in terms of their love for their children, their competence, their understanding and control of situations, the accuracy of their portrayal, or any other factors you wish. Do you personally find one more attractive than the other? Explain your answer in the concluding sentence.

George Orwell

1903–1950

Journalist, autobiographer, social critic, and novelist, George Orwell wrote prophetically of the dangers of dictatorial government. His aim was to write "prose like a window pane," an aim he achieved in both his fiction and nonfiction.

Orwell, whose real name was Eric Arthur Blair, was born in Motihāri, Bengal, where his father was an agent in the Indian Civil Service. Young Orwell was educated in England and won a scholarship to Eton, where Aldous Huxley was one of his teachers. Although Orwell was a brilliant scholar, rather than continue on to a university, he joined the Indian Imperial Police in Burma. The growing disenchantment with colonialism he developed while serving as a police officer is evident in the essay "Shooting an Elephant," which describes an episode in which he acts unwillingly as the representative of imperial authority.

In 1928 Orwell quit the Indian Imperial Police to make his living as a writer. For the next five years, he lived in the slums of Paris and London, publishing articles and working as a tutor, teacher, dishwasher, and clerk in a bookstore. Out of these varied experiences came *Down and Out in Paris and London* (1933), for which he first used the pen name George Orwell, and his early novels, *A Clergyman's Daughter* (1935) and *Keep the Aspidistra Flying* (1936).

Orwell considered himself a Socialist in the 1930's, and *The Road to Wigan Pier* (1937), an autobiographical account of his experiences living with miners in northern England, expresses his political opinions. Like many intellectuals of the time, he was drawn to the Spanish Civil War, in which the forces of Fascism, allied with Germany and Italy, were trying to take over Spain. He enlisted with the anti-Fascist forces in 1936 and was wounded in the fighting. Back in England, Orwell was rejected for military service in World War II because of recurrent tuberculosis. During the war years he wrote many articles for newspapers as well as critical essays and books about

GEORGE ORWELL.
The Bettman Archive, Inc.

England, among them *The Lion and the Unicorn* (1941).

Deeply disturbed by the spread of dictatorships, Orwell produced the works for which he is best known, *Animal Farm* (1945) and *1984* (1949). In *Animal Farm*, a fable based on the Russian revolution, farm animals act like human beings, and the pigs begin to dominate the other animals. The pigs' motto is: "All animals are equal, but some animals are more equal than others." In *1984* Orwell describes a totalitarian state that uses the tools of modern technology to keep watch on its people and to stifle any kind of individualism and protest. Part of this control is executed through the manipulation of language, a "doublespeak" of lies, propaganda, and rewritten history. An immediate sensation, *1984* sold better than any of Orwell's other books. He died less than seven months after its publication.

Shooting an Elephant

In Moulmein,[1] in Lower Burma, I was hated by large numbers of people—the only time in my life that I have been important enough for this to happen to me. I was sub-divisional police officer of the town, and in an aimless, petty kind of way anti-European feeling was very bitter. No one had the guts to raise a riot, but if a European woman went through the bazaars alone somebody would probably spit betel juice over her dress. As a police officer I was an obvious target and was baited whenever it seemed safe to do so. When a nimble Burman tripped me up on the football field and the referee (another Burman) looked the other way, the crowd yelled with hideous laughter. This happened more than once. In the end the sneering yellow faces of young men that met me everywhere, the insults hooted after me when I was at a safe distance, got badly on my nerves. The young Buddhist priests were the worst of all. There were several thousands of them in the town and none of them seemed to have anything to do except stand on street corners and jeer at Europeans.

All this was perplexing and upsetting. For at that time I had already made up my mind that imperialism was an evil thing and the sooner I chucked up my job and got out of it the better. Theoretically—and secretly, of course—I was all for the Burmese and all against their oppressors, the British. As for the job I was doing, I hated it more bitterly than I can perhaps make clear. In a job like that you see the dirty work of Empire at close quarters. The wretched prisoners huddling in the stinking cages of the lock-ups, the grey, cowed faces of the long-term convicts, the scarred buttocks of the men who had been flogged with bamboos—all these oppressed me with an intolerable sense of guilt. But I could get nothing into perspective. I was young and ill-educated and I had had to think out my problems in the utter silence that is imposed on every Englishman in the East. I did not even know that the British Empire is dying, still less did I know that it is a great deal better than the younger empires that are going to supplant it. All I knew was that I was stuck between my hatred of the empire I served and my rage against the evil-spirited little beasts who tried to make my job impossible. With one part of my mind I thought of the British Raj[2] as an unbreakable tyranny, as something clamped down, in *saecula saeculorum*,[3] upon the will of prostrate peoples; with another part I thought that the greatest joy in the world would be to drive a bayonet into a Buddhist priest's guts. Feelings like these are the normal byproducts of imperialism; ask any Anglo-Indian official, if you can catch him off duty.

One day something happened which in a roundabout way was enlightening. It was a tiny incident in itself, but it gave me a better glimpse than I had had before of the real nature of imperialism—the real motives for which despotic governments act. Early one morning the sub-inspector at a police station the other end of the town rang me up on the 'phone and said that an elephant was ravaging the bazaar. Would I please come and do something about it? I did not know what I could do,

---

1. **Moulmein** (mōōl mān').
2. **Raj** (räj): government or rule.
3. *in saecula saeculorum* (sē'koo lə sē kōō lôr' əm) *Latin:* forever and ever.

but I wanted to see what was happening and I got on to a pony and started out. I took my rifle, an old .44 Winchester and much too small to kill an elephant, but I thought the noise might be useful *in terrorem.*[4] Various Burmans stopped me on the way and told me about the elephant's doings. It was not, of course, a wild elephant, but a tame one which had gone "must."[5] It had been chained up, as tame elephants always are when their attack of "must" is due, but on the previous night it had broken its chain and escaped. Its mahout,[6] the only person who could manage it when it was in that state, had set out in pursuit, but had taken the wrong direction and was now twelve hours' journey away, and in the morning the elephant had suddenly reappeared in the town. The Burmese population had no weapons and were quite helpless against it. It had already destroyed somebody's bamboo hut, killed a cow and raided some fruit stalls and devoured the stock; also it had met the municipal rubbish van and, when the driver jumped out and took to his heels, had turned the van over and inflicted violences upon it.

The Burmese sub-inspector and some Indian constables were waiting for me in the quarter where the elephant had been seen. It was a very poor quarter, a labyrinth of squalid bamboo huts, thatched with palm-leaf, winding all over a steep hillside. I remember that it was a cloudy, stuffy morning at the beginning of the rains. We began questioning the people as to where the elephant had gone and, as usual, failed to get any definite information. That is invariably the case in the East; a story always sounds clear enough at a distance, but the nearer you get to the scene of events the vaguer it becomes. Some of the people said that the elephant had gone in one direction, some said that he had gone in another, some professed not even to have heard of any elephant. I had almost made up my mind that the whole story was a pack of lies, when we heard yells a little distance away. There was a loud, scandalized cry of "Go away, child! Go away this instant!" and an old woman with a switch in her hand came round the corner of a hut, violently shooing away a crowd of naked children. Some more women followed, clicking their tongues and exclaiming; evidently there was something that the children ought not to have seen. I rounded the hut and saw a man's dead body sprawling in the mud. He was an Indian, a black Dravidian[7] coolie, almost naked, and he could not have been dead many minutes. The people said that the elephant had come suddenly upon him round the corner of the hut, caught him with its trunk, put its foot on his back and ground him into the earth. This was the rainy season and the ground was soft, and his face had scored a trench a foot deep and a couple of yards long. He was lying on his belly with arms crucified and head sharply twisted to one side. His face was coated with mud, the eyes wide open, the teeth bared and grinning with an expression of unendurable agony. (Never tell me, by the way, that the dead look peaceful. Most of the corpses I have seen looked devilish.) The friction of the great beast's foot had stripped the skin from his back as neatly as one skins a rabbit. As soon as I saw the dead man I sent an orderly to a friend's house nearby to borrow an elephant rifle. I had already sent back the pony, not wanting it to go mad with fright and throw me if it smelled the elephant.

The orderly came back in a few minutes with a rifle and five cartridges, and meanwhile some Burmans had arrived and told us that the elephant was in the paddy fields below, only a few hundred yards away. As I started forward, practically the whole population of the quarter flocked out of the houses and followed me. They had seen the rifle and were all shouting excitedly that I was going to

---

4. *in torrorem* *Latin:* for terror.
5. **must:** a state of dangerous frenzy in animals.
6. **mahout** (mə hōōt): an elephant driver or keeper.
7. **Dravidian:** any of a group of intermixed races in southern India.

shoot the elephant. They had not shown much interest in the elephant when he was merely ravaging their homes, but it was different now that he was going to be shot. It was a bit of fun to them, as it would be to an English crowd; besides, they wanted the meat. It made me vaguely uneasy. I had no intention of shooting the elephant—I had merely sent for the rifle to defend myself if necessary—and it is always unnerving to have a crowd following you. I marched down the hill, looking and feeling a fool, with the rifle over my shoulder and an ever-growing army of people jostling at my heels. At the bottom, when you got away from the huts, there was a metaled[8] road and beyond that a miry waste of paddy fields a thousand yards across, not yet ploughed but soggy from the first rains and dotted with coarse grass. The elephant was standing eight yards from the road, his left side towards us. He took not the slightest notice of the crowd's approach. He was tearing up bunches of grass, beating them against his knees to clean them and stuffing them into his mouth.

I had halted on the road. As soon as I saw the elephant I knew with perfect certainty that I ought not to shoot him. It is a serious matter to shoot a working elephant—it is comparable to destroying a huge and costly piece of machinery—and obviously one ought not to do it if it can possibly be avoided. And at that distance, peacefully eating, the elephant looked no more dangerous than a cow. I thought then and I think now that his attack of "must" was already passing off; in which case he would merely wander harmlessly about until the mahout came back and caught him. Moreover, I did not in the least want to shoot him. I decided that I would watch him for a little while to make sure that he did not turn savage again, and then go home.

But at that moment I glanced round at the crowd that had followed me. It was an immense crowd, two thousand at the least and growing every minute. It blocked the road for a long distance on either side. I looked at the sea of yellow faces above the garish clothes—faces all happy and excited over this bit of fun, all certain that the elephant was going to be shot. They were watching me as they would watch a conjurer about to perform a trick. They did not like me, but with the magical rifle in my hands I was momentarily worth watching. And suddenly I realized that I should have to shoot the elephant after all. The people expected it of me and I had got to do it; I could feel their two thousand wills pressing me forward, irresistibly. And it was at this moment, as I stood there with the rifle in my hands, that I first grasped the hollowness, the futility of the white man's dominion in the East. Here was I, the white man with his gun, standing in front of the unarmed native crowd—seemingly the leading actor of the piece; but in reality I was only an absurd puppet pushed to and fro by the will of those yellow faces behind. I perceived in this moment that when the white man turns tyrant it is his own freedom that he destroys. He becomes a sort of hollow, posing dummy, the conventionalized figure of a sahib.[9] For it is the condition of his rule that he shall spend his life in trying to impress the "natives," and so in every crisis he has got to do what the "natives" expect of him. He wears a mask, and his face grows to fit it. I had got to shoot the elephant. I had committed myself to doing it when I sent for the rifle. A sahib has got to act like a sahib; he has got to appear resolute, to know his own mind and do definite things. To come all that way, rifle in hand, with two thousand people marching at my heels, and then to trail feebly away, having done nothing—no, that was impossible. The crowd would laugh at me. And my whole life, every white man's life in the East, was one long struggle not to be laughed at.

But I did not want to shoot the elephant. I

---

8. **metaled:** paved.
9. **sahib** (sä′ ĭb): a title formerly used in colonial India when speaking to or of a European.

watched him beating his bunch of grass against his knees, with that preoccupied grandmotherly air that elephants have. It seemed to me that it would be murder to shoot him. At that age I was not squeamish about killing animals, but I had never shot an elephant and never wanted to. (Somehow it always seems worse to kill a *large* animal.) Besides, there was the beast's owner to be considered. Alive, the elephant was worth at least a hundred pounds; dead, he would only be worth the value of his tusks, five pounds, possibly. But I had got to act quickly. I turned to some experienced-looking Burmans who had been there when we arrived, and asked them how the elephant had been behaving. They all said the same thing: he took no notice of you if you left him alone, but he might charge if you went too close to him.

It was perfectly clear to me what I ought to do. I ought to walk up to within, say, twenty-five yards of the elephant and test his behavior. If he charged, I could shoot; if he took no notice of me, it would be safe to leave him until the mahout came back. But also I knew that I was going to do no such thing. I was a poor shot with a rifle and the ground was soft mud into which one would sink at every step. If the elephant charged and I missed him, I should have about as much chance as a toad under a steamroller. But even then I was not thinking particularly of my own skin, only of the watchful yellow faces behind. For at that moment, with the crowd watching me, I was not afraid in the ordinary sense, as I would have been if I had been alone. A white man mustn't be frightened in front of "natives"; and so, in general, he isn't frightened. The sole thought in my mind was that if anything went wrong those two thousand Burmans would see me pursued, caught, trampled on, and reduced to a grinning corpse like that Indian up the hill. And if that happened it was quite probable that some of them would laugh. That would never do. There was only one alternative. I shoved the cartridges into the magazine and lay down on the road to get a better aim.

The crowd grew very still, and a deep, low, happy sigh, as of people who see the theatre curtain go up at last, breathed from innumerable throats. They were going to have their bit of fun after all. The rifle was a beautiful German thing with cross-hair sights. I did not then know that in shooting an elephant one would shoot to cut an imaginary bar running from ear-hole to ear-hole. I ought, therefore, as the elephant was sideways on, to have aimed straight at his ear-hole; actually I aimed several inches in front of this, thinking the brain would be further forward.

When I pulled the trigger I did not hear the bang or feel the kick—one never does when a shot goes home—but I heard the devilish roar of glee that went up from the crowd. In that instant, in too short a time, one would have thought, even for the bullet to get there, a mysterious, terrible change had come over the elephant. He neither stirred nor fell, but every line of his body had altered. He looked suddenly stricken, shrunken, immensely old, as though the frightful impact of the bullet had paralyzed him without knocking him down. At last, after what seemed a long time—it might have been five seconds, I dare say—he sagged flabbily to his knees. His mouth slobbered. An enormous senility seemed to have settled upon him. One could have imagined him thousands of years old. I fired again into the same spot. At the second shot he did not collapse but climbed with desperate slowness to his feet and stood weakly upright, with legs sagging and head drooping. I fired a third time. That was the shot that did for him. You could see the agony of it jolt his whole body and knock the last remnant of strength from his legs. But in falling he seemed for a moment to rise, for as his hind legs collapsed beneath him he seemed to tower upward like a huge rock toppling, his trunk reaching skyward like a tree. He trumpeted, for the first and only time. And then down he came, his belly towards me, with a crash that seemed to shake the ground even where I lay.

I got up. The Burmans were already racing past me across the mud. It was obvious that the elephant would never rise again, but he was not dead. He was breathing very rhythmically with long rattling gasps, his great mound of a side painfully rising and falling. His mouth was wide open—I could see far down into caverns of pale pink throat. I waited a long time for him to die, but his breathing did not weaken. Finally I fired my two remaining shots into the spot where I thought his heart must be. The thick blood welled out of him like red velvet, but still he did not die. His body did not even jerk when the shots hit him, the tortured breathing continued without a pause. He was dying, very slowly and in great agony, but in some world remote from me where not even a bullet could damage him further. I felt that I had got to put an end to that dreadful noise. It seemed dreadful to see the great beast lying there, powerless to move and yet powerless to die, and not even to be able to finish him. I sent back for my small rifle and poured shot after shot into his heart and down his throat. They seemed to make no impression. The tortured gasps continued as steadily as the ticking of a clock.

In the end I could not stand it any longer and went away. I heard later that it took him half an hour to die. Burmans were bringing dahs[10] and baskets even before I left, and I was told they had stripped his body almost to the bones by the afternoon.

Afterwards, of course, there were endless discussions about the shooting of the elephant. The owner was furious, but he was only an Indian and could do nothing. Besides, legally I had done the right thing, for a mad elephant has to be killed, like a mad dog, if its owner fails to control it. Among the Europeans opinion was divided. The older men said I was right, the younger men said it was a damn shame to shoot an elephant for killing a coolie, because an elephant was worth more than any damn Coringhee coolie. And afterwards I was very glad that the coolie had been killed; it put me legally in the right and it gave me a sufficient pretext for shooting the elephant. I often wondered whether any of the others grasped that I had done it solely to avoid looking a fool.

---

10. **dahs** (däz): large knives.

Getting at Meaning

1. "In a job like that," Orwell says, "you see the dirty work of Empire at close quarters." What dirty work does he refer to?

2. Trying to understand the system and his place in it, Orwell says that he had had to think out his problems "in the utter silence that is imposed on every Englishman in the East." What does he mean?

3. Describe Orwell's mixed feelings while on duty in Burma. Why are some of these feelings "the normal byproducts of imperialism"?

4. How does the death of the coolie foreshadow the death of the elephant?

5. Orwell says that the sahib, among the natives, "wears a mask, and his face grows to fit it." What process is he describing? What mask does Orwell wear?

6. In handling this situation, what was the one thing Orwell felt that he must avoid at any cost?

7. "When I pulled the trigger," Orwell says, "I did not hear the bang or feel the kick—one never does when a shot goes home. . . ." What does Orwell mean?

8. How do the reactions of the other Europeans tend to confirm Orwell's point about imperialism?

Developing Skills in Reading Literature

1. **Description.** Descriptive writing appeals to the senses, creating for the reader a vivid impression of a person, scene, object, or action. Compare the routine depiction of violence and death on television and in motion pictures with the way that Orwell has described death. What is the difference? What techniques help the reader of this selection to perceive the reality of death clearly and perhaps to feel it in a human way? Consider Orwell's reporting of objective details in describing the dead coolie. What passages most effectively convey the horror of the elephant's death?

2. **Essay: Structure.** This essay contains an interesting blend of narration, description, and exposition. Analyze the structure of the essay to determine the way that Orwell blends the three types of writing. Would you classify the essay as primarily narrative? descriptive? expository? Explain.

3. **Theme.** In the third paragraph, Orwell says that this incident "gave me a better glimpse than I had had before of the real nature of imperialism—the real motives for which despotic governments act." What are those motives, according to Orwell? Find the one sentence that most clearly states the central idea of this essay. What is ironic about this statement?

Developing Writing Skills

Explaining an Idea. Write an essay in which you demonstrate the truth of Orwell's theme in terms of some other situation, either historical or contemporary. The oppressors might be a government, a social class, or a small group.

from **1984**

The mutability of the past is the central tenet of Ingsoc.[1] Past events, it is argued, have no objective existence, but survive only in written records and in human memories. The past is whatever the records, and the memories agree upon. And since the Party is in full control of all records, and in equally full control of the minds of its members, it follows that the past is whatever the Party chooses to make it. It also follows that though the past is alterable, it never has been altered in any specific instance. For when it has been recreated in whatever shape is needed at the moment, then this new version *is* the past, and no different past can ever have existed.

This holds good even when, as often happens, the same event has to be altered out of recognition several times in the course of a year. At all times the Party is in possession of absolute truth, and clearly the absolute can never have been different from what it is now. It will be seen that the control of the past depends above all on the training of memory. To make sure that all written records agree with the orthodoxy of the moment is merely a mechanical act. But it is also necessary to *remember* that events happened in the desired

---

1. **Ingsoc:** a "Newspeak" acronym for English Socialism.

manner. And if it is necessary to rearrange one's memories or to tamper with written records, then it is necessary to *forget* that one has done so. The trick of doing this can be learned like any other mental technique. It *is* learned by the majority of Party members, and certainly by all who are intelligent as well as orthodox. In Oldspeak[2] it is called, quite frankly, "reality control." In Newspeak[3] it is called *doublethink*, although *doublethink* comprises much else as well.

Doublethink means the power of holding two contradictory beliefs in one's mind simultaneously, and accepting both of them. The Party intellectual knows in which direction his memories must be altered; he therefore knows that he is playing tricks with reality; but by the exercise of *doublethink* he also satisfies himself that reality is not violated. The process has to be conscious, or it would not be carried out with sufficient precision, but it also has to be unconscious, or it would bring with it a feeling of falsity and hence of guilt. *Doublethink* lies at the very heart of Ingsoc, since the essential act of the Party is to use conscious deception while retaining the firmness of purpose that goes with complete honesty. To tell deliberate lies while genuinely believing in them, to forget any fact that has become inconvenient, and then, when it becomes necessary again, to draw it back from oblivion for just so long as it is needed, to deny the existence of objective reality and all the while to take account of the reality which one denies—all this is indispensably necessary. Even in using the word *doublethink* it is necessary to exercise *doublethink*. For by using the word one admits that one is tampering with reality; by a fresh act of *doublethink* one erases this knowledge; and so on indefinitely, with the lie always one leap ahead of the truth. Ultimately, it is by means of *doublethink* that the Party has been able—and may, for all we know, continue to be able for thousands of years—to arrest the course of history.

All past oligarchies have fallen from power either because they ossified or because they grew soft. Either they became stupid and arrogant, failed to adjust themselves to changing circumstances, and were overthrown, or they became liberal and cowardly, made concessions when they should have used force, and once again were overthrown. They fell, that is to say, either through consciousness or through unconsciousness. It is the achievement of the Party to have produced a system of thought in which both conditions can exist simultaneously. And upon no other intellectual basis could the dominion of the Party be made permanent. If one is to rule, and to continue ruling, one must be able to dislocate the sense of reality. For the secret of rulership is to combine a belief in one's own infallibility with the power to learn from past mistakes.

It need hardly be said that the subtlest practitioners of *doublethink* are those who invented *doublethink* and know that it is a vast system of mental cheating. In our society, those who have the best knowledge of what is happening are also those who are furthest from seeing the world as it is. In general, the greater the understanding, the greater the delusion: the more intelligent, the less sane. One clear illustration of this is the fact that war hysteria increases in intensity as one rises in the social scale. Those whose attitude toward the war is most nearly rational are the subject peoples of the disputed territories. To these people the war is simply a continuous calamity which sweeps to and fro over their bodies like a tidal wave. Which side is winning is a matter of complete indifference to them.

---

2. **Oldspeak:** Standard English.
3. **Newspeak:** an "official" language devised to meet the ideological needs of Ingsoc; that is, a language meant to convey only those ideas that a "Party" member could properly express, while excluding all other meanings.

Getting at Meaning

1. What things must the Party control in order to control the past? To exercise this control, what assumption must be made about the real nature of past events?

2. If it is possible for the Party to change the past, why has it never been changed? What is the Party's definition of absolute truth?

3. Is it necessary for Party members to believe their own lies? Why or why not?

4. When history is being altered, to what extent are those responsible aware of what they are doing?

5. Under the system of *doublethink*, what is the relationship between intelligence and the ability to see the world as it is? What is the explanation for this?

6. How is *doublethink* used to promote the war effort?

7. How would you sum up the central paradox, the self-contradictory nature of *doublethink*?

Developing Skills in Reading Literature

1. **Style.** The purpose of this passage of exposition from *1984* is to set forth a complex and abstract intellectual system. It follows, therefore, that the style should be as clear as possible. To achieve clarity, balance, and coherence, Orwell has used definitions, examples, and contrasts as well as the following structural and grammatical devices.

a. **Transitional Devices.** Words such as *and*, *but*, *for*, and *also* are useful in maintaining a logical continuity between sentences. Another transitional device is the use of a pronoun whose antecedent is in the preceeding sentence. Point out several examples of these and other effective transitions in this selection.

b. **Antithesis.** In this excerpt the reasoning often involves some kind of polarity or paradox; antithetical expressions bring out these contrasting ideas. Find examples of antithesis, particularly in the last paragraph.

c. **Parallelism.** The concepts in this selection often are arranged into opposing categories, and parallel grammatical constructions function to keep the meaning clear. Look for examples of parallelism in the third paragraph. What parallelism do you find in the discussion of deliberate lies in the second paragraph?

d. **Aphorism.** Clarity is further gained by concise expressions of important concepts. An example is the definition of good rulership, which appears near the end of the selection. Identify other examples of aphoristic expressions.

2. **Theme.** Orwell's *1984* is an anti-utopian novel, the opposite of the traditional utopian novel, which dramatizes an ideal society. Orwell's projects into the future certain political trends he saw as dangerous. What are these trends, as they are implied in this excerpt? Why does the Party *need* to alter the past?

3. **Fiction and Nonfiction.** The essential difference between fiction and nonfiction is that fiction originates in the imagination of the writer while nonfiction derives from factual reality. The same techniques, however, are available to writers of both fiction and nonfiction. Notice, for example, the way that Orwell uses plot, character, point of view, and setting, which are associated with fiction, in the nonfiction piece "Shooting an Elephant." This excerpt from *1984*, on the other hand, is fiction that resembles an expository essay. What elements in the excerpt are clearly fictional? What gives it the tone of nonfiction?

Developing Writing Skills

1. **Explaining an Idea.** Without attempting something as difficult as the concept of *doublethink*, write a brief essay in which you explain an abstract idea, using some of the structural devices that Orwell uses in this selection. You might choose as your subject the rules of an organization you have belonged to, the objectives of a course you are taking, the unspoken assumptions of a social group, the justification for a particular religious doctrine, or your reasons for supporting one side of an ethical or political issue. Remember to strive for structural balance and clarity in your prose.

2. **Using Examples.** Orwell was warning against thought control and the rewriting of history by authoritarian regimes. Even in an open society, with a free flow of ideas, the historical record undergoes frequent revision and reevaluation, in an attempt to gain balance and perspective. On the basis of library research, report on such a shift in historical outlook involving one of the following: (a) John Kennedy, (b) Richard Nixon, (c) black history, (d) the place of women in history.

Aldous Huxley

1894–1963

ALDOUS HUXLEY. *The Bettmann Archive, Inc.*

Aldous Huxley addressed all the significant concerns of his day; even in fictional works, ideas and issues are as important as the characters and their emotional interplay. Critic V.S. Pritchett wrote of Huxley: "Nothing short of universal knowledge was his aim. No traveler through cultures, no connoisseur of human habits, no asker had lapped up so much. As a writer, he became [an] . . . ever-extending, ever-dramatizing encyclopedia, and he had the gaity and melancholy of mind to put it out in novels, essays, plays, and works of speculation and criticism."

Few writers have been more influenced by their families than was Huxley. His grandfather was Thomas Henry Huxley, the biologist and celebrity who popularized science and the scientific method. His father was Leonard Huxley, editor of *Cornhill Magazine*, biographer of Charles Darwin, and poet. His elder brother, Julian, was the most illustrious zoologist of the twentieth century. His mother was a niece of the poet Matthew Arnold. Young Huxley was raised in a stimulating intellectual environment, alive with exciting new ideas.

Huxley seemed destined for a career in science until an eye ailment left him virtually blind and forced him to abandon his medical studies. The profound depression he endured during this period may have contributed to the deep, unrelenting pessimism that colors his best work.

When his eyes recovered partially, Huxley finished his studies, receiving a degree in English in 1915, at which time he was well on his way to becoming a writer. By the age of seventeen, he had written an eighty-thousand-word novel that was never published. This was followed by poetry, articles in literary journals, and his first published novels, *The Defeat of Youth* (1918), *Limbo* (1920), and *Crome Yellow* (1921). In his early novels, Huxley displays the verve, wit, and wicked sense of fun that captivated the postwar generation.

Readers loved his satiric portrayals of artistic luminaries, so thinly disguised that most recognized them instantly; D.H. Lawrence and Bertrand Russell were among the figures wittily sketched.

In 1919 Huxley married Maria Nys, a Belgian refugee. The family traveled widely, living in Italy for several years, where Huxley associated with D.H. Lawrence and where he wrote *Those Barren Leaves* (1925), and *Point Counter Point* (1928). *Brave New World*, his most famous book, appeared in 1932. In it Huxley describes an anti-utopia, an ironic fantasy vision of a soullessly scientific, dehumanized future. Gone from *Brave New World* was the natural gaity of his earlier works; in its place was a serious concern with the worsening political situation.

In 1937 Huxley settled permanently in southern California, where he worked as a freelance screenwriter. He continued to pursue an interest in mysticism, evident in *Eyeless in Gaza* (1936) and *The Doors of Perception* (1954). His death in 1963 followed a long illness.

The Language of War

Words form the thread on which we string our experiences. Without them we should live spasmodically and intermittently. Hatred itself is not so strong that animals will not forget it, if distracted, even in the presence of the enemy. Watch a pair of cats, crouching on the brink of a fight. Balefully the eyes glare; from far down in the throat of each come bursts of a strange, strangled noise of defiance; as though animated by a life of their own, the tails twitch and tremble. With aimed intensity of loathing! Another moment and surely there must be an explosion. But no; all of a sudden one of the two creatures turns away, hoists a hind leg in a more than fascist salute and, with the same fixed and focused attention as it had given a moment before to its enemy, begins to make a lingual toilet. Animal love is as much at the mercy of distractions as animal hatred. The dumb creation lives a life made up of discreet and mutually irrelevant episodes. Such as it is, the consistency of human characters is due to the words upon which all human experiences are strung. We are purposeful because we can describe our feelings in rememberable words, can justify and rationalize our desires in terms of some kind of argument. Faced by an enemy we do not allow an itch to distract us from our emotions; the mere word *enemy* is enough to keep us reminded of our hatred, to convince us that we do well to be angry. Similarly the word *love* bridges for us those chasms of momentary indifference and boredom which gape from time to time between even the most ardent lovers. Feeling and desire provide us with our motive power; words give continuity to what we do and to a considerable extent determine our direction. Inappropriate and badly chosen words vitiate thought and lead to wrong or foolish conduct. Most ignorances are vincible, and in the greater number of cases stupidity is what the Buddha pronounced it to be, a sin. For, consciously, or subconsciously, it is with deliberation that we do not know or fail to understand—because incomprehension allows us, with a good conscience, to evade unpleasant obligations and responsibilities, because ignorance is the best excuse for going on doing what one likes, but ought not, to do. Our egotisms are incessantly fighting to preserve themselves, not only from external enemies, but also from the assaults of the other and better self with which they are so uncomfortably associated. Ignorance is egotism's most effective defense against that Dr. Jekyll in us who desires perfection; stupidity, its subtlest stratagem. If, as so often happens, we choose to give continuity to our experience by means of words which falsify the facts, this is because the falsification is somehow to our advantage as egotists.

Consider, for example, the case of war. War is enormously discreditable to those who order it to be waged and even to those who merely tolerate its existence. Furthermore, to developed sensibilities the facts of war are revolting and horrifying. To falsify these facts, and by so doing to make war seem less evil than it really is, and our own responsibility in tolerating war less heavy, is doubly to our advantage. By suppressing and distorting the truth, we protect our sensibilities and preserve our self-esteem. Now, language is, among other things, a device which men use for suppressing and distorting the truth. Finding the reality of war too unpleasant to contemplate, we create a verbal alternative to that reality, parallel with it, but in quality quite different from it. That which we contemplate thenceforward is not that to which we react emotionally and upon which we pass our moral judgments, is not war as it is in fact, but the fiction of war as it exists in our pleasantly falsifying verbiage. Our stupidity in using inappropriate language turns out, on analysis, to be the most refined cunning.

The most shocking fact about war is that its victims and its instruments are individual human beings, and that these individual human beings are condemned by the monstrous conventions of politics to murder or be murdered in quarrels not their own, to inflict upon the innocent and, innocent themselves of any crime against their enemies, to suffer cruelties of every kind.

The language of strategy and politics is designed, so far as it is possible, to conceal this fact, to make it appear as though wars were not fought by individuals drilled to murder one another in cold blood and without provocation, but either by impersonal and therefore wholly non-moral and impassible forces, or else by personified abstractions.

Here are a few examples of the first kind of falsification. In place of "cavalrymen" or "foot-soldiers" military writers like to speak of "sabers" and "rifles." Here is a sentence from a description of the Battle of Marengo: "The French retreat was orderly; it is certain, at any rate, that the regiments held together, for the six thousand Austrian sabers found no opportunity to charge home." The battle is between sabers in line and muskets in echelon[1]—a mere clash of ironmongery.[2]

On other occasions there is no question of anything so vulgarly material as ironmongery. The battles are between Platonic ideas, between the abstractions of physics and mathematics. Forces interact; weights are flung into scales; masses are set in motion. Or else it is all a matter of geometry. Lines swing and sweep; are protracted or curved; pivot on a fixed point.

Alternatively the combatants are personal, in the sense that they are personifications. There is "the enemy," in the singular, making "his" plans, striking "his" blows. The attribution of personal characteristics to collectivities, to geographical expressions, to institutions, is a source, as we shall see, of endless confusions in political thought, of innumerable political mistakes and crimes. Personification in politics is an error which we make because it is to our advantage as egotists to be able to feel violently proud of our country and of ourselves as belonging to it, and to believe that all the misfortunes due to our own mistakes are really the work of the Foreigner. It is easier to feel violently toward a person than toward an abstraction; hence our habit of making political personifications. In some cases military personifications are merely special instances of political personifications. A particular collectivity, the army or the warring nation, is given the name and, along with the name, the attributes of a single person, in order that we may be able to love or hate it more intensely than we could do if we thought of it as what it really is: a number of diverse individuals. In other cases personification is used for the purpose of concealing the fundamental absurdity and monstrosity of war. What is absurd and monstrous about war is that men who have no personal quarrel should be trained to murder one another in cold blood. By personifying opposing armies or countries, we are able to think of war as a conflict between individuals. The same result is obtained by writing of war as though it were carried on exclusively by the generals in command and not by the private soldiers in their armies. ("Rennenkampf had pressed back von Schubert.") The implication in both cases is that war is indistinguishable from a bout of fisticuffs in a bar room. Whereas in reality it is profoundly different. A scrap between two individuals is forgivable; mass

---

1. **echelon** (esh' ə län): a steplike formation of troops.
2. **ironmongery:** hardware.

murder, deliberately organized, is a monstrous iniquity. We still choose to use war as an instrument of policy; and to comprehend the full wickedness and absurdity of war would therefore be inconvenient. For, once we understood, we should have to make some effort to get rid of the abominable thing. Accordingly, when we talk about war, we use a language which conceals or embellishes its reality. Ignoring the facts, so far as we possibly can, we imply that battles are not fought by soldiers, but by things, principles, allegories, personified collectivities, or (at the most human) by opposing commanders, pitched against one another in single combat. For the same reason, when we have to describe the processes and the results of war, we employ a rich variety of euphemisms. Even the most violently patriotic and militaristic are reluctant to call a spade by its own name. To conceal their intentions even from themselves, they make use of picturesque metaphors. We find them, for example, clamoring for war planes numerous and powerful enough to go and "destroy the hornets in their nests"—in other words, to go and throw thermite,[3] high explosives and vesicants[4] upon the inhabitants of neighboring countries before they have time to come and do the same to us. And how reassuring is the language of historians and strategists! They write admiringly of those military geniuses who know "when to strike at the enemy's line" (a single combatant deranges the geometrical constructions of a personification); when to "turn his flank"; when to "execute an enveloping movement." As though they were engineers discussing the strength of materials and the distribution of stresses, they talk of abstract entities called "man power" and "fire power." They sum up the long-drawn sufferings and atrocities of trench warfare in the phrase, "a war of attrition"; the massacre and mangling of human beings is assimilated to the grinding of a lens.

A dangerously abstract word, which figures in all discussions about war, is *force*. Those who believe in organizing collective security by means of military pacts against a posssible aggressor are particularly fond of this word. "You cannot," they say "have international justice unless you are prepared to impose it by force." "Peace-loving countries must unite to use force against aggressive dictatorships." "Democratic institutions must be protected, if need be, by force." And so on.

Now, the word *force*, when used in reference to human relations, has no single, definite meaning. There is the "force" used by parents when, without resort to any kind of physical violence, they compel their children to act or refrain from acting in some particular way. There is the "force" used by attendants in an asylum when they try to prevent a maniac from hurting himself or others. There is the "force" used by the police when they control a crowd, and that other "force" which they used in a baton charge. And finally there is the "force" used in war. This, of course, varies with the technological devices at the disposal of the belligerents, with the policies they are pursuing, and with the particular circumstances of the war in question. But in general it may be said that, in war, "force" connotes violence and fraud used to the limit of the combatants' capacity.

Variations in quantity, if sufficiently great, produce variations in quality. The "force" that is war, particularly modern war, is very different from the "force" that is police action, and the use of the same abstract word to describe the two dissimilar processes is profoundly misleading. (Still more misleading, of course, is the explicit assimilation of a war, waged by allied League-of-Nations powers

---

3. **thermite:** a mixture of chemicals used in incendiary bombs.
4. **vesicant:** a war gas, also called blister gas because it blisters the skin.

against an aggressor, to police action against a criminal. The first is the use of violence and fraud without limit against innocent and guilty alike; the second is the use of strictly limited violence and a minimum of fraud exclusively against the guilty.)

Reality is a succession of concrete and particular situations. When we think about such situations we should use the particular and concrete words which apply to them. If we use abstract words which apply equally well (and equally badly) to other, quite dissimilar situations, it is certain that we shall think incorrectly.

Let us take the sentences quoted above and translate the abstract word *force* into language that will render (however inadequately) the concrete and particular realities of contemporary warfare.

"You cannot have international justice, unless you are prepared to impose it by force." Translated, this becomes: "You cannot have international justice unless you are prepared, with a view to imposing a just settlement, to drop thermite, high explosives and vesicants upon the inhabitants of foreign cities and to have thermite, high explosives and vesicants dropped in return upon the inhabitants of your cities." At the end of this proceeding, justice is to be imposed by the victorious party—that is, if there is a victorious party. It should be remarked that justice was to have been imposed by the victorious party at the end of the last war. But, unfortunately, after four years of fighting, the temper of the victors was such that they were quite incapable of making a just settlement. The Allies are reaping in Nazi Germany what they sowed at Versailles. The victors of the next war will have undergone intensive bombardments with thermite, high explosives and vesicants. Will their temper be better than that of the Allies in 1918? Will they be in a fitter state to make a just settlement? The answer, quite obviously, is: No. It is psychologically all but impossible that justice should be secured by the methods of contemporary warfare.

The next two sentences may be taken together. "Peace-loving countries must unite to use force against aggressive dictatorships. Democratic institutions must be protected, if need be, by force." Let us translate. "Peace-loving countries must unite to throw thermite, high explosives and vesicants on the inhabitants of countries ruled by aggressive dictators. They must do this, and of course abide the consequences, in order to preserve peace and democratic institutions." Two questions immediately propound themselves. First, is it likely that peace can be secured by a process calculated to reduce the orderly life of our complicated societies to chaos? And, second, is it likely that democratic institutions will flourish in a state of chaos? Again, the answers are pretty clearly in the negative.

By using the abstract word *force*, instead of terms which at least attempt to describe the realities of war as it is today, the preachers of collective security through military collaboration disguise from themselves and from others, not only the contemporary facts, but also the probable consequences of their favorite policy. The attempt to secure justice, peace and democracy by "force" seems reasonable enough until we realize, first, that this noncommittal word stands, in the circumstances of our age, for activities which can hardly fail to result in social chaos; and second, that the consequences of social chaos are injustice, chronic warfare, and tyranny. The moment we think in concrete and particular terms of the concrete and particular process called "modern war," we see that a policy which worked (or at least didn't result in complete disaster) in the past has no prospect whatever of working in the immediate future. The attempt to secure justice, peace and democracy by means of a "force," which means, at this particular moment of history, thermite, high explosives and vesicants, is about as reasonable as the attempt to put out a fire with a colorless liquid that happens to be, not water, but petrol.

What applies to the "force" that is war applies in large measure to the "force" that is revolution. It seems inherently very unlikely that social justice and social peace can be secured by thermite, high explosives and vesicants. At first, it may be, the parties in a civil war would hesitate to use such instruments on their fellow countrymen. But there can be little doubt that, if the conflict were prolonged (as it probably would be between the evenly balanced Right and Left of a highly industrialized society), the combatants would end by losing their scruples.

The alternatives confronting us seem to be plain enough. Either we invent and conscientiously employ a new technique for making revolutions and settling international disputes; or else we cling to the old technique and, using "force" (that is to say, thermite, high explosives and vesicants), destroy ourselves. Those who, for whatever motive, disguise the nature of the second alternative under inappropriate language, render the world a grave disservice. They lead us into one of the temptations we find it hardest to resist—the temptation to run away from reality, to pretend that facts are not what they are. Like Shelley (but without Shelley's acute awareness of what he was doing) we are perpetually weaving

> A shroud of talk to hide us from the sun
> Of this familiar life.

We protect our minds by an elaborate system of abstractions, ambiguities, metaphors, and similes from the reality we do not wish to know too clearly; we lie to ourselves, in order that we may still have the excuse of ignorance, the alibi of stupidity and incomprehension, possessing which we can continue with a good conscience to commit and tolerate the most monstrous crimes:

> The poor wretch who has learned his only prayers
> From curses, who knows scarcely words enough
> To ask a blessing from his Heavenly Father,
> Becomes a fluent phraseman, absolute
> And technical in victories and defeats,
> And all our dainty terms for fratricide;
> Terms which we trundle smoothly o'er our tongues
> Like mere abstractions, empty sounds to which
> We join no meaning and attach no form!
> As if the soldier died without a wound:
> As if the fibers of this godlike frame
> Were gored without a pang: as if the wretch
> Who fell in battle, doing bloody deeds,
> Passed off to Heaven translated and not killed;
> As though he had no wife to pine for him,
> No God to judge him.

The language we use about war is inappropriate, and its inappropriateness is designed to conceal a reality so odious that we do not wish to know it. The language we use about politics is also inappropriate; but here our mistake has a different purpose. Our principal aim in this case is to arouse and, having aroused, to rationalize and justify such intrinsically agreeable sentiments as pride and hatred, self-esteem, and contempt for others. To achieve this end we speak about the facts of politics in words which more or less completely misrepresent them. . . .

The evil passions are further justified by another linguistic error—the error of speaking about certain categories of persons as though they were mere embodied abstractions. Foreigners and those who disagree with us are not thought of as men and women like ourselves and our fellow countrymen; they are thought of as representatives and, so to say, symbols of a class. In so far as they have any personality at all, it is the personality we mistakenly attribute to their class—a personality that is, by definition, intrinsically evil. We know that the harming or killing of men and women is wrong, and we are reluctant consciously to do what we know to be wrong. But when particular men and women are thought of merely as representatives of a class, which has previously been defined as evil and personified in the shape of a devil, then the reluctance to hurt or murder disappears. Brown, Jones and Robinson are no longer thought of as Brown, Jones and Robinson, but as heretics, gentiles, Yids, niggers, barbarians, Huns, communists, capitalists, fascists, liberals—whichever the case may be. When they have been called such names and assimilated to the accursed class to which the names apply, Brown, Jones, and Robinson cease to be conceived as what they really are—human persons—and become for the users of this fatally inappropriate language mere vermin or, worse, demons whom it is right and proper to destroy as thoroughly and as painfully as possible. Wherever persons are present, questions of morality arise. Rulers of nations and leaders of parties find morality embarrassing. That is why they take such pains to depersonalize their opponents. All propaganda directed against an opposing group has but one aim: to substitute diabolical abstractions for concrete persons. The propagandist's purpose is to make one set of people forget that certain other sets of people are human. By robbing them of their personality, he puts them outside the pale of moral obligation. Mere symbols can have no rights —particularly when that of which they are symbolical is, by definition, evil.

Politics can become moral only on one condition; that its problems shall be spoken of and thought about exclusively in terms of concrete reality; that is to say, of persons. To depersonify human beings and to personify abstractions are complementary errors which lead, by an inexorable logic, to war between nations and to idolatrous worship of the State, with consequent governmental oppression. All current political thought is a mixture, in varying proportions, between thought in terms of concrete realities and thought in terms of depersonified symbols and personified abstractions. In the democratic countries the problems of internal politics are thought about mainly in terms of concrete reality; those of external politics, mainly in terms of abstractions and symbols. In dictatorial countries the proportion of concrete to abstract and symbolic thought is lower than in democratic countries. Dictators talk little of persons, much of personified abstractions, such as the Nation, the State, the Party, and much of depersonified symbols, such as Yids, Bolshies, Capitalists. The stupidity of politicians who talk about a world of persons as though it were not a world of persons is due in the main to self-interest. In a fictitious world of symbols and personified abstractions, rulers find that they can rule more effectively, and the ruled, that they can gratify instincts which the conventions of good manners and the imperatives of morality demand that they should repress. To think correctly is the condition of behaving well. It is also in itself a moral act; those who would think correctly must resist considerable temptations.

Getting at Meaning

1. "The dumb creation," says Huxley, "lives a life made up of discreet and mutually irrelevant episodes." What does this mean, and why is it not true of human beings?

2. According to Huxley, why do people find stupidity and ignorance useful? How does he apply this idea to war?

3. Huxley uses several examples to illustrate the idea that people speak of battles as if they were fought not by soldiers but by abstractions. Why do people do this?

4. According to Huxley, why can abstract words be dangerous? What is particularly dangerous about the use of the "noncommittal word" *force*? What important distinction does Huxley make between force in war and force in certain other situations?

5. Why is it all but impossible "to secure justice, peace, and democracy by the methods of contemporary warfare"?

6. Who is the "poor wretch" referred to in the first line of the poem included in this essay? What is the point of the poem?

7. In politics, what happens when the concrete "world of persons" becomes changed into "depersonified symbols" and "personified abstractions"? What examples does Huxley cite? How does he distinguish between democratic and dictatorial countries?

8. According to Huxley, what does thinking have to do with morality?

9. Both this essay and the excerpt from Orwell's *1984* consider the relationships among language, thought, and politics. To what extent do Huxley and Orwell make a similar argument?

10. Huxley wrote this essay before World War II. Does his argument apply today any more or less than it did then? Why?

Developing Skills in Reading Literature

1. **Style.** Huxley uses examples to clarify many of the ideas in this essay. In the first paragraph, what point does he illustrate by describing the behavior of cats? The second paragraph begins: "Consider, for example, the case of war." Of what is it an example? Where else in the essay does Huxley strengthen or clarify his position with examples? Why are examples particularly important in this essay?

2. **Persuasion.** Huxley's purpose in this essay is clearly persuasive as well as expository; thus he uses various techniques of argumentation, providing concrete, relevant examples and making logical connections between premises. With what other rhetorical devices does Huxley advance his argument? Look specifically for the use of questions and answers and the delineation of alternatives. How does he discredit language that does not meet his standards of accuracy?

Like all effective persuasion, this essay has both intellectual and emotional appeal. Notice, for example, how many times the phrase "thermite, high explosives, and vesicants" is repeated. What does this repetition contribute to the emotional impact of the essay? Notice, too, the kinds of words and phrases that describe war; for example, *monstrous*, *murder*, *atrocities*, and *mangling*. Find additional examples of this emotionally charged diction.

In general, does Huxley achieve his purpose? Will all readers necessarily accept his ideas? Can you think of any counterarguments that might be offered?

3. **Allusion.** Huxley writes: "Ignorance is egotism's most effective defense against that Dr. Jekyll in us who desires perfection. . . ." Identify the allusion in this sentence. Why is it particularly useful in this discussion?

Developing Vocabulary

1. **Formal Diction.** This essay is rather formal in style, with long and well developed paragraphs, complex sentences, carefully logical organization, and precise diction. Convert the following examples of formal diction into informal language. Then choose additional examples of formal diction from the essay and rewrite these as well.

a. "Watch a pair of cats, crouching on the brink of a fight. Balefully the eyes glare. . . ."

b. ". . . [the cat] begins to make a lingual toilet."

c. "Most ignorances are vincible. . . ."

d. "Our egotisms are incessantly fighting to preserve themselves, not only from external enemies, but also from the assaults of the other and better self with which they are uncomfortably associated."

e. "The battles are between Platonic ideas, between the abstractions of physics and mathematics."

f. ". . . the combatants would end by losing their scruples."

2. **Euphemism.** A euphemism is an indirect statement substituted for a direct one in an effort to avoid bluntness; for example, "passed on" for "dead." Huxley believes that euphemisms allow people to depersonalize war. Euphemisms also tend to be used in discussions of social issues such as education, housing, and health care. Provide several contemporary examples of euphemism.

Developing Writing Skills

1. **Explaining an Idea.** As an example of incorrect thinking, Huxley shows how the abstract word *force* can be highly misleading, because it can apply differently to various concrete situations. Choose another abstract word that you think might lead to confused thinking, and in a brief essay conduct a similar analysis.

2. **Writing an Explanation.** In his final paragraph, Huxley writes:

> Wherever persons are present, questions of morality arise. Rulers of nations and leaders of parties find morality embarrassing. That is why they take such pains to depersonalize their opponents. All propaganda directed against an opposing group has but one aim: to substitute diabolical abstractions for concrete persons.

Have you observed such tendency in public utterances in the nation or the world? Specify one or more examples. Then discuss how this propaganda might affect thinking on critical issues.

SQUARE MOTIF IN BROWN, WHITE, BLACK, BLUE, AND OCHRE, 1948-53.
Victor Pasmore.
Collection, The Museum of Modern Art, New York.
Gift of Mr. and Mrs. Allan D. Emil.

Virginia Woolf

1882–1941

The author of brilliantly original fiction and penetrating criticism, Virginia Woolf has achieved legendary status during the decades since her death. She was one of the most celebrated members of the Bloomsbury group, artists and writers who sought new subjects and modes of expression in the postwar years.

Woolf's father was Sir Leslie Stephen, a distinguished critic, philosopher, scholar, biographer, and abolitionist. Born in London, Woolf was raised in the cultured world of the upper-middle-class intelligentsia. Hers was a large and talented family, and her father's friends included the leading artists and thinkers of the age. Woolf's education took place at home; she read in her father's splendid library and conversed with his famous friends. After their father's death in 1904, Virginia, with two brothers and her sister Vanessa, settled in the Bloomsbury district of London. When Vanessa married art critic Clive Bell in 1907, Virginia and her brother Adrian rented another house in Bloomsbury, where they hosted literary evenings renowned for the quality of conversation. Art critic Roger Fry, novelist E. M. Forster, economist John Maynard Keynes, biographer Lytton Strachey, and poet Victoria Sackville-West were leading figures in this brilliant circle.

In 1912 Virginia married Leonard Woolf, a journalist, essayist, and political thinker who was part of the Bloomsbury group, and their home near the British Museum came to be the spiritual center of Bloomsbury. Woolf and her husband founded the Hogarth Press, which issued several literary landmarks, including Woolf's own novels and the early poetry of T. S. Eliot.

Monday or Tuesday, a collection of experimental sketches, came out in 1921 and *Jacob's Room* in 1922, but it was only with *Mrs. Dalloway* (1925) that Woolf showed complete mastery of her distinctive prose style. She was less interested in utilizing the traditional devices of the novel than in portraying subtle impressions that seemed to her to comprise true reality. Her fictional works, including *To the Lighthouse* (1927) and *The Waves*

VIRGINIA WOOLF, 1935. *Man Ray.*

(1931) are characterized by stream of consciousness narration and by the evocative detail and flowing rhythms of lyric poetry. *Orlando* (1928) evidences Woolf's fascination with female and male identity and with the interplay of past and present. When the book begins, Orlando is a young man in Elizabethan times, but by midpoint Orlando is a young woman in the 1920's.

Woolf wrote numerous reviews and critical essays, many of which were collected in *The Common Reader* (1925) and *The Common Reader: Second Series* (1932). In the long essay *A Room of One's Own* (1929), she ponders the difficulties experienced by women writers. Woolf also wrote *Flush* (1933), a fanciful "memoir" narrated by Elizabeth Barrett Browning's dog, and a biography of Roger Fry.

Woolf struggled with recurrent bouts of mental illness, and in 1941 she drowned herself. A final novel, *Between the Acts,* was published posthumously in the year of her death. *A Writer's Diary,* which contains extracts from her journals, was published in 1953 by Leonard Woolf.

Old Mrs. Grey

There are moments even in England, now, when even the busiest, most contented suddenly let fall what they hold—it may be the week's washing. Sheets and pajamas crumble and dissolve in their hands, because, though they do not state this in so many words, it seems silly to take the washing round to Mrs. Peel when out there over the fields over the hills, there is no washing; no pinning of clotheslines; mangling[1] and ironing; no work at all, but boundless rest. Stainless and boundless rest; space unlimited; untrodden grass; wild birds flying; hills whose smooth uprise continues that wild flight.

Of all this, however, only seven foot by four could be seen from Mrs. Grey's corner. That was the size of her front door which stood wide open, though there was a fire burning in the grate. The fire looked like a small spot of dusty light feebly trying to escape from the embarrassing pressure of the pouring sunshine.

Mrs. Grey sat on a hard chair in the corner looking—but at what? Apparently at nothing. She did not change the focus of her eyes when visitors came in. Her eyes had ceased to focus themselves; it may be that they had lost the power. They were aged eyes, blue, unspectacled. They could see, but without looking. She had never used her eyes on anything minute and difficult; merely upon faces, and dishes and fields. And now at the age of ninety-two they saw nothing but a zigzag of pain wriggling across the door, pain that twisted her legs as it wriggled; jerked her body to and fro like a marionette. Her body was wrapped round the pain as a damp sheet is folded over a wire. The wire was spasmodically jerked by a cruel invisible hand. She flung out a foot, a hand. Then it stopped. She sat still for a moment.

In that pause she saw herself in the past at ten, at twenty, at twenty-five. She was running in and out of a cottage with eleven brothers and sisters. The line jerked. She was thrown forward in her chair.

"All dead. All dead," she mumbled. "My brothers and sisters. And my husband gone. My daughter too. But I go on. Every morning I pray God to let me pass."

The morning spread seven foot by four, green and sunny. Like a fling of grain the birds settled on the land. She was jerked again by another tweak of the tormenting hand.

"I'm an ignorant old woman. I can't read or write, and every morning when I crawls downstairs, I say I wish it were night; and every night, when I crawls up to bed, I say I wish it were day. I'm only an ignorant old woman. But I prays to God: O let me pass. I'm an ignorant old woman—I can't read or write."

So when the color went out of the doorway, she could not see the other page which is then lit up; or hear the voices that have argued, sung, talked for hundreds of years.

The jerked limbs were still again.

"The doctor comes every week. The parish doctor now. Since my daughter went, we can't afford Dr. Nicholls. But he's a good man. He says he wonders I don't go. He says my heart's nothing but wind and water. Yet I don't seem able to die."

So we—humanity—insist that the body shall still cling to the wire. We put out the eyes and the ears; but we pinion it there, with a bottle of medicine, a cup of tea, a dying fire, like a rook on a barn door; but a rook that still lives, even with a nail through it.

---

1. **mangle:** a machine for pressing and smoothing cloth, especially flat pieces, between heated rollers.

Getting at Meaning

1. Why, sometimes, do "even the busiest, most contented suddenly let fall what they hold"? Where is "over the fields over the hills"? What part of this scene can Mrs. Grey see from her corner?

2. Notice the references to Mrs. Grey's eyes in the third paragraph. What do these references reveal about her?

3. What point in her life would you say Mrs. Grey has reached? What are her reactions?

4. Explain "the other page" that Mrs. Grey cannot see, the voices she cannot hear.

5. What point does the narrator make in the final paragraph?

Developing Skills in Reading Literature

1. **Extended Metaphor and Theme.** Woolf develops a metaphor at some length in this selection, through a variety of images that culminate in the last paragraph, when their full implication becomes clear: "So we—humanity—insist that the body shall still cling to the wire." What is Woolf saying about humanity through the comparison with old Mrs. Grey? Specifically, how is humanity's view of reality limited? How can human beings see without looking? What losses has humanity suffered? What pain must humanity endure? Who or what causes that pain? How is humanity ignorant? seemingly unable to die?

2. **Simile.** Explain these similes, and tell what each conveys or suggests about old Mrs. Grey or the human condition: (a) "jerked her body to and fro like a marionette," (b) "Her body was wrapped round the pain as a damp sheet is folded over a wire," and (c) "we pinion it there . . . like a rook on a barn door."

3. **Symbol.** Although Mrs. Grey's door stands wide open to the sunshine and to the place where there is "no work at all, but boundless rest," there is a fire burning in her grate. "The fire looked like a small spot of dusty light feebly trying to escape from the embarrassing pressure of the pouring sunshine." In the context of this selection, what might this fire symbolize? What other reference to the fire tends to confirm this interpretation?

Developing Vocabulary

Using Reference Books. The *Oxford English Dictionary*, often referred to as the *O.E.D.*, offers elaborate analyses of meanings and etymologies and includes dated quotations of actual sentences, which show the meanings of a word at various historical periods dating back to 1200.

If your library has the *O.E.D.*, find the proper volume and look up the word *pinion* in its first listing as a noun (labeled *sb* 1). How many definitions of the word are included in this first listing? What is the word's first and earliest meaning? What is the year of the earliest citation? Note that *pinion* is listed several more times, labeled *sb* 2, *sb* 3, and so forth. How many of these additional definitions are there? (Those marked with a cross are obsolete.)

Now look for *pinion* as a verb. What is its first definition? What object does the verb take? What is the earliest quotation given? Answer the same questions for the second definition of *pinion* as a verb. Write out the quotation from Swift's *Gulliver's Travels*.

Answer the following questions, even if you do not have access to the *O.E.D.* In the last paragraph of this selection, what sense of the word *pinion* is intended? How does the original or primary meaning of *pinion* give the word an added figurative sense and enrich its connotations?

William Butler Yeats
1865–1939

William Butler Yeats is considered one of the finest poets of the English language. Already an important poet in his youth, he changed his style as he matured, becoming that rare poet whose last poems are better than his first. According to critic M. L. Rosenthal, Yeats "grew at last into the boldest, most vigorous voice of this century."

Yeats was born at Sandymount, near Dublin, but much of his childhood was divided among London, Dublin, and Sligo, the wild rural area in the west of Ireland where his mother's family lived. His early poetry was inspired by his love of this region, its land and its legends. After leaving high school, Yeats studied at the Metropolitan School of Art in Dublin from 1883 to 1886, a natural choice for the son of artist John Butler Yeats and the brother of artist Jack Butler Yeats. William, however, preferred the pen to the brush. His first published poems appeared in the *Dublin University Review* in 1885. In 1887 he returned to London, where four years later he helped found the Rhymers' Club, which included many important poets.

Yeats's work cannot be properly appreciated without some awareness of his mystical bent. He was fascinated with Irish mythology and with Irish belief in the supernatural, and he was active in the Theosophical Society, whose members sought wisdom and brotherhood through mysticism. Repelled by the age of science in which he lived, Yeats was attracted to magic and to the prophetic books of William Blake and other visionaries.

As a young man, Yeats met and fell in love with the beautiful actress Maud Gonne, a fiery Irish patriot. The love affair was doomed, for Gonne respected but did not love Yeats, but she inspired many of his finest lyrics and deepened his commitment to Irish nationalism. In 1899 Yeats, along with Lady Augusta Gregory, George Moore, and Edward Martyn, founded the Irish Literary Theater (later the Abbey Theater), which was a leading force in the Irish Literary Renaissance. As director of the Abbey from 1904 until his death, Yeats was involved in the furor over John Millington Synge's *Playboy of the Western World* (1907), which caused

WILLIAM BUTLER YEATS, 1917. *Augustus John. Glasgow Art Gallery and Museum.*

riots because it dealt unsentimentally with certain traits of the Irish. This reaction increased Yeats's long-standing dislike of the middle class, whose attitudes he found conventional and materialistic.

In 1917 Yeats married Georgie Hyde-Lees, a spiritualist medium. The couple moved into a tower on the Irish coast and became parents to a son and a daughter. From 1922 to 1928, Yeats served as a senator in the new Irish Free State, delivering speeches of great eloquence. He won the Nobel Prize for Literature in 1923. Ten years later *A Vision* appeared, in which Yeats expresses his views of the relation among history, imagination, and the occult. He translated the plays of Sophocles in 1928 and compiled *The Oxford Book of Modern Verse 1892–1935* in 1936.

No summary can do justice to the impact of Yeats. He brought a new realism to the Irish stage in one generation and a new kind of symbolism to English poetry in another. His was the voice of a true genius, and he left a body of poetry unmatched in range and power. Intellectually active to the last, Yeats died in France in 1939 and according to his wishes was later buried at Sligo.

When You Are Old

When you are old and gray and full of sleep,
And nodding by the fire, take down this book,
And slowly read, and dream of the soft look
Your eyes had once, and of their shadows deep;

How many loved your moments of glad grace,   5
And loved your beauty with love false or true;
But one man loved the pilgrim soul in you,
And loved the sorrows of your changing face.

And bending down beside the glowing bars,
Murmur, a little sadly, how Love fled   10
And paced upon the mountains overhead
And hid his face amid a crowd of stars.

MAUDE GONNE. *Sarah Purser. Dublin Municipal Gallery of Modern Art.*

Getting at Meaning

1. What is "this book" referred to in line 2? What are "the glowing bars" in line 9? What is the subject of the verb "murmur" in line 10?

2. Explain in your own words what "one man" saw and loved that others did not. Who is this "one man"?

3. The speaker in this poem looks upon the present as if it is being seen from the past. How does this enhance the effect of the poem?

Developing Skills in Reading Literature

1. **Tone.** What tone does the poet achieve in this poem? Point out the particular words and phrases that contribute to the tone.

2. **Personification.** Where is personification used in this poem? Without it, what effects or qualities of the poem would be lost?

3. **Meter.** What is the dominant metrical pattern of this poem? How regular is the meter? Read the poem aloud, listening for irregularities in meter. Find four irregular lines and scan them. Do they still have the same number of feet and of strong and weak accents? Look for lines in which the grammatical pattern differs from the metrical one. Point out the caesuras, and the lines that are enjambed rather than end stopped. How would you summarize the effect of these deviations within the regularity of the poem?

4. **Diction.** The word *pilgrim* is rich in connotation. What does it suggest about the woman's soul? Think of two synonyms for *paced* in line 11 and for *crowd* in line 12. In each case what meaning or connotations would be lost if another word were used?

T. S. Eliot
1888–1965

More than any other single individual, Thomas Stearns Eliot defined the contours of modern poetry. As poet, dramatist, literary critic, and editor, he exerted an immense influence on twentieth-century culture and particularly on twentieth-century poetry. Eliot deplored the spiritual and emotional emptiness that he believed was characteristic of his time and in his later poems affirmed the value of religious, literary, and political tradition.

Born in St. Louis and educated at Harvard, Eliot studied in France and Germany, then took up residence in England in 1914. He published his first collection of poems in 1917; ten years later he became a naturalized British subject. To support himself and his wife, Eliot taught school, worked as a bank clerk, and in 1925 joined the publishing firm that later became Faber & Faber Ltd., where he worked as an editor until his death.

Eliot's early poems, including "Preludes" and "The Love Song of J. Alfred Prufrock," reflect the influence of French Symbolist poetry, of the poems of Dante and the Elizabethan and metaphysical poets, of Indian mysticism, and of the avant-garde artists who made up the London literary scene. *The Waste Land* (1922) established Eliot's international reputation. In this poem Eliot describes the spiritual infirmities of the age, creating a statement of the human condition that electrified the literary world.

Eliot's poems are highly complex and tightly structured, characterized by symbol and irony, by precise, richly suggestive diction, and by a blend of the formal and the colloquial. His are intellectual poems, which in the early twentieth century represented a sharp break with the prevailing romanticism of the prewar years. Eliot considered himself a classicist, insisting on discipline and order over mere self-expression. In the essay "Hamlet and His Problems," he explains his theory of aesthetic expression: "The one way of expressing emotion in the form of art is by finding an 'objective correlative'; in other words, a set of objects, a situation, a chain of events which shall be the formula for that particular emotion; such that, when the external

T. S. ELIOT. *Wyndham Lewis.*
The Fogg Art Museum, Cambridge, Mass.

facts, which must terminate in sensory experience, are given, the emotion is immediately evoked." Eliot also contrasted the disjointed and chaotic tenor of modern life with the "unified sensibility" art can create when that art is faithful to an unbroken tradition stretching back to the Greek myths.

The effect of Eliot's conversion to the Anglican church is evident in the verse play *Murder in the Cathedral* (1935) and in his masterpiece *The Four Quartets.* Written between 1935 and 1943, this work explores the possibility and meaning of redemptive spiritual faith within a temporal existence.

In his early poems Eliot is detached from the debilitating conditions that so paralyze Prufrock, the modern Everyman. In his later, gentler poems, Eliot speaks of the commitment to a spiritual quest for a transcendent plane of faith and renewal. In the words of the critic Hyatt Waggoner, Eliot's poems ". . . named, what had been nameless—and so only dimly known—and what they named, they brought to consciousness." As a testimonial to the significance of his achievements, Eliot was awarded the Nobel Prize for Literature in 1948.

THE ADORATION OF THE MAGI. *Hieronymous Bosch.*
The Metropolitan Museum of Art.
John Stewart Kennedy Fund, 1912.

Journey of the Magi

"A cold coming we had of it,
Just the worst time of the year
For a journey, and such a long journey:
The ways deep and the the weather sharp,
The very dead of winter."[1]   5
And the camels galled, sore-footed, refractory,
Lying down in the melting snow.
There were times we regretted
The summer palaces on slopes, the terraces,
And the silken girls bringing sherbet.   10
Then the camel men cursing and grumbling
And running away, and wanting their liquor and women,
And the night-fires going out, and the lack of shelters,
And the cities hostile and the towns unfriendly
And the villages dirty and charging high prices: 15
A hard time we had of it.
At the end we preferred to travel all night,
Sleeping in snatches,
With the voices singing in our ears, saying
That this was all folly.   20

   Then at dawn we came down to a temperate valley,
Wet, below the snow line, smelling of vegetation;
With a running stream and a water mill beating the darkness,
And three trees[2] on the low sky,
And an old white horse galloped away in the meadow.   25
Then we came to a tavern with vine leaves over the lintel,
Six hands at an open door dicing for pieces of silver,[3]
And feet kicking the empty wineskins.
But there was no information, and so we continued
And arrived at evening, not a moment too soon   30
Finding the place; it was (you may say) satisfactory.

   All this was a long time ago, I remember,
And I would do it again, but set down
This set down

---

1. **"a cold . . . winter"**: Eliot adapted this from Lancelot Andrieve's "Nativity
Sermon" (1622). Andrieves was on one of the committees that produced the *King
James Bible*.
2. **three trees:** the three crosses at the Crucifixion of Christ.
3. **Six . . . silver:** this line combines the Roman soldiers' gambling for Jesus's robe
and Judas, who betrayed Jesus for thirty pieces of silver.

This: were we led all that way for   35
Birth or Death? There was a Birth, certainly,
We had evidence and no doubt. I had seen birth and death,
But had thought they were different; this Birth was
Hard and bitter agony for us, like Death, our death.
We returned to our places, these Kingdoms,   40
But no longer at ease here, in the old dispensation,[4]
With an alien people clutching their gods.
I should be glad of another death.

---

4. **dispensation:** pagan religions in force before the coming of Christ.

Getting at Meaning

1. Who are the travelers, and where are they going? What kind of life have they been accustomed to? How is this suggested in a very few words?

2. How does the poem manage to depict the journey as arduous and prolonged? What is the journey like, especially toward the end? What are the "voices" referred to in line 19?

3. The speaker says that the travelers arrived and found the place "not a moment too soon." Explain.

4. What question lingers in the speaker's mind long after the journey? Why are these men "no longer at ease here"? Why should the speaker "be glad of another death"?

Developing Skills in Reading Literature

1. **Imagery and Symbol.** Note the succession of images that suggest the nature of the journey. What changes occur in the imagery as the travelers approach their destination, coming to the valley, the running stream, the water mill "beating the darkness"? Study the images closely, and try to pick up any suggestive overtones. What is the effect of the image "three trees on the low sky"? Could the "old white horse" symbolize anything (see Revelation 6:2 and 19:11), or is it perhaps just a fleeting glimpse, something that might have seemed significant at the time, remembered half a lifetime later? What about the tavern scene, in which people are described as "hands" or "feet": what details seem notable?

In *The Use of Poetry and the Use of Criticism* Eliot wrote:

Why, for all of us, out of all that we have heard, seen, felt, in a lifetime, do certain images recur, charged with emotion, rather than others? The song of one bird, the leap of one fish, at a particular place and time, the scent of one flower, an old woman on a German mountain path, six ruffians seen through an open window playing cards at night at a small French railway junction where there was a water mill. . . .

In the context of "Journey of the Magi," what does this passage suggest about the nature of the creative process?

2. **Tone.** Is there any contrast between the speaker's tone in describing the journey (see line 31, for example) and the remarkable effects that it had upon him? What does the speaker's tone in the last stanza reflect or suggest about him, and the point that he has reached in his life?

3. **Theme.** Consider the ambiguity of "birth" and "death" in this poem. Note that they are sometimes capitalized, sometimes not. Discuss the various meanings each of these words takes on. How was "this Birth . . . like Death"?

4. **Free Verse.** Poetry written without regular patterns of rhyme and meter is known as free verse. Free verse differs from prose in sound effects, in compression of language, and in the blend of sound and sense typical of all poetry. Eliot had this to say on the subject of poetry:

It would be convenient if poetry were always verse—either accented, alliterative, or quantitative; but that is not true. Poetry may occur, within a definite limit on one side, at any point along a line of which the formal limits are "verse" and "prose."

Is this poem closer to prose or to verse, as it is described by Eliot? What is the effect of techniques such as balanced or parallel phrases and repetition? What characteristics distinguish this poem from prose? Support your answer with quotations from the poem.

The Hollow Men

Mistah Kurtz[1]—he dead.
A penny for the Old Guy[2]

I

We are the hollow men
We are the stuffed men
Leaning together
Headpiece filled with straw. Alas!
Our dried voices, when   5
We whisper together
Are quiet and meaningless
As wind in dry grass
Or rats' feet over broken glass
In our dry cellar   10

Shape without form, shade without color,
Paralyzed force, gesture without motion;

Those who have crossed
With direct eyes, to death's other Kingdom[3]
Remember us—if at all—not as lost   15
Violent souls, but only
As the hollow men
The stuffed men.

II

Eyes[4] I dare not meet in dreams
In death's dream kingdom   20
These do not appear:
There, the eyes are
Sunlight on a broken column
There, is a tree swinging
And voices are   25
In the wind's singing
More distant and more solemn
Than a fading star.

Let me be no nearer
In death's dream kingdom   30
Let me also wear
Such deliberate disguises
Rat's coat, crowskin, crossed staves[5]
In a field
Behaving as the wind behaves   35
No nearer—

Not that final meeting
In the twilight kingdom

---

1. **Mistah Kurtz:** a character in Joseph Conrad's *Heart of Darkness* who goes to Africa to reform the natives, but because of his own weakness is corrupted by the primitive civilization.
2. **A . . . Old Guy:** a cry of English children on the streets on Guy Fawkes Day, November 5, when they carry Fawkes's effigy and beg for money for fireworks to celebrate the day. Fawkes was a traitor who attempted with conspirators to blow up both houses of Parliament in 1605; the "gunpowder plot" failed.
3. **Those . . . Kingdom:** Those who have represented something positive and direct are blessed in Paradise. The reference is to Dante's *Paradiso*.
4. **Eyes:** eyes of those in eternity who had faith and confidence and were a force that acted and were not paralyzed.
5. **crossed staves:** refers to scarecrows.

III

This is the dead land
This is cactus land   40
Here the stone images
Are raised, here they receive
The supplication of a dead man's hand
Under the twinkle of a fading star.

Is it like this   45
In death's other kingdom
Waking alone
At the hour when we are
Trembling with tenderness
Lips that would kiss   50
Form prayers to broken stone.

IV

The eyes are not here
There are no eyes here
In this valley of dying stars
In this hollow valley   55
This broken jaw of our lost kingdoms
In this last of meeting places
We grope together
And avoid speech
Gathered on this beach of the tumid river⁶   60

Sightless, unless
The eyes reappear
As the perpetual star
Multifoliate rose⁷
Of death's twilight kingdom   65
The hope only
Of empty men.

V

*Here we go round the prickly pear*⁸
Prickly pear prickly pear
Here we go round the prickly pear   70
At five o'clock in the morning.

Between the idea
And the reality
Between the motion
And the act⁹   75
Falls the Shadow
        *For Thine is the Kingdom*¹⁰
Between the conception
And the creation
Between the emotion
And the response   80
Falls the Shadow
        Life is very long
Between the desire
And the spasm
Between the potency
And the existence   85
Between the essence
And the descent
Falls the Shadow
        For Thine is the Kingdom
For Thine is
Life is   90
For Thine is the

This is the way the world ends
This is the way the world ends
This is the way the world ends
Not with a bang but a whimper.   95

---

6. **tumid river:** swollen river. The River Acheron (ak′ ə rän′) in Hell in Dante's *Inferno*. The damned must cross this river to get to the land of the dead.
7. **Multifoliate rose:** In Dante's *Divine Comedy* paradise is described as a rose of many leaves.
8. **prickly pear:** cactus.
9. **Between . . . act:** a reference to *Julius Caesar:* "Between the acting of a dreadful thing/And the first motion, all the interim is/Like a phantasma or a hideous dream."
10. **For . . . Kingdom:** the beginning of the closing words of the Lord's Prayer

Getting at Meaning

1. What qualities of the hollow men do the first ten lines suggest? What images convey these qualities?

2. How do the four images in lines 11 and 12 further characterize the hollow men?

3. Line 14 refers to "death's other Kingdom." What does the word *other* imply about the hollow men?

4. Those who have crossed to that other kingdom remember the speaker and others like him not as "lost violent souls" but only as hollow or stuffed. What does this suggest about the spiritual condition of the hollow men?

5. In Part II the direct eyes, which the speaker "dare not meet in dreams," indeed do not appear in "death's dream kingdom." What images suggest instead things reflected or remote, things perceived only indirectly?

6. Why does the speaker wish to be "no nearer" (lines 29 and 36) to avoid direct eyes? How might he be like a scarecrow "behaving as the wind behaves"? What ultimate reality or confrontation does he fear?

7. In Part III, which phrases and lines suggest a deadened kind of worship, spiritual emptiness or death, frustrated love?

8. In Part IV, what lines suggest that the place where "there are no eyes" is the "valley of the shadow of death"? Note that the "fading star" has now become "dying stars." The hollow men are "Sightless, unless/ The eyes reappear/ As the perpetual star." What do these lines mean? Why is the hope they express "the hope only/ Of empty men"?

9. Part V shows the reality rather than the hope of hollow men: the untouchable cactus rather than the rose. "Five o'clock in the morning" recalls the hour of thwarted tenderness described in Part III. How does Part V develop the theme of frustration of impulse or desire? What might be the "Shadow" that keeps intervening?

10. After each fall of the shadow is an interrupting response; the line from the Lord's Prayer is interrupted by the jingle or nursery rhyme at the end of the poem. How does the end of Part V echo its beginning? What do the jingle-like stanzas suggest about the hollow men?

11. The two final lines are among the most quoted in twentieth-century literature. What do they mean? Why are they appropriate to the hollow men?

12. The hollow men are not "lost violent souls," and their world does not end "with a bang." How are they unlike the two characters in the epigraph: Mistah Kurtz and the Old Guy?

Developing Skills in Reading Literature

1. **Sound Devices.** This poem has no clear meter or rhyme scheme. Look for effects that might take their place. Do you find any rhyme at all? Read aloud lines 4–10, and point out any assonance, consonance, and onomatopoeia that you hear. How do these sounds echo and reinforce the meaning of the lines? Find examples of alliteration, particularly in Part II. What other devices create sound effects in this poem?

2. **Extended Metaphor.** Discuss the central metaphor that extends through this poem. Why is it particularly suitable?

3. **Theme.** Eliot offered some advice about another poet's work that could be useful in reading his own:

. . . any obscurity of the poem, on first reading, is due to the suppression of "links in the chain," or explanatory and connecting matter, and not to incoherence, or to the love of the cryptogram. . . . The reader has to allow the images to fall into his memory successively without questioning the reasonableness of each at the moment; so that, at the end, a total effect is produced.

What total effect is produced by "The Hollow Men"? From this poem what might you infer about Eliot's views of the religious or spiritual condition of the modern world?

Developing Writing Skills

Explaining an Idea. The following statement is quoted from Eliot's critical writing. In a brief essay explain how it might apply to "Journey of the Magi" or "The Hollow Men."

The chief use of the "meaning" of a poem, in the ordinary sense, may be (for here again I am speaking of some kinds of poetry and not all) to satisfy one habit of the reader, to keep his mind diverted and quiet, while the poem does its work upon him: much as the imaginary burglar is always provided with a bit of nice meat for the house dog.

Dylan Thomas
1914–1953

DYLAN THOMAS. *Augustus John.*
By Permission of the National Museum of Wales.

Considered by many the most original English poet since Yeats and Eliot, Dylan Thomas wrote lyrics whose imagery is sometimes obscure but always intense. He wrote of the things closest to his heart, calling his poetry "the record of my individual struggle from darkness toward some measure of light." A performer with a great gift for reading poetry, Thomas enchanted audiences with dramatic readings of his own poems and verse plays and of the works of earlier poets such as Dryden, Pope, Blake, and Hopkins. To Thomas's fascinated public in America and Great Britain, he was the typical bohemian poet, romantic, irresponsible, and self-destructive.

Thomas was born in Swansea in southwest Wales, and his writings are rooted deep in the countryside and in the culture of Wales. Although he did not learn to speak the Welsh language, he captured its cadences and word sequences in his prose and poetry. After attending Swansea grammar school, where his father taught English, he worked as a reporter for the *Wales Daily Post*. After 1933 he lived the financially precarious life of a freelance writer. Thomas's first book was *Eighteen Poems* (1934), which was praised by many influential critics. A second volume, *Twenty-Five Poems*, appeared in 1936, and in 1938 he was given an award by *Poetry*, a prestigious American magazine.

At first Thomas was hailed as a spontaneous singer, a Celtic rhapsodist. In fact, he was a fastidious and exacting craftsman. Early in his career he experimented with surrealistic techniques. As his style matured, his poems gained in clarity, although in his later poems, too, sound often competes with sense. Thomas drew inspiration for both his poetry and prose from his own experiences, writing of childhood, holidays, nature, and death. A collection of humorous autobiographical sketches was published in 1940 as *Portrait of the Artist as a Young Dog*, and his reminiscence "A Child's Christmas in Wales" (1954) became a Christmas favorite in the years after Thomas's death. *Under Milk Wood* (performed 1953), a radio play, also attests to Thomas's keen powers of observation and his ability to shape experiences into artistic statements.

Reckless, impulsive, a brilliant talker when the spirit moved him, Thomas became a popular character, although his life was not as colorful as he led people to believe. He was often inebriated, but he was neither a Casanova nor "the drunkest man in the world," as he often claimed. Thomas, who read so beautifully that he entranced people ordinarily oblivious to poetry, brought his magic to the American lecture circuit in 1950, 1952, and 1953. He drank even more than usual in the United States, perhaps to live up to his legend. He died in New York City on his third American tour, after a drinking spree.

Do Not Go Gentle into That Good Night

Do not go gentle into that good night,
Old age should burn and rave at close of day;
Rage, rage against the dying of the light.

Though wise men at their end know dark is right,
Because their words had forked no lightning they   5
Do not go gentle into that good night.

Good men, the last wave by, crying how bright
Their frail deeds might have danced in a green bay,
Rage, rage against the dying of the light.

Wild men who caught and sang the sun in flight,   10
And learn, too late, they grieved it on its way,
Do not go gentle into that good night.

Grave men, near death, who see with blinding sight
Blind eyes could blaze like meteors and be gay,
Rage, rage against the dying of the light.   15

And you, my father, there on the sad height,
Curse, bless, me now with your fierce tears, I pray.
Do not go gentle into that good night.
Rage, rage against the dying of the light.

Getting at Meaning

1. Put into your own words the opening line of the poem. What way of facing death does the speaker urge?

2. Why do wise men resist death? Explain the line, "Because their words had forked no lightning."

3. What do good men realize when it is too late?

4. What do you think the speaker means by "Wild men who caught and sang the sun in flight"?

5. What do "Grave men . . . see with blinding sight"? How could "Blind eyes . . . be gay"?

6. How could the father's "fierce tears" both curse and bless?

Developing Skills in Reading Literature

1. **Villanelle.** A villanelle is an intricately patterned French verse form with five tercets followed by a quatrain. Thomas shows here that a villanelle can be much more than a trivial literary exercise. Study this example, and point out the rules of the villanelle form. What is the rhyme scheme? Where must lines 1 and 3 be repeated as refrains? as a couplet? Why is it extremely difficult to avoid an effect of monotony and artificiality? How does repetition give this poem added force?

2. **Meter.** What is the prevailing metrical pattern of the poem? Where do you find pronounced deviations

from that pattern, with spondees substituted for iambs? What makes these deviations particularly appropriate, given the meanings being conveyed?

3. **Assonance and Consonance.** As you know, English vowel sounds range from the high end of the scale, as in *see* and *say,* to the low end, as in *shoo* and *so.* The higher-pitched vowels are associated with greater excitement or intensity. Identify the vowel sounds that predominate in this poem. How does this use of assonance reinforce the poem's theme and mood?

Point out examples of consonance in the third tercet, assonance in the fourth, and both in the quatrain. Then comment on the specific effects created by these sound devices.

4. **Diction.** The intensity of effect in this poem results partly from words, particularly verbs, that themselves convey intensity. *Rage* is a good example. What other words in the poem have a similar effect? How do the connotations enrich the meaning of the poem? How do these intense words contrast with the words used to describe death?

And Death Shall Have No Dominion

And death shall have no dominion.
Dead men naked they shall be one
With the man in the wind and the west moon;
When their bones are picked clean and the clean bones gone,
They shall have stars at elbow and foot;   5
Though they go mad they shall be sane,
Though they sink through the sea they shall rise again;
Though lovers be lost love shall not;
And death shall have no dominion.

And death shall have no dominion.   10
Under the windings of the sea
They lying long shall not die windily;
Twisting on racks when sinews give way,
Strapped to a wheel, yet they shall not break;
Faith in their hands shall snap in two,   15
And the unicorn evils run them through;
Split all ends up they shan't crack;
And death shall have no dominion.

And death shall have no dominion.
No more may gulls cry at their ears   20
Or waves break loud on the seashores;
Where blew a flower may a flower no more
Lift its head to the blows of the rain;
Though they be mad and dead as nails,
Heads of the characters hammer through daisies;   25
Break in the sun till the sun breaks down,
And death shall have no dominion.

Getting at Meaning

1. According to the first few lines, what happens, physically, to the dead? How does this illustrate the idea that "death shall have no dominion"?

2. How is it that "Though lovers be lost love shall not"?

3. In the second stanza, how do images of violence emphasize the poem's theme?

4. In the third stanza, how does nature imagery develop the theme further? What process seems to be described in the last four lines? What is meant by "till the sun breaks down"?

Developing Skills in Reading Literature

1. **Paradox.** Point out the examples of paradox in this poem. Why is paradox an especially appropriate rhetorical device, in view of the poem's theme?

2. **Meter.** What regularities can you find in the meter? How many accents do the lines typically contain? Point out lines that begin with anapests or dactyls and end with spondees or iambs. An anapest is a metrical foot that consists of two unaccented syllables followed by an accented syllable[˘˘´]; a dactyl is a foot made up of an accented syllable followed by two unaccented syllables ['˘˘]. How do you think this mixed meter affects the sound of the poem when it is read aloud?

3. **Rhyme.** Note that in this poem there are a number of off-rhymes, with consonance or assonance substituting for true rhymes. Point out several examples of this technique. Do you find any true rhymes in the poem?

4. **Parallelism and Antithesis.** The varying meter and the off-rhymes in this poem are balanced by parallelism and by antithesis within the stanzas. How do these devices enhance the poem's effectiveness? How does the parallel structure of the stanzas heighten the impact of the poem?

5. **Allusion.** Look up *Romans* 6:9, the Biblical source for the title of this poem, and compare it with Thomas's handling of the same idea. Is the poem's philosophy Christian? Is it pantheistic? Is it basically optimistic or pessimistic?

Developing Vocabulary

Inferring Word Meaning. From the context of the poem and from your own knowledge, try to determine the meanings of the following words, as the poet used them.

dominion   blew ("where *blew* a flower")
windings   characters
unicorn

Developing Writing Skills

Using Comparisons and Contrasts. Based on Thomas's treatment of death in this poem and in "Do Not Go Gentle into That Good Night," what can you infer about his attitude toward life? How do the two poems differ in their approach? Do they complement one another? Discuss the answers to these questions in a brief expository essay.

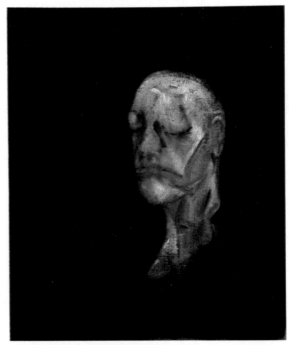

STUDY FOR PORTRAIT II (after the life mask of William Blake), 1955. *Francis Bacon. Tate Gallery, London.*

C. S. Lewis

1898–1963

C. S. LEWIS. *The Bettmann Archive, Inc.*

Novelist, essayist, poet, literary historian, and scholar, Clive Staples Lewis is best known for *The Screwtape Letters* (1942), a collection of essays in which an elderly devil instructs his nephew in the art of temptation. Most of Lewis's forty books address ethical and Christian themes, sometimes in the context of imaginative fiction.

Born in Belfast, Lewis was educated privately, except for one year at Malvern College. He served with the Somerset Light Infantry during World War I and then went on to Oxford University, where he was an exceptional scholar. From 1925 to 1954, he was a fellow at Oxford, during which time he wrote *Allegory of Love: A Study in Medieval Tradition* (1936), a lively survey of medieval literature, and *English Literature in the Sixteenth Century* (1954), the third volume of the *Oxford History of English Literature*. From 1954 until his death, he was professor of Medieval and Renaissance English at Cambridge University.

In addition to a vast number of essays, Lewis wrote fictional allegories to promote his religious beliefs. Some of these were science fiction, such as *Out of the Silent Planet* (1938) and *Perelandra* (1943), accounts of voyages in search of an unearthly utopia. Among Lewis's most popular books are the *Chronicles of Narnia* (1950–1956), a seven-volume fantasy series that begins with *The Lion, the Witch, and the Wardrobe.* These stories are glorious tales of medieval adventure, full of magic and swordplay, danger and derring-do. Written for children, they are admired by older readers as well. As the *Times Literary Supplement* said of Lewis, "He could best say what he had to say through genial fantasy or a childlike kind of romance."

The Late Passenger

The sky was low, the sounding rain was falling dense and dark,
And Noah's sons were standing at the window of the Ark.

The beasts were in, but Japhet said, "I see one creature more
Belated and unmated there come knocking at the door."

"Well let him knock," said Ham, "Or let him drown or learn to swim.   5
We're overcrowded as it is; we've got no room for him."

"And yet it knocks, how terribly it knocks," said Shem, "Its feet
Are hard as horn—but oh the air that comes from it is sweet."

"Now hush," said Ham, "You'll waken Dad, and once he comes to see
What's at the door, it's sure to mean more work for you and me."   10

Noah's voice came roaring from the darkness down below,
"Some animal is knocking. Take it in before we go."

Ham shouted back, and savagely he nudged the other two,
"That's only Japhet knocking down a brad nail in his shoe."

Said Noah, "Boys, I hear a noise that's like a horse's hoof."   15
Said Ham, "Why, that's the dreadful rain that drums upon the roof."

Noah tumbled up on deck and out he put his head;
His face went gray, his knees were loosed, he tore his beard and said,

"Look, look! It would not wait. It turns away. It takes its flight.
Fine work you've made of it, my sons, between you all tonight!   20

"Even if I could outrun it now, it would not turn again
—Not now. Our great discourtesy has earned its high disdain.

"Oh noble and unmated beast, my sons were all unkind;
In such a night what stable and what manger will you find?

"Oh golden hoofs, oh cataracts of mane, oh nostrils wide   25
With indignation! Oh the neck wave-arched, the lovely pride!

"Oh long shall be the furrows ploughed across the hearts of men
Before it comes to stable and to manger once again,

"And dark and crooked all the ways in which our race shall walk,
And shriveled all their manhood like a flower with broken stalk,   30

"And all the world, oh Ham, may curse the hour when you were born;
Because of you the Ark must sail without the Unicorn."

Getting at Meaning

1. What indications are there in the poem that the unicorn is a rather special creature? Is it significant that it is unmated?

2. Twice Noah mentions a stable and a manger. What does this reference suggest?

3. What does Noah predict will be the result of this "great discourtesy"? What curse does he foresee?

Developing Skills in Reading Literature

1. **Stanza.** The verse form of this poem has been used often for popular narrative poetry. How many accented syllables are in each line? If these rhymed couplets were printed as quatrains, what would the rhyme scheme be, and what kind of stanza, often associated with folklore, would result?

2. **Light Verse.** Light verse is characterized by grace and ease of expression and often by a fanciful wit and humor, although its intent may be serious or satirical. What makes this poem an example of light verse? How strict does the adherence to rhyme and meter seem to be in this kind of verse?

3. **Theme.** If this narrative poem is a kind of myth, what does it "explain"? What does the unicorn represent, and what are the implications of its being left behind? What elements of this narrative are reminiscent of material in both the Old and the New Testaments?

Developing Vocabulary

Words from Latin: Prefixes and Roots. From what you know of the unicorn, how do you explain its name? What do you think is the root meaning of -corn? the meaning of the prefix uni-? Using a dictionary, explain how the prefix and the root together relate to the present-day meaning of each of the following words.

uniform   unison
unify   universe

Developing Writing Skills

Writing a Narrative Poem. Try writing some light verse, following the metrical pattern of this poem. Possible topics include an encounter with a mythical creature of your own imagining, an embarrassing incident, a confrontation with a computer, and an experience with a sibling.

William Butler Yeats

An Irish Airman Foresees His Death

I know that I shall meet my fate
Somewhere among the clouds above;
Those that I fight I do not hate,
Those that I guard I do not love;[1]
My country is Kiltartan Cross,   5
My countrymen Kiltartan's poor,
No likely end could bring them loss
Or leave them happier than before.
Nor law, nor duty bade me fight,
Nor public men, nor cheering crowds,   10
A lonely impulse of delight
Drove to this tumult in the clouds;
I balanced all, brought all to mind,
The years to come seemed waste of breath,
A waste of breath the years behind   15
In balance with this life, this death.

---

1. **Those . . . love:** The Irish hated their English rulers, not the Germans.

Getting at Meaning

1. When the airman says, "No likely end could bring them loss/ Or leave them happier . . .," what point is he making?

2. What does the airman mean by "A lonely impulse of delight"? Why is it lonely? What is "this tumult"?

3. In making his decision, what factors did the airman reject as irrelevant? What exact balance did he strike? Does he accept his fate?

Developing Skills in Reading Literature

1. **Irony.** What is ironic about the airman's attitude about the war and about the results of his efforts?

2. **Style.** How does the form of this poem reinforce the feeling that the airman, although he speaks of an impulse, is not simply a wild romantic but has measured his options and has deliberated carefully? Answer this question in terms of techniques such as parallelism, antithesis, line length, and enjambment.

Developing Writing Skills

Analyzing Theme. What was it that was worth so much to the young airman? From what you know or can find out about the nature of early aviation and its use in war, explain what he meant by the understated phrase "this life" in line 16.

Alternatively, in a more philosophic vein, what in this poem helps to explain war itself and the willingness to kill and be killed for no good reason? Are men more prone to this than women? Explain your ideas in a brief essay.

Wilfred Owen

1893–1918

Enthusiasts of Wilfred Owen's work believe that he was a poet with the potential to rival T. S. Eliot in importance had he not been killed in war at an early age. His compassionate, innovative poems on the waste and "pity" of war exerted a major influence on the writers of the postwar years.

Owen was born in Shropshire, where his father worked for the railroad. Delicate and precocious as a boy, he was influenced by a natural love of poetry and by his strict Calvinist mother. He attended a technical school, studied botany, and finally enrolled at the University of London, only to withdraw for lack of funds. He was lay assistant to the vicar of Dunsden in Oxfordshire and briefly contemplated entering the priesthood. In August of 1913, he went to Bordeaux, France, to teach at the Berlitz School, eventually becoming a tutor.

At the outbreak of war, Owen returned to England to enlist in the Artist's Rifles. Commissioned in the Manchester Regiment, he was dispatched to the western front in January, 1917. The cold was nearly as savage as the fighting, and by June, Owen was so ill that he was sent back to a hospital in England. A fellow patient was Siegfried Sassoon, a war poet and outspoken pacifist. Sassoon, recognizing Owen's gift, encouraged him to continue writing poetry and introduced him to other writers.

Owen returned to France as a company commander in late August of 1918. In October he won the Military Cross, and in November he was killed in the crossing of the Sambre Canal, a week before

WILFRED OWEN. *Harold Owen.*

the armistice. Sassoon collected Owen's poems and published them in 1920.

Owen's emphasis is not the horror of war but pity for its victims, making his poetry less bitter than that of many other war poets. He balances irony with empathy and remains personally involved with his subject rather than distanced from it. Owen used flexible stanzas, harsh sounds, hesitant rhythms, and "pararhymes" (off-rhymes), techniques imitated and adapted by later poets.

Dulce et Decorum Est

Bent double, like old beggars under sacks,
Knock-kneed, coughing like hags, we cursed through sludge,
Till on the haunting flares we turned our backs
And towards our distant rest began to trudge.
Men marched asleep. Many had lost their boots   5
But limped on, blood-shod. All went lame; all blind;
Drunk with fatigue; deaf even to the hoots
Of tired, outstripped Five-Nines[1] that dropped behind.

Gas! GAS! Quick, boys!—An ecstasy of fumbling,
Fitting the clumsy helmets just in time;   10
But someone still was yelling out and stumbling
And flound'ring like a man in fire or lime . . .
Dim, through the misty panes and thick green light,
As under a green sea, I saw him drowning.

In all my dreams, before my helpless sight,   15
He plunges at me, guttering, choking, drowning.

If in some smothering dreams you too could pace
Behind the wagon that we flung him in,
And watch the white eyes writhing in his face,
His hanging face, like a devil's sick of sin;   20
If you could hear, at every jolt, the blood
Come gargling from the froth-corrupted lungs,
Obscene as cancer, bitter as the cud
Of vile, incurable sores on innocent tongues,—
My friend, you would not tell with such high zest   25
To children ardent for some desperate glory,
The old Lie: Dulce et decorum est
Pro patria mori.[2]

---

1. **Five-Nines:** gas shells.
2. **Dulce . . . mori** *Latin:* It is sweet and proper to die for one's country (the Roman poet Horace).

Getting at Meaning

1. What happens suddenly, and why are the soldiers slow in reacting to it?

2. What is done with the soldier after he is stricken? What is then the vantage point of the speaker, enabling him to witness a scene he can never forget?

3. To what sort of person is this poem addressed?

Developing Skills in Reading Literature

1. **Realism.** Realism is the truthful imitation of actual life. Given not only the subject of this poem but also its theme, why is a realistic approach particularly suitable?

2. **Simile.** In the interests of realism, the poet uses similes to convey a sense of his experience. Point out the four or five similes that seem most effective.

3. **Tone.** How would you describe the tone of this poem? What one phrase in the poem perhaps best sums up the poet's attitude toward war and death in war?

4. **Contrast.** Literature often produces dramatic effects through contrast in structure, image, or idea. What particularly ironic contrast does this poem present? How does the use of Latin reinforce the contrast?

5. **Diction.** Why is *sludge* an effective word in this poem? Is *sludge* onomatopoetic? What does "an ecstasy of fumbling" convey? Explain the phrase "misty panes." What does *guttering* suggest in this context? Identify several other words and phrases that create strong, specific impressions.

CORNISH CHURCH, 1920. *Sir Matthew Smith. Tate Gallery, London.*

Anthem for Doomed Youth

What passing-bells for these who die as cattle?
  Only the monstrous anger of the guns.
  Only the stuttering rifles' rapid rattle
Can patter out their hasty orisons.[1]
No mockeries now for them; no prayers nor bells,   5
  Nor any voice of mourning save the choirs—
The shrill, demented choirs of wailing shells;
  And bugles calling for them from sad shires.

What candles may be held to speed them all?
  Not in the hands of boys, but in their eyes   10
Shall shine the holy glimmers of goodbyes.
  The pallor of girls' brows shall be their pall;
Their flowers the tenderness of patient minds,
And each slow dusk a drawing down of blinds.

---

1. **orison:** prayer.

Getting at Meaning

1. Why are these youth not receiving a normal funeral?

2. What items or practices associated with services or observances for the dead are named in this poem? What is substituted for the usual customs?

3. Why would prayers or bells be "mockeries"?

4. Notice that the octave is concerned with the horror, noise, and confusion of the battlefield. What contrast in setting and mood is developed in the sestet? Who are the mourners?

5. What point is the speaker making about how war affects the processes and rituals of death? What is the speaker implying about war itself?

Developing Skills in Reading Literature

1. **Structure.** Aside from the octave-sestet arrangement of this sonnet, what other structural devices or regularities do you see?

2. **Sound Devices.** Identify examples of onomatopoeia in this poem. Point out the alliteration. Do any of these sounds, too, imitate what the words are describing? Which images in the poem are strongly auditory? What effect does the poet achieve through the re-creation of sounds, particularly those associated with battle?

3. **Tone.** How would you describe the tone of this poem? Is it perhaps a mixed one? What images are particularly effective in conveying tone?

Developing Vocabulary

Using a Dictionary. Look up the meanings of these words and explain their appropriateness in this poem.
anthem
passing-bells
pall (Need it always be dark?)

Rupert Brooke

1887–1915

RUPERT BROOKE (pencil drawing). *J. H. Thomas. The Bettman Archive, Inc.*

Rupert Brooke became a symbol of the generation sacrificed in World War I. His war poetry, published posthumously in 1915, captured perfectly the mood of selfless patriotism that had animated young people at the beginning of the conflict. When years of war had turned idealism into bitterness, Brooke's noble sentiments came to symbolize the values of a lost civilization.

Born at Rugby School, where his father was a housemaster, Brooke was educated there and at Cambridge University, where he concentrated on Elizabethan and early seventeenth-century drama. Brooke had written poetry from boyhood, and his first volume, *Poems*, was published in 1911, when he was twenty-four. As is typical of prewar Georgian poetry, Brooke's poems are quietly meditative, traditional rather than innovative in style.

A handsome, personable youth of brilliant promise, Brooke numbered among his friends influential figures, such as the literary historian and critic Edmund Gosse, the poet Walter de la Mare, and the Prime Minister of England. Brooke settled at the Old Vicarage, Grantchester, the subject of one of his best known poems. In 1913 and 1914 he traveled to America, Hawaii, Samoa, Fiji, New Zealand, and Tahiti, but his tour was interrupted by the outbreak of war.

Brooke obtained a commission in 1914 and was stationed with the Royal Naval Division at Antwerp. In 1915 he was ordered to the Dardanelles, but on his way there he contracted blood poisoning and died on a hospital ship off the Greek island of Skyros. He was buried on the island, the "corner of a foreign field/ that is forever England."

The Soldier

If I should die, think only this of me:
   That there's some corner of a foreign field
That is forever England. There shall be
   In that rich earth a richer dust concealed;
A dust whom England bore, shaped, made aware;   5
   Gave, once, her flowers to love, her ways to roam,
A body of England's breathing English air,
   Washed by the rivers, blest by suns of home.

And think, this heart, all evil shed away,
   A pulse in the eternal mind, no less   10
      Gives somewhere back the thoughts by England given;
Her sights and sounds; dreams happy as her day;
   And laughter, learnt of friends; and gentleness,
      In hearts at peace, under an English heaven.

Getting at Meaning

1. What is the "richer dust" referred to in line 4? "A body of England's" in line 7?

2. Explain the reference to "A pulse in the eternal mind." What is the source of the pulse, and what function would it perform?

3. What qualities does the speaker associate with England?

4. What point of view or philosophy enables the speaker to come to terms with his possible death?

Developing Skills in Reading Literature

1. **Sonnet.** What type of sonnet is this? What relation do you see between its structure and its idea?

2. **Tone.** What is the tone of this poem? Do you find it sentimental? Is it optimistic or pessimistic? How does the tone compare with that of "Anthem for Doomed Youth," which also deals with death in battle?

Developing Writing Skills

Using Contrasts. Contrast the speaker in this poem with the soldier-speaker in "Dulce et Decorum Est." What difference is apparent in their attitudes about country? about patriotic sacrifice? What might explain this difference? Answer these questions in a well developed paragraph.

Siegfried Sassoon

1886–1967

Siegfried Sassoon is best known for intense anti-war lyrics that describe the carnage and futility of war, unrelieved by glimpses of glorious moments or hints of noble purposes.

Born in Kent, England, Sassoon belonged to a prominent, artistic family of Spanish origin. More interested in poetry and sports than in his studies, he did poorly at Cambridge University. He moved to London, where he published several volumes of poetry in the pastoral mode of the prewar Georgian poets.

When World War I broke out, Sassoon enlisted and was sent to France. The experience of trench warfare affected Sassoon profoundly; although he served for four-and-a-half years and won the Military Cross, he emerged as a vocal pacifist. Because he voiced his antiwar views while still in the army, he was thought to be suffering from shell shock and was sent to a sanatorium. There he met the soldier-poet Wilfred Owen, whose works he later published, after Owen's early death.

Sassoon's first prose work, *Memoirs of a Fox-Hunting Man* (1928), was the first of three volumes in his fictionalized autobiography *The Memoirs of George Sherston* (1928–1936). Another autobiographical trilogy, *Siegfried's Journey*, appeared in 1945. In these autobiographical works, Sassoon depicts English country life and expresses the spirituality that gradually replaced the bitterness and anger of the war years.

SIEGFRIED SASSOON. *Beresford.*
The Bettman Archive, Inc.

Dreamers

Soldiers are citizens of death's gray land,
    Drawing no dividend from time's tomorrows.
In the great hour of destiny they stand,
    Each with his feuds, and jealousies, and sorrows.
Soldiers are sworn to action; they must win   5
    Some flaming, fatal climax with their lives.
Soldiers are dreamers; when the guns begin
    They think of firelit homes, clean beds and wives.

I see them in foul dugouts, gnawed by rats,
    And in the ruined trenches, lashed with rain,   10
Dreaming of things they did with balls and bats,
    And mocked by hopeless longing to regain
Bank holidays, and picture shows, and spats,
    And going to the office in the train.

Getting at Meaning

1. What kind of realm is death's "gray land"? Why do the soldiers draw "no dividend from time's tomorrows"?

2. The soldiers stand "In the great hour of destiny." Do you suppose that this refers to a national destiny or to a personal one? What is the significance of their "feuds, jealousies, and sorrows"?

Developing Skills in Reading Literature

1. **Alliteration.** In the octave of this sonnet, where is alliteration used most notably? What effect is achieved in each alliterative phrase?

2. **Meter.** When you scan this sonnet, how many lines do you find in which the iambic pentameter is regular? How many lines begin with dactyls? What is the effect of the spondee in line 1?

3. **Theme.** The poem's title directs the reader to think of the soldiers as "dreamers." As people generally dream about exotic or extraordinary things, what is sadly ironic about the soldiers' dreams?

William Butler Yeats

The Wild Swans at Coole[1]

The trees are in their autumn beauty,
The woodland paths are dry,
Under the October twilight the water
Mirrors a still sky;
Upon the brimming water among the stones   5
Are nine-and-fifty swans.

The nineteenth autumn has come upon me
Since I first made my count;
I saw, before I had well finished,
All suddenly mount   10
And scatter wheeling in great broken rings
Upon their clamorous wings.

I have looked upon those brilliant creatures,
And now my heart is sore.
All's changed since I, hearing at twilight,   15
The first time on this shore,
The bell-beat of their wings above my head,
Trod with a lighter tread.

Unwearied still, lover by lover,
They paddle in the cold   20
Companionable streams or climb the air;
Their hearts have not grown old;
Passion or conquest, wander where they will,
Attend upon them still.

But now they drift on the still water,   25
Mysterious, beautiful;
Among what rushes will they build,
By what lake's edge or pool
Delight men's eyes when I awake some day
To find they have flown away?   30

---

1. **Coole** (ko͞ol): Coole Park, the estate of Yeats's friend and
fellow playwright, Lady Augusta Gregory.

SWANS. *John Singer Sargent.*
The Metropolitan Museum of Art. Gift of Mrs. Francis Ormond, 1950.

Getting at Meaning

1. Seeing these swans for the first time, what did the speaker do? What interrupted this? How did this experience affect the speaker?

2. Since the speaker first saw the swans, what has stayed the same? What has changed?

3. What emotional qualities does the speaker associate with the swans? What words or phrases convey this?

4. What are the implications of the speaker's question at the end of the poem? What do the swans symbolize for the speaker?

Developing Skills in Reading Literature

1. **Meter and Rhyme Scheme.** What metrical regularities do you find in this poem? What is the rhyme scheme of each stanza? How do run-on lines enhance the description of the birds' movement in the second stanza?

2. **Diction.** What is the effect of the word *brimming* in line 5? (Note, incidentally, that *brim* is an Anglo-Saxon root that means "sea, surf, or edge of the sea.") In line 6, why is "nine-and-fifty" more effective than "fifty-nine"? How does the root meaning of *clamorous* "to cry out" enrich its meaning in line 12? Why is the phrase "cold/Companionable streams" particularly effective? What verbs in this poem convey the strength and energy of these birds, propelling themselves upward?

3. **Tone.** What is the tone of the poem? How does its setting, particularly the time of day and the year, contribute to this tone?

4. **Theme.** How would you express the theme of this poem? What does the theme have to do with a sense of beauty and passion and the passing of time? Why is the speaker's heart sore?

5. **Imagery.** Identify the auditory images in this poem. What produces the sound described by these images? What visual image of the birds strikes you as most impressive? How does it contrast with the image at the beginning of the last stanza? How does this contrast emphasize the poem's theme?

The Lake Isle of Innisfree

I will arise and go now, and go to Innisfree,[1]
And a small cabin build there, of clay and wattles[2] made:
Nine bean rows will I have there, a hive for the honeybee,
And live alone in the bee-loud glade.

And I shall have some peace there, for peace comes dropping slow,   5
Dropping from the veils of the morning to where the cricket sings;
There midnight's all a glimmer, and noon a purple glow,
And evening full of the linnet's wings.

I will arise and go now, for always night and day
I hear lake water lapping with low sounds by the shore;   10
While I stand on the roadway, or on the pavements gray,
I hear it in the deep heart's core.

---

1. **Innisfree:** an island in Lough Gill, County Sligo.
2. **wattles:** woven wood used for walls and roofs.

Getting at Meaning

1. How would you characterize the kind of life the speaker desires to live at Innisfree? How does "nine bean rows" suggest this kind of life? What is the pace of the life the speaker would lead?

2. What is the speaker's present life situation and state of mind? What is the "deep heart's core"?

Developing Skills in Reading Literature

1. **Meter.** Scan the metrical pattern of the first line. Which other lines in the poem echo this pattern? Which line in each stanza is different from the others? What is the effect of this shift in meter?

2. **Sound Devices.** This poem abounds with sound effects, many created by the variety of vowel sounds. In line 10, for example, how many different vowel sounds do you hear? What consonant is repeated in combination with different vowel sounds? Note the way the last three vowel sounds in the poem descend from high to low pitch. Point out a similar effect in line 5. In lines 6 and 8, why do the short *i* sounds seem appropriate for the meanings of the lines? Point out additional examples of assonance and alliteration.

3. **Diction.** "Bee-loud glade" illustrates in a small way the difference between poetry and more ordinary language. The image is intensified by the use of *loud*,

not the usual way to describe bee-sounds. The meaning of *glade* is not quite the same as the meanings of other English words that Yeats might have used; *clearing*, for example. Look up the etymologies of *glade* and of the related word *glad*. How does the root meaning of *glade* enrich its connotations, making it just the right word here? Say the words "bee-loud glade" and listen to the play of vowels and consonants. Clearly sound and sense work together; the glade resonates with sound.

In *bee-loud* Yeats combines words in an unexpected way, a characteristic of poetic language. Discuss the effect in this poem of the use of *glimmer* with *midnight*, *glow* with *noon*, *peace* with *dropping*, *veils* with *morning*, and *heart* with *core*.

4. **Theme.** What impulse motivates the speaker in this poem? It is said that Yeats was influenced by his reading of Thoreau's *Walden*. From what you know of that book, how does the poem reflect this influence?

Developing Vocabulary

1. **Word Origins.** *Glimmer* derives from a Middle English word, as does *gleam*. In your dictionary, which other words begin with *gli-*, coming from Middle English, and have to do with light?

2. **Using a Dictionary.** Dictionaries sometimes label a word such as *cricket* "of echoic origin." What does this mean? What is another word for *cricket*?

D. H. Lawrence

Hummingbird

I can imagine, in some otherworld
Primeval-dumb, far back
In that most awful stillness, that only gasped and hummed,
Hummingbirds raced down the avenues.

Before anything had a soul,   5
While life was a heave of Matter, half inanimate,
This little bit chipped off in brilliance
And went whizzing through the slow, vast, succulent stems.

I believe there were no flowers then,
In the world where the hummingbird flashed ahead of creation.   10
I believe he pierced the slow vegetable veins with his long beak.

Probably he was big
As mosses, and little lizards, they say, were once big.
Probably he was a jabbing, terrifying monster.

We look at him through the wrong end of the long telescope of Time,   15
Luckily for us.

BONAPARTE'S STAR-FRONTLET HUMMINGBIRD, 1861.
J. Gould and H. C. Richter.
Victoria and Albert Museum, Crown Copyright.

Getting at Meaning

1. According to this poem, what was the nature of the primeval world? Why is the stillness "awful"?

2. Against the backdrop of the primeval world, what particular qualities of the hummingbird stand out? What are the "avenues" referred to in line 4?

3. What qualities made the hummingbird menacing? What words indicate these qualities? What are the "little lizards" that "were once big"? Explain the meaning of "the wrong end of the long telescope of Time."

Developing Skills in Reading Literature

1. **Sound Devices.** Find three examples of onomatopoeia in the first eight lines. Is *chipped* onomatopoetic? Then read aloud lines 7 and 8. Do the vowel sounds suit the nature of the hummingbird? Do the last four words produce a different effect? Explain how the sounds in these two lines reinforce the idea of two contrasting life forms.

2. **Diction.** In line 1, what is the effect of printing *otherworld* as one word? The original sense of *awful* has been much diluted through overuse. How does it recover that earlier sense in this context? How does "heave of Matter" convey a particular sense of what life was like, except for the hummingbird? Point out how the bird's qualities are suggested through diction, particularly through verbs.

3. **Tone.** This poem magnifies the hummingbird, portraying the bird as something it might once have been. What mixture of feelings about this creature does the poem convey?

Snake

A snake came to my water-trough
On a hot, hot day, and I in pajamas for the heat,
To drink there.

In the deep, strange-scented shade of the great dark carob-tree
I came down the steps with my pitcher   5
And must wait, must stand and wait, for there he was at the trough before me.

He reached down from a fissure in the earth-wall in the gloom
And trailed his yellow-brown slackness soft-bellied down, over the edge
   of the stone trough
And rested his throat upon the stone bottom,
And where the water had dripped from the tap, in a small clearness,   10
He sipped with his straight mouth,
Softly drank through his straight gums, into his slack long body,
Silently.

Someone was before me at my water-trough,
And I, like a second comer, waiting.   15

He lifted his head from his drinking, as cattle do,
And looked at me vaguely, as drinking cattle do,
And flickered his two-forked tongue from his lips, and mused a moment,
And stooped and drank a little more,
Being earth-brown, earth-golden from the burning bowels of the earth   20
On the day of Sicilian July, with Etna[1] smoking.
The voice of my education said to me
He must be killed,
For in Sicily the black, black snakes are innocent, the gold are venomous.

And voices in me said, If you were a man   25
You would take a stick and break him now, and finish him off.

But must I confess how I liked him,
How glad I was he had come like a guest in quiet, to drink at my water-trough
And depart peaceful, pacified, and thankless,
Into the burning bowels of this earth?   30

Was it cowardice, that I dared not kill him?
Was it perversity, that I longed to talk to him?
Was it humility, to feel so honored?
I felt so honored.

---

1. **Etna:** Mount Etna, a volcano in Sicily.

And yet those voices: 35
If you were not afraid, you would kill him!

And truly I was afraid, I was most afraid,
But even so, honored still more
That he should seek my hospitality
From out the dark door of the secret earth.   40

He drank enough
And lifted his head, dreamily, as one who has drunken,
And flickered his tongue like a forked night on the air, so black;
Seeming to lick his lips,
And looked around like a god, unseeing, into the air,   45
And slowly turned his head,
And slowly, very slowly, as if thrice adream,
Proceeded to draw his slow length curving round
And climb again the broken bank of my wall-face.

And as he put his head into that dreadful hole,   50
And as he slowly drew up, snake-easing his shoulders, and entered
     farther.
A sort of horror, a sort of protest against his withdrawing into that
     horrid black hole,
Deliberately going into the blackness, and slowly drawing himself after,
Overcame me now his back was turned.
I looked round, I put down my pitcher,   55
I picked up a clumsy log
And threw it at the water-trough with a clatter.

I think it did not hit him,
But suddenly that part of him that was left behind convulsed in
     undignified haste,
Writhed like lightning, and was gone   60
Into the black hole, the earth-lipped fissure in the wall front,
At which, in the intense still noon, I stared with fascination.

And immediately I regretted it.
I thought how paltry, how vulgar, what a mean act!
I despised myself and the voices of my accursed human education.   65

And I thought of the albatross,[2]
And I wished he would come back, my snake.

---

2. **albatross:** a symbol of good luck. A reference to the bird killed by the mariner in Coleridge's
"The Rime of the Ancient Mariner."

For he seemed to me again like a king,
Like a king in exile, uncrowned in the underworld,
Now due to be crowned again.   70

And so, I missed my chance with one of the lords
Of life.
And I have something to expiate;
A pettiness.

Getting at Meaning

1. Why does the speaker, though aware of "the voice of my education," feel honored at the visit of the snake? Do the snake's movements and demeanor contribute to this feeling? Explain.

2. What impulse leads the speaker to throw the log? Does the way the snake reacts contribute to the speaker's regret? Explain.

Developing Skills in Reading Literature

1. **Sound Devices.** Point out several examples of alliteration in this poem. What repeated consonant in lines 11–13 seems appropriate in a description of a snake? Is this same consonant repeated elsewhere in the poem? Does the very sound of the word *snake* seem to suit its meaning?

2. **Imagery.** The effect of this poem results partly from the reader's perceiving the snake as the speaker does. What descriptive details and images convey the special way that the snake moves? How is the creature made to seem almost human? Comment on the color imagery in the poem. Why is the snake's tongue "like a forked night" (line 43)? What three similes in particular indicate the special status the snake has for the speaker? Why is the albatross allusion appropriate?

3. **Theme.** Having been torn between conflicting impulses, the speaker says, "I despised myself and the voices of my accursed human education." He also speaks of a missed chance with the snake, a "king in exile, uncrowned." What does this poem say about the way that human beings generally relate to the natural world? What is the conventional view of the snake? Is this the view held by the speaker? What seems to be the superior value, nature and natural instincts or society? What seems to be the effect of society on human beings?

DES CHATS. *Steinlein.*
New York Graphic Society.

T. S. Eliot

The Naming of Cats

The Naming of Cats is a difficult matter,
   It isn't just one of your holiday games;
You may think at first I'm as mad as a hatter
When I tell you, a cat must have THREE DIFFERENT NAMES.
First of all, there's the name that the family use daily,   5
   Such as Peter, Augustus, Alonzo or James,
Such as Victor or Jonathan, George or Bill Bailey—
   All of them sensible everyday names.
There are fancier names if you think they sound sweeter,
   Some for the gentlemen, some for the dames: 10
Such as Plato, Admetus, Electra, Demeter—
   But all of them sensible everyday names.
But I tell you, a cat needs a name that's particular,
   A name that's peculiar, and more dignified,
Else how can he keep up his tail perpendicular,   15
   Or spread out his whiskers, or cherish his pride?
Of names of this kind, I can give you a quorum,
   Such as Munkustrap, Quaxo, or Coricopat,
Such as Bombalurina, or else Jellylorum—
   Names that never belong to more than one cat.   20
But above and beyond there's still one name left over,
   And that is the name that you never will guess;
The name that no human research can discover—
   But THE CAT HIMSELF KNOWS, and will never confess.
When you notice a cat in profound meditation,   25
   The reason, I tell you, is always the same:
His mind is engaged in a rapt contemplation
   Of the thought, of the thought, of the thought of his name:
     His ineffable effable
     Effanineffable   30
Deep and inscrutable singular Name.

Getting at Meaning

1. Among the fancier names for cats, what kind are those in line 11? Why would they be considered "sensible everyday names"?

2. What makes the names in the second group "peculiar" (line 14)? Where might Eliot have gotten the examples he gives?

3. The names in the third group are "ineffable." Why do you suppose the poem includes no examples? What other name has sometimes been considered ineffable? Consult a dictionary if you need help.

Developing Skills in Reading Literature

1. **Meter.** What kind of meter does Eliot employ in this poem? Do some of the lines contain extra syllables? What pace does this meter create?

2. **Rhyme Scheme.** Notice that the word *name* is part of the rhyme scheme throughout the poem. What is the effect of alternating masculine rhymes, particularly in combinations with *name*, with feminine rhymes? Find the triple feminine rhymes that occur in the middle and at the end of the poem. What effect do they achieve?

3. **Light Verse.** What qualities of this poem make it an example of light verse? In what way is the form suitable to the subject matter? How important do the effects of meter and rhyme seem to be in this kind of poem?

Developing Vocabulary

Words from Latin. Both *ineffable* and *inscrutable* have negative prefixes. What do their roots mean? What is the root meaning of *rapt*? Can you find two or three other English words with the same Latin root?

Dylan Thomas

Fern Hill

Now as I was young and easy under the apple boughs
About the lilting house and happy as the grass was green,
  The night above the dingle[1] starry,
    Time let me hail and climb
  Golden in the heydays of his eyes,   5
And honored among wagons I was prince of the apple towns
And once below a time I lordly had the trees and leaves
    Trail with daisies and barley
  Down the rivers of the windfall light.

And as I was green and carefree, famous among the barns   10
About the happy yard and singing as the farm was home,
  In the sun that is young once only,
    Time let me play and be
  Golden in the mercy of his means,
And green and golden I was huntsman and herdsman, the calves   15
Sang to my horn, the foxes on the hills barked clear and cold,
    And the sabbath rang slowly
  In the pebbles of the holy streams.

All the sun long it was running, it was lovely, the hay
Fields high as the house, the tunes from the chimneys, it was air   20
  And playing, lovely and watery
    And fire green as grass.
  And nightly under the simple stars
As I rode to sleep the owls were bearing the farm away,
All the moon long I heard, blessed among stables, the nightjars[2]   25
  Flying with the ricks,[3] and the horses
    Flashing into the dark.

---

1. **dingle:** a small, deep valley.
2. **nightjars:** any nocturnal birds.
3. **ricks:** haystacks.

And then to awake, and the farm, like a wanderer white
With the dew, come back, the cock on his shoulder: it was all
  Shining, it was Adam and maiden,   30
    The sky gathered again
  And the sun grew round that very day.
So it must have been after the birth of the simple light
In the first, spinning place, the spellbound horses walking warm
  Out of the whinnying green stable   35
    On to the fields of praise.

And honored among foxes and pheasants by the gay house
Under the new made clouds and happy as the heart was long,
  In the sun born over and over,
    I ran my heedless ways,   40
  My wishes raced through the house high hay
And nothing I cared, at my sky blue trades, that time allows
In all his tuneful turning so few and such morning songs
  Before the children green and golden
    Follow him out of grace.   45

Nothing I cared, in the lamb white days, that time would take me
Up to the swallow thronged loft by the shadow of my hand,
  In the moon that is always rising,
    Nor that riding to sleep
  I should hear him fly with the high fields   50
And wake to the farm forever fled from the childless land.
Oh as I was young and easy in the mercy of his means,
    Time held me green and dying
  Though I sang in my chains like the sea.

Getting at Meaning

1. Time is mentioned often in this poem. The speaker, telling about his childhood, says, "Once below a time . . ." (line 7). What does he mean?

2. What is the setting of the speaker's remembered childhood? List two or three words and phrases from each stanza that indicate where the speaker was and the kind of things he did.

3. What does the speaker mean in the last stanza when he says that he would "wake to the farm forever fled from the childless land"?

Developing Skills in Reading Literature

1. **Motif.** A recurring image, word, or idea can help to develop the theme of a poem and to give it a unity that rhyme and meter would ordinarily provide. In the first stanza are introduced three motifs that run throughout the poem: (1) the heedless condition of being a child ("Now as I was young and easy . . ."); (2) the delighting in that condition ("honored among wagons I was prince . . ."); and (3) the controlling presence of time ("Time let me hail and climb . . ."). Where do you find these ideas repeated in the other

stanzas? How do all three come together in the last three lines of the poem?

Green and gold are recurrent color images in this poem. What associations are suggested by these colors? What makes them appropriate, particularly in relation to the three recurrent ideas?

Another recurring image is that of singing and music. What pattern of these images can you detect? How do the images change as the poem moves forward?

2. **Figurative Language.** Thomas often telescopes two images, combining their associations in a condensed simile or metaphor. For example, "fire green as grass" (line 22) might be a way of saying something like "grass that is green with the intensity of fire." Similarly, what are the layers of meaning conveyed by "the lilting house" (line 2) and "the heydays of his eyes" (line 5)? What does it mean to be moving through childhood "Down the rivers of the windfall light"?

3. **Sound Devices.** This poem lacks a patterned rhyme scheme. Nevertheless, it rings with sound and deserves, even more than most, to be read aloud. Chose one or two stanzas (four and five, for example), and point out all the sound effects you can find. Also, list what you think are the poem's most effective examples of alliteration, assonance, and consonance. Then read the entire poem aloud, experiencing the impact of these sound devices.

4. **Syllabic Verse.** This poem is an example of verse in which the measure of a line is determined not by the number of metrical feet but by the number of syllables. (Japanese *haiku* are written in syllabic verse.) In each nine-line stanza of this poem, what pattern of syllables per line has Thomas followed: Are there any examples of regular meter in the poem?

5. **Parallelism.** Which lines of the second stanza echo or parallel those of the first? This kind of parallelism, along with the repetition of key images and ideas, helps weave the poem into a unified whole. Can you find other examples of parallelism in the poem? See, for example, the first four words of lines 19 and 25.

6. **Imagery.** This poem conveys the sense that nothing is static; looking back, the speaker seems always to have been moving. What lines in particular convey this often headlong sense of movement? How does the use of present participles contribute to the effect?

Explain the image of the wanderer in the fourth stanza. Why is a "cock on his shoulder"? Explain "it was Adam and maiden." Comment on the imagery of the rest of the stanza; how do the lines convey a sense of wonder and discovery?

Examine the imagery of light and dark. How does this imagery reinforce the poem's theme? At what point does nocturnal imagery enter, with a slightly chilling effect? What contrast follows? Although the sun is "born over and over" in stanza five, in stanza six it is "the moon that is always rising." What effect is building up in this last stanza? Note the image of time taking the child "Up to the swallow thronged loft by the shadow of my hand." What might this image mean? Discuss the poem's final image. What is the significance of singing in chains? What is the effect of the comparison with the sea?

7. **Paradox and Tone.** Point out the paradoxes and contradictions in the last two lines. As a result of these contradictions, does the poem have a mixed tone? How would you compare the tone of the early part of the poem with the tone toward the end?

Developing Vocabulary

1. **Inferring Word Meaning.** In the fifth stanza of the poem is the phrase "my sky blue trades." What do you think *trades* means in this context? Does your dictionary define *trade* in its plural form?

2. **Word Origins.** What is the rather surprising etymology of *dingle*? What is the literal or original sense of *windfall*? What is the origin of *heyday*? How did the nightjar get its name?

Developing Writing Skills

Writing a Reminiscence. Is there some part of your past life, of your childhood, that will remain with you though you can never return to it? In prose, or perhaps in free verse, try to recapture that place and time through images that convey the intensity of your experience. If possible, conclude with an adult perspective, as does Thomas in his poem.

Bernard Shaw

1856–1950

A dramatist for more than half a century, Bernard Shaw challenged the complacencies of conventional thinking, with characters so original and dialogue so clever that audiences were more amused than offended. "My method is to take the utmost trouble to find the right thing to say, and then to say it with the utmost levity," Shaw said. Shaw also was an influential critic, a social reformer, a colorful eccentric, and finally an international celebrity.

Born in Dublin into an Anglo-Irish family, Shaw was influenced in distinct ways by his parents. His father drank too much, and in reaction the son became a teetotaler and a moralist; his mother, who eventually left her husband to live in London, was a gifted musician and music teacher from whom the young Shaw learned a love of music. He attended the Wesleyan School until he was fourteen, when he went to work as a cashier in a Dublin land agent's office. Five years later he moved to London, where he tried to support himself as a writer. His early novels, however, were miserable failures. In 1885 he became music critic for the London *Star* and then the *World*, writing under the pseudonym Corno di Bassetto. For more than a dozen years, he was a prolific critic of music, art, literature, and drama, respected for the breadth of his outlook and feared for his vitriolic barbs. He was also a spellbinding lecturer and incisive pamphleteer for the socialist cause. By 1895, as drama critic for the London periodical *Saturday Review*, Shaw was one of the most powerful critical voices in the English-speaking world, a writer whose reviews and essays helped alter the taste of the time. An expert on Henrik Ibsen, Shaw especially admired the Norwegian playwright for his exposure of middle-class pretension.

Shaw was determined to create as well as to criticize drama, but he had difficulty establishing himself as a playwright. Since 1884 he had been a Fabian socialist, dedicated to gradual reform of British society, and his plays dealt realistically and often shockingly with controversial issues. His first, produced in 1892, was *Widowers' Houses*, a play about slum landlords. In steady succession he wrote *Mrs. Warren's Profession* (written 1893), which the Lord Chamberlain banned because its subject was prostitution; *Arms and the Man* (performed 1894), a satiric look at military heroism; *Candida* (performed 1895), the story of a modern love triangle; and *You Never Can Tell* (performed 1899), a farce. In 1898 Shaw published these works and others as *Plays Pleasant and Unpleasant*, with long prefaces attacking hypocrisy and censorship. In the texts of these and later plays, Shaw implemented the simplifications of spelling and punctuation that he advocated in his self-proclaimed role as language reformer.

In 1925 Shaw won the Nobel Prize for Literature for *Androcles and the Lion*, Pygmalion, and *Saint Joan* (performed 1923), which is based on the paradoxical idea that society often destroys its saints and heroes. In 1931, when he was seventy-five, he traveled around the world, and at the age of ninety-three he wrote the autobiographical *Sixteen Self Sketches*. The following year he broke his leg while cutting a tree in his garden and died not long after.

BERNARD SHAW, 1925. *Bernard Partridge. National Portrait Gallery, London.*

Preface to Pygmalion

The English have no respect for their language, and will not teach their children to speak it. They spell it so abominably that no man can teach himself what it sounds like. It is impossible for an Englishman to open his mouth without making some other Englishman hate or despise him. German and Spanish are accessible to foreigners: English is not accessible even to Englishmen. The reformer England needs today is an energetic phonetic enthusiast: that is why I have made such a one the hero of a popular play. There have been heroes of that kind crying in the wilderness for many years past. When I became interested in the subject towards the end of the eighteen-seventies, the illustrious Alexander Melville Bell, the inventor of Visible Speech, had emigrated to Canada, where his son invented the telephone; but Alexander J. Ellis was still a London patriarch, with an impressive head always covered by a velvet skull cap, for which he would apologize to public meetings in a very courtly manner. He and Tito Pagliardini, another phonetic veteran, were men whom it was impossible to dislike. Henry Sweet, then a young man, lacked their sweetness of character: he was about as conciliatory to conventional mortals as Ibsen or Samuel Butler. His great ability as a phonetician (he was, I think, the best of them all at his job) would have entitled him to high official recognition, and perhaps enabled him to popularize his subject, but for his Satanic contempt for all academic dignitaries and persons in general who thought more of Greek than of phonetics. Once, in the days when the Imperial Institute rose in South Kensington, and Joseph Chamberlain was booming the Empire, I induced the editor of a leading monthly review to commission an article from Sweet on the imperial importance of his subject. When it arrived, it contained nothing but a savagely derisive attack on a professor of language and literature whose chair Sweet regarded as proper to a phonetic expert only. The article, being libellous, had to be returned as impossible; and I had to renounce my dream of dragging its author into the limelight. When I met him afterwards, for the first time for many years, I found to my astonishment that he, who had been a quite tolerably presentable young man, had actually managed by sheer scorn to alter his personal appearance until he had become a sort of walking repudiation of Oxford and all its traditions. It must have been largely in his own despite that he was squeezed into something called a Readership of phonetics there. The future of phonetics rests probably with his pupils, who all swore by him; but nothing could bring the man himself into any sort of compliance with the university to which he nevertheless clung by divine right in an intensely Oxonian way. I daresay his papers, if he has left any, include some satires that may be published without too destructive results fifty years hence. He was, I believe, not in the least an illnatured man: very much the opposite, I should say; but he would not suffer fools gladly.

Those who knew him will recognize in my third act the allusion to the patent shorthand in which he used to write postcards, and which may be acquired from a four and six-penny manual published by the Clarendon Press. The postcards which Mrs Higgins describes are such as I have received from Sweet. I would decipher a sound which a cockney would represent by *zerr*, and a Frenchman by *seu*, and then write demanding with some heat what on earth it meant. Sweet, with boundless contempt for my stupidity, would reply that it not only meant but obviously was the word Result, as no other word containing that sound, and capable of making sense with the context, existed in any language spoken on earth. That less expert mortals should require fuller indications was beyond Sweet's patience. Therefore, though the whole point of his Current Shorthand is that it can express every sound in the language perfectly, vowels as well as consonants, and that your hand has to make no stroke except the easy and current ones with which you write *m*, *n*, and *u*, *l*, *p*, and *q*, scribbling them at whatever angle comes easiest to you, his unfortunate determination to make this remarkable and quite legible script serve also as a shorthand reduced it in his own practice to the most inscrutable of cryptograms. His true objective was the provision of a full, accurate, legible script for our noble but ill-dressed language; but he was led past that by his contempt for the popular Pitman system of shorthand, which he called the Pitfall system. The triumph of Pitman was a triumph of business organization: there was a weekly paper to persuade you to learn Pitman: there were cheap textbooks and exercise books and transcripts of speeches for you to copy, and schools where experienced teachers coached you up to the necessary proficiency. Sweet could not organize his market in that fashion. He might as well have been the Sybil who tore up the leaves of prophecy that nobody would attend to. The four and sixpenny manual, mostly in his lithographed handwriting, that was never vulgarly advertized, may perhaps some day be taken up by a syndicate and pushed upon the public as The Times pushed the Encyclopædia Britannica; but until then it will certainly not prevail against Pitman. I have bought three copies of it during my lifetime; and I am informed by the publishers that its cloistered existence is still a steady and healthy one. I actually learned the system too several times; and yet the shorthand in which I am writing these lines is Pitman's. And the reason is, that my secretary cannot transcribe Sweet, having been perforce taught in the schools of Pitman. Therefore, Sweet railed at Pitman as vainly as Thersites railed at Ajax: his raillery, however it may have eased his soul, gave no popular vogue to Current Shorthand.

Pygmalion Higgins is not a portrait of Sweet, to whom the adventure of Eliza Doolittle would have been impossible; still, as will be seen, there are touches of Sweet in the play. With Higgins's physique and temperament Sweet might have set the Thames on fire. As it was, he impressed himself professionally on Europe to an extent that made his comparative personal obscurity, and the failure of Oxford to do justice to his eminence, a puzzle to foreign specialists in his subject. I do not blame Oxford, because I think Oxford is quite right in demanding a certain social amenity from its nurslings (heaven knows it is not exorbitant in its requirements!); for although I well know how hard it is for a man of genius with a seriously underrated subject to maintain serene and kindly relations with the men who underrate it, and who keep all the best places for less important subjects which they profess without originality and sometimes without much capacity for them, still, if he overwhelms them with wrath and disdain, he cannot expect them to heap honors on him.

Of the later generations of phoneticians I know little. Among them towers the Poet Laureate, to whom perhaps Higgins may owe his Miltonic sympathies, though here again I must disclaim all portraiture. But if the play makes the public aware that there are such people as phoneticians, and that they are among the most important people in England at present, it will serve its turn.

I wish to boast that Pygmalion has been an extremely successful play all over Europe and North America as well as at home. It is so intensely and deliberately didactic, and its subject is esteemed so dry, that I delight in throwing it at the heads of the wiseacres who repeat the parrot cry that art should never be didactic. It goes to prove my contention that art should never be anything else.

Finally, and for the encouragement of people troubled with accents that cut them off from all high employment, I may add that the change wrought by Professor Higgins in the flower-girl is neither impossible nor uncommon. The modern concierge's daughter who fulfils her ambition by playing the Queen of Spain in Ruy Blas at the Théâtre Français is only one of many thousands of men and women who have sloughed off their native dialects and acquired a new tongue. But the thing has to be done scientifically, or the last state of the aspirant may be worse than the first. An honest and natural slum dialect is more tolerable than the attempt of a phonetically untaught person to imitate the vulgar dialect of the golf club; and I am sorry to say that in spite of the efforts of our Royal Academy of Dramatic Art, there is still too much sham golfing English on our stage, and too little of the noble English of Forbes Robertson.

Pygmalion

CHARACTERS

Henry Higgins	Mrs. Eynsford Hill
Colonel Pickering	Miss Eynsford Hill
Freddy Eynsford Hill	Mrs. Higgins
Alfred Doolittle	Mrs. Pearce
Bystanders	Parlormaid
Eliza Doolittle	Taximan

ACT ONE

Covent Garden[1] *in London at 11.15 p.m. Torrents of heavy summer rain. Cab whistles blowing frantically in all directions. Pedestrians running for shelter into the market and under the portico of St Paul's Church, where there are already several people, among them a lady and her daughter in evening dress. They are all peering out gloomily at the rain, except one man with his back turned to the rest, who seems wholly preoccupied with a notebook in which he is writing busily.*

The church clock strikes the first quarter.

THE DAUGHTER (*in the space between the central pillars, close to the one on her left*). I'm getting chilled to the bone. What can Freddy be doing all this time? He's been gone twenty minutes.

THE MOTHER (*on her daughter's right*). Not so long. But he ought to have got us a cab by this.

A BYSTANDER (*on the lady's right*). He wont[2] get no cab not until half-past eleven, missus, when they come back after dropping their theatre fares.

THE MOTHER. But we must have a cab. We cant stand here until half-past eleven. It's too bad.

THE BYSTANDER. Well, it ain't my fault, missus.

THE DAUGHTER. If Freddy had a bit of gumption, he would have got one at the theatre door.

THE MOTHER. What could he have done, poor boy?

THE DAUGHTER. Other people got cabs. Why couldnt he?

(FREDDY *rushes in out of the rain from the Southampton Street side, and comes between them closing a dripping umbrella. He is a young man of twenty, in evening dress, very wet round the ankles.*)

THE DAUGHTER. Well, havnt you got a cab?

FREDDY. Theres not one to be had for love or money.

THE MOTHER. Oh, Freddy, there must be one. You cant have tried.

THE DAUGHTER. It's too tiresome. Do you expect us to go and get one ourselves?

FREDDY. I tell you theyre all engaged. The rain was so sudden: nobody was prepared; and everybody had to take a cab. Ive been to Charing Cross one way and nearly to Ludgate Circus the other; and they were all engaged.

THE MOTHER. Did you try Trafalgar Square?

FREDDY. There wasnt one at Trafalgar Square.

THE DAUGHTER. Did you try?

FREDDY. I tried as far as Charing Cross Station.

---

1. **Covent Garden:** the large fruit, vegetable, and flower-market district of London. The area includes St. Paul's Church (not to be confused with St. Paul's Cathedral) and a theater, the Royal Opera House, which first opened in 1732.

2. **wont:** One of Shaw's spelling reforms was to omit apostrophes in contractions unless omission would be confusing (*shell* instead of *she'll*) or omission would change pronunciation (*were* instead of *we're*).

Did you expect me to walk to Hammersmith?

THE DAUGHTER. You havnt tried at all.

THE MOTHER. You really are very helpless, Freddy. Go again; and dont come back until you have found a cab.

FREDDY. I shall simply get soaked for nothing.

THE DAUGHTER. And what about us? Are we to stay here all night in this draught,[3] with next to nothing on? You selfish pig—

FREDDY. Oh, very well: I'll go, I'll go. *(He opens his umbrella and dashes off Strandwards, but comes into collision with a flower girl, who is hurrying in for shelter, knocking her basket out of her hands. A blinding flash of lightning, followed instantly by a rattling peal of thunder, orchestrates the incident.)*

THE FLOWER GIRL. Nah then, Freddy: look wh' y' gowin, deah.

FREDDY. Sorry *(he rushes off)*.

THE FLOWER GIRL *(picking up her scattered flowers and replacing them in the basket).* Theres menners f' yer! Te-oo banches o voylets trod into the mad. *(She sits down on the plinth[4] of the column, sorting her flowers, on the lady's right. She is not at all an attractive person. She is perhaps eighteen, perhaps twenty, hardly older. She wears a little sailor hat of black straw that has long been exposed to the dust and soot of London and has seldom if ever been brushed. Her hair needs washing rather badly: its mousy color can hardly be natural. She wears a shoddy black coat that reaches nearly to her knees and is shaped to her waist. She has a brown skirt with a coarse apron. Her boots are much the worse for wear. She is no doubt as clean as she can afford to be; but compared to the ladies she is very dirty. Her features are no worse than theirs; but their condition leaves something to be desired; and she needs the services of a dentist.)*

THE MOTHER. How do you know that my son's name is Freddy, pray?

THE FLOWER GIRL. Ow, eez ye-ooa san, is e? Wal, fewd dan y' de-ooty bawmz a mather should, eed now bettern to spawl a pore gel's flahrzn than ran awy athaht pyin. Will ye-oo py me f' them? *(Here, with apologies, this desperate attempt to represent her dialect without a phonetic alphabet must be abandoned as unintelligible outside London.)*

THE DAUGHTER. Do nothing of the sort, mother. The idea!

THE MOTHER. Please allow me, Clara. Have you any pennies?

THE DAUGHTER. No. Ive nothing smaller than sixpence.

THE FLOWER GIRL *(hopefully).* I can give you change for a tanner,[5] kind lady.

THE MOTHER *(to CLARA).* Give it to me. *(CLARA parts reluctantly.)* Now *(to the girl)* this is for your flowers.

THE FLOWER GIRL. Thank you kindly, lady.

THE DAUGHTER. Make her give you the change. These things are only a penny a bunch.

THE MOTHER. Do hold your tongue, Clara. *(To the girl)* You can keep the change.

THE FLOWER GIRL. Oh, thank you, lady.

THE MOTHER. Now tell me how you know that young gentleman's name.

THE FLOWER GIRL. I didnt.

THE MOTHER. I heard you call him by it. Dont try to deceive me.

THE FLOWER GIRL *(protesting).* Who's trying to deceive you? I called him Freddy or Charlie same as you might yourself if you was talking to a stranger and wished to be pleasant. *(She sits down beside her basket.)*

THE DAUGHTER. Sixpence thrown away! Really, mamma, you might have spared Freddy that. *(She retreats in disgust behind the pillar.)*

---

3. **draught:** draft.

4. **plinth:** the square block at the base of a column.

5. **tanner** *British slang:* sixpence.

(An elderly gentleman of the amiable military type rushes into the shelter, and closes a dripping umbrella. He is in the same plight as FREDDY, *very wet about the ankles. He is in evening dress, with a light overcoat. He takes the place left vacant by the daughter's retirement.)*

THE GENTLEMAN. Phew!

THE MOTHER *(to the gentleman)*. Oh, sir, is there any sign of its stopping?

THE GENTLEMAN. I'm afraid not. It started worse than ever about two minutes ago. *(He goes to the plinth beside the flower girl; puts up his foot on it; and stoops to turn down his trouser ends.)*

THE MOTHER. Oh dear! *(She retires sadly and joins her daughter.)*

THE FLOWER GIRL *(taking advantage of the military gentleman's proximity to establish friendly relations with him)*. If it's worse, it's a sign it's nearly over. So cheer up, Captain; and buy a flower off a poor girl.

THE GENTLEMAN. I'm sorry. I havnt any change.

THE FLOWER GIRL. I can give you change, Captain.

THE GENTLEMAN. For a sovereign? Ive nothing less.

THE FLOWER GIRL. Garn! Oh do buy a flower off me, Captain. I can change half-a-crown. Take this for tuppence.

THE GENTLEMAN. Now dont be troublesome: theres a good girl. *(Trying his pockets)* I really havnt any change—Stop: heres three hapence, if thats any use to you. *(He retreats to the other pillar.)*

THE FLOWER GIRL *(disappointed, but thinking three half-pence better than nothing)*. Thank you, sir.

THE BYSTANDER *(to the girl)*. You be careful: give him a flower for it. Theres a bloke here behind taking down every blessed word youre saying. *(All turn to the man who is taking notes.)*

THE FLOWER GIRL *(springing up terrified)*. I aint done nothing wrong by speaking to the gentleman. Ive a right to sell flowers if I keep off the kerb. *(Hysterically)* I'm a respectable girl: so help me, I never spoke to him except to ask him to buy a flower off me.

(General hubbub, mostly sympathetic to the FLOWER GIRL, *but deprecating her excessive sensibility. Cries of* Dont start hollerin. Who's hurting you? Nobody's going to touch you. Whats the good of fussing? Steady on. Easy, easy, *etc., come from the elderly staid spectators, who pat her comfortably. Less patient ones bid her shut her head, or ask her roughly what is wrong with her. A remoter group, not knowing what the matter is, crowd in and increase the noise with question and answer:* What's the row? What she do? Where is he? A tec[6] taking her down. What! him? Yes: him over there: Took money off the gentleman, *etc.)*

THE FLOWER GIRL *(breaking through them to the* GENTLEMAN, *crying wildly)*. Oh, sir, dont let him charge me. You dunno what it means to me. Theyll take away my character and drive me on the streets for speaking to gentlemen. They—

THE NOTE TAKER *(coming forward on her right, the rest crowding after him)*. There, there, there, there! who's hurting you, you silly girl? What do you take me for?

THE BYSTANDER. It's all right: he's a gentleman: look at his boots. *(Explaining to the* NOTE TAKER*)* She thought you was a copper's nark, sir.

THE NOTE TAKER *(with quick interest)*. Whats a copper's nark?

THE BYSTANDER *(inapt at definition)*. It's a—well, it's a copper's nark, as you might say. What else would you call it? A sort of informer.

THE FLOWER GIRL *(still hysterical)*. I take my Bible oath I never said a word—

---

6. **tec** British slang: detective.

THE NOTE TAKER (*overbearing but good-humored*). Oh, shut up, shut up. Do I look like a policeman?

THE FLOWER GIRL (*far from reassured*). Then what did you take down my words for? How do I know whether you took me down right? You just shew me what youve wrote about me. (*The* NOTE TAKER *opens his book and holds it steadily under her nose, though the pressure of the mob trying to read it over his shoulders would upset a weaker man.*) Whats that? That aint proper writing. I cant read that.

THE NOTE TAKER. I can. (*Reads, reproducing her pronunciation exactly*) "Cheer ap, Keptin; n' baw ya flahr orf a pore gel."

THE FLOWER GIRL (*much distressed*). It's because I called him Captain. I meant no harm. (*To the* GENTLEMAN) Oh, sir, don't let him lay a charge agen me for a word like that. You—

THE GENTLEMAN. Charge! I make no charge. (*To the* NOTE TAKER) Really, sir, if you are a detective, you need not begin protecting me against molestation by young women until I ask you. Anybody could see that the girl meant no harm.

THE BYSTANDERS GENERALLY (*demonstrating against police espionage*). Course they could. What business is it of yours? You mind your own affairs. He wants promotion, he does. Taking down people's words! Girl never said a word to him. What harm if she did? Nice thing a girl cant shelter from the rain without being insulted, etc., etc., etc. (*She is conducted by the more sympathetic demonstrators back to her plinth, where she resumes her seat and struggles with her emotion.*)

THE BYSTANDER. He aint a tec. He's a blooming busybody: thats what he is. I tell you, look at his boots.

THE NOTE TAKER (*turning on him genially*). And how are all your people down at Selsey?

THE BYSTANDER (*suspiciously*). Who told you my people come from Selsey?

THE NOTE TAKER. Never you mind. They did. (*To the girl*) How do you come to be up so far east? You were born in Lisson Grove.

THE FLOWER GIRL (*appalled*). Oh, what harm is there in my leaving Lisson Grove? It wasnt fit for a pig to live in; and I had to pay four-and-six a week. (*In tears*) Oh, boo—hoo—oo—

THE NOTE TAKER. Live where you like; but stop that noise.

THE GENTLEMAN (*to the girl*). Come, come! he cant touch you: you have a right to live where you please.

A SARCASTIC BYSTANDER (*thrusting himself between the* NOTE TAKER *and the* GENTLEMAN). Park Lane, for instance. I'd like to go into the Housing Question with you, I would.

THE FLOWER GIRL (*subsiding into a brooding melancholy over her basket, and talking very low-spiritedly to herself*). I'm a good girl, I am.

THE SARCASTIC BYSTANDER (*not attending to her*). Do you know where I come from?

THE NOTE TAKER (*promptly*). Hoxton.

(*Titterings. Popular interest in the* NOTE TAKER's *performance increases.*)

THE SARCASTIC ONE (*amazed*). Well, who said I didnt? Bly me! You know everything, you do.

THE FLOWER GIRL (*still nursing her sense of injury*). Aint no call to meddle with me, he aint.

THE BYSTANDER (*to her*). Of course he aint. Dont you stand it from him. (*To the* NOTE TAKER) See here: what call have you to know about people what never offered to meddle with you? Wheres your warrant?

SEVERAL BYSTANDERS (*encouraged by this seeming point of law*). Yes: wheres your warrant?

THE FLOWER GIRL. Let him say what he likes. I dont want to have no truck with him.

THE BYSTANDER. You take us for dirt under your feet, dont you? Catch you taking liberties with a gentleman!

THE SARCASTIC BYSTANDER. Yes: tell him where he come from if you want to go fortune-telling.

THE NOTE TAKER. Cheltenham, Harrow, Cambridge, and India.

THE GENTLEMAN. Quite right.

(Great laughter. Reaction in the NOTE TAKER'S *favor. Exclamations of* He knows all about it. Told him proper. Hear him tell the toff[7] where he come from? *etc.)*

THE GENTLEMAN. May I ask, sir, do you do this for your living at a music hall?

THE NOTE TAKER. I've thought of that. Perhaps I shall some day.

(The rain has stopped; and the persons on the outside of the crowd begin to drop off.)

THE FLOWER GIRL *(resenting the reaction).* He's no gentleman, he aint, to interfere with a poor girl.

THE DAUGHTER *(out of patience, pushing her way rudely to the front and displacing the* GENTLEMAN, *who politely retires to the other side of the pillar).* What on earth is Freddy doing? I shall get pneumonia if I stay in this draught any longer.

THE NOTE TAKER *(to himself, hastily making a note of her pronunciation of "monia").* Earlscourt.

THE DAUGHTER *(violently).* Will you please keep your impertinent remarks to yourself.

THE NOTE TAKER. Did I say that out loud? I didnt mean to. I beg your pardon. Your mother's Epsom, unmistakeably.

THE MOTHER *(advancing between her daughter and the* NOTE TAKER*).* How very curious! I was brought up in Largelady Park, near Epsom.

THE NOTE TAKER *(uproariously amused).* Ha!

ha! What a devil of a name! Excuse me. *(To the* DAUGHTER*)* You want a cab, do you?

THE DAUGHTER. Dont dare speak to me.

THE MOTHER. Oh please, please, Clara. *(Her daughter repudiates her with an angry shrug and retires haughtily.)* We should be so grateful to you, sir, if you found us a cab. *(The* NOTE TAKER *produces a whistle.)* Oh, thank you. *(She joins her daughter.)*

(The NOTE TAKER *blows a piercing blast.)*

THE SARCASTIC BYSTANDER. There! I knowed he was a plainclothes copper.

THE BYSTANDER. That aint a police whistle: thats a sporting whistle.

THE FLOWER GIRL *(still preoccupied with her wounded feelings).* He's no right to take away my character. My character is the same to me as any lady's.

THE NOTE TAKER. I dont know whether youve noticed it; but the rain stopped about two minutes ago.

THE BYSTANDER. So it has. Why didnt you say so before? and us losing our time listening to your silliness! *(He walks off toward the Strand.)*

THE SARCASTIC BYSTANDER. I can tell where you come from. You come from Anwell. Go back there.

THE NOTE TAKER *(helpfully).* Hanwell.

THE SARCASTIC BYSTANDER *(affecting great distinction of speech).* Thenk you, teacher. Haw haw! So long. *(He touches his hat with mock respect and strolls off.)*

THE FLOWER GIRL. Frightening people like that! How would he like it himself?

THE MOTHER. It's quite fine now, Clara. We can walk to a motor bus. Come. *(She gathers her skirts above her ankles and hurries off toward the Strand.)*

THE DAUGHTER. But the cab—*(Her mother is out of hearing.)* Oh, how tiresome! *(She follows angrily.)*

---

7. **toff** *British slang:* a dandy.

(All the rest have gone except the NOTE TAKER, *the* GENTLEMAN, *and the* FLOWER GIRL, *who sits arranging her basket and still pitying herself in murmurs.)*

THE FLOWER GIRL. Poor girl! Hard enough for her to live without being worried and chivied.[8]

THE GENTLEMAN *(returning to his former place on the* NOTE TAKER'S *left)*. How do you do it, if I may ask?

THE NOTE TAKER. Simply phonetics. The science of speech. Thats my profession: also my hobby. Happy is the man who can make a living by his hobby! You can spot an Irishman or a Yorkshireman by his brogue. *I* can place any man within six miles. I can place him within two miles in London. Sometimes within two streets.

THE FLOWER GIRL. Ought to be ashamed of himself, unmanly coward!

THE GENTLEMAN. But is there a living in that?

THE NOTE TAKER. Oh yes. Quite a fat one. This is an age of upstarts. Men begin in Kentish Town with £80 a year, and end in Park Lane with a hundred thousand. They want to drop Kentish Town; but they give themselves away every time they open their mouths. Now I can teach them—

THE FLOWER GIRL. Let him mind his own business and leave a poor girl—

THE NOTE TAKER *(explosively)*. Woman: cease this detestable boohooing instantly; or else seek the shelter of some other place of worship.

THE FLOWER GIRL *(with feeble defiance)*. Ive a right to be here if I like, same as you.

THE NOTE TAKER. A woman who utters such depressing and disgusting sounds has no right to be anywhere—no right to live. Remember that you are a human being with a soul and the divine gift of articulate speech: that your native language is the language of Shakespear[9] and Milton and The Bible: and dont sit there crooning like a bilious pigeon.

THE FLOWER GIRL *(quite overwhelmed, looking up at him in mingled wonder and deprecation without daring to raise her head)*. Ah-ah-ah-ow-ow-ow-oo!

THE NOTE TAKER *(whipping out his book)*. Heavens! what a sound! *(He writes; then holds out the book and reads, reproducing her vowels exactly.)* Ah-ah-ah-ow-ow-ow-oo!

THE FLOWER GIRL *(tickled by the performance, and laughing in spite of herself)*. Garn!

THE NOTE TAKER. You see this creature with her kerbstone English: the English that will keep her in the gutter to the end of her days. Well, sir, in three months I could pass that girl off as a duchess at an ambassador's garden party. I could even get her a place as lady's maid or shop assistant, which requires better English. Thats the sort of thing I do for commercial millionaires. And on the profits of it I do genuine scientific work in phonetics, and a little as a poet on Miltonic lines.

THE GENTLEMAN. I am myself a student of Indian dialects; and—

THE NOTE TAKER *(eagerly)*. Are you? Do you know Colonel Pickering, the author of Spoken Sanscrit?

THE GENTLEMAN. I am Colonel Pickering. Who are you?

THE NOTE TAKER. Henry Higgins, author of Higgins's Universal Alphabet.

PICKERING *(with enthusiasm)*. I came from India to meet you.

HIGGINS. I was going to India to meet you.

PICKERING. Where do you live?

HIGGINS. 27A Wimpole Street. Come and see me tomorrow.

PICKERING. I'm at the Carlton. Come with me now and lets have a jaw over some supper.

HIGGINS. Right you are.

THE FLOWER GIRL *(to* PICKERING, *as he passes*

---

8. **worrited and chivied:** worried and tormented.
9. **Shakespear:** Shaw spells names phonetically.

her). Buy a flower, kind gentleman. I'm short for my lodging.

PICKERING. I really havnt any change. I'm sorry. *(He goes away.)*

HIGGINS *(shocked at the girl's mendacity)*. Liar. You said you could change half-a-crown.

THE FLOWER GIRL *(rising in desperation)*. You ought to be stuffed with nails, you ought. *(Flinging the basket at his feet)* Take the whole blooming basket for sixpence.

(The church clock strikes the second quarter.)

HIGGINS *(hearing in it the voice of God, rebuking him for his pharisaic want of charity to the poor girl)*. A reminder. *(He raises his hat solemnly; then throws a handful of money into the basket and follows* PICKERING.)

THE FLOWER GIRL *(picking up a half-crown)*. Ah-ow-ooh! *(Picking up a couple of florins)* Aaah-ow-ooh! *(Picking up several coins)* Aaaaaah-ow-ooh! *(Picking up a half-sovereign)* Aaaaaaaaaaaah-ow-ooh!!!

FREDDY *(springing out of a taxicab)*. Got one at last. Hallo! *(To the* GIRL) Where are the two ladies that were here?

THE FLOWER GIRL. They walked to the bus when the rain stopped.

FREDDY. And left me with a cab on my hands! Damnation!

THE FLOWER GIRL *(with grandeur)*. Never mind, young man. *I'm* going home in a taxi. *(She sails off to the cab. The driver puts his hand behind him and holds the door firmly shut against her. Quite understanding his mistrust, she shews him her handful of money)*. Eightpence aint no object to me, Charlie. *(He grins and opens the door.)* Angel Court, Drury Lane, round the corner of Micklejohn's oil shop. Lets see how fast you can make her hop it. *(She gets in and pulls the door to with a slam as the taxicab starts.)*

FREDDY. Well, I'm dashed!

Act One

Getting at Meaning

1. At first, the characters are identified by labels, suggesting that they represent various social and economic classes. Which groups are represented, and what characteristics are associated with each? What suggests that Higgins may be somewhat of a maverick?

2. Because the flower girl is so very poor, there is an unspoken assumption that she probably sells something besides flowers. In what lines does she acknowledge these suspicions and defend herself against them? Why does the sympathetic bystander urge her to give the gentleman a flower in return for the three hapence? Why is Freddy's mother so suspicious when the flower girl refers to her son by name? What does the daughter mean when she says, "Sixpence thrown away! Really, mamma, you might have spared Freddy that"? In the last speech of the act, the flower girl refers to the cab driver as Charlie. How does this confirm her virtue?

3. In this play, language symbolizes the gap between rich and poor, the social abyss between them in the England of 1912. How wide is this gap, as suggested by the communication difficulties experienced by the flower girl and the upper-class theatergoers? as indicated by Shaw's abandoning the attempt to represent the flower girl's dialect?

4. Just before the note taker and the gentleman discover each other's identity, the note taker summarizes the plot that will unfold in the succeeding acts. Quote the lines in which he does this. What seems to be Colonel Pickering's role? What questions are you left with at the end of Act One?

Developing Skills in Reading Literature

1. **Characterization.** The major and minor characters in this play begin to emerge in the first act, mainly through the following methods of characterization.

a. **Dialogue.** Which lines spoken by the flower girl demonstrate her spunk and resourcefulness? her strength of character and flair for colorful expression? her determination to better herself? Identify lines that establish the character of Higgins. Which lines indicate his attitude toward people in general? How does his attitude contrast with that of Colonel Pickering? Cite lines to support your answer. What do you learn about the mother, her daughter, and her son from what they say? How is their economic situation suggested?

b. **Dialect.** At first, Shaw renders the flower girl's dialect in phonetics, forcing the reader to say the words aloud to catch their meanings. He then switches to more conventional English. What purpose is served by the inclusion of the barely intelligible dialect? What is Shaw suggesting about the flower girl?

c. **Stage Directions.** The stage directions in this play give significant details that suggest the scene and the characters, providing just enough information for the reader to visualize the action. Notice that the flower girl is the only character whose appearance is described in any detail. What impression emerges from this description? What kinds of stage directions help to characterize Freddy? his sister? Colonel Pickering is described as "an elderly gentleman of the amiable military type." What picture do you form from this limited detail? Even fewer details are given about Higgins's appearance, but the stage directions do indicate the way he speaks his lines. Locate several examples of these directions, and discuss the qualities they reveal.

2. **Drama.** Drama, literature meant to be acted on a stage, requires a certain "willing suspension of disbelief" on the part of the audience. That is, the audience is expected to accept things that might be incredible in real life. For example, Higgins claims that he can listen to a person speak and place him within six miles, even within two streets. Could an expert truly do what Higgins does? Does it matter in the context of the play whether his skills are actually possible or in the realm of fantasy? Are there other occurrences in Act One that would be highly unlikely in real life? What dramatic purpose do they serve?

ACT TWO

Next day at 11 A.M. HIGGINS's *laboratory in Wimpole Street. It is a room on the first floor, looking on the street, and was meant for the drawing room. The double doors are in the middle of the back wall; and persons entering find in the corner to their right two tall file cabinets at right angles to one another against the walls. In this corner stands a flat writing-table, on which are a phonograph, a laryngoscope, a row of tiny organ pipes with bellows, a set of lamp chimneys for singing flames with burners attached to a gas plug in the wall by an indiarubber tube, several tuning-forks of different sizes, a life-size image of half a human head, shewing in section the vocal organs, and a box containing a supply of wax cylinders for the phonograph.*

Further down the room, on the same side, is a fireplace, with a comfortable leather-covered easy-chair at the side of the hearth nearest the door, and a coal-scuttle. There is a clock on the mantel-piece. Between the fireplace and the phonograph table is a stand for newspapers.

On the other side of the central door, to the left of the visitor, is a cabinet of shallow drawers. On it is a telephone and the telephone directory. The corner beyond, and most of the side wall, is occupied by a grand piano, with the keyboard at the end furthest from the door, and a bench for the player extending the full length of the keyboard. On the piano is a dessert dish heaped with fruit and sweets, mostly chocolates.

The middle of the room is clear. Besides the easy-chair, the piano bench, and two chairs at the phonograph table, there is one stray chair. It stands near the fireplace. On the walls, engravings: mostly Piranesis[1] and mezzotint[2] portraits. No paintings.

PICKERING *is seated at the table, putting down some cards and a tuning-fork which he has been using.* HIGGINS *is standing up near him, closing two or three file drawers which are hanging out. He appears in the morning light as a robust, vital, appetizing sort of man of forty or thereabouts, dressed in a professional-looking black frock-coat with a white linen collar and black silk tie. He is of the energetic, scientific type, heartily, even violently interested in everything that can be studied as a scientific subject, and careless about himself and other people, including their feelings. He is, in fact, but for his years and size, rather like a very impetuous baby "taking notice" eagerly and loudly, and requiring almost as much watching to keep him out of unintended mischief. His manner varies from genial bullying when he is in a good humor to stormy petulance when anything goes wrong; but he is so entirely frank and void of malice that he remains likeable even in his least reasonable moments.*

HIGGINS *(as he shuts the last drawer).* Well, I think thats the whole show.

PICKERING. It's really amazing. I havnt taken half of it in, you know.

HIGGINS. Would you like to go over any of it again?

PICKERING *(rising and coming to the fireplace, where he plants himself with his back to the fire).* No, thank you; not now. I'm quite done up for this morning.

HIGGINS *(following him, and standing beside him on his left).* Tired of listening to sounds?

PICKERING. Yes. It's a fearful strain. I rather fancied myself because I can pronounce twenty-four distinct vowel sounds; but your hundred and thirty beat me. I cant hear a bit of difference between most of them.

HIGGINS *(chuckling, and going over to the piano to eat sweets).* Oh, that comes with practice. You hear no difference at first; but

---

1. **Piranesis.** Giambattista Piranesi (1720–1778), an Italian artist.

2. **mezzotint:** a copper or steel engraving.

you keep on listening, and presently you find theyre all as different as A from B. *(MRS PEARCE looks in: she is HIGGINS's housekeeper.)* Whats the matter?

MRS PEARCE *(hesitating, evidently perplexed)*. A young woman wants to see you sir.

HIGGINS. A young woman! What does she want?

MRS PEARCE. Well, sir, she says youll be glad to see her when you know what she's come about. She's quite a common girl, sir. Very common indeed. I should have sent her away, only I thought perhaps you wanted her to talk into your machines. I hope Ive not done wrong; but really you see such queer people sometimes—youll excuse me, I'm sure, sir—

HIGGINS. Oh, thats all right, Mrs Pearce. Has she an interesting accent?

MRS PEARCE. Oh, something dreadful, sir, really. I dont know how you can take an interest in it.

HIGGINS *(to PICKERING)*. Lets have her up. Shew her up, Mrs Pearce. *(He rushes across to his working table and picks out a cylinder to use on the phonograph.)*

MRS PEARCE *(only half resigned to it)*. Very well, sir. It's for you to say. *(She goes downstairs.)*

HIGGINS. This is rather a bit of luck. I'll shew you how I make records. We'll set her talking; and I'll take it down first in Bell's visible Speech; then in broad Romic; and then we'll get her on the phonograph so that you can turn her on as often as you like with the written transcript before you.

MRS PEARCE *(returning)*. This is the young woman, sir.

(The FLOWER GIRL enters in state. She has a hat with three ostrich feathers, orange, sky-blue, and red. She has a nearly clean apron, and the shoddy coat has been tidied a little. The pathos of this deplorable figure, with its innocent vanity and consequential air, touches PICKERING, who has already straightened himself in the presence of MRS PEARCE. But as to HIGGINS, the only distinction he makes between men and women is that when he is neither bullying nor exclaiming to the heavens against some feather-weight cross,[3] he coaxes women as a child coaxes its nurse when it wants to get anything out of her.)

HIGGINS *(brusquely, recognizing her with unconcealed disappointment, and at once, babylike, making an intolerable grievance of it)*. Why, this is the girl I jotted down last night. She's no use: Ive got all the records I want of the Lisson Grove lingo; and I'm not going to waste another cylinder on it. *(To the GIRL)* Be off with you: I dont want you.

THE FLOWER GIRL. Dont you be so saucy. You aint heard what I come for yet. *(To MRS PEARCE, who is waiting at the door for further instructions)* Did you tell him I come in a taxi?

MRS PEARCE. Nonsense, girl! what do you think a gentleman like Mr Higgins cares what you came in?

THE FLOWER GIRL. Oh, we are proud! He aint above giving lessons, not him: I heard him say so. Well, I aint come here to ask for any compliment; and if my money's not good enough I can go elsewhere.

HIGGINS. Good enough for what?

THE FLOWER GIRL. Good enough for ye-oo. Now you know, dont you? I'm come to have lessons, I am. And to pay for em too: make no mistake.

HIGGINS *(stupent)*.[4] Well!!! *(Recovering his breath with a gasp)* What do you expect me to say to you?

THE FLOWER GIRL. Well, if you was a gentleman, you might ask me to sit down, I think. Dont I tell you I'm bringing you business?

HIGGINS. Pickering: shall we ask this baggage to sit down, or shall we throw her out of the window?

---

3. **feather-weight cross:** momentary inconvenience.
4. **stupent:** dumbfounded.

THE FLOWER GIRL *(running away in terror to the piano, where she turns at bay)*. Ah-ah-oh-ow-ow-ow-oo! *(Wounded and whimpering)* I wont be called a baggage when Ive offered to pay like any lady.

(Motionless, the two men stare at her from the other side of the room, amazed.)

PICKERING *(gently)*. What is it you want, my girl?

THE FLOWER GIRL. I want to be a lady in a flower shop stead of selling at the corner of Tottenham Court Road. But they wont take me unless I can talk more genteel. He said he could teach me. Well, here I am ready to pay him—not asking any favor—and he treats me as if I was dirt.

MRS PEARCE. How can you be such a foolish ignorant girl as to think you could afford to pay Mr Higgins?

THE FLOWER GIRL. Why shouldnt I? I know what lessons cost as well as you do; and I'm ready to pay.

HIGGINS. How much?

THE FLOWER GIRL *(coming back to him, triumphant)*. Now youre talking! I thought youd come off it when you saw a chance of getting back a bit of what you chucked at me last night. *(Confidentially)* Youd had a drop in, hadnt you?

HIGGINS *(peremptorily)*. Sit down.

THE FLOWER GIRL. Oh, if youre going to make a compliment of it—

HIGGINS *(thundering at her)*. Sit down.

MRS PEARCE *(severely)*. Sit down, girl. Do as youre told. *(She places the stray chair near the hearthrug between* HIGGINS *and* PICKERING, *and stands behind it waiting for the girl to sit down.)*

THE FLOWER GIRL. Ah-ah-ah-ow-ow-oo! *(She stands, half rebellious, half bewildered.)*

PICKERING (very courteous). Wont you sit down?

THE FLOWER GIRL/LIZA (coyly). Dont mind if I do. (She sits down. PICKERING returns to the hearthrug.)

HIGGINS. Whats your name?

THE FLOWER GIRL. Liza Doolittle.

HIGGINS (declaiming gravely).

Eliza, Elizabeth, Betsy and Bess,
They went to the woods to get a bird's nes':

PICKERING. They found a nest with four eggs in it:

HIGGINS. They took one apiece, and left three in it.

(They laugh heartily at their own wit.)

LIZA. Oh, dont be silly.

MRS PEARCE. You mustnt speak to the gentleman like that.

LIZA. Well, why wont he speak sensible to me?

HIGGINS. Come back to business. How much do you propose to pay me for the lessons?

LIZA. Oh, I know whats right. A lady friend of mine gets French lessons for eighteenpence an hour from a real French gentleman. Well, you wouldnt have the face to ask me the same for teaching me my own language as you would for French; so I wont give more than a shilling. Take it or leave it.

HIGGINS (walking up and down the room, rattling his keys and his cash in his pockets). You know, Pickering, if you consider a shilling, not as a simple shilling, but as a percentage of this girl's income, it works out as fully equivalent to sixty or seventy guineas from a millionaire.

PICKERING. How so?

HIGGINS. Figure it out. A millionaire has about £150 a day. She earns about half-a-crown.

LIZA (haughtily). Who told you I only—

HIGGINS (continuing). She offers me two-fifths of her day's income for a lesson. Two-fifths of a millionaire's income for a day would be somewhere about £60. It's handsome.

By George, it's enormous! it's the biggest offer I ever had.

LIZA (rising, terrified). Sixty pounds! What are you talking about? I never offered you sixty pounds. Where would I get—

HIGGINS. Hold your tongue.

LIZA (weeping). But I aint got sixty pounds. Oh—

MRS PEARCE. Dont cry, you silly girl. Sit down. Nobody is going to touch your money.

HIGGINS. Somebody is going to touch you, with a broomstick, if you dont stop snivelling. Sit down.

LIZA (obeying slowly). Ah-ah-ah-ow-oo-o! One would think you was my father.

HIGGINS. If I decide to teach you, I'll be worse than two fathers to you. Here! (He offers her his silk handkerchief.)

LIZA. Whats this for?

HIGGINS. To wipe your eyes. To wipe any part of your face that feels moist. Remember: thats your handkerchief; and thats your sleeve. Dont mistake the one for the other if you wish to become a lady in a shop.

(LIZA, utterly bewildered, stares helplessly at him.)

MRS PEARCE. It's no use talking to her like that, Mr Higgins: she doesnt understand you. Besides, youre quite wrong: she doesnt do it that way at all. (She takes the handkerchief.)

LIZA (snatching it). Here! You give me that handkerchief. He give it to me, not to you.

PICKERING (laughing). He did. I think it must be regarded as her property, Mrs Pearce.

MRS PEARCE (resigning herself). Serve you right, Mr Higgins.

PICKERING. Higgins: I'm interested. What about the ambassador's garden party? I'll say youre the greatest teacher alive if you make that good. I'll bet you all the expenses of the experiment you cant do it. And I'll pay for the lessons.

LIZA. Oh, you are real good. Thank you, Captain.

HIGGINS (tempted, looking at her). It's almost irresistible. She's so deliciously low—so horribly dirty—

LIZA (protesting extremely). Ah-ah-ah-ah-ow-ow-oo-oo!!! I aint dirty: I washed my face and hands afore I come, I did.

PICKERING. Youre certainly not going to turn her head with flattery, Higgins.

MRS PEARCE (uneasy). Oh, dont say that, sir: theres more ways than one of turning a girl's head; and nobody can do it better than Mr Higgins, though he may not always mean it. I do hope, sir, you wont encourage him to do anything foolish.

HIGGINS (becoming excited as the idea grows on him). What is life but a series of inspired follies? The difficulty is to find them to do. Never lose a chance: it doesnt come every day. I shall make a duchess of this draggle-tailed guttersnipe.

LIZA (strongly deprecating this view of her). Ah-ah-ah-ow-ow-oo!

HIGGINS (carried away). Yes: in six months—in three if she has a good ear and a quick tongue—I'll take her anywhere and pass her off as anything. We'll start today: now! this moment! Take her away and clean her, Mrs Pearce. Monkey Brand, if it wont come off any other way. Is there a good fire in the kitchen?

MRS PEARCE (protesting). Yes: but—

HIGGINS (storming on). Take all her clothes off and burn them. Ring up Whiteley or somebody for new ones. Wrap her up in brown paper til they come.

LIZA. Youre no gentleman, youre not, to talk of such things. I'm a good girl, I am; and I know what the like of you are, I do.

HIGGINS. We want none of your Lisson Grove prudery here, young woman. Youve got to learn to behave like a duchess. Take her away, Mrs Pearce. If she gives you any trouble, wallop her.

LIZA (springing up and running between PICKERING and MRS PEARCE for protection). No! I'll call the police, I will.

MRS PEARCE. But Ive no place to put her.

HIGGINS. Put her in the dustbin.

LIZA. Ah-ah-ah-ow-ow-oo!

PICKERING. Oh come, Higgins! be reasonable.

MRS PEARCE (resolutely). You must be reasonable, Mr Higgins: really you must. You cant walk over everybody like this.

(HIGGINS, thus scolded, subsides. The hurricane is succeeded by a zephyr of amiable surprise.)

HIGGINS (with professional exquisiteness of modulation). I walk over everybody! My dear Mrs Pearce, my dear Pickering, I never had the slightest intention of walking over anyone. All I propose is that we should be kind to this poor girl. We must help her to prepare and fit herself for her new station in life. If I did not express myself clearly it was because I did not wish to hurt her delicacy, or yours.

(LIZA, reassured, steals back to her chair.)

MRS PEARCE (to PICKERING). Well, did you ever hear anything like that, sir?

PICKERING (laughing heartily). Never, Mrs Pearce: never.

HIGGINS (patiently). Whats the matter?

MRS PEARCE. Well, the matter is, sir, that you cant take a girl up like that as if you were picking up a pebble on the beach.

HIGGINS. Why not?

MRS PEARCE. Why not! But you dont know anything about her. What about her parents? She may be married.

LIZA. Garn!

HIGGINS. There! As the girl very properly says, Garn! Married indeed! Dont you know that a woman of that class looks a worn out drudge of fifty a year after she's married?

LIZA. Whood marry me?

HIGGINS (suddenly resorting to the most thrilling beautiful low tones in his best elocutionary style). By George, Eliza, the streets will be strewn with the bodies of men shooting themselves for your sake before Ive done with you.

MRS PEARCE. Nonsense, sir. You mustnt talk like that to her.

LIZA (*rising and squaring herself determinedly*). I'm going away. He's off his chump, he is. I dont want no balmies teaching me.

HIGGINS (*wounded in his tenderest point by her insensibility to his elocution*). Oh, indeed! I'm mad, am I? Very well, Mrs Pearce: you neednt order the new clothes for her. Throw her out.

LIZA (*whimpering*). Nah-ow. You got no right to touch me.

MRS PEARCE. You see now what comes of being saucy. (*Indicating the door*) This way, please.

LIZA (*almost in tears*). I didn't want no clothes. I wouldnt have taken them. (*She throws away the handkerchief.*) I can buy my own clothes.

HIGGINS (*deftly retrieving the handkerchief and intercepting her on her reluctant way to the door*). Youre an ungrateful wicked girl. This is my return for offering to take you out of the gutter and dress you beautifully and make a lady of you.

MRS PEARCE. Stop, Mr Higgins. I wont allow it. It's you that are wicked. Go home to your parents, girl; and tell them to take better care of you.

LIZA. I aint got no parents. They told me I was big enough to earn my own living and turned me out.

MRS PEARCE. Wheres your mother?

LIZA. I aint got no mother. Her that turned me out was my sixth stepmother. But I done without them. And I'm a good girl, I am.

HIGGINS. Very well, then, what on earth is all this fuss about? The girl doesnt belong to anybody—is no use to anybody but me. (*He goes to* MRS PEARCE *and begins coaxing.*) You can adopt her, Mrs Pearce: I'm sure a daughter would be a great amusement to you. Now dont make any more fuss. Take her downstairs; and—

MRS PEARCE. But whats to become of her? Is she to be paid anything? Do be sensible, sir.

HIGGINS. Oh, pay her whatever is necessary: put it down in the housekeeping book. (*Impatiently*) What on earth will she want with money? She'll have her food and her clothes. She'll only drink if you give her money.

LIZA (*turning on him*). Oh you are a brute. It's a lie: nobody ever saw the sign of liquor on me. (*She goes back to her chair and plants herself there defiantly.*)

PICKERING (*in good-humored remonstrance*). Does it occur to you, Higgins, that the girl has some feelings?

HIGGINS (*looking critically at her*). Oh no, I dont think so. Not any feelings that we need bother about. (*Cheerily*) Have you, Eliza?

LIZA. I got my feelings same as anyone else.

HIGGINS (*to* PICKERING, *reflectively*). You see the difficulty?

PICKERING. Eh? What difficulty?

HIGGINS. To get her to talk grammar. The mere pronunciation is easy enough.

LIZA. I dont want to talk grammar. I want to talk like a lady.

MRS PEARCE. Will you please keep to the point, Mr Higgins? I want to know on what terms the girl is to be here. Is she to have any wages? And what is to become of her when youve finished your teaching? You must look ahead a little.

HIGGINS (*impatiently*). Whats to become of her if I leave her in the gutter? Tell me that, Mrs Pearce.

MRS PEARCE. Thats her own business, not yours, Mr Higgins.

HIGGINS. Well, when Ive done with her, we can throw her back into the gutter; and then it will be her own business again; so thats all right.

LIZA. Oh, youve no feeling heart in you: you dont care for nothing but yourself. (*She rises and takes the floor resolutely.*) Here! Ive had enough of this. I'm going. (*Making for the door*) You ought to be ashamed of yourself, you ought.

HIGGINS (*snatching a chocolate cream from the piano, his eyes suddenly beginning to twinkle with mischief*). Have some chocolates, Eliza.

LIZA (*halting, tempted*). How do I know what might be in them? I've heard of girls being drugged by the like of you.

(HIGGINS *whips out his penknife; cuts a chocolate in two; puts one half into his mouth and bolts it; and offers her the other half.*)

HIGGINS. Pledge of good faith, Eliza. I eat one half: you eat the other. (Liza *opens her mouth to retort: he pops the half chocolate into it.*) You shall have boxes of them, barrels of them, every day. You shall live on them. Eh?

LIZA (*who has disposed of the chocolate after being nearly choked by it*). I wouldnt have ate it, only I'm too ladylike to take it out of my mouth.

HIGGINS. Listen, Eliza. I think you said you came in a taxi.

LIZA. Well, what if I did? Ive as good a right to take a taxi as anyone else.

HIGGINS. You have, Eliza; and in future you shall have as many taxis as you want. You shall go up and down and round the town in a taxi every day. Think of that, Eliza.

MRS PEARCE. Mr. Higgins: youre tempting the girl. It's not right. She should think of the future.

HIGGINS. At her age! Nonsense! Time enough to think of the future when you havnt any future to think of. No, Eliza: do as this lady does: think of other people's futures; but never think of your own. Think of chocolates, and taxis, and gold, and diamonds.

LIZA. No: I dont want no gold and no diamonds. I'm a good girl, I am. (*She sits down again, with an attempt at dignity.*)

HIGGINS. You shall remain so, Eliza, under the care of Mrs Pearce. And you shall marry an officer in the Guards, with a beautiful moustache: the son of a marquis, who will disinherit him for marrying you, but will relent when he sees your beauty and goodness—

PICKERING. Excuse me, Higgins; but I really must interfere. Mrs Pearce is quite right. If this girl is to put herself in your hands for six months for an experiment in teaching, she must understand thoroughly what she's doing.

HIGGINS. How can she? She's incapable of understanding anything. Besides, do any of us understand what we are doing? If we did, would we ever do it?

PICKERING. Very clever, Higgins; but not sound sense. (To ELIZA) Miss Doolittle—

LIZA (*overwhelmed*). Ah-ah-ow-oo!

HIGGINS. There! Thats all youll get out of Eliza. Ah-ah-ow-oo! No use explaining. As a military man you ought to know that. Give her her orders: thats what she wants. Eliza: you are to live here for the next six months, learning how to speak beautifully, like a lady in a florist's shop. If youre good and do whatever youre told, you shall sleep in a proper bedroom, and have lots to eat, and money to buy chocolates and take rides in taxis. If youre naughty and idle you will sleep in the back kitchen among the black beetles, and be walloped by Mrs Pearce with a broomstick. At the end of six months you shall go to Buckingham Palace in a carriage, beautifully dressed. If the King finds out youre not a lady, you will be taken by the police to the Tower of London, where your head will be cut off as a warning to other presumptuous flower girls. If you are not found out, you shall have a present of seven-and-sixpence to start life with as a lady in a shop. If you refuse this offer you will be a most ungrateful and wicked girl; and the angels will weep for you. (To PICKERING) Now are you satisfied, Pickering? (To MRS PEARCE) Can I put it more plainly and fairly, Mrs Pearce?

MRS PEARCE (*patiently*). I think youd better let me speak to the girl properly in private. I dont know that I can take charge of her or consent to the arrangement at all. Of course I know you dont mean her any harm; but when you get what you call interested in people's accents, you never think or care what may happen to them or you. Come with me, Eliza.

HIGGINS. Thats all right. Thank you, Mrs Pearce. Bundle her off to the bath-room.

LIZA (*rising reluctantly and suspiciously*). Youre a great bully, you are. I wont stay here if I dont like. I wont let nobody wallop me. I never asked to go to Bucknam Palace, I didnt. I was never in trouble with the police, not me. I'm a good girl—

MRS PEARCE. Dont answer back, girl. You dont understand the gentleman. Come with me. (*She leads the way to the door, and holds it open for* ELIZA.)

LIZA (*as she goes out*). Well, what I say is right. I wont go near the King, not if I'm going to have my head cut off. If I'd known what I was letting myself in for, I wouldnt have come here. I always been a good girl; and I never offered to say a word to him; and I dont owe him nothing; and I dont care; and I wont be put upon; and I have my feelings the same as anyone else—

(MRS PEARCE *shuts the door; and* ELIZA'S *plaints are no longer audible.* PICKERING *comes from the hearth to the chair and sits astride it with his arms on the back.*)

PICKERING. Excuse the straight question, Higgins. Are you a man of good character where women are concerned?

HIGGINS (*moodily*). Have you ever met a man of good character where women are concerned?

PICKERING. Yes: very frequently.

HIGGINS (*dogmatically, lifting himself on his hands to the level of the piano, and sitting on it with a bounce*). Well, I havnt. I find that the moment I let a woman make friends with me, she becomes jealous, ex-acting, suspicious, and a damned nuisance. I find that the moment I let myself make friends with a woman, I become selfish and tyrannical. Women upset everything. When you let them into your life, you find that the woman is driving at one thing and youre driving at another.

PICKERING. At what, for example?

HIGGINS (*coming off the piano restlessly*). Oh, Lord knows! I suppose the woman wants to live her own life; and the man wants to live his; and each tries to drag the other on to the wrong track. One wants to go north and the other south; and the result is that both have to go east, though they both hate the east wind. (*He sits down on the bench at the keyboard.*) So here I am, a confirmed old bachelor, and likely to remain so.

PICKERING (*rising and standing over him gravely*). Come, Higgins! You know what I mean. If I'm to be in this business I shall feel responsible for that girl. I hope it's understood that no advantage is to be taken of her position.

HIGGINS. What! That thing! Sacred, I assure you. (*Rising to explain*) You see, she'll be a pupil; and teaching would be impossible unless pupils were sacred. Ive taught scores of American millionairesses how to speak English: the best looking women in the world. I'm seasoned. They might as well be blocks of wood. *I* might as well be a block of wood. It's—

(MRS PEARCE *opens the door. She has* ELIZA'S *hat in her hand.* PICKERING *retires to the easy-chair at the hearth and sits down.*)

HIGGINS (*eagerly*). Well, Mrs Pearce: is it all right?

MRS PEARCE (*at the door*). I just wish to trouble you with a word, if I may, Mr Higgins.

HIGGINS. Yes, certainly. Come in. (*She comes forward.*) Dont burn that, Mrs Pearce. I'll keep it as a curiosity. (*He takes the hat.*)

MRS PEARCE. Handle it carefully, sir, please. I

had to promise her not to burn it; but I had better put it in the oven for a while.

HIGGINS (*putting it down hastily on the piano*). Oh! thank you. Well, what have you to say to me?

PICKERING. Am I in the way?

MRS PEARCE. Not at all, sir. Mr Higgins: will you please be very particular what you say before the girl?

HIGGINS (*sternly*). Of course. I'm always particular about what I say. Why do you say this to me?

MRS PEARCE (*unmoved*). No, sir: youre not at all particular when youve mislaid anything or when you get a little impatient. Now it doesnt matter before me: I'm used to it. But you really must not swear before the girl.

HIGGINS (*indignantly*). I swear! (*Most emphatically*) I never swear. I detest the habit. What the devil do you mean?

MRS PEARCE (*stolidly*). Thats what I mean, sir. You swear a great deal too much. I dont mind your damning and blasting, and what the devil and where the devil and who the devil—

HIGGINS. Mrs Pearce: this language from your lips! Really!

MRS PEARCE (*not to be put off*).—but there is a certain word I must ask you not to use. The girl has just used it herself because the bath was too hot. It begins with the same letter as bath. She knows no better: she learnt it at her mother's knee. But she must not hear it from your lips.

HIGGINS (*loftily*). I cannot charge myself with having ever uttered it, Mrs Pearce. (*She looks at him steadfastly. He adds, hiding an uneasy conscience with a judicial air*) Except perhaps in a moment of extreme and justifiable excitement.

MRS PEARCE. Only this morning, sir, you applied it to your boots, to the butter, and to the brown bread.

HIGGINS. Oh, that! Mere alliteration, Mrs Pearce, natural to a poet.

MRS PEARCE. Well, sir, whatever you choose to call it, I beg you not to let the girl hear you repeat it.

HIGGINS. Oh, very well, very well. Is that all?

MRS PEARCE. No, sir. We shall have to be very particular with this girl as to personal cleanliness.

HIGGINS. Certainly. Quite right. Most important.

MRS PEARCE. I mean not to be slovenly about her dress or untidy in leaving things about.

HIGGINS (*going to her solemnly*). Just so. I intended to call your attention to that. (*He passes on to* PICKERING, *who is enjoying the conversation immensely.*) It is these little things that matter, Pickering. Take care of the pence and the pounds will take care of themselves is as true of personal habits as of money. (*He comes to anchor on the hearthrug, with the air of a man in an unassailable position.*)

MRS PEARCE. Yes, sir. Then might I ask you not to come down to breakfast in your dressing-gown, or at any rate not to use it as a napkin to the extent you do, sir. And if you would be so good as not to eat everything off the same plate, and to remember not to put the porridge saucepan out of your hand on the clean tablecloth, it would be a better example to the girl. You know you nearly choked yourself with a fishbone in the jam only last week.

HIGGINS (*routed from the hearthrug and drifting back to the piano*). I may do these things sometimes in absence of mind; but surely I dont do them habitually. (*Angrily*) By the way: my dressing-gown smells most damnably of benzine.

MRS PEARCE. No doubt it does, Mr Higgins. But if you will wipe your fingers—

HIGGINS (*yelling*). Oh very well, very well: I'll wipe them in my hair in future.

MRS PEARCE. I hope youre not offended, Mr Higgins.

HIGGINS (*shocked at finding himself thought capable of an unamiable sentiment*). Not at all, not at all. Youre quite right, Mrs

Culver Pictures, Inc.

Pearce: I shall be particularly careful before the girl. Is that all?

MRS PEARCE. No, sir. Might she use some of those Japanese dresses you brought from abroad? I really cant put her back into her old things.

HIGGINS. Certainly. Anything you like. Is that all?

MRS PEARCE. Thank you, sir. Thats all. (She goes out.)

HIGGINS. You know, Pickering, that woman has the most extraordinary ideas about me. Here I am, a shy, diffident sort of man. Ive never been able to feel really grown-up and tremendous, like other chaps. And yet she's firmly persuaded that I'm an arbitrary overbearing bossing kind of person. I cant account for it.

(MRS PEARCE returns.)

MRS PEARCE. If you please, sir, the trouble's beginning already. Theres a dustman downstairs, Alfred Doolittle, wants to see you. He says you have his daughter here.

PICKERING (rising). Phew! I say! (He retreats to the hearthrug.)

HIGGINS (promptly). Send the blackguard up.

MRS PEARCE. Oh, very well, sir. (She goes out.)

PICKERING. He may not be a blackguard, Higgins.

HIGGINS. Nonsense. Of course he's a blackguard.

PICKERING. Whether he is or not, I'm afraid we shall have some trouble with him.

HIGGINS (confidently). Oh no: I think not. If theres any trouble he shall have it with me, not I with him. And we are sure to get something interesting out of him.

PICKERING. About the girl?

HIGGINS. No. I mean his dialect.

PICKERING. Oh!

MRS. PEARCE *(at the door)*. Doolittle, sir. *(She admits* DOOLITTLE *and retires.)*

*(*ALFRED DOOLITTLE *is an elderly but vigorous dustman, clad in the costume of his profession, including a hat with a back brim covering his neck and shoulders. He has well marked and rather interesting features, and seems equally free from fear and conscience. He has a remarkably expressive voice, the result of a habit of giving vent to his feelings without reserve. His present pose is that of wounded honor and stern resolution.)*

DOOLITTLE *(at the door, uncertain which of the two gentlemen is his man)*. Professor Higgins?

HIGGINS. Here. Good morning. Sit down.

DOOLITTLE. Morning, Governor. *(He sits down magisterially.)* I come about a very serious matter, Governor.

HIGGINS *(to* PICKERING*)*. Brought up in Hounslow. Mother Welsh, I should think. *(*DOOLITTLE *opens his mouth, amazed.* HIGGINS *continues.)* What do you want, Doolittle?

DOOLITTLE *(menacingly)*. I want my daughter: thats what I want. See?

HIGGINS. Of course you do. Youre her father, arnt you? You dont suppose anyone else wants her, do you? I'm glad to see you have some spark of family feeling left. She's upstairs. Take her away at once.

DOOLITTLE *(rising, fearfully taken aback)*. What!

HIGGINS. Take her away. Do you suppose I'm going to keep your daughter for you?

DOOLITTLE *(remonstrating)*. Now, now, look here, Governor. Is this reasonable? Is it fairity to take advantage of a man like this? The girl belongs to me. You got her. Where do I come in? *(He sits down again.)*

HIGGINS. Your daughter had the audacity to come to my house and ask me to teach her how to speak properly so that she could get a place in a flower-shop. This gentleman

and my housekeeper have been here all the time. *(Bullying him)* How dare you come here and attempt to blackmail me? You sent her here on purpose.

DOOLITTLE *(protesting)*. No, Governor.

HIGGINS. You must have. How else could you possibly know that she is here?

DOOLITTLE. Dont take a man up like that, Governor.

HIGGINS. The police shall take you up. This is a plant—a plot to extort money by threats. I shall telephone for the police. *(He goes resolutely to the telephone and opens the directory.)*

DOOLITTLE. Have I asked you for a brass farthing? I leave it to the gentleman here: have I said a word about money?

HIGGINS *(throwing the book aside and marching down on* DOOLITTLE *with a poser)*. What else did you come for?

DOOLITTLE *(sweetly)*. Well, what would a man come for? Be human, Governor.

HIGGINS *(disarmed)*. Alfred: did you put her up to it?

DOOLITTLE. So help me, Governor, I never did. I take my Bible oath I aint seen the girl these two months past.

HIGGINS. Then how did you know she was here?

DOOLITTLE *("most musical, most melancholy")*. I'll tell you, Governor, if youll only let me get a word in. I'm willing to tell you. I'm wanting to tell you. I'm waiting to tell you.

HIGGINS. Pickering: this chap has a certain natural gift of rhetoric. Observe the rhythm of his native woodnotes wild. "I'm willing to tell you: I'm wanting to tell you: I'm waiting to tell you." Sentimental rhetoric! thats the Welsh strain in him. It also accounts for his mendacity and dishonesty.

PICKERING. Oh, please, Higgins: I'm west country myself *(To* DOOLITTLE*)* How did you know the girl was here if you didnt send her?

DOOLITTLE. It was like this, Governor. The girl took a boy in the taxi to give him a jaunt. Son of her landlady, he is. He hung about on the chance of her giving him another ride home. Well, she sent him back for her luggage when she heard you was willing for her to stop here. I met the boy at the corner of Long Acre and Endell Street.

HIGGINS. Public house. Yes?

DOOLITTLE. The poor man's club, Governor: why shouldnt I?

PICKERING. Do let him tell his story, Higgins.

DOOLITTLE. He told me what was up. And I ask you, what was my feelings and my duty as a father? I says to the boy, "You bring me the luggage," I says—

PICKERING. Why didn't you go for it yourself?

DOOLITTLE. Landlady wouldnt have trusted me with it, Governor. She's that kind of woman: you know. I had to give the boy a penny afore he trusted me with it, the little swine. I brought it to her just to oblige you like, and make myself agreeable. Thats all.

HIGGINS. How much luggage?

DOOLITTLE. Musical instrument, Governor. A few pictures, a trifle of jewelry, and a bird-cage. She said she didn't want no clothes. What was I to think from that, Governor? I ask you as a parent what was I to think?

HIGGINS. So you came to rescue her from worse than death, eh?

DOOLITTLE (appreciatively: relieved at being so well understood). Just so, Governor. Thats right.

PICKERING. But why did you bring her luggage if you intended to take her away?

DOOLITTLE. Have I said a word about taking her away? Have I now?

HIGGINS (determinedly). Youre going to take her away, double quick. (He crosses to the hearth and rings the bell.)

DOOLITTLE (rising). No, Governor. Dont say that. I'm not the man to stand in my girl's light. Heres a career opening for her, as you might say; and—

(MRS PEARCE opens the door and awaits orders.)

HIGGINS. Mrs Pearce: this is Eliza's father. He has come to take her away. Give her to him. (He goes back to the piano, with an air of washing his hands of the whole affair.)

DOOLITTLE. No. This is a misunderstanding. Listen here—

MRS PEARCE. He cant take her away, Mr Higgins: how can he? You told me to burn her clothes.

DOOLITTLE. Thats right. I cant carry the girl through the streets like a blooming monkey, can I? I put it to you.

HIGGINS. You have put it to me that you want your daughter. Take your daughter. If she has no clothes go out and buy her some.

DOOLITTLE (desperate). Wheres the clothes she come in? Did I burn them or did your missus here?

MRS PEARCE. I am the housekeeper, if you please. I have sent for some clothes for your girl. When they come you can take her away. You can wait in the kitchen. This way, please.

(DOOLITTLE, much troubled, accompanies her to the door; then hesitates; finally turns confidentially to HIGGINS.)

DOOLITTLE. Listen here, Governor. You and me is men of the world, aint we?

HIGGINS. Oh! Men of the world, are we? Youd better go, Mrs Pearce.

MRS PEARCE. I think so, indeed, sir. (She goes, with dignity.)

PICKERING. The floor is yours, Mr Doolittle.

DOOLITTLE (to PICKERING). I thank you, Governor. (To HIGGINS, who takes refuge on the piano bench, a little overwhelmed by the proximity of his visitor; for DOOLITTLE has a professional flavour of dust about him.) Well, the truth is, Ive taken a sort of fancy to you, Governor; and if you want the girl, I'm not so set on having her back home again but what I might be open to an arrangement. Regarded in the light of a young woman, she's a fine handsome girl. As a daughter she's not worth her keep; and so I tell you straight. All I ask is my rights as a father; and youre the last man alive to expect me to let her go for nothing; for I can see youre one of the straight sort, Governor. Well, whats a five-pound note to you? And whats Eliza to me? *(He returns to his chair and sits down judicially.)*

PICKERING. I think you ought to know, Doolittle, that Mr Higgins's intentions are entirely honorable.

DOOLITTLE. Course they are, Governor. If I thought they wasnt, I'd ask fifty.

HIGGINS *(revolted)*. Do you mean to say, you callous rascal, that you would sell your daughter for £50?

DOOLITTLE. Not in a general way I wouldnt; but to oblige a gentleman like you I'd do a good deal, I do assure you.

PICKERING. Have you no morals, man?

DOOLITTLE *(unabashed)*. Cant afford them, Governor. Neither could you if you was as poor as me. Not that I mean any harm, you know. But if Liza is going to have a bit out of this, why not me too?

HIGGINS *(troubled)*. I dont know what to do, Pickering. There can be no question that as a matter of morals it's a positive crime to give this chap a farthing. And yet I feel a sort of rough justice in his claim.

DOOLITTLE. Thats it, Governor. Thats all I say. A father's heart, as it were.

PICKERING. Well, I know the feeling; but really it seems hardly right—

DOOLITTLE. Dont say that, Governor. Dont look at it that way. What am I, Governors both? I ask you, what am I? I'm one of the undeserving poor: thats what I am. Think of what that means to a man. It means that he's up agen middle class morality all the time. If theres anything going, and I put in for a bit of it, it's always the same story: "Youre undeserving; so you cant have it." But my needs is as great as the most deserv-

ing widow's that ever got money out of six different charities in one week for the death of the same husband. I dont need less than a deserving man: I need more. I dont eat less hearty than him; and I drink a lot more. I want a bit of amusement, cause I'm a thinking man. I want cheerfulness and a song and a band when I feel low. Well, they charge me just the same for everything as they charge the deserving. What is middle class morality? Just an excuse for never giving me anything. Therefore, I ask you, as two gentlemen, not to play that game on me. I'm playing straight with you. I aint pretending to be deserving. I'm undeserving; and I mean to go on being undeserving. I like it; and thats the truth. Will you take advantage of a man's nature to do him out of the price of his own daughter what he's brought up and fed and clothed by the sweat of his brow until she's growed big enough to be interesting to you two gentlemen? Is five pounds unreasonable? I put it to you; and I leave it to you.

HIGGINS *(rising, and going over to* PICKERING*)*. Pickering: if we were to take this man in hand for three months, he could choose between a seat in the Cabinet and a popular pulpit in Wales.

PICKERING. What do you say to that, Doolittle?

DOOLITTLE. Not me, Governor, thank you kindly. Ive heard all the preachers and all the prime ministers—for I'm a thinking man and game for politics or religion or social reform same as all the other amusements—and I tell you it's a dog's life any way you look at it. Undeserving poverty is my line. Taking one station in society with another, it's—it's—well, it's the only one that has any ginger in it, to my taste.

HIGGINS. I suppose we must give him a fiver.

PICKERING. He'll make a bad use of it, I'm afraid.

DOOLITTLE. Not me, Governor, so help me I wont. Dont you be afraid that I'll save it and spare it and live idle on it. There wont be a penny of it left by Monday: I'll have to go to work same as if I'd never had it. It wont pauperize me, you bet. Just one good spree for myself and the missus, giving pleasure to ourselves and employment to others, and satisfaction to you to think it's not been throwed away. You couldnt spend it better.

HIGGINS *(taking out his pocket book and coming between* DOOLITTLE *and the piano).* This is irresistible. Lets give him ten. *(He offers two notes to the dustman.)*

DOOLITTLE. No, Governor. She wouldnt have the heart to spend ten; and perhaps I shouldnt neither. Ten pounds is a lot of money: it makes a man feel prudent like; and then goodbye to happiness. You give me what I ask you, Governor: not a penny more, and not a penny less.

PICKERING. Why dont you marry that missus of yours? I rather draw the line at encouraging that sort of immorality.

DOOLITTLE. Tell her so, Governor: tell her so. I'm willing. It's me that suffers by it. Ive no hold on her. I got to be agreeable to her. I got to give her presents. I got to buy her clothes something sinful. I'm a slave to that woman, Governor, just because I'm not her lawful husband. And she knows it too. Catch her marrying me! Take my advice, Governor: marry Eliza while she's young and dont know no better. If you dont youll be sorry for it after. If you do, she'll be sorry for it after; but better her than you, because youre a man, and she's only a woman and dont know how to be happy anyhow.

HIGGINS. Pickering: if we listen to this man another minute, we shall have no convictions left. *(To* DOOLITTLE*)* Five pounds I think you said.

DOOLITTLE. Thank you kindly, Governor.

HIGGINS. Youre sure you wont take ten?

DOOLITTLE. Not now. Another time, Governor.

HIGGINS *(handing him a five-pound note).* Here you are.

DOOLITTLE. Thank you, Governor. Good morning. *(He hurries to the door, anxious to get away with his booty. When he opens it he is confronted with a dainty and exquisitely clean young Japanese lady in a simple blue cotton kimono printed cunningly with small white jasmine blossoms.* MRS PEARCE *is with her. He gets out of her way deferentially and apologizes).* Beg pardon, miss.

THE JAPANESE LADY. Garn! Dont you know your own daughter?

DOOLITTLE *exclaiming* ⎰ Bly me! it's Eliza!
HIGGINS *simul-* ⎰ Whats that! This!
PICKERING *taneously* ⎰ By Jove!

LIZA. Dont I look silly?

HIGGINS. Silly?

MRS PEARCE *(at the door).* Now, Mr Higgins, please dont say anything to make the girl conceited about herself.

HIGGINS *(conscientiously).* Oh! Quite right, Mrs Pearce. *(To* ELIZA*)* Yes: damned silly.

MRS PEARCE. Please, sir.

HIGGINS *(correcting himself).* I mean extremely silly.

LIZA. I should look all right with my hat on. *(She takes up her hat; puts it on; and walks across the room to the fireplace with a fashionable air.)*

HIGGINS. A new fashion, by George! And it ought to look horrible!

DOOLITTLE *(with fatherly pride).* Well, I never thought she'd clean up as good looking as that, Governor. She's a credit to me, aint she?

LIZA. I tell you, it's easy to clean up here. Hot and cold water on tap, just as much as you like, there is. Woolly towels, there is; and a towel horse[5] so hot, it burns your fingers. Soft brushes to scrub yourself, and a wooden bowl of soap smelling like primroses. Now I know why ladies is so clean. Wash-

---

5. **towel horse:** here, a metal rack with hot water in it.

ing's a treat for them. Wish they saw what it is for the like of me!

HIGGINS. I'm glad the bathroom met with your approval.

LIZA. It didnt: not all of it; and I dont care who hears me say it. Mrs Pearce knows.

HIGGINS. What was wrong, Mrs Pearce?

MRS PEARCE *(blandly)*. Oh, nothing, sir. It doesnt matter.

LIZA. I had a good mind to break it. I didnt know which way to look. But I hung a towel over it, I did.

HIGGINS. Over what?

MRS PEARCE. Over the looking-glass, sir.

HIGGINS. Doolittle: you have brought your daughter up too strictly.

DOOLITTLE. Me! I never brought her up at all, except to give her a lick of a strap now and again. Dont put it on me, Governor. She aint accustomed to it, you see: thats all. But she'll soon pick up your free-and-easy ways.

LIZA. I'm a good girl, I am; and I wont pick up no free-and-easy ways.

HIGGINS. Eliza: if you say again that youre a good girl, your father shall take you home.

LIZA. Not him. You dont know my father. All he come here for was to touch you for some money to get drunk on.

DOOLITTLE. Well, what else would I want money for? To put into the plate in church, I suppose. *(She puts out her tongue at him. He is so incensed by this that* PICKERING *presently finds it necessary to step between them.)* Dont you give me none of your lip; and dont let me hear you giving this gentleman any of it neither, or youll hear from me about it. See?

HIGGINS. Have you any further advice to give her before you go, Doolittle? Your blessing, for instance.

DOOLITTLE. No, Governor: I aint such a mug as to put up my children to all I know myself. Hard enough to hold them in without that. If you want Eliza's mind improved, Governor, you do it yourself with a strap. So long, gentlemen. *(He turns to go.)*

HIGGINS *(impressively)*. Stop. Youll come regularly to see your daughter. It's your duty, you know. My brother is a clergyman; and he could help you in your talks with her.

DOOLITTLE *(evasively)*. Certainly. I'll come, Governor. Not just this week, because I have a job at a distance. But later on you may depend on me. Afternoon, gentlemen. Afternoon, maam. *(He takes off his hat to* MRS PEARCE, *who disdains the salutation and goes out. He winks at* HIGGINS, *thinking him probably a fellow-sufferer from* MRS PEARCE's *difficult disposition, and follows her.)*

LIZA. Dont you believe the old liar. He'd as soon you set a bull-dog on him as a clergyman. You wont see him again in a hurry.

HIGGINS. I dont want to, Eliza. Do you?

LIZA. Not me. I dont want never to see him again, I dont. He's a disgrace to me, he is, collecting dust, instead of working at his trade.

PICKERING. What is his trade, Eliza?

LIZA. Taking money out of other people's pockets into his own. His proper trade's a navvy;[6] and he works at it sometimes too—for exercise—and earns good money at it. Aint you going to call me Miss Doolittle any more?

PICKERING. I beg your pardon, Miss Doolittle. It was a slip of the tongue.

LIZA. Oh, I dont mind; only it sounded so genteel. I should just like to take a taxi to the corner of Tottenham Court Road and get out there and tell it to wait for me, just to put the girls in their place a bit. I wouldnt speak to them, you know.

PICKERING. Better wait til we get you something really fashionable.

HIGGINS. Besides, you shouldnt cut your old friends now that you have risen in the world. Thats what we call snobbery.

LIZA. You dont call the like of them my

---

6. **navvy:** an unskilled laborer.

friends now, I should hope. Theyve took it out of me often enough with their ridicule when they had the chance; and now I mean to get a bit of my own back. But if I'm to have fashionable clothes, I'll wait. I should like to have some. Mrs Pearce says youre going to give me some to wear in bed at night different to what I wear in the daytime; but it do seem a waste of money when you could get something to shew. Besides, I never could fancy changing into cold things on a winter night.

MRS PEARCE *(coming back)*. Now, Eliza. The new things have come for you to try on.

LIZA. Ah-ow-oo-ooh! *(She rushes out.)*

MRS PEARCE *(following her)*. Oh, dont rush about like that, girl. *(She shuts the door behind her.)*

HIGGINS. Pickering: we have taken on a stiff job.

PICKERING *(with conviction)*. Higgins: we have.

Act Two

Getting at Meaning

1. Liza's transformation occurs gradually throughout the play. What stage in this process is depicted in Act Two? Is the change in Liza merely external? What is Liza's goal? How does it contrast with that of Higgins and Pickering?

2. Mrs. Pearce is concerned particularly about maintaining the appearance of respectability. Is she worried that the world will think ill of her employer or that the reputation of Liza could be destroyed? Why does she urge Higgins to consider the consequences of what he is proposing?

3. Higgins scoffs at Liza's prudery. Why can he afford to be cavalier about public opinion?

4. Pickering expresses his concern about Liza, saying, "I hope it's understood that no advantage is to be taken of her position." How does Higgins respond? What is comic about his rhetorical posturing?

5. Alfred Doolittle assumes that Higgins's intentions must be dishonorable, so he hurries to blackmail the professor. Rather than coming across as an unscrupulous villain, however, Doolittle seems a charming scamp. How does Shaw manage this neat trick? As Higgins is innocent, why does he pay the blackmail?

Developing Skills in Reading Literature

1. **Title.** In Greek mythology Pygmalion was a king of Cyprus who made a statue so beautiful that he fell in love with it. He prayed to the goddess Aphrodite to transform the statue into a real woman. Aphrodite brought the statue to life as a woman named Galatea, and Pygmalion married her. In Act One of Shaw's play, the audience learns that the plot deals with a similar transformation. At the beginning of Act Two, Higgins is rude to Liza. What is the irony of this scene, when considered in light of what is going to happen? Would Higgins's insults be as amusing if the audience did not know what is in store for him? Why are his views on women and marriage so ironic, given his identity as a modern Pygmalion? What hint at the end of Act Two suggests that Higgins is beginning to change his attitude toward Liza?

2. **Characterization.** In this act the three main characters emerge more clearly than in Act One, through dialogue, through the devices of setting and stage directions, and through the use of a foil. Note, for example, the detailed description of Higgins's laboratory. What does this physical setting suggest about him as a person? What details suggest education and

culture? Why is this somewhat surprising, given the impression of Higgins created in Act One? This same passage of stage directions contains a description of Higgins's appearance and typical behavior. Notice the concluding assessment. Why might Shaw have included it at the beginning of the act rather than after Higgins has had a chance to expound on his views?

Mrs. Pearce offers her own perspective on Higgins. How does it confirm and extend the information presented in the opening stage directions? Identify passages that are particularly revealing.

Colonel Pickering is a foil for Higgins, calling attention to the professor's less desirable qualities. What are some of these qualities? What, for example, is Higgins's attitude toward Liza as opposed to Pickering's attitude? How do the two contrast in their view of men's "honor"?

The characterization of Liza builds on the groundwork laid in Act One. What qualities does she exhibit in Act Two that were first evident in Act One? What new information does the audience learn in Act Two? How is this information revealed? Is it consistent with what the audience already knows about her?

3. **Stereotype.** The characters in this play express stereotypical attitudes toward men and women, social classes, and ethnic groups. To Higgins and Doolittle, for example, Liza represents woman-as-object and woman-as-commodity. Doolittle forfeits his paternal "rights" to her reputation and her person, and Higgins buys these "rights" from Doolittle. How does the wager between Higgins and Pickering also evidence this stereotype? Cite passages in which Liza is referred to as a thing, and identify stereotypical remarks about women made by Higgins and Doolittle.

The concept of the upper class held by Liza and Doolittle is as stereotypical as Higgins's view of the lower class. What do Doolittle and Liza believe about upper class "ways"? How does Higgins conceive the lower class? On what ethnic heritage does Higgins blame Doolittle's "mendacity and dishonesty"? Cite passages to support your answers. What is Shaw's purpose in including these stereotypical references?

4. **Satire.** In the long passage spoken by Doolittle, Shaw is having fun at the expense of middle-class morality, which he finds hypocritical. What specifically does he criticize? Why might Shaw have chosen to amuse rather than to outrage his audience? What satirical commentary on marriage does Shaw present through Doolittle? What is Shaw satirizing in Higgins's glowing descriptions of Liza's future?

Developing Vocabulary

Inferring Word Meaning. Define each of the italicized words in the following sentences, using the context in which the word appears and the context of the play in general to determine the definitions.

a. "I shall make a duchess of this *draggletailed guttersnipe.*"

b. "He's off his chump, he is. I dont want no *balmies* teaching me."

c. "And you shall marry an officer in the Guards, with a beautiful moustache: the son of a *marquis.* . . ."

d. "Alfred Doolittle is an elderly but vigorous *dustman.* . . ."

e. "There can be no question that as a matter of morals it's a positive crime to give this chap a *farthing.*"

ACT THREE

It is MRS HIGGINS'*s at-home day. Nobody has yet arrived. Her drawing room, in a flat on Chelsea Embankment, has three windows looking on the river; and the ceiling is not so lofty as it would be in an older house of the same pretension. The windows are open, giving access to a balcony with flowers in pots. If you stand with your face to the windows, you have the fireplace on your left and the door in the right-hand wall close to the corner nearest the windows.*

MRS HIGGINS *was brought up on Morris[1] and Burne Jones;[2] and her room, which is very unlike her son's room in Wimpole Street, is not crowded with furniture and little tables and nicknacks. In the middle of the room there is a big ottoman; and this, with the carpet, the Morris wall-papers, and the Morris chintz window curtains and brocade covers of the ottoman and its cushions, supply all the ornament, and are much too handsome to be hidden by odds and ends of useless things. A few good oil-paintings from the exhibitions in the Grosvenor Gallery thirty years ago (the Burne Jones, not the Whistler[3] side of them) are on the walls. The only landscape is a Cecil Lawson[4] on the scale of a Rubens.[5] There is a portrait of Mrs Higgins as she was when she defied fashion in her youth in one of the beautiful Rossettian costumes which, when caricatured by people who did not understand, led to the absurdities of popular estheticism in the eighteen-seventies.*

In the corner diagonally opposite the door MRS HIGGINS, *now over sixty and long past taking the trouble to dress out of the fashion, sits writing at an elegantly simple writing-table with a bell button within reach of her hand. There is a Chippendale chair further back in the room between her and the window nearest her side. At the other side of the room, further forward, is an Elizabethan chair roughly carved in the taste of Inigo Jones.[6] On the same side a piano in a decorat-ed case. The corner between the fireplace and the window is occupied by a divan cushioned in Morris chintz.*

It is between four and five in the afternoon.

The door is opened violently; and HIGGINS *enters with his hat on.*

MRS HIGGINS *(dismayed)*. Henry *(scolding him)*! What are you doing here today? It is my at-home day: you promised not to come. *(As he bends to kiss her, she takes his hat off, and presents it to him.)*

HIGGINS. Oh bother! *(He throws the hat down on the table.)*

MRS HIGGINS. Go home at once.

HIGGINS *(kissing her)*. I know, mother. I came on purpose.

MRS HIGGINS. But you mustnt. I'm serious, Henry. You offend all my friends: they stop coming whenever they meet you.

HIGGINS. Nonsense! I know I have no small talk; but people dont mind. *(He sits on the settee.)*

MRS HIGGINS. Oh! dont they? Small talk indeed! What about your large talk? Really, dear, you mustnt stay.

HIGGINS. I must. Ive a job for you. A phonetic job.

MRS HIGGINS. No use, dear. I'm sorry; but I cant get round your vowels; and though I like to get pretty postcards in your patent shorthand, I always have to read the copies in ordinary writing you so thoughtfully send me.

HIGGINS. Well, this isnt a phonetic job.

---

1. **Morris:** William Morris (1834–1896), English poet, artist, and decorative designer.
2. **Burne-Jones:** Sir Edward Coley Burne-Jones (1833–1898), English painter and designer.
3. **Whistler:** James Abbott McNeill Whistler (1834–1903), American painter and etcher in England.
4. **Cecil Lawson:** Cecil Gordon Lawson (1851–1882), English landscape painter.
5. **Rubens:** Peter Paul Rubens (1577–1640), Flemish painter of large paintings.
6. **Inigo Jones:** English architect and stage designer (1573–1652).

would only be frank and say what they really think!

HIGGINS *(relapsing into gloom)*. Lord forbid!

MRS EYNSFORD HILL *(taking up her daughter's cue)*. But why?

HIGGINS. What they think they ought to think is bad enough, Lord knows; but what they really think would break up the whole show. Do you suppose it would be really agreeable if I were to come out now with what *I* really think?

MISS EYNSFORD HILL *(gaily)*. Is it so very cynical?

HIGGINS. Cynical! Who the dickens said it was cynical? I mean it wouldnt be decent.

MRS EYNSFORD HILL *(seriously)*. Oh! I'm sure you dont mean that, Mr Higgins.

HIGGINS. You see, we're all savages, more or less. We're supposed to be civilized and cultured—to know all about poetry and philosophy and art and science, and so on; but how many of us know even the meanings of these names? *(To MISS HILL)* What do you know of poetry? *(To MRS HILL)* What do you know of science? *(Indicating FREDDY)* What does he know of art or science or anything else? What the devil do you imagine I know of philosophy?

MRS HIGGINS *(warningly)*. Or of manners, Henry?

THE PARLORMAID *(opening the door)*. Miss Doolittle. *(She withdraws.)*

HIGGINS *(rising hastily and running to MRS HIGGINS)*. Here she is, mother. *(He stands on tiptoe and makes signs over his mother's head to ELIZA to indicate to her which lady is her hostess.)*

(ELIZA, who is exquisitely dressed, produces an impression of such remarkable distinction and beauty as she enters that they all rise, quite fluttered. Guided by HIGGINS's signals, she comes to MRS HIGGINS with studied grace.)

LIZA *(speaking with pedantic correctness of pronunciation and great beauty of tone)*.

How do you do, Mrs Higgins? *(She gasps slightly in making sure of the H in HIGGINS, but is quite successful.)* Mr Higgins told me I might come.

MRS HIGGINS *(cordially)*. Quite right: I'm very glad indeed to see you.

PICKERING. How do you do, Miss Doolittle?

LIZA *(shaking hands with him)*. Colonel Pickering, is it not?

MRS EYNSFORD HILL. I feel sure we have met before, Miss Doolittle. I remember your eyes.

LIZA. How do you do? *(She sits down on the ottoman gracefully in the place just left vacant by HIGGINS.)*

MRS EYNSFORD HILL *(introducing)*. My daughter Clara.

LIZA. How do you do?

CLARA *(impulsively)*. How do you do? *(She sits down on the ottoman beside ELIZA, devouring her with her eyes.)*

FREDDY *(coming to their side of the ottoman)*. Ive certainly had the pleasure.

MRS EYNSFORD HILL *(introducing)*. My son Freddy.

LIZA. How do you do?

(FREDDY bows and sits down in the Elizabethan chair, infatuated.)

HIGGINS *(suddenly)*. By George, yes: it all comes back to me! *(They stare at him.)* Covent Garden! *(Lamentably)* What a damned thing!

MRS HIGGINS. Henry, please! *(He is about to sit on the edge of the table.)* Dont sit on my writing-table: youll break it.

HIGGINS *(sulkily)*. Sorry.

(He goes to the divan, stumbling into the fender and over the fire-irons on his way; extricating himself with muttered imprecations; and finishing his disastrous journey by throwing himself so impatiently on the divan that he almost breaks it. MRS HIGGINS looks at him, but controls herself and says nothing. A long and painful pause ensues.)

MRS HIGGINS (at last, conversationally). Will it rain, do you think?

LIZA. The shallow depression in the west of these islands is likely to move slowly in an easterly direction. There are no indications of any great change in the barometrical situation.

FREDDY. Ha! ha! how awfully funny!

LIZA. What is wrong with that, young man? I bet I got it right.

FREDDY. Killing!

MRS EYNSFORD HILL. I'm sure I hope it wont turn cold. Theres so much influenza about. It runs right through our whole family regularly every spring.

LIZA (darkly). My aunt died of influenza: so they said.

MRS EYNSFORD HILL (clicks her tongue sympathetically)!!!

LIZA (in the same tragic tone). But it's my belief they done the old woman in.

MRS HIGGINS (puzzled). Done her in?

LIZA. Y-e-e-e-es, Lord love you! Why should she die of influenza? She come through diphtheria right enough the year before. I saw her with my own eyes. Fairly blue with it, she was. They all thought she was dead; but my father he kept ladling gin down her throat til she came to so sudden that she bit the bowl off the spoon.

MRS EYNSFORD HILL (startled). Dear me!

LIZA (piling up the indictment). What call would a woman with that strength in her have to die of influenza? What become of her new straw hat that should have come to me? Somebody pinched it; and what I say is, them as pinched it done her in.

MRS EYNSFORD HILL. What does doing her in mean?

HIGGINS (hastily). Oh, thats the new small talk. To do a person in means to kill them.

MRS EYNSFORD HILL (to ELIZA, horrified). You surely dont believe that your aunt was killed?

Culver Pictures, Inc.

LIZA. Do I not! Them she lived with would have killed her for a hat-pin, let alone a hat.

MRS EYNSFORD HILL. But it cant have been right for your father to pour spirits down her throat like that. It might have killed her.

LIZA. Not her. Gin was mother's milk to her. Besides, he'd poured so much down his own throat that he knew the good of it.

MRS EYNSFORD HILL. Do you mean that he drank?

LIZA. Drank! My word! Something chronic.

MRS EYNSFORD HILL. How dreadful for you!

LIZA. Not a bit. It never did him no harm what I could see. But then he did not keep it up regular. *(Cheerfully)* On the burst, as you might say, from time to time. And always more agreeable when he had a drop in. When he was out of work, my mother used to give him fourpence and tell him to go out and not come back until he'd drunk himself cheerful and loving-like. Theres lots of women has to make their husbands drunk to make them fit to live with. *(Now quite at her ease)* You see, it's like this. If a man has a bit of a conscience, it always takes him when he's sober; and then it makes him low-spirited. A drop of booze just takes that off and makes him happy. *(To* FREDDY, *who is in convulsions of suppressed laughter)* Here! what are you sniggering at?

FREDDY. The new small talk. You do it so awfully well.

LIZA. If I was doing it proper, what was you laughing at? *(To* HIGGINS*)* Have I said anything I oughtnt?

MRS HIGGINS *(interposing)*. Not at all, Miss Doolittle.

LIZA. Well, thats a mercy, anyhow. *(Expansively)* What I always say is—

HIGGINS *(rising and looking at his watch)*. Ahem!

LIZA *(looking round at him; taking the hint; and rising)*. Well: I must go. *(They all rise. FREDDY goes to the door.)* So pleased to have met you. Goodbye. *(She shakes hands with* MRS HIGGINS.*)*

MRS HIGGINS. Goodbye.

LIZA. Goodbye, Colonel Pickering.

PICKERING. Goodbye, Miss Doolittle. *(They shake hands.)*

LIZA *(nodding to the others)*. Goodbye, all.

FREDDY *(opening the door for her)*. Are you walking across the Park, Miss Doolittle? If so—

LIZA. Walk! Not bloody likely. *(Sensation.)* I am going in a taxi. *(She goes out.)*

*(*PICKERING *gasps and sits down.* FREDDY *goes out on the balcony to catch another glimpse of* ELIZA*).*

MRS EYNSFORD HILL *(suffering from shock)*. Well, I really cant get used to the new ways.

CLARA *(throwing herself discontentedly into the Elizabethan chair)*. Oh, it's all right, mamma, quite right. People will think we never go anywhere or see anybody if you are so old-fashioned.

MRS EYNSFORD HILL. I daresay I am very old-fashioned; but I do hope you wont begin using that expression, Clara. I have got accustomed to hear you talking about men as rotters, and calling everything filthy and beastly; though I do think it horrible and unladylike. But this last is really too much. Don't you think so, Colonel Pickering?

PICKERING. Don't ask me. Ive been away in India for several years; and manners have changed so much that I sometimes dont know whether I'm at a respectable dinnertable or in a ship's forecastle.

CLARA. It's all a matter of habit. Theres no right or wrong in it. Nobody means anything by it. And it's so quaint, and gives such a smart emphasis to things that are not in themselves very witty. I find the new small talk delightful and quite innocent.

MRS EYNSFORD HILL *(rising)*. Well, after that, I think it's time for us to go.

(PICKERING *and* HIGGINS *rise.*)

CLARA (*rising*). Oh yes: we have three at-homes to go to still. Goodbye, Mrs. Higgins. Goodbye, Colonel Pickering. Goodbye, Professor Higgins.

HIGGINS (*coming grimly at her from the divan, and accompanying her to the door*). Goodbye. Be sure you try on that small talk at the three at-homes. Dont be nervous about it. Pitch it in strong.

CLARA (*all smiles*). I will. Goodbye. Such nonsense, all this early Victorian prudery!

HIGGINS (*tempting her*). Such damned nonsense!

CLARA. Such bloody nonsense!

MRS EYNSFORD HILL (*convulsively*). Clara!

CLARA. Ha! ha! (*She goes out radiant, conscious of being thoroughly up to date, and is heard descending the stairs in a stream of silvery laughter.*)

FREDDY (*to the heavens at large*). Well, I ask you—(*He gives it up, and comes to* MRS HIGGINS.) Goodbye.

MRS HIGGINS (*shaking hands*). Goodbye. Would you like to meet Miss Doolittle again?

FREDDY (*eagerly*). Yes, I should, most awfully.

MRS HIGGINS. Well, you know my days.

FREDDY. Yes. Thanks awfully. Goodbye. (*He goes out.*)

MRS EYNSFORD HILL. Goodbye, Mr Higgins.

HIGGINS. Goodbye. Goodbye.

MRS EYNSFORD HILL (*to* PICKERING). It's no use. I shall never be able to bring myself to use that word.

PICKERING. Dont. It's not compulsory, you know. Youll get on quite well without it.

MRS EYNSFORD HILL. Only, Clara is so down on me if I am not positively reeking with the latest slang. Goodbye.

PICKERING. Goodbye. (*They shake hands.*)

MRS EYNSFORD HILL (*to* MRS HIGGINS). You mustnt mind Clara. (PICKERING, *catching from her lowered tone that this is not meant for him to hear, discreetly joins* HIGGINS *at the window.*) We're so poor! and she gets so few parties, poor child! She doesnt quite know. (MRS HIGGINS, *seeing that her eyes are moist, takes her hand sympathetically and goes with her to the door.*) But the boy is nice. Dont you think so?

MRS HIGGINS. Oh, quite nice. I shall always be delighted to see him.

MRS EYNSFORD HILL. Thank you, dear. Goodbye. (*She goes out.*)

HIGGINS (*eagerly*). Well? Is Eliza presentable? (*He swoops on his mother and drags her to the ottoman, where she sits down in* ELIZA's *place with her son on her left.*)

(PICKERING *returns to his chair on her right.*)

MRS HIGGINS. You silly boy, of course she's not presentable. She's a triumph of your art and of her dressmaker's; but if you suppose for a moment that she doesnt give herself away in every sentence she utters, you must be perfectly cracked about her.

PICKERING. But dont you think something might be done? I mean something to eliminate the sanguinary[7] element from her conversation.

MRS HIGGINS. Not as long as she is in Henry's hands.

HIGGINS (*aggrieved*). Do you mean that my language is improper?

MRS HIGGINS. No, dearest: it would be quite proper—say on a canal barge; but it would not be proper for her at a garden party.

HIGGINS (*deeply injured*). Well I must say—

PICKERING (*interrupting him*). Come, Higgins: you must learn to know yourself. I havnt heard such language as yours since we used to review the volunteers in Hyde Park twenty years ago.

HIGGINS (*sulkily*). Oh, well, if you say so, I suppose I dont always talk like a bishop.

---

7. **sanguinary:** bloody; a reference to Eliza's using "bloody," a slang term, in her conversation.

MRS HIGGINS (*quieting* HENRY *with a touch*). Colonel Pickering: will you tell me what is the exact state of things in Wimpole Street?

PICKERING (*cheerfully: as if this completely changed the subject*). Well, I have come to live there with Henry. We work together at my Indian Dialects; and we think it more convenient—

MRS HIGGINS. Quite so. I know all about that: it's an excellent arrangement. But where does this girl live?

HIGGINS. With us, of course. Where should she live?

MRS HIGGINS. But on what terms? Is she a servant? If not, what is she?

PICKERING (*slowly*). I think I know what you mean, Mrs Higgins.

HIGGINS. Well, dash me if *I* do! Ive had to work at the girl every day for months to get her to her present pitch. Besides, she's useful. She knows where my things are, and remembers my appointments and so forth.

MRS HIGGINS. How does your housekeeper get on with her?

HIGGINS. Mrs Pearce? Oh, she's jolly glad to get so much taken off her hands; for before Eliza came, she used to have to find things and remind me of my appointments. But she's got some silly bee in her bonnet about Eliza. She keeps saying "You dont think, sir": doesnt she, Pick?

PICKERING. Yes: thats the formula. "You dont think, sir." Thats the end of every conversation about Eliza.

HIGGINS. As if I ever stop thinking about the girl and her confounded vowels and consonants. I'm worn out, thinking about her, and watching her lips and her teeth and her tongue, not to mention her soul, which is the quaintest of the lot.

MRS HIGGINS. You certainly are a pretty pair of babies, playing with your live doll.

HIGGINS. Playing! The hardest job I ever tackled: make no mistake about that, mother.

But you have no idea how frightfully interesting it is to take a human being and change her into a quite different human being by creating a new speech for her. It's filling up the deepest gulf that separates class from class and soul from soul.

PICKERING (*drawing his chair closer to* MRS HIGGINS *and bending over to her eagerly*). Yes: it's enormously interesting. I assure you, Mrs Higgins, we take Eliza very seriously. Every week—every day almost—there is some new change. (*Closer again*) We keep records of every stage—dozens of gramophone disks and photographs—

HIGGINS (*assailing her at the other ear*). Yes, by George: it's the most absorbing experiment I ever tackled. She regularly fills our lives up: doesnt she, Pick?

PICKERING. We're always talking Eliza.

HIGGINS. Teaching Eliza.

PICKERING. Dressing Eliza.

MRS HIGGINS. What!

HIGGINS. Inventing new Elizas.

HIGGINS.	(*speaking together*)	You know, she has the most extraordinary quickness of ear:
PICKERING.		I assure you, my dear Mrs Higgins, that girl
HIGGINS.		just like a parrot. Ive tried her with every—
PICKERING.		is a genius. She can play the piano quite beautifully.
HIGGINS.		possible sort of sound that a human being can make—
PICKERING.		We have taken her to classical concerts and to music
HIGGINS.		Continental dialects, African dialects, Hottentot
PICKERING.		halls; and it's all the same to her: she plays everything

HIGGINS.
PICKERING.
HIGGINS.
PICKERING.
HIGGINS.
PICKERING.

{ clicks, things it took me years to get hold of; and
she hears right off when she comes home, whether it's
she picks them up like a shot, right away, as if she had
Beethoven and Brahms or Lehar and Lionel Monckton;
been at it all her life. though six months ago, she'd never as much as touched a piano— }

MRS HIGGINS (*putting her fingers in her ears, as they are by this time shouting one another down with an intolerable noise*). Sh-sh-sh—sh! (*They stop.*)

PICKERING. I beg your pardon. (*He draws his chair back apologetically.*)

HIGGINS. Sorry. When Pickering starts shouting nobody can get a word in edgeways.

MRS HIGGINS. Be quiet, Henry. Colonel Pickering: dont you realize that when Eliza walked into Wimpole Street, something walked in with her?

PICKERING. Her father did. But Henry soon got rid of him.

MRS HIGGINS. It would have been more to the point if her mother had. But as her mother didnt something else did.

PICKERING. But what?

MRS HIGGINS (*unconsciously dating herself by the word*). A problem.

PICKERING. Oh, I see. The problem of how to pass her off as a lady.

HIGGINS. I'll solve that problem. Ive half solved it already.

MRS HIGGINS. No, you two infinitely stupid male creatures: the problem of what is to be done with her afterwards.

HIGGINS. I dont see anything in that. She can go her own way, with all the advantages I have given her.

MRS HIGGINS. The advantages of that poor woman who was here just now! The manners and habits that disqualify a fine lady from earning her own living without giving her a fine lady's income! Is that what you mean?

PICKERING (*indulgently, being rather bored*). Oh, that will be all right, Mrs Higgins. (*He rises to go.*)

HIGGINS (*rising also*). We'll find her some light employment.

PICKERING. She's happy enough. Dont you worry about her. Goodbye. (*He shakes hands as if he were consoling a frightened child, and makes for the door.*)

HIGGINS. Anyhow, theres no good bothering now. The thing's done. Goodbye, mother. (*He kisses her, and follows* PICKERING.)

PICKERING (*turning for a final consolation*). There are plenty of openings. We'll do whats right. Goodbye.

HIGGINS (*to* PICKERING *as they go out together*). Let's take her to the Shakespear exhibition at Earls Court.

PICKERING. Yes: lets. Her remarks will be delicious.

HIGGINS. She'll mimic all the people for us when we get home.

PICKERING. Ripping. (*Both are heard laughing as they go downstairs.*)

MRS HIGGINS (*rises with an impatient bounce, and returns to her work at the writing-table. She sweeps a litter of disarranged papers out of her way; snatches a sheet of paper from her stationery case; and tries resolutely to write. At the third line she gives it up; flings down her pen; grips the table angrily and exclaims*). Oh, men! men!! men!!!

Act Three

Getting at Meaning

1. Describe the relationship between Higgins and his mother. How does his attitude toward his mother contrast with his view of young women? What evidence indicates that Mrs. Higgins is a sensitive, perceptive, broad-minded person?

2. What stage in the transformation of Liza is depicted in this act? What aspect of society, dealt with more subtly in Acts One and Two, comes into sharp focus in Act Three?

3. Liza's crude anecdote contrasts dramatically with her proper appearance and genteel usage. What do the Eynsford Hills assume about her? When Liza blurts out the shocking word *bloody,* what explanation does Clara provide? What type in society does Clara represent?

4. Colonel Pickering, the perfect Victorian gentleman, refers to Liza's expletive as the "sanguinary element." How else does he demonstrate his respect for propriety? Are he and Mrs. Eynsford Hill old fashioned in a negative sense? Explain.

5. Notice the interweaving dialogue in which Higgins and Pickering describe their experiences with Liza. What point are they both making, only in different ways?

6. When Freddy is introduced to Higgins, Higgins looks at him "much as if he were a pickpocket." Why do you suppose Higgins reacts to Freddy with such immediate and intense antipathy? How does his reaction connect with the idea of "woman-as-object"?

7. Mrs. Higgins calls her son and Colonel Pickering "a pretty pair of babies." Why? What idea in Act Two is echoed by her words? How are her concerns similar to those of Mrs. Pearce? How do Higgins and the Colonel respond to her concerns?

Developing Skills in Reading Literature

1. **Setting and Character.** Higgins seems to personify masculine intelligence, while his mother seems to epitomize feminine wisdom. The contrast between their rooms reflects this fundamental difference, as well as other subtle contrasts. What details of decor reflect the differences between mother and son? between the generations they represent? between male and female?

2. **Theme.** Although Mrs. Higgins is connected to Pickering and her son by ties of social class and to her son by ties of blood, she identifies strongly with Liza. She calls Pickering and her son "infinitely stupid male creatures," and her final words are, "Oh, men! men!! men!!!" Is Shaw suggesting that the bond joining women is as powerful as the bonds of economic interest and family relation? What might be the basis of the female bond? How does it relate to the male bond that allowed Doolittle to connive with Higgins to determine Liza's future?

Despite Liza's wild story about the murder of her aunt, neither Clara nor her mother recognizes Liza as the disreputable looking flower girl. The fine clothes and elegant accent make a perfect disguise. What point is Shaw making?

In the midst of the discussion about small talk, Higgins comments, "You see, we're all savages, more or less." Is Shaw being ironic?

Consider Higgins's statement regarding Liza: "But you have no idea how frightfully interesting it is to take a human being and change her into a quite different human being by creating a new speech for her. It's filling up the deepest gulf that separates class from class and soul from soul." According to Shaw, what kinds of barriers separate human beings? Are they natural or artificial? Is Shaw implying that all human beings share a common humanity? Is this humanity "savage," as Higgins suggests? Support your opinion.

Developing Writing Skills

Writing an Explanation. In *Pygmalion,* Shaw satirizes pre-war British society. Much of what he has to say, however, still applies today. In a brief essay discuss the way that Shaw's society is similar, either to American society in general or to the specific society of which you are a part. You might consider the following questions when planning your essay: Are similar character types still evident? Does stereotyping still take place? Are there constricting social conventions and an emphasis on externals? Is language still an important social determinant?

ACT FOUR

The Wimpole Street laboratory. Midnight. Nobody in the room. The clock on the mantelpiece strikes twelve. The fire is not alight: it is a summer night.

Presently HIGGINS *and* PICKERING *are heard on the stairs.*

HIGGINS *(calling down to* PICKERING*).* I say, Pick: lock up, will you? I shant be going out again.

PICKERING. Right. Can Mrs Pearce go to bed? We dont want anything more, do we?

HIGGINS. Lord, no!

*(*ELIZA *opens the door and is seen on the lighted landing in opera cloak, brilliant evening dress, and diamonds, with fan, flowers, and all accessories. She comes to the hearth, and switches on the electric lights there. She is tired: her pallor contrasts strongly with her dark eyes and hair; and her expression is almost tragic. She takes off her cloak; puts her fan and flowers on the piano; and sits down on the bench, brooding and silent.* HIGGINS, *in evening dress, with overcoat and hat, comes in, carrying a smoking jacket which he has picked up downstairs. He takes off the hat and overcoat; throws them carelessly on the newspaper stand; disposes of his coat in the same way; puts on the smoking jacket; and throws himself wearily into the easychair at the hearth.* PICKERING, *similarly attired, comes in. He also takes off his hat and overcoat, and is about to throw them on* HIGGINS'S *when he hesitates.)*

PICKERING. I say: Mrs Pearce will row if we leave these things lying about in the drawing room.

HIGGINS. Oh, chuck them over the bannisters into the hall. She'll find them there in the morning and put them away all right. She'll think we were drunk.

PICKERING. We are, slightly. Are there any letters?

HIGGINS. I didnt look. *(*PICKERING *takes the overcoats and hats and goes downstairs.* HIGGINS *begins half singing half yawning an air from La Fanciulla del Golden West.[1] Suddenly he stops and exclaims)* I wonder where the devil my slippers are!

*(*ELIZA *looks at him darkly; then rises suddenly and leaves the room.*

HIGGINS *yawns again, and resumes his song.*

PICKERING *returns, with the contents of the letter-box in his hand.)*

PICKERING. Only circulars, and this coroneted billet-doux[2] for you. *(He throws the circulars into the fender, and posts himself on the hearthrug, with his back to the grate.)*

HIGGINS *(glancing at the billet-doux)* Moneylender. *(He throws the letter after the circulars.)*

*(*ELIZA *returns with a pair of large down-at-heel slippers. She places them on the carpet before* HIGGINS, *and sits as before without a word.)*

HIGGINS *(yawning again).* Oh Lord! What an evening! What a crew! What a silly tomfoolery! *(He raises his shoe to unlace it, and catches sight of the slippers. He stops unlacing and looks at them as if they had appeared there of their own accord.)* Oh! theyre there, are they?

PICKERING *(stretching himself).* Well, I feel a bit tired. It's been a long day. The garden party, a dinner party, and the opera! Rather too much of a good thing. But youve won your bet, Higgins. Eliza did the trick, and something to spare, eh?

HIGGINS *(fervently).* Thank God it's over!

*(*ELIZA *flinches violently; but they take no notice of her; and she recovers herself and sits stonily as before.)*

---

1. **La Fanciulla del Golden West:** *The Girl of the Golden West,* an opera by Puccini (1858–1924).
2. **billet-doux** (bil′ ē d̄o̅o̅′) *French:* a love letter.

Culver Pictures, Inc.

PICKERING. Were you nervous at the garden party? *I* was. Eliza didnt seem a bit nervous.

HIGGINS. Oh, she wasnt nervous. I knew she'd be all right. No: it's the strain of putting the job through all these months that has told on me. It was interesting enough at first, while we were at the phonetics; but after that I got deadly sick of it. If I hadnt backed myself to do it I should have chucked the whole thing up two months ago. It was a silly notion: the whole thing has been a bore.

PICKERING. Oh come! the garden party was frightfully exciting. My heart began beating like anything.

HIGGINS. Yes, for the first three minutes. But when I saw we were going to win hands down, I felt like a bear in a cage, hanging about doing nothing. The dinner was worse: sitting gorging there for over an hour, with nobody but a damned fool of a fashionable woman to talk to! I tell you, Pickering, never again for me. No more artificial duchesses. The whole thing has been simple purgatory.

PICKERING. Youve never been broken in properly to the social routine. *(Strolling over to the piano)* I rather enjoy dipping into it occasionally myself: it makes me feel young again. Anyhow, it was a great success: an immense success. I was quite frightened once or twice because Eliza was doing it so well. You see, lots of the real people cant do it at all: theyre such fools that they think style comes by nature to people in their position; and so they never learn. Theres always something professional about doing a thing superlatively well.

HIGGINS. Yes: thats what drives me mad: the silly people dont know their own silly business. *(Rising)* However, it's over and done with; and now I can go to bed at last without dreading tomorrow.

(ELIZA's *beauty becomes murderous.*)

PICKERING. I think I shall turn in too. Still, it's been a great occasion: a triumph for you. Goodnight. *(He goes.)*

HIGGINS *(following him)*. Goodnight. *(Over his shoulder, at the door)* Put out the lights, Eliza; and tell Mrs Pearce not to make coffee for me in the morning; I'll take tea. *(He goes out.)*

(ELIZA *tries to control herself and feel indifferent as she rises and walks across to the hearth to switch off the lights. By the time she gets there she is on the point of screaming. She sits down in* HIGGINS's *chair and holds on hard to the arms. Finally she gives way and flings herself furiously on the floor, raging.)*

HIGGINS *(in despairing wrath outside)*. What the devil have I done with my slippers? *(He appears at the door.)*

LIZA *(snatching up the slippers, and hurling them at him one after the other with all her force)*. There are your slippers. And there. Take your slippers; and may you never have a day's luck with them!

HIGGINS *(astounded)*. What on earth—! *(He comes to her.)* Whats the matter? Get up. *(He pulls her up.)* Anything wrong?

LIZA *(breathless)*. Nothing wrong—with you. Ive won your bet for you, havnt I? Thats enough for you. *I* dont matter, I suppose.

HIGGINS. You won my bet! You! Presumptuous insect! *I* won it. What did you throw those slippers at me for?

LIZA. Because I wanted to smash your face. I'd like to kill you, you selfish brute. Why didnt you leave me where you picked me out of—in the gutter? You thank God it's all over, and that now you can throw me back again there, do you? *(She crisps her fingers[3] frantically.)*

HIGGINS *(looking at her in cool wonder)*. The creature is nervous, after all.

LIZA *(gives a suffocated scream of fury, and instinctively darts her nails at his face)*!!

HIGGINS *(catching her wrists)*. Ah! would you? Claws in, you cat. How dare you shew your temper to me? Sit down and be quiet. *(He throws her roughly into the easy-chair.)*

LIZA *(crushed by superior strength and weight)*. Whats to become of me? Whats to become of me?

HIGGINS. How the devil do I know whats to become of you? What does it matter what becomes of you?

LIZA. You dont care. I know you dont care. You wouldnt care if I was dead. I'm nothing to you—not so much as them slippers.

HIGGINS *(thundering)* Those slippers.

LIZA *(with bitter submission)*. Those slippers. I didnt think it made any difference now.

(A pause. ELIZA *hopeless and crushed.* HIGGINS *a little uneasy.)*

HIGGINS *(in his loftiest manner)*. Why have you begun going on like this? May I ask whether you complain of your treatment here?

LIZA. No.

HIGGINS. Has anybody behaved badly to you? Colonel Pickering? Mrs Pearce? Any of the servants?

LIZA. No.

HIGGINS. I presume you dont pretend that *I* have treated you badly?

LIZA. No.

HIGGINS. I am glad to hear it. *(He moderates his tone.)* Perhaps youre tired after the strain of the day. Will you have a glass of champagne? *(He moves towards the door.)*

LIZA. No. *(Recollecting her manners)* Thank you.

HIGGINS *(good-humored again)*. This has been coming on you for some days. I suppose it was natural for you to be anxious about the garden party. But thats all over now. *(He pats her kindly on the shoulder. She*

---

3. **crisps her fingers:** opens and closes her fists.

writhes.) Theres nothing more to worry about.

LIZA. No. Nothing more for you to worry about. *(She suddenly rises and gets away from him by going to the piano bench, where she sits and hides her face.)* Oh God! I wish I was dead.

HIGGINS *(staring after her in sincere surprise).* Why? In heaven's name, why? *(Reasonably, going to her)* Listen to me, Eliza. All this irritation is purely subjective.

LIZA. I dont understand. I'm too ignorant.

HIGGINS. It's only imagination. Low spirits and nothing else. Nobody's hurting you. Nothing's wrong. You go to bed like a good girl and sleep it off. Have a little cry and say your prayers: that will make you comfortable.

LIZA. I heard your prayers. "Thank God it's all over!"

HIGGINS *(impatiently).* Well, dont you thank God it's all over? Now you are free and can do what you like.

LIZA *(pulling herself together in desperation).* What am I fit for? What have you left me fit for? Where am I to go? What am I to do? Whats to become of me?

HIGGINS *(enlightened, but not at all impressed).* Oh thats whats worrying you, is it? *(He thrusts his hands into his pockets, and walks about in his usual manner, rattling the contents of his pockets, as if condescending to a trivial subject out of pure kindness.)* I shouldnt bother about it if I were you. I should imagine you wont have much difficulty in settling yourself somewhere or other, though I hadnt quite realized that you were going away. *(She looks quickly at him: he does not look at her, but examines the dessert stand on the piano and decides that he will eat an apple.)* You might marry, you know. *(He bites a large piece out of the apple and munches it noisily.)* You see, Eliza, all men are not confirmed old bachelors like me and the Colonel. Most men are the marry-ing sort (poor devils!); and youre not bad-looking: it's quite a pleasure to look at you sometimes—not now, of course, because youre crying and looking as ugly as the very devil; but when youre all right and quite yourself, youre what I should call attractive. That is, to the people in the marrying line, you understand. You go to bed and have a good nice rest; and then get up and look at yourself in the glass; and you wont feel so cheap.

(ELIZA again looks at him, speechless, and does not stir.

The look is quite lost on him: he eats his apple with a dreamy expression of happiness, as it is quite a good one.)

HIGGINS *(a genial afterthought occurring to him).* I daresay my mother could find some chap or other who would do very well.

LIZA. We were above that at the corner of Tottenham Court Road.

HIGGINS *(waking up).* What do you mean?

LIZA. I sold flowers. I didn't sell myself. Now youve made a lady of me I'm not fit to sell anything else. I wish youd left me where you found me.

HIGGINS *(slinging the core of the apple decisively into the grate).* Tosh, Eliza. Dont you insult human relations by dragging all this cant about buying and selling into it. You neednt marry the fellow if you dont like him.

LIZA. What else am I to do?

HIGGINS. Oh, lots of things. What about your old idea of a florist's shop? Pickering could set you up in one: he's lots of money. *(Chuckling)* He'll have to pay for all those togs you have been wearing today; and that, with the hire of the jewellery, will make a big hole in two hundred pounds. Why, six months ago you would have thought it the millennium to have a flower shop of your own. Come! youll be all right. I must clear off to bed: I'm devilish sleepy.

Culver Pictures, Inc.

By the way, I came down for something: I forget what it was.

LIZA. Your slippers.

HIGGINS. Oh yes, of course. You shied them at me. (*He picks them up, and is going out when she rises and speaks to him.*)

LIZA. Before you go, sir—

HIGGINS (*dropping the slippers in his surprise at her calling him Sir*). Eh?

LIZA. Do my clothes belong to me or to Colonel Pickering?

HIGGINS (*coming back into the room as if her question were the very climax of unreason*). What the devil use would they be to Pickering?

LIZA. He might want them for the next girl you pick up to experiment on.

HIGGINS (*shocked and hurt*). Is that the way you feel towards us?

LIZA. I dont want to hear anything more about that. All I want to know is whether anything belongs to me. My own clothes were burnt.

HIGGINS. But what does it matter? Why need you start bothering about that in the middle of the night?

LIZA. I want to know what I may take away with me. I dont want to be accused of stealing.

HIGGINS (*now deeply wounded*). Stealing! You shouldnt have said that, Eliza. That shews a want of feeling.

LIZA. I'm sorry. I'm only a common ignorant girl; and in my station I have to be careful. There cant be any feelings between the like of you and the like of me. Please will you tell me what belongs to me and what doesnt?

HIGGINS (*very sulky*). You may take the whole damned houseful if you like. Except the jewels. Theyre hired. Will that satisfy you? (*He turns on his heel and is about to go in extreme dudgeon.*)

LIZA (*drinking in his emotion like nectar, and nagging him to provoke a further supply*). Stop, please. (*She takes off her jewels.*) Will you take these to your room and keep them safe? I dont want to run the risk of their being missing.

HIGGINS *(furious).* Hand them over. *(She puts them into his hands.)* If these belonged to me instead of to the jeweller, I'd ram them down your ungrateful throat. *(He perfunctorily thrusts them into his pockets, unconsciously decorating himself with the protruding ends of the chains.)*

LIZA *(taking a ring off).* This ring isnt the jeweller's: it's the one you bought me in Brighton. I dont want it now. *(HIGGINS dashes the ring violently into the fireplace, and turns on her so threateningly that she crouches over the piano with her hands over her face, and exclaims)* Dont you hit me.

HIGGINS. Hit you! You infamous creature, how dare you accuse me of such a thing? It is you who have hit me. You have wounded me to the heart.

LIZA *(thrilling with hidden joy).* I'm glad. Ive got a little of my own back, anyhow.

HIGGINS *(with dignity, in his finest professional style).* You have caused me to lose my temper: a thing that has hardly ever happened to me before. I prefer to say nothing more tonight. I am going to bed.

LIZA *(pertly).* Youd better leave a note for Mrs Pearce about the coffee; for she wont be told by me.

HIGGINS *(formally).* Damn Mrs Pearce; and damn the coffee; and damn you; and damn my own folly in having lavished hard-earned knowledge and the treasure of my regard and intimacy on a heartless guttersnipe. *(He goes out with impressive decorum, and spoils it by slamming the door savagely.)*

(ELIZA smiles for the first time; expresses her feelings by a wild pantomime in which an imitation of HIGGINS's exit is confused with her own triumph; and finally goes down on her knees on the hearthrug to look for the ring.)

Act Four

Getting at Meaning

1. At the beginning of Act Four, when Liza, Higgins, and Pickering return from their evening out, can you tell who has won the bet? How does the atmosphere of this scene contrast with what might be expected on a night of triumph?

2. At the beginning of this act, how do both Higgins and Pickering show lack of respect for Liza's feelings? What might explain their behavior?

3. Liza likens an arranged marriage to the act of selling herself. Higgins responds, "Dont you insult human relations by dragging all this cant about buying and selling into it." Who has insulted human relations more, Higgins by his suggestion or Liza by her response? Why is Higgins's statement ironic, given his earlier dealings with Alfred Doolittle and his wager with Colonel Pickering?

4. Higgins seems indifferent to the prospect of Liza's marrying someone else, even suggesting that his mother "find some chap or other who would do very well." Is Shaw changing the Pygmalion myth? Is

Higgins aware of his true feelings at this point in the action? Explain.

5. Throughout most of their argument, Higgins remains coolly rational in the face of Liza's anger and despair. At the end of the act, however, Higgins is furious and Liza is triumphant. How has Liza provoked Higgins to fury? Why?

Developing Skills in Reading Literature

1. **Characterization.** In her argument with Higgins, Liza refers to herself as common and ignorant. Is she showing a lingering lack of self-esteem, or is she being sarcastic? What do these statements reveal about her mastery of the language? about her development as an individual?

At the end of the act, Higgins exits, saying, ". . . and damn my own folly in having lavished hard-earned knowledge and the treasure of my regard and intimacy on a heartless guttersnipe." Does he use *guttersnipe* in the same way that he used it earlier in the play? What character deficiencies are suggested by "the treasure of my regard and intimacy"? Higgins makes his final statement with "impressive decorum." How does this stage direction affect the way that you interpret his words?

Notice the stage directions that describe the action in this act. Liza "flinches violently," "flings herself furiously on the floor, raging," and "gives a suffocated scream of fury;" Higgins "throws her roughly into the easy-chair," "dashes the ring violently into the fire-place," and slams the door "savagely." What does the intensity of the action imply about the feelings of Liza and Higgins toward each other? Does the violence in this act confirm Higgins's view that human beings are basically savages? Explain.

2. **Character and Theme.** In drama, generalizations about life are drawn from the specific behavior of individual characters, who tend to be both larger than life and decidedly human. Liza, for example, proves to be beautiful and talented, becoming an accomplished pianist in a matter of months. She also exhibits the qualities of a normal young woman, which allows the audience to identify with her. What actions seem typical of a young woman in her predicament? What universal human qualities does she demonstrate? What might Shaw have believed to be typical female qualities? How does Shaw seem to view the position of women in post-Victorian society?

The case of Higgins is more complicated, for he is an incorrigible eccentric. After the first violent outburst, with Liza still in a state of extreme agitation, Shaw describes Higgins in these words: "The look is quite lost on him: he eats his apple with a dreamy expression of happiness, as it is quite a good one." Do you think that Shaw wants the audience to draw some conclusion about the different emotional makeup of men and women from the striking contrast between Liza and Higgins? Or is Higgins simply too idiosyncratic to represent men? Support your answer by citing incidents that highlight typical or atypical actions and responses.

ACT FIVE

MRS HIGGINS's *drawing room. She is at her writing-table as before. The* PARLORMAID *comes in.*

THE PARLORMAID *(at the door).* Mr Henry, maam, is downstairs with Colonel Pickering.

MRS HIGGINS. Well, shew them up.

THE PARLORMAID. Theyre using the telephone, maam. Telephoning to the police, I think.

MRS HIGGINS. What!

THE PARLORMAID *(coming further in and lowering her voice).* Mr Henry is in a state, maam. I thought I'd better tell you.

MRS HIGGINS. If you had told me that Mr Henry was not in a state it would have been more surprising. Tell them to come up when theyve finished with the police. I suppose he's lost something.

THE PARLORMAID. Yes, maam *(going).*

MRS HIGGINS. Go upstairs and tell Miss Doolittle that Mr Henry and the Colonel are here. Ask her not to come down til I send for her.

THE PARLORMAID. Yes, maam.

*(*HIGGINS *bursts in. He is, as the* PARLORMAID *has said, in a state.)*

HIGGINS. Look here, mother: heres a confounded thing!

MRS HIGGINS. Yes, dear. Good morning. *(He checks his impatience and kisses her, whilst the* PARLORMAID *goes out.)* What is it?

HIGGINS. Eliza's bolted.

MRS HIGGINS *(calmly continuing her writing).* You must have frightened her.

HIGGINS. Frightened her! nonsense! She was left last night, as usual, to turn out the lights and all that; and instead of going to bed she changed her clothes and went right off: her bed wasnt slept in. She came in a cab for her things before seven this morning; and that fool Mrs Pearce let her have

them without telling me a word about it. What am I to do?

MRS HIGGINS. Do without, I'm afraid, Henry. The girl has a perfect right to leave if she chooses.

HIGGINS *(wandering distractedly across the room).* But I cant find anything. I dont know what appointments Ive got. I'm— *(*PICKERING *comes in.* MRS HIGGINS *puts down her pen and turns away from the writing-table.)*

PICKERING *(shaking hands).* Good morning, Mrs Higgins. Has Henry told you? *(He sits down on the ottoman.)*

HIGGINS. What does that ass of an inspector say? Have you offered a reward?

MRS HIGGINS *(rising in indignant amazement).* You dont mean to say you have set the police after Eliza.

HIGGINS. Of course. What are the police for? What else could we do? *(He sits in the Elizabethan chair.)*

PICKERING. The inspector made a lot of difficulties. I really think he suspected us of some improper purpose.

MRS HIGGINS. Well, of course he did. What right have you to go to the police and give the girl's name as if she were a thief, or a lost umbrella, or something? Really! *(She sits down again, deeply vexed.)*

HIGGINS. But we want to find her.

PICKERING. We cant let her go like this, you know, Mrs Higgins. What were we to do?

MRS HIGGINS. You have no more sense, either of you, than two children. Why—

(The PARLORMAID *comes in and breaks off the conversation.)*

THE PARLORMAID. Mr Henry: a gentleman wants to see you very particular. He's been sent on from Wimpole Street.

HIGGINS. Oh, bother! I cant see anyone now. Who is it?

THE PARLORMAID. A Mr Doolittle, sir.

PICKERING. Doolittle! Do you mean the dustman?

THE PARLORMAID. Dustman! On no, sir: a gentleman.

HIGGINS *(springing up excitedly).* By George, Pick, it's some relative of hers that she's gone to. Somebody we know nothing about. *(To the* PARLORMAID*)* Send him up, quick.

THE PARLORMAID. Yes, sir. *(She goes.)*

HIGGINS *(eagerly, going to his mother).* Genteel relatives! now we shall hear something. *(He sits down in the Chippendale chair.)*

MRS HIGGINS. Do you know any of her people?

PICKERING. Only her father: the fellow we told you about.

THE PARLORMAID *(announcing).* Mr. Doolittle. *(She withdraws.)*

*(*DOOLITTLE *enters. He is brilliantly dressed in a new fashionable frock-coat, with white waistcoat and grey trousers. A flower in his buttonhole, a dazzling silk hat, and patent leather shoes complete the effect. He is too concerned with the business he has come on to notice* MRS HIGGINS. *He walks straight to* HIGGINS, *and accosts him with vehement reproach.)*

DOOLITTLE *(indicating his own person).* See here! Do you see this? You done this.

HIGGINS. Done what, man?

DOOLITTLE. This, I tell you. Look at it. Look at this hat. Look at this coat.

PICKERING. Has Eliza been buying you clothes?

DOOLITTLE. Eliza! not she. Not half. Why would she buy me clothes?

MRS HIGGINS. Good morning, Mr. Doolittle. Wont you sit down?

DOOLITTLE *(taken aback as he becomes conscious that he has forgotten his hostess).* Asking your pardon, maam. *(He approaches her and shakes her proffered hand.)* Thank you. *(He sits down on the ottoman, on* PICKERING's *right.)* I am that full of what has happened to me that I cant think of anything else.

HIGGINS. What the dickens has happened to you?

DOOLITTLE. I shouldnt mind if it had only happened to me: anything might happen to anybody and nobody to blame but Providence, as you might say. But this is something that you done to me: yes, you, Henry Higgins.

HIGGINS. Have you found Eliza? Thats the point.

DOOLITTLE. Have you lost her?

HIGGINS. Yes.

DOOLITTLE. You have all the luck, you have. I aint found her; but she'll find me quick enough now after what you done to me.

MRS HIGGINS. But what has my son done to you, Mr Doolittle?

DOOLITTLE. Done to me! Ruined me. Destroyed my happiness. Tied me up and delivered me into the hands of middle class morality.

HIGGINS *(rising intolerantly and standing over* DOOLITTLE*).* Youre raving. Youre drunk. Youre mad. I gave you five pounds. After that I had two conversations with you, at half-a-crown an hour. Ive never seen you since.

DOOLITTLE. Oh! Drunk! am I? Mad! am I? Tell me this. Did you or did you not write a letter to an old blighter in America that was giving five millions to found Moral Reform Societies all over the world, and that wanted you to invent a universal language for him?

HIGGINS. What! Ezra D. Wannafeller! He's dead. *(He sits down again carelessly.)*

DOOLITTLE. Yes: he's dead; and I'm done for. Now did you or did you not write a letter to him to say that the most original moralist at present in England, to the best of your knowledge, was Alfred Doolittle, a common dustman.

HIGGINS. Oh, after your last visit I remember making some silly joke of the kind.

DOOLITTLE. Ah! You may well call it a silly joke. It put the lid on me right enough. Just give him the chance he wanted to shew that Americans is not like us: that they recognize and respect merit in every class of life, however humble. Them words is in his blooming will, in which, Henry Higgins, thanks to your silly joking, he leaves me a share in his Pre-digested Cheese Trust worth three thousand a year on condition that I lecture for his Wannafeller Moral Reform World League as often as they ask me up to six times a year.

HIGGINS. The devil he does! Whew! *(Brightening suddenly)* What a lark!

PICKERING. A safe thing for you, Doolittle. They wont ask you twice.

DOOLITTLE. It aint the lecturing I mind. I'll lecture them blue in the face, I will, and not turn a hair. It's making a gentleman of me that I object to. Who asked him to make a gentleman of me? I was happy. I was free. I touched pretty nigh everybody for money when I wanted it, same as I touched you, Henry Higgins. Now I am worrited; tied neck and heels; and everybody touches me for money. It's a fine thing for you, says my solicitor. Is it? says I. You mean it's a good thing for you, I says. When I was a poor man and had a solicitor once when they found a pram in the dust cart, he got me off, and got shut of me and got me shut of him as quick as he could. Same with the doctors: used to shove me out of the hospital before I could hardly stand on my legs, and nothing to pay. Now they finds out that I'm not a healthy man and cant live unless they looks after me twice a day. In the house I'm not let do a hand's turn for myself: somebody else must do it and touch me for it. A year ago I hadnt a relative in the world except two or three that wouldnt speak to me. Now Ive fifty, and not a decent week's wages among the lot of them. I have to live for others and not for myself: thats middle class morality. You talk of losing Eliza. Dont you be anxious: I bet she's on my doorstep by this: she that could support

herself easy by selling flowers if I wasnt respectable. And the next one to touch me will be you, Henry Higgins. I'll have to learn to speak middle class language from you, instead of speaking proper English. Thats where youll come in; and I daresay thats what you done it for.

MRS HIGGINS. But, my dear Mr Doolittle, you need not suffer all this if you are really in earnest. Nobody can force you to accept this bequest. You can repudiate it. Isnt that so, Colonel Pickering?

PICKERING. I believe so.

DOOLITTLE *(softening his manner in deference to her sex)*. Thats the tragedy of it, maam. It's easy to say chuck it; but I havnt the nerve. Which of us has? We're all intimidated. Intimidated, maam: thats what we are. What is there for me if I chuck it but the workhouse in my old age? I have to dye my hair already to keep my job as a dustman. If I was one of the deserving poor, and had put by a bit, I could chuck it; but then why should I, acause the deserving poor might as well be millionaires for all the happiness they ever has. They dont know what happiness is. But I, as one of the undeserving poor, have nothing between me and the pauper's uniform but this here blasted three thousand a year that shoves me into the middle class. (Excuse the expression, maam: youd use it yourself if you had my provocation.) Theyve got you every way you turn: it's a choice between the Skilly of the workhouse and the Char Bydis[1] of the middle class; and I havnt the nerve for the workhouse. Intimidated: thats what I am. Broke. Bought up. Happier

---

1. **Skilly . . . Char Bydis:** a reference to Scylla (sil' ə) and Charybdis (kə rib' dis), a dangerous rock and whirlpool on either side of a narrow strait between Sicily and Italy. In the *Odyssey* they are portrayed as two female monsters whom Odysseus had to outwit in order to steer his ship through the strait. They symbolize equal dangers in any course of action.

men than me will call for my dust, and touch me for their tip; and I'll look on helpless, and envy them. And thats what your son has brought me to. *(He is overcome by emotion.)*

MRS HIGGINS. Well, I'm very glad youre not going to do anything foolish, Mr Doolittle. For this solves the problem of Eliza's future. You can provide for her now.

DOOLITTLE *(with melancholy resignation)*. Yes, maam: I'm expected to provide for everyone now, out of three thousand a year.

HIGGINS *(jumping up)*. Nonsense! he cant provide for her. He shant provide for her. She doesn't belong to him. I paid him five pounds for her. Doolittle: either youre an honest man or a rogue.

DOOLITTLE *(tolerantly)*. A little of both, Henry, like the rest of us: a little of both.

HIGGINS. Well, you took that money for the girl; and you have no right to take her as well.

MRS HIGGINS. Henry: dont be absurd. If you want to know where Eliza is, she is upstairs.

HIGGINS *(amazed)*. Upstairs!!! Then I shall jolly soon fetch her downstairs. *(He makes resolutely for the door.)*

MRS HIGGINS *(rising and following him)*. Be quiet, Henry. Sit down.

HIGGINS. I—

MRS HIGGINS. Sit down, dear; and listen to me.

HIGGINS. Oh very well, very well, very well. *(He throws himself ungraciously on the ottoman, with his face towards the windows.)* But I think you might have told us this half an hour ago.

MRS HIGGINS. Eliza came to me this morning. She passed the night partly walking about in a rage, partly trying to throw herself into the river and being afraid to, and partly in the Carlton Hotel. She told me of the brutal way you two treated her.

HIGGINS *(bounding up again)*. What!

PICKERING *(rising also)*. My dear Mrs Higgins, she's been telling you stories. We didnt treat her brutally. We hardly said a word to her; and we parted on particularly good terms. *(Turning on HIGGINS)* Higgins: did you bully her after I went to bed?

HIGGINS. Just the other way about. She threw my slippers in my face. She behaved in the most outrageous way. I never gave her the slightest provocation. The slippers came bang into my face the moment I entered the room—before I had uttered a word. And used perfectly awful language.

PICKERING *(astonished)*. But why? What did we do to her?

MRS HIGGINS. I think I know pretty well what you did. The girl is naturally rather affectionate, I think. Isnt she, Mr. Doolittle?

DOOLITTLE. Very tender-hearted, maam. Takes after me.

MRS HIGGINS. Just so. She had become attached to you both. She worked very hard for you, Henry! I dont think you quite realize what anything in the nature of brain work means to a girl like that. Well, it seems that when the great day of trial came, and she did this wonderful thing for you without making a single mistake, you two sat there and never said a word to her, but talked together of how glad you were that it was all over and how you had been bored with the whole thing. And then you were surprised because she threw your slippers at you! *I* should have thrown the fire-irons at you.

HIGGINS. We said nothing except that we were tired and wanted to go to bed. Did we, Pick?

PICKERING *(shrugging his shoulders)*. That was all.

MRS HIGGINS *(ironically)*. Quite sure?

PICKERING. Absolutely. Really, that was all.

MRS HIGGINS. You didnt thank her, or pet her, or admire her, or tell her how splendid she'd been.

HIGGINS *(impatiently)*. But she knew all about that. We didnt make speeches to her, if thats what you mean.

PICKERING *(conscience stricken)*. Perhaps we were a little inconsiderate. Is she very angry?

MRS HIGGINS *(returning to her place at the writing-table)*. Well, I'm afraid she wont go back to Wimpole Street, especially now that Mr Doolittle is able to keep up the position you have thrust on her; but she says she is quite willing to meet you on friendly terms and to let bygones be bygones.

HIGGINS *(furious)*. Is she, by George? Ho!

MRS HIGGINS. If you promise to behave yourself, Henry, I'll ask her to come down. If not, go home; for you have taken up quite enough of my time.

HIGGINS. Oh, all right. Very well. Pick: you behave yourself. Let us put on our best Sunday manners for this creature that we picked out of the mud. *(He flings himself sulkily into the Elizabethan chair.)*

DOOLITTLE *(remonstrating)*. Now, now, Henry Higgins! Have some consideration for my feelings as a middle class man.

MRS HIGGINS. Remember your promise, Henry. *(She presses the bell-button on the writing-table.)* Mr. Doolittle: will you be so good as to step out on the balcony for a moment. I dont want Eliza to have the shock of your news until she has made it up with these two gentlemen. Would you mind?

DOOLITTLE. As you wish, lady. Anything to help Henry to keep her off my hands. *(He disappears through the window.)*

(The PARLORMAID answers the bell. Pickering sits down in DOOLITTLE's place.)

MRS HIGGINS. Ask Miss Doolittle to come down, please.

THE PARLORMAID. Yes, maam. *(She goes out.)*

MRS HIGGINS. Now, Henry: be good.

HIGGINS. I am behaving myself perfectly.

PICKERING. He is doing his best, Mrs Higgins.

(A pause. HIGGINS throws back his head; stretches out his legs; and begins to whistle.)

MRS HIGGINS. Henry, dearest, you dont look at all nice in that attitude.

HIGGINS *(pulling himself together)*. I was not trying to look nice, mother.

MRS HIGGINS. It doesnt matter, dear. I only wanted to make you speak.

HIGGINS. Why?

MRS HIGGINS. Because you cant speak and whistle at the same time.

(HIGGINS groans. Another very trying pause.)

HIGGINS *(springing up, out of patience)*. Where the devil is that girl? Are we to wait here all day?

(ELIZA enters, sunny, self-possessed, and giving a staggeringly convincing exhibition of ease of manner. She carries a little workbasket, and is very much at home. PICKERING is too much taken aback to rise.)

LIZA. How do you do, Professor Higgins? Are you quite well?

HIGGINS *(choking)*. Am I—*(He can say no more.)*

LIZA. But of course you are: you are never ill. So glad to see you again, Colonel Pickering. *(He rises hastily; and they shake hands.)* Quite chilly this morning, isnt it? *(She sits down on his left. He sits beside her.)*

HIGGINS. Dont you dare try this game on me. I taught it to you; and it doesnt take me in. Get up and come home; and dont be a fool.

(ELIZA takes a piece of needlework from her basket, and begins to stitch at it, without taking the least notice of this outburst.)

MRS HIGGINS. Very nicely put, indeed, Henry. No woman could resist such an invitation.

HIGGINS. You let her alone, mother. Let her speak for herself. You will jolly soon see whether she has an idea that I havnt put into her head or a word that I havnt put into her mouth. I tell you I have created this thing out of the squashed cabbage leaves of Covent Garden; and now she pretends to play the fine lady with me.

MRS HIGGINS (*placidly*). Yes, dear; but youll sit down, wont you?

(HIGGINS *sits down again, savagely.*)

LIZA (*to* PICKERING, *taking no apparent notice of* HIGGINS, *and working away deftly*). Will you drop me altogether now that the experiment is over, Colonel Pickering?

PICKERING. Oh dont. You mustnt think of it as an experiment. It shocks me, somehow.

LIZA. Oh, I'm only a squashed cabbage leaf—

PICKERING (*impulsively*). No.

LIZA (*continuing quietly*).—but I owe so much to you that I should be very unhappy if you forgot me.

PICKERING. It's very kind of you to say so, Miss Doolittle.

LIZA. It's not because you paid for my dresses. I know you are generous to everybody with money. But it was from you that I learnt really nice manners; and that is what makes one a lady, isnt it? You see it was so very difficult for me with the example of Professor Higgins always before me. I was brought up to be just like him, unable to control myself, and using bad language on the slightest provocation. And I should never have known that ladies and gentlemen didnt behave like that if you hadnt been there.

HIGGINS. Well!!

PICKERING. Oh, thats only his way, you know. He doesnt mean it.

LIZA. Oh, *I* didnt mean it either, when I was a flower girl. It was only my way. But you see I did it; and thats what makes the difference after all.

PICKERING. No doubt. Still, he taught you to speak; and I couldnt have done that, you know.

LIZA (*trivially*). Of course: that is his profession.

HIGGINS. Damnation!

LIZA (*continuing*). It was just like learning to dance in the fashionable way: there was nothing more than that in it. But do you know what began my real education?

PICKERING. What?

LIZA (*stopping her work for a moment*). Your calling me Miss Doolittle that day when I first came to Wimpole Street. That was the beginning of self-respect for me. (*She resumes her stitching.*) And there were a hundred little things you never noticed, because they came naturally to you. Things about standing up and taking off your hat and opening doors—

PICKERING. Oh, that was nothing.

LIZA. Yes: things that shewed you thought and felt about me as if I were something better than a scullery-maid; though of course I know you would have been just the same to a scullery-maid if she had been let into the drawing room. You never took off your boots in the dining room when I was there.

PICKERING. You mustnt mind that. Higgins takes off his boots all over the place.

LIZA. I know. I am not blaming him. It is his way, isn't it? But it made such a difference to me that you didnt do it. You see, really and truly, apart from the things anyone can pick up (the dressing and the proper way of speaking, and so on), the difference between a lady and a flower girl is not how she behaves, but how she's treated. I shall always be a flower girl to Professor Higgins, because he always treats me as a flower girl, and always will; but I know I can be a lady to you, because you always treat me as a lady, and always will.

MRS HIGGINS. Please dont grind your teeth, Henry.

PICKERING. Well, this is really very nice of you, Miss Doolittle.

LIZA. I should like you to call me Eliza, now, if you would.

PICKERING. Thank you. Eliza, of course.

LIZA. And I should like Professor Higgins to call me Miss Doolittle.

HIGGINS. I'll see you damned first.

MRS HIGGINS. Henry! Henry!

PICKERING (laughing). Why dont you slang back at him? Dont stand it. It would do him a lot of good.

LIZA. I cant. I could have done it once; but now I cant go back to it. Last night, when I was wandering about, a girl spoke to me; and I tried to get back into the old way with her; but it was no use. You told me, you know, that when a child is brought to a foreign country, it picks up the language in a few weeks, and forgets its own. Well, I am a child in your country. I have forgotten my own language, and can speak nothing but yours. Thats the real break-off with the corner of Tottenham Court Road. Leaving Wimpole Street finishes it.

PICKERING (much alarmed). Oh! but youre coming back to Wimpole Street, arnt you? Youll forgive Higgins?

HIGGINS (rising). Forgive! Will she, by George! Let her go. Let her find out how she can get on without us. She will relapse into the gutter in three weeks without me at her elbow.

(DOOLITTLE appears at the center window. With a look of dignified reproach at HIGGINS, he comes slowly and silently to his daughter, who, with her back to the window, is unconscious of his approach.)

PICKERING. He's incorrigible, Eliza. You wont relapse, will you?

LIZA. No: not now. Never again. I have learnt my lesson. I dont believe I could utter one of the old sounds if I tried. (DOOLITTLE touches her on her left shoulder. She drops her work, losing her self-possession utterly at the spectacle of her father's splendor) A-a-a-a-a-ah-ow-ooh!

HIGGINS (with a crow of triumph). Aha! Just so. A-a-a-a-ahowooh! A-a-a-a-ahowooh! A-a-a-a-ahowooh! Victory! Victory! (He throws himself on the divan, folding his arms, and spraddling arrogantly.)

DOOLITTLE. Can you blame the girl? Dont look at me like that, Eliza. It aint my fault. Ive come into some money.

LIZA. You must have touched a millionaire this time, dad.

DOOLITTLE. I have. But I'm dressed something special today. I'm going to St George's, Hanover Square. Your stepmother is going to marry me.

LIZA (angrily). Youre going to let yourself down to marry that low common woman!

PICKERING (quietly). He ought to, Eliza. (To DOOLITTLE) Why has she changed her mind?

DOOLITTLE (sadly). Intimidated, Governor. Intimidated. Middle class morality claims its victim. Wont you put on your hat, Liza, and come and see me turned off?

LIZA. If the Colonel says I must, I—I'll (almost sobbing) I'll demean myself. And get insulted for my pains, like enough.

DOOLITTLE. Dont be afraid: she never comes to words with anyone now, poor woman! respectability has broke all the spirit out of her.

PICKERING (squeezing ELIZA's elbow gently). Be kind to them, Eliza. Make the best of it.

LIZA (forcing a little smile for him through her vexation). Oh well, just to shew theres no ill feeling. I'll be back in a moment. (She goes out.)

DOOLITTLE (sitting down beside PICKERING). I feel uncommon nervous about the ceremony, Colonel. I wish youd come and see me through it.

PICKERING. But youve been through it before, man. You were married to Eliza's mother.

DOOLITTLE. Who told you that, Colonel?

PICKERING. Well, nobody told me. But I concluded—naturally—

DOOLITTLE. No: that aint the natural way, Colonel: it's only the middle class way. My way was always the undeserving way. But dont say nothing to Eliza. She dont know: I always had a delicacy about telling her.

PICKERING. Quite right. We'll leave it so, if you dont mind.

DOOLITTLE. And youll come to the church, Colonel, and put me through straight?

PICKERING. With pleasure. As far as a bachelor can.

MRS HIGGINS. May I come, Mr Doolittle? I should be very sorry to miss your wedding.

DOOLITTLE. I should indeed be honored by your condescension, maam; and my poor old woman would take it as a tremenjous compliment. She's been very low, thinking of the happy days that are no more.

MRS HIGGINS *(rising)*. I'll order the carriage and get ready. *(The men rise, except HIG-GINS.)* I shant be more than fifteen minutes. *(As she goes to the door ELIZA comes in, hatted and buttoning her gloves.)* I'm going to the church to see your father married, Eliza. You had better come in the brougham² with me. Colonel Pickering can go on with the bridegroom.

(MRS HIGGINS goes out. ELIZA comes to the middle of the room between the centre window and the ottoman. PICKERING joins her.)

DOOLITTLE. Bridegroom! What a word! It makes a man realize his position, some-how. *(He takes up his hat and goes towards the door.)*

PICKERING. Before I go, Eliza, do forgive him and come back to us.

LIZA. I dont think papa would allow me. Would you, dad?

DOOLITTLE *(sad but magnanimous)*. They played you off very cunning, Eliza, them two sportsmen. If it had been only one of them, you could have nailed him. But you see, there was two; and one of them chaperoned the other, as you might say. *(To PICKERING)* It was artful of you, Colonel; but I bear no malice: I should have done the same myself. I been the victim of one woman after another all my life; and I dont grudge you two getting the better of Eliza. I shant interfere. It's time for us to go, Colonel. So long, Henry. See you in St George's, Eliza. *(He goes out.)*

PICKERING *(coaxing)*. Do stay with us, Eliza. *(He follows DOOLITTLE).*

(ELIZA goes out on the balcony to avoid being alone with HIGGINS. He rises and joins her there. She immediately comes back into the room and makes for the door; but he goes along the balcony quickly and gets his back to the door before she reaches it.)

HIGGINS. Well, Eliza, youve had a bit of your own back, as you call it. Have you had enough? and are you going to be reasonable? Or do you want any more?

LIZA. You want me back only to pick up your slippers and put up with your tempers and fetch and carry for you.

HIGGINS. I havnt said I wanted you back at all.

LIZA. Oh, indeed. Then what are we talking about?

HIGGINS. About you, not about me. If you come back I shall treat you just as I have always treated you. I cant change my nature; and I dont intend to change my manners. My manners are exactly the same as Colonel Pickering's.

LIZA. Thats not true. He treats a flower girl as if she was a duchess.

HIGGINS. And I treat a duchess as if she was a flower girl.

LIZA. I see. *(She turns away composedly, and sits on the ottoman, facing the window.)* The same to everybody.

HIGGINS. Just so.

LIZA. Like father.

HIGGINS *(grinning, a little taken down)*. Without accepting the comparison at all points, Eliza, it's quite true that your father is not a snob, and that he will be quite at home in any station of life to which his eccentric destiny may call him. *(Seriously)* The great secret, Eliza, is not having bad manners or good manners or any other particular sort of manners, but having the same manner for all human souls: in short, behaving as if

---

2. **brougham** (brōōm): a four-wheeled carriage.

you were in Heaven, where there are no third-class carriages, and one soul is as good as another.

LIZA. Amen. You are a born preacher.

HIGGINS (irritated). The question is not whether I treat you rudely, but whether you ever heard me treat anyone else better.

LIZA (with sudden sincerity). I dont care how you treat me. I dont mind your swearing at me. I dont mind a black eye: Ive had one before this. But (standing up and facing him) I wont be passed over.

HIGGINS. Then get out of my way; for I wont stop for you. You talk about me as if I were a motor bus.

LIZA. So you are a motor bus: all bounce and go, and no consideration for anyone. But I can do without you: dont think I cant.

HIGGINS. I know you can. I told you you could.

LIZA (wounded, getting away from him to the other side of the ottoman with her face to the hearth). I know you did, you brute. You wanted to get rid of me.

HIGGINS. Liar.

LIZA. Thank you. (She sits down with dignity.)

HIGGINS. You never asked yourself, I suppose, whether I could do without you.

LIZA (earnestly). Dont you try to get round me. Youll have to do without me.

HIGGINS (arrogant). I can do without anybody. I have my own soul: my own spark of divine fire. But (with sudden humility) I shall miss you, Eliza. (He sits down near her on the ottoman.) I have learnt something from your idiotic notions: I confess that humbly and gratefully. And I have grown accustomed to your voice and appearance. I like them, rather.

LIZA. Well, you have both of them on your gramophone and in your book of photographs. When you feel lonely without me, you can turn the machine on. It's got no feelings to hurt.

HIGGINS. I cant turn your soul on. Leave me those feelings; and you can take away the voice and the face. They are not you.

LIZA. Oh, you are a devil. You can twist the heart in a girl as easy as some could twist her arms to hurt her. Mrs Pearce warned me. Time and again she has wanted to leave you; and you always got round her at the last minute. And you dont care a bit for her. And you dont care a bit for me.

HIGGINS. I care for life, for humanity; and you are a part of it that has come my way and been built into my house. What more can you or anyone ask?

LIZA. I wont care for anybody that doesnt care for me.

HIGGINS. Commercial principles, Eliza. Like (reproducing her Covent Garden pronunciation with professional exactness) s'yollin voylets [selling violets], isn't it?

LIZA. Dont sneer at me. It's mean to sneer at me.

HIGGINS. I have never sneered in my life. Sneering doesnt become either the human face or the human soul. I am expressing my righteous contempt for Commercialism. I dont and wont trade in affection. You call me a brute because you couldnt buy a claim on me by fetching my slippers and finding my spectacles. You were a fool: I think a woman fetching a man's slippers is a disgusting sight: did I ever fetch your slippers? I think a good deal more of you for throwing them in my face. No use slaving for me and then saying you want to be cared for: who cares for a slave? If you come back, come back for the sake of good fellowship; for youll get nothing else. Youve had a thousand times as much out of me as I have out of you; and if you dare to set up your little dog's tricks of fetching and carrying slippers against my creation of a Duchess Eliza, I'll slam the door in your silly face.

LIZA. What did you do it for if you didnt care for me?

HIGGINS (heartily). Why, because it was my job.

LIZA. You never thought of the trouble it would make for me.

HIGGINS. Would the world ever have been made if its maker had been afraid of making trouble? Making life means making trouble. Theres only one way of escaping trouble; and thats killing things. Cowards, you notice, are always shrieking to have troublesome people killed.

LIZA. I'm no preacher: I dont notice things like that. I notice that you dont notice me.

HIGGINS *(jumping up and walking about intolerantly)*. Eliza: youre an idiot. I waste the treasures of my Miltonic mind by spreading them before you. Once for all, understand that I go my way and do my work without caring twopence what happens to either of us. I am not intimidated, like your father and your stepmother. So you can come back or go to the devil: which you please.

LIZA. What am I to come back for?

HIGGINS *(bouncing up on his knees on the ottoman and leaning over it to her)*. For the fun of it. Thats why I took you on.

LIZA *(with averted face)*. And you may throw me out tomorrow if I dont do everything you want me to?

HIGGINS. Yes; and you may walk out tomorrow if I dont do everything you want me to.

LIZA. And live with my stepmother?

HIGGINS. Yes, or sell flowers.

LIZA. Oh! if I only could go back to my flower basket! I should be independent of both you and father and all the world! Why did you take my independence from me? Why did I give it up? I'm a slave now, for all my fine clothes.

HIGGINS. Not a bit. I'll adopt you as my daughter and settle money on you if you like. Or would you rather marry Pickering?

LIZA *(looking fiercely round at him)*. I wouldnt marry you if you asked me; and youre nearer my age than what he is.

HIGGINS *(gently)*. Than he is: not "than what he is."

LIZA *(losing her temper and rising)*. I'll talk as I like. Youre not my teacher now.

HIGGINS *(reflectively)*. I dont suppose Pickering would, though. He's as confirmed an old bachelor as I am.

LIZA. Thats not what I want; and dont you think it. Ive always had chaps enough wanting me that way. Freddy Hill writes to me twice and three times a day, sheets and sheets.

HIGGINS *(disagreeably surprised)*. Damn his impudence! *(He recoils and finds himself sitting on his heels.)*

LIZA. He has a right to if he likes, poor lad. And he does love me.

HIGGINS *(getting off the ottoman)*. You have no right to encourage him.

LIZA. Every girl has a right to be loved.

HIGGINS. What! By fools like that?

LIZA. Freddy's not a fool. And if he's weak and poor and wants me, may be he'd make me happier than my betters that bully me and dont want me.

HIGGINS. Can he make anything of you? Thats the point.

LIZA. Perhaps I could make something of him. But I never thought of us making anything of one another; and you never think of anything else. I only want to be natural.

HIGGINS. In short, you want me to be as infatuated about you as Freddy? Is that it?

LIZA. No I dont. Thats not the sort of feeling I want from you. And dont you be too sure of yourself or of me. I could have been a bad girl if I'd liked. Ive seen more of some things than you, for all your learning. Girls like me can drag gentlemen down to make love to them easy enough. And they wish each other dead the next minute.

HIGGINS. Of course they do. Then what in thunder are we quarrelling about?

LIZA *(much troubled)*. I want a little kindness. I know I'm a common ignorant girl, and you a book-learned gentleman; but I'm not dirt under your feet. What I done *(correcting herself)* what I did was not for the dresses and the taxis: I did it because we were pleasant together and I come—came —to care for you; not to want you to make love to me, and not forgetting the difference between us, but more friendly like.

HIGGINS. Well, of course. Thats just how I feel. And how Pickering feels. Eliza: youre a fool.

LIZA. Thats not a proper answer to give me *(she sinks on the chair at the writing-table in tears.)*

HIGGINS. It's all youll get until you stop being a common idiot. If youre going to be a lady, youll have to give up feeling neglected if the men you know dont spend half their time snivelling over you and the other half giving you black eyes. If you cant stand the coldness of my sort of life, and the strain of it, go back to the gutter. Work til you are more a brute than a human being; and then cuddle and squabble and drink til you fall asleep. Oh, it's a fine life, the life of the gutter. It's real: it's warm: it's violent: you can feel it through the thickest skin: you can taste it and smell it without any training or any work. Not like Science and Literature and Classical Music and Philosophy and Art. You find me cold, unfeeling, selfish, dont you? Very well: be off with you to the sort of people you like. Marry some sentimental hog or other with lots of money, and a thick pair of lips to kiss you with and a thick pair of boots to kick you with. If you cant appreciate what youve got, youd better get what you can appreciate.

LIZA *(desperate)*. Oh, you are a cruel tyrant. I cant talk to you: you turn everything against me: I'm always in the wrong. But you know very well all the time that youre nothing but a bully. You know I cant go back to the gutter, as you call it, and that I have no real friends in the world but you and the Colonel. You know well I couldn't bear to live with a low common man after you two; and it's wicked and cruel of you to insult me by pretending I could. You think I must go back to Wimpole Street because I have nowhere else to go but father's. But dont you be too sure that you have me under your feet to be trampled on and talked down. I'll marry Freddy, I will, as soon as he's able to support me.

HIGGINS *(sitting down beside her)*. Rubbish! you shall marry an ambassador. You shall marry the Governor-General of India or the Lord-Lieutenant of Ireland, or somebody who wants a deputy-queen. I'm not going to have my masterpiece thrown away on Freddy.

LIZA. You think I like you to say that. But I havent forgot what you said a minute ago; and I wont be coaxed round as if I was a baby or a puppy. If I cant have kindness, I'll have independence.

HIGGINS. Independence? Thats middle class blasphemy. We are all dependent on one another, every soul of us on earth.

LIZA *(rising determinedly)*. I'll let you see whether I'm dependent on you. If you can preach, I can teach. I'll go and be a teacher.

HIGGINS. Whatll you teach, in heaven's name?

LIZA. What you taught me. I'll teach phonetics.

HIGGINS. Ha! ha! ha!

LIZA. I'll offer myself as an assistant to Professor Nepean.

HIGGINS *(rising in a fury)*. What! That impostor! that humbug! that toadying ignoramus! Teach him my methods! my discoveries! You take one step in his direction and I'll wring your neck. *(He lays hands on her.)* Do you hear?

LIZA *(defiantly non-resistant)*. Wring away. What do I care? I knew youd strike me some day. *(He lets her go, stamping with rage at having forgotten himself, and recoils so hastily that he stumbles back into his seat on the ottoman.)* Aha! Now I know how to deal with you. What a fool I was not to think of it before! You cant take away the knowledge you gave me. You said I had a finer ear than you. And I can be civil and kind to people, which is more than you can. Aha! Thats done you, Henry Higgins, it has. Now I dont care that *(snapping her fingers)* for your bullying and your big talk. I'll advertize it in the papers that your duchess is only a flower girl that you taught, and that she'll teach anybody to be a duchess just the same in six months for a thousand guineas. Oh, when I think of myself crawling under your feet and being trampled on and called names, when all the time I had only to lift up my finger to be as good as you, I could just kick myself.

HIGGINS *(wondering at her)*. You damned impudent slut, you! But it's better than snivelling; better than fetching slippers and finding spectacles, isn't it? *(Rising)* By George, Eliza, I said I'd make a woman of you; and I have. I like you like this.

LIZA. Yes: you turn round and make up to me now that I'm not afraid of you, and can do without you.

HIGGINS. Of course I do, you little fool. Five minutes ago you were like a millstone round my neck. Now youre a tower of strength: a consort battleship. You and I and Pickering will be three old bachelors together instead of only two men and a silly girl.

(MRS HIGGINS returns, dressed for the wedding. ELIZA instantly becomes cool and elegant.)

MRS HIGGINS. The carriage is waiting, Eliza. Are you ready?

LIZA. Quite. Is the Professor coming?

MRS HIGGINS. Certainly not. He cant behave himself in church. He makes remarks out loud all the time on the clergyman's pronunciation.

LIZA. Then I shall not see you again, Professor. Goodbye. *(She goes to the door.)*

MRS HIGGINS *(coming to* HIGGINS*)*. Goodbye, dear.

HIGGINS. Goodbye, mother. *(He is about to kiss her, when he recollects something.)* Oh, by the way, Eliza, order a ham and a Stilton cheese, will you? And buy me a pair of reindeer gloves, number eights, and a tie to match that new suit of mine, at Eale & Binman's. You can choose the color. *(His cheerful, careless, vigorous voice shows that he is incorrigible.)*

LIZA *(disdainfully)*. Buy them yourself. *(She sweeps out.)*

MRS HIGGINS. I'm afraid youve spoiled that girl, Henry. But never mind, dear: I'll buy you the tie and gloves.

HIGGINS *(sunnily)*. Oh, dont bother. She'll buy em all right enough. Goodbye.

(They kiss. MRS HIGGINS *runs out.* HIGGINS, *left alone, rattles his cash in his pocket; chuckles; and disports himself in a highly self-satisfied manner.)*

Act Five

Getting at Meaning

1. At the end of Act Four, Higgins seems resigned to Liza's departure. At the opening of Act Five, however, he and Pickering summon police help in locating Liza. Does Higgins now want Liza back? If so, what has changed his mind? If not, what does he want?

2. When Liza enters the room, is she really as at ease as she appears to be? What subtle point is she making when she comments on Higgins's health and on the weather?

3. Mrs. Higgins accuses Pickering and her son of having been brutal with Liza, a charge that they deny vehemently. Is Mrs. Higgins right to use the word *brutal*? Explain.

4. Why does Doolittle feel trapped by his good fortune? What is paradoxical about his rise in status? What parallels can be drawn between his transformation and Liza's?

5. According to Liza, why is Pickering responsible for her becoming a lady? How are Higgins, Pickering, and Doolittle alike, according to Higgins? What is his view of independence? of commercialism in human relations? Do his actions in this act or earlier in the play contradict or affirm his statements? Explain.

6. Higgins offers to adopt Liza, to settle money on her, and to arrange for her to marry Pickering. Do you think that he is being facetious? Does Liza think so? Looking fiercely at him, she says, "I wouldnt marry you if you asked me." Does she really mean that? Support your answer with evidence from the play.

7. Higgins contrasts the life of the gutter, which is real, warm, and violent, with the colder life of the intellect, which requires training and dedication. What view of human nature underlies this speech?

8. Higgins says that he admires Liza for defying him. Does he mean it, or is he shifting his approach to get his own way? What kind of life does he envision if Liza were to return to his household? Is this what Liza wants? Explain.

9. Liza talks about becoming a lady; so does Higgins as a rule. At one point, however, he says, ". . . I said I'd make a woman of you; and I have." Why is his use of *woman* significant?

Developing Skills in Reading Literature

1. **Indeterminate Ending.** When a work ends with no definite resolution, the ending is called indeterminate. At the end of Act Five, Higgins is convinced that Liza will return to his household. As the play ends, "Higgins, left alone, rattles his cash in his pocket; chuckles; and disports himself in a highly self-satisfied manner." Will Liza come back? Is Higgins self-satisfied because he has created a female version of himself? Notice that Liza does not punctuate her exit by slamming the door. Is this a hint that she might come back?

Shaw wrote an epilogue to this play in which he explains what happens to the characters. What questions might be answered in the epilogue? What do you think the future holds for each of the characters?

2. **Thematic Unity.** In Act Five, Shaw brings together the important characters and highlights the points that he has made throughout the preceding four acts. For example, Higgins ridicules as "commercialism" the traditional relation between the sexes, thus recalling earlier references to marriage as contrary to natural human impulses. Point out several other examples of ideas in this act that are introduced earlier in the play.

3. **Comedy.** Most romantic comedies end with an actual or anticipated wedding. Shaw treats this convention ironically by providing the wedding of Alfred Doolittle. How does his wedding mock the traditional romantic wedding?

From Shakespeare's time and even earlier, playwrights have used characters from the poorest classes to provide broad farcical humor. Why is it ironic that Shaw uses the same device? What makes the scenes with Doolittle so humorous? Why can Doolittle's scene in Act Five be viewed as comic relief, even though the entire play is a comedy?

4. **Character.** Shaw turns the conventions of character upside down. His hero, although charming, is nonetheless rude and disagreeable, cold, pompous, and demanding; his heroine is spunky and independent, not at all the type to be swept off her feet by romantic illusion. Comment on how these characters and Mrs. Higgins and Freddy, too, might have surprised audiences accustomed to more conventional characters. What is Shaw's satiric purpose in providing the unexpected rather than the expected?

Review the list of characters at the beginning of the play. Which are portrayed most sympathetically? In Act Five, Higgins says, "Doolittle: either youre an honest man or a rogue." Doolittle answers, "A little of both, Henry, like the rest of us: a little of both." How do Shaw's characters reflect this view of human nature? Are all the characters highly original, or are some the kinds of stock characters typical of traditional drama? Explain.

Developing Writing Skills

1. **Analyzing Character.** The characters Liza and Higgins unfold throughout the play, with each scene revealing a new dimension. Both emerge as complex, consistent characters; they behave in a way that is logical, given their basic qualities. Choose either Liza or Higgins, and in a well organized essay trace the development of the character through all five acts. In your conclusion comment on how the character as portrayed in Act Five is consistent with the character as introduced in Act One.

2. **Analyzing Theme.** In *Pygmalion,* Shaw attempts to give audiences a new perspective on society. He satirizes the class system and the prevailing and often hypocritical views of marriage, money, morality, and the relationship between men and women. Choose three of these topics, and in a well developed essay discuss for each (a) the accepted view criticized by Shaw, (b) Shaw's own ideas, and (c) the way that Shaw dramatizes his ideas. Include several quotations from the play to support your points.

3. **Writing a Review.** Imagine that you have just seen *Pygmalion* performed, and write a review of the play. In the review mention any aspects of the play that now seem dated and speculate on the reasons for the enduring popularity of the play.

4. **Writing a Play.** Write a one-act play that utilizes the Pygmalion myth. Whether you choose to write a satirical comedy or a straight drama, plan your play so that it has two main characters, one conflict, a contemporary setting, and few changes of scene. If you decide to write satire, focus clearly on one specific improvement that you would like to see made.

Unit Review *The Twentieth Century: New Directions*

Understanding the Unit

1. A major theme in the literature of this period is the isolation of human beings from one another. How is this theme treated in works such as "The Secret Sharer," "Shooting an Elephant," "Miss Brill," "The Rocking-Horse Winner," "Journey of the Magi" and *Pygmalion?*

2. In which selection in this unit is nature important either as subject or setting? What relation between human beings and the natural world is suggested in the six poems beginning with "The Wild Swans at Coole" and ending with "Fern Hill"? In which short stories does nature imagery contribute to the tone or mood?

3. Huxley writes, "The language we use about war is inappropriate." To what extent do the war poems in this unit contain language that is more appropriate? Describe the feelings about war—for example, anger, resignation, pity, disillusionment, idealism, or disgust —that are expressed in these war poems. Do you notice any examples of the dangerous abstractions that Huxley warned against? How do the two Orwell selections echo this warning?

4. E.M. Forster, distinguishing between story and plot, says: "A story is a narrative of events in their time-sequence. A plot is also a narrative of events, the emphasis falling on causality." Aristotle in his *Poetics* stresses the importance of plot as the "imitation of an action," and insists that the sequence of events should have a causal, inevitable quality: "A good plot goes from possibility to probability to necessity." Which selections do you think most closely adhere to this Aristotelian ideal? Choose one and demonstrate how each part of the action seems to lead inevitably to the next.

5. Choose a selection in which character is more interesting than plot, and analyze the means by which the main character or characters are portrayed. To what extent is the characterization of each achieved (a) through physical description, (b) through dialogue spoken by character and by other characters, (c) through the character's actions, (d) through the reactions of other characters, and (e) through the charac-ter's inner thoughts and feelings? Comment on the point of view and on whether the characters are static or dynamic (unchanged or changed by their experiences).

6. Compare and contrast several selections that develop varying or opposing views of human mortality. You might consider the following: the poetry of Thomas and Eliot, certain of the war poems, and "Old Mrs. Grey."

Writing

1. In "The Second Coming," William Butler Yeats summed up the prevailing mood of the postwar period, a sense that old values and verities had lost their hold and a foreboding of worse things to come:

Things fall apart; the center cannot hold;
Mere anarchy is loosed upon the world,
The blood-dimmed tide is loosed, and everywhere
The ceremony of innocence is drowned;
The best lack all conviction, while the worst
Are full of passionate intensity.

In a well developed essay, discuss how these preoccupations are expressed in the poetry and prose of this unit.

2. In "Preface to *The Nigger of the 'Narcissus,'*" Joseph Conrad describes the artist as follows:

[The artist] speaks to our capacity for delight and wonder, to the sense of mystery surrounding our lives; to our sense of pity, and beauty, and pain; to the latent feeling of fellowship with all creation— and to the subtle, but invincible, conviction of solidarity that knits together the loneliness of innumerable hearts, to the solidarity in dreams, in joy, in sorrow, in aspirations, in illusions, in hope, in fear, which binds men to each other, which binds together all humanity—the dead to the living and the living to the unborn.

Discuss how "The Secret Sharer" and at least three other selections in the unit exemplify these characteristics of artistic expression.

HORNED FORMS, 1944. *Graham Sutherland.*
Tate Gallery, London.

Unit 8

The Twentieth Century:
Modern Period (1939–1984)

YELLOW ATTENUATION, 1965. *Peter Sedgley.*
Tate Gallery, London.

England in the Modern Age

British life in the twentieth century has been characterized by several interrelated trends: the rising political significance of the laboring class; the decline of the wealth and influence of the upper class; repeated economic crises; and lessening prosperity due to aging industries, increasing competition in the world marketplace, and the disintegration of the great British Empire. War has been a hallmark of the age, with two great world wars, separated by only twenty years of uneasy truce and followed by years of disillusionment and uncertainty. The forces that emerged after World War I have come to fruition in the years since World War II, shaping the national character of the contemporary kingdom.

BRITAIN IN WORLD WAR II

World War II was truly a world war, fought on land and sea, in the jungles of Asia, on tiny islands in the Pacific, on the deserts of North Africa, and throughout Europe. From 1939 through most of 1941, when the United States entered the war, however, Britain stood alone against Hitler, who threatened invasion and launched intensive bombing attacks on London and other industrial cities. The entire population mobilized for war, with civilian volunteers acting as plane spotters, fire fighters, rescue and demolition workers, police officers, and ambulance drivers. Londoners slept in the subways, while incendiary bombs rained on the city above. Thousands of civilians died; precious cultural treasures and architectural landmarks were destroyed as were hundreds of thousands of homes and shops, schools, churches, and libraries. During this period, known as the Battle of Britain, a small number of well trained fighter pilots persistently battered away at the German bombers and fighter planes. Winston Churchill, Britain's courageous wartime Prime Minister, praised these heroes, saying, "Never in the field of human conflict was so much owed by so many to so few."

The spirit of determination and patriotism that inspired the British to great acts of courage during the bombing raids sustained them throughout the rest of the war. They put up with shortages and rationing, exhausting labor, and restrictive military government, and they mourned the deaths of soldiers, pilots, and sailors abroad and of more than a quarter of a million civilians at home. Finally in 1945 Germany and Japan surrendered, ending the long years of fighting.

THE AFTERMATH OF WAR

One newspaper described the people of England after World War II as weary with "forever making do, and mending in a way of life that is drab, grubby, undersoaped, and starved of color." Wracked by poverty among all classes and desperately in need of re-creating social order, the country turned to its young liberals for leadership, electing the Labor Party by an overwhelming majority.

For the next six years the Labor government implemented a policy of strict control over industry and personal economy that transformed Britain into a welfare state. Wartime rationing continued, with meat, gas, tobacco, dairy products, fruit, sheets, towels, and clothing among the restricted items. Labor-sponsored legislation extended the provisions for free medical and dental care, unemployment protection, state-built housing with regulated rents, and generous maternity and death benefits. The British government, which already owned the telephone and telegraph companies, the airlines, the trucking companies, the radio stations, docks and harbors, and public utilities, now took over, or nationalized, the steel, coal, and iron industries, the railroads and bus lines, the overseas cable and radio networks, and the Bank of England.

The British economy could ill afford to finance expensive social programs and to subsidize nationalized industries. The country was deeply in debt, forced to borrow heavily from the United States and to sell lucrative foreign investments to finance the war and to pay for imported food. The new high taxes imposed on the middle and upper classes raised the living standard of the poor and laboring classes. They were insufficient, however, to establish domestic prosperity while continuing to support troops stationed in defeated Germany and in the Balkans and colonial governments throughout the world.

The socialization and nationalization that took place in the postwar years set the direction of British society. Even under Conservative administrations, few industries were de-nationalized and few social programs were discontinued.

The early 1950's marked a turning point in the grim postwar decade. In 1953 Queen Elizabeth II was crowned queen in an elaborate ceremony filled with tradition. This event recalled England's tradition of greatness and seemed to symbolize new hope. By the mid-1950's economic recovery was evident. Food rationing was finally ended; taxes were lowered somewhat; and industries such as machinery, chemicals, appliances, automobiles, and tourism prospered. Overall, however, Britain has never regained its former position as a dominant economic power. Strikes, competition, inflation, fuel shortages, and other factors related to the international economy have limited British economic growth relative to other industrialized nations.

THE INTERNATIONAL SCENE

In the decades after World War II, Britain yielded to nationalistic and economic pressures and relinquished control of nearly all her remaining colonies. With only a few notable exceptions, the transitions from colonies and protectorates to independent nations were orderly. India, Pakistan, Ceylon (Sri Lanka), Burma, Ghana, Kenya, Nigeria, Sudan, Uganda, Rhodesia (Zimbabwe), Trinidad, Tobago, and many other former possessions joined the United Nations as independent nations, most still members of the British Commonwealth.

Relationships among the major countries of the world also were changing. The United States and the Soviet Union vied for world dominance, and Communist China emerged as a powerful new political force. An "iron curtain" divided East from West, and "cold war" threatened international security. The best hope for peace was thought to lie in a balance of power, with superior force as the major deterrent to war. Britain's foreign policy was closely aligned with that of the United States. From 1950 to 1953 British troops fought in the Korean War alongside American troops, and the British government permitted the United States to establish military bases in England, a cause for protest by anti-nuclear groups in the 1980's.

European alliances forged in the postwar years include the North Atlantic Treaty Organization (NATO) and the European Economic Community, known as the Common Market. Britain joined NATO but was at first reluctant to participate in the Common Market, fearing entanglement in Continental politics and a weakening of ties to the Commonwealth nations. Britain finally petitioned for membership in the 1960's and was accepted in 1973.

THE ROOTS OF RADICALISM

After World War II many intellectuals questioned whether western civilization could ever be reconstructed. During the 1950's they saw no hope for redemption under socialism, capitalism, or communism, and they commented on society from a position of detachment. Their view of postwar life is expressed in an editorial in the *London Times*, December 28, 1956, which describes society as "sick and convulsed as never before. . . . Never have frustrations and disloyalties been so widespread. . . . Never have law and order come into such worldwide disregard."

By the late 1950's a new movement of working-class leftists and young student radicals began to take shape. Called the "angry young men" in John Osborne's play *Look Back in Anger* (1956), they represented a mood of dissatisfaction with conservative political leadership and voiced disdain for traditional institutions and contempt for their apathetic contemporaries.

THE RADICAL REVOLT

Many of the angry young men and their heirs, the radicals of the 1960's and 1970's, were products of the new universities that were established in the two decades after the war. Overcrowded and impersonal, these institutions became hotbeds of intellectual unrest and social revolution. Young extremists created new anti-heroes and attacked everything official and traditional. Nothing associated with the "Establishment" escaped ridicule: religion, the royal family, Parliament, sexual inhibitions. Pop artists parodied traditional art by painting "portraits" of soup cans and by constructing gigantic, stuffed canvas loaves of bread. Op artists made use of geometrical patterns to create unusual effects such as the illusion of movement. Beat poets staged popular poetry readings in which they promoted individuality and personal freedom. Avant-garde musicians wrote "environmental sounds and noises," discarding tonality and experimenting with electronic music and computer composition. One dramatist illustrated the ultimate break with tradition when he wrote a play that lasted thirty seconds and that presented no actors, dialogue, or action, just a pile of trash on stage and the sounds of a baby's amplified cry and breathing.

During this same period "Beatlemania" swept the world, initiating a craze for British rock groups and for British pop culture that lasted through the 1970's.

Meanwhile, a small group of British intellectuals lamented the dissolution of art and criticized the avant-garde for re-creating what was new fifty years earlier and calling it original. The majority of the English were unaffected by experimentation, trendiness, and anti-traditionalism. They continued to attend revivals of Shakespearean and other classics and performances of classic and new ballets and operas and to enjoy the same kinds of entertainments as had their predecessors.

BRITAIN IN A TECHNOLOGICAL AGE

World War II stimulated technology, particularly in aviation, shipbuilding, communications, and weaponry. The development of the atomic bomb foreshadowed the nuclear age, and in the late 1950's and early 1960's Britain became one of the first nuclear powers. In the 1950's scientists experimented with computers, which led to a revolution in the processing of information. More recently, medical researchers have discovered the exact way in which genes transmit hereditary characteristics, which has raised the possibility of artificially determining the inherited characteristics of human beings. Laser technology has transformed fields as different as film making and brain surgery. Television has revolutionized British society, and satellite communication and jet travel have ended any lingering sense of the isolation once felt by the people of this island nation. Britain has not pioneered in all these areas, yet the achievements of technology affect profoundly the way that the British view themselves and their world.

CULTURAL REPERCUSSIONS

Britain is a relatively homogeneous society, yet the cultural unity that marked earlier historical periods no longer characterizes contemporary society. Immigrants from third-world countries have brought their own traditions and behavior patterns, often causing conflict with the established citizenry. A major contributing factor to cultural fragmentation has to do with sheer numbers. Four hundred years ago Sir Walter Raleigh boasted that he bought every book that was published. Today, publishers in Western Europe and the United States produce at least 100,000 new titles each year, more than any one person could possibly read.

Fragmentation is manifested in the destruction of standards, the breakdown of social order, and isolation among individuals and groups. Rapidly changing fashions and the rejection of tradition for novelty pervade all areas of life, resulting in the so-called generation gap. Seemingly, only people of nearly the same age can share in cultural intimacies such as songs, jokes, books, and colloquial expressions.

Despite these problems, which plague all western societies, Britain does have a cultural core, maintained through national support for the arts. Opera, ballet, and theatre companies, orchestras, and exhibits preserve British heritage, encourage the development of new talent, and constitute a major attraction for tourists and British alike.

LITERARY TRENDS

Unlike World War I, the Second World War did not signal a sharp break in literary continuity. While the writers after World War I explored new subjects, forms, and themes, the majority of those after World War II tended to be more traditional in philosophy and style. Many of the writers who had matured during the 1920's and 1930's continued to be active through the postwar decade and beyond. Among them were T. S. Eliot, W. H. Auden, Stephen Spender, Elizabeth Bowen, George Orwell, William Golding, and Aldous Huxley. These writers responded in various ways to the alienation and cynicism of the postwar period. Eliot and Auden sought alternatives in religion and spirituality; Orwell, Golding, and Huxley all projected the dire consequences of postwar trends. The dark mysteries of life and death no longer were the prime concerns of serious writers, who instead focused on personal experiences and on political and social issues.

The young poets, dramatists, and novelists who emerged during this period struggled to come to terms with a changed and changing world and explored its impact on individuals and their sustaining relationships. The "angry young men" of the 1950's articulated the resentments of the working class in plays, novels, and films. These writers were a new kind of intellectual avant-garde, who considered the innovators of earlier periods "phoney" and "high brow." Osborne's *Look Back in Anger*, John Braine's *Room at the Top* (1957), and Alan Sillitoe's *The Loneliness of the Long Distance Runner*

(1959) were a new kind of literature, traditional in structure but original in subject and point of view.

The theatre was an important forum for the "angry young men" and for their more radical contemporaries. Samuel Beckett, Harold Pinter, and others associated with the Theatre of the Absurd abandoned realism, plot, and characterization in order to communicate a sense of the emptiness and absurdity of modern existence. In Beckett's *Waiting for Godot* (1952), for example, two characters wait pointlessly for the arrival of an unknown something or someone. In more recent works, the experimenters of the 1950's and 1960's and

Literature

- Elizabeth Bowen (1899-1973) publishes first novel *The Death of the Heart* set in wartime England

- W.H. Auden (1907-1973) writes poetry and becomes associated with politics of the Left

- Winston Churchill (1874-1965) delivers "blood, toil, tears, and sweat" speech

- H.R. Trevor-Roper (b. 1914) publishes *The Last Days of Hitler*

- Judith Wright (b. 1915) publishes first book of poetry

- J.B. Priestley (b. 1984) publishes *Delight*

- Doris Lessing (b. 1919) publishes first novel *The Grass is Singing* based upon her experiences in Rhodesia

- Frank O'Connor (1903-1966) publishes collection of short stories

- Samuel Beckett (b. 1906) writes *Waiting for Godot*, creating a new "theatre of the absurd"

- Collected poems of Stephen Spender (b. 1909) published

- John Osborne (b. 1929) writes *Look Back in Anger*, introducing term "angry young men"

- John Braine (b. 1922) writes novel *Room at the Top*

- Ted Hughes (b. 1930) publishes *The Hawk in the Rain*

| 1939 | 1945 | 1950 | 1955 |

History

- Britain and France declare war on Germany

- Allied invasion of Normandy begins June 6 (D-Day), ending German offensive in Europe

- Paris Peace Treaty ends World War II

- The end of World War II is proclaimed on May 8

- General election in Britain brings Labor landslide

- U.N. Charter is signed

- British mandate over Palestine ends as Jewish State of Israel is proclaimed

- NATO is formed to safeguard West against Soviet aggression

- Korean War begins

- Queen Elizabeth II ascends throne

- Armistice ends Korean War in which Britain and America were allies

- Big Four (Britain, U.S., France, and U.S.S.R) meet to discuss German reorganization

- British conservatives win general election. Church forms government

- Six-nation treaty signed Rome begins Common Market but Britain does not join

- Russians launch *Sputnik* ushering in period of intensely competitive space technology

the new young dramatists have been less intent on pushing the limits of dramatic convention and have created more realistic drama concerned with society and the human condition.

Contemporary drama has become increasingly interrelated with motion pictures and television. Adaptations from stage to screen are common, and a new dramatic work is as likely to debut on the screen as on the stage. The impact of this trend on dramatic literature has yet to become clear, although it is likely that playwrights will continue to work out their themes within traditional structures.

- Harold Pinter (b. 1930) writes *The Birthday Party*

- Alan Sillitoe (b. 1928) writes *The Loneliness of the Long Distance Runner*

- Seamus Heaney (b.1939) publishes *Eleven Poems*

- Wole Soyinka (b. 1934) publishes first volume of collected poetry

- Arthur C. Clarke (b. 1917) writes *2001: A Space Odyssey*

- Margaret Atwood (b. 1939) publishes *The Edible Woman*

| 1960 | 1965 | 1970 | 1975 | 1980 |

- Nuclear test ban treaty is signed by U.S., Britain, and the U.S.S.R.

- Beatles gain popularity

- Prime Minister Wilson announces "standstill" in wages and prices

- Terrorism continues in Northern Ireland and spreads to London

- Wilson's Labor Party wins general elections

- British send troops to Belfast in response to violent fighting between Catholics and Protestants

- Conservative Party wins general election

- Britain imposes direct rule on Northern Ireland

- Great Britain becomes member of Common Market, joining European economic community

TRENDS IN POETRY, FICTION, AND NONFICTION

During the 1950's a group of young poets called "The Movement" introduced a new humanism and accessibility to poetic expression. Rejecting complex styles, they wrote clear, rational, understated poetry on subjects drawn from everyday experiences. "The Movement" poets, particularly Thom Gunn and Ted Hughes, have evolved as artists, moving away from the pared-down simplicity and conservative values advocated in the 1950's. On the whole, modern poets have either denounced or ignored technology, and in more recent years they have addressed the dangers of the nuclear age.

Traditional narrative structures and great variety have characterized postwar fiction, with realism and fantasy as the two distinct strains. The working-class novels of the 1950's, the spy stories of John Le Carré, and documentary-style writing that blurs the distinction between fiction and nonfiction are representative of realistic writing; the science fiction of Arthur C. Clarke and Joan Aiken and the elaborate fairy tales of J. R. R. Tolkien exemplify literary fantasy.

One significant trend that cuts across the genres has been the coming of age of regional and Commonwealth writers, thus broadening the concept of "English" literature. Seamus Heaney (Northern Ireland), Frank O'Connor (Ireland), Doris Lessing and Nadine Gordimer (southern Africa), Wole Soyinka (Nigeria), Judith Wright and Evan Jones (Australia), Margaret Atwood (Canada), and R. S. Thomas (Wales) all enrich English literature with their unique perceptions of common human experiences.

In earlier eras, writers of fiction and nonfiction from diverse fields—social critics, philosophers, scientists, politicians, economists, historians, and psychologists—contributed to the literary mainstream. Today, it is highly unusual for a person to be specialized and technically proficient and also to be a writer of literary merit. The gap widens between scientist and humanist, even as the need for mutual understanding increases.

The Development of the English Language

MODERN PERIOD

Britishers and Americans who debate the superiority of British *vs.* American English often fail to consider the importance of the English of Canada, Australia, and South Africa, of India and New Zealand; yet many popular novels, movies, and musicians come from these places, bringing their distinctive usages with them. Together with the United States, these and other nations contain the great majority of English-speaking people.

Canadian English

Canadian English is more similar to the American variety of English than to the British variety, for reasons that transcend mere proximity. Americans introduced their version of English to Canada during and after the American Revolution, when more than sixty thousand Loyalists fled to Canada. Patterns of immigration gave Canada distinct pronunciations, such as the pronunciation of *about* as "a boot," so that one waggish definition of a Canadian is a person mistaken for an Englishman in America and mistaken for an American in England.

Australian English

The Australian usage is so distinct and vivid that, like the American, it is generally accorded the scholarly status of language rather than dialect. The formal language of Australia is close to standard English, but colloquial usage is colorful and singular. The original dialect was strongly influenced by Cockney prisoners sent to the Australian penal colony, and the Aborigines contributed now common words such as *kangaroo* and *boomerang.*

The English of South Africa

The situation in South Africa illustrates the relationship between language and politics in a multilingual nation. While English remains an important tongue in India and Israel, only in South Africa is the fate of English enmeshed in a volatile political tangle. Britain fought Dutch settlers for South Africa in the Boer War of 1899–1902, after having acquired the Cape Colony from the Dutch in 1814. English was the official language, borrowing many words from native African tongues, including *gnu*, *tsetse*, and *chimpanzee*. However, the Boers clung to their language, refusing to adopt words from black tribes, while many Boer words entered English: *veld*, *spoor*, *trek*, *springbok*. When the Dutch came to political power, they created the system of racial separation known as apartheid, and they favored their Afrikaaner dialect of Dutch to English, which declined in importance. The future of English in South Africa, like the political future of South Africa, remains undecided.

The Question of Correctness

In the United States in the past half-century, attention has focused on nonstandard forms of American English. While some factions argue for more flexibility in accepting nonstandard usages, particularly those common to large ethnic and racial groups, other factions condemn the use of nonstandard English and defend the status quo. In the capitalistic American environment, they contend, a requirement of success is the mastery of standard English, whether of a formal or informal variety. On the other hand, linguistic liberals consider such language strictures prejudicial, even tyrannical.

In England as well as America, the argument between those who deplore nonstandard English and those who mock them as purists and reactionaries continues. In recent decades, the pendulum has swung to favor those who tolerate virtually any usage as appropriate. Samuel Johnson admitted that "the pen must at length comply with the tongue," a position shared by twentieth-century structural linguists who, according to *The American Heritage Dictionary of the English Language*, "would no more criticize a locution than a physicist would criticize an atom or an entomologist a cockroach."

Language and Politics

As groups gain political influence, they use language as both a weapon of the struggle and a proof of the victory. Now that change is rapid, taking place within a few years rather than over many generations, speakers of English must make quick adjustments.

Since the 1960's the women's movement has created new coinages and has attacked certain words and phrases as sexist. *Ms.* was unknown a few decades ago, when *man* and *mankind* were frequently used as synonyms for *human beings* or *humanity*, a practice many now find offensive. In 1940, *black* would have been considered racist, with *Negro* thought of as more acceptably scientific and neutral. During the civil rights movement, though, *black* came to be preferred as a parallel term to *white*.

English in an Electronic Age

The major force for language change in recent years has been the electronic media. Media theorist Marshall McLuhan asserted that life on the planet would be altered in revolutionary ways by electronic communications and described the world as a "global village" with instant communication across continents. He argued that print forces people to think with linear logic, while television leads to the use of quantum logic, a leaping from point to point with relative unconcern for transitions, just as a television program can leap from an image of one continent in one century to another continent in another century in the blink of an eye.

Is print on the way out? Will people think differently if they communicate primarily in spoken language? Will the computerized future bring new patterns of thought and language? These are not simple questions, for language is and will continue to be ever evolving, affecting the way that human beings think. The future of print is indeed uncertain, but the consequences of its decline can be assessed only by future generations of scholars.

Even as a dynamic language, English enjoys relative stability, for which its users can be grateful. English is fixed enough to allow today's readers to understand the works of Shakespeare and Dryden and still flexible enough to allow as free a range of expression as any language on earth.

Elizabeth Bowen

1899–1973

The exquisitely crafted short stories and novels of Elizabeth Bowen reveal universal truths through finely drawn depictions of personal relationships. Often compared with Virginia Woolf and Henry James, Bowen was among the finest writers to emerge after World War I.

Bowen was born in Dublin of Anglo-Irish parents. When she was seven, the family moved to the south of England, where she attended local schools. During the last year of World War I, Bowen worked in a shell-shock hospital in Dublin, and at the end of the war, she left home to live alone in London and then on the Continent. She began to write stories when she was twenty, with her first collection appearing in 1923 under the title *Encounters*. More stories were collected in 1926, a year before the appearance of her first novel, *The Hotel*.

Bowen alternated between the novel and the short story, using similar methods in each genre. She evokes a particular milieu through rich images of texture and color and re-creates impressions as experienced by her characters. A typical protagonist in Bowen's stories is from the upper middle class, innocent or inexperienced, grappling with an inexplicable world for which he or she is unprepared. Among Bowen's most highly praised novels are *The Death of the Heart* (1938), which describes the disillusionment felt by lovers, and *The Heat of the Day* (1949), set in wartime London.

Bowen's narrative style owes a great deal to Henry James. Her sentences, like his, are intricate structures that describe every nuance of a character's cultivated sensibility. Her tone is reminiscent of Jane Austen, conveying humor and common sense with delicacy and restraint.

Bowen's career was diversified as well as distinguished. She was a reviewer for *The Tatler* in 1941 and worked for the Ministry of Information during World War II. From 1954 to 1961, she was on the editorial board of *London Magazine*. Bowen's works defy easy categorization, her subject matter ranging from a history of her family in *Bowen's Court* (1942) to ruminations on her motives in *Why Do I Write? An Exchange of Views Between Elizabeth Bowen, Graham Greene, and V. S. Pritchett* (1948). She also wrote a history of Dublin's Shelbourne Hotel *(The Shelbourne)* in 1951 and a juvenile work titled *The Good Tiger* in 1965.

The Demon Lover

Towards the end of her day in London Mrs. Drover went round to her shut-up house to look for several things she wanted to take away. Some belonged to herself, some to her family, who were by now used to their country life. It was late August; it had been a steamy, showery day: at the moment the trees down the pavement glittered in an escape of humid yellow afternoon sun. Against the next batch of clouds, already piling up ink-dark, broken chimneys and parapets stood out. In her once familiar street, as in any unused channel, an unfamiliar queerness had silted up; a cat wove itself in and out of railings, but no human eye watched Mrs. Drover's return. Shifting some parcels under her arm, she slowly forced round her latchkey in an unwilling lock, then gave the door, which had warped, a push with her knee. Dead air came out to meet her as she went in.

The staircase window having been boarded up, no light came down into the hall. But one door, she could just see, stood ajar, so she went quickly through into the room and unshuttered the big window in there. Now the prosaic woman, looking about her, was more perplexed than she knew by everything that she saw, by traces of her long former habit of life—the yellow smoke stain up the white marble mantelpiece, the ring left by a vase on the top of the escritoire;[1] the bruise in the wallpaper where, on the door being thrown open widely, the china handle had always hit the wall. The piano, having gone away to be stored, had left what looked like claw marks on its part of the parquet.[2] Though not much dust had seeped in, each object wore a film of another kind; and, the only ventilation being the chimney, the whole drawing room smelled of the cold hearth. Mrs. Drover put down her parcels on the escritoire and left the room to proceed upstairs; the things she wanted were in a bedroom chest.

She had been anxious to see how the house was—the part-time caretaker she shared with some neighbors was away this week on his holiday, known to be not yet back. At the best of times he did not look in often, and she was never sure that she trusted him. There were some cracks in the structure, left by the last bombing, on which she was anxious to keep an eye. Not that one could do anything—

A shaft of refracted daylight now lay across the hall. She stopped dead and stared at the hall table—on this lay a letter addressed to her.

She thought first—then the caretaker *must* be back. All the same, who, seeing the house shuttered, would have dropped a letter in at the box? It was not a circular, it was not a bill. And the post office redirected, to the address in the country, everything for her that came through the post. The caretaker (even if he *were* back) did not know she was due in London today—her call here had been planned to be a surprise—so his negligence in the manner of this letter, leaving it to wait in the dusk and the dust, annoyed her. Annoyed, she picked up the letter, which bore no stamp. But it cannot be important, or they would know . . . She took the letter rapidly upstairs with her, without a stop to look at the writing till she reached what had been her bedroom,

---

1. **escritoire** (es′ krə twär′): a writing desk or table.
2. **parquet** (pär kā′): a flooring of inlaid woodwork in geometric forms.

where she let in light. The room looked over the garden and other gardens: the sun had gone in; as the clouds sharpened and lowered, the trees and rank lawns seemed already to smoke with dark. Her reluctance to look again at the letter came from the fact that she felt intruded upon—and by someone contemptuous of her ways. However, in the tenseness preceding the fall of rain she read it: it was a few lines.

Dear Kathleen: You will not have forgotten that today is our anniversary, and the day we said. The years have gone by at once slowly and fast. In view of the fact that nothing has changed, I shall rely upon you to keep your promise. I was sorry to see you leave London, but was satisfied that you would be back in time. You may expect me, therefore, at the hour arranged. Until then . . .

K.

Mrs. Drover looked for the date: it was to-day's. She dropped the letter on to the bed-springs, then picked it up to see the writing again—her lips, beneath the remains of lip-stick, beginning to go white. She felt so much the change in her own face that she went to the mirror, polished a clear patch in it and looked at once urgently and stealthily in. She was confronted by a woman of forty-four, with eyes starting out under a hat-brim that had been rather carelessly pulled down. She had not put on any more powder since she left the shop where she ate her solitary tea. The pearls her husband had given her on their marriage hung loose round her now rather thinner throat, slipping in the V of the pink wool jumper her sister knitted last autumn as they sat round the fire. Mrs. Drover's most normal expression was one of controlled worry, but of assent. Since the birth of the third of her little boys, attended by a quite serious illness, she had had an intermittent muscular flicker to the left of her mouth, but in spite of this she could always sustain a manner that was at once energetic and calm.

Turning from her own face as precipitately as she had gone to meet it, she went to the chest where the things were, unlocked it, threw up the lid and knelt to search. But as rain began to come crashing down she could not keep from looking over her shoulder at the stripped bed on which the letter lay. Behind the blanket of rain the clock of the church that still stood struck six—with rapidly heightening apprehension she counted each of the slow strokes. "The hour arranged . . . My God," she said, "what hour? How should I . . . ? After twenty-five years. . . ."

The young girl talking to the soldier in the garden had not ever completely seen his face. It was dark; they were saying goodbye under a tree. Now and then—for it felt, from not seeing him at this intense moment, as though she had never seen him at all—she verified his presence for these few moments longer by putting out a hand, which he each time pressed, without very much kindness, and painfully, on to one of the breast buttons of his uniform. That cut of the button on the palm of her hand was, principally what she was to carry away. This was so near the end of a leave from France that she could only wish him already gone. It was August 1916. Being not kissed, being drawn away from and looked at intimidated Kathleen till she imagined spectral glitters in the place of his eyes. Turning away and looking back up the lawn she saw, through branches of trees, the drawing room window alight: she caught a breath for the moment when she could go running back there into the safe arms of her mother and sister, and cry: "What shall I do, what shall I do? He has gone."

Hearing her catch her breath, her fiancé said, without feeling: "Cold?"

"You're going away such a long way."

"Not so far as you think."

"I don't understand?"

"You don't have to," he said. "You will. You know what we said."

"But that was—suppose you—I mean, suppose."

"I shall be with you," he said, "sooner or later. You won't forget that. You need do nothing but wait."

Only a little more than a minute later she was free to run up the silent lawn. Looking in through the window at her mother and sister, who did not for the moment perceive her, she already felt that unnatural promise drive down between her and the rest of all human kind. No other way of having given herself could have made her feel so apart, lost and foresworn. She could not have plighted a more sinister troth.

Kathleen behaved well when, some months later, her fiancé was reported missing, presumed killed. Her family not only supported her but were able to praise her courage without stint because they could not regret, as a husband for her, the man they knew almost nothing about. They hoped she would, in a year or two, console herself—and had it been only a question of consolation things might have gone much straighter ahead. But her trouble, behind just a little grief, was a complete dislocation from everything. She did not reject other lovers, for these failed to appear: for years she failed to attract men—and with the approach of her 'thirties she became natural enough to share her family's anxiousness on this score. She began to put herself out, to wonder; and at thirty-two she was very greatly relieved to find herself being courted by William Drover. She married him, and the two of them settled down in this quiet, arboreal part of Kensington: in this house the years piled up, her children were born and they all lived till they were driven out by the bombs of the next war. Her movements as Mrs. Drover were circumscribed, and she dismissed any idea that they were still watched.

As things were—dead or living the letter-writer sent her only a threat. Unable, for some minutes, to go on kneeling with her back exposed to the empty room, Mrs. Drover rose from the chest to sit on an upright chair whose back was firmly against the wall. The desuetude[3] of her former bedroom, her married London home's whole air of being a cracked cup from which memory, with its reassuring power, had either evaporated or leaked away, made a crisis—and at just this crisis the letter-writer had, knowledgeably, struck. The hollowness of the house this evening cancelled years on years of voices, habits and steps. Through the shut windows she only heard rain fall on the roofs around. To rally herself, she said she was in a mood—and, for two or three seconds shutting her eyes, told herself that she had imagined the letter. But she opened them—there it lay on the bed.

On the supernatural side of the letter's entrance she was not permitting her mind to dwell. Who, in London, knew she meant to call at the house today? Evidently, however, this had been known. The caretaker, *had* he come back, had had no cause to expect her: he would have taken the letter in his pocket, to forward it, at his own time, through the post. There was no other sign that the caretaker had been in—but, if not? Letters dropped in at doors of deserted houses do not fly or walk to tables in halls. They do not sit on the dust of empty tables with the air of certainty that they will be found. There is needed some human hand—but nobody but the caretaker had a key. Under circumstances she did not care to consider, a house can be entered without a key. It was possible that she was not alone now. She might be being waited for, downstairs. Waited for—until when? Until "the hour arranged." At least that was not six o'clock: six has struck.

She rose from the chair and went over and locked the door.

The thing was, to get out. To fly? No, not

---

3. **desuetude** (des' wi tood): disuse.

that: she had to catch her train. As a woman whose utter dependability was the keystone of her family life she was not willing to return to the country, to her husband, her little boys and her sister, without the objects she had come up to fetch. Resuming work at the chest she set about making up a number of parcels in a rapid, fumbling-decisive way. These, with her shopping parcels, would be too much to carry; these meant a taxi—at the thought of the taxi her heart went up and her normal breathing resumed. I will ring up the taxi now; the taxi cannot come too soon: I shall hear the taxi out there running its engine, till I walk calmly down to it through the hall. I'll ring up—But no: the telephone is cut off . . . She tugged at a knot she had tied wrong.

The idea of flight . . . He was never kind to me, not really. I don't remember him kind at all. Mother said he never considered me. He was set on me, that was what it was—not love. Not love, not meaning a person well. What did he do, to make me promise like that? I can't remember—But she found that she could.

She remembered with such dreadful acuteness that the twenty-five years since then dissolved like smoke and she instinctively looked for the weal left by the button on the palm of her hand. She remembered not only all that he said and did but the complete suspension of *her* existence during that August week. I was not myself—they all told me so at the time. She remembered—but with one white burning blank as where acid has dropped on a photograph: *under no conditions could she remember his face.*

So, wherever he may be waiting, I shall not know him. You have no time to run from a face you do not expect.

The thing was to get to the taxi before any clock struck what could be the hour. She would slip down the street and round the side of the square to where the square gave on the main road. She would return in the taxi, safe,

to her own door, and bring the solid driver into the house with her to pick up the parcels from room to room. The idea of the taxi driver made her decisive, bold: she unlocked her door, went to the top of the staircase and listened down.

She heard nothing—but while she was hearing nothing the *passé*[4] air of the staircase was disturbed by a draft that traveled up to her face. It emanated from the basement: down there a door or window was being opened by someone who chose this moment to leave the house.

The rain had stopped; the pavements steamily shone as Mrs. Drover let herself out by inches from her own front door into the empty street. The unoccupied houses opposite continued to meet her look with their damaged stare. Making towards the thoroughfare and the taxi, she tried not to keep looking behind. Indeed, the silence was so intense—one of those creeks of London silence exaggerated this summer by the damage of war—that no tread could have gained on hers unheard. Where her street debouched[5] on the square where people went on living, she grew conscious of, and checked, her unnatural pace. Across the open end of the square two buses impassively passed each other: women, a perambulator, cyclists, a man wheeling a barrow signalized, once again, the ordinary flow of life. At the square's most populous corner should be—and was—the short taxi rank. This evening, only one taxi—but this, although it presented its blank rump, appeared already to be alertly waiting for her. Indeed, without looking round, the driver started his engine as she panted up from behind and put her hand on the door. As she did so, the clock struck seven. The taxi faced the main road; to make the trip back to her house it would have to turn—she had settled

---

4. **passé** (pa sā′): stale, out-of-date.
5. **debouched** (di boosh′ 'd): emerged.

back on the seat and the taxi *had* turned before she, surprised by its knowing movement, recollected that she had not "said where." She leaned forward to scratch at the glass panel that divided the driver's head from her own.

The driver braked to what was almost a stop, turned round and slid the glass panel back: the jolt of this flung Mrs. Drover forward till her face was almost into the glass.

Through the aperture driver and passenger, not six inches between them, remained for an eternity eye to eye. Mrs. Drover's mouth hung open for some seconds before she could issue her first scream. After that she continued to scream freely and to beat with her gloved hands on the glass all round as the taxi, accelerating without mercy, made off with her into the hinterland of deserted streets.

Getting at Meaning

1. Why has Mrs. Drover returned to London? What is the condition of her house there? What kind of life had she led in the house?

2. What is unusual about the letter that has been delivered for Mrs. Drover? Describe her first reaction to the contents of the letter. How do her emotions change as she recalls the past?

3. What had been the nature of Mrs. Drover's relationship with the writer of the letter? What disturbing promise did he make to her? What one thing in particular is Mrs. Drover unable to remember about this young man?

4. The writer of the letter says that nothing has changed. What might he have meant? Is he referring to Mrs. Drover herself? to circumstances? to their relationship? Explain.

5. Point out the supernatural elements in this story. What do these elements contribute to the mood of the story?

6. What would you say is the moment of highest dramatic intensity in this story? Is the ending of the story believable? Explain.

Developing Skills in Reading Literature

1. **Flashback.** Various devices may be used to present a flashback within a story; for example, reminiscences by a character, dream sequences, or description by a third-person narrator. What devices does Bowen use to present the flashbacks in this story? Why are these flashbacks essential to the development of the story? How do they add to its dramatic intensity?

2. **Point of View.** This short story is presented, for the most part, by an omniscient third-person narrator who remains detached from the action. On two occasions, however, the point of view shifts to that of the central character, to an interior monologue that reveals the emotions of the character. At what points in the story do these shifts occur? How do they intensify the dramatic effect of the narration?

3. **Setting.** In this story the time of day, the season of the year, the place of the action, and particularly the descriptions of the weather all create an impact upon the reader. Describe these elements of setting, and identify specific lines and phrases that are especially effective in creating mood.

4. **Irony and Foreshadowing.** Sometimes the impact of a short story depends upon an ironic twist at the end of the story. For such an ending to be successful, readers must be surprised, yet they also must be prepared through hints or suggestions that foreshadow the ending. Look for specific examples of foreshadowing in this story. In what way does each example prepare the reader for the ironic ending of the story?

Roald Dahl

born in 1916

Roald Dahl is an enormously popular writer in two distinct genres—perversely amusing tales of terror for adults and fantastically inventive books for children. Original, exacting, tough-minded, and amusing, Dahl's works have entertained millions and are likely to endure as classics of their kind.

Dahl was born in Landaff, South Wales, and was educated at Repton School. His early writing was based on his wartime experience with the Royal Air Force. *Over to You: 10 Stories of Flyers and Flying* came out in 1946, and his first novel for adults, *Sometime Never: A Fable for Supermen* (1948), dealt with some of the same horrors and hallucinations. Dahl soon discovered his ideal form in the short, tightly plotted tale of the grotesque. In these stories he creates a world in which the familiar and the conventional are juxtaposed with the absurd and the bizarre, as when a stray cat is discovered to contain the soul of composer Franz Liszt. Dahl makes the incredible credible, creating a realistic atmosphere in which his bizarre twists seem commonplace. He was awarded the Edgar Allan Poe Award for mystery writers in 1954 and 1959.

Dahl's stories for children blend the horrible and the humorous as do his stories for adults. In *Charlie and the Chocolate Factory* (1967), the hero is matter-of-factly cheerful as nasty children and grownups are mutilated in appropriate ways, the punishment perhaps excessive but always fitting the crime. Dahl wrote the screenplay for the movie version of that book, which appeared in 1971 as *Willie Wonka and the Chocolate Factory*. Dahl had previously written the script for the James Bond film *You Only Live Twice* (1965) and for the Ian Fleming children's story *Chitty-Chitty-Bang-Bang* (1967).

ROALD DAHL.

Dahl's thirty-year marriage to actress Patricia Neal was marked by tragedy. One of their five children died of measles at the age of seven; one suffered brain damage as the result of an accident; and Ms. Neal was partially paralyzed by a succession of strokes.

The Landlady

Billy Weaver had traveled down from London on the slow afternoon train, with a change at Swindon on the way, and by the time he got to Bath it was about nine o'clock in the evening and the moon was coming up out of a clear starry sky over the houses opposite the station entrance. But the air was deadly cold and the wind was like a flat blade of ice on his cheeks.

"Excuse me," he said, "but is there a fairly cheap hotel not too far away from here?"

"Try the Bell and Dragon," the porter answered, pointing down the road. "They might take you in. It's about a quarter of a mile along on the other side."

Billy thanked him and picked up his suitcase and set out to walk the quarter-mile to The Bell and Dragon. He had never been to Bath before. He didn't know anyone who lived there. But Mr. Greenslade at the Head Office in London had told him it was a splendid city. "Find your own lodgings," he had said, "and then go along and report to the Branch Manager as soon as you've got yourself settled."

Billy was seventeen years old. He was wearing a new navy blue overcoat, a new brown trilby hat,[1] and a new brown suit, and he was feeling fine. He walked briskly down the street. He was trying to do everything briskly these days. Briskness, he had decided, was *the* one common characteristic of all successful businessmen. The big shots up at Head Office were absolutely fantastically brisk all the time. They were amazing.

There were no shops on this wide street that he was walking along, only a line of tall houses on each side, all of them identical. They had porches and pillars and four or five steps going up to their front doors, and it was obvious that once upon a time they had been very swanky residences. But now, even in the darkness, he could see that the paint was peeling from the woodwork on their doors and windows, and that the handsome white facades were cracked and blotchy from neglect.

Suddenly, in a downstairs window that was brilliantly illuminated by a street lamp not six yards away, Billy caught sight of a printed notice propped up against the glass in one of the upper panes. It said BED AND BREAKFAST. There was a vase of yellow chrysanthemums, tall and beautiful, standing just underneath the notice.

He stopped walking. He moved a bit closer. Green curtains (some sort of velvety material) were hanging down on either side of the window. The chrysanthemums looked wonderful beside them. He went right up and peered through the glass into the room, and the first thing he saw was a bright fire burning in the hearth. On the carpet in front of the fire, a pretty little dachshund was curled up asleep with its nose tucked into its belly. The room itself, so far as he could see in the half darkness, was filled with pleasant furniture. There was a baby grand piano and a big sofa and several plump armchairs; and in one corner he spotted a large parrot in a cage. Animals were usually a good sign in a place like this, Billy told himself; and all in all, it looked to him as though it would be a pretty decent house to stay in. Certainly it would be more comfortable than The Bell and Dragon.

On the other hand, a pub would be more congenial than a boardinghouse. There would be beer and darts in the evening, and lots of people to talk to, and it would probably be a

---

1. **trilby hat:** a type of soft felt hat popular in England.

good bit cheaper, too. He had stayed a couple of nights in a pub once before and he had liked it. He had never stayed in any boardinghouses, and, to be perfectly honest, he was a tiny bit frightened of them. The name itself conjured up images of watery cabbage, rapacious landladies, and a powerful smell of kippers[2] in the living room.

After dithering about like this in the cold for two or three minutes, Billy decided that he would walk on and take a look at The Bell and Dragon before making up his mind. He turned to go.

And now a queer thing happened to him. He was in the act of stepping back and turning away from the window when all at once his eye was caught and held in the most peculiar manner by the small notice that was there. BED AND BREAKFAST, it said. BED AND BREAKFAST, BED AND BREAKFAST, BED AND BREAKFAST. Each word was like a large black eye staring at him through the glass, holding him, compelling him, forcing him to stay where he was and not to walk away from that house, and the next thing he knew, he was actually moving across from the window to the front door of the house, climbing the steps that led up to it, and reaching for the bell.

He pressed the bell. Far away in a back room he heard it ringing, and then *at once*—it must have been at once because he hadn't even had time to take his finger from the bell button— the door swung open and a woman was standing there.

Normally you ring the bell and you have at least a half-minute's wait before the door opens. But this dame was like a jack-in-the-box. He pressed the bell—and out she popped! It made him jump.

She was about forty-five or fifty years old, and the moment she saw him, she gave him a warm welcoming smile.

"Please come in," she said pleasantly. She stepped aside, holding the door wide open, and Billy found himself automatically starting forward. The compulsion or, more accurately, the desire to follow after her into that house was extraordinarily strong.

"I saw the notice in the window," he said, holding himself back.

"Yes, I know."

"I was wondering about a room."

"It's *all* ready for you, my dear," she said. She had a round pink face and very gentle blue eyes.

"I was on my way to The Bell and Dragon," Billy told her. "But the notice in your window just happened to catch my eye."

"My dear boy," she said, "why don't you come in out of the cold?"

"How much do you charge?"

"Five and sixpence a night, including breakfast."

It was fantastically cheap. It was less than half of what he had been willing to pay.

"If that is too much," she added, "then perhaps I can reduce it just a tiny bit. Do you desire an egg for breakfast? Eggs are expensive at the moment. It would be sixpence less without the egg."

"Five and sixpence is fine," he answered. "I should like very much to stay here."

"I knew you would. Do come in."

She seemed terribly nice. She looked exactly like the mother of one's best school friend welcoming one into the house to stay for the Christmas holidays. Billy took off his hat, and stepped over the threshold.

"Just hang it there," she said, "and let me help you with your coat."

There were no other hats or coats in the hall. There were no umbrellas, no walking sticks—nothing.

"We have it *all* to ourselves," she said, smiling at him over her shoulder as she led the way upstairs. "You see, it isn't very often I have the pleasure of taking a visitor into my little nest."

The old girl is slightly dotty, Billy told himself. But at five and sixpence a night, who

---

2. **kippers:** smoked or dried fish.

gives a damn about that? "I should've thought you'd be simply swamped with applicants," he said politely.

"Oh, I am, my dear, I am, of course I am. But the trouble is that I'm inclined to be just a teeny weeny bit choosy and particular—if you see what I mean."

"Ah, yes."

"But I'm always ready. Everything is always ready day and night in this house just on the off chance that an acceptable young gentleman will come along. And it is such a pleasure, my dear, such a very great pleasure when now and again I open the door and I see someone standing there who is just *exactly* right." She was halfway up the stairs, and she paused with one hand on the stairrail, turning her head and smiling down at him with pale lips. "Like you," she added, and her blue eyes traveled slowly all the way down the length of Billy's body, to his feet, and then up again.

On the second-floor landing she said to him, "This floor is mine."

They climbed up another flight. "And this one is *all* yours," she said. "Here's your room. I do hope you'll like it." She took him into a small but charming front bedroom, switching on the light as she went in.

"The morning sun comes right in the window, Mr. Perkins. It *is* Mr. Perkins, isn't it?"

"No," he said. "It's Weaver."

"Mr. Weaver. How nice. I've put a water bottle between the sheets to air them out, Mr. Weaver. It's such a comfort to have a hot water bottle in a strange bed with clean sheets, don't you agree? And you may light the gas fire at any time if you feel chilly."

"Thank you," Billy said. "Thank you ever so much." He noticed that the bedspread had been taken off the bed, and that the bedclothes had been neatly turned back on one side, all ready for someone to get in.

"I'm so glad you appeared," she said, looking earnestly into his face. "I was beginning to get worried."

"That's all right," Billy answered brightly.

"You mustn't worry about me." He put his suitcase on the chair and started to open it.

"And what about supper, my dear? Did you manage to get anything to eat before you came here?"

"I'm not a bit hungry, thank you," he said. "I think I'll just go to bed as soon as possible because tomorrow I've got to get up rather early and report to the office."

"Very well, then. I'll leave you now so that you can unpack. But before you go to bed, would you be kind enough to pop into the sitting room on the ground floor and sign the book? Everyone has to do that because it's the law of the land, and we don't want to go breaking any laws at *this* stage in the proceedings, do we?" She gave him a little wave of the hand and went quickly out of the room and closed the door.

Now, the fact that his landlady appeared to be slightly off her rocker didn't worry Billy in the least. After all, she not only was harmless—there was no question about that—but she was also quite obviously a kind and generous soul. He guessed that she had probably lost a son in the war, or something like that, and had never gotten over it.

So a few minutes later, after unpacking his suitcase and washing his hands, he trotted downstairs to the ground floor and entered the living room. His landlady wasn't there, but the fire was glowing in the hearth, and the little dachshund was still sleeping soundly in front of it. The room was wonderfully warm and cozy. I'm a lucky fellow, he thought, rubbing his hands. This is a bit of all right.

He found the guest book lying open on the piano, so he took out his pen and wrote down his name and address. There were only two other entries above his on the page, and, as one always does with guest books, he started to read them. One was a Christopher Mulholland from Cardiff. The other was Gregory W. Temple from Bristol.

That's funny, he thought suddenly. Christopher Mulholland. It rings a bell.

Now where on earth had he heard that rather unusual name before?

Was it a boy at school? No. Was it one of his sister's numerous young men, perhaps, or a friend of his father's? No, no, it wasn't any of those. He glanced down again at the book.

Christopher Mulholland   *231 Cathedral Road, Cardiff*

Gregory W. Temple   *27 Sycamore Drive, Bristol*

As a matter of fact, now he came to think of it, he wasn't at all sure that the second name didn't have almost as much of a familiar ring about it as the first.

"Gregory Temple?" he said aloud, searching his memory. "Christopher Mulholland? . . ."

"Such charming boys," a voice behind him answered, and he turned and saw his landlady sailing into the room with a large silver tea tray in her hands. She was holding it well out in front of her, and rather high up, as though the tray were a pair of reins on a frisky horse.

"They sound somehow familiar," he said.

"They do? How interesting."

"I'm almost positive I've heard those names before somewhere. Isn't that odd? Maybe it was in the newspapers. They weren't famous in any way, were they? I mean famous cricketers or footballers or something like that?"

"Famous," she said, setting the tea tray down on the low table in front of the sofa. "Oh no, I don't think they were famous. But they were incredibly handsome, both of them, I can promise you that. They were tall and young and handsome, my dear, just exactly like you."

Once more, Billy glanced down at the book. "Look here," he said, noticing the dates. "This last entry is over two years old."

"It is?"

"Yes, indeed. And Christopher Mulholland's is nearly a year before that—more than *three years* ago."

"Dear me," she said, shaking her head and heaving a dainty little sigh. "I would never have thought it. How times does fly away from us all, doesn't it, Mr. Wilkins?"

"It's Weaver," Billy said. "W-e-a-v-e-r."

"Oh, of course it is!" she cried, sitting down on the sofa. "How silly of me. I do apologize. In one ear and out the other, that's me, Mr. Weaver."

"You know something?" Billy said. "Something that's really quite extraordinary about all this?"

"No, dear, I don't."

"Well, you see, both of these names—Mulholland and Temple—I not only seem to remember each one of them separately, so to speak, but somehow or other, in some peculiar way, they both appear to be sort of connected together as well. As though they were both famous for the same sort of thing, if you see what I mean—like . . . well . . . like Dempsey and Tunney, for example, or Churchill and Roosevelt."

"How amusing," she said. "But come over here now, dear, and sit down beside me on the sofa and I'll give you a nice cup of tea and a ginger biscuit before you go to bed."

"You really shouldn't bother," Billy said. "I didn't mean you to do anything like that." He stood by the piano, watching her as she fussed about with the cups and saucers. He noticed that she had small, white, quickly moving hands, and red fingernails.

"I'm almost positive it was in the newspapers I saw them," Billy said. "I'll think of it in a second. I'm sure I will."

There is nothing more tantalizing than a thing like this that lingers just outside the borders of one's memory. He hated to give up.

"Now wait a minute," he said. "Wait just a minute. Mulholland . . . Christopher Mulholland . . . wasn't *that* the name of the Eton schoolboy who was on a walking tour through the West Country, and then all of a sudden . . ."

"Milk?" she said. "And sugar?"

"Yes, please. And then all of a sudden . . ."

"Eton schoolboy?" she said. "Oh no, my dear, that can't possibly be right because *my* Mr. Mulholland was certainly not an Eton schoolboy when he came to me. He was a Cambridge undergraduate. Come over here now and sit next to me and warm yourself in front of this lovely fire. Come on. Your tea's all ready for you." She patted the empty place beside her on the sofa, and she sat there smiling at Billy and waiting for him to come over.

He crossed the room slowly, and sat down on the edge of the sofa. She placed his teacup on the table in front of him.

"*There* we are," she said. "How nice and cozy this is, isn't it?"

Billy started sipping his tea. She did the same. For half a minute or so, neither of them spoke. But Billy knew that she was looking at him. Her body was half turned toward him, and he could feel her eyes resting on his face, watching him over the rim of her teacup. Now and again, he caught a whiff of a peculiar smell that seemed to emanate directly from her person. It was not in the least unpleasant, and it reminded him—well, he wasn't quite sure what it reminded him of. Pickled walnuts? New leather? Or was it the corridors of a hospital?

At length, she said, "Mr. Mulholland was a great one for his tea. Never in my life have I seen anyone drink as much tea as dear, sweet Mr. Mulholland."

"I suppose he left fairly recently," Billy said. He was still puzzling his head about the two names. He was positive now that he had seen them in the newspapers—in the headlines.

"Left?" she said, arching her brows. "But my dear boy, he never left. He's still here. Mr. Temple is also here. They're on the fourth floor, both of them together."

Billy set his cup down slowly on the table and stared at his landlady. She smiled back at him, and then she put out one of her white hands and patted him comfortingly on the knee. "How old are you, my dear?" she asked.

"Seventeen."

"Seventeen!" she cried. "Oh, it's the perfect age! Mr. Mulholland was also seventeen. But I think he was a trifle shorter than you are; in fact I'm sure he was, and his teeth weren't *quite* so white. You have the most beautiful teeth, Mr. Weaver, did you know that?"

"They're not as good as they look," Billy said. "They've got simply masses of fillings in them at the back."

"Mr. Temple, of course, was a little older," she said, ignoring his remark. "He was actually twenty-eight. And yet I never would have guessed it if he hadn't told me, never in my whole life. There wasn't a *blemish* on his body."

"A what?" Billy said.

"His skin was *just* like a baby's."

There was a pause. Billy picked up his teacup and took another sip of his tea, then he set it down again gently in its saucer. He waited for her to say something else, but she seemed to have lapsed into another of her silences. He sat there staring straight ahead of him into the far corner of the room biting his lower lip.

"That parrot," he said at last. "You know something? It had me completely fooled when I first saw it through the window. I could have sworn it was alive."

"Alas, no longer."

"It's most terribly clever the way it's been done," he said. "It doesn't look in the least bit dead. Who did it?"

"I did."

"*You* did?"

"Of course," she said. "And have you met my little Basil as well?" She nodded toward the dachshund curled up so comfortably in front of the fire. Billy looked at it. And suddenly he realized that this animal had all the time been just as silent and motionless as the parrot. He put out a hand and touched it gently on the top of its back. The back was hard and cold, and when he pushed the hair to one side with his fingers, he could see the skin underneath, grayish-black and dry and perfectly preserved.

"Good gracious me," he said. "How absolutely fascinating." He turned away from the dog and stared with deep admiration at the little woman beside him on the sofa. "It must be most awfully difficult to do a thing like that."

"Not in the least," she said. "I stuff *all* my little pets myself when they pass away. Will you have another cup of tea?"

"No, thank you," Billy said. The tea tasted faintly of bitter almonds, and he didn't much care for it.

"You did sign the book, didn't you?"

"Oh, yes."

"That's good. Because later on, if I happen to forget what you were called, then I could always come down here and look it up. I still do that almost every day with Mr. Mulholland and Mr. . . . . Mr. . . . ."

"Temple," Billy said. "Gregory Temple. Excuse my asking, but haven't there been *any* other guests here except them in the last two or three years?"

Holding her teacup high in one hand, inclining her head slightly to the left, she looked up at him out of the corners of her eyes and gave him another gentle little smile.

"No, my dear," she said. "Only you."

Getting at Meaning

1. What qualities make Billy Weaver "just right" as the central character of a horror story?

2. How does Billy's first impression of the landlady's house give him a sense of warmth and security? Why does Billy forget about going to The Bell and Dragon?

3. Billy gradually picks up clues that eventually will lead to his understanding the reality of the situation. List as many of these clues as you can. When did you first sense that something was "wrong"?

4. How satisfactory is the end of this story? Is the outcome clear for Billy Weaver? Is the ending humorous or horrible or both? Explain.

Developing Skills in Reading Literature

1. **Irony.** Examine the landlady's remarks and find several that carry double meanings. How does the reader's interpretation of these remarks differ from that of Billy Weaver? What effect is achieved through this verbal irony?

2. **Verisimilitude.** The writer of this story presents details in such a way as to create a believable world on the basis of an unbelievable premise. Cite several details from the story that ordinarily would be dismissed as preposterous or highly unlikely. To what extent does Billy Weaver accept them as credible? To what extent are you convinced while reading the story? when thinking about the story in retrospect?

Developing Writing Skills

Extending a Story. This story has an open ending. Continuing in a similar style, write a closed ending, showing through narration, description, and dialogue what happens to Billy and to the landlady.

Frank O'Connor

1903–1966

Although he was also a novelist, playwright, and essayist, Frank O'Connor is best remembered as a short story writer. His stories describe life in Ireland with warmth and humor and are told with the seemingly effortless grace of the true storyteller. O'Connor himself said of storytelling, "It doesn't deal with problems; it doesn't have any solutions to offer; it just states the human condition."

O'Connor was the pen name of Michael O'Donovan, who was born and raised in Cork, Ireland, and attended the Christian Brothers school there. He was a boy during the time of fervent Irish nationalism, which led not only to rebellion against British rule but also to a revived interest in the nearly extinct Gaelic language and in plays, poems, and stories with Irish subjects and themes. O'Connor learned to speak Gaelic and later did many notable translations from that language.

O'Connor worked as a librarian, first in County Cork and later in Dublin. He fought for Irish freedom, using his experiences as the basis for stories collectd as *Guests of the Nation* (1931). The title piece, in which a young soldier in the Irish Republican Army develops sympathy for his two British prisoners, is among O'Connor's most famous stories.

O'Connor often wove together fact and fiction in his stories. "The Drunkard," for example, is rooted in an actual incident. This story, like O'Connor's other autobiographical fiction, is much more than a clever anecdote, for he remains objective even while shaping his material. One critic commented that O'Connor "allows the observed experience to carry its own moral, and the moral is that anything less than a profound and all-inclusive charity is madness." Many of O'Connor's best stories are told from the point of view of a child, a technique that is inherently ironic, for the mature reader necessarily interprets events differently than does the innocent narrator.

An acknowledged master of the short story, O'Connor was many other things as well. He was a playwright who directed at the Abbey Theater in the 1930's. He wrote of his travels; he was an interestingly quirky literary critic who maintained a "considered opinion in happy independence of the general consensus"; and he was a radio commentator. He also taught at various universities in the United States.

The Idealist

Reading? I was never struck on it. It never did anything for me but get me into trouble.

Adventure stories weren't so bad, but as a kid I was very serious and always preferred realism to romance. School stories were what I liked best. The trouble was that even they seemed to be a bit farfetched, judging by our standards. The schools were English and quite different to the one I attended. They were always called "the venerable pile," and there was usually a ghost in them; they were built in a square that was called the "quad," and, to judge by the pictures, were all clock towers, spires and pinnacles like the lunatic asylum with us. The fellows in the stories were all good climbers, and used to get in and out of the school at night on ropes made of knotted sheets. They dressed queerly; they wore long trousers, short black jackets and top hats. When they did anything wrong they were given "lines." When it was a bad case they were flogged, and never showed any sign of pain, only the bad fellows, and they always said "Ow! Ow!"

Mostly, they were grand chaps who always stuck together and were great at football and cricket. They never told lies, and anyone who did, they wouldn't talk to him. If they were caught out and asked a point-blank question, they always told the truth, unless someone else was in it along with them, and then wild horses wouldn't get them to split, even if the other fellow was a thief, which, as a matter of fact, he frequently was. It was surprising in such good schools, with fathers who never gave them less than five quid,[1] the number of thieves there were. The fellows I knew hardly ever stole, even though they only got a penny a week, and sometimes not even that when their fathers were on the booze and their mothers had to go to the pawn.[2]

I worked hard at the football and cricket, though, of course, we never had a proper football, and the sort of cricket we played was with a hurley stick against a wicket chalked on some wall. The officers in the barrack played proper cricket, and I used to go up on summer evenings to see them.

Even so, I couldn't help being disgusted at the bad way things were run in our school. Our venerable pile was a red brick building without tower or pinnacle a fellow could climb, and no ghost at all; we had no team, so a fellow, no matter how hard he worked, could never play for the school, and nobody had ever thought of giving us lines. Instead Murderer Molony either lifted you by the ears or bashed you with a cane.

But these were only superficial things. What was really wrong was ourselves. The fellows sucked up to the masters and told them everything that went on. If they were caught out they tried to put the blame on somebody else, even if it meant telling lies. If they were caned, they sniveled and said it wasn't fair; drew back their hands the least shade as if they were terrified, so that the cane only caught the top of their fingers, and then screamed and stood on one leg, and shook their fingers out in hopes of getting it counted as one. Finally they roared that their wrist was broken, and crawled back to their desks with their hands squeezed under their armpits, howling. I mean, you couldn't help feeling ashamed, imagining what chaps from a decent school would think if they saw it.

My way to school led me past the barrack gate. In those peaceful days the English

---

1. **quid:** one English pound sterling.
2. **pawn:** pawnshop.

sentries never minded you going past the guardroom to have a look; if you came at dinnertime they even called you in and gave you plum duff[3] and tea. Naturally, with such a temptation on my way, I was often late. When you were late, the only excuse, short of a letter from your mother, was to say you were at early Mass. The Murderer would never know whether you were or not, and if he did anything to you, you could easily get him into trouble with the parish priest. Even as kids we all knew who the real boss of the school was.

But after I had started reading school stories I was always a bit uneasy about saying I was at Mass. It was a lie, and I knew the chaps in the stories would never have told it. They were all round me like invisible presences, and I hated to do anything they wouldn't approve of.

One morning I was very late.

"What kept you till this hour, Regan?" asked Murderer Molony, looking at the clock.

I wanted to say I was at Mass but I couldn't. The invisible presences were all round me.

"I delayed at the barrack, sir," I said in panic.

There was a faint giggle from the class and Molony raised his brows in mild surprise. He was a big powerful man with fair hair and blue eyes and a manner that at times was deceptively mild.

"Oh, indeed?" he said politely enough. "And what did you do that for?"

"I was watching the soldiers drilling, sir," said I.

The class giggled again. This was a new line entirely for them. I suppose it was the first time anyone ever told the truth in that class. Besides, Molony had a dead set on the English.

"Oh," said Molony casually, "I never knew you were such a military man. Hold out your hand!"

Compared with the laughter the slaps were nothing and I did not flinch. I returned to my desk slowly and quietly without sniveling or

squeezing my hands, and the Murderer looked after me, raising his brows again as much as to say that this was a new line for him too. But the other fellows gaped and whispered as if I were some strange animal. At playtime they all gathered round me, full of excitement.

"Regan, why did you say that about the barrack?"

"Because 'twas true," I replied firmly. "I wasn't going to tell him a lie."

"What lie?"

"That I was at Mass."

"Then couldn't you say you had to go on a message?"

"That would be a lie too."

"Cripes, Regan," they said, "you'd better mind yourself. The Murderer is in an awful wax. He'll massacre you."

I knew that only too well. I could see that the man's professional pride had been deeply hurt, and for the rest of the day I was on my best behavior. But my best was not sufficient for the occasion, for I underrated the Murderer's guile. From the frown on his face he seemed to be puzzled over something in a book he was reading, and even when he spoke, in a low quiet voice, he scarcely raised his blue eyes from it.

"Regan, was that you talking?"

"'Twas, sir," I replied in consternation.

This time the whole class laughed. They couldn't believe that I wasn't deliberately trailing my coat, and, of course, the laugh must have convinced him that I was. I suppose if people do tell you lies all day and every day it soon becomes a sort of perquisite[4] and you resent being deprived of it.

"Oh," he said, throwing down the book, "we'll soon put a stop to that."

This time it was a tougher job, because he really was on his mettle. But so was I. I knew

---

3. **plum duff:** plum pudding.
4. **perquisite** (pur′ kwə zit): a privilege or benefit.

this was the testing point, and that if only I could keep my head I should provide a model for the whole class. When I had got through with it without moving a muscle and returned to my desk with my hands by my side, the invisible presences gave me a great clap, but the visible ones were nearly as annoyed as the Murderer. After school a half-dozen of them followed me down the playground through the smell of stale bread and butter.

"Go on!" they shouted truculently. "Shaping[5] as usual!"

"I was not shaping."

"You were shaping! You're always showing off. Trying to pretend he didn't hurt you—a blooming crybaby like you!"

"I wasn't trying to pretend," I shouted, even then resisting the temptation to nurse my bruised hands. "Only decent fellows don't cry over every little pain like kids."

"Go on!" they bawled after me. "You ould[6] idiot." And as I went down the school lane, still trying to keep what the stories called "a stiff upper lip" and reminding myself that my torture was over until the next morning, I heard their mocking voices after me.

"Mad Bill! Yah, Mad Bill!"

I realized that if I were to keep on terms with the invisible presences I should have to watch my step in school.

So I did, all through that year. But then, one day, an awful thing happened. I was coming in from the yard, and in the porch outside our schoolroom I saw a fellow called Gorman taking something from a coat on the rack. Gorman was a fellow I disliked and feared; a handsome, sulky, spoiled, and sneering lout. I paid no attention to him because I had escaped for a few moments into my dream world in which fathers never gave you anything less than fivers and chaps who had been ignored suddenly turned up and saved the honor of the school in the last half of the match.

"Who are you looking at?" he asked threateningly.

"I wasn't looking at anyone," I said with an indignant start.

"I was only getting a pencil out of my coat," he added, clenching his fists.

"Nobody said you weren't," said I, thinking this a very queer thing to start a row about.

"You'd better not either," he snarled. "You can mind your own business."

"You mind yours," I retorted, for the purpose of saving face. "I never spoke to you at all."

And that, so far as I was concerned, was the end of it. But after playtime, the Murderer, looking exceptionally serious, stood before the class, balancing a pencil in both hands.

"Everyone who left the classroom this morning, stand out!" he said. Then he lowered his head and looked at us from under his fair brows. "Mind, now, I said everyone!"

I stood out with the others, including Gorman.

"Did you take anything from a coat on the rack this morning?" asked the Murderer, laying a heavy, hairy paw on Gorman's shoulder and staring into his face.

"Me, sir?" Gorman asked innocently. "No, sir."

"Did you see anyone doing it?"

"No, sir."

"You?" he asked another lad, but even before he reached me at all I realized why Gorman had told the lie and wondered in panic what I should do.

"You?" he asked me, and his big red face was close to mine and his blue eyes only a couple of inches away.

"I didn't take anything, sir," I said in a low voice.

"Did you see someone else do it?" he asked, raising his brows and indicating quite plainly that he had noticed my evasion. "Have you a tongue in your head?" he shouted suddenly,

---

5. **shaping**: pretending.
6. **ould**: old.

and the whole class, electrified, stared at me. "You?" he added curtly to the next boy as though he had given me up.

"No, sir."

"Back to your desks, the rest of ye!" he ordered. "Regan, you stay here!"

He waited until everyone was seated again before he went on.

"Turn out your pockets!"

I did, and a half-stifled giggle rose which the Murderer quelled with a thunderous glance. Even for a small boy, I had pockets that were museums in themselves; the purpose of half the things I brought to light I couldn't have explained myself. They were antiques, prehistoric, and unlabeled. Among them was a school story borrowed the previous evening from another chap, a queer fellow who chewed paper as if it were gum. The Murderer reached out for it, and, holding it at arm's length, shook it out with an expression of deepening disgust as he saw the nibbled corners and margins.

"Oh," he said disdainfully, "so this is how you waste your time, is it? What do you do with these—eat them?"

"'Tisn't mine, sir," I said against the laugh that sprang up. "I borrowed it."

"Is that what you did with the money?" he added quickly, his fat head on one side.

"Money?" I said, getting confused. "What money?"

"The shilling that was stolen from Flanagan's overcoat this morning," he added—Flanagan was a little hunchback whose people coddled him: no one else in the school would have had that much money.

"I never took Flanagan's shilling," I said, beginning to cry. "And you have no right to say I did."

"I have the right to say that you're the most impudent, defiant puppy in the class," he replied, his voice hoarse with rage, "and I wouldn't put it past you. What else can anyone expect and you reading this dirty, rotten, filthy rubbish?" And he tore my school story in two halves and tossed them to the farthest corner of the schoolroom. "Dirty, filthy English rubbish! Now hold out your hand!"

This time the invisible presences deserted me. Hearing themselves described in those contemptuous terms, they fled. The Murderer went mad in the way people do whenever they're up against something they don't understand. Even the other fellows were shocked, and heaven knows they had little enough sympathy with me.

"You should put the police on him," they advised me afterwards in the playground. "He lifted the cane over his shoulder. He could get the jail for that."

"But why didn't you say you didn't see anyone?" asked one chap.

"Because I did," I said, beginning to sob all over again at the memory of my wrongs. "I saw Gorman."

"Gorman?" they echoed incredulously. "Was it Gorman took Flanagan's money? And why didn't you say so?"

"Because it wouldn't be right," I sobbed.

"Why wouldn't it be right?" one of them asked, gaping.

"Because Gorman should have told the truth himself," I said. "And if this was a decent school no one would ever speak to him again for it."

"But why would Gorman tell the truth if he took the money?" he asked, as you'd speak to a baby. "Jay, Regan," he added pityingly, "you're getting madder and madder. Now look what you're after bringing on yourself!"

Suddenly Gorman himself came lumbering up.

"Regan," he shouted threateningly, "did you say I stole Flanagan's money?"

Gorman, though, of course, I didn't realize it, was as much at sea as Molony and the rest of them. The only way he could explain my silence was by assuming that I was afraid of his threats, and now he felt the time had come to renew them. He couldn't have come at a moment when I cared less for them. Despairingly I lashed out with all my strength at his brutal face. He screamed, and his hand came away from his mouth, all blood. Then he threw off his satchel and made for me, but at the same moment a door opened behind us and a lame teacher called Murphy emerged. We all ran like mad and the fight was forgotten.

But it wasn't forgotten in other quarters. Next morning after prayers the Murderer scowled at me.

"Regan," he asked, "were you fighting in the yard after school yesterday?"

For a second or so I didn't reply. I couldn't help feeling that the game wasn't worth a candle. But before the spiritual presences fled forever I made one last effort.

"I was, sir," I said, and this time there wasn't even a titter. The whole class took it solemnly as the behavior of a chap who was quite out of his mind.

"Who were you fighting with?"

"I'd rather not say, sir," I replied, hysteria beginning to well up in me. It was all very well for the invisible presences, but they hadn't to deal with the Murderer.

"Who was he fighting with?" he asked lightly, resting his hands on the desk and studying the ceiling.

"Gorman, sir," replied three or four voices —as easy as that!

"Did Gorman hit him first?"

"No, sir. He hit Gorman first."

"Stand out," he said, taking up the cane again. "Now," he added, going up to Gorman, "you take this and hit him. And make sure you hit him hard," he added, giving Gorman's arm an encouraging squeeze. "Regan thinks he's a great fellow. You show him now what *we* think of him."

Gorman came towards me with the cane in one hand and a broad grin on his face. The whole class began to roar as if it were a great joke and even the Murderer permitted himself a modest grin at his own cleverness.

"Hold out your hand," he said to me.

I didn't. I began to feel trapped and a little crazy.

"Hold out your hand, I say!" he shouted, beginning to lose his temper again.

"I will not," I shouted back at him, losing all control of myself.

"You what?" he cried, dashing at me round the classroom with his hand raised above his head as though to strike me. "What's that you said, you dirty little thief?"

"I'm not a thief," I screamed. "And if he comes near me I'll kick the shins off him. You have no right to give him that cane. And you have no right to call me a thief either. If you do it again, I'll go down to the police and then we'll soon see who the thief is."

"You refused to answer my questions," he shouted, and if I had been in my right mind I should have known that he was suddenly frightened of something.

"No," I said through my sobs, "and I won't answer them now either. I'm not a spy."

"Oh," he retorted with a sarcastic sniff, "so that's what you call a spy?"

"Yes, and that's what they all are, all the fellows here—dirty spies!—but I'm not going to be a spy for you. You can do your own spying."

"That's enough now, that's enough!" he said, raising his fat hand almost beseechingly. "There's no need to lose control of yourself, my dear young fellow, and there's no need whatever to screech like that. 'Tis most unmanly. Go back to your seat now and I'll talk to you another time."

That day I did no work at all, and no one else did much either. The hysteria had spread to the class. I alternated between fits of exultation at the thought of how I had defied the Murderer to his face and panic at the prospect of how he'd take it out of me after, and at each change of mood I put my head in my hands and sobbed all over again. The Murderer didn't tell me to stop. He didn't even look at me. The poor unfortunate man! When I think of it now I almost feel sorry for him.

After that I was the hero of the school for a whole afternoon. Even Gorman, when he tried to resume the fight, was told by two or three of the bigger fellows to hop off; a fellow that took the cane to beat another chap, he had no status at all. But that was not the sort of hero I wanted to be. I wanted something calmer, more codified, less sensational.

Next morning I was in such a state of panic that I didn't know how to face school at all. The silence of the school lane and the yard put me into a fresh panic. I was late again!

"What kept you, Regan?" the Murderer asked quietly.

"I was at Mass, sir," said I.

"Oh, all right," he said, though he seemed a bit surprised. What I hadn't realized was the immense advantage of our system over the English one. By this time half a dozen of his pets had brought the Murderer the true story, and if he didn't feel himself a monster, he certainly felt himself a fool, which is worse.

But by that time I didn't care. In my school sack I had another story. Not a school story this time, though. School stories were a wash-out. "Bang! Bang!"—that was the only way to deal with fellows like the Murderer and Gorman. "The only good teacher is a dead teacher."

Getting at Meaning

1. According to the narrator, what are the main differences between the schools he reads about and the school he attends? What values do the students in the school stories have that Regan does not see in his fellow students? What values of the English students does he attempt to put into practice?

2. How has Murderer Molony earned his nickname? Why is he especially angry at Regan?

3. After Murderer Molony whips him, Regan says ". . . the invisible presences gave me a great clap, but the visible ones were nearly as annoyed as the Murderer." What does he mean? Where else in the story do the invisible presences appear?

4. How does the incident with Gorman complicate Regan's plan to act like the students in the school stories? Is Regan able to be true to his ideal throughout the story? Explain.

5. Do you think that Regan acts with strength or with weakness when he confronts Murderer Molony? Explain. How do the other students respond to Regan's behavior? Do you think that he has influenced them in any way? Explain.

6. How has Regan changed by the end of the story? Is he still an idealist? Explain.

Developing Skills in Reading Literature

Realism and Romanticism. The narrator in this story says that he has always preferred realism to romance. What does he mean? Are the school stories that he enjoys realistic or romantic? Is he truly a realist, according to the way that the story unfolds?

To what extent is the writer of this story a realist? Does he depict the behavior of the students realistically? Are the main characters true-to-life? Does the setting seem to be realistic, based on what you know about Ireland in the mid-twentieth century? Are the details in the story concrete or impressionistic, external or psychological? What truths about human nature does O'Connor bring out? Are these universal truths, judging from your own experience?

Developing Vocabulary

Inferring Word Meaning. Study the context in which each of the italicized words appears. Determine the meaning of the word, and suggest a synonym, using a dictionary as necessary.

a. "The schools were . . . always called 'the *venerable* pile'. . . ."

b. ". . . I underrated the Murderer's *guile*. From the frown on his face he seemed to be puzzling over something in a book he was reading, and even when he spoke, in a low quiet voice, he scarcely raised his blue eyes from it."

c. "This time it was a tougher job, because he [Molony] really was on his *mettle*."

d. ". . . a half-stifled giggle rose which the Murderer *quelled* with a thunderous glance."

e. "This time the invisible presences deserted me. Hearing themselves described in those *contemptuous* terms, they fled."

f. " 'Gorman?' they echoed *incredulously*. 'Was it Gorman took Flanagan's money? Why didn't you say so?' "

COMING OUT OF SCHOOL, 1927. L. S. Lowry. Tate Gallery, London.

Doris Lessing

born in 1919

The novels and short stories of Doris Lessing provide a vivid record of contemporary social and political movements, particularly the changing situation for women. Her intelligent exploration of feminist themes a decade and more before the re-emergence of feminism as a political force earned the admiration and loyalty of many readers.

Lessing was born in Kermanshah, Persia (Iran), where her father was a captain in the British army. Between 1924 and 1949 she lived on a farm in Rhodesia (Zimbabwe). Those colonial experiences contributed to the psychological richness of Lessing's writing. If she came to believe that women were exploited in a system dominated by men, it was part of an awareness that many kinds of exploitation exist, economic and racial as well as sexual.

Educated at a Roman Catholic convent and at the Girls' High School in Salisbury, Lessing married Frank Charles Wisdom in 1939, a childless union that ended in divorce in 1943. Shortly thereafter, she married Gottfried Anton Lessing, with whom she had two sons and a daughter before their divorce in 1949. She then settled in England and began her literary career.

Lessing's fictional heroines speak in a voice that most critics and readers consider autobiographical. Her first novel, *The Grass Is Singing* (1950), chronicles the breakup of a marriage in Rhodesia. Her second novel, *Martha Quest* (1952), was the first volume in what evolved into a five-book series with the general title *Children of Violence*. In *Martha Quest* and her next book, *A Proper Marriage* (1954), Lessing wrote with straightforward candor about the life of an independent southern African woman, recording her change and growth. The third and fourth books in the sequence, *A Ripple from the Storm* (1958) and *Landlocked* (1965), deal with political squabbles among Rhodesian radicals, while the final volume, *The Four-Gated City* (1969), recounts the story of Martha Quest's move to England after World War II. The epilogue to this book is an apocalyptic vision of twentieth-century civilization on the verge of cataclysm, in which mad characters using ESP are portrayed as more sane than those who accept the insanities of society.

Some of Lessing's work is not easily categorized. Her most widely read work, *The Golden Notebook* (1962), is a novel written in the form of interlocking diaries and notebooks. Some of her works seem significant as psychosocial documents as well as literature, for she describes her perceptions with such clarity that many readers are shocked to recognize their own feelings with new force.

A Sunrise on the Veld

Every night that winter he said aloud into the dark of the pillow: Half-past four! Half-past four! till he felt his brain had gripped the words and held them fast. Then he fell asleep at once, as if a shutter had fallen; and lay with his face turned to the clock so that he could see it first thing when he woke.

It was half-past four to the minute, every morning. Triumphantly pressing down the alarm knob of the clock, which the dark half of his mind had outwitted, remaining vigilant all night and counting the hours as he lay relaxed in sleep, he huddled down for a last warm moment under the clothes, playing with the idea of lying abed for this once only. But he played with it for the fun of knowing that it was a weakness he could defeat without effort; just as he set the alarm each night for the delight of the moment when he woke and stretched his limbs, feeling the muscles tighten, and thought: Even my brain—even that! I can control every part of myself.

Luxury of warm rested body, with the arms and legs and fingers waiting like soldiers for a word of command! Joy of knowing that the precious hours were given to sleep voluntarily!—for he had once stayed awake three nights running, to prove that he could, and then worked all day, refusing even to admit that he was tired; and now sleep seemed to him a servant to be commanded and refused.

The boy stretched his frame full length, touching the wall at his head with his hands, and the bedfoot with his toes; then he sprung out, like a fish leaping from water. And it was cold, cold.

He always dressed rapidly, so as to try and conserve his night warmth till the sun rose two hours later; but by the time he had on his clothes his hands were numbed and he could scarcely hold his shoes. These he could not put on for fear of waking his parents, who never came to know how early he rose.

As soon as he stepped over the lintel, the flesh of his soles contracted on the chilled earth, and his legs began to ache with cold. It was night: the stars were glittering, the trees standing black and still. He looked for signs of day, for the graying of the edge of a stone, or a lightening in the sky where the sun would rise, but there was nothing yet. Alert as an animal he crept past the dangerous window, standing poised with his hand on the sill for one proudly fastidious moment, looking in at the stuffy blackness of the room where his parents lay.

Feeling for the grass-edge of the path with his toes, he reached inside another window further along the wall, where his gun had been set in readiness the night before. The steel was icy, and numbed fingers slipped along it, so that he had to hold it in the crook of his arm for safety. Then he tiptoed to the room where the dogs slept, and was fearful that they might have been tempted to go before him; but they were waiting, their haunches crouched in reluctance at the cold, but ears and swinging tails greeting the gun ecstatically. His warning undertone kept them secret and silent till the house was a hundred yards back: then they bolted off into the bush, yelping excitedly. The boy imagined his parents turning in their beds and muttering: Those dogs again! before they were dragged back in sleep; and he smiled scornfully. He always looked back over his shoulder at the house before he passed a wall of trees that shut it from sight. It looked so low and small, crouching there under a tall and brilliant sky. Then he turned his back on it, and on the frowsting[1] sleepers, and forgot them.

He would have to hurry. Before the light grew strong he must be four miles away; and already a tint of green stood in the hollow of a leaf, and the air smelled of morning and the stars were dimming.

He slung the shoes over his shoulder, veld skoen[2] that were crinkled and hard with the dews of a hundred mornings. They would be necessary when the ground became too hot to bear. Now he felt the chilled dust push up between his toes, and he let the muscles of his feet spread and settle into the shapes of the earth; and he thought: I could walk a hundred miles on feet like these! I could walk all day, and never tire!

He was walking swiftly through the dark tunnel of foliage that in daytime was a road. The dogs were invisibly ranging the lower travelways of the bush, and he heard them panting. Sometimes he felt a cold muzzle on his leg before they were off again, scouting for a trail to follow. They were not trained, but free-running companions of the hunt, who often tired of the long stalk before the final shots, and went off on their own pleasure. Soon he could see them, small and wild-looking in a wild strange light, now that the bush stood trembling on the verge of color, waiting for the sun to paint earth and grass afresh.

The grass stood to his shoulders; and the trees were showering a faint silvery rain. He was soaked; his whole body was clenched in a steady shiver.

Once he bent to the road that was newly scored with animal trails, and regretfully straightened, reminding himself that the pleasure of tracking must wait till another day.

He began to run along the edge of a field, noting jerkily how it was filmed over with fresh spiderweb, so that the long reaches of great black clods seemed netted in glistening gray. He was using the steady lope he had learned by watching the natives, the run that is a dropping of the weight of the body from one foot to the next in a slow balancing movement that never tires, nor shortens the breath; and he felt the blood pulsing down his legs and along his arms, and the exultation and pride of body mounted in him till he was shutting his teeth hard against a violent desire to shout his triumph.

Soon he had left the cultivated part of the farm. Behind him the bush was low and black. In front was a long vlei,[3] acres of long pale grass that sent back a hollowing gleam of light to a satiny sky. Near him thick swathes of grass were bent with the weight of water, and diamond drops sparkled on each frond.

The first bird woke at his feet and at once a flock of them sprang into the air calling shrilly that day had come; and suddenly, behind him, the bush woke into song, and he could hear the guinea fowl calling far ahead of him. That meant they would now be sailing down from their trees into thick grass, and it was for them he had come: he was too late. But he did not mind. He forgot he had come to shoot. He set his legs wide, and balanced from foot to foot, and swung his gun up and down in both hands horizontally, in a kind of improvised exercise, and let his head sink back till it was pillowed in his neck muscles, and watched how above him small rosy clouds floated in a lake of gold.

Suddenly it all rose in him: it was unbearable. He leaped up into the air, shouting and yelling wild, unrecognizable noises. Then he began to run, not carefully, as he had before, but madly, like a wild thing. He was clean crazy, yelling mad with the joy of living and a superfluity of youth. He rushed down the vlei under a tumult of crimson and gold, while all

---

1. **frowsting:** lounging about in a hot stuffy room.
2. **veld skoen:** In South Africa, a veld (fĕlt) is open grassy country with few bushes and almost no trees. Veld skoen (fĕlt′ shūn) are rawhide homemade shoes.
3. **vlei** (flā): low-lying swampy land.

the birds of the world sang about him. He ran in great leaping strides, and shouted as he ran, feeling his body rise into the crisp rushing air and fall back surely on to sure feet; and though briefly, not believing that such a thing could happen to him, that he could break his ankle any moment, in this thick tangled grass. He cleared bushes like a duiker,[4] leaped over rocks; and finally came to a dead stop at a place where the ground fell abruptly away below him to the river. It had been a two-mile-long dash through waist-high growth, and he was breathing hoarsely and could no longer sing. But he poised on a rock and looked down at stretches of water that gleamed through stooping trees, and thought suddenly, I am fifteen! Fifteen! The words came new to him; so that he kept repeating them wonderingly, with swelling excitement; and he felt the years of his life with his hands, as if he were counting marbles, each one hard and separate and compact, each one a wonderful shining thing. That was what he was: fifteen years of this rich soil, and this slow-moving water, and air that smelled like a challenge whether it was warm and sultry at noon, or as brisk as cold water, like it was now.

There was nothing he couldn't do, nothing! A vision came to him, as he stood there, like when a child hears the word *eternity* and tries to understand it, and time takes possession of the mind. He felt his life ahead of him as a great and wonderful thing, something that was his; and he said aloud, with the blood rising to his head: all the great men of the world have been as I am now, and there is nothing I can't become, nothing I can't do; there is no country in the world I cannot make part of myself, if I choose. I contain the world. I can make of it what I want. If I choose, I can change everything that is going to happen: it depends on me, and what I decide now.

The urgency, and the truth and the courage of what his voice was saying exulted him so that he began to sing again, at the top of his voice, and the sound went echoing down the river gorge. He stopped for the echo, and sang again: stopped and shouted. That was what he was!—he sang, if he chose; and the world had to answer him.

And for minutes he stood there, shouting and singing and waiting for the lovely eddying sound of the echo; so that his own new strong thoughts came back and washed round his head, as if someone were answering him and encouraging him; till the gorge was full of soft voices clashing back and forth from rock to rock over the river. And then it seemed as if there was a new voice. He listened, puzzled, for it was not his own. Soon he was leaning forward, all his nerves alert, quite still: somewhere close to him there was a noise that was no joyful bird, nor tinkle of falling water, nor ponderous movement of cattle.

There it was again. In the deep morning hush that held his future and his past, was a sound of pain, and repeated over and over: it was a kind of shortened scream, as if someone, something, had no breath to scream. He came to himself, looked about him, and called for the dogs. They did not appear: they had gone off on their own business, and he was alone. Now he was clean sober, all the madness gone. His heart beating fast, because of that frightened screaming, he stepped carefully off the rock and went towards a belt of trees. He was moving cautiously, for not so long ago he had seen a leopard in just this spot.

At the edge of the trees he stopped and peered, holding his gun ready; he advanced, looking steadily about him, his eyes narrowed. Then, all at once, in the middle of a step, he faltered, and his face was puzzled. He shook his head impatiently, as if he doubted his own sight.

There, between two trees, against a background of gaunt black rocks, was a figure from

---

4. **duiker** (dī′ kər): a small African antelope.

a dream, a strange beast that was horned and drunken-legged, but like something he had never even imagined. It seemed to be ragged. It looked like a small buck that had black ragged tufts of fur standing up irregularly all over it, with patches of raw flesh beneath . . . but the patches of rawness were disappearing under moving black and came again elsewhere; and all the time the creature screamed, in small gasping screams, and leaped drunkenly from side to side, as if it were blind.

Then the boy understood: it *was* a buck. He ran closer, and again stood still, stopped by a new fear. Around him the grass was whispering and alive. He looked wildly about, and then down. The ground was black with ants, great energetic ants that took no notice of him, but hurried and scurried towards the fighting shape, like glistening black water flowing through the grass.

And, as he drew in his breath and pity and terror seized him, the beast fell and the screaming stopped. Now he could hear nothing but one bird singing, and the sound of the rustling whispering ants.

He peered over at the writhing blackness that jerked convulsively with the jerking nerves. It grew quieter. There were small twitches from the mass that still looked vaguely like the shape of a small animal.

It came into his mind that he should shoot it and end its pain; and he raised the gun. Then he lowered it again. The buck could no longer feel; its fighting was a mechanical protest of the nerves. But it was not that which made him put down the gun. It was a swelling feeling of rage and misery and protest that expressed itself in the thought; if I had not come it would have died like this: so why should I interfere? All over the bush things like this happen; they happen all the time; this is how life goes on, by living things dying in anguish. He gripped the gun between his knees and felt in his own limbs the myriad swarming pain of the twitching animal that could no longer feel, and set his teeth, and said over and over again under his breath: I can't stop it. I can't stop it. There is nothing I can do.

He was glad that the buck was unconscious and had gone past suffering so that he did not have to make a decision to kill it even when he was feeling with his whole body: this is what happens, this is how things work.

It was right—that was what he was feeling. *It was right and nothing could alter it.*

The knowledge of fatality, of what has to be, had gripped him and for the first time in his life; and he was left unable to make any movement of brain or body, except to say: "Yes, yes. That is what living is." It had entered his flesh and his bones and grown in to the furthest corners of his brain and would never leave him. And at that moment he could not have performed the smallest action of mercy, knowing as he did, having lived on it all his life, the vast unalterable, cruel veld, where at any moment one might stumble over a skull or crush the skeleton of some small creature.

Suffering, sick, and angry, but also grimly satisfied with his new stoicism,[5] he stood there leaning on his rifle, and watched the seething black mound grow smaller. At his feet, now, were ants trickling back with pink fragments in their mouths, and there was a fresh acid smell in his nostrils. He sternly controlled the uselessly convulsing muscles of his empty stomach, and reminded himself: the ants must eat too! At the same time he found that the tears were streaming down his face, and his clothes were soaked with the sweat of that other creature's pain.

The shape had grown small. Now it looked

---

5. **stoicism** (stō' ĭ cĭsm): indifference to pleasure or pain. The Stoics founded a Greek school of philosophy about 300 B.C., teaching that human beings should remain indifferent to the external world and to passion or emotion.

like nothing recognizable. He did not know how long it was before he saw the blackness thin, and bits of white showed through, shining in the sun—yes, there was the sun, just up, glowing over the rocks. Why, the whole thing could not have taken longer than a few minutes.

He began to swear, as if the shortness of the time was in itself unbearable, using the words he had heard his father say. He strode forward, crushing ants with each step, and brushing them off his clothes, till he stood above the skeleton, which lay sprawled under a small bush. It was clean-picked. It might have been lying there years, save that on the white bone were pink fragments of gristle. About the bones ants were ebbing away, their pincers full of meat.

The boy looked at them, big black ugly insects. A few were standing and gazing up at him with small glittering eyes.

"Go away!" he said to the ants, very coldly. "I am not for you—not just yet, at any rate. Go away." And he fancied that the ants turned and went away.

He bent over the bones and touched the sockets in the skull; that was where the eyes were, he thought incredulously, remembering the liquid dark eyes of a buck. And then he bent the slim foreleg bone, swinging it horizontally in his palm.

That morning, perhaps an hour ago, this small creature had been stepping proud and free through the bush, feeling the chill on its hide even as he himself had done, exhilarated by it. Proudly stepping the earth, tossing its horns, frisking a pretty white tail, it had sniffed the cold morning air. Walking like kings and conquerors it had moved through this free-held bush, where each blade of grass grew for it alone, and where the river ran pure sparkling water for its slaking.

And then—what had happened? Such a swift surefooted thing could surely not be trapped by a swarm of ants?

The boy bent curiously to the skeleton. Then he saw that the back leg that lay uppermost and strained out in the tension of death, was snapped midway in the thigh, so that broken bones jutted over each other uselessly. So that was it! Limping into the ant-masses it could not escape, once it had sensed the danger. Yes, but how had the leg been broken? Had it fallen, perhaps? Impossible, a buck was too light and graceful. Had some jealous rival horned it?

What could possibly have happened? Perhaps some Africans had thrown stones at it, as they do, trying to kill it for meat, and had broken its leg. Yes, that must be it.

Even as he imagined the crowd of running, shouting natives, and the flying stones, and the leaping buck, another picture came into his mind. He saw himself, on any one of these bright ringing mornings, drunk with excitement, taking a snap shot at some half-seen buck. He saw himself with the gun lowered, wondering whether he had missed or not; and thinking at last that it was late, and he wanted his breakfast, and it was not worth while to track miles after an animal that would very likely get away from him in any case.

For a moment he would not face it. He was a small boy again, kicking sulkily at the skeleton, hanging his head, refusing to accept the responsibility.

Then he straightened up, and looked down at the bones with an odd expression of dismay, all the anger gone out of him. His mind went quite empty: all around him he could see trickles of ants disappearing into the grass. The whispering noise was faint and dry, like the rustling of a cast snakeskin.

At last he picked up his gun and walked homewards. He was telling himself half defiantly that he wanted his breakfast. He was telling himself that it was getting very hot, much too hot to be out roaming the bush.

Really, he was tired. He walked heavily, not

looking where he put his feet. When he came within sight of his home he stopped, knitting his brows. There was something he had to think out. The death of that small animal was a thing that concerned him, and he was by no means finished with it. It lay at the back of his mind uncomfortably.

Soon, the very next morning, he would get clear of everybody and go to the bush and think about it.

Getting at Meaning

1. Why does the boy in this story get up at half-past four? How does he feel about himself and about his surroundings as he goes out into the veld?

2. Describe the boy's emotional reaction to the sunrise. How does he express his feelings?

3. What happens to interrupt his moment of joy? How does the imagery of the story change?

4. How does the boy feel toward the buck? How does his reaction to the buck change his entire outlook on life? What similarities between the buck and the boy are implied or stated throughout the story? Is the boy aware of these similarities? Explain.

5. Is the cause of the buck's injury made clear in this story? Why, or why not? How do you think that the experience described in this story will affect the boy in the future? What has he learned about himself and about hunting, for example?

Developing Skills in Reading Literature

1. **Imagery.** Because sight is the most highly developed sense, the majority of images in literature are visual. However, imagery may also appeal to the senses of smell (olfactory), hearing (auditory), taste (gustatory), and touch (tactile). Images that re-create a sensation of heat are called thermal; images that re-create movement are called kinetic; and images that re-create tension felt through muscles, tendons, or joints within the body are called kinesthetic.

Identify several different kinds of imagery in this selection. Examine particularly the passage describing the boy's ecstatic feelings at sunrise. How does the lavish imagery contribute to the effectiveness of this story?

2. **Naturalism.** Naturalism is an extreme form of realism in which characters exist in a harsh world, victims of environmental forces and internal drives beyond their control or comprehension. In this story the creatures of the veld act according to universal laws that apply to all life, including human life. How does the veld represent the world? What do the ants represent, from the view of a naturalistic philosophy? What causes the buck's death, in a symbolic rather than a concrete sense? Is the boy, as a character, typical of a naturalistic short story? What tempers the naturalism of this story?

3. **Title.** Think about the connotations of the word *sunrise*. Why is "A Sunrise on the Veld" an apt title for this story? In answering this question, be sure to consider the age of the main character, the change that takes place in him, and the significance of nature in the story.

Arthur C. Clarke

born in 1917

More than any other writer, Arthur C. Clarke has made science fiction intellectually respectable. While most writers of science fiction novels and short stories have modest ambitions, seeking primarily to entertain, Clarke combines a sound scientific foundation with a skillful narrative style, often writing prophetically of future explorations. As Clarke once explained, "My chief aim is . . . 'The search for wonder.' However, I am almost equally interested in style and rhythm."

Born at Minehead, Somerset, Clarke graduated with honors in physics and mathematics at King's College, London. From 1941 to 1946 he was a Flight Lieutenant in the Royal Air Force, serving as radar instructor and as technical officer on the first ground controlled approach radar. Fascinated by technology, Clarke published his first science fiction stories during this period, and in 1945 he wrote an article for *Wireless World* predicting in detail the use of satellites for communications. Clarke was an assistant editor of *Physics Abstracts* in London in 1949 and 1950, and since 1954 he has been engaged in underwater exploration and photography off the coast of Sri Lanka and the Great Barrier Reef of Australia.

Clarke has published scientific works as well as fiction, including his first book, *Interplanetary Flight: An Introduction to Astronautics* (1950). In several early novels, such as *The Sands of Mars* (1952) and *Earthlight* (1955) he describes the exploration of a new environment. Among his primarily philosophical and religious works are *Childhood's End* (1953), *The City and the Stars* (1956), and *2001: A Space Odyssey* (1968) on which he collaborated with film maker Stanley Kubrick. Clarke's

ARTHUR C. CLARKE. *Jill Krementz.*

short stories are more experimental than his novels. "Transcience" is a prose poem about three stages in human existence, while "Hate" is a moral fable.

Clarke's work describes a universe that challenges humanity by its infinite strangeness and richness, its ultimate beauty. He creates heroes who are romantic mavericks, such as might be found in westerns, detective stories, and historical adventures. Clarke says, "My main themes are exploration (space, sea, time), the position of Man in the hierarchy of the universe, and the effect of contact with other intelligences."

History Lesson

No one could remember when the tribe had begun its long journey. The land of great rolling plains that had been its first home was now no more than a half-forgotten dream.

For many years, Shann and his people had been fleeing through a country of low hills and sparkling lakes, and now the mountains lay ahead. This summer they must cross them to the southern lands. There was little time to lose. The white terror that had come down from the Poles, grinding continents to dust and freezing the very air before it, was less than a day's march behind.

Shann wondered if the glaciers could climb the mountains ahead, and within his heart he dared to kindle a little flame of hope. This might prove a barrier against which even the remorseless ice would batter in vain. In the southern lands of which the legends spoke, his people might find refuge at last.

It took weeks to discover a pass through which the tribe and the animals could travel. When midsummer came, they had camped in a lonely valley where the air was thin and the stars shone with a brilliance no one had ever seen before.

The summer was waning when Shann took his two sons and went ahead to explore the way. For three days they climbed, and for three nights slept as best they could on the freezing rocks, and on the fourth morning there was nothing ahead but a gentle rise to a cairn[1] of gray stones built by other travelers, centuries ago.

Shann felt himself trembling, and not with cold, as they walked toward the little pyramid of stones. His sons had fallen behind. No one spoke, for too much was at stake. In a little while they would know if all their hopes had been betrayed.

To east and west, the wall of mountains curved away as if embracing the land beneath. Below lay endless miles of undulating plain, with a great river swinging across it in tremendous loops. It was a fertile land, one in which the tribe could raise crops knowing that there would be no need to flee before the harvest came.

Then Shann lifted his eyes to the south, and saw the doom of all his hopes. For there at the edge of the world glimmered that deadly light he had seen so often to the north—the glint of ice below the horizon.

There was no way forward. Through all the years of flight, the glaciers from the south had been advancing to meet them. Soon they would be crushed beneath the moving walls of ice . . .

Southern glaciers did not reach the mountains until a generation later. In that last summer the sons of Shann carried the sacred treasures of the tribe to the lonely cairn overlooking the plain. The ice that had once gleamed below the horizon was now almost at their feet. By spring it would be splintering against the mountain walls.

No one understood the treasures now. They were from a past too distant for the understanding of any man alive. Their origins were lost in the mists that surrounded the Golden Age, and how they had come at last into the possession of this wandering tribe was a story that now would never be told. For it was the story of a civilization that had passed beyond recall.

---

1. **cairn:** a conical heap of stones built as a monument or landmark.

Once, all these pitiful relics had been treasured for some good reason, and now they had become sacred though their meaning had long been lost. The print in the old books had faded centuries ago though much of the lettering was still visible—if there had been any to read it. But many generations had passed since anyone had had a use for a set of seven-figure logarithms, an atlas of the world, and the score of Sibelius's[2] Seventh Symphony printed, according to the flyleaf, by H.K. Chu and Sons, at the City of Pekin in the year 2371 A.D.

The old books were placed reverently in the little crypt that had been made to receive them. There followed a motley collection of fragments—gold and platinum coins, a broken telephoto lens, a watch, a cold-light lamp, a microphone, the cutter from an electric razor, some midget radio tubes, the flotsam[3] that had been left behind when the great tide of civilization had ebbed forever.

All these treasures were carefully stowed away in their resting place. Then came three more relics, the most sacred of all because the least understood.

The first was a strangely shaped piece of metal, showing the coloration of intense heat. It was, in its way, the most pathetic of all these symbols from the past, for it told of man's greatest achievement and of the future he might have known. The mahogany stand on which it was mounted bore a silver plate with the inscription

Auxiliary Igniter from Starboard Jet
Spaceship "Morning Star"
Earth-Moon, A.D. 1985

Next followed another miracle of the ancient science—a sphere of transparent plastic with strangely shaped pieces of metal imbedded in it. At its center was a tiny capsule of synthetic radio-element, surrounded by the converting screens that shifted its radiation far down the spectrum. As long as the material remained active, the sphere would be a tiny radio transmitter, broadcasting power in all directions. Only a few of these spheres had ever been made. They had been designed as perpetual beacons to mark the orbits of the asteroids. But man had never reached the asteroids and the beacons had never been used.

Last of all was a flat, circular tin, wide in comparison with its depth. It was heavily sealed, and rattled when shaken. The tribal lore predicted that disaster would follow if it was ever opened, and no one knew that it held one of the great works of art of nearly a thousand years before.

The work was finished. The two men rolled the stones back into place and slowly began to descend the mountainside. Even to the last, man had given some thought to the future and had tried to preserve something for posterity.

That winter the great waves of ice began their first assault on the mountains, attacking from north and south. The foothills were overwhelmed in the first onslaught, and the glaciers ground them into dust. But the mountains stood firm, and when the summer came the ice retreated for a while.

So, winter after winter, the battle continued, and the roar of the avalanches, the grinding of rock and the explosions of splintering ice filled the air with tumult. No war of man's had been fiercer than this, and even man's battles had not quite engulfed the globe as this had done.

At last the tidal waves of ice began to subside and to creep slowly down the flanks of the mountains they had never quite subdued. The valleys and passes were still firmly in their grip. It was stalemate. The glaciers had met their match, but their defeat was too late to be of any use to man.

---

2. **Sibelius:** Jean Sibelius (1865–1957), Finnish composer.
3. **flotsam:** the wreckage of a ship or its cargo found floating on the sea or washed ashore.

So the centuries passed, and presently there happened something that must occur once at least in the history of every world in the universe, no matter how remote and lonely it may be.

The ship from Venus came five thousand years too late, but its crew knew nothing of this. While still many millions of miles away, the telescopes had seen the great shroud of ice that made Earth the most brilliant object in the sky next to the sun itself.

Here and there the dazzling sheet was marred by black specks that revealed the presence of almost buried mountains. That was all. The rolling oceans, the plains and forests, the deserts and lakes—all that had been the world of man was sealed beneath the ice, perhaps forever.

The ship closed in to Earth and established an orbit less than a thousand miles away. For five days it circled the planet, while cameras recorded all that was left to see and a hundred instruments gathered information that would give the Venusian scientists many years of work.

An actual landing was not intended. There seemed little purpose in it. But on the sixth day the picture changed. A panoramic monitor, driven to the limit of its amplification, detected the dying radiation of the five-thousand-year-old beacon. Through all the centuries, it had been sending out its signals with ever-failing strength as its radioactive heart steadily weakened.

The monitor locked on the beacon frequency. In the control room, a bell clamored for attention. A little later, the Venusian ship broke free from its orbit and slanted down toward Earth, toward a range of mountains that still towered proudly above the ice, and to a cairn of gray stones that the years had scarcely touched. . . .

The great disk of the sun blazed fiercely in a sky no longer veiled with mist, for the clouds that had once hidden Venus had now completely gone. Whatever force had caused the change in the sun's radiation had doomed one civilization, but had given birth to another. Less than five thousand years before, the half-savage people of Venus had seen sun and stars for the first time. Just as the science of Earth had begun with astronomy, so had that of Venus, and on the warm, rich world that man had never seen progress had been incredibly rapid.

Perhaps the Venusians had been lucky. They never knew the Dark Age that held man enchained for a thousand years. They missed the long detour into chemistry and mechanics but came at once to the more fundamental laws of radiation physics. In the time that man had taken to progress from the Pyramids to the rocket-propelled spaceship, the Venusians had passed from the discovery of agriculture to antigravity itself—the ultimate secret that man had never learned.

The warm ocean that still bore most of the young planet's life rolled its breakers languidly against the sandy shore. So new was this continent that the very sands were coarse and gritty. There had not yet been time enough for the sea to wear them smooth.

The scientists lay half in the water, their beautiful reptilian bodies gleaming in the sunlight. The greatest minds of Venus had gathered on this shore from all the islands of the planet. What they were going to hear they did not know, except that it concerned the Third World and the mysterious race that had peopled it before the coming of the ice.

The Historian was standing on the land, for the instruments he wished to use had no love of water. By his side was a large machine which attracted many curious glances from his colleagues. It was clearly concerned with optics, for a lens system projected from it toward a screen of white material a dozen yards away.

The Historian began to speak. Briefly he recapitulated what little had been discovered concerning the Third Planet and its people.

He mentioned the centuries of fruitless research that had failed to interpret a single word of the writings of Earth. The planet had been inhabited by a race of great technical ability. That, at least, was proved by the few pieces of machinery that had been found in the cairn upon the mountain.

"We do not know why so advanced a civilization came to an end," he observed. "Almost certainly, it had sufficient knowledge to survive an Ice Age. There must have been some other factor of which we know nothing. Possibly disease or racial degeneration may have been responsible. It has even been suggested that the tribal conflicts endemic to our own species in prehistoric times may have continued on the Third Planet after the coming of technology.

"Some philosophers maintain that knowledge of machinery does not necessarily imply a high degree of civilization, and it is theoretically possible to have wars in a society possessing mechanical power, flight, and even radio. Such a conception is alien to our thoughts, but we must admit its possibility. It would certainly account for the downfall of the lost race.

"It has always been assumed that we should never know anything of the physical form of the creatures who lived on Planet Three. For centuries our artists have been depicting scenes from the history of the dead world, peopling it with all manner of fantastic beings. Most of these creations have resembled us more or less closely, though it has often been pointed out that because *we* are reptiles it does not follow that all intelligent life must necessarily be reptilian.

"We now know the answer to one of the most baffling problems of history. At last, after hundreds of years of research, we have discovered the exact form and nature of the ruling life on the Third Planet."

There was a murmur of astonishment from the assembled scientists. Some were so taken aback that they disappeared for a while into the comfort of the ocean, as all Venusians were apt to do in moments of stress. The Historian waited until his colleagues re-emerged into the element they so disliked. He himself was quite comfortable, thanks to the tiny sprays that were continually playing over his body. With their help he could live on land for many hours before having to return to the ocean.

The excitement slowly subsided and the lecturer continued:

"One of the most puzzling of the objects found on Planet Three was a flat metal container holding a great length of transparent plastic material, perforated at the edges and wound tightly into a spool. This transparent tape at first seemed quite featureless, but an examination with the new subelectronic microscope has shown that this is not the case. Along the surface of the material, invisible to our eyes but perfectly clear under the correct radiation, are literally thousands of tiny pictures. It is believed that they were imprinted on the material by some chemical means, and have faded with the passage of time.

"These pictures apparently form a record of life as it was on the Third Planet at the height of its civilization. They are not independent. Consecutive pictures are almost identical, differing only in the detail of movement. The purpose of such a record is obvious. It is only necessary to project the scenes in rapid succession to give an illusion of continuous movement. We have made a machine to do this, and I have here an exact reproduction of the picture sequence.

"The scenes you are now going to witness take us back many thousands of years, to the great days of our sister planet. They show a complex civilization, many of whose activities we can only dimly understand. Life seems to have been very violent and energetic, and much that you will see is quite baffling.

"It is clear that the Third Planet was inhabited by a number of different species, none of them reptilian. That is a blow to our pride, but the conclusion is inescapable. The dominant type of life appears to have been a two-armed biped. It walked upright and covered its body with some flexible material, possibly for protection against the cold, since even before the Ice Age the planet was at a much lower temperature than our own world. But I will not try your patience any further. You will now see the record of which I have been speaking.''

A brilliant light flashed from the projector. There was a gentle whirring, and on the screen appeared hundreds of strange beings moving rather jerkily to and fro. The picture expanded to embrace one of the creatures, and the scientists could see that the Historian's description had been correct.

The creature possessed two eyes, set rather close together, but the other facial adornments were a little obscure. There was a large orifice in the lower portion of the head that was continually opening and closing. Possibly it had something to do with the creature's breathing.

The scientists watched spellbound as the strange being became involved in a series of fantastic adventures. There was an incredibly violent conflict with another, slightly different creature. It seemed certain that they must both be killed, but when it was all over neither seemed any the worse.

Then came a furious drive over miles of country in a four-wheeled mechanical device which was capable of extraordinary feats of locomotion. The ride ended in a city packed with other vehicles moving in all directions at breathtaking speeds. No one was surprised to see two of the machines meet head on with devastating results.

After that, events became even more complicated. It was now quite obvious that it would take many years of research to analyze and understand all that was happening. It was also clear that the record was a work of art, somewhat stylized, rather than an exact reproduction of life as it actually had been on the Third Planet.

Most of the scientists felt themselves completely dazed when the sequence of pictures came to an end. There was a final flurry of motion, in which the creature that had been the center of interest became involved in some tremendous but incomprehensible catastrophe. The picture contracted to a circle, centered on the creature's head.

The last scene of all was an expanded view of its face, obviously expressing some powerful emotion. But whether it was rage, grief, defiance, resignation or some other feeling could not be guessed. The picture vanished. For a moment some lettering appeared on the screen, then it was all over.

For several minutes there was complete silence, save for the lapping of the waves upon the sand. The scientists were too stunned to speak. The fleeting glimpse of Earth's civilization had had a shattering effect on their minds. Then little groups began to start talking together, first in whispers and then more and more loudly as the implications of what they had seen became clearer. Presently the Historian called for attention and addressed the meeting again.

''We are now planning,'' he said, ''a vast program of research to extract all available knowledge from this record. Thousands of copies are being made for distribution to all workers. You will appreciate the problems involved. The psychologists in particular have an immense task confronting them.

''But I do not doubt that we shall succeed. In another generation, who can say what we may not have learned of this wonderful race? Before we leave, let us look again at our remote cousins, whose wisdom may have surpassed our own but of whom so little has survived.''

Once more the final picture flashed on the screen, motionless this time, for the projector had been stopped. With something like awe, the scientists gazed at the still figure from the past, while in turn the little biped stared back at them with its characteristic expression of arrogant bad temper.

For the rest of time it would symbolize the human race. The psychologists of Venus would analyze its actions and watch its every movement until they could reconstruct its mind. Thousands of books would be written about it. Intricate philosophies would be contrived to account for its behavior.

But all this labor, all this research, would be utterly in vain. Perhaps the proud and lonely figure on the screen was smiling sardonically at the scientists who were starting on their age-long fruitless quest.

Its secret would be safe as long as the universe endured, for no one now would ever read the lost language of Earth. Millions of times in the ages to come those last few words would flash across the screen, and none could ever guess their meaning:

A Walt Disney Production.

Getting at Meaning

1. What is the setting for this story? When were the treasures first "stowed away in their resting place"? At what point in the story do you first become aware of the futuristic time frame? What is deceptive about the setting as it is described at the beginning of the story?

2. What does the motley collection of relics reveal about human civilization? In what sense was it a "great tide of civilization"? What is the implied relationship between the culture dating from 2371 and the earlier culture dating from 1985?

3. What false assumption does the historian from Venus make about the pictures of Earth's inhabitants? What clues throughout the historian's lecture suggest the actual subject matter of the film?

Developing Skills in Reading Literature

1. **Science Fiction.** Science fiction is a form of fantasy in which scientific data and theories form the basis for adventures in the future or past, on other planets, or in unknown dimensions of time and space. Science fiction is written as entertainment and also as commentary on aspects of the real world. What possible messages might Clarke be suggesting to the twentieth-century reader of this story? What is the "history lesson"?

2. **Surprise Ending.** The success of "History Lesson" depends to a great degree upon the element of surprise at the end of the story. How is the ending an example of dramatic irony? How successful is this ending, from your point of view? When did you first identify the subject of the film, for example? What happens if the reader becomes aware of the Venusians' misconception earlier in the story? For example, what happens to the reader's view of the scientists? to the dramatic irony of the final line?

Joan Aiken

born in 1924

JOAN AIKEN.

Joan Aiken is a successful writer of both juvenile and adult fiction, including gothic romances and tales of mystery and suspense for adults; plays, teleplays, and poetry; and novels and short stories for children. Her superior literary skill, fertile imagination, and willingness to take risks result in works that transcend the usual limits of the popular genres in which she works.

Born in Rye, Sussex, Aiken is the daughter of Conrad Aiken, an American poet living in England. Aiken's mother educated her at home until she was twelve, and she attended Wychwood School, Oxford, from 1936 to 1941. She worked for the British Broadcasting Corporation in 1942 and 1943. Aiken then was librarian with the United Nations Information Center in London until 1949, after which she became an editor for Amalgamated Press, an English firm that published various magazines such as *Argosy*, *Women's Journal*, *Woman & Home*, and *Suspense*.

One of Aiken's first gothic-suspense stories was serialized in *Suspense*, and soon several others appeared in *Everywoman* magazine. Her first full-length adult fiction was *The Silence of Herondale* (1964). Aiken's gift for suspense is part of what makes her books so readable. She often uses fabulously unlikely plot twists along with typical features of melodrama such as physical illness and amnesia. Avoiding the simple narrative formula characteristic of gothic romances, Aiken uses flashbacks and differing points of view. Her plots are typical of the genre, however, as Aiken's admirably independent women invariably fall helplessly in love with total cads, forcing the heroines to struggle valiantly to achieve the inevitable happy ending.

Aiken's works for children are among her best writing. Her first big success was *The Wolves of Willoughby Chase* (1963), followed by many books and short stories, including *A Necklace of Raindrops and Other Stories* (1969). Aiken develops her characters fully and constructs her plots with interlocking details that give each work a sense of shape and coherence. She uses dialect for its richness and poetry and imbues her stories with the sense of mystery that she believes essential in books for children. In *The Way To Write for Children* (1982) she discusses these and other techniques, stating that children's writing "needs to have everything that is in adult writing squeezed into a smaller compass."

Follow My Fancy

"Uranium," said the captain. "Uranium 235." The words glittered on his tongue like sparks from a gold-stopped tooth.

There was no crew. The only answer came from the wind, which sang in the rigging of his crazy old ship like the music of Orpheus.[1] Jake Brandywine looked about him thoughtfully. The decks were clear. The sails were stowed, since there would be no need for them. In so far as was possible, old *Argo*[2] was trim and ready for the voyage.

Provisions? He had laid in a thousand breakfast biscuits, a thousand tins of lunch meat, a thousand tea cakes, a thousand bottles of dinner wine; food for over three years. And if, despite this store, hunger gnawed at him like an old rat, he could munch away at his supply of charcoal, brought for sketching seascapes.

Nevertheless, the captain had a hunted, haunted look in his eye; he glanced continually about him, started at sounds and grabbed convulsively at the shrouds when sea swallows swooped past. His hand, holding the little soapstone box of uranium shook uncontrollably, white at the knuckles, and sweat darted glistening on his forehead. He had the air of a man pursued by the furies, escaping only just in time.

To learn the reason for this state of affairs we must go back some months, and shift our scene to the luxuriously appointed consulting room of a Harley Street psychosomatic[3] specialist.

Dr. Killgruel looked at his patient appraisingly, noted the fine-drawn lines round eyes and mouth, the restless movements, the unsteady hands.

"You are Jake Brandywine the artist?" he inquired.

The patient nodded.

"I admire your work," said the doctor. "I am the possessor of an early Brandywine myself." He flicked a speck from his snowy sleeve. "Now, what is your trouble precisely?"

Jake looked somewhat shamefaced.

"You need not be embarrassed," said the doctor. "I can see that you are suffering from nervous exhaustion, a state which leads people into all sorts of odd activities, of no importance in themselves. One of my patients, for instance, suffers from a compulsion to get up in the night and eat the cheese out of the mousetraps in the pantry. His fingers are terribly badly bruised and he has chronic indigestion. But I interrupt."

He placed his fingertips together and looked attentively at Jake.

"My trouble is not like that exactly," Jake said. "It undoubtedly began with exhaustion. There is, as perhaps you know, an enormous demand for my work at present, not only by private buyers, but also for tube stations, corner houses, town halls, piers, and public lavatories. About a month ago I had been rushing to finish a series of murals for restaurant cars, working nineteen and twenty hours a day, and was suffering from acute physical fatigue. I live some distance from the center

---

1. **Orpheus** (ôr′ fē əs): in Greek mythology, a poet-musician with magical musical powers.
2. **Argo:** a mythical ship on which Jason sailed to find the Golden Fleece.
3. **psychosomatic:** designating a physical disorder caused by emotional disturbance.

of London, on the 93 bus route, and just at this time the service had been cut; I used to work all night and go home in the middle of the day, and in my exhausted state it seemed to me that I spent my entire life either working or waiting for buses that failed to appear.

"Well, one day, to pass the time, I started willing the bus to come; I imagined it cruising past Woolworths, along to the Town Hall, round the corner, over the railway bridge, and down to the bus stop. When I stopped concentrating and looked up, there was a 93, sure enough. Of course I was amused, and thought it nothing but a coincidence, but the next day the same thing happened, and every day after that; it became a sort of game which I played to distract myself."

The doctor nodded.

"That was all right. I didn't really take it seriously, you understand. But one evening when I was literally staggering with fatigue, I was waiting in Oxford Street, for a bus to take me to Hyde Park corner, and unconsciously, without intending to, I started playing my game. A flash of red caught my eye, I looked up, and there was a 93—a bus which, as you know, has no right to be in Oxford Street at all."

He stopped and gazed, hollow-eyed at the doctor, who smiled sympathetically.

"It must have been a dreadful moment," he agreed. "What did you do?"

"I took a taxi."

"Very sensible." The doctor's tone was approving. "Take as many as you can while the delusion lasts."

"But Doctor, it was no delusion. It was a real bus. And since then it has happened repeatedly. I can't stop thinking about 93 buses and they keep turning up everywhere. What terrifies me is the thought that sooner or later I shall fetch one down into the underground or a turkish bath or—or a canoe in the Serpentine—"

"Come, come," said Dr. Killgruel. "These are morbid fears. We can deal with them at once, very easily. Then I'll give you a tonic to set you right. You know quite well that your subconscious won't let you will a bus to appear in an unsuitable place any more than, for example, a hypnotic subject will let himself be ordered to do something which violates his conscience. He just refuses. Now, just to convince you, and make your mind easy on this point, I order you to will a 93 bus into this room."

"No, no!" exclaimed Brandywine, white with terror. "For god's sake, Doctor, don't make me do that!"

Dr. Killgruel was implacable.

"You must put yourself in my hands or I can do nothing for you. Will the bus to appear—I command you."

Jake gave him a desperate look and then with a visible effort summoned his forces as if he were drawing a deep breath.

There was a rending sound, a frantic tooting, a screech of brakes, and with a last burst of resolution Jake dragged the doctor to one side as a 93 bus bore triumphantly down upon them.

Dr. Killgruel was in hospital for two months. Jake hardly liked to go and see him, since he himself had escaped with bruises and concussion, though his state of mind was such that the number of 93 buses on London Transport's roster was more than trebled.

But when the doctor came out he summoned Jake for another consultation.

"Your case interests me," he said. "I've been thinking a lot about it, and I can see that until you're cured, which I'm convinced is only a matter of time, we must effect a transference."

"A transference?"

"Your remarkably powerful will must be trained on some object more suitable than a 93 bus. Can you think of anything else occupying a large part of your attention? There are generally several things of the sort in one's mind such as broken shirt buttons or lost letters."

"My life was so well organized until this business began," said Jake mournfully.

"Are you married?" asked Dr. Killgruel.

Jake shook his head. "I have a char,"[4] he said with brevity.

"Is there no female person present in your thoughts?"

At this Jake paused and a shadow came over his face. Then he said slowly, "I suppose you might say that of Miss M."

Pressed to explain himself he gave an account of Miss M.

He rented his studio from the art department of a fashion magazine called *Fancy*, which had more space than it required in its offices, and where he felt comfortably anonymous among the elegancies of typists and the detached Plymouth Brotherhood of typographers. The arrangement had worked admirably for a year, but recently there had been some internal rearrangements among the personnel of *Fancy* and he discovered that the editress, Miss Milk, had been installed in the room next his.

The first intimation he had was a series of melancholy howls which began at half-past ten each morning and continued throughout the day. These were explained when he found himself being scrutinized malevolently through the window by a pair of sapphire eyes; Miss M's Siamese was outside on the sill. He opened the window but was so repelled by the neurotic clamor raised by the creature that he shot it out into the passage.

This provoked the first of a series of notes: "Dear Mr. Brandywine, if you let Judas into your room, please see that he is returned to Room 515; he must not be allowed to wander about the building, as he gets lost." It was written on *Fancy* notepaper thick as steel plate, in an arrogant black hand, and signed with the initials A.M.

Brandywine resolved that never again should Judas set foot in his room, but it was impossible to adhere to this resolution as spring turned to sweltering summer and he was obliged to leave the windows open. Judas would come in, patter superciliously round the room, making Jake nervous by long silences and sudden querulous howls; then he would disappear through the window to his owner's room, incurring a perfect torrent of notes from Miss M: could Mr. Brandywine keep his room cleaner; Judas had to be shampooed to get the charcoal dust out of his fur; could Mr. Brandywine put away his paints when not in use as Judas had returned with chrome yellow on his paws and flake white on his tail; would Mr. Brandywine please refrain from feeding Judas (this when he had been driven to the vain resort of sardine sandwiches for pacificatory purposes) as one meal a day was sufficient for any Siamese.

Each note was signed A.M. and the initials began to have a malignant significance in Jake's mind. He pictured Miss Milk as a sort of embodied capital letter, a black gallows of a woman with square upper-case shoulders and feet like serifs.[5]

"Splendid," said the doctor at the end of this recital. "She will form the nexus of an excellent fixation. You must think about her all you can, and arrange to meet her. Reality is always more useful than imagination. And move up to town, out of range of the 93 buses. Come back and see me in a fortnight."

Next morning Brandywine was in his studio meditating pretexts for meeting Miss M, when the telephone rang and a frightened voice twittered into his ear that Miss Milk would be pleased if he would step round and have coffee with her at eleven-three. His state of mind hovered between alarm and elation at this rapid development; the transference seemed to be taking place with disconcerting speed.

When he entered Miss M's room he found her sitting in an attitude that would have

---

4. **char:** a charwoman, one who cleans.
5. **serifs:** in printing, a fine line projecting from the main stroke of a letter; in this case "tiny" or "nondescript."

been inelegant in most women; she was tipped back in her chair, crossed ankles resting on the corner of her desk. But all Brandywine could think was that she resembled a swallow, with the bird's slender, elongated silhouette. She was wearing a close, dark, smoke-blue dress which heightened the impression; wings of black hair, faintly silvered, were brushed back above haughty blue eyes and an angular profile.

She nodded coldly at Brandywine, indicating a chair, and a terrified little secretary scurried forward with a cup of coffee. Jake felt that unless he asserted himself now he was lost. "I wonder if you could let me have a drop of cognac," he said hoarsely. "I find I can't get through the day unless I have one at this time."

When he returned to his studio an hour later his mind was in a ferment. Miss M had commissioned a series of illustrations for *Fancy* at less than a third of his usual price, and she had also said that they must have lunch on Tuesday, a drink on Wednesday, and dinner on Thursday.

"What was the other thing I had to do?" he wondered, leaning out of his window and distractedly tearing up little bits of paper. The sight of windows across the road ornamented with squirls of whitewash reminded him; he was supposed to find a flat in town. If that one was empty he might as well inquire about it.

His hopes were justified and he moved in without delay, the only proviso[6] from the landlord being that he must not upset the tenant on the top flat, who did not care for dogs, modern music, or late parties.

He arrived home late the following evening to find a note stuck in his letter-box, and stood reading it by the landing light. It said: "Tenant No 17. Please do not leave fish heads on the fire escape. A.M."

He was still digesting this when a perfumed, dark-blue presence rustled up the stairs to him, closely followed by a Siamese.

A fortnight later Brandywine staggered into Dr. Killgruel's room more dead than alive.

"Well," said the doctor with interest. "How are things going? Are you getting the 93's reduced?"

"93's—" Jake brushed them aside. "It's not them, Doctor, it's Atalanta. She's killing me."

"*Who?*"

"Atalanta—Miss Milk. I can't sleep, I can't work, I can't think— she's always turning up. At seven in the morning she wants to borrow my spatula, at midnight she drops in saying she's run out of olive oil. Look at me—I've lost two stone[7] already."

"Is she beautiful?" inquired Killgruel professionally.

"Beautiful?" Jake groaned furiously, "my god, Doctor, she's a fiend. You should hear her rating that unfortunate child who works for her, or blowing up the char, or chiseling some wretched author down to subsistence rates. I shall go crazy. I can't stop thinking about her."

"I'd like to see her."

Jake threw him a look of despair, the door opened, and Miss M sailed in.

"It's good of you to spare me a moment," she said to Killgruel. "It isn't for myself—my health is always excellent, naturally—but Judas has been feeling the heat and seems to be rather nervy."

Poor Jake burst into tears and ran out of the room.

When Killgruel next saw Jake he was surprisingly calm and composed.

"I've made my own plans," he said. "I must get away from everything."

"An excellent plan," agreed the doctor. "Where are you going?"

"I've applied for the job of captain on the *Argo*."

---

6. **proviso:** condition or stipulation.
7. **stone:** in Great Britain, a unit of weight equal to fourteen pounds.

"The *Argo*!" said Killgruel, startled. Recently the papers had been full of the battered old schooner which was going to be the first craft powered solely by uranium. A little piece no bigger than a hazelnut, inserted in a special chamber under the stern would, it was suggested, propel the aged ship forever, like the tiny Japanese boats which dart about saucers of warm water impelled by little bits of camphor.

The only question unsolved was whether *Argo*, once launched, could be made to stop? No anchor cable would hold her; it was possible that a negative reaction might be started to neutralize the force under her keel, but this must be a matter of speculation until the experiment was carried out. There was a chance, therefore, that the man who hazarded himself on her worm-eaten decks was due to be a second Flying Dutchman,[8] borne in a random circle round the earth's circumference forever.

Jake seemed to relish the prospect.

"Frankly, I've had enough of civilization," he said. "A life in which one can be dogged by female fashion editors and 93 buses is no life for me."

"But," Dr. Killgruel objected, "what's to stop them from following you on board?"

"Navigation," Jake answered. "My mind will be too occupied for the first year. I've never been good at mathematics and I shan't have any attention to spare."

"It will come easier after a while."

"By that time I shall have recovered, or if not," said Jake decisively, "I shall throw myself overboard."

Dr. Killgruel could not entirely approve this course but he saw that Brandywine's mind was made up.

The Press of the world waited in excitement for the launching of *Argo*, but it waited at a distance; Jake had been particular that he should be left alone on the lonely Essex beach that was the taking-off point. Also, and this was perhaps a more cogent reason, there was the possibility of a nuclear explosion when the uranium was first subjected to the activating current.

Here was Jake, then, pacing about the deck, which sparkled with February frost, and glancing from time to time along the pale deserted line of sand, fringed with a white tidemark. Gulls keened, the wind sang, sharp gusts of sand, "travelers," blew from time to time past *Argo*'s keel in an offshore wind, as she snuggled deeper and deeper into her bed of sand and ooze.

The shipping lanes had been cleared, helicopters hovered at a respectful distance, and telegrams from statesmen and heads of governments were pinned to the mast; also photographs, self-sent, by enthusiastic schoolgirls.

At length Jake's anxious vigil was at an end; glancing for a last time at his watch, he climbed awkwardly down the swinging rope ladder over the stern, with care deposited the soapstone box and its precious contents in the prepared chamber, and snapped home the protective door. Then he swung himself back on deck, checked the time again, drew a deep breath, and pulled the switch of a tiny battery lying in the fo'c'sle.[9]

There was a convulsive jerk and shudder, as *Argo* tore herself loose from the mud, and then, with an unbelievably smooth and lightning-swift motion she darted off, cutting through the choppy sea like a razor.

"We've done it!" Jake cried, his face brilliant with happiness. "I'm free!" And he patted the old ship on her carved wooden quarter-deck railings before swinging himself aft to unlash the rudder and turn her on the agreed course down-Channel.

---

8. **Flying Dutchman:** a fabled Dutch sailor condemned to sail the seas until Judgment Day.
9. **fo'c'sle** (fōk' s'l): phonetic spelling of *forecastle;* the uppermost deck of a ship in front of the foremast.

She was followed in her flight by numerous aircraft. No ship could keep her in view, though many had a brief glimpse of her, masts set back like a scalded cat, scudding through the mist on her way to the South Atlantic.

Radio stations kept track of her progress as she fled by the Argentine coast and rounded Cape Horn; storm or shine meant nothing to her, she was through all weather before it could affect her.

The sole message transmitted by her captain from time to time was, "All well." In two days he had completed his first circuit of the world, in seven the urgently repeated question "Can you stop?" was answered by a laconic "No," and *Argo* pursued her crazy course into infinity.

Scientists, distressed at the thought of Jake skating over the world's aqueous surface for the rest of his life, like a grain of sand on an eyeball, worked night and day at the problem of how to put a brake on *Argo's* career. But no signs of distress came from Jake.

On a summer day some months later Dr. Killgruel was visited by Miss M. They had become friends since the departure of Brandywine, and the visit was nothing unusual, but she was looking pale, he thought, and rather sad; she said she was run down and needed a tonic.

"You hear nothing from Mr. Brandywine, I suppose?" she asked, and he noticed a wistful tone to her voice. "You know, it's odd, but I miss him terribly. I suppose he doesn't even think of me."

For the first time since he had met her she looked human, Killgruel reflected; human and vulnerable. There were tears in her eyes, even.

"I'm tired," she said miserably. "I can't work up any enthusiasm for *Fancy* nowadays. If only I thought he sometimes remembered me it would be a little better."

"Perhaps he will later on," said the doctor gently. "He's very occupied just now you know. You must give him time—" He paused, his words hanging in mid-air. For the chair in which Miss M had been sitting was empty, and nothing of her remained in the room save a fragrance of Chanel No. 5.

Eighteen months after *Argo's* launching, Jake signaled that he was running short of food. The scientists were surprised that their calculations on the duration of his provisions should have been so wide of the mark.

"Give reason for extra consumption," they radioed, and Jake replied, "Stowaways."

Dr. Killgruel managed to secure a place on the aircraft which was to parachute fresh supplies; the area chosen was the South Pacific.

Gradually they overhauled *Argo*; she appeared first as a speck on the shining blue, then as a cobweb or skeleton leaf, and finally as her rakish self, clawing through the water with a bone in her teeth. Slowly the plane gained on her, and at last held steady over her chalk-white decks while the little dandelion-puffs fluttered down with their life-saving cargoes of soya, sago, celery, and stout.[10]

Looking through powerful glasses Dr. Killgruel saw Brandywine and his stowaways. Dressed in nothing but a pair of old jeans, with an arm round Miss M, serene in a sarong, Jake sprawled in a hammock, brown as a nut and blissfully happy. Near at hand, like a faithful dinosaur, stood an attendant 93 bus.

---

10. **soya . . . stout:** health foods and strong British ale.

Getting at Meaning

1. Who is Jake Brandywine, and what is his problem? What is the doctor's diagnosis and treatment?

2. Describe Jake's new problem in his relationship with Miss Milk. What does he eventually do to escape this problem?

3. The ancient Greeks believed that the longer a person struggles against fate, the more problems occur. Once the struggle ends, the conflict is resolved. How does this philosophy apply to Aiken's story?

Developing Skills in Reading Literature

1. **Allusion.** In Getting at Meaning, question 3, you explored a possible link between this story and Greek philosophy. This interpretation is made more plausible by several allusions to mythology: Orpheus, Argo, the Flying Dutchman, Atalanta. Using the information provided in the footnotes and a dictionary of mythology, explain what each allusion suggests about the story.

2. **Fantasy.** Fantasy describes literary works such as *Alice in Wonderland,* which takes place in a nonexistent world and features unreal characters such as Humpty Dumpty. The term also refers to science fiction and to stories such as "Follow My Fancy" in which seemingly realistic characters overstep the boundaries of reality. The purpose of a fantasy may be simply to delight the reader or it may be to offer a serious comment on reality. Identify the fantastical elements in Aiken's story. What is the absurd premise on which it is based? Which events are impossible or highly unlikely? Note the way that the names of the characters add to the sense of fantasy. Why would someone named Brandywine flee from someone named Milk? Why is Killgruel an appropriate name for a "psychosomatic specialist"? What commentary does Aiken make on the psychiatric profession? on art and society? on human nature?

3. **Flashback.** As a structural device Aiken uses flashback within flashback. Analyze the chronology of this story, and comment on what effect is achieved by showing result before cause. How does the material presented through flashbacks create the irony of the final scene?

Developing Vocabulary

Inferring Word Meaning. Locate the following sentences in this selection and study the context in which they appear. Then determine the meaning of each italicized word, and suggest a synonym, using a dictionary as necessary.

a. ". . . he found himself being *scrutinized malevolently* through the window by a pair of sapphire eyes; Miss M's Siamese was outside on the sill."

b. "Judas would come in, patter *superciliously* round the room, making Jake nervous by long silences and sudden *querulous* howls. . . ."

c. ". . . this when he had been driven to the vain resort of sardine sandwiches for *pacificatory* purposes. . . ."

d. "'She will form the *nexus* of an excellent fixation.'"

J. B. Priestley

born in 1894

Novelist, playwright, critic, essayist, and biographer, John Boynton Priestley has created a body of work impressive in its scope. His fictional work ranges from traditional novels to plays that employ experimental and imaginative techniques. His social criticism combines perception and tolerance, amusement and provocation, and has attracted a wide readership through much of the twentieth century.

Priestley was born at Bradford, Yorkshire, where his father was a schoolmaster. He served in the Devonshire Regiment during World War I, after which he studied at Cambridge University. He went to London in 1922 to work as a reviewer and critic, and in 1927 he published two novels: *Adam in Moonshine* and *The Old Dark House*. He established his reputation as a novelist with *The Good Companions* (1929), which was both a popular and a critical success. In this book the narrative unfolds in a series of letters describing the adventures of a troupe of traveling players in England during the 1920's.

In 1932 Priestley entered the field of playwriting with *Dangerous Corner*, a notable success followed by *Eden End* (1934), *Time and the Conways* (1937), and *I Have Been Here Before* (1937). In these and other plays, Priestley is often innovative, using expressionist techniques and time distortion.

As a critic and essayist, Priestley addresses the problems of contemporary society, once saying,

J. B. PRIESTLEY.
Lord Snowden.

"Just when Man thinks he can do everything, he finds himself helpless in the clutch of some unknown force. And in this ironic principle, which appears to govern so much of our lives, I find delight." His novels, too, often contain serious social criticism and attest to Priestley's breadth of experience and depth of sympathy. *Angel Pavement* (1930) portrays the anguish and fear of people isolated in a city and *Walk in the City* (1936) reveals both the gaiety and the sadness of ordinary people.

from **Delight**

The Marx Brothers

One afternoon, nearly twenty years ago, some long-forgotten business took me to Golders Green, and when I had finished and was walking towards the Tube station there came a sudden drenching downpour. I had no raincoat, so I hurried into a cinema, more for shelter than for amusement. It was a large solemn cinema, almost empty, and I felt as quiet and remote in there as if I were sitting at the bottom of the sea. The news reel came and went. There were the usual fancy tricks with the lights. The feature film noisily arrived. I stared idly at the reception desk of an hotel in Florida. A fantastic character entered, and, without speaking a word, took the letters from the rack and casually tore them up, drank the ink, and began to eat the telephone. I sat up, lost in wonder and joy. The film was *The Coconuts*, and with it the Marx Brothers had entered my life. And this was the perfect way to discover these glorious clowns, unexpectedly in the middle of a wet afternoon in Golders Green. Since then—besides making their acquaintance and actually watching them on the job—I have followed them from cinema to cinema. I like them best when they are given the largest *carte blanche*—as in the sublime *Duck Soup*—but even when they are clamped to some miserable plot, have to give place to some preposterous tenor and his simpering girl, I do not desert them but sit there, waiting for such delight as they can offer me. My family—thank heaven—share this rapture, and we often exchange memories, mere shadows and echoes, of our favorite antics at the dinner table. Friends who refuse to enjoy these inspired zanies are regarded with suspicion. I have never understood why some London cinema does not show the Marx Brothers year in and year out. We appear to be living, as so many well-informed persons have observed, in a gigantic madhouse,[1] but there are a few compensations even here, and one of them is that we have the Marx Brothers with us. Their clowning is a comment on our situation. Chico is the eternal, sulky but wistful peasant, sceptical but not without hope. Groucho is urban America, the office executive, the speculator, the publicity agent, the salesman, raised to a height at which the folly of such men blazes like a beacon. Harpo is modern man with the lid off, a symbolic figure of the masculine unconscious. Together they have worked out comic routines that may be regarded one day as a saga of satire, Rabelais[2] caught in celluloid. But even if they should be soon forgotten, some of us will remember how they dissolved us in laughter, during those evenings in the 'thirties when the fuses were already spluttering round our feet. Karl Marx showed us how the dispossessed would finally take possession. But I think the Brothers Marx do it better.

---

1. **We appear . . . gigantic madhouse:** It should be noted that this piece was written at the outset of World War II when England was already experiencing tremendous disillusionment and a loss of national and personal identity.
2. **Rabelais:** Francois Rabelais (1490?–1553), a broadly and coarsely humorous satirist.

Report Cards

We fathers of families have one secret little source of delight that is closed to other men. As we read the school reports upon our children, we realize with a sense of relief that can rise to delight that—thank heaven—nobody is reporting in this fashion upon us. What a nightmare it would be if our personalities were put through this mincing machine![1] I can imagine my own report: *"Height and weight at beginning of term—5 feet, 9 inches: 13 stone, 10 lbs. At end of term—5 feet, 8 inches: 14 stone, 2 lbs. Note: Through greed and lack of exercise, J. B. is putting on weight and is sagging. He must get out more and eat and drink less. Conduct—Not satisfactory. J. B. is increasingly irritable, inconsiderate, and uncooperative. He is inclined to blame others for faults in himself. He complains of lack of sleep but persists in remaining awake to finish rubbishy detective stories. He smokes far too much, and on several occasions has been discovered smoking in bed. There is no real harm in him but at the present time he tends to be self-indulgent, lazy, vain and touchy. He should be encouraged to spend some weeks this summer with the Sea Scouts or at a Harvest Camp. Eng. Lang. & Lit.: Fair but inclined to be careless. French: A disappointing term. History: Has not made the progress here that we expected of him. Should read more. Mathematics: Very poor. Art: Has made some attempts both at oils and watercolor but shows little aptitude. Has been slack in his Appreciation and did not attend Miss Mulberry's excellent talks on the Italian Primitives.[2] Music: Fair, but will not practice. Natural History: Still professes an interest but finds it impossible to remember names of birds, butterflies, flowers. Has not joined in the Rambles this term. Chemistry: Clearly has no interest in this subject. Physics: Poor, though occasionally shows interest. Fails to comprehend basic laws. Physical Culture: Sergeant Beefer reports that J. B. has been frequently absent and is obviously far from keen. A bad term. General Report: J. B. is not the bright and helpful member of our little community that he once promised to be. He lacks self-discipline and does not try to cultivate a cheery outlook. There are times when he still exerts himself—e.g. he made a useful contribution to the end of term production of A Comedy of Errors—but he tends to be lazy and egotistical. His housemaster has had a talk with him, but I suggest that stronger parental guidance would be helpful, and is indeed necessary."* And then I would be asked to see my father, and would find him staring and frowning at this report, and then he would stare and frown at me and would begin asking me, in his deep and rather frightening voice, what on earth was the matter with me. But it can't happen, not this side of the grave. I am knee-deep in the soggy world of graying hair and rotting teeth, of monstrous taxes and overdrafts, of vanishing friends and fading sight; but at least, I can tell myself delightedly, nobody is writing a school report on me.

---

1. **mincing machine:** meat grinder.
2. **Italian Primitives:** early Italian painters.

Getting at Meaning

THE MARX BROTHERS

1. Priestley finds the Marx Brothers to be one of the "few compensations even here." How do they comment on the madness of the modern world? What "fuses were already spluttering" in the 1930's?

2. How does Priestley compare Karl Marx and the Brothers Marx? What does he think the Marx Brothers do better?

REPORT CARDS

3. While Priestley pokes fun at himself, he reveals some of his habits and personality traits. What are some of these qualities?

Developing Skills in Reading Literature

1. **Style.** Priestley often read his essays aloud to friends and family, and he encouraged his readers to do the same. "I have always tried to write through the ear and not the eye," he said, "and if you do not enjoy my pieces, you might at least enjoy the sound of your own voice and find delight that way."

Examine these two essays and find specific examples of sound devices such as assonance, consonance, alliteration, repetition, and auditory imagery. Look also for examples of parallelism in sentence structure and of phrasing that is pleasingly rhythmic. Be prepared to discuss the dramatic effect of these sound devices.

2. **Essay.** These two essays attest to the flexibility of the essay form, for Priestley uses description, anecdote, and both personal and objective commentary to make observations about human behavior and society. What notable differences in subject and style distinguish even these two essays written by the same person? What opinions does Priestley express about society? change? himself?

Developing Writing Skills

1. **Writing an Explanation.** Priestley believes that the comedy routines of the Marx Brothers comment on the society of the 1930's and 1940's. Which comedians today do the same for contemporary society? Choose one individual or comedy group, and in a well developed paragraph describe what that person or group reveals about twentieth-century life.

2. **Writing About a Personal Experience.** In "Report Cards" Priestley rejoices in the fact that as an adult he is no longer subjected to the kind of scrutiny imposed on children. Consider some of the things that you are happy to have left behind. Perhaps, for example, you once were forced to participate in a sport or to play a musical instrument, or maybe you dreaded attending your first co-ed parties. Describe several of these activities in a well developed paragraph.

H. R. Trevor-Roper

born in 1914

Hugh Redwald Trevor-Roper is among the most famous historians in the English-speaking world. A generalist in an age of specialists, he has followed his curiosity from century to century rather than concentrating upon a single epoch. His prose is lively, his perceptions keen, his wit acerbic.

Trevor-Roper was born in Glanton, Northumberland. Educated at Charterhouse and Oxford University, he became a research fellow at Oxford in 1937 and remained associated with the university in various capacities for over forty years. Early in his career, at the age of twenty-six, he dazzled readers with *Archbishop Laud* (1940), a brilliant biography of a controversial seventeenth-century cleric.

During World War II, Trevor-Roper served with British Intelligence and was given the assignment of verifying that Hitler was truly dead. He turned the results of his investigation into *The Last Days of Hitler* (1947), a best seller that established his popular fame. The general public seemed to have an obsessive fascination with the minute details of the life of Hitler and of his Nazi entourage, and Trevor-Roper went on to edit *Hitler's Table Talk* (1953), *Hitler's War Directives* (1964), and *Goebbels' Diaries: The Last Days* (1978).

Trevor-Roper's major works include *The Gentry: 1540–1640* (1953); *The Rise of Christian Europe* (1963); and *The European Witch-Craze in the 16th and 17th Centuries* (1970), all of which are written in prose considerably more literary than that of most historians. His lively style, along with his popular success, his pugnacity, and his failure to specialize have put him at odds with his own profession. In the foreword to *Historical Essays* (1966), Trevor-Roper defended his refusal to specialize: "To me the interest of history lies not in its periods but in its problems, and, primarily, in one general problem which is its substance in all times and all places: the interplay between heavy social forces or intractable geographic facts and the creative or disruptive forces which wrestle with them: the nimble mind, the burning conscience, the blind passions of man."

The Dark Soul of Hitler

Hitler was a genius, of course; a revolutionary genius. It is useless to deny that, for no ordinary man could have achieved such a masterpiece of destruction; but to define a man as a genius doesn't bring us much nearer to understanding him. Wherein did his genius lie? In what respects was he outside ordinary human categories, in what within them?

Some people have suggested that he was himself an unimportant man, a mere symptom, a pawn, moved by impersonal economic forces or by their manipulators; by big business, heavy industry, the army, the Junkers.[1] This is an impossible doctrine. For a time all these interests thought they could manage Hitler. They helped him to power. In the end he ruled and ruined them all.

It was in his last days that his absolute personal power was exhibited most clearly. Then he no longer had any administrative machinery at his disposal. He had no army, no Gestapo,[2] no propaganda. Failure of his mission was obvious. He had ruined Germany. Yet such was the compelling power of his personality that his orders were still implicitly obeyed.

Deputy Fuehrer Martin Bormann[3] and many others wished to escape from Berlin before it was surrounded. They could easily have done so. But Hitler refused to move and they stayed. They even stayed for more than twenty-four hours after his death in order to carry out his orders and burn his body. In consequence their escape was impossible and most of them perished in Berlin. Only one man tried to make a secret escape in those days. He was Hitler's own brother-in-law. Hitler ordered him to be found, brought back and shot, and again he was obeyed.

How can we explain this extraordinary power? The habit of obedience no doubt confirmed it, but what caused it? Apart from political reasons, Hitler certainly had an extraordinary personal magnetism. He persuaded the Germans that he was inspired. All who came into his orbit were seduced away from their former loyalties; they were bewitched by him.

His eyes especially had a hypnotic effect. They weren't bright; they were a dull and opaque blue tinged with gray. But they had a dim intensity which subdued the beholder. One of the ablest of his court admitted that Hitler's mere presence left him exhausted and void. Hitler was a sorcerer who convinced a nation that he alone understood the mystery of politics.

He even convinced himself, believing to the end that he was a German messiah who alone had the willpower to carry Germany through to victory; and it was partly for this reason that he lived in fear of assassination, hiding night and day in deep underground bunkers. In other respects, too, he can be compared with a sorcerer. Like Wallenstein, the German adventurer of the Thirty Years' War,[4] he believed in astrology. Both he and Himmler[5]

---

1. **Junker** (yoon' kər): a member of the privileged landowning class in Germany. The name is a combination of the German *jung* and *herr*, literally, "young master."
2. **Gestapo** (gə stä' pō): the secret police force of the German Nazi state, notorious for its terrorism and brutality.
3. **Martin Bormann:** Bormann disappeared without a trace after the Nazi collapse.
4. **Wallenstein . . . the Thirty Years' War:** Wallenstein, an Austrian Duke and a general, was killed in 1634. The Thirty Years' War, a series of conflicts fought over political and religious issues, lasted in Europe from 1618 to 1648.
5. **Himmler:** Heinrich Himmler, chief of the SS, Hitler's militia, and organizer of the Gestapo. Attempting to escape at the end of the war, Himmler was captured by the British and committed suicide at a British intelligence center on May 23, 1945.

kept astrologers and consulted their horoscopes on important occasions.

But if a genius, Hitler was never a constructive genius. At the bottom of his heart, behind the meaningless phrases of peaceful intentions and the defense of Western civilization, he wished only to destroy. When he thought of himself as a great historical figure, it wasn't as any of the great builders of civilization; it was as one of the scourges of mankind—Alaric, Attila, Genghis Khan.[6]

In his early philosophy this nihilism was obvious to all who examined it. In his middle years it was obscured by the vested interests which rode on the Nazi tide. At the end, when all of Goebbels' tricks had been played out, it returned to prominence, and Nazism resumed its original character. The appeal to the Werewolves was an appeal for universal destruction; Germany was to go down in a Wagnerian twilight of the gods.[7] In Hitler's own character this mania for destruction was clear to those who knew him.

Though Hitler was physically afraid of blood, the thought of it excited and intoxicated him. Mere mention of the great blood purge of 1934[8] or of the slaughter in Europe would set him off into his famous tantrums. His eyes would pop from his head and his whole nature would become transformed. Nor did he mind whose blood it was that was shed.

An officer once began to explain apologetically that German losses had been severe. Hitler cut him short. "Losses can never be too high," he exclaimed eagerly. "They sow the seed of future greatness!" In his last days he ordered wholesale executions for no apparent reason. All the "prominent" war prisoners were to be murdered. Like an ancient hero, he wished to be sent with human sacrifice to his grave.

A man who seeks to change the whole world has inevitably something of the artist in him; for artists also seek to change the world, though they generally confine their ambitions to the world of ideas. Hitler always thought of himself as an artist and of politics as a form of art. He would never consider Himmler as his sucessor, because he was "so completely inartistic," and at the end he was more interested in an operatic grand finale than in the fate of Germany. Before the war he lived an "artistic life."

He kept irregular hours (his working day was from noon till four-thirty in the morning), worked erratically, played truant from his office, went picnicking in the hills ("It gave me that inner calm," he explained, "necessary for my world-shattering decisions"), and surrounded himself with people from the screen and studio.

Both Eva Braun and his physician, Dr. Morell, entered his circle in this way; and both had an important influence on his life. Hitler often persuaded himself that he wished to retire and become an artist; to live in Linz[9] alone with Eva Braun. He always thought of Linz as his home town. In his last days he was still busying himself with plans for a new opera house there. In his will he bequeathed his pictures to found an art gallery at Linz.

Both the artist and the revolutionary genius are supposed to transcend the vulgar limitations of class. If this is so, Hitler was an exception; and many of the contrasts in his

---

6. **Alaric . . . Genghis Khan:** Alaric was a king of the Visigoths who captured Rome in the fifth century; Attila, despotic king of the Huns, was known during the fifth century as "The Scourge of God"; Genghis Khan was a thirteenth century Mongol conqueror who ruled an empire that stretched from China to Bulgaria.
7. **Wagnerian . . . gods:** Richard Wagner (1813–1883) was Hitler's favorite composer. Himself a deeply troubled man, obsessed with his own sense of power, Wagner composed a gigantic series of operas called *The Ring of the Nibelung*, based on German myths and legends. The final opera is *Götterdämmerung*, or "Twilight of the Gods." The word means "utter destruction."
8. **blood . . . 1934:** When Hitler was elected Chancellor of Germany in 1933, he was given dictatorial powers. In June, 1934, he ordered a purge, or a "cleansing," of all the Nazis he suspected of disloyalty. Over 1,000 were killed.
9. **Linz:** a city in upper Austria, on the Danube.

character are due to this fact. He came from the lower middle class; and, though in his politics and his ideas he was a demonic figure, the angel of destruction, in taste and in his private life he always remained the petty bourgeois.

In some ways it was useful to him to do so; for the German workman, the German common soldier, and the German blackcoated worker, though they regarded Goering[10] and the Gauleiters[11] as bouncing tycoons and the generals as a feudal caste, never felt estranged from Hitler. He was always one of them. His life never became grand.

He lived simply and had his meals regularly, when Eva Braun was away, with his secretaries and his vegetarian cook. He was always one of them. Nevertheless, there is a somewhat macabre contrast between the revolutionary nihilism of his doctrines with his unlimited plans of conquest and the background of coziness and triviality from which they proceeded: teacups and cream buns, cuckoo clocks, and Bavarian bric-a-brac.

This cream-bun element is never entirely absent from Hitler's personality. It appears vividly in his will. While his political will dismisses Ministers, sets up governments, and declares eternal war on international Jewry, his private will empowers his executor to give his relatives only personal mementos and such assistance "as may be necessary to maintain a petty-bourgeois standard of life." But the most significant evidence of these petty-bourgeois standards is to be found in his relations with Eva Braun.

She was not a conventional tyrant's mistress. Though attractive, she was not glamorous. She had no exotic tastes, no love of power. A photographer's assistant, she came from the same class as himself; and for that reason Hitler preferred her above all the blowzy Nordic actresses whom Goebbels introduced to the chancellery. She never interfered in politics but attended quietly to the details of bourgeois life, which was exactly what he wanted.

She kept the politicians away when he wanted rest, saw that his social receptions (at 2:30 A.M.) weren't disturbed by business, and supplied him with a private world. When everyone else seemed to be deserting him, he had complete confidence in her; only Eva Braun and his Alsatian Blendi,[12] he said, would remain faithful to the end. At first Eva Braun was kept at Obersalzburg[13] and did not come to Berlin. There she skied and climbed; she danced well (she had learned dancing as a profession), and she shared his "artistic" tastes, talking with him on books and pictures and advising him in his purchases. Only in the last two years was she allowed to come to Berlin. At the end, she came unbidden and he tried to send her away; but she refused to go. She had come for the wedding.

The exact position of Eva Braun in Hitler's household will probably always be an enigma. Hitler liked to consider it ideally. He described it as "true friendship," and so that base considerations of cash should not disturb it he made her independent, giving her a share in the monopoly of his photographs.

For about fifteen years she was neither wife nor acknowledged mistress. Even her existence was a secret outside the court, and her picture was removed from his photographs before they could be published. The ambiguity of her position embarrassed the servants, who still lower their voices when they mention her. (To them she was always known as "E. B.") It evidently embarrassed her, too. It

---

10. **Goering:** Hermann Goering, Hitler's field marshal, the Commander in Chief of the German *Luftwaffe*, or Air Force. He was captured after the battle of Britain and condemned to death at the Nuremberg Trials. He committed suicide in his cell, October 15, 1946.

11. **Gauleiter** (gou' lī tər): a Nazi official.

12. **Alsatian Blendi:** Hitler's German shepherd dog, Blendi, poisoned by Hitler shortly before his own suicide.

13. **Obersalzburg:** also Berchtesgaden, a resort village in the Bavarian Alps, the site of Hitler's mountain retreat and occasionally used as his headquarters.

gave her an inferiority complex which made her seem conceited and haughty. And the unattractive elements in her character, the schoolgirl heroics and threats of suicide, probably sprang from the same cause.

Since Hitler certainly loved her, his unwillingness to give her any definite status for so long requires explanation. The easiest explanation is that their relations were platonic or at least were so represented. The status of either wife or mistress would have been inconsistent with such relations. Ultimately a ceremony was necessary; her status had to be established if she was to share in the ritual death of the Fuehrer. Hence the last-minute symbolic marriage which has so perplexed the world.

But no character remains static, especially in such a giddy position. In Hitler's last year the failure of hope and the corruption of power emphasized other characteristics. Drunk with power, he exacted oriental servility from his subordinates. All suggestions from below ceased.

His Cabinet had become a despotic court of toadies and flatterers in which he heard only the echo of his own megalomania.[14] Under the pressure of defeat he gave up all relaxation, all "artistic" activity, and irregularity and became a weary hack. Quite suddenly, from looking younger than his age, he became an old man. His hands trembled, his body stooped; he was obstinate and morose. Two causes hastened his physical and mental collapse: his own physician and the generals' plot.[15]

Hitler's relations with his physician are as extraordinary as anything in that extraordinary history. Dr. Morell was a mere quack. He arrived at Obersalzburg as a specialist in venereal disease, a necessary attendant on Hitler's court photographer; he stayed as court physician. His god was Mammon;[16] he used his position to obtain lucrative monopolies for his own proprietary medicines, and in nine years he made a large fortune.

All this time he was treating Hitler with an endless series of drugs and injections upon which, in the end, his patient became dependent. Narcotics, stimulants, aphrodisiacs, colored water—all were stuffed into Hitler by this charlatan, who succeeded in concealing his real exhaustion and preparing him for complete collapse.

Three other doctors discovered the facts and warned Hitler that he was being slowly poisoned. For their reward they were all dismissed and one of them later sentenced to death. For the last six months of his life, Hitler's health was in sole charge of Dr. Morell. By this time, though he suffered no organic complaint and had a very strong constitution, he was a physical wreck: the joint work of his own eccentricities, the failure of his ambitions, and Dr. Morell.

Meanwhile the generals' plot of July 20, 1944, also had its influence. From the physical effects of that attack Hitler soon recovered; from the mental effects, never. Thenceforth the fear of treachery obsessed him; he saw it everywhere and especially in the army.

In his private circle he had often admired Stalin for having liquidated the Russian General Staff before the war; now he made no pretense to conceal his hatred of the army which had opposed his politics, assaulted his person, and failed to win his war. "Everyone has lied to me," he would scream. "The armed forces have deceived me; even the SS has left me in the lurch!"

As defeat followed defeat, he became more hysterical in his denunciations, and Bormann, eager to eliminate all rivals for the succession, fanned his suspicions into flame.

---

14. **megalomania** (meg ə lō mā′ nē ə): a mental disorder characterized by delusions of grandeur, wealth, or power.
15. **generals' plot:** On July 20, 1944, at a high-level command conference, a bomb exploded, killing several officers and wounding others, including Hitler himself. The plotters, who included several of Hitler's top officials, were rounded up and promptly executed.
16. **Mammon:** a personification for materialism or greed. (See Matthew 6:24; Luke 16:19.)

Even in his will, meant as a dignified appeal to posterity, Hitler could not resist the temptation to fling a sidelong charge of desertion at the army. The last news from the outside world informed him of Himmler's treachery. That was the end. It was a "shattering blow"; *"der treue Heinrich"*—the faithful Heinrich — had betrayed him. He decided to postpone his death no longer. Like Caesar, Hitler died with an *"et tu, Brute!"* on his lips.

Such is the picture I have formed of Hitler's personality. It was a dual personality and cannot be contained in a single formula. As a historical figure he was a revolutionary genius, a man of destiny who in a crisis of civilization offered a new gospel to a nation and on it based a new power for himself—a barbarous and bestial gospel and a terrible destructive power.

At the same time, as a human being he remained trivial and rather mean. Power corrupted him without either softening the resentment or extending the horizon of his frustrated youth in Vienna.

However effective his appeal has been, we must not forget that it contained no constructive ideas; it was a hodgepodge of mesmerism and superstition, concealing the bitterness of the disinherited; and it was successful because it corresponded to the mood of the nation. His genius consisted in diagnosing the disease; but he did not cure it. Rather, he exploited it. As he once said, "My task is not to make men better, but to make use of their weaknesses."

DEVASTATION—EAST END STREET, 1941. *Graham Sutherland.*
Tate Gallery, London.

Getting at Meaning

1. What extraordinary quality possessed by Hitler is emphasized in the first part of this essay? According to Trevor-Roper what prevented Hitler from being a constructive genius? How did his attitude toward blood reflect his twisted psychology?

2. In what way was Hitler essentially different from most artists and revolutionary geniuses? How did this difference work to his advantage as a dictator?

3. How is Hitler's attraction to Eva Braun understandable in light of his "artistic" and bourgeois tastes?

4. What factors hastened Hitler's mental and physical collapse, according to Trevor-Roper? In what ways did Hitler's personality change during the last year he was in power? What caused the change?

5. In the final paragraphs how does Trevor-Roper summarize the duality of Hitler's personality?

Developing Skills in Reading Literature

1. **Essay: Character Sketch.** At the beginning of this character sketch, Trevor-Roper asks these rhetorical questions about his subject: "Within did his genius lie? In what respects was he outside ordinary human categories, in what within them?" Throughout the sketch, the answers to these questions take shape and form. Summarize these answers. To what extent do you think that this writer has captured the "dark soul" of Hitler? Be prepared to defend your opinion.

2. **Tone.** Hitler is perhaps the most hated human being in the twentieth century. Because of his notoriety, it would seem difficult even for a skilled biographer to remain objective in writing about him. Does the tone of this essay seem to be objective? Does Trevor-Roper attribute any positive qualities to Hitler, for example? What does Trevor-Roper's overall attitude toward Hitler seem to be? Be prepared to defend your answer.

3. **Diction.** Trevor-Roper uses many terms associated with religion, myth, and magic to describe Hitler and to explain his appeal to the German people. Examine the italicized words and phrases in the following quotations from the essay. Be prepared to discuss the kind of superhuman quality that each conveys about Hitler.

a. "He [Hitler] even convinced himself, believing to the end that he was a *German messiah.* . . ."

b. "Germany was to go down in a *Wagnerian twilight of the gods.*"

c. ". . . though in his policies and his ideas he was a *demonic figure,* the *angel of destruction.* . . ."

d. ". . . a man of destiny who . . . offered a *new gospel* to a nation. . . ."

e. ". . . his appeal . . . was a hodgepodge of *mesmerism* and superstition. . . ."

Developing Writing Skills

Writing a Report. Read an encyclopedia article on Hitler. Then choose an aspect of his life or of his regime that interests you; for example, the early life of the dictator or the social factors in Germany that contributed to his rise to power. Once you have narrowed your topic, do additional research and take careful notes, documenting your sources. Finally, write a well developed five-paragraph report on what you have learned.

Winston Churchill

1874–1965

Justly admired as the indomitable Prime Minister who led Britain to victory in World War II, Winston Churchill was also a journalist and historian of uncommon ability. His greatest genius was doubtless for oratory. "It was the British that had the lion's heart," he said; "I had the luck to be called upon to give the roar." Churchillian rhetoric roars in sonorous, majestic cadences that seem to emanate from an earlier, more heroic age.

Born to luxury and privilege at Blenheim Palace in Oxfordshire, Churchill was the son of Lord Randolph Churchill, a descendent of the Duke of Marlborough and Jennie Jerome Churchill, an American who became prominent in British society. Churchill was educated first at Harrow and then at the Royal Military College at Sandhurst, the English equivalent of West Point. As a soldier he saw action in Cuba, India, and the Sudan.

Churchill was elected to Parliament in 1900 and rose rapidly to ministerial rank, serving as Home Secretary in 1910 and in 1911 becoming First Lord of the Admiralty. Unfairly held responsible for the disastrous Gallipoli Campaign, he resigned from the cabinet in 1915. He was asked to be Minister of Munitions in Lloyd George's coalition government of 1917, but the Lloyd George government fell in 1922, and Churchill also lost his seat in Parliament that year.

Alarmed by the increasing threat of Germany under Hitler, Churchill used all his rhetorical power to support military preparedness. When war was declared, he became First Lord of the Admiralty, and when Germany invaded the Low Countries in May, 1940, he became Prime Minister at the head of the coalition government and the symbol of British valor against the Nazi onslaught. Randolph S. Churchill and Desmond Flower compiled Winston Churchill's speeches in *Blood, Sweat, and Tears* (1940).

WINSTON CHURCHILL.
Karsh, Ottawa.

Churchill wrote a magnificent history of World War II in six volumes, *The Second World War* (1948–1954), and was awarded the Nobel Prize for Literature in 1953. He served a second term as Prime Minister from 1951 until his retirement in 1955. In 1956 he began his four-volume *History of the English-Speaking Peoples*, which he completed in 1958.

A hero at a time when the world needed heroism, Churchill would be numbered among the great figures of the twentieth century even if he had never put pen to paper. Conversely, as the author of histories that capture the grandeur of the heroic past, Churchill would be an important figure in British literature even if he had never held public office.

from **The Speeches**

This speech, excerpted from Churchill's first address as Prime Minister, was delivered as Hitler's armies were approaching The Netherlands.

May 13, 1940

In this crisis I hope I may be pardoned if I do not address the House at any length today. I hope that any of my friends and colleagues, or former colleagues, who are affected by the political reconstruction, will make all allowance for any lack of ceremony with which it has been necessary to act. I would say to the House, as I said to those who have joined this Government: "I have nothing to offer but blood, toil, tears, and sweat."

We have before us an ordeal of the most grievous kind. We have before us many, many long months of struggle and of suffering. You ask, What is our policy? I will say: "It is to wage war, by sea, land and air, with all our might and with all the strength that God can give us: to wage war against a monstrous tyranny, never surpassed in the dark, lamentable catalog of human crime. That is our policy." You ask, What is our aim? I can answer in one word: Victory—victory at all costs, victory in spite of all terror, victory however long and hard the road may be; for without victory there is no survival. Let that be realized; no survival for the British Empire; no survival for all that the British Empire has stood for; no survival for the urge and impulse of the ages, that mankind will move forward towards its goal. But I take up my task with buoyancy and hope. I feel sure that our cause will not be suffered to fail among men. At this time I feel entitled to claim the aid of all, and I say, "Come, then, let us go forward together with our united strength."

March 5, 1946

A shadow has fallen upon the scenes so lately lighted by the Allied victory. Nobody knows what Soviet Russia and its Communist international organization intends to do in the immediate future, or what are the limits, if any, to their expansive and proselytizing tendencies. I have a strong admiration and regard for the valiant Russian people and for my wartime comrade, Marshal Stalin. There is deep sympathy and good will in Britain—and I doubt not here also—toward the peoples of all the Russias and a resolve to persevere through many differences and rebuffs in establishing lasting friendships. We understand the Russian need to be secure on her western frontiers by the removal of all possibility of German aggression. We welcome Russia to her rightful place among the leading nations of the world. We welcome her flag upon the seas. Above all, we welcome constant, frequent, and growing contacts between the Russian people and our own people on both sides of the Atlantic. It is my duty, however, for I am sure you would wish me to state the facts as I see them to you, to place before you certain facts about the present position in Europe.

From Stettin in the Baltic to Trieste in the Adriatic, an iron curtain has descended across the Continent. Behind that line lie all the capitals of the ancient states of central and eastern Europe. Warsaw, Berlin, Prague, Vienna, Budapest, Belgrade, Bucharest, and Sofia, all these famous cities and the populations around them lie in what I must call the Soviet sphere, and all are subject in one form or another, not only to Soviet influence, but to a very high and, in many cases, increasing measure of control from Moscow. Athens alone—Greece with its immortal glories—is free to decide its future at an election under British, American, and French observation. The Russian-dominated Polish government has been encouraged to make enormous and wrongful inroads upon Germany, and mass expulsions of millions of Germans on a scale grievous and undreamed of are now taking place. The Communist parties, which were very small in all these eastern states of Europe, have been raised to pre-eminence and power far beyond their numbers and are seeking everywhere to obtain totalitarian control. Police governments are prevailing in nearly every case, and so far, except in Czechoslovakia, there is no true democracy. . . .

Getting at Meaning

1. To what qualities of the British people does Churchill appeal in the speech given on May 3, 1940?

2. What is Churchill's essential warning in the speech given on March 5, 1946? Why does he suspect that the British people might not heed the warning at this particular time?

Developing Skills in Reading Literature

Style. Although not everyone in Churchill's audiences agreed with him, few failed to respond to the power of his rhetoric. Directness, clarity, and wit raise his oratory to a level far above that of most public speakers. Examine the two speeches given here, and find examples of the following techniques characteristic of Churchill's oratorical style: anaphora, rhetorical questions, and parallelism. Discuss the effect of these techniques within the context of the speeches and on the reader or listener. Then examine the way that Churchill creates emotional appeal through words and phrases with highly emotional connotations. Which is the more highly emotional of the two speeches? What might account for this difference in tone?

Developing Writing Skills

Supporting an Opinion. The first of the two speeches could be called an "invitation to war," a just war according to Churchill. Do you agree that this kind of war is justified? Defend your opinion in a well developed paragraph.

Arthur C. Clarke

We'll Never Conquer Space

Man will never conquer space. Such a statement may sound ludicrous, now that our rockets are already 100 million miles beyond the moon and the first human travelers are preparing to leave the atmosphere. Yet it expresses a truth which our forefathers knew, one we have forgotten—and our descendants must learn again, in heartbreak and loneliness.

Our age is in many ways unique, full of events and phenomena which never occurred before and can never happen again. They distort our thinking, making us believe that what is true now will be true forever, though perhaps on a larger scale. Because we have annihilated distance on this planet, we imagine that we can do it once again. The facts are far otherwise, and we will see them more clearly if we forget the present and turn our minds towards the past.

To our ancestors, the vastness of the earth was a dominant fact controlling their thoughts and lives. In all earlier ages than ours, the world was wide indeed, and no man could ever see more than a tiny fraction of its immensity. A few hundred miles—a thousand, at the most—was infinity. Only a lifetime ago, parents waved farewell to their emigrating children in the virtual certainty that they would never meet again.

And now, within one incredible generation, all this has changed. Over the seas where Odysseus wandered for a decade, the Rome-Beirut Comet[1] whispers its way within the hour. And above that, the closer satellites span the distance between Troy and Ithaca[2] in less than a minute.

Psychologically as well as physically, there are no longer any remote places on earth. When a friend leaves for what was once a far country, even if he has no intention of returning, we cannot feel that same sense of irrevocable separation that saddened our forefathers. We know that he is only hours away by jet liner, and that we have merely to reach for the telephone to hear his voice.

In a very few years, when the satellite communication network is established,[3] we will be able to see friends on the far side of the earth as easily as we talk to them on the other side of the town. Then the world will shrink no more, for it will have become a dimensionless point.

Forever Too Large

But the new stage that is opening up for the human drama will never shrink as the old one has done. We have abolished space here on the little earth; we can never abolish the space that yawns between the stars. Once again we are face to face with immensity and must

---

1. **Over the seas . . . Rome-Beirut Comet:** One of the tedious journeys of Odysseus, as recorded by Homer in *The Odyssey*, can be covered in less than an hour by a modern airplane such as the *Comet.*
2. **Troy . . . Ithaca:** Troy, a city in Asia Minor, was the scene of the Trojan War where Odysseus fought. Ithaca, one of the Ionian islands off the coast of Greece, was Odysseus's legendary home.
3. It was Arthur C. Clarke who in 1945 first proposed the idea of using satellites for communication. Telstar, the first commercial communications satellite for relaying microwave transmissions, was placed in earth orbit on July 10, 1962. Since 1962, many satellites have been developed, and their impact has been great, not only in communication but also in the fields of medicine and education.

accept its grandeur and terror, its inspiring possibilities and its dreadful restraints. From a world that has become too small, we are moving out into one that will be forever too large, whose frontiers will recede from us always more swiftly than we can reach out towards them.

Consider first the fairly modest solar, or planetary, distances which we are now preparing to assault. The very first Lunik[4] made a substantial impression upon them, traveling more than 200 million miles from the earth—six times the distance to Mars. When we have harnessed nuclear energy for spaceflight, the solar system will contract until it is little larger than the earth today. The remotest of the planets will be perhaps no more than a week's travel from the earth, while Mars and Venus will be only a few hours away.

This achievement, which will be witnessed within a century, might appear to make even the solar system a comfortable, homely place, with such giant planets as Saturn and Jupiter playing much the same role in our thoughts as do Africa or Asia today. (Their qualitative differences of climate, atmosphere and gravity, fundamental though they are, do not concern us at the moment.) To some extent this may be true, yet as soon as we pass beyond the orbit of the moon, a mere quarter-million miles away, we will meet the first of the barriers that will separate the earth from her scattered children.

The marvelous telephone and television network that will soon enmesh the whole world, making all men neighbors, cannot be extended into space. It will never be possible to converse with anyone on another planet.

Do not misunderstand this statement. Even with today's radio equipment, the problem of sending speech to the other planets is almost trivial. But the messages will take minutes—sometimes hours—on their journey, because radio and light waves travel at the same limited speed of 186,000 miles a second.

Twenty years from now you will be able to listen to a friend on Mars, but the words you hear will have left his mouth at least three minutes earlier, and your reply will take a corresponding time to reach him. In such circumstances, an exchange of verbal messages is possible—but not a conversation.

Even in the case of the nearby moon, the 2-1/2 second time-lag will be annoying. At distances of more than a million miles, it will be intolerable.

"Time Barrier"

To a culture which has come to take instantaneous communication for granted, as part of the very structure of civilized life, this "time barrier" may have a profound psychological impact. It will be a perpetual reminder of universal laws and limitations against which not all our technology can ever prevail. For it seems as certain as anything can be that no signal—still less any material object—can ever travel faster than light.

The velocity of light is the ultimate speed limit, being part of the very structure of space and time. Within the narrow confines of the solar system, it will not handicap us too severely, once we have accepted the delays in communication which it involves. At the worst, these will amount to 20 hours—the time it takes a radio signal to span the orbit of Pluto, the outermost planet.

Between the three inner worlds, the earth, Mars, and Venus, it will never be more than 20 minutes—not enough to interfere seriously with commerce or administration, but more than sufficient to shatter those personal links of sound or vision that can give us a sense of direct contact with friends on earth, wherever they may be.

It is when we move out beyond the confines of the solar system that we come face to face with an altogether new order of cosmic reality. Even today, many otherwise educated

---

4. **Lunik:** an unmanned prober to the moon launched by the Soviet Union in 1958.

men—like those savages who can count to three but lump together all numbers beyond four—cannot grasp the profound distinction between solar and stellar space. The first is the space enclosing our neighboring worlds, the planets; the second is that which embraces those distant suns, the stars, and it is literally millions of times greater.

There is no such abrupt change of scale in terrestrial affairs. To obtain a mental picture of the distance to the nearest star, as compared with the distance to the nearest planet, you must imagine a world in which the closest object to you is only five feet away—and then there is nothing else to see until you have traveled a thousand miles.

Many conservative scientists, appalled by these cosmic gulfs, have denied that they can ever be crossed. Some people never learn; those who sixty years ago scoffed at the possibility of flight, and ten (even five!) years ago laughed at the idea of travel to the planets, are now quite sure that the stars will always be beyond our reach. And again they are wrong, for they have failed to grasp the great lesson of our age—that if something is possible in theory, and no fundamental scientific laws oppose its realization, then sooner or later it will be achieved.

One day, it may be in this century, or it may be a thousand years from now, we shall discover a really efficient means of propelling our space vehicles. Every technical device is always developed to its limit (unless it is superseded by something better) and the ultimate speed for spaceships is the velocity of light. They will never reach that goal, but they will get very close to it. And then the nearest star will be less than five years' voyaging from the earth.

Our exploring ships will spread outwards from their home over an ever-expanding sphere of space. It is a sphere which will grow at almost—but never quite—the speed of light. Five years to the triple system of Alpha Centauri, ten to the strangely-matched dou-

blet Sirius A and B, eleven to the tantalizing enigma of 61 Cygni,[5] the first star suspected to possess a planet. These journeys are long, but they are not impossible. Man has always accepted whatever price was necessary for his explorations and discoveries, *and the price of Space is Time.*

Even voyages which may last for centuries or millenia will one day be attempted. Suspended animation has already been achieved in the laboratory, and may be the key to interstellar travel. Self-contained cosmic arks which will be tiny traveling worlds in their own right may be another solution, for they would make possible journeys of unlimited extent, lasting generation after generation.

The famous Time Dilation effect predicted by the Theory of Relativity, whereby time appears to pass more slowly for a traveler moving at almost the speed of light, may be yet a third. And there are others.

Looking far into the future, therefore, we must picture a slow (little more than half a billion miles an hour!) expansion of human activities outwards from the solar system, among the suns scattered across the region of the galaxy in which we now find ourselves. These suns are on the average five light-years apart; in other words, we can never get from one to the next in less than five years.

To bring home what this means, let us use a down-to-earth analogy. Imagine a vast ocean, sprinkled with islands—some desert, others perhaps inhabited. On one of these islands an energetic race has just discovered the art of building ships. It is preparing to explore the ocean, but must face the fact that the very nearest island is five years' voyaging away,

---

5. **Alpha Centauri . . . Cygni:** Alpha Centauri is a double star, generally held to be the star nearest to the earth (except for the sun). Serius A, or Serius Alpha, is the brightest star in the constellation Canis Major and the brightest star in the whole sky. Serius B, or Serius Beta, is next brightest. Cygni, the Swan, is the first radio star discovered; it is considered the most powerful of the thousands of radio stars that exist.

and that no possible improvement in the technique of ship-building will ever reduce this time.

In these circumstances (which are those in which we will soon find ourselves) what could the islanders achieve? After a few centuries, they might have established colonies on many of the nearby islands and have briefly explored many others. The daughter colonies might themselves have sent out further pioneers, and so a kind of chain reaction would spread the original culture over a steadily expanding area of the ocean.

But now consider the effects of the inevitable, unavoidable time-lag. There could be only the most tenuous contact between the home island and its offspring. Returning messengers could report what had happened on the nearest colony—five years ago. They could never bring information more up to date than that, and dispatches from the more distant parts of the ocean would be from still further in the past—perhaps centuries behind the times. There would never be news from the other islands, but only history.

Independent "Colonies"

All the star-borne colonies of the future will be independent, whether they wish it or not. Their liberty will be inviolably protected by Time as well as Space. They must go their own way and achieve their own destiny, with no help or hindrance from Mother Earth.

At this point, we will move the discussion on to a new level and deal with an obvious objection. Can we be sure that the velocity of light is indeed a limiting factor? So many "impassible" barriers have been shattered in the past; perhaps this one may go the way of all the others.

We will not argue the point, or give the reasons why scientists believe that light can never be outraced by any form of radiation or any material object. Instead, let us assume the contrary and see just where it gets us. We will even take the most optimistic possible case and imagine that the speed of transportation may eventually become infinite.

Picture a time when, by the development of techniques as far beyond our present engineering as a transistor is beyond a stone axe, we can reach anywhere we please instantaneously, with no more effort than by dialing a number. This would indeed cut the universe down to size and reduce its physical immensity to nothingness. What would be left?

Everything that really matters. For the universe has two aspects—its scale, and its overwhelming, mind-numbing complexity. Having abolished the first, we are now face-to-face with the second.

What we must now try to visualize is not size, but quantity. Most people today are familiar with the simple notation which scientists use to describe large numbers; it consists merely of counting zeroes, so that a hundred becomes 10^2, a million, 10^6, a billion, 10^9 and so on. This useful trick enables us to work with quantities of any magnitude, and even defense budget totals look modest when expressed as 5.76×10^9 instead of $5,760,000,000.

The number of other suns in our own galaxy (that is, the whirlpool of stars and cosmic dust of which our sun is an out-of-town member, lying in one of the remoter spiral arms) is estimated at about 10^{11}—or written in full, 100,000,000,000. Our present telescopes can observe something like 10^9 other galaxies, and they show no sign of thinning out even at the extreme limit of vision.

There are probably at least as many galaxies in the whole of creation as there are stars in our own galaxy, but let us confine ourselves to those we can see. They must contain a total of about 10^{11} times 10^9 stars, or 10^{20} stars altogether. 1 followed by 20 other digits is, of course, a number beyond all understanding.

Before such numbers, even spirits brave enough to face the challenge of the light-years must quail. The detailed examination of all the grains of sand on all the beaches of the world is a far smaller task than the exploration of the universe.

And so we return to our opening statement. Space can be mapped and crossed and occupied without definable limit; but it can never be conquered. When our race has reached its ultimate achievements, and the stars themselves are scattered no more widely than the seed of Adam, even then we shall still be like ants crawling on the face of the earth. The ants have covered the world, but have they conquered it—for what do their countless colonies know of it, or of each other?

So it will be with us as we spread outwards from Mother Earth, loosening the bonds of kinship and understanding, hearing faint and belated rumors at second—or third—or thousandth-hand of an ever-dwindling fraction of the entire human race.

Though Earth will try to keep in touch with her children, in the end all the efforts of her archivists and historians will be defeated by time and distance, and the sheer bulk of material. For the number of distinct societies or nations, when our race is twice its present age, may be far greater than the total number of all the men who have ever lived up to the present time.

We have left the realm of human comprehension in our vain effort to grasp the scale of the universe; so it must always be, sooner rather than later.

When you are next outdoors on a summer night, turn your head towards the zenith. Almost vertically above you will be shining the brightest star of the northern skies—Vega of the Lyre,[6] twenty-six years away at the speed of light, near enough the point-of-no-return for us short-lived creatures. Past this blue-white beacon, fifty times as brilliant as our sun, we may send our minds and bodies, but never our hearts.

For no man will ever turn homewards from beyond Vega, to greet again those he knew and loved on the earth.

---

6. **Vega of the Lyre:** a very bright star in the constellation Lyra, its shape suggesting a lyre or harp.

EQUIVALENTS FOR THE MEGALITHS, 1935. *Paul Nash. Tate Gallery, London.*

Getting at Meaning

1. What does Clarke mean when he says, ". . . there are no longer any remote places on earth"? What is an essential difference between exploring the earth and exploring outer space?

2. What will always make conversation impossible between a person on earth and anyone on another planet? At what point in space exploration does he believe that this barrier will cause almost insurmountable difficulties?

3. According to Clarke anything that is possible can be realized if it does not violate a fundamental scientific law. What are some of the unrealized possibilities mentioned in this essay that probably will become accomplishments in time?

4. How could the Time Dilation effect make space travel over great distances more feasible? In spite of this possibility, Clarke says that human beings can never "catch up" to the movement of the universe. On what basis does he make such a statement?

5. Even if scientists learn to reach any destination instantaneously, what remains as a barrier to the conquest of space?

6. Clarke concludes this essay by affirming a human need for sustained relationships. What factors in space exploration cited by Clarke would interfere with this need?

Developing Skills in Reading Literature

Essay. In this expository essay Clarke presents a thesis, then defends his position, using the techniques of restatement, definition, classification, analogy and other comparisons, and contrast to support and clarify his explanation. Identify the thesis statement of the essay, and find examples of the various methods of development utilized by Clarke. What seems to be his main purpose: to convince, to inform, or to astound the reader? to provoke thought about a contemporary issue? Does the essay accomplish a combination of primary and secondary purposes? Explain.

Developing Writing Skills

Explaining a Process. In this essay Clarke provides scientific explanations understandable to the general reader. Choose a scientific process with which you are familiar; for example, photosynthesis or osmosis. Then in one well developed paragraph explain the process clearly and succinctly.

Stephen Spender

born in 1909

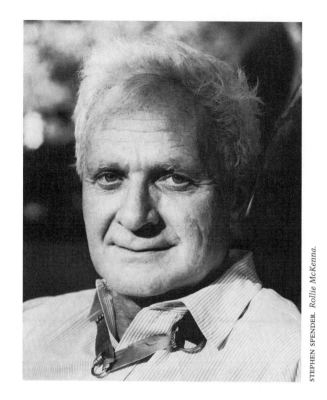

Poet, critic, editor, and translator, Stephen Spender has traveled widely as a lecturer and visiting professor. He serves as a tireless cultural representative, working to remind people that the artistic and the intellectual dimensions of life are essential complements to its economic and political concerns. Reacting to a world that he believes lacks values and belief, Spender writes polished poetry that is consistently humanistic and that strikes a balance between bleak pessimism and unfailing optimism.

Spender was born in London, the son of a distinguished liberal journalist. After attending University College School in London, Spender went to Oxford University, where he summoned up his courage to show his poetry to a slightly older student, W. H. Auden. Spender later published Auden's first book, as well as his own, on a small handpress. At Oxford Spender was part of the so-called English Group, along with Auden, poet Louis MacNeice, and C. Day Lewis.

After graduation Spender traveled extensively, frequently with the writer Christopher Isherwood, and he lived for a time in Germany. He eventually did significant work as a translator, particularly of the works of German writers Schiller and Rilke. When the Spanish Civil War broke out, Spender went to Spain where he wrote propaganda for the anti-fascist government. The experience of war left him somewhat disillusioned but provided the stuff of some of his best poems, among them "Port Bou" and "The Generous Years." These poems and others show the influence of the poetry of T. S. Eliot and Wilfred Owen and of the novels and stories of James Joyce, while offering Spender's own unique perception of human life and its relation to technological society. The poems also show Spender to be a meticulous craftsman, committed to his art. Of "The Generous Years," he said, "It is also a poem which I have taken exceptional pains over (I must have written at least 100 attempts at it), and that, of course, attaches one to a poem."

In 1939 Spender and essayist and critic Cyril Connelly founded and edited *Horizon*, a literary magazine, and *Poems for Spain* came out that same year. During the 1950's Spender co-founded *Encounter*, another important literary magazine.

Spender was a frequent visiting professor at American universities, including Northwestern and the University of Connecticut. Eventually he accepted a chair in English literature at University College, University of London, a post from which he retired in 1975.

Spender's autobiography, *World Within World*, came out in 1951. An additional memoir, *The Thirties and After*, came out in 1978, while *Letters to Christopher* appeared in 1981. His collected poems were published in 1955, and *Selected Poems* followed in 1964. With American poet Donald Hall, Spender edited *The Concise Encyclopedia of English and American Poets and Poetry* (1963). He wrote a perceptive study of Anglo-American sensibilities titled *Love-Hate Relations* in 1974, and the following year he edited a work on T. S. Eliot and a tribute to W. H. Auden.

What I Expected

What I expected was
Thunder, fighting,
Long struggles with men
And climbing.
After continual straining   5
I should grow strong;
Then the rocks would shake
And I should rest long.

What I had not foreseen
Was the gradual day   10
Weakening the will
Leaking the brightness away,
The lack of good to touch
The fading of body and soul
Like smoke before wind   15
Corrupt, unsubstantial.

The wearing of Time,
And the watching of cripples pass
With limbs shaped like questions
In their odd twist,   20
The pulverous[1] grief
Melting the bones with pity,
The sick falling from earth—
These, I could not foresee.

For I had expected always   25
Some brightness to hold in trust,
Some final innocence
To save from dust;
That, hanging solid,
Would dangle through all   30
Like the created poem
Or the dazzling crystal.

Getting at Meaning

1. What is the subject of this poem? What is the speaker saying about the process of aging? about the forces to which all humans are subject?

2. How does the speaker feel about life at the present moment? How had the speaker expected to respond to the passage of time? How did he or she actually respond?

Developing Skills in Reading Literature

1. **Free Verse.** Free verse is a common means of poetic expression among twentieth-century poets, who tend to believe that conventional verse forms stifle spontaneity and individuality. "What I Expected" is written in free verse. Comment on the way that free verse reinforces the concept of life expressed in the poem. How would you characterize the overall rhythm of the poem? How does rhythm, too, relate to the content of the poem?

2. **Simile.** Notice the similes at the end of the second and fourth stanzas. How do these contrasting images relate to the central conflict expressed in the poem?

3. **Imagery.** Examine the two kinds of images in this poem: those that describe the speaker's expectations and those that describe the speaker's actual experiences. What is the difference between these two groups of images? What age-old question is recalled by the image in line 19? What is the effect of the many participles used in this poem? Is there a relationship between the use of participles and the image of "dazzling crystal" in the closing line? Explain.

---

1. **pulverous:** disintegrating, crushing.

The Silent Crowd

Moving through the silent crowd
Who stand behind dull cigarettes
These men who idle in the road,
I have the sense of falling light.

They lounge at corners of the street   5
And greet friends with a shrug of shoulder
And turn their empty pockets out,
The cynical gestures of the poor.

Now they've no work, like better men
Who sit at desks and take much pay   10
They sleep long nights and rise at ten
To watch the hours that drain away.

I'm jealous of the weeping hours
They stare through with such hungry eyes.
I'm haunted by these images,   15
I'm haunted by their emptiness.

Getting at Meaning

1. What images haunt the speaker of this poem? What mood is created by these images?

2. What social class do the men described in the poem represent? Can you tell if the speaker belongs to the same class? What attitude does the speaker convey toward the silent crowd?

Developing Skills in Reading Literature

1. **Literal and Figurative Language.** A number of images in this poem can be taken literally. For example, the speaker could move "through the silent crowd" and see men "greet friends with a shrug of shoulders." Images such as these also can convey subtle figurative meanings, such as the loss of hope or indifference to human ties. Other images in the poem, however, must be interpreted figuratively. For example, the images of "falling light" and "hours that drain away" make sense only on a figurative level. Identify other phrases and lines that must be taken figuratively and those that can be interpreted on both a literal and a figurative level. Be prepared to explain each example. What theme is conveyed by the interweaving of literal and figurative language in this poem?

2. **Meter.** Although the meter of this poem is fairly regular, the poet occasionally varies this regularity in order to emphasize an idea or to convey an impression. The last two lines of the poem, for example, end with a metrical unit known as a pyrrhic foot (˘ ˘). How do these "weak" endings reflect the meaning of these lines? Why is it appropriate that the third stanza be the only stanza with an absolutely regular meter and rhyme scheme?

NIGHT FACADE, 1955. *Ben Nicholson.*
The Solomon R. Guggenheim Museum, New York.

W. H. Auden
1907–1973

Generally regarded as the foremost English poet since T.S. Eliot, Wystan Hughes Auden produced a large and complex body of work. At times obscure, his poetry defies easy description or categorization, for it is satirical and lyrical, religious and concerned with the individual in contemporary society.

Auden was born the son of a doctor in York, England, and in his childhood was influenced by the inquisitive, logical atmosphere of science. He soon discovered his talent for poetry, however, and by the time he attended Oxford (1925–1928) he was a recognized poet. At college he exerted a significant influence on the group of young poets who became the literary leaders of the 1930's: Christopher Isherwood, Stephen Spender, Louis MacNeice, and C. Day Lewis. It was Spender who published Auden's first book, *Poems*, in 1928 on a hand-operated printing press. At Oxford Auden also read widely in psychology, particularly the writings of Freud, and he came to regard poetry as a kind of therapy that can cure people's souls.

Auden visited Germany directly after college, and he became fascinated with the German language and culture. He later incorporated Icelandic and German sagas into his poetry. Auden was especially attracted to the vitality and variety of American life. In 1939 he moved to the United States, and he became an American citizen in 1946. For most of the rest of his life Auden split his time between Greenwich Village in New York City and country homes in Italy and Austria. A year before his death, however, he joined a cooperative group community at Christ Church, Oxford.

Auden divides his career into four periods. The first, which begins with his undergraduate career and extends to the publication of *The Orators* in 1937, includes the volume that established Auden's reputation, *Paid on Both Sides* (1930). Uneven and at times obscure, these poems reveal Auden's concern with the social, political, and psychological aspects of human existence.

During the second period, which extended from 1933 to 1938, Auden became associated with the politics of the left. His verse from this time includes *On This Island* (1937). He also wrote, with Isherwood, three plays, including *The Dog beneath the Skin* (1935). The third period begins in 1939, when Auden moved to the United States, and is marked by his increasingly Christian orientation. *Another Time* (1940) is from this period. During the fourth period, beginning in 1948, Auden produced his longer works, including *The Shield of Achilles* (1955) and *City Without Walls* (1969) as well as a book of criticism, *The Dyer's Hand* (1970).

Auden wanted the style of his poetry to reflect his concern with the common person and strove to write simply and avoid the finery of "grand poetry." To this end he constantly revised his poems, even those made famous many years before. He also provided easier access to his verse by reordering his poems in his later years, publishing them as *Collected Shorter Poems 1927–57* (1966) and *Collected Longer Poems* (1968).

The Unknown Citizen

(To JS/07/M/378
**This Marble Monument
Is Erected by the State)**

He was found by the Bureau of Statistics to be
One against whom there was no official complaint,
And all the reports on his conduct agree
That, in the modern sense of an old-fashioned word, he was a saint,
For in everything he did he served the Greater Community.   5
Except for the War till the day he retired
He worked in a factory and never got fired,
But satisfied his employers, Fudge Motors Inc.
Yet he wasn't a scab[1] or odd in his views,
For his Union reports that he paid his dues,   10
(Our report on his Union shows it was sound)
And our Social Psychology workers found
That he was popular with his mates and liked a drink.
The Press are convinced that he bought a paper every day
And that his reactions to advertisements were normal in every way.   15
Policies taken out in his name prove that he was fully insured,
And his Health-card shows he was once in hospital but left it cured.
Both Producers Research and High-Grade Living declare
He was fully sensible to the advantages of the Installment Plan
And had everything necessary to the Modern Man,   20
A phonograph, a radio, a car and a frigidaire.
Our researchers into Public Opinion are content
That he held the proper opinions for the time of year;
When there was peace, he was for peace; when there was war, he went.
He was married and added five children to the population,   25
Which our Eugenist[2] says was the right number for a parent of his generation,
And our teachers report that he never interfered with their education.
Was he free? Was he happy? The question is absurd:
Had anything been wrong, we should certainly have heard.

---

1. **scab:** a scoundrel.
2. **Eugenist:** a specialist in genetics, one dedicated to
improving the human species through the control of
hereditary factors.

Getting at Meaning

1. Why do you suppose that "no official complaint" was brought against the unknown citizen? What is the poet's apparent attitude toward conformity?

2. In the next to the last line, the speaker asks, "Was he free? Was he happy?" How does the speaker answer these questions? Is the speaker's answer the same as one that might have been given by the poet? Explain.

Developing Skills in Reading Literature

1. **Eulogy.** A eulogy is a public speech or written tribute praising the virtues and accomplishments of a person, generally one who has died recently. What is unusual about this eulogy? Does the poet praise his subject? Explain.

2. **Rhyme.** Rhyme performs several valuable functions in poetry. It gives pleasure through the senses; it unifies and distinguishes the divisions of a poem; and it can contribute to the establishment of tone. Examine "The Unknown Citizen," then explain how rhyme reinforces the sarcastic attitude of the poet toward blind conformity. Do the rhymes also add humor to the poem? Cite examples to illustrate your point.

3. **Speaker.** Sometimes a poet creates a "voice" in a poem in order to criticize a naive point of view or to present alternative attitudes toward a particular subject. For "The Unknown Citizen" Auden has created a speaker whose attitudes are quite different from his own. What do you think was Auden's purpose in speaking through this voice? Point out specific lines throughout the poem in which the speaker says something that the poet most likely does not agree with.

4. **Theme.** Throughout this poem the speaker comments on contemporary society and on the role of the individual within that society. What does the poet imply about bureaucracy and industrialization? about their effect on individuals? on creativity and personal integrity?

Who's Who

A shilling life[1] will give you all the facts:
How Father beat him, how he ran away,
What were the struggles of his youth, what acts
Made him the greatest figure of his day:
Of how he fought, fished, hunted, worked all night,   5
Though giddy, climbed new mountains; named a sea:
Some of the last researchers even write
Love made him weep his pints like you and me.

With all his honors on, he sighed for one
Who, say astonished critics, lived at home;   10
Did little jobs about the house with skill
And nothing else; could whistle; would sit still
Or potter around the garden; answered some
Of his long marvelous letters but kept none.

---

1. **A shilling life:** a short biography popular in England and available for a shilling or 1/20 of a pound.

Getting at Meaning

1. What difficulties has the subject had to overcome, according to the octave of this sonnet?

2. Who is described in the sestet? Why do you think that the subject wrote "long marvelous letters" to this person? Why do you suppose that this person kept none of them?

3. What is the significance of the poem's title? What is the poet's attitude toward fame and public acclaim, as indicated by mention in a Who's Who?

Developing Skills in Reading Literature

Sonnet. Comment on the relation between the octave and the sestet in this sonnet. Notice the off-rhymes in the sestet. Does this imperfect rhyme seem to echo an idea contained within the poem? Explain.

Developing Vocabulary

Word Origins. The words *giddy* and *potter* derive from Old English. Look up both words in an etymological dictionary to determine their original meanings. Then be prepared to explain their connotations in modern usage and the relation between their original and current meanings.

R. S. Thomas

born in 1913

R. S. THOMAS.

A Christian minister in the hill country of Wales, Ronald Stuart Thomas writes poems that express his love for the Welsh people and the country of Wales. Thomas was born in Cardiff, Glamorgan, Wales, and was educated in several local schools, earning a degree in classics at the University of Wales in 1935. He became a deacon the following year and was ordained a priest in the Anglican church in 1937.

Thomas's first volume of poetry was *Stones of the Field*, which appeared in 1947. Other works include *Poetry for Supper* (1958), *The Bread of Truth* (1963), and *Pietà* (1966). He has published twenty books of poetry, and some of his poems are collected in *Selected Poems 1946-1968* (1973).

Thomas writes about rough farming life, the difficulty of digging a living out of the soil, and the quiet routines that such a life imposes. His poetry also warns of the threat that modern technology and the machine bring to the values of life and speaks of the exploitation of the Welsh country-side. Thomas portrays the priest as a figure as isolated as the farmer, but with the same gifts for re-creating life and faith and the same aspirations for spiritual life. His most recent books to deal with this are *H'm* (1972) and *Laboratories of the Spirit* (1975).

The Word

A pen appeared, and the god said:
"Write what it is to be
man." And my hand hovered
long over the bare page,

until there, like footprints   5
of the lost traveler, letters
took shape on the page's
blankness, and I spelled out

the word "lonely." And my hand moved
to erase it; but the voices   10
of all those waiting at life's
window cried out loud: "It is true."

Getting at Meaning

1. What freedom does the god give to the human being in this poem? Describe the speaker's response to this freedom. Why does the speaker move to erase the word?

2. Whose are the voices of all those "waiting at life's/window"? What is the tone of their response? What does this response imply about their attitude toward life?

Developing Skills in Reading Literature

1. **Concrete Universal.** Concrete universal is a critical term meaning that a work of art expresses a universal idea or concept through the use of particular images. In this short poem each object, character, and action possesses a symbolic meaning independent from its literal meaning. What might the god, the speaker, and the voices symbolize? What about the pen, the page, and the window? What universal aspects of human life are suggested by the actions depicted in the poem? What view of the world is represented by the poem as a whole?

2. **Enjambment.** Notice the way that the lines and the stanzas of this poem flow together. How is this appropriate to a narrative? to a speaker who represents the ordinary person? Why might the poet have decided to break the poem into three stanzas rather than to arrange the lines as one stanza?

Children's Song

We live in our own world,
A world that is too small
For you to stoop and enter
Even on hands and knees,
The adult subterfuge.   5
And though you probe and pry
With analytic eye,
And eavesdrop all our talk
With an amused look,
You cannot find the center   10
Where we dance, where we play,
Where life is still asleep
Under the closed flower,
Under the smooth shell
Of eggs in the cupped nest   15
That mock the faded blue
Of your remoter heaven.

Getting at Meaning

1. What attitude does the speaker in this poem take toward the adult world?

2. What is the "adult subterfuge"? In what sense is this subterfuge bound to fail?

3. What does the image in the last two lines suggest about the poet's view of the adult world? Why is it a "remoter heaven"?

Developing Skills in Reading Literature

1. **Extended Metaphor.** This poem compares childhood with an actual world, distinct from the world of adults. The two worlds are portrayed as physically separate, an idea that must be interpreted in a figurative sense. What do the images in the poem imply about the world of childhood? about the adult world?

2. **Repetition.** Notice the frequent repetition of words and phrases throughout this poem. How does the use of repetition reinforce both tone and mood in the poem?

Developing Vocabulary

Word Origins. Look up the word *eavesdrop* in a dictionary. Be prepared to give the original meaning of the word and to explain the derivation of the modern-day expression.

Developing Writing Skills

Writing a Definition. "Children's Song" deals in a way with the generation gap that seems to plague so many teenagers and their parents. In a well developed paragraph define the term "generation gap" and cite some possible causes.

Vernon Scannell

born in 1922

An acute observer of twentieth-century urban life, Vernon Scannell writes of violence, war, and the "sense of danger" that is part of the modern experience. Scannell was born in Spilsby, Lincolnshire, and served in the Gordon Highlanders during World War II. He worked as a professional boxer and then as an English teacher for seven years and is now a freelance writer and broadcaster in Dorset, England. Scannell has written three plays for British radio and seven novels in addition to his sixteen books of poetry. His books of verse include *Walking Wounded* (1965), *Mastering the Craft* (1970), and *The Winter Man* (1973).

Scannell's poetry deals with the threatening aspects of city life. His most polished and accomplished work, *A Sense of Danger* (1962), describes urban sights and sounds as well as psychopaths, suicides, and the strange characters found walking the streets. In contrast, his more private poems express a belief in the essential indestructible quality that insures humanity's survival and in the importance of art as the expression of this fundamental quality.

Incendiary

That one small boy with a face like pallid cheese
And burnt-out little eyes could make a blaze
As brazen, fierce and huge, as red and gold
And zany yellow as the one that spoiled
Three thousand guineas'[1] worth of property   5
And crops at Godwin's Farm on Saturday
Is frightening, as fact and metaphor:
An ordinary match intended for
The lighting of a pipe or kitchen fire
Misused may set a whole menagerie   10
Of flame-fanged tigers roaring hungrily.
And frightening, too, that one small boy should set
The sky on fire and choke the stars to heat
Such skinny limbs and such a little heart
Which would have been content with one warm kiss,   15
Had there been anyone to offer this.

---

1. **guinea:** a gold coin last minted in England in 1813, equal to twenty-one shillings.

Getting at Meaning

1. What do you know about the physical and emotional health of the small boy from the description of his face and eyes?

2. What is the frightening fact referred to in line 7? What is the equally frightening metaphor?

3. What was the boy's apparent motivation for starting the fire, as implied by the poem? What is the boy's hunger?

Developing Skills in Reading Literature

Figurative Language. Find examples of metaphor, simile, and hyperbole in this poem. Be prepared to explain how these figures of speech heighten the impact of the poem.

Developing Vocabulary

Adjectives. Scannell makes use of vivid, precise adjectives in this poem in order to create clear pictoral images in the mind of the reader. Using a dictionary if necessary, define each of the following italicized adjectives. Describe the color and the texture of the visual image that it creates.

a. "a face like *pallid* cheese"
b. "a blaze/ As *brazen*"
c. "*zany* yellow"
d. "*flame-fanged* tigers"

Philip Hobsbaum

born in 1932

Philip Hobsbaum's blunt poetry captures the awkwardness and pain of life. A ruthlessly honest observer of himself and others, he creates scenes and atmospheres of memorable reality.

Although Hobsbaum was born in London and studied at Cambridge University, he has taught in Belfast, Northern Ireland, and now lives in Glasgow, Scotland, where he has also taught. While at college he studied under the prominent literary critic F.R. Leavis. With Edward Lucie-Smith and others, he founded the "Group," poets who met to promote and analyze each others' poetry. Hobsbaum has taught creative writing, edited literary magazines, written criticism and radio plays, and published half a dozen books of poetry. He also studied at the Royal Academy of Music, and his recent work includes dramatic monologues about composer Frédéric Chopin and other artists.

The central images in Hobsbaum's poetry are those that reflect his own experiences, and he expresses especially well the doubts and fears arising from his failing eyesight, the weakening of his religious faith, and his love life and divorce. His work is characterized by honesty and by a belief in the continuation of humanity despite its shortcomings.

The Place's Fault

Once, after a rotten day at school—
Sweat on my fingers, pages thumbed with smears,
Cane smashing down to make me keep them neat—
I blinked out to the sunlight and the heat
And stumbled up the hill, still swallowing tears.   5
A stone hissed past my ear—"yah! gurt[1] fat fool!"

Some urchins waited for me by my gate.
I shouted swearwords at them, walked away.
"Yeller," they yelled, "'e's yeller!" And they flung
Clods, stones, bricks—anything to make me run.   10
I ran, all right, up hill all scorching day
With "yeller" in my ears. "I'm not, I'm not!"

Another time, playing too near the shops—
Oddly no doubt, I'm told I was quite odd,
Making, no doubt, a noise—a girl in slacks   15
Came out and told some kids "Run round the back,
Bash in his back door, smash up his back yard,
And if he yells I'll go and fetch the cops."

And what a rush I had to lock those doors
Before that rabble reached them! What desire   20
I've had these twenty years to lock away
That place where fingers pointed out my play,
Where even the grass was tangled with barbed wire,
Where through the streets I waged continual wars!

We left (it was a temporary halt)   25
The knots of ragged kids, the wired-off beach,
Faces behind the blinds. I'll not return;
There's nothing there I haven't had to learn,
And I've learned nothing that I'd care to teach—
Except that I know it was the place's fault.   30

---

1. **gurt:** stupid.

Getting at Meaning

1. What humiliating experiences does the speaker remember from his childhood? How have these experiences affected him?

2. What does the speaker mean in the last stanza when he says, ". . . (it was a temporary halt)"? Does he suggest any insight into his real problem in this line? Explain.

3. What is ironic about the speaker's assertion, "I'll not return" in line 27?

4. What does the last line reveal about the speaker's emotional maturity? What is the overall tone of the poem?

Developing Skills in Reading Literature

1. **Rhyme Scheme.** Which stanzas of this poem exhibit a regular rhyme scheme? How is this pattern varied in the other stanzas? In which lines does assonance substitute for true rhyme? How does rhyme reinforce the content of this poem?

2. **Dialect.** Note the effective use of dialect in this poem. How does dialect help to characterize the speaker's attackers? the nature of his early environment? How does the speaker's own language contrast with that of the other children? How does this relate to the content of the poem?

Developing Writing Skills

Analyzing Theme. Both "Incendiary" and "The Place's Fault" deal with themes of isolation and loneliness. Consider the way that these themes are treated in each poem, keeping in mind the following questions: What causes these feelings? How are they manifested? Who is the speaker? Is place equally important in the two poems? In a brief essay contrast the way that poets Scannell and Hobsbaum develop similar themes.

Ted Hughes

born in 1930

Considered one of the most distinguished poets of his generation, Ted Hughes fills his poems with images of violence, often writing of the savage, predatory aspects of nature. Hughes contends, however, that his work is "not about violence but vitality."

Hughes was born in Mytholmroyd, Yorkshire, in England, and served in the Royal Air Force. In 1954 he earned a bachelor's degree at Cambridge University, where he met the American poet Sylvia Plath. After marrying in 1956, the couple lived in the United States for two years before returning to England. Plath committed suicide in 1963.

Hughes has supported himself at times as a gardener, a night watchman, and the editor of a poetry magazine. He remarried in 1970 and now makes his home in London.

Hughes's first book of poetry, *The Hawk in the Rain*, appeared in 1957. In it he introduces themes that are typical of his work, as he focuses on the violence in legend and in nature, especially on the predator in the wild. In *Crow* (1970) the title character is a pessimistic observer of the human condition, yet a survivor, who reappears in later works such as *Crow Wakes* (1971) and *Eat Crow* (1972). Hughes has been compared with Aesop and George Orwell in the way that he uses animals as representative of mankind.

TED HUGHES. *Rollie McKenna.*

Hughes's poems are sparse and blunt, full of surprising rhymes and direct vocabulary. Although his more recent work has been calmer, his earlier work makes clear his commitment to presenting the physical side of nature without sentimentality. His other works include *Wodwo* (1967), a compilation of poetry and prose; verse for children, including *The Earth-Owl and Other Moon-People* (1963); and many plays for radio and television.

Thistles

Against the rubber tongues of cows and the hoeing hands of men
Thistles spike the summer air
Or crackle open under a blue-black pressure.

Every one a revengeful burst
Of resurrection, a grasped fistful   5
Of splintered weapons and Icelandic frost thrust up

From the underground stain of a decayed Viking.
They are like pale hair and the gutturals of dialects.
Every one manages a plume of blood.

Then they grow gray, like men.   10
Mown down, it is a feud. Their sons appear,
Stiff with weapons, fighting back over the same ground.

Getting at Meaning

1. Point out images of violence and death in this poem. What are the thistles "warring" against? Who "wins" the war?

2. Apparently indestructible, thistles reappear in a "revengeful burst/Of resurrection." What does this image suggest about the ability of human beings to battle the forces of nature? Explain.

Developing Skills in Reading Literature

1. **Imagery.** A major strength in the poetry of Ted Hughes is his use of vivid, concrete images. Identify several powerful images in this poem, and describe for each the sharply defined mental picture and also the feeling, impression, and/or abstract concept that it creates.

2. **Oxymoron.** The phrase "a revengeful burst/Of resurrection" is an oxymoron that expresses both the pain and the joy of new life and the vindictiveness and renewal associated with natural forces. How does this oxymoron reflect the tone of the poem?

Hawk Roosting

I sit in the top of the wood, my eyes closed.
Inaction, no falsifying dream
Between my hooked head and hooked feet:
Or in sleep rehearse perfect kills and eat.

The convenience of the high trees!   5
The air's buoyancy and the sun's ray
Are of advantage to me;
And the earth's face upward for my inspection.

My feet are locked upon the rough bark.
It took the whole of Creation   10
To produce my foot, my each feather:
Now I hold Creation in my foot

Or fly up, and revolve it all slowly—
I kill where I please because it is all mine.
There is no sophistry in my body: 15
My manners are tearing off heads—

The allotment of death.
For the one path of my flight is direct
Through the bones of the living.
No arguments assert my right: 20

The sun is behind me.
Nothing has changed since I began.
My eye has permitted no change.
I am going to keep things like this.

Getting at Meaning

1. How does the hawk view itself within the "whole of Creation"?

2. In the fourth stanza the hawk compares its own "manners" to those of humans. What does it imply about each?

3. What typical human weakness is implied by the arrogant assertion in the last line of the poem? What references in the fifth stanza prepare the reader to question the validity of the assertion?

Developing Skills in Reading Literature

Speaker and Theme. What are the advantages of the poet's use of a created speaker in this poem? What qualities generally are associated with the hawk? How is the hawk analogous to the human being? Why is it ironic that the hawk cannot really control the forces of nature? What might the poet be saying about violence

and human cruelty? about the inevitability of change and of death?

Developing Vocabulary

Words from Greek. Look up the word *sophistry* in an etymological dictionary. Who were the Sophists, and what was their role in Greek society? After examining the derivation of the word, determine how the poet meant the word in this poem.

Developing Writing Skills

Poetry: Creating a Speaker. Imagine a scene in which an animal is in conflict with human beings in some way; for example, a caged animal tormented by visitors at a zoo or a pet dog defending a home from intruders. Write a poem in which you describe the scene from the point of view of the animal.

Norman MacCaig

born in 1910

NORMAN MACCAIG

Although Norman MacCaig was born and raised in Edinburgh, the capital city of Scotland, his poetry seems to be that of a country boy from the Highlands. His poems abound in the physical detail of the nature poet, and he makes it clear that an urban writer can capture the beauty in homely objects and quiet moments.

In 1932 MacCaig received a master's degree in classics from Edinburgh University. He has spent much of his life educating young people, teaching at Edinburgh University from 1934 until 1967 and serving as a headmaster after that. He has also taught creative writing at Edinburgh University and has served as a Reader in Poetry at the University of Stirling.

After publishing two books in the 1940's (his first was *Far Cry* in 1943), almost a decade passed before MacCaig's next book, *Riding Lights* (1956), appeared. From the beginning he drew from the local countryside for his subjects, writing poetry that deals with the geography of Scotland and with family relationships. Throughout his work there is a concern with the relation of observer to observed, with the speakers in his poems representing the perspective of the artist.

In the 1960's MacCaig traveled extensively in the United States and Italy, and he also began to broaden his writing and increase his output. His recent work is less embellished than his earlier style, but he has not departed from his original subjects and themes. He still watches and remembers and creates descriptions that give the reader a sense of the world's beauty.

Aunt Julia

Aunt Julia spoke Gaelic[1]
very loud and very fast.
I could not answer her—
I could not understand her.

She wore men's boots   5
when she wore any.
—I can see her strong foot,
stained with peat,[2]
paddling the treadle of the spinningwheel
while her right hand drew yarn   10
marvelously out of the air.

Hers was the only house
where I lay at night
in the absolute darkness
of the box bed, listening to   15
crickets being friendly.

She was buckets
and water flouncing into them.
She was winds pouring wetly
round house-ends.   20
She was brown eggs, black skirts
and a keeper of threepennybits
in a teapot.

Aunt Julia spoke Gaelic
very loud and very fast.   25
By the time I had learned
a little, she lay
silenced in the absolute black
of a sandy grave

at Luskentyre.[3]   30
But I hear her still, welcoming me
with a seagull's voice
across a hundred yards
of peatscrapes and lazybeds[4]
and getting angry, getting angry   35
with so many questions
unanswered.

1. **Gaelic** (gā′ lĭk): a Celtic language still spoken in parts
of Scotland and Ireland.
2. **peat:** a piece of turf, commonly used as a mulch.
3. **Luskentyre:** a village in the western isles of Scotland.
4. **peatscrapes and lazybeds:** peat marshes and swampy
bogs. Dried blocks of peat gathered from these places are
commonly used as fuel in parts of the British Isles.

THE GIRL AT THE GATE, 1889. *Sir George Clausen.*
Tate Gallery, London.

Getting at Meaning

1. Why might Aunt Julia have spoken so loud and fast? What overall impression of her emerges from this poem?

2. How does the speaker feel about the visits to Aunt Julia? about Aunt Julia herself? Do you think that the speaker regrets not having answered Aunt Julia's questions? Why, or why not?

Developing Skills in Reading Literature

1. **Metaphor.** In the fourth stanza MacCaig uses a number of metaphors to characterize Aunt Julia. What human qualities do each of these metaphors suggest?

2. **Connotation.** The speaker describes the "absolute darkness" of a box bed and the "absolute black"

of Aunt Julia's grave. What are the differing connotations of these two phrases, out of context and within the context of the poem?

Developing Writing Skills

Writing a Poem. Think of a person you knew as a child, someone whose appearance and mannerisms you can recall vividly. List images that describe that person and his or her characteristic activities. Also list several metaphors that capture the spirit of the person and the sense of the scenes you want to re-create. Use these preliminary notes to create a poem, incorporating the images and the metaphors that seem most appropriate.

Tony Connor

born in 1930

Poet and playwright Tony Connor writes of ordinary, everyday experiences in his economical, conventionally constructed poetry. Because he is closely identified with his native city and because he is compared with Robert Frost, Connor is often thought of as a regional poet. Although he uses his region as a source for details and scene, like Frost, he doesn't limit himself to folksy or sentimental subjects.

Connor was born in Manchester, a factory city and port in northwest England. After quitting school at fourteen, he worked as a textile designer until 1960, interrupting that occupation to serve as a tank driver in the Dragoon Guards from 1948 to 1950. In 1967 he began teaching as a visiting poet at Amherst College in the United States, a school with which Frost was closely associated. Since 1971 Connor has lived in the United States and has taught English at Wesleyan University in Connecticut. The subjects and tone of his poems, however, are still more British than American.

Connor's poetry recalls the meter and rhyme of ballads and treats subjects that are rooted in the earth and in his memory. Also characteristic of his poetic style is precise detail, the touch of irony, the off-rhyme, and the memory that turns shocking or ludicrous.

TONY CONNOR.

Connor's early works include *With Love Somehow* (1962), *Lodgers* (1965), and *12 Secret Poems* (1965). In the 1970's his poems and plays moved to darker subjects of disaster and brushes with death. As in the poem "End of the World," Connor writes of the individual who has survived and who finds a source of strength in the small tasks and rituals of everyday life.

Elegy for Alfred Hubbard

Hubbard is dead, the old plumber;
who will mend our burst pipes now,
the tap that has dripped all the summer,
testing the sink's overflow?

No other like him. Young men with knowledge   5
of new techniques, theories from books,
may better his work straight from college,
but who will challenge his squint-eyed looks

in kitchen, bathroom, under floorboards,
rules of thumb which were often wrong;   10
seek as erringly stopcocks in cupboards,
or make a job last half as long?

He was a man who knew the ginnels,[1]
alleyways, streets,—the whole district;
family secrets, minor annals,   15
time-honored fictions fused to fact.

Seventy years of gossip muttered
under his cap, his tufty thatch,
so that his talk was slow and clotted,
hard to follow, and too much.   20

As though nothing fell, none vanished,
and time were the maze of Cheetham Hill,[2]
in which the dead,—with jobs unfinished—,
waited to hear him ring the bell.

For much he never got round to doing,   25
but meant to, when the weather bucked up,
or worsened, or when his pipe was drawing,
or when he'd finished this cup.

I thought time, he forgot so often,
had forgotten him, but here's Death's pomp   30
over his house, and by the coffin
the son who will inherit his blowlamp,

---

1. **ginnel:** a narrow passage or entry between buildings.
2. **Cheetham Hill:** the cemetery in the town where Alfred Hubbard lived.

tools, workshop, cart, and cornet,
(pride of Cheetham Prize Brass Band),—
and there's his mourning widow, Janet,   35
stood at the gate he'd promised to mend.

Soon he will make his final journey;
shaved and silent, strangely trim,
with never a pause to talk to any-
body: how arrow-like, for him!   40

In St Mark's Church,—whose dismal tower
he pointed and painted when a lad—,
they will sing his praises amidst flowers,
while, somewhere, a cellar starts to flood,

and the housewife banging his front-door knocker   45
is not surprised to find him gone,
and runs for Thwaite, who's a better worker,
and sticks at a job until it's done.

Getting at Meaning

1. What qualities characterize Alfred Hubbard's ability as a plumber? What hint of his boyhood activities suggests that he was ill-suited to this job?

2. Paraphrase lines 21–24. What do these lines reveal about Alfred Hubbard's past reputation?

3. What is ironic about the way that Alfred Hubbard appears in death? How is "Death's pomp" incongruous or inappropriate for the man?

4. What has the town lost with the passing of Alfred Hubbard?

Developing Skills in Reading Literature

1. **Elegy.** An elegy usually is written to praise a person whom the poet respects. What is unusual about this elegy? Is the overall tone of the poem elegaic?

2. **Rhyme.** Cite examples of off-rhyme in this poem. Why is this device particularly effective for a poem about a man like Alfred Hubbard?

Developing Vocabulary

Compound Adjectives. Connor uses four hyphenated adjectives in this poem, among them *squint-eyed, time-honored,* and *arrow-like*. Discuss the meanings and connotations of these three adjectives within the context of the poem.

Charles Causley

born in 1917

CHARLES CAUSLEY. *Nicholas Elder. Photo Trends.*

Using the traditional ballad form, Charles Causley writes verse characterized by humor and memorable images and by the absence of the poet's personal voice. His poetry is meant to be spoken aloud and performed publicly before large audiences.

Causley lives now where he was born, in Launceston, Cornwall, in the west of England. He served in the Royal Navy during World War II, worked as a literary editor for the British Broadcasting Corporation, and has taught since 1947. His first book of poetry, *Farewell, Aggie Weston,* was published in 1951. He has produced more than twenty books, and his eleven plays and many short stories include a number written for young people. He also has edited many anthologies.

Causley's song-like verses depend on sound devices, ironic turns, and tall-tale exaggerations for humor. His direct style is easily accessible, even to children. Causley's subjects include his experience of childhood, teaching, and his years in the navy, and he also employs the ballad method of creating "legends" out of local characters.

Timothy Winters

Timothy Winters comes to school
With eyes as wide as a football pool,[1]
Ears like bombs and teeth like splinters:
A blitz of a boy is Timothy Winters.

His belly is white, his neck is dark,   5
And his hair is an exclamation mark.
His clothes are enough to scare a crow
And through his britches the blue winds blow.

When teacher talks he won't hear a word
And he shoots down dead the arithmetic bird,   10
He licks the patterns off his plate
And he's not even heard of the Welfare State.

Timothy Winters has bloody feet
And he lives in a house on Suez Street,
He sleeps in a sack on the kitchen floor   15
And they say there aren't boys like him any more.

Old Man Winters likes his beer
And his missus ran off with a bombardier,
Grandma sits in the grate with a gin
And Timothy's dosed with an aspirin.   20

The Welfare Worker lies awake
But the law's as tricky as a ten-foot snake,
So Timothy Winters drinks his cup
And slowly goes on growing up.

At Morning Prayers the Master helves[2]   25
For children less fortunate than ourselves,
And the loudest response in the room is when
Timothy Winters roars "Amen!"

So come one angel, come on ten: 30
Timothy Winters says "Amen
Amen amen amen amen."
Timothy Winters, Lord.
                              Amen.

---

1. **football pool:** a bomb crater. A football is a British sixty pound
trench mortar shell.
2. **helves:** prays.

Getting at Meaning

1. How does the speaker feel about Timothy Winters? What qualities does Timothy Winters exhibit that are not usually considered admirable?

2. What problems plague the Winters family? How has Timothy resolved many of these problems, at least in his own mind?

Developing Skills in Reading Literature

1. **Figurative Language.** Causley begins this poem with a series of similes that are also hyperboles. What is the effect of these unusual figures of speech and of the metaphor-hyperbole in the final line of the first stanza? What other exaggerations are found in the poem?

2. **Meter.** The meter of this poem is produced by a combination of trochaic, iambic, dactylic, and anapestic feet. Scan either the first four or the last four stanzas of the poem, marking the accented and unaccented syllables. Then answer the following questions.

a. Does each line contain an equal number of metrical feet?

b. What is the predominant type of foot?

c. Is there an overall pattern in the use of two-syllable and three-syllable feet? in the blend of trochees and dactyls, iambs and anapests?

d. Did your scansion reveal any partial feet or extra syllables?

e. Is the rhythm fairly regular throughout the poem, or does it vary significantly among lines and stanzas?

f. How does the rhythm contrast with the subject matter of the poem? How is it appropriate to the content?

3. **Theme.** What is the poet's attitude toward the welfare state? What is ironic about line 17? What troubles the welfare worker, according to the poem? What does the welfare worker's frustration indicate about government bureaucracy? Does the poet seem to be critical of the ideals of social service organizations? Explain. What does the poet imply about the individual in this social setting? Compare the theme of this poem with that of "The Unknown Citizen" by W.H. Auden. What similarities and differences do you find in the poets' attitudes toward society and toward the individual?

Developing Writing Skills

Description: Using Figures of Speech. Causley has made effective use of hyperbole, metaphor, and simile in this poem in order to emphasize Timothy Winters's expansive personality. Think of a person you know or would like to know who is a "real character." Then write a paragraph or a poem in which you exaggerate that person's uniqueness through figures of speech.

Seamus Heaney

born in 1939

Seamus Heaney is influenced by the political climate of his native Northern Ireland, and his perceptions are those of a person caught in a world changing from rustic to modern, from peaceful to violent.

Heaney's clear, terse poems tell of times when life was harder and seemed simpler and show the influence of the past on the present. Heaney's message is that the poet, as witness, is partly responsible for the condition of the modern world, but that the poet also bridges the gap between past and present and offers through art a quiet and resigned redemption.

Heaney was born a Catholic, in County Derry, and spent his boyhood on a farm. He attended Queen's University in Belfast, where he received a bachelor's degree in English in 1961. He has taught, both in Ireland and in the United States, ever since, and now teaches and lives in Dublin.

Heaney's first book was *Eleven Poems*, published in 1965, but his first major work was *Death of a Naturalist*, which appeared the following year. In it he celebrates the rustic life, one of nearly unceasing toil, as well as the pleasures of fishing and berrypicking. The values of skill, work well done, and the cooperation of the community are extolled. In "Digging," one of his earliest poems, Heaney compares writing poetry to digging with a shovel as he says, "Between my finger and my thumb/The squat pen rests./I'll dig with it."

SEAMUS HEANEY. *Thomas Victor.*

Although he has made it clear that he is not a political poet, the recent subject of Heaney's poetry is the history of northern Europe, which he explores in his acclaimed book *North* (1975). His view is comprehensive, as he writes about history from the Stone Age, including a series of poems about the primitive bog people.

A Drink of Water

She came every morning to draw water
Like an old bat staggering up the field:
The pump's whooping cough, the bucket's clatter
And slow diminuendo as it filled,
Announced her. I recall   5
Her gray apron, the pocked white enamel
Of the brimming bucket, and the treble
Creak of her voice like the pump's handle.
Nights when a full moon lifted past her gable
It fell back through her window and would lie   10
Into the water set out on the table.
Where I have dipped to drink again, to be
Faithful to the admonishment on her cup,
Remember the Giver fading off the lip.

Getting at Meaning

1. What does the water set out on the table symbolize for the speaker?

2. Which words and phrases in the first part of the poem convey pain, sickness, and decay? What quality of the woman does the speaker portray through these images?

3. What lesson has the speaker learned from the "admonishment on her cup"?

Developing Skills in Reading Literature

1. **Sonnet.** Examine the octave and the sestet of this contemporary sonnet. What difference in imagery do you find between these two sections of the poem? Does the octave state a problem and the sestet resolve that problem, as in the Elizabethan sonnet? Explain.

2. **Imagery.** Much of the impact of this poem is achieved through the skillful use of imagery. Identify words and phrases that appeal particularly to the sense of hearing. What is the effect of this auditory imagery? What other senses are aroused through the images in this poem?

Thom Gunn

born in 1929

THOM GUNN.
Rollie McKenna.

One of the most significant English poets to emerge since World War II, Thom Gunn writes poetry characterized by intellectual complexity and powerful images. Gunn's verse deals with such varied subjects as love, modern urban life, and the effects of atomic war.

Gunn was born Thomson William Gunn in Gravesend, England. His family moved often as his father, a journalist, changed jobs. After serving in the British Army for two years, from 1948 to 1950, Gunn went to France, where he worked on a novel. He returned to England and attended Cambridge University, where he received a bachelor's degree in 1953. During this time he published his poetry in pamphlet form, and in 1954 his first book, *Fighting Terms*, appeared. From 1954 to 1958 Gunn studied and taught at Stanford University, and from 1958 to 1966 he taught at the University of California, Berkeley. Since that time he has been a freelance writer living in San Francisco.

Gunn's second book, *The Sense of Movement* (1957), won the Somerset Maugham Award. *Touch* (1967) includes his powerful sequence "Misanthropos," in which Gunn treats, with unsentimental humanism, the situation of the last human survivor of atomic war.

Much of Gunn's work has been described as an attempt to find the right character, attitude, and perception from which to face the world. During the 1960's he plunged spiritedly into the California counter-culture, and his poetry moved from the disciplined verse of the 1950's to looser forms and from an expression of middle-class values to a more liberal stance. The range of Gunn's work is demonstrated in a recent volume, *Selected Poems 1950-1975* (1979).

Taylor Street

The small porch of imitation
marble is never sunny, but
outside the front door he
sits on his kitchen chair facing
the street. In the bent yellowish   5
face, from under the brim
of a floppy brown hat,
his small eyes watch what
he is not living. But he
lives what he can: 10
watches without a smile, with
a certain strain, the warmth
of his big crumpled
body anxiously cupped
by himself in himself, as   15
he leans over himself not
over the cold railing, unmoving but carefully getting
a little strength from the sight of the
passers-by. He has it   20
all planned: he will live
here morning by morning.

Getting at Meaning

1. In spite of the stillness of the man sitting on the porch, he possesses a certain life and vitality. Point out words and phrases that suggest this vitality. What is the relationship between the man and the passers-by?

2. What feeling do you think that the poet wishes to evoke in the reader: admiration, guilt, pity, sorrow, or something else? Explain your answer.

Developing Skills in Reading Literature

Diction: Connotation. What unique qualities do the following phrases connote about the person and the place described in this poem?
   a. "imitation/marble"
   b. "bent yellowish/face"
   c. "floppy brown hat"
   d. "anxiously cupped/by himself in himself"
   e. "the cold railing"
   f. "morning by morning"

In Praise of Cities

I

Indifferent to the indifference that conceived her,
Grown buxom in disorder now, she accepts
—Like dirt, strangers, or moss upon her churches—
Your tribute to the wharf of circumstance,
Rejected side street, formal monument . . .   5
And, irresistible, the thoroughfare.

You welcome in her what remains of you;
And what is strange and what is incomplete
Compels a passion without understanding,
For all you cannot be.   10

II

                    Only at dawn
You might escape, she sleeps then for an hour:
Watch where she hardly breathes, spread out and cool,
Her pavements desolate in the dim dry air.

III

You stay. Yet she is occupied, apart.   15
Out of a mist the river turns to see
Whether you follow still. You stay. At evening
Your blood gains pace even as her blood does.

IV

Casual yet urgent in her lovemaking,
She constantly asserts her independence: 20
Suddenly turning moist pale walls upon you
—Your own designs, peeling and unachieved—
Or her whole darkness hunching in an alley.
And all at once you enter the embrace
Withheld by day while you solicited.   25
She wanders lewdly, whispering her given name,
Charing Cross Road, or Forty-second Street:
The longest streets, desire that never ends,
Familiar and inexplicable, wearing
Cosmetic light a fool could penetrate.   30
She presses you with her hard ornaments,
Arcades, late movie shows, the piled lit windows
Of surplus stores. Here she is loveliest;
Extreme, material, and the work of man.

Getting at Meaning

1. Who might be the "you" addressed by the speaker in this poem? What relationship between the "you" and the city does the speaker suggest?

2. What different impressions does the city convey at different times of day?

3. When the "you" in the poem has an opportunity to escape the city, he, she, or they do not. Why?

4. The city as described in the last six lines is cheap and garish. What then does the speaker mean by "Here she is loveliest"? For what qualities is the speaker praising cities?

Developing Skills in Reading Literature

1. **Figurative Language.** Throughout this poem, the poet personifies the city as a woman, and in doing so he creates an extended metaphor. What are the qualities of this woman? What qualities of the city are comparable? Cite evidence from the poem to support your answers.

2. **Structure: Stanza.** Notice that the stanzas of this poem vary considerably in length. What relationship do you see between the length of each stanza and its content?

Developing Vocabulary

Suffixes. In the first line of this poem, both the adjective *indifferent* and the noun *indifference* are used. The following adjectives and verbs also are found in the poem. What noun can be formed from each word or from the root of the word? What various suffixes are used in creating these nouns?

rejected	solicited
irresistible	familiar
desolate	inexplicable
urgent	cosmetic
moist	penetrate

From the Wave

It mounts at sea, a concave wall
   Down-ribbed with shine,
And pushes forward, building tall
   Its steep incline.

Then from their hiding rise to sight   5
   Black shapes on boards
Bearing before the fringe of white
   It mottles towards.

Their pale feet curl, they poise their weight
   With a learn'd skill.   10
It is the wave they imitate
   Keeps them so still.

The marbling bodies have become
   Half wave, half men,
Grafted it seems by feet of foam   15
   Some seconds, then.

Late as they can, they slice the face
   In timed procession:
Balance is triumph in this place,
   Triumph possession.   20

The mindless heave of which they rode
   A fluid shelf
Breaks as they leave it, falls and, slowed,
   Loses itself.

Clear, the sheathed bodies slick as seals   25
   Loosen and tingle;
And by the board the bare foot feels
   The suck of shingle.[1]

They paddle in the shallows still;
   Two splash each other;   30
Then all swim out to wait until
   The right waves gather.

---

1. **shingle:** waterworn gravel found on a beach.

Getting at Meaning

1. Which lines do you think mark the dramatic high point, the point of highest tension in the poem? At what point does this tension relax?

2. Although human beings are described in this poem, they are without faces and personalities. Why is this lack of individuality appropriate to the poem? Explain.

Developing Skills in Reading Literature

1. **Extended Metaphor.** This poem is based on an extended comparison between the wave and the surfers. Trace this metaphor throughout the poem, pointing out various characteristics that the two have in common.

2. **Onomatopoeia.** The alliteration and consonance in the phrase "sheathed bodies slick as seals" creates an onomatopoetic effect because the sound of the words echoes the sleekness and the speed of the surfers. Find other similar phrases in the poem, and describe the impression that each creates.

3. **Imagery.** Much of the success of this lyric depends upon images of power and grace. In which stanzas do these images prevail? Although the surfers move at tremendous speeds, notice how their movement is described in the third and fourth stanzas. How does this description suggest the classical ideals of beauty and grace?

4. **Form and Meaning.** Sometimes the topography of a poem, or the way that the lines are arranged on the printed page, enhances its meaning. What visual image do the alternating line lengths provide in this poem? How does the topography reflect an idea contained within the poem? Do alternating rhymes also contribute to this effect? Explain.

Seamus Heaney

Follower

My father worked with a horse plough,
His shoulders globed like a full sail strung
Between the shafts and the furrow.
The horses strained at his clicking tongue.

An expert. He would set the wing   5
And fit the bright steel-pointed sock.[1]
The sod rolled over without breaking.
At the headrig,[2] with a single pluck

Of reins, the sweating team turned round
And back into the land. His eye   10
Narrowed and angled at the ground,
Mapping the furrow exactly.

I stumbled in his hobnailed wake,[3]
Fell sometimes on the polished sod;
Sometimes he rode me on his back   15
Dipping and rising to his plod.

I wanted to grow up and plough,
To close one eye, stiffen my arm.
All I ever did was follow
In his broad shadow round the farm.   20

I was a nuisance, tripping, falling,
Yapping always. But today
It is my father who keeps stumbling
Behind me, and will not go away.

---

1. **set the wing . . . sock:** fasten the wing nut to tighten the "socket" on the plowshare.
2. **headrig:** the carriage and saw used in cutting logs into slabs.
3. **hobnailed wake:** in the path of his hobnailed boots, boots with broad-headed nails put on the soles to prevent wear or slipping.

THE CORNFIELD, 1918. *John Nash. Tate Gallery, London.*

1. What contrast between the speaker and the father is developed throughout the poem? In what way does this contrast prepare the reader for the impact of the last two lines?

2. What change of mood occurs in the final stanza of the poem? Does the father literally become the follower at this point? Explain.

3. What does the speaker mean by "I wanted . . . / To close one eye, stiffen my arm"?

Developing Skills in Reading Literature

1. **Diction.** The choice of words is vital to the strong simplicity of this poem. What meanings are suggested by the following phrases? How does each of them relate to the overall tone of the poem?

    a. "shoulders globed like a full sail"

    b. "An expert"

    c. "a single pluck/Of reins"

    d. "In his broad shadow"

    e. "Yapping always"

    f. "my father who keeps stumbling"

2. **Theme.** The speaker experiences an ironic reversal of roles in this poem. What universal theme is suggested by this reversal?

Digging

Between my finger and my thumb
The squat pen rests; snug as a gun.

Under my window, a clean rasping sound
When the spade sinks into gravelly ground:
My father, digging. I look down   5

Till his straining rump among the flowerbeds
Bends low, comes up twenty years away
Stooping in rhythm through potato drills
Where he was digging.

The coarse boot nestled on the lug, the shaft   10
Against the inside knee was levered firmly.
He rooted out tall tops, buried the bright edge deep
To scatter new potatoes that we picked
Loving their cool hardness in our hands.

By God, the old man could handle a spade.   15
Just like his old man.

My grandfather cut more turf in a day
Than any other man on Toner's bog.
Once I carried him milk in a bottle
Corked sloppily with paper. He straightened up   20
To drink it, then fell to right away

Nicking and slicing neatly, heaving sods
Over his shoulder, going down and down
For the good turf. Digging.

The cold smell of potato mould, the squelch and slap   25
Of soggy peat, the curt cuts of an edge
Through living roots awaken in my head.
But I've no spade to follow men like them.

Between my finger and my thumb
The squat pen rests.   30
I'll dig with it.

Getting at Meaning

1. In what ways is the speaker "digging" in this poem? What reminds the speaker of the past? What is meant by "My father . . . bends low, comes up twenty years away"?

2. What differences exist between past and present in this poem? What is the significance of this contrast?

3. The speaker describes the grandfather "going down and down/For the good turf. Digging." How does this idea of digging relate to the kind of digging done by the speaker?

Developing Skills in Reading Literature

Imagery. The poet makes effective use of tactile images throughout this poem. Find several examples, and be prepared to discuss how this type of imagery enhances the tone and the mood of the poem.

An image that describes one sensation in terms of another is an example of the technique known as synesthesia. For example, the "cold smell of potato mould" is an olfactory image described in terms of temperature. Another illustration of synesthesia is an image in which the texture of an object is described in terms of its temperature. What is this image? How does the use of synesthesia strengthen the overall effect of the poem?

Developing Writing Skills

Analyzing Style. Examine the three poems by Seamus Heaney included in this unit. List the stylistic characteristics that mark all three poems, noting elements such as diction, structure, imagery, figurative language, tone, and mood. Then write an essay in which you describe Heaney's style and the overall impression created by his poems.

Judith Wright

born in 1915

Noted for her technical skill and intense evocation of the Australian landscape, Judith Wright sees the poet's role as that of observer and commenter on human social roles. She draws on her own life concerns for her poetry, her main themes being the preservation of her native Australia and the relations between women and the people in their lives—lovers, husbands, children. She is the most widely read contemporary Australian poet.

Wright was born in Armidale, New South Wales, Australia, and was educated at the University of Sydney. From 1938 to 1949 she worked as a secretary, a clerk, and a statistician, and since that time she has lectured at various universities in Australia. Since 1967 she has been an Honors Tutor in English at the University of Brisbane.

Wright traces her roots to the English settlers of Australia and prefers the rural and farming past to city life. Many of her poems deal with the Australian aborigines, the rugged and beautiful frontier, and the destruction of these by pollution and urbanization. Another significant influence on Wright's poetry was the philosophical investigations of Western thought she shared with her husband, writer J.P. McKinney.

Wright's first book of poetry, *The Moving Image*, was published in Melbourne in 1946. Other works include *Woman to Man* (1949) and *City Sunrise* (1964). She has also written books for children and a history of her family's settlement and life in Australia, *The Generations of Men* (1959).

Eve to Her Daughters

It was not I who began it.[1]
Turned out into draughty caves,
hungry so often, having to work for our bread,
hearing the children whining,
I was nevertheless not unhappy.   5
Where Adam went I was fairly contented to go.
I adapted myself to the punishment: it was my life.

But Adam, you know . . . !
He kept on brooding over the insult,
over the trick They had played on us, over the scolding.   10
He had discovered a flaw in himself
and he had to make up for it.
Outside Eden the earth was imperfect,
the seasons changed, the game was fleet-footed,
he had to work for our living, and he didn't like it.   15
He even complained of my cooking
(it was hard to compete with Heaven).

So, he set to work.
The earth must be made a new Eden
with central heating, domesticated animals,   20
mechanical harvesters, combustion engines,
escalators, refrigerators,
and modern means of communication
and multiplied opportunities for safe investment
and higher education for Abel and Cain[2]   25
and the rest of the family.
You can see how his pride had been hurt.

In the process he had to unravel everything,
because he believed that mechanism
was the whole secret—he was always mechanical-minded.   30
He got to the very inside of the whole machine
exclaiming as he went, So this is how it works!

---

1. **it:** See Genesis, Chapter 3. Adam and Eve are sent from the Garden of Eden because they disobey God's command not to eat fruit from the Tree of Knowledge.
2. **Abel and Cain:** twin sons of Adam and Eve. See Genesis, Chapter 4.

And now that I know how it works, why, I must have
   invented it.
As for God and the Other, they cannot be demonstrated,
and what cannot be demonstrated   35
doesn't exist.
You see, he had always been jealous.

Yes, he got to the center
where nothing at all can be demonstrated.
And clearly he doesn't exist; but he refuses   40
to accept the conclusion.
You see, he was always an egotist.

It was warmer than this in the cave;
there was none of this fallout.
I would suggest, for the sake of the children,   45
that it's time you took over.

But you are my daughters, you inherit my own faults
   of character;
you are submissive, following Adam
even beyond existence.
Faults of character have their own logic   50
and it always works out.
I observed this with Abel and Cain.

Perhaps the whole elaborate fable
right from the beginning
is meant to demonstrate this; perhaps it's the whole secret. 55
Perhaps nothing exists but our faults?

But it's useless to make
such a suggestion to Adam.
He has turned himself into God,
who is faultless, and doesn't exist.   60

Getting at Meaning

1. What is Eve's attitude toward Adam and toward her life after the fall? How does she feel about the mechanized world that Adam creates?

2. In what sense does Adam's attitude ultimately lead to his loss of religious faith? Has Eve lost her faith in God, too? How do you know?

3. How is Eve essentially different from Adam?

4. Who or what is responsible for the fallout that Eve mentions in line 44? When Eve says, ". . . you are my daughters, . . . /you are submissive, following Adam," does she mean "daughters" in a literal or a figurative sense? Is Adam an individual or the representative of all men? Explain.

Developing Skills in Reading Literature

1. **Allusion.** Read the account of Adam and Eve's fall and the story of Cain and Abel in Genesis, Chapters 3 and 4. What references in the poem are true to the Biblical account? What liberties does Wright take?

2. **Tone and Theme.** Through sarcastic remarks, writers express disapproval under the guise of approval or praise. Look for examples of sarcasm in this poem and also for comments that are more directly critical. Of what does the speaker disapprove? What is she implying about contemporary society? In what sense is this a feminist poem? Explain.

3. **Diction.** Examine the use of the words *mechanism, mechanical* and *machine* in lines 29–31 of this poem. Do these words have differing connotations? How do the words relate to Adam's personality, according to Eve?

Developing Vocabulary

Words from Latin. The speaker in this poem calls her daughters submissive. Look up the word *submissive* in a dictionary. What is the meaning of the prefix *sub-*? What does the root word mean? Does Eve seem entirely submissive as she is characterized in this poem? Explain.

Edward Lucie-Smith

born in 1933

EDWARD LUCIE-SMITH.
Rollie McKenna.

Edward Lucie-Smith has involved himself in many facets of art, as poet, publisher, and art critic. His poetry has changed markedly over the course of his career, becoming increasingly simple and direct.

Lucie-Smith was born in Kingston, Jamaica, but moved to England and earned his B.A. at Oxford in 1954. He served in the Royal Air Force for two years in the 1950's and thereafter turned his efforts entirely to writing, earning his living as a freelance writer and journalist in London. He is also a co-founder of Turret Press, through which he pursues his interest in publishing and promoting other poets. Lucie-Smith was one of the founders of "The Group," a society of writers who met to discuss their poetry and the poetry of others and to consider the possibilities of art.

Lucie-Smith has published more than two dozen books of poetry. He first wrote about subjects from his childhood, speaking of the small ironies and betrayals of children, but he soon moved on to freer, less conventional forms and a variety of subjects. His themes include love, religion, history, and especially matters of art. He attempts to preserve the rhythms of prose in his poetry, to say things in the most natural and direct way possible.

The long list of Lucie-Smith's books includes many critical and historical studies of visual art, including *What Is a Painting?* (1966) and *Symbolist Art* (1972). He has also edited and translated many books on art and poetry. His own books of poetry include *A Tropical Childhood and Other Poems* (1961), *Confessions and Histories (1964), Towards Silence (1968),* and *The Well-Wishers* (1974).

The Lesson

"Your father's gone," my bald headmaster said.
His shiny dome and brown tobacco jar
Splintered at once in tears. It wasn't grief.
I cried for knowledge which was bitterer
Than any grief. For there and then I knew   5
That grief has uses—that a father dead
Could bind the bully's fist a week or two;
And then I cried for shame, then for relief.

I was a month past ten when I learned this:
I still remember how the noise was stilled   10
In school assembly when my grief came in.
Some goldfish in a bowl quietly sculled
Around their shining prison on its shelf.
They were indifferent. All the other eyes
Were turned towards me. Somewhere in myself   15
Pride, like a goldfish, flashed a sudden fin.

Getting at Meaning

1. What experience is described in the first three lines of this poem? What "splintered"?

2. What is the bitter knowledge that causes the speaker to cry? For what other reasons does he cry? Explain each of these reasons in terms of the speaker's experience.

3. Although the speaker in this poem makes use of his father's death, does he also feel real grief? Explain.

4. What is paradoxical about the lesson that the speaker learns?

Developing Skills in Reading Literature

Figurative Language. Explain the figurative language in the second stanza. How are the boy's feelings similar to a goldfish in a bowl?

Developing Writing Skills

1. **Analyzing Theme.** Both this poem and "My Grandmother" by Elizabeth Jennings deal with the subjects of death and grief. In a well developed paragraph compare and contrast the poets' treatment of these subjects, concentrating on the similarities and differences between the two speakers.

2. **Writing a Definition.** A quality such as pride can be both a negative and a positive force in a person's life. Look up this word in a dictionary. Then in a well developed paragraph write a clear definition of the word, noting both its positive and its negative consequences.

Evan Jones

born in 1931

The poems of Evan Jones describe the influence of time and location on people. He has experimented with portraying the sound of localities and has made extensive use of traditional poetic forms, such as the sestina, a complex pattern of rhyme and meter.

Jones was born in Melbourne, Australia. He attended the University of Melbourne, earning a master's degree in history in 1957, and Stanford University, where he received a master's degree in English in 1959. He has taught at the University of Melbourne since 1955.

Inside the Whale, Jones's first book of poetry, was published in 1960. It includes verses written in forms from earlier times as well as the well known "Noah's Song." In the next twenty years Jones published only two more collections of verse. The poems in *Understandings* (1967), the first of these two collections, examine the experiences of early adulthood: love, marriage, and estrangement. Jones works carefully, incorporating the speech patterns of his speakers into the sound of his poetry.

EVAN JONES.

Lament of the Banana Man

Gal, I'm tellin' you, I'm tired fo' true,
Tired of Englan', tired o' you.
But I can' go back to Jamaica now. . . .

I'm here in Englan', I'm drawin' pay,
I go to de underground[1] every day—   5
Eight hours is all, half-hour fo' lunch,
M' uniform's free, an' m' ticket punch—
Punchin' tickets not hard to do,
When I'm tired o' punchin', I let dem through.

I get a paid holiday once a year.   10
Ol' age an' sickness can' touch me here.

I have a room o' m' own, an' a iron bed,
Dunlopillo[2] under m' head,
A Morphy-Richards[3] to warm de air,
A formica table, an easy chair.   15
I have summer clothes, an' winter clothes,
An' paper kerchiefs to blow m' nose.

My yoke is easy, my burden is light,[4]
I know a place I can go to, any night.
Dis place Englan'! I'm not complainin',   20
If it col', it col', if it rainin', it rainin'.
I don' min' if it's mostly night,
Dere's always inside, or de sodium light.[5]

I don' min' white people starin' at me
Dey don' want me here? Don't is deir country?[6]   25
You won' catch me bawlin' any homesick tears
If I don' see Jamaica for a t'ousand years!

. . . Gal, I'm tellin' you, I'm tired fo' true,
Tired of Englan', tired o' you,
I can' go back to Jamaica now—   30
But I'd want to die there, anyhow.

---

1. **underground:** the subway in London.
2. **Dunlopillo:** brand name for a foam pillow.
3. **Morphy-Richards:** brand name for a space heater.
4. **My yoke . . . light:** See Jeremiah 6:16 and Matthew 11:30.
5. **sodium light:** a street light, fitted with electrodes and filled with sodium vapor, that gives off a soft yellow light.
6. **Don't . . . country:** Isn't this their country?

Getting at Meaning

1. What are the apparent advantages of being in England, according to the speaker? What is ironic about the speaker's description of his lifestyle? What does he imply about Jamaica?

2. What is the attitude of the "white people" toward the speaker?

3. What is the significance of referring to the speaker as "the banana man" in the title of the poem?

Developing Skills in Reading Literature

1. **Dialect and Tone.** Examine the following examples of the Jamaican dialect used in this poem. How does each example differ from standard English in pronunciation, vocabulary, colloquial expression, grammatical construction, or in a combination of these?

a. "I'm tired fo' true"
b. "Punchin' tickets not hard to do"
c. "If it col', it col', if it rainin', it rainin'."
d. "Dere's always inside"
e. "Don't is deir country?"

How does the speaker feel about England? How does the use of the Jamaican dialect reinforce this tone?

2. **Allusion.** Find in the book of Matthew the reference quoted in line 18. Who speaks these words in the Bible? What do they mean? How do the words relate to the experience of the banana man? Is the line in the poem ironic? Explain.

3. **Lament.** A lament is traditionally a poem that expresses great grief and a sense of personal loss. It is commonly written as a monologue addressed to an identifiable but silent listener. Is this a poem of great grief? Which lines convey the most intense feelings of loss? What is implied about the speaker's relationship with the "gal" addressed in this lament?

Wole Soyinka

born in 1934

Perhaps the best known of all African writers, Wole Soyinka writes plays, poems, and novels that deal with the themes of death and self-sacrifice, with African politics and society, and with the struggle for human dignity. His work can be seen as an attempt to find meaning in the contradictory forces that govern human life and actions.

Soyinka was born Akinwande Oluwole Soyinka in Abeokuta, Nigeria. His mother was a strictly religious Christian, and his father was the head-master at a Christian school for children. The story of Soyinka's first eleven years, *Ake*, was published in the United States in 1982. In it Soyinka tells of the clash he felt as a child between the Christian teachings and the traditional Yoruba tribal customs.

Between 1954 and 1957 Soyinka attended the University of Leeds, in Yorkshire, England, earning a bachelor's degree in English. Taking a job as a play reader at the Royal Court Theater in London, Soyinka was exposed to the latest in European drama as well as the classics of the English stage and was able to have his own first play, *The Inventor*, performed. In 1958 his verse play *The Swamp Dwellers*, a tragedy about impoverished swamp farmers, was produced in London.

In 1960 Soyinka returned to Africa as a Research Fellow in Drama at the University of Ibadan. At this time he founded an amateur theatrical company, the Masks, which had an enormous influence on the theatre of West Africa.

The early 1960's was a time when many African countries were gaining independence, and Soyinka was involved in the accompanying political unrest. He was arrested in 1965 for his connection with a radio broadcast that denounced a disputed election. During the bloody Nigerian civil war, he was

WOLE SOYINKA.
Jill Krementz.

imprisoned from 1967 to 1969, spending a good part of the time in solitary confinement. *A Shuttle in the Crypt* (1972) is Soyinka's poetic record of this experience. He now teaches as a professor of comparative literature at the University of Ife, in Nigeria.

Soyinka first became famous as a writer of satirical poems such as "Telephone Conversation," but he then moved into plays and more serious verse. His first volume of collected poems, *Idanre and Other Poems* (1967), in fact excludes his lighter poetry. He has published several books of poetry, more than seventeen plays, novels, auto-biographical works, and literary criticism. His recent work, which effects a reconciliation of Western and African influences, deals with African politics and the contradictory relationship between death and growth.

Telephone Conversation

The price seemed reasonable, location
Indifferent. The landlady swore she lived
Off premises. Nothing remained
But self-confession. "Madam," I warned,
"I hate a wasted journey—I am African."   5
Silence. Silenced transmission of
Pressurized good breeding. Voice, when it came,
Lipstick coated, long gold-rolled
Cigarette holder pipped. Caught I was, foully.
"HOW DARK?" . . . I had not misheard. . . . "ARE YOU LIGHT   10
OR VERY DARK?" Button B. Button A. Stench
Of rancid breath of public hide-and-speak.
Red booth. Red pillar box.[1] Red double-tiered
Omnibus[2] squelching tar. It *was* real! Shamed
By ill-mannered silence, surrender   15
Pushed dumbfounded to beg simplication.
Considerate she was, varying the emphasis—
"ARE YOU DARK? OR VERY LIGHT?" Revelation came.
"You mean—like plain or milk chocolate?"
Her assent was clinical, crushing in its light   20
Impersonality. Rapidly, wave-length adjusted,
I chose. "West African sepia"[3]—and as afterthought,
"Down in my passport." Silence for spectroscopic
Flight of fancy, till truthfulness clanged her accent
Hard on the mouthpiece. "WHAT'S THAT?" conceding   25
"DON'T KNOW WHAT THAT IS." "Like brunette."
"THAT'S DARK, ISN'T IT?" "Not altogether.
Facially, I am brunette, but madam, you should see
The rest of me. Palm of my hand, soles of my feet
Are a peroxide blonde. Friction, caused—   30
Foolishly madam—by sitting down, has turned
My bottom raven black—One moment madam!"—sensing
Her receiver rearing on the thunderclap
About my ears—"Madam," I pleaded, "wouldn't you rather
See for yourself?"   35

---

1. **pillar box:** a mail collection box.
2. **Omnibus:** a two-tiered bus, commonly used in England.
3. **sepia:** a rich brown color.

Getting at Meaning

1. What do the following lines reveal about the social values of the landlady in this poem?

a. "Silenced transmission of/Pressurized good breeding."

b. "Lipstick coated, long gold-rolled/Cigarette-holder pipped."

What other lines reinforce these values? Does the poet approve or disapprove of her? How do you know?

2. What emotions does the speaker express in lines 12–14? What is the tone of the speaker's response to the landlady throughout the remainder of the poem? What is her response?

Developing Skills in Reading Literature

Stream of Consciousness. The series of seemingly random words and phrases in lines 12–15 of this poem illustrates stream of consciousness as a poetic technique through which the thoughts and sensations of the speaker are captured at different levels of awareness. "Button," for example, is probably meant to suggest something like "panic button." What do "stench" and "rancid breath" seem to suggest about the speaker's feelings? What does the color red symbolize? Find other lines in the poem that illustrate stream of consciousness. What do they reveal about the speaker's perceptions and feelings?

Developing Writing Skills

Using Contrasts. Both "Lament of the Banana Man" and "Telephone Conversation" were written by members of minority groups. Both deal with the subject of discrimination and racial prejudice. In spite of these similarities, however, the poems evidence distinct differences in the treatment of subject, particularly in the kind of speaker chosen to convey the theme. In a well developed paragraph contrast the two poems, focusing on the characteristics of each speaker and on other literary devices that communicate the poets' message.

Margaret Atwood

born in 1939

MARGARET ATWOOD.
Thomas Victor.

As the writer of literary criticism, several well known novels, and more than a dozen books of poetry, Margaret Atwood is one of Canada's most visible authors. She has distinguished herself as an artist who describes the ironies and difficulties of women in contemporary society.

Atwood was born in Ottawa, Ontario, Canada, and was educated at the University of Toronto. She did graduate work at Harvard University and received a master's degree from Radcliffe College in Massachusetts in 1962. She has taught at the University of British Columbia in Vancouver and at Sir George Williams University in Montreal. She now lives in Ontario and writes full time.

Atwood's novels, including *The Edible Woman* (1969), *Surfacing* (1972), and *Lady Oracle* (1976), usually portray women moving through a period of adjustment, from being victimized by the patterns of social correctness to achieving a sense of independence. Often, they are liberated by a symbolic act, such as embarking on a dangerous wilderness expedition. Although Atwood's stories are serious in subject and theme, they are typically told with humor and optimism.

Atwood's poetry tends to be lean and conversational, expressing calmly the poignancy, failures, and hopes involved in human relationships. Feminism imbues her poetry as it does her prose and is evident in books of verse such as *The Circle Game* (1964), *The Animals in That Country* (1968), and *You Are Happy* (1974).

I Can Change Myself

I can change my-
self more easily
than I can change you

I could grow bark and
become a shrub   5

or switch back in time
to the woman image left
in cave rubble, the drowned
stomach bulbed with fertility,
face a tiny bead, a   10
lump, queen of the termites

or (better) speed myself up,
disguise myself in the knuckles
and purple-veined veils of old ladies,
become arthritic and genteel   15

or one twist further:
collapse across your
bed clutching my heart
and pull the nostalgic sheet up over
my waxed farewell smile   20

which would be inconvenient
but final.

GIRL BEFORE A MIRROR, 1932. *Pablo Picasso.*
Collection, The Museum of Modern Art, New York.
Gift of Mrs. Simon Guggenheim.

Getting at Meaning

1. In the second, third, and fourth stanzas, the speaker speculates about various ways that she might change herself. What are these ways? Is the change that she suggests in the fifth stanza any more possible than those she suggests earlier?

2. What conclusion is implied in the last two lines of the poem? How might these lines relate to the opening three lines?

Developing Skills in Reading Literature

1. **Structure.** This poem begins with a three-line assertion by the speaker. The assertion is followed by a two-line stanza that provides an example. How do the next three stanzas develop the idea further? What effect is created by the repetition of *or* at the beginning of each of these stanzas? What is the function of the final stanza? When looking at the entire poem as it appears on the page, what ideas seem to stand out?

2. **Tone.** The tone at the beginning of this poem seems rather light hearted, although the subject itself is serious. What, however, is the speaker's underlying attitude, which becomes apparent only after reading the entire poem? Is her attitude one of anger, frustration, annoyance, bravado, resignation, or something else? What is the overall tone of the poem? Is it ironic? bitter? melodramatic? sarcastic? self-righteous? humorous? Be prepared to defend your answer.

Edwin Morgan

born in 1920

In his traditional poems of Scottish childhood as well as in his humorous verse and poems that are games, Edwin Morgan seems to be exploring just what poetry is capable of expressing. A versatile writer, his work includes translations, science fiction poems, poems written as though by a machine, and some of the finest examples of concrete poetry in any language.

Born in Glasgow, Scotland, Morgan was educated at Glasgow University, where he now teaches. He entered the university in 1937, interrupted his education to spend six years in the Royal Army Medical Corps in World War II, and received a master's degree in 1947. Morgan's first book of poems, a small paperback titled *The Vision of Cathkin Braes*, was published in 1952. Very much a Scottish writer, Morgan has always written about Glasgow, the decline of life in Scotland, and the plight of the poor; and he has translated *Beowulf*, passages from Shakespeare, and Russian, Spanish, and German poetry into the Scots dialect.

Unlike some contemporary writers, Morgan believes that poetry can be both fun and serious, and he uses humor and experimentation in his poetry. Influenced by the word play of Irish writer James Joyce, Morgan often makes his poems into games. Other examples of his ingenuity include "The Computer's First Christmas Card," a lyric that is written as if by a computer, and "The Loch Ness Monster's Song," which appears to be a series of sounds and animal grunts.

Morgan's collection *From Glasgow to Saturn* (1973) includes poems about local people and places and speculations about time and space, as did perhaps his finest collection of verse, *The Second Life* (1968). Other titles include *The Cape of Good Hope* (1955), *Proverbfolder* (1969), *Twelve Songs* (1970), and *Glasgow Sonnets* (1972). Despite all his variety and experimentation Morgan has never abandoned the traditional forms, continuing to write sonnet sequences and poems that tell of everyday life.

The Computer's First Christmas Card

jollymerry
hollyberry
jollyberry
merryholly
happyjolly   5
jollyjelly
jellybelly
bellymerry
hollyheppy
jollyMolly   10
marryJerry
merryHarry
hoppyBarry
heppyJarry
boppyheppy   15
berryjorry
jorryjolly
moppyjelly
Mollymerry
Jerryjolly   20
bellyboppy
jorryhoppy
hollymoppy
Barrymerry
Jarryhappy   25
happyboppy
boppyjolly
jollymerry
merrymerry
merrymerry   30
merryChris
ammerryasa
Chrismerry
asMERRYCHR
YSANTHEMUM   35

Getting at Meaning

1. What mood is created by this poem?

2. What does the last line imply about the "success" of the computer's attempt to write a Christmas card? How do you think that this poet feels about the value of the computer? Explain.

Developing Skills in Reading Literature

Concrete Poetry. A concrete poem is one in which form and meaning are inseparable. How are both the form and the meaning of this poem made clear by its title?

Developing Writing Skills

Writing a Concrete Poem. Find additional examples of concrete poetry in anthologies and other reference books, and study the way that form and meaning are interrelated in these poems. Then write a sentence or a phrase that expresses a strong emotion, such as anger, hatred, joy, or determination. Arrange the words or the letters (or repetitions of them) into a form that suggests the reason for the emotion.

Unit Review   *The Twentieth Century: Modern Period*

Understanding the Unit

1. Most twentieth-century critics find fault with the Romantic excess that characterizes much nineteenth-century writing. Most modern writers, too, insist that disciplined forms, fully visualized scenes, and concrete images must provide the basis for literary expression. In spite of its fundamental realism, however, contemporary literature does contain Romantic elements. You have already discussed Realism and Romanticism in relation to Frank O'Connor's "The Idealist." Now identify one or two other stories and several poems in the unit that seem to illustrate qualities typical of Romanticism. Be prepared to point out characteristics of Realism and Romanticism in each.

2. Personal courage, human relationships, the process of physical and emotional growth, the impact of death, the individual and society, nature, mechanization and technology: all these ideas are explored by the writers in this unit. Review the selections, and find examples that illustrate each of these broad themes. What thematic links can you make between the literature in this unit and that of earlier units? In what periods, for example, are writers primarily concerned with human relationships? In what periods do they seem more preoccupied with social issues?

3. Several of the poems in this unit comment on contemporary social problems such as poverty, unemployment, and the plight of minority groups. Review the poems by Spender, Scannell, Hobsbaum, Causley, Jones, and Soyinka. Which poets seem most similar in attitude? most different? Do any of them seem to offer solutions, or do they simply present problems? Which of the poems seems most poignant? most bitter? most humorous? Be prepared to defend your opinions.

4. Some contemporary writers seem to champion the cause of technological development, while others lament the depersonalization and the pervasive sense of powerlessness within modern technological society. Examine both the essay and the story by Arthur C. Clarke and the poems by Auden, Thomas, Connor, Wright, and Morgan. Discuss both obvious and subtle contrasts in attitude toward technology.

5. Many postwar writers did not even attempt to deal directly with the realities of the postwar world. Discuss the ways that the short stories in the unit exemplify this kind of withdrawal from society. Do these writers allude even indirectly to the war or its aftermath? Which take refuge in the past or in the future? Which selections are the most pure escapist?

6. Doris Lessing and Ted Hughes employ vivid imagery to convey the power of nature. They also use nature as a means of commenting on life in general and on human life in particular. Compare and contrast the impression of nature that emerges from Lessing's story and the impression created by Hughes's poems. Cite images and passages to support your statements.

Writing

1. Several poems in the unit deal with alienation from society or with the rejection of social values. Choose two poems that convey this similar theme. Write a composition describing the techniques used to develop the theme. Consider for each: structure, imagery, figurative language, connotations, sound devices, and the use of irony, satire, and humor.

2. As is typical of the entire period, the writers of fiction represented in this unit all utilize traditional narrative methods. Choose two short stories from the unit, and for each analyze the plot structure and the techniques of characterization.

3. In the following excerpt from "On Teaching Modern Poetry," Stephen Spender asks several thought-provoking questions:

A poem has many levels of meaning, and none of them is prose. Are some of these "righter" than others? Is it altogether "wrong" to think that a poem may be paraphrased? Can an appreciation of poetry be acquired? Does poetry have educational value for the student who is incapable of a complete experience of poetry but who can acquire a limited appreciation which may not seem to survive his years at school or college?

What do you think? Present your opinions in a well developed essay.

Handbook of Literary Terms

Alliteration. Alliteration is the repetition of initial consonant sounds, as in "sweet spring." Alliteration occurs in both prose and poetry, as well as in everyday speech. Writers use alliteration to help create mood, to emphasize words, to unify a passage, to reinforce meaning, and to impart a pleasant sound. Often alliteration is reinforced by repeating the same consonant sound within and at the ends of other words. Notice the alliteration of the s sound in these lines, as well as the reinforcement of that alliteration in other words.

> When Stella strikes the tuneful string
> In scenes of imitated spring,
> Where Beauty lavishes her powers
> On beds of never-fading flowers,
> and pleasure propagates around
> Each charm of modulated sound,
>
> SAMUEL JOHNSON
"To Miss—"

See *Consonance*.

Allusion. An allusion is a reference to an historical or literary person, place, or event with which the reader is assumed to be familiar. Many works of literature contain allusions to the Bible or to classical mythology. The title of Bernard Shaw's drama, *Pygmalion*, for example, is an allusion to a woman-hating character in a Greek myth who fashioned a statue of the ideal woman. Understanding an allusion gives the reader deeper understanding of the work. In the following lines Matthew Prior alludes to Falstaff, a character in Shakespeare's *Henry IV*, and to Venus, the Roman goddess of beauty.

> Dear Cloe, how blubbered is that pretty face!
>   Thy cheek all on fire, and thy hair all uncurled!
> Prithee quit this caprice; and (as old Falstaff says)
>   Let us e'en talk a little like folks of this world.
>
> How canst thou presume thou hast leave to destroy
>   The beauties which Venus but lent to thy keeping?
> Those looks were designed to inspire love and joy;
>   More ordinary eyes may serve people for weeping.
>
> "A Better Answer"

Analogy. An analogy is a point by point comparison between two dissimilar things for the purpose of clarifying the less familiar of the two things. In purpose and structure, the analogy differs from the figures of speech that are also comparisons: simile, metaphor, and personification. In "We'll Never Conquer Space," Arthur C. Clarke compares the colonizing of distant planets and galaxies to the colonizing of distant islands by primitive island-dwellers. The analogy clarifies his point about the unconquerable nature of space. Analogy often is used in persuasion as a kind of reasoning. For the purpose of convincing readers of a course of action, for example, Thomas Carlyle likens the position of human beings to that of soldiers at war.

> . . . let that vain struggle to read the mystery of the Infinite cease to harass us . . . . Do we not already know that the name of the Infinite is GOOD, is GOD? Here on Earth we are as Soldiers, fighting in a foreign land; that understand not the plan of the campaign, and have no need to understand it; seeing well what is at our hand to be done. Let us do it like Soldiers; with submission, with courage, with a heroic joy.
>
> *Characteristics*

Anaphora. In rhetoric, anaphora is the repetition of a word or word group, often at the beginnings of successive sentences, clauses, paragraphs, or poetic lines. One type of repetition, anaphora is used by speakers and writers to unify a work and to create a dramatic effect that calls attention to certain ideas. For example, in these poetic lines anaphora adds impact to the stated contrast:

> Let Fortune lay on me her worst disgrace;
> Let folk o'ercharged with brain against me cry;
> Let clouds bedim my face, break in mine eye;
> Let me no steps but of lost labor trace;
> Let all the earth with scorn recount my case;
> But do not will me from my Love to flie.
>
> SIR PHILP SIDNEY
Astrophel and Stella

Anglo-Saxon Poetry. Anglo-Saxon poetry is characterized by a strong rhythm, or cadence, that makes it easily chanted or sung. Lines are unified through alliteration and through use of the same number of accented syllables in each line. Typically, a line of Anglo-Saxon poetry is divided by a caesura, or pause, into two parts, each part having two accented syllables. Usually, an accented syllable in the first part alliterates with one or both accented syllables in the second part. This passage from *Beowulf*, an Anglo-Saxon poem, illustrates these characteristics:

And Beowulf uttered ‖ his final boast:
"I've never known fear; ‖ as a youth I fought
In endless battles. ‖ I am old, now,
But I will fight again, ‖ seek fame still,
If the dragon ‖ hiding in his tower dares
To face me." ‖
    Then he said farewell to his followers,
Each in his turn, ‖ for the last time:

See *Kenning*.

Antagonist. The antagonist of a novel, drama, short story, or narrative poem is the character or force against which the protagonist is pitted. An antagonist may be another character, as it is for Henry Higgins in *Pygmalion*. The antagonist also may be society, nature, or one side of a character that wars against other impulses in an internal conflict.

See *Conflict*.

Antithesis. Antithesis is a figure of speech in which sharply contrasting words, phrases, clauses, or sentences are juxtaposed. Antithesis is used to emphasize a point. In true antithesis, both the ideas and the grammatical structure are balanced. Notice the balanced opposition in this line from "The Rape of the Lock" by Alexander Pope: "Charms strike the sight, but merit wins the soul." These lines present examples of antithesis.

Raised in extremes, and in extremes decried;
With oaths affirmed, with dying vows denied;
Not weighed or winnowed by the multitude;
But swallowed in the mass, unchewed and crude.
Some truth there was, but dashed and brewed with
    lies,
To please the fools, and puzzle all the wise.
Succeeding times did equal folly call,
Believing nothing, or believing all.
            JOHN DRYDEN
            Absalom and Achitophel

Aphorism. An aphorism is a brief statement that expresses a general truth about life. A succinct expression of a principle, the aphorism is usually witty and pointed. Unlike a proverb, which may stem from oral folk tradition, the term *aphorism* implies a specific author.

'Tis better to have loved and lost
Than never to have loved at all.
            ALFRED, LORD TENNYSON
            In Memoriam

The better part of valor is discretion.
            WILLIAM SHAKESPEARE
            King Henry IV

The busy bee has no time for sorrow.
            WILLIAM BLAKE
            The Marriage of Heaven and Hell

There is only one thing in the world worse than being talked about, and that is not being talked about.
            OSCAR WILDE
            The Picture of Dorian Gray

Apostrophe. An apostrophe is a figure of speech in which a thing, an abstract quality, or an absent or imaginary person is addressed as if present and able to understand. Writers use apostrophe for emotional effect. In poetry, a characteristic example of apostrophe is an invocation of a muse.

O, thou! in Hellas deemed of heavenly birth,
Muse! formed or fabled at the minstrel's will!
            GEORGE GORDON, LORD BYRON
            Childe Harold's Pilgrimage

Following are two other examples of apostrophe. In the first the speaker addresses the abstract quality of quiet; in the second the essayist addresses Shakespeare.

Fair Quiet, have I found thee here,
And Innocence, thy sister dear?
            ANDREW MARVELL "The Garden"

O mighty poet! Thy works are not as those of other men, simply and merely great works of art, but are also like the phenomena of nature. . . .
            THOMAS DE QUINCEY
            "On the Knocking at the Gate in
            Macbeth"

Aside. In drama, an aside is a remark spoken in an undertone by one character either to the audience or to another character, which the remaining characters supposedly do not hear. The aside is a traditional dramatic convention, a device that the audience accepts even though it is obviously unrealistic. The aside can be used to express a character's feelings, opinions, and reactions, and thus functions as a method of characterization.

PETKOFF (*Aside to Catherine, beaming with parental pride*). Pretty, isn't it? She always appears at the right moment.
BERNARD SHAW *Arms and the Man*

KING (*Aside*). Oh, 'tis too true!
How smart a lash that speech doth give my conscience!
WILLIAM SHAKESPEARE *Hamlet*

Assonance. Assonance is the repetion of a vowel sound within words. In poetry and prose, writers use assonance to emphasize certain words, impart a musical quality, create a mood, or unify a passage. Notice the assonance of the long *e* and *a* sounds in these lines from "A Dirge":

Deep caves and dreary main—
Wail, for the world's wrong!
PERCY BYSSHE SHELLEY

In the following lines, assonance of the long *e* sound predominates:

She bound her green sleeve on my helm,
Sweet pledge of love's sweet meed;
DANTE GABRIEL ROSSETTI
"She Bound Her Green Sleeve"

See *Consonance*.

Autobiography. An autobiography is the story of a person's life written by that person. While a formal autobiography implies a sustained, lengthy narrative of a person's history, other autobiographical narratives are less formal and often briefer. Under this general category are autobiographical writings such as diaries, journals, memoirs, and letters. Both diaries and journals are day-by-day accounts of events and personal impressions; diaries usually are considerd the more intimate of the two. A good example of a diary is *The Diary of*

Samuel Pepys excerpted in Unit 4, and an example of a journal is the excerpt from *The Journal* by Mary Shelley in Unit 5. Diaries, journals, and most letters are not written for public reading, while autobiographies and memoirs are intended for a wide audience. Both formal and informal autobiographies provide revealing insights into the writer's character, attitudes, and motivations, as well as some understanding of the society in which the writer lived.

Ballad. A ballad is a narrative poem that was originally intended to be sung. Preserved by oral transmission, the anonymous folk ballad is one of the earliest forms of literature. Folk ballads often depict tragic events that befall common people, include supernatural elements, and treat themes related to love, adventure, and bravery.

The ballad is characterized by simplicity. The action is straightforward, the dialogue direct. The stanza form typical of the ballad is four lines rhyming *a b c b*, the first and third lines being slightly longer than the second and fourth lines. Repetition of words, phrases, lines, and ideas is common in ballads. Some ballads use incremental repetition, which is the repetition of a line or lines with slight changes. If a refrain, or repetition of lines, occurs, it is usually at the ends of stanzas. These sound devices make the early folk ballads musically appealing and memorable.

Folk ballads have been traced back to the early fifteenth century. Here are two stanzas from an early English ballad about an old woman whose three sons return from the dead:

There lived a wife at Usher's Well,	a
And a wealthy wife was she;	b
She had three stout and stalwart sons,	c
And sent them o'er the sea.	b
They hadna' been a week from her,	a
A week but barely ane,	b
When word came to the carlin wife	c
That her three sons were gane.	b

"The Wife of Usher's Well"

A literary ballad is a ballad with a single author. Modeled on the early English and Scottish folk ballads, literary ballads became popular during the Romantic Period. Samuel Taylor Coleridge's "The Rime of the Ancient Mariner" (Unit 5) is an example of a Romantic literary ballad.

For more information on folk ballads, and for several examples, see pages 108-120 in Unit 2.

See *Narrative Poem, Refrain*.

Biography. A biography is a narrative about a person's life written by another person. Since the eighteenth century, biography has been conceived as a comprehensive, unified, accurate history of a person, with emphasis on interpreting facts to present a full picture of the subject's personality. One of the greatest biographies of all time is James Boswell's *The Life of Johnson*, part of which appears in Unit 4; it contains a rich texture of details that reveal the life of author and lexicographer Samuel Johnson.

While early biographies were written to eulogize heroes or to instruct on morality, the modern biography tends to be more objective and psychologically probing. The skilled biographer synthesizes information from sources such as letters, journals, interviews, and documents. Attempting objectivity and avoiding editorial commentary, the good biographer presents a balanced portrayal through detailed anecdotes, reconstructed dialogue, description, quotations, and interpretive passages.

While full-length biographies cover the life history of a person from birth to death, less extensive writings also may be considered biographical. These include the anecdote, which relates a revealing incident in a person's life, and the character sketch, a brief descriptive essay that highlights certain qualities of the subject.

Blank Verse. Blank verse is unrhymed poetry written in iambic pentameter. Each line has five metrical feet, and each foot consists of an unstressed syllable followed by a stressed syllable. Because it resembles the natural rhythm of spoken English, iambic pentameter has been considered most suitable for dramatic verse in English. All of William Shakespeare's plays, including *Macbeth*, were written largely in blank verse. Blank verse also was used frequently for long poems, whether narrative, dramatic, or philosophical. Here is an example of blank verse from *Othello*:

Good name in man and woman, dear my lord,
Is the immediate jewel of their souls.
Who steals my purse steals trash—'tis something,
nothing;

But he that filches from me my good name
Robs me of that which not enriches him
And makes me poor indeed.

See *Meter*.

Caesura. A caesura is a pause in the meter of a line of poetry. The position of a caesura usually is determined by the natural flow of the language and often is marked by punctuation. While the classic use of caesura is at the middle of a line, the pause may fall toward the beginning or the end as well. Note the caesuras in these lines of blank verse.

To die, ‖ to sleep,
To sleep—perchance to dream. ‖ Aye, there's the rub,
For in that sleep of death ‖ what dreams may come
When we have shuffled off this mortal coil
Must give us pause. ‖ There's the respect
That makes calamity of so long life.
　　　　　WILLIAM SHAKESPSEARE *Hamlet*

Caesura is one device that poets use to create variety within a formal meter. Poets also use caesura to reinforce the meaning of a poem through its rhythm, as in the lines from *Hamlet*.

See *Anglo-Saxon Poetry*.

Character. Characters are the people and sometimes the animals who participate in the action of a literary work. For example, in *Beowulf* the characters include Beowulf as well as Grendel and Grendel's mother. A character may be main or minor, depending on his or her role in the short story, novel, play, or narrative poem. A character may be underdeveloped, with one or two dominant traits, or fully developed, exhibiting a unique complex of traits. In longer works of fiction, main characters often change as the plot unfolds. Such characters are called dynamic, the opposite of static characters, who remain the same. Successful characters are not only individuals but also in some way examples of the universal human condition.

See *Antagonist, Characterization, Foil, Protagonist, Stereotype*.

Characterization. Characterization refers to the techniques employed by writers to develop characters. There are five basic methods.

1. The writer may present direct description of a character's physical appearance or personal traits. In The "Prologue" to *The Canterbury Tales*, Chaucer characterizes the pilgrims as individuals primarily through the use of this technique. He describes the monk, for example, as "a fat and personable priest," "a manly man," and "a leader of fashions."

2. Creating dialogue to be spoken by the characters is another means of characterization. For example, "The Nun's Priest's Tale" reveals the priest's holiness and concern for saving souls. The priest says, ". . . gracious Father, if it be thy will/ As saith my Savior, make us all good men,/ And bring us to heavenly bliss."

The dialogue that develops a character also may be spoken by another character. For example, the host says of the nun's priest: "Just look what brawn he has, this gentle priest."

3. Portraying a character's actions may be a means of characterization. For example, in *Macbeth* Macbeth's murder of King Duncan reveals the side of his character that is violent and ambitious.

4. The reactions of another character also may be revealing. For example, King Duncan's awarding a title to Macbeth at the beginning of the play reveals Macbeth as a respected soldier and a loyal subject.

5. A character's thoughts and feelings also may be presented as a means of characterization. For example, the horrifying visions that Macbeth suffers show him to be essentially principled and conscience-stricken over his betrayal of Duncan and Banquo.

See *Character, Narrator, Point of View.*

Climax. In dramatic or narrative literature, the climax is the turning point of the action as well as the moment when interest and intensity reach their peak. The climax of *Beowulf*, for example, is the slaying of the fire dragon. All episodes lead to this emotional scene, when the dying Beowulf reviews his life, and parts with warriors after rescuing them from the dreaded monster. In the short story "Miss Brill" in Unit 7, the climax occurs when Miss Brill overhears a young couple mocking her; the humiliation alters her image of herself. The climax of "Shooting an Elephant," Unit 7, occurs when the narrator succumbs to the natives' expectations and shoots the elephant.

See *Conflict, Plot.*

Comic Relief. Comic relief is a humorous scene, incident, or speech that is included in a serious drama to provide respite from emotional intensity. Because it breaks the tension, comic relief allows an audience to internalize preceding plot events and to prepare emotionally for events to come. The sharp contrasts afforded by comic relief may intensify the themes of a literary work. In many of Shakespeare's plays, a scene involving a fool or bawdy interplay among common folks provides comic relief. Comic relief in *Macbeth* is provided by Macbeth's garrulous, vulgar porter at the beginning of Act II, Scene 3, just after Duncan's murder. This scene is needed to relax the tension built up in the preceding scenes.

Complication. See *Plot.*

Conceit. See *Extended Metaphor.*

Concrete Poem. A concrete poem presents something important about the poem's meaning in a visual way. In concrete poetry, a direct and often obvious relationship exists between form and meaning. An example of concrete poetry is Edwin Morgan's "The Computer's First Christmas Card," which is the final selection in this book.

Conflict. Conflict is a struggle between opposing forces that is the basis of plot in dramatic and narrative literature. The conflict provides the interest or suspense in a short story, drama, novel, narrative poem, or nonfiction narrative. Conflict may be one of five kinds:

1. A character may struggle against nature. In Samuel Taylor Coleridge's "The Rime of the Ancient Mariner," for example, the old sailor comes into conflict with forces of nature at sea after he kills an albatross. In Daniel Defoe's classic adventure tale *Robinson Crusoe*, a man cast ashore on a desert island struggles with the elements of nature. In Arthur C. Clarke's "History Lesson" in Unit 8, Shann's tribe struggles against the encroaching ice.

2. One character may struggle against another. In the short story "The Boarding House" in Unit 7, Mrs. Moody manipulates her daughter's suitor into marriage, and in the short story "The Idealist" in Unit 8 a young schoolboy comes into conflict with an authoritarian teacher.

3. A conflict may occur between a person and the forces of society, as in "Shooting an Elephant" in Unit 7. In that narrative essay, a British law-enforcement officer in colonial Burma clashes with Burmese society; at the same time, he opposes his own country's imperialism.

4. A character may be pitted against supernatural forces, as in Greek and Roman mythology. In *Beowulf*, for instance, the hero struggles against various monsters, including Grendel, Grendel's mother, and the fire dragon. Gawain in *Sir Gawain and the Green Knight* comes into conflict with the magic of Morgan le Fay. Sometimes a conflict against the supernatural is interpreted as a struggle against fate.

5. A conflict may occur within a character, between opposing tendencies in the individual's makeup. An example is the internal struggle in "The Secret Sharer" of the sea captain who undergoes deep inner torment over his identification with a sailor guilty of murder. Macbeth, too, is torn between elements in his nature that struggle for mastery. His ambition to be king, for example, wars against his basic compassion and his loyalty for King Ducan.

The first four types of conflicts are external; that is, they occur between a character and some outside force. The fifth type of conflict differs because it is internal, occurring within one character. In long narratives there is rarely only one conflict. For example, while the basic conflict in "Shooting an Elephant" is between the main character and society, the character also comes into conflict with nature as he struggles to kill an elephant and with his own impulses to leave the elephant alone.

See *Antagonist, Climax, Plot*.

Connotation. The emotional response evoked by a word is its connotation, as distinguished from the word's denotation, which is the objective dictionary definition of the word. Connotations for a word may be personal and individual, or they may be general and even universal. Connotations for words may be different even when their denotations are quite similar. For example, the denotations of the words *cuisine* and *food* are similar, but their connotations are quite different. While the word *food* suggests simplicity, plainness, and nourishment, *cuisine* carries connotations of elegance and culture.

See *Diction*.

Consonance. Consonance is the repetition of consonant sounds within and at the ends of words, as in dow<u>n</u> and mi<u>n</u>e. Consonance differs from rhyme in that the vowels that precede the like consonants differ, as in r<u>oll</u> and b<u>ill</u>. Consonance may be used instead of rhyme to link words at the ends of lines. Consonance is often used together with alliteration to create a musical quality, to emphasize certain words, or to unify a poem or a passage. Notice the repetition of the <u>s</u> and <u>r</u> sounds in these lines:

> The force that through the green fuse drives the
>   flower
> Drives my green age; that blasts the roots of trees
> Is my destroyer.
> And I am dumb to tell the crooked rose
> My youth is bent by the same wintry fever.
>   DYLAN THOMAS
>   "The Force That Through the
>   Green Fuse Drives the Flower"

See *Alliteration, Assonance*.

Contrast. Contrast is a stylistic device in which one element is put into opposition with another. The opposing elements might be contrasting structures, such as sentences of varying lengths or stanzas of different configurations, or they might be contrasting ideas or images juxtaposed within phrases, sentences, paragraphs, stanzas, or sections of a longer work of literature. Writers use contrast to clarify or emphasize ideas, as well as to elicit emotional responses from the reader. In *Macbeth*, for example, Shakespeare heightens the gloom by contrasting the youthful innocence of Macduff's son with the murderous intentions of Macbeth's soldiers. Notice the contrasting images in this stanza:

> For winter's rains and ruins are over,
>   And all the season of snows and sins;
> The days dividing lover and lover,
>   The light that loses, the night that wins;
> And time remembered is grief forgotten,
> And frosts are slain and flowers begotten,
> And in green underwood and cover
>   Blossom by blossom the spring begins.
>   ALGERNON CHARLES SWINBURNE
>   *Atalanta in Calydon*

See *Antithesis*.

Couplet. A couplet is two consecutive lines of poetry that end with rhyming words. A simple couplet may be written in any rhythmic pattern. The following couplet is written in iambic heptameter.

In the spring a livelier iris changes on the burnished dove;
In the spring a young man's fancy lightly turns to thoughts of love.

ALFRED, LORD TENNYSON
"Locksley Hall"

A closed couplet is two rhymed lines of verse that comprise in themselves a complete statement:

He was in logic a great critic,
Profoundly skilled in analytic.

SAMUEL BUTLER "Hubridas"

See *Heroic Couplet, Stanza.*

Denotation. See *Connotation.*

Dénouement. See *Plot.*

Description. Description is writing that appeals to the senses. Effective description enables a reader to see, hear, smell, taste, and/or feel the subject, which may be a single person, place, or thing, or a combination of these. Along with precise adverbs, adjectives, nouns, and verbs, carefully selected detail creates successful description. Description may be used with, and is often subordinated to, other types of writing, including narration, exposition, and argumentation. The following is a descriptive passage from *Hard Times* by Charles Dickens.

It was a town of red brick, or of brick that would have been red if the smoke and ashes had allowed it; but, as matters stood, it was a town of unnatural red and black, like the painted face of a savage. It was a town of machinery and tall chimneys, out of which interminable serpents of smoke trailed themselves for ever and ever, and never got uncoiled. It had a black canal in it, and a river that ran purple with ill-smelling dye, and vast piles of building full of windows where there was a rattling and a trembling all day long, and where the piston of the steam engine worked monotonously up and down, like the head of an elephant in a state of melancholy madness. It contained several large streets all very

like one another, and many small streets still more like one another, inhabited by people equally like one another, who all went in and out at the same hours, with the same sound upon the same pavements, to do the same work, and to whom every day was the same as yesterday and tomorrow, and every year the counterpart of the last and the next.

Dialect. Dialect is the particular variety of language spoken in one place by a distinct group of people. Dialects reflect the colloquialisms, grammatical constructions, distinctive vocabulary, and pronunciations that are typical of a region. At times writers use dialect to establish or emphasize a setting, as well as to develop characters. The Scottish dialect that Robert Burns uses in the following lines is manifested mainly in regional pronunciations.

Ye flowery banks o' bonnie Doon,
How can ye blume sae fair?
How can ye chant, ye little birds,
And I sae fu' o' care?

"Ye Flowery Banks"

For another example of a poem written in dialect, see Evan Jones's "Lament of the Banana Man" in Unit 8. Also, Bernard Shaw attempts to reproduce a Cockney dialect in the first act of *Pygmalion.*

Dialogue. Dialogue is written conversation between two or more characters. Although dialogue is most common in novels, short stories, and dramas, it is also used in other forms of prose, as well as in poetry. Realistic, well-paced dialogue advances the plot in a narrative. It also reveals the traits of the characters, for the language and rhythm varies for different speakers.

See *Characterization, Drama.*

Diary. See *Autobiography.*

Diction. Diction is a writer's choice of words, a significant component of his or her style. Effective diction involves carefully selecting precise and appropriate words, as well as employing an acceptable level of usage. The diction of a poem or prose selection encompasses both the denotations and connotations of words. Diction may be formal or informal, technical or common, abstract or concrete.

See *Connotation, Style.*

Drama. Drama is literature that develops plot and character through dialogue and action; in other words, drama is literature in play form. Dramas are intended to be performed by actors and actresses who appear on a stage or before cameras or microphones.

According to Aristotle's definition, drama is an imitation of life. However, because the imitation cannot be a true representation of reality, the audience must accept certain artificial devices, called dramatic conventions. The audience must accept the actors, for example, as representations of the characters and the stage as the representational setting for the action. Likewise, the audience may be expected to accept the use of poetic languages by common people. Other conventions include monologues, or soliloquys, which are lengthy speeches generally delivered when a character is alone on stage, and asides, which are remarks made supposedly without other characters hearing. To accept such stage conventions as real, the reader or spectator must bring to a drama what Samuel Taylor Coleridge called the "willing suspension of disbelief."

Most plays are divided into acts, with each act having a climax. Sometimes the acts of a play are subdivided into scenes, with each scene limited to a particular time and place. While Shakespeare's plays have five acts, modern dramas usually have two or three acts. Some plays are brief one-act plays.

The script for a play contains stage directions, instructions that help the reader to visualize the stage setting and the characters' movements and to "hear" the dialogue as it might be spoken. Stage directions may also provide suggestions for staging, lighting, music, and sound effects.

See *Aside, Dialogue, Soliloquy.*

Dramatic Irony. See *Irony.*

Dramatic Lyric. See *Dramatic Monologue, Lyric.*

Dramatic Monologue. A dramatic monologue is a lyric poem in which a speaker addresses a silent listener in a moment of high intensity or deep emotion. To increase the dramatic impact of the poem, the poet often reveals the motivations as well as the feelings, personality, and circumstances of the speaker. Calling his poems *dramatic*

lyrics, Robert Browning established the importance of the dramatic monologue in poems such as "My Last Duchess," which is in Unit 6. Alfred, Lord Tennyson used the form in "Ulysses," also in Unit 6. Following is a stanza from another dramatic monologue, in which the speaker is a spiteful monk.

> Gr-r-r—there go, my heart's abhorrence!
>   Water your damned flowerpots, do!
> If hate killed men, Brother Lawrence,
>   God's blood, would not mine kill you!
> What? your myrtle bush wants trimming?
>   Oh, that rose has prior claims—
> Needs its leaden vase filled brimming?
>   Hell dry you up with its flames!
>   ROBERT BROWNING
>   "Soliloquy of the Spanish Cloister"

See *Speaker.*

Echoing. Echoing is the repetition of certain words and phrases, sometimes with slightly different meanings. Echoing reinforces important ideas and entertains with the delight of word play, as in the following lines from Shakespeare's plays.

> The fool doth think he is wise, but the wise
> Man knows himself to be a fool.
>   *As You Like It*

> And my kingdom for a little grave
> A little, little grave, an obscure grave
>   *King Richard II*

> Some are born great, some achieve greatness, and
>   some have
> Greatness thrust upon them.
>   *Twelfth Night*

> Love goes toward love, as schoolboys from their
>   books,
> But lover from love, toward school with heavy looks.
>   *Romeo and Juliet*

Sometimes echoing occurs throughout a work, as in the recurrence of *done* throughout *Macbeth.*

See *Repetition.*

Elegy. An elegy is a lyric poem about death or another solemn subject, usually written in tribute to a person who has died recently. In its broadest terms, an elegy is a meditative poem with a serious mood or theme. An elegy is formal and dignified in tone. Samuel Taylor Coleridge described the elegy as the kind of poetry "natural to a reflective mind." Famous English elegies include "The Seafarer" in Unit 1, Thomas Gray's "Elegy Written in a Country Churchyard" in Unit 4, and Alfred, Lord Tennyson's *In Memoriam*, part of which is included in Unit 6.

Elizabethan (Shakespearean) Sonnet. See *Sonnet*.

End Rhyme. See *Rhyme, Rhyme Scheme*.

English (Shakespearean) Sonnet. See *Sonnet*.

Enjambment. Enjambment is the continuation of the sense and grammatical construction of a line of poetry onto the next line or of a couplet or stanza onto the succeeding couplet or stanza. In poetry with regular meter, enjambment is used to add variety to the rhythm as well as to emphasize ideas. The run-on lines created by enjambment contrast with the end-stopped lines characteristic of eighteenth-century couplets. The first and second lines of the following three-line excerpt are examples of enjambment.

> Well I remember how you smiled
>   To see me write your name upon
> The soft sea-sand . . .
>> WALTER SAVAGE LANDOR
>> "Well I Remember How You Smiled."

Likewise, the two couplets that follow use enjambment.

> A thing of beauty is a joy forever:
> Its loveliness increases; it will never
> Pass into nothingness; but still will keep
> A bower quiet for us, and a sleep
> Full of sweet dreams . . .
>> JOHN KEATS *Endymion*

Epic. An epic is a long narrative poem on a serious subject, presented in an elevated style and concerned with a heroic character or characters whose actions speak for a particular group of people, such as a nation or race. The earliest epics, which may have evolved through the contributions of various poets, were Homer's *Iliad* and *Odyssey*, as well as the Old English *Beowulf*. Epics without known authors are called folk epics. Art epics, such as John Milton's *Paradise Lost*, part of which appears in Unit 3, have a single author.

Among the characteristics that epics share are the following.

1. The hero has high status and is a prominent historical or legendary figure.

2. The epic has a vast setting that ranges over many locales.

3. The action consists of courageous, even superhuman, deeds.

4. Supernatural forces often are operative.

Certain devices are also common to epics, including an opening statement of theme or invocation of a muse or higher power. The epic typically begins *in medias res*, immediately plunging the reader into the middle of the action without any background information. Epics often include long formal speeches by the main character and catalogues, or lists, of ships, warriors, or battles.

An epic addresses universal concerns, such as good and evil, life and death, sin and redemption.

See *Hero*.

Epigram. An epigram originally was a memorial inscription for a tombstone; the term came to mean a short poem notable for its conciseness, balance, wit, and clarity in making a point. A classic epigram is written in two parts, the first establishing the occasion or setting the tone and the second stating the main point. A few lines taken from a longer poem can also be an epigram. For examples of such epigrams, see the excerpts from Alexander Pope's *Essay on Criticism* in Unit 4.

The epigram is used for many purposes, including the expression of friendship, grief, criticism, praise, and philosophy. The following is an epigram of praise.

> Three poets, in three distant ages born,
> Greece, Italy, and England did adorn.
> The first in loftiness of thought surpassed,
> The next in majesty, in both the last:
> The force of Nature could no farther go:
> To make a third, she joined the former two.
>> JOHN DRYDEN
>> "Epigram on Milton"

*The Rubáiyát of Omar Khayyá*m, translated by Edward FitzGerald, is a collection of epigrams:

The Moving Finger writes, and, having writ,
Moves on; nor all your Piety nor Wit
  Shall lure it back to cancel half a Line,
Nor all your Tears wash out a Word of it.

In modern usage, *epigram* has also come to mean a pointed saying.

Epistle. An epistle is a formal literary letter addressed to a specific person but intended for a wide audience. In contrast to an informal letter, an epistle is a consciously public or literary effort rather than a spontaneous, private communication. An epistle may concern subjects such as love, politics, philsophy, art, or social customs. Most epistles are written in prose, although they also may be written in poetry. Alexander Pope, for example, considered the epistle a formal letter in verse, used for the purpose of satirizing society. Such an epistle is Pope's "Epistle to Miss Blount" in Unit 4.

Epitaph. An epitaph is the inscription on a tombstone or monument written in memory of the person or people buried there. Sometimes these commemorative verses or lines are merely written as if they were intended to mark a grave. The following is an example of an epitaph.

Wouldst thou hear what man can say
In a little? Reader, stay.
Underneath this stone doth lie
As much beauty as could die;
Which in life did harbor give
To more virtue than doth live.
If at all she had a fault,
Leave it buried in this vault.
One name was Elizabeth;
Th' other, let it sleep with death:
Fitter, where it died, to tell,
Than that it lived at all. Farewell!
               BEN JOHNSON
       "Epitaph on Elizabeth, L. H."

The earliest epitaphs were serious, but some later ones have been written with a humorous tone. For example, John Dryden wrote the following epitaph for his wife.

Here lies my wife: here let her lie!
Now she's at rest, and so am I.

Essay. The essay is a brief, nonfiction composition that offers an opinion on a subject. The purpose of an essay may be to inform, to persuade, or to entertain the reader or to analyze a subject. An example of an informative essay is Arthur C. Clarke's "We'll Never Conquer Space" in Unit 8. An example of an essay that intends to persuade is Jane Anger's "Her Protection for Women" in Unit 3, which argues that men subjugate women unjustly. Another persuasive essay is John Milton's famous "Areopagitica," which defends freedom of the press. An example of an essay that entertains while making a wry comment on a social issue is J. B. Priestley's "Report Cards" in Unit 8. That essay delights readers with its humorous parody of a report card. An example of an essay that analyzes a subject is H. R. Trevor-Roper's "The Dark Soul of Hitler" in Unit 8, which examines the character of Adolf Hitler.

A useful distinction with regard to essays can be made between formal and informal essays. Formal essays are serious in tone and subject matter, and they are tightly organized and objective. Informal essays are looser in structure, lighter in tone, and generally briefer than formal essays. The informal essay takes a personal approach to a subject and often may be humorous, as in Charles Lamb's "Dissertation upon Roast Pig" in Unit 5. The essays of Joseph Addison and Richard Steele in Unit 4 also are examples of informal essays.

Essays also can be classified as descriptive, narrative, or expository. Most essays, however, combine all three types of writing. While Lamb's "Dissertation upon Roast Pig," for example, is primarily expository in its explanation of the origins and benefits of cooked pork, it also includes several narrative passages such as the story of Bo-Bo's discovery of charred pork flesh and an anecdote about a sweetcake given to Lamb by his aunt. Furthermore, Lamb's essay also includes descriptive passages about the smell and taste of roast pork.

Eulogy. A eulogy is a public speech or formal written tribute praising the virtues or achievements of a person, especially one who has recently died. In Unit 8, "Elegy for Alfred Hubbard" is a mock eulogy that humorously points out the failings of a deceased plumber, and "The Unknown Citizen" by W. H. Auden is an ironic eulogy, written as an epitaph for an imaginary citizen who has achieved the distinction of being pathetically "normal."

Exaggeration. See *Hyperbole*.

Exposition. Exposition is a detailed explanation, often at the beginning of a literary work, that provides pertinent background information. This introductory material usually presents the setting, introduces the characters, establishes the tone, and otherwise reveals facts necessary for understanding the narrative.

In dramatic structure, the opening scenes present the exposition. In *Macbeth*, for example, the first two scenes of Act One tell the reader that Macbeth has been awarded the title Thane of Cawdor by King Duncan and establish Macbeth's loyalty to the king and the ominous atmosphere of the play, along with the reason for King Duncan's visit to Macbeth's castle. After the exposition, the plot events get underway. In Bernard Shaw's *Pygmalion* the first act establishes the occupations, interests, and situations of the main characters; it reveals the setting to be London and the tone to be light-hearted.

In a short story, the exposition usually appears in the opening paragraphs. The first three paragraphs of "The Rocking-Horse Winner," for instance, introduce Paul's mother, suggest the family's precarious finances, and establish the tense atmosphere of the story.

While the exposition usually occurs at the beginning of a narrative, it may be interspersed throughout with the use of flashbacks.

See *Flashback, Plot*.

Extended Metaphor. In an extended metaphor, two unlike things are compared at some length and in several ways. Sometimes the comparison is carried throughout a paragraph, a stanza, or an entire selection. Extended metaphors may be used in both poetry and prose.

Like an extended metaphor, a conceit parallels two essentially dissimilar things on several points. A *conceit*, though, is a more elaborate, formal, and ingenious comparison than the ordinary extended metaphor. Sometimes a conceit forms the framework of an entire poem, as in the following stanzas, in which John Donne describes his own and his lover's souls as the two legs of a mathematician's compass.

Our two souls therefore, which are one,
　Though I must go, endure not yet
A breach, but an expansion,
　Like gold to airy thinness beat.

If they be two, they are two so
　As stiff twin compasses are two;
Thy soul, the fix'd foot, makes no show
　To move, but doth, if th' other do.
And though it in the center sit,
　Yet when the other far doth roam,
It leans and hearkens after it,
　And grows erect, as that comes home.

Such wilt thou be to me, who must
　Like th' other foot, obliquely run;
Thy firmness makes my circle just,
And makes me end where I begun.

　　　　"A Valediction: Forbidding Mourning"

External Conflict. See *Conflict*.

Fable. A fable is a brief tale told to illustrate a moral or principle of behavior. While the characters in a fable may be human, usually they are animals who speak and act as humans do. The most famous fables are those of Aesop, a Greek slave who lived about 600 B.C. Fables often are based on folklore and may contain supernatural elements. "The Nun's Priest's Tale" by Chaucer is based on a fable about a fox and a rooster. The narrator of the tale, the nun's priest, used the fable to teach a religious moral.

Falling Action. See *Climax, Conflict, Plot*.

Fantasy. The term *fantasy* is applied to a work of fiction characterized by extravagant imagination and disregard for the restraints of reality. The aim of a fantasy may be purely to delight or may be to make a serious comment on reality. One type of fantasy is represented by *Alice in Wonderland* in which Lewis Carroll creates a nonexistent, unreal, imaginary world. Fiction that depicts utopian societies is also fantasy of this type. Such fantasies may have grotesque or unbelievable characters. A less extreme form of fantasy portrays characters who, within a realistic world, marginally overstep the bounds of reality. For example, in Unit 8,

"Follow My Fancy" by Joan Aiken, depicts the uncanny mental powers of a man haunted by a bus. Finally, science fiction is a form of fantasy, for it extends scientific principles to new realms of time or place. An example is Arthur Clarke's "History Lesson" in Unit 8, set in the distant future.

See *Science Fiction*.

Feminine Rhyme. See *Rhyme*.

Fiction. Fiction refers to imaginative works of prose, including the novel and the short story. While fiction sometimes draws on actual events and real people, it stems primarily from the imagination of the writer. The purpose of fiction is to entertain, but it also enlightens by providing a deeper understanding of the human condition.

The basic elements of fiction are plot, character, setting, and theme. Fictional forms include science fiction, fable, and fantasy.

See *Character, Fable, Nonfiction, Plot, Science Fiction, Setting, Short Story, Theme*.

Figurative Language. Language that communicates ideas beyond the ordinary, literal meanings of the words is called figurative language. Writers use figurative language to create effects, to emphasize ideas, and to evoke emotions. As opposed to literal truth, figurative language expresses fresh or vivid meanings in an original, imaginative way. For example, Robert Browning in "Meeting at Night" describes "startled little waves that leap." While the waves are not literally startled nor do they actually leap, Browning's figurative language contributes to a striking impression of the sea as well as to the tensely expectant mood of the poem. Likewise, A. E. Housman in "With Rue My Heart is Laden," describes "rose-lipped girls." Clearly, the literal meaning of the phrase, that girls have roses for lips, is absurd. Housman's language is figurative, suggesting in an original way the maidens' fresh and youthful beauty.

Figurative language is used in both prose and poetry, as well as in oral expression. Common figures of speech, or kinds of figurative language, include simile, metaphor, personification, hyperbole, apostrophe, and metonymy.

See *Apostrophe, Hyperbole, Metaphor, Metonymy, Personification, Simile*.

First-Person Narration. See *Point of View*.

Flashback. A flashback is a plot device used in drama and fiction through which a writer presents a scene or incident that occurred chronologically before the beginning of a story or at an earlier point in the narrative. The scene or event reveals character or presents background information in a dramatic way. Flashbacks may be presented as a character's recollections, as a narrator's commentary, or as a dream episode. For example, in Katherine Mansfield's "Miss Brill" in Unit 7, Miss Brill recalls her English students and her reading to an invalid. In Unit 8, "The Demon Lover" has a flashback to a time twenty-five years earlier when Mrs. Drover parted with her fiancé.

See *Exposition, Plot*.

Foil. A foil is a character who provides a striking contrast to another character. By using a foil, a writer calls attention to certain traits possessed by a main character or simply enhances a character by contrast. For example, in *Pygmalion*, Colonel Pickering, genteel, tolerant, and controlled, is a foil for Henry Higgins, who is frank, temperamental, and sometimes abusive. In *The Canterbury Tales*, many of the characters act as foils for each other. For example, the generous, virtuous Parson is a foil for the carousing, corrupt, conniving Friar. Likewise, the lowly Plowman is a foil for the distinguished Knight, and the coarse, thieving Miller contrasts with the affectedly dainty and tenderhearted Nun. The poor, bookish Scholar is a foil for the richly-dressed, high-living Monk.

Folk Ballad. See *Ballad*.

Foreshadowing. Foreshadowing is a writer's use of hints or clues to indicate events that will occur later in a narrative. For example, in *Macbeth*, the witches' warnings foreshadow the fate of Macbeth. The use of foreshadowing creates suspense. It may also help to make a plot resolution more believable. In "The Rocking-Horse Winner," for instance, the strange, mad frenzy with which Paul rides his rocking horse early in the story foreshadows his final, fatal ride.

Free Verse. Poetry written without regular patterns of rhyme and meter is known as free verse.

Like most poetry, free verse is usually more rhythmic than ordinary language. Free verse, which initially was a protest against the strict conventions of earlier forms, allows the poet the freedom to use various rhythmic effects. A great deal of poetry written in the twentieth century is free verse. Poems in Unit 8 that are free verse include Ted Hughes's "Thistles" and "Hawk Roosting," Norman MacCaig's "Aunt Julia," Thom Gunn's "Taylor Street," and Margaret Atwood's "I Can Change." Following are two stanzas in free verse.

> While my hair was still cut straight across my
>   forehead
> Played I about the front gate, pulling flowers.
> You came by on bamboo stilts, playing horse,
> You walked about my seat, playing with blue plums.
> And we went on living in the village of Chokan:
> Two small people, without dislike or suspicion.
>
> At fourteen I married My Lord you.
> I never laughed, being bashful.
> Lowering my head, I looked at the wall.
> Called to, a thousand times, I never looked back.
>   EZRA POUND
>   "The River Merchant's Wife: A Letter"

Hero. The hero, or protagonist, is the central character in a work of fiction, drama, or epic poetry. A traditional hero possesses "good" qualities that enable him or her to triumph over an antagonist who is "bad."

The term *tragic hero*, first used by Greek philosopher Aristotle, refers to a central character who is dignified or noble. However, because of a character defect, or tragic flaw, the character makes a definite choice that brings about his or her own downfall. Tragic flaws may be caused by poor judgment, bad character, inborn weakness, or an excess of an admirable quality. For example, idealism might become vain foolhardiness or naive gullibility, and pride might become greedy ambition. According to Aristotle's classic definition, tragic heroes, before their downfalls, realize how they have caused their own destruction. Macbeth is an example of a tragic hero.

Another important type of hero is the epic hero, a worthy, noble figure who has a high position in society. The epic hero usually is important in a nation's history or legends. Through remarkable deeds, the epic hero demonstrates great courage and often even superhuman abilities. Beowulf, king of the Geats and supremely strong against all foes, is an example of an epic hero.

See *Epic, Tragedy.*

Heroic Couplet. When the meter of a couplet, which is two consecutive rhyming lines of poetry, is iambic pentameter, the lines constitute a heroic couplet. Geoffrey Chaucer introduced the heroic couplet into English literature, and in the seventeenth century heroic couplets became popular for poetic dramas. In the Neoclassical Period, the heroic couplet was usually composed of two end-stopped lines. In other words, at the ends of the lines were pauses, and each couplet formed a unit. The following is an example of heroic couplets.

> All human things are subject to decay,
> And when fate summons, monarchs must obey.
>   JOHN DRYDEN "Mac Flecknoe"

Humor. See *Hyperbole, Irony, Tone.*

Hyperbole. Hyperbole is a figure of speech in which the truth is exaggerated for emphasis or for a humorous effect. For example, in "The Demon Lover" in Unit 8, Elizabeth Bowen creates a jarring effect with this hyperbole: "Through the aperture driver and passenger, not six inches between them, remained for an eternity eye to eye." The following example of hyperbole has a humorous effect.

> Who ever would love or be tied to a wife
> When it makes a man mad all the days of his life?
>   JOHN CLARE "Song"

The speaker in these lines emphasizes his love through hyperbole:

> And I will luve thee still, my dear,
>   Till a' the seas gang dry.
>   ROBERT BURNS
>   "A Red, Red Rose"

Iambic Pentameter. See *Blank Verse, Heroic Couplet, Meter, Sonnet.*

Imagery. The term *imagery* refers to words and phrases that create vivid sensory experiences for the reader. While the majority of images are visual, imagery also may appeal to the senses of smell (olfactory), hearing (auditory), taste (gustatory), and touch (tactile). Images may re-create sensations of heat (thermal), movement (kinetic), and bodily tension (kinesthetic). When an image describes one sensation in terms of another, the technique is called synesthesia. For example, the "cold smell of potato mould" is an olfactory image described in terms of temperature.

Effective writers of both prose and poetry frequently use imagery that appeals to more than one sense simultaneously. Notice the appeals to the senses of sight, hearing, taste, smell, and touch in the following lines.

> You strange, astonished-looking, angle-faced,
> Dreary-mouthed, gaping wretches of the sea,
> Gulping salt-water everlastingly,
> Cold-blooded, though with red your blood be graced,
> And mute, though dwellers in the roaring waste;
> And you, all shapes beside, that fishy be—
> Some round, some flat, some long, all devilry,
> Legless, unloving, unfamously chaste—
>
> O scaly, slippery, wet, swift, staring wights,
> What is't ye do? what life lead? eh, dull goggles?
> LEIGH HUNT
> "The Fish, the Man, and the Spirit"

In many cases, recurring imagery within a literary work adds to the plot, theme, or mood of the work. For example, in *Macbeth* the images of blood, darkness, and water pervade the play and emphasize its themes.

Incremental Repetition. See *Ballad, Refrain, Repetition.*

Internal Conflict. See *Conflict.*

Internal Rhyme. See *Rhyme.*

Irony. Irony is a contrast between appearance and actuality, or between expectation and reality. This incongruity often has the effect of surprising the reader or viewer or of creating humorous or satirical effects. The techniques of irony include hyperbole, understatement, and sarcasm. For example, the hyperbole, or exaggeration, in these stanzas makes them ironic.

> Out upon it! I have loved
> Three whole days together;
> And am like to love three more,
> If it prove fair weather.
>
> Time shall molt away his wings
> Ere he shall discover
> In the whole wide world again
> Such a constant lover.
> SIR JOHN SUCKLING "The Constant Lover"

The three main types of irony are situational, verbal, and dramatic. An ironic situation occurs when something happens that is entirely different from what is expected. For example, "The Idealist" in Unit 8 presents the ironic situation of a schoolboy who is punished whenever he behaves virtuously and then emerges victorious when he lies. In "The Nun's Priest's Tale," it is ironic that Chanticleer escapes from the fox when the fox begins to boast about catching Chanticleer. The poem "Who's Who" in Unit 8 expresses the ironic situation of a person who achieves worldwide fame yet pines for the admiration of a simple homebody. Likewise, the following comments by Jonathan Swift reflect ironic situations.

> We all behold with envious eyes
> Our equal raised above our size. . . .
> No enemy can match a friend.
> "Verses on the Death of Dr. Swift"

> Every man desires to live long, but no man would be old.
> *Thoughts on Various Subjects*

In verbal irony, a writer or character says one thing, but means something entirely different. With verbal irony, words of praise convey criticism, and criticism conveys praise. For example, in Shakespeare's *Julius Caesar*, when Antony says contemptuously, "Brutus was an honorable man," he means just the opposite. Another example of verbal irony is the final two lines of W.H. Auden's "The Unknown Citizen." After describing the quintessential conformist who leads a dully "normal" life, the speaker concludes with biting irony, "Was he free? Was he happy? The question is absurd:/Had anything been wrong, we should certainly have heard." A famous example of verbal irony is Johathan Swift's contention in "A Modest Proposal" that to alleviate the poverty in Ireland, children should "at a year old, be offered in sale to the persons of quality and fortune through the kingdom; always advising the mother to let them suck plentifully in the last month, so as to render them plump and fat for a good table."

Dramatic irony occurs when the reader or audience understands meanings that one or more characters do not. The plot of *Morte d'Arthur*, for example, involves dramatic irony, for the reader—but not Arthur—is aware before Arthur pulls the sword from the stone that he is the son of King Uther. The dramatic irony in *Pygmalion* results from the audience's knowledge that Liza is not the duchess that her admirers take her to be.

See *Hyperbole, Sarcasm, Understatement.*

Italian (Petrarchan) Sonnet. See *Sonnet.*

Journal. See *Autobiography.*

Literal and Figurative Meaning. See *Figurative Language.*

Kenning. A kenning is a compressed metaphor often substituted for a noun in Anglo-Saxon poetry. The phrase is a miniature riddle that implies a comparison in a picturesque way. The kenning usually has two parts and is often hyphenated. The following are kennings from one translation of *Beowulf:* "wave-way," "swan's road," and "whale's way" for the sea; "word-hoard" for thoughts; "battle-blade" for a sword; "folk-hammer" and "war flier" for the dragon; and "war-prince," "shield-warrior," "folk-king," and "gold-friend" for Beowulf.

Light Verse. Light verse is a general term describing poetry that is characterized by grace and ease of expression and often by fanciful wit and humor, even when the purpose is serious or satirical. C. S. Lewis's "The Late Passenger" in Unit 7 is an example of light verse.

Literary Ballad. See *Ballad.*

Literary Letter. See *Epistle.*

Lyric. The lyre was a musical instrument in ancient Greece, and *lyric* became the name for a song accompanied by music. In common speech,

the words of songs are still called lyrics. In literary terminology, a lyric is any short poem that presents a single speaker who expresses thoughts and feelings. Love lyrics are common, but lyric poems have also been written on subjects as different as religion and reading. In Unit 3, the poems of Robert Herrick, Richard Lovelace, John Suckling, and Andrew Marvell are lyrics. Lyrics of the Romantic Period include the poems by William Wordsworth, John Keats, and Percy Bysshe Shelley. Early lyrics, such as this one from the sixteenth century, were intended to be sung:

When to her lute Corinna sings,
Her voice revives the leaden strings,
And doth in highest notes appear
As any challenged echo clear;
But when she doth of mourning speak,
Ev'n with her sighs the strings do break.

And as her lute doth live or die,
Led by her passion, so must I:
For when of pleasure she doth sing,
My thoughts enjoy a sudden spring,
But if she doth of sorrow speak,
Ev'n from my heart the strings do break.

THOMAS CAMPION
"When to Her Lute Corinna Sings"

See *Ode, Sonnet.*

Masculine Rhyme. See *Rhyme.*

Metaphor. A metaphor is a figure of speech that implies or states a comparison between two unlike things that have something in common. While similes use the words *like* or *as,* metaphors do not. The basic figure of speech in poetry, metaphors are used to present fresh insights, to arouse strong feelings, and to establish ideas. Metaphors are used in prose and everyday speech as well as in poetry. The following poems present metaphors for life and for death.

Life is but a day;
A fragile dewdrop on its perilous way
From a tree's summit.

JOHN KEATS "Sleep and Poetry"

Strange, is it not? that of the myriads who
Before us passed the door of Darkness through,
Not one returns to tell us of the Road,
Which to discover we must travel too.

EDWARD FITZGERALD
The Rubáiyát of Omar Khayyám

Notice the ingenious metaphors for learning and for evening in these lines:

> your wisdom's golden mine
> Dig deep with learning's spade;
> > SIR PHILIP SIDNEY
> > *Astrophel and Stella*

> Though evening, with her richest dye,
> Flames o'er the hills of Ettrick's shore.
> > SIR WALTER SCOTT
> > "The Dreary Change"

See *Extended Metaphor, Figurative Language, Simile.*

Meter. Meter is the repetition of a regular rhythmic unit in a line of poetry. The meter of a poem emphasizes the musical quality of the language and often relates directly to the subject matter of the poem.

Each unit of meter is known as a foot, with each foot having one stressed and one or two unstressed syllables. The four basic types of metrical feet are the iamb, an unstressed syllable followed by a stressed syllable (˘ ´); the trochee, a stressed syllable followed by an unstressed syllable (´ ˘); the anapest, two unstressed syllables followed by a stressed syllable (˘ ˘ ´); and the dactyl, a stressed syllable followed by two unstressed syllables (´ ˘ ˘).

Two words are used to identify the meter of a line of poetry. The first word describes the predominant type of metrical foot in the line. The second word describes the number of feet in the line: dimeter (two feet), trimeter (three feet), tetrameter (four feet), pentameter (five feet), hexameter (six feet), and so forth. Thus, the meter of a poem might be trochaic trimeter or anapestic tetrameter.

The following excerpt is an example of iambic tetrameter. Notice the variation in this basic meter in the fourth line.

> The butterfly, a cabbage-white,
> (His honest idiocy of flight)
> Will never now, it is too late,
> Master the art of flying straight,
> Yet has—who knows so well as I?—
> A just sense of how not to fly:
> > ROBERT GRAVES "Flying Crooked"

Most modern poems are not written in precise meters, but rather in a combination of meters. Alternate lines may have different meters, for example, or iambic lines may end with trochaic feet. The fourth line in the sample, for instance, opens with a trochaic foot. Variations in meter are conscious choices made by poets to achieve desired effects, such as an emphasis on certain words or interestingly textured rhythms.

See *Pyrrhic Rhythm, Spondee.*

Metonymy. Metonymy is a figure of speech that substitutes for a word something closely associated with that word. For example, the figurative meaning of the statement "The pen is mightier than the sword" is that written words can be more influential than violent deeds. *Pen* stands for writing and *sword* for action. A common example of metonymy is the use of the word *heart*, as in "from the heart," to refer to deep-felt emotions. Wordsworth uses this figure of speech in the poetic line "We have given our hearts away." The following lines provide additional examples of metonymy.

> Milton! Thou shouldst be living at this hour:
> England hath need of thee: she is a fen
> Of stagnant waters: altar, sword, and pen,
> Fireside, the heroic wealth of hall and bower,
> Have forfeited their ancient English dower
> Of inward happiness.
> > WILLIAM WORDSWORTH "London, 1802"

> The hand that signed the paper felled a city
> > DYLAN THOMAS
> > "The Hand That Signed the Paper"

Mock Epic. An epic is a long narrative poem in which the characters and the action are of heroic proportions. A mock epic is a form of satire that treats a trivial matter on a heroic plane, generally with a humorous effect. Lowly characters and insignificant events are mocked by their incongruous presentation with the elevated style of the epic. In "The Nun's Priest's Tale," for example, Chaucer describes a scuffle between a fox and a rooster with the grandiose style used in epics such as *Beowulf.*

Monologue. See *Dramatic Monologue, Soliloquy.*

Mood. Mood is the feeling, or atmosphere, that a writer creates for the reader. Connotative words, sensory images, figurative language, and precise diction contribute to the mood of a literary work, as do sound techniques and the rhythm of the language. In this sentence, for example, the writer uses all of these techniques to create a peaceful mood:

> Sulaco had found an inviolable sanctuary from the temptations of a trading world in the solumn hush of the deep Golfo Placido as if within an enormous semicircular and unroofed temple open to the ocean, with its walls of lofty mountains hung with the mourning draperies of cloud.
>
> JOSEPH CONRAD *Nostromo*

Motif. A recurring word, phrase, image, object, idea, or action in a work of literature is called a motif. Motifs function as unifying devices and often relate directly to one or more major themes. Motifs in "The Prologue" to *The Canterbury Tales*, for example, include images of earthly love along with images of spiritual devotion. In *Macbeth*, references to blood, sleep, and water form motifs in the play.

Narration. See *Narrator, Point of View.*

Narrative Poem. A narrative poem is a poem that tells a story. Like a short story, a narrative poem has the following elements: characters; a setting, or time and place of action; a plot, or plan of action, which builds to a climax; and a point of view, all of which combine to develop a theme. "The Lady of Shalott" in Unit 6 is an example of a narrative poem. Epics, such as *Beowulf*, as well as ballads and verse romances, are specific types of narrative poems.

See *Ballad, Epic, Romance.*

Narrator. The narrator of a literary work is the person from whose point of view events are related. The narrator may be a main or a minor character in a work of fiction; an external witness to events, a witness created by the writer; or the writer presenting and commenting on the action. The unique personality and vantage point of the narrator profoundly affect a work of fiction. For example, the events related in *Beowulf* take on an entirely different nature when they are related by the monster himself in John Gardner's *Grendel*.

See *Point of View.*

Naturalism. An extreme form of realism, naturalism in fiction presents life objectively and precisely, without idealizing. Like the realist, the naturalist accurately portrays the world. However, the naturalist creates characters who are victims of environmental forces and internal drives beyond their comprehension and control. Naturalistic fiction conveys the belief that everything that exists is part of the scheme of nature, explainable entirely by natural and physical, rather than spiritual, causes. In Unit 8, Doris Lessing's "A Sunrise on the Veld," which depicts a boy who encounters death and brutality in nature, has naturalistic aspects.

See *Realism.*

Neoclassicism. Neoclassicism refers to the attitudes toward life and art that dominated English literature during the Restoration Period and the eighteenth century. As opposed to the intensity, individuality, and optimism of the Renaissance, Neoclassicism respected order, reason, and rules and viewed humans as limited and imperfect. Imitating classical literature, Neoclassical writers developed a style that was characterized by good form, logic, symmetry, grace, good taste, restraint, clarity, and conciseness. Because they believed that literature should serve mankind, these writers created literary works that were meant not only to delight readers but also to instruct them in moral virtues and the art of "correct" social behavior. To the Neoclassicists, the intellect was more important than the emotions, and society was more important than the individual. Their prose and poetry are coolly polite, witty, and unemotional and are concerned with public rather than private issues. Among the literary forms that flourished during the Neoclassical Period were the essay, the literary letter, and the epigram. The heroic couplet was the dominant verse form, and satire and parody prevailed in both prose and poetry. For examples of Neoclassical writing, refer to selections by Alexander Pope, John Dryden, Jonathan Swift, and Samuel Johnson in Unit 4.

Nonfiction. Nonfiction is prose writing about real people, places, and events. Unlike fiction, nonfiction is largely concerned with factual information, although the writer selects and interprets the information according to his or her purpose and may reveal a viewpoint in the presentation of facts.

While the subject matter of nonfiction is not imaginative, the writer's style may be individualistic and innovative. Types of nonfiction include autobiographies, biographies, letters, essays, diaries, journals, and speeches.

See *Autobiography, Biography, Epistle, Essay, Fiction.*

Nonsense Verse. Nonsense verse is a type of humorous verse characterized by strong rhythm and lack of logic. Typical devices in nonsense verse are coined words, tongue twisters, unusual type arrangement, and foreign words. Among the most famous writers of nonsense verse are two Victorians: Edward Lear, who developed the nonsense verse form known as the limerick, and Lewis Carroll, whose "Jabberwocky" appears in Unit 6. Following is another example of nonsense verse, a stanza from Edward Lear's "The Jumblies."

> They went to sea in a sieve, they did;
>   In a sieve they went to sea;
> In spite of all their friends could say,
> On a winter's morn, on a stormy day,
>   In a sieve they went to sea.
> And when the sieve turned round and round,
> And everyone cried, "You'll be drowned!"
> They called aloud, "Our sieve ain't big,
> But we don't care a button; we don't care a fig—
>   In a sieve we'll go to sea!"
>   Far and few, far and few,
>   Are the lands where the Jumblies live.
>   Their heads are green, and their hands are blue;
>   And they went to sea in a sieve.

Octave. See *Sonnet.*

Ode. In its original Greek form, an ode was a choral work; it was associated with movement, for the members of the chorus moved dramatically from one side to another to emphasize the rise and fall of emotion. Later, *ode* came to mean any exalted, complex lyric, written for a specific purpose, that develops one dignified theme. An ode appeals to both the imagination and the intellect and often commemorates an event or praises a person or an element of nature. In structure, an ode is divided into stanzas that may be identical in form or that may show patterned variations in form. Following is an ode written to praise those who died defending England in 1745.

> How sleep the brave who sink to rest
> By all their country's wishes blest!
> When Spring, with dewy fingers cold,
> Returns to deck their hallowed mold,
> She there shall dress a sweeter sod
> Than Fancy's feet have ever trod.
>
> By fairy hands their knell is rung,
> By forms unseen their dirge is sung;
> There Honor comes, a pilgrim gray,
> To bless the turf that wraps their clay,
> And Freedom shall awhile repair,
> To dwell a weeping hermit there!
>
> WILLIAM COLLINS
> "Ode Written in the Beginning of
> the Year 1746"

Onomatopoeia. Onomatopoeia refers to the use of echoic words, such as *crash, tap, groan, chatter,* and *boom,* whose pronunciations suggest their specific meanings. These words, which may be coined or actual, imitate sounds. Notice John Dryden's use of onomatopoeia to recreate sounds in these lines:

> The trumpet's loud *clangor*
>   Excites us to arms,
>   "A Song for St. Cecilia's Day"

> Break his bands of sleep asunder,
> And rouse him, like a *rattling* peal of thunder.
>   "Alexander's Feast"

Onomatopoeia as a literary technique goes beyond the use of simple echoic words. Skilled writers, especially poets, choose words whose sounds suggest their denotations and connotations. Notice the use of melodious words that echo meaning in these poems:

> So smooth, so sweet, so silv'ry is thy voice,
> As, could they hear, the Damned would make no
>   noise,
> But listen to thee (walking in thy chamber)
> Melting melodious words to Lutes of Amber.
>   ROBERT HERRICK
>   "Upon Julia's Voice"

> The moan of doves in immemorial elms,
> And murmuring of innumerable bees.
>   ALFRED, LORD TENNYSON
>   "Come Down, O Maid"

In this stanza, onomatopoeia helps to recreate the sound of a storm:

> The candle slanting sooty wicked,
>   The thuds upon the thatch,
> The eaves-drops on the window flicked,
>   The clacking garden-hatch,
> THOMAS HARDY
"She Hears the Storm"

Oxymoron. See *Paradox*.

Parable. A parable is a brief tale that teaches a lesson or illustrates a moral truth. The characters in a parable are developed as individuals, in contrast with the characters in an allegory who represent abstract qualities. Some critics view "The Rime of the Ancient Mariner" by Samuel Taylor Coleridge (Unit 5) as a Christian parable of sin and redemption. Alfred, Lord Tennyson's "The Lady of Shalott" (Unit 6) has been considered a parable.

Paradox. A paradox is a statement that seems to be contradictory or ridiculous but is actually quite true. For example, the following statement from one of Shakespeare's sonnets is paradoxical.

> When my love swears that she is made of truth,
> I do believe her, though I know she lies,

The seemingly contradictory statement expresses the speaker's willingness to be flattered by his lover and, in that sense, is logical. Another example of paradox is William Wordworth's line "The child is father to the man." Upon analysis, the truth behind the apparent contradiction becomes clear. Wordsworth is suggesting that the experiences and tendencies of childhood shape the adult person, or as he puts it, "So was it when my life began;/So is it now I am a man."

A special kind of succinct paradox is the oxymoron, which brings together two contradictory terms. Examples are "cruel kindness," or "brave fear," and Milton's "darkness visible." Notice the example of oxymoron in the final line of this stanza:

> Yes, I'm in love, I feel it now,
>   And Celia has undone me;
> And yet I'll swear I can't tell how
>   The pleasing plague stole on me.
> WILLIAM WHITEHEAD "The 'Je Ne Sais Quoi'"

Parallelism. The technique of parallelism, or parallel construction, is the expression of ideas of equal worth with the same grammatical form. Effective use of parallel arrangement can make both writing and speeches more forceful, unified, and clear, as in this example:

> Unlearn'd, he knew no schoolman's subtle art,
> No language but the language of the heart.
> By nature honest, by experience wise,
> Healthy by temperance, and by exercise;
> His life, though long, to sickness passed unknown,
> His death was instant, and without a groan.
> Oh grant me thus to live, and thus to die!
> ALEXANDER POPE
"Epistle to Dr. Arbuthnot"

In prose, parallelism can occur within a sentence or in succeeding sentences of identical construction. Parallelism is used within each of the sentences in the following paragraph.

> Men in great place are thrice servants: servants of the sovereign or state, servants of fame, and servants of business. So as they have no freedom, neither in their persons, nor in their actions, nor in their times. It is a strange desire, to seek power and lose liberty, or to seek power over others and to lose power over a man's self.
> FRANCIS BACON "Of Great Place"

Parody. A parody imitates, mocks, or burlesques another, usually serious, work or type of literature. Like the caricature in art, the parody in literature mimicks a subject or a style. The purpose of a parody may be to ridicule through broad humor. On the other hand, a parody may broaden understanding or add insight to the original work. Some parodies are even written in tribute to a work of literature. *Grendel*, John Gardner's parody of the epic *Beowulf*, for example, has the primary effect of enlightening the reader through its new viewpoint on the events in the original tale.

See *Satire*.

Pastoral. A pastoral is a poem that portrays shepherds and rustic life, usually in an idealized manner. The speaker of the conventional pastoral refers to himself and his friends as poetic shepherds or rustic folks. The form of the pastoral is artificial, for its meters and rhyme schemes are characteristic of formal poetry. The language is similarly unnatural, for the rustics often speak in courtly language rather than in the language of common speech. Christopher Marlowe's "The Passionate Shepherd to His Love" in Unit 3 is an example of a pastoral poem. Loosely, the term *pastoral* has come to mean any poem with a rural setting or about country people. Following is a stanza from a nineteenth-century pastoral.

> Too rare, too rare, grow now my visits here,
>> But once I knew each field, each flower, each
>> stick;
>> And with the countryfolk acquaintance made
> By barn in threshing time, by new-built rick.
> Here, too, our shepherd pipes we first assayed.
>> Ah me! this many a year
> My pipe is lost, my shepherd's holiday!
>> Needs must I lose them, needs with heavy heart
> Into the world and wave of men depart;
> But Thyrsis of his own will went away.
>> MATTHEW ARNOLD
>> "Thyrsis"

Pathetic Fallacy. A pathetic fallacy is the attribution of human traits and emotions to nature. Coined by critic John Ruskin in the nineteenth century, the term combines *pathetic*, meaning "pertaining to the feelings," and *fallacy*, meaning "false notion." In Shakespeare's *Julius Caeser*, the day and the night before the fatal Ides of March, the heavens rain fire, an owl shrieks at noonday, and a lionness gives birth in the streets, all unnatural events that portend the assassination of Caesar. This is an example of pathetic fallacy, for nature is neither in sympathy with nor opposition to human behavior. The distinction between pathetic fallacy and personification is arbitrary, as interpretation and response vary among readers and literary periods.

Pathos. Derived from the Greek word for suffering or deep feeling, pathos is the quality in literature that stimulates pity, sorrow, sympathy, or compassion in the reader. Although pathos is associated with tragedy, a pathetic figure usually is a helpless victim, ignorant of the cause of his or her pain, who suffers undeservedly. A pathetic figure lacks the insight and stature of the justly punished tragic hero. In this sense, because she lacks vision and imagination, Lady Macbeth is merely pathetic,

while Macbeth alone is the tragic figure. Miss Brill in "Miss Brill," and Paul in "The Rocking-Horse Winner," both characters in Unit 7, are other examples of pathetic figures.

Persona. See *Speaker*.

Personification. Personification is a figure of speech in which human qualities are attributed to an object, an animal, or an idea. Like the simile and the metaphor, personification allows a writer to communicate emotions and sensory images to the reader in a concise way. The following examples personify moon, stars, and sea.

> That orbéd maiden with white fire laden,
>> Whom mortals call the Moon,
> Glides glimmering o'er my fleecelike floor,
>> By the midnight breezes strewn;
> And wherever the beat of her unseen feet,
>> Which only the angels hear,
> May have broken the woof of my tent's thin roof,
>> The stars peep behind her and peer;
>> PERCY BYSSHE SHELLEY
>> "The Cloud"

> . . . the tide was flowing in fast to the land with a low whisper of her waves, islanding a few last figures in distant pools.
>> JAMES JOYCE
>> *A Portrait of the Artist as a Young Man*

Persuasion. Persuasion is a technique used by speakers and writers to convince an audience to adopt a particular opinion, perform an action, or both. Effective persuasion appeals to both the intellect and the emotions. The most common form of persuasion is the oration, or speech, as in Winston Churchill's speech of May 13, 1940, in Unit 8. An early example of persuasive prose is the excerpt from Jane Anger's "Her Protection for Women," in Unit 3, which argues that men wrong women.

Petrarchan (Italian) Sonnet. See *Sonnet*.

Plot. A plot is the planned series of interrelated actions and events that take place in a narrative work. The action of the plot progresses because of a conflict, or struggle between opposing forces. The conflict usually builds to the emotional peak of a climax, and a dénouement follows, when the conflict is resolved in some way.

The complications that build to the climax, known also as the crisis, or turning point, are described as the rising action. The events that take place after the climax are called the falling action.

Long works of literature frequently have subplots, which are minor plots subordinate to the overall story. The main plot in *Pygmalion*, for example, centers on the conflict between Liza and Henry Higgins. However, a subplot is the story of Alfred Doolittle, Liza's father. After the climax of the play, the argument between Liza and Higgins at the end of Act Four, both the plot and the subplot are resolved in the play's falling action during Act Five.

See *Climax, Conflict.*

Poetry. Poetry is an arrangement of lines in which form and content fuse to suggest meanings beyond the literal meanings of the words. The language of poetry is more compressed than that of prose and also more musical, enhancing meaning through the sounds of words and phrases, as well as through the sound patterns of lines and stanzas. Sound techniques are crucial to poetry not only for pure pleasure but also as reinforcement of the meaning of the poem. As Alexander Pope writes in "True Ease in Writing," "The sound must seem as echo to the sense."

The purpose of poetry is to create an experience, and that experience is inherently emotional. William Wordsworth defined poetry as "the imaginative experience of strong feeling, usually rhythmical." Other famous definitions of poetry include Samuel Taylor Coleridge's: "the best words in the best order." Thomas Carlyle defined poetry as "musical thought" and Percy Bysshe Shelley as "the record of the best and happiest moments of the best and happiest minds."

Characteristic of poetry is the use of imagery, language that appeals to the senses. Poetry is also rich in connotative words and figurative language, although some poems contain more imaginative language than others.

Certain poems, especially those of earlier ages, conform to traditional patterns of rhyme, meter, and stanza form. Others rely more on sounds and rhythms and less on fixed meters and rhyme schemes. Experimentation with flexible and unconventional forms is especially characteristic of twentieth-century poets.

Point of View. Point of view refers to the method of narrating a short story, novel, narrative poem, or nonfiction selection. The three most common points of view are first-person, third-person omniscient, and third-person limited. The point of view that a writer employs determines to a great degree the reader's view of the action and the characters; manipulation of point of view creates many striking effects in fiction.

When the narrator is a character in the story, narrating the action as he or she perceives and understands it, the writer is using first-person point of view. This type of narration is indicated by the pronoun *I.* A first-person narrator may be either the main character or a minor character. First-person narration imparts an immediacy to the narrative and usually leads to involvement with the narrating character. Two selections related in the first-person by the main character are "The Secret Sharer" and "Shooting an Elephant," in Unit 7. Nearly all autobiographies employ first-person point of view, although some early ones, such as *The Book of Margery Kempe* excerpted in Unit 2, use an artificial third-person point of view.

Third-person point of view is indicated by the third-person pronouns *he, she,* and *they.* A third-person narrator is not a participant in the action and thus maintains a certain distance from the characters. The writer can adjust that distance to range from closeness to complete detachment.

In third-person omniscient point of view, the narrator is all-knowing about the thoughts and feelings of all the characters. This point of view gives the writer the freedom to reveal the inner responses of the characters and to comment freely on the plot events. In "The Boarding House" in Unit 7, for example, the narrator sees into the minds of Mrs. Moody, her daughter Polly, and her boarder Mr. Doran. This omniscient point of view gives the story psychological depth that would be impossible with a different point of view. Another densely psychological story in Unit 7, "The Rocking-Horse Winner," is also told by an omniscient narrator.

If a writer tells a story in the third person but limits the narrator to the awareness of a single character, the point of view is called third-person limited. Because the writer presents events only as experienced by one character, a subjective, one-sided view of events emerges, as in Katherine Mansfield's "Miss Brill" in Unit 7, told entirely from Miss Brill's viewpoint. Another example is "The Landlady" in Unit 8, told in third person from Billy's viewpoint.

Two terms related to narrative method are *panoramic* and *scenic*. In a panoramic presentation, the writer summarizes events and conversations rather than presenting them in detail. In a scenic presentation, on the other hand, actions are presented as they are imagined to occur, sometimes as they are perceived by a single character.

Two terms used frequently in discussing point of view in nonfiction are *objectivity* and *subjectivity*. Objectivity means describing events without showing feelings and imposing judgements. The modern-day news reporter strives for objectivity in reporting news events. Subjectivity, on the other hand, means that a writer reveals his or her personal responses. In Unit 8, Arthur C. Clarke in "We'll Never Conquer Space" objectively reports many facts about outer space. His point of view, however, is overridingly subjective as he advances his own opinion about the futility of efforts to master the universe. Similarly, while Samuel Pepys in his *Diary*, excerpted in Unit 3, reports objectively at times, his viewpoint is primarily subjective.

See *Narrator*.

Prose. Generally, prose means all forms of written or spoken expression that are consciously organized and that lack regular rhythmic patterns. Prose implies logical order, continuity of thought, and individual style and, therefore, does not include haphazard remarks, lists, or catalogues. The work considered most influential in shaping English prose style is the King James version of the Bible.

The distinction between prose and poetry is sometimes difficult to draw, for some prose is highly poetic, while some poetry is quite prosaic.

See *Poetry*.

Protagonist. The main character in a literary work is called the protagonist. The protagonist may be heroic or common, virtuous or evil, forceful or weak. The protagonist is always involved in the central conflict of the story and often changes after the climax of the plot. The force or person who opposes the protagonist in a conflict is the antagonist. In *Beowulf*, for example, Beowulf is the protagonist, and his antagonists are the monsters that threaten the Geats. The narrator may be the protagonist if the story is told in first-person by the main character.

See *Antagonist, Character, Hero*.

Pyrrhic. In poetry, a pyrrhic is a metrical foot consisting of two unaccented syllables. It is the opposite of a spondee, which consists of two accented syllables. The pyrrhic is used to bring variety and freshness to a regular metric pattern such as iambic pentameter. Another effect is to quicken the pace of a line, thereby reinforcing meaning. Notice the pyrrhic in one critic's scansion:

When tŏ thĕ séssĭons ŏf swéet sílĕnt thóught
WILLIAM SHAKESPEARE "Sonnet 30"

See *Meter*.

Quatrain. A standard quatrain is a stanza of four lines of approximately the same metrical length. In other words, it is four lines set off as a unit, having about the same number of feet in each line. The quatrain is common in English poetry. The Shakespearean (English) sonnet is composed of three quatrains and a couplet. Following is an example of a quatrain that is written in iambic pentameter.

Cold in the earth—and the deep snow piled above thee,
Far, far removed, cold in the dreary grave!
Have I forgot, my only Love, to love thee,
Severed at last by Time's all-severing wave?
EMILY BRONTË "Remembrance"

See *Sonnet, Stanza*.

Realism. As a way of handling material in fiction, Realism is the truthful imitation of actual life. Realism is manifested in three ways: in the method of writing, in the choice of subject matter, and in a pragmatic, democratic attitude. The Realist tends to use clear, direct prose to present the ordinary, everyday events of a particular milieu.

Realism became an important literary movement in the latter half of the nineteenth century, developed by writers such as George Eliot, Jane Austen, and H. G. Wells. In part, Realism arose as a reaction against the sentimentality of most Romantic fiction. Avoiding the traditional approach to fiction, the modern-day Realist centers on char-

acterization and avoids conventional plot structure as too contrived to reflect real life. Early stirrings of Realism are apparent in the writing of Charles Dickens in Unit 6. Nearly all of the major short story writers of the twentieth century incorporate aspects of Realism into their writing, as evidenced by the short stories in Units 7 and 8.

See *Naturalism*.

Refrain. A refrain is part of a stanza, consisting of one or more lines that are repeated in a regular pattern throughout a poem, often at the ends of succeeding stanzas. Sometimes the line or lines that are repeated are altered somewhat each time they appear. Most ballads contain some kind of refrain. The following two stanzas illustrate the use of a two-line refrain at the end of each stanza.

"Why weep ye by the tide, ladie?
  Why weep ye by the tide?
I'll wed ye to my youngest son,
  And ye sall be his bride:
And ye sall be his bride, ladie,
  Sae comely to be seen"—
But ay she loot the tears down fa'
  For Jock of Hazeldean.

"Now let this willfu' grief be done,
  And dry that cheek so pale;
Young Frank is chief of Errington
  And lord of Langley Dale;
His step is first in peaceful ha',
  His sword in battle keen"—
But ay she loot the tears down fa'
  For Jock of Hazeldean.

SIR WALTER SCOTT "Jock of Hazeldean"

See *Ballad, Repetend*.

Repetend. Repetend refers to a word or phrase that is repeated fairly frequently throughout part or all of a poem. In contrast to the refrain, which appears in set positions, a repetend creates a pleasant effect by appearing irregularly. The repetends in this stanza are *come*, *come away*, and *call*.

Come, dear children, come away down;
Call no more!
One last look at the white-walled town,
And the little gray church on the windy shore,
Then come down!
She will not come though you call all day,
Come away, come away!

MATTHEW ARNOLD "The Forsaken Merman"

Repetition. Repetition is a literary technique in which a sound, word, phrase, line, or grammatical construction is repeated for the purpose of emphasis or unity. Repetition is a general term that includes specific devices associated with both prose and poetry, such as refrain, alliteration, anaphora, and parallelism.

See *Alliteration, Anaphora, Assonance, Consonance, Parallelism, Refrain, Repetend*.

Resolution. See *Plot*.

Rhetorical Question. A question that is intended to produce an effect, usually emotional, and not an answer is called a rhetorical question. The device is effectively used for emphasis in both prose and poetry; it is common in persuasion and oratory. Thomas Henry Huxley, for example, uses rhetorical questions to make a point as he compares a liberal education to a game of chess.

Suppose it were perfectly certain that the life and fortune of every one of us would, one day or other, depend upon his winning or losing a game of chess. Don't you think that we should all consider it to be a primary duty to learn at least the names and the moves of the pieces; to have a notion of a gambit, and a keen eye for all the means of giving and getting out of check? Do you not think that we should look with a disapprobation amounting to scorn, upon the father who allowed his son, or the state which allowed its members, to grow up without knowing a pawn from a knight?
"A Liberal Education"

Rhyme. Words rhyme when the sound of their accented vowels and all succeeding sounds are identical. In true rhyme, the consonant sounds that precede the vowels must be different, as in *aside* and *divide*.

One distinction in rhyme is between masculine rhyme and feminine rhyme. When rhyme occurs in two or three consecutive syllables, the first of which is stressed, it is called feminine, imperfect, or multiple rhyme. An example is *remember* and *December* or *waken* and *shaken*. When only the final accented syllables rhyme, the rhyme is called masculine or perfect rhyme, as in *pursue* and *renew*.

When rhyme comes at the ends of lines of poetry, it is called end rhyme, as in this example:

Sweet Auburn! loveliest village of the plain,
Where health and plenty cheered the laboring swain,
Where smiling spring its earliest visit paid,
And parting summer's lingering blooms delayed:
OLIVER GOLDSMITH
"The Deserted Village"

Rhyme that occurs within a line, as in the following example, is called internal rhyme.

The splendor falls on castle walls
    And snowy summits old in story;
The long light shakes across the lakes,
ALFRED, LORD TENNYSON
"The Splendor Falls"

End rhymes that are approximate rather than exact are called imperfect rhymes, near rhymes, off-rhymes, sprung rhymes, or slant rhymes. Many twentieth-century poets prefer off-rhyme to exact rhyme. The third and fourth lines that follow illustrate slant rhyme.

Fish say, they have their Stream and Pond;
But is there anything Beyond?
This life cannot be All, they swear,
For how unpleasant, if it were!
RUPERT BROOKE "Heaven"

Some off-rhymes result from changes in pronunciations over the years, while others result from a poet's intention to vary a regular pattern.

Rhyme Scheme. A rhyme scheme is the pattern of end rhyme in a poem. The pattern is charted by assigning a letter of the alphabet, beginning with *a*, to each line. Lines that rhyme are assigned the same letter. The rhyme scheme of a couplet, for example, is *aa*. Another common rhyme scheme has rhyme in alternating lines and is charted *a b a b*. In the twentieth century, poets have experimented freely with rhyme schemes, while in early centuries poets conformed more closely to established patterns. The rhyme scheme for the following stanza is identified at the right.

She that but little patience knew,	a
From childhood on, had now so much	b
A gray gull lost its fear and flew	a
Down to her cell and there alit,	c
And there endured her fingers' touch	b
And from her fingers ate its bit.	c

W. B. YEATS "On a Political Prisoner"

Rhythm. Rhythm refers to the cadence of poetic lines or prose passages, often denoting the regular, patterned recurrence of strong and weak elements. A poem without a regular meter may still have a strong rhythm. Along with stressed and unstressed syllables, devices such as alliteration, rhyme, assonance, consonance, and parallelism often contribute to a musical beat. Writers use rhythm to unify a literary work, to emphasize ideas, to create mood, to reinforce content, and to heighten emotional response.

See *Meter*.

Rising Action. See *Climax, Conflict, Plot*.

Romance. As a general term, *romance* refers to any imaginative narrative concerned with noble heroes, gallant love, chivalry, or daring deeds. Romances usually have faraway settings and depict events unlike those of ordinary life. They idealize their heroes as well as the eras in which they live.

Early medieval romances tell the adventures of knights and their brave deeds. Examples of medieval romances in this text are *Sir Gawain and the Green Knight*, which idealizes Sir Gawain as the epitome of the virtuous and chivalric knight, and *Morte d' Arthur*, written by Thomas Malory, which is based on the Arthurian legend. The earliest romances were in verse. In contrast with an epic, a romance is light-hearted in tone and loose in structure; it involves fantasy and recounts aimless adventures rather than great attainment.

During the Renaissance, the romantic epic, or *romance*, combined aspects of the medieval romance, including the love element, loose organization, and large number of characters, with structural elements of the epic. These included the invocation, statement of theme, speeches by the main character, and supernatural elements. Edmund Spenser's *The Faerie Queene* is an example of a romantic epic, having an Arthurian setting and epic characteristics.

The term *romance* also is applied to romantic tales of the early nineteenth century. Influenced by medieval romances, these stories, many of them in verse, have remote settings, sentimental tone, and episodic structures.

Romanticism. Romanticism is a movement in the arts that flourished in Europe and America throughout much of the nineteenth century. Romantic writers glorified nature, idealized the past, and celebrated the individual. In reaction against Neoclassicism, their treatment of subject was emotional rather than rational, imaginative rather than analytical. Instead of the ode and the heroic couplet, the forms favored by Romantic poets included the lyric, ballad, and sonnet. For a more detailed explanation of Romanticism, see the introduction to Unit 5.

Sarcasm. Sarcasm, a type of verbal irony, refers to a remark in which the literal meaning is complimentary but the actual meaning is critical. One such contemptuous remark is this one in Jonathan Swift's *Gulliver's Travels*:

> You have clearly proved that ignorance, idleness, and
>   vice are
> the proper ingredients for qualifying a legislator.

Sarcasm is personal and biting. In "The Prologue" to *The Canterbury Tales*, Chaucer sarcastically describes the corrupt, greedy Friar:

> He knew the taverns well in every town
> And every innkeeper and barmaid too
> Better than lepers, beggars and that crew,
> For in so eminent a man as he
> It was not fitting with the dignity
> Of his position dealing with such scum. . . .
> Natural gifts like his were hard to match.
> He was the finest beggar of his batch,

See *Irony*.

Satire. Satire is a literary technique used both in poetry and prose that combines a critical attitude with wit and humor for the purpose of improving society. Short stories, poems, novels, essays, and plays may be vehicles for satire. For example, Jonathan Swift's essay "A Modest Proposal" (Unit 4) satirizes human morality and political institutions, and Alexander Pope's poem "Epistle to Miss Blount" (Unit 4) satirizes both the country squire and the city fop.

The two basic types of satire in English literature are distinct in tone. Horatian satire, named after the Roman poet Horace, is gentle, wry, and urbane, seeking to correct foolish customs or ideas through sympathetic laughter. On the other hand, Juvenalian satire, named after the Roman poet Juvenal, is biting and angry; it criticizes corrupt individuals and institutions with bitterness and indignation.

See *Irony, Mock Epic, Parody, Sarcasm, Understatement.*

Science Fiction. Science fiction is prose writing that presents the possibilities of the past or the future, using known scientific data and theories as well as the creative imagination of the writer. Most science fiction comments on present-day society through the writer's fictional conception of a past or future society. For instance, George Orwell's *1984* presents a frightening society in which government suppresses all freedom, even freedom of thought. Orwell is warning readers against the dangers of modern totalitarian regimes by projecting extreme consequences.

See *Fantasy*.

Sestet. See *Sonnet*.

Setting. Setting is the time and place of the action in a short story, novel, play, narrative poem, or nonfiction narrative. *Beowulf*, for example, is set during the third or fourth century in the area that is now northern Germany, Denmark, and southern Sweden. Setting also includes the social and moral environment that form the background for a narrative. As such, the setting of *Beowulf* is the bleak atmosphere of the warlike Germanic tribes with their emphasis on loyalty, courage, strength, and adventure.

Setting, along with plot, character, and theme, is one of the main elements in fiction. While setting is extremely important in some works of literature, sometimes serving as a source of conflict, it is incidental and only vaguely defined in others.

Shakespearean (English) Sonnet. See *Sonnet*.

Short Story. A short story is a work of fiction that can be read at one sitting. Usually it develops one primary conflict and produces a single effect. The four basic elements of a short story are its plot, characters, setting, and theme. The plot is the story that unfolds as the result of a struggle between opposing forces. The characters are the people or animals who take part in the action. The setting is the time and place in which the action occurs. An outgrowth of these three, the theme is the central truth about human nature or about life conveyed by the writer.

See *Fiction*.

Simile. A simile is a figure of speech that states a comparison between two things that are essentially unlike but similar in some way. While a metaphor implies a comparison or states it directly, a simile expresses the comparison by the use of the words *like* or *as*.

Both poets and prose writers use similes to itensify emotional response, stimulate vibrant images, provide imaginative delight, and concentrate the expression of ideas. Notice the effects of similes in the following examples.

We watched the ghostly dancers spin.
To sound of horn and violin,
Like black leaves wheeling in the wind.

OSCAR WILDE

There was not a light, not a stir, not a sound. The
  mysterious East
faced me, perfumed like a flower, silent like death,
  dark like a grave.

JOSEPH CONRAD
"Youth"

A heavy fall aroused us: John had gone down like a
  stone.

THOMAS HARDY
"The Rash Bride"

Her pretty feet
Like snails did creep

ROBERT HERRICK
"Upon Mistress Susanna
Southwell, Her Feet"

See *Figurative Language, Metaphor*.

Situational Irony. See *Irony*.

Soliloquy. In drama, a soliloquy is a speech given by a character while he or she is either alone on stage or among characters who are ignored temporarily. The purpose of a soliloquy is to let the audience know the character's thoughts and plans. Soliloquys are characteristic of Elizabethan drama; *Macbeth* has several soliloquys. Following is part of Hamlet's famous soliloquy.

To be, or not to be—that is the question.
Whether 'tis nobler in the mind to suffer
The slings and arrows of outrageous fortune,
Or to take arms against a sea of troubles,
And by opposing end them. To die, to sleep—
No more, and by a sleep to say we end
The heartache and the thousand natural shocks
That flesh is heir to. 'Tis a consummation
Devoutly to be wished. To die, to sleep,
To sleep—perchance to dream. Aye, there's the rub,
For in that sleep of death what dreams may come
When we have shuffled off this mortal coil
Must give us pause.

WILLIAM SHAKESPEARE
Hamlet

Sonnet. A sonnet is a lyric poem of fourteen lines, commonly written in iambic pentameter. For centuries the sonnet has been a popular form, for it is long enough to permit development of a complex idea yet short and structured enough to challenge any poet's artistic skills. Sonnets written in English usually follow one of two forms.

The Petrarchan, or Italian, sonnet, introduced into English by Sir Thomas Wyatt, is named after Petrarch, a fourteenth-century Italian poet. This type of sonnet consists of two parts, called the octave (the first eight lines) and the sestet (the last six lines). The usual rhyme scheme for the octave is *a b b a a b b a*. The rhyme scheme for the sestet may be *c d e c d e, c d c c d e*, or a similar variation. The octave generally presents a problem or raises a question while the sestet resolves or comments on the problem. Following is an example of a Petrarchan sonnet by John Milton.

Methought I saw my late espousèd saint	a
Brought to me like Alcestis from the grave,	b
Whom Jove's great son to her glad husband gave,	b
Rescued from Death by force though pale and faint.	a
Mine, as whom washed from spot of childbed taint,	a
Purification in the old law did save,	b
And such, as yet once more I trust to have	b
Full sight of her in Heaven without restraint,	a
Came vested all in white, pure as her mind.	c
Her face was veiled, yet to my fancied sight,	d
Love, sweetness, goodness, in her person shined	c
So clear, as in no face with more delight	d
But O, as to embrace me she inclined,	c
I waked, she fled, and day brought back my night	d

"Methought I Saw My Late
Espoused Saint"

The Shakespearean, or English, sonnet is sometimes called the Elizabethan sonnet. It consists of three quatrains, or four-line units, and a final couplet. The typical rhyme scheme is *a b a b c d c d e f e f g g*. In the English sonnet, the rhymed couplet at the end of the sonnet provides a final commentary on the subject developed in the three quatrains. Following is an example of an English sonnet.

Not marble, nor the gilded monuments	a
Of princes, shall outlive this powerful rhyme.	b
But you shall shine more bright in these contents	a
Than unswept stone, besmeared with sluttish time.	b
When wasteful war shall statues overturn,	c
And broils root out the work of masonry,	d
Nor Mars his sword nor war's quick fire shall burn	c
The living record of your memory.	d
'Gainst death and all-oblivious enmity	e
Shall you pace forth. Your praise shall still find room	f
Even in the eyes of all posterity	e
That wear this world out to the ending doom.	f
So, till the judgment that yourself arise,	g
You live in this, and dwell in lovers' eyes.	g

WILLIAM SHAKESPEARE
"Sonnet 55"

Edmund Spenser created a third type of sonnet by adapting the Shakespearean quatrains with an interlocking rhyme scheme. The rhyme scheme for the Spenserian sonnet is *a b a b b c b c c d c d e e*.

Some poets have written a series of related sonnets that have the same subject. These are called sonnet sequences, or sonnet cycles. Toward the end of the fifteenth century, writing sonnet sequences became fashionable, with a common subject being love for a beautiful but unattainable woman. The sonnets in this text by Edmund Spenser, Philip Sidney, William Shakespeare, and Elizabeth Barrett Browning, are poems from sonnet sequences.

See *Lyric*, *Quatrain*.

Sonnet Sequence. See *Sonnet*.

Sound Devices. See *Alliteration*, *Assonance*, *Consonance*, *Meter*, *Onomatopoeia*, *Repetition*, *Rhyme*, *Rhyme Scheme*, *Rhythm*.

Speaker. In poetry, the speaker is the voice that "talks" to the reader; the speaker in poetry is

analogous to the narrator in a work of fiction. Speaker and poet are not necessarily synonymous, although a poet may choose to speak in his or her own voice. Often, a poet creates a speaker, or persona, with a distinct identity in order to achieve a particular effect. For example, in Judith Wright's "Eve to Her Daughters," the speaker of the poem is the Biblical Eve. In the lines that follow, the speaker is a dead soldier.

That night your great guns, unawares,
Shook all our coffins as we lay,
And broke the chancel window-squares,
We thought it was the Judgment Day
And sat upright.

THOMAS HARDY
"Channel Firing"

Spenserian Stanza. The Spenserian stanza is a stanza form invented by Edmund Spencer for his epic *The Faerie Queene*. Each stanza has nine lines with eight lines of iambic pentameter followed by a ninth line containing two additional syllables. The rhyme scheme follows the pattern *a b a b b c b c c*. Like Spenser's sonnet form, the Spenserian stanza has an interlocking rhyme scheme, which creates a unified impression and a tight expression of ideas. Other poets, including Robert Burns, John Keats, and George Gordon, Lord Byron, also used the form. The following is a stanza from Spenser's *The Faerie Queene*.

Then mounted he upon his Steede againe,	a
And with the Lady backward sought to wend;	b
That path he kept, which beaten was most plaine,	a
Ne ever would to any by-way bend,	b
But still did follow one unto the end,	b
The which at last out of the wood them brought.	c
So forward on his way (with God to frend)	b
He passéd forth, and new adventure sought;	c
Long way he travelled, before he heard of ought.	c

Spondee. In poetry, a metrical foot consisting of two accented syllables is called a spondee. Spondees are used occasionally to produce variety within the regular meter of blank verse or any other conventional meter. John Milton uses the spondee "déep péace" in the line "Silence, ye troubled waves and thee, deep peace!" In the following lines, the opening repetition of *she* comprises a spondee.

Shé, she hersélf, and ónlÿ she,
Shone thróugh hér bodÿ visíblÿ.

SAMUEL TAYLOR COLERIDGE "Phantom"

This line too opens with a spondee within a line of iambic pentameter:

Lóve, faíthfúl lóve, recálléd theé tó mÿ mínd—

WILLIAM WORDSWORTH "Surprised by Joy"

See *Meter*.

Sprung Rhythm. Sprung rhythm is a term invented by Gerard Manley Hopkins to describe his own metrical system. It is a type of irregular meter in which each foot has one stressed syllable or else one stressed syllable and then one, two, or three unstressed syllables. Following is a line from Hopkins' poetry that uses sprung rhythm. Notice that in sprung rhythm a foot may begin on one line and continue onto the following line.

Dówn in dím wóods the díamŏnd delves! the
    elvés'-eyés!
The gréy láwns cóld where góld, where quíckgold
    líes!

"The Starlight Night"

Stage Directions. See *Drama*.

Stanza. A stanza is a group of lines that form a unit of poetry. The stanza is roughly comparable to the paragraph in prose. In traditional poems, the stanzas usually have the same number of lines and often have the same rhyme scheme and meter as well. Twentieth-century poets have experimented more freely with stanza forms than did earlier poets, sometimes writing poems that have no stanza breaks at all.

The quatrain, or four-line stanza, is common in English poetry. A three-line stanza is called a tercet. A couplet set off by itself functions as a two-line stanza.

Thomas Gray's "Elegy Written in a Country Churchyard" in Unit 4 is structured in quatrains. "Ode to the West Wind" by Percy Bysshe Shelley in Unit 5 repeats a stanza pattern of four tercets followed by a couplet. In Unit 7, "The Hollow Men" by T. S. Eliot and "Dulce et Decorum Est" by Wilfred Owen contain stanzas of varying lengths, from couplets to stanzas of more than ten lines.

See *Couplet, Quatrain*.

Stereotype. In everyday speech and in literature, the term *stereotype* refers to something that conforms to a fixed or general pattern, without individuating marks or qualities. Often a stereotype is a standardized mental picture, held in common by members of a group, which represents an oversimplified opinion, such as of a race or national group. Sweeping generalizations about "all Irish people" or "every Southerner" are stereotypes.

In literature, simplified or stock characters who represent a recognizable type of person often are called stereotypes. Such characters do not usually demonstrate the complexities of real people. Familiar stereotypes in popular literature include the absent-minded professor, the dumb athlete, and the busybody. In *Beowulf*, Grendel, Grendel's mother, and the fire dragon are stereotypical villains.

Stream of Consciousness. The technique of presenting the flow of thoughts, responses, and sensations of one or more characters is called stream of consciousness. A stream-of-consciousness narrative is not structured into a coherent, logical presentation of ideas. The connections between ideas are associative, with one idea suggesting another, as in T. S. Eliot's "The Hollow Men" in Unit 7.

Often a character's interior monologue is integrated into a more traditional narrative, as in "The Demon Lover" by Elizabeth Bowen in unit 7. Sometimes writers, such as James Joyce in *Ulysses*, rely entirely on the technique. The following passage by Virginia Woolf shows how she uses stream of consciousness to develop a character.

The tree outside the window taps very gently on the pane. . . . I want to think quietly, calmly, spaciously, never to be interrupted, never to have to rise from my chair, to slip easily from one thing to another, without any sense of hostility, or obstacle. I want to sink deeper and deeper, away from the surface, with its hard separate facts. To steady myself, let me catch hold of the first idea that passes . . . Shakespeare . . . Well, he will do as well as another. A man who sat himself solidly in an armchair, and looked into the fire, so—A shower of ideas fell perpetually from some very high Heaven down through his mind. He leant his forehead on his hand,

and people, looking in through the open door—for this scene is supposed to take place on a summer's evening—But how dull this is, this historical fiction! It doesn't interest me at all. I wish I could hit upon a pleasant track of thought, a track indirectly reflecting credit upon myself, for those are the pleasantest thoughts. . . .

"The Mark on the Wall"

See *Characterization, Point of View.*

Structure. Structure is the way in which the parts of a work of literature are put together. Paragraphs are a basic unit in prose, as are chapters in novels and scenes and acts in plays. A prose selection can be structured by idea or incident, as are most essays, short stories, and one-act plays. In poetry, structure refers to the arrangement of words and lines to produce a desired effect. A common structural unit in poetry is the stanza. Samuel Taylor Coleridge's "Kubla Khan" in Unit 5, for example, is structured with three parts: a thesis in the first stanza, its antithesis, or opposite, in the second stanza, and a synthesis of the two in the final stanza. Chaucer's *The Canterbury Tales* is structured with a framing narrative, a story about a pilgrimage that connects a series of tales told by the individual travelers.

The structure of a poem, short story, novel, play, or nonfiction selection usually emphasizes certain important aspects of content. For example, the structure of Jonathan Swift's "A Modest Proposal" in Unit 4, with its rational statement of problem, followed by an ironic solution and then devastatingly ironic arguments, brings the full force of its satire to a crescendo at the end of the essay.

Structure is also a means through which the writer adds layers of psychological complexity to the characters. For example, "The Secret Sharer" is structured so that the central action both begins and ends with the mysterious Leggatt swimming in the sea. The intervening sea journey, symbolic of a journey into the narrator's subconscious, identifies the sea captain, and by interpolation all humans, with the lawlessness and irrationality of the "proud swimmer striking out for a new destiny."

Style. Style is the way in which a piece of literature is written. Style refers not to what is said, but to how it is said. Many elements contribute to style, such as diction, syntax, imagery, rhythm, figurative language, tone, point of view, and techniques of characterization. A literary style may be described as formal, conversational, journalistic, wordy, ornate, poetic, or dynamic, to name just a few examples.

Style expresses the individuality of a writer for it is the writer's uniquely personal way of communicating ideas. The styles of some writers are so consistent and recognizable that their names have become associated with the general characteristics of their styles. For example, Virginia Woolf and James Joyce are associated with the stream-of-consciousness technique, while Bernard Shaw is associated with wit and Jonathan Swift with satire.

Surprise Ending. A surprise ending is an unexpected twist at the conclusion of a story. The surprise may be a sudden turn in the action, as in "The Demon Lover" in Unit 8, or a revelation that gives a different perspective to the entire story, as in "History Lesson," also in Unit 8.

Syllabic Verse. Syllabic verse is poetry measured by the number of syllables in each line, rather than by the number of feet or the number of accents in a line. An example of syllabic verse is Dylan Thomas's "Fern Hill" in Unit 7.

Symbol. A symbol is a person, place, or object that represents something beyond itself. Symbols can succinctly communicate abstract, complex ideas. Certain symbols are commonly used in literature, such as a journey to represent life or night to represent death. Other symbols acquire meaning only through a particular literary work. For example, in John Keats's "Ode on a Grecian Urn" in Unit 5, the urn with its sculpted figures symbolizes static perfection, which also implies an absence of vitality and fulfillment. Other examples are the lamb in William Blake's "The Tyger" in Unit 4, which represents innocence, and the lady in Alfred, Lord Tennyson's "The Lady of Shalott" in Unit 6, who symbolizes the poet. Besides functioning as symbols, symbolic elements also relate to other elements in a literary work.

Synesthesia. See *Imagery.*

Terza Rima. Terza rima is a three-line stanza form with a rhyme scheme of *a b a, b c b, c d c, d e* *d*, and so forth. In terza rima, the middle rhyme-sound of one tercet, or three-line stanza, rhymes with the first and third lines of the succeeding tercet. Terza rima was originally an Italian stanza form but became popular with English poets, such as John Milton, Percy Bysshe Shelley, and George Gordon, Lord Byron. The following is an example of terza rima.

As in that trance of wondrous thought I lay	a
This was the tenor of my waking dream.	b
Methought I sate beside a public way	a
Thick strewn with summer dust, & a great stream	b
Of people there was hurrying to & fro	c
Numerous as gnats upon the evening gleam,	b
All hastening onward, yet none seemed to know	c
Whither he went, or whence he came, or why	d
He made one of the multitude, yet so	c
Was borne amid the crowd as through the sky	d
One of the million leaves of summer's bier.—	e
Old age & youth, manhood & infancy,	d

PERCY BYSSHE SHELLEY
"The Triumph of Life"

Thematic Unity. See *Unity.*

Theme. A theme is the main idea or message communicated by a work of literature. It is a writer's perception about life or human nature shared with a reader. Some works of literature are intended as light entertainment only and as such have no underlying messages. Most serious writing, however, comments in some way on life or the human condition. Themes seldom are stated directly and may reveal themselves only through careful reading and thought. In *Macbeth*, for example, the themes include the corrupting effect of unbridled ambition, the corrosiveness of guilt, the lure and power of inscrutable supernatural forces, and the tragedy of psychological disintegration. The theme of "The Rime of the Ancient Mariner" by Samuel Taylor Coleridge has been interpreted as the transformation of the human personality through a loss of innocence and youth; another interpretation of theme concerns the effects of sin and spiritual redemption.

Third-Person Narration. See *Point of View.*

Title. The distinguishing name attached to any piece of writing is its title. Frequently writers use the title of a work of literature to highlight its theme, as Joseph Conrad does in *"The Secret Sharer."* That title suggests the mysterious, dark side of human nature that the narrator of the tale comes to accept.

A poet may provide in the title significant information necessary for understanding a poem. For example, a reader of the "Journey of the Magi" by T. S. Eliot in Unit 7 might not recognize the situation described in the poem without the clue in the title.

Tone. Tone is the attitude that a writer takes toward his or her subject. The details in a work of literature and the way that these details are presented work together to imply the tone. A writer's tone may be comic, bitter, angry, objective, casual, or passionate, among many other possibilities. The tone of "A Modest Proposal" by Jonathan Swift in Unit 4, for example, is searingly ironic, while Arthur C. Clarke's tone in "We'll Never Conquer Space" in Unit 8 is logical and scientific. Chaucer's tone in "The Prologue" to *The Canterbury Tales* is restrained and detached, accounting for much of its humor. While Chaucer could have attacked the scoundrels of his age with vehement indignation, he instead chose the ironic, subdued tone that allows the reader to form his or her own conclusions, as in this example, which describes the deceitful, swindling Pardoner:

> There was no pardoner of equal grace,
> For in his trunk he had a pillow-case
> Which he asserted was Our Lady's veil.
> He said he had a gobbet of the sail
> Saint Peter had the time when he made bold
> To walk the waves, till Jesus Christ took hold.
> He had a cross of metal set with stones
> And, in a glass, a rubble of pig's bones.
> And with these relics, any time he found
> Some poor up-country parson to astound,
> On one short day, in money down, he drew
> More than the parson in a month or two

Tone is different from mood, which refers to the way that a reader responds to a literary work. For example, the mood in the short story "The Demon Lover" in Unit 8 is tense, ominous, and sinister; the tone, however, is serious but detached. The mood of the poem "Dulce et Decorum Est" in Unit 7 is horrifying; Wilfred Owen's tone, though, might be described as bitter, angry, and ironic.

Tragedy. A tragedy is a literary work that recounts the downfall of a dignified, superior character who is involved in historically or socially significant events. The main character, or tragic hero, has a tragic flaw, the quality that leads to his or her destruction. The events in a tragic plot are set in motion by a decision that is often an error in judgment caused by the tragic flaw. Succeeding events are linked in a cause-effect relationship and lead inevitably to a disastrous conclusion. Tragedy arouses both pity and fear, pity for the doomed hero and fear for all humans, who are subject to the same forces and weaknesses as the tragic hero. Shakespeare's *Macbeth* is a famous tragedy.

Tragic Hero. See *Hero*.

Tragic Flaw. See *Hero, Tragedy*.

Understatement. The technique of creating emphasis by saying less than is actually or literally true is understatement. An example from everyday speech is the use of "not bad" to mean "pretty good." Understatement is the opposite of hyperbole, or exaggeration. One of the primary devices of irony, understatement can be used for humorous effect. Understatement also may be used to create biting satire or to achieve a restrained tone. Chaucer employs humorous understatement in "The Prologue" to *The Canterbury Tales*, as in this comment on the womanly Nun: "She was by no means undergrown." Another example of understatement is the last two lines of this poem:

> Give me for life the honest name,
> Then take my due arrears of fame.
> I am grown deaf, and shall become
> A trifle deafer in the tomb.
> WALTER SAVAGE LANDOR
"Give Me for Life"

Unity. Unity refers to the harmonious blend of elements in a literary work. Almost any technique used in fiction, nonfiction, and poetry can function as a unifying device. Consistency of tone, mood, character, and diction, for example, contribute to unity, as do foreshadowing, balanced structure, and parallelism. In poetry, sound devices such as rhythm, meter, rhyme, alliteration, assonance, and consonance, along with repetition in the form of repetend and refrain all create and reinforce unity. Thematic unity, which is characteristic of longer works of fiction and drama, occurs when an idea presented in one part of a literary work is further developed later in the work.

Verbal Irony. See *Irony*.

Verisimilitude. The appearance or semblance of truth in literature is called verisimilitude. Verisimilitude is achieved when a writer presents details, however far-fetched, in such a way as to give them the appearance of truth and to sweep the reader, for the moment at least, into an acceptance of them. In "A Modest Proposal" in Unit 4, for example, Jonathan Swift imbues a semblance of logic to the preposterous idea that the children of the poor should be marketed as food. Likewise, in the short story "Follow My Fancy, in Unit 4, Joan Aiken makes fantastic events plausible.

Villanelle. A villanelle is an intricately patterned French verse form, planned to give the impression of simplicity. The villanelle has nineteen lines, composed of five tercets followed by a quatrain. The first line is repeated as a refrain at the ends of the second and fourth stanzas. The last line of the first stanza is repeated at the ends of the third and fifth stanzas. Both lines reappear as the final two lines of the poem. The rhyme scheme of a villanelle is *a b a* for each tercet and then *a b a a* for the quatrain. In Unit 7, Dylan Thomas's "Do Not Go Gentle into That Good Night" is an example of a villanelle.

Glossary

The glossary is an alphabetical listing of words from the selections, along with their meanings. If you are not familiar with a word as you read, look it up in the glossary.

The glossary gives the following information:

1. **The pronunciation of each word.** For example, **turbulent** (tʉr′ byələnt). If there is more than one way to pronounce a word, the most common pronunciation is listed first. For example, **status** (stā′ təs, stat′ əs).

   A primary accent ′ is placed after the syllable that is stressed the most when the word is spoken. **A secondary accent** ′ is placed after a syllable that has a lighter stress. For example, **imitation** (im′ə tā′shən). The Pronunciation Key below shows the symbols for the sounds of letters, and key words that contain those sounds. Also, there is a short pronunciation key at the bottom of each right-hand page in the glossary.

2. **The part of speech of the word.** The following abbreviations are used:

adj. adjective	*conj.* conjunction	*pro.* pronoun	*prep.* preposition
adv. adverb	*n.* noun	*v.* verb	*interj.* interjection

3. **The meaning of the word.** The definitions listed in the glossary are the ones that apply to the way a word is used in these selections.

4. **Related forms.** Words with suffixes such as *-ing*, *-ed*, *-ness*, and *-ly* are listed under the base word. For example, **decisive** *adj.* . . . **decisively** *adv.*, **decisiveness** *n.*

Pronunciation Key

Symbol	Key Words	Symbol	Key Words	Symbol	Key Words	Symbol	Key Words
a	ask, fat, parrot	oi	oil, point, toy	b	bed, fable, dub	t	top, cattle, hat
ā	ape, date, play	ou	out, crowd, plow	d	dip, beadle, had	v	vat, hovel, have
ä	ah, car, father	u	up, cut, color	f	fall, after, off	w	will, always, swear
		ʉr	urn, fur, deter	g	get, haggle, dog	y	yet, onion, yard
e	elf, ten, berry			h	he, ahead, hotel	z	zebra, dazzle, haze
ē	even, meet, money	ə	a in ago	j	joy, agile, badge		
i	is, hit, mirror		e in agent	k	kill, tackle, bake	ch	chin, catcher, arch
ī	ice, bite, high		i in sanity	l	let, yellow, ball	sh	she, cushion, dash
			o in comply	m	met, camel, trim	th	thin, nothing, truth
ō	open, tone, go		u focus	n	not, flannel, ton	*th*	then, father, lathe
ô	all, horn, law			p	put, apple, tap	zh	azure, leisure
o͞o	ooze, tool, crew			r	red, port, dear	ŋ	ring, anger, drink
oo	look, pull, moor	ər	perhaps, murder	s	sell, castle, pass	′	able (ā′b′l)
yo͞o	use, cute, few						
yoo	united, cure, globule						

A

abasement (ə bās′ mənt) n. Degradation, humiliation.

abdicate (ab′ də kāt′) v. To give up (a high office, throne, etc.).

ablution (ab lōō′ shən) n. A washing of the body, especially as a religious ceremony.

absolution (ab′ sə lōō′ shən) n. Forgiveness of sins.

abstemious (əb stē′ mē əs) adj. Characterized by abstinence, that is, voluntarily doing without some or all food, drink, or other pleasures.

abstruse (ab strōōs′) adj. Hard to understand.

access (ak′ ses) n. [Archaic] An attack of disease, usually a malarial fever.

accession (ak sesh′ ən) n. The act of coming to or attaining a throne or power.

acerbic (ə sur′ bik) adj. Sharp, bitter, or harsh.

admonishment (ad män′ ish mənt) n. A caution, warning, or reminder.

adroit (ə droit′) adj. Clever, expert.

aëry (er′ ē) adj. [Poetic] Airy.

affectation (af′ ek tā′ shən) n. Artificial behavior meant to impress others.

affinity (ə fin′ ə te) n. A close relationship; natural liking.

agape (ə gāp′) adj. With or as with the mouth wide open, in surprise or wonder.

aggrieve (ə grēv′) v. To offend.

agrarian (ə grer′ ē ən) adj. Of agriculture or farmers generally.

alchemy (al′ kə mē) n. An early form of chemistry.

allay (ə lā′) v. To lessen, alleviate.

allegorical (al′ ə gôr′ i k′l) adj. Characteristic of a story in which people, things, and happenings have a hidden or symbolic meaning: allegories are used for teaching or explaining principles or ideas.

alms (ämz) n. Money, food, or clothes given to poor people.

altercation (ôl′ tər kā′ shən) n. An angry or heated argument.

ambrosian (am brō′ zhən) adj. Delicious, fragrant.

anarchic (an är′ kik) adj. Of, like, or involving political disorder and violence.

animosity (an′ ə mäs′ ə tē) n. Hatred, hostility.

annals (an′ ′lz) n. Historical records.

anthem (an′ thəm) n. A song of praise or devotion.

aperture (ap′ ər chər) n. An opening.

apocalyptic (ə päk′ ə lip′ tik) adj. Prophetic; predicting the future.

apothecary (ə päth′ ə ker′ ē) n. A pharmacist or druggist.

apparition (ap′ ə rish′ ən) n. Anything that appears unexpectedly or in an extraordinary way, especially a strange figure appearing suddenly and thought to be a ghost.

apprehend (ap′ rə hend′) v. **1.** To dread; anticipate with anxiety. **2.** To perceive, understand.

apprise (ə prīz′) v. To inform or notify.

approbation (ap′ rə bā′ shən) n. Official approval, sanction, or commendation.

aqueous (ā′ kwē əs) adj. Watery; of, like, or containing water.

arbiter (är′ bə tər) n. A person fully authorized or qualified to judge or decide.

arboreal (är bôr′ ē al) adj. Of or like a tree.

archivist (är′ kə vist) n. A person in charge of public records.

arduous (är′ joo wəs) adj. Using much energy; strenuous; difficult to do.

argot (är′ gō) n. The specialized idioms and vocabulary of those in the same work, way of life, etc., as the secret jargon of criminals.

arrears (ə rirz′) n. Unpaid and overdue debts.

asceticism (ə set′ ə siz′m) n. The religious doctrine that one can reach a higher spiritual state by rigorous self-discipline and self-denial.

asperity (as per′ ə tē) n. Harshness or sharpness of temper.

aspirant (as′ pər ənt) n. A person who aspires, seeks, or is ambitious (to get or do something).

assail (ə sāl′) v. To have a forceful effect on; attack.

assiduous (ə sij′ oo wəs) adj. Done with constant and careful attention; diligent.—**assiduously** adv.

assize (ə sīz′) n. A court session held periodically in each county of England to try civil and criminal cases.

assuage (ə swāj′) v. [Archaic] To abate, subside, or calm.

asunder (ə sun′ dər) adv. Apart or separate.

athwart (ə thwôrt′) prep. Across; from one side to the other of.

attrition (ə trish′ ən) n. Any gradual wearing or weakening, especially to the point of exhaustion.

autocratic (ôt′ ə krat′ ik) adj. Ruling with absolute power; dictatorial, domineering.

aver (ə vur′) v. To declare to be true.

avouch (ə vouch′) v. To guarantee.

axiom (ak′ sē əm) n. A statement universally accepted as true; maxim.

azure (azh′ ər) n. Sky blue. adj. Of or like the color of a clear sky; sky blue.

B

baldric (bôl′ drik) n. A belt worn over one shoulder and across the chest to support a sword.

baleful (bāl′ fəl) adj. Deadly, harmful, or threatening evil.—**balefully** adv.

balmy (bäm′ ē) adj. [British slang] Crazy or foolish.

bandy (ban′ dē) adj. Bent or curved outward; bowed.

barbarism (bär′ bər iz′m) n. The use of words and expressions not standard in a language.

bark (bärk) n. A sailing vessel.

base (bās) adj. Having or showing little or no honor, courage or decency; contemptible.

battlement (bat′ ′l mənt) n. A low wall with open spaces for shooting, built on top of a castle wall, tower, or fort.

bdellium (del′ ē əm) n. A jewel interpreted as being a carbuncle, crystal, or pearl.

beguile (bi gīl′) v. To mislead by cheating or tricking; deceive.

belligerent (bə lij′ ər ənt) n. A person, group, or nation seeking a fight or war.

benefice (ben′ ə fis) n. An endowed church office providing a living for a vicar, rector, etc.

benevolent (bə nev' ə lənt) *adj.* Kindly, charitable.

benign (bi nīn') *adj.* Good-natured, kindly.

bereft (bi reft') *adj.* Deprived, robbed, dispossessed.

besot (bi sät') *v.* To stupefy or confuse, make silly.

betel (bēt' 'l) *n.* A tropical Asiatic plant whose leaf is chewed by some Asian peoples.

betide (bi tīd') *v.* To befall or happen to.

betimes (bi tīmz') *adv.* Early or early enough.

bide (bīd) *v.* To stay, wait, reside.

bier (bir) *n.* A coffin and its supporting platform.

billow (bil' ō) *n.* A large wave; great swell of water.

biped (bī' ped) *n.* Any two-footed animal.

blackguard (blag' ərd) *n.* Scoundrel, villain.

blanch (blanch) *v.* To whiten, turn pale.

blasphemer (blas fēm' ər) *n.* One who speaks irreverently of or to God or anything held as divine.—**blasphemy** *n.*

blood (blud) *v.* [Archaic] To bleed.

blowzy (blou' zē) *adj.* Fat, coarse-looking, sloppy.

bohemian (bō hē' mē ən) *adj.* Characteristic of a person, especially an artist or poet, who lives in an unconventional, nonconforming way.

bombardier (bäm' bə dir') *n.* A member of the crew of a bomber.

bonnie, bonny (bän' ē) *adj.* Handsome or pretty, with a healthy, cheerful glow.

boracic (bə ras' ik) *adj.* Of or containing boron, which is used in boric acid, a mild antiseptic.

bourgeois (boor zhwä') *n.* A person whose beliefs, attitudes, and practices are conventionally middle-class.

brandish (bran' dish) *v.* To wave, shake, or exhibit in a menacing way.

bravado (brə vä' dō) *n.* Pretended courage or defiant confidence where there is really little or none.

brazen (brā' z'n) *adj.* Of brass.—**brazen it out** To act in a bold way as if one need not be ashamed.

buckler (buk' lər) *n.* A small, round shield held by a handle or worn on the arm.

buffoon (bə fōōn') *n.* A clown.

burgeon (bʉr' jen) *v.* To grow or develop rapidly.

burgess (bʉr' jis) *n.* [Now Rare] A citizen of a British borough.

burlesque (bər lesk') *n.* Any broadly comic or satirical imitation, as of a writing or play.

burnish (bʉr' nish) *v.* To polish or make shiny by rubbing.

buss (bus) *n.* A kiss.

C

cadaverous (kə dav' ər əs) *adj.* Like a corpse; especially pale, ghastly, and gaunt.

canker (kan' kər) *n.* A disease of plants that causes local decay of bark and wood.

cant (kant) *n.* Insincere or almost meaningless talk used merely from convention or habit.

caper-spurge (kā' pər spʉrj) *n.* A medicinal plant.

caprice (kə prēs') *n.* A sudden, impulsive change in the way one thinks or acts.

capstan (kap' stən) *n.* An apparatus around which cables are wound for hoisting anchors.

carbuncle (kär' buŋ k'l) *n.* A painful inflammation of the tissue beneath the skin, more severe than a boil.

carcass (kär' kəs) *n.* A dead body.

career (kə rir') *v.* To move at full speed; rush wildly.

carte blanchen (kärt' blänsh) Freedom to do as one wishes.

castigate (kas' tə gāt') *v.* To punish or blame severely, especially by harsh public criticism.

cataclysm (kat' ə kliz'm) *n.* Any great upheaval that causes sudden and violent changes, as earthquake, war, etc.

cataract (kat' ə rakt') *n.* A large waterfall.

catholic (kath' ə lik) *adj.* All-inclusive; of general scope.

cavalier (kav' ə lir') *adj.* Casual or indifferent toward matters of some importance.

celibate (sel' ə bət) *n.* An unmarried person or one who abstains from sexual activity.

censorious (sen sôr' ē əs) *adj.* Inclined to find fault; harshly critical.

censure (sen' shər) *v.* To express strong disapproval of; condemn as wrong; blame.

centaury (sen' tôr ē) *n.* A medicinal plant.

chaffy (chaf' ē) *adj.* Full of the husks or worthless part of grain.

chamberlain (chām' bər lin) *n.* The bedchamber attendant of a ruler or lord.

chancel (chan' s'l) *n.* The part of a church around the altar.

chancellery (chan' sə lə rē) *n.* The office of a high government official.

charlatan (shär' lə t'n) *n.* A fake; person who pretends to have expert knowledge but does not.

chasm (kaz' 'm) *n.* **1.** A deep crack in the earth's surface. **2.** Any break or gap.

chaste (chāst) *adj.* Pure, decent, or modest in nature or behavior.

chasten (chās' 'n) *v.* To restrain from excess.

chide (chīd) *v.* To scold.

chimerical (ki mir' i k'l) *adj.* Fantastic, unreal, absurd, impossible.

choler (käl' ər) *n.* [Obsolete] Bile: in medieval times yellow bile was considered one of the four humors of the body, the source of anger and irritability.

choleric (käl' ər ik) *adj.* **1.** Having or showing a quick temper or irritable nature. **2.** Having the appearance of one who has a liver ailment; bilious.

chronometer (krə näm' ə tər) *n.* An instrument for measuring time precisely.

circumscribe (sʉr' kəm skrīb') *v.* To limit, confine.

circumspect (sʉr' kəm spekt') *adj.* Cautious; careful to consider all related circumstances before acting.—**circumspection** *n.*

circumstantial (sʉr' kəm stan' shəl) *adj.* Full or complete in detail.

cistern (sis' tərn) *n.* A large receptacle for storing water; especially a tank, usually underground, in which rain water is collected for use.

---

fat, āpe, cär; ten, ēven; is, bīte; gō, hôrn, tōōl, look; oil, out; up, fʉr; get; joy; yet; chin; she; thin, *th*en; zh, leisure; ŋ, ring; ə for *a* in *ago*, *e* in *agent*, *i* in *sanity*, *o* in *comply*, *u* in *focus*; ' as in *able* (ā'b'l)

citadel (sit' ə d'l) *n.* A fortress on a commanding height for defense of a city.

clarion (klar' ē ən) *n.* A trumpet of the Middle Ages producing clear, sharp, shrill tones.

cleave (klēv) *v.* **1.** To adhere, cling (to). **2.** To be faithful (to). **3.** To split, separate.

cleric (kler' ik) *n.* A clergyman, minister, priest, or rabbi.

cloister (klois' tər) *v.* To seclude or confine in or as in a cloister or convent.

cloven (klō' v'n) *adj.* Divided, split.

cloy (kloi) *v.* To make weary or displeased by too much of something.

cob (käb) *n.* A short, thickset horse with a high gait.

collateral (kə lat' ər əl) *adj.* Parallel in importance.

collectivity (käl' ek tiv' ə tē) *n.* The people as a whole.

colloquial (kə lō' kwē əl) *adj.* Conversational, informal.

comely (kum' lē) *adj.* Attractive, fair.

complicity (kəm plis' ə tē) *n.* The fact or state of being an accomplice; partnership in wrongdoing.

concierge (kän' sē ʉrzh') *n.* A doorkeeper or head porter of a hotel or apartment house.

conciliate (kən sil' ē āt) *v.* To win over; soothe the anger of.—**conciliatory** *adj.*

concubine (käŋ' kyə bīn') *n.* A woman who cohabits with a man although not legally married to him.

confabulation (kən fab' yə lā' shən) *n.* An informal talk; chat.

confute (kən fyoot') *v.* To prove wrong.

congeal (kən jēl') *v.* To solidify; thicken by cooling or freezing.

conjugal (kän' jə gəl) *adj.* Of marriage or the relation between husband and wife.

consort (*v.* kən sôrt' *n.* kän' sôrt) *v.* To associate. *n.* **1.** A spouse. **2.** A ship that travels along with another.

constabulary (kən stab' yə ler' ē) *n.* A police force characterized by a military organization but distinct from the regular army.

consternation (kän' stər nā' shən) *N.* Great fear or shock that makes one feel helpless or bewildered.

consummate (kən sum' it) *adj.* Complete or perfect in every way.

converse (kän' vərs) *n.* Informal talk, conversation.

corporeal (kôr pôr' ē əl) *adj.* Of, for, or having the nature of the body; bodily; not spiritual.

cosmos (käz' məs) *n.* The universe.

coterie (kōt' ər ē) *n.* A close circle of friends who share a common interest or background.

countenance (koun' tə nəns) *n.* The face; facial features. *v.* To approve, support, or tolerate.

courtier (kôr' tē ər) *n.* An attendant at a royal court.

covenant (kuv' ə nənt) *n.* A binding agreement.

covert (kuv' ərt) *n.* A hiding place, such as underbrush.

covetousness (kuv' it əs nis) *n.* Greed, envy.

cower (kou' ər) *v.* To shrink and tremble, as from someone's anger.

cranny (kran' ē) *n.* A small, narrow opening; crack, as in a wall.

credulous (krej' oo ləs) *adj.* Tending to believe too readily; easily convinced.

crestfallen (krest' fôl' ən) *adj.* Dejected, disheartened, humbled.

cryptogram (krip' tə gram') *n.* Something written in code.

cud (kud) *n.* A mouthful of previously swallowed food regurgitated from the first stomach of cattle back to the mouth where it is chewed a second time.

cudgel (kuj' əl) *n.* A short, thick stick or club.

D

dais (dā' is) *n.* A platform raised above the floor at one end of a room as for a throne, speaker's stand, etc.

dalliant (dal' ē ənt) *adj.* Careless, trifling.

dandify (dan' də fī') *v.* To make look like a man who pays too much attention to his clothes and appearance.

darkling (där' kliŋ) *adj.* [Poet.] Dark, dim, obscure.

dauntless (dônt' lis) *adj.* That cannot be discouraged or intimidated; fearless.

dear (dir) *adv.* Much valued; costly.

dearth (dʉrth) *n.* Famine, scarcity of food supply.

debar (dē bär') *v.* To keep (from some right or privilege); exclude.

decimate (des' ə māt') *v.* To destroy or kill a large part of.

declamation (dek' lə mā' shən) *n.* The act or art of reciting a speech, poem, etc. with studied or artificial eloquence.—**declaim** *v.*

decorum (di kôr' əm) *n.* Propriety and good taste in behavior, speech, dress, etc.

deference (def' ər əns) *n.* Courteous regard or respect.—**deferentially** *adv.*

deign (dān) *v.* To condescend.

denigrate (den' ə grāt') *v.* To disparage the character or reputation of.

deportment (di pôrt' mənt) *n.* The manner of conducting or bearing oneself; behavior.

deprave (di prāv') *v.* To lead into bad habits; pervert, corrupt.

depraved (di prāvd') *adj.* Morally bad, corrupt, perverted.

deprecate (dep' rə kāt') *v.* To express disapproval of; belittle.—**deprecation** *n.*

deputy (dep' yə tē) *n.* A person appointed to act as a substitute or assistant.

derisive (di rī' siv) *adj.* Ridiculing, contemptuous.

descant (des' kant) *v.* To talk or write at length.

desist (di zist') *v.* To cease, stop.

desolation (des' ə lā' shən) *n.* Lonely grief; misery.

despoil (di spoil') *v.* To deprive (of something) by force; rob, plunder, ravage.

despond (di spänd') *v.* To lose courage or hope; become disheartened.

despotic (de spät' ik) *adj.* Autocratic, tyrannical; like an absolute ruler.

destitute (des' tə toot') *adj.* Living in poverty.

desultory (des' 'l tôr' ē) *adj.* Aimless.

didactic (dī dak' tik) *adj.* Intended for teaching.

diffident (dif' ə dənt) *adj.* Lacking self-confidence; timid, shy.

diffusive (di fyoo' siv) *adj.* Characterized by spreading out, not being concentrated.

dilation (dī lā' shən) *n.* A stretching or expanding.

diminuendo (də min' yoo wen' dō) *n.* A gradual decrease in loudness.

dirge (dʉrj) *n.* A slow, sad song, poem, or musical composition expressing grief or mourning.

discernment (di surn' mənt) n. Keen perception or judgment; insight.

discomfit (dis kum' fit) v. To defeat or frustrate the plans or expectations of.—**discomfiture** n.

discreditable (dis kred' it ə b'l) adj. Damaging to one's reputation or status.

disoblige (dis' ə blīj') v. To slight, offend.

disport (dis pôrt') v. To indulge in amusement.

disquiet (dis kwī' ət) 1. n. Uneasiness, anxiety, restlessness. 2. v. To make anxious, uneasy, or restless.

dissemble (di sem' b'l) v. To conceal the truth or one's true feelings or motives by pretense; behave hypocritically.

dissident (dis' ə dənt) n. A person who dissents or disagrees.

dissipate (dis' ə pāt') v. To break up and scatter; dispel, disperse.

dissipated (dis' ə pāt' id) adj. Characterized by, or showing the harmful effects of, over-indulgence in pleasure, especially drinking, gambling, etc., to the point of harming oneself.—**dissipation** n.

dissolute (dis' ə lo͞ot') adj. Immoral; indulging in pleasure to the point of harming oneself.

dissolution (dis' ə lo͞o' shən) n. Decomposition into fragments or parts; disintegration.

distaff (dis' taf) n. A staff on which flax or wool is wound for spinning.

distension (dis ten' shən) n. A swelling, expansion.

divertisement (də vur' tiz mənt) n. Diversion, amusement, or recreation.

divine (də vīn') v. To guess, conjecture.

dogmatically (dôg mat' i k'l ē) adv. In a positive or arrogant manner.

doleful (dōl' fəl) adj. Full of or causing sorrow or sadness.

domiciliate (däm 'ə sil' ē āt') v. To establish in a home or residence.

dominion (də min' yən) n. 1. Power to rule; sovereign authority. 2. (D-) Formerly, any of certain self-governing member nations of the British Commonwealth of Nations.

dower (dou' ər) n. A natural gift or endowment.

dowry (dou' rē) n. The property that a woman brings to her husband at marriage.

draught (draft) n. The amount taken at one drink.

dudgeon (duj' ən) n. Anger or resentment.

dulcet (dul' sit) adj. [Archaic] Sweet to taste or smell.

dustman (dust' mən) n. [Brit.] A man whose work is removing rubbish, ashes, garbage, etc.

E

ecclesiast (i klē' zē ast) n. [Archaic] A priest or clergyman.

ecclesiastical (i klē' zē as' ti k'l) adj. Of the church.

eddy (ed' ē) n. A current of air or water moving against the main current; a little whirlpool. v. To move with a circular motion against the current.

edification (ed' ə fi kā' shən) n. Instruction, enlightenment.

efface (i fās') v. To erase.

effectually (ə fek' cho͞o wə lē) adv. With the desired effect; completely, effectively.—**effectual** adj.

effigy (ef' ə jē) n. A portrait, statue, or the like, especially of a person.

egalitarian (i gal' ə ter' ē ən) adj. Of the belief that all people should have equal political, social, and economic rights.

eglantine (eg' lən tīn') n. A European rose.

egregious (i grē' jəs) adj. Remarkably bad; outstanding for undesirable qualities.

ejaculation (i jak' yə lā' shən) n. A sudden vehement utterance; exclamation.

elegiac (el' ə jī' ək) adj. Of a poem or song of mourning or in a mournfully contemplative tone.

elocutionary (el' ə kyo͞o' shən ər ē) adj. Of the art of public speaking.—**elocution** n.

elusive (i lo͞o' siv) adj. Tending to escape notice or understanding.

embower (im bou' ər) v. To enclose or shelter in or as in a bower or arbor.

eminent (em' ə nənt) adj. Distinguished, renowned.

emplacement (im plās' mənt) n. The position in which something is placed.

emulate (em' yə lāt') v. To imitate or copy.—**emulation** n.

encroach (in krōch') v. To advance beyond the proper or customary limits.

encumber (in kum' bər) v. To burden, hinder, hamper.

endemic (en dem' ik) adj. Native to a country or region.

enigma (ə nig' mə) n. A perplexing, baffling, or seemingly inexplicable matter or person; puzzle.

enjoin (in join') v. To urge or impose with authority; order.

entail (in tāl') v. To cause or require as a necessary consequence.

entreat (en trēt') v. To beg, plead, or urge earnestly.

entreaty (in trēt' ē) n. An earnest request.

epicure (ep' i kyo͞or') n. A person who enjoys and has a discriminating taste for fine foods and drinks.

epitomize (i pit' ə mīz) v. To make or be representative of the quality of a whole class.

equably (ek' wə blē) adv. Steadily, uniformly, equally.

equanimity (ek' wə nim' ə tē) n. The quality of remaining calm and undisturbed.

equinoctial (ē' kwə näk' shəl) adj. Relating to either of the equinoxes; that is, the time when the sun crosses the equator making day and night of equal length.

equivocal (i kwiv' ə k'l) adj. Uncertain, undecided, doubtful.

erudite (er' yo͞o dīt) adj. Learned, scholarly.

estheticism (es thet' ə siz'm) n. The artificial cultivation of artistic sensitivity.

ethereal (i thir' ē əl) adj. Heavenly.

etymology (et' ə mäl' ə jē) n. The origin and development of a word.

fat, āpe, cär; ten, ēven; is, bīte; gō, hôrn, to͞ol, look; oil, out; up, fur; get; joy; yet; chin; she; thin, then; zh, leisure; η, ring; ə for a in ago, e in agent, i in sanity, o in comply, u in focus; ' as in able (ā'b'l)

GLOSSARY 971

euphemism (yōō′ fə miz′m) *n.* A word or phrase that is less expressive or direct but considered less offensive or distasteful.

evanescent (ev′ ə nes′ ′nt) *adj.* Tending to fade from sight; vanishing.

evangelical (ē′ van jel′ i k′l) *adj.* Concerning a preaching of, or zealous effort to spread, the gospel, as in revival meetings.

evensong (ē′ vən sôŋ′) *n.* An evening prayer.

evocative (i väk′ ə tiv) *adj.* Tending to draw forth or elicit (a particular image, reaction, etc.).

exaltation (eg′ zəl tā′ shən) *n.* A feeling of great joy, pride, or power.

excoriate (ik skôr′ ē āt′) *v.* To strip, scratch, or rub off the skin of; whip, scrape, chafe.

exemplary (ig zem′ plə rē) *adj.* Serving as a model or example.

exhortation (eg′ zôr tā′ shən) *n.* A plea that urges strongly.

exigence (ek′ sə jəns) *n.* A situation calling for immediate attention or action.

expansively (ik span′ siv lē) *adv.* Freely, generously, openly, sympathetically.

expediency (ik spē′ dē ən sē) *n.* The doing of what is of selfish use or advantage rather than of what is right or just; self-interest.

expedient (ik spē′ dē ənt) *n.* A means to an end.

expiate (ek′ spē āt′) *v.* To make amends or reparation for (wrongdoing or guilt); atone for.

expostulate (ik späs′ chə lāt′) *v.* To reason with a person earnestly, objecting to his actions or intentions.

extant (ek′ stənt) *adj.* Still existing.

extort (ik stôrt′) *v.* To get from someone by violence or threats; exact or wrest from.

exult (ig zult′) *v.* To rejoice greatly.

F

facetious (fə sē′ shəs) *adj.* Joking or trying to be funny.

facile (fas′ ′l) *adj.* **1.** [Now Rare] Easy to influence or persuade. **2.** Acting or working in a quick, smooth way; fluent.

fain (fān) *adv.* [Archaic] Gladly, with eagerness.

fallow (fal′ ō) *adj.* Left unplanted or uncultivated.

farrow (far′ ō) *v.* To give birth (to a litter of pigs).

farthing (fär′ thiŋ) *n.* A former small British coin, equal to one fourth of a penny.

fastidious (fas tid′ ē as) *adj.* Very critical or discriminating.

fatalistic (fa′ t′l is′ tik) *adj.* Characterized by the belief that all events are determined by fate and are hence inevitable.—**fatalism** *n.*

fatuously (fach′ ᴏᴏ wəs lē) *adv.* Foolishly.

felicitous (fə lis′ ə təs) *adj.* Used or expressed in a way suitable to the occasion; appropriate.

felicity (fə lis′ ə tē) *n.* Happiness; bliss.

feral (fir′ əl) *adj.* Savage.

festal (fes′ t′l) *adj.* Festive; of a joyous celebration.

fetter (fet′ ər) *v.* To bind, shackle, or chain.

fidelity (fə del′ ə tē) *n.* Faithfulness.

filial (fil′ ē əl) *adj.* Of, suitable to, or due from a son or daughter.

firmament (fur′ mə mənt) *n.* The sky.

fissure (fish′ ər) *n.* A long, narrow, deep crack.

fisticuffs (fis′ ti kufs′) *n.* A fist fight.

fixation (fik sā′ shən) *n.* An exaggerated preoccupation; obsession.

florid (flôr′ id) *adj.* Flushed red or pink; rosy or ruddy: said of the complexion.

flout (flout) *v.* To mock or show scorn for.

foppish (fäp′ ish) *adj.* Affected.

forbear (fôr ber′) *v.* To refrain from doing.

forebitt (fôr′ bit) *n.* One of the timbers at the foremast around which cables or lines may be secured.

forebrace (fôr′ brās) *n.* A rope by which a rod is swung and secured on a forward sail of a square-rigged ship.

forsooth (fər sōōth′) *adv.* In truth; indeed; no doubt.

franchise (fran′ chīz) *n.* The right to vote; suffrage.

fraught (frôt) *adj.* Filled, charged, or loaded.

fumitory (fyōō′ mə tor′ ē) *n.* A medicinal plant.

furrow (fur′ ō) *n.* **1.** A narrow groove made in ground by a plow. **2.** Anything resembling such a groove.

G

gable (gā′ b′l) *v.* To make or have gables, which are triangular walls enclosed by sloping roof sections.

gall (gôl) *v.* To injure or make sore by rubbing.

gambol (gam′ b′l) *n.* A jumping and skipping about in play.

gamesome (gām′ səm) *adj.* Playful.

garner (gär′ nər) *n.* A place for storing grain; granary.

gauntlet (gônt′ lit) *n.* A glove.

gelding (gel′ diŋ) *n.* A castrated animal, especially a castrated male horse.

gibbet (jib′ it) *n.* A gallows.

gimlet (gim′ lit) *n.* A small boring tool.

glean (glēn) *v.* To collect or find out gradually or bit by bit.

gleaner (glēn′ ər) *n.* One who collects the remaining grain, etc. from a harvested field.

gregarious (grə ger′ ē əs) *adj.* Fond of the company of others; sociable.

gridiron (grid′ ī′ ərn) *n.* A grill.

guile (gīl) *n.* Cunning in dealing with others; craftiness.

guttersnipe (gut′ ər snīp′) *n.* A slum child who spends most of the time in the streets: contemptuous term applied to anyone having the manners, morals, etc. of the gutter.

guttural (gut′ ər əl) *adj.* Characterized by harsh sounds produced in the throat. *n.* A sound produced in the throat.

gyroscope (jī′ rə skōp′) *n.* A wheel mounted in a ring so that its axis is free to turn in any direction.

H

habitation (hab′ ə tā′ shən) *n.* **1.** A place in which to live; a dwelling, home. **2.** The act of inhabiting; occupancy.

habituate (hə bich′ ᴏᴏ wāt′) *v.* To make used (to); accustom, familiarize.

haft (haft) *n.* A handle or hilt.

hallow (hal′ ō) *v.* To make holy or sacred.

hapless (hap′ lis) *adj.* Unfortunate, unlucky.

haply (hap' lē) *adv.* [Archaic] By chance; perhaps.

hearken (här' kən) *v.* To give careful attention; listen carefully.

heathen (hē' thən) *adj.* Pagan or irreligious.

hedonistic (hēd' 'n is' tik) *adj.* Characterized by the belief that pleasure is the principal good and the proper aim of action.

hegemony (hi jem' ə nē) *n.* Leadership or dominance, especially that of one state or nation over others.

hellebore (hel' ə bôr') *n.* A medicinal plant.

heretic (her' ə tik) *n.* One who holds beliefs opposed to the official or established doctrines.

hermitage (hur' mit ij) *n.* A secluded retreat.

hew (hyoo) *v.* To chop or hack with an ax, knife, etc.

hireling (hīr' liŋ) *adj.* Mercenary; like one who will follow anyone's orders for pay.

hoarfrost (hôr' frôst') *n.* White, frozen dew; white frost.

hoary (hôr' ē) *adj.* **1.** Having white or gray hair because very old. **2.** White, gray, or grayish–white.—**hoar** *n.*

hostelry (häs' t'l rē) *n.* A lodging place; inn, hotel.

hyperbolical (hī' pər bäl' i kal) *adj.* Exaggerated.

I

idiosyncratic (id' ē ə sin krat' ik) *adj.* Having personal peculiarities or mannerisms.

idyllic (ī dil' ik) *adj.* Pleasing and simple; rural or picturesque.

ignominious (ig' nə min' ē əs) *adj.* Degrading, humiliating.

illumine (i loo' min) *v.* To light up.

imbrue (im broo') *v.* To soak, stain, or saturate.

imbue (im byoo') *v.* To permeate or inspire.

immutable (i myoo' ə b'l) *adj.* Never changing or varying; unchangeable.

imparadise (im par' ə dīs) *v.* To make as happy as though in paradise; enrapture.

impassible (im pas' ə b'l) *adj.* Unfeeling.

impassive (im pas' iv) *adj.* Not feeling or showing emotion.

impediment (im ped' ə mənt) *n.* Anything that obstructs or hinders progress.

impenetrability (im pen' i trə bil' ə tē) *n.* The condition of being unsolvable or unfathomable; inability to penetrate or pass through.

imperialism (im pir' ē əl iz'm) *n.* The policy and practice of forming and maintaining an empire in seeking to control raw materials and world markets by the conquest of other countries, the establishment of colonies, etc.

impertinent (im pur' t'n ənt) *adj.* **1.** Not showing proper respect; overstepping the bounds of propriety. **2.** Irrelevant; inappropriate.

impetuous (im pech' oo wəs) *adj.* Acting or doing suddenly with little thought; rash, impulsive.

impiety (im pī' ə tē) *n.* **1.** A lack of reverence for God. **2.** A disrespectful act or remark.

implacable (im plak' ə b'l) *adj.* That cannot be appeased or pacified.

implicit (im plis' it) *adj.* Without reservation or doubt; unquestioning, absolute.

importune (im' pôr toon') *v.* **1.** [Obsolete] To annoy. **2.** To trouble with requests or demands; urge or beg persistently or repeatedly.

imposture (im päs' chər) *n.* The act or practice of an impostor; fraud, deception.

imprecation (im' prə kā' shən) *n.* A curse.

impressment (im pres' mənt) *n.* The practice or act of drafting men or property into public service.

impudence (im' pyoo dəns) *n.* Shamelessly bold or disrespectful behavior.—**impudent** *adj.*

impute (im pyoot') *v.* To attribute to another.

incantation (in' kan tā' shən) *n.* The chanting of magical words or formulas that are supposed to cast a spell or perform other magic.

incarnation (in' kär nā' shən) *n.* Any person or thing serving as the type or embodiment of a quality or concept.

incendiary (in sen' dē er' ē) *adj.* Causing or designed to cause fires. *n.* A person who willfully destroys property by fire.

incertitude (in sur' tə tood') *n.* An uncertain state of mind; doubt.

incessantly (in ses' 'nt lē) *adv.* Endlessly, constantly.

incisive (in sī' siv) *adj.* Sharp, penetrating.

inclemency (in klem' ən sē) *n.* Roughness, severeness.

incorrigible (in kôr' i jə b'l) *adj.* That cannot be corrected, improved, or reformed.

incredulous (in krej' oo ləs) *adj.* Showing doubt or disbelief.—**incredulously** *adv.* **incredulity** *n.*

inculcate (in kul' kāt) *v.* To impress upon the mind by frequent repetition or persistent urging.

incumbrance (in kum' brəns) *n.* A burden, hindrance, or obstruction.

indocility (in' dä sil' ə tē) *n.* The condition of being not easy to teach or discipline.

indolence (in' də ləns) *n.* Idleness.

indomitable (in däm' it ə b'l) *adj.* Not easily discouraged or defeated.

inebriated (in ē' brē āt' id) *adj.* Drunk.

ineffable (in ef' ə b'l) *adj.* Too overwhelming to be described in words; inexpressible.

inexorable (in ek' sər ə b'l) *adj.* That cannot be altered or checked.

infidelity (in' fə del' ə tē) *n.* Unfaithfulness or disloyalty to another.

infraction (in frak' shən) *n.* A breaking of a law, pact, or rule; violation.

infrastructure (in' frə struk' chər) *n.* An underlying foundation, especially the basic facilities and installations on which the continuance of a community depend.

ingenuous (in jen' yoo wəs) *adj.* Frank, open, candid.

iniquity (in ik' wə tē) *n.* Wickedness

inscrutable (in skroot' ə b'l) *adj.* That cannot be easily understood; completely obscure or mysterious.

---

fat, āpe, cär; ten, ēven; is, bīte; gō, hôrn, tool, look; oil, out; up, fur; get; joy; yet; chin; she; thin, then; zh, leisure; ŋ, ring; ə for a in ago, e in agent, i in sanity, o in comply, u in focus; ' as in able (ā'b'l)

insensibility (in sen′ sə bil′ i tē) *n.* **1.** [Obsolete] Sense-lessness, stupidity. **2.** Unawareness, indifference; lack of emotional response.

insensible (in sen′ sə b′l) *adj.* Unconscious.

insensibly (in sen′ sə blē) *adv.* So gradually as to be virtually imperceptible.

insidious (in sid′ ē əs) *adj.* Characterized by treachery or slyness; crafty, wily.

intelligentsia (in tel′ ə jent′ sē ə) *n.* The educated and enlightened class; intellectuals collectively.

intenerate (in ten′ ə rāt′) *v.* [Rare] To make tender or soft.

inter (in tʉr′) *v.* To bury.

interfuse (in′ tər fyōōz′) *v.* To combine by mixing, blending, or fusing together.

intermit (in′ tər mit′) *v.* To stop for a time.

interpenetration (in′ tər pen′ ə trā′ shən) *n.* The act of permeating, penetrating, or spreading through.

interpolation (in tʉr′ pə lā′ shən) *n.* An alteration or insertion, as in a book or manuscript.

interpose (in′ tər pōz′) *v.* To intervene or mediate.

intimation (in′ tə mā′ shən) *n.* A hint or indirect suggestion.

intractable (in trak′ tə b′l) *adj.* Hard to manage.

invective (in vek′ tiv) *n.* A violent verbal attack.

inviolably (in vī′ ə lə blē) *adv.* In a way that cannot be violated or destroyed.

invoke (in vōk′) *v.* **1.** To call on for blessing, help, inspiration, or support. **2.** To beg for or ask solemnly for.—**invocation** *n.*

irksome (ʉrk′ səm) *adj.* Tiresome or annoying.

irrevocable (i rev′ ə kə b′l) *adj.* That cannot be revoked, recalled, or undone.

itinerant (ī tin′ ər ənt) *adj.* Traveling from place to place or on a circuit.

J

jade (jād) *n.* A horse, especially a worn-out, worthless one.

jingoism (jiŋ′ gō izm) *n.* Patriotism that favors an aggressive, warlike foreign policy.

jocund (jäk′ ənd) *adj.* Cheerful, genial, gay.

jow (jou) *n.* [Archaic] A stroke, toll, or ring.

joyance (joi′ əns) *n.* [Archaic] Joy, rejoicing.

K

keen (kēn) *v.* To wail, cry.

ken (ken) *n.* **1.** [Rare] Range of vision. **2.** Mental perception; range of understanding.

ketch (kech) *n.* A small sailboat.

kindred (kin′ drid) *adj.* Of like nature; similar.

kith (kith) *n.* Friends, acquaintances.

knavery (nāv′ ərē) *n.* Behavior characteristic of a rogue; rascality; dishonesty.

knavish (nāv′ ish) *adj.* Dishonest, tricky.

knell (nel) *v.* [Obsolete] To ring or toll (a bell).

knotty (nät′ ē) *adj.* Covered with knots or knotlike bunches.

L

labyrinth (lab′ ə rinth′) *n.* A structure containing an intricate network of winding passages hard to follow without losing one's way; maze.

lacerate (las′ ə rāt′) *v.* To wound or hurt (one's feelings, etc.) deeply.

laconic (lə kän′ ik) *adj.* Brief or terse.

lament (lə ment′) *n.* An outward expression of sorrow, especially a weeping or wailing.—**lamentation** *n.* **lamentably** *adv.*

lamentably (lam′ ən tə blē) *adv.* Unfortunately, grievously; in a distressing way.

lampoon (lam pōōn′) *v.* To attack or ridicule by means of a piece of strongly satirical writing.

languid (laŋ′ gwid) *adj.* Without interest, vigor, or spirit; weak, sluggish.—**languidly** *adv.*

languish (laŋ′ gwish) *v.* **1.** To be in a state of lessened strength or vitality because of outward circumstances. **2.** To suffer with longing; pine. **3.** To put on an air of sentimental tenderness or wistful melancholy.—**languishment** *n.*

languor (laŋ′ gər) *n.* Lack of interest or spirit; feeling of listlessness; indifference.

laryngoscope (lə riŋ′ gə skōp′) *n.* An instrument for examining the interior of the larynx.

latent (lāt′ 'nt) *adj.* Present but invisible or inactive; lying hidden and undeveloped.

lavish (lav′ ish) *adj.* Very generous, extravagant.

lawn (lôn) *n.* A fine sheer cloth of linen or cotton.

lay (lā) *n.* **1.** [Archaic] A song or melody. **2.** A short poem.

lea (lē) *n.* A meadow or grassy field.

lees (lēz) *n.* Dregs or sediment, as of wine.

lethargy (leth′ ər jē) *n.* A great lack of energy; sluggishness, dullness, apathy.

lexicographer (lek′ sə käg′ rə fər) *n.* A person who writes or compiles a dictionary.

lexicon (lek′ si kən) *n.* The total stock of words and other linguistic forms in a language.

liberality (lib′ ə ral′ ə tē) *n.* Generosity.

licentious (lī sen′ shəs) *adj.* Morally unrestrained.

liege (lēj) *adj.* Entitled to the service and loyalty of his or her subjects.

lin (lin) *v.* [Archaic] To stop.

lintel (lin′ t'l) *n.* The horizontal crosspiece over a door or window.

litigious (li tij′ əs) *adj.* Given to carrying on lawsuits.

livid (liv′ id) *adj.* Black-and-blue.

loath (lōth) *adj.* Unwilling, reluctant.

loathsome (lōth′ səm) *adj.* Disgusting, abhorrent, detestable.

loth (lōth) *adj. Alternate spelling of* **loath:** Unwilling, reluctant.

lugubrious (loo gōō′ brē əs) *adj.* Very sad or mournful, especially in a way that seems exaggerated or ridiculous.

luminary (lōō′ mə ner′ ē) *n.* A famous intellectual; any famous person.

M

macabre (mə käb′ rə) *adj.* Gruesome, grim, and horrible; ghastly.

madrigal (mad′ ri gəl) *n.* A type of song with parts for several voices singing without accompaniment common in the fifteenth, sixteenth, and seventeenth centuries.

magisterially (maj′ is tir′ ē əl ē) *adv.* Authoritatively, pompously.

malevolently (mə lev′ ə lənt lē) *adv.* Having or showing ill will.

manifest (man′ ə fest′) *adj.* Evident, obvious, clear.

manifestation (man′ ə fes tā′ shən) *n.* An appearance to the senses; something shown.

manifesto (man′ ə fes′ tō) *n.* A public declaration of motives and intentions.

manna (man′ ə) *n.* In the Bible, food miraculously provided for the Israelites in the wilderness.

marshal (mär′ shəl) *v.* To manage, direct, guide.

matins (mat′ ′nz) *n.* A morning prayer or morning song.

maverick (mav′ ər ik) *n.* [Colloquial] A person who takes an independent stand.

mawkish (mô′ kish) *adj.* Sentimental in a weak, insipid way, so as to be sickening.

maxim (mak′ sim) *n.* A principle or rule of conduct; a statement of general truth.

maze (māz) *v.* To confuse, bewilder.

mead (mēd) *n. poetic variant of* **meadow.**

mélange (mā länzh′) *n.* A mixture.

menace (men′ is) *v.* To threaten or be a danger to.— **menacingly** *adv.*

menagerie (mə naj′ ər ē) *n.* A collection of wild or strange animals kept in cages or enclosures for exhibition.

mendacity (men das′ ə tē) *n.* The state or quality of being not truthful.

mercenary (mur′ sə ner′ ē) *n.* A person who will do anything for money.

mesmerism (mez′ mər iz′m) *n.* Hypnotic or irresistible attraction; fascination.

mettle (met′ ′l) *n.* Quality of character; spirit—**on one's mettle** Prepared to do one's best.

mezzotint (mez′ ō tint′) *n.* A copper or steel engraving.

millenium (mi len′ ē əm) *n.* **1.** In theology, the period of one thousand years during which Christ will reign on earth. **2.** Any period of great happiness, peace, and prosperity. **3.** Any period of one thousand years.

mire (mīr) *n.* An area of wet, soggy ground; bog.—**miry** *adj.*

mischance (mis chans′) *n.* Bad luck; misadventures.

miter (mīt′ ər) *n.* A tall cap with peaks in front and back worn by bishops, etc.

mizzen (miz′ ′n) *adj.* Of the mast closest to the stern of a ship.

modulation (mäj′ ə lā′ shən) *n.* A variation in stress or pitch in speaking.

molder (mōl′ dər) *v.* To crumble into dust; decay.

mollify (mäl′ ə fī′) *v.* To soothe the temper of; pacify.

moor (moor) *n.* A tract of open, rolling wasteland, usually covered with heather and often marshy or peaty.

mortification (môr′ tə fi kā′ shən) *n.* Shame, humiliation, loss of self-respect.—**mortify** *v.*

mottle (mät′ ′l) *v.* To mark with blotches, streaks, and spots of different shades or colors.

munificence (myoo nif′ ə səns) *n.* Generosity.

mutability (myoot′ ə bil′ ə tē) *n.* The tendency to frequent change; inconstancy.

mysticism (mis′ tə siz′m) *n.* The doctrine that it is possible to achieve communion with God through contemplation and love without the medium of human reason.

N

necromancy (nek′ rə man′ sē) *n.* Black magic, sorcery; communicating with the dead.

nexus (nek′ səs) *n.* A connection, tie, or link between individuals of a group.

nigh (nī) *adv.* Near.

nihilism (nī′ ə liz′m) *n.* In politics, the doctrine that existing social, political, and economic institutions must be completely destroyed in order to make way for new institutions.

nunnery (nun′ ər ē) *n.* A convent.

O

obdurate (äb′ door ət) *adj.* Not giving in readily; stubborn.

obliterate (ə blit′ ə rāt′) *v.* To blot out, erase, destroy.

obstinate (äb′ stə nit) *adj.* Stubborn.

odious (ō′ dē əs) *adj.* Disgusting, offensive.

odoriferous (ō′ də rif′ ər əs) *adj.* Giving off an odor, often specifically a fragrant one.

officious (ə fish′ əs) *adj.* Offering unnecessary and unwanted advice or services.

oleaginous (ō′ lē aj′ i nəs) *adj.* Oily, greasy.

oligarchy (äl′ ə gär′ kē) *n.* A form of government in which the ruling power belongs to a few persons.

omnivorous (äm niv′ ər əs) *adj.* Taking in everything indiscriminately, as with the intellect.

operative (äp′ ər rā tiv) *n.* A worker, especially one skilled in industrial work.

opulent (äp′ yə lənt) *adj.* Characterized by abundance or profusion.

oracle (ôr′ ə k′l) *n.* Among the ancient Greeks and Romans, the place where, or medium by which, deities were consulted.

orifice (ôr′ ə fis) *n.* An opening, mouth.

orthodoxy (ôr′ thə däk′ sē) *n.* The beliefs or established doctrines.

ossify (äs′ ə fī′) *v.* To change or develop into bone; to settle rigidly into a practice.

ostensibly (äs ten′ sə blē) *adv.* Apparently, seemingly.

ostentatious (äs′ tən tā′ shəs) *adj.* Showy and pretentious. —**ostentatiously** *adv.*

overcloy (ō′ vər kloi) *v.* To overindulge, or make weary and displeased by too much of something.

overture (ō′ vər chər) *n.* Introductory proposal or offer.

P

pacificatory (pə sif′ ə kə tôr′ ē) *adj.* Calming or tranquilizing.

pall (pôl) *n.* A cover for a coffin.

palpitate (pal′ pə tāt′) *v.* To beat rapidly or flutter.

paltry (pôl′ trē) *adj.* Contemptible, petty.

panacea (pan′ ə sē′ ə) *n.* A cure-all or supposed remedy.

pantheistic (pan′ thē is′ tik) *adj.* Of the doctrine that God is not a personality, but that all laws, forces, and images of the self-existing universe are God.

---

fat, āpe, cär; ten, ēven; is, bīte; gō, hôrn, tool, look; oil, out; up, fur; get; joy; yet; chin; she; thin, then; zh, leisure; ŋ, ring; ə for *a* in *ago, e* in *agent, i* in *sanity, o* in *comply, u* in *focus;* ′ as in *able* (ā′b′l)

papist (pā' pist) *n*. A Roman Catholic.

paradigm (par' ə dim) *n*. A pattern, example, or model.

paramour (par' ə moor') *n*. A sweetheart, lover.

parry (par' ē) *v*. To turn aside as by a clever or evasive reply.

parsimony (pär' sə mō' nē) *n*. A tendency to be over-careful in spending.

partake (pär tāk') *v*. [Rare] To have or take a share in.

pastoral (pas' tər əl) *adj*. Characteristic of rural life, idealized as peaceful, simple, and natural.

patent (pat' 'nt) *adj*. Open to examination by the public.

pathos (pā' thäs) *n*. The quality in something which arouses feelings of pity, sorrow, sympathy, or compassion.

patriarch (pā' trē ärk') *n*. A man of great age and dignity.

pauperize (pô' pə rīz) *v*. To make a poor person of.

pavilion (pə vil' yən) *v*. To shelter as in a tent or building.

pedantic (pi dan' tik) *adj*. Laying stress on minor or trivial points of learning or displaying a scholarship lacking in judgment.—**pedant** *n*.

penury (pen' yə rē) *n*. Lack of money, property, or necessities; extreme poverty.

perambulator (pər am' byoo lāt' ər) *n*. A baby carriage.

per annum (pər an' əm) [Latin] By the year; annually.

perdition (pər dish' ən) *n*. Hell, damnation.

peremptorily (pə remp' tər i lē) *adv*. Imperiously, dictatorially.

perforce (pər fôrs') *adv*. By or through necessity.

perfunctory (pər funk' tər ē) *adj*. Done without care or interest or merely as a form or routine.—**perfunctorily** *adv*.

pernicious (pər nish' əs) *adj*. Causing great injury, destruction, or ruin.

perpetuate (pər pech' oo wāt') *v*. To cause to continue or be remembered.

persona (pər sō' nə) *n*. The personality or façade presented to others.

perturbation (pur' tər bā' shən) *n*. Disturbance, alarm, agitation.

pestiferous (pes tif' ər əs) *adj*. Dangerous to the welfare of society; evil.

pestilence (pes' t'l əns) *n*. An epidemic, plague, or infectious disease.

petulance (pech' oo ləns) *n*. Irritability, especially over a petty annoyance.

Pharisaic (far' ə sā' ik) *adj*. Self-righteous; emphasizing the letter but not the spirit of religious law.

philistinism (fil' is tēn iz'm) *n*. Smug conventionality; indifference to culture or aesthetic values.

phonetician (fō' nə tish' ən) *n*. An expert in phonetics, the system of sounds of a language.

phosphorescent (fäs' fə res' 'nt) *adj*. Giving off a lingering emission of light.—**phosphorescence** *n*.

physic (fiz' ik) *n*. A medicine or remedy.

piety (pī' ə tē) *n*. Devotion to religious duties.

pilgrimage (pil' grəm ij) *n*. A journey, especially to a shrine or holy place.

pinion (pin' yən) *v*. To confine or shackle.

pinnacle (pin' ə k'l) *n*. A small turret or spire.

pique (pēk) *v*. To excite, arouse, provoke.

plaint (plānt) *n*. A complaint or grievance.

platonic (plə tän' ik) *adj*. Of a relationship between a man and a woman that is purely spiritual or intellectual and without sexual activity.

plight (plīt) *v*. To pledge or promise.

plover (pluv' ər) *n*. Any of a number of related wading or shore birds.

plunder (plun' dər) *v*. To rob.

ply (plī) *v*. **1.** To do work with; use. **2.** To keep busy or work (at something).

poach (pōch) *v*. To hunt on another's territory; steal.

polemic (pə lem' ik) *n*. An argument or controversial discussion.

poltroon (päl troon') *n*. A coward.

ponderous (pän' dər əs) *adj*. Very heavy.

portico (pôr' tə kō') *n*. A porch or covered walk.

portmanteau (pôrt man' tō) *n*. A suitcase that opens like a book into two compartments.

poser (pō' zər) *n*. A baffling question or problem.

postern (pōs' tərn) *n*. A private entrance at the side or rear.

posthumously (päs' choo məs lē) *adv*. **1.** After the author's death. **2.** In continuation after death.—**posthumous** *adj*.

posture (päs' chər) *v*. To pose, assume an attitude merely for effect.

potable (pōt' ə b'l) *adj*. Fit to drink; drinkable.

prattle (prat' 'l) *n*. Idle chatter.

precept (prē' sept) *n*. A rule of moral conduct.

precipice (pres' ə pis) *n*. A steep cliff.

precipitately (pri sip' ə tāt lē) *adv*. Very suddenly, unexpectedly, or abruptly.

predestination (prē des' tə na' shən) *n*. The doctrine that God predetermined everything that would happen; fate.

preeminence (prē em' ə nəns) *n*. The quality of surpassing or excelling others.—**preeminent** *adj*.

prelate (prel' it) *n*. A high-ranking clergyman, as a bishop.

premonitory (pri män' ə tôr' ē) *adj*. Warning in advance.

presumptuous (pri zump' choo wəs) *adj*. Showing overconfidence.

prevarication (pri var' ə kā' shən) *n*. A lie or evasion of the truth.

primeval (prī mē' v'l) *adj*. Of the earliest of times or ages.

prithee (prith' ē) *interj*. [Archaic] I pray thee.

privation (prī vā' shən) *n*. Lack of the ordinary necessities or comforts of life; want.

privily (priv' i lē) *adv*. [Archaic] Secretly, furtively.

prodigious (prə dij' əs) *adj*. Enormous, huge.

proffer (präf' ər) *v*. To offer.

profiteer (präf' ə tir') *n*. A person who makes excessive profits, especially by taking advantage of a shortage of supply to charge exorbitant prices. *v*. To be a profiteer.

profligate (präf' lə git) *adj*. Extremely wasteful.

progeny (präj' ə nē) *n*. Children, descendants, or offspring.

prologue (prō' lôg) *n*. An introduction.

promontory (präm' ən tôr' ē) *n*. A peak of high land that juts out over water.

propagate (präp' ə gāt') *v*. To spread from one person or place to another.

propagation (präp' ə gā' shən) *n*. Reproduction or multiplication, as of a plant or animal.

prophetic (prə fet′ ik) *adj.* Characterized by the ability to predict the future.

propound (prə pound′) *v.* To put forward for consideration; propose.

proprietary (prə prī′ ə ter′ ē) *adj.* Held under patent, trademark, or copyright by a private person or company.

prosaic (prō zā′ ik) *adj.* Matter-of-fact, commonplace, dull, and ordinary.

proselytize (präs′ ə li tīz′) *v.* To persuade to do or join something.

prostrate (präs′ trāt) *adj.* Lying face down in demonstration of great humility or abject submission.

prototypical (prō′ tə tip′ i k′l) *adj.* Characteristic of a person or thing that serves as a model or perfect example.

protract (prō trakt′) *v.* To draw out; lengthen in duration.

provinciality (prō vin′ shē al′ ə tē) *n.* Narrowness of outlook.

pugnacious (pug nā′ shəs) *adj.* Eager and ready to fight.— **pugnacity** *n.*

punctilious (puŋk til′ ē as) *adj.* Very careful about every detail of behavior, ceremony, etc.

punitive (pyoo′ nə tiv) *adj.* Inflicting punishment.

purge (pʉrj) *v.* To cleanse or rid of undesirable elements.

Q

quail (kwāl) *v.* To draw back in fear; lose heart or courage.

quell (kwel) *v.* To subdue.

querulous (kwer′ ə ləs) *adj.* Complaining, peevish.

quiescent (kwī es′ ′nt) *adj.* Quiet, still, inactive.

quintessential (kwin′ tə sen′ shəl) *adj.* Pure; perfect in manifesting a quality or thing.—**quintessentially** *adv.* **quintessence** *n.*

quire (kwīr) *n. Archaic variant of* **choir:** A part of a church.

quitclaim (kwit′ klām′) *v.* To give up claim or title to.

quoth (kwōth) *v.* [Archaic] Said.

R

rail (rāl) *v.* **1.** To speak bitterly or reproachfully; complain violently. **2.** To scoff or ridicule.—**raillery** *n.*

raiment (rā′ mənt) *n.* [Archaic or Poetic] Clothing.

rake (rāk) *n.* An immoral or depraved man.—**rakish** *adj.*

rapacious (rə pā′ shəs) *adj.* Greedy or grasping.

ratiocination (rash′ ē ō′ sə nā′ shən) *n.* The act or process of reasoning, especially using formal logic.

ravenous (rav′ ə nəs) *adj.* Greedily or wildly hungry.

ravish (rav′ ish) *v.* To violate.

ravishing (rav′ ish iŋ) *adj.* Causing great joy or delight; entrancing.

reactionary (rē ak′ shə ner′ ē) *n.* A person who advocates return to a former condition; extremely conservative person.

reanimation (rē an′ i mā′ shən) *n.* To give new life, power, etc., to.

rebuff (ri buf′) *n.* A blunt refusal; any check or repulse.

rebuke (ri byook′) *n.* A sharp reprimand. *v.* To blame, scold, or reprimand.

recapitulate (rē′ kə pich′ ə lāt′) *v.* To summarize, repeat briefly.

reciprocal (ri sip′ rə k′l) *adj.* Present or existing on both sides; mutual.

recoil (ri koil′) *v.* To start or shrink back.

recompense (rek′ əm pens′) *n.* Something given or done in return for something else; repayment or reward.

redress (ri dres′) *v.* To set right, rectify.

refractory (ri frak′ tər ē) *adj.* Hard to manage; stubborn.

regicide (rej′ ə sīd′) *n.* A person who kills, or is responsible for the killing of, a king.

remonstrate (ri män′ strāt) *v.* To protest, object.— **remonstrance** *n.*

rend (rend) *v.* To tear or rip.

reparation (rep′ ə rā′ shən) *n.* Anything paid or done to make up for something else.

repartee (rep′ ər tē) *n.* A quick, witty reply or a series of such rejoinders.

repast (ri past′) *n.* A meal.

repine (ri pīn′) *v.* To feel or express unhappiness or discontent; complain.

replenish (ri plen′ ish) *v.* To fill or make complete again.

repletion (ri plē′ shan) *n.* The state of having eaten or drunk to excess.—**replete** *adj.*

reprisal (ri prī′ z′l) *n.* Injury done in return for injury received; retaliation.

reproach (ri prōch′) *n.* Blame, shame, disgrace.

reprobate (rep′ rə bāt′) *v.* To disapprove of strongly; condemn.

reproof (ri proof′) *n.* Rebuke, censure; the act of expressing disapproval.

reprove (ri proov′) *v.* To rebuke; express disapproval.

respite (res′ pit) *n.* A postponement or delay.

retributory (ri trib′ yoo tôr ē) *adj.* Of or for punishing evil done.

reverie (rev′ ər ē) *n.* A daydream.

revile (ri vīl′) *v.* To use abusive or contemptuous language in speaking to or about.

rhapsodist (rap′ sə dist) *n.* A person who speaks or writes in an extravagantly enthusiastic manner.

rhapsody (rap′ sə dē) *n.* A part of an epic poem suitable for recitation.

rhetorician (ret′ ə rish′ ən) *n.* One who speaks effectively.

rivulet (riv′ yoo lit) *n.* A little stream, brook.

roe (rō) *n.* A type of small, agile, graceful European and Asiatic deer.

roguishly (rō′ gish lē) *adv.* Mischievously, playfully.

rook (rook) *n.* A European bird similar to the crow.

roundelay (roun′ də lā′) *n.* A simple song.

ruck (ruk) *n.* A mass or crowd.

rudiment (roo′ də mənt) *n.* A first principle, element, or fundamental, as of a subject to be learned.

rue (roo) *v.* To be sorrowful or regretful. *n.* **1.** A type of strong-scented plant with yellow flowers. **2.** [Archaic] Sorrow, regret.

ruffian (ruf′ ē ən) *n.* A brutal, violent, lawless person.

rumination (roo′ mə na′ shən) *n.* Meditation.

---

fat, āpe, cär; ten, ēven; is, bīte; gō, hôrn, tool, look; oil; out; up; fʉr; get; joy; yet; chin; she; thin, then; zh, leisure; ŋ, ring; ə for a in ago, e in agent, i in sanity, o in comply, u in focus; ′ as in able (ā′b′l)

sacrosanct (sak' rō saŋkt') *adj.* Very sacred or holy.

salutary (sal' yoo ter' ē) *adj.* Beneficial.

sanctitude (saŋk' tə tood) *n.* Saintliness, holiness, sacredness.

sanguine (saŋ' gwin) *adj.* **1.** Reddish in complexion. **2.** Cheerful and confident.

sardonically (sär dän' i k'l ē) *adv.* Disdainfully, ironically, sarcastically, sneeringly.

satiety (sə tī' ə tē) *n.* The state of being satisfied.

savour (sā' vər) *n.* A particular smell, taste, or characteristic quality.

scabbard (skab' ərd) *n.* A sheath to hold the blade of a sword.

scourge (skʉrj) *n.* Any cause of serious trouble or affliction.

scrabblings (skrab' 'liŋz) *n.* Scrapings; things scratched together.

scrofula (skräf' yə lə) *n.* Tuberculosis of the lymphatic glands, especially of the neck, characterized by the enlargement of the glands.

scruple (skroo' p'l) *v.* To hesitate from doubt or uneasiness; be unwilling because of one's conscience. *n.* A qualm, misgiving, or uneasiness about something one thinks is wrong.

scrupulosity (skroo' pyə läs' ə tē) *n.* Consciously honest or proper behavior.—**scrupulous** *adj.*

scrutinize (skroot' 'n īz') *v.* To examine closely; look at very carefully.

scud (skud) *v.* To glide or skim along easily.

scurrilous (skʉr' ə ləs) *adj.* Using abusive language.

secularism (sek' yə lər iz'm) *n.* Wordly spirit or views, especially in disregarding religious faith and worship.

seemly (sēm' lē) *adj.* **1.** Suitable, proper, becoming. **2.** Pleasing in appearance; handsome.

semblance (sem' bləns) *n.* Outward appearance.

sensibility (sen' sə bil' ə tē) *n.* **l.** The capacity to respond perceptively to intellectual, moral, or aesthetic values. **2.** The capacity for emotion or physical sensation.

sensualist (sen' shoo wəl ist) *n.* One who indulges in pleasures of the senses.

sentinel (sen' ti n'l) *n.* A person or animal set to guard something.

sepulcher (sep' 'l ker) *n.* A vault for burial; grave, tomb.

sepulchral (sə pul' krəl) *adj.* Gloomy, dismal; suggestive of the grave.

sequestered (si kwes' tərd) *adj.* Removed from others; secluded.

serpentine (sʉr' pən tēn') *adj.* Winding; coiled or twisted.

servile (sʉr' v'l) *adj.* Characteristic of a slave; humbly yielding or submissive.

shire (shīr) *n.* Any of the counties of England.

shoal (shōl) *n.* A large group, mass, crowd.

shrive (shrīv) *v.* [Archaic] To hear the confession of and, usually after penance, give absolution to.

shroud (shroud) *n.* A burial cloth.

signification (sig' nə fi kā' shən) *n.* Significance, meaning.

similitude (sə mil' ə tood') *n.* Similarity, likeness, resemblance.

simper (sim' pər) *v.* To smile in a silly, affected way.

sinew (sin' yoo) *n.* A tendon.

sire (sīr) *n.* A father.

sloth (slôth) *n.* Laziness.

slovenly (sluv' ən lē) *adj.* Careless in appearance, habits, work, etc.—**sloven** *n.*

smite (smīt) *v.* **1.** To punish or destroy; defeat. **2.** To hit or strike hard. **3.** To disturb mentally.

snivel (sniv' 'l) *v.* To cry and sniffle.

soirée (swä rā') *n.* A party or gathering in the evening.

solace (säl' is) *n.* Comfort, consolation. *v.* To comfort, console.

solicitor (sə lis' it ər) *n.* In England, a member of the legal profession who is not a barrister.

solicitous (sə lis' ə təs) *adj.* Showing care or concern.—**solicitude** *n.*

sonorous (sə nôr' əs) *adj.* Full, deep, or rich in sound; having a powerful, impressive sound.

sophistry (säf' is trē) *n.* Clever, plausible, and subtle reasoning.

sordid (sôr' did) *adj.* Base, ignoble, mean.

sovereign (säv' rən) *n.* A ruler or monarch. *adj.* Greatest or supreme; outstanding.

sovereignty (säv' rən tē) *n.* **1.** A quality of susperiority. **2.** Supreme and independent political authority.

spasmodically (spaz mäd' i k'l ē) *adv.* In a way that is like a spasm; suddenly, violently, and temporarily.

spectral (spek' trəl) *adj.* Having the nature of a phantom or ghost.

sporadically (spô rad' ik lē) *adv.* Occasionally; from time to time.

sportively (spôr' tiv lē) *adv.* Playfully.

spraddle (sprad' 'l) *v.* To spread (the legs) in a sprawling or straddling way.

spurious (spyoor' ē əs) *adj.* **1.** [Now Rare] Illegitimate. **2.** Not true or genuine; false.

squalid (skwäl' id) *adj.* Foul or unclean, especially as the result of neglect or unsanitary conditions.

squalor (skwäl' ər) *n.* Filth and wretchedness.

squander (skwän' dər) *v.* To spend or use wastefully.

stagflation (stag flā' shən) *n.* An economic condition marked by a continuing inflation together with a decline in business activity and an increase in unemployment.

stint (stint) *v.* [Archaic] To stop.

stolidly (stäl' id lē) *adv.* In a way that shows little or no emotion; impassively.

stopcock (stäp käk') *n.* A pipe valve.

straiten (strāt' 'n) *v.* To bring into difficulties; cause to be in distress or want.

stratagem (strat' ə jəm) *n.* A trick, scheme, or plan.

stricture (strik' chər) *n.* A limiting or restricting condition.

stringent (strin' jənt) *adj.* Rigidly controlled.

sublime (sə blīm') *adj.* Noble, exalted, majestic.

submission (səb mish' ən) *n.* **1.** The quality of being submissive; resignation. **2.** The act of submitting, yielding, or surrendering.

subsistence (səb sis' təns) *n.* Means of support or livelihood.

subterfuge (sub' tər fyooj') *n.* Any plan or action used to hide one's true objective.

subtile (sut' 'l) *adj. Now rare variant of* **subtle:** Capable of making fine distinctions; skillful and clever.

succulent (suk' yoo lənt) *adj.* Full of juice.

suckle (suk' 'l) *v.* To bring up; rear.

sumptuously (sump' choo wəs lē) *adv.* Magnificently or splendidly.

sundry (sun' drē) *adj.* Various.

superciliously (soo' pər sil' ē əs lē) *adv.* Disdainfully, haughtily, contemptuously.

superfluity (soo' pər floo' ə tē) *n.* Excess or superabundance.

supplication (sup' lə kā' shən) *n.* A humble request, prayer, or petition.

surfeit (sur' fit) *v.* To overindulge or be supplied to excess. *n.* Overindulgence.

surliness (sur' lē nes) *n.* Sullen rudeness, hostility.— **surlily** *adv.*

sustenance (sus' ti nəns) *n.* That which sustains life; nourishment, food.

swain (swān) *n.* **1.** [Archaic] A country youth. **2.** A lover.

swathe (swāth) *n.* A long strip, track, or belt of land.

sycophant (sik' ə fənt) *n.* A person who seeks favor by flattering people of wealth or influence.

sylvan (sil' vən) *adj.* Living, found, or carried on in the woods or forest.

T

tarry (tar' ē) *v.* To wait.

tegument (teg' yoo mənt) *n.* Hide or skin.

temperate (tem' pər it) *adj.* Moderate in indulging the appetites.

tempered (tem' pərd) *adj.* Modified by addition of or mixture with other qualities.

tenacity (tə nas' ə tē) *n.* Persistence, stubbornness.— **tenacious** *adj.*

tenor (ten' ər) *n.* General character or nature.

tenuous (ten' yoo wəs) *adj.* Not substantial; slight, flimsy.

terrestrial (tə res' trē əl) *adj.* Of this world; earthly.

timorous (tim ər əs) *adj.* Timid, fearful.

tincture (tiŋk' chər) *n.* A trace or tinge.

tithe (tīth) *n.* A tax or levy, especially one tenth of one's income paid to the church or clergy.

toady (tōd' ē) *n.* A servile or slavelike flatterer; parasite.

torrid (tôr' id) *adj.* Subjected to intense heat, especially of the sun; parched, arid.

totalitarian (tō tal' ə ter' ē ən) *adj.* Characteristic of a government in which one political party maintains complete control under a dictatorship and bans all others.

transcendent (tran sen' dənt) *adj.* Excelling, extraordinary.

transgress (trans gres') *v.* To break a law; sin.— **transgression** *n.*

transient (tran' shənt) *adj.* Not permanent; temporary.

transitory (tran' sə tôr' ē) *adj.* Of a passing nature; temporary.

transmute (trans myoot') *v.* To transform.

travail (trav' āl) *n.* Toil; very hard work.

travesty (trav' is tē) *n.* A crude, distorted, or ridiculous representation.

treachery (trech' ər ē) *n.* Treason, betrayal of trust.

treble (treb' 'l) *n.* A high-pitched voice or sound. *adj.* High-pitched or shrill.

tremulous (trem' yoo ləs) *adj.* Trembling, quivering, palpitating.

tribulation (trib' yə lā' shən) *n.* A trial or affliction.

troth (trôth) *n.* One's pledged word or promise.

truculently (truk' yoo lənt lē) *adv.* Rudely, harshly, scathingly.

turbid (tur' bid) *adj.* Thick, dense, or dark, as clouds or smoke.

turpitude (tur' pə tood') *n.* Baseness, vileness, depravity.

twain (twān) *n. Archaic variant of* **two.**

U

unabashed (un' ə bash't') *adj.* Unashamed; not embarrassed.

unassailable (un' ə sāl' ə b'l) *adj.* That cannot be successfully attacked or assaulted.

uncloistered (un klois' tər'd) *adj.* Not secluded or living in a monastery.

uncouth (un kooth') *adj.* Uncultured, crude.

undulate (un' joo lāt) *v.* To move as in waves; have a wavy surface.

unfetter (un fet' ər) *v.* To free from chains or restraint of any kind; liberate.

unflagging (un flag' iŋ) *adj.* Not losing strength or growing weak.

ungainly (un gān' lē) *adj.* Awkward, clumsy.

unrebuked (un' ri byookt') *adj.* Not reprimanded or scolded.

unrequited (un ri kwīt' id) *adj.* Not returned.

unseemly (un sēm' lē) *adv.* In a manner that is not decent or proper; improperly.

unslaked (un slāk'd') *adj.* Not lessened or satisfied.

upbraid (up brād') *v.* To rebuke or scold severely.

urbanity (ur ban' ə tē) *n.* The quality of being polite and courteous in a smooth, polished way; refinement.— **urbane** *adj.* **urbanely** *adv.*

utopian (yoo tō' pē ən) *adj.* Founded on ideas envisioning perfection in social and political organization.

V

vanquish (vaŋ' kwish) *v.* To conquer or defeat in battle.

vassal (vas' 'l) *n.* A subject, subordinate.

vaunt (vônt) *v.* To boast or brag.

venerable (ven' ər ə b'l) *adj.* Worthy of respect or reverence by reason of age and dignity, character, etc.

veneration (ven' ə rā' shən) *n.* A feeling of deep respect.

venerian (və ner' ē ən) *n.* [Archaic] One inclined to the indulgence of sexual desire.

verbiage (vur' bē ij) *n.* **1.** An excess of words beyond those needed to express concisely what is meant. **2.** Style of expression.

verge (vurj) *n.* The edge.

---

fat, āpe, cär; ten, ēven; is, bīte; gō, hôrn, tool, look; oil, out; up, fur; get; joy; yet; chin; she; thin, *th*en; zh, leisure; ŋ, ring; ə for *a* in *ago, e* in *agent, i* in *sanity, o* in *comply, u* in *focus*; ' as in *able* (ā'b'l)

verily (ver′ ə lē) *adv.* In very truth; truly.

verity (ver′ ə tē) *n.* A truth; a principle taken to be fundamentally and permanently true.

vermin (vʉr′ min) *n.* Any of various insects, bugs, or small animals regarded as objectionable because destructive or disease-carrying, as flies, lice, rats, or weasels.

vernal (vʉr′ n′l) *adj.* Relating to or occurring in the spring.

vex (veks) *v.* To disturb, annoy, irritate, trouble.—**vexation** *n.*

vicissitudes (vi sis′ ə toodz′) *n.* Unpredictable changes or variations that keep occurring in life, fortune, etc.; shifting circumstances.

victual (vit′ ′l) *n.* Food or other provisions.

vigilance (vij′ ə ləns) *n.* The quality or state of being alert and watchful.—**vigilant** *adj.*

vilify (vil′ ə fī′) *v.* **1.** To use abusive or slanderous language about. **2.** [Rare] To degrade.

vincible (vin′ sə b′l) *adj.* That can be overcome or defeated; conquerable.

vindicate (vin′ də kāt) *v.* To defend or maintain (a cause, claim, etc.) against opposition.

vintner (vint′ nər) *n.* A wine merchant.

virtuosity (vʉr′ choo wäs′ ə tē) *n.* Great technical skill in some fine art.

visage (viz′ ij) *n.* The face.

vitiate (vish′ ē āt′) *v.* To make faulty, corrupt.

vitriolic (vit′ rē äl′ ik) *adj.* Extremely biting or caustic; sharp and bitter.

W

wanton (wän′ t′n) *adj.* **1.** Undisciplined, capricious. **2.** Indecent. **3.** [Rare] Luxuriant: said of vegetation.—**wantonness** *n.*

wassail (wäs′ ′l) *n.* A celebration with much drinking, especially at Christmas time.

weal (wēl) *n.* A mark or line; welt.

wend (wend) *v.* [Archaic] to go, journey, travel.

whelp (hwelp) *n.* **1.** The young of any of various flesh-eating animals. **2.** A youth or child: a contemptuous usage.

whet *(hwet)* *v.* To stimulate.

wimple (wim′ p′l) *v.* To cover or clothe with a woman's head covering of medieval times, consisting of a cloth arranged about the head, cheeks, chin, and neck.

winnow (win′ ō) *v.* To blow the chaff from (grain) by wind.

withal (with ôl′) *adv.* In addition, besides.

wont (wōnt) *adj.* Accustomed.

wrest (rest) *v.* To turn or twist violently.

Y

yawl (yôl) *n.* A small sailboat.

yeoman (yō′ mən) *n.* **1.** An attendant or manservant. **2.** An independent farmer or landholder.

Z

zenith (zē′ nith) *n.* **1.** The highest point; peak. **2.** The point in the sky directly overhead.

zephyr (zef′ ər) *n.* A soft gentle breeze.

Index of Titles and Authors

Index of Fine Art

The Museum of Modern Art

Square Motif in Brown, White, Black, Blue, and Ochre, 1948–53. Victor Pasmore.
Collage and oil on canvas, 25 × 30".

Girl Before a Mirror, 1932. Pablo Picasso.
Oil on canvas, 64 × 51¼".

Art Credits

Cover

Square Motif: Blue and Gold: The Eclipse, 1950.
Tate Gallery, London.

Photographs

Michael Holford, 10, 42, 47, 50, 91, 135; Robert C. Ragsdale, 198, 203, 216, 233, 243, 247, 260, 262; Ray Gardner, 308, 407; Sally Chappell, 361, 730, 737; Eileen Tweedy, 493, 571; John Webb, 548, 573, 608, 609, 802, 803, 876; New Directions/© copyright Harold Owen, 718; Derek Bayes, Click/Aspect, 815; Colin Davey/Photo Trends, 821; W. Suschitsky/Knopf, 828; Lionel Cherrualt/Photo Trends, 836; © 1984 by Jill Krementz, 843, 927; Alex Gotfryd/Brandt & Brandt, 850; Camera Press/Photo Trends, 858; © 1984 by Thomas Victor, 862, 907, 930; © 1984 by ADAGP, Paris, 867; Woodfin Camp, Assoc., 869; Carmelo Guadagno, 881; Photo Trends, 886, 904, 918; Layle Silbert, 889; Shana Sureck/Wesleyan University, 901; Bassano/Photo Trends, 924; Carcanet Press, Ltd., 932.

Index of Skills

Reading and Literary Skills

Act 240

Alexandrine 485, 487

Alliteration 41, 288, 310, 350, 457, 482, 487, 497, 508, 595, 606, 709, 721, 725, 728, 733, 739, 861, 914

Allusion 133, 272, 296, 299, 323, 452, 649, 696, 713, 857, 921, 926

Analogy 51, 301, 500, 877

Anapestic Meter 713, 906

Anaphora 277, 288, 871

Anglo-Saxon Poetry 41, 54

Antagonist 209, 240

Antithesis 369, 688, 713, 717

Aphorism 277, 688

Apostrophe 170, 567

Aside 209

Assonance 288, 310, 350, 457, 482, 487, 497, 606, 709, 712, 713, 728, 739, 861, 893

Audience 186

Autobiography 123, 362, 517

Ballad 63, 108, 115, 116, 118, 119, 479

Biography 397

Blank Verse 208, 330, 444

Caesura 41, 444, 498, 702

Character 40, 90, 123, 133, 144, 223, 251, 273, 330, 526, 563, 648, 667, 672, 678–679, 752, 779, 786, 799–800, 868
  Dynamic, 801
  Foil, 648, 768–769
  Hero, 40, 273, 487
  Main and Minor Characters, 752
  Protagonist, 209, 240
  Static, 801
  Stereotype, 41, 526, 769, 800
  Tragic Hero, 40, 273

Characterization 90, 223, 563, 589, 648, 667, 672, 752, 768, 786, 801
  Through Actions, 90
  Through Dialogue, 223, 563, 589, 752, 768, 786
  Through Physical Description, 90, 648
  Through Reactions and Comments of Other Characters, 90
  Through Reactions and Thoughts, 672

Climax 240, 580, 667

Comedy 799

Comic Relief 223

Comparison. See **Analogy.**

Conceit 307

Concrete Poetry 934

Concrete Universal 887

Conflict 240, 580
  Conflict with Another Character, 580
  Conflict with Nature, 580
  Conflict with Society, 580
  Internal Conflict, 580

Connotation 51, 330, 403, 452, 487, 497, 498, 500, 504, 595, 702, 712, 842, 871, 885, 900, 903, 910, 921

Consonance 288, 310, 350, 457, 482, 487, 497, 508, 709, 712, 713, 733, 739, 861, 914

Contrast 223, 331, 385, 444, 497, 504, 526, 565, 594, 595, 597, 648, 712, 720, 727
  Foil, 648, 768, 769

Couplet 90, 162, 170, 184, 303, 306, 369, 451, 508, 711
  Heroic Couplet, 90, 306, 369

Dactylic Meter 713, 725, 906

Dénouement 273

Description 686

Dialect 416, 752, 893, 926

Dialogue 208, 209, 223, 272, 589

Diary 362

Diction 330, 386, 446, 447, 490, 497, 500, 504, 592, 594, 595, 599, 696, 702, 712, 720, 727, 729, 730, 801, 868, 910, 916, 921

Drama 63–64, 155, 186, 209, 340–342, 539, 563, 619, 752, 799, 810–811
  Act, 240
  Aside, 209
  Comedy, 799
  Scene, 257
  Stage Directions, 752, 768–769, 786
  Tragedy, 273

Dramatic Irony 209, 563, 849

Dramatic Lyric 307

Dramatic Monologue 553, 563

Echoing 208

Elegy 51, 306, 556, 903

Enjambment 424, 444, 593, 702, 717, 887

Epic 40, 107, 330

Epigram 184, 368

Epistle 366, 377

Epitaph 368

Essay 136, 277, 373, 526, 686, 696, 861, 868, 877
  Descriptive, 136, 686
  Expository, 136, 686, 877
  Formal, 277, 373, 696

Vocabulary and Language Skills

Writing Skills